EXCELLENCE IN
BUSINESS COMMUNICATION

FIFTH EDITION

John V. Thill

Chief Executive Officer
Communication Specialists of America

Courtland L. Bovée

Professor of Business Communication
C. Allen Paul Distinguished Chair
Grossmont College

Prentice
Hall

Upper Saddle River, New Jersey 07458

Library of Congress Cataloging-in-Publication Data
Thill, John V.
  Excellence in business communication / John V. Thill, Courtland L. Bovée.—5th ed.
    p. cm.
  Includes bibliographical references and index.
  ISBN 0-13-090947-5
  1. Business communication—United States—Case studies. I. Bovée, Courtland L. II.
Title.

HF5718.2.U6 T45 2001
658.4'5--dc21   2001021273

Editor-in-Chief: Jeff Shelstad
Assistant Editor: Jennifer Surich
Editorial Assistant: Virginia Sheridan
Media Project Manager: Cindy Harford
Senior Marketing Manager: Debbie Clare
Managing Editor (Production): Judy Leale
Production Editor: Cindy Spreder
Permissions Coordinator: Suzanne Grappi
Associate Director, Manufacturing: Vincent Scelta
Production Manager: Arnold Vila
Art Director: Cheryl Asherman
Interior Design: Jill Little
Cover Design: Jill Little
Cover Illustration: Theo Rudnak/Stock Illustration Source
Illustrator (Interior): Electra Graphics
Assoc. Director, Multimedia Production: Karen Goldsmith
Manager, Multimedia Production: Christy Mahon
Page Formatter II: Ashley Scattergood
Composition: Carlisle Communications
Full-Service Project Management: Lynn Steines, Carlisle Communications
Printer/Binder: Courier

Credits and acknowledgments borrowed from other sources and reproduced, with permission, in this textbook appear on page R1.

10 9 8 7 6 5 4 3 2
ISBN 0-13-090947-5

CONTENTS IN BRIEF

CONTENTS

8 WRITING BAD-NEWS MESSAGES 197

9 WRITING PERSUASIVE MESSAGES 230

11 WRITING BUSINESS REPORTS AND PROPOSALS   315

12 COMPLETING FORMAL REPORTS AND PROPOSALS   358

13   GIVING SPEECHES AND ORAL PRESENTATIONS   403

PART V   *Employment Messages*   431

14   WRITING RÉSUMÉS AND APPLICATION LETTERS   432

Appendix A FORMAT AND LAYOUT OF BUSINESS DOCUMENTS 491

Appendix B DOCUMENTATION OF REPORT SOURCES 513

Appendix C FUNDAMENTALS OF GRAMMAR AND USAGE 519

PREFACE

Only One Text Gives Students Experience *"On the job"*

Each chapter opens with an exclusive feature, *"On the job:* FACING A COMMUNICATION DILEMMA." This slice-of-life vignette summarizes a communication problem being faced by an actual company, such as American Express, Home Depot, the U.S. Mint, Patagonia, and Dell Computer. The solution to the dilemma is found in the concepts presented in the chapter, and the featured company reappears from time to time throughout the chapter to dramatize the connection between chapter principles and life on the job.

But we don't stop there. Each chapter ends with another exclusive feature, *"On the job:* SOLVING A COMMUNICATION DILEMMA." These simulations expand on the chapter-opening dilemma and are set within the featured company. Students are asked to solve situational problems by applying the principles discussed in the text, by making decisions about the communication process, and by selecting the best alternatives from the choices offered.

Not only do these simulations give students the opportunity to practice real-world decision making, they also tie the textual information to real-life examples, providing a concrete basis for analyzing the chapter principles. This feature provides a dimension of reality unmatched by other textbooks in the field.

New Features in This Edition

A Greater Emphasis on Process and Product

We have reorganized the material in many of the text's chapters into a series of three easy-to-follow steps: planning, writing, and completing business messages. Students will appreciate this practical strategy for solving communication problems and creating well-crafted communication products. The three-step process is explained in detail (Chapters 4–6) before it is applied to specific types of business messages: letters, memos, and e-mail messages (Chapters 7–9); reports and proposals (Chapters 10–12), and speeches and oral presenta-tions (Chapter 13). The three-step writing process even serves as the frame-work for writing employment messages (Chapters 14–15).

Writing for the Web

Writing for the Web is quite different from writing for print, so anyone who wants to be an effective Web writer must learn new skills. Discussed briefly in Chapters 1 and 4, writing for the Web is covered more fully in Chapter 5, which also includes a checklist. In addition, an "Effective E-Business Communication" feature is included in each chapter of the text. Using real-company Web pages as examples, these features present important Web-writing guidelines and include two discussion questions. Topics include:

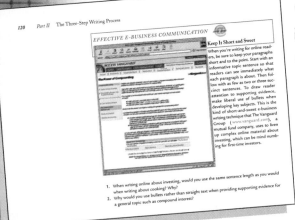

- Get to the Point—Quickly (Southwest Airlines)
- Calling a Meeting in Cyberspace (WebEx)
- Putting the World in the Web (REI)
- Design Messages for Easy Navigation (UPS)
- Annual Reports in Cyberspace (Compaq)
- Speeches That Live On and On (Sears)

Special Feature Sidebars

Boxed and strategically placed within each chapter, special-feature sidebars extend the chapter material. We've included discussion questions at the end of each special fea-ture to give students numerous opportunities to analyze business communication prin-ciples and practices. These special features center on four well-integrated themes:

Achieving Intercultural Communication Tested techniques help students communicate successfully in the global arena and in the culturally diverse business world at home. Cultural issues are well explored in special features such as:

- Test Your Intercultural Knowledge
- Communicating with a Global Audience on the Web
- Good Ways to End Bad News Around the World

Promoting Workplace Ethics By examining critical ethical issues that face business communicators in today's workplace, students gain instruction on how to identify areas of ethical vulnerability, how to steer clear of ethical perils, and when to seek ethical advice. Special features include a wide range of topics such as:

- Spin Cycle: Deciphering Corporate Doublespeak
- Recommendation Letters: What's Right to Write?
- Inflating Your Résumé: Is It Worth the Risk?

Sharpening Your Career Skills Practical pointers and confidence-building guidelines help students improve their writing and speaking skills. Special features help students strengthen their career skills by exploring such topics as:

- Beating Writer's Block: Nine Workable Ideas to Get Words Flowing
- How to Proofread Like a Pro
- Interview Strategies: Answering the 16 Toughest Questions

Using the Power of Technology Specific techniques offer students guidance for using technological applications to improve business communication. Special features present a well-balanced selection of technological topics, including:

- Elements of Cyberstyle
- Spam: Putting a Lid on It
- Netting a Job on the World Wide Web

Streamlined and Reorganized Text

This edition streamlines and reorganizes the text, reducing the number of regular chapters from 18 to 15, making it easier to cover the entire text in one term. Material previously covered in Chapters 1 and 2 has been combined into Chapter 1. The chapter on writing direct requests has been combined with the chapter on writing routine, good-news, and goodwill letters—shortening the letter-writing chapters from four to three. The discussion of interpersonal communication skills such as listening and working in teams has been expanded and moved to Chapter 2. And the discussion of the writing process now begins one chapter earlier.

Trademark Features — All Updated for This Edition

Up-to-Date Internet Resources

The World Wide Web contains a wealth of valuable resources. To acquaint students with Web sites that relate to the content of *Excellence in Business Communication*, each chapter includes a Going Online feature that describes an especially useful Web site.

Students can access the site by using the URL provided or by visiting the Web site for this text (www.prenhall.com/thill), where live links take students straight to the site of their choice.

Examples of the Going Online feature include:

- Write Is Right: Rethink and Revise
- Announcing an Employee Layoff: How to Write a Termination Notice

- Influence an Official and Promote Your Career
- Pointers for Business Plans
- Post an Online Résumé

To give students practice exploring the rich resources of the Web, Going Online Exercises are included at the end of each chapter. These exercises are directly tied to the Going Online sites showcased within the chapters. Moreover, students can access online instructions for completing these exercises.

Gallery of Business Communication Professionals

Another unique feature of this text is the inclusion of full-color photographs with incisive captions that focus on 30 highly successful communication professionals from business, industry, government, and the media. Among the new individuals featured are Meg Whitman (eBay), Martha Stewart (Martha Stewart Living Omnimedia), Gerald Levin (AOL Time Warner), Andrea Jong (Avon), Carly Fiorina (Hewlett-Packard), and Sherry Lansing (Paramount Studios).

Strategically placed in the margins throughout each chapter, these captions with accompanying photographs expand the amount of insight to be gained from this book. Each caption relates specifically to the text and adds a new dimension to student learning by giving a communication expert's view about a particular aspect of business communication.

Example After Example of Letters, Memos, E-Mail Messages, and Reports

This text contains outstanding examples of documents from numerous types of organizations and from people working in a variety of functional areas. Many of these documents are fully formatted, and some are presented on the letterhead of well-known companies. Accompanying analyses help students see precisely how to apply the principles discussed in the text. Poor and improved examples illustrate common errors and effective techniques for correcting them.

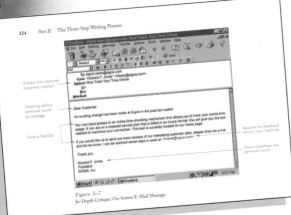

Figure 5–7
In-Depth Critique: On-Screen E-Mail Message

The report-writing chapters give numerous examples too. And the last chapter of the report unit illustrates the step-by-step development of a long report, which appears in its entirety to show how all the parts fit together.

Real-World Issues

The boundaries of business communication are always expanding. In addition to covering all the traditional subjects, *Excellence in Business Communication*, Fifth Edition, provides material to help students manage these important current issues in business communication:

- ◆ *Ethics.* Taking an ethical position in the face of pressures and temptations requires more than courage—it requires strong communication skill.
- ◆ *Communication Barriers.* The shift toward a service economy means that more and more careers will depend on interpersonal skills, making it vital for people to overcome communication barriers.
- ◆ *Cultural Diversity.* The changing nature of the domestic work force requires strong communication skills to relate to older workers, women, members of various socioeconomic groups, immigrants, and others. Also, strong skills are needed to communicate effectively with people from other cultures.
- ◆ *Communication Technology.* More and more face-to-face interactions are giving way to interactions with and through computers. And this trend will continue. To survive in today's business world, students must master high-tech communication skills.
- ◆ *Law.* The increasing tendency of people to sue makes it important to understand the legal implications of written and oral communication.
- ◆ *Employment Search.* More and more people are making radical mid-career job changes, whether by choice or because their companies are downsizing and

flattening hierarchies. These people need to master new communication skills to compete in today's job market.

◆ **Communication Versatility.** Small businesses create most of the new jobs and employ more people than large corporations do. Since these small businesses are unable to support communication specialists for specific jobs, people working for them need to be versatile in their communication skills.

Real-World Competencies—SCANS (Secretary's Commission on Achieving Necessary Skills)

Like no other business communication text, this edition emphasizes the skills and competencies necessary for students to make the transition from academia to the workplace. As described in the SCANS report from the Department of Labor, it is essential that students meet national standards of academic and occupational skill. To help accomplish the SCANS goal, this text offers a wide variety of interactive pedagogy (much of which is grounded in real-world situations).

Checklists

To help students organize their thinking when they begin a communication project, make decisions as they write, and check their own work, we've included numerous checklists throughout the book. In the Fifth Edition, we've streamlined and condensed them to increase their usefulness. Appearing as close as possible to the related discussion, these check-lists are reminders, not "recipes." They provide useful guidelines for writing, without limiting creativity.

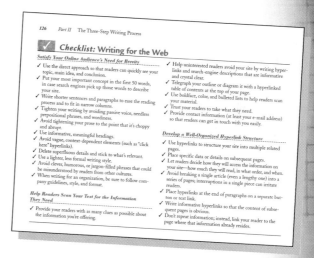

Documents for Analysis

In this textbook we have provided a wide selection of documents that students can cri-tique and revise. Documents include letters, memos and e-mail messages, a letter of application, and a résumé. This hands-on experience in analyzing and improving sam-ple documents will help students revise their own business messages.

In-Depth Critiques

You will find up-to-date sample documents, many collected in our consulting work. All In-Depth Critiques are introduced in the text (identifying the particular business situation being illustrated), and all are accompanied by margin comments that point to specific letter parts to help students see precisely how to apply the principles discussed in the text. Many samples are also accompanied by a three-step-writing-process graphic that gives students important insights into planning, writing, and completing the specific document shown.

Additional documents are displayed in text, some including poor and improved examples to illustrate common errors and effective techniques for correcting them.

Exercises and Cases

A wealth of new exercises and cases (almost all companies featured are real) provide assignments like those that students will most often face at work. Many of them are memo-writing and e-mail tasks. New in the Fifth Edition, each exercise is labeled as to its type, such as "Team," "Ethical Choices," "Self-Assessment," or "Internet." The exercises and cases deal with all types and sizes of organizations, both domestic and international. Each chapter also includes exercises and cases that require access to the

World Wide Web, giving students practice with this fast-growing communication technology.

The cases are yet another tool for demonstrating the role of communication in the real business world. Examples include:

- ◆ Midnight mission: Thank-you letter at The Blue Marble Bookstore
- ◆ Reverse migration: Letter requesting letter of recommendation for "dot-com" dropout
- ◆ Tethered SwimCords: Letter to Italian sports retailer returning order

♦ Air rage fiasco: Letter requesting refund from British Airways
♦ Travel turnaround: E-mail message at Travelfest convincing your boss to expand client services

Learning Objectives

Chapter-opening learning objectives are clearly stated to signal important concepts that students are expected to master. In addition, the numbered objectives reappear in the text margins, close to the relevant material. Moreover, the end-of-chapter "Summary of Learning Objectives" reinforces basic concepts by capsulizing chapter highlights for students.

Margin Notes

To reinforce learning, the book's margins contain short summary statements that highlight key points of *Excellence in Business Communication*, Fifth Edition. These notes are no substitute for reading the chapters, but they help students quickly get the gist of a section, review a chapter, and locate areas of greatest concern.

End-of-Chapter Questions

The end-of-chapter questions (225) are divided into two types: Test Your Knowledge (review questions), and Apply Your Knowledge (application questions). One application question in each chapter focuses on ethics and is labeled "Ethical Choices."

The end-of-chapter questions are designed to get students thinking about the concepts introduced in each chapter. The questions may also prompt students to stretch their learning beyond the chapter content. Not only will students find them useful in studying for examinations, but the instructor may also draw on them to promote classroom discussion of issues that have no easy answers.

TEST YOUR KNOWLEDGE

1. What are the three steps in the writing process?
2. What two types of purposes do all business messages have?
3. What do you need to know in order to develop an audience profile?
4. How can you test the thoroughness of the information you include in a message?
5. What is media richness and how is it determined?
6. What is the "you" attitude and how does it differ from an "I" attitude?
7. Why is it important to establish your credibility when communicating with an audience of strangers?
8. How does using bias-free language help communicators to establish a good relationship with their audiences?
9. What are the main advantages of oral communication? Of written media?
10. What is boilerplate, and how is it used?

INTERACTIVE LEARNING

USE THIS TEXT'S ONLINE RESOURCES

Visit the myPHLIP Web site at www.prenhall.com/thill. For Chapter 4, take advantage of the interactive "Study Guide" to test your chapter knowledge. Get instant feedback on whether you need additional studying. Read the "Current Events" articles to get the latest on chapter topics, and complete the exercises—as specified by your instructor.

This site's "Study Hall" helps you succeed in this course. "Talk in the Hall" lets you leave messages and meet new friends online. If you have a question, you can "Ask the Tutor." And to get a better grade in this course, you can find more help at "Writing Skills," "Study Skills," and "Study Tips."

The "Research Area" helps you locate a wealth of information to use in course assignments. Plus, you can send a message to online research experts, who will help you find exactly the information you need.

APPLY YOUR KNOWLEDGE

1. Some writers argue that planning messages wastes time because they inevitably change their plans as they go along. How would you respond to this argument? Briefly explain.
2. As a member of the public relations department, what medium would you recommend using to inform the local community that your toxic-waste cleanup program has been successful? Why?
3. When composing business messages, how can you be yourself and project your company's image at the same time?
4. Considering how fast and easy it is, should e-mail replace meetings and other face-to-face communication in your company? Why or why not?
5. **Ethical Choices** The company president has asked you to draft a memo to the board of directors informing them that sales in the newly acquired line of gourmet fruit jams have far exceeded anyone's expectations. As purchasing director, you happen to know that sales of moderately priced jams have declined substantially (many customers have switched to the more expensive jams). You were not directed to add that tidbit of information. What should you do?

Appendixes

Excellence in Business Communication, Fifth Edition, contains four appendixes: Appendix A, "Format and Layout of Business Documents," discusses in one convenient place the formatting for all types of documents. Appendix B, "Documentation of Report Sources," gives basic guidelines for handling reference citations, bibliographies, and source notes. Appendix C, "Fundamentals of Grammar and Usage," is a primer in brief, presenting the basic tools of language. Appendix D, "Correction Symbols," provides convenient symbols for students to use when revising documents.

Indexes

To assist students and instructors in locating information as conveniently as possible, two types of indexes are included in the book: an Organization/Company/Brand Index and a Subject Index.

Book Design

This book's state-of-the-art design is based on extensive research and invites students to delve into the content. It also makes reading easier, reinforces learning, and increases comprehension. For example, the special features do not interfere with the flow of text material, a vital factor in maintaining attention and concentration. The design of this book, like much communication, has the simple objective of gaining interest and making a point.

An Unparalled Supplements Package Offers a Fully Integrated Teaching System

The instructional resource package accompanying this text is specially designed to simplify the task of teaching and learning. Several new and exciting items have been added.

All-New! Instructor's Resource Manual

This comprehensive paperback book is an instructor's tool kit. Among its many teaching aids, this manual provides a section about collaborative writing, suggested solutions to exercises, suggested solutions and fully formatted letters for *every* case in the letter-writing chapters, and a grammar pretest and posttest.

   This all-new, comprehensive manual contains a set of completely integrated support materials. It is designed to assist instructors in quickly finding and assembling the resources available for each chapter of the text and includes the following new material:

   ◆ Course planning guide
   ◆ Collaborative writing guide
   ◆ Diagnostic tests of English skills
   ◆ Chapter outline
   ◆ Changes to the new edition
   ◆ Detailed lecture outlines keyed to the transparency acetates
   ◆ Answers to all end-of-chapter questions and assignments
   ◆ Solutions to all cases and exercises

Test Item File

The **Test Item File** contains approximately 1,500 questions, all of which have been carefully reviewed to provide a fair, structured program of evaluation. The questions for each chapter consist of a comprehensive set of multiple-choice, true/false, and fill-in questions. The ***Test Item File*** reinforces students' understanding of key terms and concepts and requires them to apply their critical-thinking and analytical skills.

All New! Prentice Hall's Computerized Test Manager *4.2—ESATEST 2000 (Windows Version)*

Our user-friendly software allows you to generate error-free tests quickly and easily by previewing questions individually on the screen and then selecting randomly by query or by number. The *Computerized Test Manager* allows you to generate random tests with our extensive bank of questions. You can also edit our questions/answers and even add some of your own. You can create an exam, administer it traditionally or online, and analyze your success with the simple click of the mouse. The newest version of our *Computerized Test Manager*, **ESATEST 2000**, has been improved to provide users with a vast array of new options. Enhancements now allow you to:

- Import Test Questions from Word Processors
- Import/Export Tests
- Correlate Charts
- Select by Query
- Select by Review (redesigned)
- Select by Criteria
- Archive Database Capability
- Analyze Test Bank Items
- Export Grades to Excel
- Weight Grades
- Record Grades in a New Spreadsheet Format and Create a Grade Database
- Control Online Testing

All-New! Telephone Test Preparation

For those instructors who prefer not to use the *Computerized Test Manager*, Prentice Hall provides a special 800 call-in service for ease of use. All you need to do is call the **800 Testing Help Desk** to have a customized test created. The test can then be delivered by e-mail, U.S. mail, or overnight carrier.

All-New! Color Acetate Transparency Program

A set of 140 large-type transparency acetates are available to instructors on request. These visuals help bring concepts alive in the classroom and provide a starting point for discussing communication techniques. All transparencies are keyed to the *Instructor's Resource Manual*. Many contrast poor and improved solutions to featured cases from the textbook.

All-New! PowerPoint Presentation

Enhance your classroom presentations with this well-developed PowerPoint presentation set created by Jimidene Murphey, Clarendon College. The colorful text-specific electronic slides highlight and reinforce the important concepts of the text. Free to adopters, PowerPoint slides are available on CD or can be downloaded from the Instructor's Resource Web site at www.prenhall.com/thill.

Study Guide

A *Study Guide for Excellence in Business Communication* by Jimidene Murphy, Clarendon

College, is designed to increase your students' comprehension of the concepts presented in this text. The guide provides chapter-by-chapter explanations and exercises designed to reinforce comprehension of key terms and concepts and to promote concept-application skills.

Mastering Business Communication: The Perils of Pauline, 2.0

Let students learn valuable lessons about communicating effectively in a variety of business situations prior to experiencing them first-hand. The Perils of Pauline is an exciting interactive CD that uses custom video scenarios linked with exercises and activities. These tools allow your students to help Pauline, a recent college graduate, deal with real-world communication predicaments on her first job. Twelve individual episodes are featured, each including unique video scenarios that set up the episode, interactive exercises that offer feedback based on student decisions, video conclusions for both good and bad endings, and stimulating discussion questions. This CD can be packaged with the text for a nominal fee.

Communication Briefings Video Series and Video Guide

Accompanying the text is a series of videos from Communication Briefings, a firm known for its monthly newsletter and its informative videos. The video set is available without charge to adopters of *Excellence in Business Communication*. Included in the series are the following videos:

Everyone's Teamwork Role

Communicating for Results: How to Be Clear,
    Concise, and Credible

Better Business Grammar

Make the Phone Work for You

Listen and Win: How to Keep Customers Coming Back

How to See Opportunity in a Changing Workplace

Resolving Conflict: Strategies for a Winning Team

Make Presentations Work for You

In addition, a separate video guide is available. Features include synopses of each video and discussion questions. To order the set, please call 1-800-388-8433.

Business Communication Update *Newsletter for Faculty*

Delivered exclusively by e-mail every month, this newsletter provides interesting materials that can be used in class and offers a wealth of practical ideas about teaching methods. To receive a complimentary subscription, send an e-mail to bovee-thill@uia.net. In the subject line, put "BCU Subscription Request." In the message area, please list your name and institutional affiliation.

Authors' E-Mail Hotline for Faculty

Integrity, excellence, and responsiveness are our hallmarks. This means providing you with the textbooks that are academically sound, creative, timely, and sensitive to instructor and student needs. As an adopter of *Excellence in Business Communication*, you are invited to use our E-Mail Hotline. We want to be sure you're completely satisfied, so if you ever have a question or concern related to the text or its supplements, please e-mail us at bovee-thill@uia.net. We'll get back to you as quickly as possible.

Introducing the myPhlip Companion Web Site for *Excellence in Business Communication*, Fifth Edition

The myPhlip (Prentice Hall's Learning on the Internet Partnership) Companion Web site is your personal guide to the free online resources for your book and is located at www.prenhall.com/thill. It's the most advanced, text-specific site available on the Web!

Featuring one-click access to all of the resources created by an award-winning team of educators, here is a preview of its exciting features.

- **myPHLIP pages**—Your personal access page unites all your myPHLIP texts.
- **Notes**—Add personal notes to our resources for personal reminders and references.
- **Messages**—Instructors can send messages to individual students or to all students linked to a course.
- **Student Resources**—Add premium PHLIP resources for your students to view and download (such as PowerPoint slides, videos, and spreadsheets).

◆ **Business Headlines**—Check out links to articles in today's business news.

◆ **Search**—Search all PHLIP resources for relevant articles and exercises.

◆ **Instructor's Manual**—For instructors, the myPHLIP Instructor's Manual provides tips and suggestions from our PHLIP faculty for integrating PHLIP resources into your course.

◆ **Current Events**—These articles and exercises, linked to relevant chapters, are added throughout the year. Each article is summarized by our team of expert professors. Group activities, critical thinking questions, discussion questions, and reference citations follow each article, all supported by instructor materials.

◆ **Study Guide**—An interactive, online study guide written by William Peirce, Prince Georges Community College, offers a wide variety of self-assessment questions for every chapter. Results from the automatically graded questions for every chapter provide immediate feedback for students that can be e-mailed to the instructor for extra credit or serve as practice exams.

◆ **Research Area**—Let myPHLIP save you time finding the most valuable and relevant material available on the Web. With a compilation of the best search tools currently available, plus links to virtual libraries, students and instructors can quickly and efficiently search the Web for just the right piece of information.

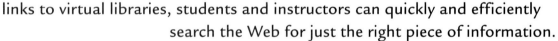

◆ **Internet Resources**—Links connect you to discipline-specific sites, including preview information that allows you to review site information before viewing the site, ensuring that you visit the best available business resources found by our learning community.

For the Student

◆ **Talk to the Tutor** has virtual office hours that allow students to post questions from any supported discipline and receive responses from the dedicated PHLIP/CW faculty team.

- **Writing Resource Center** is an online writing center that provides links to online directories, thesauruses, writing tutors, style and grammar guides, and additional tools.
- **Career Resource Center** helps students access career information, view sample résumés, even apply for jobs online.
- **Study Tips** is an area for students to learn to develop better study skills.

For the Instructor

- **Syllabus Manager**—An improved online syllabus manager is an easy-to-use program that allows faculty to create online custom syllabuses hosted by Prentice Hall servers. Syllabus Manager provides instructors with a step-by-step process to create and revise syllabuses, with direct links into Companion Web Sites and other online content. Changes you make to your syllabus are immediately available to your students at their next login. Your students need only know the Web address for the Companion Web site, and the password you've assigned to your syllabus, and they may log on to your syllabus during any study session.

- **Teaching Resources** include resources contributed by professors throughout the world, including teaching tips, techniques, academic papers, and sample syllabuses.

- **Talk to the Team** is a moderated faculty chat room.
- **Online Faculty Support** is a password-protected area that provides faculty with the most current and advanced support material available, including downloadable supplements, additional cases, articles, links, and suggested answers to Current Events Activities.
- **What's New** gives you one-click access to all newly posted PHLIP resources.

Offering *Excellence in Business Communication*, Fifth Edition, as an Online Course

WebCT

Now you have the freedom to personalize your own online course materials! Prentice Hall Business Publishing provides the content and support you need to create and manage your own online course materials in WebCT. With quality materials and the best support package available, we make it easy for you to use WebCT's course management tools.

WebCT is a course management system with robust course management tools, including page tracking, progress tracking, class and student management, grade book, communication, calendar, reporting tools, and more.

The Excellence in Business Communication, *Fifth Edition, online course provides:*

Customizable Content   Use Prentice Hall materials created by professors for professors and their students.

Our development team:
- checks course material and tests for accuracy;
- clears permission for content and images; and
- edits material for consistency with the supported title.

An example of content created for the course includes
   Tests and Quizzes created for each chapter give instructors hundreds of questions to select and customize for every chapter.

Support   Prentice Hall Business Publishing provides the best support package available for a WebCT course:
- Business Publishing in-print *Instructor's Manual*
- Course-specific online instructor's manual
- Course-specific online student manual
- Gold Level Technical Support hotline

Blackboard

Blackboard's simple templates and tools make it easy to create, manage, and use online course materials.

Course Management Tools   Include progress tracking, class and student management, grade book, communication, assignments, and reporting tools.

Communication Tools   Blackboard offers communication tools such as the Virtual Classroom (chat rooms, whiteboard, and slides), document sharing, and bulletin boards.

Testing   Testing programs include the abilty for the instructor to create online quizzes and tests, and to automatically grade and track results.

Design Tools   Blackboard's design tools and pre-set designs help customize your course.

Content   Prentice Hall content is available for each course, including additional course material, exercises, and tests.

Service
- ◆ Online Instructor and Student Manuals
- ◆ Downloadable Instructor and Student Manuals
- ◆ Online Tutorials
- ◆ CD Tutorials
- ◆ On-site Training

CourseCompass

CourseCompass makes putting your course online as easy as opening a textbook. Combining Prentice Hall's flexible content with Blackboard's flexible tools gives you an easy way to preview, customize, and manage your online course materials.

Personal Acknowledgments

Excellence in Business Communication, Fifth Edition, is the product of the concerted efforts of a number of people. A heartfelt thanks to our many friends, acquaintances, and business associates who agreed to be interviewed so that we could bring the real world into the classroom.

Our thanks to Terry Anderson, whose outstanding communication skills, breadth of knowledge, and organizational ability assured this project's clarity and completeness.

We are grateful to Barbara Schatzman for her remarkable talents; to Marian Burk Wood for her valuable contributions; to Susan Sawyer for her noteworthy skills; to Lianne Downey for her unique contributions; to Stef Gould for her artistry; to Jackie Estrada for her astute attention to detail; to Kathy Mooney for her specialized knowledge; and to Joe Glidden for his research efforts and database supervision.

We also appreciate the notable talents and distinguished contributions of Deborah Valentine, Emory University; Anne Bliss, University of Colorado, Boulder; Carolyn A. Embree, University of Akron; Carla L. Sloan, Liberty University; Doris A. Van Horn Christopher, California State University, Los Angeles; and Susan S. Rehwaldt, Southern Illinois University.

We also feel it is important to acknowledge and thank the Association for Business Communication, an organization whose meetings and publications provide a valuable forum for the exchange of ideas and for professional growth.

Thanks to the many individuals whose valuable suggestions and constructive comments contributed to the success of this book. The authors are deeply grateful to **Anita S. Bednar**, Central State University; **Donna Cox**, Monroe Community College; **Sauny Dills**, California Polytechnic State University—San Luis Obispo; **Charlene A. Gierkey**, Northwestern Michigan College; **Sue Granger**, Jacksonville State University; **Bradley S. Hayden**, Western Michigan University; **Michael Hignite**, Southwest Missouri State; **Cynthia Hofacker**, University of Wisconsin—Eau Claire; **Louise C. Holcomb**, Gainesville College; **Larry Honl**, University of Wisconsin—Eau Claire; **Kenneth Hunsaker**, Utah State University; **Robert O. Joy**, Central Michigan University; **Paul Killorin**, Portland Community College; **Al Lucero**, East Tennessee State University; **Rachel Mather**, Adelphi University; **Betty Mealor**, Abraham Baldwin College; **Mary Miller**, Ashland University; **Richard Profozich**, Prince George's Community College; **Brian Railsback**, Western Carolina University; **John Rehfuss**, California State University—Sacramento; **Joan C. Roderick**, Southwest Texas State University; **Jean Anna Sellers**, Fort Hays State University; **Carla L. Sloan**, Liberty University; **Michael Thompson**, Brigham Young University;

Betsy Vardaman, Baylor University; **Billy Walters**, Troy State University; **George Walters**, Emporia State University; **F. Stanford Wayne**, Southwest Missouri State; **Robert Wheatley**, Troy State University; **Rosemary B. Wilson**, Washtenaw Community College; and **Beverly C. Wise**, SUNY—Morrisville.

We especially want to thank the reviewers of this new, fifth edition. Their detailed and perceptive comments resulted in excellent refinements. These reviewers include: **Janet Adams,** Minnesota State University—Mankato; **Gus Amaya,** Florida International University; **Ruthann Dirks,** Emporia State University; **Mary DuBoise,** DeVry Institute of Technology—Dallas; **Lindsay S. English,** Ursuline College; **Mike Flores,** Wichita State University; **Paula R. Kaiser,** University of North Carolina—Greensboro; **Linda M. LaDuc,** University of Massachusetts—Amherst; **Linda McAdams,** Westark Community College; **Jeanne Stannard,** Johnson County Community College; **John L. Waltman,** Eastern Michigan University; **Aline Wolff,** New York University; **Bonnie Yarbrough,** University of North Carolina—Greensboro.

We want to extend our warmest appreciation to the devoted professionals at Prentice Hall. They include Jerome Grant, president; Jeff Shelstad, editor-in-chief; Elisa Adams, editor; Debbie Clare, senior marketing manager; Jennifer Surich, supplements manager; Amy Whitaker, supplements assistant; and Virginia Sheridan, editorial assistant, all of Prentice Hall Business Publishing, and the outstanding Prentice Hall sales representatives. Finally, we thank Judy Leale, managing editor of production, and Cindy Spreder, production editor, for their dedication, and we are grateful to Lynn Steines, project manager at Carlisle Communications; Suzanne Grappi, permissions editor; Melinda Alexander, photo researcher; and Cheryl Asherman, creative director, for their superb work.

John V. Thill
Courtland L. Bovée

Foundations of Business Communication

chapter 1

Understanding Business Communication

chapter 2

Communicating in Teams: Collaboration, Listening, Nonverbal, and Meeting Skills

chapter 3

Communicating Interculturally

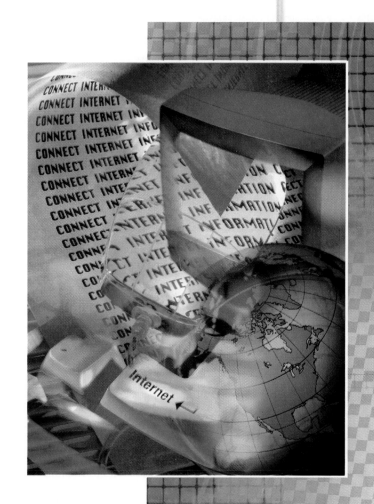

chapter 1

After studying this chapter, you will be able to

1 Explain why effective communication is important to organizations and how it can help you succeed in business

2 Discuss four changes in the workplace that are intensifying the need to communicate effectively

3 Describe how organizations share information internally and externally

4 List and briefly define the six phases of the communication process

5 Identify and briefly discuss four types of communication barriers

6 Discuss four guidelines for overcoming communication barriers

7 Differentiate between an ethical dilemma and an ethical lapse; then list four questions that will help you decide what is ethical

When people browse through Hallmark greeting cards, they are looking for the best way to express a sentiment—whether with joy, sympathy, or humor. Strong communication is the key to success at Hallmark, whether helping people share their thoughts and feelings or conducting operations within the organization.

On the job:

FACING A COMMUNICATION DILEMMA AT HALLMARK

When You Care Enough to Send the Very Best—Inside or Outside the Company

www.hallmark.com

Have you ever needed to discuss a sensitive topic with someone and been unsure of how to start the conversation? Chances are you could find a Hallmark card to help you. Hallmark is in the communication business, helping people share their thoughts and feelings. The company introduces thousands of new paper cards each year and has recently introduced CD greeting cards, online greeting cards, and software for customers to design their own greeting cards. With more than 12,000 employees and such a diverse range of products, communicating within the company is at least as important as communicating with customers.

As Hallmark's internal communications and publications manager, Andy McMillen is responsible for ensuring that employees receive all the information they need to be both productive and satisfied. Most Hallmark employees are organized in teams, and the company's success depends heavily on information flowing freely within and between all its teams, as well as between these teams and upper management. McMillen is responsible for maintaining this open communication climate, and he encourages feedback whenever possible. McMillen knows that Hallmark's teams have their own responsibilities and are immersed in their own work. To avoid overloading people with too many distractions, he sends only necessary messages. A message about changes in employee benefits would be distributed to everyone, but information about a specific project would be sent only to the team involved.

McMillen also understands that every person and each team has a unique personality. For example, the teams of writers and artists who come up with new ideas for cards require a unique combination of individual creativity and team cooperation. On the other hand, cross-functional teams of people from marketing, sales, customer service, and operations tend to make decisions by reaching a consensus rather than by relying on decisions passed down from upper management. McMillen keeps these and other differences in mind when communicating with his colleagues.

Hallmark works hard to attract and keep high-quality employees, viewing them as the company's most important resource. It's up to McMillen to make sure that internal communication not only keeps employees informed but also makes them feel like part of the company. If you were in McMillen's position, what would you do to keep communication flowing throughout the organization smoothly and efficiently? How would you ensure that everyone receives necessary information? How would you overcome all the possible barriers to communication as you prepare the many different messages you need to share with the people inside Hallmark?[1]

ACHIEVING CAREER SUCCESS THROUGH EFFECTIVE COMMUNICATION

Organizations such as Hallmark understand that achieving success in today's workplace is closely tied to the ability of their employees and managers to communicate effectively. **Communication** is the process of sending and receiving messages. However, communication is effective only when people understand each other, stimulate others to take action, and encourage others to think in new ways.

Effective communication offers you and your organization many benefits. When you communicate effectively, you increase productivity, both yours and that of the people around you. Effective communication helps you anticipate problems, make decisions, coordinate work flow, supervise others, develop relationships, and promote products. It helps you shape the impressions you make on your colleagues, employees, supervisors, investors, and customers. It helps you understand and respond to the needs of these **stakeholders** (the various groups you interact with).[2]

Without effective communication, people misunderstand each other and misinterpret information. Ideas misfire or fail to gain attention, and people and companies flounder.[3] Fourteen percent of each 40-hour work week is wasted because of poor communication between staff and management.[4] Whether you are pitching a business proposal, responding to a customer inquiry, or explaining a new process to your teammates, your ability to communicate effectively increases your chance for career success (see Figure 1–1).[5] Moreover, improving your communication skills will help you adapt to the changes occurring in today's workplace.

Adapting to the Changing Workplace

Good communication skills have always been important in the workplace. They are even more vital today. Effective communication helps us adapt to the continuing advances in technology, the globalization of the marketplace, the ability to access vast amounts of information, and the increased use of teams.

Communicating at Internet Speed   Technology brings new and better tools to the workplace, increasing the speed and frequency of communication and allowing people from opposite ends of the world to work together seamlessly, 24 hours a day. The Internet, e-mail, voice mail, faxes, and pagers make it possible for more and more people to telecommute from home, from the road, and from satellite offices around the globe. Depending on which study you read, between 20 and 58 percent of employers now offer telecommuting arrangements for their employees. In fact, current estimates put the number of U.S. telecommuters at about 16 million.[6] (See "Using the Power of Technology— Is Telecommuting Right for You?")

Objective

1

Explain why effective communication is important to organizations and how it can help you succeed in business.

Communication enables organizations to function.

Effective communication helps you and your organization succeed.

Objective

2

Discuss four changes in the workplace that are intensifying the need to communicate effectively.

Figure 1–1
The Benefits of Effective Communication

Using the Power of Technology

Is Telecommuting Right for You?

Telecommuting seems like the perfect life. No commute. No morning rush to get ready for. No expensive wardrobe. No day care for kids. But for many people, telecommuting also means no social life.

Many home-based workers soon find that they miss interacting with colleagues. Some worry that if they're not in the office—if they're not seen—they'll be forgotten. Others find that they actually put in longer hours or they encounter too many distractions, such as young children requiring attention. Still others discover that it takes a lot of willpower and self-discipline to be productive when the refrigerator and a nice warm bed are just a few feet away.

Is telecommuting right for you? Here's a checklist to help you determine whether you'd be a good candidate. If you answer "yes" to all the questions, go for it. But if you answer "no" to any of them, you need to think the issue through carefully before taking the leap.

❑ Have you worked at your company long enough to thoroughly understand its culture and expectations?

❑ Does your home have a separate room in which to work, with a door that shuts?

❑ Can others perform their jobs without you being physically available?

❑ Does you home work space have a separate phone line for a fax/modem, computer, and other equipment?

❑ Are you content to work in isolation?

❑ If you have a child, will you have day care available while you work?

❑ Can you perform your job, complete projects, and meet your deadlines without supervision?

❑ If you live with someone else who works at home, will this pose any problems?

❑ Can you physically take your work home with you in a briefcase?

❑ Are you disciplined enough to stop working at the end of the day?

❑ Can you communicate everything you need for your daily workload via phone or e-mail?

❑ If you were your boss, would you let you telecommute?

CAREER APPLICATIONS

1. Based on your answers to the telecommuting questions, do you think telecommuting is right for you? Why or why not?
2. What sort of person do you think would be happy as a telecommuter?

Meg Whitman, President and CEO of eBay Inc., has made her online auction company profitable because she knows the value of two-way communication. Whitman attracts and keeps customers by focusing on them, informing them of site changes, and welcoming their feedback. "What we've basically done is put in place a venue where people can be successful dealing and communicating with one another," says Whitman.

Electronic commerce intensifies the need to communicate effectively.

The increased use of technology in the workplace not only facilitates new working arrangements but also requires employees to communicate more effectively and efficiently. Technology showcases your communication skills—your writing skills are revealed in every e-mail message, and your verbal skills are revealed in audio and video teleconferences.[7] Technology also increases the frequency with which you communicate, and it extends the reach of your messages. *Intranets* are private corporate networks based on Internet technology, and *extranets* are the extension of private networks to certain outsiders such as suppliers. Both facilitate communication among employees, managers, customers, suppliers, and investors. Moreover, the need to communicate effectively with people outside the organization is magnified as more and more businesses transact **electronic commerce (e-commerce),** buying and selling goods and services over the Internet.

For example, during their first Internet Christmas season in 1999, customers flocked to Web sites to do their shopping, but these companies were unprepared to handle the flood of orders that poured in. When employees explained that they could not guarantee product delivery by Christmas day, angry customers from all over the world complained by phone and e-mail. Then, when employees tried to explain the company's position and offer possible remedies, they faced another wave of customer inquiries, and so on.[8]

Communicating With a Culturally Diverse Work Force More and more businesses today are crossing national boundaries to compete on a global scale. Over 2 million North Americans now work for foreign employers, and the number of foreign companies that have built plants in the United States is increasing.[9] A growing percentage of the U.S. work force is made up of people with diverse cultural and ethnic backgrounds, a trend that will continue in the years ahead. In the United States, for example, women and ethnic minorities are entering the work force in record numbers (see Figure 1–2). By 2010 Hispanic Americans will become the largest minority group, and by 2050 the number of minority workers will almost equal that of white workers.[10]

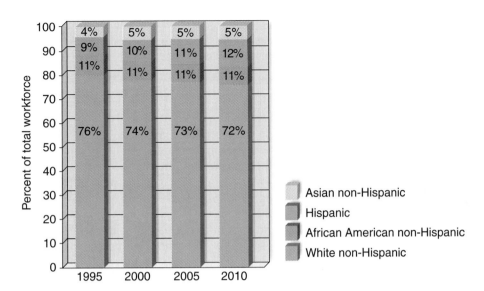

Figure 1–2
Ethnic Composition of the
U.S. Work Force

Increased globalization and work force diversity mean that employees must understand the laws, customs, and business practices of many countries besides being able to communicate with people who speak different languages. Take 3Com's sprawling modem factory in Chicago. The plant employs 1,200 people, and the vast majority are immigrants. Urbane Asians with multiple college degrees work alongside people only recently arrived from Central American villages. Serbs work with Bosnian Muslims and with Iraqis, Peruvians, and South Africans. The employees speak more than 20 different languages, including Tagalog, Gujarati, and Chinese. English skills of varying degrees tie them together.[11]

Overcoming language barriers is just one of the many communication challenges employees face in today's workplace. Chapter 3 discusses intercultural communication in detail and explains how understanding other backgrounds, personalities, and perceptions helps you become a more effective communicator.

Communicating in the Age of Information   In the age of information, "organizations will live or die, depending on their ability to process raw data, transform the data into information, distribute the information appropriately, and use it speedily to make decision," notes professor Fernando Bartolome in his book *The Articulate Executive*.[12] In other words, to be successful in today's workplace, employees must know how to find, evaluate, and process information effectively and efficiently, and they must be able to communicate this information to others. As one project manager at NASA's Marshall Space Flight Center put it, "Knowledge may be power, but communication skills are the primary raw materials of good client relationships." Every job description for a new position on this manager's staff includes the following line: "Required—effective organization skills and mastery of the English language in written and oral forms."[13] Because ideas and data are replacing natural resources and physical materials, communication skills are even more necessary in this information age.

Communicating in Team-Based Organizations   The command-and-control style of traditional management structures is ineffective in today's fast-paced, e-commerce environment.[14] Successful companies such as Hallmark no longer limit decisions to a few managers at the top of a formal hierarchy. Instead, organizations use teams and collaborative work groups to make the fast decisions required to succeed in a global and competitive marketplace. As Andy McMillen knows, the challenges of working in teams increase as more and more team members come from different departments, perform different functions, and have diverse cultural backgrounds. As Chapter 2 discusses in detail, in order to function in a team-based organization, you must be able to clarify, confirm, listen to and understand others, give balanced feedback, explore ideas, keep everyone involved, and credit others' work.[15] Moreover, you must understand how groups interact, reach decisions, work collaboratively,

The increases in international business dealings and in the diversity of the workforce create communication challenges.

Today's employees must communicate with people who speak English as a second language.

The ability to find and communicate information is a requirement for most jobs.

When working in teams you should be able to clarify, confirm, give feedback, explore ideas, and credit others.

Raychem Training Center employees work in teams, collaborating to insure their company's success. Functioning in a team requires that all employees communicate effectively so that they can make decisions efficiently, solve problems quickly, and achieve their company's goals.

and resolve conflict. Clearly, working in teams requires effective communication, but understanding this need is only the first step toward developing effective communication skills.

Setting Your Course for Effective Communication

Many companies provide employees a variety of opportunities for communication skills training. Some companies offer seminars and workshops on handling common oral communication situations (dealing with customers, managing subordinates, getting along with co-workers); others offer training in computers and other electronic means of communication. But even though you may ultimately receive training on the job, don't wait. Start mastering business communication skills right now, in this course. People with good communication skills have an advantage in today's workplace.

Practice helps you improve your communication skills.

One way to improve your communication skills is to practice. Lack of experience may be the only obstacle between you and effective messages, whether written or spoken. Perhaps you have a limited vocabulary, or maybe you're uncertain about questions of grammar, punctuation, and style. Perhaps you're simply frightened by the idea of writing something or of appearing before a group. People aren't "born" writers or speakers. The more they speak and write the more their skills improve. Someone who has written ten reports is usually better at it than someone who has written only two.

Constructive criticism also helps you improve your communication skills.

You learn from experience, and some of the most important lessons are learned through failure. Learning what *not* to do is just as important as learning what *to* do. One of the great advantages of taking a course in business communication is that you get to practice in an environment that provides honest and constructive criticism. A course of this kind also gives you an understanding of acceptable techniques, so you can avoid making costly mistakes on the job.

This course prepares you to handle communication tasks on the job.

No matter what career you pursue, this course prepares you to handle the communication tasks that await you. This book helps you discover how to collaborate in teams, how to listen well, how to master nonverbal communication, and how to ensure successful meetings. You'll also learn about communicating across cultures and through the Internet. This book presents a three-step process for composing business messages. It gives tips for writing letters, memos, e-mail messages, reports, and oral presentations, and it provides a collection of good and bad communication examples with annotated comments to guide you with your own communication efforts. Finally, it explains how to write effective résumés and application letters and how to handle employment interviews. But before you delve into those topics, it's important that you understand what it's like to communicate in an organizational setting.

COMMUNICATING IN ORGANIZATIONS

Whether an organization is large, small, or virtual, sharing information among its parts and with the outside world is the glue that binds the organization together. When you join a company such as Hallmark, you become a link in its information chain. Whether you're a top manager or an entry-level employee, you have information that others need to perform their jobs, and others have information that is crucial to you.

In a business with only five or six employees, much information can be exchanged casually and directly by phone, e-mail, fax, or interoffice memo. For example, Personalized Products, Inc. (PPI) produces souvenirs and toys for vacation spots such as Disney theme parks. PPI Sales Manager Tom Beatty used an interoffice memo to report first-quarter sales to PPI's vice president of finance (see Figure 1–3).

Giant organizations such as PepsiCo have hundreds of thousands of employees scattered around the world, and transmitting the right information to the right people at the right time is a real challenge. To meet this challenge, organizations rely on internal and external communication.

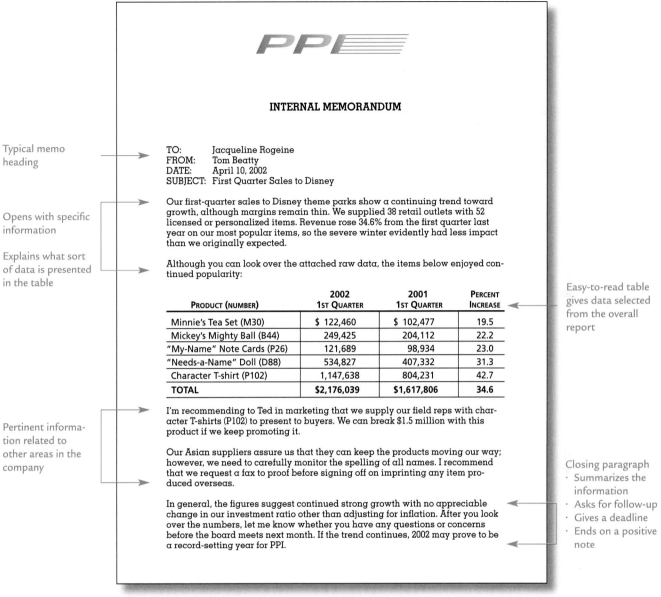

INTERNAL MEMORANDUM

Typical memo heading →

TO: Jacqueline Rogeine
FROM: Tom Beatty
DATE: April 10, 2002
SUBJECT: First Quarter Sales to Disney

Opens with specific information →

Our first-quarter sales to Disney theme parks show a continuing trend toward growth, although margins remain thin. We supplied 38 retail outlets with 52 licensed or personalized items. Revenue rose 34.6% from the first quarter last year on our most popular items, so the severe winter evidently had less impact than we originally expected.

Explains what sort of data is presented in the table →

Although you can look over the attached raw data, the items below enjoyed continued popularity:

Easy-to-read table gives data selected from the overall report →

Product (number)	2002 1st Quarter	2001 1st Quarter	Percent Increase
Minnie's Tea Set (M30)	$ 122,460	$ 102,477	19.5
Mickey's Mighty Ball (B44)	249,425	204,112	22.2
"My-Name" Note Cards (P26)	121,689	98,934	23.0
"Needs-a-Name" Doll (D88)	534,827	407,332	31.3
Character T-shirt (P102)	1,147,638	804,231	42.7
TOTAL	$2,176,039	$1,617,806	34.6

Pertinent information related to other areas in the company →

I'm recommending to Ted in marketing that we supply our field reps with character T-shirts (P102) to present to buyers. We can break $1.5 million with this product if we keep promoting it.

Our Asian suppliers assure us that they can keep the products moving our way; however, we need to carefully monitor the spelling of all names. I recommend that we request a fax to proof before signing off on imprinting any item produced overseas.

Closing paragraph
· Summarizes the information
· Asks for follow-up
· Gives a deadline
· Ends on a positive note

In general, the figures suggest continued strong growth with no appreciable change in our investment ratio other than adjusting for inflation. After you look over the numbers, let me know whether you have any questions or concerns before the board meets next month. If the trend continues, 2002 may prove to be a record-setting year for PPI.

Figure 1–3
In-Depth Critique: Internal Communication by Memo

Internal Communication

Internal communication refers to the exchange of information and ideas within an organization. Communication among the members of an organization is essential for effective functioning. As an employee, you are in a position to observe firsthand things that your supervisors and co-workers cannot see: a customer's first reaction to a product display, a supplier's brief hesitation before agreeing to a delivery date, an odd whirring noise in a piece of equipment, or a slowdown in the flow of customers. Managers and co-workers need these little gems of information in order to do their jobs. If you don't pass that information along, nobody will—because nobody else knows. Communicating freely helps employees develop a clear sense of the organization's mission and helps managers identify and react quickly to potential problems. To maintain a healthy flow of information within the organization, effective communicators use both formal and informal channels.

You are a contact point in both the external and internal communication networks.

Formal Communication Network   The **formal communication network** is typically shown as an organization chart such as the one in Figure 1–4. Such charts summarize the

The formal flow of information follows the official chain of command.

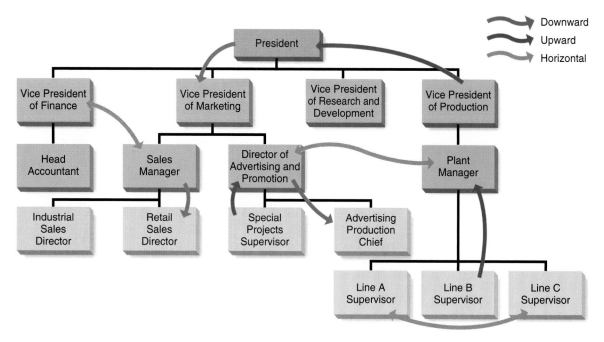

Downward
Upward
Horizontal

President

Vice President of Finance

Vice President of Marketing

Vice President of Research and Development

Vice President of Production

Head Accountant

Sales Manager

Director of Advertising and Promotion

Plant Manager

Industrial Sales Director

Retail Sales Director

Special Projects Supervisor

Advertising Production Chief

Line A Supervisor

Line B Supervisor

Line C Supervisor

Figure 1–4
Formal Communication

lines of authority; each box represents a link in the chain of command, and each line represents a formal channel for the transmission of official messages. Information may travel down, up, and across an organization's formal hierarchy.

Information flows up, down, and across the formal hierarchy.

◆ **Downward flow.** Organizational decisions are usually made at the top and then flow down to the people who will carry them out. Most of what filters downward is geared toward helping employees do their jobs. From top to bottom, each person must understand each message, apply it, and pass it along.

◆ **Upward flow.** To solve problems and make intelligent decisions, managers must learn what's going on in the organization. Because they can't be everywhere at once, executives depend on lower-level employees to furnish them with accurate, timely reports on problems, emerging trends, opportunities for improvement, grievances, and performance.

◆ **Horizontal flow.** Communication also flows from one department to another, either laterally or diagonally. This horizontal communication helps employees share information and coordinate tasks, and it is especially useful for solving complex and difficult problems.[16]

Formal organization charts illustrate how information is supposed to flow. In actual practice, however, lines and boxes on a piece of paper cannot prevent people from talking with one another.

The informal communication network carries information along the organization's unofficial lines of activity and power.

Informal Communication Network   Every organization has an **informal communication network**—a *grapevine*—that supplements official channels. As people go about their work, they have casual conversations with their friends in the office. Although many of these conversations deal with personal matters, about 80 percent of the information that travels along the grapevine pertains to business.[17]

Some executives are wary of the informal communication network, possibly because it threatens their power to control the flow of information. However, savvy managers tap into the grapevine, using it to spread and receive informal messages.[18] Because eliminating the grapevine is virtually impossible, sophisticated companies minimize its importance by making certain that the official word gets out.

The grapevine is an important source of information in most organizations.

Typical inside address

Opening tells what prompted the letter and clearly states the purpose

Seeks to establish a special rapport with the magazine's readers

Save the Wolves Foundation
4542 Audubon Highway • Viper, MT 32400
(406) 266-6223 • Fax (406) 723-3229
www.wolves.org

March 13, 2002

Mr. Sam Davis, Managing Editor
Montana Times Magazine
468 West Times Drive
Helena, Montana 59601

Dear Mr. Davis:

Thank you for your recent editorial supporting the Montana wolf relocation program. We are as dedicated to preserving domestic livestock herds as are the ranchers who own them. However, killing the wolf predators is both a short-term and a short-sighted solution. We'd like your readers to have some additional information, besides the excellent points you made.

Every one of the 32 wolves we've captured and relocated this year has been examined by a veterinarian. The wolves receive inoculations to prevent rabies, among other diseases. Therefore, the relocated wolves pose little threat of disease to wildlife, their pack, or the occasional domestic animal or human who might encounter them.

In the wilderness areas where they will be relocated, wolves help keep the population of caribou, moose, and deer under control, and they cull injured or sick animals from the herd. However, wolves fear human beings and will avoid people whenever possible. Our North American wolves do not attack humans.

In addition, your readers will be interested to know a little more about wolves in general. Wolves have strong family ties and often mate for life. Female wolves give birth to about four to six pups, and both parents supply food and help train the pups. In fact, the wolf pack is usually a family group. And just as families call to their children, wolves sometimes howl to keep their pack together.

We invite those of your readers who would like to join our efforts to call 1-800-544-8333 to receive more information.

Sincerely,

Carroll Paulding

Carroll Paulding
President

sg

Identifies two audiences for this information: the magazine editor and his readers

Provides specific information on the relocation program and reassures readers of their personal safety

Clearly states the invitation where reader will notice it

Figure 1–5
In-Depth Critique: External Communication by Letter

External Communication

Just as internal communication carries information up, down, and across the organization, **external communication** carries it into and out of the organization. Companies constantly exchange messages with customers, vendors, distributors, competitors, investors, journalists, and community representatives. Sometimes this external communication is carefully orchestrated—especially during a crisis. At other times it occurs informally as part of routine business operations.

Formal Outside Communication   Carefully constructed letters convey an important message to outsiders about the quality of your organization. For example, Montana's Save the Wolves Foundation seeks to raise funds for relocating wolves from other states into selected wilderness areas of Montana. To try to educate the public and garner support, the foundation communicates externally, sending a letter to representatives of the mass media (see Figure 1–5).

The external communication network links the organization with the outside world of customers, suppliers, competitors, and investors.

Companies use external communication to create a favorable impression.

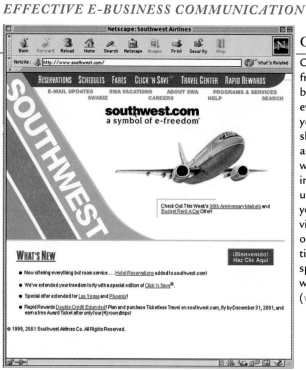

EFFECTIVE E-BUSINESS COMMUNICATION

Get to the Point—Quickly

Online audiences can click away from your Web site in an instant, so be sure your Web-based material is even leaner and more efficient than your printed material. Provide short but descriptive headings for all links so that readers can find what they want right away. Just as important, position the most popular or critical links at the top of your page or along one side so that visitors waste no time scrolling up or down. Help regular visitors identify updates by grouping them in a special "What's New" section, the way it's done at Southwest Airlines (www.southwest.com).

1. How can you plan your Web site to avoid the problem of information overload?
2. How can you minimize home-page distractions that can prevent effective communication?

One important form of communication is the Internet. A company Web site can impart crucial information both inside the organization (using an intranet) and outside (via the Internet). Web sites can communicate a company's image to the outside world and a company's culture to employees.

Whether by letter, Web, phone, fax, or videotape, good communication is the first step in creating a favorable impression. Extremely careful planning is required for messages such as statements to the press, letters to investors, advertisements, price announcements, and litigation updates. Therefore, such documents are often drafted by a marketing or public relations team—a group of individuals whose sole job is creating and managing the flow of formal messages to outsiders.

The way a company handles a crisis can have a profound effect on the organization's subsequent performance.

One of the most visible tasks of professional business communicators is to help management plan for and respond to crises—which can range from environmental accidents or sabotage situations to strikes, massive product failure, major litigation, or even an abrupt change in management. To minimize the impact of any crisis, expert communicators advise managers to communicate honestly, openly, and often (see Table 1–1).[19]

Informal Outside Communication   Although companies often communicate with outsiders in a formal manner, informal contacts with outsiders are important for learning about customer needs. As a member of an organization, you are an important informal conduit for communicating with the outside world. In the course of your daily activities, you unconsciously absorb bits and pieces of information that add to the collective knowledge of your company. What's more, every time you speak for or about your company, you send a message. Many outsiders may form their impression of your organization on the basis of the subtle, unconscious clues you transmit through your tone of voice, facial expression, and general appearance.

Every employee informally accumulates facts and impressions that contribute to the organization's collective understanding of the outside world.

Top managers rely heavily on informal contacts with outsiders to exchange information that might be useful to their companies. Much of their networking involves interaction with fellow executives. However, plenty of high-level managers recognize the value of keeping in touch with "the real world" by creating opportunities to talk with and get

Table 1-1   What to Do in a Crisis
When a Crisis Hits:

Do	Don't
Do prepare for trouble ahead of time by identifying potential problems, appointing and training a response team, and preparing and testing a crisis management plan.	**Don't** blame anyone for anything.
	Don't speculate in public.
Do get top management involved as soon as the crisis hits.	**Don't** refuse to answer questions.
Do set up a news center for company representatives and the media, equipped with phones, computers, and other electronic tools for preparing news releases.	**Don't** release information that will violate anyone's right to privacy.
· Issue at least two news updates a day, and have trained personnel on call to respond to questions around the clock.	**Don't** use the crisis to pitch products or services.
· Provide complete information packets to the media as soon as possible.	**Don't** play favorites with media representatives.
· Prevent conflicting statements and provide continuity by appointing a single person, trained in advance, to speak for the company.	
· Tell receptionists to direct all calls to the news center.	
Do tell the whole story—openly, completely, and honestly. If you are at fault, apologize.	
Do demonstrate the company's concern by your statements and your actions.	

feedback from customers and frontline employees. To facilitate this exchange of information, companies strive to minimize disruptions to the communication process. For the remainder of this chapter we will explain the communication process, the barriers that can block it, and how to overcome these barriers.

UNDERSTANDING THE COMMUNICATION PROCESS

Communication doesn't occur haphazardly. Nor does it happen all at once. It is more than a single act. Communication is a dynamic, transactional (two-way) process that can be broken into six phases (See Figure 1–6).

1. **The sender has an idea.** You conceive an idea and want to share it.

2. **The sender encodes the idea.** When you put your idea into a message that your receiver will understand, you are **encoding** it, deciding on the message's form (word, facial expression, gesture), length, organization, tone, and style—all of which depend on your idea, your audience, and your personal style or mood.

3. **The sender transmits the message.** To physically transmit your message to your receiver, you select a **medium** (telephone, letter, memo, e-mail, report, face-to-face exchange). These choices depend on your message, your audience's location, your need for speed, and the formality required.

4. **The receiver gets the message.** For communication to occur, your receiver must first get the message. If you send a letter, your receiver has to read it before understanding it. If you're giving a speech, your listeners have to be able to hear you, and they have to be paying attention.

5. **The receiver decodes the message.** Your receiver must **decode** (absorb and understand) your message. The decoded message must then be stored in the receiver's mind. If all goes well, the receiver interprets your message correctly; that is, the receiver assigns the same meaning to your words as you intended and responds in the desired way.

Objective

4

List and briefly define the six phases of the communication process.

The communication process consists of six phases linking sender and receiver.

Figure 1–6
The Communication Process

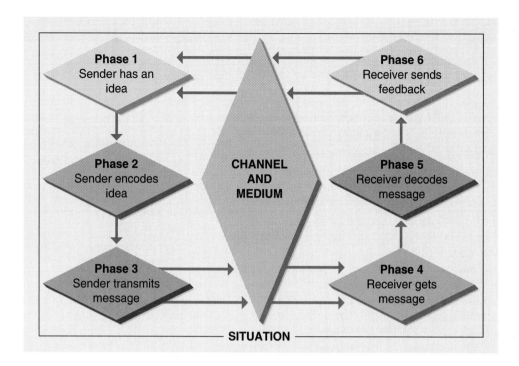

6. **The receiver sends feedback. Feedback** is your receiver's response. After decoding your message, the receiver responds in some way and signals that response to you. Feedback enables you to evaluate the effectiveness of your message: If your audience doesn't understand what you mean, you can tell by the response and refine your message.

As Figure 1–6 illustrates, the communication process is repeated until both parties have finished expressing themselves.[20]

Feedback is your audience's response; it enables you to evaluate your message's effectiveness.

RECOGNIZING COMMUNICATION BARRIERS

Objective

5

Identify and briefly discuss four types of communication barriers.

When you send a message, you intend to communicate meaning, but the message itself contains no meaning. The meaning exists in your mind and in the mind of your receiver. To understand each other, you and your receiver must share similar meanings for words, gestures, tone of voice, and other symbols.

The communication process is effective only when each step is successful. Ideas cannot be communicated if any step in this process is blocked (skipped or completed incorrectly). When interference in the communication process distorts or obscures the sender's meaning, it is called a **communication barrier,** or **noise.** Recognizing communication barriers is the first step in overcoming them. Examples of barriers to effective communication include perceptual differences, restrictive environments, distractions, and deceptive communication tactics.

Communication barriers block the communication process.

Perceptual Differences

Perception is people's individual interpretation of the sensory world around them.

Even when two people experience the same event, their mental images are not identical. When sending a message, you choose the details that seem important to you. However, when receiving a message, you try to fit new details into your existing pattern, and if a detail doesn't quite fit, you're inclined to distort the information rather than rearrange your pattern.

Our perception affects how we see the world and even how we develop language. For example, consider the word *cookie.* You might think of oatmeal, chocolate chip, and sugar cookies. However, someone from Europe may think of meringues, florentines, and spritz. You both agree on the general concept of *cookie,* but your precise images differ.

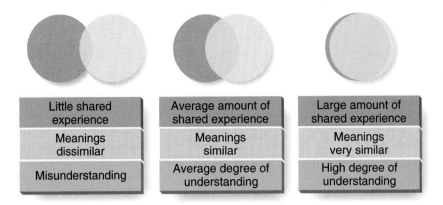

Figure 1–7
How Shared Experience
Affects Understanding

Language is only one of the many differences that exist between cultures. Communicating with someone from another country may be the most extreme example of how different cultures can block communication. But even in your own culture, you and your receiver may differ in age, education, social status, economic position, religion, and life experience. The more experiences you share with another person, the more likely you are to share perception and thus share meaning (see Figure 1–7).

Perception is strongly influenced by cultural differences.

Restrictive Environments

Every link in the communication chain is open to error. By the time a message travels all the way up or down the chain, it may bear little resemblance to the original idea. If a company's formal communication network limits the flow of information in any direction (upward, downward, or horizontal), then communication becomes fragmented. Lower-level employees may obtain only enough information to perform their own isolated tasks, learning little about other areas, so only the people at the very top of the organization can see "the big picture."

When managers use a directive and authoritarian leadership style, information moves down the chain of command but not up. In a recent poll of 638 employees, 90 percent said they had good ideas on how their companies could run more successfully. Yet more than 50 percent said they were prevented from communicating these thoughts because of a lack of management interest and a lack of effective means for sharing their ideas.[21]

At Staples, managers must communicate clearly with the employees they supervise, regardless of differences in their age, gender, culture, or ethnic background.

Distractions

Communication barriers are often physical distractions: bad connections, poor acoustics, or illegible copy. Although noise of this sort seems trivial, it can block an otherwise effective message. Your receiver might be distracted by an uncomfortable chair, poor lighting, health problems, or some other irritating condition.

Your audience is more likely to receive your message accurately if nothing physical interrupts or distorts the message.

Another kind of distraction is poor listening. We all let our minds wander now and then, and we are especially likely to drift off when we are forced to listen to information that is difficult to understand or that has little direct bearing on our own lives. We are even more likely to lose interest if we are tired or concerned about other matters.

Listening ability decreases when information is difficult to understand and when it has little meaning for the listener.

Emotional distractions can be difficult to overcome. When you are upset, hostile, or fearful, you have a hard time shaping a message objectively. If your receiver is emotional, he or she may ignore or distort your message. It's practically impossible to avoid all communication when emotions are involved, but you must recognize that emotional messages have a greater potential for misunderstanding.

Emotions block the communication process.

The sheer number of messages can also be distracting. A recent study by the Gallup organization found that, on a typical day, the average white-collar worker sends and receives as many as 190 messages (see Figure 1–8).[22] With phone calls, e-mail, faxes, and

Today's businesspeople are plagued by message overload.

Figure 1–8
Message Mania

Average number of messages received daily
(per employee)

Going Online

Using the Internet to Explore International Business Communication

↓

Among its many advantages, the International Association of Business Communicators (IABC) offers analyses of issues, case studies, models of communication practices, and advice. All of these can help you develop strategies for managing communication in international business. The IABC is a source for real-world examples, as well as manuals and handbooks on a variety of topics. For students, communicators seeking jobs, and employers, IABC provides a "career and job posting area." And when you log on to this site, you'll find an updated list of topics on the IABC homepage, including news items and announcements of conferences and workshops.

www.iabc.com

To reach this Web site, go to www.prenhall.com/thill *(the Web site for this text). Select Chapter 1, then select "Student Resources." There, you'll find a current live link that will take you straight to the site.*

voice mail—not to mention printed research, reports, and industry news—many executives are overwhelmed by information overload (the increased volume of messages from all sources).[23]

Deceptive Tactics

Language itself is made up of words that carry values. So merely by saying things a certain way, you influence how others perceive your message, and you shape expectations and behaviors.[24] An organization cannot create illegal or unethical messages and still be credible or successful in the long run. Still, some business communicators try to manipulate their receivers by using deceptive tactics.

Deceptive communicators may exaggerate benefits, quote inaccurate statistics, or hide negative information behind an optimistic attitude. They may state opinions as facts, leave out crucial information, or portray graphic data unfairly. Unscrupulous communicators may seek personal gain by making others look better or worse than they are. And they may allow personal preferences to influence their own perception and the perception of others.

OVERCOMING BARRIERS TO IMPROVE COMMUNICATION

Effective communicators work hard at perfecting the messages they deliver. When they make mistakes, they learn from them. If a memo they've written doesn't get the response they hoped for, they change their approach the next time around. If a meeting they're running gets out of control or proves unproductive, they do things differently at the next one. If they find that they have to explain themselves over and over again, they reevaluate their choice of communication medium or rework their message.

Just think about the people you know. Which of them would you call successful communicators? What do these people have in common? Chances are, the individuals on your list share these five traits:

◆ **Perception.** They are able to predict how you will receive their message. They anticipate your reaction and shape the message accordingly. They read your response correctly and constantly adjust to correct any misunderstanding.

◆ **Precision.** They create a "meeting of the minds." When they finish expressing themselves, you share the same mental picture.

◆ **Credibility.** They are believable. You have faith in the substance of their message. You trust their information and their intentions.

◆ **Control.** They shape your response. Depending on their purpose, they can make you laugh or cry, calm down, change your mind, or take action.

◆ **Congeniality.** They maintain friendly, pleasant relations with you. Regardless of whether you agree with them, good communicators command your respect and goodwill. You are willing to work with them again, despite your differences.

In the coming chapters we present real-life examples of both good and bad communication and explain what's good or bad about them. After a while you'll notice that four themes keep surfacing: (1) adopting an audience-centered approach; (2) fostering an open communication climate; (3) creating lean, efficient messages, and (4) committing to ethical communication. These guidelines will help you overcome barriers and improve your communication. Here's a closer look at them.

Objective **6**
Discuss four guidelines for overcoming communication barriers.

Effective communication requires perception, precision, credibility, control, and congeniality.

Guideline 1: Adopt an Audience-Centered Approach

When you adopt an **audience-centered approach** to communication, you focus on and care about your audience, making every effort to get your message across in a way that is meaningful to your audience. To create an effective message, you need to learn as much as possible about the biases, education, age, status, and style of your receiver. When you address strangers, try to find out more about them; if that's impossible, try to project yourself into their position by using your common sense and imagination. Whatever the tactic, you need to write and speak from your audience's point of view to help your audience understand and accept your message.

Centering on your audience is paramount because it facilitates the fulfillment of the three other guidelines that help you overcome communication barriers and send effective messages. Because you want to know what your audience's needs are and what they think of your message, you work for an open communication climate inside and outside your organization. Because you value your audience's time and anticipate your audience's expectations, you create lean, efficient messages and use communication technology responsibly. And because you sincerely wish to satisfy your audience's needs, you approach communication situations with good intentions and high ethical standards. Throughout this book, you'll find important advice on how best to use the audience-centered approach to communication. For example, Chapter 4 (Planning Business Messages) presents in-depth information on learning about your audience and focusing on your audience's needs.

NBC Nightly News anchor Tom Brokaw excels at communicating in this age of information. He covers news events across the country and around the world. He conducts one-on-one interviews and reports from the scene of dramatic events. No matter what the situation, Brokaw's calm delivery and straightforward style help him develop rapport with his audience and overcome communication barriers. As a successful communicator, Brokaw is perceptive, precise, credible, controlled, and congenial.

Using an audience-centered approach means keeping your audience in mind at all times when communicating.

Guideline 2: Foster an Open Communication Climate

An organization's communication climate is a reflection of its **corporate culture:** the mixture of values, traditions, and habits that give a company its atmosphere or personality. Successful companies such as Hallmark encourage employee contributions by making sure that communication flows freely down, up, and across the organization chart. They encourage candor and honesty, and their employees feel free to confess their mistakes, disagree with the boss, and express their opinions. These companies create an open climate in two ways: by modifying the number of organizational levels and by facilitating feedback.

The organization's communication climate affects the quantity and quality of the information exchanged.

Modifying the Number of Organizational Levels One way to foster an open communication climate is to reduce the number of levels in the organization's structure. The fewer the links in the communication chain, the less likely it is that misunderstandings will occur.[25] In other words, a flat structure (having fewer levels) and a wide span of control (having more people reporting to each supervisor) is less likely to introduce distortion than a tall structure and a narrow span of control.

As a $1.5 billion global manufacturer of electronic-connector products, Molex keeps its organization relatively flat to encourage communication at all levels. Officers at Molex work in cubicles, just as regular employees do, and they are accessible to everyone.[26] Although flat is not necessarily better, more and more companies are flattening their structure in an effort to cut costs, boost productivity, and get closer to customers. Flatter

Adjusting organizational levels can improve the communication climate.

organizations enable managers not only to share information with colleagues and employees but also to include employees in decision making, goal setting, and problem solving.[27] Still, designing too few formal channels and having too many people report to a single individual can block effective communication by overburdening that key individual.

Facilitating Feedback   Giving your audience a chance to provide feedback is crucial to maintaining an open communication climate. According to a recent American Express survey, the thing employees want the most from employers is personal feedback (money was rated second). But many managers are eager to avoid conflict, so they avoid giving frank feedback to underperforming employees until it's too late.[28]

Encourage feedback by
- *Asking specific questions*
- *Encouraging your audience to express general reactions*
- *Being receptive to your audience's responses*

To encourage feedback, many companies use techniques such as employee surveys, open-door policies, company newsletters, memos, e-mail, and task forces. Still feedback, it isn't always easy to get. You may have to draw out the other person by asking specific questions. Also encourage your audience to express general reactions; you can gain useful information that way. Long-time General Electric CEO Jack Welch used this process successfully. A fierce believer in the power of his people, Welch encouraged near-brutal candor in meetings. He not only collected unfiltered information but also ensured that GE's triumphs and failures were shared openly.[29]

Guideline 3: Create Lean, Efficient Messages

You must distinguish between necessary and unnecessary information.

Too much information is as bad as too little; it reduces the audience's ability to concentrate on the most important data. You must realize that some information is unnecessary, and you must make necessary information easily available. Try to give information meaning, rather than just passing it on, and set priorities for dealing with the overall message flow. Successful communicators overcome information overload and other communication barriers by reducing the number of messages, decreasing possible distractions, and using technology wisely.

Organizations save time and money by sending only necessary messages.

Reducing the Number of Messages   A good way to make your messages more effective is to send fewer of them. Think twice before sending one. For example, if a written message merely adds to the information overload, it's probably better left unsent or handled some other way—say, by a quick telephone call or a face-to-face chat. Holding down the number of messages reduces the chance of information overload.

Control physical distractions such as a messy appearance of written messages and poor acoustics in oral presentations.

Minimizing Distractions   Although you don't have power over every eventuality, the key to overcoming distracting barriers is control. To overcome physical barriers, exercise as much control as possible over the physical transmission link: If you're preparing a written document, make sure its appearance doesn't detract from your message. If you're delivering an oral presentation, choose a setting that permits the audience to see and hear you without straining. When you're the audience, learn to concentrate on the message rather than on any distractions.

Do your best to control emotions before they block the communication process.

Overcome emotional barriers by recognizing the feelings that arise in yourself and in others as you communicate and by attempting to control these emotions. For example, choose neutral words to avoid arousing strong feelings unduly. Avoid affecting attitudes, placing blame, and generally reacting subjectively. Most important, be aware of the greater potential for misunderstanding that accompanies emotional messages.

Overcome listening barriers by doing everything you can to understand and provide feedback.

As a listener, overcome listening barriers by paraphrasing what you've understood. Try to view the situation through the speaker's eyes, and resist jumping to conclusions. Listen without interrupting, and clarify meaning by asking nonthreatening questions. As a speaker, help listeners by connecting your subject to their needs, using language that is clear and vivid, and relating your subject to familiar ideas. The greater part of this book focuses on how to control your message and the communication process.

Technology has such an impact on business communication that you have no choice but to master it.

Using Technology Responsibly   The Internet is just one part of the technological advance in electronic communication. Together with voice mail, teleconferencing, e-mail,

Promoting Workplace Ethics

Ethical Boundaries: Where Would You Draw the Line?

At the very least, you owe your employer an honest day's work for an honest day's pay: your best efforts, obedience to the rules, a good attitude, respect for your employer's property, and a professional appearance. Such duties and considerations seem clear-cut, but where does your obligation to your employer end? For instance, where would you draw the line in communication situations such as the following?

❏ Writing your résumé so that an embarrassing two-year lapse won't be obvious

❏ Telling your best friend about your company's upcoming merger right after mailing the formal announcement to your shareholders

❏ Hinting to a co-worker (who's a close friend) that it's time to look around for something new, when you've already been told confidentially that she's scheduled to be fired at the end of the month

❏ Saying nothing when you witness one employee taking credit for another's successful idea

❏ Preserving your position by presenting yourself to supervisors as the only person capable of achieving an objective

❏ Buying one software package for use by three computer operators

❏ Making up an excuse when (for the fourth time this month) you have to pick up your child from school early and miss an important business meeting

❏ Calling in sick because you're taking a few days off and you want to use up some of the sick leave you've accumulated.

The ethics involved in these situations may seem perfectly umambiguous . . . until you think about them. But, wherever you are, whatever the circumstances, you owe your employer your best efforts. And time and again, it will be up to you to decide whether those efforts are ethical.

CAREER APPLICATIONS

1. List ethical behaviors you would expect from your employees, and compare your list with those of your classmates.
2. As the supervisor of the office typing pool, you must deal with several typists who have a tendency to gossip about their co-workers. List five things you might do to resolve the situation.

---

and wireless technology, the Internet has revolutionized both oral and written communication. Electronic communication has become a vital element in achieving organizational goals; however, each form of communication has its limitations. Protocols must be followed, and individuals must learn when it is appropriate to use each form.[30] You have to think not only about what you are going to say and how you are going to say it but also about which technological tools you'll use to do so. Throughout this book we present numerous examples of the types of technological tools you'll encounter on the job and how to use those tools effectively and wisely.

Guideline 4: Commit to Ethical Communication

Ethics are the principles of conduct that govern a person or a group. Unethical people are essentially selfish and unscrupulous, saying or doing whatever it takes to achieve an end. Ethical people are generally trustworthy, fair, and impartial, respecting the rights of others and concerned about the effects of their actions on society. Former Supreme Court Justice Potter Stewart defined ethics as "knowing the difference between what you have a right to do and what is the right thing to do."[31]

> Ethics are the principles of conduct that govern a person or a group.

Ethical communication includes all relevant information, is true in every sense, and is not deceptive in any way. When sending an ethical message, you are accurate and sincere. You avoid language that manipulates, discriminates, or exaggerates. You do not hide negative information behind an optimistic attitude, you don't state opinions as facts, and you portray graphic data fairly. You are honest with employers, co-workers, and clients, never seeking personal gain by making others look better or worse than they are. You don't allow personal preferences to influence your perception or the perception of others, and you act in good faith. On the surface, such ethical practices appear fairly easy to recognize. But deciding what is ethical can be quite complex (see "Promoting Workplace Ethics—Ethical Boundaries: Where Would You Draw the Line?").

> Ethical communication is truthful and relevant.

Recognizing Ethical Choices   Every company has responsibilities to various groups: customers, employees, shareholders, suppliers, neighbors, the community, and the nation.

O b j e c t i v e   **7**
Differentiate between an ethical dilemma and an ethical lapse; then list four questions that will help you decide what is ethical.

Conflicting priorities and the vast gray areas between right and wrong create ethical dilemmas for an organization's communicators.

Unfortunately, what's right for one group may be wrong for another.[32] Moreover, as you attempt to satisfy the needs of one group, you may be presented with an option that seems right on the surface but somehow feels wrong. When people must choose between conflicting loyalties and weigh difficult trade-offs, they are facing a dilemma.

An **ethical dilemma** involves choosing among alternatives that aren't clear-cut (perhaps two conflicting alternatives are both ethical and valid, or perhaps the alternatives lie somewhere in the vast gray area between right and wrong). Suppose you are president of a company that's losing money. You have a duty to your shareholders to try to cut your losses and to your employees to be fair and honest. After looking at various options, you conclude that you'll have to lay off 500 people immediately. You suspect you may have to lay off another 100 people later on, but right now you need those 100 workers to finish a project. What do you tell them? If you confess that their jobs are shaky, many of them may quit just when you need them most. However, if you tell them that the future is rosy, you'll be stretching the truth.

Unlike a dilemma, an **ethical lapse** is making a clearly unethical or illegal choice. Suppose you have decided to change jobs and have discreetly landed an interview with your boss's largest competitor. You get along great with the interviewer, who is impressed enough with you to offer you a position on the spot. The new position is a step up from your current job, and the pay is double what you're getting now. You accept the job and agree to start next month. Then, as you're shaking hands with the interviewer, she asks you to bring along profiles of your current company's 10 largest customers when you report for work. Do you comply with her request? How do you decide between what's ethical and what is not?

Laws provide ethical lines for certain types of messages.

Making Ethical Choices   One place to look for guidance is the law. If saying or writing something is clearly illegal, you have no dilemma: You obey the law. However, even though legal considerations will resolve some ethical questions, you'll often have to rely on your own judgment and principles. If your intent is honest, the statement is ethical, even though it may be factually incorrect; if your intent is to mislead or manipulate the audience, the message is unethical, regardless of whether it is true. You might look at the consequences of your message and opt for the solution that provides the greatest good to the greatest number of people, and one that you can live with.[33] You might ask yourself a set of questions[34]:

Asking the right questions can help you decide what is ethical.

- ◆ **Is this message legal?** Does it violate civil law or company policy?

- ◆ **Is this message balanced?** Does it do the most good and the least harm? Is it fair to all concerned in the short term as well as the long term? Does it promote positive win-win relationships?

- ◆ **Is it a message you can live with?** Does it make you feel good about yourself? Does it make you proud? Would you feel good about your decision if a newspaper published it? If your family knew about it?

- ◆ **Is this message feasible?** Can it work in the real world? Have you considered your position in the company? Your company's competition? Its financial and political strength? The likely costs or risks of your decision? The time available?

Organizations can foster ethical behavior
- By formalizing a written code of ethics
- By using ethics audits
- By setting a good ethical example

Motivating Ethical Choices   Some companies lay out an explicit ethical policy by using a written **code of ethics** to help employees determine what is acceptable. In addition, many managers use *ethics audits* to monitor ethical progress and to point up any weaknesses that need to be addressed. They know that being ethical is simply the right thing to do. Plus, it's contagious. Others will follow your example when they observe you being ethical and see the success you experience both in your interpersonal relationships and in your career.[35]

STRENGTHENING YOUR COMMUNICATION SKILLS

Focus on building skills in the areas where you've been weak.

Perhaps the best place to begin strengthening your communication skills is with an honest assessment of where you stand. In the next few days, watch how you handle the communication situations that arise. Try to figure out what you're doing right and what you're doing wrong. Then, as you progress through this course in the months ahead, focus on those areas in which you need the most work.

This book has been designed to provide the kind of communication practice that will prepare you to get the job you want, to boost your chances for a promotion, to start your own business, or to succeed at whatever you choose to do in the future. As you proceed through this book, you'll meet many business communicators, such as Andy McMillen of Hallmark. Their experiences will give you an insight into what it takes to communicate effectively on the job.

APPLYING WHAT YOU'VE LEARNED

In this chapter, you've met Hallmark's Andy McMillen, and throughout the book you'll meet a cross section of real people—men and women who work for some of the most fascinating organizations around. At the beginning of this chapter, you read about the challenge McMillen faced as he tried to keep communication flowing smoothly and efficiently inside Hallmark. Every chapter begins with similar slice-of-life vignette titled "On the Job: Facing a Communication Dilemma." As you read through each chapter, think about the communication problems faced by the person and the company highlighted in the vignette. Become familiar with the various concepts presented in the chapter, and imagine how they might apply to the featured scenario.

At the end of each chapter, you'll take part in an innovative simulation called "On the Job: Solving a Communication Dilemma." Each simulation starts by explaining how the highlighted company actually solved the communication dilemma you read about. Then you'll play the role of a person working in that organization, and you'll face a situation you'd encounter there. You will be presented with several communication scenarios, each with several possible courses of action. It's up to you to recommend one course of action from the simulations as homework, as teamwork, as material for in-class discussion, or in a host of other ways. These scenarios let you explore various communication ideas and apply the concepts and techniques from the chapter.

Now you're ready for the first simulation on page 20. As you tackle each problem, think about the material you covered in this chapter and consider your own experience as a communicator. You'll probably be surprised to discover how much you already know about business communication.

SUMMARY OF LEARNING OBJECTIVES

1 **Explain why effective communication is important to organizations and how it can help you succeed in business.** Communication is the lifeblood of organizations, and effective communication improves an organization's productivity, image, and responsiveness. Communication is effective when it helps people understand each other, stimulates others to take action, and encourages others to think in new ways. It helps you speed problem solution, strengthen decision making, coordinate work flow, cement business relationships, clarify promotional materials, enhance your professional image, and improve your response to stakeholders. Good communication skills increase your chances for career success and your ability to adapt to the changing workplace.

2 **Discuss four changes in the workplace that are intensifying the need to communicate effectively.** Technological advances such as the Internet and portable communication devices make it possible for employees to telecommute; using such devices also highlights employees' ability to write and speak clearly. Increased cultural diversity in the workforce requires employees to adapt their communication so that they can be understood by different cultures. An abundance of information and the need to share knowledge with others places a greater demand on the ability to organize and communicate one's thoughts. Increased use of teams requires mastery of interpersonal skills such as listening, giving feedback, working collaboratively, and resolving conflict.

3 **Describe how organizations share information internally and externally.** Within an organization, communication occurs formally or informally. The formal communication network can be depicted as an organization chart, with information flowing downward from managers to employees, upward from employees to managers, and horizontally between departments. The informal communication network, or grapevine, follows the path of casual conversation and has no set pattern of flow. Communication between organizations and the outside world can be as formal as a news release carefully prepared by a marketing or public relations team or as informal as talking with a customer or letting one's appearance transmit an impression of the organization.

4 **List and briefly define the six phases of the communication process.** The communication process occurs in six phases: First, the sender has an idea (conceives a thought and wants to share it). Second, the sender encodes the idea (puts it into message form). Third, the sender transmits the message (sends the message using a specific channel and medium). Fourth, the receiver gets the message (receives the physical message by hearing or reading it). Fifth, the receiver decodes the message (absorbs and understands the meaning). And sixth, the receiver sends feedback (responds to the message and signals that response to the sender).

5 **Identify and briefly discuss four types of communication barriers.** First, perceptual differences affect how we see the world; no two people perceive things exactly the same way. Perception also influences how we develop language, which depends on shared definitions for meaning and is shaped by our culture. Second, restrictive structures and management block effective communication. Formal channels tend to cause distortion, as each link in the communication channel holds the potential for misinterpretation. Similarly, if managers aren't diligent in their efforts to communicate down the formal network, their messages can become fragmented so that employees never get the "big picture." Third, distractions can be physical (from poor acoustics to illegible copy), emotional, attributed to poor listening, or the result of information overload. And fourth, deceptive communication tactics are used by unethical communicators to manipulate their receivers.

6 **Discuss four guidelines for overcoming communication barriers.** First, adopting an audience-centered approach to communication means focusing on your audience and caring about their needs—which means finding out as much as you can about audience members, especially if your audience is from a different culture. Second, fostering an open communication climate means encouraging employee contributions, candor, and honesty. You can create an open climate by modifying the number of organizational levels and by facilitating feedback. Third, creating lean and efficient messages means not communicating unnecessary information and making necessary information easy to get. You can send better messages by reducing the number of messages, minimizing distractions, and using technology responsibly. And fourth, committing to ethical communication means including relevant information that is true in every sense and not deceptive in any way.

7 **Differentiate between an ethical dilemma and an ethical lapse; then list four questions that will help you decide what is ethical.** An ethical dilemma involves choosing between two or more alternatives that are neither clearly ethical nor clearly unethical, such as alternatives that are all ethical but conflicting or alternatives that lie somewhere in the gray areas between right and wrong. An ethical lapse involves choosing an alternative that is clearly unethical or illegal, perhaps placing your own desire or ambition above the welfare of others. One way to decide whether a decision is ethical is to ask yourself four questions: (1) Is this decision legal? (2) Is this decision balanced? (3) Is it a decision you can live with? (4) Is it feasible?

SOLVING A COMMUNICATION DILEMMA AT HALLMARK

Hallmark relies on effective communication to keep employees informed about new products, the company's financial status, changes in employee benefits, and so on. To keep Hallmark's communication climate open and to ensure that all employees receive the information they need, McMillen uses every tool available to him in the formal communication network.

Focusing on all the various audiences at Hallmark, McMillen oversees several company publications. *Noon News* is a professionally designed and produced newsletter for all company employees. It's published every day and, much like a small-town newspaper, fosters a sense of community with personal bits of information (such as birthdays and anniversaries), want ads, reminders of such things as health plan enrollment deadlines, and information on company products and finances. Another internal publication is *Directions,* which distributes information to managers. It has no established publication schedule, since its purpose is to give managers important company information before it becomes public. McMillen keeps up with technology by using several computer-monitor signboards (in various locations throughout the headquarters building) to display information that was too late for print deadlines.

To facilitate feedback from employees, McMillen schedules regular face-to-face meetings with company president and CEO Irvine Hockaday. Several times a year McMillen schedules CEO Forums, at

which Hockaday meets with about 50 employees selected at random from all company divisions. For 90 minutes employees can discuss their concerns directly with the head of the company. With no predetermined agenda, the participants are free to bring up anything they want to discuss. Says McMillen, "The forums are purely for mid-management and below so there's no intimidation factor. You can talk to Irv about anything, and you don't have to worry about your VP sitting there taking notes. It's a terrific opportunity for dialogue." Four times a year McMillen arranges a Corporate Town Hall, at which Hockaday holds sessions for 400 employees. Unlike the CEO Forums, these meetings have an agenda and a specific topic. For the first 30 minutes, Hockaday talks about a specific company issue, and then he opens the meeting for an hour of discussion.

Communication also occurs throughout the informal network when people chat together or talk by telephone, in memos, and by electronic mail. Whether the communication is formal or informal, Hallmark cares enough to strive for the very best, and it's McMillen's job to make sure that all necessary information is delivered effectively and efficiently.

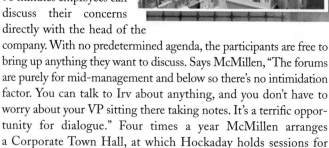

Your Mission You are manager of communications at Hallmark's corporate headquarters. In this position, you're responsible for both internal and external communication. Use your knowledge of communication to choose the best response for each of the following situations. Be prepared to explain why your choice is best.

1. The company's medical insurance plan for the next year contains substantial changes from this year's plan. To maintain Hallmark's open communication climate, how should this information be distributed to employees?

   a. Have the company president present the information at Corporate Town Hall meetings so that employees can give him feedback on their reactions to the changes.
   b. Detail the changes in *Noon News*.
   c. Publish details in *Directions*, so that managers will be able to answer any questions from employees, and summarize the major changes in *Noon News*, so that employees get the overall picture.
   d. Describe the changes in the annual benefits statement sent to each employee.

2. A manager has asked for your help. Her team is responsible for shipping party products, but shipments have been falling behind schedule. She confides that many team members are just going through the motions and not giving their best to the job. As one way of improving performance, she wants to send a memo to everyone in the department, and she's asked you to recommend an approach. Which of the following approaches would be the most ethical and effective?

   a. Tell employees that the team's performance is not as good as it could be, and ask for ideas on how to improve the situation.
   b. Explain that you'll have to fire the next person you see giving less than 100 percent (even though you know company policy prevents you from actually doing so).

   c. Ask employees to monitor one another and report problems to the department manager.
   d. Tell all employees that if team performance does not improve, wages will be reduced and evaluations will not be positive.

3. A rumor begins circulating that a major product line will be dropped and the workers in that area will be laid off. The rumor is false. What is the first action you should take?

   a. Put a notice on the computer-monitor signboards denying the rumor.
   b. Publish a denial in *Directions* asking all managers to tell their employees that the rumor is false.
   c. Schedule a meeting with all employees on the affected product line. At the meeting have the company president explain the facts and publicly state that the rumor is false.
   d. Ignore the rumor. Like all false rumors it will eventually die out.

4. In collaboration with a software company, Hallmark has developed PC software that helps users design their own greeting cards. Hallmark's development team wants employees to try out the new product and make comments. What is the best way for the team to get feedback from fellow employees?

   a. Announce the product in *Noon News*, ask for volunteers to test the software, and include a detailed survey to be returned to the development team.
   b. Publish an edition of *Directions* that explains the new product and asks managers to recruit employee testers and to get their feedback.
   c. Have the president announce the introduction at a Corporate Town Hall session and ask for help in getting the needed feedback.
   d. Send all employees an e-mail message that asks for volunteers and directs interested employees to a download site on the intranet (which includes a detailed survey to be filled out online).[36]

TEST YOUR KNOWLEDGE

1. Define *communication* and list four of the eight benefits of effective communication.

2. How is technology changing communication in the workplace?

3. How does internal communication differ from external communication?

4. In what directions can information travel within an organization's formal hierarchy?

5. What is the grapevine, and why should managers know how it works?

6. In which of the six phases of the communication process do messages get encoded and decoded?

7. How can information overload affect communication?

8. Why should communicators take an audience-centered approach to communication?

9. How does corporate culture affect the communication climate within an organization?

10. Define *ethics*, and explain what ethical communication covers.

INTERACTIVE LEARNING

USE THIS TEXT'S ONLINE RESOURCE

Visit the myPHLIP Web site at www.prenhall.com/thill. For Chapter 1, take advantage of the interactive "Study Guide" to test your chapter knowledge. Get instant feedback on whether you need additional studying. Read the "Current Events" articles to get the latest on chapter topics, and complete the exercises—as specified by your instructor.

This site's "Study Hall" helps you succeed in this course. "Talk in the Hall" lets you leave messages and meet new friends online. If you have a question, you can "Ask the Tutor." And to get a better grade in this course, you can find more help at "Writing Skills," "Study Skills," and "Study Tips."

The "Research Area" helps you locate a wealth of information to use in course assignments. Plus, you can send a message to online research experts, who will help you find exactly the information you need.

APPLY YOUR KNOWLEDGE

1. Why do you think good communication in an organization improves employees' attitudes and performance? Explain briefly.

2. Under what circumstances might you want to limit the feedback you receive from an audience of readers or listeners? Explain briefly.

3. Would written or spoken messages be more susceptible to noise? Why?

4. As a manager, how can you impress on your employees the importance of including both negative and positive information in messages?

5. **Ethical Choices** Because of your excellent communication skills, your boss always asks you to write his reports for him. When you overhear the CEO complimenting him on his logical organization and clear writing style, he responds as if he'd written all those reports himself. What kind of ethical choice does this represent? What can you do in this situation? Briefly explain your solution and your reasoning.

PRACTICE YOUR KNOWLEDGE

DOCUMENT FOR ANALYSIS

Read the following document; then (1) analyze the strengths and weaknesses of each sentence and (2) revise the document so that it follows this chapter's guidelines.

It has come to my attention that many of you are lying on your time cards. If you come in late, you should not put 8:00 on your card. If you take a long lunch, you should not put 1:00 on your time card. I will not stand for this type of cheating. I simply have no choice but to institute a time-clock system. Beginning next Monday, all employees will have to punch in and punch out whenever they come and go from the work area.

The time clock will be right by the entrance to each work area, so you have no excuse for not punching in. Anyone who is late for work or late coming back from lunch more than three times will have to answer to me. I don't care if you had to take a nap or if you girls had to shop. This is a place of business, and we do not want to be taken advantage of by slackers who are cheaters to boot.

It is too bad that a few bad apples always have to spoil things for everyone.

EXERCISES

1–1. **Internal Communication: Planning the Flow** For the following tasks, identify the necessary direction of communication (downward, upward, horizontal), suggest an appropriate type of communication (casual conversation, formal interview, meeting, workshop, videotape, newsletter, memo, bulletin board notice, and so on), and briefly explain your suggestion.

   a. As personnel manager, you want to announce details about this year's company picnic.

   b. As director of internal communication, you want to convince top management of the need for a company newsletter.

   c. As production manager, you want to make sure that both the sales manager and the finance manager receive your scheduling estimates.

   d. As marketing manager, you want to help employees understand the company's goals and its attitudes toward workers.

1–2. **Communication Networks: Formal or Informal?** An old college friend phoned you out of the blue to say: "Truth is, I had to call you. You'd better keep this under your hat, but when I heard my company was buying you guys out, I was dumbfounded. I had no idea that a company as large as yours could sink so fast. Your group must be in pretty bad shape over there!" Your stomach turned suddenly queasy, and you felt a chill go up your spine. You'd heard nothing about any buyout, and before you could even get your college friend off the phone, you were wondering what you should do. Of the following, choose one course of action and briefly explain your choice.

   a. Contact your CEO directly and relate what you've heard.

   b. Ask co-workers whether they've heard anything about a buyout.

   c. Discuss the phone call confidentially with your immediate supervisor.

   d. Keep quiet about the whole thing (there's nothing you can do about the situation anyway).

1–3. Ethical Choices In less than a page, explain why you think each of the following is or is not ethical.

    a. De-emphasizing negative test results in a report on your product idea

    b. Taking a computer home to finish a work-related assignment

    c. Telling an associate and close friend that she'd better pay more attention to her work responsibilities or management will fire her

    d. Recommending the purchase of excess equipment to use up your allocated funds before the end of the fiscal year so that your budget won't be cut next year

1–4. The Changing Workplace: Always in Touch Technological devices such as faxes, cell phones, e-mail, and voice mail are making businesspeople easily accessible at any time of day or night, at work and at home. What effects might frequent intrusions have on their professional and personal lives? Please explain your answer in less than a page.

1–5. Internet As a manufacturer of aerospace, energy, and environmental equipment, Lockheed Martin has developed a code of ethics that it expects employees to abide by. Visit Lockheed Martin's Web site at www.lockheedmartin.com/exeth/ethset.html and review the six important virtues and the company's code of ethics (scroll down). In a brief paragraph, describe three specific examples of things you could do that would violate these provisions. Now scroll down and study the list of "Warning Signs" of ethics violations and take the "Quick Quiz." In another brief paragraph, describe how you could use this advice to avoid ethical problems as you write business letters, memos, and reports. Submit both paragraphs to your instructor.

1–6. Communication Process: Know Your Audience Top management has asked you to speak at an upcoming executive meeting to present your arguments for a more open communication climate. Which of the following would be most important for you to know about your audience before giving your presentation? (Briefly explain your choice.)

    a. How many top managers will be attending

    b. What management style members of your audience prefer

    c. How firmly these managers are set in their ways

1–7. Ethical Choices Your boss often uses you as a sounding board for her ideas. Now she seems to want you to act as an unofficial messenger, passing her ideas along to the staff without mentioning her involvement and informing her of what staff members say without telling them you're going to repeat their responses. What questions should you ask yourself as you consider the ethical implications of this situation? Write a short paragraph explaining the ethical choice you will make in this situation.[37]

1–8. Formal Communication: Self-Introduction Write a memo or prepare an oral presentation introducing yourself to your instructor and your class. Include information such as your background, interests, achievements, and goals. If you write a memo, keep it under one page, and use Figure 1–3 as a model for the format. If you prepare an oral presentation, plan to speak for no more than 2 minutes.

1–9. Teamwork Your boss has asked your work group to research and report on corporate child-care facilities. Of course, you'll want to know who (besides your boss) will be reading your report. Working with two team members, list four or five other things you'll want to know about the situation and about your audience before starting your research. Briefly explain why the items on your list are important.

1–10. Communication Process: Analyzing Miscommunication Use the six phases of the communication process to analyze a miscommunication you've recently had with a co-worker, supervisor, classmate, teacher, friend, or family member. What idea were you trying to share? How did you encode and transmit it? Did the receiver get the message? Did the receiver correctly decode the message? How do you know? Based on your analysis, identify and explain the barriers that prevented your successful communication in this instance.

1–11. Ethical Choices You've been given the critical assignment of selecting the site for your company's new plant. After months of negotiations with landowners, numerous cost calculations, and investments in ecological, social, and community impact studies, you are about to recommend building the new plant on the Lansing River site. Now, just 15 minutes before your big presentation to top management, you discover a possible mistake in your calculations; site-purchase costs appear to be $50,000 more than you calculated, nearly 10 percent over budget. You don't have time to recheck all your figures, so you're tempted to just go ahead with your recommendation and ignore any discrepancies. You're worried that management won't approve this purchase if you can't present a clean, unqualified solution. You also know that many projects run over their original estimates, so you can probably work the extra cost into the budget later. On your way to the meeting room, you make your final decision. In a few paragraphs, explain the decision you made.

1–12. Communication Barriers: Eliminating Noise Whenever you report negative information to your boss, she never passes it along to her colleagues or supervisors, even though you think the information is important and should be shared. What barriers to communication are operating in this situation? What can you do to encourage more sharing of this kind of information?

GOING ONLINE EXERCISES

Using the Internet to Explore International Business Communication, page 14

Skillful communication is critical to the success of your business or organizational relationships. To help you communicate more effectively, explore IABC's resources, including its links to a global network of communicators.

1. Describe several of IABC's resources. How could the manual "Business Management for Communicators" be useful to you in public relations or organizational communication?
2. What professional benefits does IABC offer to business communicators?
3. What is the IABC Code of Ethics?

To complete this exercise, log on to this text's Web site at www.prenhall.com/thill. Select Chapter 1, then select "Student Resources," click on the name of the featured Web site, and follow the detailed navigational directions.

Tips on Using the Web

To reach any of the Web sites listed in this book, you need not type the URLs into your browser. Just go to the Web site for this book at www.prenhall.com/thill. There, you'll find live links that take you straight to the site of your choice.

If you get an error message when you try to get to a site mentioned in this text, go to www.ixquick.com. Insert the name of the site in the space provided, and press "search." If the site you're seeking is still operating, the results of the search will usually provide a live link to it.

If you're new to using the Web, you can learn more by taking an Internet tour at www.lib.berkeley.edu/TeachingLib/Guides/Internet/FindInfo.html, at www.provide.net/~bfield/polaris/tour0000.htm, or at www.learnthenet.com.

As you visit sites around the Internet, be sure to evaluate your online sources before making use of the information you find. For an exhaustive list of sites pertaining to this topic, go to www.surfwax.com, and enter "evaluation of information sources" and related phrases in the search box.

COMMUNICATING IN TEAMS: COLLABORATION, LISTENING, NONVERBAL, AND MEETING SKILLS

chapter 2

After studying this chapter, you will be able to

1 Highlight the advantages and disadvantages of using teams

2 Identify the characteristics of effective teams

3 Discuss the tasks involved in preparing team messages and list nine guidelines for improvement

4 Describe the listening process and discuss three barriers that interfere with this process

5 Clarify the importance of nonverbal communication and briefly describe six categories of nonverbal expression

6 Explain how you can improve meeting productivity through preparation, leadership, and participation

On the job:

FACING A COMMUNICATION DILEMMA AT AMERICAN EXPRESS

Taking Charge of Business through Teamwork

www.americanexpress.com

Don't leave home without it! That says it all—a powerful message about the dangers of traveling without an American Express Card tucked into your pocket. Millions of customers heed that advice each day, relying on the company to meet their financial and travel needs and, in the process, making American Express not only the world's largest travel agency but also a leading provider of global financial services.

However, the slogan could as easily apply to the 84,000 American Express employees who must work together on behalf on their customers. Wherever they go, whatever they do on the job, American Express employees need one crucial element at all times—teamwork—and they better not leave home without it. Managers are leaders, not bosses. Employees are partners, not competitors. The team concept permeates American Express. Just ask David House, president of American Express Worldwide Establishment Services, the division that signs up merchants to accept the American Express card.

To ensure the success of his division, House relies heavily on effective communication among team members and between teams and upper management. It's up to House to get all employees to contribute to and participate in the team approach, whether they're telecommuting from home in Los Angeles or working from company offices in London or Lisbon. If you were David House, how would you develop an effective team? What would you need to know about getting team members to collaborate? And how could you help your team members improve their listening, nonverbal communication, and meeting skills?[1]

With over 58,000 employees in the United States, American Express is recognized as a top corporate employer (in leading publications such as Fortune's "100 Best Companies to Work For"). American Express helps its employees succeed in their jobs by encouraging teamwork and free-flowing communication throughout the organization. As a financial services giant and as the world's number one travel agency, the company issues travelers checks, publishes magazines, and provides financial advisory services.

WORKING IN TEAMS

American Express's David House knows that working in teams and small groups puts people's communication skills to the test. A **team** is a unit of two or more people who work together to achieve a goal. Team members have a shared mission and are collectively responsible for their work.[2]

Team members may be responsible for writing reports, giving oral presentations, and attending meetings. Whether the goal is to solve a problem, monitor a process, or investigate an opportunity, team members must communicate effectively among themselves and with people outside their team. Thus companies are looking for people who can interact successfully in teams and make useful contributions while working together. Some companies even base pay raises and promotions on an employee's effectiveness as a team player.

In a recent survey of Fortune 1000 executives, 83 percent said their firms are working in teams or moving in that direction.[3] Why are teams so important in today's workplace? One reason is performance. A recent study of 232 organizations across 16 countries and

Studies show that teams contribute to an organization's performance.

more than eight industries revealed that organizations working in teams experience the highest improvement in performance.[4] Another reason is creativity. Teams encourage creativity in workers through **participative management,** involving employees in the company's decision making. At Kodak, for example, using teams has allowed the company to reduce by 50 percent the amount of time it takes to move a new product from the drawing board to store shelves.[5]

Types of Teams

The type, structure, and composition of individual teams varies within an organization. Companies can create *formal teams* that become part of the organization's structure, or they may establish *informal teams,* which aren't part of the formal organization but are formed to solve a problem, work on a specific activity, or encourage employee participation.

Two popular types of informal teams are problem-solving teams and task forces.

Problem-solving teams and task forces are informal teams that assemble to resolve specific issues and disband once their goal has been accomplished. Team members often include representatives of many departments so that those who have a stake in the outcome are allowed to provide input.[6] When Saint Francis Hospital in Tulsa, Oklahoma established a task force to find ways to reduce the cost of supplies, team members came from departments such as surgery, laboratory, nursing, financial planning, administration, and food service. This cross-department team not only helped the hospital save money by curbing supply waste but also generated excitement among hospital employees about working together for common goals.[7]

Committees are long-term teams.

In contrast to problem-solving teams and task forces, a committee usually has a long life span and may become a permanent part of the organizational structure. Committees typically deal with regularly recurring tasks. For example, a grievance committee may be formed as a permanent resource for handling employee complaints and concerns.

Virtual teams conduct their business by using advanced communication technology.

Virtual teams bring together geographically distant employees to accomplish goals. A company may have plants and offices around the world, but it can use computer networks, teleconferencing, e-mail, and global transportation to build teams that are as effective as those in organizations functioning under a single roof. At British Petroleum, for example, virtual teams link workers in the Gulf of Mexico with teams working in the eastern Atlantic and around the globe. By using a virtual team network, the company decreased the number of helicopter trips to offshore oil platforms, avoided refinery shutdowns (because technical experts at other locations were able to handle problems remotely), and experienced a significant reduction in construction rework, among other benefits.[8]

Objective 1

Highlight the advantages and disadvantages of using teams.

Teams can play a vital role in helping an organization reach its goals. However, they are not appropriate for every situation. When deciding whether to use teams, managers must weigh both the advantages and disadvantages of doing so.[9]

Advantages and Disadvantages of Teams

At their best, teams can be an extremely useful forum for making key decisions. The interaction of the participants leads to good decisions based on the combined intelligence of the group. An organization's decision making can benefit from the team approach in the following ways:[10]

- ◆ **Increased information and knowledge.** By aggregating the resources of several individuals, teams bring more information to the decision process.

- ◆ **Increased diversity of views.** Teams bring many different perspectives to the decision process.

- ◆ **Increased acceptance of a solution.** Team members who participate in making a decision are more likely to enthusiastically support the decision and encourage others to accept it. Because they share in the final product, they are committed to seeing it succeed.

Teams generally achieve performance levels that exceed what would have been accomplished had the members worked independently, perhaps because teams have the potential to unleash vast amounts of creativity and energy in workers. Motivation and

Going Online

Participate in a Team-Based Organization

At the Center for the Study of Work Teams (CSWT) you'll learn about "collaborative work systems." The site's advantages include links to many other sites about working in teams, a newsletter with articles on teaming tips and communication techniques, and research projects on theoretical and applied knowledge about teams. CSWT lists free publications and information on conferences and workshops. Log on to see what sources are available for career opportunities.

www.workteams.unt.edu

To reach this Web site, go to www.prehall.com/thill *(the Web site for this text). Select Chapter 2, then select "Student Resources." There you'll find a current live link that will take you straight to the site.*

performance are often increased because workers share a sense of purpose and mutual accountability. Teams can also fill the individual worker's need to belong to a group. Furthermore, they can reduce employee boredom, increase feelings of dignity and self-worth, and reduce stress and tension between workers.

Although teamwork has many advantages, it also has a number of potential disadvantages. At their worst, teams are unproductive and frustrating, and they waste everyone's time. Some may actually be counterproductive, because they may arrive at bad decisions. For instance, when people are pressured to conform, they may abandon their sense of personal responsibility and agree to ill-founded plans. Similarly, a team may develop **groupthink,** the willingness of individual members to set aside their personal opinions and go along with everyone else, even if everyone else is wrong, simply because belonging to the team is more important to them than making the right decision. Groupthink can lead to poor-quality decisions and ill-advised actions, even inducing people to act unethically.

Some team members may have a **hidden agenda**—private motives that affect the group's interaction. Sam might want to prove that he's more powerful than Sherry; Sherry might be trying to share the risk of making a decision; and Don might be looking for a chance to postpone doing "real" work. Each person's hidden agenda can detract from the team's effectiveness.

And the potential disadvantages don't stop there. **Free riders** are team members who don't contribute their fair share to the group's activities because they aren't being held individually accountable for their work. The free-ride attitude can lead to certain tasks going unfulfilled. Still another drawback to teamwork is the high cost of coordinating group activities. Aligning schedules, arranging meetings, and coordinating individual parts of a project can eat up a lot of time and money. Finally, teams simply aren't effective for all situations. As management guru Peter Drucker puts it, "When the ship goes down, you don't call a meeting. The captain gives an order or everybody drowns."[11]

As CEO of Andes Chemical Corporation, Fernando Espinosa encourages teamwork and welcomes employee involvement. When workers contribute and share ideas, the company meets its goals, employees feel motivated by their common sense of purpose, and they stay with the company longer. *Hispanic Business* magazine named Espinosa Entrepreneur of the Year for his team philosophy and business success.

Group members' personal motives can interfere with the group's efforts to accomplish its mission.

Group Dynamics

The interactions and processes that take place in a team are called **group dynamics.** Some teams are more effective than others simply because the dynamics of the group facilitate member input and the resolution of differences. To keep things moving forward, productive teams also tend to develop rules that are conducive to business. Often these rules are unstated; they just become standard group practice, or **norms**—informal standards of conduct that members share and that guide member behavior. For example, there may be an unspoken agreement that it's okay to be 10 minutes late for meetings but not 15 minutes late.

When a team has a strong identity, the members observe team rules religiously: They're upset by any deviation and feel a great deal of pressure to conform. This loyalty can be positive, giving members a strong commitment to one another and highly motivating them to see that the team succeeds. However, an overly strong identity could lead to negative conditions such as groupthink.

Group dynamics are the interactions and processes that take place in a team.

Team Roles Members of a team can play various roles, which fall into three categories (see Table 2–1). Members who assume **self-oriented roles** are motivated mainly to fulfill personal needs, so they tend to be less productive than other members. Far more likely to contribute to team goals are those members who assume **team-maintenance roles** to help everyone work well together and those members who assume **task-facilitating roles** to help solve problems or make decisions.

To a great extent, the roles that individuals assume in a group depend on their status in that group and their reasons for joining the group. Status depends on many variables, including personal attractiveness, competence in a particular field, past successes, education, age, social background, and organizational position. A person's status also varies from team to team. In most teams, as people try to establish their relative status, an undercurrent of tension can get in the way of the real work. Until roles and status have stabilized, a team may have trouble accomplishing its goals.

Each member of a group plays a role that affects the outcome of the group's activities.

Roles are often determined by status, which can vary from team to team.

Table 2–1 Team Roles People Play		
Self-Oriented Roles	*Team-Maintenance Roles*	*Task-Facilitating Roles*
Controlling: dominating others by exhibiting superiority or authority	**Encouraging:** drawing out other members by showing verbal and nonverbal support, praise, or agreement	**Initiating:** getting the team started on a line of inquiry
Withdrawing: retiring from the team either by becoming silent or by refusing to deal with a particular aspect of the team's work	**Harmonizing:** reconciling differences among team members through mediation or by using humor to relieve tension	**Information giving or seeking:** offering (or seeking) information relevant to questions facing the team
Attention seeking: calling attention to oneself and demanding recognition from others	**Compromising:** offering to yield on a point in the interest of reaching a mutually acceptable decision	**Coordinating:** showing relationships among ideas, clarifying issues, summarizing what the team has done
Diverting: focusing the team's discussion on topics of interest to the individual rather than on those relevant to the task		**Procedure setting:** suggesting decision-making procedures that will move the team toward a goal

Five Phases of Team Decisions   While teams grow and evolve in their own ways, research shows that most teams typically reach a decision by passing through five phases:[12]

Group decision making passes through five phases: orientation, conflict, emergence, and reinforcement.

- ◆ **Orientation.** Team members socialize, establish their roles, and begin to define their task or purpose.

- ◆ **Conflict.** Team members begin to discuss their positions and become more assertive in establishing their roles. If members have been carefully selected to represent a variety of viewpoints and expertise, disagreements are a natural part of this phase.

- ◆ **Brainstorm.** Team members air all the options and discuss the pros and cons fully. At the end of this phase, members begin to settle on a single solution to the problem.

- ◆ **Emergence.** Team members reach a decision. Consensus is reached when the team finds a solution that is acceptable enough for all members to support (even if they have reservations). This consensus happens only after all members have had an opportunity to communicate their positions and feel that they have been listened to.

- ◆ **Reinforcement.** Group feeling is rebuilt and the solution is summarized. Members receive their assignments for carrying out the group's decision, and they make arrangements for following up on those assignments.

These five phases almost always occur regardless of what task or what type of decision is being considered. Moreover, team members naturally use this process, even when they lack experience or training in team communication.

DEVELOPING AN EFFECTIVE TEAM

Objective

2

Identify the characteristics of effective teams.

In effective collaborative relationships, all team members recognize that each individual brings valuable assets, knowledge, and skills to the team, says American Express's David House. They are willing to exchange information, examine issues, and work through conflicts that arise. They trust each other, looking toward the greater good of the team and organization rather than focusing on personal agendas, making unilateral decisions, or pulling power plays.[13]

Developing an effective team is an ongoing process. The characteristics of effective teams include the following:[14]

Effective teams
- understand their purpose
- communicate openly
- build consensus
- think creatively
- stay focused

- ◆ **Clear sense of purpose.** Team members clearly understand the task at hand, what is expected of them, and their role on the team.

Checklist: Developing an Effective Team

Build a Sense of Fairness in Decision Making

✓ Encourage debate and disagreement without fear of reprisal
✓ Allow members to communicate openly and honestly
✓ Consider all proposals
✓ Build consensus by allowing team members to examine, compare, and reconcile differences
✓ Avoid quick votes
✓ Keep everyone informed
✓ Present all the facts

Select Team Members Wisely

✓ Involve stakeholders
✓ Limit size to no more than 12 to 15 members
✓ Select members with a diversity of views
✓ Select creative thinkers

Make Working in Teams a Top Management Priority

✓ Recognize and reward individual and group performance

✓ Provide ample training opportunities for employees to develop interpersonal, decision-making, and problem-solving skills
✓ Allow enough time for the team to develop and learn how to work together

Manage Conflict Constructively

✓ Share leadership
✓ Encourage equal participation
✓ Discuss disagreements
✓ Focus on the issues, not the people
✓ Don't let things get out of hand

Stay on Track

✓ Make sure everyone understands the team's purpose
✓ Communicate what is expected of team members
✓ Don't deviate from the core assignment
✓ Develop and adhere to a schedule
✓ Develop rules and obey norms

◆ **Open and honest communication.** The team culture encourages discussion and debate. Team members speak openly and honestly, without the threat of anger, resentment, or retribution. They listen to and value feedback from others. As a result, all team members participate.

◆ **Decision by consensus.** All decisions are arrived at by consensus. No easy, quick votes are taken.

◆ **Creative thinking.** Effective teams encourage original thinking, considering options beyond the usual.

◆ **Focused.** Team members get to the core issues of the problem and stay focused on key issues.

Learning these team skills takes time and practice, so many companies now offer employees training in building their team skills. At Saturn, for example, every team member goes through a minimum of 92 hours of training in problem solving and people skills. Saturn teaches team members how to reach a consensus point they call "70 percent comfortable but 100 percent supportive." At that level of consensus, everybody supports the solution.[15] For a brief review of characteristics of effective teams, see this chapter's "Checklist: Developing an Effective Team."

Employees can learn effective team skills on the job.

Understanding Conflict

Functioning effectively in teams requires many skills. However, none is more important than the ability to handle conflict—clashes over differences in ideas, opinions, goals, or procedures. Conflict can be both constructive and destructive to a team's effectiveness. Conflict is constructive if it increases the involvement of team members and results in the solution to a problem. Conflict is destructive if it diverts energy from more important issues, destroys the morale of teams or individual team members, or polarizes or divides the team.[16]

 Conflict can arise for any number of reasons. Teams and individuals may believe they are competing for scarce or declining resources, such as money, information, and supplies. Team members may disagree about who is responsible for a specific task (usually the

Conflict is not necessarily bad, as long as it is handled in a constructive fashion.

result of poorly defined responsibilities and job boundaries). Poor communication can lead to misunderstandings and misperceptions about other team members, and intentionally withholding information can undermine member trust. Basic differences in values, attitudes, and personalities may lead to arguments. Power struggles may result when one party questions the authority of another or when people or teams with limited authority attempt to increase their power or exert more influence. And conflict can also arise because individuals or teams are pursuing different goals.[17]

Resolving Conflict

Effective teams know how to manage conflict so that it makes a positive contribution.[18] The following measures can help team members successfully resolve conflict:

- ◆ **Proaction.** Deal with minor conflict before it becomes major conflict.
- ◆ **Communication.** Get those directly involved in the conflict to participate in resolving it.
- ◆ **Openness.** Get feelings out in the open before dealing with the main issues.
- ◆ **Research.** Seek factual reasons for the problem before seeking solutions.
- ◆ **Flexibility.** Don't let anyone lock into a position before considering other solutions.
- ◆ **Fair play.** Don't let anyone avoid a fair solution by hiding behind the rules.
- ◆ **Alliance.** Get parties to fight together against an "outside force" instead of against each other.

Overcoming Resistance

Part of dealing with conflict is learning how to persuade other people to accept your point of view. In a business situation, reason usually prevails. However, you sometimes encounter people who react emotionally. When you face irrational resistance, try to remain calm and detached so that you can avoid destructive confrontations and present your position in a convincing manner.

When you encounter resistance or hostility, try to maintain your composure and address the other person's emotional needs.

- ◆ **Express understanding.** Most people are ashamed of reacting emotionally in business situations. Show that you sympathize. You might say, "I can understand that this change might be difficult, and if I were in your position, I might be reluctant myself." Help the other person relax and talk about his or her anxiety so that you have a chance to offer reassurance.[19]
- ◆ **Make people aware of their resistance.** When people are noncommittal and silent, they may be tuning you out without even knowing why. Continuing with your argument is futile. Deal directly with the resistance, without being accusing. You might say, "You seem cool to this idea. Have I made some faulty assumptions?" Such questions force people to face and define their resistance.[20]
- ◆ **Evaluate others' objections fairly.** Don't simply repeat yourself. Focus on what the other person is expressing, both the words and the feelings. Get the person to open up so that you can understand the basis for the resistance. Others' objections may raise legitimate points that you'll need to discuss, or they may reveal problems that you'll need to minimize.[21]
- ◆ **Hold your arguments until the other person is ready for them.** Getting your point across depends as much on the other person's frame of mind as it does on your arguments. You can't assume that a strong argument will speak for itself. By becoming more audience-centered, you will learn to address the other person's emotional needs first.

The whole purpose of developing a team that's effective is to get members to collaborate on necessary tasks. One of those tasks is communication. Team members must often work together on preparing messages.

COLLABORATING ON TEAM MESSAGES

Collaborative messages, or team messages, involve working with other writers to produce a single document or presentation. For instance, you might sit down with your boss to plan a memo, work independently during the writing phase, and then ask your boss to review the message and suggest revisions. On the other hand, you might participate in an all-out team effort to write your company's business plan or prepare and present a major report.

Collaborative messages can involve a project manager, researchers, writers, typists, graphic artists, and editors. Because team messages bring multiple perspectives and various skills to a project, the result is often better than could have been produced by an individual working alone. Still, collaborative messages have their challenges. To begin with, team members often come from different backgrounds and have different work habits or concerns: A technical expert may focus on accuracy and scientific standards; an editor on organization and coherence; and a manager on schedules, cost, and corporate goals. Team members also differ in writing styles and personality traits.

Hewlett-Packard's Industrial Lab investigative team collaborated to write a major report on research-and-development (R&D) contributions to the company. Their team effort produced a document that assessed the impact and value of all future R&D.

Using Technology to Collaborate

Videoconferencing allows people in several locations to "meet" via video and audio links. In fact, a job candidate may be asked to sit down on the spur of the moment for an interview via videoconference with a prospective employer in another city. Similarly, a salesperson may be required to make a videoconference presentation to a roomful of customers, or a newly formed work team with members in offices around the world may be asked to brainstorm on camera.[22]

One form of videoconferencing technology is decision-making software (also called *groupware* or *electronic meeting systems*). This software offers distinct advantages. For example, participants can anonymously type any message they want, and it flashes on the screen for all to see. Such anonymity allows people to be brutally honest without penalty. In addition, this approach is as much as 55 percent faster than face-to-face meetings because chitchat is eliminated. Still, videoconferencing has its drawbacks. First, you must be a good typist. Also, those with the best ideas don't get credit for them. Finally, the process lacks the rich nonverbal feedback of face-to-face communication. For a closer look at electronic decision making, see "Using the Power of Technology—Electronic Meetings: Work Together—Wherever You Are—to Get the Results You Want."

Web technology also helps team members collaborate. More and more companies are developing large-scale work spaces on the Internet for online discussions, videoconferencing, and data sharing. The primary benefits of Web-based collaboration are that it's easy, it's cost effective, and it allows you to do multiple activities in a seamless fashion. For example, at KPMG Consulting, eight employees scattered around the globe wrote, edited, and commented on a report, using WebFlow Corp's SamePage. This software allows users to draft different sections of a document while editing other sections and participating in a Web-based discussion—all at the same time.[23] Whether sharing information, reaching decisions, or making recommendations, team members can use technology to compose, exchange, and present effective messages.

Collaborative messages benefit from multiple perspectives and various skills; however, team members may have to work hard to overcome differences in background and working habits.

Decision-making software offers anonymity, allows honesty, and saves time.

Web-based collaboration is easy, cost-effective, and efficient.

Preparing Effective Team Messages

To prepare effective team messages, you must be flexible and open to the opinions of others—focusing on your team's objectives instead of your own.[24] You must also get organized. Select a leader and clarify goals.[25] Before anyone begins to write, team members must agree on the purpose of the project and the audience. Your team must also plan

O b j e c t i v e

3

Discuss the tasks involved in preparing team messages and list nine guidelines for improvement.

Using the Power of Technology

Electronic Meetings: Work Together—Wherever You Are—to Get the Results You Want

Imagine a meeting where everyone shares ideas, but no one knows who contributed them: a meeting in which people aren't talking, but typing. Computer-supported (or electronic) meetings have been popular with big corporations since IBM introduced the technology in the 1980s. Thanks to computer conferencing, the Internet, groupware, and a variety of new, affordable software packages, you can attend a virtual meeting in the morning and, in the afternoon, enter the electronic decision room to brainstorm ideas with colleagues.

Here's How It Works

Attending a *virtual meeting* means joining (by computer) an ongoing dialogue between two or more individuals communicating over telephone lines via computer modems. The exchange is similar to e-mail, but it's interactive (like chat rooms); that is, everyone sees everyone else's message as soon as it's sent. Participants may be separated by miles, but they can exchange ideas as if they were in the same room.

Electronic meeting rooms go one step further with special electronic meeting systems (EMS), group decision support systems, and electronic voting systems. The simplest of these setups includes a large viewing screen, personal computers, and individual keypads (one for each participant). In general, the participants are all together, and the meeting is led by a trained facilitator who asks questions while participants type their responses.

With a simple keypad system, participants can view all responses, vote on an idea, and see the results immediately displayed on the large screen—whether as a graph, a simple number tally, or a complex breakdown of categories and voting trends. Discussion follows, along with subsequent votes on every aspect of the issues at hand. At the end of the meeting, the system provides a printed summary for everyone.

Are Electronic Meetings More Productive?

Electronic meetings are up to 55 percent faster than traditional meetings. Participants stay focused on the issues, and detailed statistical data help guide decision making. Plus, everyone speaks at the same time (typing responses simultaneously).

"It's the great equalizer," notes one communication expert. "Employees can share opinions anonymously—and honestly—without fear of displeasing superiors." Many employees are more candid in computer conferences than in traditional meetings or memos. Furthermore, because electronic meetings engender a true sense of shared decision making, participants are more satisfied with the results.

Still, electronic meetings can't replace the synergy and spontaneity of face-to-face meetings. In fact, electronic-meeting keyboards are sometimes set aside for vigorous group discussion. After all, the purpose of electronic meetings isn't to dwell on the technology but to enhance the group process, gather information, elicit honest thoughts and ideas, and engage members in dialogue.

CAREER APPLICATIONS

1. What advantages do in-person, face-to-face meetings have over electronic meetings?
2. What potential risks face employees and companies that don't keep up with trends in electronic meeting technology?

Make sure the final document "speaks with one voice."

the organization, format, and style of the document—after all, the final message must look and sound as if one writer prepared it. The following guidelines will help you produce team messages that are clear, seamless, and successful:[26]

- ◆ **Select team members wisely.** Choose team members who have strong interpersonal skills, understand team dynamics, and care about the project.
- ◆ **Select a responsible leader.** Identify a group leader who will keep members informed and intervene when necessary.
- ◆ **Promote cooperation.** Establish communication standards that motivate accuracy, openness, and trust.
- ◆ **Clarify goals.** Make sure team goals are aligned with individual expectations.
- ◆ **Elicit commitment.** Create a sense of ownership and shared responsibility for the document.
- ◆ **Clarify responsibilities.** Assign specific roles and establish clear lines of reporting.
- ◆ **Instill prompt action.** Establish a timeline and deadlines for every part of the project.
- ◆ **Apply technology.** Use electronic tools to communicate quickly and effectively with other team members.
- ◆ **Ensure technological compatibility.** Use the same word-processing program to facilitate combining files.

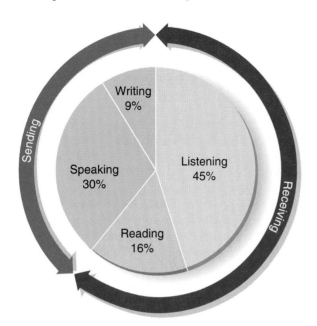

Keep in mind that team presentations can give an organization the opportunity to show off its brightest talent while capitalizing on each person's unique presentation skills. The real advantage is that you can take the collective energy and expertise of the team and create something that transcends what you could do otherwise.[27]

SPEAKING WITH TEAM MEMBERS

Given a choice, people would rather talk to each other than write to each other (see Figure 2–1). Talking takes less time and needs no composing, keyboarding, rewriting, duplicating, or distributing. Even more important, oral communication provides the opportunity for feedback. When people communicate orally, they can ask questions and test their understanding of the message; they can share ideas and work together to solve problems.

However, speaking is such an ingrained activity that we tend to do it without much thought, and that casual approach can be a problem in business. You have far less opportunity to revise your spoken words than to revise your written words. You can't cross out what you just said and start all over.

To improve your speaking skills, advises American Express's David House, be more aware of using speech as a tool for accomplishing your objectives in a business context. Break the habit of talking spontaneously, without planning *what* you're going to say or *how* you're going to say it. Before you speak, think about your purpose, your main idea, and your audience. Organize your thoughts, decide on a style that suits the occasion and your audience, and edit your remarks mentally.

Perhaps the most important thing you can do is to focus on your audience. Try to predict how your audience will react, and organize your message accordingly. As you speak, watch the other person and judge from verbal and nonverbal feedback whether your message is making the desired impression. If it isn't, revise it and try again.

Now look again at Figure 2–1. In addition to underscoring the importance of oral communication, it illustrates that people spend more time *receiving* information than transmitting it. Listening and reading are every bit as important as speaking and writing.

Listening to Team Members

Because listening is such a routine, everyday activity, few people think of developing their listening skills. Unfortunately, most of us aren't very good listeners. We may hear the words, but that doesn't mean we're actually listening to the message.[28] Most of us face so

Most people would rather talk than write.

Spoken words are more difficult to revise than written ones.

Whether speaking or writing, try to predict your audience's reaction.

The ability to listen is a vital skill in business.

Most people need to improve their listening skills.

Whether interacting with customers or with fellow employees, people at Whole Foods must know how to listen. Developing good listening skills helps team members overcome distractions so that they can work together successfully and respond to customers' needs.

many distractions that we often give speakers less than our full attention. In fact, businesses lose millions of dollars each year because of a failure to listen to and understand customers' needs.[29]

Effective listeners welcome new information and new ideas. The payoff is that they stay informed, up to date, and out of trouble. Good listening gives you an edge and increases your impact when you speak. It strengthens organizational relationships, enhances product delivery, alerts the organization to innovation from both internal and external sources, and allows the organization to manage growing diversity both in the workforce and in the customers it serves.[30]

Even so, most people listen poorly. In fact, people listen at or below a 25 percent efficiency rate, remember only about half of what's said during a 10-minute conversation, and forget half of that within 48 hours.[31] Furthermore, when questioned about material they've just heard, people are likely to get the facts mixed up. That's because effective listening requires a conscious effort and a willing mind. Learning to listen effectively can be a difficult skill, but it's one of the best ways to improve your communication skills. It enhances your performance, which leads to raises, promotions, status, and power.[32]

Types of Listening   Three types of listening differ not only in purpose but also in the amount of feedback or interaction that occurs. You can improve relationships and productivity by matching your listening style to the speaker's purpose.[33] For example, the goal of **content listening** is to understand and retain the speaker's message. You may ask questions, but basically information flows from the speaker to you. It doesn't matter that you agree or disagree, approve or disapprove—only that you understand.[34] When you listen to a regional sales manager's monthly report on how many of your products sold that month, you are listening for content.

> To be a good listener, vary the way you listen to suit the situation.

The goal of **critical listening** is to understand and evaluate the meaning of the speaker's message on several levels: the logic of the argument, the strength of the evidence, the validity of the conclusions, the implications of the message for you and your organization, the speaker's intentions and motives, and the omission of any important or relevant points. Critical listening generally involves interaction as you try to uncover the speaker's point of view and credibility.[35] When the regional sales manager presents sales projections for the next few months, you listen critically, evaluating whether the estimates are valid and what the implications are for your manufacturing department.

The goal of **empathic listening** is to understand the speaker's feelings, needs, and wants so that you can appreciate his or her point of view, regardless of whether you share that perspective. By listening in an empathic way, you help the individual vent the emotions that prevent a dispassionate approach to the subject. Avoid the temptation to give advice. Try not to judge the individual's feelings. Just let the other person talk.[36] You listen empathically when your regional sales manager tells you about the problems he had with his recreational vehicle while vacationing with his family.

Each type of listening is most effective in particular situations. To gain better control of your listening skill, examine what happens when you listen.

The Listening Process   By understanding the process of listening, you begin to understand why oral messages are so often lost. Listening involves five related activities, which usually occur in sequence:[37]

> *Objective*
>
> **4**
>
> Describe the listening process and discuss three barriers that interfere with this process.
>
> Listening involves five steps: receiving, interpreting, remembering, evaluating, and responding.

◆ **Receiving:** Physically hearing the message and taking note of it. Physical reception can be blocked by noise, impaired hearing, or inattention.

◆ **Interpreting:** Assigning meaning to sounds according to your own values, beliefs, ideas, expectations, roles, needs, and personal history. The speaker's frame of reference may be quite different from yours, so you may need to determine what the speaker really means.

◆ **Remembering:** Storing a message for future reference. As you listen, you retain what you hear by taking notes or by making a mental outline of the speaker's key points.

Table 2–2 Giving Constructive Feedback

To Give Constructive Feedback

- **Focus on particular behaviors.** Feedback should be specific rather than general.

- **Keep feedback impersonal.** No matter how upset you are, keep feedback job related, and never criticize someone personally.

- **Use "I" statements.** Instead of saying, "You are absent from work too often," say, "I feel annoyed when you miss work so frequently."

- **Keep feedback goal oriented.** If you have to say something negative, make sure it's directed toward the recipient's goals. Ask yourself whom the feedback is supposed to help. If the answer is essentially you, bite your tongue.

- **Make feedback well timed.** Feedback is most meaningful when there is a short interval between the recipient's behavior and the receipt of feedback about that behavior.

- **Ensure understanding.** If feedback is to be effective, you need to make sure the recipient understands it.

- **Direct negative feedback toward behavior that is controllable by the recipient.** There's little value in reminding a person of some shortcoming over which he or she has no control.

◆ **Evaluating:** Applying critical thinking skills to weigh the speaker's remarks. You separate fact from opinion and evaluate the quality of the evidence.

◆ **Responding:** Reacting once you've evaluated the speaker's message. If you're communicating one-on-one or in a small group, the initial response generally takes the form of verbal feedback (see Table 2–2). If you're one of many in an audience, your initial response may take the form of applause, laughter, or silence. Later on, you may act on what you have heard.

Because listening requires a mix of physical and mental activities, it is subject to a variety of physical and mental barriers. A large part of becoming a good listener is the ability to recognize and overcome these barriers.

Barriers to Effective Listening Prejudgment is one of the most common barriers to listening. It can be difficult to overcome because it is an automatic process. To operate in life, people must hold some assumptions. However, in new situations, these assumptions can often be incorrect. Moreover, some people listen defensively, viewing every comment as a personal attack. To protect their self-esteem, they distort messages by tuning out anything that doesn't confirm their view of themselves.

When you jump to conclusions, you close your mind to additional information.

Self-centeredness causes people to take control of conversations, rather than listening to what's being said. For example, if a speaker mentions a problem (perhaps a manager is trying to deal with conflict between team members), self-centered listeners eagerly relate their own problems with team conflict. They trivialize the speaker's concerns by pointing out that their own difficulties are twice as great. And they can top positive experiences as well. No matter what subject is being discussed, they know more than the speaker does—and they're determined to prove it.

Self-centered listeners shift their attention from the speaker to themselves.

When you listen selectively (also known as *out-listening*), you let your mind wander to things such as whether you brought your dry-cleaning ticket to work. You stay tuned out until you hear a word or phrase that gets your attention once more. The result is that you don't remember what the speaker *actually* said; instead, you remember what you *think* the speaker probably said.[38]

Selective listeners tune the speaker out.

One reason our minds tend to wander is that we think faster than we speak. Most people speak at about 120 to 150 words per minute. However, studies indicate that, depending on the subject and the individual, people can process information at 500 to 800 words per minute.[39] This disparity between rate of speech and rate of thought can be used to pull your arguments together, but some listeners let their minds wander and just tune out.

Your mind can process information more than four times faster than the rate of speech.

Table 2–3 Distinguishing Good Listeners from Bad Listeners		
The Bad Listener	**The Good Listener**	**To Listen Effectively**
Tunes out dry subjects	Opportunizes; asks "What's in it for me?"	1. Find areas of interest
Tunes out if delivery is poor	Judges content; skips over delivery errors	2. Judge content, not delivery
Tends to enter into argument	Doesn't judge until comprehension is complete; interrupts only to clarify	3. Hold your fire
Listens for facts	Listens for central themes	4. Listen for ideas
Takes extensive notes	Takes fewer notes	5. Take selective notes
Fakes attention	Works hard; exhibits active body state	6. Work at listening
Is distracted easily	Fights or avoids distractions; knows how to concentrate	7. Block out competing thoughts
Resists difficult expository material	Uses heavier material as exercise for the mind	8. Paraphrase the speaker's ideas
Reacts to emotional words	Interprets emotional words; does not get hung up on them	9. Stay open-minded
Tends to daydream with slow speakers	Listens between the lines; weighs the evidence; mentally summarizes	10. Capitalize on the fact that thought is faster than speech

The important thing is to recognize these counterproductive tendencies as barriers and to work on overcoming them. Becoming a good listener will help you in many business situations—especially those that are emotion laden and difficult (see Table 2–3). You can assess your listening skills by paying attention to how you listen. Are you really hearing what is said? Or are you mentally rehearsing how you will respond? For a summary of how to listen better, see this chapter's "Checklist: Improving Your Listening Skills."

Understanding Nonverbal Communication

Objective **5**

Clarify the importance of nonverbal communication and briefly describe six categories of nonverbal expression.

Nonverbal signals often occur unconsciously.

Nonverbal communication is more reliable and more efficient than verbal communication.

Good listeners pay attention to more than just verbal communication: They look for unspoken messages, the most basic form of communication. Such **nonverbal communication** consists of all the cues, gestures, facial expressions, spatial relationships, and attitudes toward time that enable people to communicate without words. And it differs from verbal communication in terms of intent and spontaneity. When you say, "Please get back to me on that order by Friday," you have a conscious purpose; you think about the message, if only for a moment. However, you don't mean to raise an eyebrow or to blush. Those actions come naturally. Without a word, and without your consent, your face reveals your emotions. Good communicators recognize the value of nonverbal communication and use it to enhance the communication process.

The Importance of Nonverbal Communication   The old maxim is true: People's actions often do speak louder than their words. In fact, most people can deceive others much more easily with words than they can with their bodies. Words are relatively easy to control; body language, facial expressions, and vocal characteristics are not. By paying attention to these nonverbal cues, you can detect deception or affirm a speaker's honesty.

Because nonverbal communication is so reliable, people generally have more faith in nonverbal cues than they do in verbal messages. If a person says one thing but transmits a conflicting message nonverbally, listeners almost invariably believe the nonverbal signal.[40] Chances are, if you can read other people's nonverbal messages correctly, you can interpret their underlying attitudes and intentions and respond appropriately.

Nonverbal communication is also important because it is efficient. You can transmit a nonverbal message without even thinking about it, and your audience can register the

Checklist: Improving Your Listening Skills

Look Beyond the Speaker's Style

✓ Don't judge the message by the speaker but by the argument.
✓ Ask yourself what the speaker knows that you don't.
✓ Depersonalize your listening.
✓ Decrease the emotional impact of what's being said.

Fight Distractions

✓ Close doors.
✓ Turn off radios or televisions.
✓ Move closer to the speaker.
✓ Stay ahead of the speaker by anticipating what will be said next and summarizing what's already been said.
✓ Don't interrupt—avoid sidetracking solutions and throwing the speaker off course.
✓ Hold your rebuttal until you've heard the entire message.

Provide Feedback

✓ Let the speaker know you're paying attention.
✓ Maintain eye contact.

✓ Offer appropriate facial expressions.
✓ Paraphrase what you've heard when the speaker reaches a stopping point.
✓ Keep all criticism and feedback positive.

Listen Actively

✓ Listen for concepts, key ideas, and facts.
✓ Be able to distinguish between evidence and argument, idea and example, fact and principle.
✓ Analyze the key points—whether they make sense and are supported by facts.
✓ Look for unspoken messages in the speaker's tone of voice or expressions.
✓ Keep an open mind.
✓ Ask questions that clarify.
✓ Reserve judgment until the speaker has finished.
✓ Take meaningful notes that are brief and to the point.

---

meaning unconsciously. At the same time, when you have a conscious purpose, you can often achieve it more economically with a gesture than you can with words. A wave of the hand, a pat on the back, a wink—all are streamlined expressions of thought. However, nonverbal communication usually blends with speech to carry part of the message—to augment, reinforce, and clarify that message.

> People use nonverbal signals to support and clarify verbal communication.

The Types of Nonverbal Communication   According to one estimate, there are more than 700,000 forms of nonverbal communication.[41] For discussion purposes, however, these forms can be grouped into the following general categories: facial expression, gesture and posture, vocal characteristics, personal appearance, touching behavior, and use of time and space.

Facial Expression   Your face is the primary site for expressing your emotions; it reveals both the type and the intensity of your feelings.[42] Your eyes are especially effective for indicating attention and interest, influencing others, regulating interaction, and establishing dominance. In fact, eye contact is so important in the United States that even when your words send a positive message, averting your gaze can lead your audience to perceive a negative one.[43] Of course, people sometimes manipulate their expressions to simulate an emotion they do not feel or to mask their true feelings. Just remember, the interpretation of facial expressions, and of all nonverbal signals, varies from culture to culture (as discussed in Chapter 3). However, even though many nonverbal gestures and expressions are interpreted differently in different cultures, six facial expressions are understood around the globe (see Figure 2–2).

> The face and eyes command particular attention as sources of nonverbal messages.

Gesture and Posture   By moving your body, you can express both specific and general messages, some voluntary and some involuntary. Many gestures—a wave of the hand, for example—have a specific and intentional meaning, such as "hello" or "good-bye." Other types of body movement are unintentional and express a more general message. Slouching, leaning forward, fidgeting, and walking briskly are all unconscious signals that reveal whether you feel confident or nervous, friendly or hostile, assertive or passive, powerful or

> Body language and tone of voice reveal a lot about a person's emotions and attitudes.

Figure 2–2
Facial Expressions Around
the World

FEAR

ANGER

SURPRISE

DISGUST

SORROW

JOY

powerless (see "Achieving Intercultural Communication—Actions Speak Louder than Words All Around the World.")

Vocal Characteristics   Like body language, your voice carries both intentional and unintentional messages. On a conscious level, we can use our voices to create various impressions. Consider the sentence "What have you been up to?" If you repeat that question four or five times, changing your tone of voice and stressing various words, you can convey quite different messages. However, your vocal characteristics also reveal many things that you are unaware of. The tone and volume of your voice, your accent and speaking pace, and all the little *um*'s and *ah*'s that creep into your speech say a lot about who you are, your relationship with the audience, and the emotions underlying your words.

> Physical appearance and personal style contribute to one's identity.

Personal Appearance   People respond to others on the basis of their physical appearance. Because you see yourself as others see you, their expectations are often a self-fulfilling prophecy; that is, when people think you're capable and attractive, you feel good about yourself, and that feeling affects your behavior, which in turn affects other people's perceptions of you. Although an individual's body type and facial features impose limitations, most people are able to control their attractiveness to some degree. Grooming, clothing, accessories, "style"—all modify a person's appearance. If your goal is to make a good impression, adopt the style of the people you want to impress.

Touching Behavior   Touch is an important vehicle for conveying warmth, comfort, and reassurance. Perhaps because it implies intimacy, touching behavior is governed in various circumstances by relatively strict customs that establish who can touch whom and how. The accepted norms vary, depending on the gender, age, relative status, and cultural background of the persons involved. In business situations, touching suggests dominance, so a higher-status person is more likely to touch a lower-status person than the other way around. Touching has become controversial, however, because it can sometimes be interpreted as sexual harassment.

> Punctuality and comfort zones vary by culture and authority.

Use of Time and Space   Like touch, time and space can be used to assert authority. Some people demonstrate their importance by making other people wait; others show respect by being on time. People can also assert their status by occupying the best space. In U.S. companies, the chief executive usually has the corner office and the prettiest view. Apart from serving as a symbol of status, space can determine how comfortable people feel talking with each other. When others stand too close or too far away, we are likely to feel ill at ease.

Achieving Intercultural Communication

Actions Speak Louder than Words All Around the World

"He wouldn't look me in the eye. I found it disconcerting that he kept looking all over the room but rarely at me," said Barbara Walters after her interview with Libya's Colonel Muamar el-Qaddafi. Like many people in the United States, Walters was associating eye contact with trustworthiness, so when Qaddafi withheld eye contact, she felt uncomfortable. In fact, Qaddafi was paying Walters a compliment. In Libya, *not* looking conveys respect, and looking straight at a woman is considered nearly as serious as physical assault.

Nonverbal communication varies widely between cultures, even between subcultures, and the differences strongly affect communication in the workplace. Whether you're trying to communicate with your new Asian American assistant, the Swedish managers who recently bought out your company, the young African American college student who won a summer internship with your firm, or representatives from the French company you hope will buy your firm's new designs, your efforts will depend as much on physical cues as on verbal ones. Most Americans aren't usually aware of their own nonverbal behavior, so they have trouble understanding the body language of people from other cultures. The list of differences is endless:

❑ In Thailand it's rude to place your arm over the back of a chair in which another person is sitting.

❑ Finnish female students are horrified by Arab girls who want to walk hand in hand with them.

❑ Canadian listeners nod to signal agreement.

❑ Japanese listeners nod to indicate only that they have understood.

❑ British listeners stare at the speaker, blinking their eyes to indicate understanding.

❑ People in the United States are taught that it's impolite to stare.

❑ Saudis accept foreigners in Western business attire but are offended by tight-fitting clothing and by short sleeves.

❑ Spaniards indicate a receptive friendly handshake by clasping the other person's forearm to form a double handshake.

❑ Canadians consider touching any part of the arm above the hand intrusive, except in intimate relationships.

It may take years to adjust your nonverbal communication to other cultures, but many options can help you prepare. Books and seminars on cultural differences are readily available, as are motion pictures showing a wide range of cultures. You can always rent videos of films and TV shows from other countries. Examining the illustrations in news and business magazines can give you an idea of expected business dress and personal space. Finally, remaining flexible and interacting with people from other cultures who are visiting or living in your country will go a long way toward lowering the barriers presented by nonverbal communication.

CAREER APPLICATIONS

1. Explain how watching a movie from another country might help you prepare to correctly interpret nonverbal behavior from that culture.
2. One of your co-workers is originally from Saudi Arabia. You like him, and the two of you work well together. However, he stands so close when you speak with him that it makes you very uncomfortable. Do you tell him of your discomfort, or do you try to cover it up?

Again, attitudes toward punctuality and comfort zones vary from culture to culture (see Chapter 3). See this chapter's "Checklist: Improving Nonverbal Communication Skills."

INCREASING MEETING PRODUCTIVITY

Objective **6**
Explain how you can improve meeting productivity through preparation, leadership, and participation.

Meetings help teams solve problems by providing the opportunity for giving and getting feedback, whether your goal is to develop ideas, identify opportunities, or decide how to maximize resources. The number of meetings necessary to solve problems and collaborate on projects is increasing. In the world of business, more than 25 million meetings are already taking place every day.[44]

Unfortunately, many meetings are unproductive. In a recent study, senior and middle managers reported that only 56 percent of their meetings were actually productive and that 25 percent of them could have been handled by a phone call or a memo.[45] Meeting productivity is affected by the way you prepare for them and the way you conduct and participate in them.

Preparing for Meetings

The biggest mistake in holding meetings is not having a specific goal. So before you call a meeting, satisfy yourself that one is truly needed. Perhaps you could communicate more

The best preparation for a meeting is having a specific goal that would be best handled in a face-to-face situation.

✓ *Checklist:* Improving Nonverbal Communication Skills

Receiving Nonverbal Signals

✓ Pay more attention to the nonverbal signals of others.
✓ Be aware that people may give false nonverbal cues.

Sending Nonverbal Signals

✓ Avoid giving conflicting signals.
✓ Try to be as honest as possible in communicating your emotions.
✓ Smile genuinely. Faking a smile is obvious to observers.
✓ Maintain the eye contact your audience expects.
✓ Be aware of your posture and of the gestures you use.
✓ Try to use appropriate vocal signals while minimizing unintentional messages.

✓ Imitate the appearance of the people you want to impress.
✓ Respect your audience's comfort zone.
✓ Adopt a handshake that matches your personality and intention.
✓ Be aware of varying attitudes toward time.
✓ Use touch only when appropriate.

Interpreting Nonverbal Signals

✓ Remember that few gestures convey meaning in and of themselves.
✓ Nonverbal signals must be interpreted by an observer in the context of situation and culture.

Hewlett-Packard's President and CEO Carly Fiorina believes teamwork gets the job done in meetings too. Her leadership helps team members solve problems, brings out the best in each employee, and results in productive meetings. Fiorina understands that successful meetings need a clearly defined purpose. "The people of HP are very smart," she says. "They're pretty clear on the things they need to work on."

effectively in a memo or through individual conversations. If you do require the interaction of a group, you want to bring the right people together in the right place for just enough time to accomplish your goals. The key to productive meetings is careful planning of purpose, participants, location, and agenda.

Decide on Your Purpose   Although many meetings combine purposes, most are usually either informational or decision making. Informational meetings allow participants to share information and perhaps coordinate action. Briefings may come from each participant or from the leader, who then answers questions from attendees. Decision-making meetings mainly involve persuasion, analysis, and problem solving. They often include a brainstorming session, followed by a debate on the alternatives, and they require that each participant is aware of the nature of the problem and the criteria for its solution.

Select Participants   Being invited to this or that meeting can be a mark of status, and you may be reluctant to leave anyone out. Nevertheless, try to invite only those people whose presence is essential. If the session is purely informational and one person will be doing most of the talking, you can include a relatively large group. However, if you're trying to solve a problem, develop a plan, or reach a decision, try to limit participation to between 6 and 12 people.[46] The more participants, the more comments and confusion you're likely to get, and the longer the whole thing will take. But even as you try to limit participation, be sure to include key decision makers and those who can contribute. Holding a meeting is pointless if the people with necessary information aren't there.

Choose an Appropriate Location   Decide where you'll hold the meeting, and reserve the location. For work sessions, morning meetings are usually more productive than afternoon sessions. Also, consider the seating arrangements. Are rows of chairs suitable, or do you need a conference table? Plus, give some attention to details such as room temperature, lighting, ventilation, acoustics, and refreshments. These things may seem trivial, but they can make or break a meeting.

You might also consider calling a meeting in cyberspace. Companies such as WebEx offer facilities in cyberspace for meeting with colleagues, customers, and other stakeholders. Cyberspace meetings are how Siebel Systems and other e-businesses streamline meeting planning and team discussions.

Set and Follow an Agenda   Although the nature of a meeting may sometimes prevent you from developing a fixed agenda, at least prepare a list of matters to be discussed. Distribute the agenda to the participants several days before the meeting so that they will know what to expect and can come prepared to respond to the issues at hand.

Distribute the agenda ahead of time.

EFFECTIVE E-BUSINESS COMMUNICATION

Calling a Meeting in Cyberspace

Working with team members in different locations is less of a challenge when you bridge the distance with WebEx (www.webex.com) or a similar Web-based service. Say you're going to call a cyberspace meeting. Following the WebEx prompts, you simply enter the meeting date and time, send e-mail announcements to attendees, and request features such as online polling. Then, at meeting time, participants log onto WebEx, click "Join Meeting," and enter a special code to attend your meeting.

1. What information should you include in your premeeting e-mail announcements to cyber-space meeting attendees?
2. Why would a company encourage teams to meet in cyberspace rather than travel to one central location for a meeting?

Agendas include the names of the participants, the time, the place, and the order of business (see Appendix A for agenda format). Make sure the agenda is specific. For example, the phrase "development budget" doesn't reveal much, whereas the longer explanation "Discussion: Proposed reduction of 1999–2000 development budget due to our new product postponement" helps all committee members prepare in advance with facts and figures.

Agendas help you start and end your meetings on time. Starting and ending on time sends a signal of good organization and allows attendees to meet other commitments. In fact, one solution for improving meetings is simply telling people what time the meeting will end. A productive agenda should answer three key questions: (1) What do we need to do in this meeting to accomplish our goals? (2) What conversations will be of greatest importance to all the participants? (3) What information must be available in order to have these conversations?[47]

Conducting and Participating in Meetings

Whether a meeting is conducted electronically or conventionally, its success depends largely on how effective the leader is. If the leader is prepared and has selected participants carefully, notes American Express's David House, the meeting will generally be productive, especially if the leader has good listening skills.

Keep the Meeting on Track   A good meeting is not a series of dialogues between individual members and the leader. Instead, it's a cross-flow of discussion and debate, with the leader occasionally guiding, mediating, probing, stimulating, and summarizing, but mostly letting the others thrash out their ideas. That's why it's important for leaders to avoid being so domineering that they close off suggestions. Of course, they must not be so passive that they lose control of the group.

Don't be so rigid that you cut off discussion too quickly.

Checklist: Improving Meeting Productivity

Preparation

✓ Determine the meeting's objectives.
✓ Work out an agenda that will achieve your objectives.
✓ Select participants.
✓ Determine the location and reserve a room.
✓ Arrange for light refreshments, if appropriate.
✓ Determine whether the lighting, ventilation, acoustics, and temperature of the room are adequate.
✓ Determine seating needs: chairs only or table and chairs.

Conduct

✓ Begin and end the meeting on time.

✓ Control the meeting by following the announced agenda.
✓ Encourage full participation, and either confront or ignore those who seem to be working at cross-purposes with the group.
✓ Sum up decisions, actions, and recommendations as you move through the agenda, and restate main points at the end.

Follow-Up

✓ Distribute the meeting's notes or minutes on a timely basis.
✓ Take the follow-up action agreed to.

As leader, you're responsible for keeping the meeting moving along. If the discussion lags, call on those who haven't been heard from. Pace the presentation and discussion so that you'll have time to complete the agenda. As time begins to run out, interrupt the discussion and summarize what has been accomplished. However, don't be too rigid. Allow enough time for discussion, and give people a chance to raise related issues. If you cut off discussion too quickly or limit the subject too narrowly, no real consensus can emerge.

Follow Parliamentary Procedure   One way you can improve the productivity of a meeting is by using **parliamentary procedure,** a time-tested method for planning and running effective meetings. Anyone belonging to a team should understand the basic principles of parliamentary procedure. Used correctly, it can help teams[48]

◆ Transact business efficiently

◆ Protect individual rights

◆ Maintain order

◆ Preserve a spirit of harmony

◆ Accomplish team and organizational goals

Robert's Rules of Order is the most common guide to parliamentary procedure.

The most common guide to parliamentary procedure is *Robert's Rules of Order,* available in various editions and revisions. Also available are less technical guides based on "Robert's Rules." You can determine how strictly you want to adhere to parliamentary procedure. For small groups you may be quite flexible, but for larger groups you'll want to use a more formal approach.

Encourage Participation   As the meeting gets under way, you'll discover that some participants are too quiet and others are too talkative. To draw out the shy types, ask for their input on issues that particularly pertain to them. You might say something like, "Roberto, you've done a lot of work in this area. What do you think?" For the overly talkative, simply say that time is limited and others need to be heard from. The best meetings are those in which everyone participates, so don't let one or two people dominate your meeting while others doodle on their notepads. As you move through your agenda, stop at the end of each item, summarize what you understand to be the feelings of the group, and state the important points made during the discussion.

Don't let one or two members dominate the meeting.

If you're a meeting participant, try to contribute to both the subject of the meeting and the smooth interaction of the participants. Use your listening skills and powers of observation to size up the interpersonal dynamics of the people, then adapt your behavior to help the group achieve its goals. Speak up if you have something useful to say, but don't monopolize the discussion.

Close and Follow Up   At the conclusion of the meeting, tie up the loose ends. Either summarize the general conclusion of the group or list the suggestions. Wrapping things up ensures that all participants agree on the outcome and gives people a chance to clear up any misunderstandings. Before the meeting breaks up, briefly review who has agreed to do what by what date.

Finally, be sure to follow up. As soon as possible after the meeting, make sure all participants receive a copy of the minutes or notes, showing recommended actions, schedules, and responsibilities (see Appendix A for minutes format). The minutes will remind everyone of what took place and will provide a reference for future actions. To review the tasks that contribute to productive meetings, see this chapter's "Checklist: Improving Meeting Productivity."

> Following up with minutes of the meeting allows you to remind everyone of what happened and who needs to take action.

SUMMARY OF LEARNING OBJECTIVES

1 **Highlight the advantages and disadvantages of using teams.** Teams can achieve a higher level of performance than individuals because of the combined intelligence and energy of the group. Motivation and creativity flourish in team settings. Moreover, individuals tend to perform better because they achieve a sense of purpose by belonging to a group. Teams also bring more input and a greater diversity of views, which tends to result in better decisions. And because team members participate in the decision process, they are committed to seeing the results succeed. Teams are not without disadvantages, however. If poorly managed, teams can be a waste of everyone's time. If members are pressured to conform, they may develop groupthink, which can lead to poor-quality decisions and ill-advised actions; some members may let their private motives get in the way. Others may not contribute their fair share, so certain tasks may not be completed.

2 **Identify the characteristics of effective teams.** Effective team members interact openly and recognize the value that others bring to the group. Members are willing to exchange information, examine issues, and work though conflicts. They focus on the greater good of the team instead of personal agendas. As a group, they understand what is expected of them, stick to the task at hand, and reach decisions by consensus after open, honest debate. All members are encouraged to think creatively and participate. They listen to and value feedback from others, and they don't feel threatened by taking an unpopular stance.

3 **Discuss the tasks involved in preparing effective team messages, and list nine guidelines for improvement.** Effective team messages require team members to be flexible and open-minded so that they can focus on the team's objectives rather than their own. Team members need to get organized, select a leader, and clarify goals. They must agree on the purpose of their project and on who their audience is. Members must plan how the document will be organized and formatted, and they must choose a writing style. To prepare effective messages, team members can use guidelines such as the following: (1) Select team members wisely, (2) select a responsible leader, (3) promote cooperation, (4) clarify goals, (5) elicit commitment, (6) clarify responsibilities, (7) instill prompt action, (8) apply technology, (9) ensure technological compatibility.

4 **Describe the listening process, and list three barriers that interfere with this process.** The listening process involves five activities: (1) receiving (physically hearing the message), (2) interpreting (assigning meaning to what you hear), (3) remembering (storing the message for future reference), (4) evaluating (thinking about the message), and (5) responding (reacting to the message, taking action, or giving feedback). Three barriers can interfere with the listening process. Prejudgment involves holding assumptions, right or wrong, sometimes even distorting messages if they don't conform with what you want to hear. Self-centeredness involves people monopolizing a conversation with their own experience rather than listening to what someone else has to say. And, finally, selective listening (or out-listening) involves letting your mind wander away from the speaker and not paying close attention.

5 **Clarify the importance of nonverbal communication, and briefly describe six categories of nonverbal expression.** Nonverbal communication is important because actions speak louder than words. Body language is more difficult to control than words and may reveal a person's true feelings, motivation, or character. Because of this, people believe nonverbal signals over words. In addition, nonverbal communication is more efficient; with a wave of your hand or a wink, you can streamline your thoughts and do so without much thought. Types of nonverbal expression include facial expression, gesture and posture, vocal characteristics, personal appearance, touching behavior, and use of time and space.

6 **Explain how you can improve meeting productivity through preparation, leadership, and participation.** When preparing to have a meeting, be sure that your purpose cannot be accomplished better by some other means (e-mail, phone calls, etc.). Plan effectively by deciding on your purpose, selecting participants who really need to be there, choosing a location and time that are conducive to your goals, and developing an agenda that is specific and thorough. Conduct productive meetings by guiding, mediating, and summarizing. Pace the discussion, and encourage everyone to participate. Before the end, summarize conclusions and review who has agreed to do what by what deadline. Follow up with minutes that show recommended actions, schedules, and responsibilities. As a participant in any meeting, do everything you can to contribute to the smooth interaction of attendees as well as to the subject.

SOLVING A COMMUNICATION DILEMMA AT AMERICAN EXPRESS

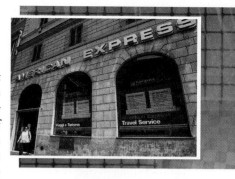

David House believes that all employees in his division must work together as a team if they are to contribute to the company's success. House does everything he can to encourage teamwork. Each year, he commends outstanding team effort, awarding lavish prizes to the top 75 sales reps for their contributions. But it takes more than an impressive sales record to be recognized. Representatives must follow House's agenda for building a winning team: (1) staying close to the customer, (2) having a commitment to excellence, (3) making a difference every day, (4) being accountable for results, and (5) sharing with peers. For example, House recognized one sales rep who focused on her team's regional sales objectives instead of her own quotas and made an effort to share her winning strategies with her peers. In addition to accompanying other reps on sales calls in her region, she distributed copies of her winning presentation to every sales rep in the country.

To promote communication within each team, House makes sure that every employee has access to the company's highly efficient computer network. Team members conduct virtual meetings with colleagues around the world, and they take advantage of e-mail and videoconferencing to brainstorm and collaborate on projects. Several units in House's division use a buddy system that requires remote workers to chat with on-site colleagues by phone every morning, covering topics ranging from new customers to office politics. Other telecommuters report to a local or regional office several times each week, meeting with co-workers for specific purposes. Office meetings have predetermined agendas and follow regular schedules to reduce wasted meeting time and to allow team members to communicate face to face.

House also introduces new employees to the team concept right away. On their first day of work, new recruits are assigned tasks that involve a team effort. If one team member needs help, the new employee is asked to pitch in. From the newest recruits to top executives, House makes sure that everyone at American Express contributes to the company's success through effective teamwork.

Your Mission You have recently been promoted to sales manager for the Northwest region of American Express Worldwide Establishment Services. Your responsibilities include (1) promoting the team concept among all sales representatives in your region, and (2) serving as a team leader on special projects that involve sales managers throughout the country. Choose the best alternatives for handling the following situations, and be prepared to explain why your choice is best.

1. David House has asked you and four other employees to find solutions to the lack of sufficient office space for the growing number of employees in the Northwest region. As leader, you schedule team meetings on Thursday afternoons for five weeks to address the problem. After two meetings with your co-workers, you notice that everyone is making vital contributions to the group's efforts—except Jane. During the meetings, she displays very poor listening skills. She often jumps ahead of the topic or interrupts a speaker's train of thought. At other times, she doodles on her notepad instead of taking constructive notes. And she remains silent after team members deliver lengthy reports about possible solutions to the office space problem. What can you do as team leader to help Jane improve her listening skills?

   a. Ask Jane to take extensive notes during each meeting. The process of taking detailed notes will improve her concentration and force her to listen more carefully to team members. After the meeting, she can use her notes as a reference to clarify any questions about team decisions or the nature of assignments to individual team members.

   b. Suggest that Jane mentally summarize the speaker's ideas—or verbally rephrase the ideas in her own words—during the meeting. With some practice, Jane should be able to focus on the topics under discussion and block out distracting thoughts.

   c. Schedule future team meetings for Thursday mornings instead of Thursday afternoons. After devoting most of the workday to her regular duties, Jane may be feeling tired or sluggish by the time your team meeting rolls around.

   d. Prepare a detailed, written summary of each meeting. The summary will clarify any points that Jane may have missed during the meeting and provide her with a complete reference of team decisions and assignments.

2. As leader of a team of regional sales managers, you schedule a team meeting to discuss new methods of inspiring and motivating sales representatives to achieve their quarterly sales goals. During the meeting, one regional sales manager disagrees with every suggestion offered by team members, often reacting with a sneer on his face and a belligerent tone of voice. Which of the following strategies is the best way to overcome the manager's resistance?

   a. Ignore his remarks. Keep the meeting on track and avoid destructive confrontations by asking for input from other team members.

   b. Directly confront the sales manager's concerns. Point out the flaws in his arguments, and offer support for the opinions of other team members.

   c. Remain calm and try to understand his point of view. Ask him to clarify his points, and solicit his suggestions for motivating sales representatives.

   d. Politely acknowledge his opinions, then repeat the most valid suggestions offered by other team members in a convincing manner.

3. Some employees of American Express Worldwide Establishment Services have been pushing the company to adopt a corporate statement of goals. In response, David House has

decided to call an executive meeting. Which purpose should House focus on during the meeting?

    a. To find out about competitors' goals and determine whether they are appropriate for American Express

    b. To inform top managers of his intention to evaluate all employees on the basis of their contributions to corporate goals

    c. To decide which managers/employees should be asked to come to a meeting about corporate goals

    d. To reach an agreement about the company's primary corporate goals

4. The manager of the Southeast region realizes his communication skills are important for several reasons: He holds primary responsibility for successful communication in the region; he needs to communicate with the sales representatives who report to him; and his style sets an example for other employees in the region. He asks you to sit in on face-to-face meetings for several days to observe his nonverbal messages. You witness four habits. Which of the following habits do you think is the most negative?

    a. He rarely comes out from behind his massive desk when meeting people; at one point, he offered a congratulatory handshake to a sales representative, and the sales rep had to lean way over his desk just to reach him.

    b. When a sales rep hands him a report and then sits down to discuss it, he alternates between making eye contact and making notes on the report.

    c. He is consistently pleasant, even if the person he is meeting is delivering bad news. He interrupts meetings to answer the phone, rather than letting an assistant get the phone; then he apologizes to visitors for the interruption.[49]

TEST YOUR KNOWLEDGE

1. What are three ways in which an organization's decision making can benefit from teams?

2. What are the main activities that make up the listening process?

3. In what six ways can an individual communicate nonverbally?

4. What questions should an effective agenda answer?

5. How do self-oriented team roles differ from team-maintenance roles and task-facilitating team roles?

6. What is groupthink, and how can it affect an organization?

7. How can organizations help team members successfully resolve conflict?

8. What role does the leader play in helping a team produce effective messages?

9. How does content listening differ from critical listening and empathic listening?

10. What is the purpose of using parliamentary procedure?

INTERACTIVE LEARNING

USE THIS TEXT'S ONLINE RESOURCES

Visit the myPHLIP Web site at www.prenhall.com/thill. For Chapter 2, take advantage of the interactive "Study Guide" to test your chapter knowledge. Get instant feedback on whether you need additional studying. Read the "Current Events" articles to get the latest on chapter topics, and complete the exercises—as specified by your instructor.

    This site's "Study Hall" helps you succeed in this course. "Talk in the Hall" lets you leave messages and meet new friends online. If you have a question, you can "Ask the Tutor." And to get a better grade in this course, you can find more help at "Writing Skills," "Study Skills," and "Study Tips."

    The "Research Area" helps you locate a wealth of information to use in course assignments. Plus, you can send a message to online research experts, who will help you find exactly the information you need.

APPLY YOUR KNOWLEDGE

1. How can nonverbal communication help you run a meeting? How can it help you call a meeting to order, emphasize important topics, show approval, express reservations, regulate the flow of conversation, and invite a colleague to continue with a comment?

2. Whenever your boss asks for feedback, she blasts anyone offering criticism, which causes people to agree with everything she says. You want to talk to her about it, but what should you say? List some of the points you want to make when you discuss this issue with your boss.

3. Is conflict in a team good or bad? Explain your answer.

4. At your last department meeting, three people monopolized the entire discussion. What might you do at the next meeting to encourage other department members to voluntarily participate?

5. **Ethical Choices** You've just come from a meeting of your project team, where the marketing representative kept raising objections to points of style in a rough draft of your group's report. Instead of focusing on recommendations, the team spent precious time debating individual words and even punctuation. After the meeting, two members asked you to join them in going to management to request that the marketing rep be removed from the team. You don't want to make this member look bad, nor do you want to stifle constructive comments and participation. On the other hand, you're concerned about completing the project on time. What should you do? Explain your choice.

PRACTICE YOUR KNOWLEDGE

DOCUMENT FOR ANALYSIS

A project leader has made notes about covering the following items at the quarterly budget meeting. Prepare a formal agenda by putting these items into a logical order and rewriting, where necessary, to give phrases a more consistent sound. (See Appendix A for agenda format.)

Budget Committee Meeting to be held on December 12, 2001 at 9:30 a.m.

- I will call the meeting to order.
- Site director's report: A closer look at cost overruns on Greentree site.
- The group will review and approve the minutes from last quarter's meeting.
- I will ask the finance director to report on actual vs. projected quarterly revenues and expenses.
- I will distribute copies of the overall divisional budget and announce the date of the next budget meeting.
- Discussion: How can we do a better job of anticipating and preventing cost overruns?
- Meeting will take place in Conference Room 3.
- What additional budget issues must be considered during this quarter?

EXERCISES

2-1. **Listening Skills: Overcoming Barriers** Identify some of your bad listening habits and make a list of some ways you could correct them. For the next 30 days, review your list and jot down any improvements you've noticed as a result of your effort.

2-2. **Teamwork** With a classmate, attend a local community or campus meeting where you can observe group discussion as well as voting or another group action. Take notes individually during the meeting and then work together to answer the following questions.

a. What is your evaluation of this meeting? In your answer, consider (1) the leader's ability to clearly articulate the meeting's goals, (2) the leader's ability to engage members in a meaningful discussion, (3) the group's dynamics, and (4) the group's listening skills.

b. How did group members make decisions? Did they vote? Did they reach decisions by consensus? Did the naysayers get an opportunity to voice their objections?

c. How well did the individual participants listen? How could you tell?

d. Did any participants change their expressed views or their votes during the meeting? Why might that have happened?

e. Did you observe any of the communication barriers discussed in Chapter 1? Identify them.

f. Compare the notes you took during the meeting with those of your classmate. What differences do you notice? How do you account for these differences?

2-3. **Team Communication: Overcoming Barriers** Every month, each employee in your department is expected to give a brief oral presentation on the status of his or her project. However, your department has recently hired an employee with a severe speech impediment that prevents people from understanding most of what he has to say. As department manager, how will you resolve this dilemma? Please explain.

2-4. **Nonverbal Communication: Analyzing Written Messages** Select a business letter and envelope that you have received at work or home. Analyze their appearance. What nonverbal messages do they send? Are these messages consistent with the content of the letter? If not, what could the sender have done to make the nonverbal communication consistent with the verbal communication?

2-5. **Internet** Visit the PolyVision Web site at www.ibidwhiteboards.com/index.shtml and read about electronic whiteboards. What advantages do you see in using this kind of whiteboard during a meeting? Draft a short internal memo to your boss outlining the product's advantages, using the memo format in Figure 1–3 on page 7.

2-6. **Team Development: Resolving Conflict** Describe a recent conflict you had with a team member at work or at school, and explain how you resolved it. Did you find a solution that was acceptable to both of you and to the team?

2-7. **Listening Process: Giving Feedback** Review the guidelines for developing effective feedback skills in Table 2–2 and write a brief explanation of why it's important to adopt an audience-centered approach when giving feedback to others.

2-8. **Ethical Choices** During team meetings, one member constantly calls for votes before all the members have voiced their views. As the leader, you asked this member privately about his behavior. He replied that he was trying to move the team toward its goals, but you are concerned that he is really trying to take control. How can you deal with this situation without removing the member from the group?

2–9. **Meeting Productivity: Analyzing Agendas** Obtain a copy of the agenda from a recent campus or work meeting. Does this agenda show a start time or end time? Is it specific enough that you, as an outsider, would be able to under-

stand what was to be discussed? If not, how would you improve the agenda?

2–10. **Listening Skills: Self-Assessment** How good are your listening skills? Rate yourself on each of the following elements of good listening; then examine your ratings to identify where you are strongest and where you can improve, using the tips in this chapter.

ELEMENT OF LISTENING	ALWAYS	FREQUENTLY	OCCASIONALLY	NEVER
1. I look for areas of interest when people speak.	_____	_____	_____	_____
2. I focus on content rather than delivery.	_____	_____	_____	_____
3. I wait to respond until I understand the content.	_____	_____	_____	_____
4. I listen for ideas and themes, not isolated facts.	_____	_____	_____	_____
5. I take notes only when needed.	_____	_____	_____	_____
6. I really concentrate on what speakers are saying.	_____	_____	_____	_____
7. I stay focused even when the ideas are complex.	_____	_____	_____	_____
8. I keep an open mind despite emotionally charged language.	_____	_____	_____	_____

GOING ONLINE EXERCISES

Participate in a Team-Based Organization, page 26

Working in teams to set goals and meet objectives requires cooperation. Collaboration is more than a skill, it's an art. Draw on what you've learned in this chapter and what you find at CSWT to improve your teaming skills.

1. Describe what makes a good or effective team.

2. What information did you learn from a research project about the value of effective teamwork? What was the purpose of the study?

3. In an organizational setting, what is the purpose of dialogue? What did you learn about the benefits of a team approach to solving problems in an organization?

To complete this exercise, log on to this text's Web site at www.prenhall.com/thill. Select Chapter 2, then select "Student Resources," click on the name of the featured Web site, and follow the detailed navigational directions.

chapter 3

One key to Target's success is its commitment to training employees in the subtleties of intercultural exchanges. Training sessions may stress differences in social as well as business customs to encourage understanding, communication, and cooperation.

On the job:

FACING A COMMUNICATION DILEMMA AT TARGET STORES

Taking Aim at Cultural Diversity

www.target.com

Rafael Rodriguez is a stock clerk supervisor at the Target store in Pasadena, California. Supervising people in the fast-paced world of retailing is demanding under any circumstances, and the rich cultural mix of Rodriguez's team makes his job even more challenging. Rodriguez is Hispanic, and his manager is African American. The employees that Rodriguez supervises have cultural backgrounds that are as diverse as the communities served by the nearly 700 Target retail outlets across the United States. Moreover, as in most other Target stores, some of Rodriguez's employees have grown up in the United States, whereas others have recently immigrated and speak English as a second language.

The unique combination of influences present in one culture can condition people to think, feel, and behave quite differently from people in another culture. Some of these differences are dramatic, such as in the importance placed on social status. Other differences can be more subtle and more difficult to perceive, such as variations in personal values and decision-making approaches. Rodriguez finds that basic language barriers often prevent employees from understanding each other, but the potential for problems goes beyond differences in language. In one case, a recently immigrated employee was inadvertently making some female co-workers uncomfortable by asking personal questions about hair styles and nose piercing. His questions were innocent, but because of his cultural background, he couldn't see the invisible boundary that his colleagues had built around their personal lives.

Variations in culture—and the misunderstandings that result from them—can affect teamwork, productivity, and job satisfaction. If you were Rafael Rodriguez, what steps would you take to foster a productive and satisfying work environment? How would you make sure your employees improve their intercultural sensitivity so that they can communicate effectively and work together efficiently?[1]

UNDERSTANDING THE IMPORTANCE OF COMMUNICATING ACROSS CULTURES

Like Target, more and more companies are facing the challenges of communicating across cultures. **Intercultural communication** is the process of sending and receiving messages between people whose cultural background leads them to interpret verbal and nonverbal signs differently. Two trends contributing to the rapidly increasing importance of intercultural communication are market globalization and cultural diversity.

The Global Marketplace

Market globalization is the increasing tendency of the world to act as one market. Domestic markets are opening to worldwide competition to provide growth opportuni-

Figure 3–1
What Languages Do Current
Internet Users Speak?

ties for a company's goods and services. Technological advances in travel and telecommunications are the driving force behind market globalization. New communication technologies allow teams from all over the world to work on projects and share information without leaving their desks. At the same time, advanced technologies allow manufacturers to produce their goods in foreign locations that offer an abundant supply of low-cost labor.[2] Natural boundaries and national borders have disappeared, for the most part, as increasing numbers of people work in multicultural settings. Even firms that once thought they were too tiny to expand into a neighboring city have discovered that they can tap the sales potential of overseas markets with the help of fax machines, overnight delivery services, e-mail, and the Internet. To be successful in the global marketplace, e-commerce companies must consider offering Web sites in the languages that current Internet users speak (see Figure 3–1).

Outdoor-equipment retailer REI uses custom-designed international Web sites to recognize and accommodate cultural differences in the global marketplace. Similarly, UPS has expanded its Web-based tracking services so that customers in 13 European countries can check—in their own language—to see whether packages have reached their destinations around the world. But you need not "go global" or launch a Web site to interact with someone who speaks a foreign language or who thinks, acts, or transacts business differently than you do.[3] Even if your company transacts business locally, chances are you will be communicating at work with people who come from various national, religious, and ethnic backgrounds.

O b j e c t i v e
1

Discuss two trends that
have made intercultural
business communication
so important.

Advances in technology help
companies cross national borders to
find customers, materials, and
money, leading to market
globalization.

A company's cultural diversity
affects how its business messages are
conceived, composed, delivered,
received, and interpreted.

The Multicultural Work Force

Today's work force is made up of more and more people who differ in race, gender, age, culture, family structure, religion, and educational background. Such **cultural diversity** is the second trend contributing to the importance of intercultural communication. It affects how business messages are conceived, planned, sent, received, and interpreted in the workplace.

The U.S. work force is partly composed of immigrants (new arrivals from Europe, Canada, Latin America, and Asia) and people from various ethnic backgrounds (such as African Americans, Hispanic Americans, and Asian Americans)—all of whom bring their own language and culture to the workplace. For example, foreign-born engineers jam the corridors of Silicon Valley, hoping to reap the benefits of the U.S. information technology boom. By 2010 minorities will account for 50 percent of the U.S. population, and immigrants will account for half of all new U.S. workers.[4] Which is why Target offers its employees classes that help them understand and accept cultural differences. Such diversity training is also considered a competitive advantage at Allstate Insurance, which invests in excess of 540,000 hours of classroom time.[5]

Like Target's Rafael Rodriguez, you will be exchanging business messages with co-workers, customers, suppliers, investors, and competitors. To be successful, you must be sensitive to cultural differences

IBM's corporate work force diversity staff is sensitive to cultural differences both inside and outside the company. An important goal for staff members is to ensure that company employees recognize how cultural differences can affect communication with co-workers and customers.

EFFECTIVE E-BUSINESS COMMUNICATION

Putting the World in the Web

Because the Web is truly world-wide, think carefully about different cultures and subcultures when planning your online material. For example, Recreational Equipment Inc. (REI) sells outdoor equipment through stores, catalogs, and a Web site that offers information in five languages. Noticing many orders from Japan, REI hired native speakers to develop a site for that country (www.japan.rei.com) and to adjust the graphics, as well as the words. For example, when an item is out of stock, the U.S. site displays a "sorry" message with a person shrugging and holding hands palms up. Knowing this is impolite in Japan, the developers substituted a graphic of someone politely bowing.

1. How did REI use its knowledge of different cultures and subcultures in presenting information on its Japanese Web site?
2. When REI's developers replaced the shrugging figure with a bowing figure, how did they demonstrate their understanding of Japan as a high-context culture?

as you communicate with people around the world and within your organization. Glance at the job ads in newspapers and you will find that employment opportunities are everywhere if you have good intercultural communication skills. In fact, you will be left behind if you do not develop these skills. However, to do so you must first understand some basics about culture.

IMPROVING INTERCULTURAL SENSITIVITY

Objective

2

Define *culture* and *sub-culture,* and list culture's four basic characteristics.

Culture is a shared system of symbols, beliefs, attitudes, values, expectations, and norms for behavior.

Culture is a shared system of symbols, beliefs, attitudes, values, expectations, and norms for behavior. All members of a culture have similar assumptions about how people should think, behave, and communicate, and they all tend to act on those assumptions in much the same way. You belong to the culture you share with all the people who live in your own country.

Subcultures are distinct groups that exist within a major culture.

In addition, you also belong to other cultural groups, including an ethnic group, probably a religious group, and perhaps a profession that has its own special language and customs. Distinct groups that exist within a major culture are referred to as **subcultures.** For example, Indonesia is home to a wide variety of ethnic and religious subcultures, whereas Japan is much more homogeneous, having only a few subcultures.[6] Groups that might be considered subcultures in the United States are Mexican Americans, Mormons, wrestling fans, Russian immigrants, disabled individuals, and Harvard graduates.

In order to communicate more effectively, you need to understand a few basics about culture:

To better understand culture, remember that culture is learned and that it varies in stability, complexity, and tolerance.

◆ **Culture is learned.** As we grow up in a culture, we are sometimes told which behaviors are acceptable, and we sometimes observe which values work best in our particular society. But whether conscious or unconscious, culture is transmitted from person to person, from generation to generation, teaching us who we are and how best to function in our society.[7]

◆ **Cultures vary in stability.** All cultures are changing, but at different rates. Rapid change can interfere with receiving and decoding messages, which requires adjustment from all communicators, both insiders and outsiders. For example, Japan's culture has come to expect the security of lifelong employment. But today's stagnating economy is forcing employees to face the possibility of developing their own benefits and even of being laid off.[8]

◆ **Cultures vary in complexity.** The accessibility of information in a culture ranges from explicit verbal codes to implicit body language. Some complex cultures require much more effort from outsiders who wish to communicate clearly with insiders.

◆ **Cultures vary in tolerance.** Some cultures are openly hostile toward outsiders, some maintain a detached aloofness, and others are friendly and cooperative toward strangers. These attitudes can affect the level of trust and open communication that you can achieve with people of other cultures.

As you can see, communication is strongly affected by culture. You can improve your ability to communicate effectively across cultures by recognizing cultural differences and then overcoming ethnocentrism.

Recognize Cultural Differences

When you write to or speak with someone from another culture, you encode your message using the assumptions of your own culture. However, members of your audience decode your message according to the assumptions of their culture, so your meaning may be misunderstood. The greater the difference between cultures, the greater the chance for misunderstanding.[9] For instance, a nodding gesture indicates understanding in the United States, but in Japan it means only that the person is listening.[10]

Cultural differences often surface in our assumptions. When Japanese auto manufacturer Mazda opened a plant in the United States, officials passed out company baseball caps and told U.S. employees that they could wear the caps at work, along with their mandatory company uniform (blue pants and khaki shirts). The employees assumed that the caps were a *voluntary* accessory, and many decided not to wear them. Japanese managers were upset, regarding the decision as a sign of disrespect and believing that employees who really cared about the company would want to wear the caps. However, the U.S. employees resented being told what they should want to do.[11] Similarly, exhibitors at a trade show could not understand why Chinese visitors were not stopping by their booth. Exhibitors were wearing green hats and giving them away as promotional items. But they soon discovered that for many Chinese, green hats are associated with infidelity; the Chinese expression "He wears a green hat" indicates that a man's wife has been cheating on him. So they discarded the green hats (giving out T-shirts instead) and the Chinese visited the booth.[12]

Problems such as these arise when we assume, wrongly, that other people's attitudes and lives are like ours (see "Achieving Intercultural Communication—Test Your Intercultural Knowledge"). As a graduate of one intercultural training program said, "I used to think it was enough to treat people the way I wanted to be treated. But [after taking the course] . . . I realized you have to treat people the way *they* want to be treated."[13] You can improve intercultural sensitivity, by recognizing and accommodating cultural differences, which can be examined in four major categories: contextual, ethical, social, and nonverbal.

Contextual Differences   **Cultural context** is the pattern of physical cues, environmental stimuli, and implicit understanding that convey meaning between two members of the same culture. However, from culture to culture, people convey contextual meaning differently. In fact, correct social behavior and effective communication can be defined by how much a culture depends on contextual cues (see Table 3–1 on page 53).

In a **high-context culture** such as South Korea or Taiwan, people rely less on verbal communication and more on the context of nonverbal actions and environmental setting to convey meaning. A Chinese speaker expects the receiver to discover the essence of a message and uses indirectness and metaphor to provide a web of meaning.[14] In high-context cultures, the rules of everyday life are rarely explicit; instead, as individuals grow

CEO Gerald Levin developed "Vision and Values," a company-wide initiative at AOL Time Warner to discuss issues such as diversity and integrity. "I've been building networks all my life," says Levin. His vision creates the potential not only of committing his global media giant to public service but also of bridging gaps and encouraging ties between people from different cultural and ethnic backgrounds.

O b j e c t i v e

3

Explain the importance of recognizing cultural differences, delineate the differences between high- and low-context cultures, and list four categories of cultural differences.

Effective intercultural communication depends on recognizing ways in which people differ.

It's best to treat people the way they expect to be treated.

Cultural context is the pattern of physical cues, environmental stimuli, and implicit understanding that conveys meaning between members of the same culture.

High-context cultures rely on implicit nonverbal actions and environmental setting to convey meaning, unlike low-context cultures, which rely heavily on explicit verbal communication.

Achieving Intercultural Communication

Test Your Intercultural Knowledge

Never take anything for granted when you're doing business in a foreign country. All sorts of assumptions that are valid in one place can trip you up elsewhere if you fail to consider that customs may vary. Here are several true stories about businesspeople who blundered by overlooking some simple but important cultural differences. Can you spot the erroneous assumptions that led these people astray?

1. You're tired of the discussion and you want to move on to a new topic. You ask your Australian business associate, "Can we table this for a while?" To your dismay, your colleague keeps right on discussing just what you want to put aside. Are Australians that inconsiderate?

2. You finally made the long trip overseas to meet the new German director of your division. Despite slow traffic, you arrive only four minutes late. His door is shut, so you knock on it and walk in. The chair is too far away from the desk, so you pick it up and move it closer. Then you lean over the desk, stick out your hand and say, "Good morning, Hans, it's nice to meet you." Of course, you're baffled by his chilly reaction. Why?

3. Your meeting went better than you'd ever expected. In fact, you found the Japanese representative for your new advertising agency to be very agreeable; she said yes to just about everything. When you share your enthusiasm with your boss, he doesn't appear very excited. Why?

4. You've finally closed the deal, after exhausting both your patience and your company's travel budget. Now, two weeks later, your Chinese customers are asking for special considerations that change the terms of the agreement. How could they do this? Why are they doing it? And, most important, what should you do?

In each case the problems have resulted from inaccurate assumptions. Here are the explanations of what went wrong:

1. To "table" something in Australia means to bring it forward for discussion. This is the opposite of what Americans usually mean. The English that's spoken in Australia is closer to British than to American English. If you are doing business in Australia, become familiar with the local vocabulary. Note the tendency to shorten just about any word whenever possible, and adding "ie" to it is a form of familiar slang: for example, *brolly* (umbrella) and *lollie* (candy). And yes, it's true: "G'day" is the standard greeting. Use it.

2. You've just broken four rules of German polite behavior: punctuality, privacy, personal space, and proper greetings. In time-conscious Germany, you should never arrive even a few minutes late. Also, Germans like their privacy and space, and they adhere to formal greetings of "Frau" and "Herr," even if the business association has lasted for years.

3. The word *yes* may not always mean "yes" in the Western sense. Japanese people may say *yes* to confirm they have heard or understood something but not necessarily to indicate that they agree with it. You'll seldom get a direct no. Some of the ways that Japanese people say no indirectly include "It will be difficult," "I will ask my supervisor," "I'm not sure," "We will think about it," and "I see."

4. For most U.S. businesspeople, the contract represents the end of the negotiation. For Chinese businesspeople, however, it's just the beginning. Once a deal is made, Chinese negotiators view their counterparts as trustworthy partners who can be relied on for special favors—such as new terms in the contract.

---

up, they learn how to recognize situational cues (such as gestures and tone of voice) and how to respond as expected.[15]

In a **low-context culture** such as the United States or Germany, people rely more on verbal communication and less on circumstances and cues to convey meaning. An English speaker feels responsible for transmitting the meaning of the message and often places sentences in chronological sequence to establish a cause-and-effect pattern.[16] In a low-context culture, rules and expectations are usually spelled out through explicit statements such as "Please wait until I'm finished" or "You're welcome to browse."[17] Contextual differences are apparent in the way cultures approach situations such as negotiating, decision making, and problem solving.

Differences in Negotiating Styles   U.S., Canadian, and German negotiators tend to take a relatively impersonal view of negotiations. Members of these low-context cultures see their goals in economic terms and usually presume trust of the other party, at least at the outset. In contrast, high-context Japanese negotiators prefer a more sociable negotiating atmosphere that is conducive to forging personal ties as the basis for trust. To high-context negotiators, achieving immediate economic gains are secondary to establishing and maintaining a long-term relationship.[18]

Differences in Decision-Making Practices   In lower-context cultures, executives try to reach decisions as quickly and efficiently as possible. They are concerned with reaching an

High-context cultures emphasize relationships and a sociable atmosphere when negotiating, whereas low-context cultures view negotiations impersonally and focus on economic goals.

Table 3-1   How Cultural Context Affects Business

In Low-Context Companies	In High-Context Companies
Executive offices are separate with controlled access.	Executive offices are shared and open to all.
Workers rely on detailed background information.	Workers do not expect or want detailed information.
Information is highly centralized and controlled.	Information is shared with everyone.
Objective data are valued over subjective relationships.	Subjective relationships are valued over objective data.
Business and social relationships are discrete.	Business and social relationships overlap.
Competence is valued as much as position and status.	Position and status are valued more than competence.
Meetings have fixed agendas and plenty of advance notice.	Meetings are often called on short notice, and key people always accept.

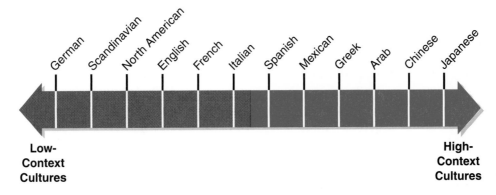

German   Scandinavian   North American   English   French   Italian   Spanish   Mexican   Greek   Arab   Chinese   Japanese

Low-Context Cultures ————————————————————————→ **High-Context Cultures**

agreement on the main points, leaving the details to be worked out later by others. However, this approach would backfire in higher-context Greece, because Greek executives assume that anyone who ignores the details is being evasive and untrustworthy. Spending time on each little point is considered a mark of good faith.

> High-context cultures encourage lengthy decision making, concentrating on every detail, whereas low-context cultures emphasize quick, efficient decisions on major points while leaving the details to be worked out later.

Differences in Problem-Solving Techniques   Cultures differ in their tolerance for open disagreement. Low-context U.S. businesspeople typically enjoy confrontation and debate, but high-context Japanese executives shun such tactics. To avoid the unpleasant feelings that might result from open conflict, Japanese companies may use a go-between or third party. Chinese businesspeople also try to prevent public conflict, making concessions slowly and staying away from proposal-counterproposal methods. If you try to get members of a Chinese team to back down from their position, you will cause them to lose face—very likely ruining the relationship.

> High-context cultures avoid confrontation and debate, whereas low-context cultures encourage open disagreement.

Ethical Differences   Cultural context influences many other cultural areas, including legal and ethical behavior. For example, because low-context cultures value the written word, they consider written agreements binding. But high-context cultures put less emphasis on the written word and consider personal pledges more important than contracts. They also have a tendency to view law with flexibility, whereas low-context cultures would adhere to the law strictly.[19]

> High-context cultures view laws as being more flexible, whereas low-context cultures tend to value written agreements and interpret laws strictly.

As you conduct business around the world, you'll find that legal systems differ from culture to culture. In the United Kingdom and the United States, someone is presumed innocent until proved guilty, a principle rooted in English common law. However, in Mexico and Turkey, someone is presumed guilty until proved innocent, a principle rooted in the Napoleonic code.[20] These distinctions can be particularly important if your firm must communicate about a legal dispute in another country.

> Legal systems differ from culture to culture.

As discussed in Chapter 1, making ethical choices can be difficult, even within your own culture. When communicating across cultures, ethics can be even more complicated. What does it mean for a business to do the right thing in Thailand? In Africa? In Norway? What happens when a certain behavior is unethical in the United States but an accepted practice in another culture? For example, in the United States, bribing officials

> Ethical choices can be even more complicated when communicating across cultures; for example, bribing officials is viewed differently from culture to culture.

is illegal, but Kenyans consider paying such bribes a part of life. To get something done right, they pay *kitu kidogo* (or "something small"). In China businesses pay *huilu*, in Russia they pay *vzyatka*, in the Middle East it's *baksheesh*, and in Mexico it's *una mordida* ("a small bite").[21] The United States has lobbied other nations for 20 years to outlaw bribery, and at last the industrialized nations have signed a treaty that makes payoffs to foreign officials a criminal offense. Of course, bribery won't end just because a treaty has been signed, but supporters are optimistic that countries will ratify the treaty, pass legislation, and enforce the new laws stringently.[22] Making ethical choices across cultures can seem incredibly complicated, but doing so actually differs little from the way you choose the most ethical path in your own culture (see Chapter 1).

When communicating across cultures, keep your messages ethical by applying four basic principles:[23]

> Keep your messages ethical by actively seeking mutual ground, exchanging messages without judgment, sending messages that are honest, and showing respect for cultural differences.

◆ **Actively seek mutual ground.** To allow the clearest possible exchange of information, both parties must be flexible and avoid insisting that an interaction take place strictly in terms of one culture or another.

◆ **Send and receive messages without judgment.** To allow information to flow freely, both parties must recognize that values vary from culture to culture, and both must trust one another.

◆ **Send messages that are honest.** To ensure that the information is true, both parties must see things as they are—not as we would like them to be. In the interest of honesty, we must be fully aware of our personal and cultural biases.

◆ **Show respect for cultural differences.** To protect the basic human rights of both parties, each must understand and acknowledge the other's needs and preserve each other's dignity by communicating without deception.

Social Differences   In any culture, rules of social etiquette may be formal or informal. Formal rules are the specifically taught "rights" and "wrongs" of how to behave in common social situations, such as table manners at meals. When formal rules are violated, members of a culture can explain why they feel upset. In contrast, informal social rules are more difficult to identify and are usually learned by watching how people behave and then imitating that behavior. Informal rules govern how males and females are supposed to behave, when it is appropriate to use a person's first name, and so on. When informal rules are violated, members of a culture are likely to feel uncomfortable, although they may not be able to say exactly why.[24]

> Formal rules of etiquette are explicit and well defined, but informal rules are learned through observation and imitation.

Although the United States is home to millions of people having different religions and values, the major social influence is the Puritan work ethic. The predominant U.S. view is that money solves many problems, that material comfort (earned by individual effort) is a sign of superiority, and that people who work hard are better than those who don't. By and large, people in the United States assume that people from other cultures also dislike poverty and value hard work. However, many societies condemn materialism, and some prize a more carefree lifestyle. For example, U.S. workers annually put in almost 300 more hours at work than West Germans and 60 more hours than their Japanese peers (see Figure 3–2). Such social values are apparent in the way cultures recognize status, define manners, and think about time.

> People from the United States emphasize hard work, material success, and efficiency more than many people in other countries do.

Differing Attitudes Toward Status   Culture dictates how people show respect and signify rank. For example, people in the United States show respect by addressing top managers as "Mr. Roberts" or "Ms. Gutierrez." However, people in China address businesspeople according to their official titles, such as "President" or "Manager."[25] In addition, a U.S. executive's rank may be reflected by a large corner office, deep carpets, an expensive desk, and handsome accessories. But the highest-ranking executives in France sit in the middle of an open area, surrounded by lower-level employees. And in the Middle East, fine possessions are reserved for the home, while business is conducted in cramped and modest quarters.

> Respect and rank are reflected differently from culture to culture in the way people are addressed and in their working environment.

Differing Attitudes Toward Manners   What is polite in one culture may be considered rude in another. In Arab countries it's impolite to take gifts to a man's wife, but it's acceptable to

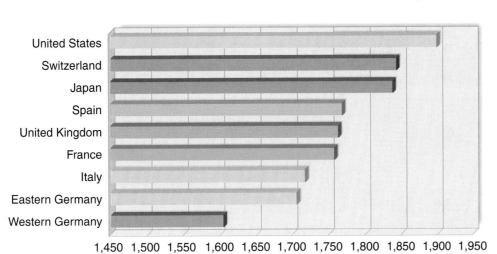

Figure 3–2
Working Hours Vary from
Culture to Culture

take gifts to his children. In Germany giving a woman a red rose is considered a romantic invitation—inappropriate if you're trying to establish a business relationship with her. In India, if you're invited to visit someone's home "any time," you should make an unexpected visit without waiting for a definite invitation. Failure to take the "any time" invitation literally would be an insult, a sign that you don't care to develop the friendship.

The rules of polite behavior vary from country to country.

Differing Attitudes Toward Time   Conducting business entails schedules, deadlines, and appointments, but these matters are regarded differently from culture to culture. German and U.S. executives see time as a way to plan the business day efficiently, focusing on only one task during each scheduled period and viewing time as limited. However, executives from Latin America and Asia see time as more flexible. Meeting a deadline is less important than building a business relationship. So the workday isn't expected to follow a rigid, preset schedule.[26]

Although businesspeople in the United States, Germany, and some other nations see time as a way to organize the business day efficiently, other cultures see time as more flexible.

Nonverbal Differences   As discussed in Chapter 2, nonverbal communication is extremely reliable when determining meaning, but that reliability is valid only when the communicators belong to the same culture. The simplest hand gestures change meaning from culture to culture, so interpreting nonverbal elements according to your own culture can be dangerous. Nonverbal elements are apparent in attitudes toward personal space and in body language.

Variations in the meaning of nonverbal communication can cause problems because people are unaware of the messages they are transmitting.

Attitudes Toward Personal Space   People in Canada and the United States usually stand about five feet apart during a business conversation. However, this distance is uncomfortably close for people from Germany or Japan and uncomfortably far for Arabs and Latin Americans. Because of these differing concepts of personal space, a Canadian manager may react negatively (without knowing exactly why) when an Arab colleague moves closer during their conversation. And the Arab colleague may react negatively (again, without knowing why) when the Canadian manager backs away.

People from various cultures have different "comfort zones."

Use of Body Language   Gestures help members of a culture clarify confusing messages, but differences in body language are a major source of misunderstanding during intercultural communication. Don't assume that someone from another culture who speaks your language has mastered your culture's body language. For example, people in the United States and Canada say no by shaking their heads back and forth; people in Bulgaria nod up and down; people in Japan move their right hand; and people in Sicily raise their chin. Similarly, U.S. businesspeople assume that a person who won't meet their gaze is evasive and dishonest. However, in many parts of Asia, keeping your eyes lowered is a sign of respect.[27]

    People from different cultures may misread an intentional nonverbal signal, may overlook the signal entirely, or may assume that a meaningless gesture is significant. For

Learning the verbal language of a culture does not mean you understand the body language of that culture.

Figure 3–3
Components of Successful
Intercultural Communication

example, an Arab man indicates a romantic interest in a woman by running a hand backward across his hair, but most Westerners would not see the gesture as significant. Conversely, an Egyptian might mistakenly assume that a Westerner who exposes the sole of his or her shoe is offering a grave insult.[28]

Recognizing cultural differences helps you avoid sending inappropriate signals and helps you correctly interpret the signals from others—an important step toward improving intercultural sensitivity. But simple recognition isn't the whole story. Being aware of cultural differences is only the first step in improving your intercultural communication. To achieve intercultural sensitivity, you need to balance cultural awareness with cultural flexibility. The diagram in Figure 3–3 shows the relationship of language, exposure, and technique to communication skill (all of which are covered in detail in this chapter). To communicate across cultures successfully, you must be able to accommodate these differences without judging them, which means you must be able to overcome the human tendency toward ethnocentrism.

> Recognizing cultural differences must be followed by the sincere attempt to accommodate those differences.

Overcome Ethnocentrism

When communicating across cultures, your effectiveness depends on maintaining an open mind. Unfortunately, many people lapse into **ethnocentrism,** the belief that one's own cultural background—including ways of analyzing problems, values, beliefs, and verbal and nonverbal communications—is superior.[29] Enthnocentrists lose sight of the possibility that their words and actions can be misunderstood, and they forget that they are likely to misinterpret the actions of others.

When you first begin to investigate the culture of another group, you may attempt to understand the common tendencies of that group's members by **stereotyping**—predicting individuals' behavior or character on the basis of their membership in a particular group or class. For example, Japanese visitors often stereotype Americans as people who walk fast, are wasteful in utilizing space, speak directly, ask too many questions in the classroom and don't respect professors, are disrespectful of age and status, lack discipline, and are extravagant.[30]

Although stereotyping may be useful in the beginning, your next step is to move beyond the stereotypes to relationships with real people. Unfortunately, when ethnocen-

> *Objective*
> **4**
> Define *ethnocentrism* and *stereotyping;* then discuss three suggestions for overcoming these limiting mind sets.

> Ethnocentrism is the tendency to judge all other groups according to one's own group's standards, behaviors, and customs and to see other groups as inferior by comparison.

> Stereotyping is the attempt to categorize individuals by trying to predict their behavior or character on the basis of their membership in a particular group.

tric people stereotype, they tend to do so on the basis of limited, general, or inaccurate evidence. They frequently develop biased attitudes toward the group, and they fail to move beyond that initial step.[31] So instead of talking with Abdul Karhum, unique human being, ethnocentric people are talking to "an Arab." They may believe that all Arabs are, say, hagglers, so Abdul Karhum's personal qualities cannot alter such preconceptions. His every action is forced to fit the preconceived image, even if that image is wrong.

In order to overcome ethnocentrism, follow a few simple suggestions:

◆ **Acknowledge distinctions.** Don't ignore the differences between another person's culture and your own.

◆ **Avoid assumptions.** Don't assume that others will act the same way you do, that they will operate from the same assumptions, or that they will use language and symbols the same way you do.

◆ **Avoid judgments.** When people act differently, don't conclude that they are in error, that their way is invalid, or that their customs are inferior to your own.

At Target, Rafael Rodriguez works hard to move his people away from ethnocentrism and toward understanding and tolerance. Too often, both parties in an intercultural exchange are guilty of ethnocentrism and prejudice. Little wonder, then, that misunderstandings arise when communicating across cultures.

IMPROVING COMMUNICATION ACROSS CULTURES

Once you can recognize cultural elements and overcome ethnocentrism, you're ready to focus directly on your intercultural communication skills. To communicate more effectively with people from other cultures, you need to overcome language barriers, study other cultures, develop effective written skills, and develop effective oral skills.

Overcome Language Barriers

By choosing specific words to communicate, you signal that you are a member of a particular culture or subculture and that you know the code. The nature of your code—your language and vocabulary—imposes its own barriers on your message. For example, the language of a lawyer differs from that of an accountant or a doctor, and the difference in their vocabularies affects their ability to recognize and express ideas. Barriers also exist because words can be interpreted in more than one way. In fact, it's often said that the United States and the United Kingdom are two countries divided by a common language (see Table 3–2).

You can overcome ethnocentrism by acknowledging distinctions, avoiding assumptions, and avoiding judgments.

Colin Powell, the first African American to serve as Secretary of State, is a former chairman of the Joint Chiefs of Staff, and has chaired America's Promise—The Alliance for Youth. Early in his career, Powell rejected the limits of racial stereotyping. As the son of Jamaican immigrants, he grew up in the racially integrated South Bronx, where sheer determination drove him to succeed. Today, both by example and in speeches to diverse audiences, Powell promotes the value of cultural difference and the importance of moving beyond labels to break down the barriers that prevent communication.

Objective
5

Discuss three ways to improve communication with people who speak English as a second language; then discuss three ways to improve communication with people who don't speak your language at all.

Table 3–2　U.S. versus British English	
U.S. English	**British English**
apartment	flat
eggplant	auberg
cleaning lady	charwoman
elevator	lift
first floor	ground level
long-distance call	trunk call
organization	organisation
pharmacist	chemist
rare	underdone
roast	joint
string bean	French bean
sweater	pullover

The barriers become greater still when you're communicating across cultures. You must be able to communicate effectively both with people who speak English as a second language (ESL) and with people who don't speak your language at all.

Breaking Through ESL Barriers   Of the many millions of people who use English as a second language, some are extremely fluent, and others have only an elementary command. When dealing with those less fluent in your own language, you may miss a few subtleties, but you are still able to communicate. Even so, don't assume that the other person understands everything you say. Your message can be mangled by slang and idioms, by local accents, and by vocal variations.

> English is the most prevalent language in international business, but it's a mistake to assume that everyone understands it.

> Slang and idioms, local accents and pronunciation, and vocal variations can pose problems when you're speaking to people from other cultures.

Avoid Using Slang and Idioms   Languages never translate word for word. They are idiomatic—constructed with phrases that mean more than the sum of their literal parts. For example, if a U.S. executive tells an Egyptian executive that a certain product "doesn't cut the mustard" or that making the monthly sales quota will be "a piece of cake," chances are that the communication will fail. When speaking to people less fluent in your language, try to choose words carefully to convey only their most specific denotative meaning. Use words that have singular rather than multiple meanings. The word *high* has 20 meanings; the word *expensive* has one.[32]

Overcoming language barriers by avoiding slang and idioms is a constant pursuit in a company like NEC Corporation, which has offices in North America, South America, Europe, Asia, Africa, and Oceania. NEC is recognized as a world leader in high technology, and its goal is to link the world and transform it into a cooperative global village.

Pay Attention to Local Accents and Pronunciation   Even when people speak your language, you may have a hard time understanding their pronunciation. After transferring to Toyota's U.S. office, some English-speaking Japanese employees had to enroll in a special course to learn that "Jeat yet?" means "Did you eat yet?" and that "Cannahepya?" means "Can I help you?" Some nonnative English speakers don't distinguish between the English sounds *v* and *w*, so they say "wery" for "very." At the same time, many people from the United States are unable to pronounce the French *r* or the German *ch*.

Be Aware of Vocal Variations   Some people use their voices differently from culture to culture. Russian speakers tend to use a flat, level tone, so to some U.S. listeners they sound bored or rude. Middle Easterners tend to speak more loudly than Westerners and may therefore mistakenly be considered more emotional. On the other hand, people from Japan are soft-spoken, a characteristic that implies politeness or humility to Western listeners.

Breaking Through Foreign Language Barriers   Even though English is widely spoken in the global business marketplace, the language of business is the language of the customer. Increasingly, that language may not be English.[33] So U.S. companies are realizing that they can no longer get by speaking only English—even in the United States. One of every seven people in the United States speaks a language other than English when at home. After English, Spanish is by far the most commonly spoken language in the United States, followed by French, German, Italian, and Chinese.[34] When communicating with people who don't speak your language at all, you have three options: You can learn their language, use an intermediary or a translator, or teach them your language. However you choose to overcome language barriers, remember that effective communication requires a major commitment—even on the Web (see "Achieving Intercultural Communication—Communicating with a Global Audience on the Web").

> Many companies recognize that they must be able to conduct business in languages other than English.

Learn a Foreign Language   If you're planning to live in another country or to do business there repeatedly, you might want to learn the language. The same holds true if you'll be working closely with a subculture that has its own language, such as Vietnamese Americans. Even if you're doing business in your own language, you show respect by making the effort to learn the subculture's language, or at least to learn a few words. One problem is that language courses may take more time and more money than you can afford.

> If you have a long-term business relationship with people of another culture, it is helpful to learn their language.

Achieving Intercultural Communication

Communicating with a Global Audience on the Web

With growing global access to the World Wide Web, some U.S. corporate sites are already reporting that foreign visitors account for as much as 30 percent of their traffic and 10 percent of their commerce. Nevertheless, reaching an international audience on the Web involves more than simply offering translations of the English language. Successful global sites address the needs of international customers in five ways:

1. **Consider the reader's viewpoint.** Assume your audience is unfamiliar with common American phrases and references. To avoid confusion, provide both American units and metric equivalents for weights, measures, sizes, and temperatures. Also, use universal terms for times, dates, and geographical names. For example, consider expressing time in military format ("16:00" for 4 p.m.). Since Europeans read "10/04/2002" as April 10, 2002, be sure you spell out the month and year. And offer complete location descriptions, such as "Kansas City, MO, USA."

2. **Be sensitive to cultural differences.** Since humor is rooted in cultural norms, a touch of American humor may not be so funny to Asian or European readers. Don't risk offending or slighting your audience with cultural stereotypes or expressions. Avoid idioms and references that aren't universally recognized, such as "putting all your eggs in one basket" or "jumping out of the frying pan into the fire."

3. **Keep the message clear.** Use simple words and write in the active voice. Avoid complicated sentence structure to achieve a simple, straightforward tone. And don't forget to define abbreviations and acronyms.

4. **Break through language barriers with graphics.** Clarify written concepts with graphics. However, even though most graphical icons are internationally recognized, some images are more widely accepted than others. In some countries, for example, a mailbox doesn't necessarily convey the idea of sending mail. So an envelope might be a more appropriate symbol to reinforce the message "Contact Us."

5. **Consult local experts.** Work with local experts and webmasters to develop native-language keywords that will direct international customers to your site. Seek the advice of local experts about customary phrases and references. Even simple terms such as "home page" differ from country to country. Spanish readers refer to the "first page," or *pagina inicial*, whereas the French term is "welcome page," or *page d'accuei.*

CAREER APPLICATIONS

1. Visit the World of Sony Music Entertainment at www.sonymusic.com/world and examine Sony's sites for Argentina, France, and Germany. How does Sony "localize" each country's site?

2. Compare Sony Music's international sites to IBM's global Web pages at www.ibm.com. How does Sony's approach differ from IBM's? Do both corporations successfully address the needs of a global audience? Write a two-paragraph summary that compares the international sites of both companies.

Use an Intermediary or a Translator   Because so many international business letters are written in English, U.S. firms don't always worry about translating their correspondence. However, many other forms of written communication must be translated. Advertisements are almost always translated into the customer's language. Warranties, repair and maintenance manuals, and product labels also require translation. For example, the warranty for a Hewlett-Packard laser jet printer cartridge is written in English, French, Spanish, Italian, and Japanese. In addition, many multinational companies translate policy and procedure manuals for use in overseas offices. Reports from foreign branches to the home office may be written in one language and then translated into another. One multinational company, E. I. Du Pont de Nemours & Company, translates roughly 70,000 pages of documents each year. [35]

> Many companies use translators to help them communicate with people who don't speak English.

An experienced translator can analyze a message, understand its meaning in the cultural context, consider how to convey the meaning in another language, and then use verbal and nonverbal signals to encode or decode the message for someone from another culture. Whenever possible, arrange to meet translators ahead of time to give them a sense of what you are presenting and to discuss specific words or concepts that could be confusing.[36] Some companies use *back-translation* to ensure accuracy. Once a translator encodes a message into another language, a different translator retranslates the same message into the original language. This back-translation is then compared with the original message to discover any errors or discrepancies.

> Back-translation helps ensure accuracy by allowing translators to check a second translation against the original message.

Some companies find it useful to teach their employees to speak English.

Offer English-Language Training Programs for Employees   The option of teaching other people to speak your language doesn't appear to be very practical at first glance. However, many companies find it beneficial to offer language-training programs. For example, Tenneco instituted an English language-training program in New Jersey for its Spanish-speaking employees. The training concentrated on practical English for use on the job, and thanks to the classes, accidents and grievances declined and productivity improved.[37] Some multinational companies ask all their employees to use English when writing to employees in other countries, regardless of where they're located. For example, Nissan employees use English for internal memos to colleagues around the world, even though the corporation is based in Japan.[38] Of course, requiring employees to use a specific language when they're on the job can create tension and may be considered discriminatory.

Study Other Cultures

Objective

6

Explain why studying other cultures helps you communicate more effectively, and list at least 7 of the 15 tips offered by successful intercultural businesspeople.

Learning as much as possible about another culture will enhance your ability to communicate with its members.

Learning all you can about a particular culture is a good way to figure out how to send and receive intercultural messages effectively. Read books and articles about these cultures, and talk to people who have done business with members of these cultures. Concentrate on learning something about each culture's history, religion, politics, values, and customs. Find out about a country's subcultures, especially its business subculture, and any special rules or protocol. Studying culture is especially important if you interact with people from a variety of cultures or subcultures, like Target's Rodriguez.

"In dealing with American businesspeople," says Y. A. Cho, chief operating officer of Korean Airlines, "I'm amazed at how naive most are about other cultures and the way that others do business."[39] Something as simple as a handshake differs from culture to culture. For example, in Spain a proper handshake must last five to seven strokes, and pulling away too soon may be interpreted as rejection. However, in France the preferred handshake is only a single stroke. In Arab countries, you'll insult your hosts if you turn down food, drink, or hospitality of any kind. But don't accept too quickly, either. A polite refusal (such as "I don't want to put you to any trouble") is expected before you finally accept.

This chapter's "Checklist: Doing Business Abroad" can help you start your investigation of another culture. However, don't expect ever to understand another culture completely. No matter how much you study German culture, for example, you'll never be a German or share the experiences of having grown up in Germany. The trick is to learn useful general information while remaining aware of and open to variations and individual differences. You can communicate more effectively if you follow the tips from successful intercultural businesspeople:[40]

◆ **Assume differences until similarity is proved.** Don't assume that others are more similar to you than they actually are.

◆ **Take responsibility for communication.** Don't assume it's the other person's job to communicate with you.

◆ **Withhold judgment.** Learn to listen to the whole story and accept differences in others without judging them.

◆ **Show respect.** Learn how respect is communicated in various cultures (through gestures, eye contact, and so on).

◆ **Empathize.** Before sending a message, put yourself in the receiver's shoes. Imagine the receiver's feelings and point of view.

◆ **Tolerate ambiguity.** Learn to control your frustration when placed in an unfamiliar or confusing situation.

◆ **Look beyond the superficial.** Don't be distracted by things such as dress, appearance, or environmental discomforts.

◆ **Be patient and persistent.** If you want to communicate with someone from another culture, don't give up easily.

◆ **Recognize your own cultural biases.** Learn to identify when your assumptions are different from the other person's assumptions.

Going Online

Hone Your Skills for International Business

→

What do you need to know about international business practices and different social customs? For crucial information that will help you successfully conduct business abroad, preview "Going Global" at americanexpress.com. Learn about appropriate business etiquette by accessing information such as negotiation strategies, international business regulations, and reference sources for 78 countries. If you want details on business travel, visa requirements, appropriate attire, accommodations, and language fluency, the research reports at this site will help prepare you to deal internationally.

www.americanexpress.
com/smallbusiness

To reach the Web site above, go to www.prenhall.com/thill *(the Web site for this text). Select Chapter 3, then select "Student Resources." There you'll find a current live link that will take you straight to the site.*

Checklist: Doing Business Abroad

Understand Social Customs

- ✓ How do people react to strangers? Are they friendly? Hostile? Reserved?
- ✓ How do people greet each other? Should you bow? Nod? Shake hands?
- ✓ How are names used for introductions?
- ✓ What are the attitudes toward touching people?
- ✓ How do you express appreciation for an invitation to lunch or dinner or to someone's home? Should you bring a gift? Send flowers? Write a thank-you note?
- ✓ How, when, or where are people expected to sit in social or business situations?
- ✓ Are any phrases, facial expressions, or hand gestures considered rude?
- ✓ How close do people stand when talking?
- ✓ How do you attract the attention of a waiter? Do you tip the waiter?
- ✓ When is it rude to refuse an invitation? How do you refuse politely?
- ✓ What are the acceptable patterns of eye contact?
- ✓ What gestures indicate agreement? Disagreement? Respect?
- ✓ What topics may or may not be discussed in a social setting? In a business setting?
- ✓ How is time perceived?
- ✓ What are the generally accepted working hours?
- ✓ How do people view scheduled appointments?

Learn About Clothing and Food Preferences

- ✓ What occasions require special clothing? What colors are associated with mourning? Love? Joy?
- ✓ Are some types of clothing considered taboo for one sex or the other?
- ✓ What are the attitudes toward human body odors? Are deodorants or perfumes used?
- ✓ How many times a day do people eat?
- ✓ How are hands or utensils used when eating?
- ✓ What types of places, food, and drink are appropriate for business entertainment?
- ✓ Where is the seat of honor at a table?

Assess Political Patterns

- ✓ How stable is the political situation? Does it affect businesses in and out of the country?
- ✓ How is political power manifested? Military power? Economic strength?
- ✓ What are the traditional government institutions?

What Channels are Used for Expressing Official and Unofficial Political Opinion?

- ✓ What information media are important? Who controls them?
- ✓ Is it appropriate to talk politics in social or business situations?

Understand Religious and Folk Beliefs

- ✓ To which religious groups do people belong?
- ✓ How do religious beliefs influence daily activities?
- ✓ Which places, objects, and events are sacred?
- ✓ Is there a tolerance for minority religions?
- ✓ How do religious holidays affect business and government activities?
- ✓ Does religion affect attitudes toward smoking? Drinking? Gambling?
- ✓ Does religion require or prohibit eating specific foods? At specific times?
- ✓ Which objects or actions portend good luck? Bad luck?

Learn About Economic and Business Institutions

- ✓ Is the society homogeneous?
- ✓ What minority groups are represented?
- ✓ What languages are spoken?
- ✓ Do immigration patterns influence work force composition?
- ✓ What are the primary resources and principal products?
- ✓ What vocational/technological training is offered?
- ✓ What are the attitudes toward education?
- ✓ Are businesses generally large? Family controlled? Government controlled?
- ✓ Is it appropriate to do business by telephone? By fax? By e-mail?
- ✓ Do managers make business decisions unilaterally or do they involve employees?
- ✓ How are status and seniority shown in an organization? In a business meeting?
- ✓ Must people socialize before conducting business?

Appraise the Nature of Ethics, Values, and Laws

- ✓ Is money or a gift expected in exchange for arranging business transactions?
- ✓ What ethical or legal issues might affect business transactions?
- ✓ Do people value competitiveness or cooperation?
- ✓ What are the attitudes toward work? Toward money?
- ✓ Is politeness more important than factual honesty?
- ✓ What qualities are admired in a business associate?

- ◆ **Be flexible.** Be prepared to change your habits and attitudes when communicating with someone from another culture.
- ◆ **Emphasize common ground.** Look for similarities to work from.
- ◆ **Send clear messages.** Make both your verbal and nonverbal signals clear and consistent.

Learning general intercultural communication skills will help you adapt in any culture, an ability that is especially important if you interact with people from a variety of cultures or subcultures.

Checklist: **Communicating with a Culturally Diverse Work Force**

Accept Cultural Differences

✓ Adjust your message to employees' education level.
✓ Encourage employees to discuss their culture's customs.
✓ Create a formal forum to teach employees about the customs of all cultures represented in the firm.
✓ Train employees to see and overcome ethnocentric stereotyping.
✓ Provide books, articles, and videos about various cultures.
✓ Stamp out negative labels by observing how people identify their own groups.

Improve Oral and Written Communications

✓ Define the terms people need to know on the job.
✓ Emphasize major points with repetition and recap.
✓ Use familiar words whenever possible.
✓ Don't cover too much information at one time.
✓ Be specific and explicit—using descriptive words, exact measurements, and examples when possible.
✓ Give the reason for asking employees to follow a certain procedure and explain what will happen if the procedure is not followed.
✓ Use written summaries and visual aids (when appropriate) to clarify your points.

✓ Demonstrate and encourage the right way to complete a task, use a tool, and so on.
✓ Reduce language barriers: Train managers in the language of their employees, train employees in the language of most customers and of most people in the company, ask bilingual employees to serve as translators, print important health and safety instructions in as many languages as necessary.

Assess How Well You've Been Understood

✓ Research the nonverbal reactions of other cultures; then be alert to facial expressions and other nonverbal signs that indicate confusion or embarrassment.
✓ Encourage employees to ask questions in private and in writing.
✓ Observe how employees use the information you've provided, and review any misunderstood points.

Offer Feedback to Improve Communication

✓ Focus on the positive by explaining what *should* be done rather than what *shouldn't* be done.
✓ Discuss a person's behaviors and the situation, rather than making a judgment about the person.
✓ Be supportive as you offer feedback, and reassure individuals that their skills and contributions are important.

◆ **Deal with the individual.** Communicate with each person as an individual, not as a stereotypical representative of another group.

◆ **Learn when to be direct.** Investigate each culture so that you'll know when to send your message in a straightforward manner and when to be indirect.

◆ **Treat your interpretation as a working hypothesis.** Once you think you understand a foreign culture, carefully assess the feedback provided by recipients of your communication to see if it confirms your hypothesis.

This advice will help you communicate with anybody, regardless of culture. For more ideas on how to improve communication in the workplace, see this chapter's "Checklist: Communicating with a Culturally Diverse Work Force."

O b j e c t i v e

7

Illustrate how word choice affects communication with people in other cultures; then list six recommendations for writing more effectively and nine guidelines for speaking across cultures more effectively.

Whether you choose written or oral channels to communicate your message across cultures, you must adapt your style.

Develop Effective Intercultural Skills

Only after you've studied other cultures can you truly begin to develop effective intercultural skills. Once you discover which language barriers must be overcome, and once you understand what sort of cultural differences you'll be facing, you must decide how best to communicate your message, whether using written or oral channels would be best. Then you must adapt your style to make the right impression. For example, your choice of words reflects the relationship between you and your audience. So whether writing or speaking across cultures, be sure to use the appropriate level of formality.

Improve Your Written Skills   In general, U.S. businesspeople will want to be somewhat more formal in their international correspondence than they would be when writing to people in their own country. In many cultures, writers use a more elaborate style, so your audience will expect more formal language in your letter. The letter in Figure 3–4 was

Furtwangen Handcrafts
Kussenhofstrasse 150
Furtwangen, Germany

Geschäfts-fürer literally means "business leader": A common English translation would be "managing director."

Mister
Karl Wieland
Business Leader
Black Forest Gifts
Friedrichstrasse 98
70174 Stuttgart
GERMANY

May 15, 2002

Very honorable Mister Wieland,

Refers to the ongoing business relationship

Because the tourist season will begin soon, we would like to seize the opportunity to introduce our new line of hand-carved cuckoo clocks to you. Last year you were so friendly as to buy two dozen of our clocks. In recognition of our good business relationship, we now offer you the opportunity to select the new models before we offer this line to other businesses for purchase.

Shows concern for the audience

Language a bit more formal than in U.S. letters

As you know, our artisans use only the best wood. According to time-honored patterns that are passed on from generation to generation, they carefully carve every detail by hand. Our clockworks are of superior quality, and we test every clock before it is painted and shipped. We give you a guarantee of five years on all Furtwangen Handcrafts clocks.

Enclosed you will find a copy of our newest brochure and an order form. To express our appreciation, we take over the shipping costs if you order before June 15.

We continue to wish you a lot of success in your new Stuttgart location. We are convinced that you will satisfy your regular clientele with your larger exhibition area and expanded stock and will gain many new visitors.

Ends with a compliment to the recipient

Complimentary close typical of German business letters

With friendly greetings

Frederick Semper

Frederick Semper

Typed name includes no title

Figure 3–4
In-Depth Critique: Translated German Business Letter

written by a supplier in Germany to a nearby retailer. The tone is more formal than would be used in the United States, but the writer clearly focuses on his audience. In Germany, business letters usually open with a reference to the business relationship and close with a compliment to the recipient. Of course, be careful not to carry formality to extremes, or you'll sound unnatural.

International business letters generally have a formal tone and a relatively elaborate style.

Letter writers in other countries also use various techniques to organize their thoughts. If you are aware of some of these practices, you'll be able to concentrate on the message without passing judgment on the writers. Letters from Japanese businesspeople, for example, are slow to come to the point. They typically begin with a remark about the season or weather, which is followed by an inquiry about your health or congratulations on your success. A note of thanks for your patronage might come next. After these preliminaries, the main idea is introduced. The letter in Figure 3–5 was written by a Japanese banker to a large business customer. Notice how the banker emphasizes developing a long-term business relationship.

Be aware of various cultures' tendency to organize thoughts differently.

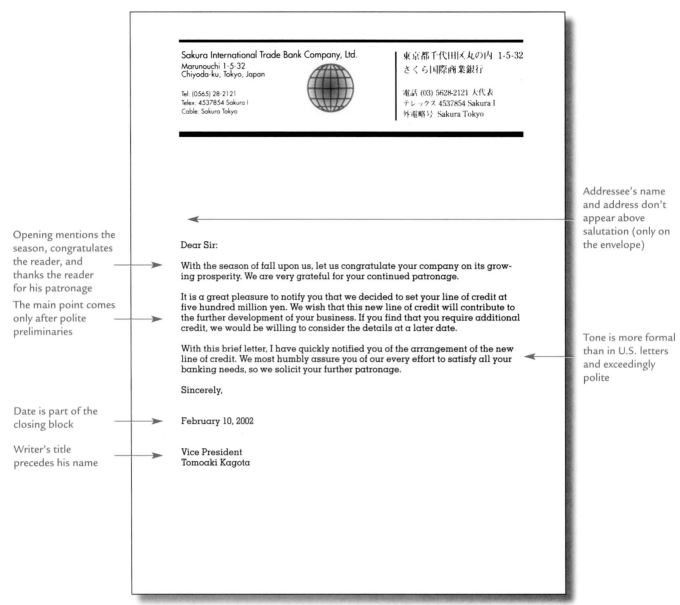

The following callouts appear around the letter:

- Opening mentions the season, congratulates the reader, and thanks the reader for his patronage
- The main point comes only after polite preliminaries
- Date is part of the closing block
- Writer's title precedes his name
- Addressee's name and address don't appear above salutation (only on the envelope)
- Tone is more formal than in U.S. letters and exceedingly polite

Letter content:

Sakura International Trade Bank Company, Ltd.
Marunouchi 1-5-32
Chiyoda-ku, Tokyo, Japan

Tel: (0565) 28-2121
Telex: 4537854 Sakura I
Cable: Sakura Tokyo

東京都千代田区丸の内 1-5-32
さくら国際商業銀行

電話 (03) 5628-2121 大代表
テレックス 4537854 Sakura I
外電略号 Sakura Tokyo

Dear Sir:

With the season of fall upon us, let us congratulate your company on its growing prosperity. We are very grateful for your continued patronage.

It is a great pleasure to notify you that we decided to set your line of credit at five hundred million yen. We wish that this new line of credit will contribute to the further development of your business. If you find that you require additional credit, we would be willing to consider the details at a later date.

With this brief letter, I have quickly notified you of the arrangement of the new line of credit. We most humbly assure you of our every effort to satisfy all your banking needs, so we solicit your further patronage.

Sincerely,

February 10, 2002

Vice President
Tomoaki Kagota

Figure 3–5
In-Depth Critique: Translated Japanese Business Letter

To ensure effective written communication, follow these recommendations (all of which are discussed in more detail in Chapter 5, "Composing Business Messages"):[41]

◆ **Use plain English.** Use short, precise words that say exactly what you mean.

◆ **Be clear.** Rely on specific terms and concrete examples to explain your points.

◆ **Avoid slang and idioms.** Avoid using slang, idioms, jargon, and buzzwords. Abbreviations, acronyms (such as CAD/CAM), and unfamiliar product names may also lead to confusion.

◆ **Be brief.** Construct sentences that are shorter and simpler than those you might use when writing to someone fluent in your own language.

◆ **Use short paragraphs.** Each paragraph should stick to one topic and be no more than eight to ten lines long.

◆ **Use transitional elements.** Help readers follow your train of thought by using transitional phrases. Precede related points with expressions such as *in addition* and *first, second, third.*

Improve Your Oral Skills   If you've ever studied another language, you know it's easier to write in that language than to conduct a conversation. However, some transactions simply cannot be handled without face-to-face contact. In many countries, business relationships are based on personal relationships, and until you establish rapport, nothing happens. When speaking in English to people who speak English as a second language, you may find these guidelines helpful:

Face-to-face communication lets you establish a personal relationship with people from other cultures and gives you the benefit of immediate feedback.

- **Try to eliminate noise.** Pronounce words clearly, stop at distinct punctuation points, and make one point at a time.

- **Look for feedback.** Be alert to signs of confusion in your listener. Realize that nods and smiles don't necessarily mean understanding. Recognize that gestures and expressions mean different things in different cultures. If the other person's body language seems at odds with the message, take time to clarify the meaning.

- **Rephrase your sentence when necessary.** If someone doesn't seem to understand you, choose simpler words; don't just repeat the sentence in a louder voice.

- **Clarify your true intent with repetition and examples.** Try to be aware of unintentional meanings that may be read into your message.

- **Don't talk down to the other person.** Try not to overenunciate, and don't "blame" the listener for not understanding. Use phrases such as "Am I going too fast?" rather than "Is this too difficult for you?"

- **Use objective, accurate language.** Avoid throwing around adjectives such as *fantastic* and *fabulous*, which people from other cultures might consider unreal and overly dramatic.

- **Listen carefully and patiently.** Let other people finish what they have to say. If you interrupt, you may miss something important. You'll also show a lack of respect. If you do not understand a comment, ask the person to repeat it.

- **Adapt your conversation style to the other person's.** For instance, if the other person appears to be direct and straightforward, follow suit.

- **Clarify what will happen next.** At the end of the conversation, be sure that you and the other person agree on what has been said and decided. If appropriate, follow up by writing a letter or a memo summarizing the conversation and thanking the person for meeting with you.

In short, take advantage of the other person's presence to make sure that your message is getting across and that you understand his or her message too.

SUMMARY OF LEARNING OBJECTIVES

1 **Discuss two trends that have made intercultural business communication so important.** Two trends have made intercultural business communication important. *Market globalization*, the first trend, is brought about by improvements in communication and transportation technology. Such technological advancements allow companies to sell and produce goods all over the world. As a result, more and more people are working in companies whose employees come from various national, ethnic, racial, and religious backgrounds. This, of course, affects a country's *cultural diversity*, the second trend contributing to the importance of intercultural business communication. The U.S. workforce includes recent immigrants (from Europe, Canada, Latin America, and Asia), people from various ethnic backgrounds (such as African Americans, Hispanic Americans, and Asian Americans), and people who differ in other characteristics (such as gender, age, family status, and educational background). Thus, to be successful in today's workplace, you must be sensitive to cultural differences and possess good intercultural skills.

2 **Define *culture* and *subculture*, and list culture's four basic characteristics.** *Culture* is a shared system of symbols, beliefs, attitudes, values, expectations, and norms for behavior. A *subculture* is a distinct group existing within a major culture, such as Russian immigrants or disabled individuals existing within the United States. Culture has four basic characteristics: (1) culture is learned, (2) cultures vary in stability, (3) cultures vary in complexity, and (4) cultures vary in tolerance.

3 **Explain the importance of recognizing cultural differences, delineate the differences between high- and low-context cultures, and list four categories of cultural differences.** People from different cultures encode and decode messages differently, increasing the chances of misunderstanding. By recognizing cultural differences, we don't automatically assume that everyone's thoughts and actions are just like ours. For example, *high-context cultures* convey meaning by relying less on verbal communication and more on nonverbal actions and environmental setting. They expect the audience to discover the meaning of a message, and they rarely state the rules of everyday life explicitly. Conversely, *low-context cultures* convey meaning by relying more on verbal communication and less on circumstances and cues. They expect the speaker to transmit the meaning of a message, and they usually spell out rules and expectations in explicit statements. The four categories of cultural differences are contextual differences, ethical differences, social differences, and nonverbal differences.

4 **Define *ethnocentrism* and *stereotyping*; then discuss three suggestions for overcoming this limiting mind set.** *Ethnocentrism* is the tendency to judge all other groups according to one's own standards, behaviors, and customs. *Stereotyping* is predicting individuals' behavior or character on the basis of their membership in a particular group or class. To overcome ethnocentrism, follow three suggestions: (1) acknowledge distinctions, (2) avoid assumptions, and (3) avoid judgments.

5 **Discuss three ways to improve communication with people who speak English as a second language; then discuss three ways to improve communication with people who don't speak your language at all.** When communicating with people who speak English as a second language, clarify your meaning in three ways. First, since language never translates word for word, avoid using slang and idioms. Choose words that will convey only the most specific denotative meaning. Second, listen carefully and pay close attention to local accents and pronunciation. Third, don't assume that people from different cultures use their voice the same way you do. Be aware of vocal variations across cultures. When communicating with someone who doesn't speak your language at all, you have three choices. First, you can learn a foreign language or at least show respect by learning a few words. Second, you can use an intermediary or a translator to analyze a message, understand its cultural context, and convey its meaning in another language. Back translation helps ensure accuracy and avoid embarrassing mistakes. Third, you can teach others your language. Many companies offer language-training programs to employees who speak little or no English.

6 **Explain why studying other cultures helps you communicate more effectively, and list at least 7 of the 15 tips offered by successful intercultural businesspeople.** Studying other cultures helps you send and receive intercultural messages more effectively. Even though you can't expect to understand another culture completely, you can increase your intercultural knowledge by reading books and articles about other cultures and by talking to people who do business in other cultures. Tips offered by successful intercultural businesspeople include the following: (1) take responsibility for communication, (2) withhold judgment, (3) show respect, (4) empathize, (5) look beyond the superficial, (6) be patient and persistent, (7) be flexible.

7 **Illustrate how word choice affects communication with people from other cultures; then list six recommendations for writing more effectively and nine guidelines for speaking across cultures more effectively.** Word choice reflects the relationship between you and your audience; for example, the appropriate level of formality is achieved by word choice. To write more effectively, follow six recommendations: (1) use plain English, (2) be clear, (3) avoid slang and idioms, (4) be brief, (5) use short paragraphs, and (6) use transitional elements. To speak across cultures more effectively, follow these nine guidelines: (1) try to eliminate noise, (2) look for feedback, (3) rephrase your sentence when necessary, (4) clarify your true intent with repetition and examples, (5) don't talk down to the other person, (6) use objective and accurate language, (7) listen carefully and patiently, (8) adapt your conversation style to the other person's, and (9) clarify what will happen next.

On the job: SOLVING A COMMUNICATION DILEMMA AT TARGET STORES

Besides ensuring that his team members stock shelves efficiently, Rafael Rodriguez makes sure they work and communicate well with each other and with him. Because English is a second language for some team members, Rodriguez guarantees that each employee understands his instructions by using easily understood vocabulary, avoiding idioms, and encouraging questions. He's patient when resolving problems and misunderstandings based on cultural differences, and he follows company policy about providing plenty of opportunity for team members to learn about the cultures of their co-workers.

When Patrick Navarez immigrated to the United States from the Philippines, he was the only Asian on Rodriguez's team. Navarez quickly ran into problems when he tried to start conversations with some of his female co-workers by asking questions about their hair, nose rings, and other fashion choices. When other co-workers realized he was invading personal territory without knowing it, they explained that his questions were too personal. The whole team was eventually able to laugh with him about his cultural blunder, and not long after, Navarez had a chance to educate his co-workers. When a Vietnamese employee joined the team, other team members expected Navarez and the new employee to feel a sense of camaraderie based on their shared culture. But Navarez explained that even though they were both Asian, their languages and cultures were very different.

All levels of management at Target are ethnically diverse, and the company offers diversity training to help employees understand

and work better with their co-workers. When Rodriguez visited corporate headquarters in Minneapolis, he met many executives who were Hispanic, Asian, and African American, confirming his belief that his ethnicity would not prevent his being promoted if he performed well on the job.

For many of Rodriguez's team members, the stock clerk job is their first real exposure to cultural differences. At Target they're motivated to communicate across cultures and to cooperate in order to get the job done. They all realize that they can move up in the company, and they each have an evaluation twice a year, receiving constructive feedback on job performance. Team members who communicate well are likely to receive higher evaluations, and with Rodriguez's help, the stock clerks on his team are learning early how to succeed in a diverse work force.

Your Mission Like Rodriguez, you supervise a culturally diverse team of Target stock clerks. You want to foster cooperation among your team members and encourage them to perform well. Use your skill in intercultural communication to choose the best response in each of the following situations. Be prepared to explain why your choice is best.

1. One of your Hispanic American team members, Miguel Gomez, has started making derogatory remarks about team members who are African American. Gomez is refusing to work with them and tells you that he would rather work with other team members who are Hispanic American. How do you resolve the problem?

    a. To avoid conflict, let him work with the co-workers who make him most comfortable.
    b. Tell him he has to work with whomever you assign him to. If he refuses, fire him.
    c. Schedule a time for him to sit down with you and the African American team members so that all of you can discuss cultural differences.
    d. Speak with him privately about the company's goals regarding a diverse work force, and then sign him up for the company diversity training program.

2. Amy Tam is not stocking shelves correctly: she's stacking cans too high and mixing brands in the displays. You think language may be a problem; perhaps she does not comprehend all your instructions. How do you make sure that she understands you?

    a. Write everything down in a list so that Tam can refer to it if she has questions.
    b. Have Tam repeat what you have said. If she can repeat it, she must understand it.
    c. Speak slowly and clearly, using simple terms. Pause often, repeating or writing down phrases or instructions that Tam does not seem to understand.
    d. To get and keep Tam's attention and to clarify your meaning, speak a bit more loudly and exaggerate your hand motions.

3. You have hired a new stock clerk. Vasily Pevsner has recently immigrated from Russia. He works well alone, but he resists working together with other team members. How do you handle the situation?

    a. Stay uninvolved and let the situation resolve itself. Pevsner has to learn how to get along with the other team members.
    b. Tell the rest of the team to work harder at getting along with Pevsner.
    c. Tell Pevsner he must work with others or he will not progress in the company.
    d. Talk privately with Pevsner to find out why he doesn't want to work with others. Then help him understand the importance of working together as a team.

4. Your employees are breaking into ethnically based cliques. Members of ethnic groups eat together, socialize together, and chat in their native language while they work. Some other team members feel left out and alienated. How do you encourage a stronger team attitude?

    a. Ban the use of languages other than English at work.
    b. Do nothing. This is normal behavior.
    c. Have regular team meetings and encourage people to mingle and get to know each other better.
    d. Send all of your employees to diversity training classes.[42]

TEST YOUR KNOWLEDGE

1. How have market globalization and cultural diversity contributed to the increased importance of intercultural communication?

2. What is the relationship between culture and subculture?

3. What are the four basic characteristics of culture?

4. How do high-context cultures differ from low-context cultures?

5. In addition to contextual differences, what other categories of cultural differences exist?

6. What four principles apply to ethical intercultural communication?

7. What is ethnocentrism, and how can it be overcome in communication?

8. Why is it a good idea to avoid slang and idioms when addressing a multicultural audience?

9. What are some ways to improve oral skills when communicating with people of other cultures?

10. What is the purpose of back-translation when preparing a message in another language?

INTERACTIVE LEARNING

USE THIS TEXT'S ONLINE RESOURCES

Visit the myPHLIP Web site at www.prenhall.com/thill. For Chapter 3, take advantage of the interactive "Study Guide" to test your chapter knowledge. Get instant feedback on whether you need additional studying. Read the "Current Events" articles to get the latest on chapter topics, and complete the exercises—as specified by your instructor.

This site's "Study Hall" helps you succeed in this course. "Talk in the Hall" lets you leave messages and meet new friends online. If you have a question, you can "Ask the Tutor." And to get a better grade in this course, you can find more help at "Writing Skills," "Study Skills," and "Study Tips."

The "Research Area" helps you locate a wealth of information to use in course assignments. Plus, you can send a message to online research experts, who will help you find exactly the information you need.

APPLY YOUR KNOWLEDGE

1. What are some of the intercultural differences that managers of a U.S.-based firm might encounter during a series of business meetings with a China-based company whose managers speak English fairly well?

2. What are some of the intercultural communication issues to consider when deciding whether to accept an overseas job with a firm that's based in your own country? A job in your own country with a local branch of a foreign-owned firm? Explain.

3. How do you think company managers from a country that has a relatively homogeneous culture might react when they do business with the culturally diverse staff of a company based in a less homogeneous country? Explain your answer.

4. Your company has relocated to a U.S. city where a Vietnamese subculture is strongly established. Many of your employees will be from this subculture. What can you do to improve communication between your management and the Vietnamese Americans you are currently hiring?

5. **Ethical Choices** Your office in Turkey desperately needs the supplies that have been sitting in Turkish customs for a month. Should you bribe a customs official to speed up delivery? Explain your decision.

PRACTICE YOUR KNOWLEDGE

DOCUMENT FOR ANALYSIS

Your boss wants to send a brief e-mail message welcoming employees recently transferred to your department from your Hong Kong branch. They all speak English, but your boss asks you to review his message for clarity. What would you suggest your boss change in the following e-mail message—and why? Would you consider this message to be audience centered? Why or why not?

I wanted to welcome you ASAP to our little family here in the states. It's high time we shook hands in person and not just across the sea. I'm pleased as punch about getting to know you all, and I for one will do my level best to sell you on America.

EXERCISES

3-1. **Intercultural Sensitivity: Recognizing Differences** You represent a Canadian toy company that's negotiating to buy miniature truck wheels from a manufacturer in Osaka, Japan. In your first meeting, you explain that your company expects to control the design of the wheels as well as the materials that are used to make them. The manufacturer's representative looks down and says softly, "Perhaps that will be difficult." You press for agreement, and to emphasize your willingness to buy, you show the prepared contract you've brought with you. However, the manufacturer seems increasingly vague and uninterested. What cultural differences may be interfering with effective communication in this situation? Explain.

3-2. **Ethical Choices** A U.S. manager wants to export T-shirts to a West African country, but a West African official expects a special payment before allowing the shipment into his country. How can the two sides resolve their different approaches without violating U.S. rules against bribing foreign officials? On the basis of the information presented in Chapter 1, would you consider this situation an ethical dilemma or an ethical lapse? Please explain.

3–3. **Teamwork** Working with two other students, prepare a list of ten examples of slang (in your own language) that would probably be misinterpreted or misunderstood during a business conversation with someone from another culture. Next to each example, suggest other words you might use to convey the same message. Do the alternatives mean *exactly* the same as the original slang or idiom?

3–4. **Intercultural Communication: Studying Cultures** Choose a specific country, such as India, Portugal, Bolivia, Thailand, or Nigeria, with which you are not familiar. Research the culture and write a brief summary of what a U.S. manager would need to know about concepts of personal space and rules of social behavior in order to conduct business successfully in that country.

3–5. **Multicultural Work Force: Bridging Differences** Differences in gender, age, and physical abilities contribute to the diversity of today's work force. Working with a classmate, role-play a conversation in which

   a. A woman is being interviewed for a job by a male personnel manager
   b. An older person is being interviewed for a job by a younger personnel manager
   c. A person using a wheelchair is being interviewed for a job by a person who can walk

   How did differences between the applicant and the interviewer shape the communication? What can you do to improve communication in such situations?

3–6. **Intercultural Sensitivity: Understanding Attitudes** As the director of marketing for a telecommunications firm based in Germany, you're negotiating with an official in Guangzhou, China, who's in charge of selecting a new telephone system for the city. You insist that the specifications be spelled out in detail in the contract. However, your Chinese counterpart argues that in developing a long-term business relationship, such minor details are unimportant. What can you do or say to break this intercultural deadlock and obtain the contract without causing the official to lose face?

3–7. **Culture and Language: Understanding Differences** Germany is a low-context culture; by comparison, France and England are more high context. These three translations of the same message were posted on a lawn in Switzerland: the German sign read, "Walking on the grass is forbidden"; the English sign read, "Please do not walk on the grass"; and the French sign read, "Those who respect their environment will avoid walking on the grass."[43] How does the language of each sign reflect the way information is conveyed in the cultural context of each nation? Write a brief (two- to three-paragraph) explanation.

3–8. **Culture and Time: Dealing with Differences** When a company knows that a scheduled delivery time given by an overseas firm is likely to be flexible, managers may buy in larger quantities or may order more often to avoid running out of product before the next delivery. Identify three other management decisions that may be influenced by differing cultural concepts of time, and make notes for a short (two-minute) presentation to your class.

3–9. **Intercultural Communication: Using Translators** Imagine that you're the lead negotiator for a company that's trying to buy a factory in Prague, capital of the Czech Republic. Your parents grew up near Prague, so you understand and speak the language fairly well. However, you wonder about the advantages and disadvantages of using a translator anyway. For example, you may have more time to think if you wait for an intermediary to translate the other side's position. Decide whether to hire a translator, and then write a brief (two- or three-paragraph) explanation of your decision.

3–10. **Internet** Some companies are experimenting with software that automatically translates business messages and Web sites. To see how this works, go to the AltaVista site at www.altavista.com. Click on "translate" and enter a sentence such as "We are enclosing a purchase order for four dozen computer monitors." Select "English to Spanish" and click to complete the translation. Once you've read the Spanish version, cut and paste it into the "text for translation" box, select "Spanish to English," and click to translate. Try translating the same English sentence into German, French, or Italian and then back into English. How do the results of each translation differ? What are the implications for the use of automated translation services and back-translation? How could you use this Web site to sharpen your intercultural communication skills?

3–11. **Intercultural Communication: Improving Skills** You've been assigned to host a group of Swedish college students who are visiting your college for the next two weeks. They've all studied English but this is their first trip to your area. Make a list of at least eight slang terms and idioms they are likely to hear on campus. How will you explain each phrase? When speaking with the Swedish students, what word or words might you substitute for each slang term or idiom?

GOING ONLINE EXERCISES

Hone Your Skills for International Business, page 60

Procedures and protocol for conducting international business are diverse. Go to the global resources at americanexpress.com to learn why an awareness of differences in business practices is important and how to be culturally correct.

1. Describe several business customs pertaining to etiquette in Korea that differ from customs in the United States. Why is your negotiating style particularly important in establishing a business relationship?

2. What did you discover about cultural differences in Russia that might make it difficult to adapt to Russian business customs such as a dinner meeting?

3. Select a country you might travel to and investigate its customs: what tips and specific information about doing international business did you learn?

To complete this exercise, log on to this text's Web site at www.prenhall.com/thill. Select Chapter 3, then select "Student Resources," click on the name of the featured Web site, and follow the detailed navigational directions.

The Three-Step Writing Process

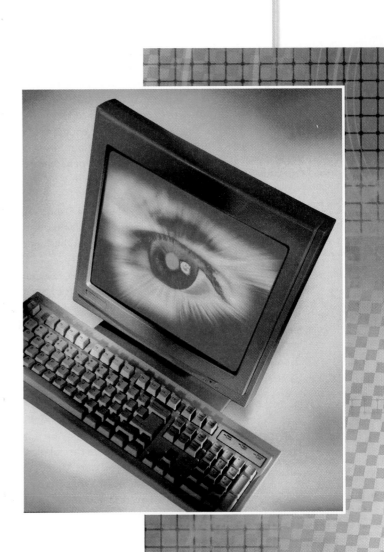

chapter 4

After studying this chapter, you will be able to

1 Describe the three-step writing process

2 Explain why it's important to define your purpose carefully and then list four questions that can help you test that purpose

3 Justify the importance of analyzing your audience profile and then list four ways of developing a profile

4 Outline how you can collect information informally, clarify what your audience wants to know, and test the thoroughness of your information

5 Define media richness and then list other factors to consider when choosing the most appropriate channel and medium for your message

6 Discuss how you can establish a good relationship with your audience

As the world's largest home-improvement retailer, Home Depot currently operates in 46 U.S. states, Canadian provinces, Chile, Puerto Rico, and Argentina—with plans to expand even more. Employing more than 230,000 people, the company must keep operations running smoothly by constantly refining its communication, much of which must be in writing.

On the job:

FACING A COMMUNICATION DILEMMA AT HOME DEPOT
Designing a Blueprint for Success
www.homedepot.com

Whether you need a few tips on installing curtain rods or some expert guidance on kitchen remodeling, Bernie Marcus and Arthur Blank want to lend a helping hand. As co-founders of Home Depot, these business partners have worked hard to create a retail culture that encourages homeowners to tackle their own home improvement and repair projects without hiring contractors. Since launching Home Depot in 1979, Marcus and Blank have opened more than 900 stores throughout the United States, Canada, Puerto Rico, and Chile. And they plan to open 900 more, doubling the size of Home Depot by the end of 2003.

But Home Depot's future success centers on Marcus and Blank's ability to communicate effectively with employees, customers, and suppliers. To keep operations running smoothly, they need to establish good working relationships with all three audiences. They must find out what each audience needs to know, and they must determine the right way to communicate that information. For example, before Marcus and Blank can stock a new product, they must analyze the needs of their audiences and plan appropriate messages for each one. They must assess customer demand, educate employees about product use, and seek vendors that can deliver the right amount of merchandise in a timely manner.

Planning effective messages wasn't as difficult when Marcus and Blank opened their first four stores in Atlanta. Working in the stores each day, they personally trained every employee, helped customers find the right tools and supplies for their projects, and dealt directly with every supplier. But opening a new store every 53 hours means that Marcus and Blank can no longer depend on oral messages to communicate with their various audiences. Establishing relationships with 200,000 employees, 25,000 suppliers, and millions of customers has complicated matters. And adapting their messages to serve the needs of each Home Depot audience requires careful planning.

If you were Marcus and Blank, how would you plan your business messages to various audiences? What factors would you consider as you plan your messages? How would you analyze each audience? And how would you choose the best channel and medium for each of your messages?[1]

UNDERSTANDING THE THREE-STEP WRITING PROCESS

Like Home Depot founders Marcus and Blank, you'll face a variety of communication assignments in your career, both oral and written. Some of your tasks will be routine, needing little more than jotting down a few sentences on paper or keyboarding a brief e-mail message; others will be more complex, requiring reflection, research, and careful document preparation. The number of business messages is increasing daily, each one competing for your audience's attention. So your messages must be livelier, easier to read, more concise, and more interesting than ever before.

Of course, making your business messages interesting doesn't mean using the dramatic techniques of creative writing. Your purpose is not to dazzle your readers with your extensive knowledge or powerful vocabulary. Instead, your messages must be

- **Purposeful.** Business messages provide information, solve a problem, or request the resources necessary to accomplish a goal. Every message you prepare will have a specific purpose.
- **Audience-centered.** Business messages help audiences understand an issue, collaborate on accomplishing a goal, or take some action. So every message you prepare must consider the audience's point of view.
- **Concise.** Business messages respect everyone's time by presenting information clearly and efficiently. Every message you prepare will be as short as it can be without detracting from the subject.

The goal of effective business writing is to express your ideas rather than to impress your audience. One of the best ways to do so is to follow a systematic writing process.

What Is the Three-Step Process?

The specific actions you take to write business messages will vary with each situation, audience, and purpose. However, following a process of generalized steps will help you write more effective messages. As Figure 4–1 shows, this **writing process** may be viewed as comprising three simple steps: (1) planning, (2) writing, and (3) completing your business messages.

- **Planning.** Think about the fundamentals of your message. Clarify your purpose in communicating, and analyze audience members so that you can tailor your message to their needs and expectations. Gather the information that will inform, persuade, or motivate your audience. Then adapt your message by selecting the channel and medium that both suit your needs and meet your audience's expectations. And finally, establish a good relationship with your audience. Planning business messages is the focus of this chapter.
- **Writing.** Once you've planned your message, organize your ideas and begin composing your first draft. This is when you commit your thoughts to words, create sentences and paragraphs, and select illustrations and details to support your main idea. Writing business messages is discussed in Chapter 5.
- **Completing.** Now that you have your first draft, step back to review the content and organization for overall style, structure, and readability. Revise and rewrite until your message comes across clearly and effectively; then edit your message for details such as

1 Planning

Analyze: Study your purpose, lay out your writing schedule, and then profile your audience.

Investigate: Gather information through formal or informal research methods.

Adapt: Choose the right channel and medium; then establish a good relationship with your audience.

2 Writing

Organize: Define your main idea, limit the scope, group your points, and choose the direct or indirect approach.

Compose: Control your style through level of formality and conversational tone. Choose your words carefully so that you can create effective sentences and paragraphs.

3 Completing

Revise: Evaluate content and review readability, editing and rewriting for conciseness and clarity.

Produce: Use effective design elements and suitable delivery methods.

Proofread: Review for errors in layout, spelling, and mechanics.

Figure 4–1
The Three-Step Writing Process

Andrea Jung is the first female CEO in Avon's 114-year history. Called a "great marketer," Jung set out to change the company image and reach new consumers with well-planned business messages. Her general purpose is twofold: to inform current customers and to persuade a more upscale audience to try Avon products.

grammar, punctuation, and format. Next produce your message, putting it into the form that your audience will receive. And finally, proof the final draft for typos, spelling errors, and other mechanical problems. Completing business messages is discussed in Chapter 6.

How Does the Three-Step Process Work?

Because so many of today's business messages are composed under pressure and on a schedule that is anything but realistic, allocating your time among these three steps can be a challenge. In some cases, your audience may expect you to get your message out in record time—sometimes only minutes after speaking with a client or attending a meeting. But whether you have 30 minutes or two days, try to give yourself enough time to plan, write, and complete your message.

As a general rule, try using roughly half of your time for planning—for deciding on your purpose, getting to know your audience, and immersing yourself in your subject matter. Use less than a quarter of your time for writing your document. Then use more than a quarter of your time for completing the project (so that you don't shortchange important final steps such as revising and proofing).[2]

Home Depot's Marcus and Blank understand that there is no right or best way to write all business messages. As you work through the writing process presented in Chapters 4, 5, and 6, try not to view it as a list of how-to directives but as a way to understand the various tasks involved in effective business writing.[3] The three-step process will help you avoid the risky "rush in and start writing" routine. Effective communicators complete all three steps, although they may not necessarily complete them in 1-2-3 order. Some jump back and forth from one step to another; some compose quickly and then revise; others revise as they go along. But for the sake of organization, we'll start with planning, the first step of the writing process.

ANALYZING YOUR PURPOSE AND AUDIENCE

2

For a business message to be effective, its purpose and its audience must complement one another. You must know enough about your purpose and audience to shape your message in a way that serves both. So you begin planning your message by being as specific as you can about the purpose of your message. Then you analyze your audience as thoroughly as possible.

Define Your Purpose

Your general purpose may be to inform, to persuade, or to collaborate.

The general purpose of a message influences how much your audience will participate in your message and how much you will control it.

When planning a business message, you must decide on the general and specific purpose of the message. All business messages have a **general purpose:** to inform, to persuade, or to collaborate with your audience. This overall purpose determines both the amount of audience participation you need and the amount of control you have over your message. To inform your audience, you need little interaction. Audience members absorb the information and accept or reject it, but they don't contribute to message content; you control the message. To persuade your audience, you require a moderate amount of participation, and you need to retain a moderate amount of message control. Finally, to collaborate with audience members, you need maximum participation. Your control of the message is minimal because you must adjust to new input and unexpected reactions.

To determine the specific purpose, think of how the audience's ideas or behavior should be affected by the message.

Business messages also have a **specific purpose.** That purpose may be clear and straightforward (such as placing an order) or it may be more encompassing (such as convincing management to hire more part-time employees during the holiday season). To help you define the specific purpose of your message, ask yourself what your audience should do or think after receiving your message. Then state your specific purpose as precisely as possible, even identifying which audience members should respond.

You must also consider whether your purpose is worth pursuing at this time. Too many business messages serve no practical purpose, and writing useless memos can destroy your **credibility,** your believability—based on how reliable you are and how much trust you evoke in others. If you suspect that your ideas will have little impact, wait until you have a more practical purpose. To help you decide whether to proceed, ask yourself four questions:

◆ **Is your purpose realistic?** If your purpose involves a radical shift in action or attitude, go slowly. Consider proposing the first step and viewing your message as the beginning of a learning process.

◆ **Is this the right time?** If an organization is undergoing changes of some sort, you may want to defer your message until things stabilize and people can concentrate on your ideas.

◆ **Is the right person delivering your message?** Even though you may have done all the work, achieving your objective is more important than taking the credit. You may want to play a supporting role in delivering your message if, for example, your boss's higher status could get better results.

◆ **Is your purpose acceptable to your organization?** If you receive an abusive letter that unfairly attacks your company, you might wish to fire back an angry reply. But your supervisors might prefer that you regain the customer's goodwill. Your response must reflect the organization's priorities.

Once you are satisfied that you have a legitimate purpose in communicating, you must take a good look at your intended audience.

Develop an Audience Profile

Who are your audience members? What are their attitudes? What do they need to know? And why should they care? The answers to such questions will indicate which material you'll need to cover and how to cover it.

If you're communicating with someone you know well, perhaps your boss or a co-worker, audience analysis is relatively easy. You can predict this person's reaction pretty well, without a lot of research. On the other hand, your audience could be made up of strangers—customers or suppliers you've never met, a new boss, or new employees. So just like Home Depot's Marcus and Blank, you'll have to learn about the members of your audience before you can adjust your message to serve them (see Figure 4–2).

◆ **Identify the primary audience.** If you can reach the decision makers or opinion molders in your audience, other audience members will fall into place. Key people ordinarily have the most organizational clout, but occasionally a person of relatively low status may have influence in one or two particular areas.

◆ **Determine audience size.** A report for wide distribution requires a more formal style, organization, and format than one directed to three or four people in your department. Also, be sure to respond to the particular concerns of key individuals. The head of marketing would need different facts than the head of production or finance would need.

◆ **Determine audience composition.** Look for common denominators that tie audience members together across differences in culture, education, status, or attitude. Include evidence that touches on everyone's area of interest. To be understood across cultural barriers, consider how audience members think and learn, as well as what style they expect.[4]

◆ **Gauge your audience's level of understanding.** If audience members share your general background, they'll understand your material without difficulty. If not, you must educate them. But deciding how much information to include can be a challenge. As a guideline, include only enough information to accomplish your objective. Everything else is irrelevant and must be eliminated; otherwise it will overwhelm your audience and divert attention from the important points. If audience members do not have the same level of understanding, gear your coverage to your primary audience (the key decision makers).

◆ **Estimate your audience's probable reaction.** Chapter 5 discusses how audience reaction affects message organization. If you expect a favorable response, you can state

---

Defer a message, or do not send it at all if
- The purpose is not realistic
- The timing is not right
- You are not the right person to deliver the message
- The purpose is not acceptable to the organization

O b j e c t i v e

3

Justify the importance of analyzing your audience profile and then list four ways of developing a profile.

Ask yourself some key questions about your audience:
- Who are they?
- What is their probable reaction to your message?
- How much do they already know about the subject?
- What is their relationship to you?

Focus on the common interests of the audience, but be alert to their individual concerns.

Going Online

Learn About Your Audience

↓

How can you use an audience profile to write a message that promotes your product? What type of information would you need about your audience? What audience characteristics would be most helpful? Asking the right questions is one way to analyze a specific group. You can learn what sources of information people use, where they live, and what they do for a living. You can learn their age, sex, educational level, marital status, economic level, and cultural background. At the Games.net Audience Profile, you'll learn about the characteristics of Games.net customers.

Marketing.pcworld.com/
surveys/gamesnetaudience
profile.html

To reach this Web site, go to www.prenhall.com/thill *(the Web site for this text). Select Chapter 4, then select "Student Resources." There, you'll find a current live link that will take you straight to the site.*

Figure 4–2
Audience Analysis Helps
You Plan Your Message

A gradual approach and plenty of evidence are required to win over a skeptical audience.

conclusions and recommendations up front and with less evidence. If you expect skepticism, you can introduce conclusions gradually, with more proof. By anticipating the primary audience's response to certain points, you can include evidence to address those issues.

INVESTIGATING NECESSARY INFORMATION

O b j e c t i v e
4

Outline how you can collect information informally, clarify what your audience wants to know, and test the thoroughness of your information.

When writing long, formal reports, you'll need to conduct formal research to locate and analyze all the information relevant to your purpose and your audience. Formal techniques for finding, evaluating, and processing information are discussed in Chapter 10 (Planning Business Reports and Proposals). However, many other kinds of business messages require much less formal information-gathering techniques.

For many messages, you may need to collect information only informally.

Whether you're preparing for an informational interview with your supervisor, writing an e-mail message to a close colleague, or gathering opinions for an article to appear in your organization's monthly newsletter, you can collect information informally by

- **Considering others' viewpoints.** You might put yourself in someone else's position to consider what others might be thinking, feeling, or planning.

- **Browsing through company files.** Your own filing cabinet may be a rich source of the information you need for a particular memo or e-mail message.

- **Chatting with supervisors or colleagues.** Fellow workers may have information you need, or they may know what your audience will be interested in.

- **Asking your audience for input.** If you're unsure of what audience members need from your message, ask them—whether through casual conversation (face-to-face or over the phone), informal surveys, or unofficial interviews.

Gathering information from coworkers in conversations or informal interviews helps Levi Strauss editors determine how much detail about a project their audience expects in the company newsletter.

The key to effective communication is determining your reader's informational needs and then responding to them. A good message answers all audience questions. But if you don't know what audience members want to know, you're likely to serve them fruit punch and peanut butter when they're expecting champagne and caviar.

Find Out Exactly What Your Audience Wants to Know

In many cases your audience's information needs are readily apparent; for example, a consumer may send you a letter asking a specific question. In other cases, your audience may not be particularly good at telling you what's needed. When your audience makes a vague request, try restating the request in more specific terms. If your boss says, "Find out everything you can about Polaroid," you might respond, "You want me to track down their market position by product line and get sales and profit figures by division for the past five years, right?" Another way to handle a vague request is to get a fix on its priority. You might ask, "Should I drop everything else and devote myself to this for the next week?" Asking a question or two forces the person to think through the request and define more precisely what is required.

Also, try to think of information needs that your audience may not even be aware of. Suppose your company has just hired a new employee from out of town, and you've been assigned to coordinate this person's relocation. At a minimum, you would write a welcoming letter describing your company's procedures for relocating employees. With a little extra thought, however, you might include some information about the city: perhaps a guide to residential areas, a map or two, brochures about cultural activities, or information on schools and transportation facilities. In some cases, you may be able to tell your audience something they consider important but wouldn't have thought to ask. Although adding information of this sort lengthens your message, doing so creates goodwill.

Provide All Required Information

Once you've defined your audience's information needs, be sure you satisfy those needs completely. One good way to test the thoroughness of your message is to use the journalistic approach: Check to see whether your message answers *who, what, when, where, why,* and *how.* Many messages fail to pass the test—such as this letter requesting information from a large hotel:

Dear Ms. Hill:

I just got back from a great vacation in Hawaii. However, this morning I discovered that my favorite black leather shoes are missing. Since I wore them in Hawaii, I assume I left them at the Hawaii Sands Hotel. Please check the items in your "lost and found" and let me know whether you have the missing shoes.

The letter fails to tell Hill everything she needs to know. The *what* could be improved by a detailed description of the missing shoes (size, brand, distinguishable style or trim). Hill doesn't know *when* the writer stayed at the Hawaii Sands, *where* (in what room) the writer stayed, or *how* to return the shoes. Hill will have to write or call the writer to get the missing details, and the inconvenience may be just enough to prevent her from complying with the request.

Be Sure the Information Is Accurate   There's no point in answering all your audience's questions if the answers are wrong. Your organization is legally bound by any promises you make, so be sure your company is able to follow through. Whether you're promising delivery by a given date or agreeing to purchase an item, if you have any doubt about the organization's ability or willingness to back up your promises, check with the appropriate people *before* you make the commitment.

You can minimize mistakes by double-checking everything you write or say. If you are using outside sources, ask yourself whether they are current and reliable. If your sources are international, remember that various cultures can view accuracy differently. A German bank may insist on balancing the books to the last penny, whereas an Italian bank may be more lenient.[5] Be sure to review any mathematical or financial calculations. Check all dates and schedules, and examine your own assumptions and conclusions to be certain they are valid.

Be Sure the Information Is Ethical   Honest mistakes are certainly possible. You may sincerely believe that you have answered someone's questions correctly and then later realize that your information was incorrect. If that happens, the most ethical thing for you to do is to contact the person immediately and correct the error. Most people will respect you for your honesty.

> Good ethics will help you determine how much detail to include in your message.

Messages can be unethical simply because information is omitted. Of course, as a business professional, you may have legal or other sound business reasons not to include every detail about every matter. So just how much detail should you include? Even though most people don't want to be buried in an avalanche of paperwork, include enough detail to avoid misleading your audience. If you're unsure about how much information your audience needs, offer as much as you believe best fits your definition of complete, and then offer to provide more upon request.

> Try to figure out what points will especially interest your audience; then give those points the most attention.

Be Sure the Information Is Pertinent   Remember that some information will be of greater interest and importance to your audience. If you're summarizing a recent conversation you had with one of your company's oldest and best customers, the emphasis you give each point of the conversation will depend on your audience's concerns. The head of engineering might be most interested in the customer's reaction to your product's new design features. The shipping manager might be most concerned about the customer's comments on recent delivery schedules. In other words, you must choose and emphasize the points that will have the most impact on your audience.

> Your knowledge of your audience members can help you figure out what will most interest them.

If you don't know your audience, or if you're communicating with a large group of people, use your common sense to identify points of particular interest. Audience factors such as age, job, location, income, or education can give you a clue. If you're trying to sell memberships in the Book-of-the-Month Club, you would adjust your message for college students, suburban homemakers, retired people, traveling sales representatives, and auto mechanics. All these people would need to know the same facts about membership,

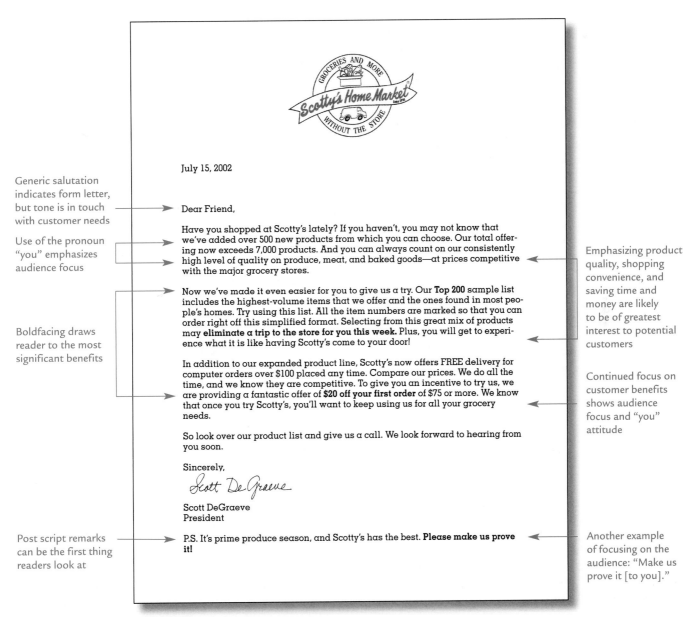

Generic salutation indicates form letter, but tone is in touch with customer needs

Use of the pronoun "you" emphasizes audience focus

Boldfacing draws reader to the most significant benefits

Post script remarks can be the first thing readers look at

Emphasizing product quality, shopping convenience, and saving time and money are likely to be of greatest interest to potential customers

Continued focus on customer benefits shows audience focus and "you" attitude

Another example of focusing on the audience: "Make us prove it [to you]."

Figure 4–3
In-Depth Critique: An Audience-Centered Letter

but each group would be more interested in some facts than in others. Economy might be important to college students or retired people, and convenience might attract sales reps or homemakers. Remember that your main goal is to tell audience members what they need to know. As President of Scotty's Home Market, Scott DeGraeve knows his audience is made up of busy people who prefer to spend their time doing something other than pushing a grocery cart down supermarket aisles (see Figure 4–3).

ADAPTING YOUR MESSAGE TO SERVE YOUR AUDIENCE AND PURPOSE

By now you know why you're writing, you know the audience you're writing to, and you have most of the information you need. But before actually beginning to write your message, you need to figure out how to make it serve both your audience and your purpose. To adapt your message, you may need to decide matters as detailed as whether to include a date on your Web site materials. Mainly, you need to select a

Using the Power of Technology

Elements of Cyberstyle

In cyberspace, "you are what you write," says Charles Rubin, author of 30 books about technology. People's opinion of you online is determined to a large extent by your command of the written word. And writing for the Web is indeed different.

People go to the Web because they want to get information efficiently. Ninety percent of the people reading Web pages don't scroll down, which is why you need to grab the reader's attention and make your main points on the first screen. Furthermore, Web readers have short attention spans, so you must hook them quickly.

To hook readers and keep them, experts suggest that you use a more conversational tone and that you keep words, sentences, and paragraphs short. Many readers will just scan a Web page, so use meaningful—not clever—subheads to break up text. Use lists whenever possible, and cut excess verbiage. Accuracy is also important. People have a zillion other sites to choose from. If the first thing a reader sees has an error in it, you may lose the reader forever.

Along with conciseness and accuracy comes comprehensiveness. While Web surfers may be in a hurry, if they like what they see,

they'll want as much of it as they can get. The Web allows you to be concise and comprehensive at the same time. You do this by using your first Web page to present the big picture. Then you unfold the rest of your story through links to other pages. But be sure to make it clear how many links are involved. Readers like to know what they are getting into. They don't like to be forced into following one path, but at the same time, subdividing pages too much and forcing readers to tunnel through too many links will only frustrate them. Moreover, readers like to be in control. If you don't let them take control, they will anyway. But they'll do so by clicking to another site.

CAREER APPLICATIONS

1. Do you notice any elements of cyberstyle that also apply to business messages? Make a list, and discuss why each element is important in business.
2. Visit any two Web sites and compare their cyberstyles. Do both Web sites contain all the elements recommended here? If not, briefly outline how the sites might be improved by applying good cyberstyle.

---

channel and a medium that fit your purpose and satisfy your audience's expectations. In addition, you need to make plans for establishing a good relationship with your audience.

Objective **5**

Define media richness and then list other factors to consider when choosing the most appropriate channel and medium for your message.

Different types of messages require different communication channels and media.

Select the Appropriate Channel and Medium

Selecting the best channel and medium for your message can make the difference between effective and ineffective communication.[6] When selecting a channel, you must consider the media within each channel. For example, the oral channel includes media such as face-to-face conversations, speeches, videotapes, voice mail, phone conversations, and so on. A written channel includes media such as letters, reports, e-mail, faxes, flyers, and so on. No matter what channel and medium you choose, do your best to match your selection to your message and your intention.

Your channel and medium choices also govern the style and tone of your message (see "Using the Power of Technology—Elements of Cyberstyle"). For instance, you wouldn't write an e-mail message with the same level of formality that you would use in a memo. When Glenda Anderson, a General Mills consumer services representative, responds to a customer, she is careful to maintain a tone of courtesy and friendliness (see Figure 4–4). Or if your purpose were to notify employees of a new procedure, you would probably write it in an e-mail message rather than send a formal letter or make a lengthy face-to-face presentation. Similarly, drafting a few notes for a conversation with an employee would be less formal than drafting a letter of reprimand. So before you begin writing, make sure your channel and medium match your purpose and your audience, and then tailor your message accordingly.

Media richness is the value of a medium in a given communication situation. Richness is determined by a medium's ability to

◆ Convey a message by means of more than one informational cue (visual, verbal, vocal)

◆ Facilitate feedback

◆ Establish personal focus

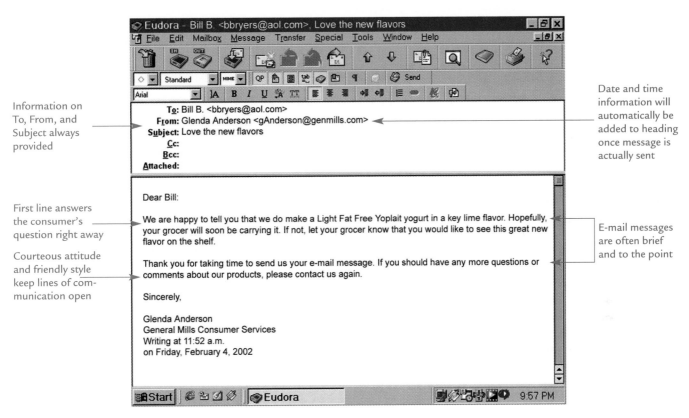

Information on To, From, and Subject always provided

Date and time information will automatically be added to heading once message is actually sent

First line answers the consumer's question right away

Courteous attitude and friendly style keep lines of communication open

E-mail messages are often brief and to the point

Figure 4–4
In-Depth Critique: A Typical E-Mail Message

Choose the richest media for nonroutine, complex messages (see Figure 4–5). Use rich media to extend and humanize your presence throughout the organization, to communicate caring to employees, and to gain employee commitment to organizational goals. Marcus and Blank use satellite video broadcasts to educate employees and to introduce new hires to the Home Depot culture. Use leaner media to communicate simple, routine messages. Face-to-face communication is the richest medium because it is personal, it provides both immediate verbal and nonverbal feedback, and it conveys the emotion behind the message. But it's also one of the most restrictive media because you and your audience must be in the same place at the same time.[7]

Keep in mind that every medium has limitations that filter out parts of the message. For example, flyers and bulletin boards are nondynamic and ineffective for communicating extremely complex messages, but they're perfect for simple ones. Moreover, every medium influences your audience's perception of your intentions. If you want to emphasize the formality of your message, use a more formal medium, such as a memo or a letter. If you want to emphasize the confidentiality of your message, use voice mail rather than a fax, send a letter rather than a memo, or address the matter in a private

The more complicated the message, the richer the medium necessary.

The richest media aren't always the best choice for every situation.

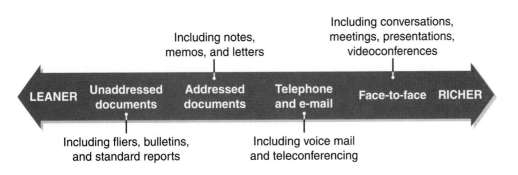

Including conversations, meetings, presentations, videoconferences

Including notes, memos, and letters

Figure 4–5
Media Richness

LEANER   Unaddressed documents   Addressed documents   Telephone and e-mail   Face-to-face   RICHER

Including fliers, bulletins, and standard reports

Including voice mail and teleconferencing

Table 4–1   Choosing the Most Appropriate Channel and Medium

A Written Channel Is Best When	*An Oral Channel Is Best When*
You need no immediate feedback	You want immediate feedback from the audience
Your message is detailed and complex, and it requires careful planning	Your message is relatively simple and easy to accept
You need a permanent, verifiable record	You need no permanent record
Your audience is large and geographically dispersed	You can assemble your audience conveniently and economically
You want to minimize the distortion that can occur when a message passes orally from person to person	You want to encourage interaction to solve a problem or reach a decision

Written Media Include	*Oral Media Include*
• Letters and memos	• Face-to-face conversation, speeches, meetings
• Reports and proposals	• Telephone and voice mail
• Electronic mail	• Audiotape and videotape
• Faxes	• Teleconferences and videoconferences

Your intentions heavily influence your choice of medium.

conversation rather than during a meeting. If you want to instill an emotional commitment to corporate values, consider a visual medium (videotape or videoconference). If you require immediate feedback, face-to-face conversation is your best choice.[8] However, if you'll need a written record, you'll probably want to write a memo or a letter.

Time and cost also affect medium selection.

Time is another factor you must consider when selecting a medium. If your message is urgent, you'll probably choose to use the phone, fax, or next-day mail. Plus you'll need to consider cost. There is usually a trade-off between time and cost. For instance, you wouldn't think twice about telephoning an important customer overseas if you just discovered your company erroneously sent the customer the wrong shipment. But you'd probably choose to fax or e-mail a routine order acknowledgment to your customer in Australia.

When choosing the appropriate medium, don't forget to consider your audience's expectations.

In addition to complexity, formality, confidentiality, feedback, time, and cost, you'll need to consider which media your audience expects or prefers and whether you'll need a permanent record of the communication.[9] What would you think if your college tried to deliver your diploma by fax? You'd expect the college to hand it to you at graduation or mail it to you. In addition, some cultures tend to favor one channel over another. For example, the United States, Canada, and Germany emphasize written messages, whereas Japan emphasizes oral messages—perhaps because its high-context culture carries so much of the message in nonverbal cues and "between the lines" interpretation.[10]

Oral Media   Primary oral communication media include face-to-face conversation (the richest medium), telephone calls, speeches, presentations, and meetings. Your choice between a face-to-face conversation and a telephone call would depend on audience location, message importance, and your need for the sort of nonverbal feedback that only body language can reveal.

In general, use an oral channel if your purpose is to collaborate with the audience.

The chief advantage of oral communication is the opportunity it provides for immediate feedback. This is the channel to use when you want the audience to ask questions and make comments or when you're trying to reach a group decision. It's also the best channel if there's an emotional component to your message and you want to read the audience's body language or hear the tone of their response (see Table 4–1).[11]

If you need to reach a decision or solve a problem, stick with a smaller audience to get things done.

Small Meetings, Conversations, and Interviews   In general, the smaller the audience, the more interaction among the members. If your purpose involves reaching a decision or solving a problem, select an oral medium geared toward a small audience. Be sure the program is relatively informal and unstructured so that ideas can flow freely. Gatherings of this sort can be arranged quickly and economically.

Large Meetings, Conventions, and Presentations At the opposite extreme are formal presentations to large audiences, which are common at events such as sales conventions, shareholder meetings, and ceremonial functions. Often, these major presentations take place in a big facility, where the audience can be seated auditorium style. Their formality makes them unsuitable for collaborative purposes that require audience interaction.

If your purpose is strictly to inform, a larger audience may be appropriate.

Written Media Written messages take many forms. At one end are the scribbled notes people use to jog their own memories; at the other are elaborate, formal reports that rival magazines in graphic quality. Regardless of the form, written messages have one big advantage: They let you plan and control the message. A written format is appropriate when the information is complex, when a permanent record is needed for future reference, when the audience is large and geographically dispersed, and when immediate interaction with the audience is either unimportant or undesirable.

A written channel increases the sender's control but eliminates the possibility of immediate feedback.

Although many types of written communication are specialized, the most common are letters, memos, and reports. Component Chapter A discusses accepted formats for business documents.

Letters and Memos Most letters and memos are relatively brief documents, generally one or two pages. Memos are the workhorses of business communication, used for the routine, day-to-day exchange of information within an organization. In general, memos lack a salutation. They use a TO, FROM, DATE, and SUBJECT heading to emphasize the needs of readers who usually have time only to skim messages. Good memos discuss only one topic, and their tone is conversational. Because of their open construction and informal method of delivery (e-mail or interoffice mail), memos are less private than letters.

Letters frequently go to outsiders, and they perform an important public relations function in addition to conveying a particular message. Many organizations rely on form letters (and sometimes form memos) to save time and money on routine communication. A variation of the form letter is the **boilerplate,** a standard paragraph that can be selected to suit an occasion or audience.

Both letters and memos can be classified by function into three categories: (1) routine, good-news, and goodwill messages; (2) bad-news messages; and (3) persuasive messages. (Chapters 7 to 9 elaborate on the function and nature of each of these message types.)

Reports and Proposals Reports and proposals are factual, objective documents that may be distributed to insiders or outsiders, depending on their purpose and subject. They come in many formats, including preprinted forms, letters, memos, and manuscripts. In length, they range from a few to several hundred pages, and they are generally more formal in tone than a typical business letter or memo. (Chapters 10 to 13 discuss reports and proposals in detail.)

Reports are generally longer and more formal than letters and memos, and they have more components.

Electronic Forms Both oral and written media have electronic forms. In addition to the traditional forms of meetings, conversations, interviews, and conventions, oral media also include electronic forms such as voice mail, audiotape and videotape, teleconferencing and videoconferencing, closed-circuit television, and many more. In addition to the traditional forms of letters and memos, reports and proposals, written media also include electronic forms such as e-mail, faxing, computer conferencing (with groupware), Web sites, and more.

The trick is to pick the tool that does the best overall job in each situation. Electronic forms are useful when you need speed, when you're physically separated from your audience, when time zones differ, when you must reach a dispersed audience personally, and

In general, use electronic forms of communication for speed, to overcome time-zone barriers, and to reach a widely dispersed audience personally.

when you're unconcerned about confidentiality. Although no hard rules dictate which tool to use in each case, here are a few pointers that will help you determine when to select electronic over more traditional forms:[12]

♦ **Voice mail.** Can be used to replace short memos and phone calls that need no response. It is most effective for short, unambiguous messages. It solves time-zone difficulties and reduces a substantial amount of interoffice paperwork.[13]

♦ **Teleconferencing.** Best for informational meetings, but ineffective for negotiation. It's an efficient alternative to a face-to-face meeting, but it discourages the "secondary" conversations that occur during a meeting of more than four or five people—which helps participants focus on a topic but prevents them from sharing valuable information.

♦ **Videotape.** Often effective for getting a motivational message out to a large number of people. By communicating nonverbal cues, it can strengthen the sender's image of sincerity and trustworthiness; however, it offers no opportunity for immediate feedback.

♦ **Computer conferencing.** Allows users to meet and collaborate in real time while viewing and sharing documents electronically. It offers democracy because more attention is focused on ideas than on who communicates them. But overemphasizing a message (to the neglect of the person communicating it) can threaten corporate culture, which needs a richer medium.

♦ **Faxing.** Can be used to overcome time-zone barriers when a hard copy is required. It has all the characteristics of a written message, except that (1) it may lack the privacy of a letter, and (2) the message may appear less crisp, even less professional, depending on the quality of the audience's machine.

♦ **E-mail.** Offers speed, low cost, increased access to other employees, portability, and convenience (not just overcoming time-zone problems but carrying a message to many receivers at once). It's best for communicating brief, noncomplex information that is time sensitive, but its effectiveness depends on user skill.

♦ **Web site.** Offers interactive communication through hyperlinks, allowing readers to absorb information nonsequentially: they can take what they need and skip everything else. A Web site can tailor the same information for numerous readers by breaking up the information into linked pages. Writing for the Web can be a specialized skill (see Chapter 5).

Electronic forms also have disadvantages, such as tactless remarks causing tension and overuse leading to information overload.

Even though electronic messages offer innumerable advantages, they aren't problem-free. Consider e-mail, for example. People sometimes include things in e-mail messages that they wouldn't dream of saying in person or typing in a document. So although this new openness can help companies get input from a wider variety of people, it can also create tension and interpersonal conflict. Furthermore, because e-mail is so cheap and easy to send, people tend to overuse it, distributing messages more widely than necessary and contributing to the hundreds of junk-mail messages that some executives receive every day. Overusing e-mail can also overload company networks, resulting in lost messages or even system crashes.

Electronic forms lack privacy.

Another drawback is lack of privacy. Some people negate their own privacy by being careless about screening their electronic distribution lists and sending information to receivers who shouldn't have it or don't need it. Of course, even if your message goes only where you originally intended, any recipient can easily forward it to someone else. In addition, e-mail and voice mail can legally be monitored by employers, and both can be subpoenaed for court cases.

Electronic forms can reduce productivity.

Furthermore, employee productivity is constantly interrupted by e-mail, voice mail, conference calls, and faxes. Chat or real-time conversation windows can pop up on computer screens and demand immediate conversation. On the other hand, some employees are cutting productivity by misusing Internet privileges—surfing the Web and visiting non–business-related Web sites during working hours. In one report, 31 percent of the

Checklist: **Observing High-Tech Etiquette**

Leaving Messages on Answering Machines and Voice Mail

✓ State whom you are calling, your first and last name, your company and title, the reason for your call, and your phone number (with area code and extension).
✓ Be brief when stating your message, and indicate specific callback times.
✓ Speak slowly.
✓ Deliver bad news personally.
✓ Follow up on important messages to make sure they were received.

Recording Messages on Answering Machines and Voice Mail

✓ Limit menus and options.
✓ Give callers an easy way to reach a live person.
✓ Test your message.
✓ Update greetings frequently and change your message when going on vacation.

Faxing Messages

✓ Fax nonpersonal messages only.
✓ Use a cover sheet stating the date, number of pages, recipient's name, sender's name, and a phone number to call if there is a transmission error.
✓ Sign your fax for a more personal message.

✓ Call before faxing urgent messages or before faxing long documents.
✓ Check your fax machine regularly to make sure it has adequate paper and cartridges.

Sending E-mail

✓ Respect other people's electronic space by sending messages only when necessary.
✓ Respond to messages quickly.
✓ Read, write, and edit your messages offline (before you connect to the Internet).
✓ Make your subject line informative.
✓ Change the subject line when replying.
✓ Avoid overusing the label "urgent."
✓ Use short paragraphs.
✓ Refrain from using all capital letters (shouting).
✓ Quote a previous e-mail when responding to questions or requests.
✓ Don't send large files (including large attachments) without prior notice.
✓ Proofread every message.
✓ Be careful about using the "reply all" button.
✓ Check your e-mail often, and clean out your e-mailbox regularly.
✓ Remember that e-mail isn't always private.

---

businesses surveyed cited financial losses from reduced employee productivity as a result of Internet misuse alone.[14]

The drawbacks of electronic forms are often outweighed by the advantages, so businesses are selecting electronic forms over traditional ones more and more often. (See this chapter's "Checklist: Observing High-Tech Etiquette.") But whatever medium you choose, you're not yet ready to draft your message. Once you've chosen an appropriate channel and medium, you must do more than simply convey information. You need to establish a good relationship with your audience.

Establish a Good Relationship with Your Audience

Think about who you are and who your audience is. Are you old friends with common interests, or are you total strangers? Are you equal in status, experience, and education, or are you clearly unequal? Your answers to these questions will help you give the right impression in your message.

Perhaps the most important thing you can do to establish a good relationship with your audience is to avoid trying to be someone you're not. People can spot falseness very quickly, so just be yourself and be sincere. Home Depot's Marcus and Blank will tell you that as in any undertaking, a good relationship is based on respect and courtesy. So when trying to establish good relationships in your business messages, remember to use the "you" attitude, emphasize the positive, establish your credibility, be polite, use bias-free language, and project the company's image.

Use the "You" Attitude   You are already becoming familiar with the audience-centered approach, trying to see a subject through your audience's eyes. Now you want

O b j e c t i v e **6**

Discuss how you can establish a good relationship with your audience.

To establish a good relationship, be yourself.

As managing editor and anchor of CBS Evening News, Dan Rather is a leader in electronic news reporting. He has a reporter's knack for knowing how to inform audiences. For example, Rather says that his audience expects "hard news"; they want to be informed, not entertained, and he resists pressures to "soften it up" to attract more viewers. Establishing a good relationship with your audience helps your messages succeed.

The "you" attitude is best implemented by expressing your message in terms of the audience's interests and needs.

Don't overdo the "you" attitude.

Avoid using *you* and *yours* when doing so
• Makes you sound dictatorial
• Make someone else feel guilty
• Goes against your organization's style

to project this approach in your messages by adopting a **"you" attitude**—that is, by speaking and writing in terms of your audience's wishes, interests, hopes, and preferences. When you talk about the other person, you're talking about the thing that most interests him or her.

On the simplest level, you can adopt the "you" attitude by replacing terms that refer to yourself and your company with terms that refer to your audience. In other words, use *you* and *yours* instead of *I, me, mine, we, us,* and *ours:*

INSTEAD OF THIS	USE THIS
To help us process this order, we must ask for another copy of the requisition.	So that your order can be filled promptly, please send another copy of the requisition.
We are pleased to announce our new flight schedule from Atlanta to New York, which is any hour on the hour.	Now you can take a plane from Atlanta to New York any hour on the hour.
We offer the printer cartridges in three colors: black, blue, and green.	Select your printer cartridge from three colors: black, blue, and green.

Too many business messages have an "I" or "we" attitude, which sounds selfish and uninterested in the audience. The message tells what the sender wants, and the audience is expected to go along with it. However, using *you* and *yours* requires finesse. If you overdo it, you're likely to create some rather awkward sentences, and you run the risk of sounding like a high-pressure carnival barker.[15] The "you" attitude is not intended to be manipulative or insincere. It's an extension of the audience-centered approach. In fact, the best way to implement the "you" attitude is to be sincere in thinking about your audience.

The "you" attitude isn't just a matter of using one pronoun rather than another; it's a matter of genuine empathy. You can use *you* 25 times in a single page and still ignore your audience's true concerns. Look back at the letter in Figure 4–3. The first paragraph uses the pronoun *you* correctly and effectively. But the second paragraph also displays the "you" attitude by explaining how potential customers will benefit from Scotty's service.

It's the thought and sincerity that count, not the pronoun. If you're talking to a retailer, try to think like a retailer; if you're dealing with a production supervisor, put yourself in that position; if you're writing to a dissatisfied customer, imagine how you would feel at the other end of the transaction. The important thing is your attitude toward audience members and your appreciation of their position.

In fact, on some occasions you'll do better to avoid using *you*. For instance, using *you* in a way that sounds dictatorial is impolite. Or, when someone makes a mistake, you may want to minimize ill will by pointing out the error impersonally. You might say, "We have a problem," instead of "You caused a problem."

INSTEAD OF THIS	USE THIS
You should never use that type of paper in the copy machine.	That type of paper doesn't work very well in the copy machine.
You must correct all five copies by noon.	All five copies must be corrected by noon.

As you practice using the "you" attitude, be sure to consider the attitudes and policies of your organization, as well. Some companies have a tradition of avoiding references to *you* and *I* in their memos and formal reports. If you work for a company that expects a formal, impersonal style, confine your use of personal pronouns to informal letters and memos.

Emphasize the Positive   Another way of establishing a good relationship with your audience is to emphasize the positive side of your message.[16] Focus on the silver lining, not on the cloud. Stress what is or will be instead of what isn't or won't be. Most information, even bad news, has some redeeming feature. If you can make your audience aware of that feature, your message will be more acceptable.

INSTEAD OF THIS	USE THIS
It is impossible to repair your vacuum cleaner today.	Your vacuum cleaner will be ready by Tuesday.
We apologize for inconveniencing you during our remodeling.	The renovations now under way will help us serve you better.
We never exchange damaged goods.	We are happy to exchange merchandise that is returned to us in good condition.

Explain what you have done, what you can do, and what you will do—not what you haven't done, can't do, or won't do.

In addition, when you're criticizing or correcting, don't hammer on the other person's mistakes. Avoid referring to failures, problems, or shortcomings. Focus instead on what the person can do to improve:

INSTEAD OF THIS	USE THIS
The problem with this department is a failure to control costs.	The performance of this department can be improved by tightening up cost controls.
You filled out the order form wrong. We can't send you the paint until you tell us what color you want.	So that your order can be processed properly, please check your color preferences on the enclosed card.

When you are offering criticism or advice, focus on what the person can do to improve.

If you're trying to persuade the audience to buy a product, pay a bill, or perform a service for you, emphasize what's in it for them. Don't focus on why *you* want them to do something. An individual who sees the possibility for personal benefit is more likely to respond positively to your appeal.

INSTEAD OF SAYING	SAY
Please buy this book so that I can make my sales quota.	The plot of this novel will keep you in suspense to the last page.
We need your contribution to the Boys and Girls Club.	You can help a child make friends and build self-confidence through your donation to the Boys and Girls Club.

Show your audience how they will benefit from complying with your message.

In general, try to state your message without using words that might hurt or offend your audience. Substitute mild terms (euphemisms) for those that have unpleasant connotations. You can be honest without being harsh. Gentle language won't change the facts, but it will make them more acceptable:

Avoid words with negative connotations; use meaningful euphemisms instead.

INSTEAD OF THIS	USE THIS
cheap merchandise	bargain prices
toilet paper	bathroom tissue
used cars	resale cars
high-calorie food	high-energy food
elderly	senior citizen
pimples and zits	complexion problems

On the other hand, don't carry euphemisms to extremes. If you're too subtle, people won't know what you're talking about. "Derecruiting" workers to the "mobility pool" instead of

Promoting Workplace Ethics

Spin Cycle: Deciphering Corporate Doublespeak

If there's one product U.S. businesses can produce in large amounts, it's doublespeak. Doublespeak is language that only pretends to say something but that in reality hides, evades, or misleads. Like most products, doublespeak comes in many forms, from the popular buzzwords that everyone uses but no one really understands—such as *competitive dynamics* and *empowerment*—to words that try to hide meaning, such as *reengineering, synergy,* and *restructure.*

With doublespeak, bribes and kickbacks are called *rebates* or *fees for product testing;* junk and used-car-parts dealers have become *auto dismantlers and recyclers;* and travel agents are called *vacation specialists, destination counselors,* or *reservation specialists.* Plus, just about everyone's job title has the word *chief* in it: Chief Nuclear Officer, Chief Learning Officer, Chief Cultural Officer, Chief Ethics Officer, Chief Turnaround Officer, and Chief Creative Officer. After all the "operations improvement" that corporations have undergone, you have to wonder who all those "chiefs" are leading. Never before have so many led so few.

With doublespeak, banks don't have *bad loans* or *bad debts;* they have *nonperforming credits* that are *rolled over* or *rescheduled.* And corporations never lose money; they just experience *negative cash flow, deficit enhancement,* or *negative contributions to profits.*

Of course, no one gets fired these days. If you're high enough in the corporate pecking order, you *resign for personal reasons.* But for those below the lofty heights of corporate power, you're *involuntarily terminated* as the result of *downsizing, work force adjustments,* and *headcount reductions.* Some companies even *assign candidates to a*

mobility pool, implement a skills mix adjustment, or *eliminate redundancies in the human resources area.* One automobile company (which closed an entire assembly plant and eliminated over 8,000 jobs) calls it *a volume-related production schedule adjustment.*

But don't worry, if you're *dehired, deselected, surplused,* or *uninstalled,* corporations will offer you a *career change opportunity* or *vocational relocation.* In fact, hardly anyone is laid off these days. "We don't characterize it as a layoff," said one corporate doublespeaker (sometimes called a spin doctor). "We're managing our staff resources. Sometimes you manage them up, and sometimes you manage them down."

CAREER APPLICATIONS

1. The president of one company just learned that some of his employees have been playing a popular game called "buzzword bingo," in which participants ridicule doublespeak by tracking the jargon their bosses use during staff meetings on bingo-like cards. Some managers are complaining that it's getting out of control. In fact, as one meeting dragged on, employees tried to steer the conversation to use all the buzzwords on their cards. What can managers do to avoid these silly games?

2. Visit one of the following buzzword bingo Web sites and print out a card or two. Read the current business section of your favorite newspaper. How many buzzwords did you find?
   www.ksquared.net/~key/ietf-bingo.cgi
   Buzzword-bingo.com/play/index.htm

---

telling them that they have six weeks to find another job isn't really very helpful. When using euphemisms, you walk a fine line between softening the blow and hiding the facts. It would be unethical to speak to your community about relocating refuse when you're really talking about your plans for disposing of toxic waste. Such an attempt to hide the facts would very likely backfire, damaging your business image and reputation. In the end, people respond better to an honest message delivered with integrity than they do to sugar-coated double-talk (see "Promoting Workplace Ethics—Spin Cycle: Deciphering Corporate Doublespeak").

Establish Your Credibility   If you're unknown to your audience members, you'll have to earn their confidence before you can win them to your point of view. Their belief in your competence and integrity is important. You want people to trust that your word is dependable and that you know what you're doing.

> People are more likely to react positively to your message when they have confidence in you.

If you're communicating with a familiar group, your credibility has already been established, so you can get right down to business. Of course, even in this case some audience members may have preconceptions about you and may have trouble separating your arguments from your personality or your field. If they think of you as, say, a "numbers person," they may question your competence in other areas. You can overcome these prejudices as you develop your message by providing ample evidence for any material outside your usual area of expertise.

But what if audience members are complete strangers? Or worse, what if they start off with doubts about you? In a new or hostile situation, devote the initial portion of your message to gaining credibility. First, show an understanding of your audience's situation by calling attention to the things you have in common. If you're communicating with someone who shares your professional background, you might say, "As a fellow engineer (lawyer, doctor, teacher, or whatever), I'm sure you can appreciate this situation." Another approach is to use technical or professional terms that identify you as a peer.

You can also gain your audience's confidence by explaining your credentials, but be careful not to sound pompous. Mentioning one or two aspects of your background is enough. Your title or the name of your organization might be enough to impress your audience with your abilities. If not, you might mention the name of someone who carries some weight with your audience. You might begin a letter with "Professor Goldberg suggested that I contact you," or you could quote a recognized authority on your subject, even if you don't know the authority personally. The fact that your ideas are shared by a credible source adds prestige to your message.

Your credibility is enhanced by the quality of the information you provide. If you support your points with evidence that can be confirmed through observation, research, experimentation, or measurement, audience members will recognize that you have the facts, and they'll respect you. On the other hand, exaggerated claims are unethical and do more harm than good. A mail-order catalog promised: "You'll be absolutely amazed at the remarkable blooms on this healthy plant. Gorgeous flowers with brilliant color and an intoxicating aroma will delight you week after week." Terms such as *amazing, incredible, extraordinary, sensational,* and *revolutionary* exceed the limits of believability, unless they're supported with some sort of proof.

You also risk losing credibility if you seem to be currying favor with insincere compliments. So support compliments with specific points:

Instead of This	Use This
My deepest heartfelt thanks for the excellent job you did. It's hard these days to find workers like you. You are just fantastic! I can't stress enough how happy you have made us with your outstanding performance.	Thanks for the fantastic job you did filling in for Gladys at the convention with just an hour's notice. Despite the difficult circumstances, you managed to attract several new orders with your demonstration of the new line of coffeemakers. Your dedication and sales ability are truly appreciated.

Another threat to credibility is too much modesty and not enough confidence. You express a lack of confidence when you use words such as *if, hope,* and *trust.* Try not to undermine your credibility with vague sentiments:

Instead of This	Use This
We hope this recommendation will be helpful.	We're glad to make this recommendation.
If you'd like to order, mail us the reply card.	To order, mail the reply card.
We trust that you'll extend your service contract.	By extending your service contract, you can continue to enjoy top-notch performance from your equipment.

If you lack faith in yourself, you're likely to communicate an uncertain attitude that undermines your credibility. The key to being believable is to believe in yourself. If you are convinced that your message is sound, you can state your case with authority so that your audience has no doubts.

Be Polite   Being polite is another good way to earn your audience's respect. By being courteous to members of your audience, you show consideration for their needs and feelings. Express yourself with kindness and tact.

To enhance your credibility
- Show that you understand the other person's situation
- Explain your own credentials or ally yourself with a credible source
- Back up your claims with evidence, not exaggerations
- Use words that express confidence
- Believe in yourself and your message

You will undoubtedly be frustrated and exasperated by other people many times in your career. When that happens, you'll be tempted to say what you think in blunt terms. But venting your emotions rarely improves the situation and can jeopardize your audience's goodwill. Instead, be gentle when expressing yourself:

Although you may be tempted now and then to be brutally frank, try to express the facts in a kind and thoughtful manner.

INSTEAD OF THIS	USE THIS
You really fouled things up with that last computer run.	Let's go over what went wrong with the last computer run so that the next run goes smoothly.
You've been sitting on my order for two weeks, and we need it now!	We are eager to receive our order. When can we expect delivery?

Of course, some situations require more diplomacy than others. If you know your audience well, you can get away with being less formal. However, when you are communicating with people who outrank you or with people outside your organization, an added measure of courtesy is usually needed.

Use extra tact when writing and when communicating with higher-ups and outsiders.

In general, written communication requires more tact than oral communication. When you're speaking, your words are softened by your tone of voice and facial expression. Plus, you can adjust your approach according to the feedback you get. But written communication is stark and self-contained. If you hurt a person's feelings in writing, you can't soothe them right away. In fact, you may not even know that you have hurt the other person, because the lack of feedback prevents you from seeing his or her reaction.

Promptness is a form of courtesy.

Another simple but effective courtesy is to be prompt in your correspondence. If possible, answer your mail within two or three days. If you need more time to prepare a reply, call or write a brief note to say that you're working on an answer. Most people are willing to wait if they know how long the wait will be. What annoys them is the suspense.

Use Bias-Free Language   Most of us think of ourselves as being sensitive, unbiased, ethical, and fair. But being fair and objective isn't enough; to establish a good relationship with your audience, you must also *appear* to be fair.[17] **Bias-free language** avoids unethical, embarrassing blunders in language related to gender, race, ethnicity, age, and disability. Good communicators make every effort to change biased language (see Table 4–2).

Avoid biased language that might offend your audience.

Replace words that inaccurately exclude women or men.

- **Gender bias.** Avoid sexist language by using the same label for everyone (don't call a woman chairperson and then call a man chairman). Reword sentences to use *they* or to use no pronoun at all. Vary traditional patterns by sometimes putting women first (*women and men, she and he, her and his*). And finally, the preferred title for women in business is Ms., unless the individual asks to be addressed as Miss or Mrs. or has some other title, such as Dr.

Eliminate references that reinforce racial or ethnic stereotypes.

- **Racial and ethnic bias.** The central principle is to avoid language suggesting that members of a racial or an ethnic group have stereotypical characteristics. The best solution is to avoid identifying people by race or ethnic origin unless such a label is relevant.

Avoid references to an individual's age or physical limitations.

- **Age bias.** As with gender, race, and ethnic background, mention the age of a person only when it is relevant. When referring to older people, avoid such stereotyped adjectives as *spry* and *frail.*

Always refer to people first and their disabilities second.

- **Disability bias.** No painless label exists for people with a physical, mental, sensory, or emotional impairment. Avoid mentioning a disability unless it is pertinent. However, if you must refer to someone's disability, avoid terms such as *handicapped, crippled,* or *retarded.* Put the person first and the disability second.[18] Present the whole person, not just the disability, by showing the limitation in an unobtrusive manner.

Project the Company's Image   Even though establishing a good relationship with the audience is your main goal, give some thought to projecting the right image for your company. When you communicate with outsiders, on even the most routine matter, you

Table 4–2 Overcoming Bias in Language		
Examples	*Unacceptable*	*Preferable*
GENDER BIAS		
Using words containing "man"	Mankind	Humanity, human beings, human race, people
	Man-made	Artificial, synthetic, manufactured, constructed
	Manpower	Human power, human energy, workers, work force
	Businessman	Executive, business manager, businessperson
	Salesman	Sales representative, salesperson, clerk, sales agent
	Foreman	Supervisor
Using female-gender words	Authoress, actress, stewardess	Author, actor, cabin attendant
Using special designations	Woman doctor, male nurse	Doctor, nurse
Using "he" to refer to "everyone"	The average worker . . . he	The average worker . . . he or she
Identifying roles with gender	The typical executive spends four hours of his day in meetings.	Most executives spend four hours a day in meetings.
	the consumer . . . she	Consumers . . . they
	the nurse/teacher . . . she	nurses/teachers . . . they
Identifying women by marital status	Phil Donahue and Marlo	Phil Donahue and Ms. Thomas
	Phil Donahue and Ms. Thomas	Mr. Donahue and Ms. Thomas
RACIAL/ETHNIC BIAS		
Assigning stereotypes	My black assistant speaks more articulately than I do.	My assistant speaks more articulately than I do.
	Jim Wong is an unusually tall Asian.	Jim Wong is tall.
Identifying people by race or ethnicity	Mario M. Cuomo, Italian American politician and ex-governor of New York	Mario M. Cuomo, politician and ex-governor of New York
AGE BIAS		
Including age when irrelevant	Mary Kirazy, 58, has just joined our trust department.	Mary Kirazy has just joined our trust department.
DISABILITY BIAS		
Putting the disability before the person	Crippled workers face many barriers on the job.	Workers with physical disabilities face many barriers on the job.
	An epileptic, Tracy has no trouble doing her job.	Tracy's epilepsy has no effect on her job performance.

serve as the spokesperson for your organization. The impression you make can enhance or damage the reputation of the entire company. Thus your own views and personality must be subordinated, at least to some extent, to the interests and style of your company.

Say you've just taken a job with a hip, young retail organization called Rappers. One of your first assignments is to write a letter canceling additional orders for clothing items that haven't been selling well.

> Subordinate your own style to that of the company.

Dear Ms. Bataglia:

I am writing to cancel our purchase order 092397AA for the amount of $12,349. Our contract with your organization specifies that we have a 30-day cancellation clause, which we wish to invoke. If any shipments went out before you received this notification, they will be returned; however, we will remunerate freight charges as specified in the contract.

I am told we have ordered from you since our inception in 1993. Your previous service to us has been quite satisfactory; however, recent sales of the "Colored Denim"

Checklist: **Planning Business Messages**

Analyze Your Purpose and Audience

✓ Determine whether the purpose of your message is to inform, persuade, or collaborate.
✓ Identify the specific behavior you hope to induce in the audience.
✓ Make sure that your purpose is worthwhile and realistic.
✓ Make sure that the time is right for your purpose.
✓ Make sure the right person is delivering your message.
✓ Make sure your purpose is acceptable to your organization.
✓ Identify the primary audience.
✓ Determine the size of your audience.
✓ Determine the composition of your audience.
✓ Determine your audience's level of understanding.
✓ Estimate your audience's probable reaction to your message.

Investigate Necessary Information

✓ Decide whether to use formal or informal techniques for gathering information.
✓ Find out what your audience wants to know.
✓ Provide all required information and make sure it's accurate, ethical, and pertinent.

Adapt Your Message to Serve Your Audience and Your Purpose

✓ Select a channel and medium for your message by matching media richness to your audience and purpose.
✓ Select the right medium for your message by considering factors such as urgency, formality, complexity, confidentiality, emotional content, cost, audience expectation, and your need for a permanent record.
✓ Consider the problems as well as the advantages of using electronic forms.
✓ Adopt an audience-centered approach by using the "you" attitude.
✓ Emphasize the positive aspects of your message.
✓ Gain audience confidence by establishing your credibility.
✓ Show respect for your audience by using a polite tone.
✓ Show your sensitivity and fairness by using bias-free language.
✓ Project your company's image to make sure your audience understands that you are speaking for your organization.

---

line have been less than forecast. We realize that our cancellation may have a negative impact, and we pledge to more accurately predict our needs in the future.

We maintain positive alliances with all our vendors and look forward to doing further business with you. Please keep us informed of new products as they appear.

After reading your draft, you realize that its formal tone may leave a feeling of ill will. Moreover, it certainly doesn't reflect the corporate culture of your new employer. You try again.

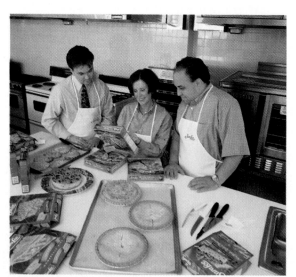

Before writing a letter or e-mail message on behalf of your company, think about how you project the company image, says Elizabeth Tanis (center), manager of consumer affairs at Sara Lee Bakery. "We want everyone to understand about the high quality and high standards at Sara Lee—that's how we made our good name, and that's how we're going to keep it."

Dear Ms. Bataglia:

We appreciate the relationship we've had with you since 1993. Your shipments have always arrived on time and in good order.

However, our recent store reports show a decline in sales for your "Colored Denim" line. Therefore, we're canceling our purchase order 092397AA for $12,349. If you'll let us know the amounts, we'll pay the shipping charges on anything that has already gone out.

We're making a lot of changes at Rappers, but one thing remains the same—the positive relationship we have with vendors such as you. Please keep us informed of your new lines as they appear. We look forward to doing business with you in the future.

This version reflects the more relaxed image of your new company. You can save yourself a great deal of time and frustration if you master your company's style early in your career.

The three stages of planning help you get ready to write business messages. This chapter's "Checklist: Planning Business Messages" is a reminder of the tasks and choices you address during the planning process.

SUMMARY OF LEARNING OBJECTIVES

1 Describe the three-step writing process. (1) Planning consists of analyzing your purpose and your audience, investigating necessary information (whether formally or informally), and adapting your message by selecting the appropriate channel and medium and by establishing a good relationship with your audience. (2) Writing consists of organizing your ideas and actually composing words, sentences, paragraphs, and visual graphics. (3) Completing your message consists of revising your message by evaluating content and then rewriting and editing for clarity, producing your message by using effective design elements and suitable delivery methods, and proofreading your message for typos and errors in spelling and mechanics.

2 Explain why it's important to define your purpose carefully, and list four questions that can help you test that purpose. You must know enough about the purpose of your message to shape that message in a way that will achieve your goal. To decide whether you should proceed with your message, ask four questions: (1) Is my message realistic? (2) Is my message acceptable to my organization? (3) Is my message being delivered by the right person? (4) Is my message being delivered at the right time?

3 Justify the importance of analyzing your audience profile, and list four ways of developing a profile. Analyzing your audience helps you discover who the members of your audience are, what their attitudes are, what they need to know, and why they should care about your purpose in communicating. An effective profile helps you predict how your audience will react to your message. It also helps you know what to include in your message and how to include it. To develop an audience profile, you need to determine your primary audience (key decision makers), the size of your audience, the make-up of your audience, the level of your audience's understanding, and your audience's probable reaction.

4 Outline how you can collect information informally, clarify what your audience wants to know, and test the thoroughness of your information. You can collect necessary information informally by considering others' viewpoints, browsing through company files, chatting with supervisors or colleagues, or asking your audience for input. You can clarify what your audience wants to know by restating questions, establishing assignment priorities, and trying to think of information needs that your audience may not even be aware of. Finally, you can test the thoroughness of your information by checking whether your message answers *who, what, when, where, why,* and *how.* You also want to be sure that your information is accurate, ethical, and pertinent.

5 Define media richness and list other factors to consider when choosing the most appropriate channel and medium for your message. Media richness is the value of a medium for communicating a message. Richness is determined by the medium's ability to (1) convey a message using more than one informational cue (visual, verbal, vocal), (2) facilitate feedback, and (3) establish personal focus. Other factors to consider when selecting media include complexity, formality, confidentiality, emotional commitment, feedback needs, whether a written record is needed, urgency, cost, and audience expectation. Electronic forms are best for speed, to overcome physical separation and differing time zones, to reach a dispersed audience personally, and when confidentiality is not an issue.

6 Discuss how you can establish a good relationship with your audience. Most important, be yourself and be sincere so that your audience won't be put off by falseness. Use the "you" attitude to project your audience focus and highlight audience benefits. Emphasize the positive by talking about what is possible, by not focusing on another person's mistakes, and by using euphemisms when appropriate. Establish your credibility by providing ample evidence for material outside your expertise, calling attention to what you have in common with your audience, explaining your credentials when necessary, and always providing the highest-quality information. Be polite by expressing yourself with courtesy, kindness, and tact and by being prompt in your correspondence. Use bias-free language to avoid blunders with respect to gender, race and ethnicity, age, and disability. And finally, be sure that you establish the right relationship with your audience by projecting your company's image.

On the job:
SOLVING A COMMUNICATION DILEMMA AT HOME DEPOT

Home Depot co-founders Bernie Marcus and Arthur Blank carefully plan their many messages to various audiences. They are also careful to select just the right medium for each message they send. For example, Marcus and Blank realize that face-to-face communication with customers is a vital element in Home Depot's success, so they train employees to ask specific questions about their customers' needs. This input allows Marcus and Blank to gauge their audience's level of understanding so that they can educate their customers about different repair techniques.

Marcus and Blank use various media for this customer education. They invite people to attend small-group in-store meetings, known as "how-to clinics," where live presentations demonstrate repair techniques and product installations. They also use written media, distributing free product literature, installation instructions, and informational brochures throughout the stores. Plus they offer a toll-free customer service number, staffed by home improvement experts and company managers who answer questions and handle customer complaints immediately.

Home Depot's books, *Home Improvement 1-2-3* and *Outdoor Projects 1-2-3,* feature the expertise of store employees and educate consumers about home and garden projects. Customers can also review how-to articles either in Home Depot's magazine, *Weekend,* or on a Home Depot CD-ROM. Home Depot's television program, *House Smart,* is a regular feature on the Discovery Channel, showing viewers how to handle home improvement projects and problems.

To establish and maintain good relationships with their employees, Marcus and Blank use *Doings at the Depot,* a bimonthly print newsletter that covers company operations and features articles written by the co-founders. Marcus and Blank educate their employees about company values and industry developments by broadcasting live videoconferences via satellite to all store locations. In fact, the company's closed-circuit satellite television network (Home Depot Television) produces *Breakfast with Bernie and Arthur,* which includes news segments about company events and employee training. Satellite telecasts are also used to introduce Home Depot's philosophies to new associates. Also, Home Depot University conducts in-depth employee training sessions in specific areas of home improvement (such as flooring or lighting) and in the fundamentals of customer service.

Marcus and Blank must also establish and maintain effective communication with more than 25,000 North American suppliers. Twice each year, they sponsor week-long vendor conferences, holding the events in large arenas throughout the country. During these conferences, Marcus and Blank interact in small groups to become better acquainted with new suppliers and to learn about new product offerings from current suppliers. They also make presentations to large audiences, informing suppliers about which products customers want, which ones aren't selling, and which need to be changed or dropped.

Your Mission You have recently joined Home Depot's community relations department in the company's Atlanta headquarters, known as the Store Support Center. Two of your major functions in this position are (1) helping store managers and other company executives plan effective business messages for a variety of audiences, and (2) responding to press inquiries about Home Depot. Choose the best alternatives for handling the following situations, and be prepared to explain why your choice is best:

1. You have received a phone call from Ann Mason, a reporter for a small Idaho newspaper. She is planning to write an article about Home Depot's recent decision to open a store in her community, a small town in a rural area of Idaho. Mason has asked you for information about the economic impact of Home Depot stores in other small communities across the nation. When responding to Mason's request, what should the purpose of your letter be?

   a. The general purpose is to inform. The specific purpose is to provide Mason with a brief summary of the evolution of Home Depot over the past 20 years.

   b. The general purpose is to persuade. The specific purpose is to convince Mason that Home Depot creates hundreds of jobs within a community, and that small, existing merchants should not feel threatened by the arrival of the home improvement giant in rural Idaho.

   c. The general purpose is to collaborate. The specific purpose is to work with Mason to develop an article that examines the history of Home Depot's entry into new markets.

   d. The general purpose is to respond. The specific purpose is to convey details requested by a journalist.

2. Assume that your purpose is to convince Mason of Home Depot's abilities to create new jobs and increase economic activity in small communities. Is your purpose worth pursuing at this time?

   a. Yes. The purpose is realistic, the timing is right, you are the right person to send the message, and the purpose is acceptable to the organization.

   b. Not completely. Realistically, many readers of Mason's newspaper may dread the arrival of Home Depot in their small community, fearing that the giant retailer may force small retailers out of business.

   c. The purpose is fine, but you are not the right person to send this message. Home Depot's chief executive officer should respond.

   d. The timing is right for this message. Stress Home Depot's involvement in small communities, citing contributions to social causes in other rural areas. Show how Home Depot cares about customers on a personal basis.

3. When planning your reply to Mason, what assumptions can you make about your audience?

   a. The audience includes not only Ann Mason but also the readers of the community's newspaper. Given their bias for a simple, rural lifestyle, the readers will probably be hostile to big business in general and to Home Depot in particular. They probably know little about large retail operations. Furthermore, they probably mistrust you because you are a Home Depot employee.

   b. Ann Mason will probably be the only person who reads the letter directly. She is the primary audience; the readers of her article are the secondary audience. Mason will be happy to hear from Home Depot and will read the information with an open mind. However, she may not know a great deal about Home Depot. Although she is a stranger to you, she trusts your credibility as a Home Depot spokesperson.

   c. Ann Mason is probably the sole and primary audience for the letter. The fact that she is writing an article about Home Depot suggests that she already knows a great deal about the company and likes the idea of Home Depot's entry into her community. In all likelihood, she will respond positively to your reply and will trust your credibility as a Home Depot representative.

   d. Ann Mason may be an industrial spy working for a rival home improvement center. She will show your reply to people who work for your competitor; they will analyze the information and use it to improve their market share of the home improvement industry.

4. A light bulb manufacturer is unable to keep up with consumer demand for light bulbs in Home Depot stores. Customers and store managers are complaining about the shortage of light bulbs on the shelves. Home Depot's merchandising manager decides that the manufacturer must correct the supply problem within 30 days or Home Depot will have to find another, more reliable supplier that can meet the high demand. The merchandising manager asks you to suggest the best method of communicating this message to the light bulb manufacturer. Which communication medium would you recommend?

a. Call the manufacturer on the phone to discuss the problem; then follow up with a letter that summarizes the conversation.
b. Call the manufacturer on the phone to discuss the issue, and inform the company of Home Depot's course of action if the problem cannot be corrected within 30 days.
c. Send a fax asking for correction of the problem within 30 days, explaining the consequences of noncompliance.
d. Send a form letter that states the consequences of failing to meet Home Depot's demand for products.[19]

TEST YOUR KNOWLEDGE

1. What are the three steps in the writing process?

2. What two types of purposes do all business messages have?

3. What do you need to know in order to develop an audience profile?

4. How can you test the thoroughness of the information you include in a message?

5. What is media richness and how is it determined?

6. What is the "you" attitude and how does it differ from an "I" attitude?

7. Why is it important to establish your credibility when communicating with an audience of strangers?

8. How does using bias-free language help communicators to establish a good relationship with their audiences?

9. What are the main advantages of oral communication? Of written media?

10. What is boilerplate, and how is it used?

INTERACTIVE LEARNING

USE THIS TEXT'S ONLINE RESOURCES

Visit the myPHLIP Web site at www.prenhall.com/thill. For Chapter 4, take advantage of the interactive "Study Guide" to test your chapter knowledge. Get instant feedback on whether you need additional studying. Read the "Current Events" articles to get the latest on chapter topics, and complete the exercises—as specified by your instructor.

This site's "Study Hall" helps you succeed in this course. "Talk in the Hall" lets you leave messages and meet new friends online. If you have a question, you can "Ask the Tutor." And to get a better grade in this course, you can find more help at "Writing Skills," "Study Skills," and "Study Tips."

The "Research Area" helps you locate a wealth of information to use in course assignments. Plus, you can send a message to online research experts, who will help you find exactly the information you need.

APPLY YOUR KNOWLEDGE

1. Some writers argue that planning messages wastes time because they inevitably change their plans as they go along. How would you respond to this argument? Briefly explain.

2. As a member of the public relations department, what medium would you recommend using to inform the local community that your toxic-waste cleanup program has been successful? Why?

3. When composing business messages, how can you be yourself and project your company's image at the same time?

4. Considering how fast and easy it is, should e-mail replace meetings and other face-to-face communication in your company? Why or why not?

5. **Ethical Choices** The company president has asked you to draft a memo to the board of directors informing them that sales in the newly acquired line of gourmet fruit jams have far exceeded anyone's expectations. As purchasing director, you happen to know that sales of moderately priced jams have declined substantially (many customers have switched to the more expensive jams). You were not directed to add that tidbit of information. What should you do?

PRACTICE YOUR KNOWLEDGE

DOCUMENT FOR ANALYSIS

Read the following document; then (1) analyze the strengths and weaknesses of each sentence and (2) revise the document so that it follows this chapter's guidelines.

I am a new publisher with some really great books to sell. I saw your announcement in *Publishers Weekly* about the bookseller's show you're having this summer, and I think it's a great idea. Count me in, folks! I would like to get some space to show my books. I thought it would be a neat thing if I could do some airbrushing on T-shirts live to help promote my hot new title, *T-Shirt Art*. Before I got into publishing, I was an airbrush artist, and I could demonstrate my techniques. I've done hundreds of advertising illustrations and have been a sign painter all my life, so I'll also be promoting my other book, hot off the presses, *How to Make Money in the Sign Painting Business*.

I will be starting my PR campaign about May 2002 with ads in *PW* and some art trade papers, so my books should be well known by the time the show comes around in August. In case you would like to use my appearance there as part of your publicity, I have enclosed a biography and photo of myself.

P.S. Please let me know what it costs for booth space as soon as possible so that I can figure out whether I can afford to attend. Being a new publisher is mighty expensive!

EXERCISES

4–1. **Planning Messages: Specific Purpose** For each of the following communication tasks, state a specific purpose (if you have trouble, try beginning with "I want to . . .").

   a. A report to your boss, the store manager, about the outdated items in the warehouse
   b. A memo to clients about your booth at the upcoming trade show
   c. A letter to a customer who hasn't made a payment for three months
   d. A memo to employees about the office's high water bills
   e. A phone call to a supplier checking on an overdue parts shipment
   f. A report to future users of the computer program you have chosen to handle the company's mailing list

4–2. **Planning Messages: General and Specific Purpose** Make a list of communication tasks you'll need to accomplish in the next week or so (for example, a job application, a letter of complaint, a speech to a class, an order for some merchandise). For each, determine a general and a specific purpose.

4–3. **Adapting Messages: Media and Purpose** List five messages you have received lately, such as direct-mail promotions, letters, e-mail messages, phone solicitations, and lectures. For each, determine the general and the specific purpose; then answer the following questions: (a) Was the message well timed? (b) Did the sender choose an appropriate medium for the message? (c) Did the appropriate person deliver the message? (d) Was the sender's purpose realistic?

4–4. **Adapting Messages: Media Selection** Barbara Marquardt is in charge of public relations for a cruise line that operates out of Miami. She is shocked to read a letter in a local newspaper from a disgruntled passenger, complaining about the service and entertainment on a recent cruise. Marquardt will have to respond to these publicized criticisms in some way. What audiences will she need to consider in her response? What medium should she choose? If the letter had been published in a travel publication widely read by travel agents and cruise travelers, how might her course of action differ?

4–5. **Planning Messages: Audience Profile** For each communication task below, write brief answers to three questions: Who is my audience? What is my audience's general attitude toward my subject? What does my audience need to know?

   a. A final-notice collection letter from an appliance manufacturer to an appliance dealer, sent 10 days before initiating legal collection procedures
   b. An unsolicited sales letter asking readers to purchase computer disks at near-wholesale prices
   c. An advertisement for peanut butter
   d. Fliers to be attached to doorknobs in the neighborhood, announcing reduced rates for chimney lining or repairs
   e. A cover letter sent along with your résumé to a potential employer
   f. A request (to the seller) for a price adjustment on a piano that incurred $150 in damage during delivery to a banquet room in the hotel you manage

4–6. **Teamwork** Your team has been studying a new method for testing the durability of your company's electric hand tools. Now the team needs to prepare three separate reports on the findings: first, a report for the administrator who will decide whether to purchase the equipment needed for this new testing method; second, a report for the company's engineers who design and develop the hand tools; and third, a report for the trainers who will be showing workers how to use the new equipment. To determine the audience's needs for each of these reports, the team has listed the following questions: (1) Who are the readers? (2) Why will they read my report? (3) Do they need introductory or background material? (4) Do they need definitions of terms? (5) What level or type of language is needed? (6) What level of detail is needed? (7) What result does my report aim for? Working with two other students, answer the questions for each of these audiences:

a. The administrator
b. The engineers
c. The trainers

4–7. Meeting Audience Needs: Necessary Information Choose an electronic device (videocassette recorder, personal computer, telephone answering machine) that you know how to operate well. Write two sets of instructions for operating the device: one set for a reader who has never used that type of machine and one set for someone who is generally familiar with that type of machine but has never operated the specific model. Briefly explain how your two audiences affect your instructions.

4–8. Internet More companies are reaching out to audiences through their Web sites. Go to the PepsiCo Web site at www.pepsico.com and follow the link to the latest annual report. Then locate and read the chairman's letter. Who is the audience for this message? What is the general purpose of the message? What do you think this audience wants to know from the chairman of PepsiCo? How does the chairman emphasize the positive in this letter? Summarize your answers in a brief (one page) memo or oral presentation.

4–9. Audience Relationship: Courteous Communication Substitute a better phrase for each of the following:

a. You claim that
b. It is not our policy to
c. You neglected to
d. In which you assert
e. We are sorry you are dissatisfied
f. You failed to enclose
g. We request that you send us
h. Apparently you overlooked our terms
i. We have been very patient
j. We are at a loss to understand

4–10. Audience Relationship: The "You" Attitude Rewrite these sentences to reflect your audience's viewpoint.

a. We request that you use the order form supplied in the back of our catalog.
b. We insist that you always bring your credit card to the store.
c. We want to get rid of all our 15-inch monitors to make room in our warehouse for the 19-inch screens. Thus we are offering a 25 percent discount on all sales this week.
d. I am applying for the position of bookkeeper in your office. I feel that my grades prove that I am bright and capable, and I think I can do a good job for you.
e. As requested, we are sending the refund for $25.

4–11. Audience Relationship: Emphasize the Positive Revise these sentences to be positive rather than negative.

a. To avoid the loss of your credit rating, please remit payment within 10 days.
b. We don't make refunds on returned merchandise that is soiled.
c. Because we are temporarily out of Baby Cry dolls, we won't be able to ship your order for 10 days.
d. You failed to specify the color of the blouse that you ordered.
e. You should have realized that waterbeds will freeze in unheated houses during winter. Therefore, our guarantee does not cover the valve damage and you must pay the $9.50 valve-replacement fee (plus postage).

4–12. Audience Relationship: Emphasize the Positive Provide euphemisms for the following words and phrases:

a. stubborn
b. wrong
c. stupid
d. incompetent
e. loudmouth

4–13. Audience Relationship: Bias-Free Language Rewrite each of the following to eliminate bias:

a. For an Indian, Maggie certainly is outgoing.
b. He needs a wheelchair, but he doesn't let his handicap affect his job performance.
c. A pilot must have the ability to stay calm under pressure, and then he must be trained to cope with any problem that arises.
d. Candidate Renata Parsons, married and the mother of a teenager, will attend the debate.
e. Senior citizen Sam Nugent is still an active salesman.

4–14. Ethical Choices Your supervisor, whom you respect, has asked you to withhold important information that you think should be included in a report you are preparing. Disobeying him could be disastrous for your relationship and your career. Obeying him could violate your personal code of ethics. What should you do? On the basis of the discussion in Chapter 1, would you consider this situation to be an ethical dilemma or an ethical lapse? Please explain.

4–15. Three-Step Process: Other Applications How can the material discussed in this chapter also apply to meetings as discussed in Chapter 2? (Hint: Review the section headings in Chapter 4 and think about making your meetings more productive.)

4–16. Message Planning Skills: Self-Assessment How good are you at planning business messages? Use the chart on the next page to rate yourself on the elements of planning an audience-centered business message. Then examine your ratings to identify where you are strongest and where you can improve, using the tips in this chapter.

ELEMENT OF PLANNING	ALWAYS	FREQUENTLY	OCCASIONALLY	NEVER
1. I start by defining my purpose.	_____	_____	_____	_____
2. I analyze my audience before writing a message.	_____	_____	_____	_____
3. I investigate what my audience wants to know.	_____	_____	_____	_____
4. I check that my information is accurate, ethical, and pertinent.	_____	_____	_____	_____
5. I consider my audience and purpose when selecting media.	_____	_____	_____	_____
6. I adopt the "you" attitude in my messages.	_____	_____	_____	_____
7. I emphasize the positive aspects of my message.	_____	_____	_____	_____
8. I establish my credibility with audiences of strangers.	_____	_____	_____	_____
9. I express myself politely and tactfully.	_____	_____	_____	_____
10. I use bias-free language.	_____	_____	_____	_____
11. I am careful to project my company's image.	_____	_____	_____	_____

GOING ONLINE EXERCISES

Learn About Your Audience, page 75

Messages that produce results require audience analysis. You need to know who your audience members are, determine their interests, and satisfy their needs. Practice using data from audience profiles. Log on to Games.net Audience Profile.

1. To get information to the Games.net audience, would it be effective to place a message in the *Wall Street Journal?* Explain your answer.

2. Check out PC World's summary of its own audience at marketing.pcworld.com/temp/main8audprofsummary.html. Based on the information listed, give reasons why you'd develop a Web site to reach an audience rather than send a mass mailing.

3. The URL for PC World's audience profile indicates that it is located in the marketing pages of the magazine's Web site. How do you think PC World uses the data in its audience profile? How might it help PC World attract new readers? New advertisers?

To complete this exercise, log on to this text's Web site at www.prenhall.com/thill. Select Chapter 4, then select "Student Resources," click on the name of the featured Web site, and follow the detailed navigational directions.

WRITING BUSINESS MESSAGES

5
chapter

On the job:

FACING A COMMUNICATION DILEMMA AT THE U.S. MINT

Making Money by Making Change

www.usmint.gov

It's a nickel-and-dime operation—literally—producing all those coins that jingle in your pockets. But the U.S. Mint does more than manufacture and distribute pocket change for U.S. commerce. As an agency of the U.S. Treasury Department, the Mint has a legal mission not only to serve but also to educate the public about U.S. coins. In addition, the Mint operates a mail-order business, with distributors in 45 countries selling coins, medals, and coin-based consumer products.

When Philip Diehl took charge of the agency in the mid-1990s, the Mint was struggling to overcome a tarnished image. Most of the Mint's commemorative coins weren't compelling enough to excite coin collectors or the general public, and what orders did come in took months to fill. Diehl worked hard to streamline internal operations and improve customer service, but that wasn't enough. He also had to rejuvenate interest in coin collecting. First, Diehl and his team solicited input from the public and from avid coin collectors. Then they created two exciting new products: the 50 State Quarters Program (which honors each state with its own special quarter) and the golden dollar coin (featuring Sacagawea—the Shoshone woman who played a strategic role in Lewis and Clark's 1804 expedition from the Ohio River Valley to the Pacific Ocean).

Now Diehl must educate the public about the Mint's fascinating new products and do what he can to stimulate interest in coin collecting. He must compose effective messages to create a desire for the new coins, and he must appeal to audience members ranging from coin distributors to vending machine owners to parents helping their children with school projects.

If you were Philip Diehl, how would you go about writing these messages? How would you organize your messages? Would you use an outline? What style and tone would you use?[1]

ORGANIZING YOUR MESSAGE

Like Philip Diehl, all business communicators face the problem of conveying a complicated web of ideas in an understandable fashion. People don't remember separate facts and figures, so successful communicators rely on organization to make their messages meaningful (take another look at Figure 4.1).[2] However, before thinking about *how* to achieve good organization, let's look at *what* it means and *why* it's important.

What Good Organization Means

The definition of good organization varies from country to country. But in the United States and Canada, it generally means creating a linear message that proceeds point by point. If you've ever received a disorganized message, you're familiar with the frustration

After studying this chapter, you will be able to

1 Explain why good organization is important to both the communicator and the audience

2 Summarize the process for organizing business messages effectively

3 Discuss two ways of achieving a tone that is businesslike and a style that is clear and concise

4 Briefly describe how to select words that are not only correct but also effective

5 Explain four guidelines that help you achieve clarity and efficiency in your sentences

6 List five ways to develop a paragraph and discuss three factors that increase paragraph readability

As head of the U.S. Mint, Philip Diehl communicates about coins. Whether soliciting input from the public, educating the public about U.S. Mint products, or writing catalogs to create demand for commemorative coins, Diehl and his staff must compose messages that are clear, concise, and well organized.

As chairman and CEO of Living Omnimedia, Martha Stewart publishes two magazines, numerous books, and a newspaper column. Her creative, practical ideas on cooking, gardening, crafts, holidays, and home improvement have made Stewart trusted guide to stylish living. Stewart's messages are a prime example of good organization: the subject and purpose are clear; information relates to the subject and purpose; and good organization allows the audience to receive only the information they need.

Most disorganized communication suffers from problems with clarity, relevance, grouping, and completeness.

A message is well organized when all the pieces fit together in a coherent pattern.

O b j e c t i v e

1

Explain why good organization is important to both the communicator and the audience.

of trying to sort through a muddle of ideas. Consider this letter from Jill Saunders, the office manager at Boswell & Sons, mapmakers:

> Our president, Mr. Boswell, was in an accident last year, and he hasn't been able to work full-time. His absence has affected our business, so we don't have the budget we used to. His two sons are working hard, so we aren't bankrupt by any means, and soon Mr. Boswell will be coming back full-time.
>
> Boswell & Sons has been doing business with ComputerTime since I was hired six years ago. Your building was smaller then, and it was located on the corner of Federal Avenue and 2nd N.W. Mr. Boswell bought our first laser printer there. I still remember the day. It was the biggest check I'd ever written. Of course, over the years, I've gotten used to larger purchases.
>
> We have seven employees. Although not all of them are directly involved in producing the maps we sell, they all need to have their computers working so that they can do their jobs. The CD-ROM drive we bought for my assistant, Suzanne, has been a problem. We've taken it in for repairs three times in three months to the authorized service center, and Suzanne is very careful with the machine and hasn't abused it. She does like playing interactive adventure games on lunch breaks. Anyway, it still doesn't work right, and she's tired of hauling it back and forth. We're all putting in longer hours to make up for Mr. Boswell's not being here, and none of us has a lot of spare time.
>
> This is the first time we've returned anything to your store, and I hope you'll agree that we deserve a better deal.

This letter displays a lack of organization that U.S. and Canadian readers find frustrating. By taking a closer look at what's wrong, you can distinguish four of the most common organization problems:

◆ **Taking too long to get to the point.** Saunders didn't introduce her topic, the faulty CD-ROM drive, until the third paragraph. Then she waited until the final paragraph to state her purpose: requesting an adjustment. *Solution:* Make the subject and purpose clear.

◆ **Including irrelevant material.** Does it matter that ComputerTime used to be smaller or that it was in a different location? Is it important that Saunders's boss is working only part-time or that her assistant likes playing computer games during lunch? *Solution:* Include only information that is related to the subject and purpose.

◆ **Getting ideas mixed up.** Saunders tries to make six points: (1) Her company has money to spend, (2) it's an old customer, (3) it pays by check, (4) it has purchased numerous items at ComputerTime, (5) the CD-ROM drive doesn't work, and (6) Saunders wants an adjustment. However, the ideas are mixed up and located in the wrong places. *Solution:* Group the ideas and present them in a logical way. For example, begin with the fact that the drive doesn't work, and group some ideas to show that the company is a valuable customer.

◆ **Leaving out necessary information.** ComputerTime may want to know the make, model, and price of the CD-ROM drive; the date of purchase; the specific problems the machine has had; and whether the repairs were covered by the warranty. Saunders also failed to say what she wants the store to do: send her a new CD-ROM drive of the same type, send her a different model, or simply refund her money. *Solution:* Include all the necessary information.

Achieving good organization can be a challenge. However, solving these common problems can help you communicate clearly. Saunders can make her letter more effective by organizing all the necessary information in a sequence that helps ComputerTime understand the message (see Figure 5–1).

Why Good Organization Is Important

Does it matter whether a message is well organized as long as its point is eventually made? Why not just let your ideas flow naturally and trust your audience to grasp your

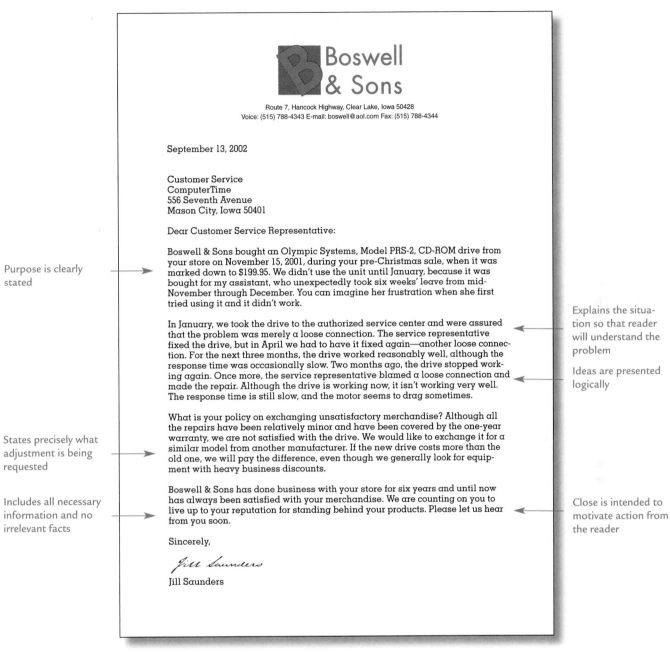

Purpose is clearly stated →

States precisely what adjustment is being requested →

Includes all necessary information and no irrelevant facts →

← Explains the situation so that reader will understand the problem

← Ideas are presented logically

← Close is intended to motivate action from the reader

Figure 5–1
In-Depth Critique: Letter with Improved Organization

meaning? Misinterpreted messages lead to wasted time reading and rereading, poor decision making, and shattered business relationships. When you consider such costs, you begin to realize the value of clear writing and good organization.[3]

In business, the objective is to get work done, not to produce messages. When chief executives were asked what they would most like to improve about their own business writing, they mentioned speed of composition more often than any other factor.[4] Being well organized helps you compose your messages more quickly and efficiently.

Before you begin to write, think about what you're going to say and how you're going to say it. Good organization will save you time. Your draft will go more quickly because you won't waste time putting ideas in the wrong places or composing material you don't need. In addition, you can use your organizational plan to get some advance input from your audience. That way, you can be sure you're on the right track *before* you spend hours working on your draft. If you're working on a large, complex project, you can use your

Good organization saves time, strengthens relationships, and improves efficiency.

Good organization helps audience members understand your message, accept your message, and save time.

organization plan to divide the writing job among co-workers. Good organization also helps your audience understand your message, helps your audience accept your message, and saves your audience time:

◆ **Good organization helps your audience understand your message.** As the Mint's Philip Diehl points out, successful organization makes your message "user friendly and understandable." By making your main point clear at the outset, and by stating your needs precisely, your well-organized message will satisfy your audience's need for information.

◆ **Good organization helps your audience accept your message.** Even when your message is logical, you need to select and organize your points in a diplomatic way. Softening refusals and leaving a good impression enhances your credibility and adds authority to your messages. When ComputerTime responds to the Boswell & Sons inquiry, the message is negative, but the letter is diplomatic and positive (see Figure 5–2).

◆ **Good organization saves your audience time.** Well-organized messages are efficient. They contain only relevant ideas, and they are brief. Moreover, all the information in a well-organized message is in a logical place. Audience members receive only the information they need, and because that information is presented as accessibly and succinctly as possible, audience members can follow the thought pattern without a struggle.

Objective **2**

Summarize the process for organizing business messages effectively.

How Good Organization Is Achieved

Understanding the *need* for good organization is half the battle. Knowing *how* to organize your messages well is the other half. When writing messages at the U.S. Mint, Philip Diehl achieves good organization by defining the main idea, limiting the scope, grouping supporting points, and establishing their sequence by selecting either a direct or an indirect approach.

To organize a message
• Define your main idea
• Limit the scope
• Group your points
• Choose the direct or indirect approach

Define the Main Idea   In addition to having a general purpose and a specific purpose, all business messages can be boiled down to one main idea—one central point that sums up everything. The rest of your message supports, explains, or demonstrates this point. Your main idea is not the same as your topic. The broad subject of your message is the **topic,** and your **main idea** makes a statement about that topic. Consider the examples in Table 5–1.

The topic is the broad subject; the main idea makes a statement about the topic.

Your main idea may be pretty obvious when you're preparing a brief message with simple facts that have little emotional impact on your audience. If you're responding to a request for information, your main idea may be simply, "Here is what you wanted." However, defining your main idea is more complicated when you're trying to persuade someone or when you have disappointing information to convey. In these situations, try to define a main idea that will establish a good relationship between you and your audience. For example, you may choose a main idea that highlights a common interest you share with your audience or that emphasizes a point that you and your audience can agree on.

Table 5–1 Defining Business Messages			
General Purpose	**Specific Purpose**	**Topic**	**Main Idea**
To inform	Teach customer service reps how to file insurance claims	Insurance claims	Proper filing by reps saves the company time and money.
To persuade	Get top managers to approve increased spending on research and development	Funding for research and development	Competitors spend more than we do on research and development.
To collaborate	Get personnel and accounting to devise an incentive system that ties wages to profits	Incentive pay	Tying wages to profits motivates employees and reduces compensation in tough years.

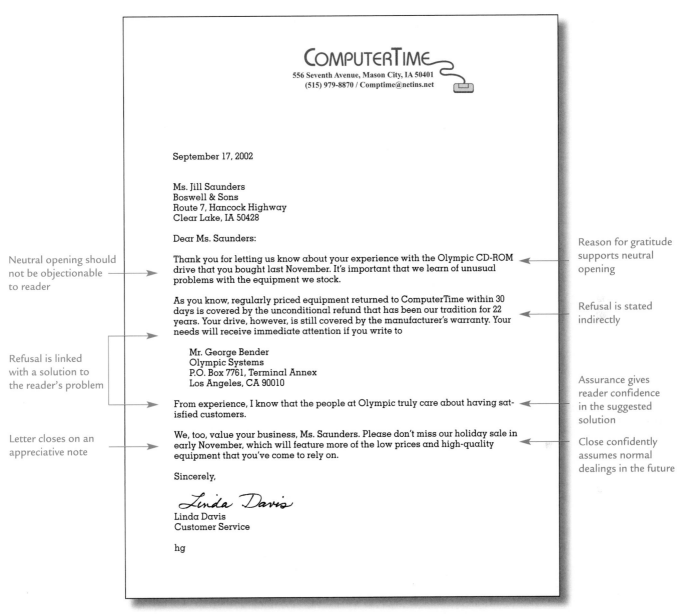

Neutral opening should not be objectionable to reader

Refusal is linked with a solution to the reader's problem

Letter closes on an appreciative note

Reason for gratitude supports neutral opening

Refusal is stated indirectly

Assurance gives reader confidence in the suggested solution

Close confidently assumes normal dealings in the future

Figure 5–2
In-Depth Critique: Letter Demonstrating a Diplomatic Organization Plan

In longer documents and presentations, you'll need to unify a mass of material, so you'll need to define a main idea that encompasses all the individual points you want to make. For tough assignments like these, you may want to take special measures to define your main idea. One great way to generate ideas is to **brainstorm**—letting your mind wander over the possibilities and testing various alternatives against your purpose, your audience, and the facts you've gathered. The important thing to remember about brainstorming is to be completely uncensored and to leave editing and polishing until later (see "Sharpening Your Career Skills—Beating Writer's Block: Nine Workable Ideas to Get Words Flowing"). Successful communicators use a number of approaches to define the main idea in a message.

For longer messages, determining the main idea often requires creative thinking.

Storyteller's Tour   Turn on your tape recorder and pretend that you've just run into an old friend on the street. Give an overview of your message, focusing on your reasons for communicating, your major points, your rationale, and the implications for your intended audience. Listen critically to the tape, then repeat the exercise until you are able to give a

Some techniques for establishing the main idea:
• Storyteller's tour
• Random list
• FCR worksheet
• Journalistic approach
• Question-and-answer chain

Sharpening Your Career Skills

Beating Writer's Block: Nine Workable Ideas to Get Words Flowing

Putting words on a page or on screen can be a real struggle. Some people get stuck so often that they develop a mental block. If you get writer's block, here are some ways to get words flowing:

❑ *Use positive self-talk.* Stop worrying about how well or easily you write, and stop thinking of writing as difficult, time consuming, or complicated. Tell yourself that you're capable and that you can do the job. Also, recall past examples of your writing that were successful.

❑ *Know your purpose.* Be specific about what you want to accomplish with this particular piece of writing. Without a clear purpose, writing can indeed be impossible.

❑ *Visualize your audience.* Picture audience backgrounds, interests, subject knowledge, and vocabulary (including the technical jargon they use). Such visualization can help you choose an appropriate style and tone for your writing.

❑ *Create a productive environment.* Write in a place that's for writing only, and make that place pleasant. Set up "writing appointments." Scheduling a session from 9:30 to noon is less intimidating than an indefinite session. Also, keep your mind fresh with scheduled breaks.

❑ *Make an outline or a list.* Even if you don't create a formal outline, at least jot down a few notes about how your ideas fit together. As you go along, you can revise your notes, as long as you end up with a plan that gives direction and coherence.

❑ *Just start.* Put aside all worries, fears, distractions—anything that gives you an excuse to postpone writing. Then start putting down any thoughts you have about your topic. Don't worry about whether these ideas can actually be used; just let your mind range freely.

❑ *Write the middle first.* Start wherever your interest is greatest and your ideas are most developed. You can follow new directions, but note ideas to revisit later. When you finish one section, choose another without worrying about sequence. Just get your thoughts down.

❑ *Push obstacles aside.* If you get stuck at some point, don't worry. Move past the thought, sentence, or paragraph, and come back to it later. Prime the pump simply by writing or talking about why you're stuck: "I'm stuck because . . ." Also try brainstorming. Before you know it, you'll be writing about your topic.

❑ *Read a newspaper or magazine.* Try reading an article that uses a style similar to yours. Choose one you'll enjoy so that you'll read it more closely.

When deadlines loom, don't freeze in panic. Concentrate on the major ideas first, and save the details for later, after you have something on the page. If you keep things in perspective, you'll succeed.

CAREER APPLICATIONS

1. List the ways you procrastinate, and discuss what you can do to break these habits.
2. Analyze your own writing experiences. What negative self-talk do you use? What might you do to overcome this tendency?

---

smooth, two-minute summary that conveys the gist of your message. The summary should reveal your main idea.

Random List   On a computer screen or a clean sheet of paper, list everything you can think of that pertains to your message. Once you begin your list, your thoughts will start to flow. When you've exhausted the possibilities, study the list for relationships. Sort the items into groups, as you would sort a deck of cards into suits. Look for common denominators; the connection might be geographic, sequential, spatial, chronological, or topical. Part of the list might break down into problems, causes, and solutions; another part, into pros and cons. Regardless of what categories finally emerge, the sorting process will help you sift through your thoughts and decide what's important—thus clarifying your main idea. The best way to decide importance is to concentrate on the points that will benefit your audience most.

FCR Worksheet   If your subject involves the solution to a problem, you might try using an FCR worksheet to help you visualize the relationships among your findings (F), your conclusions (C), and your recommendations (R). For example, you might find that you're losing sales to a competitor who offers lower prices than you do (F). From this information, you might conclude that your loss of sales is due to your pricing policy (C). This conclusion would lead you to recommend a price cut (R). To make an FCR worksheet, divide a computer screen or a sheet of paper into three columns. List the major findings in the first column, then extrapolate conclusions and write them in the second column. These conclusions form the basis for the recommendations, which are listed in the third column. An analysis of the three columns should help you define the main idea.

Journalistic Approach For informational messages, the journalistic approach may provide a good point of departure. Find the answers to six questions—who, what, when, where, why, and how. The answers you come up with should clarify your main idea.

Question-and-Answer Chain Perhaps the best approach is to look at the subject of your message from your audience's point of view. Ask yourself: "What is the audience's main question? What do audience members need to know?" Write down and examine your answers. As additional questions emerge, write down and examine those answers. Follow the chain of questions and answers until you have replied to every conceivable question that might occur to your audience. By thinking about your material from your audience's perspective, you are likely to define your main idea.

Limit the Scope The scope of your message (its length and detail) must match your main idea. Whether your audience expects a one-page memo or a one-hour speech, you must develop your main idea within that framework. Once you have a tentative statement of your main idea, test it against the length limitations that have been imposed for your message. If you lack the time and space to develop your main idea fully, or if your main idea won't fill up the time and space allotted, you'll need to redefine the main idea of your message.

> Gear your main idea to the length of the message.

How much you can communicate in a given number of words depends on the nature of the subject, your audience members' familiarity with the topic, their receptivity to your conclusions, and your credibility. You'll need fewer words to present routine information to a knowledgeable audience that already knows and respects you. You'll need more time to build consensus about a complex and controversial subject, especially if the audience is composed of skeptical or hostile strangers.

As you adjust your message to fit the time or space available, don't change the number of major points. Regardless of how long the message will be, stick with three or four major points—five at the very most. According to communication researchers, that's all your audience will remember.[5]

> Deal with three or four major points (not more than five), regardless of message length.

If your message is brief (four minutes or one page), you'll have only a minute or a paragraph each for the introduction, conclusion, and major points. Because the amount of evidence you can present is limited, your main idea will have to be both easy to understand and easy to accept. However, if you're delivering a long message (say, a 60-minute presentation or a 20-page report), you can develop the major points in considerable detail. You can spend about 10 minutes or 10 paragraphs (more than three pages of double-spaced, typewritten text) on each of your key points, and you'll still have room for your introduction and conclusion. Instead of introducing additional points, you can deal more fully with complex issues, offer a variety of evidence, and overcome resistance.

The overall scope of your message also determines the amount and depth of investigation you can conduct. You may need only to glance at your calendar to confirm a meeting, or you may need to spend weeks conducting formal research for a complicated report. Gathering information for reports and proposals is thoroughly discussed in Chapter 10.

Michael Eisner is chairman and CEO of Walt Disney Company and thus a leading figure in the international communications industry. As such, he pays close attention to detail. For example, he adjusts his messages to fit the time or space available so that his associates will be more receptive to his ideas. Whether he uses a brief memo or a long report, three or four major points are what his audience will remember.

Group Your Points Although these techniques will help generate your main idea, they won't necessarily tell you how to develop it or how to group the supporting details in the most logical and effective way. To decide on the final structure of your message, you need to visualize how all the points fit together. One way to do so is to construct an outline. Whether you use the outlining features provided with word-processing software or simply jot down three or four points on the back of an envelope, making a plan and sticking to it will help you cover the important details.

> An outline or a schematic diagram will help you visualize the relationship among parts of a message.

When you're preparing a longer, more complex message, an outline is indispensable because it helps you visualize the relationships among the various parts. Without an outline, you may be inclined to ramble. As you're describing one point, another point may occur to you, so you describe it. One detour leads to another, and before you know it, you've forgotten the original point. With an outline to guide you, however, you can communicate in a more systematic way. Following an outline also helps you insert transitions so that your message is coherent and your audience can understand the relationships among your ideas.

Figure 5–3
Two Common Outline Forms

ALPHANUMERIC OUTLINE

I. First Major Part
   A. First subpoint
   B. Second subpoint
      1. Evidence
      2. Evidence
         a. Detail
         b. Detail
      3. Evidence
   C. Third subpoint
II. Second Major Point
   A. First subpoint
      1. Evidence
      2. Evidence
   B. Second subpoint

DECIMAL OUTLINE

I.0 First Major Part
   1.1 First subpoint
   1.2 Second subpoint
      1.2.1 Evidence
      1.2.2 Evidence
         1.2.2.1 Detail
         1.2.2.2 Detail
      1.2.3 Evidence
   2.0 Third subpoint
2.0 Second Major Point
   2.1 First subpoint
      2.1.1 Evidence
      2.1.2 Evidence
   2.2 Second subpoint

Outlines can appear in various formats.

You're no doubt familiar with the basic outline formats, which (1) use numbers or numbers and letters to identify each point and (2) indent points to show which ideas are of equal status. A good outline divides a topic into at least two parts, restricts each subdivision to one category, and ensures that each group is separate and distinct (see Figure 5–3).

A more schematic format illustrates the structure of your message in an "organization chart" similar to the charts used to show a company's management structure (see Figure 5–4). The main idea is shown in the highest-level box, and like a top executive it establishes the big picture. The lower-level ideas, like lower-level employees, provide the details. All the ideas are logically organized into divisions of thought, just as a company is organized into divisions and departments.[6] To develop this type of outline, you must start with the main idea, state the major supporting points, then illustrate these points with evidence.

The main idea is the starting point for constructing an outline.

Start with the Main Idea   The main idea, placed at the top of an organization chart, helps you establish the goals and general strategy of the message. This main idea summarizes two things: (1) what you want your audience to do or think and (2) why they should do so. Everything in the message should either support the main idea or explain its implications.

Major supporting points clarify your main idea.

State the Major Points   In an organization chart, the boxes directly below the top box represent the major supporting points (corresponding to the main headings in a conventional outline). These are the "vice presidential" ideas that clarify the message by expressing it in more concrete terms. When breaking the main idea into these smaller units, try to identify between three and five major points. If you come up with more, go back and look for opportunities to combine some of your ideas.

Sometimes the points that go into these boxes are fairly obvious. But at other times, you may have hundreds of ideas to sort through and group together. Be sure to keep in mind your purpose and the nature of the material.

The division of major points may be based on physical relationships, the description of a process, the components of an object, or a historical chronology.

If your purpose is to inform and the material is factual, divisions are generally suggested by the subject itself. Major points are often based on something physical—something you can visualize or measure, such as activities to be performed, functional units, spatial or chronological relationships, or parts of a whole. When you're describing a process, the major points are almost inevitably steps in the process. When you're describing an object, the major points correspond to the components of the object. When you're giving a historical account, major points represent events in the chronological chain.

If your purpose is to persuade or to collaborate, the major supporting points may be more difficult to identify. Instead of relying on a natural order imposed by the subject, develop a line of reasoning that proves your central message and motivates your audience

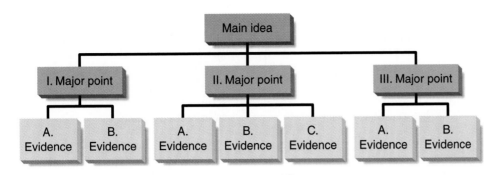

Figure 5–4
"Organization Chart" for
Organizing a Message

to act. The boxes on the organization chart then correspond to the major elements in a logical argument. The supporting points are the main reasons your audience should accept your message.

Illustrate with Evidence   The third level on the organization chart shows the specific evidence you'll use to illustrate your major points. This evidence is the flesh and blood that helps your audience understand and remember the more abstract concepts you're presenting. For example, if you're advocating that your company increase its advertising budget, you can support your major point by providing evidence that your most successful competitors spend more on advertising than you do. You can also describe a case in which a particular competitor increased its ad budget and achieved an impressive sales gain. And then you can show that over the past five years, your firm's sales have gone up and down in response to the amount spent on advertising.

If you're developing a long, complex message, you may need to carry the organization chart (or outline) down several levels. Remember that every level is a step along the chain from the abstract to the concrete, from the general to the specific. The lowest level contains the individual facts and figures that tie the generalizations to the observable, measurable world. The higher levels are the concepts that reveal why those facts are significant.

The more evidence you provide, the more conclusive your case will be. If your subject is complex and unfamiliar or if your audience is skeptical, you'll need a lot of facts and figures to demonstrate your points. On the other hand, if your subject is routine and the audience is positively inclined, you can be more sparing with the evidence. You want to provide enough support to be convincing but not so much that your message becomes boring or inefficient.

Choose Between the Direct and Indirect Approaches   Once you've defined and grouped your ideas, you're ready to decide on their sequence. When you're addressing a U.S. or Canadian audience with minimal cultural differences, you have two basic options:

◆ **Direct approach (deductive).** The main idea comes first, followed by the evidence. Use this approach when your audience will be neutral about your message or pleased to hear from you.

◆ **Indirect approach (inductive).** The evidence comes first, and the main idea comes later. Use this approach when your audience will be displeased about what you have to say.

To choose between these two alternatives, you must analyze your audience's likely reaction to your purpose and message. Audience reaction will fall somewhere between being eager to accept your message and being unwilling to accept your message (see Figure 5–5). The direct approach is generally fine when audience members will be receptive—if they are eager, interested, pleased, or even neutral. But you may have better results with the indirect approach if audience members are likely to resist your message— if they are displeased, uninterested, or unwilling.

Bear in mind, however, that each message is unique. No simple formula will solve all your communication problems. For example, if you're sending bad news to outsiders, an indirect approach may be best. On the other hand, if you're writing a memo to an associate, you may want to get directly to the point, even if your message is unpleasant. The direct approach might also be a good choice for long messages, regardless of your audience's attitude, because

Major points may also be based on the elements of a logical argument.

Each major point must be supported with enough specific evidence to be convincing, but not so much that it's boring.

Use direct order if the audience's reaction is likely to be positive and indirect order if it is likely to be negative.

Audience reaction can range from eager to unwilling.

Figure 5–5
Audience Reaction Affects
Organizational Approach

Audience reaction

| Eager | Interested | Pleased | Neutral | Displeased | Uninterested | Unwilling |

Direct approach   **Indirect approach**

delaying the main idea could cause confusion and frustration. To summarize, your choice of a direct or an indirect approach depends on the following factors:

- ◆ **Audience reaction:** (1) positive, (2) neutral, or (3) negative

Choice of approach also depends on message length and type.

- ◆ **Message length:** (1) short (memos and letters), or (2) long (reports, proposals, and presentations—discussed in Part 4)

- ◆ **Message type:** (1) routine, good-news, and goodwill messages, (2) bad-news messages, or (3) persuasive messages

When used with good judgment, the three basic types of business messages can be powerful tools of communication.[7] Just remember, cautions Philip Diehl of the U.S. Mint, your first priority is to make your message clear. In the following brief discussions, note how the opening, body, and close all play an important role in getting your message across, regardless of message type.

The direct approach is effective for messages that will please the audience or will cause no particular reaction.

Routine, Good-News, and Goodwill Messages   The most straightforward business messages are routine, good-news, and goodwill messages. If you're inquiring about products or placing an order, your audience will usually want to comply. If you're announcing a price cut, granting an adjustment, accepting an invitation, or congratulating a colleague, your audience will most likely be pleased to hear from you. If you're providing routine information as part of your regular business, your audience will probably be neutral, neither pleased nor displeased.

Aside from being easy to understand, these kinds of messages are easy to prepare. In most cases you get right down to business. In the opening, you state your main idea directly, without searching for some creative introduction. The body of your message can then provide all necessary detail. The close is cordial and emphasizes your good news or makes a statement about the specific action desired.

By starting off with your positive idea, you put your audience in a good frame of mind and encourage them to be receptive to whatever else you have to say. This approach also emphasizes the pleasing aspect of your message by putting it right up front, where it's the first thing recipients see. Routine, good-news, and goodwill messages are discussed in greater detail in Chapter 7.

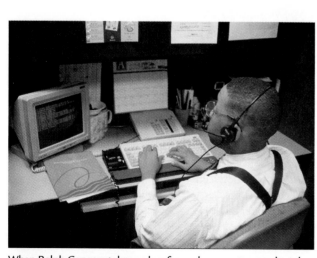

When Ralph Congers takes orders from phone customers, he asks for the same information that a writer would need to include in an order letter: contact information (name, address, phone, e-mail), payment information (check, credit card type and number), and item information (item description, how many, etc.). Because such orders are routine, the information is presented in a direct and straightforward manner.

Bad-News Messages   If you're turning down a job applicant, refusing credit, or denying a request for an adjustment, your audience will be disappointed. In such cases, it may be best to use the indirect approach—putting the evidence first and the main idea later. For example, by blurting out an unpleasant message, you may think that you're just being businesslike or that your audience is too far away or too unimportant to matter. However, astute businesspeople know that every person they encounter could be a potential customer, supplier, or contributor or could influence someone who is a customer, a supplier, or a contributor.

Successful communicators take a little extra care with their bad-news messages. They open with a neutral statement that acts as a transition to the reasons for the bad news.

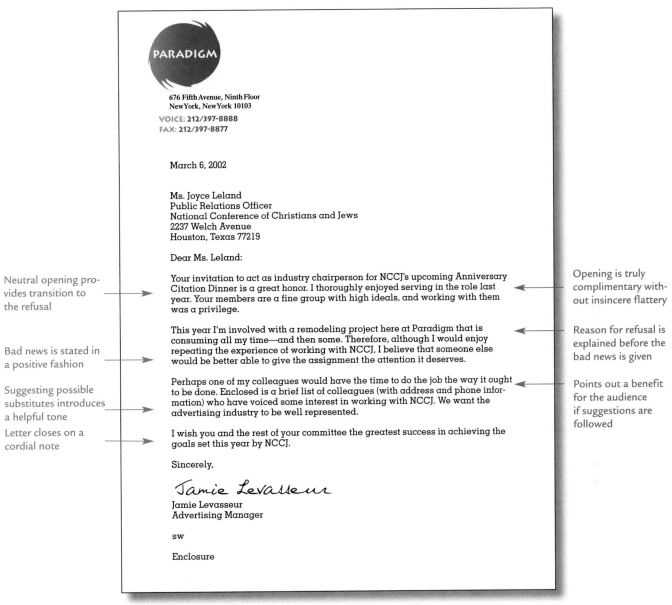

Figure 5–6
In-Depth Critique: Letter Delivering Bad News

In the body they give the reasons that justify a negative answer before stating or implying the bad news. And they are always careful to close cordially.

The challenge lies in being honest but kind. You don't want to sacrifice ethics and mislead your audience; nor do you want to be overly blunt. To achieve a good mix of candor and kindness, focus on some aspect of the situation that makes the bad news a little easier to take. As advertising manager at Paradigm Enterprises, Jamie Levasseur wrote a letter declining a request (Figure 5–6). Note how she cushions the bad news.

The first and last sections of any message make the biggest impression. If Levasseur had refused in the first sentence of her letter, the reader might never have bothered to go on to the reasons or might have been in the wrong frame of mind to consider them. By putting the explanation before the refusal, Levasseur focused attention on the reasons. To use this approach effectively, you have to be sincere about your reasons. A reader can spot a phony excuse in a minute.

The indirect approach is neither manipulative nor unethical. As long as you can be honest and reasonably brief, you're better off opening a bad-news message with a neutral

> If you have bad news, try to put it somewhere in the middle, cushioned by other, more positive ideas.

> The indirect approach should not be used to manipulate.

Checklist: Organizing Business Messages

Recognize Good Organization	*Decide What to Say*
✓ Subject and purpose are clear.	✓ Start with the main idea.
✓ Information is directly related to subject and purpose.	✓ State the major points.
✓ Ideas are grouped and presented logically.	✓ Illustrate with evidence.
✓ All necessary information is included.	
	Organize the Message to Respond to the Audience's Probable Reaction
Define the Main Idea	
✓ Stimulate your creativity with brainstorming techniques.	✓ Use the direct approach when your audience will be neutral, pleased, interested, or eager.
✓ Identify a "hook" to motivate your audience to respond in the way you intend.	✓ Use the indirect approach when your audience will be displeased, uninterested, or unwilling.
✓ Evaluate whether the main idea is realistic, given the imposed length limitations.	
✓ Collect any necessary information.	

point and putting the negative information after the explanation. Then, if you can close with something fairly positive, you're likely to leave the audience feeling okay—not great, but not hostile either (which is often about all you can hope for when you must deliver negative messages). Bad-news messages are discussed further in Chapter 8.

Using the indirect approach gives you an opportunity to get your message across to an uninterested or skeptical audience.

Persuasive Messages   The indirect approach is also useful when you know that your audience will resist your message (will be uninterested in your request or unwilling to comply without extra coaxing). You might find an audience resistant to a sales letter, a collection letter, an unsolicited job application, or a request for a favor of some kind. In such cases, you have a better chance of getting through to the person if you lead off with something catchy. This doesn't mean that you should go in for gimmicks, but try to think of something that will make your audience receptive to what you have to say.

You have to capture people's attention before you can persuade them to do something. You have to get your audience to consider with an open mind what you have to say. So you have to make an interesting point and provide supporting facts that encourage the audience to continue paying attention.

Persuasive messages have their own indirect pattern.

The opening begins by mentioning a possible benefit, referring to a problem that the recipient might have, posing a question, or mentioning an interesting statistic. Then the body builds interest in the subject and arouses your audience members' desire to comply. Once you have them thinking, you can introduce your main idea. The close is cordial and requests the desired action. Persuasive messages are discussed at greater length in Chapter 9. For a reminder of the organization tasks involved in preparing your messages, see "Checklist: Organizing Business Messages."

COMPOSING YOUR MESSAGE

Once you've completed the planning process and organized your message, you're ready to begin composing your first draft. If your schedule permits, put aside your outline or organization chart for a day or two. Then review it with a fresh eye, looking for opportunities to improve the flow of ideas.

Composition is the process of drafting your message; polishing it is a later step.

Composition is easiest if you've already figured out what to say and in what order, although you may need to pause now and then to find the right word. You may also discover as you go along that you can improve on your outline. Feel free to rearrange, delete, and add ideas, as long as you don't lose sight of your purpose.

As you compose your first draft, pay attention to your style and tone, and try to select words that match the tone you want to achieve. Try to create effective sentences and to develop coherent paragraphs. But don't worry about getting everything perfect. Just put down your ideas as quickly as you can. You'll have time to revise and refine the material later.

Remember, good business writing is learned by imitation and practice. As you read business journals, newspapers, and even novels, make a note of the words, phrases, or paragraphs you think are effective, and keep them in a file. Then look through the file before you draft your next letter or report. Try using some of these ideas in your document. You may be surprised how helpful they are.

Control Your Style and Tone

Style is the way you use words to achieve a certain **tone,** or overall impression. You can vary your style—your sentence structure and vocabulary—to sound forceful or objective, personal or formal, colorful or dry. The right choice depends on the nature of your message and your relationship with the reader. Although style can be refined during the revision phase (see Chapter 6), you'll save time and a lot of rewriting if you use a style that allows you to achieve the desired tone from the start.

Your use of language is one of your credentials, a badge that identifies you as being a member of a particular group. Try to make your style clear, concise, and grammatically correct, and try to make it conform to the norms of your group. Every organization has its own stylistic conventions, and many occupational groups share a particular vocabulary. In general, try to make your tone conversational, and keep your message clear by using plain English.

Use a Conversational Tone The tone of your business messages may span a continuum from informal to conversational to formal. Most business messages aim for a conversational tone, using plain language that sounds businesslike without being stuffy, stiff, wordy, or full of jargon. Rather than trying to impress audiences with an extensive vocabulary, good communicators focus on being sensible, logical, and objective; they provide supporting facts and a rationale. To achieve such a conversational tone in your messages, try to avoid obsolete and pompous language, intimacy, humor, and preaching or bragging:

◆ **Avoid obsolete and pompous language.** Business language used to be much more formal than it is today, and some out-of-date phrases still remain. Avoid using such obsolete language by asking yourself, "Would I say this if I were talking with someone face to face?" Similarly, avoid using big words, trite expressions, and overly complicated sentences to impress others. Such pompous language sounds puffed up and roundabout (see Table 5–2).

◆ **Avoid intimacy.** Don't mention anything about anyone's personal life unless you know the individual very well. Avoid phrases that imply intimacy, such as "just between you and me" and "as you and I are well aware." Be careful about sounding too folksy or chatty; such a familiar tone may be seen as an attempt to seem like an old friend when, in fact, you're not.

◆ **Avoid humor.** Using humor can backfire, especially if you don't know your audience very well. What seems humorous to you may be deadly serious to others. And when you're communicating across cultures, chances are slim that your audience will appreciate your humor or even realize that you're trying to be funny.[8] Also, humor changes too quickly. What's funny today may not be in a week or a month from now.

◆ **Avoid preaching and bragging.** Few things are more irritating than people who think they know everything and others know nothing. If you must tell your audience something obvious, place the information in the middle of a paragraph, where it will sound like a casual comment rather than a major revelation. Also, avoid bragging about your accomplishments or about the size or profitability of your organization (unless your audience is a part of your organization).

Your conversational tone may become less or more formal, depending on the situation. For instance, if you're addressing an old friend, your conversational tone may lean more toward an informal level. In business messages, however, your tone would never be as informal as it would with family members or school friends. On the other hand, if you're in a large organization and you're communicating with your superiors or if you're

Objective

3

Discuss two ways of achieving a tone that is businesslike and a style that is clear and concise.

When composing your message, you can vary the style to create a tone that suits the occasion.

Your composition style says a lot about you.

Most business messages aim for a conversational style. To achieve a warm but businesslike tone
• Don't use obsolete language.
• Don't use pompous phrases.
• Don't be too familiar.
• Use humor only with great care.
• Don't preach.
• Don't brag.

Going Online

Compose a Better Business Message
◆
At Purdue's Online Writing Lab (OWL) you'll find tools to help you improve your business messages. For advice on composing written messages, for help with grammar, and for referrals to other information sources, you'll be wise to visit this site. Purdue's OWL offers online services and an introduction to Internet search tools. You can also download a variety of handouts on writing skills. Check out the resources at the OWL home page and learn how to write a professional business message.

owl.english.purdue.edu

To reach this Web site, go to www.prenhall.com/thill (the Web site for this text). Select Chapter 5, then select "Student Resources." There, you'll find a current live link that will take you straight to the site.

Table 5-2   Staying Up to Date and Down to Earth

Obsolete	*Up to Date*
in due course	today, tomorrow (or a specific time)
permit me to say that	(permission is not necessary)
we are in receipt of	we have received
pursuant to	(omit)
in closing, I'd like to say	(omit)
the undersigned	I; me
kindly advise	please let us know
we wish to inform you	(just say it)
attached please find	enclosed is
it has come to my attention	I have just learned; or, Ms. Garza has just told me
our Mr. Lydell	Mr. Lydell, our credit manager
please be advised that	(omit)

Pompous	*Down to Earth*
Upon procurement of additional supplies, I will initiate fulfillment of your order.	I will fill your order when I receive more supplies.
Perusal of the records indicates a substantial deficit for the preceding accounting period due to the utilization of antiquated mechanisms.	The records show a company loss last year due to the use of old equipment.

communicating to customers, your conversational tone would tend to be more formal and respectful.

Use Plain English   Plain English is a way of writing and arranging technical materials so that your audience can understand your meaning. Because it's close to the way people normally speak, plain English is easily understood by anyone with an eighth- or ninth-grade education. If you've ever tried to make sense of an overwritten or murky passage in a legal document or credit agreement, you can understand why governments and corporations today are endorsing the plain-English movement.[9]

This movement has already led to the use of plain English in loan and credit card application forms, insurance policies, investment documents, and real estate contracts (see "Sharpening Your Career Skills—No Need to Explain It, Just Say It in Plain English"). Even software programmers are trying to simplify their language. They need to communicate clearly with product users who may not understand what it means to "pop out to DOS."[10]

Of course, plain English has some limitations. It lacks the precision necessary for scientific research, intense feeling, and personal insight. Moreover, it fails to embrace all cultures and dialects equally. But even though it's intended for audiences who speak English as their primary language, plain English can also help you simplify the messages you prepare for audiences who speak English only as a second or even third language. For example, by choosing words that have only one interpretation, you will surely communicate more clearly with your intercultural audience.[11]

Select the Best Words

To compose effective messages, you must choose your words carefully.[12] First, pay close attention to correctness. The "rules" of grammar and usage are constantly changing to reflect changes in the way people speak. So even editors and grammarians occasionally have questions about correct usage, and they sometimes disagree about the answers. For

Plain English is close to spoken English and can be easily understood.

Plain English is already being used in many areas.

Not every application is appropriate for plain English.

Objective
4
Briefly describe how to select words that are not only correct but also effective.

Correctness is the first consideration when choosing words.

Sharpening Your Career Skills

No Need to Explain It, Just Say It in Plain English

The goal of good writing is to communicate, not to confuse; to be understood, not to hide behind words. Look at this confusing excerpt from an investment document:

> The applicability of the general information and administrative procedures set forth below accordingly will vary depending on the investor and the record-keeping system established for a shareholder's investment in the Fund. Participants in 401(k) and other plans should first consult with the appropriate persons at their employer or refer to the plan materials before following any of the procedures below.

No wonder investors turn to brokers, accountants, and lawyers for help. As chairman of the Security and Exchange Commission (SEC), Arthur Levitt Jr. found that even he couldn't understand some investment documents: "I realized the SEC did a good job requiring disclosure, but not enough to make sure documents were in a form most investors could understand."

Today's consumers want to understand the investments and the insurance policies they purchase, as well as the leases, mortgages, and sales contracts they sign. And in January 1998, the SEC began requiring companies to write all investment documents in plain English—following six basic writing principles:

- ❏ Use active voice.
- ❏ Use short sentences.
- ❏ Use everyday words.
- ❏ Use lists to present complex material.
- ❏ Avoid legal jargon.
- ❏ Do not use multiple negatives.

Restating our excerpt in plain English reveals one simple thought: "If you are investing through a large retirement plan or other special program, follow the instructions in your program material."

Some companies are concerned that writing documents in plain English will increase their liability, but many companies are finding just the opposite. "In many ways," notes one Bell Atlantic employee, "we reduced our liability because we have created a document that is much clearer and less ambiguous." Similarly, when Citibank introduced promissory notes written in plain English, the number of collection lawsuits fell dramatically. The clearer writing simply made it easier for borrowers to understand their obligations.

Some lawyers may purposely choose obscure language to control vital information, to take advantage of those who don't know what they're signing, or to profit from people who call them to interpret the gobbledegook. But many legal professionals strongly endorse the plain-English movement. The State Bar of Texas offers sarcastic "legaldegook" awards for especially atrocious writing. And law schools are investing in programs designed to teach students how to write in plain English.

The plain-English movement has generated such momentum that in 1998, President Clinton signed an executive order requiring federal agencies to communicate in language that is "clearer and easier to understand." Agencies must now use plain English in any new document explaining how to get a benefit or comply with a requirement, all new regulations must use simple wording, and all existing letters and notices must be revised by 2002. Clearly, confusing language is becoming obsolete.

CAREER APPLICATIONS

1. How does writing in plain English affect a company's image?
2. Why don't more companies draft their documents using plain English?

---

example, the word *data* is the plural form of *datum,* yet some experts now prefer to treat *data* as a singular noun when it's used in nonscientific material to refer to a body of information. You be the judge: Which of the following sentences sounds better?

> The data on our market share is consistent from region to region.
> The data on our market share are consistent from region to region.

Although debating the finer points of usage may seem like nitpicking, using words correctly is important. If you make grammatical or usage errors, you lose credibility with your audience. Poor grammar implies that you're unaware or uninformed, and audiences put little faith in an uninformed source. Even if an audience is broad-minded enough to withhold such a judgment, grammatical errors are distracting.

Correct grammar enhances your image.

If you have doubts about what is correct, don't be lazy. Look up the answer and use the proper form of expression. Check the grammar and usage guide in Appendix C, or consult any number of special reference books and resources available in libraries, in bookstores, and on the Internet. Most authorities agree on the basic conventions.

If in doubt, check it out.

Just as important as selecting the correct word is selecting the most suitable word for the job at hand. Word effectiveness is generally more difficult to achieve than correctness, particularly in written communication. Writers such as the U.S. Mint's Philip Diehl have

Effectiveness is the second consideration when choosing words.

to work at their craft, using functional and content words correctly and finding the words that communicate.

Functional words (conjunctions, prepositions, articles, and pronouns) express relationships among content words (nouns, verbs, adjectives, and adverbs).

Use Functional and Content Words Correctly   Words can be divided into two main categories. *Functional words* express relationships and have only one unchanging meaning in any given context. They include conjunctions, prepositions, articles, and pronouns. Your main concern with functional words is to use them correctly. *Content words* are multidimensional and therefore subject to various interpretations. They include nouns, verbs, adjectives, and adverbs. These words carry the meaning of a sentence. In your sentences, content words are the building blocks, and functional words are the mortar that holds them together. In the following sentence, all the content words are underlined:

> <u>Some objective observers</u> of the <u>cookie market give Nabisco</u> the <u>edge</u> in <u>quality</u>, but <u>Frito-Lay is lauded</u> for <u>superior distribution</u>.

Both functional words and content words are necessary, but your effectiveness as a communicator depends largely on your ability to choose the right content words for your message. Content words can be classified (1) by denotation and connotation and (2) by abstraction and concreteness.

Content words have both a denotative (explicit, specific) meaning and a connotative (implicit, associative) meaning.

Denotation and Connotation   Content words have both a denotative and a connotative meaning. The **denotative meaning** is the literal, or dictionary, meaning. The **connotative meaning** includes all the associations and feelings evoked by the word.

The denotative meaning of *desk* is "a table used for writing." Some desks may have drawers or compartments, and others may have a flat top or a sloping top, but the literal meaning is generally well understood. The connotative meaning of *desk* may include thoughts associated with work or study, but the word *desk* has fairly neutral connotations—neither strong nor emotional. However, some words have much stronger connotations than others. For example, if you say that a student *failed* to pass a test, the connotative meaning suggests that the person is inferior, incompetent, below some standard of performance. The connotations of the word *fail* are negative and can carry strong emotional meaning.

Business communicators avoid words with negative connotations.

In business communication, avoid using terms that are high in connotative meaning. By saying that a student achieved a score of 65 percent, you communicate the facts and avoid a heavy load of negative connotations. If you use words that have relatively few possible interpretations, you are less likely to be misunderstood. In addition, because you are trying to communicate in an objective, rational manner, you want to avoid emotion-laden comments.

The more abstract a word, the more it is removed from the tangible, objective world of things that can be perceived with the senses.

Abstraction and Concreteness   An *abstract word* expresses a concept, quality, or characteristic. Abstractions are usually broad, encompassing a category of ideas. They are often intellectual, academic, or philosophical. *Love, honor, progress, tradition,* and *beauty* are abstractions.

A *concrete word* stands for something you can touch or see. Concrete terms are anchored in the tangible, material world. *Chair, table, horse, rose, kick, kiss, red, green,* and *two* are concrete words; they are direct, clear, and exact.

You might assume that concrete words are better than abstract words, because they are more precise, but you would sometimes be wrong. For example, try to rewrite this sentence without using the underlined abstract words:

> We hold these <u>truths</u> to be <u>self-evident</u>, that all men are <u>created equal</u>, that they are <u>endowed</u> by their <u>Creator</u> with certain <u>unalienable Rights</u>, that among these are <u>Life</u>, <u>Liberty</u>, and the <u>Pursuit of Happiness</u>.

As you can see, the Declaration of Independence needs abstractions, and so do business messages. Abstractions permit us to rise above the common and tangible. They allow us to refer to concepts such as *morale, productivity, profits, quality, motivation,* and *guarantees.*

Even though they're indispensable, abstractions can be troublesome. They tend to be fuzzy and subject to many interpretations. They also tend to be boring. It isn't always

Table 5–3 Thinking Like a Wordsmith	
Avoid Weak Phrases	*Use Strong Terms*
Wealthy businessperson	Tycoon
Business prosperity	Boom
Hard times	Slump
Avoid Unfamiliar Words	*Use Familiar Words*
Ascertain	Find out, learn
Consummate	Close, bring about
Peruse	Read, study
Circumvent	Avoid
Increment	Growth, increase
Unequivocal	Certain
Avoid Clichés	*Use Plain Language*
Scrape the bottom of the barrel	Strain shrinking resources
An uphill battle	A challenge
Writing on the wall	Prediction
Call the shots	Be in charge
Take by storm	Attack
Cost an arm and a leg	Expensive
A new ballgame	Fresh start
Worst nightmare	Strong competitor, disaster
Fall through the cracks	Be overlooked

easy to get excited about ideas, especially if they're unrelated to concrete experience. The best way to minimize such problems is to blend abstract terms with concrete ones, the general with the specific. State the concept, then pin it down with details expressed in more concrete terms. Save the abstractions for ideas that cannot be expressed any other way.

> In business communication, use concrete, specific terms whenever possible; use abstractions only when necessary.

Take a moment to look at a sample of your writing. Circle all the nouns. How many of them stand for a specific person, place, or object? The ones that do are concrete. Look at the vague nouns; can you replace them with terms that are more vivid? Now underline all the adjectives. How many of them describe the exact color, size, texture, quantity, or quality of something? Remember that words such as *small, numerous, sizable, near, soon, good,* and *fine* are imprecise. Try to replace them with terms that are more accurate. Instead of referring to a *sizable loss,* talk about a *loss of $32 million.*

Find Words That Communicate   Anyone who earns a living by crafting words is a *wordsmith*—including journalists, public relations specialists, editors, and letter and report writers. Unlike poets, novelists, or dramatists, wordsmiths don't strive for dramatic effects. Instead, they are concerned with using language to be clear, concise, and accurate. To reach their goal, they emphasize words that are strong and familiar. When you compose your business messages, do your best to think like a wordsmith (See Table 5–3).

> Business communicators aim for clarity and accuracy rather than dramatic effect.

◆ **Choose strong words.** Choose words that express your thoughts most clearly, specifically, and dynamically. Nouns and verbs are the most concrete, so use them as much as you can. Adjectives and adverbs have obvious roles, but use them sparingly—they often evoke subjective judgments. Verbs are especially powerful because they tell what's happening in the sentence, so make them dynamic and specific (replace *rise* or *fall* with *soar* or *plummet*).

> Wordsmiths choose strong words, choose familiar words, avoid clichés, and use jargon carefully.

◆ **Choose familiar words.** You'll communicate best with words that are familiar to your readers. However, keep in mind that words familiar to one reader might be unfamiliar to another.

◆ **Avoid clichés.** Although familiar words are generally the best choice, beware of terms and phrases so common that they have become virtually meaningless. Because clichés are used so often, readers tend to slide right by them to whatever is coming next. Most people use these phrases not because they think it makes their message more vivid and inviting but because they don't know how to express themselves otherwise.[13]

◆ **Use jargon carefully.** Handle technical or professional terms with care. These words can add precision and authority to a message, but many people don't understand them (even a sophisticated audience can be lulled to sleep by too many). Let your audience's vocabulary guide you. When addressing a group of engineers or scientists, refer to *meteorological effects on microwave propagation;* otherwise, refer to the *effects of weather on radio waves.*

Create Effective Sentences

In English, word order is important when constructing sentences. Every sentence contains a subject (noun or noun equivalent) and a predicate (verb and related words).

In English, words don't make much sense until they're combined in a sentence to express a complete thought. Thus the words *Jill, receptionist, the, smiles,* and *at* can be organized into "Jill smiles at the receptionist." Now that you've constructed the sentence, you can begin exploring the possibilities for improvement, looking at how well each word performs its particular function. Nouns and noun equivalents are the topics (or subjects) you're communicating about, and verbs and related words (or predicates) make statements about those subjects. In a complicated sentence, adjectives and adverbs modify the subject and the statement, and various connectors hold the words together.

The Four Types of Sentences   Sentences come in four basic varieties: simple, compound, complex, and compound-complex. A **simple sentence** has one main clause (a single subject and a single predicate), although it may be expanded by nouns and pronouns serving as objects of the action and by modifying phrases. Here's a typical example (with the subject underlined once and the predicate verb underlined twice):

A simple sentence has one main clause.

<u>Profits</u> <u>have increased</u> in the past year.

A compound sentence has two main clauses.

A **compound sentence** has two main clauses that express two or more independent but related thoughts of equal importance, usually joined by *and, but,* or *or.* In effect, a compound sentence is a merger of two or more simple sentences (independent clauses) that are related. For example:

Wage <u>rates</u> <u>have declined</u> by 5 percent, and employee <u>turnover</u> <u>has been</u> high.

The independent clauses in a compound sentence are always separated by a comma or by a semicolon (in which case the conjunction—*and, but, or*—is dropped).

A complex sentence has one main clause and one subordinate clause.

A **complex sentence** expresses one main thought (the independent clause) and one or more subordinate thoughts (dependent clauses) related to it, often separated by a comma. The subordinate thought, which comes first in the following sentence, could not stand alone:

Although you may question Gerald's conclusions, <u>you</u> <u>must admit</u> that his research is thorough.

A compound-complex sentence has two main clauses and at least one dependent clause.

A **compound-complex sentence** has two main clauses, at least one of which contains a subordinate clause:

<u>Profits</u> <u>have increased</u> in the past year, and although you may question Gerald's conclusions, <u>you</u> <u>must</u> admit that his research is thorough.

When constructing a sentence, choose the form that matches the relationship of the ideas you want to express. If you have two ideas of equal importance, express them as two simple sentences or as one compound sentence. However, if one of the ideas is less important than the other, place it in a dependent clause to form a complex sentence. For example, although the following compound sentence uses a conjunction to join two ideas, they aren't truly equal:

> The chemical products division is the strongest in the company, and its management techniques should be adopted by the other divisions.

By making the first thought subordinate to the second, you establish a cause-and-effect relationship. So the following complex sentence is much more effective:

> Because the chemical products division is the strongest in the company, its management techniques should be adopted by the other divisions.

In complex sentences, the placement of the dependent clause hinges on the relationship between the ideas expressed. If you want to emphasize the idea, put the dependent clause at the end of the sentence (the most emphatic position) or at the beginning (the second most emphatic position). If you want to downplay the idea, bury the dependent clause within the sentence.

> **Most emphatic:** The electronic parts are manufactured in Mexico, *which has lower wage rates than the United States.*
> **Emphatic:** *Because wage rates are lower there,* the electronic parts are manufactured in Mexico.
> **Least emphatic:** Mexico, *which has lower wage rates,* was selected as the production point for the electronic parts.

To make your writing as effective as possible, balance all four sentence types. If you use too many simple sentences, you won't be able to properly express the relationships among your ideas. If you use too many long, compound sentences, your writing will sound monotonous. On the other hand, an uninterrupted series of complex or compound-complex sentences is hard to follow.

Sentence Style   Sentence style varies from culture to culture. German sentences are extremely complex, with lots of modifiers and appositives; Japanese and Chinese languages don't even have sentences in the same sense that Western languages do.[14] However, in English try to make your sentences grammatically correct, efficient, readable, interesting, and appropriate for your audience. In general, strive for straightforward simplicity. For most business audiences, clarity and efficiency take precedence over literary style. The following guidelines will help you achieve these qualities in your own writing.

Select Active or Passive Voice   You're using **active voice** when the subject (the "actor") comes before the verb and the object of the sentence (the "acted upon") follows the verb: "John rented the office." You're using **passive voice** when the subject follows the verb and the object precedes it: "The office was rented by John." As you can see, the passive voice combines the helping verb *to be* with a form of the verb that is usually similar to the past tense.

Active verbs produce shorter, stronger sentences, making your writing more vigorous and concise and generally easier to understand (see Table 5–4).[15] Passive verbs make sentences longer and de-emphasize the subject. Nevertheless, because you always focus on your audience and demonstrate the "you" attitude, using the passive voice makes sense in some situations:

1. When you want to be diplomatic about pointing out a problem or error of some kind (the passive version seems less like an accusation)

2. When you want to point out what's being done without taking or attributing either the credit or the blame (the passive version leaves the actor completely out of the sentence)

3. When you want to avoid personal pronouns in order to create an objective tone (the passive version may be used in a formal report, for example)

Dependent clauses can determine emphasis.

O b j e c t i v e **5**
Explain four guidelines that help you achieve clarity and efficiency in your sentences.

Business communicators strive for a clear and efficient style.

Active sentences are stronger than passive ones.

Use passive sentences to soften bad news, to put yourself in the background, or to create an impersonal tone.

Table 5–4 Choosing Active or Passive Voice	
Avoid Passive Voice in General	*Use Active Voice in General*
The new procedure is thought by the president to be superior.	The president thinks the new procedure is superior.
There are problems with this contract.	This contract has problems.
It is necessary that the report be finished by next week.	The report must be finished by next week.
Sometimes Avoid Active Voice	*Sometimes Use Passive Voice*
1. You lost the shipment.	1. The shipment was lost.
2. I am analyzing the production line to determine the problem.	2. The production line is being analyzed to determine the problem.
3. We have established criteria to evaluate capital expenditures.	3. Criteria have been established to evaluate capital expenditures.

Emphasize parts of a sentence by
• Giving them more space
• Putting them at the beginning or at the end of the sentence
• Making them the subject of the sentence

Emphasize Key Thoughts   In every message, some ideas are more important than others. You can emphasize these key ideas through your sentence style. One obvious technique is to give important points the most space. When you want to call attention to a thought, use extra words to describe it. Consider this sentence:

> The chairperson of the board called for a vote of the shareholders.

To emphasize the importance of the chairperson, you might describe her more fully:

> Having considerable experience in corporate takeover battles, the chairperson of the board called for a vote of the shareholders.

You can increase the emphasis even more by adding a separate, short sentence to augment the first:

> The chairperson of the board called for a vote of the shareholders. She has considerable experience in corporate takeover battles.

You can also call attention to a thought by making it the subject of the sentence. In the following example, the emphasis is on the person:

> *I* can write letters much more quickly using a computer.

However, by changing the subject, the computer takes center stage:

> The *computer* enables me to write letters much more quickly.

Of course, another way to emphasize an idea is to place it at either the beginning or the end of a sentence:

> **Less Emphatic:** We are cutting the *price* to stimulate demand.
> **More Emphatic:** To stimulate demand, we are cutting the *price*.

Techniques like these give you a great deal of control over the way your audience interprets what you have to say.

Vary Sentence Length   Variety is the key to making your message interesting. With your words and sentence structure, you create a rhythm that emphasizes important points, enlivens your writing style, and makes your information appealing to your reader. Although good business writers use short sentences most of the time, too many short sentences in a row can make your writing choppy. Conversely, if all your sentences move at the same plodding gait, you're likely to lull your reader to sleep. So to be interesting, use a variety of both short and long sentences.

To keep readers' interest, use both long and short sentences.

Long sentences are usually harder to understand than short sentences because they are packed with information that must all be absorbed at once. On the other hand, long sentences are especially well suited for grouping or combining ideas, listing points, and summarizing or previewing information. Medium-length sentences (those with about 20 words) are useful for showing the relationships among ideas. Short sentences emphasize important information. Most good business writing has an average sentence length of 20 words or fewer. This figure is the average, not a ceiling. (For audiences abroad, varying sentence length can create translation problems for the reader, so stick to short sentences in international messages.)[16]

Use Bullets and Lists   An effective alternative to using straight sentences is to set off important ideas in a **list**—a series of words, names, or items. Lists can show the sequence of your ideas or heighten their impact visually. In addition, they ease the skimming process for busy readers, simplify complex subjects, highlight the main point, break up the page visually, and give the reader a breather.

Lists are effective tools for highlighting and simplifying material.

When creating a list, you can separate items with numbers, letters, or bullets (a general term for any kind of graphical element that precedes each item). Bullets are generally preferred over numbers, unless the sequence of events is critical (if the steps in a process must be completed in a specific order, for example). The following three steps need to be performed in the order indicated, and the numbers make that clear:

1. Find out how many employees would like on-site day care facilities.

2. Determine how much space the day care center would require.

3. Estimate the cost of converting a conference room for the on-site facility.

When using lists, make sure to introduce them clearly so that people know what they're about to read. Consider the following example:

The board of directors met to discuss the revised annual budget. To keep expenses in line with declining sales, the directors voted to

◆ Cut everyone's salary by 10 percent

◆ Close the employee cafeteria

◆ Reduce travel expenses

One thing that Jerry Blount depends on when making a sale is contract clarity. He doesn't want his customers to feel confused about what services they're purchasing from his home security company. That's why Blount's contracts break out specific security services in bulleted lists that are easy to locate, read, and understand.

Note that the items in the sample lists are phrased in parallel form. In other words, if one item begins with a verb, all subsequent items begin with a verb. If one is a noun phrase, all should be noun phrases.

Develop Coherent Paragraphs

A paragraph is a cluster of sentences all related to the same general topic. It is a unit of thought. A series of paragraphs makes up an entire composition. Each paragraph is an important part of the whole, a key link in the train of thought. As you compose your message, think about the paragraphs and their relationship to one another.

Paragraphs are functional units that revolve around a single thought.

When you're talking with someone face to face, you develop your paragraphs informally, using tone of voice and gestures to signal the relationships among ideas. You pause to indicate that you have completed one topic and are ready to begin another, a new "paragraph." In a written document, on the other hand, paragraphs are developed more formally. Each paragraph is separated from other units of thought by skipping a line or indenting the first line.

Elements of the Paragraph   Paragraphs vary widely in length and form. You can communicate effectively in one short paragraph or in pages of lengthy paragraphs, depending on

EFFECTIVE E-BUSINESS COMMUNICATION

Keep It Short and Sweet

When you're writing for online readers, be sure to keep your paragraphs short and to the point. Start with an informative topic sentence so that readers can see immediately what each paragraph is about. Then follow with as few as two or three succinct sentences. To draw reader attention to supporting evidence, make liberal use of bullets when developing key subjects. This is the kind of short-and-sweet e-business writing technique that The Vanguard Group (www.vanguard.com), a mutual fund company, uses to liven up complex online material about investing, which can be mind numbing for first-time investors.

1. When writing online about investing, would you use the same sentence length as you would when writing about cooking? Why?
2. Why would you use bullets rather than straight text when providing supporting evidence for a general topic such as compound interest?

Most paragraphs consist of a topic sentence, related sentences, and transitional elements.

your purpose, your audience, and your message. The typical paragraph contains three basic elements: a topic sentence, related sentences that develop the topic, and transitional words and phrases.

The topic sentence
- **Reveals the subject of the paragraph**
- **Indicates how the subject will be developed**

Topic Sentence Every properly constructed paragraph is *unified;* it deals with a single topic. The sentence that introduces that topic is called the **topic sentence.** In informal and creative writing, the topic sentence may be implied rather than stated. In business writing, the topic sentence is generally explicit and is often the first sentence in the paragraph. The topic sentence gives readers a summary of the general idea that will be covered in the rest of the paragraph. The following examples show how a topic sentence can introduce the subject and suggest the way that subject will be developed:

> The medical products division has been troubled for many years by public relations problems. [In the rest of the paragraph, readers will learn the details of the problems.]

> Relocating the plant in New York has two main disadvantages. [The disadvantages will be explained in subsequent sentences.]

> To get a refund, you must supply us with some additional information. [The details of the necessary information will be described in the rest of the paragraph.]

Paragraphs are developed through a series of related sentences that provide details about the topic sentence.

Related Sentences The sentences that explain the topic sentence round out the paragraph. These related sentences must all have a bearing on the general subject and must provide enough specific details to make the topic clear:

> The medical products division has been troubled for many years by public relations problems. Since 1997 the local newspaper has published 15 articles that portray the division in a negative light. We have been accused of every-

thing from mistreating laboratory animals to polluting the local groundwater. Our facility has been described as a health hazard. Our scientists are referred to as "Frankensteins," and our profits are considered "obscene."

The developmental sentences are all more specific than the topic sentence. Each one provides another piece of evidence to demonstrate the general truth of the main thought. Also, each sentence is clearly related to the general idea being developed; the relation between the sentences and the idea is what gives the paragraph its unity. A paragraph is well developed when it contains enough information to make the topic sentence convincing and interesting.

Transitional Elements　In addition to being unified and well developed, effective paragraphs are *coherent;* that is, they are arranged in a logical order so that the audience can understand the train of thought. When you complete a paragraph, your readers automatically assume that you've finished with a particular idea. You achieve coherence by using **transitions** that show the relationship between paragraphs and among sentences within paragraphs. Transitions show how one thought is related to another, and they help readers understand the connections you're trying to make. You can establish transitions in various ways:

Because each paragraph covers a single idea, use transitional words and phrases to show readers how paragraphs relate to each other.

◆ Use connecting words: *and, but, or, nevertheless, however, in addition,* and so on.

◆ Echo a word or phrase from a previous paragraph or sentence: "A system should be established for monitoring inventory levels. *This system* will provide . . ."

◆ Use a pronoun that refers to a noun used previously: "Ms. Arthur is the leading candidate for the president's position. *She* has excellent qualifications."

◆ Use words that are frequently paired: "The machine has a *minimum* output of . . . Its *maximum* output is . . ."

Some transitional devices include
• Connecting words (conjunctions)
• Repeated words or phrases
• Pronouns
• Words that are frequently paired

Some transitional elements serve as mood changers; that is, they alert the reader to a change in mood from the previous paragraph. Some announce a total contrast with what's gone on before; some announce a causal relationship; and some signal a change in time. They prepare your reader for the change. At least a dozen words will do this job for you: *but, yet, however, nevertheless, still, instead, thus, therefore, meanwhile, now, later, today, subsequently,* and several more. Use them.[17]

Five Ways to Develop a Paragraph　Paragraphs can be developed in many ways. Five of the most common techniques are illustration, comparison or contrast, cause and effect, classification, and problem and solution (see Table 5–5). Your choice of technique depends on your subject, your intended audience, and your purpose.

Objective

6

List five ways to develop a paragraph and discuss three factors that increase paragraph readability.

In actual practice, you'll often combine two or more methods of development in a single paragraph. To add interest, you might begin by using illustration, shift to comparison or contrast, and then shift to problem and solution. However, before settling for the first approach that comes to mind, consider the alternatives. Think through various methods before committing yourself. If you fall into the easy habit of repeating the same old paragraph pattern time after time, your writing will be boring.

Five ways to develop paragraphs:
• Illustration
• Comparison or contrast
• Cause and effect
• Classification
• Problem and solution

Paragraph Readability　Making your message easier to read helps audience members move through your material more quickly and helps them understand what you're trying to say. To increase readability, consider using shorter paragraphs, effective headings, and occasional questions.

Length　Short paragraphs (of 100 words or fewer) are easier to read than long ones, and they make your writing look inviting. Direct-mail letters almost always use very short paragraphs because the writers know that their letters will be read more carefully that way. Even in memos, letters, and reports, you may want to emphasize an idea from time to time by isolating it in a short, forceful paragraph.

Short paragraphs are easier to read than long ones.

However, some ideas are simply too big to be handled conveniently in one paragraph. Unless you break up your thoughts somehow, you'll end up with a three-page

Table 5–5   Five Techniques for Developing Paragraphs

Technique	Description	Sample
Illustration	Giving examples that demonstrate the general idea	Some of our most popular products are available through local distributors. For example, Everett & Lemmings carries our frozen soups and entrees. The J. B. Green Company carries our complete line of seasonings, as well as the frozen soups. Wilmont Foods, also a major distributor, now carries our new line of frozen desserts.
Comparison or Contrast	Using similarities or differences to develop the topic	In previous years, when the company was small, the recruiting function could be handled informally. The need for new employees was limited, and each manager could comfortably screen and hire her or his own staff. Today, however, Gambit Products must undertake a major recruiting effort. Our successful bid on the Owens contract means that we will be doubling our labor force over the next six months. To hire that many people without disrupting our ongoing activities, we will create a separate recruiting group within the human resources department.
Cause and Effect	Focusing on the reasons for something	The heavy-duty fabric of your Wanderer tent probably broke down for one of two reasons: (1) a sharp object punctured the fabric, and without reinforcement, the hole was enlarged by the stress of erecting the tent daily for a week or (2) the fibers gradually rotted because the tent was folded and stored while still wet.
Classification	Showing how a general idea is broken into specific categories	Successful candidates for our supervisor trainee program generally come from one of several groups. The largest group, by far, consists of recent graduates of accredited data-processing programs. The next largest group comes from within our own company, as we try to promote promising clerical workers to positions of greater responsibility. Finally, we do occasionally accept candidates with outstanding supervisory experience in related industries.
Problem and Solution	Presenting a problem and then discussing the solution	Selling handmade toys by mail is a challenge because consumers are accustomed to buying heavily advertised toys from major chains. However, if we develop an appealing catalog, we can compete on the basis of product novelty and quality. In addition, we can provide craftsmanship at a competitive price: a rocking horse of birch, with a hand-knit tail and mane; a music box with the child's name painted on the top; a real Indian teepee, made by Native American artisans.

paragraph that's guaranteed to intimidate even the most dedicated reader. When you want to package a big idea in short paragraphs, break the idea into subtopics and treat each subtopic in a separate paragraph—being careful to provide plenty of transitional elements.

By breaking a large single paragraph into several shorter ones, a writer can make the material more readable. Of course, many other approaches might be as effective. There is no "right" way to develop a paragraph. As you write your message, try to use a variety of paragraph lengths. But be careful to use one-sentence paragraphs only occasionally and only for emphasis.

Use headings to grab the reader's attention and divide material into short sections.

Headings   Headings are another effective tool for organizing your material into short sections. They act as labels to group related paragraphs together. They not only help the reader understand you but can also serve as shortcuts, highlighting material so that your reader can decide whether to read or skip it. Effective headings grab the reader's attention and make the copy easier to read. They are informative, inviting, and in some cases intriguing.

Headings are similar to the subject line in memos and e-mail correspondence. However, subject lines merely identify the purpose of the memo or e-mail, whereas headings also advise the reader about the material included in the paragraph. Keep your headings brief, and try to put your reader right into the context of your message.

✓ *Checklist:* Composing Business Messages

Generate Ideas

✓ Get ideas down as quickly as you can.
✓ Rearrange, delete, and add ideas without losing sight of your purpose.

Vary the Style to Create a Tone That Suits the Occasion

✓ Use the appropriate level of formality.
✓ Avoid being overly familiar, using inappropriate humor (including obvious flattery), sounding preachy, bragging, or trying to be something you're not.
✓ Avoid obsolete and pompous language.

Select the Best Words

✓ Use plain English.
✓ Use concrete words that avoid negative connotations.
✓ Rely on nouns, verbs, and specific adjectives and adverbs.
✓ Choose words that are strong and familiar while avoiding clichés.

Create Effective Sentences

✓ Use simple, compound, and complex sentences, choosing the form that best fits the thought you want to express.
✓ Write mainly in the active voice, but use the passive voice to achieve specific effects.
✓ Emphasize key points through sentence style; give important points the most space.
✓ Vary the sentence length, but aim for an average of 20 words.
✓ Use lists.

Create Effective Paragraphs

✓ Be sure each paragraph contains a topic sentence, related sentences, and transitional elements.
✓ Choose a method of development that suits the subject: illustration, comparison or contrast, cause and effect, classification, problem and solution.
✓ Vary the length and structure of sentences within paragraphs.
✓ Mix paragraphs of different lengths, but aim for an average of 100 words.

Questions   Questions are another way to punch up your writing. They stop the motion, and then the answer starts it up again. By asking questions of your readers, you engage their interest and help them make their way through your message. Consider the following:

> Frank Deitch is an excellent employee who fully deserves the Employee of the Year Award. Why? The answer is simple. He understands every aspect of his position and is results driven.

Together with paragraph length and descriptive headings, questions make your message more readable and thus more effective. For a reminder of the tasks involved in composing your message, see "Checklist: Composing Business Messages."

Questions help readers by increasing their interest.

Compose Elegant E-Mail Messages

E-mail has a reputation for speed and informality. Nevertheless, you'll want to take time to compose your e-mail messages carefully. Even though e-mail seems transitory, organization and style are just as important for these messages as for any other type of business message.

E-mail can be as informal and casual as a conversation between old friends. But it can also emulate "snail mail" by using conventional business language, a respectful style, and a more formal format—such as a traditional greeting, formalized headings, and a formal closing and signature.[18] (For an in-depth discussion of e-mail etiquette, see Chapter 4, "Checklist: Observing High-Tech Etiquette"). As with any business communication, how formal you make your message depends on your audience and your purpose. Just be sure that the style you select is appropriate for the situation.

Also, be sure you use correct spelling and proper grammar in these electronic messages. Some e-mail old-timers insist that spelling, grammar, capitalization, and punctuation take a backseat in cyberspace.[19] But in business communication, e-mail needs to be as clear and as easy to understand as possible.

E-mail messages need as much care and attention as other business messages.

The formality of your e-mail depends on your audience and your purpose.

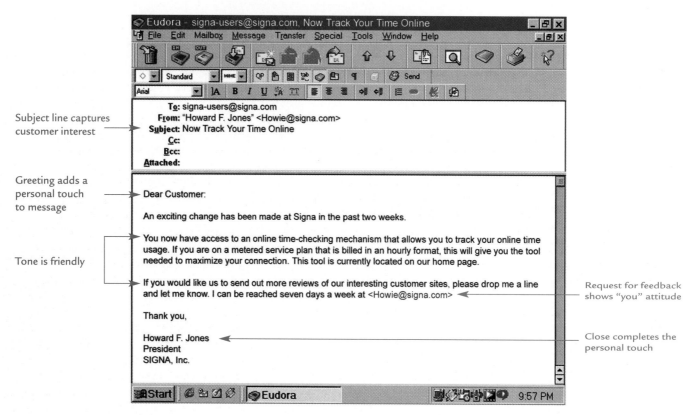

Subject line captures customer interest

Greeting adds a personal touch to message

Tone is friendly

Request for feedback shows "you" attitude

Close completes the personal touch

Figure 5-7
In-Depth Critique: On-Screen E-Mail Message

Make responding easy.

In addition, make responding to your message easy by clearly stating the type of response you need. Word your message so that your audience can respond as briefly as possible, perhaps with a yes or a no. Also, ask for your audience's response early in your message, perhaps even in your subject line.[20]

Above all, concentrate on grabbing your audience's attention. When e-mail receivers are deciding which messages to spend time on, they look at who sent each message, they check the subject line, and then they may scan the first screen. If your message can't attract your reader's attention by that time, your e-mail will probably go unread and will perhaps be deleted.[21] To capture audience attention, make your subject line informative, personalize your message, and make your message easy to follow (see Figure 5-7):

Make your e-mail interesting by making your subject line informative, personalizing your message, and making it easy to follow.

◆ **Make your subject line informative.** Do more than just describe or classify message content. You have 25 to 30 characters to build interest with key words, humor, quotations, or questions.[22] Word subject lines to tell readers what to do: Saying *Send figures for July sales* is more informative than saying just *July sales figures*. Finally, don't put *urgent* in your subject line too often; doing so will soon have an effect quite different from the one intended.

◆ **Personalize your e-mail message.** Adding a greeting and a closing makes your e-mail more personal.[23] Greeting formality (*Hi Marty, Dear Dr. Jones:*) depends on your audience. Close simply (*Thanks* or *Regards*). For your signature, type your name on a new line, use a *signature file* (that includes your name, company, address, fax, etc.) or a digital copy of your handwritten signature (which is becoming accepted as legal for business transactions).

◆ **Make your e-mail easy to follow.** Avoid lines that run off screen or wrap oddly by using the *Enter* key to limit lines to 80 characters (60 if e-mail will be forwarded). Avoid styled text (boldface, italics), unless your receiver's system can read it.[24] Write short, focused, logically organized paragraphs. And try to limit e-mail to one screen; otherwise, write like a reporter—starting with the "headline" and adding detail in descending order of importance.[25]

Build Effective Web Content with Hyperlinks

The Internet is unlike any other medium you may be required to write for. First of all, the Web is overwhelmingly competitive. Whenever readers visit a Web site they have more than 5,000,000 other cyber-places they could be.[26] More than any other medium, the Web demands that you grab reader attention quickly, write concisely, and get directly to your point.

But most important of all, the Web is interactive.[27] This capability offers readers the opportunity to absorb information in an order and at a speed that is most convenient and comfortable for each individual. The tool that makes this possible is the **hyperlink**—the in-text "tag" that allows online readers to click on a screen element and be instantly transported to related information on another section of the same Web page, on another Web page within the same site, or even on a completely different site. Using hyperlinks, Web writers can minutely tailor their messages to various members of their audience, and they can involve their readers in the written message itself. When writing for the Web, you either use hyperlinks or lose readers.

The pace of business today and the sheer amount of available information have made readers hungry for immediate results. They want the information they're looking for, and they want it in the blink of an eye. To find what they need, they want the ability to scan online documents without actually having to read them. Once they find a document, they want to sort through it, take what they need, and get out. To be effective on the Web, you must give online audiences what they want; to do that, you must use hyperlinks.

To write successfully for the Web, you need to follow all the guidelines detailed in this chapter. Moreover, you need to be aware that the quick-fix, skim-and-scan style of today's online reader demands extreme brevity, scannability, and a well-organized structure of links:[28]

◆ **Write 50 percent less text.** Reading a message on a computer screen is more difficult and less pleasant than reading it in hard copy—plus, it's 25 percent slower. In addition, readers don't like to scroll through text on screen. So, successful online documents give readers less to read at a time and present that material in a shorter space (less than one screen if possible).

◆ **Write for scannability.** On-screen reading is unpleasant, and readers are impatient. So rather than read text, they scan it. Successful online documents help readers skim text. Text is broken up with headings (at least a page title and two levels of subheads). Headings are informative (rather than cute or meaningless). Important concepts are highlighted (with graphics, boldfaced or colorized key words, lists, etc.).

◆ **Structure text around hyperlinks.** For brevity and scannability, use hyperlinks. Successful online documents split information into readable chunks (or pages) and connect these pages with hyperlinks that are convenient, recognizable, and informative. This way, each separate page is brief while all the pages together can cover extensive and detailed information. Plus, only interested readers need pursue any given hyperlink.

For a review of the tasks that make Web documents successful, see "Checklist: Writing for the Web."

Checklist: Writing for the Web

Satisfy Your Online Audience's Need for Brevity

✓ Use the direct approach so that readers can quickly see your topic, main idea, and conclusion.

✓ Put your most important concept in the first 50 words, in case search engines pick up those words to describe your site.

✓ Write shorter sentences and paragraphs to ease the reading process and to fit in narrow columns.

✓ Tighten your writing by avoiding passive voice, needless prepositional phrases, and wordiness.

✓ Avoid tightening your prose to the point that it's choppy and abrupt.

✓ Use informative, meaningful headings.

✓ Avoid vague, context-dependent elements (such as "click here" hyperlinks).

✓ Delete superfluous details and stick to what's relevant.

✓ Use a lighter, less formal writing style.

✓ Avoid clever, humorous, or jargon-filled phrases that could be misunderstood by readers from other cultures.

✓ When writing for an organization, be sure to follow company guidelines, style, and format.

Help Readers Scan Your Text for the Information They Need

✓ Provide your readers with as many clues as possible about the information you're offering.

✓ Help uninterested readers avoid your site by writing hyperlinks and search-engine descriptions that are informative and crystal clear.

✓ Telegraph your outline or diagram it with a hyperlinked table of contents at the top of your page.

✓ Use boldface, color, and bulleted lists to help readers scan your material.

✓ Trust your readers to take what they need.

✓ Provide contact information (at least your e-mail address) so that readers can get in touch with you easily.

Develop a Well-Organized Hyperlink Structure

✓ Use hyperlinks to structure your site into multiple related pages.

✓ Place specific data or details on subsequent pages.

✓ Let readers decide how they will access the information on your site—how much they will read, in what order, and when.

✓ Avoid breaking a single article (even a lengthy one) into a series of pages; interruptions in a single piece can irritate readers.

✓ Place hyperlinks at the end of paragraphs on a separate button or text link.

✓ Write informative hyperlinks so that the content of subsequent pages is obvious.

✓ Don't repeat information; instead, link your reader to the page where that information already resides.

SUMMARY OF LEARNING OBJECTIVES

1 **Explain why good organization is important to both the communicator and the audience.** Audiences benefit from good organization in several ways. When audience members receive a message that is well organized, they don't have to read and reread a message to make sense of it, so they save time. They are also better able to understand the content, so they can accept the message more easily and can make better decisions based on its information. Communicators also benefit from good organization. When a message is well organized, communicators save time because preparing the message is quicker. Communicators can also use their organization plan to get advance input from their audience members, making sure they're on the right track. Finally, good organization allows communicators to divide portions of the writing assignment among co-workers.

2 **Summarize the process for organizing business messages effectively.** The process for organizing messages effectively has four parts, or steps. First, define the main idea of the message by making a specific statement about the topic. Second, limit the scope of the message by adjusting the space and detail you allocate to major points (which should number three to five, regardless of message length). Third, group the points by constructing an outline to visualize the relationship between the ideas and the supporting material. Fourth, choose either a direct or an indirect approach by anticipating the audience's reaction to the message (positive, neutral, or negative) and by matching the approach to message length (short or long) and message type (routine, good-news, and goodwill; bad-news; or persuasive).

3 **Discuss two ways of achieving a businesslike tone with a style that is clear and concise.** To ensure that messages are businesslike, clear, and concise, start by using a conversational tone: (1) focus on the facts, (2) construct rational arguments, and (3) try to avoid obsolete and pompous language, intimacy, humor, and preaching and bragging. Support this conversational tone by using plain English, which is easily understood by anyone with an eighth- or ninth-grade education.

4 **Briefly describe how to select words that are not only correct but also effective.** To select the best words, first make sure they are correct by checking grammar and usage guides. Next, make sure the words you select are effective by knowing how to use functional and content words. Choose words that have fewer connotations and no negative connotations. Blend abstract words with concrete ones, narrowing from the general to the specific, and select words that communicate clearly, specifically, and dynamically. Choose words that are strong, choose words that are familiar, avoid clichés, and use jargon only when your audience will understand it.

5 Explain four guidelines that help you achieve clarity and efficiency in your sentences. To create effective sentences, follow four guidelines: First, use the active voice to produce shorter, stronger sentences, and use the passive voice to be diplomatic, to avoid taking credit or placing blame, or to create an objective tone. Second, emphasize key ideas by using more words to describe them, by making them the subject of sentences, or by placing them at the beginning or end of sentences. Third, vary sentence length to emphasize points, to enliven the writing, and to make information more appealing to readers. And, fourth, use lists and bullets to set off important ideas, to show the sequence of a process, or to heighten visual impact.

6 List five ways to develop a paragraph and discuss three factors that increase paragraph readability. Paragraphs can be developed by illustration (giving examples), by comparison and contrast (pointing out similarities or differences), by focusing on cause and effect (giving reasons), by classification (discussing categories), and by focusing on the solution to a problem (stating a problem and showing how to solve it). Paragraphs are easier to read when they are short (100 words or fewer), when they are broken up by headings (which highlight and summarize the material covered), and when they occasionally contain questions (which engage reader interest).

On the job: SOLVING A COMMUNICATION DILEMMA AT THE U.S. MINT

Phillip Diehl needs to create and maintain demand for the Mint's 50 State Quarters Program and the golden dollar coin. He has to compose messages that educate the public about coins and that revive interest in coin collecting. Diehl's messages must also be well organized in order to communicate all relevant product information in a logical manner to coin distributors, banks, and the retail industry.

Diehl and his staff write seasonal catalogs featuring the Mint's new products along with a wide range of coin collectibles, gifts, and coin-based jewelry. To capture reader interest, these catalogs are audience-centered. They maintain a conversational tone, and they use strong words to formulate appealing product descriptions and clear ordering procedures.

With the help of his e-commerce staff, Diehl has created a well-organized Web site at www.usmint.gov—both to accept online catalog orders and to educate visitors about the Mint's history, the State Quarters Program, the golden dollar, and other relevant information of interest to coin enthusiasts and collectors. To establish and maintain long-term relationships with online customers, Diehl's staff formulates well-organized, courteous e-mail messages to promote new products, respond to customer inquiries, and process orders. Moreover, Diehl's team composes electronic newsletters and frequently updates the Web site to provide customers with prompt, accurate information about the Mint and its products.

In order to prepare coin distributors, banks, and the retail industry for the Mint's new product releases, Diehl's staff writes educational materials. Writers are careful to outline the coins' major features and to provide strong support for each aspect. The staff also composes letters that use a direct approach to encourage businesses to order this free educational information—and some 2,600 institutions have responded.

Finally, Diehl appeals to a new generation of coin enthusiasts by expanding www.usmint.gov to include "History in Your Pocket," an educational tool for teaching kids about American history, math, and language arts as they enjoy coin-related games and activities. Known as *h.i.p. pocket,* the Mint's Web site for kids features a lively, entertaining style and a tone much different from the one used for adult coin collectors. Written with the help of educators, *h.i.p. pocket* also includes

a "Teacher's Lounge" that provides lesson plans and additional exercises for the classroom.

From all indications, Diehl's business messages have been successful in creating demand for the Mint's products and have sparked new interest in coin collecting. Within three months after launching www.usmint.gov, the Mint fulfilled more than $7 million in online coin sales, generating 40 percent of its orders from new customers. To meet the high demand for the golden dollar, the Mint was forced to double its production within the first month of release. Overall, mail-order sales surpass $1 billion each year. In addition, the Mint estimates that over 100 million kids and adults are actively collecting the 50 state quarters—and 150 million more people are expected to become collectors by the time the last state quarter is minted in 2008.

Your Mission As assistant director at the U.S. Mint's Office of Electronic Products and Information, you are responsible for promoting *h.i.p. pocket,* the Mint's Web site for kids at www.usmint. gov/kids. You know that teachers are your best source for introducing kids to coins and to the fun of coin collecting, and you want teachers to support your site. You plan to send them brochures describing the Web site, and you have drafted a letter to introduce yourself and encourage teachers to use the site as an educational tool. Here is a copy of your draft:

Dear Educator:

What do your students know about coins? Our Web site, *www.usmint.gov,* is one of the most popular sites on the Internet, but that is not the only online source of information about American coins.

I'm sure it isn't news to you that coin collecting is a popular hobby today. Kids are always looking for new and different hobbies, and we think they would enjoy learning about coins and the value of coin collecting. Our "History in Your Pocket" (*h.i.p. pocket*) Web site is geared to kids 12 and under. The enclosed brochure describes the Web site at www.usmint.gov/kids, and I'm sure you'll find that *h.i.p. pocket* provides a great educational tool for teaching your students about coins.

I am excited about working with you to introduce American coins to a new generation of collectors. Please feel free to call me if I can be of any assistance to you.

Now select the best responses to the questions that follow. Be prepared to explain why your choice is best.

1. Does the letter conform to the guidelines for good organization?

   a. No. The opening paragraph does not directly state the purpose of the message. The letter does not get to the point until the end of the second paragraph, and even then it is vague. There is not enough information to support the main purpose, and the information is poorly organized. The first paragraph should introduce the new Web site, then subsequent paragraphs should contain supporting information, describing how the program meets the needs of students and teachers.

   b. The letter includes unnecessary information. You are including a brochure, so you just need to refer the reader to the brochure.

   c. The letter is basically well organized, but there is not enough information to support the main point. It says that kids would enjoy coin collecting, but it does not have enough detail to convince teachers that the site would be beneficial to students.

   d. The letter is well organized. The subject and purpose are clear. All necessary information is included, and the information is directly related to subject and purpose. Information is grouped and presented logically.

2. You decide to rewrite the draft. Your first step is to develop an outline. What should you use as your main idea?

   a. Kids are a rapidly growing part of the market for collectible coins.

   b. Coin collecting is not just for adults who are interested in making smart investments.

   c. The Mint's Web site has been expanded to include an educational tool for teachers and students.

   d. The Mint's Web site for kids, www.usmint.gov/kids, is a valuable educational resource for teachers and a fun educational tool for generating kids' interest in coins, the Mint, and U.S. history.

3. What basic points will you use to develop and support the main idea?

   a. Kids like to play games on the computer, and they will be attracted to *h.i.p. pocket* because of the online games and activities.

   b. Because the Mint generates a large portion of its revenue from the sale of coins and coin-related products, the Mint is putting a lot of effort into creating a new generation of coin collectors. The success of *h.i.p. pocket* depends on teacher support.

   c. The Mint's Web site for kids provides entertaining games and activities that make learning fun and encourage students to think about the hobby of coin collecting.

   d. The Mint's Web site for kids benefits both students and teachers. Kids can learn about coins and coin collecting while enjoying games and other online activities. Teachers have access to a wealth of coin-related lesson plans and classroom activities covering history, language arts, and mathematics.

4. Which organizational plan should the letter follow?

   a. Direct. Open by asking teachers to use *h.i.p. pocket* as an educational tool for their students. Inform teachers that part of the Mint's mission is to educate the public about coins and that the site was developed with the help of educators. Include information on how *h.i.p. pocket* not only entertains but also educates kids, and describe how teachers have direct access to coin-related lesson plans on the Web site. Close by providing your phone number and e-mail address so that the teachers can contact you for assistance or more information.

   b. Indirect. You are targeting a totally different market than typical adult customers who visit the Mint's main Web page, so teachers may be skeptical about the value of *h.i.p. pocket*. Open by saying the Mint wants to expand its customer base and explain why. Refer the teachers to the brochure for information on *h.i.p. pocket*. Close by asking teachers to recommend *h.i.p. pocket* to their students.

   c. Indirect. Start by mentioning the rapid growth in collectibles market. Describe what kind of coins kids like to collect. Refer teachers to the brochure for information on *h.i.p. pocket*. Close by asking teachers to recommend the site to their students.

   d. Direct. The Mint's Web site for kids will benefit teachers as well as the Mint, so teachers will be eager to recommend the site to their students. State in the first paragraph that you want to generate kids' interest in coins and in the Mint. Then explain why doing so is a good idea because it generates interest in U.S. history. Finish by providing your phone number so that the teachers can contact you for assistance or more information.[29]

TEST YOUR KNOWLEDGE

1. What are the four steps in the process for organizing messages?

2. How does the denotative meaning of a word differ from its connotative meaning?

3. What three elements do you consider when choosing between a direct and an indirect approach?

4. How does the audience benefit from a well-organized message?

5. What is style, and how do you decide on the appropriate style for a message?

6. How does an abstract word differ from a concrete word?

7. In what three situations is passive voice appropriate?

8. What is the purpose of the topic sentence?

9. How do you use the subject line in an e-mail?

10. How can you increase the readability of your paragraphs?

INTERACTIVE LEARNING

USE THIS TEXT'S ONLINE RESOURCES

Visit the myPHLIP Website at www.prenhall.com/thill. For Chapter 5, take advantage of the interactive "Study Guide" to test your chapter knowledge. Get instant feedback on whether you need additional studying. Read the "Current Events" articles to get the latest on chapter topics, and complete the exercises—as specified by your instructor.

This site's "Study Hall" helps you succeed in this course. "Talk in the Hall" lets you leave messages and meet new friends online. If you have a question, you can "Ask the Tutor." And to get a better grade in this course, you can find more help at "Writing Skills," "Study Skills," and "Study Tips."

The "Research Area" helps you locate a wealth of information to use in course assignments. Plus, you can send a message to online research experts, who will help you find exactly the information you need.

APPLY YOUR KNOWLEDGE

1. When organizing the ideas for your business message, how can you be sure that what seems logical to you will also seem logical to your audience?

2. Would you use a direct or an indirect approach to ask employees to work overtime to meet an important deadline? Please explain.

3. Which approach would you use to let your boss know that you'll be out half a day this week to attend your father's funeral—direct or indirect? Why?

4. Is it ever okay to use an indirect approach when writing e-mail? How can you put off the bad news when you have to state your purpose in the subject line? Explain.

5. **Ethical Choices** Do you think that using an indirect approach to cushion bad news is manipulative? Discuss the ethical issues in your answer.

PRACTICE YOUR KNOWLEDGE

DOCUMENT FOR ANALYSIS

A writer is working on an insurance information brochure and is having trouble grouping the ideas logically into an outline. Prepare the outline, paying attention to appropriate subordination of ideas. If necessary, rewrite phrases to give them a more consistent sound.

Accident Protection Insurance Plan
- Coverage is only pennies a day
- Benefit is $100,000 for accidental death on common carrier
- Benefit is $100 a day for hospitalization as result of motor vehicle or common carrier accident
- Benefit is $20,000 for accidental death in motor vehicle accident
- Individual coverage is only $17.85 per quarter; family coverage is just $26.85 per quarter

- No physical exam or health questions
- Convenient payment—billed quarterly
- Guaranteed acceptance for all applicants
- No individual rate increases
- Free, no-obligation examination period
- Cash paid in addition to any other insurance carried
- Covers accidental death when riding as fare-paying passenger on public transportation, including buses, trains, jets, ships, trolleys, subways, or any other common carrier
- Covers accidental death in motor vehicle accidents occurring while driving or riding in or on automobile, truck, camper, motor home, or nonmotorized bicycle

EXERCISES

5–1. **Message Organization: Limiting Scope** Suppose you are preparing to recommend that top management install a new heating system (using the cogeneration process). The following information is in your files. Eliminate topics that aren't essential; then arrange the other topics so that your report will give top managers a clear understanding of the heating system and a balanced, concise justification for installing it.

> History of the development of the cogeneration heating process
> Scientific credentials of the developers of the process
> Risks assumed in using this process
> Your plan for installing the equipment in your building
> Stories about its successful use in comparable facilities
> Specifications of the equipment that would be installed
> Plans for disposing of the old heating equipment
> Costs of installing and running the new equipment
> Advantages and disadvantages of using the new process
> Detailed 10-year cost projections
> Estimates of the time needed to phase in the new system
> Alternative systems that management might wish to consider

5–2. **Message Organization: Choosing the Approach**   Indicate whether the direct or the indirect approach would be best in each of the following situations; then briefly explain why. Would any of these messages be inappropriate for e-mail? Explain.

a. A letter asking when next year's automobiles will be put on sale locally

b. A letter from a recent college graduate requesting a letter of recommendation from a former instructor

c. A letter turning down a job applicant

d. An announcement that because of high air-conditioning costs, the plant temperature will be held at 78 degrees during the summer

e. A final request to settle a delinquent debt

5–3. **Message Organization: Planning Persuasive Messages**   If you were trying to persuade people to take the following actions, how would you organize your argument?

a. You want your boss to approve your plan for hiring two new people.

b. You want to be hired for a job.

c. You want to be granted a business loan.

d. You want to collect a small amount from a regular customer whose account is slightly past due.

e. You want to collect a large amount from a customer whose account is seriously past due.

5–4. **Message Composition: Creating Sentences**   Suppose that end-of-term frustrations have produced this e-mail message to Professor Anne Brewer from a student who believes he should have received a B in his accounting class. If this message were recast into three or four clear sentences, the teacher might be more receptive to the student's argument. Rewrite the message to show how you would improve it:

> I think that I was unfairly awarded a C in your accounting class this term, and I am asking you to change the grade to a B. It was a difficult term. I don't get any money from home, and I have to work mornings at the Pancake House (as a cook), so I had to rush to make your class, and those two times that I missed class were because they wouldn't let me off work because of special events at the Pancake House (unlike some other students who just take off when they choose). On the midterm examination, I originally got a

75 percent, but you said in class that there were two different ways to answer the third question and that you would change the grades of students who used the "optimal cost" method and had been counted off 6 points for doing this. I don't think that you took this into account, because I got 80 percent on the final, which is clearly a B. Anyway, whatever you decide, I just want to tell you that I really enjoyed this class, and I thank you for making accounting so interesting.

5–5. **Message Composition: Controlling Style**   Rewrite the following letter to Mrs. Bruce Crandall (1597 Church Street, Grants Pass, Oregon 97526) so that it conveys a helpful, personal, and interested tone:

> We have your letter of recent date to our Ms. Dobson. Owing to the fact that you neglected to include the size of the dress you ordered, please be advised that no shipment of your order was made, but the aforementioned shipment will occur at such time as we are in receipt of the aforementioned information.

5–6. **Message Composition: Selecting Words**   Write a concrete phrase for each of these vague phrases:

a. sometime this spring

b. a substantial saving

c. a large number attended

d. increased efficiency

e. expanded the work area

5–7. **Message Composition: Selecting Words**   List terms that are stronger than the following:

a. ran after

b. seasonal ups and downs

c. bright

d. suddenly rises

e. moves forward

5–8. **Message Composition: Selecting Words**   As you rewrite these sentences, replace the clichés with fresh, personal expressions:

a. Being a jack-of-all-trades, Dave worked well in his new selling job.

b. Moving Leslie into the accounting department, where she was literally a fish out of water, was like putting a square peg into a round hole, if you get my drift.

c. I knew she was at death's door, but I thought the doctor would pull her through.

d. Movies aren't really my cup of tea; as far as I am concerned, they can't hold a candle to a good book.

e. It's a dog-eat-dog world out there in the rat race of the asphalt jungle.

5–9. **Message Composition: Selecting Words**   Suggest short, simple words to replace each of the following.

a. inaugurate

b. terminate

c. utilize

d. anticipate

e. assistance

f. endeavor

g. ascertain

h. procure

i. consummate

j. advise

k. alteration

l. forwarded

m. fabricate

n. nevertheless

o. substantial

5-10. Message Composition: Creating Sentences Rewrite each sentence so that it is active rather than passive:

 a. The raw data are submitted to the data processing division by the sales representative each Friday.
 b. High profits are publicized by management.
 c. The policies announced in the directive were implemented by the staff.
 d. Our computers are serviced by the Santee Company.
 e. The employees were represented by Janet Hogan.

5-11. Message Composition: Selecting Words Write up-to-date versions of these phrases; write *none* if you think there is no appropriate substitute:

 a. as per your instructions
 b. attached herewith
 c. in lieu of
 d. in reply I wish to state
 e. please be advised that

5-12. Message Composition: Writing Paragraphs Rewrite the following paragraph to vary the length of the sentences and to shorten the paragraph so it looks more inviting to readers.

Although Major League Baseball remains popular, more people are attending minor league baseball games because they can spend less on admission, snacks, and parking and still enjoy the excitement of America's pastime. Connecticut, for example, has three AA minor league teams, including the New Haven Ravens, who are affiliated with the St. Louis Cardinals; the Norwich Navigators, who are affiliated with the New York Yankees; and the New Britain Rock Cats, who are affiliated with the Minnesota Twins. These teams play in relatively small stadiums, so fans are close enough to see and hear everything, from the swing of the bat connecting with the ball to the thud of the ball landing in the outfielder's glove. Best of all, the cost of a family outing to see rising stars play in a local minor league game is just a fraction of what the family would spend to attend a major league game in a much larger, more crowded stadium.

5-13. Message Composition: Writing Paragraphs In the following paragraph, identify the topic sentence and the related sentences (those that support the idea of the topic sentence):

Each year McDonald's sponsors the All-American Band, made up of two high school students from each state. The band marches in Macy's Thanksgiving Day parade in New York City and the Rose Bowl Parade in Pasadena. Franchisees are urged to join their local Chamber of Commerce, United Way, American Legion, and other bastions of All-Americana. McDonald's tries hard to project an image of almost a charitable organization. Local outlets sponsor campaigns on fire prevention, bicycle safety, and litter cleanup, with advice from Hamburger Central on how to extract the most publicity from their efforts.[30]

Now add a topic sentence to this paragraph:

Your company's image includes what a person sees, hears, and experiences in relation to your firm. Every business letter you write is therefore important. The quality of the letterhead and typing, the position of the copy on the page, the format, the kind of typeface used, and the color of the typewriter ribbon—all these factors play a part in creating an impression of you and your company in the mind of the person you are writing to.[31]

5-14. Teamwork Working with four other students, divide the following five topics and write one paragraph on your selected topic. Be sure one student writes a paragraph using the illustration technique, one using the comparison-or-contrast technique, one using a discussion of cause and effect, one using the classification technique, and one using a discussion of problem and solution. Then exchange paragraphs within the team and pick out the main idea and general purpose of the paragraph one of your teammates wrote. Was everyone able to correctly identify the main idea and purpose? If not, suggest how the paragraph might be rewritten for clarity.

 a. Types of cameras (or dogs or automobiles) available for sale
 b. Advantages and disadvantages of eating at fast-food restaurants
 c. Finding that first full-time job
 d. Good qualities of my car (or house, or apartment, or neighborhood)
 e. How to make a dessert recipe (or barbecue a steak or make coffee)

5-15. Internet Visit the Security Exchange Commission's (SEC) plain-English Web site at www.sec.gov, click on "Online Publications," and review the online handbook. In one or two sentences, summarize what the SEC means by the phrase "plain English." Now read the SEC's online advice about how to invest in mutual funds. Does this document follow the SEC's plain-English guidelines? Can you suggest any improvements to organization, words, sentences, or paragraphs?

5-16. Message Composition: Using Bullets Rewrite the following paragraph using a bulleted list:

With our alarm system, you'll have a 24-hour security guard who signals the police at the suggestion of an intruder. You'll also appreciate the computerized scanning device that determines exactly where and when the intrusion occurred. No need to worry about electrical failure, either, thanks to our backup response unit.[32]

5-17. Message Organization: Grouping Points Using the Boswell & Sons letter in Figure 5-1, draw an organizational chart similar to the one shown in Figure 5-4, filling in the main idea, the major points, and the evidence provided in this letter. (Note: Your diagram may be smaller.)

5-18. Ethical Choices Under what circumstances would you consider the use of terms that are high in connotative meaning to be ethical? When would you consider it to be unethical? Explain your reasoning.

GOING ONLINE EXERCISES

Compose a Better Business Message, page 111

To be effective, the ideas you express in a written message must be logically organized. The style and tone of your business message are equally important and should fit the occasion and the intended audience. To reinforce what you've learned in this chapter about writing a business message, log on to Purdue University's OWL.

1. Explain why positive wording in a message is more effective than negative wording. Why should you be concerned about the position of good news or bad news in your written message?
2. What six factors of tone should you consider when conveying your message to your audience?
3. What points should you include in the close of your business message? Why?

Hot links and detailed instructions for Going Online exercises are provided at the Web site for this book, www.prenhall.com/thill. Log on to the Web site, select the chapter, then click on the Going Online feature for navigational directions and up-to-date links.

COMPLETING BUSINESS MESSAGES

chapter 6

After studying this chapter, you will be able to

1 Explain why revision is so important in business, list its three main tasks, and discuss when revision is performed

2 Discuss why it's important to make your message more concise and give four tips on how to do so

3 List nine tips for making your writing clear

4 Identify seven issues to keep in mind when critiquing someone else's writing

5 Describe five design elements, explain how they can change a document's appearance, and tell how to use them effectively

6 Outline some of the ways technology helps you produce and distribute your messages

7 Define the types of errors to look for when proofreading

On the job:

FACING A COMMUNICATION DILEMMA AT MCDONALD'S

A Little More Polish on the Golden Arches, Please

www.mcdonalds.com

If you hanker for a Big Mac, a Coke, and some fries, here's a job for you: being a quality control representative for McDonald's. David Giarla has been one for 10 years, and he still loves the smell of Egg McMuffins in the morning. On a typical day, he visits seven or eight McDonald's, samples the food, inspects the kitchen, surveys the storeroom, and chats with the manager and employees. If he likes what he eats and sees, everybody breathes a sigh of relief and goes back to flipping burgers and wiping tables. But if the food, service, or facilities are not up to snuff, watch out. Giarla might file a negative report with headquarters. And if enough negative reports pile up, McDonald's might cancel the franchisee's license.

Giarla's aim, however, is not to get people into trouble. On the contrary, he wants the store managers to succeed. He believes that by holding them to McDonald's high standards, he can help them build their businesses. When he spots a problem, he always points it out and gives the manager a chance to fix it before he files a negative report. His aim is to offer criticism in a diplomatic and constructive manner, and he usually succeeds.

Next time you're in a McDonald's, put yourself in Giarla's position. What would you tell the manager and employees to help them improve their operation? How would you phrase your suggestions? What words would you choose, and how would you arrange them in sentences and paragraphs?[1]

_____

MOVING BEYOND YOUR FIRST DRAFT

Once you've completed the first draft of your message, you may be tempted to breathe a sigh of relief and get on with the next project. Resist the temptation. As professional communicators such as David Giarla are aware, the first draft is rarely good enough. In a first attempt, most writers don't say what they want to say—or don't say it as well as they could. You owe it to yourself and to your audience to review and refine your messages before sending them. In fact, many writing authorities suggest that you plan to go over a document at least three times: one pass for content and organization, one for style and readability, and—after producing your message—one for mechanics and format.

You might wonder whether all this effort to fine-tune a message is worthwhile. The fact is, people in business care very much about saying precisely the right thing in precisely the right way. Their willingness to go over the same document at least three times shows just how important it is to communicate effectively.

REVISING YOUR MESSAGE

Although the tendency is to separate revision from composition, revision is an ongoing activity that occurs throughout the writing process. You revise as you go along; then you revise again after you've completed the first draft. You constantly search for the best way to

Professionals such as David Giarla at McDonald's understand the importance of careful revision. The most successful communicators make sure their messages are the best they can be.

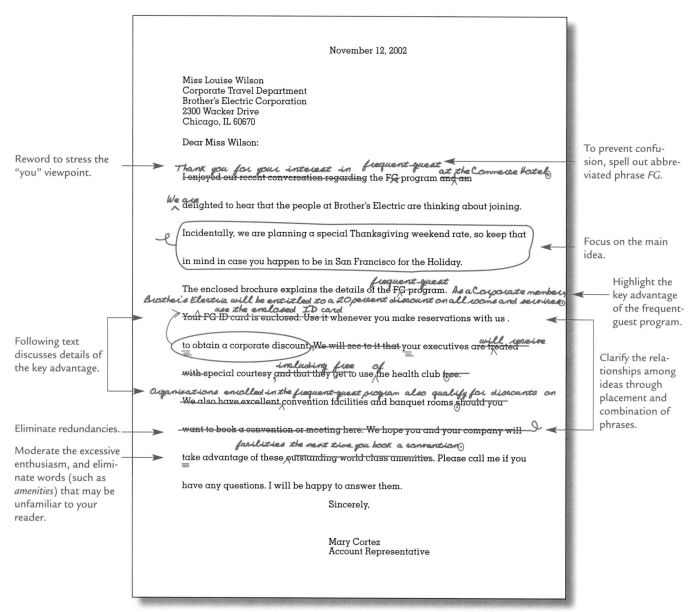

Figure 6–1
In-Depth Critique: Sample Edited Letter

Objective

1

Explain why revision is so important in business, list its three main tasks, and discuss when revision is performed.

say something, probing for the right words, testing alternative sentences, reshaping, tightening, and juggling elements that already exist. The draft in Figure 6–1 responds to Louise Wilson's request for information about the Commerce Hotel's frequent-guest program. It has been edited using the proofreading marks shown in Appendix D. Figure 6–2 shows how the letter looks with all the revisions incorporated—providing the requested information in a more organized fashion, in a friendlier style, and with clearer mechanics.

Evaluate Your Content and Organization

After a day or two, review your message for content and organization.

Ideally, let your draft age a day or two before you begin the revision process so that you can approach the material with a fresh eye. Then read through the document quickly to evaluate its overall effectiveness. You're mainly concerned with content, organization, and flow. Compare the draft with your original plan. Have you covered all your points in the most logical order? Is there a good balance between the general and the specific? Do the most important ideas receive the most space, and are they placed in the most prominent positions? Have you provided enough support and double-checked the facts? Would the

Now displays a "you" attitude.

Contains no irrelevant material.

Personalizes benefits by using the "you" attitude.

Combines a final benefit with more information about services available.

Spells out what was previously abbreviated.

Clarifies the benefits of the frequent-guest program.

Concludes with a friendly tone.

Commerce Hotel
333 Sansome Street · San Francisco, CA 94104
(800) 323-7347 · (415) 854-2447 · Fax (415) 854-7669
www.CommerceHotel.com

November 12, 2002

Miss Louise Wilson
Corporate Travel Department
Brother's Electric Corporation
2300 Wacker Drive
Chicago, IL 60670

Dear Miss Wilson:

Thank you for your interest in the frequent-guest program at the Commerce Hotel. We are delighted to hear that the people at Brother's Electric are thinking about joining.

The enclosed brochure explains the details of the frequent-guest program. As a corporate member, Brother's Electric will be entitled to a 20 percent discount on all rooms and services. To obtain your corporate discount, use the enclosed ID card whenever you make reservations with us. Your executives will receive special courtesy, including free use of the health club.

Organizations enrolled in the frequent-guest program also qualify for discounts on convention facilities and banquet rooms. We hope you and your company will take advantage of these facilities the next time you book a convention. Please call me if you have any questions. I will be happy to answer them.

Sincerely,

Mary Cortez

Mary Cortez
Account Representative

Figure 6–2
In-Depth Critique: Final Revised Letter

message be more convincing if it were arranged in another sequence? Do you need to add anything? Be sure to consider the effect your words will actually have on readers (not just the effect you *plan* for them to have).

In this first pass, spend a few extra moments on the beginning and ending of the message. These are the sections that have the greatest impact on the audience. Be sure that the opening of a letter or memo is relevant, interesting, and geared to the reader's probable reaction. In longer messages, check to see that the first few paragraphs establish the subject, purpose, and organization of the material. Review the conclusion to be sure that it summarizes the main idea and leaves the audience with a positive impression.

The beginning and end of a message have the greatest impact on readers.

Review Your Style and Readability

Once you're satisfied with the content and structure of your message, make a second pass to look at its style and readability, editing for conciseness and clarity. Ask yourself whether you have achieved the right tone for your audience. Look for opportunities to

Make sure you achieve the right tone and interest level.

make the material more interesting through the use of strong, lively words and phrases (as discussed in Chapter 5).

At the same time, be particularly conscious of whether your message is readable. You want your audience to understand you with a minimum of effort. Check your vocabulary and sentence structure to be sure you're relying mainly on familiar terms and simple, direct statements. You might even apply a readability formula to gauge the difficulty of your writing.

Gauge Reading Level   The most common readability formulas measure the length of words and sentences to give you a rough idea of how well educated your audience must be to understand your message. Figure 6–3 shows how one readability formula, the Fog Index, has been applied to an excerpt from a memo. (For more on this topic, visit www.profusion.com, and enter "Fog Index" in the search box.) As the calculation shows, anyone who reads at a ninth-grade level should be able to read this passage with ease. For technical documents, you can aim for an audience that reads at a twelfth- to fourteenth-grade level; for general business messages, your writing should be geared to readers at the eighth- to eleventh-grade level. The Fog Index of popular business publications such as the *Wall Street Journal* and *Forbes* magazine is somewhere between 10 and 11.

Of course, readability indexes can't be applied to languages other than English. Counting syllables makes no sense in other languages. For example, compare the English *forklift driver* with the German *Gabelstaplerfahrer.* Also, Chinese and Japanese characters don't lend themselves to syllable counting at all.[2]

Readability formulas are easy to apply; many are commonly done by computer. However, they ignore some important variables that contribute to reading ease, such as sentence structure, the organization of ideas, and the appearance of the message on the page.[3] To fully evaluate the readability of your message, ask yourself whether you have effectively emphasized the important information. Are your sentences easy to decipher? Do your paragraphs have clear topic sentences? Are the transitions between ideas obvious?

Edit and Rewrite Your Message   Ernest Hemingway once said, "There's no such thing as writing—only rewriting." Yet, once most businesspeople have a first draft, they make one of two mistakes: They shuffle words around on the page rather than actually make improvements, or they think rewriting is too time consuming and send the document out the moment that last period hits the page.[4]

With a minimal amount of solid rewriting, you'll end up with a stronger document. As you edit your business message, you'll find yourself rewriting sentences, passages, and even whole sections to improve their effectiveness. Of course, you're probably also facing a deadline, so try to stick to the schedule you set during the planning stage of the project. Do your best to revise and rewrite thoroughly but also economically.

As you rewrite, concentrate on how each word contributes to an effective sentence and how that sentence develops a coherent paragraph. Sometimes you'll find that the most difficult problem in a sentence can be solved by simply removing the problem itself. When you find yourself with a troublesome element, ask, "Do I need it at all?" Probably not. In fact, you may find that it was giving you so much grief because it was trying to do an unnecessary job.[5] Once you remove the troublesome element, the afflicted sentence will spring to life and breathe normally. Of course, before you delete anything, you'll probably want to keep copies of your previous versions. Professional communicators such as McDonald's David Giarla know how important it is to keep a paper trail for future reference.

Revise for Conciseness   Clutter is the disease of writing. Three-fourths of the executives who participated in one survey complained that most written messages are too long.[6] Many business documents are swollen with words and phrases that do no new work. In fact, most first drafts can be cut by 50 percent.[7]

Executives are more likely to read documents that efficiently say what needs to be said, so it's especially important to weed out unnecessary material. Examine every word you put on paper, and strip every sentence to its cleanest components: Eliminate every word that serves no function, replace every long word that could be a short word, and

---

Margin notes:

Readability formulas gauge reading level.

Readability depends on word choice, sentence length, sentence structure, organization, and the message's physical appearance.

Paramount Pictures Chair and CEO Sherry Lansing started as a script reader, became a story editor, and climbed the ranks to become an independent producer. Legendary for her polite, prompt communication, Lansing rebuilt Paramount into Hollywood's top studio with a successful string of movie hits. From editing to completing business messages, Lansing is skilled at simplifying: eliminating words that serve no function. People are more likely to read a message if you weed out unnecessary material.

Objective **2**

Discuss why it's important to make your message more concise and give four tips on how to do so.

Conciseness means efficiency.

EXCERPT

I called Global Corporation to ask when we will receive copies of its <u>insurance</u> <u>policies</u> and <u>engineering</u> reports. Cindy Turner of Global said that they are putting the <u>documents</u> <u>together</u> and will send them by Express Mail next week. She told me that they are late because most of the <u>information</u> is in the hands of Global's <u>attorneys</u> in Boston. I asked why it was in Boston; we had <u>understood</u> that the account is serviced by the <u>carrier's</u> Dallas branch. Turner explained that the account <u>originally</u> was sold to Global's Boston <u>division</u>, so all paperwork stays there. She promised to phone us when the package is ready to ship.

1. **SELECT WRITING SAMPLE**
   Keep the sample between 100 and 125 words long. (See excerpt.)

2. **DETERMINE AVERAGE SENTENCE LENGTH**
   Count the number of words in each sentence. Treat independent clauses (stand-alone word groups containing subject and predicate) as separate sentences. For example, "In school we studied; we learned; we improved" counts as three sentences. Then add all word counts for each sentence to get the total word count, and divide that by the number of sentences. This excerpt has an average sentence length of 14:

   $$18 + 21 + 21 + 7 + 13 + 12 + 5 + 12 = 109 \text{ words} \div 8 \text{ sentences} = 14$$

3. **DETERMINE PERCENTAGE OF LONG WORDS**
   Count the number of long words—that is, all words that have three or more syllables (underlined in the excerpt). Omit proper nouns, combinations of short words (such as *butterfly* and *anyway*), and verbs that gain a third syllable by adding *-es* or *-ed* (as in *trepasses* and *created*). Divide the number of long words by the total number of words in the sample. The percentage of long words in this excerpt is 10 percent:

   $$11 \text{ long words} \div 109 \text{ total words} = 10 \text{ percent}$$

4. **DETERMINE GRADE LEVEL REQUIRED TO READ EXCERPT**
   Add the numbers for average sentence length and percentage of long words. Multiply the sum by 0.4, and drop the number after the decimal point. The number of years of schooling required to easily read this excerpt is 9:

   14 words per sentence + 10 percent long words =
   $$24 \times 0.4 = 9.6 - 0.6 = 9 \text{ (Fog Index)}$$

Figure 6–3
The Fog Index

remove every adverb that adds nothing to the meaning already carried in the verb. For instance, *very* can be a useful word to achieve emphasis, but more often it's clutter. There's no need to call someone very methodical. Either someone is methodical or not. As you begin your editing task, simplify, prune, and strive for order. See Table 6–1 for examples of the following tips:

◆ **Delete unnecessary words and phrases.** Some combinations of words have more efficient, one-word equivalents. In addition, too many or poorly placed relative pronouns (*who, that, which*) can cause clutter. Even articles can be excessive (mostly too many *the*'s). However, well-placed relative pronouns and articles prevent confusion.

> Be on the lookout for inefficient phrases and excessive or confusing relative pronouns and articles.

◆ **Shorten long words and phrases.** Short words are generally more vivid and easier to read than long ones are. The idea is to use short, simple words, *not* simple concepts.[8] Also, by using infinitives in place of some phrases, you not only shorten your sentences but also make them clearer.

> Short words and infinitives are generally more vivid than long words and phrases, and they improve the readability of a document.

◆ **Eliminate redundancies.** In some word combinations, the words tend to say the same thing. For instance, "visible to the eye" is redundant because *visible* is enough; nothing can be visible to the ear.

> Remove unneeded repetition.

Table 6–1   Revising for Conciseness

Examples	*Unacceptable*	*Preferable*
UNNECESSARY WORDS AND PHRASES		
Using wordy phrases	for the sum of	for
	in the event that	if
	on the occasion of	on
	prior to the start of	before
	in the near future	soon
	have the capability of	can
	at this point in time	now
	due to the fact that	because
	in view of the fact that	because
	until such time as	when
	with reference to	about
Using too many relative pronouns	Cars that are sold after January will not have a six-month warranty.	Cars sold after January will not have a six-month warranty.
	Employees who are driving to work should park in the underground garage.	Employees driving to work should park in the underground garage.
Using too few relative pronouns	The project manager told the engineers last week the specifications were changed.	The project manager told the engineers last week *that* the specifications were changed.
		The project manager told the engineers *that* last week the specifications were changed.
LONG WORDS AND PHRASES		
Using overly long words	During the preceding year, the company accelerated productive operations.	Last year the company sped up operations.
	The action was predicated on the assumption that the company was operating at a financial deficit.	The action was based on the belief that the company was losing money.
Using wordy phrases rather than infinitives	If you want success as a writer, you must work hard.	To be a successful writer, you must work hard.
	He went to the library for the purpose of studying.	He went to the library to study.
	The employer increased salaries so that she could improve morale.	The employer increased salaries to improve morale.
REDUNDANCIES		
Repeating meanings	absolutely complete	complete
	basic fundamentals	fundamentals
	follows after	follows
	reduce down	reduce
	free and clear	free
	refer back	refer
	repeat again	repeat
	collect together	collect
	future plans	plans
	return back	return
	important essentials	essentials
	midway between	between
	end result	result
	actual truth	truth
	final outcome	outcome
	uniquely unusual	unique
	surrounded on all sides	surrounded
Using double modifiers	modern, up-to-date equipment	modern equipment
"IT IS/THERE ARE" STARTERS		
Starting sentences with *it* or *there*	It would be appreciated if you would sign the lease today.	Please sign the lease today.
	There are five employees in this division who were late to work today.	Five employees in this division were late to work today.

◆ **Recast "It is/There are" starters.** If you start a sentence with an indefinite pronoun (an expletive) such as *it* or *there,* odds are that the sentence could be shorter.

Revise for Clarity   Good writing doesn't come naturally, though most people think it does. Writers must constantly ask, "What am I trying to say?" Surprisingly, they often don't know. Then they must look at what they have written and ask, "Have I said what I wanted to say? Will the message be clear to someone encountering the subject for the first time?" If either answer is no, it's usually because the writer hasn't been careful enough.[9]

Carelessness can take any number of forms. Perhaps the sentence is so cluttered that the reader can't unravel it; perhaps it's so shoddily constructed that the reader can interpret it in several ways; perhaps the writer switches pronouns or tense midsentence so that the reader loses track of who is talking or when the event took place; perhaps sentence B is not a logical sequel to sentence A; or perhaps the writer uses an important word incorrectly by not taking the trouble to look it up.[10]

Writing is hard work and takes actual practice. The more you write (whether on the job or for pleasure), the better writer you'll become. A clear sentence is no accident. Few sentences come out right the first time, or even the third time. See Table 6–2 for examples of the following tips:

◆ **Break up overly long sentences.** Don't connect too many clauses by *and*. If you find yourself stuck in a long sentence, you're probably trying to make the sentence do more than it can reasonably do, such as express two dissimilar thoughts. You can often clarify your writing style by separating the string into individual sentences.

◆ **Rewrite hedging sentences.** Sometimes you have to write *may* or *seems* to avoid stating a judgment as a fact. Nevertheless, when you have too many such hedges, you aren't really saying anything.

◆ **Impose parallelism.** When you have two or more similar (parallel) ideas to express, use the same grammatical pattern for each related idea—parallel construction. Repeating the pattern makes your message more readable by telling readers the ideas are comparable and adding rhythm. Parallelism can be achieved by repeating the pattern in words, phrases, clauses, or entire sentences (see Table 6–3).

◆ **Correct dangling modifiers.** Sometimes a modifier is not just an adjective or an adverb but an entire phrase modifying a noun or a verb. Be careful not to leave this type of modifier dangling with no connection to the subject of the sentence. The first unacceptable example under "Dangling Modifiers" in Table 6–2 implies that the red sports car has both an office and the legs to walk there. The second example shows one frequent cause of dangling modifiers: passive construction.

◆ **Reword long noun sequences.** When nouns are strung together as modifiers, the resulting sentence is hard to read. You can clarify the sentence by putting some of the nouns in a modifying phrase. Although you add a few more words, your audience won't have to work as hard to understand the sentence.

◆ **Replace camouflaged verbs.** Watch for word endings such as *-ion, -tion, -ing, -ment, -ant, -ent, -ence, -ance,* and *-ency*. Most of them change verbs into nouns and adjectives. Get rid of them. Another bad habit is to transform verbs into nouns (writing "we performed an analysis of" rather than "we analyzed"). To prune and enliven your messages, use verbs instead of noun phrases.

◆ **Clarify sentence structure.** Keep the subject and predicate of a sentence as close together as possible. When subject and predicate are far apart, readers have to read the sentence twice to figure out who did what. Similarly, adjectives, adverbs, and prepositional phrases usually make the most sense when they're placed as close as possible to the words they modify.

◆ **Clarify awkward references.** To save words, business writers sometimes use expressions such as *the above-mentioned, as mentioned above, the aforementioned, the former, the latter,* and *respectively*. These words cause readers to jump from point to point, which hinders effective communication. Use specific references, even if you must add a few more words.

Sidebar notes:

Avoid starting sentences with *it* and *there.*

Objective **3**
List nine tips for making your writing clear.

Clarity avoids confusion.

In many cases, the parts of a compound sentence should be separated into two sentences.

Don't be afraid to present your opinions without qualification.

When you use the same grammatical pattern to express two or more ideas, you show that they are comparable thoughts.

Make sure that modifier phrases are really related to the subject of the sentence.

Stringing together a series of nouns may save a little space, but it causes confusion.

Turning verbs into nouns or adjectives weakens your writing style.

Subject and predicate should be placed as close together as possible, as should modifiers and the words they modify.

Be specific in your references.

Table 6–2   Revising for Clarity

Examples	Unacceptable	Preferable
OVERLY LONG SENTENCES Taking compound sentences too far	The magazine will be published January 1, and I'd better meet the deadline if I want my article included.	The magazine will be published January 1. I'd better meet the deadline if I want my article included.
HEDGING SENTENCES Overqualifying sentences	I believe that Mr. Johnson's employment record seems to show that he may be capable of handling the position.	Mr. Johnson's employment record shows that he is capable of handling the position.
UNPARALLEL SENTENCES Using dissimilar construction for similar ideas	Miss Simms had been drenched with rain, bombarded with telephone calls, and her boss shouted at her.	Miss Sims had been drenched with rain, bombarded with telephone calls, and shouted at by her boss.
	Ms. Reynolds dictated the letter, and next she signed it and left the office.	Ms. Reynolds dictated the letter, signed it, and left the office.
	To waste time and missing deadlines are bad habits.	Wasting time and missing deadlines are bad habits.
	Interviews are a matter of acting confident and to stay relaxed.	Interviews are a matter of acting confident and staying relaxed.
DANGLING MODIFIERS Placing modifiers close to the wrong nouns and verbs	Walking to the office, a red sports car passed her.	A red sports car passed her while she was walking to the office.
	Working as fast as possible, the budget was soon ready.	Working as fast as possible, the committee soon had the budget ready.
	After a 3-week slump, we increased sales.	After a 3-week slump, sales increased.
LONG NOUNS SEQUENCES Stringing too many nouns together	The window sash installation company will give us an estimate on Friday.	The company that installs window sashes will give us an estimate on Friday.
CAMOUFLAGED VERBS Changing verbs and nouns into adjectives	The manager undertook implementation of the rules.	The manager implemented the rules.
	Verification of the shipments occurs weekly.	Shipments are verified weekly.
Changing verbs into nouns	reach a conclusion about make a discovery of give consideration to	conclude discover consider
SENTENCE STRUCTURE Separating subject and predicate	A 10 percent decline in market share, which resulted from quality problems and an aggressive sales campaign by Armitage, the market leader in the Northeast, was the major problem in 2001.	The major problem in 2001 was a 10 percent loss of market share, which resulted from both quality problems and an aggressive sales campaign by Armitage, the market leader in the Northeast.
Separating adjectives, adverbs, or prepositional phrases from the words they modify	Our antique desk is suitable for busy executives with thick legs and large drawers.	With its thick legs and large drawers, our antique desk is suitable for busy executives.
AWKWARD REFERENCES	The Law Office and the Accounting Office distribute computer supplies for legal secretaries and beginning accountants, respectively.	The Law Office distributes computer supplies for legal secretaries; the Accounting Office distributes those for beginning accountants.
TOO MUCH ENTHUSIASM	We are extremely pleased to offer you a position on our staff of exceptionally skilled and highly educated employees. The work offers extraordinary challenges and a very large salary.	We are pleased to offer you a position on our staff of skilled and well-educated employees. The work offers challenges and an attractive salary.

Table 6–3 Achieving Parallelism	
Method	*Example*
Parallel words:	The letter was approved by Clausen, Whittaker, Merlin, and Carlucci.
Parallel phrases:	We have beaten the competition in supermarkets, in department stores, and in specialty stores.
Parallel clauses:	I'd like to discuss the issue after Vicki gives her presentation but before Marvin shows his slides.
Parallel sentences:	In 1998 we exported 30 percent of our production. In 1999 we exported 50 percent.

◆ **Moderate your enthusiasm.** An occasional adjective or adverb intensifies and emphasizes your meaning, but too many can ruin your writing.

Give Others Specific, Constructive Criticism

In Chapter 2, we discuss guidelines and challenges for effective team writing. We explain that before you begin writing collaboratively, your team must agree on the purpose of the project and on the audience, as well as on the organization, format, and style of the document.

Whether you're writing in teams or reviewing a document prepared by someone else for your signature, you will sometimes need to critique the writing of another. When you do, be sure to provide specific, constructive comments. To help the writer make meaningful changes, you need to say more than simply "This doesn't work" or "This isn't what I wanted" or "I don't see what you're trying to say."[11] When critiquing a document, concentrate on four elements:[12]

◆ **Are the assignment instructions clear?** Be sure to determine whether the directions given with the initial assignment were clear and complete. Making sure that directions are specific and understandable saves time for both the writer and the person giving the critique.

◆ **Does the document accomplish the intended purpose?** Is the purpose clearly stated? Does the body support the stated purpose? You might outline the key points to see whether they support the main idea. Is the conclusion supported by the data? Are the arguments presented logically? If the document fails to accomplish its purpose, it must be rewritten.

◆ **Is the factual material correct?** A proposal to provide nationwide computer-training services for $15 million would be disastrous if your intention was to provide those services for $150 million. Be sure you pay strict attention to detail. Professionals such as McDonald's David Giarla know that all factual errors must be corrected.

◆ **Does the document use unambiguous language?** Readers must not be allowed to interpret the meaning in any way other than intended. If you interpret a message differently from what a writer intended, the writer is at fault, and the document must be revised to clarify problem areas.

If any of these elements needs attention, the document must be rewritten or revised. However, once these elements are deemed satisfactory, the question is whether to request other changes. Minor changes can be made at any time in the critiquing process. But if these criteria are in fact met, consider these additional points before requesting a major revision:[13]

◆ **Can the document truly be improved?** The answer to this question is usually yes—given enough time.

◆ **Can you justify the time needed for a rewrite or a revision?** Will deadlines be missed? Will other priorities suffer from a delay? For example, if a production line is

Business writing shouldn't be gushy.

Objective **4**
Identify seven issues to keep in mind when critiquing someone else's writing.

When Starbucks Coffee Company Chairman and CEO Howard Schultz announced that Starbucks would expand beyond the coffee business, his message got the attention of customers and analysts alike. But Schultz has more than one message. He's launched a program to support literacy in children, and he's written a book (*Pour Your Heart Into It*). In interviews, Schultz's excitement shows through, but in writing, he moderates his enthusiasm. He knows that using too many adjectives and adverbs spoils good writing, so he uses just a few to intensify the meaning.

When critiquing the writing of another, make constructive comments in four areas:
• Assignment instructions
• Intended purpose
• Factual material
• Language clarity

Going Online

**Write It Right:
Rethink and Revise**

➡

Are you sure that readers perceive your written message as you intended? If you want help revising a message that you're completing, use the Paradigm Online Writing Assistant (POWA). With this interactive writer's guide, you can select topics to get tips on how to edit your work, reshape your thoughts, and rewrite for clarity. Read discussions about perfecting your writing skills, and for practice, complete one of the many online activities provided to reinforce what you've learned. Or select the Forum to "talk" about writing. At POWA's Web site, you'll learn how to improve the final draft of your message.

www.powa.org

To reach this Web site, go to www.prenhall.com/thill *(the Web site for this text). Select Chapter 6, then select "Student Resources." There, you'll find a current, live link that will take you straight to the site.*

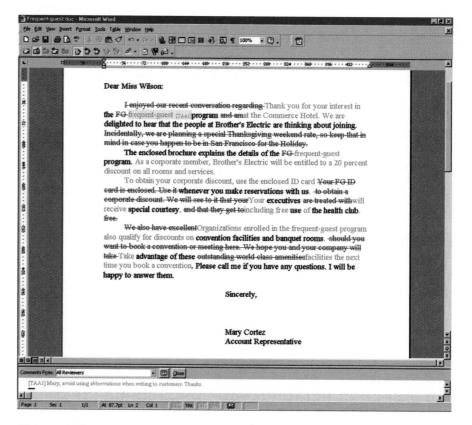

Figure 6–4
Revision Marks

down and the document in question is a description of what's wrong or how to fix it, any polishing beyond accuracy and clarity is secondary to getting the production line running again.

◆ **Will your request have a negative impact on morale?** Are the changes to be made a purely personal preference? If you regularly make unexplained or inconsistent changes to a person's writing efforts, that writer can become demoralized. (Of course, consistent style preferences can always be suggested for future use.)

Critiquing the work of another is often accomplished using *groupware*. As mentioned in Chapter 2, this sort of software allows many people to compose and edit a single document at the same time from different locations. In addition, groupware tracks each person's revisions so that if you later have a question or recommendation, you can easily identify the author of that revision. Figure 6–4 shows a screen of text using revision marks, which keep track of proposed editing changes and provide a history of a document's revisions. For a reminder of the tasks involved in revision, see this chapter's "Checklist: Revising Business Messages."

PRODUCING YOUR MESSAGE

Even after you have rewritten your message from start to finish, you're not done yet. Once you're satisfied with your message's content and organization, style and readability, word choice, sentence style, and paragraph development, you'll want to produce your message in some form that allows you to check it for appearance, accuracy, and mechanics.

Objective

5

Describe five design elements, explain how they can change a document's appearance, and tell how to use them effectively.

Design Your Message Carefully

An attractive, contemporary appearance can help you get your message across effectively. When designing your message, balancing graphics and text is important. Consider the

Checklist: Revising Business Messages

Evaluate Content and Organization

✓ Review your draft against the message plan.
✓ Check that all necessary points appear in logical order.
✓ Make sure your message is organized according to the audience's probable reaction.
✓ Verify that you present enough support to make the main idea convincing and interesting.
✓ Eliminate unnecessary material, and add useful material.
✓ Be sure the beginning and ending are effective.

Review Style and Readability

✓ Make sure you've achieved the right tone.
✓ Increase interest with lively words and phrases.
✓ Make sure your message is readable (check vocabulary and sentence structure).
✓ Consider using a readability index.

Edit for Conciseness

✓ Delete unnecessary words and phrases.
✓ Shorten long words and phrases.
✓ Eliminate redundancies.
✓ Recast "It is/There are" starters.
✓ Clarify awkward references.

Edit for Clarity

✓ Break up overly long sentences.
✓ Rewrite hedging sentences.
✓ Impose parallelism.
✓ Correct dangling modifiers.
✓ Reword long noun sequences.
✓ Replace camouflaged verbs.
✓ Clarify sentence structure.
✓ Moderate your enthusiasm.

---

memo in Figure 6–5. The bar chart in this memo is centered to give a formal impression, and the color used in the graphic is balanced by the letterhead logo.

The way you package your ideas has a lot to do with how successful your communication will be. The first thing your readers will notice about your message is its appearance. If your document looks tired and out of date, it will give that impression to your readers—even if your ideas are innovative. So choose design elements that will help your message look professional, interesting, and up to date.

Design affects the impression your message makes.

Select the Right Design Elements   Most readers have trouble comprehending long, uninterrupted pages of text. Design elements such as white space, headings, and boldface type help readers by providing visual clues to the importance and relationship of various ideas.[14] Of course, always keep in mind that if you're composing a half-page memo, too many design elements will only confuse your audience.

White Space   Space free of text or artwork is known as **white space.** It provides contrast, and perhaps even more important, it gives readers a resting point. White space includes the open area surrounding headings, the margin space, the vertical space between columns, the space created by ragged line endings, the paragraph indents or extra space between unindented paragraphs, and the horizontal space between lines of type. You need to decide how much white space to allow for each of these areas.

White space is free of text and artwork.

Margins and Line Justification   Margins define the space around your text and between text columns. They're influenced by the way you place lines of type, which can be set (1) justified (flush on the left and flush on the right), (2) flush left with a ragged right margin, (3) flush right with a ragged left margin, or (4) centered.

Margins frame your text.

Justified type "darkens" your message's appearance, because the uniform line lengths lack the white space created by ragged margins. It also tends to make your message look more like a form letter and less like a customized message. Justified type is often considered more difficult to read, because large gaps can appear between words and because more words are hyphenated. Excessive hyphenation is distracting and hard to follow. Even so, many magazines and newspapers use justified type because word density is higher.

Flush-left–ragged-right type "lightens" your message's appearance. It gives a document an informal, contemporary feeling of openness. The space between words is the same, and only long words that fall at the ends of lines are hyphenated.

Flush-left–ragged-right type gives your message an open feeling.

Balancing graphics, text, and color creates a polished appearance and lends credibility to your message.

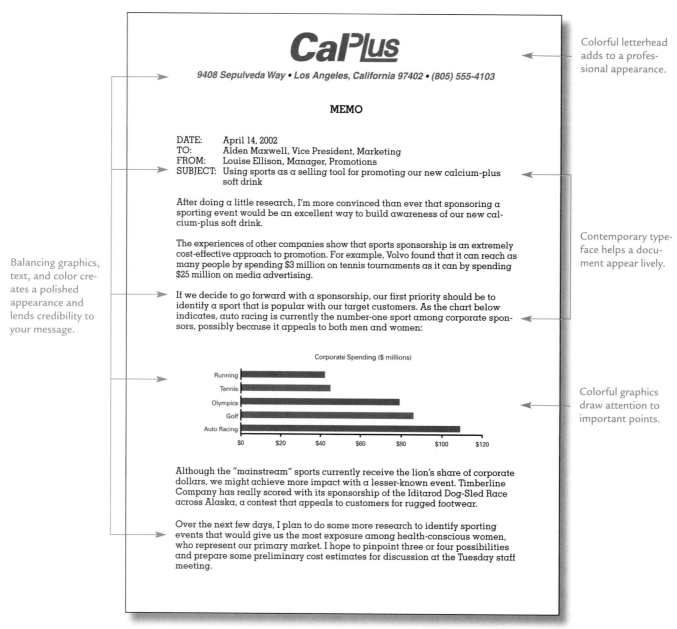

Colorful letterhead adds to a professional appearance.

Contemporary typeface helps a document appear lively.

Colorful graphics draw attention to important points.

Figure 6–5
In-Depth Critique: The Importance of Appearance

Centered type lends a formal tone to your message. However, centering long blocks of type slows reading because your audience has to search for the beginning of each line. The same problem is true of flush-right–ragged-left type. These two approaches are usually avoided for passages of text.

Headings help your readers quickly identify the content and organization of your message.

Headings and Captions Headings and subheadings are usually set larger than the type used for text and are often set in a different typeface. They invite readers to become involved in your message, so avoid centering heads that contain more than two lines. Like centered text, centered headings slow your readers as they search for the beginning of each line; flush-left heads are better. Because headings and subheadings clue readers into the organization of your message's content, you want to link them as closely as possible to the text they introduce. You can do so by putting more space above the heading than below it.

Next to headings, captions are the most widely read part of a document. They tie photographs and illustrations into the rest of your message. Although usually placed

EFFECTIVE E-BUSINESS COMMUNICATION

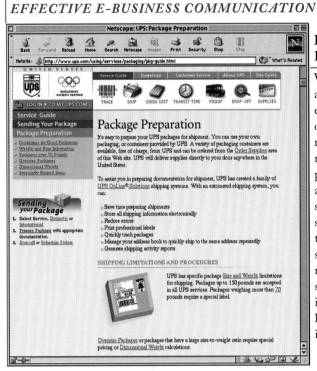

Design Messages for Easy Navigation

When you write messages for online audiences, you'll want to create an easy-to-navigate design. Use plenty of white space to make your main message stand out, and use narrow margins so that readers can see complete sentences without scrolling across the screen. If readers have to scroll down to read the entire message, provide a "top of page" link at the end to bring readers back to the start. To help readers follow the message organization, use one type style for the title, another for headings, and a third for buttons that lead to new topics, as UPS does on its Web site at www.ups.com.

1. Would you recommend setting margins as justified, flush left, or flush right in online messages? Why?
2. What other design elements should UPS incorporate in online messages to enhance readability and attract reader interest?

below the exhibits they describe, captions can also be placed beside or above their exhibits. Make sure that the width of your captions is pleasing in proportion to the width of the exhibit, the surrounding white space, and the text.

Typefaces   **Typeface** refers to the physical design of letters, numbers, and other characters. Most computers offer innumerable choices of typefaces. Each typeface influences the tone of your message, making it look authoritative, friendly, expensive, classy, casual, and so on. So choose typefaces that are appropriate for your message.

Serif typefaces have small crosslines (called serifs) at the ends of each letter stroke.[15] (See Table 6–4.) Serif faces such as Times Roman (packaged with most laser printers) are commonly used for text; they tend to look busy and cluttered when set in large sizes for headings or other display treatments. Typefaces with rounded serifs can look friendly; those with squared serifs can look official.

> Serif typefaces are commonly used for text.

Sans serif typefaces have no serifs. Faces such as Helvetica (packaged with most laser printers) are ideal for display treatments that use larger type. Sans serif faces can be difficult to read in long blocks of text. They look best when surrounded by plenty of white space—as in headings or in widely spaced lines of text.

> Sans serif typefaces are commonly used for headings.

Limit the number of typefaces used in a single document.[16] In general, avoid using more than two typefaces on a page. Many great-looking documents are based on a single sans serif typeface for heads and subheads, with a second serif typeface for text and captions. Using too many typefaces clutters the document and reduces your audience's comprehension.

Type Styles   *Type style* refers to any modification that lends contrast or emphasis to type. Most computers offer not only underlining but also boldface, italic, and other highlighting and decorative styles. Using boldface type for subheads breaks up long expanses of

Table 6–4 Common Typefaces	
Sample Serif Typeface	*Sample Sans Serif Typeface*
Times Roman is often used for text.	Helvetica is often used for headings.
TIMES ROMAN IS HARDER TO READ IN ALL CAPS.	HELVETICA IS A CLEANER FACE, EVEN IN ALL CAPS.

text. Just remember that too much boldfacing will darken the appearance of your message and make it look heavy. You can set isolated words in boldface type in the middle of a text block to draw more attention to them. If you draw more attention than a word warrants, however, you might create a "checkerboard" appearance.

Use italic type for emphasis. Although italics are sometimes used when irony or humor is intended, quotation marks are usually best for that purpose. Italics can also be used to indicate a quote and are often used in captions.

Avoid using type styles that slow your readers down.

McDonald's David Giarla recommends avoiding any style that slows your audience's progress through your message. Underlining can interfere with your reader's ability to recognize the shapes of words, and using all capitals slows reading.[17] Shadowed or outlined type can seriously hinder legibility, so use these styles judiciously.

Make sure the size of your type is proportionate to the importance of your message and the space allotted. Small type in a sea of white space appears lost. Large type squeezed into a small area is hard to read and visually claustrophobic.

For effective design, pay attention to
- Consistency
- Balance
- Restraint
- Detail

Make Design Elements Effective   Effective design guides your readers through your message, so be sure to be consistent, balanced, restrained, and detail-oriented:

◆ **Consistency.** Throughout a message (and sometimes even from message to message), be consistent in your use of margins, typeface, type size, and spacing (for example, in paragraph indents, between columns, and around photographs). Also be consistent when using recurring design elements, such as vertical lines, columns, and borders.

◆ **Balance.** To create a pleasing design, balance the space devoted to text, artwork, and white space.

◆ **Restraint.** Strive for simplicity in design. Don't clutter your message with too many design elements, too much highlighting, or too many decorative touches.

◆ **Detail.** Track all details that affect your design and thus your message. Headings and subheadings that appear at the bottom of a column or a page can offend readers when the promised information doesn't appear until the next column or page. A layout that appears off balance can be distracting, and any typographical errors can sabotage an otherwise good-looking design.

Avoid last-minute compromises. Don't reduce type size or white space to squeeze in text. On the other hand, avoid increasing type size or white space to fill space. If you've planned your message so that your purpose, your audience, and your message are clear, you can design your document to be effective.[18] Start by thinking about your medium: press release, magazine or newsletter article, brochure, direct-mail package, slide presentation, formal report, business letter, or internal memo. Once you've decided on a medium, try to make it look as interesting as you can while making it as easy as possible to read and understand.

Objective   **6**
Outline some of the ways technology helps you produce and distribute your messages.

USE TECHNOLOGY TO PRODUCE AND DISTRIBUTE YOUR MESSAGES

The most common means for creating printed documents is word-processing software.

Word-processing software is the dominant tool for creating printed documents. Composing a document on your computer involves keyboarding, of course, but that's just the beginning. Technology offers many ways to get text, graphics, sound, and even hypertext links into your document.

Using the Power of Technology

Warding Off Digital Disaster

Today's data are being threatened. Some 20 percent of the information carefully collected on Jet Propulsion Laboratory computers during NASA's 1976 Viking mission to Mars has been lost. And Defense Department computers can no longer read some POW and MIA records from the Vietnam War. Not only can computer viruses turn detailed records into electronic confetti, but the very media carrying our precious bits of information aren't lasting as long as we had expected. Moreover, chances are good that the software (or even the hardware) needed to get at today's data might not be readily available in 10 years. Anyone who has tried wresting information from a 5¼-inch floppy disk knows that.

You can help prevent your digits from turning to dust by taking these precautions:

❏ *Keep your PC clean.* Keep food and drink away from your equipment.

❏ *Maintain your hard drive.* Scan your drive for errors often, and correct them. Defragment your hard drive once a year (but only after performing a complete system backup).

❏ *Install surge protectors.* Make sure your protectors have a UL1449 rating of 330 volts or less, and install a backup power supply.

❏ *Exit your system correctly.* Shut down all applications before you turn off your computer; then shut down your computer in proper sequence.

❏ *Register your hardware and software.* Send in registration cards so that you are eligible for customer support and are notified about major problems or upgrades.

❏ *Install antivirus programs.* Use a good virus-scanning program, and update it at least quarterly. Run a virus scan on everything that comes into your computer: new software, new floppy disks, and Internet downloads. Don't open e-mail attachments from strangers.

❏ *Back up your system regularly.* Make sure you flag all important files and keep a regular backup schedule. Backup your entire system before installing any new software.

❏ *Store your backups properly.* Store your backup media offsite in a cool, dry cabinet away from heat, humidity, light, dust, and smoke. Keep them away from electric motors, speakers, phone handsets, monitors, TV screens, and transformers (which can cause electromagnetic radiation and erasure). Serious PC users may want to consider online backup services, a safe and inexpensive option.

❏ *Keep your copies clean and organized.* Label your backup media clearly. Twice a year buy and use new backup media, and clean the magnetic heads on your backup hardware. Do a test restore monthly to make sure your backups are usable.

By taking these steps, you can substantially reduce your risk should a data disaster strike.

CAREER APPLICATIONS

1. Your office has just decided to electronically store all written communications, reports, policies, and so on. Express your concerns about this policy in a brief memo to the president of the company.
2. Trade memos with a classmate. Review and edit each other's writing. Then answer the bulleted questions appearing in the section "Give Others Specific, Constructive Criticism."

Entering Text   Word processors help make entering text as painless as possible, giving you the ability to delete and move text easily. For example, when you compose a numbered list, the software will automatically renumber the remaining segments if an entry is removed. Other helpful features include automatic page numbering and dating. When you insert a date code into a document, the software automatically fills in today's date each time you open or print that document. This feature is especially handy if you use form letters. Be careful, though; sometimes you'll want to keep the original date intact, especially if you're keeping a history of your correspondence. (See "Using the Power of Technology—Warding Off Digital Disaster.")

Rapid progress is being made in developing technology that lets you enter text without keyboarding: Pen-based computers let you hand-write your text, and voice-activated computers let you speak your text. Of course, scanners let you enter text straight from a printed page. However, scanners produce just a visual image of the document, so you need to use optical character recognition (OCR) to get your computer to "read" the scanned image and pick out the letters and words that make up the text.

Some of the text that business communicators use in their documents is "prewritten." For example, say that you want to announce to the media that you've developed a new product or hired an executive. Such announcements—called press releases—usually end with a standard paragraph about the company and its line of business. Any standard block of text used in various documents without being changed is called a *boilerplate*. With a good word processor, you simply store the paragraph the first time you write it and then

Technology provides several options for entering text into a document:
- Keyboarding (typing)
- Pen-based computers
- Voice recognition systems
- Scanning and OCR

A boilerplate is any standard block of text used in various documents without being changed.

When creating these appealing sculptures, Monita Somers and Ann Carlson cut, paste, and polish to put the finishing touches on them—much the same way that you can revise and polish your business messages using computer tools such as *cut and paste* and *search and replace.*

Spell checkers, grammar checkers, and computerized thesauruses can all help with the revision process, but they can't take the place of good writing and editing skills.

pop it into a document whenever you need it. Using boilerplates saves time and reduces mistakes because you're not retyping the paragraph every time you use it. A related concept applies to manipulating existing text. If you're a national sales manager compiling a report that includes summaries from your four regional managers, you can use your word processor's *file merge* capability to combine the four documents into one, saving yourself the trouble of retyping all four.

Revising Text

When it's time to revise and polish your message, your word processor helps you add, delete, and move text with functions such as *cut and paste* (taking a block of text out of one section of a document and pasting it in somewhere else) and *search and replace* (tracking down words or phrases and changing them if you need to). Be careful, though; choosing the "replace all" option can result in some unintended errors. For example, finding *power* and replacing all occurrences with *strength* will also change the word *powerful* to *strengthful.* In addition, the AutoCorrect feature allows you to store words you commonly misspell or mistype, along with their correct spelling. So if you frequently type *teh* instead of *the,* AutoCorrect will automatically correct your typo for you.

In addition to the many revision tools, three advanced software functions can help bring out the best in your documents. First, a *spell checker* compares your document with an electronic dictionary stored on your disk drive, highlights unrecognized words, and suggests correct spelling. Spell checkers are a wonderful way to weed major typos out of your documents, but it's best not to use them as replacements for good spelling skills. For example, if you use *their* when you mean to use *there,* your spell checker will fly right past the error, because *their* is spelled correctly. If you're in a hurry and accidentally omit the *p* at the end of *top,* your spell checker will read *to* as correct. Or if you mistakenly type the semicolon instead of the *p,* your spell checker will read *to;* as a correctly spelled word. Plus, some of the "errors" detected may actually be proper names, technical words, words that you misspelled on purpose, or simply words that weren't included in the spell checker's dictionary. It's up to you to decide whether each flagged word should be corrected or left alone, and it's up to you to find the errors that your spell checker has overlooked.

Second, a computer *thesaurus* gives you alternative words, just as your printed thesaurus does. Not only can a computer thesaurus give you answers faster and more easily than a printed thesaurus, but it may be able to do things that your printed thesaurus could never do. The electronic version of the *American Heritage Dictionary* provides a thesaurus and a special WordHunter function that gives you a term when all you know is part of the definition. If you're racking your brain to remember the word that means a certain quantity of paper, you simply type *quantity AND paper* and then WordHunter searches for every definition in the dictionary that includes those two terms. In a few seconds, the word *ream* pops into view—"Aha! That's the word I was looking for."

Third, the *grammar checker* tries to do for your grammar what a spell checker does for your spelling. The catch is that checking your spelling is much easier than checking your grammar. A spell checker simply compares each word in your document with a list of correctly spelled words. A grammar checker has to determine whether you're using words correctly and constructing sentences according to the complex rules of composition. Because the program doesn't have a clue about what you're trying to say, it can't tell whether you've said it correctly. Moreover, even if you've used all the rules correctly, a grammar checker still can't tell whether your document communicates clearly. However, grammar checkers can perform some helpful review tasks and point out things you should consider changing, such as passive voice, long sentences, and words that tend to be misused or overused. Some programs even run readability formulas for you. Figure 6–6 shows the readability statistics that Grammatik computed for a paragraph in one document.

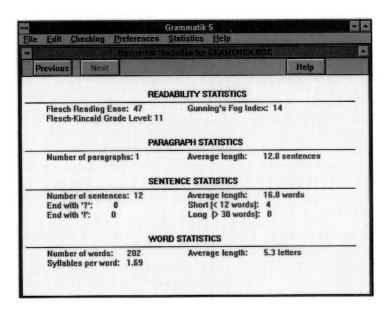

Figure 6–6
Readability Indexes Using a Grammar Checker

By all means, use any software that you find helpful when revising your documents. Just remember that it's unwise to rely on grammar or spell checkers to do all your revision work. What these programs can do is identify "mistakes" you may overlook on your own. It's up to you to decide what, if anything, needs to be done, and it's up to you to catch the mistakes that these computer programs can't.[19]

Spell checkers and grammar checkers have their limitations.

Adding Graphics, Sound, and Hypertext

With the recent advances in computer technology, it's becoming easier and easier to illustrate and enliven your text with full-color pictures, sound recordings, and hypertext links. The software for creating business visuals falls into two basic groups: *Presentation software* helps you create overhead transparencies and computerized slide shows (presentations are discussed in Chapter 13). *Graphics software* ranges from products that can create simple diagrams and flowcharts (see Chapter 11) to comprehensive tools geared to artists and graphic designers. You can create your pictures from scratch, use *clip art* (collections of uncopyrighted images), or scan in drawings or photographs.

You can use graphics software to add visual elements to your message.

Adding sound bites to your documents is an exciting new way to get your message across. Several systems now allow you to record a brief message or other sound and attach it to particular places in a document. For instance, you can add sound annotations, instead of written ones. Then, clicking on the special speaker icon plays a recorded comment, such as "Please convert this paragraph to a bulleted list." To actually hear the sound, the person receiving the memo has to load the memo into his or her computer and have a sound card installed.

You can also use HyperText Markup Language (HTML) to insert hyperlinks into your message. Readers can easily jump from one document to another by clicking on such a link. They can go directly to a Web site (provided you have an active Internet hookup), jump to another section of your document, or go to a different document altogether. For example, say you're preparing a report on this year's budget. Rather than include pages and pages of budget details from prior years, you can submit your report on disk and include a hyperlink in the file. Then, when readers click on the hyperlink, they enter a document containing details of the prior years' budget. By using hyperlinks, you can customize your documents to meet the individual information needs of your readers—just as you can on a Web page. Of course, you'll have to make sure that the file, or the software program used to open that file, is either included with your electronic document or installed on the recipient's computer. (Electronic reports are discussed in Chapter 10.)

Your document can have live links to other documents and to the Internet.

In general, the software most appropriate for assembling finished pages with graphics elements is desktop publishing (DTP), although word-processing software can handle graphics to a limited extent.

Computer software can help you add a first-class look to your most important business documents.

Using Desktop Publishing   Most word-processing programs include several elements to help you assemble your finished pages, combining text and graphics so that the appearance is both professional and inviting. But if you want a first-class report with photos and drawings, consider **desktop publishing (DTP)** software, which includes additional specialized tools for formatting, drawing, design, and layout. Today's computer software makes it easy for anyone to produce great-looking documents in a hurry. Both word processors and desktop publishing software can help you in three ways:

◆ **Adding a first-class finish.** From selecting attractive typefaces to adding color graphics, technology can help you turn a plain piece of text into a dazzling and persuasive document. Used improperly, however, the same technology can turn your document into garish, high-tech rubbish. Knowing how to use technological tools is critical for business communicators.

◆ **Managing document style.** To maintain consistent style in your document, most word processors and DTP packages use *styles,* formatting commands that you can save and apply as needed. High-end packages collect these commands into *style sheets* that save formatting effort, ensure consistency in each section you add to your report, and ensure a consistent look for all documents created in a department or even in an entire company.

◆ **Generating supporting elements.** If you've ever written a report with footnotes or endnotes, an index, and a table of contents, you know how much work creating such supporting elements can be. Fortunately, computers can help you keep track of notes, renumbering them every time you add or delete references. For indexes and tables of contents, you simply flag the items you want to include, and the software assembles the lists for you.

Technology can also help you distribute your message in the most appropriate fashion.

Distributing Your Message   Technology does some of its most amazing feats when it's time to distribute your documents. For multiple copies of your document, you can print as many as you like on your office printer, or you can print a single copy and reproduce it with a *photocopier.* For high-volume and complex reproduction (involving colors or photographs, for instance), you'll want to take your document to a *print shop,* a company that has the special equipment needed for such jobs.

When you need to send the same document (sales letter, invoice, or other customer communication) to a large number of people, *mail merge* automatically combines a standard version of the document with a list of names and addresses. It will produce one copy for each person on your mailing list, saving you the trouble of inserting the name and address each time. The names and addresses can come from your own customer databases or from mailing lists you rent from firms that specialize in collecting names and addresses.

Similarly, *broadcast faxing* allows you to enter mailing lists into your fax machine and transmit your document to the fax machines of all members on the list. Fax machines are indispensable for international business, particularly because they overcome the delay problems of regular mail and the time-zone problems of trying to contact someone by telephone.[20]

Many companies now distribute information on CD-ROM or computer disk rather than on paper. For instance, several of Hewlett-Packard's product catalogs are available either on CD-ROM or in printed form. CD-ROMs hold a large amount of information, and their small size saves money in postage and shipping.

Of course, one of the most popular methods for distributing documents is over the Internet. Most Internet browser software allows you to attach documents of all sizes and types to e-mail messages. If

Cushcity.com owners Gwen and Willie Richardson are e-tailers, selling Afrocentric books, videos, calendars, collectibles, toys, and educational items over the Internet. They also distribute business documents over the Internet, routinely sending e-mail messages and attachments of all sizes to employees and often to customers. This method of distribution is popular because of the speed. Mrs. Richardson says, "We have a very responsive e-mail system." Customers are especially impressed with the two-hour response time from Cushcity.

you are sending multiple documents or long documents over the Internet, you can use special software to encode or compress your message, reducing the file size so that it can be transmitted faster. Before doing that, however, make sure your recipients have similar software so that they can decode or uncompress the message and convert it back into its original file format.

PROOFREADING YOUR MESSAGE

Although spelling, punctuation, and typographical errors seem trivial to some people, most readers view your attention to detail as a sign of your professionalism. As McDonald's Giarla points out, whether you're writing a one-paragraph memo or a 500-page report, if you let mechanical errors slip through, your readers wonder whether you're unreliable in more important ways. Companies such as the *New Yorker* magazine take great pride in their editorial standards: When *New Yorker* misspelled *Tucson* as "Tuscon," it gave Arizona $66,000 worth of free advertising to set things right.[21]

> Your credibility is affected by your attention to the details of mechanics and form.

What to Look for When Proofreading

Proofread your message to ensure that it's letter perfect. Begin by refreshing your memory about the details of grammar, usage, and punctuation (by reviewing Appendix C). Then, in addition to these language errors, be on the lookout for common spelling errors and typos—not to mention missing material: a missing source note, a missing exhibit, or even a missing paragraph. Look for design errors. For example, some headings and text might appear in the wrong typeface (Helvetica rather than Times New Roman, or Arial Black rather than Arial Narrow). One or two special elements may appear in the wrong type style (boldface instead of italic, or italic instead of underlined). Columns within tables and exhibits on a page might be misaligned. Graphic characters such as ampersands and percent signs may appear when they should be spelled out, and numerical symbols might be incorrect. Also look for typographical errors, such as extra spacing between lines or between words, crowded type, a short line of type carried over to the top of a new page, a heading left hanging at the bottom of a page, or incorrect hyphenation. (See "Sharpening Your Career Skills—How to Proofread Like a Pro: Tips for Creating the Perfect Document").

> *Objective*
> **7**
> Define the types of errors to look for when proofreading.
>
> The types of details to look for when proofreading include language errors, missing material, design errors, and typographical errors.

Also, give some attention to your overall format. Have you followed accepted conventions and company guidelines for laying out the document on the page (margin width, number of columns, running heads)? Have you included all the traditional elements that belong in documents of the type you're creating? Have you been consistent in handling page numbers, heading styles, exhibits titles, source notes, and other details? (To resolve questions about format and layout, see Appendix A.)

How to Adapt the Proofreading Process

How many and what sort of errors you catch when proofreading depends on how much time you have and what sort of document you are preparing. The more routine your document the less time you'll need to spend. Routine documents have fewer elements to check. Moreover, the more often you prepare one type of document, the more you'll know about what sorts of errors to look for.

Longer, more complex documents can have many more components that need checking. For complicated documents, you may feel pressed for enough time to do a good proofreading job. But back in step one of the writing process (look back at Figure 4–1), you planned out how you would approach this message and you allotted a certain amount of time for each task. Try your best to stick to your schedule. You want to do your very best to create a letter-perfect document, but you also want to meet your deadline and turn your work in promptly. As with every task in the writing process, practice helps—you not only become more familiar with what errors to look for, but you also become more skilled in identifying those errors.

> Even when you're pressed for time, try to maintain the schedule you laid out during the planning step of the writing process.

Sharpening Your Career Skills

How to Proofread Like a Pro: Tips for Creating the Perfect Document

You've carefully revised and polished your document, and it's been sent off to the word-processing department to be put into final form. You can breathe a sigh of relief, but only for the moment: You'll still be proofreading what comes out of the printer. To ensure that any document is error free, always proofread the final version. Following are some hints to help make your proofreading more effective.

❑ **Multiple passes.** Go through the document several times, focusing on a different aspect each time. The first pass might be to look for omissions and errors in content; the second pass could be for layout, spacing, and other aesthetic features; a final pass might be to check for typographical, grammatical, and spelling errors.

❑ **Perceptual tricks.** Your brain has been trained to ignore transposed letters, improper capitalization, and misplaced punctuation. Try (1) reading each page from the bottom to the top (starting at the last word in each line), (2) placing your finger under each word and reading it silently, (3) making a slit in a sheet of paper that reveals only one line of type at a time, and (4) reading the document aloud and pronouncing each word carefully.

❑ **Impartial reviews.** Have a friend or colleague proofread the document for you. Others are likely to catch mistakes that you continually fail to notice. (All of us have blind spots when it comes to reviewing our own work.)

❑ **Typos.** Look for the most common typographical errors (typos): transposition (such as *teh*), substitution (such as *ecomonic*), and omission (such as *productvity*).

❑ **Mechanics.** When looking for errors in spelling, grammar, punctuation, and capitalization, if you're unsure about something, look it up in a dictionary, a usage book, or another reference work.

❑ **Accuracy.** Double-check the spelling of names and the accuracy of dates, addresses, and all numbers (quantities ordered, prices, and so on). It would not do to order 500 staplers when you want only 50.

❑ **Distance.** If you have time, set the document aside and proofread it the next day.

❑ **Vigilance.** Avoid reading large amounts of material in one sitting, and try not to proofread when you're tired.

❑ **Focus.** Concentrate on what you're doing. Try to block out distractions, and focus as completely as possible on your proofreading task.

❑ **Caution.** Take your time. Quick proofreading is not careful proofreading.

Proofreading may require patience, but it adds credibility to your document.

CAREER APPLICATIONS

1. What qualities does a person need to be a good proofreader? Are such qualities inborn, or can they be learned?
2. Proofread the following sentence:

   aplication of thse methods in stores in San Deigo nd Cinncinati have resultted in a 30 drop in roberies an a 50 percent decling in violnce there, acording ot thedevelpers if the securty sytem, Hanover brothrs, Inc.

SUMMARY OF LEARNING OBJECTIVES

1 Explain why revision is so important in business, list its three main tasks, and discuss when revision is performed. Revision consists of three main tasks: (1) evaluating content and organization, (2) reviewing style and readability, and (3) proofreading the final version after it has been produced. Revision is an ongoing activity. It occurs throughout the writing process, again after you complete the first draft of your business message, and again after you produce the final version.

2 Discuss why it's important to make your message more concise, and give four tips on how to do so. Businesspeople are more likely to read documents that give information efficiently. So to make business messages more concise, try to include only necessary material and write clean sentences by (1) deleting unnecessary words and phrases, (2) shortening overly long words and phrases, (3) eliminating redundancies, and (4) recasting "It is" and "There are" starters.

3 List nine tips for making your writing clear. Clear writing doesn't happen the first time, so you need to revise your work. As you try

to clarify your message, (1) break up overly long sentences, (2) rewrite hedging sentences, (3) impose parallelism, (4) correct dangling modifiers, (5) reword long noun sequences, (6) replace camouflaged verbs, (7) clarify sentence structure, (8) clarify awkward references, and (9) moderate your enthusiasm.

4 Identify seven issues to keep in mind when critiquing someone else's writing. When critiquing someone else's writing style, you should first make sure that the document accomplishes its intended purpose, verify that the factual material is correct, and point out all ambiguous language so that it can be eliminated. Then ask yourself whether the document can truly be improved, whether the time needed to rewrite it can be justified, and whether asking for a rewrite could have a negative effect on morale. Finally, make sure your comments are specific and constructive.

5 Describe five design elements, explain how they can change a document's appearance, and tell how to use them effectively. White space provides contrast and gives readers a resting point.

Margins define the space around the text and contribute to the amount of white space. Headings and captions invite readers to become involved in the message. Typefaces influence the tone of the message. Type styles provide contrast or emphasis. When selecting and applying design elements, you can ensure their effectiveness by being consistent throughout your document; balancing your space between text, art, and white space; showing restraint in the number of elements you use; and paying attention to every detail.

6 **Outline some of the ways technology helps you produce and distribute your messages.** Word processors help you enter, delete, replace, and move text easily. They can automatically number lists, notes, and pages, and they can even fill in the current date for you. If you don't want to use a keyboard, you can try a pen-based or voice-activated system, or you can use a scanner. Computers store boilerplate material and help you merge files. As you revise messages, computers help you manipulate text with *cut and paste* as well as *search and replace* commands. Revision tools include the spell checker, thesaurus, and grammar checker. Technology helps you illustrate your text with presentation software, graphic software, and HTML. Overall, word processors and DTP systems add a first-class finish, help you manage document style, and generate supporting elements (such as endnotes, indexes, and tables of contents). Technology also helps you distribute messages with photocopiers, mail merge, broadcast faxing, CD-ROMs, and e-mail.

7 **Define the types of errors to look for when proofreading.** When proofreading the final version of your document, always keep an eye out for errors in grammar, usage, and punctuation. In addition, watch for spelling errors and typos. Make sure that nothing is missing (whether a source note, an exhibit, or text). Correct design errors such as elements that appear in the wrong typeface, elements that appear in the wrong type style, misaligned elements (columns in a table, exhibits on a page, etc.), and graphical characters (such as ampersands and percent signs) that appear in both symbol and spelled-out form. Look for typographical errors such as uneven spacing between lines and words, a short line of type at the top of a page, a heading at the bottom of a page, or incorrect hyphenation. In addition, make sure your layout conforms to company guidelines.

SOLVING A COMMUNICATION DILEMMA AT MCDONALD'S

Over the past 10 years, David Giarla has learned a great deal about the art of communication. By nature, he is a positive individual, and his communication style reflects that fact. Although his job is to spot problems, you're more likely to hear him use words such as *outstanding, terrific,* and *delicious* rather than *bad, dreadful,* or *unacceptable.* Perhaps that's why the managers and employees on his regular route always greet him with a smile.

Giarla calls on seven or eight McDonald's every day. If you work in one of his restaurants, you have a good chance of serving Giarla breakfast, lunch, a snack, or dinner on any given day. You know he's coming, but you don't know when—and that keeps you on your toes.

On a typical visit, Giarla pulls into the parking lot and checks for rubbish. The ideal McDonald's is blindingly clean from the street to the storeroom. He enters the restaurant. Are the lines moving quickly? They'd better be. Are the order takers smiling? You bet. A perky teenager behind the counter recognizes Giarla and asks, "Big Breakfast and a regular Diet Coke?" "Correctomundo," he replies.

He carries his tray to a table. Is it spotless? Yup. He inspects his food. Hmm. The biscuit looks a little small. He nibbles a hash brown, then heads for the kitchen. "Great hash browns," he says to the person at the deep fryer. "You should get a raise." He pauses a minute to inspect the dates stamped on the hamburger wrappers. Good. They're fresh. So are the cucumbers, cheese, and milk shake mix.

Business is picking up, so Giarla pitches in to help make Egg McMuffins. "These are going to be terrific," he announces. He finds that helping out builds rapport. He tries hard to cultivate goodwill between McDonald's headquarters and the restaurant's managers and employees. He does not view himself as "the enemy spy." On the contrary, McDonald's is a team effort, and he is a coach—one of 300 field consultants who spend their days happily checking out the Golden Arches from coast to coast.

When Giarla spots the restaurant manager, he mentions the small-biscuit problem. Could someone be overkneading the dough, he wonders. He recommends that the biscuit maker review the McDonald's videotape that provides instructions for preparing biscuits and other items.

On to the next stop, where a helper crams too much food into a bag. More stops reveal more opportunities for improvement: a ceiling tile is stained and needs to be replaced; a cheeseburger bun is dented—probably because someone wrapped it too tightly; a storeroom is messy; a soft-serve cone is six inches high instead of the recommended three inches. Giarla calls attention to all these problems. You might expect the restaurant managers and employees to resent the criticism, but by and large they welcome his suggestions. Why? Because Giarla knows how to communicate.

Your Mission You have recently joined McDonald's as a quality control representative. Like David Giarla, you cover seven or eight restaurants a day. Most of the managers are very cooperative, and most of the restaurants maintain very high standards. But there is one exception. Over the past few months, you have pointed out a variety of problems to a particular McDonald's manager. You have been friendly, polite, and constructive in your suggestions, but nothing has been done to correct most of the problems. On your last visit, you warned the manager that you would have to file a negative report with headquarters if you didn't see some improvement immmediately. You have decided to put your suggestions in writing and give the manager one week to take action. Here is the first draft of your letter. Using the questions that follow, analyze it according to the material in this chapter. Be prepared to explain your analysis.

> Please correct the problems listed below. I will visit your facility within the next few days to monitor your progress. If nothing has been done toward rectifying these infractions of McDonald's principles of operation, you will be reported to headquarters for noncooperation and unsatisfactory levels of performance. As you know, I have mentioned these deviations from acceptable practice on previous visits. You have been given ample opportunity to comply with my suggestions. Your failure to comply suggests that you lack the necessary commitment to quality that has long been the hallmark of McDonald's restaurants.

> On two occasions, I have ascertained that you are using expired ingredients in preparing hamburgers. On February 14, a package of buns with a freshness date of January 31 was used in your facility. Also, on March 2, you were using cheese that had expired by at least 10 days. McDonald's is committed to freshness. All our ingredients are freshness dated. Expired ingredients should be disposed of, not used in the preparation of products for sale to the public. For example, you might contact local charities and offer the expired items to them free of charge, provided, of course, that the ingredients do not pose a health hazard (e.g., sour milk should be thrown out). The Community Resource Center in your area can be reached by calling 555-0909. Although I have warned you before about using old ingredients, the last time I visited your facility, I found expired ingredients in the storeroom.

> Your bathrooms should be refurbished and cleaned more frequently. The paper towel dispenser in the men's room was out of towels the last time I was there, and the faucet on the sink dripped. This not only runs up your water bill but also creates a bad impression for the customer. Additionally, your windows need washing. On all my visits, I have noticed fingerprints on the front door. I have never, in fact, seen your door anything but dirty. This, too, creates a negative impression. Similarly, the windows are not as clean as they might be. Also, please mop the floors more often. Nobody wants to eat in a dirty restaurant.

> The most serious infraction pertains to the appearance of store personnel. Dirty uniforms are unforgivable. Also, employees, particularly those serving the public, must have clean fingernails and hands. Hair should be neatly combed, and uniforms should be carefully pressed. I realize that your restaurant is located in an economically depressed area, and I am aware that

> many of your employees are ethnic minorities from impoverished backgrounds and single-parent families. Perhaps you should hold a class in basic cleanliness for these people. It is likely that they have not been taught proper hygiene in their homes.

> In addition, please instruct store personnel to empty the trash more frequently. The bins are constantly overflowing, making it difficult for customers to dispose of leftover food and rubbish. This is a problem both indoors and outdoors.

> Also bear in mind that all patrons should be served within a few minutes of their arrival at your place of business. Waiting in line is annoying, particularly during the busy lunch hour when people are on tight schedules. Open new lines when you must in order to accommodate the flow of traffic. In addition, instruct the order takers and order fillers to work more rapidly during busy times. Employees should not be standing around chatting with each other while customers wait in line.

> As I mentioned above, I will visit your facility within a few days to check on your progress toward meeting McDonald's criteria of operation. If no visible progress has been made, I will have no alternative other than to report you to top management at headquarters. If you have any questions or require clarification on any of these items, please feel free to contact me. I can be reached by calling 555-3549.

1. How would you rate this draft in terms of its content and organization?

   a. Although the style of the letter needs work, the content and organization are basically okay.
   b. The draft is seriously flawed in both content and organization. Extensive editing is required.
   c. The content is fine, but the organization is poor.
   d. The organization is fine, but the content is poor.

2. What should be done to eliminate the biased tone of the fourth paragraph?

   a. Omit the last three sentences of the paragraph.
   b. Omit the last three sentences and add something like the following: "Please have your employees review the videotape that deals with McDonald's standards of personal appearance."
   c. Revise the last three sentences along the following lines: "Given the composition of your labor force, you may need to stress the basics of personal hygiene."

3. Which of the following is the best alternative to this sentence: "If nothing has been done toward rectifying these infractions of McDonald's principles of operation, you will be reported to headquarters for noncooperation and unsatisfactory levels of performance."

a. "If nothing has been done to correct these infractions, you will be reported to headquarters for noncompliance."

b. "If you don't shape up immediately, headquarters will hear about it."

c. "By correcting these problems promptly, you can avoid being reported to headquarters."

d. "You can preserve your unblemished reputation by acting immediately to bring your facility into compliance with McDonald's principles of operation."

4. Take a look at the third paragraph of the letter. What is its chief flaw?

a. There is no topic sentence.

b. The topic sentence is too narrow for the ideas encompassed in the paragraph.

c. The transition from the previous paragraph is poor.

d. The paragraph deals with more than one subject.

e. The topic sentence is not adequately developed with specific details in subsequent sentences.[22]

TEST YOUR KNOWLEDGE

1. What are the three main tasks involved in revising a business message?

2. How do readers benefit from white space and headings?

3. What computer tools can you use when revising messages?

4. What is the purpose of the Fog Index and similar formulas?

5. What is parallel construction, and why is it important?

6. What are some of the issues to focus on when critiquing someone else's document?

7. What are some ways you can make a document more concise?

8. Why is proofreading an important part of the writing process?

9. What happens when you use too many hedging sentences in one document?

10. Why is it a good idea to use verbs instead of noun phrases?

INTERACTIVE LEARNING

USE THIS TEXT'S ONLINE RESOURCES

Visit the myPHLIP Web site at www.prenhall.com/thill. For Chapter 6, take advantage of the interactive "Study Guide" to test your chapter knowledge. Get instant feedback on whether you need additional studying. Read the "Current Events" articles to get the latest on chapter topics, and complete the exercises—as specified by your instructor.

This site's "Study Hall" helps you succeed in this course. "Talk in the Hall" lets you leave messages and meet new friends online. If you have a question, you can "Ask the Tutor." And to get a better grade in this course, you can find more help at "Writing Skills," "Study Skills," and "Study Tips."

The "Research Area" helps you locate a wealth of information to use in course assignments. Plus, you can send a message to online research experts, who will help you find exactly the information you need.

APPLY YOUR KNOWLEDGE

1. Why is it important to let your draft "age" a day before you begin the editing process?

2. What are some challenges you might encounter when critiquing the work of others?

3. Given the choice of only one, would you prefer to use a grammar checker or a spell checker? Why?

4. When you are designing a formal business letter, which design elements do you have to consider and which are optional?

5. **Ethical Choices** What are the ethical implications of using underlining, all capitals, and other hard-to-read type styles in a document explaining how customers can appeal the result of a decision made in the company's favor during a dispute?

PRACTICE YOUR KNOWLEDGE

DOCUMENTS FOR ANALYSIS

Read the following documents; then (1) analyze the strengths and weaknesses of each sentence and (2) revise each document so that it follows the guidelines in Chapters 4 through 6.

Document 6.A

The move to our new offices will take place over this coming weekend. For everything to run smooth, everyone will have to clean out their own desk and pack up the contents in boxes that will be provided. You will need to take everything off the walls too, and please pack it along with the boxes.

If you have alot of personal belongings, you should bring them home with you. Likewise with anything valuable. I do not mean to infer that items will be stolen, irregardless it is better to be safe than sorry.

On Monday, we will be unpacking, putting things away, and then get back to work. The least amount of disruption is anticipated by us, if everyone does their part. Hopefully, there will be no negative affects on production schedules, and current deadlines will be met.

Document 6.B

Dear Ms. Giraud:

Enclosed herewith please find the manuscript for your book, *Careers in Woolgathering*. After perusing the first two chapters of your 1,500-page manuscript, I was forced to conclude that the subject matter, handicrafts and artwork using wool fibers, is not coincident with the publishing program of Framingham Press, which to this date has issued only works on business endeavors, avoiding all other topics completely.

Although our firm is unable to consider your impressive work at the present time, I have taken the liberty of recording some comments on some of the pages. I am of the opinion that any feedback that a writer can obtain from those well versed in the publishing realm can only serve to improve the writer's authorial skills.

In view of the fact that your residence is in the Boston area, might I suggest that you secure an appointment with someone of high editorial stature at the Cambridge Heritage Press, which I believe might have something of an interest in works of the nature you have produced.

Wishing you the best of luck in your literary endeavors, I remain

Arthur J. Cogswell
Editor

Document 6.C

For delicious, air-popped popcorn, please read the following instructions: The popper is designed to pop 1/2 cup of popcorn kernels at one time. Never add more than 1/2 cup. A half cup of corn will produce three to four quarts of popcorn. More batches may be made separately after completion of the first batch. Popcorn is popped by hot air. Oil or shortening is not needed for popping corn. Add only popcorn kernels to the popping chamber. Standard grades of popcorn are recommended for use. Premium or gourmet type popping corns may be used. Ingredients such as oil, shortening, butter, margarine, or salt should never be added to the popping chamber. The popper, with popping chute in position, may be preheated for two minutes before adding the corn. Turn the popper off before adding the corn. Use electricity safely and wisely. Observe safety precautions when using the popper. Do not touch the popper when it is hot. The popper should not be left unattended when it is plugged into an outlet. Do not use the popper if it or its cord has been damaged. Do not use the popper if it is not working properly. Before using the first time, wash the chute and butter/measuring cup in hot soapy water. Use a dishcloth or sponge. Wipe the outside of the popper base. Use a damp cloth. Dry the base. Do not immerse the popper base in water or other liquid. Replace the chute and butter/measuring cup. The popper is ready to use.

Exercises

6-1. **Revising Messages: Conciseness** Revise the following sentences, using shorter, simpler words:

   a. The antiquated calculator is ineffectual for solving sophisticated problems.

   b. It is imperative that the pay increments be terminated before an inordinate deficit is accumulated.

   c. There was unanimity among the executives that Ms. Jackson's idiosyncrasies were cause for a mandatory meeting with the company's personnel director.

   d. The impending liquidation of the company's assets was cause for jubilation among the company's competitors.

   e. The expectations of the president for a stock dividend were accentuated by the preponderance of evidence that the company was in good financial condition.

6-2. **Revising Messages: Camouflaged Verbs** Rewrite each sentence so that the verbs are no longer camouflaged:

   a. Adaptation to the new rules was performed easily by the employees.

   b. The assessor will make a determination of the tax due.

   c. Verification of the identity of the employees must be made daily.

   d. The board of directors made a recommendation that Mr. Ronson be assigned to a new division.

   e. The auditing procedure on the books was performed by the vice president.

6-3. **Revising Messages: Clarity** Break these sentences into shorter ones by adding more periods:

   a. The next time you write something, check your average ... ar sen- ... ner you

   price increase is visoble

   ... en he ... ke the ... n I nod ... ice did ... ith.

   b.i b puy. inu. s/p to

   ... ng, but ... deposts

   6l.a iscut effectne

   ... its two ... vords.

   d. Know the flexibility of the written word and its power to convey an idea, and know how to make your words behave so that your readers will understand.

   e. Words mean different things to different people, and a word such as *block* may mean city block, butcher block, engine block, auction block, or several other things.

6-4. Revising Messages: Conciseness Cross out unnecessary words in the following phrases:

    a. consensus of opinion
    b. new innovations
    c. long period of time
    d. at a price of $50
    e. still remains

6-5. Revising Messages: Conciseness Use infinitives as substitutes for the overly long phrases in these sentences:

    a. For living, I require money.
    b. They did not find sufficient evidence for believing in the future.
    c. Bringing about the destruction of a dream is tragic.

6-6. Revising Messages: Conciseness Rephrase the following in fewer words:

    a. in the near future
    b. in the event that
    c. in order that
    d. for the purpose of
    e. with regard to
    f. it may be that
    g. in very few cases
    h. with reference to
    i. at the present time
    j. there is no doubt that

6-7. Revising Messages: Conciseness Condense these sentences to as few words as possible:

    a. We are of the conviction that writing is important.
    b. In all probability, we're likely to have a price increase.
    c. Our goals include making a determination about that in the near future.
    d. When all is said and done at the conclusion of this experiment, I'd like to summarize the final windup.
    e. After a trial period of three weeks, during which time she worked for a total of 15 full working days, we found her work was sufficiently satisfactory so that we offered her full-time work.

6-8. Revising Messages: Modifiers Remove all the unnecessary modifiers from these sentences:

    a. Tremendously high pay increases were given to the extraordinarily skilled and extremely conscientious employees.
    b. The union's proposals were highly inflationary, extremely demanding, and exceptionally bold.

6-9. Revising Messages: Hedging Rewrite these sentences so that they no longer contain any hedging:

    a. It would appear that someone apparently entered illegally.
    b. It may be possible that sometime in the near future the situation is likely to improve.
    c. Your report seems to suggest that we might be losing money.
    d. I believe Nancy apparently has somewhat greater influence over employees in the word-processing department.
    e. It seems as if this letter of resignation means you might be leaving us.

6-10. Revising Messages: Indefinite Starters Rewrite these sentences to eliminate the indefinite starters:

    a. There are several examples here to show that Elaine can't hold a position very long.
    b. It would be greatly appreciated if every employee would make a generous contribution to Mildred Cook's retirement party.
    c. It has been learned in Washington today from generally reliable sources that an important announcement will be made shortly by the White House.
    d. There is a rule that states that we cannot work overtime without permission.
    e. It would be great if you could work late for the next three Saturdays.

6-11. Revising Messages: Parallelism Present the ideas in these sentences in parallel form:

    a. Mr. Hill is expected to lecture three days a week, to counsel two days a week, and must write for publication in his spare time.
    b. She knows not only accounting, but she also reads Latin.
    c. Both applicants had families, college degrees, and were in their thirties, with considerable accounting experience but few social connections.
    d. This book was exciting, well written, and held my interest.
    e. Don is both a hard worker and he knows bookkeeping.

6-12. Revising Messages: Awkward Pointers Revise the following sentences to delete the awkward pointers:

    a. The vice president in charge of sales and the production manager are responsible for the keys to 34A and 35A, respectively.
    b. The keys to 34A and 35A are in executive hands, with the former belonging to the vice president in charge of sales and the latter belonging to the production manager.
    c. The keys to 34A and 35A have been given to the production manager, with the aforementioned keys being gold embossed.
    d. A laser printer and a dot-matrix printer were delivered to John and Megan, respectively.
    e. The walnut desk is more expensive than the oak desk, the former costing $300 more than the latter.

6-13. Revising Messages: Dangling Modifiers Rewrite these sentences to clarify the dangling modifiers:

    a. Running down the railroad tracks in a cloud of smoke, we watched the countryside glide by.
    b. Lying on the shelf, Ruby saw the seashell.
    c. Based on the information, I think we should buy the property.
    d. Being cluttered and filthy, Sandy took the whole afternoon to clean up her desk.
    e. After proofreading every word, the memo was ready to be signed.

6-14. Revising Messages: Noun Sequences Rewrite the following sentences to eliminate the long strings of nouns:

    a. The focus of the meeting was a discussion of the bank interest rate deregulation issue.

b. Following the government task force report recommendations, we are revising our job applicant evaluation procedures.

c. The production department quality assurance program components include employee training, supplier cooperation, and computerized detection equipment.

d. The supermarket warehouse inventory reduction plan will be implemented next month.

e. The State University business school graduate placement program is one of the best in the country.

6–15. **Revising Messages: Sentence Structure** Rearrange the following sentences to bring the subjects closer to their verbs:

a. Trudy, when she first saw the bull pawing the ground, ran.

b. It was Terri who, according to Ted, who is probably the worst gossip in the office (Tom excepted), mailed the wrong order.

c. William Oberstreet, in his book *Investment Capital Reconsidered,* writes of the mistakes that bankers through the decades have made.

d. Judy Schimmel, after passing up several sensible investment opportunities, despite the warnings of her friends and family, invested her inheritance in a jojoba plantation.

e. The president of U-Stor-It, which was on the brink of bankruptcy after the warehouse fire, the worst tragedy in the history of the company, prepared a press announcement.

6–16. **Internet** Visit the stock market page of Bloomberg's Web site at www.bloomberg.com/bbn/snapshot.html and evaluate the use of design in presenting the latest news. What design improvements can you suggest to enhance readability of the information posted on this page?

6–17. **Teamwork** Team up with another student and exchange your revised versions of Document 6.A, 6.B, or 6.C (see exercise under Documents for Analysis). Review the assignment to be sure the instructions are clear. Then read and critique your teammate's revision to see whether it can be improved. After you have critiqued each other's work, take a moment to examine the way you expressed your comments and the way you felt listening to the other student's comments. Can you identify ways to improve the critiquing process in situations such as this?

6–18. **Producing Messages: Design Elements** Look back at your revised version of Document 6.C (see exercise under Documents for Analysis). Which design elements could you use to make this document more readable? Produce your revision of Document 6.C using your selected design elements. Then experiment by changing one of the design elements. How does the change affect readability? Exchange documents with another student and critique each other's work.

6–19. **Proofreading Messages: E-Mail** Proofread the following e-mail message and revise it to correct any problems you find: Our final company orientation of the year will be held on Dec. 20. In preparation for this sesssion, please order 20 copies of the Policy handbook, the confidentiality agreement, the employee benefits Manual, please let me know if you anticipate any delays in obtaining these materials.

6–20. **Ethical Choices** Three of your company's five plants exceeded their expense budgets last month. You want all the plants to operate within their budgets from now on. You were thinking of using broadcast faxing to let all five plants see the memo you are sending to the managers of the three over-budget plants. Is this a good idea? Why or why not?

GOING ONLINE EXERCISES

Write It Right: Rethink and Revise, page 142

Before completing a message, go to www.powa.org for advice on organizing ideas, choosing the best word and appropriate style, and placing each paragraph effectively so that your message achieves its purpose.

1. Why is it better to write out ideas in a rough format and later reread your message to revise its content? When revising your message, what two questions can you ask about your writing?

2. Name the four elements of the "writing context." Imagine that you're the reader of your message. What questions might you ask?

3. When you revise a written message, what is the purpose of "tightening"? What is one way to tighten your writing as you complete a message?

To complete this exercise, log on to this text's Web site at www.prenhall.com/thill. Select Chapter 6, then select "Student Resources," click on the name of the featured Web site, and follow the detailed navigational directions.

Letters, Memos, E-Mail, and Other Brief Messages

chapter 7

After studying this chapter, you will be able to

1 Apply the three-step writing process to routine positive messages

2 Illustrate the strategy for writing routine requests

3 Discuss the differences among four types of routine requests

4 Explain the main differences in messages granting a claim when the company, the customer, or a third party is at fault

5 Outline how best to protect yourself when referring to a candidate's shortcoming in a recommendation letter

6 Clarify the importance of goodwill messages, and describe how to make them effective

The people at Campbell Soup do their best to communicate positive messages to consumers and strive to maintain good relationships with fellow employees and outside contacts. All their messages focus on clearly stating the main idea while showing a genuine understanding of the audience.

On the job:

FACING A COMMUNICATION DILEMMA AT CAMPBELL SOUP

Keeping Millions of People Happy, One Spoonful at a Time

www.campbellsoup.com

You might say that Karen Donohue is in the problem business. As supervisor of consumer response at Campbell Soup Company, she's in charge of answering consumer questions and responding to consumer complaints. Without question, she needs strong communication skills, and she must have a special talent for working with people—a lot of people.

In addition to the well-known soup brands, Campbell's also markets Pace picante sauce, Pepperidge Farm cookies, Prego pasta sauces, V8 vegetable juice, Franco-American pasta, and Spaghetti-Os, among others. So every second of every hour, consumers around the world buy 100 packages of Campbell's products—that's more than 8.6 million purchases every day. Walk into just about any kitchen in the country, and you'll find a Campbell's brand on the shelf. Working with customers can be a challenge in any business, but Donohue and her team of specialists are responsible for communicating with a huge customer base. And Campbell wants that base to keep growing.

The company has a history of high-quality products stretching back nearly to the Civil War. Soup sales took off after 1897, when a company chemist figured out how to remove most of the water from soup, making it easier and cheaper to ship long distances. In the 1980s, consumer tastes began to change, and Campbell stumbled a bit. However, the company maximized consumer feedback and began offering new products that were tailored to local markets. The attention to consumer needs, along with new management and a narrower focus on key products, has put Campbell back on track through the late 1990s and into the new millennium.

To maintain its market in the United States and to grow overseas, Campbell relies on its in-house consumer advocates, such as Karen Donohue. She is an important link between the public and the research kitchens. She is the company's eyes and ears, and in her key position she not only relays important information to company managers but also makes sure that consumers are satisfied. If you were Karen Donohue, how would you answer consumer inquiries and complaints? How would you go about writing positive business messages both inside and outside the company?[1]

USING THE THREE-STEP WRITING PROCESS FOR ROUTINE MESSAGES

Whether you're answering consumer correspondence, like Campbell's Karen Donohue, congratulating an employee on a job well done, or requesting information from another firm, chances are that in the course of everyday business you'll compose a lot of routine, good-news, and goodwill messages. In fact, most of a typical employee's communication is about routine matters: orders, information, claims, credit, employees, products, operations, and so on. These messages are rarely long or complex. Even so, to produce the best messages possible, you'll want to apply the three-step writing process.

Step 1: Planning Routine Messages

As with longer, complex messages, you need to analyze, investigate, and adapt. However, for routine messages, this planning step may take only a few moments. First, analyze your purpose to make sure that (1) it's specific, (2) it should indeed be sent, and (3) it should be written (rather than handled in a quick phone call or by walking down the hall for a brief chat). Also, think a moment about your readers. Are you sure they'll receive your message positively (or at least neutrally)? Most routine messages are of interest to your readers because they contain information necessary to conduct day-to-day business. Even so, you may need to discover more about audience attitudes or needs.

Second, investigate to learn exactly what your audience needs to know. Do you have all the relevant information? Do you need to take a little time to gather more?

Third, adapt your routine messages to your readers. Select the most appropriate medium, and establish or maintain a good relationship with them. Use the "you" attitude and be sure to keep your language positive and polite.

Step 2: Writing Routine Messages

Organizing and composing routine messages can go rather quickly. Your main idea may already be fairly well defined. Just be sure you stick to it by limiting the scope of your message. Cover only relevant points, and group them in the most logical fashion. Because your readers will be interested or neutral, you can usually adopt the direct approach for routine messages: Open with a clear statement of the main idea, include all necessary details in the body, and then close cordially.

However, even though these messages are the least complicated business messages to write, communicating across cultural boundaries can be frustrating, especially if you're not familiar with the cultural differences involved. So before selecting the direct approach for your message, verify the customs of your audience, and make sure your readers prefer direct organization. (See "Achieving Intercultural Communication—How Direct Is Too Direct?") When you're addressing an audience with minimal cultural differences, keep your tone conversational and use plain English.

Step 3: Completing Routine Messages

No matter how short or straightforward your message, make it professional by allowing plenty of time to revise, produce, and proofread it. First, revise your routine message for overall effect. Evaluate your content and organization to make sure you've said what you want in the order you wanted to say it. Review your message's readability. Edit and rewrite routine messages for conciseness and clarity. Second, design your document to suit your audience. Choose effective design elements and appropriate delivery methods. Finally, proofread the final version of your routine message. Look for typos, errors in spelling and mechanics, alignment problems, poor print quality, and so on.

MAKING ROUTINE REQUESTS

Whenever you ask for something—information, action, products, adjustments, references—you are making a request. A request is routine if it's part of the normal course of business and you anticipate that your audience will want to comply. Be careful not to make unnecessary requests. If you can find information yourself, don't burden others and risk your credibility by asking someone else to find it for you. But when you must make a routine request, make sure it's efficient and effective.

Strategy for Routine Requests

Like all routine messages, routine requests may be thought of as having three parts: an opening, a body, and a close. Using the direct approach, you place your main idea (the

Perry Klebahn's company, Atlas Snowshoe, sells high-end showshoes in more than 1,000 stores across the United States, ringing in annual sales of about $12 million. Klebahn tells his employees to establish a good relationship with their audience by learning what readers need to know and by using language that is positive and polite.

Organize your routine messages according to the direct approach.

Just as you do for other messages, you need to revise, produce, and proofread routine messages.

Achieving Intercultural Communication

How Direct Is Too Direct?

Being direct is civil, considerate, and honest—or so say people in the United States. Other folks view that same directness as being abrupt, rude, and intrusive—even dishonest and offensive. Countries such as France, Mexico, Japan, Saudi Arabia, Italy, and the Philippines all tend toward high-context cultures (see discussion in Chapter 3). That is, the people in these countries depend on shared knowledge and inferred messages to communicate; they gather meaning more from context and less from direct statement.

Offering a little constructive criticism may actually hurt your Mexican assistant's dignity. In fact, in high-context cultures, avoid saying outright, "You are wrong." You could cause the other person to lose face. When making requests, determine whether to use a direct or an implied approach by considering audience attitudes toward destiny, time, authority, and logic:

❏ *Destiny.* Do audience members believe they can control events themselves? Or do they see events as predetermined and uncontrollable? If you're supervising employees who believe that fate controls a construction deadline, your crisp e-mail message requesting them to stay on schedule may be hard for them to understand; it may even be insulting.

❏ *Time.* Do audience members view time as exact, precise, and not to be wasted? Or do they see time as relative, relaxed, and necessary for developing interpersonal relationships? If you see time as money and you get straight to business in your memo to your Mexican manager, your message may be overlooked in the confusion over your disregard for social propriety.

❏ *Authority.* Do audience members conduct business more autocratically or more democratically? In Mexico, rank and status are highly valued, so when communicating downward, you may need to be even more direct than you're used to being in the United States. And when communicating upward, you may need to be much less direct than usual.

❏ *Logic.* Do audience members pursue logic in a straight line, from point A to point B? Or do they communicate in circular or spiral patterns of logic? If you organize a speech or letter in a straightforward and direct manner, your message may be considered illogical, unclear, and disorganized.

You may want to decide not only how direct to be in written messages but also whether to write at all; perhaps a phone call or a visit would be more appropriate. By finding out how much or how little a culture tends toward high-context communication, you'll know whether to be direct or to rely on nuance when communicating with the people of that culture.

CAREER APPLICATIONS

1. Research a high-context culture such as Japan, Korea, or China, and write a one- or two-paragraph summary of how someone in that culture would go about requesting information.
2. When you are writing in American English to someone in a high-context culture, would it be better to (a) make the request directly in the interest of clarity or (b) try to match your audience's unfamiliar logic and make your request indirectly? Explain your answer.

Going Online

The Medium and the Message

Explore About.com's numerous links to sources of information on a variety of subjects. You can find tips on business writing with examples of letters, memos, and press releases. You'll find Web-design ideas and help from numerous guides on many business-related topics. You can even get online help with setting standards for a company's online communication.

www.about.com

To reach this Web site, go to www.prenhall.com/thill *(the Web site for this text). Select Chapter 7, then select "Student Resources." There, you'll find a current, live link that will take you straight to the site.*

request) in the opening. You use the middle to explain details and justify your request. Then you close by requesting specific action and concluding cordially (see Figure 7–1).

State Your Request Up Front   Begin routine requests by placing your request first. Up front is where it stands out and gets the most attention. Of course, getting right to the point should not be interpreted as a license to be abrupt or tactless:

◆ **Pay attention to tone.** Even though you expect a favorable response, the **tone** of your initial request is important. Instead of demanding action ("Send me your catalog no. 33A"), soften your request with words such as *please* and *I would appreciate.*

◆ **Assume your audience will comply.** An impatient demand for rapid service isn't necessary. Generally make the assumption that your audience will comply with your request once the reason for it is clearly understood.

◆ **Avoid beginning with personal introductions.** Don't be tempted to begin your request with a personal introduction such as "I am the supervisor of consumer response at Campbell Soup Company, and I am looking for information that . . . " Karen Donohue knows that this type of beginning buries the main idea, so the request may get lost.

◆ **Punctuate questions and polite requests differently.** A polite request in question form requires no question mark ("Would you please help us determine whether Kate Kingsley is a suitable applicant for this position.") A direct question within your message does require a question mark ("Did Kate Kingsley demonstrate an ability to work smoothly with clients?")

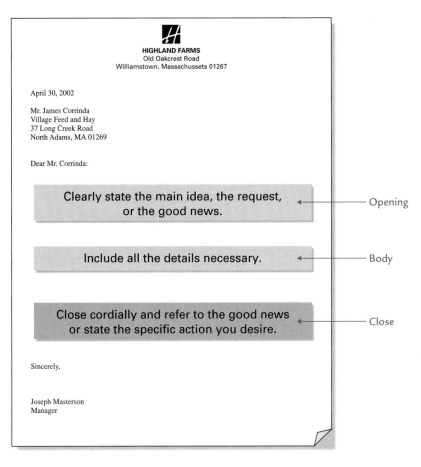

HIGHLAND FARMS
Old Oakcrest Road
Williamstown, Massachussets 01267

April 30, 2002

Mr. James Corrinda
Village Feed and Hay
37 Long Creek Road
North Adams, MA 01269

Dear Mr. Corrinda:

Clearly state the main idea, the request, or the good news. ———— Opening

Include all the details necessary. ———— Body

Close cordially and refer to the good news or state the specific action you desire. ———— Close

Sincerely,

Joseph Masterson
Manager

Figure 7–1
The Parts of Routine, Good-News, and Goodwill Messages

◆ **Be specific.** State precisely what you want. For example, if you request "the latest census figures" from a government agency, be sure to say whether you want a page or two of summary figures or a detailed report running several thousand pages.

Explain and Justify Your Request   Use the middle section of your message to explain your initial request. Make the explanation a smooth and logical outgrowth of your opening remarks. For example, you might show how your readers could benefit from complying. When The Nature Company's Silva Raker writes letters to potential suppliers, she's looking for product information, but she's also telling her unknown readers why she needs the information, and she's explaining how long-term business and personal relationships might evolve. For instance, Raker might write, "By keeping The Nature Company informed about your products, you can help create a new distribution channel for your business."[2]

The middle section of routine requests can also be handled as a series of questions—a method particularly useful if your inquiry concerns machinery or complex equipment. For instance, you might ask about technical specifications, exact dimensions, and the precise use of a complex tool. Even if your request is relatively simple, such as inquiring about the shipping options when ordering a book or compact disk from Amazon.com, you can use listed questions in the middle section of your message. Be sure to break down multiple requests. When requesting several items or answers, number the items and list them in logical order or in descending order of importance. When using a series of questions, just keep a few basics in mind:

◆ **Ask the most important questions first.** If cost is your main concern, you might begin with a question such as "What is the cost for shipping the CDs by Priority Mail?" Then you may want to ask more specific but related questions about the cost of shipping partial orders.

◆ **Ask only relevant questions.** So that your request can be handled quickly, ask only questions central to your main request. If your questions require simple yes-or-no

In the middle section of the request, give the details of your request.

Numbered lists may help readers sort through multiple related items or multiple requests.

Checklist: **Writing Routine Requests**

Direct Statement of the Request

✓ Use the direct approach, since your audience will respond favorably to your request.
✓ Phrase the opening clearly and simply so that the main idea cannot be misunderstood.
✓ Write in a polite, undemanding, personal tone.
✓ Preface complex requests with a sentence or two of explanation.

Justification, Explanation, and Details

✓ Justify the request or explain its importance.
✓ Explain the benefit of responding.
✓ State desired actions in a positive and supportive (not negative or dictatorial) manner.

✓ Itemize parts of a complex request in a logical or numbered series.
✓ List specific questions that you can't answer through your own efforts.
✓ Limit any question to one topic.
✓ Word any questions to get the type of answers you need.

Courteous Close with Request for Specific Action

✓ Courteously request a specific action.
✓ Make it easy to comply by including your contact information: name, address, phone and fax numbers (with area code), and e-mail address.
✓ Indicate gratitude.
✓ Clearly state any important deadline or time frame for the request.

---

answers, you might provide readers with a form or with boxes to check. If you need more elaborate answers, pose open-ended questions. "How fast can you ship the CDs?" is more likely to elicit the information you want than "Can you ship the CDs?"

◆ **Deal with only one topic per question.** If you have an unusual or complex request, list the request and provide supporting details in a separate, short paragraph. You may even use paragraph headings to make your reader's job easier.

Close with
• A request for some specific response
• An expression of appreciation
• Information about how you can be reached

Request Specific Action in a Courteous Close   Close your letter with three important elements: (1) a specific request, (2) information about how you can be reached, and (3) an expression of appreciation or goodwill. Use the closing to request a specific action, and ask that readers respond by a specific and appropriate time limit ("Please send the figures by April 5 so that I can return quarter results to you before the May 20 conference"). Help your reader respond easily by including your phone number, office hours, and other contact information.

Conclude your message by sincerely expressing your goodwill and appreciation. However, don't thank the reader "in advance" for cooperating. If the reader's reply warrants a word of thanks, send it after you've received the reply. To review, see this chapter's "Checklist: Writing Routine Requests."

Objective
3
Discuss the differences among four types of routine requests.

Types of Routine Requests

The various types of routine requests are innumerable, from asking favors to requesting credit. However, many of the routine messages that you'll be writing will likely fall into major categories. The following sections discuss four of these categories: placing orders, requesting information and action, making claims and requesting adjustments, and requesting recommendations and references.

Placing Orders   Messages placing orders are considered some of the simplest types of routine messages. When placing an order, you need not excite your reader's interest; just state your needs clearly and directly. Most orders refer to a product that the reader knows about, so these messages are usually processed without objection.

Most companies today use computer-generated order forms.

Most companies today use computer-generated order forms that provide a list of products with a description of each item and information such as the catalog number, name or trade name, color, size, and unit price. Your job is simple: Fill in the quantity, compute the total amount due, and provide the shipping address.

Companies are generally moving toward paperless ordering. Still, if you need to draft an order letter, follow the same format as you would on an order blank. Open with the

Checklist: **Placing Orders, Making Claims, and Requesting Adjustments***

Placing Orders

- ✓ Provide a general description of the order in the opening.
- ✓ Include all order specifications in the body: quantity, price (including discounts), size, catalog or product number, product description, delivery instructions, arrangements for payment (method, time, deposits), and cost totals.
- ✓ Indicate how and where to send the shipment (sometimes billing and delivery addresses are different).
- ✓ Use a format that presents information clearly and makes it easy to total amounts.
- ✓ Double-check the completeness of your order and the cost totals.
- ✓ Mention any payment you've enclosed, along with check number and amount.
- ✓ In the close, state when you expect delivery and specify any time limits in the closing.

Making Claims and Requesting Adjustments

- ✓ Write a claim letter as soon as possible after the problem has been identified.
- ✓ Maintain a confident, factual, fair, unemotional tone.
- ✓ Present facts honestly, clearly, and politely.
- ✓ Eliminate threats, sarcasm, exaggeration, and hostility, and use a nonargumentative tone to show confidence in the reader's fairness.
- ✓ Make no accusation against any person or company, unless you can back it up with facts.
- ✓ To gain the reader's understanding, praise some aspect of the good or service, or at least explain why the product was originally purchased.
- ✓ If appropriate, clearly state what you expect as a fair settlement, or ask the reader to propose a fair adjustment.
- ✓ Provide copies of necessary documents (invoices, canceled checks, confirmation letters, and the like); keep the originals.
- ✓ In the closing, briefly summarize desired action.

*These items are in addition to the basic tasks associated with writing routine requests.

general request. In the middle, include specific information about the items you want. Present this information in column form, double-space between the items, and total the price at the end. In the close be sure to specify the delivery address, since it may differ from the billing address. Also indicate how the merchandise is to be shipped: by truck, air freight, parcel post, air express, or delivery service. Otherwise, the seller chooses the mode of transportation. In any letter including a payment, mention the amount enclosed, explain how the amount was calculated, and if necessary, explain to what account the amount should be charged. Here's an example:

When placing orders, be thorough and clear.

Please send the following items to the above address by air freight. I am ordering from your current spring-summer catalog:

General request is stated first.

COUNT	STOCK I.D.	DESCRIPTION	ITEM PRICE	TOTAL PRICE
3	139-24	Daily appointment books (black)	$ 8.95	$ 26.85
50	289-90	Mechanical pencils (0.5 mm/black)	1.69	84.50
5	905-18	Wrist pads (gray)	6.99	34.95
10	472-67	Bulk IBM-format 3" diskettes (50/box)	17.99	179.90
		TOTAL SALE		**$326.20**
		SHIPPING		FREE
		AMOUNT DUE		**$326.20**

All necessary details provided in a format similar to an order form.

Writer calculates amount due (information on tax and shipping was provided in catalog).

My check #1738 for $326.20 is enclosed. Please ship these supplies UPS ground to the address in the letterhead.

Additional important information is included in the close.

When placing orders with international companies, remember that in most countries, the day is placed before the month: 15 March 2002 (15.3.02) rather than March 15, 2002 (3/15/02). To review the tasks involved in placing orders, see this chapter's "Checklist: Placing Orders, Making Claims, and Requesting Adjustments."

When placing international orders, use the transposed format: day/month/year.

Requesting Information and Action   When you need to know about something, to elicit an opinion from someone, or to suggest a simple action, you usually need only ask. In essence, simple requests say, "This is what I want to know or what I want you to do, why I'm making the request, and why it may be in your interest to help me." If your reader can do what you want, such a straightforward request gets the job done with a minimum of fuss.

When making a routine request, say
- What you want to know
- Why you want to know
- Why it is in the reader's interest to help you

Follow the direct approach: Start with a clear statement of your reason for writing. In the middle, provide whatever explanation is needed to justify your request. Then close with a specific account of what you expect, and include a deadline if appropriate.

Despite the simple organization of routine requests, they can cause ill will through ambiguous wording or a discourteous tone. When you prepare your request, remember that even the briefest note can create confusion and hard feelings. As with any business message, keep your purpose in mind. Ask yourself what you want readers to do or to understand as a result of reading your message.

Asking Company Insiders   Requests to fellow employees are often oral and rather casual. However, as long as you avoid writing frequent, long, or unneeded messages, a clear, thoughtfully written memo or e-mail message can save time and questions by helping readers understand precisely what is required. Both memos and e-mail messages have efficient headings that spell out who the message is for (TO:), who wrote it (FROM:), when it was written (DATE:), and what it's about (SUBJECT:). For more information on formatting memos and other business messages, see Appendix A.

As president and CEO of Charley's Steakery, Inc., Charley Shin provides company associates with the support they need to make decisions and grow with the company. Shin routinely sends memos to staff members, offering them the information they need for day-to-day operations. The tone of Shin's messages is matter-of-fact, but always sincere and polite.

The memo in Figure 7–2 was sent to all employees of a relatively small interior design firm. It seeks employee input about a new wellness and benefits program and about a new fee. The tone is matter-of-fact, and the memo assumes some shared background, which is appropriate when you're communicating about a routine matter to someone in the same company.

Asking Company Outsiders   Business writers often ask businesses, customers, or others outside their organization to provide information or to take some simple action: attend a meeting, return an information card, endorse a document, confirm an address, or supplement information on an order. Such requests are often in letter form (see Appendix A), although some are sent via e-mail. These messages are usually short and simple, like this request for information:

Makes overall request in polite question form (requiring no question mark).

Would you please supply me with information about the lawn services you provide. Pralle Realty owns approximately 27 pieces of rental property in College Station, and we're looking for a lawn service to handle all of them. We are making a commitment to provide quality housing in this college town, and we are looking for an outstanding firm to work with us.

Keeps reader's interest by hinting at possibility of future business.

1. Lawn care: What is your annual charge for each location for lawn maintenance, including mowing, fertilizing, and weed control?

Series of specific questions avoids making an overly broad request.

2. Shrubbery: What is your annual charge for each location for the care of deciduous and evergreen bushes, including pruning, fertilizing, and replacing as necessary?

Questions are itemized in a logical sequence.

3. Contract: How does Agri-Lawn Service structure such large contracts? What additional information do you need from us?

Open-ended questions avoid useless yes-or-no answers.

Please let us hear from you by February 15. We want to have a lawn-care firm in place by March 15.

The courteous close specifies a time limit.

Requests to outsiders often spell out in detail how filling the request will benefit readers.

In more complex situations, readers might be unwilling to respond unless they understand how the request benefits them. Be sure to include this information in your explanation.

The purpose of some routine requests to customers is to reestablish communication.

Sometimes businesses need to reestablish a relationship with former customers or suppliers, as Campbell's Karen Donohue knows well. Frequently, customers don't complain when they are unhappy about some purchase or about the way they were treated: They simply stay away from the offending business. A letter of inquiry might, for example, encourage readers to use idle credit accounts, offering them an opportunity to register their displeasure

1 Planning

Analyze: Purpose is to request feedback from fellow employees.

Investigate: Gather accurate, complete information on program benefits and local gym.

Adapt: Office memo or e-mail is appropriate medium. Use "you" attitude, and make responding easy.

2 Writing

Organize: Main idea is saving money while staying healthy. Save time and meet audience expectations using the direct approach.

Compose: Keep style informal but businesslike. Using a "we" attitude includes readers in the decision-making process.

3 Completing

Revise: Keep it brief—weed out overly long words and phrases. Avoid unnecessary detail.

Produce: No need for fancy design elements in this memo. Include a response form.

Proofread: Review carefully for both content and typographical errors.

Interior Design Solutions

INTERNAL MEMORANDUM

To: All Employees
From: Tony Ramirez, Human Resources
Date: October 15, 2002
Subj: New Wellness Program Opportunity

Routes message efficiently, with all needed information.

The benefits package committee has asked me to contact everyone about an opportunity to save money and stay healthier in the bargain. As you know, we've been meeting to decide on changes in our benefits package. Last week, we sent you a memo detailing the Synergy Wellness Program.

States purpose in opening to avoid wasting busy readers' time.

In addition to the package as described in the memo (life, major medical, dental, hospitalization), Synergy has sweetened the pot by offering IDD a 10 percent discount. To meet the requirements for the discount, we have to show proof that at least 25 percent of our employees participate in aerobic exercise at least three times a week for at least 20 minutes. (Their actuarial tables show a resulting 10 percent reduction in claims.)

Presents the situation that makes the inquiry necessary.

After looking around, we discovered a gymnasium just a few blocks south on Haley Boulevard. Sports Midwest will give our employees unlimited daytime access to their indoor track, gym, and pool for a group fee that comes to approximately $4.50 per month per employee if at least half of us sign up.

In addition to using the track and pools, we can play volleyball, jazzercise, form our own intramural basketball teams, and much more. Our spouses and children can also participate at a deeply discounted monthly fee. If you have questions, please e-mail or call me (or any member of the committee). Let us know your wishes on the following form.

Lists reader benefits and requests action.

Sign and return the following no later than Friday, October 29.

===

_____ Yes, I will participate in the Synergy Wellness program and pay $4.50 a month.
_____ Yes, I am interested in a discounted family membership.
_____ No, I prefer not to participate.

Provides an easy-to-use response form.

Signature _____

Employee ID Number _____

Figure 7–2
In-Depth Critique: Memo Requesting Action from Company Insiders

and then move on to a good relationship. In addition, a customer's response to such an inquiry may provide the company with insights into ways to improve its products and customer service. Even if they have no complaint, customers still welcome the personal attention. Such an inquiry to a customer might begin this way:

When a good charge customer like you has not bought anything from us in six months, we wonder why. Is there something we can do to serve you better?

Similar inquiry letters are sent from one business to another. For example, a sales representative of a housewares distributor might send the same type of letter to a retailer. To review the tasks involved in requesting information and action, see this chapter's "Checklist: Writing Routine Requests."

Making Claims and Requesting Adjustments   When you're dissatisfied with a company's product or service, you make a **claim** (a formal complaint) or request an **adjustment** (a claim settlement). Although a phone call or visit may solve the problem, a written claim letter is better because it documents your dissatisfaction. Moreover, even though your first reaction to a clumsy mistake or a defective product is likely to be anger or frustration, the person reading your letter probably had nothing to do with the problem. So a courteous, clear, concise explanation will impress your reader much more favorably than an abusive, angry letter.

> Putting your claim in writing
> • Documents your dissatisfaction
> • Requires courtesy, clarity, and conciseness

In most cases, and especially in your first letter, assume that a fair adjustment will be made, and follow the plan for direct requests. Begin with a straightforward statement of the problem. In the middle section, give a complete, specific explanation of the details. Provide any information an adjuster would need to verify your complaint about faulty merchandise or unsatisfactory service. In your closing, politely request specific action or convey a sincere desire to find a solution. And don't forget to suggest that the business relationship will continue if the problem is solved satisfactorily.

> In your claim letter
> • Explain the problem and give details
> • Provide backup information
> • Request specific action

Companies usually accept the customer's explanation of what's wrong, so ethically it's important to be entirely honest when filing claims. Also, be prepared to back up your claim with invoices, sales receipts, canceled checks, dated correspondence, catalog descriptions, and any other relevant documents. Send copies and keep the originals for your files.

> Be prepared to document your claim. Send copies and keep the original documents.

If the remedy is obvious, tell your reader exactly what will return the company to your good graces—for example, an exchange of merchandise for the right item or a refund if the item is out of stock. In some cases you might ask the reader to resolve the problem. If you're uncertain about the precise nature of the trouble, you could ask the company to make an assessment. But be sure to supply your contact information and the best time to call so that the company can discuss the situation with you if necessary.

> Be as specific as possible about what you want to happen next.

The following letter was written to a gas and electric company. As you read it, compare the tone with that in Figure 7–3. If you were the person receiving the complaint, which version would you respond to more favorably?

First Draft

We have been at our present location only three months, and we don't understand why our December utility bill is $115.00 and our January bill is $117.50. Businesses on both sides of us, in offices just like ours, are paying only $43.50 and $45.67 for the same months. We all have similar computer and office equipment, so something must be wrong.

Small businesses are helpless against big utility companies. How can we prove that you read the meter wrong or that the November bill from before we even moved in here got added to our December bill? We want someone to check this meter right away. We can't afford to pay these big bills.

Most people would react much more favorably to the version in Figure 7–3. A rational, clear, and courteous approach is best for any routine request. To review the tasks involved in making claims and requesting adjustments, see this chapter's "Checklist: Placing Orders, Making Claims, and Requesting Adjustments."

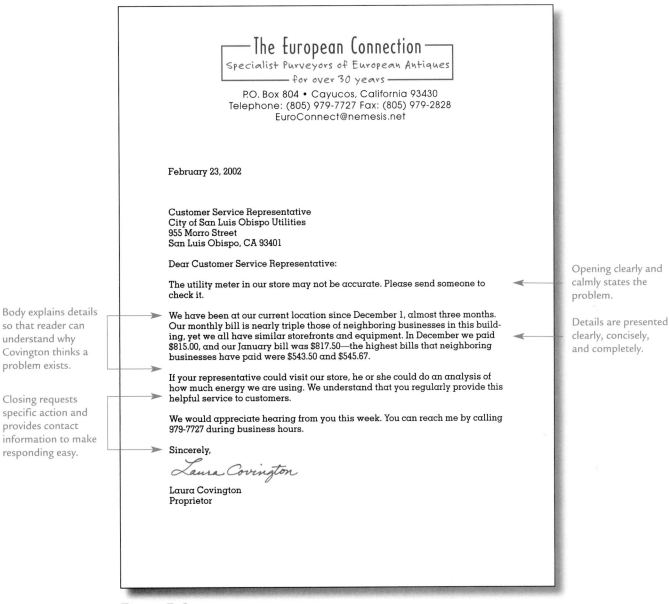

Opening clearly and calmly states the problem.

Details are presented clearly, concisely, and completely.

Body explains details so that reader can understand why Covington thinks a problem exists.

Closing requests specific action and provides contact information to make responding easy.

Figure 7–3
In-Depth Critique: Claim Letter

Requesting Recommendations and References   The need to inquire about people arises often in business. For example, before awarding credit, contracts, jobs, promotions, scholarships, and so on, some companies ask applicants to supply references. If you're applying for a job and your potential employer asks for references, you may want to ask a close personal or professional associate to write a letter of recommendation. Or, if you're an employer considering whether to hire an applicant, you may want to write directly to the person the applicant named as a reference.

Companies ask applicants to supply references who can vouch for their ability, skills, integrity, character, and fitness for the job. Before you volunteer someone's name as a reference, ask that person's permission. Some people won't let you use their names, perhaps because they don't know enough about you to feel comfortable writing a letter or because they have a policy of not providing recommendations. In any event, you are likely to receive the best recommendation from persons who agree to write about you, so check first.

Because requests for recommendations and references are routine, you can assume your reader will honor your request and organize your inquiry using the direct approach. Begin your message by clearly stating that you're applying for a position and that you

Always ask for permission before using someone's name as a reference.

would like your reader to write a letter of recommendation. If you haven't had contact with the person for some time, use the opening to recall the nature of the relationship you had, the dates of association, and any special events that might bring a clear, favorable picture of you to mind.

Refresh the memory of any potential reference you haven't been in touch with for a while.

If you're applying for a job, a scholarship, or the like, include a copy of your résumé to give the reader an idea of the direction your life has taken. After reading the résumé, your reader will know what favorable qualities to emphasize and will be able to write the recommendation that best supports your application. If you don't have a résumé, use the middle of your letter to include any information about yourself that the reader might use to support a recommendation, such as a description of related jobs you've held.

Provide your reader with as much information as possible about your qualifications.

Close your letter with an expression of appreciation and the full name and address of the person to whom the letter should be sent. When asking for an immediate recommendation, you should also mention the deadline. You'll make a response more likely if you enclose a stamped, preaddressed envelope. The letter in Figure 7–4 covers all these points and adds important information about some qualifications that might be of special interest to her potential employer.

Sending Routine Replies and Positive Messages

When responding positively to a request or sending a good-news or goodwill message, you have several goals: to communicate the good news, answer all questions, provide all required details, and leave your reader with a good impression of you and your firm. This sort of message can be quite brief and to the point. However, even though you may be doing someone a favor by responding to a request, you want to be courteous and upbeat and maintain a you-oriented tone.

Strategy for Routine Replies and Positive Messages

Like requests, routine replies and positive messages have an opening, a body, and a close. Readers receiving these messages will generally be interested in what you have to say, so you'll usually use the direct approach. Place your main idea (the positive reply or the good news) in the opening. Use the middle to explain all the relevant details, and close cordially, perhaps highlighting a benefit to your reader.

Use the direct organizational plan for positive messages.

Start with the Main Idea   By beginning your positive message with the main idea or good news, you're preparing your audience for the detail that follows. Try to make your opening clear and concise. Although the following introductory statements make the same point, one is cluttered with unnecessary information that buries the purpose, whereas the other is brief and to the point:

INSTEAD OF THIS	WRITE THIS
I am pleased to inform you that after deliberating the matter carefully, our human resources committee has recommended you for appointment as a staff accountant.	Congratulations! You've been selected to join our firm as a staff accountant, beginning March 20.

Before you begin, have a clear idea of what you want to say.

The best way to write a clear opening is to have a clear idea of what you want to say. Before you put one word on paper, ask yourself, "What is the single most important message I have for the audience?"

Provide Necessary Details and Explanation   The middle part of a positive message is typically the longest. You need the space to explain your point completely so that the audience will experience no confusion or lingering doubt. In addition to providing details in the middle section, maintain the supportive tone established at the

Analyze: Purpose is to request a recommendation letter from your college professor.

Investigate: Gather information to help reader recall you and to clarify the position you want.

Adapt: A letter format will give your message the formality you need. Be polite.

Organize: Main idea is to convince your professor to send a glowing recommendation to potential employer. Use the direct approach.

Compose: Make message friendly but businesslike and slightly more formal than usual. Use plain English and an active voice.

Revise: Be concise but thorough. Make sure that concrete detail flows logically.

Produce: Use simple typeface with ample margins and spacing between text. Enclose SASE and perhaps your résumé.

Proofread: Review letter and enclosures for errors.

Joanne Tucker
1181 Ashport, Tate Springs, Tennessee 38101
(901) 369-2093

March 14, 2001

Professor Lyndon Kenton
School of Business
University of Tennessee, Knoxville
Knoxville, Tennessee 37916

Dear Professor Kenton:

May I have a letter of recommendation from you? I recently interviewed with Strategic Investments and have been called for a second interview for their Analyst Training Program (ATP). They have requested at least one recommendation from a professor, and I immediately thought of you.

As you may recall, I took BUS 485, Financial Analysis, from you in the fall of 2000. I enjoyed the class and finished the term with an "A." Professor Kenton, your comments on assertiveness and cold-calling impressed me beyond the scope of the actual course material. In fact, taking your course helped me decide on a future as a financial analyst.

My enclosed résumé includes all my relevant work experience and volunteer activities. But I'd also like to add that I've handled the financial planning for our family since my father passed away several years ago. Although initially, I learned by trial and error, I have increasingly applied my business training in deciding what stocks or bonds to trade. This, I believe, has given me a practical edge over others who may be applying for the same job.

If possible, Ms. Blackmon in Human Resources needs to receive your letter by March 30. For your convenience, I've enclosed a preaddressed, stamped envelope.

I appreciate your time and effort in writing this letter of recommendation for me. It will be great to put my education to work, and I'll keep you informed of my progress.

Sincerely,

Joanne Tucker

Joanne Tucker

Enclosure

Opening includes information to refresh reader's memory about this former student.

Closing gives a deadline for response and includes information about the person expecting the recommendation.

Opening starts with the request, assumes the reader will honor the request, and names the potential employer.

Body refers to résumé and mentions experience that could set applicant apart from other candidates.

Figure 7–4
In-Depth Critique: Letter Requesting a Recommendation

Checklist: Writing Routine Replies and Positive Messages

Initial Statement of the Good News or Main Idea

- ✓ If the message is mixed, present the good news first.
- ✓ Respond promptly.
- ✓ Avoid trite and obvious statements such as "I am pleased to," "We have received," "This is in response to," or "Enclosed please find."
- ✓ Convey an upbeat, courteous, you-oriented tone.

Middle, Informational Section

- ✓ Imply or express interest in the request, or provide details of the good news.
- ✓ List all information in an orderly manner.
- ✓ If possible, answer all questions and requests in the order posed.
- ✓ Adapt replies to the reader's needs.
- ✓ Indicate what you have done and what you will do.
- ✓ Include any necessary details or interpretations that the reader may need in order to understand your answers.

- ✓ If you cannot comply with part of the request (perhaps because the information is unavailable or confidential), tell the reader why and then offer other assistance.
- ✓ Embed negative statements in positive contexts or balance them with positive alternatives.
- ✓ Inform or remind the reader of the general benefits of doing business with your firm. Avoid exaggerations or flamboyant language.

Warm, Courteous Close

- ✓ If further action is required, tell the reader how to proceed and encourage the reader to act promptly.
- ✓ Avoid clichés (such as "Please feel free to").
- ✓ Offer additional service, but avoid implying that your answer is inadequate (by using doubtful statements such as "I trust that" or "I hope").
- ✓ Express goodwill or take an optimistic look into the future, if appropriate.

Embed negative information in a positive context.

Make sure the audience understands what to do next and how that action will benefit them.

Rosie O'Donnell has won several Daytime Emmy awards as best TV talk show host. She's funny, gracious, and frank; audiences identify with her laughter and goodwill. O'Donnell also demonstrates good writing skills. For example, to help reduce anxiety about serious disease, she has written humorous material to accompany medical information. She's also established a foundation to support nonprofit organizations that provide childcare and education programs for children. Using positive messages, O'Donnell can help people feel better and convince them to comply with her requests.

beginning. This tone is easy to continue when your message is purely good news, as in this example:

Your educational background and internship have impressed us, and we believe you would be a valuable addition to Green Valley Properties. As discussed during your interview, your salary will be $3,300 per month, plus benefits. In that regard, you will meet with our benefits manager, Paula Sanchez, at 8:00 a.m. on Monday, March 20. She will assist you with all the paperwork necessary to tailor our benefit package to your family situation. She will also arrange various orientation activities to help you acclimate to our company.

However, if your routine message is mixed and must convey mildly disappointing information, put the negative portion of your message into as favorable a context as possible:

INSTEAD OF THIS	WRITE THIS
No, we no longer carry the Sportsgirl line of sweaters.	The new Olympic line has replaced the Sportsgirl sweaters that you asked about. Olympic features a wider range of colors and sizes and more contemporary styling.

The more complete description is less negative and emphasizes how the audience can benefit from the change. Be careful, though: You can use negative information in this type of message *only* if you're reasonably sure the audience will respond positively. Otherwise, use the indirect approach (discussed in Chapter 8).

End with a Courteous Close   Your message is most likely to succeed if your readers are left feeling that you have their personal welfare in mind. You accomplish this either by highlighting a benefit to the audience or by expressing appreciation or goodwill. If follow-up action is required, clearly state who will do what next. See this chapter's "Checklist: Writing Routine Replies and Positive Messages" to review the primary tasks involved in this type of business message.

Types of Routine Replies and Positive Messages

Innumerable types of routine replies and positive messages are used in business every day. Many of the routine positive messages that you'll be writing will likely fall into major categories. Take a moment to consider five such categories: granting requests for information and action, granting claims and requests for adjustments, providing recommendations and references, announcing good news, and sending goodwill messages.

Granting Requests for Information and Action   If your answer to a request is yes or is straightforward information, the direct plan is appropriate. Your prompt, gracious, and thorough response will positively influence how people think about your company, its products, your department, and you. Readers' perceptions are the reason that Karen Donohue of Campbell Soup is so sensitive to the tone of her memos, letters, and other messages. Donohue makes it a point to adopt the "you" attitude in all her business correspondence.

Many requests are similar. For example, a human resources department gets a lot of routine inquiries about job openings. To handle repetitive queries like these, companies usually develop form responses. Although these messages are often criticized as being cold and impersonal, you can put a great deal of thought into wording them, and you can use computers to personalize and mix paragraphs. Thus, a computerized form letter prepared with care may actually be more personal and sincere than a quickly dictated, hastily typed "personal" reply. Julian Zamakis wrote to McBride Department Stores for information on employment opportunities and received the encouraging reply in Figure 7–5.

When you're answering requests and a potential sale is involved, you have three main goals: (1) to respond to the inquiry and answer all questions, (2) to leave your reader with a good impression of you and your firm, and (3) to encourage the future sale. The following letter succeeds in meeting all three objectives:

> Many companies use form responses to reply to similar requests.

> Three main goals when a potential sale is involved:
> • Respond to the immediate request
> • Convey a good impression of you and your firm
> • Encourage a sale

You requested a copy of our brochure "Entertainment Unlimited," and Blue Ocean Communications is pleased to send it to you. This booklet describes the vast array of entertainment options available to you with an Ocean Satellite Device (OSD).

> Starts with a clear, conversational statement of the main point.

On page 12 of "Entertainment Unlimited," you'll find a list of the 138 channels that the OSD brings into your home. You'll have access to movie, sport, and music channels; 24-hour news channels; local channels; and all the major television networks. OSD gives you a clearer picture and more precise sound than those old-fashioned dishes that took up most of your yard—and OSD uses only a small dish that mounts easily on your roof.

> Presents key information immediately, along with resale and sales promotion.

More music, more cartoons, more experts, more news, and more sports are available to you with OSD than with any other cable or satellite connection in this region. Yes, it's all there, right at your fingertips.

> Encourages readers to take one more step toward a purchase by highlighting product benefits.

Just call us at 1-800-786-4331, and an OSD representative will come to your home to answer your questions. You'll love the programming and the low monthly cost. Call us today!

> Confidently points toward the sale.

Granting Claims and Requests for Adjustment   Satisfied customers bring additional business to a firm; angry or dissatisfied customers do not. In addition, angry customers complain to anyone who'll listen, creating poor public relations. So even though claims and adjustments may seem unpleasant, progressive businesspeople such as Campbell Soup's Karen Donohue treat claims and requests for adjustment as golden opportunities to build customer loyalty.[3]

Few people go to the trouble of requesting an adjustment unless they actually have a problem. So the most sensible reaction to a routine claim is to assume that the claimant's account of the transaction is an honest statement of what happened—unless the same customer repeatedly submits dubious claims or the dollar amount is very large. When you receive a complaint, respond promptly. You'll want to investigate the problem first to determine what went wrong and why. You'll also want to determine whether your company, your customer, or a third party is at fault.

> *Objective*
> **4**
> Explain the main differences in messages granting a claim when the company, the customer, or a third party is at fault.

> In general, it pays to give customers the benefit of the doubt.

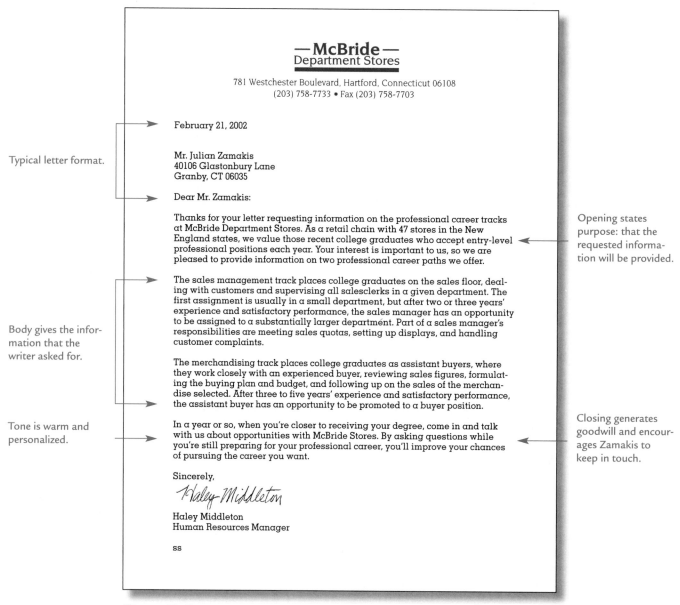

Typical letter format.

Body gives the information that the writer asked for.

Tone is warm and personalized.

Opening states purpose: that the requested information will be provided.

Closing generates goodwill and encourages Zamakis to keep in touch.

Figure 7–5
In-Depth Critique: Letter Replying to Request for Information

An ungracious adjustment may increase customer dissatisfaction.

When Your Company Is at Fault   The usual human response to a bad situation is to say, "It wasn't my fault!" However, businesspeople can't take that stance. When your company is at fault and your response to a claim is positive, you must protect your company's image and try to regain the customer's goodwill by referring to company errors carefully. Don't blame an individual or a specific department. And avoid lame excuses such as "Nobody's perfect" or "Mistakes will happen." Don't promise that problems will never happen again; such guarantees are unrealistic and often beyond your control. Instead, explain your company's efforts to do a good job, implying that the error was an unusual incident.

For example, a large mail-order clothing company has created the following form letter to respond to customers who claim they haven't received exactly what was ordered. The form letter can be customized through word processing and then individually signed:

Starts with a "good attitude" statement (not the usual good-news statement), because it goes to people with various complaints.

Puts customer at ease with "you" attitude.

Never suggests that customer was wrong to write to Klondike.

Your letter concerning your recent Klondike order has arrived and has been forwarded to our director of order fulfillment. Your complete satisfaction is our goal; when you are satisfied, we are satisfied. Our customer service representative will contact you soon to assist with the issues raised in your letter.

Whether you're skiing or driving a snowmobile, Klondike Gear offers you the best protection from wind, snow, and cold—and Klondike has been taking care of your outdoor needs for over 27 years! Because you're a loyal customer, enclosed is a $5 gift certificate. You may wish to consider our new line of quality snow goggles.

Includes resale and sales promotion.

Thank you for taking the time to write to us. Your input helps us better serve you and all our customers.

Closes with statement of company's concern for all its customers.

In contrast, a response letter written as a personal answer to a unique claim would start with a clear statement of the good news: the settling of the claim according to the customer's request. Here is a more personal response from Klondike Gear:

Here is your heather-blue wool-and-mohair sweater (size large) to replace the one returned to us with a defect in the knitting on the left sleeve. Thanks for giving us the opportunity to correct this situation. Customers' needs have come first at Klondike Gear for 27 years. Our sweaters are handmade by the finest knitters in this area.

Our newest catalog is enclosed. Browse through it and see what wonderful new colors and patterns we have for you. Whether you are skiing or driving a snowmobile, Klondike Gear offers you the best protection available from wind, snow, and cold. Let us know how we may continue to serve you and your sporting needs.

When the Customer Is at Fault   When your customer is at fault (perhaps washing a dry-clean-only sweater in hot water), you can (1) refuse the claim and attempt to justify your refusal or (2) simply do what the customer asks. But remember, if you refuse the claim, you may lose your customer—as well as many of the customer's friends, who will hear only one side of the dispute. You must weigh the cost of making the adjustment against the cost of losing future business from one or more customers.

If you choose to grant the claim, you can start off with the good news: You're replacing the merchandise or refunding the purchase price. However, the middle section needs more attention. Your job is to make the customer realize that the merchandise was mistreated, but you want to avoid being condescending ("Perhaps you failed to read the instructions carefully") or preachy ("You should know that wool shrinks in hot water").

When complying with an unjustified claim, let the customer know that the merchandise was mistreated, but maintain a respectful and positive tone.

The dilemma is this: If the customer fails to realize what went wrong, you may commit your firm to an endless procession of returned merchandise; but if you insult the customer, your cash refund will have been wasted because you'll lose your customer anyway. Without being offensive, the letter in Figure 7–6 educates a customer about how to treat his in-line skates.

When a Third Party Is at Fault   Sometimes neither you nor the claimant is at fault. Perhaps the carrier damaged merchandise in transit. Or perhaps the original manufacturer is responsible for some product defect. When a third party is at fault, you have three options:

You have three options when a third party is at fault.

◆ **Simply honor the claim.** This option is the most attractive. You can satisfy your customer with the standard good-news letter and no additional explanation. This way you maintain your reputation for fair dealing and bear no cost (because the carrier, manufacturer, or other third party will reimburse you for the damage).

◆ **Honor the claim, but explain you're not at fault.** This option corrects any impression that the damage was caused by your *negligence*. You can still write the standard good-news letter, but stress the explanation.

◆ **Refer the claimant to the third party.** This option is almost always a bad choice. When you suggest filing a claim with the firm that caused the defect or damage, you fail to satisfy the claimant's needs. The exception is when you're trying to dissociate yourself from any legal responsibility for the damaged merchandise, especially if it has caused a personal injury, in which case you would send a bad-news message (see Chapter 8).

This chapter's "Checklist: Granting Claims and Adjustment Requests, and Sending Goodwill Messages" reviews the tasks involved in granting claims and requests for adjustments.

1 Planning

Analyze: Purpose is to grant a customer's claim, gently educate him, and encourage further business.

Investigate: Gather information on product care, warranties, and resale information.

Adapt: Use letter format to reinforce businesslike tone. Give customer relationship utmost attention.

2 Writing

Organize: Main idea is that you're replacing the wheel assembly—even though you are not required to do so.

Compose: Use an upbeat conversational style, but remain businesslike. Choose words carefully, especially when educating customer. Include resale information to reinforce future business.

3 Completing

Revise: Revise for tone, focusing on conciseness, clarity, and the "you" attitude.

Produce: Avoid confusing your positive message with fussy design elements. Keep it simple.

Proofread: Review for the usual errors, and include all promised enclosures.

Skates Alive!

20901 El Dorado Hills
Laguna Niguel, CA 92677
(714) 332-7474 • Fax: (714) 336-5297
skates@speed.net

February 7, 2002

Mr. Steven Cox
1172 Amber Court
Jacksonville, FL 32073

Dear Mr. Cox:

Thank you for letting us know about the problem with your in-line skates. Although your six-month warranty has expired, we are mailing you a complete wheel assembly replacement free of charge. The enclosed instructions make removing the damaged wheel line and installing the new one relatively easy.

The "Fastrax" (model NL 562) you purchased is our best selling and most reliable skate. However, wheel jams may occur when fine particles of sand block the smooth rotating action of the wheels. These skates perform best when used on roadways and tracks that are relatively free of sand. We suggest that you remove and clean the wheel assemblies (see enclosed directions) once a month and have them checked by your dealer about every six months.

Because of your Florida location, you may want to consider our more advanced "Glisto" (model NL 988) when you decide to purchase new skates. Although more expensive than the Fastrax, the Glisto design helps shed sand and dirt quite efficiently and should provide years of trouble-free skating.

Enjoy the enclosed copy of "Rock & Roll," with our compliments. Inside, you'll read about new products, hear from other skaters, and have an opportunity to respond to our customer questionnaire.

We love hearing from our skaters, so keep in touch. All of us at Skates Alive! wish you good times and miles of healthy skating.

Sincerely,

Candace Parker

Candace Parker
Customer Service Representative

Enclosure

Opening acknowledges the problem and conveys the good news.

Body explains problem without blaming customer, suggesting ways to avoid future problems.

Body also includes resale information, encouraging the customer to "trade up."

Adds value by enclosing a newsletter that invites future response from customer.

Close is positive, ending on a "feel good" note that conveys an attitude of excellent customer service.

Figure 7–6
In-Depth Critique: Letter Responding to a Claim When the Buyer Is at Fault

Checklist: **Granting Claims and Adjustment Requests, and Sending Goodwill Messages***

Granting Claims and Adjustment Requests

✓ In the opening, state your willingness to honor the reader's claim, without negative comment.

✓ Thank the claimant for taking the time to write.

✓ In the body, explain how you will remedy the problem.

✓ Minimize or, if possible, omit any disagreements with your reader's interpretation of events.

✓ Make your explanation objective, nonvindictive, and impersonal.

✓ Apologize only when appropriate; then do so crisply and without an overly dramatic tone.

✓ Maintain a supportive tone: "Thank you for," "May we ask," and "We are glad to work with you."

✓ Admit your firm's faults carefully: Don't shift blame, imply inefficiency, or make unrealistic promises.

✓ Be careful when discussing the claimant's role in creating the problem.

✓ In the closing, remind the reader how you are honoring the claim.

✓ Encourage the claimant to look favorably on your company or the product in question.

✓ Clarify any actions that your reader must take.

Sending Goodwill Messages

✓ Be prompt when sending out goodwill messages so that they lose none of their impact.

✓ Send a written message whenever possible (it can be savored more than once), but a telephone call is better than no message at all.

✓ Use letter format for all condolences and any other goodwill message sent to outsiders or mailed to an employee's home.

✓ Except for condolences, use the memo format for any goodwill messages sent through interoffice mail, except for condolences.

✓ Hand-write condolences and replies to handwritten invitations.

✓ Use special stationery, if available.

✓ For added impact, present congratulations in a folder with a clipping or photo commemorating the special event.

✓ In the beginning, incorporate a friendly statement that builds goodwill.

✓ Focus on the good qualities of the person or situation.

✓ In the middle, express personalized details in sincere, not gushy, language.

✓ Be warm but concise.

✓ Make the reader the focus of all comments.

✓ Close with a positive or forward-looking statement.

✓ Restate the important idea in the close, when appropriate.

---

*These items are in addition to the basic tasks associated with writing positive responses.

Providing Recommendations and References   When writing a letter of recommendation, you want to convince readers that the person being recommended has the characteristics necessary for the job or benefit being sought. Your letter must contain all the relevant details:

◆ Candidate's full name

◆ Job or benefit being sought

◆ Nature of your relationship with the candidate

◆ Whether you're answering a request or taking the initiative

◆ Facts relevant to the position or benefit sought

◆ Your overall evaluation of candidate's suitability for the job or benefit

Oddly enough, the most difficult recommendation letters to write are those for truly outstanding candidates. Your audience will have trouble believing uninterrupted praise for someone's talents and accomplishments. So illustrate your general points with a specific example or two that point out the candidate's abilities. Be sure to discuss the candidate's abilities in relation to the "competition."

> Two devices for convincing the reader when the candidate is outstanding:
> • Use examples
> • Use comparisons with the "competition"

Most candidates aren't perfect, however. Omitting reference to a candidate's shortcomings may be tempting, especially if the shortcomings are irrelevant to the demands of the job in question. Even so, you have an obligation to refer to any shortcoming that is serious and related to job performance. You owe it to your audience, to your own conscience, and even to the better-qualified candidate who's relying on honest references.

Objective

Outline how best to protect yourself when referring to a candidate's shortcoming in a recommendation letter.

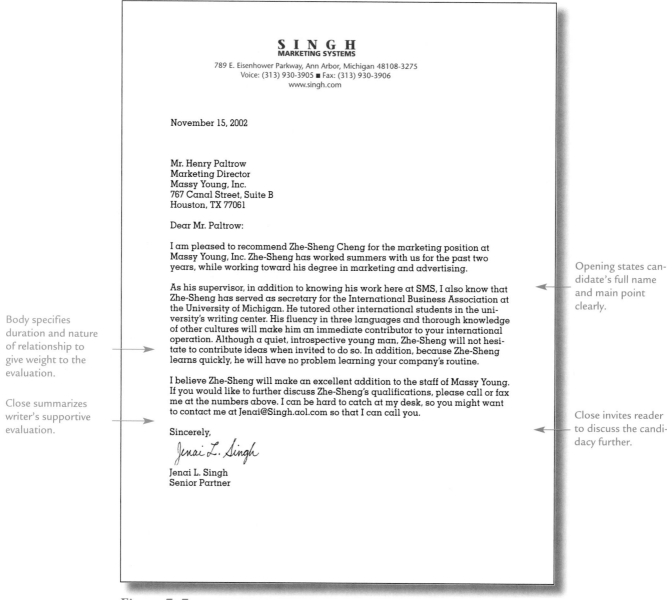

Body specifies duration and nature of relationship to give weight to the evaluation.

Close summarizes writer's supportive evaluation.

Opening states candidate's full name and main point clearly.

Close invites reader to discuss the candidacy further.

Figure 7–7
In-Depth Critique: Recommendation Letter

A serious shortcoming cannot be ignored, but beware of being libelous:
- Include only relevant, factual information
- Avoid value judgments
- Balance criticisms with favorable points

Of course, the danger in writing a critical letter is that you might engage in libel (making a false and malicious written statement that injures the candidate's reputation). On the other hand, if that negative information is truthful and relevant, it may be unethical and illegal to omit it from your recommendation. So if you must refer to a shortcoming, you can best protect yourself by sticking to the facts, avoiding value judgments, and placing your criticism in the context of a generally favorable recommendation, as in Figure 7–7. In this letter, the writer supports her statements with facts and steers clear of vague, critical judgments.

Recommendation letters are usually confidential; that is, they're sent directly to the person or committee who requested them and are not shown to the candidate. However, recent litigation has made it advisable in some situations to prepare a carefully worded letter that satisfies both parties. To explore the topic further, see "Promoting Workplace Ethics— Recommendation Letters: What's Right to Write?" You can also avoid trouble by asking yourself the following questions before mailing a recommendation letter:

◆ Does the person receiving this personal information have a legitimate right to it?

◆ Does all the information I've presented relate directly to the job/benefit being sought?

Promoting Workplace Ethics

Recommendation Letters: What's Right to Write?

You were Frank Walker's supervisor for four years. When he left the company recently, he asked you to write a letter of recommendation for him. However, your company's legal experts said no.

Why Not Give Recommendations?

Thousands of lawsuits have been filed (and won) by employees, charging former employers with making slanderous (oral) and libelous (written) statements in job recommendations. During one seven-year period in California, employees won 72 percent of the libel and related suits they brought against employers, and their average award was $582,000. One employer lost for saying an employee had "suddenly resigned," which implied the employee had resigned under "a veil of suspicion," said the court. Another employer lost for saying an employee was fired "for causes." Plus, when employees prove actual malice, damage awards skyrocket.

To complicate matters, a recent court ruling held an employer liable for *omitting* information about a former employee. So what sort of information should or should not be included in a recommendation? Even though some states have passed laws protecting companies against lawsuits when the employer acts in good faith, legal and human resources experts often advise companies to control what's being said by centralizing all recommendations. The cautious approach is to supply only dates of employment and titles of positions held—and to give that information only to people who have written authorization from former employees.

But What If You Want to Give a Recommendation?

Even so, Frank Walker was a terrific employee—a good friend—and you believe he really deserves a recommendation. You have two options. The first is to write the letter with Walker so that the contents satisfy you both and then to discuss the letter with your human resources department before releasing it. The second option is to ask Walker to list you as a *personal* reference, which removes your company from any responsibility for statements you make. But be careful—you can still be held personally responsible for your comments.

Of course, if it had been Sharon Brown who had asked for your recommendation, you'd be facing a different dilemma. Brown wasn't the greatest employee. So would you owe her potential employer the whole story? Including negative information could get you sued by Brown, and omitting negative information could get you sued by the hiring company for "failure to disclose" or "negligent referral."

Regardless of the circumstances, consult your human resources or legal department, and be sure to (1) comment only on your own experience working with a former employee, (2) make all comments in writing, and (3) limit your remarks to provable facts (don't exaggerate).

CAREER APPLICATIONS

1. A former employee was often late for work but was an excellent and fast worker who got along well with everyone. Do you think it's important to mention the tardiness to potential employers? If so, how will you handle it?
2. Step outside yourself for a moment and write a letter of recommendation about you from a former employer's perspective. Practice honesty, integrity, and prudence.

- ◆ Have I put the candidate's case as strongly and honestly as I can?
- ◆ Have I avoided overstating the candidate's abilities or otherwise misleading the reader?
- ◆ Have I based all my statements on firsthand knowledge and provable facts?

Announcing Good News   To develop and maintain good relationships, savvy companies such as Campbell Soup recognize that it's good business to spread the word about positive developments such as opening new facilities, appointing a new executive, introducing new products or services, or sponsoring community events. Because good news is welcome by all, use the direct approach.

About Employment   Writing a letter to the successful job applicant is a pleasure. Such a letter is eagerly awaited, so the direct approach is appropriate:

Welcome to Lake Valley Rehabilitation Center. A number of excellent candidates were interviewed, but your educational background and recent experience at Memorial Hospital make you the best person for the position of medical records coordinator.

← Announces news in a friendly, welcoming tone.

Explains all necessary details.

As we discussed, your salary is $26,200 a year. We would like you to begin on Monday, February 1. Please come to my office at 8:00 a.m. I will give you an in-depth orientation to Lake Valley and discuss the various company benefits available to you. You can also sign all the necessary employment documents.

Explains first day's routine to ease new employee's uncertainty.

After lunch, Vanessa Jackson will take you to the medical records department and help you settle into your new responsibilities at Lake Valley Rehabilitation Center. I look forward to seeing you first thing on February 1.

A letter telling someone that she or he got the job is a legal document, so make sure all statements are accurate.

Although letters like these are pleasant to write, they constitute a legal job offer. You and your company may be held to any promises you make. So attorneys sometimes recommend stating salary as a monthly amount and keeping the timing of performance evaluations and raises vague; you want to avoid implying that the newly hired employee will be kept on, no matter what, for a whole year or until the next scheduled evaluation.[4]

About Products and Operations   A company announcing a new discount program to customers would begin the letter by trumpeting the news. The middle section would fill in the details of the discount program, and the close would include a bit of resale information and a confident prediction of a profitable business relationship.

Specially formatted news releases convey good news to the media, which in turn disseminate it to the public.

However, when the audience for a good-news message is large and scattered, companies often communicate through the mass media. When McDonald's opened its first restaurant in Moscow, it sent announcements to newspapers, magazines, radio stations, and television networks. The specialized documents used to convey such information to the media are called **news releases.** Written to match the style of the medium they are intended for, news releases are typed on plain 8½-by-11-inch paper or on special letterhead (not on regular letterhead). They are double spaced for print media or triple spaced for electronic media.

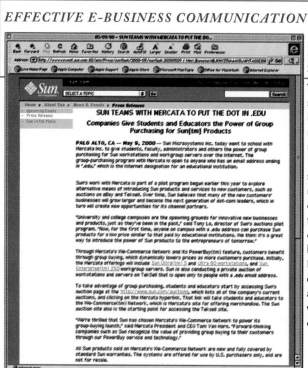

EFFECTIVE E-BUSINESS COMMUNICATION

Links and More Links for Media Use

When you write a positive message such as an online news release, include lots of links so that reporters can get additional information with just a click or two. Printed news releases offer limited space for details, but links in Web releases are a convenient way to direct reporters to online sources for more particulars. However, don't simply tell reporters to "click here" for more information. Instead, follow Sun Microsystem's example (www.sun.com): indicate active links by highlighting specific words, phrases, and URLs with color or underlining.

1. How are you demonstrating a "you" attitude when you include appropriate links in a news release?

2. Do you think reporters reading an online news release will consider multiple links as extraneous clutter? Why?

Figure 7–8
In-Depth Critique: News Release Format

Figure 7–8 illustrates the correct format for print media. The content follows the customary pattern for a good-news message: good news, followed by details and a positive close. However, it avoids explicit references to any reader and displays the "you" attitude by presenting information presumed to be of interest to all readers. To write a successful news release, keep the following points in mind:[5]

◆ Include no marketing or sales material in your news release.

◆ Put your most important idea first (Don't say "Calco's president James Grall announced today that the company will move its headquarters to the Main Street office." Instead, start with the news: "Calco will move its headquarters to the Main Street office, President James Grall announced today.").

◆ Be brief: break up long sentences and keep paragraphs short.

◆ Eliminate clutter such as redundancy and extraneous facts.

◆ Be as specific as possible.

◆ Avoid adjectives and adverbs (understatement goes a long way with the media).

In addition to issuing written news releases, many large companies hold news conferences or create their own videotapes, which are sent to television stations and networks.

Sending Goodwill Messages   You can enhance your relationships with customers, colleagues, and other businesspeople by sending friendly, unexpected notes with no direct business purpose. Jack Welch, former CEO of General Electric, is known for his handwritten notes to all employees, from managers to hourly workers. He once wrote a congratulatory note to one manager who had turned down a promotion because he didn't want to move his teenager to a different school: "Bill," wrote Welch, "we like you for a lot of reasons—one of them is that you are a very special person. You proved it again this morning. Good for you and your lucky family . . ."[6]

Effective goodwill messages must be sincere and honest. Otherwise, the writer appears interested in personal gain rather than in benefiting customers or fellow workers. To come across as sincere, avoid exaggeration and back up any compliments with specific points. In addition, readers often regard more restrained praise as being more sincere:

INSTEAD OF THIS	WRITE THIS
Words cannot express my appreciation for the great job you did. Thanks. No one could have done it better. You're terrific! You've made the whole firm sit up and take notice, and we are ecstatic to have you working here.	Thanks again for taking charge of the meeting in my absence. You did an excellent job. With just an hour's notice, you managed to pull the legal and public relations departments together so that we could present a united front in the negotiations. Your dedication and communication abilities have been noted and are truly appreciated.

Both oral and written messages from organizations can promote good relationships with colleagues, customers, and the community. For example, Ronald McDonald House has become known worldwide as a home away from home for the families of seriously ill children. But when employees of the global office send congratulations, thank-you notes, or condolences to associates inside or outside the organization, they don't boast about all the good their organization accomplishes; they focus on the situation of the person receiving the message.

Congratulations   One prime opportunity for sending goodwill messages is to congratulate someone for a significant business achievement—perhaps for being promoted or for attaining an important civic position. The congratulatory note in Figure 7–9 moves swiftly to the subject: the good news. It gives reasons for expecting success and avoids extravagances such as "Only you can do the job!"

Other reasons for sending congratulations include the highlights in people's personal lives—weddings, births, graduations, success in nonbusiness competitions. You may congratulate business acquaintances on their own achievements or on the accomplishments of a spouse or child. You may also take note of personal events, even if you don't know the reader well. Of course, if you're already friendly with the reader, you can get away with a more personal tone.

Some companies even develop a mailing list of potential customers by assigning an employee to clip newspaper announcements of births, engagements, weddings, and graduations or to obtain information on real estate transactions in the local community. Then they introduce themselves by sending out a form letter that might read like this:

Congratulations on your new home! Our wish is that it brings you much happiness.

To help you commemorate the occasion, we've enclosed a key chain with your new address engraved on the leather tab. Please accept this with our best wishes.

In this case, the company's letterhead and address are enough of a sales pitch. This simple message has a natural, friendly tone, even though the sender has never met the recipient.

1 Planning

Analyze: Purpose is to create goodwill with industry business associates.

Investigate: Gather information on specific accomplishments of the reader's firm.

Adapt: A letter format lets reader use your message (perhaps reproduce it) as an industry testimonial.

2 Writing

Organize: Main idea is to congratulate the reader. The direct approach is perfect for this welcome news.

Compose: A conversational tone compliments the slightly formal style, since this is your first contact with the reader. Avoid generalized praise by mentioning specific, concrete accomplishments.

3 Completing

Revise: Review for consistency in tone, word choice, and sentence structure.

Produce: A simple design avoids distracting your reader from the message.

Proofread: Create a positive first impression by being especially careful to send an error free message.

Office DEPOT, Inc.

2200 Old Germantown Road, Delray Beach, FL 33445   407/278-4800

March 3, 2002

Mr. Ralph Lambert, President
Lambert, Cutchen & Browt, Inc.
14355 Pasadena Parkway
Pasadena, TX 74229

Dear Mr. Lambert:

Congratulations on your firm's recent selection to design and print media advertisements for the National Association of Business Suppliers (ABS). We learned of your success at our convention in Atlanta last month.

We have long believed that the success of individual franchises is directly linked to the healthy growth of the industry at large. We can think of no better firm to help our industry achieve wide recognition than Lambert, Cutchen & Browt.

We have admired your success in promoting associations of other industries such as soft drinks, snack foods, and recycling. Your "Dream Vision 2001" ads for the bottling industry were both inspirational and effective in raising consumer awareness, and we look for similar positive responses to your ABS campaign.

Again, accept our warm congratulations. We look forward to seeing the results of the survey you conducted during our convention. And we will follow your media campaign with great interest.

Sincerely,

Janice McCarthy

Janice McCarthy
Director, Media Relations

tw

Body makes compliment more effective by showing knowledge of the reader's work.

Close includes a personal note of congratulations.

Opening immediately expresses the reason for congratulating the reader.

Close also expresses interest in following the future success of the firm.

Figure 7–9
In-Depth Critique: Letter Congratulating a Business Acquaintance

A message of appreciation documents a person's contributions.

Messages of Appreciation An important business quality is the ability to recognize the contributions of employees, colleagues, suppliers, and other associates. Your praise doesn't just make the person feel good; it also encourages further excellence. Moreover, a message of appreciation may become an important part of someone's personnel file. So when you write a message of appreciation, try to specifically mention the person or people you want to praise. The brief message that follows expresses gratitude and reveals the happy result:

Thank you for sending the air-conditioning components via overnight delivery. You allowed us to satisfy the needs of two customers who were getting very impatient with the heat.

Special thanks to Susan Brown, who took our initial call and never said, "It can't be done." Her initiative on our behalf is greatly appreciated.

Condolences In times of serious trouble and deep sadness, written condolences and expressions of sympathy leave their mark. Granted, this type of message is difficult to write, but don't let the difficulty of the task keep you from responding promptly. Those who have experienced a health problem, the death of a loved one, or a business misfortune like to know that they're not alone.

Begin condolences with a brief statement of sympathy, such as "I was deeply sorry to hear of your loss." In the middle, mention the good qualities or the positive contributions made by the deceased. State what the person or business meant to you. In closing, you can offer your condolences and your best wishes. One considerate way to end this type of message is to say something that will give the reader a little lift, such as a reference to a brighter future. Here are a few general suggestions for writing condolence messages:

In condolence messages, try to find a middle path between being superficial and causing additional distress.

◆ **Keep reminiscences brief.** Recount a memory or an anecdote (even a humorous one), but don't dwell on the details of the loss, lest you add to the reader's anguish.

◆ **Write in your own words.** Write as if you were speaking privately to the person. Don't quote "poetic" passages or use stilted or formal phrases. If the loss is a death, refer to it as such rather than as "passing away" or "departing."

◆ **Be tactful.** Mention your shock and dismay, but remember that bereaved and distressed loved ones take little comfort in lines such as, "Richard was too young to die" or "Starting all over again will be so difficult." Try to strike a balance between superficial expressions of sympathy and heart-rending references to a happier past or the likelihood of a bleak future.

◆ **Take special care.** Be sure to spell names correctly and to be accurate in your review of facts. Try to be prompt.

◆ **Write about special qualities of the deceased.** You may have to rely on reputation to do this, but let the grieving person know you valued his or her loved one.

◆ **Write about special qualities of the bereaved person.** A pat on the back helps a bereaved family member feel more confident about handling things during such a traumatic time.[7]

Supervisor George Bigalow sent the following condolence letter to his administrative assistant, Janice Case, after learning of the death of Janice's husband:

My sympathy to you and your children. All your friends at Carter Electric were so very sorry to learn of John's death. Although I never had the opportunity to meet him, I do know how very special he was to you. Your tales of your family's camping trips and his rafting expeditions were always memorable.

To review the tasks involved in writing goodwill messages, see the "Checklist: Granting Claims and Adjustment Requests, and Sending Goodwill Messages."

SUMMARY OF LEARNING OBJECTIVES

1 Apply the three-step writing process to routine positive messages. Even though routine messages are usually short and simple, they benefit from the three-step writing process. Planning routine messages may take only a few moments to (1) analyze your purpose and audience, (2) investigate your readers' needs and make sure that you have all the facts to satisfy them, and (3) adapt your message through your *choice* of medium and your "you" attitude. When writing routine messages, use the direct approach, as long as your readers will be positive (or neutral) and have minimal cultural differences. Completing routine messages means making them as professional as possible by (1) revising for clarity and conciseness; (2) selecting appropriate design elements and delivery methods; and (3) careful proofreading.

2 Illustrate the strategy for writing routine requests. When writing a routine request, open by stating your specific request. At the same time, avoid being abrupt or tactless: pay attention to tone, assume your audience will comply, avoid personal introductions, end polite requests with a period, and be specific. Use the middle of a routine request to justify your request and explain its importance. Close routine requests by asking for specific action (including a deadline as often as possible), and expressing goodwill. Be sure to include all contact information so that your reader can respond easily.

3 Discuss the differences among four types of routine requests. Each type of routine request has distinguishing features. All start with a statement of the main idea. But when placing orders, the body includes columns for product information, just like any good order blank. The close includes the delivery address, the preferred method of shipment, and information about any enclosed payment. When the request is for information or action, the middle explains or justifies your request and the close specifies what you need and when you need it. When the message is a claim or request for an adjustment, the middle includes whatever facts your reader needs to verify your complaint. The close requests a specific solution or conveys a sincere desire to find one, and it suggests that future business depends on a satisfactory resolution. In a request for a recommendation, the opening states the position or award being applied for and, if necessary, recalls the nature and dates of your relationship with the reader. The middle refers to your résumé or includes information that would support a recommendation, and the appreciative close includes the name and address of the person to whom the recommendation will be sent.

4 Explain the main differences in messages granting a claim when the company, the customer, or a third party is at fault. In messages granting a claim, the explanatory section differs, depending on who is at fault. If your company is at fault, avoid reacting defensively, and be careful when referring to company errors. Rather than placing blame, explain your company's efforts to do a good job. Remember not to make any unrealistic promises or guarantees. If your customer is at fault, you must help your reader realize what went wrong so that it won't happen again and again. However, you don't want to sound condescending, preachy, or insulting. If a third party is at fault, you can honor the claim with no explanation, or you can honor the claim and explain that the problem was not your fault.

5 Outline how best to protect yourself when referring to a candidate's shortcoming in a recommendation letter. When you find that you must refer to a candidate's shortcoming, stick to the facts. Try to give your criticism in the context of a generally favorable recommendation. Also ask yourself the following questions: Does the person receiving this personal information have a legitimate right to it? Does all the information I've presented relate directly to the job/benefit being sought? Have I put the candidate's case as strongly and as I honestly can? Have I avoided overstating the candidate's abilities or otherwise misleading the reader? Have I based all my statements on firsthand knowledge and provable facts?

6 Clarify the importance of goodwill messages, and describe how to make them effective. Goodwill messages are important for building relationships with customers, colleagues, and other businesspeople. These friendly, unexpected notes have no direct business purpose, but they make people feel good about doing business with the sender. To make goodwill messages effective, be honest and sincere. Avoid exaggerating, back up compliments with specific points, and give restrained praise.

SOLVING A COMMUNICATION DILEMMA AT CAMPBELL SOUP COMPANY

Campbell Soup continued its solid performance throughout the 1990s by matching products to local and regional tastes and by carefully choosing acquisitions. For example, Germany and France are two of the largest soup-consuming markets in the world (the French consume four times as much soup per capita as people in the United States do), and Campbell made major acquisitions in both countries. The company barely turned a profit in 1990 but earned more than $800 million in 1996 (on sales of $7.7 billion).

With growth come more customers, of course, and more customers mean more questions for consumer response supervisor Karen Donohue. Whenever people write, phone, or send e-mail,

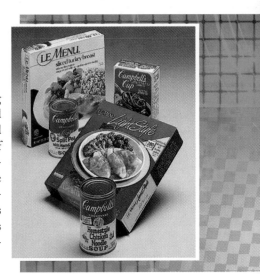

she's in charge of making sure their questions and complaints are answered satisfactorily. Many of these questions are routine and repetitive ("What are the more popular flavors of Campbell's Soup?"), but many others require special, personalized replies.

Like so many other companies these days, Campbell uses the World Wide Web as a two-way communication vehicle between the company and its customers. The company's homepage provides links to recipes, financial and investment news, educational support programs, and an online store, as well as to Donohue's consumer response center. Donohue answers some of the most frequently asked questions (for example: How many Os are in a 15-ounce can of Spaghetti-Os? Answer: 1,750) and invites consumers to e-mail other questions and comments. Consumers who wish to speak with a Campbell representative instead of sending e-mail can call a toll-free number listed on-screen.

Not surprisingly, Karen Donohue plays a major role in Campbell's efforts to better meet the needs of its millions of customers worldwide. Whether she's responding to dissatisfied customers or answering simple requests for information, Donohue is in a position to help satisfy consumers while gaining important insights into their needs and purchase behaviors. As Campbell moves into the next century, Donohue will be communicating with consumers and employees to make sure the giant food producer keeps sales and profits cooking.

Your Mission You have joined Campbell's consumer marketing staff. As an assistant to Karen Donohue, you are responsible for handling correspondence with consumers and with Campbell employees. Your objective is to improve the flow of communication between the public and the company so that Campbell can respond quickly and knowledgeably to changing consumer needs. Choose the best alternatives for responding to the situations described below and be prepared to explain why your choice is best:

1. Donohue has received a letter from a Mrs. Felton who is pleased that Campbell offers a line of Healthy Request reduced-sodium soups but would like to see more flavors added. Which of the following is the best opening paragraph for your reply?

   a. The Campbell Soup Company was founded in 1869 in Camden, New Jersey. The Dorrance family took control from the founders in 1894. At the turn of the century, John Dorrance invented the soup condensation process, which enabled the company to sell a 10-ounce can for a dime. He was a conservative man and a stickler for quality. His only son, the late Jack Dorrance, followed his father into the business and had a similar management philosophy. As chairman of the company, he used to pinch the tomatoes and taste the carrots occasionally to be sure that the folks in the factory were maintaining high standards. Mr. Dorrance took personal interest in the development of the low-salt line and would be pleased to know that it appeals to you.

   b. Thank you for your enthusiastic letter about Campbell's Healthy Request soups. We are delighted that you enjoy the flavors currently available, and we are working hard to add new varieties to the line.

   c. Good news! Our world-renowned staff of food technologists is busy in the test kitchen at this very moment, experimenting with additional low-sodium recipes for Healthy Request soups. Hang on to your bowl, Mrs. Felton, more flavors are on the way!

2. Which of the following versions is preferable for the body of the letter to Mrs. Felton?

   a. You can expect to see several exciting new Healthy Request soups on your supermarket shelf within the next year. Before the new flavors make their debut, however, they must undergo further testing in our kitchens and in selected markets across the country. We want to be sure our soups satisfy consumer expectations.

      While you're waiting for the new flavors of Healthy Request, you might like to try some of Campbell's other products designed especially for people like you who are concerned about health and nutrition. I'm enclosing coupons that entitle you to sample both Pepperidge Farm Five-Star Fibre bread and Pace picante sauce "on the house." We hope you enjoy them.

   b. We are sorry that the number of Healthy Request flavors is limited at this time. Because of the complexities of testing flavors both in the Campbell kitchens and in test markets around the country, we are a bit behind schedule in releasing new varieties. But several new flavors should be available by the end of the year, if all goes according to plan.

      In the meantime, please accept these coupons; they can be redeemed for two other fine Campbell products designed for the health-conscious consumer.

   c. Additional flavors of Healthy Request reduced-sodium soups are currently in formulation. They will arrive on supermarket shelves soon. In the meantime, why not enjoy some of Campbell's other fine products designed for the health-conscious consumer? The enclosed coupons will allow you to sample Pace picante sauce and Pepperidge Farm Five-Star Fibre bread at our expense.

3. Campbell has received a letter from the American Heart Association asking for information on the fat and sodium content of Campbell's products. Your department has developed a brochure that provides the necessary data, and you plan to send it to the association. Which of the following cover letters should you send along with the brochure?

   a. Please consult the enclosed brochure for answers to your questions regarding the composition of Campbell's products. The brochure provides detailed information on sodium and fat content of all Campbell's products, which include such well-known brands such as V-8, Pepperidge Farm, and Franco-American, as well as Campbell's Soups.

   b. Thanks for your interest in Campbell's products. We are concerned about nutrition and health issues and are trying to reduce the salts and fats in our products. At the same time, we are striving to retain the taste that consumers have come to expect from Campbell. In general, we feel very good about the nutritional value of our products and think that after you read the enclosed brochure, you will too.

   c. Thank you for your interest in Campbell's Soup. The enclosed brochure provides the information you requested about the fat and sodium content of our products. Over the past 10 years, we have introduced a number of reduced-sodium and low-fat products designed specifically for consumers on restricted diets. In addition, we've reformulated many of our regular products to reduce the salt and fat content. We have also revised our product labels so that information on sodium and fat content is readily apparent to health-conscious consumers. If you have any questions about our products, please contact our consumer information specialists at 1-800-227-9876.

4. Campbell has received a letter from a disgruntled consumer, Mr. Max Edwards, who was disappointed with his last can of Golden Classic beef soup with potatoes and mushrooms. It appears that the can contained an abundance of potatoes, little beef, and few mushrooms. You have been asked to reply to Mr. Edwards. Which of the following drafts is best?

    a. We are extremely sorry that you did not like your last can of Golden Classic beef soup with potatoes and mushrooms. Although we do our very best to ensure that all our products are of the highest quality, occasionally our quality-control department slips up and a can of soup comes out a bit short on one ingredient or another. Apparently you happened to buy just such a can—one with relatively few mushrooms, not much beef, and too many potatoes. The odds against that ever happening to you again are probably a million to one. And to prove it, here's a coupon that entitles you to a free can of Golden Classic soup. You may pick any flavor you like, but why not give the beef with potatoes and mushrooms another try? We bet it will meet your standards this time around.

    b. You are right, Mr. Edwards, to expect the highest quality from Campbell's Golden Classic soups. And you are right to complain when your expectations are not met. Our goal is to provide the best, and when we fall short of that goal, we want to know about it so that we can correct the problem.

    And that is exactly what we have done. In response to your complaint, our quality-control department is reexamining its testing procedures to ensure that all future cans of Golden Classic soup have an even blend of ingredients. Why not see for yourself by taking the enclosed coupon to your supermarket and redeeming it for a free can of Golden Classic soup? If you choose beef with potatoes and mushrooms, you can count on getting plenty of beef and mushrooms this time.

    c. Campbell's Golden Classic soups are a premium product at a premium price. Our quality-control procedures for this line have been carefully devised to ensure that every can of soup has a uniform distribution of ingredients. As you can imagine, your complaint came as quite a surprise to us, given the care that we take with our products. We suspect that the uneven distribution of ingredients was just a fluke, but our quality-control department is looking into the matter to ensure that the alleged problem does not recur.

    We would like you to give our Golden Classic soup another try. We are confident that you will be satisfied, so we are enclosing a coupon that entitles you to a free can. If you are not completely happy with it, please call me at 1-800-227-9876.[8]

TEST YOUR KNOWLEDGE

1. Should you use the direct or indirect approach for most routine messages? Why?

2. Where in a routine message should you state your actual request?

3. How does the question of fault affect what you say in a message granting a claim?

4. What is the appropriate strategy for responding to a request for a recommendation about a job candidate whose performance was poor?

5. When is a request routine?

6. What are some of the guidelines for asking a series of questions in a routine request?

7. What information should be included in an order request?

8. How does a claim differ from an adjustment?

9. How can you avoid sounding insincere when writing a goodwill message?

10. What are some of the guidelines for writing condolence messages?

INTERACTIVE LEARNING

USE THIS TEXT'S ONLINE RESOURCES

Visit the myPHLIP Web site at www.prenhall.com/thill. For Chapter 7, take advantage of the interactive "Study Guide" to test your chapter knowledge. Get instant feedback on whether you need additional studying. Read the "Current Events" articles to get the latest on chapter topics, and complete the exercises as specified by your instructor.

This site's "Study Hall" helps you succeed in this course. "Talk in the Hall" lets you leave messages and meet new friends online. If you have a question, you can "Ask the Tutor." And to get a better grade in this course, you can find more help at "Writing Skills," "Study Skills," and "Study Tips."

The "Research Area" helps you locate a wealth of information to use in course assignments. Plus, you can send a message to online research experts, who will help you find exactly the information you need.

APPLY YOUR KNOWLEDGE

1. When organizing your requests, why is it important to know whether any cultural differences exist between you and your audience? Explain.

2. Your company's error cost an important business customer a new client; you know it and your customer knows it. Do you apologize or do you refer to the incident in a positive light without admitting any responsibility? Briefly explain.

3. You've been asked to write a letter of recommendation for an employee who is disabled and uses a wheelchair. The disability has no effect on the employee's ability to do the job, and you feel confident about writing the best recommendation possible. Nevertheless, you know the prospective company and its facilities aren't well suited to wheelchair access. Do you mention the employee's disability in your letter? Explain.

4. Every time you send a direct-request memo to Ted Jackson, he delays or refuses to comply. You're beginning to get impatient. Should you send Jackson a memo to ask what's wrong? Complain to your supervisor about Jackson's uncooperative attitude? Arrange a face-to-face meeting with Jackson? Bring up the problem at the next staff meeting? Explain.

5. **Ethical Choices** You have a complaint against one of your suppliers, but you have no documentation to back it up. Should you request an adjustment anyway? Why or why not?

PRACTICE YOUR KNOWLEDGE

DOCUMENTS FOR ANALYSIS

Read the following documents; then (1) analyze the strengths and weaknesses of each sentence and (2) revise each document so that it follows this chapter's guidelines.

Document 7.A: Requesting Routine Information from a Business

Our college is closing its dining hall for financial reasons, so we want to do something to help the students prepare their own food in their dorm rooms if they so choose. Your colorful ad in *Collegiate Magazine* caught our eye. We need the following information before we make our decision.

1. Would you be able to ship the microwaves by August 15th? I realize this is short notice, but our board of trustees just made the decision to close the dining hall last week and we're scrambling around trying to figure out what to do.
2. Do they have any kind of a warranty? College students can be pretty hard on things, as you know, so we will need a good warranty.
3. How much does it cost? Do you give a discount for a big order?
4. Do we have to provide a special outlet?
5. Will students know how to use them, or will we need to provide instructions?

As I said before, we're on a tight time frame and need good information from you as soon as possible to help us make our decision about ordering. You never know what the board might come up with next. I'm looking at several other companies, also, so please let us know ASAP.

Document 7.B: Making Claims and Requests for Adjustment

At a local business-supply store, I recently purchased your "Negotiator Pro" for my computer. I bought the CD because I saw your ad for it in *MacWorld* magazine, and it looked as if it might be an effective tool for use in my corporate seminar on negotiation.

Unfortunately, when I inserted it in my office computer, it wouldn't work. I returned it to the store, but since I had already opened it, they refused to exchange it for a CD that would work or give me a refund. They told me to contact you and that you might be able to send me a version that would work with my computer.

You can send the information to me at the letterhead address. If you cannot send me the correct disk, please refund my $79.95. Thanks in advance for any help you can give me in this matter.

Document 7.C: Responding to Claims and Adjustment Requests When the Customer Is at Fault

We read your letter requesting your deposit refund. We couldn't figure out why you hadn't received it, so we talked to our maintenance engineer as you suggested. He said you had left one of the doors off the hinges in your apartment in order to get a large sofa through the door. He also confirmed that you had paid him $5.00 to replace the door since you had to turn in the U-Haul trailer and were in a big hurry.

This entire situation really was caused by a lack of communication between our housekeeping inspector and the maintenance engineer. All we knew was that the door was off the hinges when it was inspected by Sally Tarnley. You know that our policy states that if anything is wrong with the apartment, we keep the deposit. We had no way of knowing that George just hadn't gotten around to replacing the door.

But we have good news. We approved the deposit refund, which will be mailed to you from our home office in Teaneck, New Jersey. I'm not sure how long that will take, however. If you don't receive the check by the end of next month, give me a call.

Next time, it's really a good idea to stay with your apartment until it's inspected as stipulated in your lease agreement. That way, you'll be sure to receive your refund when you expect it. Hope you have a good summer.

Document 7.D: Letter of Recommendation

Your letter to Tanaka Asata, President of SONY, was forwarded to me because I am the human resources director. In my job as head of HR, I have access to performance reviews for all of the SONY employees in the United States. This means, of course, that

I would be the person best qualified to answer your request for information on Nick Oshinski.

In your letter of the 15th, you asked about Nick Oshinski's employment record with us because he has applied to work for your company. Mr. Oshinski was employed with us from January 5, 1992 until March 1, 1997. During that time, Mr. Oshinski received ratings ranging from 2.5 up to 9.6 with 10 being the top score. As you can see, he must have done better reporting to some managers than to others. In addition, he took all vacation days, which is a bit unusual. Although I did not know Mr. Oshinski personally, I know that our best workers seldom use all the vacation time they earn. I do not know if that applies in this case.

In summary, Nick Oshinski performed his tasks well depending on who managed him.

EXERCISES

7–1. Revise the following short e-mail messages so that they are more direct and concise; develop a subject line for each revised message.

a. I'm contacting you about your recent order for a High Country backpack. You didn't tell us which backpack you wanted, and you know we make a lot of different ones. We have the canvas models with the plastic frames and vinyl trim and we have the canvas models with leather trim, and we have the ones that have more pockets than the other ones. Plus they come in lots of different colors. Also they make the ones that are large for a big-boned person and the smaller versions for little women or kids.

b. Thank you for contacting us about the difficulty you had collecting your luggage at the Denver airport. We are very sorry for the inconvenience this has caused you. As you know, traveling can create problems of this sort regardless of how careful the airline personnel might be. To receive compensation, please send us a detailed list of the items that you lost and complete the following questionnaire. You can e-mail it back to us.

c. Sorry it took us so long to get back to you. We were flooded with résumés. Anyway, your résumé made the final ten, and after meeting three hours yesterday, we've decided we'd like to meet with you. What is your schedule like for next week? Can you come in for an interview on June 15 at 3:00 p.m? Please get back to us by the end of this work week and let us know if you will be able to attend. As you can imagine, this is our busy season.

d. We're letting you know that because we use over a ton of paper a year and because so much of that paper goes into the wastebasket to become so much more environmental waste, starting Monday, we're placing white plastic bins outside the elevators on every floor to recycle that paper and in the process, minimize pollution.

7–2. Rewrite the following sentences so that they are direct and concise.

a. We wanted to invite you to our special 40% off by-invitation-only sale. The sale is taking place on November 9.

b. We wanted to let you know that we are giving a tote bag and a free Phish CD with every $50 donation you make to our radio station.

c. The director planned to go to the meeting that will be held on Monday at a little before 11:00 a.m.

d. In today's meeting, we were happy to have the opportunity to welcome Paul Eccelson. He reviewed some of the newest types of order forms. If you have any questions about these new forms, feel free to call him at his office.

7–3. **Internet** Visit the business section of the Blue Mountain site at www.bluemountain.com/eng3/business/and analyze one of the electronic greeting cards bearing a goodwill message of appreciation for good performance. Under what circumstances would you send this electronic message? How could you personalize it for the recipient and the occasion? What would be an appropriate close for this message?

7–4. **Teamwork** With another student, identify the purpose and select the most appropriate format for communicating these written messages. Next, consider how the audience is likely to respond to each message. Based on this audience analysis, determine whether the direct or indirect approach would be effective for each message, and explain your reasoning.

a. A notice to all employees about the placement of recycling bins by the elevator doors

b. The first late-payment notice to a good customer who usually pays his bills on time

7–5. Critique the following closing paragraphs. How would you rewrite each to be concise, courteous, and specific?

a. I need your response sometime soon so I can order the parts in time for your service appointment. Otherwise your air conditioning system may not be in tip-top condition for the start of the summer season.

b. Thank you in advance for sending me as much information as you can about your products. I look forward to receiving your package in the very near future.

c. To schedule an appointment with one of our knowledgeable mortgage specialists in your area, you can always call our hotline at 1-800-555-8765. This is also the number to call if you have more questions about mortgage rates, closing procedures, or any other aspect of the mortgage process. Remember, we're here to make the home-buying experience as painless as possible.

7–6. **Ethical Choices** Your small supermarket chain has received dozens of complaints about the watery consistency of the ketchup sold under the chain's brand name. You don't want your customers to stop buying other store-brand foods, which are made and packaged for your chain by various suppliers, but you do want to address their concerns about the ketchup. In responding to these complaints, should you explain that the ketchup is actually manufactured by a local supplier and then name the supplier, who has already started bottling a thicker ketchup?

CASES

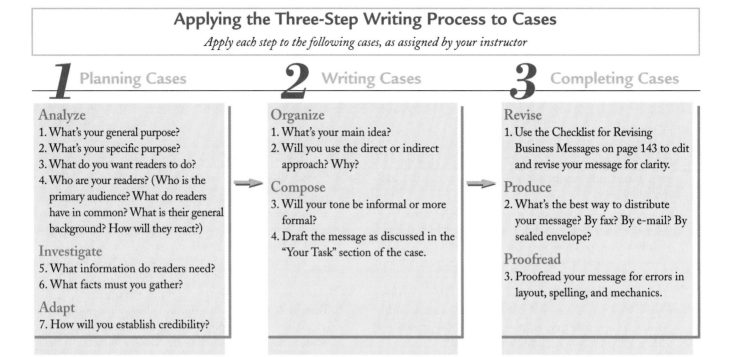

ROUTINE REQUESTS

1. Canary cam: E-mail order across the border When you bought your first canary, you had no inkling the little guy might lead you to a new job. You put "Sam" in your bedroom, feeding him the seed you gave your parakeet when you were a kid. Almost immediately, Sam stopped singing and flumped down on his perch, looking miserable. You were worried, so you turned to the Internet to find help.

First you found the Canary List users group. Mostly breeders with large flocks to tend, they nevertheless directed you to Canadian "Robirda" McDonald, owner of www.robirda.com, Web home of the Canary Cam, *Flock Talk* e-zine, and the Birds Board. At robirda.com, no question is too trivial for Robirda's personal attention. You quickly discovered why some call her the "Canary Godmother."

With her special combination of TLC and straight-shooting education, Robirda had Fluffy perked up in no time and you out in the kitchen chopping greens, grating carrots, and baking "birdie muffins." Sam has now taken over your bedroom, where you've installed a larger cage, a full-spectrum light that keeps pace with sunrise and sunset, and a radio to keep Sam company when you're gone. But he's rewarding you. He warbles opera with Andrea Bocelli and chirps along with Garth Brooks, changing keys and matching rhythms as if he were reading a score. Truly amazing.

Feeling grateful, you wrote to ask Robirda how you could help her campaign to save canaries from ignorant owners and thoughtless breeders. She put you to work answering e-mail—mostly directing worried new owners to information on her site and responding to the schoolchildren who enjoy visiting the live Canary Cam to watch canary moms and dads hatching chicks in Robirda's bird room.

Today, the good news is that Robirda's applied for status as a Canadian nonprofit educational society, and you might be her first employee! The bad news is that her local supplier went out of business, and she urgently needs 50 pounds each of canary 80/20 seed mix and soak seed. She sent you e-mail, "Can you help me find a new source?" with a reminder, "One that will ship grains to Canada?"

Your task: You've located Herman Brothers Pet Products in Detroit, and their Web address is www.hermanbros-seed.com. The company has assured you it can legally ship across the border, and president Richard Herman (rcherman@ddc.com) asks you to e-mail him the complete order so that he can calculate shipping charges. His site lists the 80/20 canary seed mix at $15.45 for 50 lbs. The soak seed is $20.25. Seeds need to be shipped to Roberta C. McDonald, 1725 E. 3rd Avenue, Vancouver, BC, V5M-5R6.[9]

2. Blockbuster shake-up: Memo requesting info from retail managers Everyone knew there was trouble at Blockbuster's new headquarters in Dallas when CEO Bill Fields, a former Wal-Mart whiz, suddenly resigned. Then Sumner Redstone and Tom Dooley (chairman and deputy chairman of Blockbuster's parent company, Viacom) flew in to assess the damage wrought by Fields's departure. They started by giving orders—particularly to you, Fields's former executive assistant.

Before Fields resigned to take a position with Hudson's Bay Company, in Canada, his strategy had been to boost Blockbuster's sagging video rentals by establishing a new niche as a "neighborhood entertainment center." Using tricks he'd learned at Wal-Mart, he ordered the reconfiguration of more than 1,000 Blockbuster outlets, surrounding the cash registers with flashy displays of candy, potato chips, new and used videotapes for sale, magazines, and tie-in toys. His stated goal was to add $1 in retail purchases to every rental transaction. Meanwhile, he also relocated Blockbuster's headquarters from Florida to Dallas, losing 75 percent of the company's top staff when they declined to make the move. Then, Fields initiated the construction of an 818,000-square-foot warehouse 25 miles outside Dallas to centralize a new, highly sophisticated distribution operation (Fields's special expertise) for Blockbuster's 3,600 North American outlets. But revenues were still falling.

Redstone and Dooley's new plan is to get Blockbuster back into its core business—video rentals—ignoring gloomy analysts who say satellite dishes and cheap tape sales are slowly sinking the rental industry. "This is still a healthy, growing business," Dooley insists. He believes that consumers coming in to rent videos were confused by the array of retail products that greeted them. "We want people to think of Blockbuster as the place to go to rent tapes," he says.

Dooley and Redstone have been hiring new headquarters staff at the rate of about 50 people per week; they've been to the warehouse construction site; they've ordered outlets to rearrange merchandise to emphasize tape rentals; and now they've turned to you. "We've got a job you'll love," Dooley smiles. "We know you can handle it."

Your task: Briefly state the purpose of your message. Then draft a memo that will pick the brains of retail managers in the stores that Fields reconfigured. Dooley wants to know whether customers walk out when current hits aren't available, whether the emphasis on retail products affected cash flow, and whether sales and rental figures have changed now that the clutter has been removed. Ask them: Where's the cash coming from—tape rentals, tape sales, or candy bars? Dooley says, "I want a full report from every manager by the end of next week!" To get that kind of cooperation, you'd better organize your questions effectively.[10]

3. Training is murder: Letter to Norwest Banks requesting information on Red Herring mystery troupe As a sales training manager for Jarvis Office Products in Denver, you've tried just about everything to get your sales reps' attention during train-

ing seminars. Usually their eyes glaze over within the first hour. After a seminar, sales figures rise slightly for a while; then they slump back to the normal average. This year you're determined to try something new.

Recently, a friend of yours mentioned an idea that's so outlandish, it might work. She'd heard of a theatrical troupe in Colorado Springs, Red Herring Productions, that performs murder mysteries for company seminars, helping management put points across with a certain unforgettable "zing." They call this "pointimation," your friend said. She thought their Web address was something like "Red Herring Productions-dot-com."

Turns out she was right. The approach looks promising. Cast members show up in character to schmooze with your participants for a while. Then they hook them with a staged murder and a subsequent team organization to decipher clues and solve the "whodunnit" mystery.

The company writes its own scripts, everything from the Wild West "Murder at the Buffalo Chip," with gunslingers, church ladies, and gamblers, to the Rockin' '50s "Murder on Location" of a movie set. "The CEO Murder" sounds a little too close to home, but surely something like "Invaded by Murder," with an alien landing in the middle of your meeting, would wake up your staff!

You click to the "Red Herring Educational Services Products" page and discover a special-purpose mystery on "Selling to Your Client's View of the World." It promises to cover nine common client personality types. Another click and you find a list of Red Herring's customers and some testimonials: "You made me look great as a meeting planner . . ."; "It was a roaring success . . ."; "I haven't laughed so hard in a long time. The performers stayed in character all day! I didn't want to stop; not even for breaks!"

That one, from a meeting planner at Norwest Banks, is the one that gets you. You try to imagine your cynical sales pros being that captivated by *anything*.

Your task: Write a letter to the meeting planning department (no name is given) at Norwest Banks (887 Dove Creek Drive, Colorado Springs, CO 80901), asking for comments on Red Herring's services. You don't want to look like a fool; after all, once Lizzie the gun moll comes swaggering into your meeting room, there'll be no turning back![11]

4. Please tell me: Letter requesting routine information about a product As a consumer, you've probably seen hundreds of products that you'd like to buy (if you haven't, look at the advertisements in your favorite magazine for ideas). Choose a big-ticket item that is rather complicated, such as a stereo system or a vacation in the Caribbean.

Your task: You surely have some questions about the features of your chosen product or about its price, guarantees, local availability, and so on. Write to the company or organization that's offering it, and ask four questions that are important to you. Be sure to include enough background information that the reader can answer your questions satisfactorily.

If requested to do so by your instructor, mail a copy of your letter (after your instructor has had an opportunity to review it) to the company or organization. After a few weeks, you and your classmates may wish to compare responses and to answer this question: How well do companies or organizations respond to unsolicited inquiries?

5. Air rage fiasco: Letter requesting refund from British Airways "There we were, cruising over the Atlantic, and the guy just went berserk! I couldn't believe it!" Samantha Alberts, vice president of sales at Richter Office Solutions, is standing over your desk, describing the scene for you. You notice that your boss is still pale and shaky, even though it's Monday and the "incident" happened last Friday.

She was flying back from a conference in London to make a presentation at your New York branch, before heading back home to San Francisco on Saturday. She admits it was a crushing schedule and probably foolish to plan to prepare her notes on the plane, but she never expected this.

"So how did it start?" you ask mildly, hoping your calm will help steady her nerves. She's got another meeting in two hours.

"Well, I didn't notice anything until this guy leaped up and lunged for the flight attendant with both fists flailing. But later I heard that he'd been viewing 'offensive images' on his laptop and that other passengers complained that they could see the screen. When the steward politely asked him to stop, the guy went nuts! He was a stocky, red-faced, bull-necked guy, and it took six crew members to handcuff him and strap him into a back-row seat. Maybe he was drunk or on drugs, I don't know, but he just kept screaming, 'I'm going to kill you!' and hitting people with his head, which was bleeding everywhere.

"Finally a passenger who was a pediatrician came forward and offered to inject the guy with a sedative for the rest of the flight. Thank goodness. Otherwise we would've been listening to his profanity for the next 10 hours . . ." she trails off. "You know, I thought he was a hijacker and I was going to die on that plane."

You pat her soothingly. "So did they arrest him?"

"As soon as we got on the ground. Police cars were everywhere. He just kept mumbling, 'I thought they were going to kill me.'" She shudders. "But the flight attendants and airline officials were wonderful. They told us to write to the airline, explain the details, and ask for a refund. Of course, I was late and unprepared for my meeting. Thank goodness it wasn't a client! When they heard about my 'air rage' encounter, the folks in our home office just handed me a cup of strong coffee and sat me on a couch with a blanket."

Your task: You always handle Samantha's travel arrangements, and she's left you with her ticket stubs and other documents. Write the letter requesting a refund to British Airways Ticket Refunds USA, 75-20 Astoria Blvd., Jackson Heights, NY 11370. (Make up any necessary times, dates, or flight numbers.)[12]

6. Reverse migration: Letter requesting letter of recommendation for "dot-com" dropout You really wanted to join the so-called "Great Migration" of executive talent to online companies. You'd seen colleagues become overnight millionaires by abandoning their jobs at big companies and plunging into the world of Internet commerce. Employee stock options and inflated IPOs offered a lure they couldn't resist, and neither could you. So

you contacted Michele James, a head-hunter specializing in finding executives for online start-ups. James went to work and quickly landed you a lucrative offer at a well-funded "dot-com" company in your industry (travel services). You took it.

The first week as Creative Services Director wasn't so bad. You learned tons of new things and adapted readily to the seat-of-the-pants work style. You discovered with delight that at your new company, creativity and vision weren't considered terrifying traits of overachievers who had to be kept on a short leash; instead, these traits were cultivated prerequisites. The more "out there" your ideas, the more attention they merited. That's because e-business moves fast and everybody needs to move fast with it.

You just didn't realize how long and how often you'd be expected to keep moving. That first week was only 50 hours. The second was 60. By the third week, 70 hours wasn't considered outlandish. Anyone who went home before 7 p.m. or who didn't show up on Saturday or Sunday was considered a loser and quickly disappeared from your workscape.

Your spouse was soon complaining about not recognizing you any more; your children told people at school functions that you were in the hospital; and you couldn't remember the last time you ate a meal without a computer screen, cell phone, or beeper a few inches from your plate. You love the fast decision making, and your CEO loves your exemplary work, but you are exhausted. One day, you pick up your briefcase and leave at 5 p.m. Horror registers on the few faces that lift to see you go. Then their weary eyes shift back to their computer screens.

Money is nice, you muse. But when will you enjoy the things it can buy? When will you live your life?

You find courage in the story of Mohan Gyani. He had also taken the Internet plunge and had gotten right back out again. Now he's CEO of wireless services at AT&T and the first hero of the "Reverse Migration." You've decided to follow his lead.

Your task: You've already resigned. Now write a hard-copy letter to Glenna Evans, CEO of Yourtravel.com, asking for a letter of recommendation.[13]

ROUTINE REPLIES

7. Window shopping at Wal-Mart: Writing a positive reply via e-mail The Wal-Mart chain of discount stores is one of the most successful in the world: designing, importing, and marketing across national borders. In particular, Wal-Mart rarely fails to capitalize on a marketing scheme, and its online shopping page is no exception. To make sure the Web site remains effective and relevant, the Webmaster asks various people to check out the site and give their feedback. As administrative assistant to Wal-Mart's director of marketing, you have just received a request from the Webmaster to visit Wal-Mart's Web site and give feedback on the shopping page.

Your task: Visit Wal-Mart at www.wal-mart.com and do some online "window shopping." As you browse through the shopping page, consider the language, layout, graphics, ease of use, and background noise. Compose a positive reply to the

Webmaster, and send your feedback to cserve@wal-mart.com. Print a copy of your e-mail message for submission to your instructor.

8. Red dirt to go: Positive reply by e-mail from Paradise Sportswear Robert Hedin would agree with whoever said that it's possible to turn a failure into a success. But he'd probably add with a chuckle that it could take several failures before you finally hit "pay dirt." As the owner of Paradise Sportswear in Hawaii, Hedin was nearly done in by Hurricane Iniki in 1992, which wiped out his first silk-screened and airbrushed T-shirt business. He tried again, but then Hawaii's red dirt started seeping into his warehouse and ruining his inventory. Finally, a friend suggested that he stop trying to fight Mother Nature. Hedin took the hint: He mortgaged his condo and began producing Red Dirt Shirts, all made with dye created from the troublesome local dirt.

Bingo: So popular are Hedin's Red Dirt Sportswear designs, they're being snapped up by locals and tourists in Hedin's eight Paradise Sportswear retail outlets and in every Kmart on the islands. Last year Hedin added a new line: Lava Blues, made with real Hawaiian lava rock.

"You can make 500 shirts with a bucket of dirt," grins Hedin as he shows you around the operation on your first day. He's just a few years away from the usual retirement age, but he looks like a kid who's finally found the right playground.

Recently Hedin decided to capitulate to all the requests he's received from retail outlets on the mainland. Buyers kept coming to the islands on vacation, discovering Hedin's "natural" sportswear, and plaguing him in person, by mail, and by e-mail, trying to set up a deal. For a long time, his answer was no; he simply couldn't handle the extra work. But now he's hired you.

As special sales representative, you'll help Hedin expand slowly into this new territory, starting with one store. Wholesaling to the local Kmarts is easy enough, but handling all the arrangements for shipping to the mainland would be too much for the current staff. So you'll start with the company Hedin has chosen to become the first mainland retailer to sell Red Dirt and Lava Blues sportswear: Surf's Up in Chicago, Illinois—of all places. The boss figures that with less competition than he'd find on either coast, his island-influenced sportswear will be a big hit in Chicago, especially in the dead of winter.

Your task: Write a positive response to the e-mail received from Surf's Up buyer Ronald Draeger, who says he fell in love with the Paradise clothing concept while on a surfing trip to Maui. Let him know he'll have a temporary exclusive and that you'll be sending a credit application and other materials by snail mail. His e-mail address is surfsup@insnet.com.[14]

9. Satellite farming: Letter granting credit from Deere & Company This is the best part of your job with Deere & Co. in Moline, Illinois: saying yes to a farmer. In this case, it's Arlen Ruestman in Toluca, Illinois. Ruestman wants to take advantage of new farming technology. Your company's new GreenStar system uses satellite technology originally developed by the defense department: the Global Positioning System (GPS). By using a series of satellites orbiting Earth, the system can pinpoint (to the

meter) exactly where a farmer is positioned at any given moment as he drives his GreenStar-equipped combine over a field. For farmers like Reustman, that means a new ability to micromanage even 10,000 acres of corn or soybeans.

For instance, using the GreenStar system, farmers can map and analyze characteristics such as acidity, soil type, or crop yields from a given area. Using this information, they know exactly how much herbicide or fertilizer to spread over precisely which spot—eliminating waste and achieving better results. With cross-referencing and accumulated data, farmers can analyze why crops are performing well in some areas and not so well in others. Then they can program farm equipment to treat only the problem area, for example, spraying a new insect infestation two meters wide, 300 yards down the row.

Some farms have already saved as much as $10 an acre on fertilizers alone. For 10,000 acres, that's $100,000 a year. Once Ruestman retrofits your GreenStar precision package on his old combine and learns all its applications, he should have no problem saving enough to pay off the $7,350 credit account you're about to grant him.

Your task: Write a letter to Mr. Ruestman (P.O. Box 4067, Toluca, Illinois 61369), informing him of the good news.[15]

10. Online expertise: Letter of recommendation for LifeSketch.com executive Mike Smith is founder, president, and CEO of LifeSketch.com (www.lifesketch.com). As his assistant, you've seen a lot of people come and go—but no one you'd rather see stay than Creative Director Becky Sharp. When you overheard her ask Smith for a letter of recommendation, you sat up and took notice. Was Becky leaving?

"She just wants to be prepared," Smith assures you. "You know how startups go: work hard, attract investors, make a good showing with your IPO—and then it's up to the world to find you and embrace you or send you off to another job as fast as you can say 'e-business.'"

LifeSketch is a good concept—good enough to attract Smith. As former president and CEO of apparel retailer Lands' End, Smith succeeded in building Landsend.com into one of the only retail sites on the Web to actually make a profit. Smith brought Becky Sharp with him from Lands' End (www.landsend.com), where she had been creative director and had done a terrific job revamping the Landsend.com site.

But now Sharp's challenge is even more difficult. The Lands' End consumers had been accustomed to buying clothes from the retailer. Now Sharp must develop a market for an entirely new product. LifeSketch.com must convince visitors to preserve their memories in digital format. By becoming members, visitors can upload their family photographs in digital format and store them online (20 MB free, 100 MB at $29.95/year, 250 MB at $49.95/year). Members can also turn these photos into a multimedia digital photo album, the Sketchbook, using free art, backgrounds, audio clips, and text. Plus, for just $19.95, members can buy a CD of the finished product. So far, Sharp has designed a site that's entertaining and easy to navigate. She's been working long, hard hours to do it, and Smith is thrilled by the results.

Smith has every intention of fulfilling Sharp's request for a letter of recommendation, but his schedule is packed, so he asks you to write the first draft. "She's wise to keep her résumé polished at all times," he explains to you, "and we owe her at least that much. She's already made us look good at two companies!"

"You know her work as well as I do," he continues. "Just don't forget to mention the way she collected 3,000 photos and then featured online those few that convey exactly the 'nostalgic hip family' feeling that LifeSketch needs to evoke." He sighs as he turns back to his office, "What would we do without her?"

 Your task: Try to capture Smith's appreciation in your recommendation draft, but make sure it's believable.[16]

POSITIVE MESSAGES

11. Cold comfort: E-mail offering a regional sales position with Golight Winter in Nebraska ranch country is something to sneeze at—and to shiver over. That's why rancher Jerry Gohl invented the Golight, a portable spotlight that can be mounted on a car or truck roof and rotated 360 degrees horizontally and 70 degrees vertically *by remote control.* No more getting out of the truck in freezing, predawn temperatures to adjust a manual spotlight in order to check on his livestock in the dark. In fact, for Gohl, there's hardly any time left to check the livestock at all these days: His invention has become so popular that Golight, Inc., expects to sell more than $2 million worth of the remote-controlled lights next year.

The company expanded fast, with Golights becoming popular all over the world among hunters, boaters, commuters who fear dark-of-night roadside tire changes, and early-morning fishing enthusiasts who can scope out the best shoreline sites by controlling the spotlight from inside their warm and cozy vehicles. Sales reps have been hired for every part of the country and overseas, but Gohl has been holding out for just the right person to replace him in the Nebraska territory. After all, the company president knows better than anyone what the local ranchers need and how they think—that's why his invention was such a success there. He doesn't want to jinx his good fortune by choosing the wrong replacement.

Finally, last week he met a young man named Robert Victor who seems to fit the bill. Robert grew up on a Nebraska ranch, helping his dad with those 4 a.m. chores. He's young, but he's felt the bite of Nebraska's cold, he knows the rancher mind, and best of all, he's been bringing in top dollar selling agricultural equipment in Montana for the past few years. Now he wants to return to his home state. Gohl liked him from the first moment they shook hands. "He's got the job if he wants it," the boss tells you. "Better send him some e-mail before someone else grabs him. He can start as soon as he's settled."

Your task: Compose the message communicating Gohl's offer to Robert Victor: salary plus commission as discussed, full benefits (paid vacation, health and dental insurance) if he's still around in six months. His e-mail address is rvictor@ism.net. Sign with your name, as Gohl's personnel manager.[17]

12. Learn while you earn: Memo announcing Burger King's educational benefits Your boss, Herb Schervish, owner of a Burger King store in Detroit's downtown Renaissance Center, is worried about employee turnover. He needs to keep 50 people on his payroll to operate the outlet, but recruiting and retaining those people is tough. The average employee leaves after about seven months, so Schervish has to hire and train 90 people a year just to maintain a 50-person crew. At a cost of $1,500 per hire, the price tag for all that turnover is approximately $62,000 a year.

Schervish knows that a lot of his best employees quit because they think that flipping burgers is a dead-end job. But what if it weren't a dead end? What if a person could really get someplace flipping burgers? What if Schervish offered to pay his employees' way through college if they remained with the store? Would that keep them behind the counter?

He's decided to give educational incentives a try. Employees who choose to participate will continue to earn their usual salary, but they will also get free books and college tuition, keyed to the number of hours they work each week. Those who work from 10 to 15 hours a week can take one free course at nearby Wayne County Community College; those who work 16 to 25 hours can take two courses; and those who work 26 to 40 hours can take three courses. The program is open to all employees, regardless of how long they have worked for Burger King, but no one is obligated to participate.

Your task: Draft a memo for Mr. Schervish to send out announcing the new educational incentives.[18]

13. Midnight mission: Thank-you letter at The Blue Marble bookstore As owner of The Blue Marble bookstore in Fort Thomas, Kentucky, Tina Moore won't be outdone this time. You are store manager, and along with the rest of the staff, you've been working hard to prepare for the biggest book sales party your store has ever hosted. Tonight's the night.

Last time you blew it with the popular *Harry Potter* series (about a boy who discovers he's not only a wizard-in-training, but a famous one). Book #4 was to be released at 12:01 A.M. on Saturday, July 8, a "strict on sale" date in the United States and Britain. Like thousands of other adults, you've enjoyed the cleverly written stories of Harry and his friends at Hogwarts school of wizardry. But you and Moore agreed that customers would probably be content to come in for a copy on Saturday morning. Who would let their kids stay up past midnight for a book party?

Apparently, tens of thousands of parents did—all grateful to see their kids reading so avidly. On Friday night, bookstores all over the country opened up at midnight—especially the chains, your biggest competitors. By morning, very few copies of "HP4" were left, and within days the entire, record-breaking first U.S. press run of 3.8 million copies was gone. British author J. K. Rowling had done it again. Even well-known adult critics loved the new book. Rowling's U.S. publisher, Scholastic, called it a "phenomenon" in publishing history, "beyond anything we imagined."

Of course, that morning you still had copies available, but your customers felt cheated. "Why didn't you have a pajama party last night?" they complained. "My kids saw the crowds on TV and wanted to go—but the nearest chain store is miles from here!" Some fans even called your staff "clueless muggles!" (nonwizards—usually the last to know about anything truly interesting). But that was last time.

This time, when the clock chimes midnight and you're allowed to sell Harry Potter #5, your customers will be ushered in by staff members in costume. A local trainer will stroll the store with a pet owl (favorite messengers in Harry's world). From the big black cauldrons your staff built, you'll serve oatmeal and Harry's favorite "butter beer" (apple juice and ginger ale over dry ice). The first kids in line will get free lightning-bolt stickers to create forehead scars like Harry's, and some will receive black, round-rimmed imitation "Harry Potter spectacles." It's going to be great fun.

Your task: Your staff has been working on their own time sewing costumes, making hats, and inventing butter-beer recipes. Write a thank-you letter to them from both you and Moore, and enclose a $25 gift certificate in each one. You plan to distribute the letters before tonight's party.[19]

14. Intercultural condolences: Letter conveying sympathy at IBM You've been working for two years as administrative assistant to J. T. "Ted" Childs, Jr., vice president of global work force diversity at IBM's Learning Center in Armonk, New York.

Chana Panichpapiboon has been with Childs even longer than you have, and, sadly, her husband was killed (along with 19 others) in a bus accident yesterday. The bus skidded on icy pavement into a deep ravine, tipping over and crushing the occupants before rescue workers could get to them.

You met Surin last year at a company banquet. You can still picture his warm smile and the easy way he joked with you and others over chicken Florentine, even though you were complete strangers to him. He was only 32 years old, and he left Chana two children,

a 12-year-old boy, Arsa, and 10-year-old girl, Veera. His death is a terrible tragedy.

Normally, you'd write a condolence letter immediately. But Chana is a native of Thailand, and so was Surin. In the past two years, you've listened many times to Childs's rousing, two-hour lecture to new managers on the benefits and demands of a multicultural work force. You know you'd better do a little research first. Is Chana Buddhist or Catholic? Is there anything about the typical Western practice of expressing sympathy that might be inappropriate? Offensive?

After making some discreet inquiries among Chana's closest friends at work, you've learned that she is Theravada Buddhist, as are most people in Thailand. From a reference work in the company library about doing business around the world, you've gleaned only that in Thailand, "the person takes precedence over rule or law" and "people gain their social position as a result of karma, not personal achievement," which means Chana may believe in reincarnation. But the book also says that Theravada Buddhists are free to choose which precepts of their religion, if any, they will follow. So Chana's beliefs are still a mystery.

You do know that her husband was very important to her and much loved by all their family. That, at least, is universal. And you're toying with a phrase you once read, "The hand of time lightly lays, softly soothing sorrow's wound." Is it appropriate?

Your task: You've decided to handwrite the condolence note on a blank greeting card you've found that bears a peaceful, "Eastern-flavor" image. You know you're risking a cultural gaffe, but you won't commit the offense of not writing at all. Choose the most sincere wording you can, which should ring through any differences in custom or tradition.[20]

GOING ONLINE EXERCISES

The Medium and the Message, page 162

Choosing what to include in a message, deciding how to effectively express it, and selecting an appropriate format are all important considerations when you write. Go to www.about.com and add to what you've already learned in this chapter about writing requests and other messages.

1. Both the chapter and this site offer guidelines for writing effective messages. List the "seven C's" that characterize good letters and memos. If you use clear language in a routine message, is it still important to restrict yourself to one topic? Why or why not?

2. Even the best-run businesses sometimes disappoint their customers. Imagine that you have been asked to write a response to an angrily worded e-mail message that charges your company with fraud because a product ordered through the Web has not arrived. Which of the ten "secrets" of writing business letters do you think would be most useful in shaping your reply?

3. Describe some similarities and differences between a memo and a letter.

   To complete this exercise, log on to this text's Web site at www.prenhall.com/thill. Select Chapter 7, then select "Student Resources," click on the name of the featured Web site, and follow the detailed navigational directions.

WRITING BAD-NEWS MESSAGES

chapter 8

ON THE JOB: FACING A COMMUNICATION DILEMMA AT AMERICAN AIRLINES

When Saying "No" Is Part of Your Job

www.aa.com

Few businesspeople enjoy saying no to well-meaning potential partners, but for Donna Burnley of American Airlines, saying "no" is a necessary part of ensuring top-quality customer service. As a senior commodity manager, she spends $23 million a year on in-flight food service supplies such as glasses, china, silverware, and napkins. In addition, Burnley manages two warehouses and oversees the maintenance and repair of the in-flight food preparation and serving equipment.

Naturally, many companies would like a part of that business, but few can meet Burnley's strict criteria. The biggest challenge these suppliers face is meeting the complicated demands of an airline that flies to more than 170 locations across the Americas, Europe, Asia, Africa, and Australia. As Burnley puts it, "There are relatively few suppliers capable of manufacturing the volume of custom catering equipment required." She can't choose suppliers based solely on their price or quality; she needs partners who can also manufacture and distribute reliably on a global scale.

If you were in Donna Burnley's shoes, how would you respond to requests from well-meaning companies who offer good products but can't meet all of American's requirements? What would you say to a supplier whose quality or customer service had slipped below acceptable levels? How would you deliver these bad-news messages in a professional manner without offending your readers, but still getting your point across?[1]

After studying this chapter, you will be able to

1 Apply the three-step writing process to bad-news messages

2 Show how to achieve an audience-centered tone and explain why it helps readers

3 Differentiate between the direct and indirect organizational approaches to bad-news messages and discuss when it's appropriate to use each one

4 Discuss the three techniques for saying "no" as clearly and kindly as possible

5 Define *defamation* and explain how to avoid it in bad-news messages

6 List three guidelines for delivering bad news to job applicants and give a brief explanation of each one

7 Outline the main purpose of performance reviews, give three ways to accomplish that purpose, and list five guidelines to follow when giving negative reviews

USING THE THREE-STEP WRITING PROCESS FOR BAD-NEWS MESSAGES

As Donna Burnley can attest, nobody likes bad news. People don't like to get it, and they don't like to give it. Saying "no" to an idea, a proposition, or a request from a customer, an employee, a shareholder, a salesperson—or even your boss—can put knots in your stomach and cost you hours of sleep.

The word *no* is terse and abrupt, so negative that a lot of people have trouble saying it. And for most, it's the toughest word to hear or understand. The delivery can be far more damaging than the answer itself. The most dangerous *no* is usually the one you don't explain.[2] That's why you must be careful whenever you deliver bad news. The three-step process can help you write bad-news messages that are more effective and less dangerous.

Step 1: Planning Your Bad-News Messages

When your message is a negative one, analysis becomes extremely important. If your purpose is specific, you are able to word it in the best possible way. You want to be sure that a bad-news message should indeed be sent and should definitely be sent in writing. And

One way American Airlines builds and retains strong relationships with its customers, employees, and investors is by focusing on audience feelings. By explaining the reasons for any bad news and by focusing on the positive aspects of a negative situation, people at American Airlines communicate their understanding and demonstrate their goodwill.

O b j e c t i v e   **1**

Apply the three-step writing process to bad-news messages.

Analysis, investigation, and adaptation help you avoid alienating your readers.

more than ever, you need to know how your audience will receive your message. Do readers prefer to receive negative news up front, without delay? Or would they accept the news more readily if you explained your reasons first?

Any investigation or research must yield reliable, unmistakable facts that will support your negative decision. You'll want to be sure that you have all the facts your audience will need. After sending your bad news, you don't want to face a barrage of questions from confused readers.

Finally, you'll want to pay particular attention to maintaining a good relationship with your audience. Be sure to adapt your medium and tone to your audience. Careful attention to adaptation can help you avoid alienating your readers.

Step 2: Writing Your Bad-News Messages

The appropriate organization helps readers accept your negative news.

In a bad-news message, your main idea is a refusal, a rejection, or a negative announcement, so you want to be careful about defining that main idea and about covering relevant points thoroughly and logically. Choosing between the direct and indirect approaches takes on added importance in bad-news messages. You need to know whether it will be better to open with the bad news or to prepare your readers with a cogent explanation before giving them the negative bits. You also need to pay special attention to word choice so that you can create your sentences and paragraphs carefully.

Step 3: Completing Your Bad-News Messages

Revision is as important as the other steps in the writing process; it helps you make sure that your bad-news messages are organized properly, that they say what you want them to say, and that they do so concisely and clearly. You'll want to make sure that your design doesn't detract from the bad news or from your efforts to be sensitive. And as always, proofreading bad-news messages guarantees that there are no misunderstandings from typos or from errors in spelling, mechanics, alignment, and so on.

SENDING BAD-NEWS MESSAGES

It's bad news when you refuse to grant a claim, encounter problems filling an order, announce that quarter profits are down, or give an employee a negative performance review. Whatever the details of your particular message, when you have bad news, make your readers feel that they have been taken seriously. You want them to agree that your news is fair and reasonable.

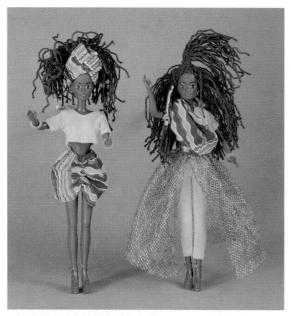

As a small company specializing in ethnic toys, Olmec Toys strives to convey bad news in the most positive light possible. Maintaining goodwill with its audience and keeping its image intact are second only to making sure the bad news is understood and accepted.

Five goals of bad-news messages:
• Give the bad news
• Ensure its acceptance
• Maintain reader's goodwill
• Maintain organization's good image
• Reduce future correspondence on the matter

Strategies for Bad-News Messages

When delivering bad news, you have five main goals: (1) to convey the bad news, (2) to gain acceptance for it, (3) to maintain as much goodwill as possible with your audience, (4) to maintain a good image for your organization, and (5) to reduce or eliminate the need for future correspondence on the matter. Accomplishing so many goals in a single message is not easy. But you can make your bad-news messages effective. First, adopt an audience-centered tone. Second, organize your message to meet your audience's needs and expectations by using either the direct approach, which presents the main idea before the supporting data (fully described in Chapter 7), or the indirect approach, which presents the supporting data before the main idea.

Creating an Audience-Centered Tone   You've heard it before: It's not *what* you say but *how* you say it that counts. That adage couldn't be truer with bad-news messages. Your tone contributes to your message's effectiveness by helping your readers

Objective **2**
Show how to achieve an audience-centered tone and explain why it helps readers.

When establishing tone, strive for
• Firmness
• Fairness
• Goodwill
• Respect

◆ Accept that your bad-news represents a firm decision

◆ Understand that, under the circumstances, your decision was fair and reasonable

◆ Remain well disposed toward your business

◆ Preserve their pride

If you are communicating across cultures, you'll want to use the tone, organization, and other cultural conventions that your audience expects. Only then can you avoid the inappropriate or even offensive approaches that could jeopardize your business relationship.[3] However, if you're communicating bad news to a U.S. or Canadian audience with minimal cultural differences, be sure to use the "you" attitude, choose positive words, and use respectful language.

Use the "You" Attitude   Using the "you" attitude is crucial to every message you write, but it's especially important in bad-news messages. For example, point out how your decision might actually further your audience's goals. Convey concern by looking for the best in your audience. And assume that your audience is interested in being fair, even when they are at fault.

The "you" attitude is especially important in bad-news messages.

Choose Positive Words   You can ease disappointment by using positive words rather than negative, counterproductive words. Just be sure that your positive tone doesn't hide the bad news behind difficult language.[4] Remember, you want to convey the bad news, not cover it up.

Use positive rather than negative phrasing in bad-news messages.

INSTEAD OF THIS	SAY THIS
I *cannot understand* what you mean.	Please clarify your request.
The *damage* won't be fixed for a week.	The item will be repaired next week.
There will be a *delay* in your order.	We will ship your order as soon as possible.
You are clearly *dissatisfied*.	We are doing what we can to make things right.
Your account is in *error*.	Corrections have been made to your account.
The breakage was not our *fault*.	The merchandise was broken during shipping.
Sorry for your inconvenience.	The enclosed coupon will save you $5 next time.
We *regret* the misunderstanding.	I'll try my best to be more clear from now on.
I was *shocked* to learn that you're unhappy.	Your letter reached me yesterday.
Unfortunately, we haven't received it.	It hasn't arrived yet.
The enclosed statement is *wrong*.	Please recheck the enclosed statement.

Use Respectful Language   When you use language that conveys respect and avoids an accusing tone, you protect your audience's pride. For instance, when refusing an adjustment or a claim, try using third-person, impersonal, passive language to explain your audience's mistakes in an inoffensive way. This approach downplays the doer of the action because the doer is not specified. Say, "The appliance won't work after being immersed in water" instead of "You shouldn't have immersed the appliance in water." When your audience is at fault, the "you" attitude is better observed by avoiding the word *you*.

Sometimes the "you" attitude is best observed by avoiding the word *you*.

Objective **3**
Differentiate between the direct and indirect organizational approaches to bad-news messages and discuss when it's appropriate to use each one.

Using the Direct Approach   As with most business messages, the key to choosing the best approach for bad-news messages is to analyze audience members first. Try to put yourself in their shoes. What is their likely reaction to the news? How important is the message? How well do you know them? Some people like to know the bad news right away. Similarly, some situations are more appropriate for directness than others. If you know that your audience is likely to prefer the bad news first, or if the situation is minor and the news will cause your audience little pain or disappointment, then use the direct approach.

Audience analysis is crucial for determining organization of bad-news messages.

Figure 8–1
Differences between the Indirect
and Direct Organizational Plans
for Bad-News Messages

Sara Tatchio is news executive
producer for Ford Communications
Network (FCN). FCN's philosophy is
that it's better for employees to hear
negative news from the company.
Whether announcing good news or
bad, FCN's internal newscast delivers the truth. Tatchio insists that
employees know what's going on
before they go home. In keeping
with this philosophy, FCN uses the
direct approach, even with a negative announcement about company
business.

Use the direct approach when your
negative answer or information will
have little personal impact.

Use the indirect approach when
some preparation will help your
audience accept your bad news.

A bad-news message organized using the direct approach starts with a clear statement of the bad news, proceeds to the reasons for the decision (perhaps offering alternatives), and ends with a positive statement aimed at maintaining a good relationship with the audience (see Figure 8–1). Stating the bad news at the beginning can have two advantages: (1) It makes a shorter message possible, and (2) the audience needs less time to reach the main idea of the message, the bad news itself.

Memos are often organized so that the bad news comes before the reasons. Some managers expect all internal correspondence to be brief and direct, regardless of whether the message is positive or negative. Routine bad-news messages to other companies often follow the direct approach, especially if they relay decisions that have little or no personal impact. The indirect approach can actually cause ill will in people who see bad news frequently (such as people searching for employment).[5] In addition, you'll sometimes know from experience that your audience simply prefers reading the bad news first in any message. The direct approach is also appropriate when you want to present an image of firmness and strength; for example, the last message in a debt collection series (just before the matter is turned over to an attorney) usually gets right to the point.

You may want to use the direct approach in a variety of circumstances, saving your positive comments for the close. Even so, remember that a tactful tone and a focus on reasons will help make any bad-news message easier to accept. (For an idea of how some other cultures handle bad news, see "Achieving Intercultural Communication—Good Ways to Send Bad News Around the World"). However, you'll find that many business communicators prefer using an indirect approach for delivering bad news.

Using the Indirect Approach   Beginning a bad news message with a blunt "no" could well prevent your audience from reading or listening to your reasons. Some prefer some preparation or explanation first. So the indirect approach eases your audience into your message by explaining your reasons before delivering the bad news. Presenting the reasons first increases your chances of gaining audience acceptance by gradually preparing readers for the negative news to come. The indirect approach follows a four-part sequence (as shown in Figure 8–1): (1) Open with a buffer, (2) continue with a logical, neutral explanation of the reasons for the bad news, (3) follow with a clear but diplomatic statement of the bad news (emphasizing any good news, and de-emphasizing the bad), and (4) close with a positive forward-looking statement that is helpful and friendly.

Begin with a Buffer   The first step in using the indirect approach is to make a neutral, noncontroversial statement that is closely related to the point of the message; this state-

Achieving Intercultural Communication

Good Ways to Send Bad News Around the World

Bad news is unwelcome in any language, but the conventions for passing it on to business associates can vary considerably from country to country. For instance, all French business letters are very formal and writer oriented (without reference to audience needs or benefits). That's because French businesses traditionally write for one purpose: to establish evidence for any future litigation. The preferred style is prudent, precise, and respectful, even if the writer and reader know each other very well. Letters begin with courteous titles ("Monsieur," "Madame," but not "Dear ___") and close with flowery salutations ("With our anticipated thanks, we beg you to accept, Sir, our sincere greetings," or "Awaiting your reply, we offer you, Sirs, our assiduous greetings"). French business letters never become personal or friendly, and U.S. audiences sometimes misinterpret this formal tone as coolness, nonchalance, or indifference.

When the news is bad, French writers take a direct approach. They open with a reference to the problem or previous correspondence and then state the bad news clearly. They don't try to avoid negative words, nor do they refer to the audience's needs, but they often do apologize and express regret for the problem. A bad-news letter in France won't necessarily end on a positive note, but the close remains gracious: "Accept, Sirs, our distinguished greetings."

In Japan all letter writing is regarded as a troublesome task, even when the news is good. Japanese letters traditionally open with remarks about the season ("The season for cherry blossoms is here with us and everybody is beginning to feel refreshed"). This opening remark is followed by a reference to the reader's business prosperity or health.

When the message is bad news, these opening formalities serve as a buffer. Explanations and apologies follow, and then comes the bad news or the refusal. Japanese writers protect their reader's feelings by wording the bad news ambiguously. Western readers may even misinterpret this vague language as a condition of acceptance rather than as the refusal it truly is.

In Britain, centuries of business tradition dictate a direct approach for all business letters, even when the message is unsettling. A typical bad-news letter opens with a reference to the subject and continues with a few paragraphs explaining the bad news in a blunt, but logical, sequence. The writer then expresses apology and regret, which further emphasizes the bad news. Some British letters end there; others close with a few words wishing the reader success or hoping for continued goodwill. Recently, however, some leading British companies have begun using the indirect approach.

CAREER APPLICATIONS

1. Select a bad-news message and see whether you can redesign it for Japan, France, and Great Britain. How would you change the format for each country? What would you add or delete?
2. Which is more important: (a) learning the language of the customers you do business with or (b) learning their customs? Please explain.

---

ment is called a **buffer.** A good buffer is tricky to write. Some critics believe that using a buffer is manipulative, dishonest, and thus unethical. In fact, buffers are unethical only if they're insincere. Breaking bad news with kindness and courtesy is the humane way. Consideration for the feelings of others is never dishonest, and that consideration helps your audience accept your message.

A buffer is a neutral lead-in to bad news.

A good buffer expresses your appreciation for being thought of, assures the reader of your attention to the request, compliments the reader, or indicates your understanding of the reader's needs. A buffer must not insult the audience with insincere flattery or self-promoting blather. It sets the stage for the bad news to follow, and it must be both sincere and relevant so that readers don't feel they are being set up or "snowed." For example, in a memo telling another supervisor that you can't spare anyone from your staff for a temporary assignment to the order fulfillment department, you might begin with a sentence like this:

Use a buffer that is
- *Neutral*
- *Relevant*
- *Not misleading*
- *Assertive*
- *Succinct*

Our department shares your goal of processing orders quickly and efficiently.

If possible, base your buffer on statements made by the person you're responding to. This type of buffer shows the person that you have listened well. If you use an unrelated buffer, you will seem to be "beating around the bush"; that is, you'll appear manipulative and unethical, and you'll lose your audience's respect.

Another goal when composing your buffer is to avoid giving the impression that good news will follow. Building up your audience's expectations at the beginning only

To write an effective buffer, avoid giving the impression that good news will follow.

makes the actual bad news even more surprising. Imagine your reaction to the following openings:

Your résumé indicates that you would be well suited for a management trainee position with our company.

Your résumé shows very clearly why you are interested in becoming a management trainee with our company.

The second opening emphasizes the applicant's interpretation of her qualifications rather than the company's evaluation, so it's less misleading but still positive. Here are some other things to avoid when writing a buffer:

- **Avoid saying "no."** An audience encountering the blunt refusal right at the beginning usually reacts negatively to the rest of the message, no matter how reasonable and well phrased it is.
- **Avoid using a know-it-all tone.** When you use phrases such as "you should be aware that," readers expect your lecture to lead to a negative response, so they resist the rest of your message.
- **Avoid wordy and irrelevant phrases and sentences.** Sentences such as "We have received your letter," "This letter is in reply to your request," and "We are writing in response to your request" are irrelevant. Make better use of the space by referring directly to the subject of the letter.
- **Avoid apologizing.** Unless warranted by extreme circumstances, an apology only weakens the following explanation of your unfavorable news.
- **Avoid writing a buffer that is too long.** Be brief. Identify something that both you and your audience are interested in and agree on before proceeding in a businesslike way.

Table 8–1 shows several types of buffers you could use to open a bad-news message tactfully.

Table 8–1   Types of Buffers

Buffer	Strategy	Example
Agreement	Find a point on which you and the reader share similar views.	We both know how hard it is to make a profit in this industry.
Appreciation	Express sincere thanks for receiving something.	Your check for $127.17 arrived yesterday. Thank you.
Cooperation	Convey your willingness to help in any way you realistically can.	Employee Services is here to smooth the way for all of you who work to achieve company goals.
Fairness	Assure the reader that you've closely examined and carefully considered the problem, or mention an appropriate action that has already been taken.	For the past week, we have carefully monitored those using the photocopying machine to see whether we can detect any pattern of use that might explain its frequent breakdowns.
Good news	Start with the part of your message that is favorable.	A replacement knob for your range is on its way, shipped February 10 via UPS.
Praise	Find an attribute or an achievement to compliment.	Your résumé shows an admirable breadth of experience, which should serve you well as you progress in your career.
Resale	Favorably discuss the product or company related to the subject of the letter.	With their heavy-duty, full-suspension hardware and fine veneers, the desks and file cabinets in our Montclair line have become a hit with value-conscious professionals.
Understanding	Demonstrate that you understand the reader's goals and needs.	So that you can more easily find the printer with the features you need, we are enclosing a brochure that describes all the Panasonic printers currently available.

After you've composed a buffer, evaluate it by asking yourself four questions: Is it pleasant? Is it relevant? Is it neutral, saying neither yes nor no? Does it provide for a smooth transition to the reasons that follow? If you can answer yes to every question, you can proceed confidently to the next section of your message.

Follow with Reasons   If you've done a good job of composing the buffer, the reasons will follow naturally. Cover the more positive points first; then move to the less positive ones. Provide enough detail for the audience to understand your reasons, but be concise; a long, roundabout explanation may make your audience impatient. Your goal is to explain *why* you have reached your decision before you explain *what* that decision is. If you present your reasons effectively, they should convince your audience that your decision is justified, fair, and logical.

> Present reasons to show that your decision is reasonable and fair.

One way to be tactful when giving your reasons is to highlight how your negative decision benefits your readers (rather than focusing on why the decision is good for you or your company). For example, when denying a credit request, you can show how your decision will keep the person from becoming overextended financially. Facts and figures are often helpful in convincing members of your audience that you're acting in their best interests.

> Focus on how the audience might benefit from your negative message.

Avoid hiding behind company policy to cushion the bad news. If you say, "Company policy forbids our hiring anyone who does not have two years' management experience," you seem to imply that you haven't considered the person on her or his own merits. Skilled and sympathetic communicators explain company policy (without referring to it as "policy") so that the audience can try to meet the requirements at a later time.

Similarly, avoid apologizing when giving your reasons. Apologies are appropriate only when someone in your company has made a severe mistake or has done something terribly wrong. If no one in the company is at fault, an apology gives the wrong impression. For example, say that you're refusing the application of a management trainee. A tactfully worded letter might give these reasons for the decision not to hire:

Because these management trainee positions are quite challenging, our human relations department has researched the qualifications needed to succeed in them. The findings show that the two most important qualifications are a bachelor's degree in business administration and two years' supervisory experience.

The paragraph does a good job of stating the reasons for the refusal:

◆ It provides enough detail to make the reason for the refusal logically acceptable.

◆ It implies that the applicant is better off avoiding a program in which he or she would probably fail, given the background of potential co-workers.

◆ It explains the company's policy as logical rather than rigid.

◆ It offers no apology for the decision.

◆ It avoids negative personal expressions ("You do not meet our requirements").

> Well-written reasons are
> • Detailed
> • Tactful
> • Individualized
> • Unapologetic
> • Positive

At American Airlines, Donna Burnley has learned that even though specific reasons help audiences accept bad news, reasons cannot always be given. Don't include reasons when they involve confidential, excessively complicated, or purely negative information or when they benefit only you or your firm (by enhancing the company's profits, for example). Instead, move directly to the next section.

> Sometimes detailed reasons should not be provided.

> *Objective* **4**
> Discuss the three techniques for saying "no" clearly and kindly as possible.

State the Bad News   When the bad news is a logical outcome of the reasons that come before it, the audience is psychologically prepared to receive it. However, the audience may still reject your message if the bad news is handled carelessly. Three techniques are especially useful for saying no as clearly and as kindly as possible. First, de-emphasize the bad news:

> To handle bad news carefully
> • De-emphasize the bad news visually and grammatically
> • Use a conditional statement
> • Tell what you did do, not what you didn't do

◆ Minimize the space or time devoted to the bad news.

◆ Subordinate bad news in a complex or compound sentence ("My department is

Laura Washington is editor and publisher of *The Chicago Reporter* and a prize-winning investigative journalist. She's an expert on urban affairs and highly respected for her reporting and analysis of race and poverty questions. Washington understands that de-emphasizing explosive news keeps her readers from rejecting a story.

Don't let the bad news get lost by overemphasizing the positive.

already shorthanded, so I'll need all my staff for at least the next two months"). This construction pushes the bad news into the middle of the sentence, the point of least emphasis.

◆ Embed bad news in the middle of a paragraph or use parenthetical expressions ("Our profits, which are down, are only part of the picture").

Second, use a conditional (*if* or *when*) statement to imply that the audience could have received, or might someday receive, a favorable answer ("When you have more managerial experience, you are welcome to reapply"). Such a statement could motivate applicants to improve their qualifications.

Third, tell the audience what you did do, can do, or will do rather than what you did not do, cannot do, or will not do. Say "We sell exclusively through retailers, and the one nearest you that carries our merchandise is . . ." rather than "We are unable to serve you, so please call your nearest dealer." By implying the bad news, you may not need to actually state it ("The five positions currently open have been staffed with people whose qualifications match those uncovered in our research"). By focusing on the positive and implying the bad news, you soften the blow.

When implying bad news, be sure your audience understands the entire message—including the bad news. It would be unethical to overemphasize the positive. So if an implied message might leave doubt, state your decision in direct terms. Just be sure to avoid overly blunt statements that are likely to cause pain and anger:

INSTEAD OF THIS	USE THIS
I *must refuse* your request.	I won't be in town on the day you need me.
We *must deny* your application.	The position has been filled.
I *am unable to* grant your request.	Contact us again when you have established . . .
We *cannot afford to* continue the program.	The program will conclude on May 1.
Much as I would like to attend . . .	Our budget meeting ends too late for me to attend.
We *must reject* your proposal.	We've accepted the proposal from AAA Builders.
We *must turn down* your extension request.	Please send in your payment by June 14.

End with a Positive Close   After giving your audience the bad news, your job is to end your message on an upbeat note. You might propose an attainable solution to the audience's problem ("The human resources department has offered to bring in temporary workers when I need them, and they would probably consider doing the same for you"). In a message to a customer or potential customer, an off-the-subject ending that includes resale information or sales promotion may also be appropriate. If you've asked readers to decide between alternatives or to take some action, make sure that they know what to do, when to do it, and how to do it with ease. Whatever type of close you choose, follow these guidelines:

◆ **Keep it positive.** Don't refer to, repeat, or apologize for the bad news, and refrain from expressing any doubt that your reasons will be accepted (avoid statements such as "I trust our decision is satisfactory").

◆ **Limit future correspondence.** Encourage additional communication *only* if you're willing to discuss your decision further (avoid phrases such as "If you have further questions, please write").

◆ **Be optimistic about the future.** Don't anticipate problems (avoid statements such as "Should you have further problems, please let us know").

◆ **Be sincere.** Steer clear of clichés that are insincere in view of the bad news (avoid saying, "If we can be of any help, please contact us").

◆ **Be confident.** Don't show any doubt about keeping the person as a customer (avoid phrases such as "We hope you will continue to do business with us").

Checklist: Bad-News Messages

Overall Strategy

✓ Use the direct approach when the situation is routine (between employees of the same company), when the reader is not emotionally involved in the message, when you know that the reader would prefer the bad news first, or when you know that firmness is necessary.
✓ Use the indirect approach in all other cases.
✓ Adopt an audience-centered tone by being sincere, being aware of cultural differences, using the "you" attitude, choosing positive words, and using respectful language.

Buffer

✓ Express appreciation, cooperation, fairness, good news, praise, resale, or understanding.
✓ Introduce a topic that is relevant to the subject and that both you and the reader can agree on.
✓ Avoid apologies and negative-sounding words (*won't, can't, unable to*).
✓ Be brief and to the point.
✓ Maintain a confident, positive, supportive tone.

Reasons

✓ Check the lead-in from the buffer for a smooth transition from the favorable to the unfavorable.
✓ Show how the decision benefits your audience.

✓ Avoid apologies and expressions of sorrow or regret.
✓ Offer enough detail to show the logic of your position.
✓ Include only factual information.
✓ Include only business reasons, not personal ones.
✓ Carefully word the reasons so that readers can anticipate the bad news.
✓ Work from the general to the specific.

Bad News

✓ State the bad news as positively as possible, using tactful wording.
✓ De-emphasize bad news by minimizing the space devoted to it, subordinating it, or embedding it.
✓ Emphasize what the firm did do or is doing rather than what it can't or won't do.

Positive, Friendly, Helpful Close

✓ Remind the reader of how his or her needs are being met.
✓ Keep the close as positive as possible by eliminating any reference to the bad news, avoiding apologies and words of regret, and eliminating words suggesting uncertainty.
✓ Suggest actions the reader might take.
✓ Keep a positive outlook on the future.
✓ Be confident about keeping the person as a customer.

If you are the one who has to reject the applicant for the management trainee position, you can observe these guidelines by writing a close like this:

Many companies seek other qualifications in management trainees, so I urge you to continue your job search. You'll certainly find an opening in which your skills and aspirations match the job requirements exactly.

Keep in mind that the close is the last thing the audience has to remember you by. Try to make the memory a positive one. For a reminder of the strategies for delivering bad-news messages, see this chapter's "Checklist: Bad-News Messages."

Types of Bad-News Messages

The various types of bad-news messages are uncountable, from refusing credit to giving negative performance reviews. Many of the routine messages that you'll be writing will probably fall into major categories. In the following sections, we discuss some specific examples within three major categories: sending negative answers to routine requests, sending negative organizational news, and sending negative employment messages.

Sending Negative Answers to Routine Requests   The businessperson who tries to say "yes" to everyone probably won't win many promotions or stay in business for long. Occasionally, your response to requests must simply be "no." It's a mark of your skill as a communicator to be able to say "no" clearly yet not cut yourself off from future dealings with other people.

Use either the direct or the indirect approach to tell someone you cannot provide what has been requested.

Refusing Requests for Information When people ask you for information and you can't honor the request, you may answer with either the direct approach or the indirect approach. Say that you've asked a company to participate in your research project concerning sales promotion. However, that company has a policy against disseminating any information about projected sales figures. In the following letter, the direct approach is used even though the reader is outside the company and may be emotionally involved in the response. This letter would offend most readers:

Poor First Draft

The writer hides behind the blanket "company policy," a policy that the reader may find questionable.

Tone is unnecessarily negative and abrupt.

> Our company policy prohibits us from participating in research projects where disclosure of discretionary information might be necessary. Therefore, we decline your invitation to our sales staff to fill out questionnaires for your study.

The offer to help is an unpleasant irony, given the writer's unwillingness to help in this instance.

> Thank you for trying to include Qualcomm Corporation in your research. If we can be of further assistance, please let us know.

As American Airlines' Donna Burnley can tell you, wording and tone conspire to make a letter either offensive or acceptable. The letter that follows conveys the same negative message as the previous letter but without sounding offensive:

Buffer is supportive and appreciative.

> We at Qualcomm Corporation appreciate and benefit from the research of companies such as yours. Your study sounds interesting, and we certainly wish we could participate.

Bad news is implied, not stated explicitly.

Fully explains reason for decision without falling back on a blanket reference to company policy.

> However, our board requires strict confidentiality of all sales information until quarterly reports are mailed to stockholders. We release press reports at the same time the quarterly reports go out, and we'll be sure to include you in all our future mailings.

Close is friendly, positive, and helpful.

> Although we cannot release projected figures, we are more than willing to share information that is part of the public record. I've enclosed several of our past earnings reports for your inspection. We look forward to seeing the results of your study. Please let us know if there is any additional way we can help.

As you think about the different impact those two letters might have on you, you can see why effective business writers like American Airlines' Donna Burnley take the time and the trouble to give negative messages the attention they deserve.

When turning down an invitation or a request for a favor, consider your relationship to the reader.

Refusing Invitations and Requests for Favors When you must say "no" to an invitation or a requested favor, your use of the direct or the indirect approach depends on your relationship with the reader. For example, suppose the president of the local community college asks your company to host graduation on your corporate grounds, but your sales meetings will be taking place at the same time. If you don't know the president well, you'll probably use the indirect approach. See Figure 8–2, in which May Yee Kwan delivers this bad news in a helpful and supportive way. If you are friends with the president and work frequently on projects for the college, you might use the direct approach:

> Sandra, thanks for asking us to host your graduation. You know we've always supported the college and would love to do this for you. Unfortunately, our company sales meetings will be going on during the same time. We'll have so many folks tied up with logistics, we won't have the personnel to adequately take care of the graduation.

> Have you called Jerry Kane over at the Botanical Gardens? I can't think of a prettier site for graduation. Roberta in my office volunteers over there and knows Jerry. She can fill you in on the details, if you'd like to talk to her first.

> Thanks again for considering us. Let's have lunch in mid-June to plan our involvement with the college for the next school year. You can think of all kinds of ways to make me sorry I had to say no! I'll look forward to seeing you and catching up on family news.

1 Planning

Analyze: Gauge audience's reaction to refusal; gear level of formality to reader familiarity.

Investigate: Collect information on possible alternatives.

Adapt: For a more formal response, letterhead is best. Maintain the relationship with the "you" attitude, and focus on the reader's problem.

2 Writing

Organize: Main idea is to refuse a request. Respect your reader by showing that the request received serious consideration. Use an indirect approach.

Compose: Make your style conversational but keep it businesslike. Keep the letter brief, clear, and helpful.

3 Completing

Revise: Maintain a friendly tone by eliminating overly formal words and phrases. Ensure your tone is positive.

Produce: Use letterhead with a straightforward format.

Proofread: Be careful to review for accuracy, spelling, and mechanics.

927 Dawson Valley Road, Tulsa, Oklahoma 74151
Voice: (918) 669-4428 Fax: (918) 669-4429
www.infotech.com

March 5, 2002

Dr. Sandra Wofford, President
Whittier Community College
333 Whittier Avenue
Tulsa, OK 74150

Dear Dr. Wofford:

Because we appreciate Whittier Community College and the many opportunities you have provided to deserving students over the years, we at Infotech have supported the college in many ways. Thank you for considering our grounds for your graduation ceremony.

Buffers bad news by demonstrating respect and recapping request.

Our company-wide sales meetings will be held during the weeks of May 29th and June 5th. We will host over 200 sales representatives and their families, and activities will take place at both our corporate campus and the Ramada Renaissance. Therefore, we will be unable to devote an adequate support staff for your graduation.

States reason for the bad news explicitly and in detail.

My assistant, Roberta Seagers, suggests you contact the Municipal Botanical Gardens as a possible graduation site. She recommends calling Jerry Kane, director of public relations. If we can help in any other way with graduation, please let us know.

Suggests an alternative—showing that Kwan cares about the college and has given the matter some thought.

Even though our annual meeting will most likely prevent us from ever hosting graduation, we remain firm in our commitment to you, President Wofford, and to the fine students you represent. We will continue to be a corporate partner to Whittier College and will support your efforts as you move forwards.

Close renews the corporation's future support.

Sincerely,

May Yee Kwan

May Yee Kwan
Public Relations Director

lc

Figure 8–2
In-Depth Critique: Letter Declining a Favor

EFFECTIVE E-BUSINESS COMMUNICATION

Transforming Wrongs into Rights

"Problems are opportunities in disguise"—an apt description of how savvy e-businesses approach customer service. Every complaint gives you a chance to strengthen your customer's loyalty, if you make full use of Internet technology to show that you're really interested in making things right. Web-based businesses can offer customers a wider choice of contact methods: phone, mail, fax, e-mail, or instant online customer-service chat, just the way Lands' End does (see www.landsend.com). Online customers expect speed, so respond quickly, ideally within 24 hours. If you need more time to resolve sticky problems, send prompt e-mail updates to let customers know you're working on their behalf.

1. When you send an e-mail message to update a customer whose problem will take several days to resolve, what can you say to maintain his or her goodwill?
2. When you send an e-mail message to update customers whose problems are taking more time to resolve, would the direct or the indirect approach be more appropriate? Why?

This letter gets right to the point but still uses some blow-softening techniques: It compliments the person and organization making the request, suggests an alternative, and looks toward future opportunities for cooperation.

The basic goal of a bad-news letter about orders is to protect or make a sale.

Handling Bad News About Orders For several reasons, businesses must sometimes convey bad news concerning orders. Also, when delivering bad news to existing or would-be customers, you have an additional challenge—resale. To make readers feel good about continuing to do business with your firm, you want to

◆ Work toward an eventual sale along the lines of the original order

◆ Keep instructions or additional information as clear as possible

◆ Maintain an optimistic, confident tone so that your reader won't lose interest

Reinforcing the customer's confidence in your service or product is an effective way to meet the resale challenge. Just don't overdo it.

Use the indirect approach for both types of bad news about orders.

When you must back order for a customer, you have one of two types of bad news to convey: (1) You're able to send only part of the order, or (2) you're able to send none of the order. When sending only part of the order, you actually have both good news and bad news. In such situations, the indirect approach works very well. The buffer contains the good news (that part of the order is en route) along with a resale reminder of the product's attractiveness. After the buffer come the reasons for the delay of the remainder of the shipment. A strong close encourages a favorable attitude toward the entire transaction. For a customer whose order for a recliner and ottoman will be only partially filled, your letter might read like the one in Figure 8–3.

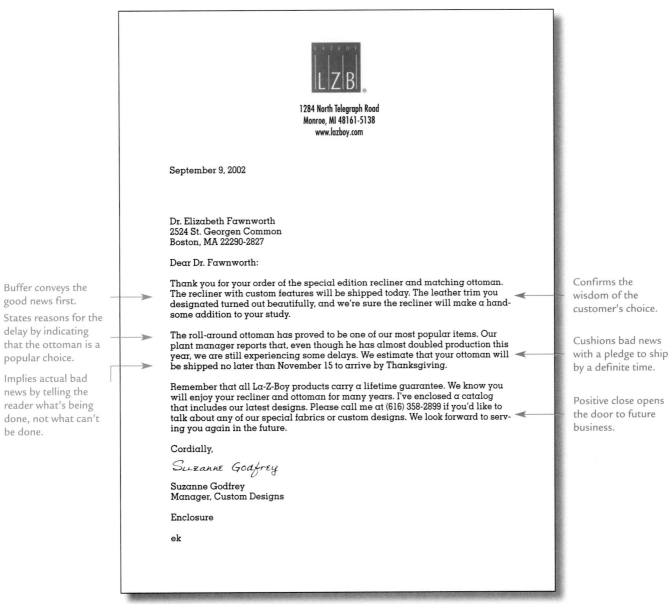

Buffer conveys the good news first.

States reasons for the delay by indicating that the ottoman is a popular choice.

Implies actual bad news by telling the reader what's being done, not what can't be done.

[Letter content:]

1284 North Telegraph Road
Monroe, MI 48161-5138
www.lazboy.com

September 9, 2002

Dr. Elizabeth Fawnworth
2524 St. Georgen Common
Boston, MA 22290-2827

Dear Dr. Fawnworth:

Thank you for your order of the special edition recliner and matching ottoman. The recliner with custom features will be shipped today. The leather trim you designated turned out beautifully, and we're sure the recliner will make a handsome addition to your study.

The roll-around ottoman has proved to be one of our most popular items. Our plant manager reports that, even though he has almost doubled production this year, we are still experiencing some delays. We estimate that your ottoman will be shipped no later than November 15 to arrive by Thanksgiving.

Remember that all La-Z-Boy products carry a lifetime guarantee. We know you will enjoy your recliner and ottoman for many years. I've enclosed a catalog that includes our latest designs. Please call me at (616) 358-2899 if you'd like to talk about any of our special fabrics or custom designs. We look forward to serving you again in the future.

Cordially,

Suzanne Godfrey

Suzanne Godfrey
Manager, Custom Designs

Enclosure

ek

Confirms the wisdom of the customer's choice.

Cushions bad news with a pledge to ship by a definite time.

Positive close opens the door to future business.

Figure 8–3
In-Depth Critique: Letter Advising of a Back Order

When you're unable to send the customer any portion of an order, you still use the indirect approach. However, because you have no good news to give, your buffer only confirms the sale, and the explanation section states your reasons for not filling the order promptly. For a brief outline of back-order tasks, see this chapter's "Checklist: Bad News About Orders."

Refusing Claims and Requests for Adjustment   Almost every customer who makes a claim is emotionally involved; therefore, the indirect approach is usually the best approach for a refusal. Your job as a writer is to avoid accepting responsibility for the unfortunate situation and yet avoid blaming or accusing the customer. To steer clear of these pitfalls, pay special attention to the tone of your letter. Keep in mind that a tactful and courteous letter can build goodwill even while denying the claim. For example, Village Electronics recently received a letter from Daniel Lindmeier, who purchased a portable CD player a year ago. He wrote to say that the unit doesn't work correctly and to inquire about the

Use the indirect approach in most cases of refusing a claim.

Checklist: Bad News About Orders*

Buffer

✓ Include any details identifying the order.

✓ Extend a welcome to a new customer.

✓ Use resale information on the ordered merchandise to build the customer's confidence in the original choice (except for unfillable orders).

✓ For partial shipments, include the good news about the fulfilled part.

Reasons

✓ State the facts without laying blame.

✓ Specify shipping dates.

✓ Explain why the item is out of stock, such as high popularity or exceptional demand, which may stimulate the customer's desire for the item.

✓ Reinforce the customer's confidence (for consumers, emphasize resale information such as personal attention,

credit, repair services, free delivery, special discounts, telephone shopping, and other services; for dealers, emphasize free counter and window displays, advertising materials, sales manuals, factory guarantees, and nearby warehousing).

✓ Refer to sales promotion material, if desirable.

The Bad News

✓ Stress the reader benefit of the decision to buy.

✓ Offer a substitute product, if available.

Positive, Friendly, Helpful Close

✓ Adopt a tone that shows you remain in control of the situation and will continue to give customers' orders personal attention.

✓ Use resale information to clinch the sale, especially for back orders.

*These items are in addition to the material included in "Checklist: Bad-News Messages."

---

warranty. Lindmeier believes that the warranty covers one year, when it actually covers only three months (see Figure 8–4).

When refusing a claim, avoid language that might have a negative impact on the reader. Instead, demonstrate that you understand and have considered the complaint. Then, even if the claim is unreasonable, rationally explain why you are refusing the request. Remember, don't apologize, and don't rely on company policy. End the letter on a respectful and action-oriented note.

You may be tempted to respond to something particularly outrageous by calling the person responsible a crook, a swindler, or an incompetent. Resist! If you don't, you could be sued for **defamation,** a false statement that tends to damage someone's character or reputation. (Written defamation is called *libel;* spoken defamation is called *slander.*) By this definition, someone suing for defamation would have to prove (1) that the statement is false, (2) that the language is injurious to the person's reputation, and (3) that the statement has been "published."

If you can prove that your accusations are true, you haven't defamed the person. The courts are likely to give you the benefit of the doubt because our society believes that ordinary business communication should not be hampered by fear of lawsuits. However, beware of the irate letter intended to let off steam: If the message has no necessary business purpose and is expressed in abusive language that hints of malice, you'll lose the case. To avoid being accused of defamation, follow these guidelines:

◆ Avoid using any kind of abusive language or terms that could be considered defamatory.

◆ If you wish to express your own personal opinions about a sensitive matter, use your own stationery (not company letterhead), and don't include your job title or position. Take responsibility for your own actions without involving your company.

◆ Provide accurate information and stick to the facts.

◆ Never let anger or malice motivate your messages.

◆ Consult your company's legal department or an attorney whenever you think a message might have legal consequences.

◆ Communicate honestly, and make sure that what you're saying is what you believe to be true.

Margin notes:

When refusing a claim
• Demonstrate your understanding of the complaint
• Explain your refusal
• Suggest alternative action

Objective

5

Define *defamation* and explain how to avoid it in bad-news messages.

Avoid defamation by not responding emotionally.

1 Planning

Analyze: Purpose is to explain that warranty has expired and to offer repairs that the reader can pay for.

Investigate: Briefly gather information on product warranties, terms for repair, and resale information.

Adapt: Use letter format and focus on customer relationship.

2 Writing

Organize: Main idea is that you're offering repairs, even though the warranty has expired. Use the indirect approach to help reader accept your message.

Compose: Make the style conversational. Choose your words carefully, and enclose a catalog to encourage future business.

3 Completing

Revise: Review for logical order and tone. Be clear but friendly.

Produce: Use a clean letter format on letterhead.

Proofread: Review for accuracy and correctness. Be sure to include promised enclosures.

NUMBER ONE IN ENTERTAINMENT

Village Electronics

68 Lake Itasca Boulevard • Hannover, MN 55341
Voice: (612) 878-1312 • Fax: (612) 878-1316

May 3, 2002

Mr. Daniel Lindmeier
849 Cedar Street
Lake Elmo, MN 55042

Dear Mr. Lindmeier:

Thank you for your letter describing the problem with your portable Sony CD Walkman. We believe, as you do, that electronic equipment should be built to last. That's why we stand behind our products with a 90-day warranty.

Even though your Walkman is a year old and therefore out of warranty, we can still help. Please package your CD player carefully and ship it to our store in Hannover. Include your complete name, address, phone number, and a brief description of the problem along with a check for $35. After examining the unit, we will give you a written estimate of the needed parts and labor. Then just let us know—either by phone or by filling out the prepaid card we will provide—whether you want us to make the repairs.

If you choose to repair the unit, the $35 will be applied toward your bill, payable by check or major credit card. If you decide not to repair the unit, the $35 will pay for the technician's time in examining the unit. Sony also has service centers available in your area. If you would prefer to take the unit to one of them, please see the enclosed list.

Thanks again for inquiring about our service. I've also enclosed a catalog of our latest high-tech electronic gear. For the month of June, Sony is offering a "Trade-Up Special," at which time you can receive trade-in credit for your Walkman when you purchase a newer model. Please visit Village Electronics very soon.

Sincerely,

Walter Brodie

Walter Brodie
President

mk

Enclosure

Annotations (left margin):
- Buffer emphasizes a point that reader and writer both agree on.
- States bad news indirectly, tactfully leaving the repair decision to the customer.
- Close blends sales promotion with acknowledgment of the customer's interests.

Annotations (right margin):
- Puts company's policy in a favorable light.
- Helps soothe the reader with a positive alternative action.

Figure 8-4
In-Depth Critique: Letter Refusing a Claim

Checklist: Refusing Claims*

Buffer

✓ Indicate your full understanding of the nature of the complaint.
✓ Avoid all areas of disagreement.
✓ Avoid any hint of your final decision.

Reasons

✓ Provide an accurate, factual account of the transaction.
✓ Emphasize ways things should have been handled, rather than dwelling on reader's negligence.
✓ Avoid using a know-it-all tone.
✓ Use impersonal, passive language.
✓ Avoid accusing, preaching (*you should have*), blaming, or scolding the reader.
✓ Do not make the reader appear or feel stupid.

The Bad News

✓ Make the refusal clear, using tactful wording.
✓ Avoid any hint that your decision is less than final.

✓ Avoid words such as *reject* and *claim*.
✓ Make a counterproposal, offer a compromise, or make a partial adjustment (if desirable).
✓ Make your tone willing, not begrudging, in a spirit of honest cooperation.
✓ Include resale information for the company or product.
✓ Emphasize a desire for a good relationship in the future.
✓ Extend an offer to replace the product or to provide a replacement part at the regular price.

Positive, Friendly, Helpful Close

✓ Make no reference to your refusal.
✓ Refer to enclosed sales material.
✓ Make any suggested action easy for readers to comply with.

---

*These items are in addition to the material included in the "Checklist: Bad-News Messages."

For a brief review of the tasks involved when refusing claims, see this chapter's "Checklist: Refusing Claims."

Sending Negative Organizational News   Bad news doesn't only result from refusing requests. At times you may have bad news about your company's products or about its operations. Whether you're reporting to a supervisor or announcing your news to the media, the particular situation dictates whether you will use the direct or the indirect approach.

Providing Bad News About Products   Say that you must provide bad news about a product. If you were writing to tell your company's bookkeeping department about increasing product prices, you'd use the direct approach. Your audience would have to make some arithmetical adjustments once the increases are put into effect, but readers would presumably be unemotional about the matter. On the other hand, if you were writing to convey the same information to customers or even to your own sales department, you would probably use the indirect approach. Customers never like to pay more, and your sales reps would see the change as weakening your products' competitive edge, threatening their incomes, and possibly threatening their jobs.

> Use either the direct or the indirect approach when providing bad news about a product.

For example, when Sybervantage pursued licensing agreements with Warner, it expected to be entering into a lucrative arrangement in which both companies would profit. But Warner rejected the request, and now Sybervantage must adjust its strategic planning and must keep its sales force both motivated and involved (see Figure 8–5). The middle section of the e-mail message presents an honest statement of the bad news. However, the effect of the bad news is diminished by the problem-solving tone, by the lack of any overt statement that such a setback may affect commissions, and by the upbeat close.

Handling Bad News About Company Operations   At least three situations require bad-news letters about company operations or performance: (1) a change in company policy that will have a negative effect on the reader, (2) problems with company performance, and (3) controversial or unpopular company operations. In trying situations, apologies may be in order. If an apology is appropriate, good writers usually make it brief and bury

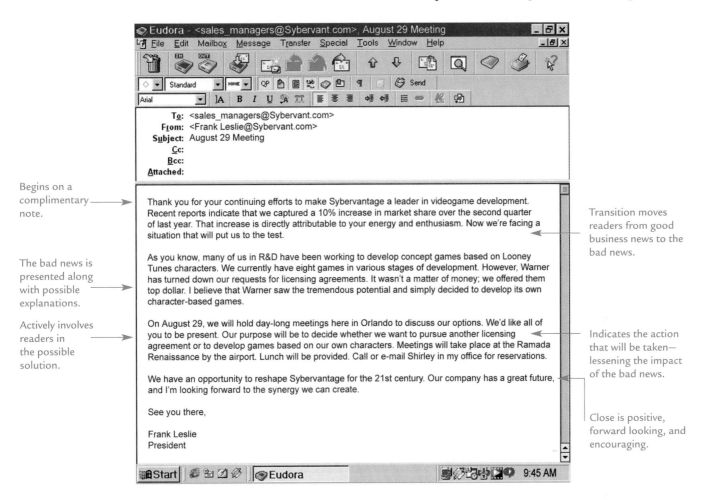

Begins on a complimentary note. →

The bad news is presented along with possible explanations. →

Actively involves readers in the possible solution. →

Transition moves readers from good business news to the bad news.

Indicates the action that will be taken—lessening the impact of the bad news.

Close is positive, forward looking, and encouraging.

To: <sales_managers@Sybervant.com>
From: <Frank Leslie@Sybervant.com>
Subject: August 29 Meeting
Cc:
Bcc:
Attached:

Thank you for your continuing efforts to make Sybervantage a leader in videogame development. Recent reports indicate that we captured a 10% increase in market share over the second quarter of last year. That increase is directly attributable to your energy and enthusiasm. Now we're facing a situation that will put us to the test.

As you know, many of us in R&D have been working to develop concept games based on Looney Tunes characters. We currently have eight games in various stages of development. However, Warner has turned down our requests for licensing agreements. It wasn't a matter of money; we offered them top dollar. I believe that Warner saw the tremendous potential and simply decided to develop its own character-based games.

On August 29, we will hold day-long meetings here in Orlando to discuss our options. We'd like all of you to be present. Our purpose will be to decide whether we want to pursue another licensing agreement or to develop games based on our own characters. Meetings will take place at the Ramada Renaissance by the airport. Lunch will be provided. Call or e-mail Shirley in my office for reservations.

We have an opportunity to reshape Sybervantage for the 21st century. Our company has a great future, and I'm looking forward to the synergy we can create.

See you there,

Frank Leslie
President

Figure 8–5
In-Depth Critique: E-Mail Message Providing Bad News About Products

it somewhere in the middle of the letter. Moreover, they try to leave readers with a favorable impression by closing on a positive note.

When a change in company policy will have a negative effect on your audience, state the reasons for the change clearly and carefully. The explanation section of the letter convinces readers that the change was necessary and, if possible, explains how the change will benefit them. For example, if your company decided to drop orthodontic coverage from its employee dental plan, you could explain the decision this way:

By eliminating this infrequently used benefit we will not have to increase the monthly amount withheld from your paycheck for insurance coverage.

If your company is having serious performance problems, your customers and shareholders want to learn of the difficulty from you, not from newspaper accounts or from rumors. Even if the news leaks out, counter it with your own explanation as soon as possible. Business is based on mutual trust; if your customers and shareholders can't trust you to inform them of your problems, they may choose to work with someone they can trust. When you do inform stakeholders, use your common business sense and present the bad news in as favorable a light as possible. If your company lost a major business customer, you could present the bad news as an opportunity to focus on smaller, growing businesses or on new products.

When Denver International Airport's automatic baggage system damaged hundreds of passengers' bags, the marketing department developed a message that uses the indirect approach to explain the problem to customers.

When conveying bad news about your company, focus on the reasons and on possible benefits.

Companies that produce unpopular products or have controversial operations can find themselves caught in a political crossfire. In such cases, your general strategy might be to explain the reasons your company is manufacturing the controversial item or providing the unpopular service. You want to show that reason and need are behind your operation (not villainy, carelessness, or greed).

Sending Negative Employment Messages   Most managers must convey bad news about people. You can use the direct approach when communicating with other companies; for example, if you're sending a negative reference to a prospective employer. But use the indirect approach when writing to job applicants and employees, because your readers will most certainly be emotionally involved.

Refusing Requests for Recommendation Letters   Even though many states have passed laws to protect employers who provide open and honest job references for former employees, legal hazards persist.[6] That's why many former employers still refuse to write recommendation letters—especially for people whose job performance has been unsatisfactory. When sending refusals to prospective employers, your message may be brief and direct:

> We received your request for a recommendation for Yolanda Johnson. According to guidelines from our human resources department, we are authorized to confirm only that Ms. Johnson worked for Tandy, Inc., for three years from June 1996 to July 1999. Best of luck as you interview the administrative applicants.

This message doesn't need to say, "We cannot comply with your request." It simply gets down to the business of giving readers the information that is allowable.

Letters to the applicants themselves are another matter. Any refusal to cooperate may seem a personal slight and a threat to the applicant's future. Diplomacy and preparation help readers accept your refusal:

> Thank you for letting me know about your job opportunity with Coca-Cola. Your internship there and the MBA you've worked so hard to earn should place you in an excellent position to land the marketing job.
>
> Although we send out no formal recommendations here at PepsiCo, I can certainly send Coke a confirmation of your employment dates. For more in-depth recommendations, be sure to ask the people you worked with during your internship to write evaluations of your work performance, and don't forget to ask several of your professors to write evaluations of your marketing skills. Best of luck to you in your career.

This letter deftly and tactfully avoids hurting the reader's feelings because it makes positive comments about the reader's recent activities, implies the refusal, suggests an alternative, and uses a polite close.

Rejecting Job Applications   It's also difficult to tactfully tell job applicants that you won't be offering them employment. But don't let the difficulty stop you from communicating the bad news. Rejecting an applicant with silence is unacceptable. At the same time, poorly written rejection letters do have negative consequences, ranging from the loss of qualified candidates for future openings to the loss of potential customers (not only the rejected applicants but also their friends and family).[7] When delivering bad news to job applicants, follow three guidelines:[8]

◆ **Open with the direct approach.** Job applicants know that good news will most likely come by phone and that bad news will most likely come by letter. If you try to buffer the bad news that your reader is expecting, you will seem manipulative and insincere.

Use the direct approach when giving readers bad news about someone else's job; use the indirect approach when giving readers bad news about their own jobs.

In letters informing prospective employers that you will not provide a recommendation, be direct, brief, and factual (to avoid legal pitfalls).

O b j e c t i v e
6
List three guidelines for delivering bad news to job applicants and give a brief explanation of each one.

Direct opening avoids postponing the bad news that the recipient expects.

The positive close offers specific praise, helping the candidate finish the message with her self-confidence intact.

Implies the bad news and emphasizes that the deciding factor was experience, not poor qualifications.

Further explanation immediately follows the bad news.

Bradley & Jackson
CERTIFIED PUBLIC ACCOUTANTS

223 Brandon Street • Biloxi, Mississippi 39530 • (601) 446-9810 • (601) 466-6235

May 7, 2002

Ms. Carol Lou DeCicco
472 Bellville Way
Biloxi, MS 39530

Dear Ms. DeCicco:

We appreciate your application for the position of tax accountant. After much consideration, we have decided to hire an applicant with over 10 years' experience in tax accounting. With more than 30 applicants for this position, the selection process was quite difficult.

Your résumé and credentials show you to be a deserving candidate, and your academic record and previous accounting experience certainly indicate your willingness to work hard. Those of us who had the opportunity to talk with you believe that your ability to communicate will certainly help you achieve an excellent position in a recognized accounting firm.

Thank you for thinking of us.

Sincerely,

Marvin R. Fichter

Marvin R. Fichter
Human Resources Director

bl

Figure 8–6
In-Depth Critique: Letter Rejecting a Job Application

◆ **Clearly state why the applicant was not selected.** Make your rejection less personal by stating that you hired someone with more experience or whose qualifications match the position requirements more closely.

◆ **Close by suggesting alternatives.** If you believe the applicant is qualified, mention other openings within your company. You might suggest professional organizations that could help the applicant find employment. Or you might simply mention that the applicant's résumé will be considered for future openings. Any of these positive suggestions may help the applicant be less disappointed and view your company more positively.

A rejection letter need not be long. Remember, sending a well-written form letter that follows these three guidelines is better than not sending one at all. After all, the applicant wants to know only one thing: Did I land the job? Your brief message conveys the information clearly and with tactful consideration for the applicant's feelings. After Carol DeCicco interviewed with Bradley & Jackson, she was hopeful about receiving a job offer. Everything went well, and her résumé was in good shape. The letter in Figure 8–6 helps

Sharpening Your Career Skills

Mastering the Art of Constructive Criticism

To improve, people need to be evaluated, but criticism from others is often hard to take. The way you tell someone "You did it wrong" can destroy goodwill and cooperation, or it can build the relationship and help the person retain self-esteem, learn from the mistake, and improve performance. To criticize more constructively, follow these suggestions:

❏ **Get all the facts first.** Don't accept hearsay or rumors. Find out who did or said what, when, where, why, and how—and be specific.

❏ **Don't act in haste.** Never act while you're angry. Think things out before you write or speak, and then explain your criticism calmly, rationally, and objectively.

❏ **Phrase your remarks impersonally.** Criticize the mistake, not the person. Focus your remarks on the action only, and analyze it thoughtfully.

❏ **Never criticize in an offhand manner.** Treat the situation seriously. Take the time to state the problem in detail, explaining what was wrong and why.

❏ **Don't ridicule, talk down, or use sarcasm.** An abusive tone prevents people from accepting what you have to say. Respect readers and listeners, giving them the benefit of the doubt.

❏ **Make the offense clear.** Don't talk in generalities. Be specific about exactly what was done wrong.

❏ **Preface the criticism with a kind word or a compliment.** Start with a few words of praise or admiration, saying how much you value the person. First the good news; then the bad.

❏ **Supply the answer.** Explain how to do things right. Don't dwell on the mistake; emphasize how to correct it, and avoid repeating it.

❏ **Ask for cooperation.** Don't demand cooperation. Asking makes the person feel like a team member and provides an incentive to improve.

❏ **Limit yourself to one criticism for each offense.** Don't dredge up or rehash past mistakes. Focus on the current problem.

❏ **End on a friendly note.** Don't leave things up in the air, to be discussed again later. Settle them now, and make the close friendly. Give the other person a pat on the back. Let the last memory of the matter be a good one.

❏ **Forgive and forget.** Once the criticism has been made, let the person start with a clean slate. Avoid looking for more mistakes, and give the person a chance to improve.

❏ **Take steps to prevent a recurrence.** Follow up to make sure the person is acting on your suggestions and doing things right.

If you follow these guidelines, constructive criticism can benefit you, your company, and—most important—the person you're criticizing.

CAREER APPLICATIONS

1. Think back over the lessons you've learned in life. How did you benefit from someone telling you the truth about something you were doing wrong?
2. With a partner, role-play a situation in which one of you is the boss and the other an employee. The boss is angry because the employee repeatedly arrives late for work, takes long lunches, and leaves 5 to 10 minutes early. However, the employee's work is always excellent. After the role-play, analyze what the boss did right and what could be improved.

DeCicco understand that (1) she would have been hired if she'd had more tax experience and (2) she shouldn't be discouraged.

Objective **7**

Outline the main purpose of performance reviews, give three ways to accomplish that purpose, and list five guidelines to follow when giving negative reviews.

Giving Negative Performance Reviews   A performance review is a manager's formal or informal evaluation of an employee. Few other communication tasks require such a broad range of skills and strategy as that needed for performance reviews, whether positive or negative. The main purpose of these reviews is to improve employee performance by (1) emphasizing and clarifying job requirements, (2) giving employees feedback on their efforts toward fulfilling those requirements, and (3) guiding continued efforts by developing a plan of action, along with its rewards and opportunities. (See "Sharpening Your Career Skills—Mastering the Art of Constructive Criticism.") In addition to improving employee performance, performance reviews help companies set organizational standards and communicate organizational values.[9]

Positive and negative performance reviews share several characteristics: The tone is objective and unbiased, the language is nonjudgmental, and the focus is problem resolution.[10] To increase objectivity, more organizations are giving their employees feedback from multiple sources. In these "360-degree reviews," employees get feedback from all directions in the organization: above, below, and horizontally.[11]

Be aware that employee performance reviews can play an important role in lawsuits. It's difficult to criticize employees face-to-face, and it's just as hard to include criticism in written performance evaluations. Nevertheless, if you fire an employee for incompetence and the performance evaluations are all positive, the employee can sue your company, maintaining you had no cause to terminate employment.[12] Also, your company could be sued for negligence if an injury is caused by an employee who received a negative evaluation but received no corrective action (such as retraining).[13] So, as difficult as it may be, make sure your performance evaluations are well balanced and honest.

When you need to give a negative performance review, remember these guidelines: [14]

◆ **Confront the problem right away.** Avoiding performance problems only makes them worse. The one acceptable reason to wait is to allow you time to calm down and regain your objectivity.

◆ **Plan your message.** Be clear about your concerns, and include examples of the employee's specific actions. Think about any possible biases you may have, and get feedback from others. Collect all relevant facts (both strengths and weaknesses).

◆ **Deliver the message in private.** Whether in writing or in person, be sure to address the performance problem privately. Don't send performance reviews by e-mail or fax. If you're reviewing an employee's performance face-to-face, conduct that review in a meeting arranged expressly for that purpose and consider holding that meeting in a conference room, the employee's office, or some other neutral area.

◆ **Focus on the problem.** Discuss the problems caused by the employee's behavior (without attacking the employee). Compare the employee's performance with what's expected, with company goals, or with job requirements (not with the performance of other employees). Identify the consequences of continuing poor performance, and show that you're committed to helping solve the problem.

◆ **Ask for a commitment from the employee.** Help the employee understand that planning for and making improvements are the employee's responsibility. However, finalize decisions jointly so that you can be sure any action to be taken is achievable. Set a schedule for improvement and for following up with evaluations of that improvement.

Donna Burnley would recommend that even if your employee's performance has been disappointing, you would do well to mention some good points in your performance review. Then, you must clearly and tactfully state how the employee can better meet the responsibilities of the job. If the performance review is to be effective, be sure to suggest ways that the employee can improve.[15] For example, instead of telling an employee only that he damaged some expensive machinery, suggest that he take a refresher course in the correct operation of that machinery. The goal is to help the employee succeed.

Terminating Employment   When writing a termination letter, you have three goals: (1) present the reasons for this difficult action, (2) avoid statements that might involve the company in legal action, and (3) leave the relationship between the terminated employee and the firm as favorable as possible. For both legal and personal reasons, present specific justification for asking the employee to leave.[16]

Make sure that all your reasons are accurate and verifiable. Avoid words that are open to interpretation, such as *untidy* and *difficult*. Make sure the employee leaves with feelings that are as positive as the circumstances allow. You can do this by telling the truth about the termination and by helping as much as you can to make the employee's transition as smooth as possible.[17] To review the tasks involved in this type of message, see this chapter's "Checklist: Negative Employment Messages."

Carefully word a termination letter to avoid creating undue ill will and grounds for legal action.

Going Online

Announcing an Employee Layoff: How to Write a Termination Notice

◆

What are some of the problems that job cuts or downsizing might pose for a company, its managers, and its employees? For news stories, editorials, and background material about layoffs, visit the "Downsizing and Layoffs" site at Yahoo!. "Related Web Sites" provide evaluations of the impact of downsizing on employees and on net profits, as well as offering advice for executives and HR managers who deal with company layoffs. Learn about your legal and social responsibilities toward employees, and find out what policies and procedures to address when preparing for a layoff. What laws and regulations might affect a downsizing decision? What assistance can you offer to maintain morale? Find out.

www.yahoo.com

To reach this Web site, go to www.prenhall.com/thill *(the Web site for this text). Select Chapter 8, then select "Student Resources." There you'll find a current live link that will take you straight to the site.*

Checklist: Negative Employment Messages*

Buffer

✓ Identify the applicant or employee clearly when writing to a third party.

✓ Express the reasons for writing—clearly, completely, and objectively.

✓ Avoid insincere expressions of regret.

✓ Avoid impersonal business clichés.

Reasons

✓ Avoid terms with legal definitions (*slanderous, criminal*).

✓ Avoid negative terms with imprecise definitions (*lazy, sloppy*).

✓ Whenever possible, embed negative comments in favorable or semifavorable passages.

✓ Avoid generalities, and explain the limits of your observations about the applicant's or employee's shortcomings.

✓ Eliminate secondhand information.

✓ Stress the confidentiality of your letter.

✓ Avoid negative personal judgments.

✓ For letters refusing to supply a recommendation to job seekers, suggest another avenue for getting a recommendation.

✓ For rejection letters, emphasize the positive qualities of the person hired rather than the shortcomings of the rejected applicant.

✓ For performance reviews, describe the employee's limitations and suggest methods for improving performance.

The Bad News

✓ Imply negative decisions whenever possible.

✓ Avoid statements that might involve the company in legal action.

Positive, Friendly, Helpful Close

✓ For refusals to supply recommendations and for rejection letters, extend good wishes.

✓ For performance reviews, express a willingness to help further.

✓ For termination letters, make suggestions for finding another job, if applicable.

*These items are in addition to the material included in the "Checklist: Bad-News Messages."

SUMMARY OF LEARNING OBJECTIVES

1 Apply the three-step writing process to bad-news messages. Because the way you say "no" can be far more damaging than the fact that you're saying it, planning your bad-news messages is crucial. Make sure your purpose is specific, necessary, and appropriate for written media. Find out how your audience prefers to receive bad news. Collect all the facts necessary to support your negative decision, and adapt your tone to the situation as well as to your audience. Bad-news messages may be organized according to the direct or the indirect approach, and your choice depends on audience preference as well as on the situation. In addition, carefully choose positive words to construct diplomatic sentences. Finally, revision, design, and proofreading are necessary to ensure that you are saying exactly what you want to say in the best possible way.

2 Show how to achieve an audience-centered tone, and explain why it helps readers. To create an audience-centered tone, be aware of and use the cultural conventions that your audience expects. For U.S. audiences with few cultural differences, use the "you" attitude, choose positive words, and use language that is respectful. Adopting this tone helps your readers accept that your decision is firm, understand that your decision is fair and reasonable, remain well-disposed toward your company, and preserve their pride.

3 Differentiate between the direct and indirect organizational approaches to bad-news messages, and discuss when it's appropriate to use each one. The direct approach to bad-news messages puts the bad news up front, follows with the reasons

(and perhaps offers an alternative), and closes with a positive statement. On the other hand, the indirect approach begins with a buffer (a neutral or positive statement), explains the reasons, clearly states the bad news (de-emphasizing it as much as possible), and closes with a positive statement. It's best to use the direct approach when you know your audience prefers receiving bad news up front or if the bad news will cause readers little pain or disappointment. Otherwise, the indirect approach is best.

4 Discuss the three techniques for saying "no" as clearly and kindly as possible. To say "no" and still be diplomatic, use three techniques. First, de-emphasize the bad news by minimizing the space (or time) devoted to it, subordinating it in a complex or compound sentence, or embedding it mid-paragraph. Second, relate the bad news in a conditional (*if* or *when*) statement to imply that readers could have received or might someday receive a favorable answer. Third, imply the bad news by saying what you will do, not what you won't do.

5 Define *defamation*, and explain how to avoid it in bad-news messages. *Defamation* is a false statement that is damaging to a person's character or reputation. When written, defamation is called libel. When spoken, it's called slander. To avoid being accused of defamation, (1) never use abusive language, (2) express personal opinions without involving your company (using your own personal letterhead and excluding your title or position), (3) stick to the facts, (4) never write a message in anger, (5) seek legal advice about questionable messages, and (6) communicate honestly.

6 **List three guidelines for delivering bad news to job applicants, and give a brief explanation of each one.** When rejecting job applicants, Follow three guidelines: (1) Use the direct approach. Your readers probably assume that a letter from you is bad news, so don't build their suspense. (2) State clearly why your reader was not selected. This explanation can be specific without being personal if you explain that you hired someone with more experience or with qualifications that more closely match position requirements. (3) Suggest alternatives. Perhaps your company has other openings or you would be willing to consider the applicant for future openings.

7 **Outline the main purpose of performance reviews, give three ways to accomplish that purpose, and list five guidelines to follow when giving negative reviews.** The main purpose of a performance review is to improve employee performance. To accomplish this purpose, be sure to emphasize and clarify job requirements, give feedback on employee efforts, and develop a plan of action to guide continuing efforts. When giving negative reviews, confront the problem immediately, plan your message carefully, deliver your message in private, focus on the problem (not on the employee), and ask for a commitment from the employee.

SOLVING A COMMUNICATION DILEMMA AT AMERICAN AIRLINES

Donna Burnley knows that saying "no" is never pleasant, but her professional responsibilities require her to be selective. Even though she is responsible for getting supplies and equipment to more than 170 locations worldwide, she relies on only a few suppliers. Narrowing the field means having no choice but to say "no"—even to nice, ethical people who come to her with nothing but good intentions.

However, Burnley does have a choice about *how* she says "no." She follows a thorough, objective decision-making process. She says that American's purchasing process "is designed to maximize total value by having me identify product specifications, assess supplier capabilities, research industry and raw material trends, understand the production process, and monitor the quality of end-products and services." When she makes a decision, she knows what she's talking about.

Because her decision process is so methodical and thorough, Burnley has clear, objective reasons to present when she has to say "no." For example, she and her team hire independent testing laboratories to evaluate the quality of the supplies and equipment they buy, so it's relatively easy to explain to rejected suppliers why they were rejected. Such explanations not only help rejected suppliers accept Burnley's messages but also provide the suppliers with the concrete, factual information necessary to improve their products and perhaps be reconsidered in the future.

Burnley uses her communication skills to convey negative messages in a professional and courteous manner. She says that effective communication is one of her primary responsibilities when working with outside suppliers.

Your Mission You're on the purchasing staff at American Airlines, working as an assistant to Donna Burnley. Your job includes responding to requests and proposals from the airline's current suppliers and from companies that would like to become suppliers. These requests cover a variety of topics, from meetings to making sales presentations.

1. Your glassware supplier has announced a dramatic price increase that affects all of the products that American buys from the company. The increase averages 12 percent, which is a lot of money in a tight-margin business such as air travel. In all other respects, this company has been a stellar performer, offering great products with superb customer service. However, this price increase is both unexpected and unacceptable. As much as everyone likes working with this company, either it will have to cancel the price increase, or American will be forced to find a new glassware supplier. You do have some room for compromise, however. An increase of only 3 or 4 percent would be acceptable. Which of the following paragraphs does the best job of presenting the bad news and the reasons?

   a. It's too bad that this is such a penny-pinching business, but that's the way things are. We can live with your current prices, but not the proposed increase. We'd love to go along with you, but I'm afraid we just can't.

   b. Because the airline industry competes primarily on price, we have no choice but to manage our costs carefully—it is our only hope of maintaining a minimal level of profitability. Your current prices fit our cost structure well. Unfortunately, the proposed 12 percent increase does not, leaving us no choice but to find another supplier.

   c. As you are probably aware, the airline industry competes primarily on price, so managing our costs carefully is about the only option we have for maintaining a minimal level of profitability. Your current prices fit our cost structure well. Unfortunately, the proposed 12 percent increase does not, and we would be unable to continue purchasing from you if the increase goes into effect.

2. Continuing with the case of the glassware price increase, which of the following closing paragraphs would you choose and why?

   a. We do appreciate quality and service, but we are not going to pay ridiculous prices to get it. I am confident that we can use American's vast buying power to find a more reasonable supplier somewhere in the world.

b. Although the 12 percent increase is unacceptable, we do respect your need to be profitable in a tough business environment. Consequently, we are open to some negotiation about a smaller price increase, if you would consider that.

c. We are saddened by our decision, let me assure you. We'll not only miss the quality of your products, but the quality of the people we've dealt with at your firm as well. We've come to know many of them almost as personal friends. Please give my best wishes to everyone in your office.

3. The company that has supplied you with plastic drinking glasses for several years has suffered some quality and service problems in recent months. The problems include cracked glasses and late deliveries that leave some airplanes with too few glasses to serve all their passengers. The supplier has been very dependable up to this point, and you're not sure whether your counterparts are even aware of the problems. The problems haven't caused any significant trouble yet, but you're afraid they might if the situation isn't corrected. You and your colleagues have a good working relationship with your counterparts in the supplier organization, even socializing with them when you're in the same city. How should you start a letter to the supplier informing management of the need to address these problems?

a. This is just a quick note to thank you for the great service you've provided us over the years. American Airlines always tries to offer the best to its customers, and your company's products have played a key role in that effort.

b. I enjoyed that round of golf last time you were in town. I only wish your company was as good as your golf game. You guys used to be one of our star performers, but you've really been dropping the ball lately. I don't mean to sound too harsh, but you've got some problems that must be fixed immediately.

c. You have always shared American's high standards for quality and service, so I know you'll be interested in some feedback that we've received from several of our field offices.

4. Personal contacts are an important source of new business opportunities in many industries. In some cases, businesspeople develop contacts through active participation in industry or professional groups, visits to trade shows, alumni societies, and other groups. You've recently received a request from a former college classmate (Marcia DeLancey) who is now a sales manager for a plastics manufacturer. She wants to visit your office to present her company's plastic containers. However, you are already familiar with the company, and you know that it is too small to meet your needs for on-time global deliveries. You didn't know DeLancey all that well in school; in fact, you had to think for a minute to remember who she was (this is the first contact you've had with her since

you both graduated five years ago). Which of the following openings would be most appropriate, keeping in mind that you know her company can't make the grade?

a. Congratulations on reaching such an impressive position at your new company. I hope you enjoy your work as much as I do. Thank you for your recent inquiry—evaluating such requests is one of my key responsibilities.

b. Great to hear from you; I'd love to catch up on old times with you and find out how you're doing in your new job. I bounced around a bit after college, but I really feel that I've found my niche here at American.

c. I'm sorry to say that American has already evaluated your company and found its resources were not a good match for our international delivery needs. However, I do appreciate your getting in touch, and I hope all is well with you.

5. Like many corporate buyers, American wants to establish stable, dependable relationships with suppliers. Having a supplier falter on the job or even go out of business without warning would be a huge disruption for you. As a result, your department is concerned about every supplier's financial health. The company that provides American with napkins and paper towels has done a good job for years, but recent events have left the company in precarious financial shape. Your office has already told the company that American would be forced to find another paper source if the company's finances didn't improve. Unfortunately, it's finances have grown even worse, and now you must act. You've already written the buffer, reasons, and bad news, and now you need a positive close for your message. Which of these would you choose?

a. Thank you very much for the service you've provided in the past. All of us here at American Airlines wish you the best in resolving your current situation. If you are able to meet these financial criteria in the future, by all means please get back in touch with us.

b. I understand that you're bound to be disappointed by our decisions. If you don't think our decision was valid or if there is more information that you believe we need to evaluate, please feel free to call me or my immediate supervisor to discuss the situation. We have to deal with quite a few suppliers, as you know, and I suppose there is a chance that we missed something in our initial evaluation.

c. I'm very sorry that we have to terminate our purchasing agreement with you. We relied on your company's products for many years, and it's a shame that we won't be able to in the future. I hope this decision doesn't affect your work force too negatively. If there's anything we can do to help, please don't hesitate to call.[18]

TEST YOUR KNOWLEDGE

1. Why is it particularly important to adapt your medium and tone to your audience's needs and preferences when writing a bad news message?

2. What are the five main goals in delivering bad news?

3. What are the advantages of using the direct approach to deliver the bad news at the beginning of a message?

4. What is the sequence of elements in a bad-news message organized using the indirect approach?

5. What is a buffer, and why do some critics consider it unethical?

6. When using an indirect approach to announce a negative decision, what is the purpose of presenting your reasons before explaining the decision itself?

7. What are three techniques for de-emphasizing bad news?

8. What is defamation, and how does libel differ from slander?

9. What are three guidelines for writing rejection letters to job applicants?

10. When giving a negative review to an employee, what five steps should you follow?

INTERACTIVE LEARNING

USE THIS TEXT'S ONLINE RESOURCES

Visit the myPHLIP Web site at www.prenhall.com/thill. For Chapter 8, take advantage of the interactive "Study Guide" to test your chapter knowledge. Get instant feedback on whether you need additional studying. Read the "Current Events" articles to get the latest on chapter topics, and complete the exercises—as specified by your instructor.

This site's "Study Hall" helps you succeed in this course. "Talk in the Hall" lets you leave messages and meet new friends online. If you have a question, you can "Ask the Tutor." And to get a better grade in this course, you can find more help at "Writing Skills," "Study Skills," and "Study Tips."

The "Research Area" helps you locate a wealth of information to use in course assignments. Plus, you can send a message to online research experts, who will help you find exactly the information you need.

APPLY YOUR KNOWLEDGE

1. Why is it important to end your bad-news message on a positive note? Explain.

2. If company policy changes, should you explain those changes to employees and customers at about the same time, or should you explain them to employees first? Why?

3. If the purpose of your letter is to convey bad news, should you take the time to suggest alternatives to your reader? Why or why not?

4. When a company suffers a setback, should you soften the impact by letting out the bad news a little at a time? Why or why not?

5. **Ethical Choices** Is intentionally de-emphasizing bad news the same as distorting graphs and charts to de-emphasize unfavorable data? Why or why not?

PRACTICE YOUR KNOWLEDGE

DOCUMENTS FOR ANALYSIS

Read the following documents; then (1) analyze the strengths and weaknesses of each sentence and (2) revise each document so that it follows this chapter's guidelines.

Document 8.A: Providing Bad News About Products

Your spring fraternity party sounds like fun. We're glad you've again chosen us as your caterer. Unfortunately, we have changed a few of our policies, and I wanted you to know about these changes in advance so that we won't have any misunderstandings on the day of the party.

We will arrange the delivery of tables and chairs as usual the evening before the party. However, if you want us to set up, there is now a $100 charge for that service. Of course, you might want to get some of the brothers and pledges to do it, which would save you money. We've also added a small charge for cleanup. This is only $3 per person (you can estimate because I know a lot of people come and go later in the evening).

Other than that, all the arrangements will be the same. We'll provide the skirt for the band stage, tablecloths, bar setup, and of course, the barbecue. Will you have the tubs of ice with soft drinks again? We can do that for you as well, but there will be a fee.

Please let me know if you have any problems with these changes and we'll try to work them out. I know it's going to be a great party.

Document 8.B: Refusing Requests for Claims and Adjustments

I am responding to your letter of about six weeks ago asking for an adjustment on your fax/modem, model FM39Z. We test all our products before they leave the factory; therefore, it could not have been our fault that your fax/modem didn't work.

If you or someone in your office dropped the unit, it might have caused the damage. Or the damage could have been caused by the shipper if he dropped it. If so, you should file a claim with the shipper. At any rate, it wasn't our fault. The parts are already covered by warranty. However, we will provide labor for the repairs for $50, which is less than our cost since you are a valued customer.

We will have a booth at the upcoming trade fair there and hope to see you or someone from your office. We have many new models of office machines that we're sure you'll want to see. I've enclosed our latest catalog. Hope to see you there.

EXERCISES

8–1. Select which approach you would use (direct or indirect) for the following bad-news messages:

   a. A memo to your boss informing her that one of your key clients is taking its business to a different accounting firm

   b. An e-mail message to a customer informing her that one of the books she ordered over the Internet is temporarily out of stock

   c. A letter to a customer explaining that the tape backup unit he ordered for his new custom computer is on back order and that, as a consequence, the shipping of the entire order will be delayed

   d. A letter from the telephone company rejecting a customer's claim that the phone company should reimburse the customer for the costs of a new high-speed modem (apparently, the phone lines will carry data at only half the modem's speed)

   e. A memo to all employees notifying them that the company parking lot will be repaved during the first week of June and that the company will provide a shuttle service from a remote parking lot during that period

   f. A letter from a travel agent to a customer stating that the airline will not refund her money for the flight she missed but that her tickets are valid for one year

   g. A form letter from a U.S. airline to a customer explaining that they cannot extend the expiration date of the customer's frequent flyer miles even though the customer was living overseas for the past three years

   h. A letter from an insurance company to a policyholder denying a claim for reimbursement for a special medical procedure that is not covered under the terms of the customer's policy

   i. A letter from an electronics store stating that the customer will not be reimbursed for a malfunctioning cell phone still under warranty (the terms of the warranty do not cover damages to phones that were accidentally placed in the freezer overnight)

   j. An announcement to the repairs department listing parts that are on back order and will be three weeks late

Document 8.C: Rejecting Job Applications

I regret to inform you that you were not selected for our summer intern program at Equifax. We had over a thousand résumés and cover letters to go through and simply could not get to them all. We have been asked to notify everyone that we have already selected students for the 25 positions based on those who applied early and were qualified.

We're sure you will be able to find a suitable position for summer work in your field and wish you the best of luck. We deeply regret any inconvenience associated with our reply.

8–2. **Teamwork** Working alone, revise the following statements to de-emphasize the bad news. (*Hint:* Minimize the space devoted to the bad news, subordinate it, embed it, or use the passive voice.) Then team up with a classmate and read each other's revisions. Did you both use the same approach in every case? Which approach seems to be most effective for each of the revised statements?

   a. The airline can't refund your money. The "Conditions" segment on the back of your ticket states that there are no refunds for missed flights. Sometimes the airline makes exceptions, but only when life and death are involved. Of course, your ticket is still valid and can be used on a flight to the same destination.

   b. I'm sorry to tell you, we can't supply the custom decorations you requested. We called every supplier and none of them can do what you want on such short notice. You can, however, get a standard decorative package on the same theme in time. I found a supplier that stocks these. Of course, it won't have quite the flair you originally requested.

   c. We can't refund your money for the malfunctioning lamp. You shouldn't have placed a 250-watt bulb in the fixture socket; it's guaranteed for a maximum of 75 watts.

8–3. Answer the following questions pertaining to buffers:

   a. You have to tell a local restaurant owner that your plans have changed and you have to cancel the 90-person banquet scheduled for next month. Do you need to use a buffer? Why or why not?

   b. Write a buffer for a letter declining an invitation to speak at the association's annual fund-raising event. Show your appreciation for being asked.

   c. Write a buffer for a letter rejecting a job applicant who speaks three foreign languages fluently. Include praise for the applicant's accomplishments.

8–4. **Internet** Public companies sometimes have to issue news releases announcing or explaining downturns in sales, profits, demand, or other business factors. Visit the Xerox Web site and read the press release from October 2, 2000, discussing the background of its financial results. You'll find the site at www.xerox.com/go/xrx/about_xerox/AX_4.jsp. (If this announcement isn't available, look for a company that recently reported lower earnings or other bad news, and access the news release on that firm's Web site.) How does the headline relate to the main message of the release? Is the release organized according to the direct or the indirect approach? What does the company do to present the bad news in a favorable light?

8–5 Ethical Choices The insurance company where you work is planning to raise all premiums for health-care coverage. Your boss has asked you to read a draft of her letter to customers announcing the new, higher rates. The first two paragraphs discuss some exciting medical advances and the expanded coverage offered by your company. Only in the final paragraph do customers learn that they will have to pay more for coverage starting next year. What are the ethical implications of this draft? What changes would you suggest?

CASES

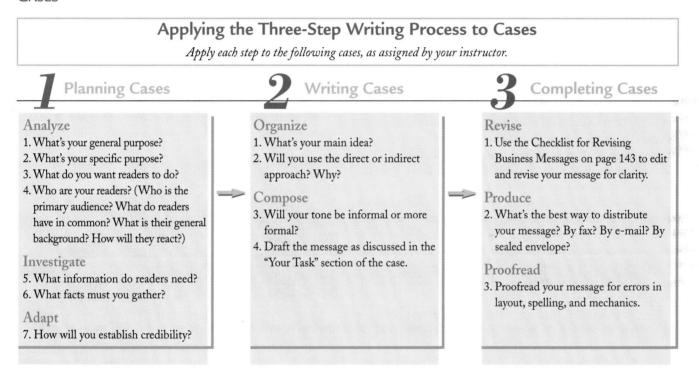

Applying the Three-Step Writing Process to Cases

Apply each step to the following cases, as assigned by your instructor.

1 Planning Cases

Analyze
1. What's your general purpose?
2. What's your specific purpose?
3. What do you want readers to do?
4. Who are your readers? (Who is the primary audience? What do readers have in common? What is their general background? How will they react?)

Investigate
5. What information do readers need?
6. What facts must you gather?

Adapt
7. How will you establish credibility?

2 Writing Cases

Organize
1. What's your main idea?
2. Will you use the direct or indirect approach? Why?

Compose
3. Will your tone be informal or more formal?
4. Draft the message as discussed in the "Your Task" section of the case.

3 Completing Cases

Revise
1. Use the Checklist for Revising Business Messages on page 143 to edit and revise your message for clarity.

Produce
2. What's the best way to distribute your message? By fax? By e-mail? By sealed envelope?

Proofread
3. Proofread your message for errors in layout, spelling, and mechanics.

NEGATIVE ANSWERS TO ROUTINE REQUESTS

1. Tethered SwimCords: Letter to Italian sports retailer returning order Kelly Greene loved to swim; more than that, she loved the all-over exercise that swimming provides, without the joint hammering of jogging or aerobics. Trouble was, it took only six strokes to swim across the small pool at her apartment complex. She spent most of her time turning and pushing off, so she was actually gliding most of the time and she wasn't getting much exercise. What could she do? She invented SwimCords.

Taking her cue from surfers who use ankle tethers to keep their boards from getting lost in the waves, Greene developed an elastic, Bungee-like leash she could attach to her ankle and the pool's edge. She could swim and swim—and go nowhere. After a few design improvements and an enthusiastic endorsement from the UCLA swim team, Greene opened her new manufacturing business.

As she explained when she hired you to help process orders, it wasn't an overnight success. She first spent two years as a member of an inventors' guild, learning her way through the patenting process. But now orders for the $29.95 SwimCords are pouring in from all over the United States.

Today you opened a letter from Isabella Caparelli, owner of Sports Italia in Milan, eagerly requesting a sizable shipment of SwimCords. Caparelli spotted them in a U.S. sporting goods store and "has to have them," she writes. You took the letter straight to Greene's office.

"Oh, dear," the inventor fretted. "We're not ready to ship overseas. I knew it would happen soon, but right now—you'll just have to tell her no." She hesitated for a moment, glanced at the letter again, then added, "But mention that we're growing fast and we might be ready to ship them internationally in, say," she glanced at the calendar on her wall, "six months. I just hate to lose an order that big. Do what you can to keep her interest, but don't mislead her, either. I'm learning that honesty pays off faster than any big-ticket sales in this business," she smiled. "Oh, and be sure to send her a free sample."

Your task: Back at your desk, write a polite and encouraging refusal to Isabella Caparelli, the owner of Sports Italia, Via Arimondi 29-20121, Milan, Italy. Enclose a sample SwimCord.[19]

2. Disappearing soaps: E-mail from Craftopia.com At Craftopia.com, based in West Chester, Pennsylvania, orders for the Seaside Soaps kit have been flying in faster than you can fill them. Consumers are ordering the kit over your 800-line and from your Web site, through the SSL (Secure Socket Layering) encrypted ordering service. The frenzy started with a national magazine ad campaign—Craftopia's first.

The print ad for the "soap-making" kits featured a luscious summer beach scene with a sun-drenched little girl playing in the surf. Next to this warm image, an inset photo displayed the translucent blue, yellow, and green "sea-life" soaps spilling from a bucket onto the sand like colored ice cubes. The kit includes molds (for conch and scallop shells, bubbles, starfish, and a porpoise), a two-pound block of glycerine soap (enough for 52 soaps), lavender scent, color dyes, and eyedroppers. Although your site sells some 75,000 products for creative crafts projects, the soap kit is the biggest seller the company has had since its springtime launch by former QVC executive Harold Poliskin.

With deep-pocketed funding from an impressive array of investors, Craftopia.com offers an extensive variety of products for the growing number of crafters now shopping online. "We're seeing people order 50 of something at once," Poliskin proudly told the *Philadelphia Inquirer* shortly after Craftopia's debut. "A lot of stores wouldn't have that much in stock."

At www.craftopia.com, consumers can read Craftopia's online magazine, share tips and ideas with others on the bulletin board, search for projects by level of skill required, and read instructions and tips for using the products they order. If they're reluctant to transmit credit card information over the Internet, they can call 1-800-373-0343, Monday through Friday, 9 a.m. to 5 p.m. ET, and speak to an operator.

Yarn, ribbon, candles, stencils; you name it, Craftopia.com can deliver it to your door. Everything a creative dabbler could ask for—except for those cool Seaside Soap kits so enticingly displayed on your Web site "for the hot price of just $39.01." You've just been informed by your supplier, which drop-ships the merchandise directly, that the stock has run out. Regardless of the scramble to speed up production, the new kits won't be ready to ship until six weeks from today.

  Your task: As customer service supervisor (www. craftopia.com/shop/customercare/customercare.asp), you've been asked to break the bad news in an e-mail message notifying customers of the delay. Craftopia will offer refunds or merchandise credit to customers who make such a request. Also, because the soap kits are hitting the kind of numbers that investors want to see, your message will be reviewed by CEO Poliskin before it's released. Better make it your best work.[20]

3. A taxing matter: Letter from O&Y Tax Service refusing to pay for another's mistake During the mid-April rush at tax time last year, Hilda Black phoned to ask whether she could roll over funds from one retirement account into another without paying taxes on any gain. You answered that such a rollover was not considered a tax event, as long as the transaction was completed in 60 days. You also informed her that when she eventually draws out the funds to supplement her retirement income, she will pay taxes on the portion that represents interest earned on the account.

Today Ms. Black has phoned to say that she is being billed by the Internal Revenue Service for $1,309.72 in penalties and back interest because she failed to declare interest income earned when she cashed in "those bonds that I told you about last April." You explain that bonds are not the same thing as a retirement account. One difference, unfortunately, is that people are required to pay taxes the following April on any interest income or capital gains earned by cashing in bonds.

Your client is not satisfied. She demands "something in writing" to show to her lawyer. Her position is that you misled her, so you should pay the penalties and interest charges, which, of course, are getting larger every day. She is willing to pay the actual tax on the transaction.

Your task: Write to Hilda Black (622 N. Bank Lane, Park Forest, IL 60045), explaining why you are unwilling to pay the penalties and interest charges requested by the IRS. Your position should be that you have done nothing to make yourself vulnerable in this transaction.

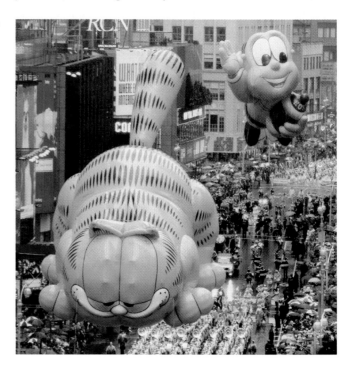

4. Cyber-surveillance: Memo refusing claim from "Silent Watch" victim Next week you're going to write a thank-you letter to Roy Young of Adavi, Inc., makers of "Silent Watch" software, for solving an impossible management task. But right now you've got an employee's claim on your desk, and you're trying to calm yourself before you reply.

Your business is called Advertising Inflatables, and your specialty is designing and building the huge balloon replicas used for advertising atop retail stores, tire outlets, used car lots, fast-food outlets, fitness clubs, etc. You've built balloon re-creations of everything from a 50-foot King Kong to a "small" 10-foot pizza. When your business grew from 2 employees to 25, you thought your biggest concern would be finding enough work to support them.

Your fame spread after local newspapers wrote about your company building giant soft drink "cans" for a Pepsi Superbowl commercial, set in outer space with real cosmonauts. The commercial never aired, but your business boomed. You hired more designers, salespeople, customer service reps, and additional painters and builders to work in the shop. Today, even design work is done on computers, and it turns out the hardest part of your job is managing the people who run them.

As business increased, you started spending your days outside the office, attending business events and making presentations. That's when productivity began to slip. If you showed up at the office unexpectedly, you noticed computer screens suddenly switching to something else. You got suspicious.

You decided to install the "cyber-surveillance" software, "Silent Watch," to record your employees' every keystroke. You sent around a memo informing your staff that their computer use should be limited to work projects only and that their e-mail should not include personal messages. You also informed them that their work would be monitored. You didn't tell them that "Silent Watch" would record their work while you were gone or that you could now monitor them from a screen in your office.

Sure enough, "Silent Watch" caught two of your sales staff spending between 50 and 70 percent of their time surfing Internet sites unrelated to their jobs. You docked their pay accordingly, without warning. You notified them that they were not fired but were on probation. You considered this extremely generous, but also wise. When they work, both of them are very good at what they do, and talent is hard to find.

Now salesman Jarod Harkington is demanding reinstatement of his pay because he claims you "spied on him illegally." On the contrary, your attorneys have assured you that the courts almost always side with employers on this issue, particularly after employees receive a warning such as the one you gave your workers. The computer equipment is yours, and you're paying a fair price for your employees' time.

Your task: Write a memo refusing Mr. Harkington's claim.[21]

5. No nukes: Letter from SDG&E refusing adjustment request "I will not support nuclear power and I demand that you remove this 'nuclear decomissioning' charge from my bill," wrote Walter Wittgen to the president of San Diego Gas and Electric Company (SDG&E). The president has turned the letter over to you.

As a supervisor in customer service, your life has recently been filled with stress, overtime, and pressure from above. Between angry customers on overloaded phone lines and company directors under pressure from the news media, Mr. Wittgen is a minor problem. But he's part of your job. And his letter came to you all the way from president Edwin A. Guiles.

The larger crisis began when summer heat struck California. As the first former power monopoly in the country to fulfill deregulation requirements, SDG&E was required by law to pass on actual electricity costs to its customers. SDG&E no longer produces or prices electricity but purchases it from a new, open-market Power Exchange (PX). Prices fluctuate with supply and demand, and they had doubled with the heat wave. Customer bills doubled and just

kept climbing. Even worse, SDG&E had failed to warn the public, so customers were stunned and angry.

The media descended, and politicians responded. With similar deregulation planned throughout the country, the governor and even the President of the United States have gotten involved, but no solution has emerged yet. Too late, SDG&E's marketing department tried to publicize that the utility's operations are still controlled by a government agency, the California Public Utilities Commission (CPUC). The new laws meant that SDG&E became only an "energy delivery service provider," selling off its generating plants. It passes on but does not set prices. Nevertheless, people saw SDG&E's name on huge bills, and a few started attacking employees and destroying property.

Then Mr. Wittgen called. Your phone operators pointed out the explanation for "nuclear decommissioning" charges on the back of his bill: "This charge pays for the retirement of nuclear power plants." The wording, like the fee itself, was ordered by the CPUC. When Wittgen called again, he was told that SDG&E bills more than a million customers every month, using a sophisticated software system. It would take a highly paid specialist more than an hour to hand-calculate Wittgen's bill every month, given all the complex line-items and formulas involved. For a 50-cent charge, that's unreasonable; plus, it could introduce errors that would cost him more. And the PUC requires that you charge him this fee.

How you handle the smallest customer problem in this volatile atmosphere could easily make tonight's news. It wouldn't be the first time.

Your task: Write a polite refusal to Mr. Walter Wittgen (732 La Cresta Boulevard, El Cajon, CA 92021), explaining why his bill will not be adjusted. SDG&E asks employees to word and sign their letters personally. Your contact number is 1-800-411-SDG&E (7343).[22]

6. It's legal: Memo to Salem State College employee defending video surveillance Maybe it was an example of bad employee relations, but it was legal. That's what your school's lawyers told you, as human resources director for Salem State College, after you passed along an angry memo from an employee in the college's Small Business Development Center (SBDC).

In her memo, Nancy Kim expressed her horror and outrage at discovering, too late, that when she slipped behind a divider after hours to change from her office attire into her jogging outfit for the trek home, she had been recorded on videotape by cameras installed in the department for security reasons. The SBDC houses a lot of expensive computer equipment, and your security department believed that the video surveillance was warranted; they had suspicions about a night intruder. However, no one informed the employees who work in the department that the cameras had been installed and were operating 24 hours a day. Your security department may have thought that was a good strategy for catching any dishonest employees red-handed, so to speak. But in light of what happened to Kim, it just seems like a rude and embarrassing misjudgment.

Kim has demanded an apology and $5,000 in damages for the indignity she suffered. Although she hasn't yet contacted her union representatives or a lawyer, she does hint that those will be her next steps. Your legal department insists she has no claim; employees relinquish their privacy rights the minute they step into the workplace. The only federal law limiting employer surveillance is the 1986 Electronic Communications Privacy Act, which prohibits employers from listening in on spoken personal conversations. Otherwise, they can tally phone numbers and call duration, videotape employees, and review e-mail, Internet access, and computer files. Only the state of Connecticut has passed a law also limiting employer surveillance in bathrooms and other areas designated for "health and personal comfort."

The college's attorneys have provided you with a copy of an article quoting Robert Ellis Smith, publisher of *Privacy Journal.* He says, "Employees are at the mercy of employers. . . . There is no protection in the workplace." According to the article, 63 percent of employers in an American Management Association survey of 900 midsize and large companies use some kind of employee surveillance, and 23 percent of them don't tell workers. Moreover, 16 percent use video cameras for their employee monitoring.

Legally, it sounds as if the college is in the right. But personally, you can't help but agree that Kim was wronged. Nevertheless, the legal department wants to discourage Kim from any form of litigation or pursuit of the case with her union representatives or the Massachusetts Labor Relations Committee. In hopes of downplaying the college's concern about the incident, the legal department wants you to handle the response. Go ahead and apologize, say the lawyers, but don't invite further action. This is not going to be easy, you think with a sigh.

Your task: Write an answering memo to Nancy Kim, denying her request for monetary compensation.[23]

7. Suffering artists: Memo declining high-tech shoes at American Ballet Theater Here at the American Ballet Theater (ABT), where you're serving as assistant to Artistic Director Kevin McKenzie, the notion of suffering for the art form

has been ingrained since the early 1800s, when the first ballerina rose up *en pointe.* Many entrepreneurs are viewing this painful situation with hopeful enthusiasm, especially when they discover that dancers worldwide spend about $150 million annually on their shoes—those "tiny torture chambers" of cardboard and satin (with glued linen or burlap to stiffen the toes). The pink monstrosities (about $50 a pair) rarely last beyond a single hard performance.

A company the size of ABT spends about $500,000 a year on ballet slippers—plus the cost of their staff physical therapist and all those trips to chiropractors, podiatrists, and surgeons to relieve bad necks, backs, knees, and feet. Entrepreneurs believe there must be room for improvement, given the current advantages of orthopedics, space-age materials, and high-tech solutions for contemporary athletes. There's no denying that ballerinas are among the hardest-working athletes in the world.

The latest entrepreneur to approach ABT is Eliza Minden of Gaynor Minden, Inc. No one in the ballet company blames her for wanting to provide a solution to the shoe problem. She buttonholed Michael Kaiser, executive director and a member of ABT's Board of Governing Trustees, with a proposal for providing new, high-performance pointe shoes in exchange for an endorsement. It truly is a good idea. It's just a hard sell among the tradition-oriented dancers.

Minden's alternative pointe shoes offer high-impact support and toe cushions. They're only $70 a pair, and supposedly they can be blow dried (like Birkenstocks) back into shape after a performance. When the cost-conscious board member urged the company to give them a try, you were assigned to collect feedback from dancers.

So far, not good. For example, principal ballerina Christine Dunham: She'd rather numb her feet in icy water, dance through "zingers" of toe pain, and make frequent visits to the physical therapist than wear Minden's shoes, she insisted after a brief trial. The others agree. Apparently, they *like* breaking in the traditional satin models with hammers and door slams and throwing them away after a single *Coppelia.* Too stiff, they say of the new shoes. Adds Dunham, "I'm totally settled into what I'm doing."

You've seen those sinewy, wedge-shaped feet bleeding backstage. You feel sorry for Minden; it *was* a good idea. Maybe she should try younger dancers.

Your task: McKenzie has asked you to write an internal memo in his name to Michael Kaiser, executive director of the American Ballet Theater, explaining the dancers' refusal to use the new high-tech Gaynor Minden pointe shoes. In your memo be sure to include the dancers' reasons as well as your own opinion regarding the matter. You'll need to decide whether to use the direct or the indirect approach; include a separate short note to your instructor justifying your selection.[24]

NEGATIVE ORGANIZATIONAL NEWS

8. The check's in the mail—almost: Letter from Sun Microsystems explaining late payments You'd think that a computer company could install a new management information system without a hitch, wouldn't you? The people at Sun Microsystems thought so too, but they were wrong. When they installed their own new computerized system for getting information to management, a few things, such as payments to vendors, fell through the cracks.

It was embarrassing when Sun's suppliers started clamoring for payment. Terence Lenaghan, the corporate controller, found himself in the unfortunate position of having to tell 6,000 vendors why Sun Microsystems had failed to pay its bills on time—and why it might be late with payments again. "Until we get these bugs ironed out," Lenaghan confessed, "we're going to have to finish some of the accounting work by hand. That means that some of our payments to vendors will probably be late next month too. We'd better write to our suppliers and let them know that there's nothing wrong with the company's financial performance. The last thing we want is for our vendors to think our business is going down the tubes."

Your task: Write a form letter to Sun Microsystem's 6,000 vendors explaining that bugs in their new management information system are responsible for the delays in payment.[25]

9. Everything old is new again: E-mail message reporting polyester findings Polyester got a bad rap in the 1980s. Now it's making a comeback in both fashion and food. What? Eat and drink from polyester containers? It's an idea whose time has come, according to chemical companies ranging from Dow to Amoco. An ice-cold Coke sipped from a polyester container may be tough for some Americans to swallow, but experts predict that a new generation of plastic may solve many of the problems, such as carbonation loss and heat sensitivity, caused by the containers now being used.

Today's drink bottles use a plastic called PET (polyethylene terephthalate). When stressed by heat, PET is too porous to contain the "fizz." But PET can now be mixed with a recently developed polyester called PEN (polyethylene naphthalate) to create a new generation of tougher plastic. Shell Chemical's director of polyester research and development, David Richardson, believes in the product. "In a few years, I'll be able to fix you a nice meal, and everything in it will come out of a polyester container."

Why make the switch from aluminum or glass to plastic? "Plastic is less deadly than glass when you throw it at a soccer match," says Richard Marion, an executive at Amoco Corporation's Amoco Chemical Company. Airlines like it because it's lightweight. Their little jelly containers used in First Class will weigh less. Consumers like it because it's clear, resealable, lightweight, and easily recycled. Polyester is definitely making a comeback. But one segment of the population is proving resistant to the trend: young adults. In a market research study, students preferred aluminum cans: Of all the container materials, aluminum ranked highest, achieving an 84 percent acceptance rate.

According to the study, students like the feel of the aluminum cans (plastic feels slippery and is harder to hold) and believe that aluminum keeps drinks colder. They also believe that aluminum keeps the carbonation longer, creating a "mouth buzz," whereas plastic lets the fizz out. And finally, they think that aluminum cans look "cool" and that plastic containers look "dorky."

Your market research team has come up with a couple of ways to deal with these perceptions. One approach would be an ad campaign showing "cool" young adults drinking from plastic bottles. Another would be ads showing that new technology is helping the plastic containers to hold in the "fizz."

Your task: As assistant director of marketing for Coca-Cola, write an e-mail message to your boss, Tom Ruffenbach, TomRuf@marketing.coca-cola.com, in which you report your findings and suggest ways to overcome this consumer bias.[26]

NEGATIVE EMPLOYMENT MESSAGES

10. Survive this: Recommendation refusal at Bank of America Rogan Halliwell is highly intelligent, quick with his work, handsome, accurate, and one of the most conceited individuals you've ever met. As manager of a Bank of America branch office, you've never had an employee irritate you like Halliwell. But he charmed his way through the interview with agile diplomacy, and you made the mistake of hiring him.

You were dazzled at first, like his co-workers. But in the eight months he worked for you, you had to call him in three times and remind him of new harrassment laws, which prohibit any behavior that distracts or irritates others. Among the complaints about him was one from a woman who said he kept calling her "Babe."

"But a 60-year-old woman should be flattered!" he argued.

Most of his co-workers complained as well: his overbearing ego disgusted them and his steady chatter about his personal life ruined their days. He made jokes about customers behind their backs, and he amused himself by stirring up conflicts among employees. Morale was rapidly disintegrating.

The problem was that, despite his abysmal interpersonal skills, Halliwell was a good teller. His cash drawer almost always balanced perfectly. He was fast, he was charming to customers while they were present, and he learned quickly. You got so many compliments about that "nice young man" from older customers that you couldn't believe they were talking about the same Rogan Halliwell. How could you fire him?

One bright morning, Halliwell solved your problem. "I've decided to move to Hollywood," he announced, loudly enough for his co-workers to hear. "I think they're ready for me." You said a silent "thank-you" as you accepted his notice.

Today you received a letter from Halliwell. He writes that he expects to be hired by one of those *Survivor*-type reality TV shows. He wants a character reference.

You blanch. He may have the right qualities to make reality TV interesting, but listing them would sound slanderous coming from a bank manager. Moreover, you can't in good conscience recommend that anyone work with him. Yet his demonstrated skills make it risky for you to refuse.

Your task: Using techniques you've learned in this chapter, write a refusal that won't expose you or Bank of America to legal repercussions. Send it to Rogan Halliwell, 2388 Pitt Avenue, Apt. 4, Hollywood, CA 90028.[27]

11. Try ladybugs: Letter rejecting an application at Fluker Farms cricket ranch It seemed almost like a joke to Richard Fluker back in 1953 when a co-worker invited him to buy into a cricket ranch in Port Allen, Louisiana. Back then, $300 was nothing to sneeze at. But Fluker thought it over and finally agreed to give it a go; after all, crickets were good fishing bait, and fishing was a long-entrenched Louisiana pastime.

Surely the elder Fluker didn't know then that the company he passed on to his son, David Fluker, would one day be looking at a balance sheet showing upward of $6 million in annual sales. That's not only from crickets, mind you. Fluker Farms has grown along with a general interest in pets (particularly reptiles). The company now ships live crickets, mealworms, and iguanas to pet stores, zoos, and universities around the world, and it has also moved into "dry goods" (as in freeze-dried crickets), as well as reptile leashes and other accessories. Fluker Farms even markets chocolate-covered crickets for brave humans—a big hit at trade shows, especially when the samplers get an "I Ate A Bug Club" button.

But Fluker Farms is no joke, and the number of applicants who want to work for you has increased as the business has grown. As human resources manager for the company, it's your job to screen them.

Last week you interviewed about a dozen candidates for a job in research and development. The company is looking for other bugs it can profit from, testing them as pet food and evaluating their "shelf-life" potential in both live and freeze-dried forms. With pet stores expanding into superstores, the demand for new food varieties is also growing. So the researcher you hire has to understand the feeding habits of reptiles and birds, must be acquainted with insect life cycles, and must possess the kind of imagination that can come up with a new idea and figure out how to make it profitable. That's not an easy spot to fill.

Your task: The candidates you saw all carried excellent credentials, every one of them with multiple degrees and a research background. But only one, Maria Richter, had the right personality for Fluker Farms: the combination of imagination, knowledge, and resourcefulness you're looking for. In addition, she has five years of reptile research, a doctorate in zoology, and a bachelor's degree in marketing. Now you have the onerous task of writing rejection letters to the other candidates. Start with a letter to Werner Speker, whom you liked personally but whose postgraduate work has been mostly with felines, not reptiles. He's at 4265 Broadview Road, Baton Rouge, LA 70815.[28]

12. All in the family: E-mail message resigning a position
Your brother, Ruben N. Rodriguez Jr., started the family-owned Los Amigos Tortilla Manufacturing, Inc., in 1969 with only $12,000. While Los Amigos developed, you were able to help support the family with your income as marketing director for the Latin American Division of IBM. Today, the Atlanta-based Los Amigos enjoys annual sales of about $4.5 million and its prospects look bright.

Ruben asked you to resign from your position at IBM and work full-time for Los Amigos. You decided to do some research before answering. You found that Hispanic-owned businesses have outperformed U.S. business growth in general. You also learned that many Hispanic corporate executives are leaving big companies to start their own business. You want to be a part of this amazing trend, not only because of the profit potential but also because you love your family and want to help your brother develop the company. You hope your son will become a part of the organization some day. After considering all aspects, you made your decision: You submitted your letter of resignation to IBM. Today, you received e-mail from the division vice president urging you to stay and offering a lucrative incentive package, including an additional week's vacation, an upgrade on your company car, and an increase of $10,000 a year.

Your task: Write an e-mail message to George Packard, your division vice president, at GPackard@lad.ibm.com, thanking him for his offer. Explain the reasons behind your decision to resign and suggest that Consuela Vargas, who has worked with you for five years, would make an excellent marketing director. Vargas not only speaks Spanish and Portuguese but has played a key role in closing deals for IBM in several Latin American countries. Plus, she's a terrific strategic thinker.[29]

GOING ONLINE EXERCISES

Announcing an Employee Layoff: How to Write a Termination Notice, p. 217

How would you notify employees about a company's plan to downsize? When drafting a memo to announce a layoff, you need to consider both existing company policy and the potential legal liability of your action. How could you minimize the threat of a frivolous lawsuit and still meet your employees' needs for information assistance? Log on to this site to learn about writing a termination notice.

1. What steps can a company take to prepare for laying off workers? List the items and advice that you could incorporate into a written notice about a potential layoff.
2. Using the information in the "Dealing with Downsizing" article and in the government report on "Best Practices in Downsizing" to help you formulate your ideas, compose an announcement of a company-wide layoff. (Remember that bad-news messages are most effective when the wording is positive and the tone supportive. Remember also that you need to be truthful as well as tactful. Avoid statements that could insult employees' intelligence or heighten their vulnerability. Balance the hard facts of termination with details about the company's layoff-related services and benefits.)
3. What other issues or resources did you learn about from this site and its related links?

   To complete this exercise, log on to this text's Web site at www.prenhall.com/thill. Select Chapter 8, then select "Student Resources," click on the name of the featured Web site, and follow the detailed navigational directions.

chapter **9**

WRITING PERSUASIVE MESSAGES

After studying this chapter, you will be able to

1 Discuss the planning tasks that need extra attention when preparing persuasive messages

2 Distinguish between emotional and logical appeals, and discuss how to balance them

3 Describe the AIDA plan for persuasive messages

4 Explain the best way to overcome resistance to your persuasive message, and list four common mistakes

5 Compare sales messages with fundraising messages

6 List eight guidelines that will help you strengthen your fundraising messages

Producing quality outdoor clothing and gear, Patagonia describes itself as having a dirtbag culture—"Seeking out places where diversity and fullness of life may still be found, mostly in the mountains, deserts, and waters." But Patagonia's culture is also one of serious responsibility. It does its best to persuade consumers not only to buy its environmentally safe clothing but also to actively protect and support the earth's environment.

FACING A COMMUNICATION DILEMMA AT PATAGONIA

Gearing Up to Save the Environment

www.patagonia.com

He's a man with a mission. He's committed to saving the earth's resources, and he believes that everyone—from consumers to corporations—should practice environmental protection. Yvon Chouinard founded Patagonia, a leading outdoor gear and apparel company, and he incorporates his personal passion for the environment into the operating values of his company. Under Chouinard's direction, Patagonia rigorously pursues a high standard of environmental responsibility while producing high-quality goods for extreme sports enthusiasts.

Chouinard works hard to develop production techniques that reduce the environmental impact of Patagonia's operations. For example, working with outside contractors, Patagonia developed Synchilla fleece, a fabric made from recycled plastic soda bottles—some 8 million bottles each year. Patagonia also introduced a line of clothing made from organic cotton, which is grown without artificial pesticides or fertilizers, and the company discovered ways to eliminate toxic dyes from its products. In addition, Patagonia created its own "earth tax," giving environmental groups about $1 million each year—more money than it allocates for advertising.

But Patagonia's continued success hinges on Chouinard's ability to convince consumers about the importance of practicing environmental responsibility. In addition to creating a desire for Patagonia's products, Chouinard wants to educate the public about the benefits of environmentally safe production. He wants to persuade consumers not only to buy Patagonia products but also to support environmental responsibility in other areas of their lives.

If you were Yvon Chouinard, how would you convince your audience that environmental responsibility is important? What sort of persuasive messages would you send to consumers? How would you organize these messages to be effective? What would you do to get your audience's attention?[1]

USING THE THREE-STEP WRITING PROCESS FOR PERSUASIVE MESSAGES

Savvy businesspeople such as Yvon Chouinard know that people today not only ask "What should I do?" but also ask "Why should I do it?" To accomplish his goals, Chouinard often employs **persuasion**—the attempt to change an audience's attitudes, beliefs, or actions.[2] The most effective business leaders have a knack for putting together a persuasive argument. They know how to take the pulse of a group and communicate with people in terms they can both understand and embrace.[3] So whether you're selling real estate or just trying to sell your idea to your boss, writing effective persuasive messages is an important skill. In today's competitive marketplace, applying the three-step writing process to your persuasive messages will help you make them as effective as possible.

Step 1: Planning Persuasive Messages

Unlike routine positive messages (discussed in Chapter 7), persuasive messages aim to influence audiences who are inclined to resist. Therefore, persuasive messages are generally longer, are usually more detailed, and often depend heavily on strategic planning. Persuasive messages require that you pay particular attention to several planning tasks. For example, because your purpose is to persuade, you must be absolutely sure that it's clear, necessary, and appropriate for written media. When analyzing your audience for a persuasive message, you may want to delve more deeply than you would for other messages. Your credibility takes on extra importance in a persuasive message. So whenever you're trying to persuade someone, you must make sure your ethics are above reproach.

Analyze Your Purpose   Although most business messages are routine, some circumstances require messages designed to motivate or persuade others. An external persuasive message is one of the most difficult tasks you could undertake. For one thing, people are busy, so they're reluctant to do something new, especially if it takes time and offers no guarantee of any reward in return. For another, competing requests are plentiful. The public relations departments of many large corporations receive so many persuasive requests for donations that they must sometimes use lotteries to decide which worthy cause to support. Given the complexity and sensitivity of persuasive messages, making sure of your purpose is perhaps the most important planning task.

Analyze Your Audience   Chapter 4 discusses the basics of audience analysis, but the process can become much more involved for persuasive messages. Learning about your audience and the position you intend to argue can take weeks—even months. Why? Because everyone's needs differ, so everyone responds differently to any given message. For instance, not every reader is interested in economy or even in fair play; you may even find that satisfying someone's need for status or appealing to someone's greed may at times be much more effective than emphasizing human generosity or civic duty.

Gauging Audience Needs   The best persuasive messages are closely connected to your audience's existing desires and interests.[4] Consider these important questions: Who is my audience? What are their needs? What do I want them to do? How might they resist? Are there alternative positions I need to examine? What does the decision maker consider the most important issue? How might the organization's culture influence my strategy?

Some theorists believe that certain needs have priority. Figure 9–1 represents psychologist Abraham Maslow's hierarchy of needs, with the most basic needs appearing at the bottom of the figure. Maslow suggests that only after lower-level needs have been met will a person seek to fulfill needs on higher levels.[5] For example, suppose you supervise someone who consistently arrives late for work. You must either persuade

Figure 9–1
Maslow's Hierarchy of Needs

him to change or fire him. First, find out why he's coming in late. Is he oversleeping because he has a second job to support his family (a safety and security need)? Is he coming in late because of a misguided desire to have people notice his arrival (an esteem and status need)? Once you've analyzed the need motivating him to arrive late, you can craft an appeal, a "hook" that will interest him in your message about changing his behavior. If the need for safety and security is behind his tardiness, you might say, "Your job is very important to you, I know." If he craves esteem and status, you could say, "You've always seemed interested in being given more responsibility, perhaps even a promotion."

Demographics include characteristics such as age, gender, occupation, income, and education.

To assess various individual needs, you can refer to specific information such as **demographics** (the age, gender, occupation, income, education, and other quantifiable characteristics of the people you're trying to persuade) and **psychographics** (the personality, attitudes, lifestyle, and other psychological characteristics of an individual). Both types of information are strongly influenced by culture. When analyzing your audience, take into account their cultural expectations and practices so that you don't undermine your persuasive message by using an inappropriate appeal or by organizing your message in a way that seems unfamiliar or uncomfortable to your audience.

Psychographics include characteristics such as personality, attitudes, and lifestyle.

Cultural differences influence your persuasion attempts.

Considering Cultural Differences   Your understanding and respect for cultural differences will help you satisfy the needs of your audience and will help your audience respect you. That's because persuasion is different in different cultures. In France, using an aggressive, hard-sell technique is no way to win respect. Such an approach would probably antagonize your audience. In Germany, where people tend to focus on technical matters, plan on verifying any figures you use for support, and make sure they are exact. In Sweden, audiences tend to focus on theoretical questions and strategic implications, whereas U.S. audiences are usually concerned with more practical matters.[6]

Every message written for a corporation adds to the corporate tradition.

As with individuals, an organization's culture or subculture heavily influences the effectiveness of messages. All the previous messages in an organization have established a tradition that defines persuasive writing within that culture. When you accept and use these traditions, you establish one type of common ground with your audience. If you reject or never learn these traditions, you'll have difficulty achieving that common ground, which damages both your credibility and your persuasion attempts.

With retail stores in 40 countries, The Body Shop demands a lot of attention from owner Anita Roddick, who is also dedicated to large-scale social causes. With a mission to provide learning and promote action, Roddick believes that business can influence the world's views of nature and people. In fact, her stores are "arenas of education." Without credibility, Roddick's efforts would seem manipulative. But her sincerity in promoting environmental issues wins people's trust and changes attitudes.

Establish Your Credibility   To persuade a skeptical or hostile audience, you must convince people that you know what you're talking about and that you're not trying to mislead them. Your *credibility* is your capability of being believed because you're reliable and worthy of confidence. Without such credibility, your efforts to persuade will seem manipulative. Research strongly suggests that most managers overestimate their own credibility—considerably.[7] Patagonia's Chouinard cautions you that establishing your credibility is a process, so it takes time to earn your audience's respect. Some of the best ways to gain credibility include the following:

◆ **Support your message with facts.** Testimonials, documents, guarantees, statistics, and research results all provide seemingly objective evidence for what you have to say, which adds to your credibility. The more specific and relevant your proof, the better.

◆ **Name your sources.** Telling your audience where your information comes from and who agrees with you always improves your credibility, especially if your sources are already respected by your audience.

◆ **Be an expert.** Your knowledge of your message's subject area (or even of some other area) helps you give your audience the quality information necessary to make a decision.

◆ **Establish common ground.** Those beliefs, attitudes, and background experiences that you have in common with members of your audience will help them identify with you.

◆ **Be enthusiastic.** Your excitement about your subject can infect your audience.

EFFECTIVE E-BUSINESS COMMUNICATION

Building Credibility Online

When you use printed messages to build credibility, you generally have limited space for testimonials and other persuasive evidence. On the Internet, however, space is never a problem—you can easily add pages of evidence to convince your audience of your expertise and reliability. Businesspeople and consumers often browse Web sites to find out more before contacting potential suppliers. You can build credibility by conspicuously posting detailed problem-solution case studies and satisfied customer testimonials. When IBM uses this technique (www.ibm.com), it also includes special links for readers to offer feedback, ask questions, and request additional information.

1. You can use case studies and testimonials to build credibility. Would this technique be best for persuasive messages that use logical appeals or those that use emotional appeals?
2. How do case studies and testimonials help reinforce your position in a persuasive message?

◆ **Be objective.** Your understanding of and willingness to acknowledge all sides of an issue help you present fair and logical arguments in your persuasive message.

◆ **Be sincere.** Your concern, genuineness, good faith, and truthfulness help you focus on your audience's needs.

◆ **Be trustworthy.** Your honesty and dependability help you earn your audience's respect.

◆ **Have good intentions.** Your willingness to keep your audience's best interests at heart helps you create persuasive messages that are ethical.

> Your credibility is improved if you are an expert, enthusiastic, objective, sincere, and trustworthy and if your intentions are good and you establish common ground.

Strive for High Ethical Standards The word *persuasion* is viewed by some as negative. They associate persuasion with dishonest and unethical practices, such as coaxing, urging, and sometimes even tricking people into accepting an idea, buying a product, or taking an unwanted or unneeded action. However, the best businesspeople make persuasion positive. They influence audience members by providing information and aiding understanding, which allows audiences the freedom to choose.[8] Ethical businesspeople inform audiences of the benefits of an idea, an organization, a product, a donation, or an action so that these audiences can recognize just how well the idea, organization, product, donation, or action will satisfy a need they truly have.

> Positive persuasion leaves your audience free to choose.

For anyone trying to influence people's actions, knowing the law is crucial. However, merely avoiding what is illegal may not always be enough. To maintain the highest standards of business ethics, make every attempt to persuade without manipulating. Choose words that won't be misinterpreted, and be sure you don't distort the truth. Adopt the "you" attitude by showing honest concern for your audience's needs and interests. Your consideration of audience needs is more than ethical; it's the proper use of persuasion. That consideration is likely to achieve the response you intended and to satisfy your audience's needs.

> To maintain the highest ethics, try to persuade without manipulating.

Step 2: Writing Persuasive Messages

When applying Step 2 to your persuasive messages, you will define your main idea, limit the scope of your message, and group your points in a meaningful way. But you must focus even more effort on choosing the direct or indirect approach.

As with routine and bad-news messages, the best organizational approach is based on your audience's likely reaction to your message. However, because the nature of persuasion is to convince your audience or to change their attitudes, beliefs, or actions, most persuasive messages use the indirect approach. So you'll want to explain your reasons and build interest before revealing your purpose. Nevertheless, many situations do call for the direct approach.

If audience members are objective, or if you know they prefer the "bottom line" first (perhaps because it saves them time), the direct approach might be the better choice. You'll also want to use the direct approach when your corporate culture encourages directness. In addition, when a message is long or complex, your readers may become impatient if the main idea is buried seven pages in, so you may want to choose the direct approach for these messages as well.

Bette McGiboney is administrative assistant to the athletic director of Auburn University. Each year, after season tickets have been mailed, the cost of the athletic department's toll-free phone number skyrockets as fans call with questions about their seats, complaints about receiving the wrong number of tickets, or orders for last-minute tickets. The August phone bill is usually over $3,000, in part because each customer is put on hold while operators serve others. McGiboney came up with an idea that could solve the problem, so she composed an e-mail message that uses the direct approach (see Figure 9–2).

If you use the direct approach, keep in mind that even though your audience may be easy to convince, you'll still want to include at least a brief justification or explanation. Don't expect your reader to accept your idea on blind faith. For example, consider the following two openers:

POOR	IMPROVED
I recommend building our new retail outlet on the West Main Street site.	After comparing the four possible sites for our new retail outlet, I recommend West Main Street as the only site that fulfills our criteria for visibility, proximity to mass transportation, and square footage.

Your choice between the direct and indirect approach is also influenced by the extent of your authority, expertise, or power in an organization. As a first-line manager writing a persuasive message to top management, you may try to be diplomatic and use an indirect approach. But your choice could backfire if some managers perceive your indirectness as manipulative and time wasting. On the other hand, you may consciously try to save your supervisors time by using a direct approach, which might be perceived as brash and presumptuous. Similarly, when writing a persuasive message to employees, you may use the indirect approach to ease into a major change, but your audience might see your message as weak, even wishy-washy. You need to think carefully about your corporate culture and what your audience expects before you select your approach.

Step 3: Completing Persuasive Messages

The length and complexity of persuasive messages makes applying Step 3 even more crucial to your success. When you evaluate your persuasive content, judge your argument objectively and seriously appraise your credibility. When revising persuasive messages and rewriting them for clarity and conciseness, you must carefully match purpose and organization to audience needs.

Margin notes:

Use the indirect approach when your audience will react unfavorably to your message. Use the direct approach when your message is long or complex, or when your reader prefers directness.

Choice of approach is also influenced by your position (or authority within the organization) relative to your audience's.

As with other business messages, step 3 of the writing process helps guarantee the success of your persuasive messages.

The writer uses the subject line to announce that the proposal will save money.

Follows the direct approach, yet still introduces the idea briefly.

Creates more interest in the idea with an explanation of how the new plan will work.

Takes care of a chore that might have caused the reader to delay.

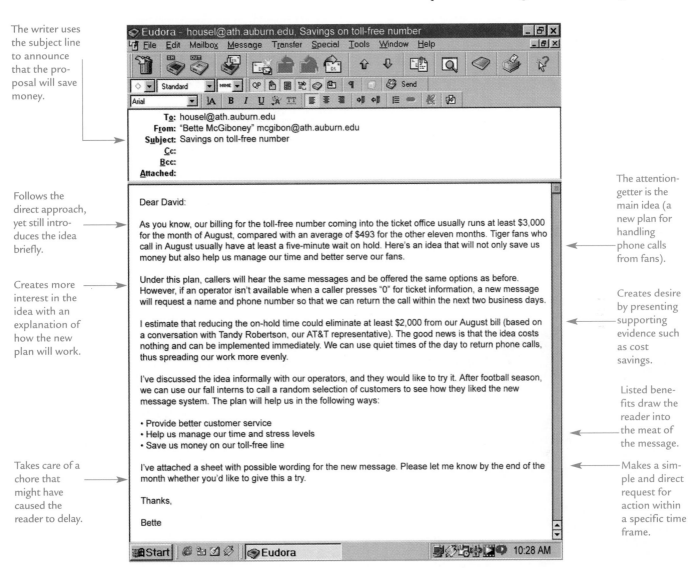

The attention-getter is the main idea (a new plan for handling phone calls from fans).

Creates desire by presenting supporting evidence such as cost savings.

Listed benefits draw the reader into the meat of the message.

Makes a simple and direct request for action within a specific time frame.

Figure 9–2
In-Depth Critique: E-Mail Message Selling an Idea to a Boss

Your design elements must complement (not detract from) your argument. In addition, make sure your delivery methods fit your audience's expectations as well as your purpose. Finally, meticulous proofreading will identify any mechanical or spelling errors that would weaken your persuasive message.

SENDING PERSUASIVE MESSAGES

Persuasion involves a bit more than routine communication. Persuasive messages differ from routine messages in one important way: in addition to communicating your main idea and reasons, you need to motivate your audience to do something. So before looking at specific types of persuasive messages, let's examine some special persuasive strategies.

Strategies for Persuasive Messages

Whether you use a direct or an indirect approach, you must convince your reader that your request or idea is reasonable. Effective persuasion involves four distinct and essential strategies: balancing emotional and logical appeals, framing your arguments, reinforcing

Four essential persuasion strategies:
- Balancing your appeals
- Framing your argument
- Reinforcing your position
- Overcoming audience resistance

your position, and dealing with resistance. The amount of detail you pursue in each of these strategies varies according to the complexity of your idea or request.

Balancing Emotional and Logical Appeals   How do you actually convince an audience that your position is the right one, that your plan will work, or that your company will do the most with readers' donations? One way is to appeal to the audience's minds and hearts. Most persuasive messages include both emotional and logical appeals. Together, these two elements have a good chance of persuading your audience to act.

Finding the right balance between the two types of appeals depends on four factors: (1) the actions you wish to motivate, (2) your reader's expectations, (3) the degree of resistance you must overcome, and (4) how far you feel empowered to go in selling your point of view.[9] When you're persuading someone to accept a complex idea, take a serious step, or make a large and important decision, lean toward logic and make your emotional appeal subtle. However, when you're persuading someone to purchase a product, join a cause, or make a donation, you'll rely a bit more heavily on emotion.

Emotional Appeals   An **emotional appeal** calls on human feelings, basing the argument on audience needs or sympathies; however, such an appeal must be subtle.[10] For instance, you can make use of the emotion surrounding certain words. The word *freedom* evokes strong feelings, as do words such as *success, prestige, credit record, savings, free, value,* and *comfort.* Words such as these put your audience in a certain frame of mind and help them accept your message. At Patagonia, Yvon Chouinard uses words and pictures to help people make an emotional connection with the environment. But be careful. Emotional appeals aren't necessarily effective by themselves. Emotion works with logic in a unique way: People need to find rational support for an attitude they've already embraced emotionally.

Appealing to your audience's emotions is a legitimate way to persuade them to support your position. As founder and president of the Children's Defense Fund, Marian Wright Edelman frequently addresses large audiences both in speeches and in fundraising letters. To spur her audience to take action, she frequently appeals to her audience's emotions by telling inspiring stories about the girls and boys her fund is trying to help.

Logical Appeals   A **logical appeal** calls on human reason. In any argument you might use to persuade an audience, you make a claim and then support your claim with reasons or evidence. When appealing to your audience's logic, you might use three types of reasoning:

- **Analogy.** You might reason from specific evidence to specific evidence. In order to persuade employees to attend a planning session, you might use a town meeting analogy, comparing your company to a small community and your employees to valued members of that community.

- **Induction.** You might reason from specific evidence to a general conclusion. To convince potential customers that your product is best, you might report the results of test marketing in which individuals preferred your product over others. After all, if some individuals prefer it, so will others.

- **Deduction.** You might reason from a generalization to a specific conclusion. To persuade your boss to hire additional employees, you might point to industry-wide projections and explain that industry activity (and thus your company's business) will be increasing rapidly over the next three months, so you'll need more employees to handle increased business.

No matter what reasoning method you use, any argument or statement can easily appear to be true when it's actually false. Whenever you appeal to your audience's reason, do everything you can to ensure that your arguments are logically sound. To avoid faulty logic, practice the following guidelines:[11]

- **Avoid hasty generalizations.** Make sure you have plenty of evidence before drawing conclusions.

Table 9-1   The AIDA Organizational Plan

Phase	Objective
Attention	Get the reader's attention with a benefit that is of real interest or value.
Interest	Build the reader's interest by further explaining benefits and appealing to his or her logic or emotions.
Desire	Build desire by showing how your offer can really help the reader.
Action	Give a strong and simple call to action and provide a convenient means for the reader to take the next step.

- **Avoid begging the question.** Make sure you can support your claim without simply restating it in different words.

- **Avoid attacking your opponent.** Be careful to address the real question. Attack the argument your opponent is making, not your opponent's character.

- **Avoid oversimplifying a complex issue.** Make sure you present all the facts rather than relying on an "either/or" statement that makes it look as if only two choices are possible.

- **Avoid assuming a false cause.** Use cause-and-effect reasoning correctly; do not assume that one event caused another just because it happened first.

- **Avoid faulty analogies.** Be sure that the two objects or situations being compared are similar enough for the analogy to hold. Even if A resembles B in one respect, it may not in all respects.

- **Avoid illogical support.** Make sure the connection between your claim and your support is truly logical and not based on a leap of faith, a missing premise, or irrelevant evidence.

Framing Your Arguments   Whether you emphasize emotion or logic, and whether you decide to use a direct or an indirect approach, you still need to frame your argument in the most effective way. You want to present the advantages of your decision, idea, or product. You want to support your main point. You need room to anticipate and answer any objections, as well as to motivate action at the close.

Using the AIDA Plan   Most persuasive messages follow an organizational plan that goes beyond the indirect approach used for negative messages. The opening does more than serve as a buffer; it grabs your audience's attention. The explanation section does more than present reasons, and it is expanded to two sections. The first incites your audience's interest, and the second changes your audience's attitude. Finally, your close does more than end on a positive note with a statement of what action is needed; it emphasizes reader benefits and motivates readers to take specific action. Although similar to the indirect approach of negative messages, this new persuasive approach pushes the envelope in each of four phases: (1) Attention, (2) Interest, (3) Desire, and (4) Action. Table 9–1 summarizes this AIDA plan.

- **Attention.** Make your audience want to hear about your problem or idea. Write a brief and engaging opening sentence, with no extravagant claims or irrelevant points. And be sure to find some common ground on which to build your case. Randy Thumwolt uses the AIDA plan in a persuasive memo about his program to reduce Host Marriott's annual plastics costs and to curtail consumer complaints about the company's recycling record (see Figure 9–3).

- **Interest.** Explain the relevance of your message to your audience. Continuing the theme you started with, paint a more detailed picture with words. Get your audience thinking, "This is an interesting idea; could it possibly solve my problems?" In Figure 9–3, Thumwolt's interest section ties a factual description to the benefits of instituting his new recycling plan. Also, Thumwolt relates benefits specifically to the attention phase that precedes this section.

Objective   **3**
Describe the AIDA plan for persuasive messages.

Organize persuasive messages using the AIDA plan:
- Attention
- Interest
- Desire
- Action

Begin every persuasive message with an attention-getting statement that is
- Personalized
- "You"-oriented
- Straightforward
- Relevant

In the interest section
- Continue the opening theme in greater detail
- Relate benefits specifically to the attention-getter

1 Planning

Analyze: The purpose is to help solve an ongoing problem. The audience will be receptive.

Investigate: Gather information on recycling problem areas.

Adapt: Use a memo, and strengthen the point by reviewing the bulk-purchase idea, which has already been instituted.

2 Writing

Organize: Follow the indirect approach by using background information to introduce the continuing problems. Then list the new recycling ideas.

Compose: Make your style businesslike and your appeal logical. Use a conversational tone, and respect the reader's time by avoiding wordiness.

3 Completing

Revise: Be sure the flow of this memo is logical. Edit and rewrite for conciseness and clarity.

Produce: Minimal design is needed for an internal memo. Send the message either as a printed memo or via e-mail.

Proofread: Review for accuracy and typos.

HOST MARRIOTT SERVICES

INTERNAL MEMORANDUM

To: Eleanor Tran, Comptroller
From: Randy Thumwolt, Purchasing Director
Date: August 22, 2002
Subject: Cost Cutting in Plastics

Grabs reader's attention with background information and specific numbers.

As you know, we purchase five tons of plastic product containers each year. The price of polyethylene terephthalate (PET), the plastic used for these containers, tends to rise and fall as petroleum costs fluctuate. You asked me earlier to find some ways to cut our annual costs for plastics. In my memo of January 5, I suggested that we bulk-purchase plastics during winter months, when petroleum prices tend to be lower. Thanks for approving that suggestion. So far, I estimate that we will realize a 10 percent savings this year.

Even so, our costs for plastic containers are exorbitant ($2 million annually). In addition, we have received an increasing number of consumer letters complaining about our lack of a recycling program for the PET plastic containers both on the airplanes and in the airport restaurants. I've done some preliminary research and have come up with the following ideas:

Clearly describes the problems Host Marriott is still facing.

Makes suggestions in an easy-to-read list, providing detailed support in an attachment.

- Provide recycling containers at all Host Marriott airport restaurants.
- Offer financial incentives for the airlines to collect and separate PET containers.
- Set up a specially designated dumpster at each airport for recycling plastics.
- Contract with A-Batt Waste Management for collection.

I've attached a detailed report of the costs involved. As you can see, our net savings the first year should run about $500,000. I've spoken to Ted Macy in marketing. If we adopt the recycling plan, he wants to build a PR campaign around it.

Provides another reader benefit.

The PET recycling plan will help build our public image while improving our bottom line. If you agree, let's meet with Ted next week to get things started.

Urges action within a specific time frame.

Figure 9–3
In-Depth Critique: Persuasive Letter Using the AIDA Plan

◆ **Desire.** Make audience members want to change by explaining how the change will benefit them. Reduce resistance by thinking up and answering in advance any questions your audience might have. If your idea is complex, explain how you would implement it. Back up your claims to increase audience willingness to take the action that you suggest in the next section. Just remember to make sure that all evidence is directly relevant to your point.

In the desire section
• Provide evidence to prove your claim
• Draw attention to any enclosures

◆ **Action.** Suggest the action you want readers to take. Make it more than a statement such as "Please institute this program soon" or "Send me a refund." This is the opportunity to remind readers of the benefits of taking action. The secret of a successful action phase is making the action easy. Ask readers to call a toll-free number for more information, to use an enclosed order form, or to use a prepaid envelope for donations. Include a deadline when applicable.

End by
• Suggesting a specific step the audience can take
• Restating how the audience will benefit by acting as you wish
• Making action easy

Making the AIDA Plan Work   The AIDA plan is tailor-made for using the indirect approach, allowing you to save your main idea for the action phase. However, it can also be used for the direct approach. In this case, you use your main idea as an attention-getter. You build interest with your argument, create desire with your evidence, and emphasize your main idea in the action phase with the specific action you want your audience to take.

Using AIDA with the indirect approach allows you to save your idea for the action phase; using it with the direct approach allows you to use your main idea as your attention-getter.

When your AIDA message uses an indirect approach and is delivered by memo or e-mail, keep in mind that your subject line usually catches your readers' eye first. Your challenge is to make it interesting and relevant enough to capture reader attention without revealing your proposal. If you put your request in the subject line, you're likely to get a quick "no" before you've had a chance to present your arguments.

When using the indirect approach, make subject lines interesting without revealing your purpose.

INSTEAD OF THIS	TRY THIS
Proposal to Install New Phone Message System	Savings on Toll-Free Number

Another thing to keep in mind when using the AIDA plan is to narrow your objectives. Focus on your primary goal when presenting your case, and concentrate your efforts on accomplishing that one goal. For example, if your main idea is to convince your company to install a new phone messaging system, leave discussions about switching long-distance carriers until another day—unless it's relevant to your argument.

To make the AIDA plan more successful, focus closely on one goal only.

Reinforcing Your Position   The facts alone may not be enough to persuade your audience. Effective persuaders such as Patagonia's Yvon Chouinard supplement numerical data with examples, stories, metaphors, and analogies to make their position come alive. They use language to paint a vivid picture of the persuader's point of view.[12]

Your language helps reinforce your position.

Semantics   Say that you're trying to build your credibility. How do you let your audience know that you're enthusiastic and trustworthy? Simply making an outright claim that you have these traits is sure to raise suspicion. However, you can use *semantics* (the meaning of words and other symbols) to do much of the job for you. The words you choose to state your message say much more than their dictionary definition.[13]

Semantics is the meaning of words and other symbols.

INSTEAD OF THIS	SAY THIS
I think we should attempt to get approval on this before it's too late.	Let's get immediate approval on this.
It seems to me that . . .	I believe . . .
I've been thinking lately that maybe someone could . . .	After careful thought over the past two months, I've decided that . . .
This plan could work if we really push it.	With our support, this plan will work.

Another way semantics can affect persuasive messages is in the variety of meanings that people attribute to certain words. As discussed in Chapter 5, abstract words are subject to interpretation because they refer to things that people cannot experience with their senses. So you can use abstractions to enhance the emotional content of a persuasive message. For example, you may be able to sell more flags by appealing to your audience's patriotism than by describing the color and size of the flags. You may have better luck collecting an overdue bill by mentioning honesty and fair play than by repeating the sum owed and the date it was due. However, be sure to include the details along with the abstractions; the very fact that you're using abstract words leaves room for misinterpretation.

Two ways of using semantics are choosing your words carefully and using abstractions to enhance emotional content.

Other Tools   Using semantics skillfully isn't your only persuasive tool. Here are some additional techniques you can use to strengthen your persuasive messages:[14]

In addition to semantics, you have other persuasive tools at your disposal.

- ◆ **Be moderate.** Asking your audience to make major changes in attitudes or beliefs will most likely evoke a negative response. However, asking audience members to take one step toward that change may be a more reasonable goal.

- ◆ **Focus on your goal.** Your message will be clearest if you shift your focus away from changing minds and emphasize the action you want your audience to take.

- ◆ **Use simple language.** In most persuasive situations, your audience will be cautious, watching for fantastic claims, insupportable descriptions, and emotional manipulation. So speak plainly and simply.

- ◆ **Anticipate opposition.** Think of every possible objection in advance. In your message, you might raise and answer some of these counterarguments.

- ◆ **Provide sufficient support.** It is up to you to prove that the change you seek is necessary.

- ◆ **Be specific.** Back up your claims with evidence, and when necessary cite actual facts and figures. Let your audience know that you've done your homework.

- ◆ **Create a win-win situation.** Make it possible for both you and your audience to gain something. Audience members will find it easier to deal with change if they stand to benefit.

- ◆ **Time your messages appropriately.** The time to sell roofs is right after the tornado. Timing is crucial in persuasive messages.

- ◆ **Speak metaphorically.** Metaphors create powerful pictures. One metaphor can convey a lifetime of experience or a head full of logic.

- ◆ **Use anecdotes and stories to make your points.** Anecdotes tie it all together—the logic and the emotions. Don't tell your audience what kinds of problems they can have if their system crashes. Tell them what happened to Jeff Porte when his hard drive crashed in the middle of his annual sales presentation.

All of these tools will help your persuasive message be accepted, but none of them will actually overcome your audience's resistance. Whether based on emotion or logic, your argument must be strong enough to persuade people to act.

Objective

4

Explain the best way to overcome resistance to your persuasive message, and list four common mistakes.

Dealing with Resistance   The best way to deal with audience resistance is to eliminate it. If you expect a hostile audience, one biased against your plan from the beginning, present all sides—cover all options, explaining the pros and cons of each. You'll gain additional credibility if you present these options before presenting the decision.[15]

You can overcome resistance by presenting the pros and cons of all sides of your argument.

To uncover audience objections, try some "What if?" scenarios. Poke holes in your own theories and ideas before your audience does. Then find solutions to the problems you've uncovered. Recognize that people support what they help create, and ask your audience for their thoughts on the subject before you put your argument together. Let your audience recommend some solutions. With enough thought and effort, you may even be able to turn problems into opportunities; for example, you may show how your proposal will be more economical in the long run, even though it may cost more now. Just

"What if?" scenarios help you see the holes in your argument.

Checklist: **Developing Persuasive Messages**

Balance Emotional and Logical Appeals

✓ Use emotional appeals to help the audience accept your message.
✓ Use logical appeals when presenting facts and evidence for complex ideas or recommendations.
✓ Avoid faulty logic.

Get Your Reader's Attention

✓ Open with a reader benefit, a stimulating question, a problem, or an unexpected statement.
✓ Discuss something your audience can agree with (establishing common ground).
✓ Demonstrate that you understand the audience's concerns.

Build Your Reader's Interest

✓ Elaborate on the main benefit.
✓ Explain the relevance of your message to your audience.

Increase Your Reader's Desire

✓ Make audience members want to change by explaining how the change will benefit them.
✓ Back up your claims with relevant evidence.

Reinforce Your Position

✓ Use semantics to build credibility and enhance the emotional content of your message.

✓ Use a variety of critical thinking and effective writing tools to strengthen your case.

Deal with Resistance

✓ Anticipate and answer possible objections. Turn them into opportunities when possible. Otherwise, give assurance that you will handle them as best you can.
✓ Try "What if?" scenarios to poke holes in your theories and then find solutions.
✓ Let others help you find solutions to problems that you uncover.
✓ Present the pros and cons of all options.
✓ Avoid common mistakes such as using a hard sell up front, resisting compromise, relying solely on great arguments, and assuming persuasion is a one-shot effort.

Motivate Your Reader to Take Action

✓ Confidently ask for the audience's cooperation.
✓ Stress the positive results of the action.
✓ Include the due date (if any) for a response, and tie it in with audience benefits.
✓ Include one last reminder of the audience benefit.
✓ Make the desired action clear and easy.

Increase the Effectiveness of Your AIDA Plan

✓ Use the AIDA plan for both direct and indirect approaches.
✓ Be careful not to give your message away in the subject line.
✓ Limit your objectives by focusing on your primary goal.

---

be sure to be thorough, open, and objective about all the facts and alternatives. When putting together persuasive arguments, avoid common mistakes such as these:[16]

◆ **Don't use an up-front hard sell.** Setting out a strong position at the start of a persuasive message gives potential opponents something to grab onto—and fight against.

◆ **Don't resist compromise.** Persuasion is a process of give and take. As one expert points out, a persuader rarely changes another person's behavior or viewpoint without altering his or her own in the process.

◆ **Don't rely solely on great arguments.** In persuading people to change their minds, great arguments matter, but they are only one part of the equation. Your ability to create a mutually beneficial framework for your position, to connect with your audience on the right emotional level, and to communicate through vivid language are all just as important; they bring your argument to life.

◆ **Don't assume persuasion is a one-shot effort.** Persuasion is a process, not a one-time event. More often than not, persuasion involves listening to people, testing a position, developing a new position that reflects new input, more testing, more compromise, and so on.

Remember, successful persuasive messages depend on your ability to balance emotional and logical appeals, frame your argument, reinforce your position, and overcome resistance. Using these strategies will help you craft strong persuasive messages, no matter what the situation. To review the steps involved in developing persuasive messages, see this chapter's "Checklist: Developing Persuasive Messages."

Avoiding common mistakes helps you overcome resistance.

Types of Persuasive Requests

People write innumerable persuasive messages within an organization: selling a supervisor on an idea for cutting costs, suggesting more efficient operating procedures, eliciting cooperation from competing departments, winning employee support for a new benefits package, requesting money for new equipment or funding for a special project, or requesting a favor. Similarly, people may send a variety of persuasive messages to people outside the organization: requesting favors, demanding adjustments, asking for information, or soliciting funds and cooperation.

The most important thing to remember when preparing a persuasive request is to keep your request within bounds. Nothing is as distressing as a request so general, so all encompassing, or so inconsiderate that it seems impossible to grant, no matter how worthy the cause. Therefore, when making a persuasive request, take special care to highlight both the direct and the indirect benefits of fulfilling the request.

For example, if you want to persuade your supervisor to institute flextime, a direct benefit for that person might be the reduced workload or the enhanced prestige. An indirect benefit might be better employee morale, once flextime is instituted. If you are asking someone to respond to a survey, you might offer a premium as the direct benefit and a chance to make a meaningful contribution as the indirect benefit. As examples of persuasive requests, let's look at two specific types: persuasive requests for action and persuasive claims and requests for adjustments.

Persuasive Requests for Action   Whether you're requesting a favor or a budget increase, remember to use the AIDA plan to frame your message. Begin with an attention-getting device. Show readers that you know something about their concerns and that you have some reason for making such a request. In this type of persuasive message, more than in most others, a flattering comment about your reader is acceptable, as long as it's sincere.

Use the interest and desire sections of your message to cover what you know about the situation you're requesting action on: the facts and figures, the benefits of helping, and any history or experience that will enhance your appeal. Your goals are (1) to gain credibility for you and your request and (2) to make your readers believe that helping you will indeed help solve a significant problem. Be careful not to doom your request to failure by asking your reader to do all your work for you. For example, don't ask your readers to

◆ Provide information that you were too lazy to seek

◆ Take action that will save you from embarrassment or inconvenience

◆ Provide total financial support for a cause that nobody else is supporting

Once you've demonstrated that your message is relevant to your reader, you can close with a request for some specific action. Be aware, however, that a persuasive memo to a colleague is somewhat more subdued than a persuasive letter to an outsider would be. Ed Alvarez wrote the memo in Figure 9–4. He's excited about a new method of packaging bananas to decrease shipping damage and reduce costs. He not only needs his boss's approval to proceed but also needs her cooperation in coordinating with another department.

When requesting a favor that is routine (such as asking someone to attend a meeting in your absence), use the direct approach and the format for routine messages (see Chapter 7). However, when asking for a special favor (such as asking someone to chair an event or to serve as the team leader because you can no longer fill that role), use persuasive techniques to convince your reader of the value of the project. Include all necessary information about the project and any facts and figures that will convince your reader that his or her contribution will be enjoyable, easy, important, and of personal benefit.

Persuasive Claims and Requests for Adjustments   Although persuasive claims and adjustment requests are sometimes referred to as complaint letters, your goal is to persuade someone to make an adjustment in your favor; you're not merely getting a com-

---

Persuasive requests are used both inside and outside the organization.

Make only reasonable requests.

Highlight the direct and indirect benefits of complying with your request.

When making a persuasive request for action, be sure to use the AIDA plan to frame your argument.

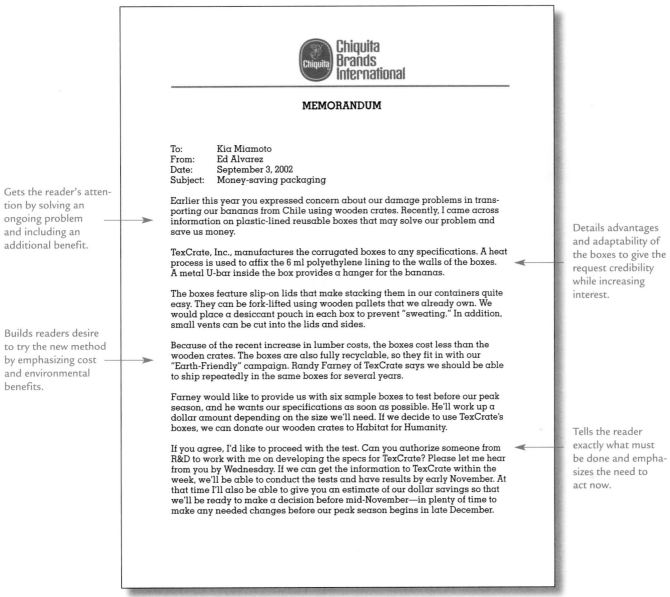

Gets the reader's attention by solving an ongoing problem and including an additional benefit.

Builds readers desire to try the new method by emphasizing cost and environmental benefits.

Details advantages and adaptability of the boxes to give the request credibility while increasing interest.

Tells the reader exactly what must be done and emphasizes the need to act now.

MEMORANDUM

To: Kia Miamoto
From: Ed Alvarez
Date: September 3, 2002
Subject: Money-saving packaging

Earlier this year you expressed concern about our damage problems in transporting our bananas from Chile using wooden crates. Recently, I came across information on plastic-lined reusable boxes that may solve our problem and save us money.

TexCrate, Inc., manufactures the corrugated boxes to any specifications. A heat process is used to affix the 6 ml polyethylene lining to the walls of the boxes. A metal U-bar inside the box provides a hanger for the bananas.

The boxes feature slip-on lids that make stacking them in our containers quite easy. They can be fork-lifted using wooden pallets that we already own. We would place a desiccant pouch in each box to prevent "sweating." In addition, small vents can be cut into the lids and sides.

Because of the recent increase in lumber costs, the boxes cost less than the wooden crates. The boxes are also fully recyclable, so they fit in with our "Earth-Friendly" campaign. Randy Farney of TexCrate says we should be able to ship repeatedly in the same boxes for several years.

Farney would like to provide us with six sample boxes to test before our peak season, and he wants our specifications as soon as possible. He'll work up a dollar amount depending on the size we'll need. If we decide to use TexCrate's boxes, we can donate our wooden crates to Habitat for Humanity.

If you agree, I'd like to proceed with the test. Can you authorize someone from R&D to work with me on developing the specs for TexCrate? Please let me hear from you by Wednesday. If we can get the information to TexCrate within the week, we'll be able to conduct the tests and have results by early November. At that time I'll also be able to give you an estimate of our dollar savings so that we'll be ready to make a decision before mid-November—in plenty of time to make any needed changes before our peak season begins in late December.

Figure 9–4
In-Depth Critique: Persuasive Memo Requesting Action

plaint off your chest. You reach your goal by demonstrating the difference between what you expected and what you actually got.

Most claim letters are routine messages and use the direct approach discussed in Chapter 7. However, suppose you purchase something, and after the warranty expires, you discover that it was defective. You write the company a routine request asking for a replacement, but your request is denied. You're not satisfied, and you still feel you have a strong case. Perhaps you just didn't communicate it well enough the first time. Persuasion is necessary in such cases.

You can't threaten to withhold payment, so try to convey the essentially negative information in a way that will get positive results. Fortunately, most people in business are open to settling your claim fairly. It's to their advantage to maintain your goodwill and to resolve your problem quickly.

The key ingredients of a good persuasive claim are a complete and specific review of the facts and a confident and positive tone. Assume that the other person is not trying to cheat you but that you also have the right to be satisfied with the transaction. Talk only about the complaint at hand, not about other issues involving similar products or other

The goal of a persuasive claim or request for adjustment is to convince someone to make an adjustment in your favor.

Make your persuasive claims
• Complete and specific when reviewing the facts
• Confident and positive in tone

A mix-up with employer identification numbers left optometrist F. Barry Jacobs and his wife Nancy in a drawn-out battle with the IRS. To resolve the situation, the couple focused on providing the IRS with plenty of history, facts, and figures—enough to persuade the government that an honest error had been made.

complaints about the company. Your goal is to solve a particular problem, and your audience is most likely to help if you focus on the audience benefits of doing so (rather than focusing on the disadvantages of neglecting your complaint).

Begin persuasive claims by stating the basic problem (or with a sincere compliment, rhetorical question, agreeable assertion, or brief review of what's been done about the problem). Include a statement that both you and your audience can agree with or that clarifies what you wish to convince your audience about. Be as specific as possible about what you want to happen.

Next, give your reader a good reason for granting your claim. Show how your audience is responsible for the problem, and appeal to your readers' sense of fair play, goodwill, or moral responsibility. Tell your audience how you feel about the problem, but don't get carried away, don't complain too much, and don't make threats. Make sure your request is calm and reasonable.

Finally, state your request specifically and confidently. Make sure your request proceeds logically from the problem and the facts you've explained. Remember to specify a deadline for action (when necessary or desirable). And don't forget to remind your audience of the main benefit of granting your claim. Look at the following letter, and note the improvements that could be made:

Opening fails to clarify the details of the purchase, the exact product involved, and the problem.

I bought an Audio-Tech sound system a few months ago to provide background music at my gift shop. Now one of the components, the CD player, does not work right. When we play a CD, it repeats and repeats. This is very irritating to me and my customers, and Audio-Tech needs to fix this problem.

Doesn't include any acceptable reasons for Audio-Tech to consider making an adjustment.

My clerks and I noticed this major mess about a month or so after I bought this fancy unit at the McNally Sound and Light Store in St. Louis, where I buy most of my video and CD stuff—although sometimes I buy through catalogs. When one of the clerks first heard the CD repeat, she tried another CD, and sure enough, it did the same thing, so it is a player problem, not a CD problem. Then we set the CD player on digital so that we could see visually what was going on, and sure enough, the sound was repeating and even skipping.

Captures the store owner's frustration, but fails to persuade the reader—who is still trying to grasp the dimensions of the problem.

When I finally brought the unit back to the store, Henry McNally said that the 60-day warranty had expired, and it was my gift shop's problem, but definitely not his problem. He said I probably had a "lemon."

Touches on what the writer expected from the product, but doesn't state what she wants done; contains only additional complaining and a vague threat.

This CD unit probably never did work right. I would think that, since I paid hundreds of dollars for this component, it would work for many years. Other stores here on Main Street cannot believe what a bummer it is to hear irritating background music on this Audio-Tech player. They say they will not buy the Audio-Tech brand if you don't replace my unit.

Figure 9–5 is a revised version of this letter that should yield much more favorable results. As the figure illustrates, resolving problems is more a reasonable exchange than a struggle between adversaries. For a review of the tasks involved here, see this chapter's "Checklist: Persuasive Claims and Requests for Adjustments."

O b j e c t i v e

5

Compare sales messages with fundraising messages.

Sales and fundraising letters are distinctive types of persuasive messages that often come in special direct-mail packages.

SENDING SALES AND FUNDRAISING MESSAGES

Two distinctive types of persuasive messages are sales and fundraising messages. These messages are often sent in special direct-mail packages that can include brochures, reply forms, or other special inserts. Both types of messages are often written by specialized and highly skilled professionals.

How do sales messages differ from fundraising messages? Sales messages are usually sent by for-profit organizations persuading readers to spend money on products for them-

Clearly describes the problem, the product involved, how the product is used, and what adjustment is requested.

Thoroughly explains the involvement of a third party (the dealer).

Restates the adjustment being requested.

ellie's special place

2201 main street, suite D • chesterfield, missouri 63071 • (314) 778-3345 • fax: (314) 778-3346

January 19, 2002

Mr. Allen Fenwick, Customer Relations
Audio-Tech Electronics
5054 Wicker Place
Chicago, IL 60622

Dear Mr. Fenwick:

As the owner of a small gift shop, I try to provide a pleasant ambiance for customers, so I play "easy listening" and classical music on my Audio-Tech Pro III sound system. I play both CDs and tapes, but the CD player is not working properly. Please replace this CD unit at no charge.

I purchased the Audio-Tech Pro III system on November 15, 2001, from McNally Sound and Light (16325 Lincoln Drive, St. Louis, Missouri 63158). All parts of the unit worked well for a month or so. I first noticed the problem on December 22: the CD would repeat a phrase two or three times in succession before moving on to the rest of the selection.

At first I assumed it was a defective CD. On December 23, two customers asked me to turn the background music off because it was repeating one phrase sporadically throughout a classical selection. The next day I checked the unit by setting it on "digital," and sure enough, every CD I played repeated phrases intermittently.

I called McNally, but I couldn't take the unit back until after the holidays, on January 5. When I returned on January 17 to pick it up, McNally told me that he could hear the problem but was unable to fix it. He said it was a manufacturing problem, but my warranty had expired, so he could not replace the unit free of charge.

Enclosed are the CD component, copies of my original sales form, and McNally's January repair order. Please replace the defective CD unit at no charge to me. Although the 60-day warranty expired on January 1, I discovered the problem well within the warranty period.

My decision to purchase Audio-Tech products was motivated by your reputation for both quality products and exceptional service. So I know you will stand behind your product and replace the faulty machine.

Sincerely,

Ellie Chambers

Ellie Chambers

Enclosure

Explains the details of purchase and how and when the problem was discovered.

Refers to attached receipts.

Provides the reader with a reason to grant the adjustment (the company's reputation for quality and customer service).

Figure 9–5
In-Depth Critique: Letter Making a Persuasive Claim

selves. However, fundraising messages are usually sent by nonprofit organizations persuading readers to donate money or time to help others. In other words, sales and fundraising messages are quite similar: Both compete for business and public attention, time, and dollars.[17] Both attempt to persuade readers to spend their time or money on the value being offered—whether that value is the convenience of a more efficient vacuum cleaner or the satisfaction of helping save children's lives. Both require a few more steps than other types of persuasive messages, and both generally use the AIDA sequence to deliver their message.

Sales and fundraising messages compete for readers' attention, time, and dollars.

Strategies for Sales Messages

Your purpose in writing a sales message is to sell a product. One of the first things to do is gain a thorough understanding of that product. What does it look like? How does it work? How is it priced? Are there any discounts? How is it packaged? How is it delivered?

When planning a sales message, know your product.

Checklist: **Persuasive Claims and Requests for Adjustments**

Attention

✓ For your opening, use one of the following: sincere compliment, rhetorical question, agreeable comment or assertion, statement of the basic problem, or brief review of what has been done about the problem.

✓ At the beginning, state something that you and the audience can agree on or what you wish to convince the audience about.

Interest and Desire

✓ Provide a description that shows the members of your audience that their firm is responsible for the problem.

✓ Make your request factual, logical, and reasonable.

✓ Appeal to the audience's sense of fair play, desire for customer goodwill, need for a good reputation, or sense of legal or moral responsibility.

✓ Emphasize your goal of having the adjustment granted.

✓ Present your case in a calm, logical manner.

✓ Tell the audience how you feel; your disappointment with the products, policies, or services provided may well be the most important part of your argument.

Action

✓ Make sure the action request is a logical conclusion based on the problem and the stated facts.

✓ State the request specifically and confidently.

✓ Specify a due date for action (when desirable).

✓ State the main audience benefit as a reminder of benefits in earlier statements.

Before writing your sales message, decide what sort of campaign you'll conduct.

In order to make campaign decisions, you need to know your audience.

Amazon.com's CEO Jeffrey Bezos knows how to determine his central selling point. He has convinced stockholders that the company's book division is profitable, and he's persuaded customers that the Internet superstore is convenient. Now his aim is to re-create that small-town store experience, where the owner knows you and what you like. To keep customers returning, the Web site is personalized. It suggests new products to you on the basis of what you have previously purchased, and it helps you provide friends accessing the site with a list of what you've already bought and what you want to buy.

You'll also need to think about the type of sales campaign you'll conduct. Will you send a letter only, or will you include brochures, samples, response cards, and the like? If you send a brochure, how many pages will it run? Will you conduct a multistage campaign, with several mailings and some sort of telephone or in-person follow-up? Or will you rely on a single hard-hitting mailing? Expensive items and hard-to-accept propositions call for a more elaborate campaign than low-cost products and simple actions.

All these decisions depend on the audience you're trying to reach—their characteristics and their likely acceptance of or resistance to your message. You must analyze your audience and focus on their needs, interests, and emotional concerns—just as you would for any persuasive message. Try to form a mental image of the typical buyer for the product you wish to sell. But in addition to the usual questions, also ask yourself: What might audience members want to know about this product? How can your product help them? Are they driven by bottom-line pricing, or is quality more important to them?

In addition to learning about your product, performing a more in-depth audience analysis, and planning your sales campaign, you need a few other sales letter strategies: You need to determine selling points and benefits; you want to be sure that you stay within the law; and you must know how to use action terms, talk about price, and support your claims. In addition, it helps to know how each phase of the AIDA plan differs in sales letters.

Determining Selling Points and Benefits   Sales letters require you to know your product's selling points and how each one benefits your particular audience. You'll need to highlight these points when you compose your persuasive message. For example, at Patagonia, sales letters emphasize the confidence that people can place not only in Patagonia's quality-made products but also in the company's environmentally safe production.

As Table 9–2 shows, selling points are the most attractive features of an idea or product; benefits are the particular advantages that readers will realize from those features. Selling points focus on the product. Benefits focus on the user. For example, if you say that your shovel has "an ergonomically designed handle," you've described a good feature. But to persuade someone to buy that shovel, say "the ergonomically designed handle will reduce your risk of back injury." That's a benefit. For your letter and your overall sales efforts to be successful, your product's distinguishing benefit must correspond to your readers' primary needs or emotional concerns.

Table 9–2 Features versus Benefits	
Product Feature (Selling Point)	**Consumer Benefit**
No money down, no interest payments for 24 months.	You can buy what you want right now at no additional costs.
This printer prints 17 pages a minute.	This printer can turn out one of your 100-page proposals in six minutes.
Our shelter provides 100 adult beds and 50 children's beds for the needy.	Your donation will provide temporary housing for 100 women who don't want to return to abusive husbands.
Your corporate sponsorship of the seminar will pay for the keynote speaker's travel and lodging.	Your corporate sponsorship of the seminar will allow your site manager a five-minute introduction at the beginning of the program to summarize your services.

Take a look at Figure 9–6. The sales letter for SecureAbel Alarms uses the AIDA plan to persuade students to buy its dorm-room alarm system. The features of the system are that it can be installed with a screwdriver, has an activator that hooks to your key chain or belt loop, and has a blinking red light to warn intruders to stay away. The benefits are ease of installation, ease of activation, and a feeling of safety and security—all obtainable without investing in a full-blown permanently installed alarm system. When composing sales messages, be sure to focus on relatively few product benefits. Ultimately, you'll single out one benefit, which will become the hallmark of your campaign. Safety seems to be the key benefit emphasized by SecureAbel Alarms.

Selling points focus on the product; benefits focus on the user.

Staying Within the Law   As with other persuasive messages, following the letter of the law isn't always enough. Whether you're selling a good, a service, or your company's image, you want to write sales letters of the highest ethical character, so focus on solving your readers' problem rather than on selling your product. When you're genuinely concerned about your audience's needs and interests, you'll find it easier to avoid legal or ethical pitfalls. Even so, to avoid serious legal problems, you need to know the law (see "Promoting Workplace Ethics—What You May Legally Say in a Sales Letter").

You can avoid both legal and ethical pitfalls by being genuinely concerned about your audience's needs, but you must also know the law.

Letters as Contracts   In many states, sales letters are considered binding contracts. You must be able to do what you say you can do. So avoid even implying offers or promises that you can't deliver.

Facts About Fraud   Misrepresenting the price, quality, or performance of a product in a sales letter is fraud. Fraud also includes using a testimonial by a person misrepresented as being an expert. Making a false statement in a sales letter is fraud if the recipient can prove the following:

◆ You intended to deceive.

◆ You made your statement regarding a fact (not an opinion or a speculation).

◆ The recipient was justified in relying on your statement.

◆ The recipient was damaged by your statement (in a legal sense).

Invasion of Privacy   Using a person's name, photograph, or other identity in a sales letter without permission constitutes invasion of privacy—with some exceptions. Using a photo of the members of a local softball team in a chamber of commerce mailer may be perfectly legal if team members are public figures in the community and if using the photo doesn't falsely imply their endorsement. On the other hand, using a photo of your governor, without consent, on a letter about the profits to be made in worm farming could be deemed an invasion of privacy.

In addition, publicizing a person's private life in a sales letter can result in legal problems. For example, stating that the president of a local bank (mentioned by name) served six months in prison for income tax evasion is a potentially damaging fact that may be

1 Planning

Analyze: The purpose here is to persuade readers to buy the portable alarm system. The audience will be neutral—or even resistant.

Investigate: Gather information on product's features and benefits, as well as on audience needs.

Adapt: Use a typical sales letter format.

2 Writing

Organize: Make safety the central selling point. Follow the indirect AIDA approach. Important to get the reader's attention right away.

Compose: Use both logical and emotional appeals. Use a friendly, conversational tone. Include a response card to make reader action easy.

3 Completing

Revise: Don't emphasize emotional appeals. The point is to help readers, not threaten them. Edit for focus and clarity.

Produce: Use a simple design for the letter and any brochures (in line with reasonable pricing).

Proofread: Be accurate. Remove all typographical distractions.

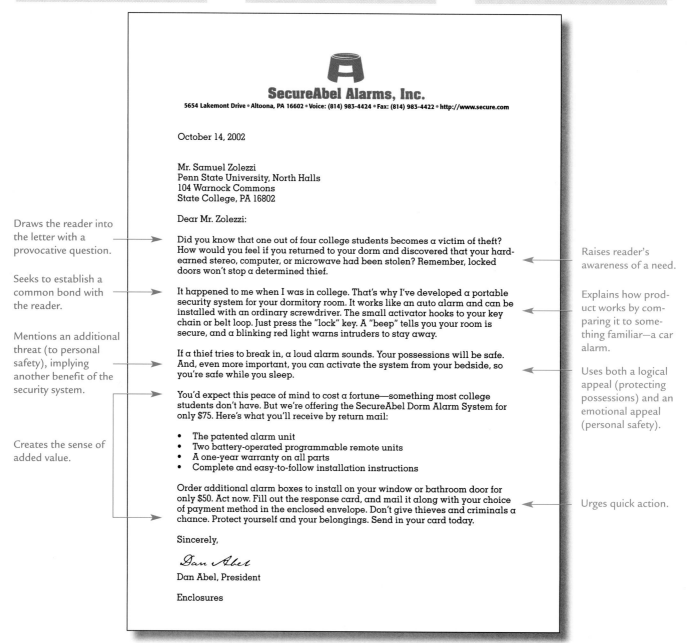

Draws the reader into the letter with a provocative question.

Seeks to establish a common bond with the reader.

Mentions an additional threat (to personal safety), implying another benefit of the security system.

Creates the sense of added value.

Raises reader's awareness of a need.

Explains how product works by comparing it to something familiar—a car alarm.

Uses both a logical appeal (protecting possessions) and an emotional appeal (personal safety).

Urges quick action.

SecureAbel Alarms, Inc.

5654 Lakemont Drive • Altoona, PA 16602 • Voice: (814) 983-4424 • Fax: (814) 983-4422 • http://www.secure.com

October 14, 2002

Mr. Samuel Zolezzi
Penn State University, North Halls
104 Warnock Commons
State College, PA 16802

Dear Mr. Zolezzi:

Did you know that one out of four college students becomes a victim of theft? How would you feel if you returned to your dorm and discovered that your hard-earned stereo, computer, or microwave had been stolen? Remember, locked doors won't stop a determined thief.

It happened to me when I was in college. That's why I've developed a portable security system for your dormitory room. It works like an auto alarm and can be installed with an ordinary screwdriver. The small activator hooks to your key chain or belt loop. Just press the "lock" key. A "beep" tells you your room is secure, and a blinking red light warns intruders to stay away.

If a thief tries to break in, a loud alarm sounds. Your possessions will be safe. And, even more important, you can activate the system from your bedside, so you're safe while you sleep.

You'd expect this peace of mind to cost a fortune—something most college students don't have. But we're offering the SecureAbel Dorm Alarm System for only $75. Here's what you'll receive by return mail:

- The patented alarm unit
- Two battery-operated programmable remote units
- A one-year warranty on all parts
- Complete and easy-to-follow installation instructions

Order additional alarm boxes to install on your window or bathroom door for only $50. Act now. Fill out the response card, and mail it along with your choice of payment method in the enclosed envelope. Don't give thieves and criminals a chance. Protect yourself and your belongings. Send in your card today.

Sincerely,

Dan Abel

Dan Abel, President

Enclosures

Figure 9–6
In-Depth Critique: Letter Selling a Product

Promoting Workplace Ethics

What You May Legally Say in a Sales Letter

As you prepare to write your sales letter, think carefully about your choice of words. False or misleading statements could land you in court, so make sure your language complies with legal and ethical standards. To keep your sales letters within the limits of the law, review the legal considerations of these typical sales phrases:

❏ **"Our product is the best on the market."** This statement is acceptable for a sales letter because the law permits you to express an opinion about your product. In the process of merchandising a product, statements of opinion are known as "puffery," which is perfectly legal as long as you make no deceptive or fraudulent claims.

❏ **"Our product will serve you well for many years to come."** This statement from a sales brochure triggered a lawsuit by a disgruntled customer who claimed the manufacturer's product lasted only a few years. The courts ruled that the statement was an acceptable form of puffery because the manufacturer did not promise that the product would last for a specific number of years.

❏ **"We're so confident you'll enjoy our products that we've enclosed a sample of our most popular line. This sample can be yours for only $5.00! Please send your payment in the enclosed, prepaid envelope."** If you include a product sample with your sales letter, your readers may keep the merchandise without paying for it. Under the law, consumers may consider unordered goods as gifts.

They are not obligated to return the items to you or submit payments for unsolicited merchandise.

❏ **"Thousands of high school students—just like you—are already enjoying this fantastic CD collection! Order before March 1 and save!"** If your sales letter appeals to minors, you are legally obligated to honor their contracts. At the same time, however, the law permits minors to cancel their contracts and return the merchandise to you. Sellers are legally obligated to accept contracts voided by minors and any goods returned by them. Legal adult status is defined differently from state to state, ranging from age 18 to age 21.

❏ **"You'll find hundreds of bargains at our annual "scratch and dent" sale! All sales are final on merchandise marked "as is."** When you use the term *as is* in your sales letter, you are not misleading customers about the quality of your products. By warning consumers that the condition of sales items is less than perfect, you are not legally obligated to issue refunds to customers who complain about defects later on.

CAREER APPLICATIONS

1. Review two sales letters for content. List the "puffery" statements in each letter.
2. Note any statements in these sales letters that appear questionable to you. Rewrite one of the statements, carefully choosing words that won't be misleading to consumers.

---

considered an invasion of privacy. You would also risk a lawsuit by publicizing another person's past-due debts or by publishing without consent another person's medical records or x-rays.

Using Action Terms Action words give strength to any business message, but they are especially important in sales letters. Compare the following:

> To give force to a message
> • Use action terms.
> • Use colorful verbs and adjectives.

INSTEAD OF THIS	WRITE THIS
The NuForm desk chair is designed to support your lower back and relieve pressure on your legs.	The NuForm desk chair supports your lower back and relieves pressure on your legs.

The second version says the same thing in fewer words and emphasizes what the chair does for the user ("supports") rather than the intentions of the design team ("is designed to support").

Use colorful verbs and adjectives that convey a dynamic image. Be careful, however, not to overdo it: "Your factory floors will sparkle like diamonds" is hard to believe and may prevent your audience from believing the rest of your message.

Talking About Price The price that people are willing to pay for a product depends on several factors: the prices of similar products, the general state of the economy, and the psychology of the buyer. Price is a complicated issue and often a sensitive one. So you need to be careful whenever you talk about price in your sales messages.

You can prepare readers for your product's price by subtle choice and arrangement of words.

Whether you highlight or downplay the price of your product, prepare your readers for it. Words such as *luxurious* and *economical* provide unmistakable clues about how your price compares with that of competitors. Such words help your readers accept your price when you finally state it. Here's an example from a sales letter offering a product at a bargain price:

All the Features of Name-Brand Pantyhose at Half the Price!
Why pay for fancy packaging or that little tag with a famous name on it when you can enjoy cotton lining, reinforced toes, and matchless durability for only $1.99?

If the price is an attractive feature, emphasize it by displaying it prominently.

In this excerpt the price falls right at the end of the paragraph, where it stands out. In addition, the price issue is featured in a bold headline. This technique may even be used as the opening of a letter, if (1) the price is the most important feature and (2) the audience for the letter is value conscious.

To de-emphasize price
- Bury actual figures in the middle of a paragraph near the end.
- Mention benefits and favorable money matters before the actual price.
- Break a quantity price into units.
- Compare the price with the cost of some other product or activity.

If price is not a major selling point, you can handle it in several ways. You could leave the price out altogether or mention it only in an accompanying brochure. You could de-emphasize the price by putting the actual figures in the middle of a paragraph that comes close to the end of your sales letter, well after you've presented the benefits and selling points.

Emphasizing the rarity of the edition signals value and thus prepares the reader for the big-ticket price that follows.

The actual price is buried in the middle of a sentence and is tied in with another reminder of the exclusivity of the offer.

Only 100 prints of this exclusive, limited-edition lithograph will be created. On June 15, they will be made available to the general public, but you can reserve one now for only $350, the special advance reservation price. Simply rush the enclosed reservation card back today so that your order is in before the June 15 publication date.

The pros also use two other techniques for minimizing price. One technique is to break a quantity price into units. Instead of saying that a case of wine costs $144, you might say that each bottle costs $12. The other technique is to compare your product's price with the cost of some other product or activity: "The cost of owning your own spa is less than you'd pay for a health-club membership." Your aim is to make the cost seem as small and affordable as possible, thereby eliminating price as a possible objection.

Supporting Your Claims You can't assume that people will believe what you say about your product just because you've said it in writing. You'll have to prove your claims. Support is especially important if your product is complicated, costs a lot, or represents some unusual approach.

Types of support for product claims:
- Samples
- Brochures
- Examples
- Testimonials
- Statistics
- Guarantees

Support for your claims may take several forms. Samples and brochures, often with photographs, are enclosed in a sales package and are referred to in the letter. The letter also describes or typographically highlights examples of how the product has benefited others. It includes testimonials (quotations from satisfied customers) or cites statistics from scientific studies of the product's performance. Guarantees of exchange or return privileges may be woven into the letter or set off in a special way, indicating that you have faith in your product and are willing to back it up.

It's almost impossible to provide too much support. Try to anticipate every question your audience may want to ask. Put yourself in your audience's place so that you can discover, and solve, all the "what if" scenarios.[18]

Using the AIDA Plan in Sales Messages Most sales letters are prepared according to the AIDA plan used for any persuasive message. You begin with an attention-getting device, generate interest by describing some of the product's unique features, increase the desire for your product by highlighting the benefits that are most appealing to your audience, and close by suggesting the action you want the audience to take.

Getting Attention Like other persuasive messages, sales letters start with an attention-getting device; however, the emphasis of the attention phase is slightly different. Sales-letter professionals use some common techniques to attract their audience's attention. One popular technique is opening with a provocative question. Look closely at the following three examples. Which seems most interesting to you?

How would you like straight A's this semester?
Get straight A's this semester!
Now you can get straight A's this semester, with . . .

If you're like most people, you'll find the first option the most enticing. The question invites your response—a positive response designed to encourage you to read on. The second option is fairly interesting too, but its commanding tone may make you wary of the claim. The third option is acceptable, but it certainly conveys no sense of excitement. Its quick introduction of the product may lead you to a snap decision against reading further.

Other techniques can also help you open your sales letters with excitement. You can grab your audience's attention by emphasizing

- **A piece of genuine news.** "In the past 60 days, mortgage rates have fallen to a 30-year low."

- **A personal appeal to the reader's emotions and values.** "The only thing worse than paying taxes is paying taxes when you don't have to."

- **Your product's most attractive feature along with the associated benefit.** "New control device ends problems with employee pilferage!"

- **An intriguing number.** "Here are three great secrets of the world's most-loved entertainers."

- **A sample of the product.** "Here's your free sample of the new Romalite packing sheet."

- **A concrete illustration with story appeal.** "In 1985 Earl Colbert set out to find a better way to process credit applications. After 10 years of trial and error, he finally developed a procedure so simple and yet thorough that he was cited for service to the industry by the American Creditors Association."

- **A specific trait shared by the audience.** "Busy executives need another complicated 'time-saving' device like they need a hole in the head!"

- **A challenge.** "Don't waste another day wondering how you're going to become the success you've always wanted to be!"

- **A solution to a problem.** "Tired of arctic air rushing through the cracks around your windows? Stay warm and save energy with StormSeal Weather-stripping."

Look at your own mail to see how many sales messages use these few techniques. Such attention-getting devices will give your sales letters added impact. Look back at Figure 9–6 for a typical example.

Sales-message professionals know that textual openings aren't the only way to get attention. In ads and catalogs, Patagonia's Chouinard captures attention and heightens emotional desire by featuring lush, vibrant photographs of nature. Professionals also use a variety of formatting devices to get attention. You can grab your audience by using personalized salutations, special sizes or styles of type, underlining, bullets, color, indentions, and so on. Even so, not all attention-getting devices are equally effective. The best is the one that makes your audience read the rest of your message.

Building Interest In the interest section of your message, highlight your product's key selling point. Say that your company's alarm device is relatively inexpensive, durable, and tamperproof. Although these are all attractive features, you want to focus on only one. Ask what the competition has to offer, what most distinguishes your product, and what most concerns potential buyers. The answers to these questions will help you select the **central selling point,** the single point around which to build your sales message. Build your audience's interest by highlighting this point, and make it stand out through typography, design, or high-impact writing.[19]

Determining the central selling point will also help you define the benefits to potential buyers. Perhaps your company built its new alarm to overcome competing products' susceptibility to tampering. Being tamperproof is the feature you choose as your central selling point, and its benefit to readers is that burglars won't be able to break in so easily.

Certain tried-and-true attention-getting devices are used in sales letters for a wide variety of products.

Choose an attention-getter that encourages the reader to read more.

To determine your product's central selling point, ask
- What does the competition offer?
- What is special about my product?
- What are potential buyers really looking for?

To increase desire, expand your main benefit while adding others.

Increasing Desire   In the desire section, mention your main benefit repeatedly, expanding and explaining as you go. Use both words and pictures, if possible. This main benefit is what will entice recipients to read on and take further action.

As you continue to stress your main benefit, weave in references to other benefits. ("You can get this worry-free protection for much less than you might think," and "The same technology that makes it difficult for burglars to crack your alarm system makes the device durable, even when it must be exposed to the elements.") Remember, sales letters reflect the "you" attitude through references to benefits, so always phrase the selling points in terms of what your product's features can do for potential customers.

Keep in mind that you don't need to provide every last detail as you explain product benefits. The best letters are short (preferably one but no more than two pages). They include enough detail to spur the reader's interest, but they don't try to be the sole source of information. Also, remember to use bullet points to highlight details whenever possible. You have to assume that your readers are pressed for time and are interested only in what matters most to them.[20]

Motivating Action   In the last section, you explain clearly how to take the next step. After all, the overriding purpose of a sales letter is to get your reader to do something. Many consumer products sold through the mail simply ask for a check—in other words, an immediate decision to buy. On the other hand, companies selling big-ticket and more complex items frequently ask for just a small step toward the final buying decision, such as sending for more information or authorizing a call by a sales representative.

Aim to get the reader to act as soon as possible.

Whatever you ask readers to do, try to persuade them to do it right away. Convince them that they must act now, perhaps to guarantee a specific delivery date. If there's no particular reason to act quickly, many sales letters offer discounts for orders placed by a certain date or prizes or special offers to, say, the first 500 people to respond. Others suggest that purchases be charged to a credit card or be paid off over time. Still others offer a free trial, an unconditional guarantee, or a no-strings request card for information—all in an effort to overcome readers' natural inertia.

Of course, adding a P.S. is one of the most effective ways to boost audience response. This is the place to make your final impression, so be sure the information is noteworthy. Use the P.S. to reiterate your primary benefit, make an additional offer, or compel the reader to act quickly by emphasizing a deadline.[21]

Finally, use good judgment when distributing your messages to would-be customers (see "Using the Power of Technology—Spam: Putting a Lid on It"). Motivating action is a challenge for the best sales letters. Even more of a challenge is motivating action when you're trying to raise funds.

Strategies for Fundraising Messages

Fundraising letters use many of the same techniques that are used in sales letters.

Most of the techniques used to write sales letters can also be used to write fundraising letters, as long as your techniques match your audience, your goals, and the cause or organization you're representing. Be careful to establish value in the minds of your donors. Above all, don't forget to include the "what's in it for me?" information: for example, telling your readers how good they'll feel by making a donation.[22]

To make sure that your fundraising letters outshine the competition's letters, take some time to get ready before you actually begin writing.[23] You can begin by reading the mail you receive from donors. Learn as much as you can about your audience by noting the tone of these letters, the language used, and the concerns raised. This exercise will help you write letters that donors will both understand and relate to.

You might also keep a file of competing fundraising letters. Study these samples to find out what other fundraisers are doing and what new approaches they're taking. Most important, find out what works and what doesn't. Then you can continue with your other research efforts, such as conducting interviews, holding focus groups, and reading trade journals to find out what people are concerned about, what they're interested in, and what gets their attention.

Using the Power of Technology

Spam: Putting a Lid on It

From exasperated consumers to giant online services, everyone is trying to stamp out irritating electronic junk mail called spam. Even the U.S. Senate is trying to regulate this scourge of cyberspace. But if spam is jamming your mailbox, don't wait for the government to step in. You can wage your own counterassault.

Keep a Low Profile

The best way to avoid junk e-mail is to stay off the spammers' lists—which can be difficult. Some marketers use automated "robot" programs. But savvy surfers can use a few tricks of their own to fool the robots:

❑ **When possible, use an online alias.** Many Internet service providers (ISPs) allow users to create multiple screen names. Create one to use only in chat rooms and forums, thus hiding your original e-mail address from spammers.

❑ **Keep your e-mail address unlisted.** Don't list yourself in your ISP's member directory.

❑ **Alter your e-mail address on bulletin boards.** Use an e-mail address that is recognizable to humans but imperceptible to stupid robot programs. For example, instead of using your real address (Jason@msn.com) disguise it (Jason NOSPAM@NOSPAM.msn.com).

Don't Reply to Spam

No matter how careful you are, you will end up on some spammers' lists. Some junk mail even offers you a civil choice: "If you don't wish to receive any more e-mail, click on the reply button and ask to be removed." But experts warn that replying to spammers is the worst possible reaction. Doing so can actually promote your address to a "premium" spam list—because it's clear that someone is actually reading the e-mail at that account.

Drown Out the Noise

When the barrage of junk e-mail gets to be too much, you can use technology to trash some of it. Most e-mail packages and online services offer filtering programs that try to get rid of stuff you don't want. You can set up a filter by instructing it to (1) accept e-mail from a list of specified users or services or (2) weed out specific people or services. No filter is perfect, though, and some desirable e-mail may get tossed out in the process.

Fight Back

You can even take more extreme steps. You might file a complaint with the Federal Trade Commission, which is vigorously campaigning to quash the worst spammers. Or you might send a complaint to the spammer's ISP. When service providers get a lot of complaints about a mass marketer on their system, they can shut down the account and put the spammer out of business—at least temporarily. Spammers can always use another ISP or even relocate offshore and out of the reach of U.S. laws.

CAREER APPLICATIONS

1. Do you think a law curbing unsolicited e-mail is a violation of free speech? Why or why not?
2. Recent legislation requires senders of unsolicited commercial e-mail to include their name, phone, and address. Do you think such legislation actually legitimizes spamming—making it okay to spam as long as you include your contact information? Why or why not?

Finally, before you start writing, know whose benefits to emphasize. Make a two-column list; on one side, list what your organization does, and on the other side, list what your donors want. You'll discover that the two columns are quite different. Make sure that the benefits you emphasize are related to what your donors want, not to what your organization does. Then you can work on stating those donor benefits in specific detail. For example: "Your donation of $100 will provide 15 people with a Christmas dinner."

Be sure to focus on the concerns of your readers, not on the concerns of your organization.

Personalizing Fundraising Messages   Because fundraising letters depend so heavily on emotional appeals, keep your message personal. A natural, real-life lead-in is usually the best. People seem to respond best to slice-of-life stories. Storytelling is perfect when your narrative is unforced and goes straight to the heart of the matter.[24] Professional fundraiser Conrad Squires advises you to "find and use relevant human-interest stories," to "show donors the faces of the people they are helping," and to "make the act of sending a contribution as real and memorable and personal" as you can.[25] Such techniques make people feel the warmth of other lives.[26]

Human interest stories are the best way to interest your readers in fundraising letters.

So that your letters remain personal, immediate, and effective, steer clear of three common mistakes: [27]

◆ Avoid letting your letter sound like a business communication of any kind.

◆ Avoid wasting space on warm-up (the things you write while you're working up to your real argument).

◆ Avoid assuming that the goals of your organization are more important than your readers' concerns (a deadly mistake).

The last item is crucial when writing fundraising letters. Squires suggests that "the more space you spend writing about the reader, the better response you're likely to get."[28] Here are some examples:

> "You've proven you are somebody who really cares about what happens to children, Mr. Jones."
>
> "Ms. Smith, your company's kindness can change the world for Meta Singh and his family."

It's also up to you to help your donors identify with recipients. A busy company executive may not be able to identify with the homeless man she passes on the street every day. But every human being understands pain; we've all felt it. So do your best to portray that homeless man's pain using words that the busy executive can understand.[29]

Strengthening Fundraising Messages The best fundraising letters do four things: (1) thoroughly explain a specific need, (2) show how important it is for readers to help, (3) spell out exactly what amount of help is being requested, and (4) describe in detail the benefits of helping.[30] To help you accomplish these four major tasks, here are some fundraising guidelines:[31]

◆ **Interest your readers immediately.** If you don't catch your readers' interest at the absolute beginning of your letter, you never will.

◆ **Use simple language.** Tell your story with simple, warm, and personal language. Nothing else is as effective in getting people to empathize.

◆ **Give readers an opportunity to accomplish something important.** Donors want to feel needed. They want the excitement of coming to your rescue.

◆ **Make it hard to say "no."** Make the need so urgent and strong that your readers will find it difficult to turn you down. "Won't you send a gift now, knowing that children's lives are on the line?"

◆ **Make your needs clear.** Leave no doubt about the amount of money that you want. Be absolutely clear, and be sure the amount requested is appropriate for your audience. Explain why the money is needed as soon as possible. Also, make it extremely easy to respond by asking for a small gift.

◆ **Write no longer than you have to.** If you use a telegram-type format, keep your message short. However, longer messages are usually best for fundraising. Just keep sentences and paragraphs short, maximize content, and minimize wordiness.

◆ **Make your reply form complete and thorough.** Include all the basics: your name, address, and telephone number; a restatement of your request and the gift amount; your donor's name and address (or space enough for a label); information on how to make out the check; and information on tax deductibility.

◆ **Use interesting enclosures.** Enclosures that simply give more information will decrease returns. Instead, use enclosures that are fun or that give the donor something to do, sign, return, or keep.

These guidelines should help you reach the humanity and compassion of your readers by focusing on specific reader benefits, detailing the unique need, emphasizing the urgency of the situation, and spelling out the exact help needed.

As president of the nonprofit Decatur High School Band Parents Association, Monty Nichols has the daunting task of raising half a million dollars to send the band to

---

Margin notes:

Personalize fundraising letters by
• Writing about your readers
• Helping your readers identify with recipients

O b j e c t i v e

6

List eight guidelines that will help you strengthen your fundraising messages.

Strong fundraising letters
• Explain a specific need thoroughly
• Show how important it is for readers to help
• Spell out exactly what amount of help is being requested
• Describe in detail the benefits of helping

Grabs attention with a "you"-oriented opening that focuses on the reader's generosity.

Creates interest by emphasizing benefits of the reader and by providing details of the trip and costs.

Creates the desire to participate in a worthwhile project.

Urges action by naming additional reader benefits and enclosing a response card.

Figure 9–7
In-Depth Critique: Letter to Raise Funds

Osaka, Japan, for an international band festival. Nichols and his board have decided to contact local businesses for help. His letter in Figure 9–7 makes a compelling case for donations.

Like sales letters, fundraising letters are simply particular types of persuasive messages. Both categories have their unique requirements, some of which only professional writers can master. (See this chapter's "Checklist: Composing Sales and Fundraising Letters" as a reminder of the tasks involved in writing these messages.)

Checklist: Composing Sales and Fundraising Letters

Attention

✓ Design a positive opening that awakens a favorable association with the product, need, or cause.

✓ Write the opening so that it's appropriate, fresh, honest, interesting, specific, and relevant.

✓ Promise a benefit to the reader.

✓ Keep the first paragraph short, preferably two to five lines, and sometimes only one.

✓ For sales letters, get attention with a provocative question, a significant/starting fact, a solution to a problem, a special offer/gift, a testimonial, a current event, an illustration, a comparison, an event in the reader's life, a problem the reader may face, or a quotation.

✓ For fundraising letters, design an attention-getter that uses a human-interest story.

Interest

✓ State information clearly, vividly, and persuasively, and relate it to the reader's concerns.

✓ Develop the central selling point.

✓ Feature the product or charitable need in two ways: physical description and reader benefits.

✓ Place benefits first, or interweave them with a physical description.

✓ Describe objective details of the need or product (size, shape, color, scent, sound, texture, etc.).

✓ Use psychological appeals to present the sensation, satisfaction, or pleasure readers will gain.

✓ Blend cold facts with warm feelings.

Desire

✓ Enlist one or more appeals to support the central idea (selling point or fundraising goal).

✓ If the product is valued mainly because of its appearance, describe its physical details.

✓ If the product is machinery or technical equipment, describe its sturdy construction, fine crafting, and other

technical details in terms that help readers visualize themselves using it.

✓ Include technical sketches and meaningful pictures, charts, and graphs, if necessary.

✓ For sales letters, provide test results from recognized experts, laboratories, or authoritative agencies.

✓ To raise funds, detail how donations are spent, using recognized accounting/auditing firms.

✓ To elicit donations, use strong visual details, good narrative, active verbs, and limited adjectives.

✓ Emphasize reader benefits.

✓ Anticipate and answer the reader's questions.

✓ Use an appropriate form of proof.

✓ Include verifiable reports/statistics about users' experience what the product or organization.

✓ Provide names (with permission only) of satisfied buyers, users, or donors.

✓ Present unexaggerated testimonials from persons or firms whose judgment readers respect.

✓ In sales letters, offer a free trial or a guarantee, and refer to samples if they are included.

✓ Note any enclosures in conjunction with a selling point or a reader benefit.

Action

✓ Clearly state the action you desire.

✓ Provide specific details on how to order the product, donate money, or reach your organization.

✓ Ease action with reply cards, preaddressed envelopes, phone numbers, follow-up phone calls.

✓ Offer a special inducement to act now: time limit or situation urgency, special price for a limited time, premium for acting before a certain date, gift for acting, free trial, no obligation to buy with more information or demonstration, easy payments with no money down, credit-card payments.

✓ Supply a final reader benefit.

✓ In a postscript, convey important donation information or an important sales point (if desired).

SUMMARY OF LEARNING OBJECTIVES

1 Discuss the planning tasks that need extra attention when preparing persuasive messages. Because persuasive messages can be complicated and sensitive, several planning tasks need extra attention. You'll be persuading people to take action that they probably wouldn't have taken without your message, so analyzing your purpose is crucial. In addition, audience analysis may be more detailed for persuasive messages, gauging psychological and social needs in addition to cultural differences. Also, when persuading a skeptical audience, your credibility must be unquestionable, so you may need to spend some extra effort to establish it. Since your attempts to persuade could be viewed by some as manipulative, you need to strive for the highest ethical standards.

2 Distinguish between emotional and logical appeals, and discuss how to balance them. Emotional appeals call on human feelings, using arguments that are based on audience needs or sympathies. However, these appeals aren't effective by themselves. Logical appeals call on human reason (whether using analogy, induction, or deduction). If you're careful to avoid faulty logic, you can use logic together with emotion, thereby supplying rational support for an idea that readers have already embraced emotionally. In general, logic will be your strongest appeal, with only subtle emotion. However, when persuading someone to purchase a product, join a cause, or make a donation, you can heighten emotional appeals a bit.

3 Describe the AIDA plan for persuasive messages. When using the AIDA plan, you open your message by getting *attention* with a reader benefit, a problem, a stimulating question, a piece of news, or an unexpected statement. You build *interest* with facts, details, and additional reader benefits. You increase *desire* by providing more evidence and reader benefits and by anticipating and answering possible objections. You conclude by motivating a specific *action*, emphasizing the positive results of that action, and making it easy for the reader to respond.

4 Explain the best way to overcome resistance to your persuasive message, and list four common mistakes. The best way to overcome resistance is to think of all the objections your audience could possibly have and then explain the pros and cons of all sides. Provide solutions to all the problems your audience might perceive. In addition, make sure you do not (1) use an up-front hard sell, (2) rule out compromise, (3) rely solely on great arguments while ignoring how you present them, and (4) assume your persuasive attempt is a one-time effort.

5 Compare sales messages with fundraising messages. Sales messages are used by for-profit companies to persuade readers to make a purchase for themselves. In contrast, fundraising messages are used by nonprofit organizations to persuade readers to donate their time or their money to help others. However, these two types of persuasive messages have a lot in common. Primarily, they both try to persuade readers to "buy" (with time or money) the value that is being offered (the product or the cause). In addition, both types of persuasive message generally use the AIDA plan.

6 List eight guidelines that will help you strengthen your fundraising messages. To strengthen your fundraising messages, follow these guidelines: (1) interest your readers immediately, (2) use simple language, (3) give your readers the chance to do something important, (4) make it hard to say no, (5) make your needs clear, (6) write no longer than you have to, (7) make your reply form complete and thorough, (8) use interesting enclosures.

SOLVING A COMMUNICATION DILEMMA AT PATAGONIA

Yvon Chouinard knows that Patagonia's success depends on strong persuasive messages that educate consumers about environmental protection and that convince readers to think about long-term sustainability issues when choosing the products they will purchase. Chouinard takes every opportunity to inform the public about the company's techniques for reducing the environmental impact of its operations, and he uses a combination of emotional and logical appeals. For example, Patagonia's catalogs capture attention and create an emotional desire for environmental responsibility by featuring lush, full-page scenic photos that resemble *National Geographic* layouts. On the other hand, the catalogs' environmental essays have a logical appeal, informing readers about the company's philosophies and environmental values. Written by Chouinard, these essays explain Patagonia's rationale for developing environmentally sensitive production techniques, and delineate the long-term benefits of investing in organically grown products and recycled materials. In addition, the catalogs are printed on recycled paper that is 50 percent chlorine-free.

The company also uses logical appeals in its environmental reports. Patagonia's internal assessment group studies the environmental impact of the company's operating procedures. The company then publishes these findings in public reports and welcomes suggestions from outside sources for refining procedures. Patagonia's annual "Earth Tax Report" invites customers to apply for grants for local environmental projects, demonstrating its support for environmental causes and establishing its creditability as an environmentally responsible company. Moreover, Chouinard does his best to persuade in-store customers about the value of environmental responsibility by using interactive displays of the earth's processes and by using garment hangtags that highlight merchandise made from organically grown cotton, Synchilla fleece, and natural dyes. Aligning his company and his environmental philosophy hasn't been easy, but Chouinard continues to get his message across.

Your Mission As Vice President for Corporate Communications, you are responsible for handling a wide range of correspondence for Patagonia's managers and executives. Use your knowledge of persuasive messages to choose the best alternative in each of the following situations. Be prepared to explain why your choice is best.

1. Every year, Patagonia awards about 350 grants from its "Earth Tax" fund to support worthy environmental causes. But several customers have complained that Patagonia's earth tax often supports radical environmental groups. In response to these complaints, you have been asked to draft a persuasive letter for Chouinard that explains Patagonia's position on supporting environmental causes. Which of the following appeals would be the most effective in such a letter?

   a. An entirely emotional appeal stressing Patagonia's commitment to support worthy environmental causes, regardless of a group's tactics for achieving environmental goals.
   b. An entirely logical appeal stressing the application process for grants, Patagonia's criteria for selecting earth tax recipients, and a brief history of Patagonia's contributions to environmental causes.
   c. A combination of emotional and logical appeals, stressing both the need to support worthy environmental causes and Patagonia's rationale for awarding grants based on the worthiness of the cause, not the tactics of the cause's supporters.
   d. A combination of emotional and logical appeals, stressing the need to save the earth's resources at any cost and stressing the importance of supporting any group that is attempting to save the environment for future generations.

2. An environmental activist is scheduled to speak at a Patagonia retail store about the importance of saving an ancient redwood forest in Northern California. The store manager hopes the speaking venue will increase awareness and educate customers about the need for saving the forest and will raise money for the "Save the Redwood Forest" group. You have been asked to draft a letter for the store manager that will persuade customers to attend the store lecture. The manager plans to send the letter to a mailing list of customers who have supported environmental causes in the past, but you're not sure if all of those customers will support the "Save the Redwood Forest" cause. Brochures about the need for saving the forest are available for distribution with the letter. Which of the following choices would be the most effective approach for the manager's letter?

   a. Use a direct approach, announcing the time, date, place, and purpose of the lecture and inviting customers to attend. Refer customers to the enclosed brochure for details about the cause and state that you've conveniently enclosed a self-addressed, stamped envelope for contributions to the "Save the Redwood Forest" group.
   b. Use an indirect approach, attracting readers' attention by naming the benefits of saving the ancient redwood forest. Encourage customers to learn more about the cause by

attending the lecture at the Patagonia store. Don't include the brochure or a self-addressed envelope for contributions with your mailing; customers who are truly interested can pick up the brochure or make contributions while attending the seminar.
   c. Use a detailed, indirect approach, creating desire to save the forest by pointing out the direct and indirect benefits of supporting the cause. Include facts about the importance of saving the redwoods for future generations, and refer readers to the enclosed brochure for more information. Invite customers to take action by attending the lecture, but don't include a self-addressed envelope in your mailing. Instead, inform customers that their contributions will be welcomed at the store lecture.
   d. Follow the detailed, indirect approach outlined above, but include a self-addressed envelope for contributions. Make an appeal for contributions at the end of your letter and ask customers to send their donations in the enclosed envelope.

3. As human resource director, Jana Thomas wants to convince a promising job candidate to accept Patagonia's job offer. She wants (1) to emphasize the advantages of working for a company that practices environmental responsibility and (2) to show that many of Patagonia's employee benefits support the company's environmental values. Thomas has asked for your advice on writing a persuasive letter to the job candidate. Which of the following choices would you recommend?

   a. Recommend that Thomas send an employee handbook to the job candidate with a short cover letter. The job candidate can study the employee handbook and review all of Patagonia's employee benefits for himself.
   b. Offer to write a persuasive letter to the job candidate, based on your experiences at Patagonia. In your letter, describe how you've benefited from participating in a two-month internship at an environmental nonprofit organization, fully paid by Patagonia, and how much you enjoy taking off two days with pay each year to test expensive Patagonia products that you could not otherwise afford to buy. With your enthusiasm for Patagonia's environmental programs, your testimonial will present a more convincing case to the job candidate than an employee handbook.
   c. You are not the right person to write the letter. As human resources director, Thomas is a more credible source. Suggest that Thomas write a persuasive letter outlining the personal benefits the job candidate will enjoy as a Patagonia employee, addressing his personal environmental concerns and creating desire for him to become part of the organization.
   d. Advise Thomas to write a letter that emphasizes the company's selling points. Her letter should describe Patagonia's policies of offering two-month paid internships at nonprofit organizations, paying employees to test new products, and making generous contributions to environmental groups.

4. The marketing department has asked you to review the copy for Patagonia's fall catalog. Which of the following sentences is the most effective for persuading customers to order Patagonia merchandise?

a. Patagonia sweaters are made from 100 percent organic cotton, meaning that the cotton is organically grown without fertilizers or pesticides.

b. By ordering Patagonia products with Synchilla fleece, you're helping to recycle more than eight million plastic soda bottles every year!

c. Editors of *Rod & Reel* insist that our fishing vest is "one of the best fishing accessories to come along in years."

d. Made from durable mesh, this Patagonia fishing vest features pockets that won't sag.[32]

TEST YOUR KNOWLEDGE

1. How do emotional appeals differ from logical appeals?

2. What is the AIDA plan, and how does it apply to persuasive messages?

3. What are four common mistakes to avoid when developing a persuasive message to overcome resistance?

4. What are the similarities and differences between sales messages and fundraising messages?

5. What are some questions to ask when gauging the audience's needs during the planning of a persuasive message?

6. What role do demographics and psychographics play in audience analysis during the planning of a persuasive message?

7. What are four of the ways you can build credibility with an audience when planning a persuasive message?

8. What three types of reasoning can you use in logical appeals?

9. How can semantics affect a persuasive message?

10. How do benefits differ from features?

INTERACTIVE LEARNING

USE THIS TEXT'S ONLINE RESOURCES

Visit the myPHLIP Web site at www.prenhall.com/thill. For Chapter 9, take advantage of the interactive "Study Guide" to test your chapter knowledge. Get instant feedback on whether you need additional studying. Read the "Current Events" articles to get the latest on chapter topics, and complete the exercises—as specified by your instructor.

This site's "Study Hall" helps you succeed in this course. "Talk in the Hall" lets you leave messages and meet new friends online. If you have a question, you can "Ask the Tutor." And to get a better grade in this course, you can find more help at "Writing Skills," "Study Skills," and "Study Tips."

The "Research Area" helps you locate a wealth of information to use in course assignments. Plus, you can send a message to online research experts, who will help you find exactly the information you need.

APPLY YOUR KNOWLEDGE

1. Why is it important to present both sides of an argument when writing a persuasive message to a potentially hostile audience?

2. How are persuasive messages different from routine messages?

3. When is it appropriate to use the direct organizational approach in persuasive messages?

4. As an employee, how many of your daily tasks require persuasion? List as many as you can think of. Who are your audiences, and how do their needs and characteristics affect the way you develop your persuasive messages at work?

5. **Ethical Choices** Are emotional appeals ethical? Why or why not?

PRACTICE YOUR KNOWLEDGE

DOCUMENTS FOR ANALYSIS

Read the following documents, then (1) analyze the strengths and weaknesses of each sentence and (2) revise each document so that it follows this chapter's guidelines.

Document 9.A: Writing Persuasive Requests for Action

At Tolson Auto Repair, we have been in business for over 25 years. We stay in business by always taking into account what the customer wants. That's why we are writing. We want to know your opinions to be able to better conduct our business.

Take a moment right now and fill out the enclosed questionnaire. We know everyone is busy, but this is just one way we have of making sure our people do their job correctly. Use the enclosed envelope to return the questionnaire.

And again, we're happy you chose Tolson Auto Repair. We want to take care of all your auto needs.

Document 9.B: Writing Persuasive Claims and Requests for Adjustment

Dear Gateway:

I'm writing to you because of my disappointment with my new TelePath X2 Faxmodem. The modem works all right, but the volume is set wide open and the volume knob doesn't turn it down. It's driving us crazy. The volume knob doesn't seem to be connected to anything but simply spins around. I can't believe you would put out a product like this without testing it first.

I depend on the modem to run my small business and want to know what you are going to do about it. This reminds me of every time I buy electronic equipment from what seems like any company. Something is always wrong. I thought quality was supposed to be important, but I guess not.

Anyway, I need this fixed right away. Please tell me what you want me to do.

Document 9.C: Writing Sales and Fundraising Letters

We know how awful dining hall food can be, and that's why we've developed the "Mealaweek Club." Once a week, we'll deliver food to your dormitory or apartment. Our meals taste great. We have pizza, buffalo wings, hamburgers and curly fries, veggie roll-ups, and more!

When you sign up for just six months, we will ask what day you want your delivery. We'll ask you to fill out your selection of meals. And the rest is up to us. At "Mealaweek," we deliver! And payment is easy. We accept MasterCard and VISA or a personal check. It will save money especially when compared with eating out.

Just fill out the enclosed card and indicate your method of payment. As soon as we approve your credit or check, we'll begin delivery. Tell all your friends about Mealaweek. We're the best idea since sliced bread!

EXERCISES

9–1. What type of reasoning is at work in the following statement: "We've lost money on 48 of the 52 power plants we've constructed in South America in the last 10 years. It's obvious that it's impossible to turn a profit in that market." In which persuasive messages would this type of reasoning be appropriate?

9–2. **Teamwork** With another student, analyze the persuasive memo at Host Marriott (Figure 9–3 on page 238) by answering the following questions:

   a. What techniques are used to capture the reader's attention?

   b. Does the writer use the direct or the indirect organizational approach? Why?

   c. Is the subject line effective? Why or why not?

   d. Does the writer use an emotional or a logical appeal? Why?

   e. What reader benefits are included?

   f. How does the writer establish credibility?

   g. What tools does the writer use to reinforce his position?

9–3. Compose effective subject lines for the following persuasive memos:

   a. A request to your supervisor to purchase a new high-speed laser printer for your office. You've been outsourcing quite a bit of your printing to AlphaGraphics and you're certain this printer will pay for itself in six months.

   b. A direct mailing to area residents soliciting customers for your new business "Meals à la Car," a carryout dining service that delivers from most local-area restaurants. All local restaurant menus are on the Internet. Mom and Dad can dine on egg rolls and chow mein while the kids munch on pepperoni pizza.

   c. A special request to the company president to allow managers to carry over their unused vacation days to the fol-

lowing year. Apparently, many managers canceled their fourth-quarter vacation plans to work on the installation of a new company computer system. Under their current contract, vacation days not used by December 31 aren't accruable.

9–4. **Ethical Choices** Your boss has asked you to draft a memo asking everyone in your department to donate money to the company's favorite charity, an organization that operates a special summer camp for physically challenged children. You wind up writing a three-page memo packed with facts and heartwarming anecdotes about the camp and the children's experiences. When you must work that hard to persuade your audience to take an action such as donating money to a charity, aren't you being manipulative and unethical? Explain.

9–5. Determine whether the following sentences focus on features or benefits; rewrite as necessary to focus all the sentences on benefits.

   a. All-Cook skillets are coated with a durable, patented nonstick surface.

   b. You can call anyone and talk as long you like on Saturdays and Sundays with this new mobile telephone service.

   c. We need to raise $25 to provide each needy child with a backpack filled with school supplies.

9–6. **Internet** Visit the Federal Trade Commission Web site and read the "Catch the Bandit In Your Mailbox" consumer warning at www.ftc.gov/bcp/conline/pubs/tmarkg/bandit. htm. Select one or two sales or fundraising letters you've recently received and see whether they contain any of the suspicious content mentioned in the FTC warning. What does the FTC suggest you do with any materials that don't sound legitimate?

CASES

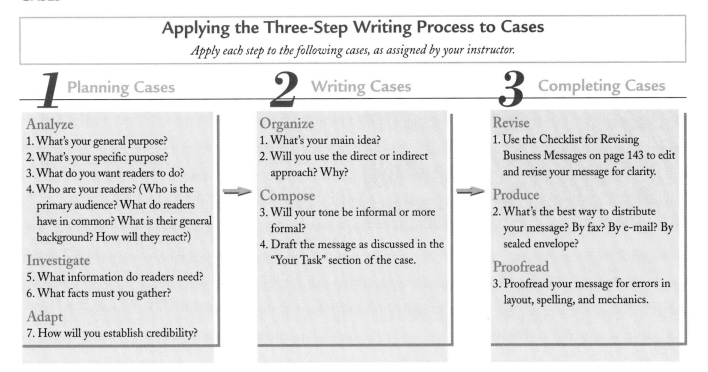

Applying the Three-Step Writing Process to Cases

Apply each step to the following cases, as assigned by your instructor.

1 Planning Cases

Analyze
1. What's your general purpose?
2. What's your specific purpose?
3. What do you want readers to do?
4. Who are your readers? (Who is the primary audience? What do readers have in common? What is their general background? How will they react?)

Investigate
5. What information do readers need?
6. What facts must you gather?

Adapt
7. How will you establish credibility?

2 Writing Cases

Organize
1. What's your main idea?
2. Will you use the direct or indirect approach? Why?

Compose
3. Will your tone be informal or more formal?
4. Draft the message as discussed in the "Your Task" section of the case.

3 Completing Cases

Revise
1. Use the Checklist for Revising Business Messages on page 143 to edit and revise your message for clarity.

Produce
2. What's the best way to distribute your message? By fax? By e-mail? By sealed envelope?

Proofread
3. Proofread your message for errors in layout, spelling, and mechanics.

PERSUASIVE REQUESTS FOR ACTION

1. Where teens gather: Memo urging partnership with Goosehead.com   Your company, Blue Nitro, sells sports shoes—at least it hopes to, as soon as your fledgling company makes enough commotion in the ever-fickle teen marketplace. As marketing director, it's your job to find out where to position the company's advertising resources to best advantage. Sure, MTV—but television chews up your budget faster than you can say "blue-soled shoes."

Early on, you hired a teen-market consultant, with disappointing results. Today you think you've hit the jackpot. You've discovered Goosehead.com, a Web site started by an 11-year-old girl. This young entrepreneur has been basking in the kind of media attention you'd kill for: a feature story in *People* magazine.

Pretty, blonde, green-eyed Ashley Power is now 15 and president of Goosehead.com, Inc. Her site flies the banner "Goosehead Teen Entertainment Network" and has spawned its own clothing line, in addition to the live video chats, games, advice columns, and other entertainment featured online. Ashley's newest partner? Academy Award-winning actor Richard Dreyfuss, father of teens himself. He's helping Ashley improve her teenage cyber-sitcom, *Whatever*, which she originated on the site. The actor will also help her develop new shows. Meanwhile, she's fielding offers to take *Whatever* to television.

Admittedly, Ashley's stepdad helped her get started. He's a television-commercial director, and he co-writes the sitcom. Ashley's stepdad introduced her to the William Morris agent who

first encouraged *Whatever*. Ashley's mom, a commercial artist, helped Ashley learn Photoshop to develop the site's alluring graphics.

But it was Ashley's original vision that won attention. She wanted "a Web site that won't talk down to teens as if they're little kids." After she listed the new site with search engines, she started getting 45,000 hits a day. Now Goosehead.com averages 100,000 visitors a day, and Ashley personally supervises the work of 30 adult staffers to make sure the content satisfies her own tastes and measures up to the feedback from her audience.

That's *your* audience she's got there. You could easily sign up to trade links with www.goosehead.com. But you're thinking that Blue Nitro needs to become an investment partner to buy more visibility on the site—probably as a sponsor for *Whatever* episodes. Or you might be able to get in on the bottom rung of future Goosehead-inspired shows. You've already seen impressive partners on the site, including some in your industry, such as Quiksilver, Oakley, Kipling. You need to act fast.

   Your task: Write a persuasive memo to your Blue Nitro president, Kevin Hawkins, convincing him that Ashley Power's site is hot and that your company should make this move. The first step will be to begin partnership discussions with Power and company.[33]

2. From horses to humans: Memo requesting trip to Flag Is Up Farms As vice president of human resources for Kingston Manufacturing in Atlanta, you try to keep up with new ideas. That's why you bought *The Man Who Listens to Horses,* the autobiography of horse trainer Monty Roberts.

Roberts grew up with horses in the 1930s—champ at age 4, stunt double for Elizabeth Taylor at age 8. But wild mustangs in Nevada taught him what he calls the silent language of "Equus." As a kid, he was fascinated by the patterns of motions, poses, and eye contact a herd's lead mare would use to communicate with the others—even to discipline rowdy youngsters. So he studied and copied her moves and tried them on unbroken horses at home—and it worked beautifully. He spoke their language and they responded.

Roberts, now in his sixties, can achieve "join up" with an untamed horse—saddling and riding it for the first time—in less than half an hour. That's a miracle compared with the brutal methods normally used to "break" a horse's spirit over the course of weeks so that it obeys—but also fears—humans. Using Equus, Roberts establishes complete rapport—within minutes—so that human and horse work with mutual respect and willing cooperation forever after. This approach is not only faster, it's more humane, safer for handlers, and smarter.

Roberts's horse-trainer father violently opposed this "radical" idea, so Roberts kept his method quiet for decades. Then in 1989, Queen Elizabeth II of England invited him to give a demonstration at the royal stables. She was stunned and impressed. Now all her horses are trained by his method, and he's gone on to demonstrate join-up to thousands of amazed witnesses.

Lives have been changed by the powerful sight of a wild horse—or, more poignantly, a "mad" one—ready to be euthanized who walks over and voluntarily nuzzles Roberts's shoulder after only a few minutes of nonverbal communication. Physically abused women and children (and their abusers) have wept or fainted as Roberts explained what a horse was "telling him" about how it had been beaten or mistreated. And many a tough horse handler and business administrator has come away from these demonstrations with new ideas. Disney, Texaco, Merrill Lynch, and Jaguar have all sent executives to Roberts's 110-acre Flag Is Up Farms in the Santa Ynez Valley (about 30 miles from Santa Barbara).

This is the radical treatment your company needs, you decide. For months, you've been fielding too many complaints from your increasingly multicultural workforce about old-school managers. Neither side is "wrong," but they aren't communicating. What managers need is a dramatic demonstration that nonverbal behaviors can be more important than all the words in the world.

Your task: Write a memo to Kingston president Marvin Montgomery, urging him to send you to visit Flag Is Up Farms as a preview before sending managers to California. Just in case Montgomery calls you into his office after he reads your memo, you'd better be prepared to discuss why nonverbal behaviors can be more important than words. What will you tell Montgomery if he asks? [34]

3. Ouch, that hurts! Persuasive memo at Technology One requesting equipment retrofit Mike Andrews leaves your office, shutting the door behind him. The pain in his arm is reflected on his face. He's about to file a worker's compensation claim—your third this month. As human resources director for Technology One, a major software development firm, you're worried not only about costs but also about the well-being of your employees.

Mike's complaints are much the same as those already reported by two other computer technicians: sharp pains in the wrist, numbness, and decreased range of motion. You know that the average technician spends at least six hours a day working on the computer, yet you've never had this many complaints in a short time, and the severity of the symptoms seems to be increasing.

You decide to seek the advice of experts. A local sports and orthopedic medicine clinic gives you a detailed description of repetitive strain injuries, or RSIs. The symptoms they describe are virtually identical to those exhibited by your technicians. You're distressed to learn that, if the cause of these injuries is not found and corrected, your technicians could require surgery or could even become permanently disabled.

The physical therapist at the clinic believes that exercises and wrist splints may help relieve symptoms and could even prevent new injuries. However, she also recommends that you consult an ergonomic analyst who can evaluate the furniture and equipment your technicians are using.

On her advice, you bring in an analyst who spends an entire day at your facility. After measuring desk and chair height, watching technicians at work, and conducting a detailed analysis of all your equipment, he makes two recommendations: (1) Throw out all your computer keyboards and replace them with ergonomic keyboards, and (2) replace every mouse with a trackball. Suddenly you realize that the RSI complaints began shortly after your controller and purchasing manager bought a truckload of new computer equipment at a local merchant's going-out-of-business sale. You begin to wonder about the quality and design of that equipment, and you ask the analyst what benefits the changes will provide.

The ergonomic keyboard actually splits the traditional rows of keys in half and places the rows of keys at different angles, allowing the wrists to stay straight and relieving pressure on the forearm. The repetitive motions involved in using a mouse further aggravate the symptoms created by use of the traditional keyboard. Using a trackball does not require the repetitive clicking motion of the forefinger.

Your task: You know that replacing peripheral equipment on more than 50 computers will be costly, especially when the existing equipment is nearly new. However, increasing RSIs and disability claims could be even more costly. Write a persuasive memo to Katherine Wilson, your controller, and convince her of the immediate need to retrofit the technicians' computer equipment.[35]

4. Travel turnaround: E-mail message at Travelfest convincing your boss to expand client services As a successful travel agent with Travelfest, Inc., you have been both amazed and troubled by the recent changes in the travel industry. The upset started more than a year ago, when airlines stopped paying the customary 10 percent commission on airline tickets. Instead, airlines paid a flat $25 on one-way domestic flights and $50 on round-trip domestic flights. International flights were not affected.

Travelfest is located in Austin, Texas. It has four offices and more than 80 employees. Headquarters are in the center of downtown, in the lobby of a 35-story office tower. The other three offices are located in major shopping centers in upscale suburbs. The company's business is made up of about 70 percent corporate and business travel and 30 percent leisure travel. However, much of the leisure business comes from corporate customers.

Your boss, Gary Hoover, has been working night and day to make up for declining revenues brought about by the loss of airline commissions. He has tried everything, from direct-mail campaigns to discount coupons to drawings for cruises and weekend getaways. Still, revenues remain flat, and there seems to be no solution in sight.

You've been doing some research and analysis of your office's existing customer profiles. You find that many of your customers are middle- to high-income sophisticated travelers and that, with the expansion of the global economy, foreign travel has increased dramatically in the past 12 months. Your research has triggered some ideas that you believe could substantially increase your revenue from existing customers.

You envision turning your suburban mall office into a travel supermarket. First, since there's such a growth in foreign travel, you'd like to sell videos and audiotape courses in Spanish, Japanese, French, and other languages. You'd like to introduce a line of travel products, including luggage, maps, travel guides, and electronics. You visualize a room with computer terminals where customers would have direct access to the Internet so that they could obtain up-to-date weather reports, currency-exchange rates, and other important information about travel destinations. You're even thinking about a special area for kids, with videos and other educational materials.

You realize your ideas won't generate a lot of direct profit. However, you believe they will get customers in the door, where you and other agents can sell them travel, particularly leisure travel to foreign destinations. If Hoover is willing to try it in your office and it works, he may want to do the same in his other two locations.

Your task: E-mail Gary Hoover at Travelfest's downtown office. Outline your ideas and suggest a meeting to discuss them further and determine what market research he'd like you to perform. Hoover's e-mail address is GHoover@travelnet.com.[36]

5. Customer crunch: Letter from Ed's food servers requesting relief Working as a food server at Ed's, a health-conscious eatery on famous Old Highway 101 in Cardiff, California, is a great way to supplement your sparse financial resources as a business student at San Diego State University. From upstairs, you can see the ocean, and during big storms you can even see the waves breaking across the sea-level highway. Last winter, when El Niño lashed the coastline relentlessly, the view was amazing. For weeks, nearly every high tide closed the flooded highway. Before it could open again, bulldozers had to clear the wave-deposited cobbles from the road, pushing back along the shore big mounds that were supposed to help stave off the salty onslaught.

Actually, El Niño was good for Ed's winter business. Lots of San Diegans came out to watch the excitement while your competitors across the highway, who are directly on the shore, lost huge picture windows to the crashing waves. Ed's offered a safe vantage point.

But now it's summer. The waves are still breaking, but now they're much smaller. And the state beach parking lots that were washed away during the storms have been restored. However, there's hardly any beach left—just a narrow strip of mostly rocks with very little sand. Ed's owners are worried.

Normally, beach crowds would cross the highway in the late afternoons for Ed's $4 smoothies and gourmet organic dinners. But there aren't any huge beach crowds this year. As far as you can tell, the locals and some tourists still turn up in healthy numbers for the sunset dinner specials, gazing out to watch dolphins playing in the surf. Nevertheless, your manager has started using what you call a "U.S. West" tactic (in honor of a short-staffing, forced-overtime policy at the telecommunications giant that led to a major strike). As so many companies are doing now, Ed's is saving on overhead by cutting back on the number of servers and kitchen staff. Because of the cutback, customers are waiting longer for their food and for their tables (especially during rush periods), so many are leaving in anger while orders are backing up in the kitchen. You're running twice as hard and getting smaller tips—especially from diners who have to wait up to half an hour for their dinner. No matter how nice you are, it's hard to smooth their ruffled feathers. You've even lost some faithful regulars who'd been coming to the restaurant for years, bringing all their out-of-town visitors and leaving you healthy tips.

This can't possibly be good for Ed's in the long term. And it's certainly not good for you and your co-workers in the short term!

Your task: Since you're the business major, your fellow servers have nominated you to write a persuasive letter to Ed's owner, Mary Fenwick, explaining why the low-overhead policy should be abandoned. If you write it, they'll sign it, they've promised. Make up any circumstantial details you need. Before you begin, however, jot down the main idea of your message. Then list the major points and supporting evidence you'll include to persuade Fenwick.[37]

6. Life's little hassles: Request for satisfaction It's hard to go through life without becoming annoyed at the way some things work. You have undoubtedly been dissatisfied with a product you've bought, a service you've received, or an action of some elected official or government agency.

Your task: Write a three- to five-paragraph persuasive request expressing your dissatisfaction in a particular case. Specify the action you want the reader to take.

PERSUASIVE REQUESTS FOR CLAIMS AND ADJUSTMENTS

7. Too good to be true: E-mail to Page South requesting adjustment Page South offered its pager services for a mere $5 a month. You purchased an inexpensive pager and signed a contract for two years. You thought your pager phone number was up and running for two weeks, but your co-workers and clients say they repeatedly get a busy signal when dialing your pager number. You call Page South and get the problem resolved, but this takes an additional week. You don't want to be charged for the time the pager wasn't in service. After discussing the situation with the local manager, she asks you to contact Judy Hinkley at the company's regional business office.

Your task: Send an e-mail message to Hinkley at <Judy@pgsouth.com> and request an adjustment to your account. Request credit or partial credit for one month of service. Remember to write a summary of events in chronological order, supplying exact dates for maximum effectiveness.

8. Phone frustration: Persuasive letter to Pacific Bell requesting resolution of telephone service overcharges As a freelance business researcher, your time is valuable, especially when you're using online research sources. These valuable resources are becoming more and more important in your work, so you can't afford to sit around waiting for files to download at 14,400 bits per second (14.4 kbps) or even at 28.8 kbps. You often deal with massive files that can take forever to transfer at these rates. You've determined that an Integrated Services Digital Network (ISDN) connection would be a faster alternative for your online work. You contacted Pacific Bell Telephone in November and requested residential ISDN service (because you work from home).

When the confirming work order arrived, you discovered that PacBell had set up your account as a business service, so you called the service representative to change it to the lower residential rate. As a result, your business service was disconnected, and it took PacBell two weeks to reconnect you. On top of that, when the initial bill arrived, there was a $125 charge for disconnecting the business service and another $75 charge for reinstallation, and no credit for the two weeks of downtime. You have made at least 13 calls to the customer service department about this problem, both locally and at the company's headquarters in Sacramento. You even left a message on the customer feedback section of PacBell's Internet home page. But none of these actions have resolved the situation.

Your task: Compose a persuasive letter to Ms. Claire Abell (PacBell's director of consumer affairs) at 6640 Rosecrans Road, Sacramento, CA 99054, explaining your frustration with this billing problem and asking for an immediate adjustment.[38]

9. Endless trouble: Claim letter to Abe's Pool Installation As chief administrator, you worked hard to convince the board of directors of Westlake Therapy and Rehabilitation Center that a small, 8-by-15-foot Endless Pool would be a wonderful addition to the facility. Because the pool produces an adjustable current flow, a swimmer can swim "endlessly" against it, never reaching the pool's edge. With this new invention by a Philadelphia manufacturer, your patients could experience a complete range of water therapy, in a year-round, indoor pool small enough to fit in a standard living room!

The board agreed, choosing the optional six-foot depth, which would allow for additional therapeutic uses but would require (1) a special platform and (2) installation in a room with a high ceiling. The old gymnasium would become your new Water Therapy Pavilion. Total cost with custom features: $20,080, plus $8,000 budgeted for installation.

According to the manufacturer, "The Endless Pool has been designed as a kit for bolt-together assembly. It can be assembled by two reasonably handy people with no prior installation experience following detailed procedural videos." You can do it yourself, they proclaim, or hire a local contractor.

You've hired Abe's Pool Installation, which will build the special access platform and install the pool. You passed along the instructional videos, along with the manufacturer's hotline numbers. They've offered a pre-installation engineering consultation for your customized pool, without additional charge, as you told Abe. They'll also be glad to help determine whether the planned site can handle the pool's 10-ton filled weight. Abe nodded and told you not to worry.

Finally, Abe's crew completed the platform and amid much excitement from your staff, assembled the galvanized steel pool. At a grand, ribbon-cutting dedication ceremony, you personally flipped the switch.

Immediately the hydraulic motor began moving 5,000 gallons of water a minute through a grill at the front, which smoothes and straightens the current. Everyone's excitement grew as the first wave of water washed down the center of the pool. But instead of entering the turning vane arrays (which were supposed to recirculate the water through hidden channels back to the front of the pool), the water kept going, splashing out the back of the pool onto the platform and the gathered onlookers . . . at 5,000 gallons a minute. Panic and shouts erupted as you fumbled quickly to turn the thing off.

Final damage included a collapsed platform, a ruined floor, an incorrectly installed pool, and numerous dry-cleaning bills from onlookers. Fortunately, no one was hurt. Estimated cost with floor repair: $10,000. Abe is not returning your phone calls. But local reporters are coming to film the damage tomorrow, and it's your job to conduct their tour.

Your task: Write a claim letter to Abe Hanson, Owner, Abe's Pool Installation, 2525 Rocket Lane, Manchester, Maryland 21088.[39]

10. Secondhand smoke: Letter requesting rent refund from Kuykendahl Joint, Inc. Last January in Harris County, Texas, your branch of Contract Management Services, Inc., (CMSI) signed a lease with Kuykendahl Joint, Inc. for new office space at 3638 University Blvd., Suite 302, Houston, TX 77005-3396. No one anticipated the nightmare that would follow. You have been assistant manager since before the move. But after relocating, you've threatened to quit many times—and so has your manager, Kathleen Thomas.

The problem is secondhand smoke invading your offices from other tenants. The Environmental Protection Agency calls this ETS (environmental tobacco smoke) and classifies it as a Group A (known human) carcinogen. There is no safe level of exposure to Group A toxins. The Surgeon General says the 4,600 chemicals in ETS (including cyanide, arsenic, formaldehyde, carbon monoxide, and ammonia) are "a cause of disease, including lung cancer, in healthy nonsmokers."

The smoke wafts in the front door of your office and seeps through openings in hollow walls shared with tenants on either side of CMSI. You and others have suffered bronchitis, migraines, and respiratory infections since the move. One of your most valuable employees, a star performer responsible for landing many new contracts, quit last week. "I can't risk this," she said. "I've had asthma since I was little, and it's getting worse."

Another employee is worried about his heart; he's in the high-risk category and there's evidence ETS can trigger heart attacks. Pneumonia, allergies, ear infections, other forms of cancer (including breast, cervical, endocrine, etc.)—all are "causally associated" with ETS, according to the EPA. In fact, secondhand smoke is

more dangerous than what smokers inhale. That's because the heat of the draw burns off some of the toxins, which are also filtered by the cigarette or cigar.

Last month CMSI spent $3,000 hiring contractors to weather-strip around vents, electrical outlets, and other built-in fixtures—even to spray polyurethane foam around the pipes that are under sinks and behind toilets. But you're still choking and gagging on smelly carcinogens. By the end of the day, you've got red eyes, a runny nose, often a headache—and you smell like a poker game.

Thomas says it's no use talking to the offending smokers. She's collected a list (from Americans for Nonsmokers' Rights) that cites legal precedents around the country, in which courts have held landlords responsible both for eliminating ETS and for compensating tenants.

Your task: Thomas has asked you to write a persuasive letter for her signature to Robert Bechtold, Manager, Kukyendahl Joint, Inc. (88 North Park Road, Houston, TX 77005). Insist that the landlord (1) improve the air quality immediately, (2) refund lease payments totaling $9,000 from January 1, and (3) reimburse CMSI for the improvements made in an attempt to solve the problem. "If this doesn't work, we're moving," she says grimly. "And then we'll sue."[40]

SALES AND FUNDRAISING MESSAGES

11. The bride wore hiking boots: Persuasive letter to We Do bridal superstore When Shari and Randy Almsburg of Dublin, Ohio, decided to tie the knot, they knew just what they wanted. "We always enjoyed hiking. In fact, we met each other on a hike. That's why we wanted to wrap our wedding plans around our favorite hobby." Enter Tie the Knot, a one-owner company specializing in bizarre wedding plans.

"Actually, the bride wearing a white dress and a pair of hiking boots was *not* our most unusual wedding," explains owner and wedding consultant Todd Dansing (whose own wedding took place a mile high just before the happy couple plunged to earth by parachute). "We recently helped plan an underwater wedding in a shark tank at the aquarium in Chicago for two marine biologists whose work involved feeding the fish. Our main problem there was this huge turtle that kept bumping into the preacher." Dansing tells you of other unusual weddings that took place in airplanes, on boats, under water, and in exotic locations such as Arizona's Painted Desert. Whatever a couple's wedding plans, Todd believes he can find the necessary resources and save them time and money in the process.

Todd's marketing efforts to date have involved mostly word of mouth and free press coverage of his unusual weddings (although reporters kept their distance when two snake handlers from the zoo exchanged vows). But his brother-in-law has invested capital in the business, so Todd hires you to help him tell the world about his services. You suggest that he consider affiliating with an established wedding service or store.

You and Todd visit We Do, a bridal superstore in Dublin, Ohio, and you help Todd see the potential for marketing his offbeat wedding service to this large company. We Do is a 26,000-square-foot matrimonial mecca that sells 600 styles of bridal gowns and everything else couples need for a traditional wedding. The franchise hopes to open 40 stores eventually, so if Todd can strike a deal with We Do, his future profit potential will be high.

Your task: Write a letter for Todd's signature to Carol Feinberg, CEO of We Do. Suggest that Tie the Knot would make a great consultant for couples with offbeat wedding tastes. Emphasize Todd's experience, and point out the ways this venture will provide additional market share for We Do. Think of possible objections, such as Todd's lack of capital and small company size, and try to assure Feinberg that Tie the Knot is the right business to help capitalize on a unique opportunity.[41]

12. Greener cleaners: Letter promoting "environmentally sound" franchise When you told everyone you aspired to work for an environmentally responsible business, you didn't imagine you'd be hanging your hat in the dry-cleaning business. But now that you are director of franchise development for Hangers Cleaners, you go home every night with a "clean conscience" (your favorite new pun).

Micell Technologies, Inc., in Raleigh, North Carolina, is the parent company of the new Hangers chain. Micell was established in 1995 after research by co-founders Joseph DeSimone, James McClain, and Timothy Romack resulted in the first breakthrough in dry-cleaning technology in nearly 50 years. They developed a cleaning process, now called Micare, which uses liquid carbon dioxide (CO_2) and specially developed detergents to clean clothes. There's no heat required, and no further need for

the toxic perchloroethylene (perc) or petroleum traditionally used in dry cleaning.

Hangers franchise owners don't have to deal with regulatory paperwork, zoning restrictions, or expensive insurance and taxes for hazardous waste disposal. And unlike petroleum-based solvents, the CO_2 that Micare uses is noncombustible. It's the same substance that carbonates beverages, and it's captured from the waste stream of industries that produce it as a by-product. Moreover, 98 percent of the CO_2 used in a Hangers outlet is recycled and used again, which helps keep prices competitive.

You've already sold franchises in 23 states. Customers love the fact that their clothes don't carry toxic fumes after cleaning, and employees are happy to be working in a safe and cool environment. The process is actually gentler on clothes (no strong solvents or heat), reducing fading and shrinking and helping them last longer. You aren't dry cleaners; you're "garment care specialists." And in addition to giving customers what they want, Micell executives talk about the "triple bottom line," a standard for success that emphasizes profit, ecology, and social responsibility.

And beyond the progressive corporate atmosphere, you simply love the design of Hangers stores. Micell hired dry-cleaning experts and architects alike to come up with a sleek, modern, high-end retail "look" that features a cool, clean, light-filled interior and distinctive signage out front. It's more akin to a Starbucks than the overheated, toxic-smelling storefront most customers associate with dry cleaning. This high-end look is making it easier to establish Hangers as a national brand, attracting investors and franchisees rapidly as word spreads about the new "greener cleaner."

Your Task: Develop a sales letter that can be mailed in response to preliminary inquiries from potential franchise owners. You'll include brochures covering franchise agreements and Micare specifics, so focus instead on introducing and promoting the unique benefits of Hangers Cleaners. Your contact information is Micell Technologies Franchise Development Department, Micell Technologies, Inc., 7516 Precision Drive, Raleigh, NC 27617, 919-313-2102, Ext. 129, or www.micell.com.[42]

13. Quotesmith.com: E-mail extolling a better way to buy insurance The great thing about Quotesmith.com is that no one is obligated to buy a thing. Consumers can log on to your Web site and ask for dozens of free insurance quotes, and then go off and buy elsewhere. They can look at instant price-comparison quotes (from more than 300 insurers) for term life, dental, individual and family medical insurance, small group medical insurance, workers' compensation, short-term medical insurance, Medicare supplement insurance, "no-exam" whole life insurance, fixed annuity insurance, and (in a click-through arrangement with Progressive) private passenger automobile insurance. All rates are up-to-the-day accurate, and Quotesmith is the largest single source for comprehensive insurance price comparisons in the United States.

Once consumers see your price-comparison charts, many choose to fill out an easy insurance application request right on your site. Why deal with an insurance salesperson when you can see the price differences for yourself—especially over such a broad range of companies? Quotesmith backs up this application with toll-free customer-service lines operated by salaried representatives. They're not working on commission, but they know about insurance. And Quotesmith has based its new online service on a long history of serving the insurance industry.

The product pretty much sells itself, and that's what you love about your marketing job with Quotesmith. Consumers and computers do most of the work—and the results are at lightning speed, especially compared with what the insurance business was like just a few years ago. During peak periods, the site has been processing one quote request every four seconds, which leads, ultimately, to increased policy sales without an agent or intermediary.

Quotesmith advertises both in print and on TV, saying that it provides "the lowest term life rates in America or we'll overnight you $500." Your company also guarantees the accuracy of quotes against a $500 reward. Final rates depend on variables such as age, sex, state availability, hazardous activities, personal and family health history, driving records, and so on.

You're proud of the fact that Quotesmith has received positive press from *Nation's Business, Kiplinger's Personal Finance, Good Housekeeping,* the *Los Angeles Times, Money, U.S. News & World Report,* and *Forbes* ("Quotesmith.com provides rock-bottom quotes")—your favorite. For every term-life quote, you even provide consumers with a look at how each insurer's ability to pay claims is rated by A.M. Best, Duff & Phelps, Moody's, Standard & Poor's, and Weiss Ratings, Inc.

And all of this is free. Too bad more people don't know about your services.

Your task: It's your job to lure more insurance customers to Quotesmith. You've decided to use direct e-mail marketing (like cold-calling without the telephone). Write a pitch extolling the benefits of Quotesmith's services, and focus on consumers who are unfa-

miliar with the site. Be sure your message is suited to an e-mail format, with an appropriate subject heading.[43]

14. Buses for seniors: Fundraising letter from Morris County Senior Center The Morris County Senior Center is one of New Jersey's oldest nonprofit institutions for the elderly. Over the past 50 years, it has relied on financial support from government, businesses, and individuals.

Unfortunately, recent state and federal cutbacks have dug into the organization's budget. In addition, in the last five years two of the county's largest companies, Hardwick Industries and McCarthy Electrical Motors, have moved offshore and shut down local operations. Both businesses were supporters of the center, as were many of the workers who lost jobs.

However, the needs of the center keep growing. For many of the county's roughly 1,000 seniors who live alone, it's the only place where they can meet their peers, use a special library, avoid extreme weather, or get a well-balanced meal. The center is not a nursing home and has no overnight facilities. Most individuals get to the facility on one of the three shuttle-type buses belonging to the center. The buses are also used for various day trips to museums, plays, and similar functions. Occasionally, they are used to help the temporarily disabled get to doctors' offices or pharmacists.

Each bus is more than eight years old. Although not quite unsafe, the buses are showing their age. The constant repairs are stopgap measures at best, and most weeks at least one of the vehicles is inoperable. Monthly repairs are averaging a total of $300 for the three vehicles. In addition, when the vans aren't working, the clients, staff, and budget all suffer. Seniors can't get to the center, trips are canceled, and drivers are sometimes paid for coming to work even though they aren't able to drive.

Conservatively, it would cost about $28,000 to replace each van with a new one: $84,000 total. This includes estimates on how much the center could gain from selling the old vans. It's a fair amount of money, but in the opinion of your board of directors, buying new vans would be better than continuously repairing the old ones or risking the purchase of used ones.

Your task: As director of the center, draft a fundraising letter to send to all of the businesses in the county. Stress the good work the center does and the fact that this is a special fundraising effort. Mention that all the money collected will go directly toward the purchase of the vans.

GOING ONLINE EXERCISES

Influence an Official and Promote Your Cause, page 242

The strategies you use to lobby a government representative and to seal a business transaction are similiar. Both tasks require the art of persuasion to convince someone to take action on your behalf. Explore the data at the Thomas site, and find an issue you can use to practice your skills at writing a persuasive message.

1. What key ideas would you include in an e-mail message to persuade your congressional representative to support an issue important to you?
2. In a letter to a senator or member of congress, what information would you include to convince the reader to vote for an issue supporting small business?
3. When sending a message to someone who daily receives hundreds of written appeals, what attention-getting techniques can you use? How can you get support for a cause that concerns you as a business person?

   To complete this exercise, log on to this text's Web site at www.prenhall.com/thill. Select Chapter 9, then select "Student Resources," click on the name of the featured Web site, and follow the detailed navigational directions.

Reports and Oral Presentations

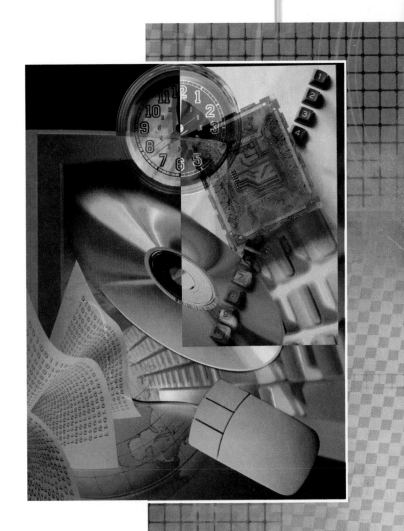

PLANNING BUSINESS REPORTS AND PROPOSALS

After studying this chapter, you will be able to

1 Discuss why businesses need reports and how these documents can be classified.

2 Distinguish between informational and analytical reports.

3 Explain the difference between a problem statement and a statement of purpose, and then identify five other elements often included in a formal work plan.

4 Describe six tasks necessary to doing research for business reports.

5 Define information interviews, and list four types of interview questions.

6 Clarify what it means to adapt your report to your audience.

Dell Computer Corporation is the world's leading direct computer systems company. It designs, manufactures, and customizes products and services to customer requirements, offering an extensive selection of hardware, software, and peripherals. In the fast-paced world of computer technology, the company relies on reports to keep up with current industry trends, statistics, and issues.

On the job:

FACING A COMMUNICATION DILEMMA AT DELL COMPUTER CORPORATION

Staying on Top of the Computer World
www.dell.com

Remember the sluggish performance of early computers? When Michael Dell entered the University of Texas at Austin in 1983, everyone on campus wanted faster personal computers. So the enterprising freshman began a lucrative business from his dorm room, selling upgraded PCs and add-on components. The rest is history. Since Michael Dell founded Dell Computer Corporation in 1984, his business has become the largest computer manufacturer in the United States and the fastest-growing computer systems company in the world.

However, as his company doubled in size every year throughout the 1990s, Dell learned some hard lessons. At one point, technological advancements in memory chips decreased the value and usefulness of his company's existing inventory. Dell was stuck with a large inventory of chips that nobody wanted, which crystallized the company's need to establish inventory controls and especially to analyze developments in the computer industry. Later on, Dell's company briefly experimented with selling computers in retail outlets. But after studying retail sales reports that were based on careful data analysis, Dell was able to determine that selling directly to consumers was the most profitable approach for his company.

Dell pulled out of the retail market and focused on selling desktop and notebook computers directly to consumers through the company's Web site, dell.com. Now Dell faces two challenges: (1) attracting new customers to dell.com and (2) satisfying the needs of existing clients. To succeed, Dell must constantly track and understand industry innovations. He must be able to inform customers about new products and trends, determine customer preferences, and respond to these preferences with appropriate products and services. He needs information. But "information in its raw form doesn't present itself in neat and tidy packages," notes Dell. "When a customer says, 'I want a notebook computer that lasts the whole day,' we have to translate that desire into relevant technology."

The reports at Dell Computer must do more than simply summarize and present carefully researched data. These reports must analyze the data to identify and discuss pertinent issues. Suppose you were in charge of writing reports for Michael Dell—reports on issues such as industry trends, inventory control, customer preferences, and employee needs. How would you go about planning these reports? What steps would you take to define each problem? Conduct the research? Analyze the data?[1]

WHY BUSINESSES NEED REPORTS

Even the most capable managers, such as Michael Dell, must rely on other people to observe events or collect information for them. Some managers are often too far away to oversee everything themselves; some are responsible for preparing the reports needed by others. Whether you prepare or receive them, reports are the basis of effective decisions and solutions.

Using the Power of Technology

Minding Your Business with Online Reporting

Mrs. Fields uses them. Mrs. Paul's uses them. However, you don't have to be in the cookie or fish business to work with electronic reports. FedEx uses online reporting to track customer shipments. More and more managers and employees are using computers to write and send reports for virtually every business purpose.

Computerized cash registers in Mrs. Fields cookie outlets are the heart of a sophisticated reporting system for monitoring and controlling operations. Rather than taking the time to write reports by hand, store managers enter data into the computer system by following report formats on their screen. Then they electronically transmit these reports to corporate headquarters in Park City, Utah. The computer system also serves as a two-way communication device, allowing store and corporate personnel to send messages back and forth in seconds. So Mrs. Fields corporate managers can quickly receive the information they need in order to track sales and productivity trends—and to spot potential problems—in more than 500 outlets around the world.

At Mrs. Paul's, a computerized reporting system allows production managers to continuously monitor and control the yield from the company's fish-processing operation. The system calculates the production yield using the weight of the fish before it's processed, the weight of any scraps, and the weight of the finished fish meals. If the

reports show that the actual yield drops below the expected yield, the managers can immediately adjust the equipment to improve the yield. The production managers have instant access to electronically monitor and control reports at each stage of the operation, so they can find and fix problems more quickly than if they had to wait for printed reports.

FedEx, the well-known package-shipping firm, uses electronic reporting to let customers know the status of their shipments at any time. It has one of the most popular sites on the World Wide Web. The company uses extensive satellite and computer technologies to track the location of every package in the system, and customers can log onto the FedEx site to find out where their packages are. This tracking system not only helps the company serve its customers better but also cuts down on costs because FedEx doesn't need to have so many people on the phones answering customer questions.

CAREER APPLICATIONS

1. What advantages and disadvantages do you see in asking store managers at Mrs. Fields to file troubleshooting reports immediately by entering data into the computerized cash register system?
2. How would an electronic reporting system help a company track the activity of personnel who frequently travel to customer sites or other locations?

Reports are like bridges, spanning time and space. Organizations use them to provide a formal, verifiable link between people, places, and times. Some reports are for internal communication; others are for corresponding with outsiders. Some serve as a permanent record; others solve an immediate problem or answer a passing question. Many reports travel upward to help managers monitor various organizational units; some travel downward to explain managerial decisions to the employees responsible for day-to-day operations.

Because business reports are intended to inform and to aid the decision-making and problem-solving process, they must be accurate, complete, and unbiased. Your goal in writing reports is to make your information as clear and convenient to use as possible. Time is precious, so tell your readers what they need to know—no more, no less—and present the information in a way that is geared to their needs.

Reports come in all shapes and sizes, from formal three-volume bound manuscripts to a fleeting image on a computer screen. Like other messages in business, reports are strongly influenced by the advances in technology. Virtually all of the reports discussed in this chapter can be adapted to computerized formats.

How Electronic Technology Affects Business Reports

Businesses have envisioned the *paperless office* for years, and it's finally coming true for many organizations. People in the United States can now file their taxes electronically, the SEC actually requires corporations to file reports electronically, and thousands of companies have set up electronic reporting procedures to communicate with employees, customers, and suppliers.[2] (See "Using the Power of Technology—Minding Your Business with Online Reporting.")

Electronic reports fall into two basic categories: First are those that essentially replace paper reports. You simply draft a report using your word processor as usual, but

Objective

1

Discuss why businesses need reports and how these documents can be classified.

Business reports help companies make decisions and solve business problems.

Make your business reports
• Accurate
• Complete
• Unbiased
• Clear
• Convenient to use
• Relevant

Electronic reports are becoming more popular.

1. Why would a company want shareholders to get in the habit of reading its annual report online?

2. What reader benefits could a company stress to encourage readership of this legally mandated report?

instead of printing it and making copies, you distribute the file electronically. The other category includes reports that are unique to the electronic format. For example, an intranet site can offer text, video, and sound in a single integrated "report."

When compared with their paper counterparts, electronic reports offer both advantages and disadvantages. The advantages include cost savings, space savings, faster distribution, multimedia communication, and easier maintenance. However, electronic reports are not a cure-all. Disadvantages include hardware and software costs (for computer purchase, installation, and maintenance), computer system incompatibility, training needs, and risks to data security and integrity.[3]

> Electronic reports have distinct advantages, but they have disadvantages as well.

How Reports Are Classified

Whether electronic, printed, or oral (see Chapter 13), reports are factual accounts that objectively communicate information about some aspect of a business. Therefore, a report is commonly classified by factors such as who initiates it (source), how often it's needed (frequency), and where it's being sent (destination). A report's medium, format, style, and organization are frequently dictated by its classification (see Table 10–1).

Keep in mind that a single report may have several classifications. For instance, a monthly sales report is generally authorized, routine, and internal. In addition to these classifications, reports can be short or long, formal or informal. Regardless of the source, frequency, or destination of reports, they vary by type. Most are either informational or analytical.

TYPES OF BUSINESS REPORTS

Informational reports focus on facts and are intended mainly to educate readers. In contrast, **analytical reports** provide data analyses, interpretation, and conclusions. In analyt-

> *Objective*
>
> **2**
>
> Distinguish between informational and analytical reports.
>
> The purpose of informational reports is to explain, whereas analytical reports are meant to convince the audience that the conclusions and recommendations developed in the text are valid.

Table 10–1   Common Report Classifications

Determinant	Class	Description
Source	Authorized	• Prepared at the request of someone else • Organized to respond to the reader's wishes
	Voluntary	• Prepared on your own initiative • Require more support, more background detail, and more careful explanation of purpose
Frequency	Special	• Prepared for unique situations or one-time (nonrecurring) events • Form and organization depend on purpose
	Routine	• Prepared for recurring events (daily, weekly, monthly, quarterly, annually) • Organized in a standard way (often on preprinted or computerized forms that the writer can simply fill in) • Require less introductory and transitional material
Destination	Internal	• Used within the organization • Often in memo format (especially if they're less than 10 pages)
	External	• Sent to people outside the organization • Often in letter format (5 pages or less) or manuscript format (more than 5 pages)
Length	Short	• Prepared as a letter, memo, or e-mail report of 10 pages or less • Usually prepared as a routine report
	Long	• Prepared as a manuscript report of more than 10 pages • Usually prepared as a special report
Formality	Informal	• Usually prepared as a routine, internal report • Includes less formal tone, fewer introductory and transitional materials
	Formal	• Usually prepared as a special internal or external report • Includes more formal tone, more introductory and transitional materials
Type	Informational	• Prepared to inform and educate • Can be either internal or external
	Analytical	• Prepared to analyze data, draw conclusions, and sometimes make recommendations • Can be either internal or external

ical reports, the information plays a supporting role—it's a means to an end rather than an end itself.

No matter what type of report you need to write, if you're new in an organization, model your documents on previous company reports. Shape your report's appearance, style, and organization to match previous reports of the same type. By using a form your boss and colleagues are familiar with, you make your information easier for them to absorb.

Informational Reports

Informational reports are used to educate and inform, not to persuade. Their uses and topics are innumerable. However, we focus here on four types: those for monitoring and controlling operations, implementing policies and procedures, complying with government regulations, and documenting progress.

Reports for Monitoring and Controlling Operations   Because managers cannot be everywhere at once, they rely on reports to find out what's happening to the operations under their control. These *monitor/control reports* focus on data, so they require special attention to accuracy, thoroughness, and honesty of content. Don't cover up bad news and emphasize only accomplishments. Such distortion defeats the purpose of these reports. Be objective. The problems will show up anyway, so you might as well get them out in the open. Following are three examples of reports used for monitoring and controlling operations.

Plans   Plans establish guidelines for future action. *Strategic plans* document an organization's overall goals and the methods it will use to reach them.[4] *Business plans* help

Fast-food entrepreneur La-Van Hawkins has opened doors for many African Americans. As CEO and owner of UrbanCityFoods and Wolverine Pizza, Hawkins has made millions of dollars in sales and hired a work force of 20,000 to help him meet his goals. But without strategic plans, his success would have been impossible. What's more, Hawkins is successful at identifying and serving customers because he uses marketing plans, which set up guidelines for future operations.

Plans help managers
- Coordinate the various activities of a business
- Guide the distribution of resources
- Motivate employees

Personal activity reports describe the facts and decisions that emerge during conversations, trips, and business meetings.

Policy/procedure reports help managers communicate the company's standards.

companies obtain financing or contract for managerial support services.[5] *Marketing plans* identify a firm's customers and detail how to serve them. Other plans include annual budgets, five-year plans, sales plans, recruiting plans, production plans, and so on. Internal audiences generally use such plans (1) to improve organizational coordination, (2) to guide the distribution of money and material, and (3) to motivate employees. However, plans are also written for external audiences.

Operating Reports   Operating reports provide managers with detailed information from a management information system (MIS), which captures statistics about everything happening in the organization (sales, production, inventory, shipments, backlogs, costs, personnel, etc.). The MIS is usually computerized, but operating reports can also be created manually. Information can be included in its raw state or analyzed and reported in paragraph form.

Periodic operating reports describe what's happened during a particular period. The report in Figure 10–1 was prepared by Roger Watson, real estate director for a San Francisco coffee retailer. "My manager needs to know that my department is making good decisions when we select new store locations," says Watson. However, he avoids burdening his boss with details about every potential site by making his report concise and presenting information in summary format.

Personal Activity Reports   Personal activity reports describe what occurred during a conference, convention, trip, or other activity. They're intended to provide important information or decisions that emerged during the activity. These reports also help companies track what's happening in the marketplace or with customers. Examples include sales-call reports, expense reports, performance reviews, and recruiting reports.

Figure 10–2 is a personal activity report prepared by Carrie Andrews, human resources manager of a small Indianapolis insurance firm. Her report summarizes the highlights of a seminar on legal issues in employee recruiting and interviewing. Says Andrews, "I prepared this report for my boss, the company president, and the four people who work for me. We can't afford to send everyone to seminars, so it's important that I share the information I received."

Case Study: Juan Martinez's Annual Recruiting Report   Juan Martinez is in charge of hiring for a Seattle-based software company. One of his responsibilities is to organize on-campus recruiting interviews. Every summer, after company representatives have visited several colleges and universities to interview and recruit new employees, Martinez analyzes statistics about the interviews and prepares his annual report for the human resources director (see Figure 10–3).

His report tracks how many students applied, interviewed on campus, flew to headquarters for further interviews, and were eventually hired. The Seattle company has divisions in Europe and Asia, so Martinez also tracks language fluency. In addition, he includes recruiting costs (by college, company department, and new employee), so his report not only documents expenses but also helps the company decide which institutions are best for future recruiting. Because the director already knows the report's purpose and content, Martinez spends little time on extensive introductory material and organizes all the data in tables.

Reports for Implementing Policies and Procedures   Reports for implementing policies and procedures are necessary because managers can't talk firsthand with everyone in an organization. Written reports are available to be read and reread by anyone with a question. These reports present their information in a straightforward manner. Even so, writers can have difficulty keeping the policies broad and the procedures simple. Highly respected retailer Nordstrom limited its policy manual to one sentence: "Use your best judgment at all times."[6] Some policy/procedure reports are preserved as lasting guidelines; others are one-time position papers.

Orients the reader but doesn't waste time with unnecessary explanations.

Headings stand out to make report easier to read.

Organizes summary information in the most time-saving format.

Helps the reader maintain a timely overview of progress.

Figure 10–1
In-Depth Critique: Roger Watson's Periodic Operating Report

Lasting Guidelines   Lasting guidelines comprise the rules of an organization. For example, the production supervisor might develop guidelines for standardizing quality-control procedures, or the office manager might issue a memo explaining how to reserve the conference room for special meetings. Such policy/procedure reports then become part of the company's large body of lasting guidelines for doing things a certain way.

Some policies and procedures provide lasting "recipes" for how things should be done.

Position Papers   In contrast to lasting guidelines, position papers treat less-permanent issues. They explain management's views on particular nonrecurring issues or problems as they arise. For example, an office manager might write a report on the need for extra security precautions after a rash of burglaries in the area.

Other policies and procedures explain management's position on passing events.

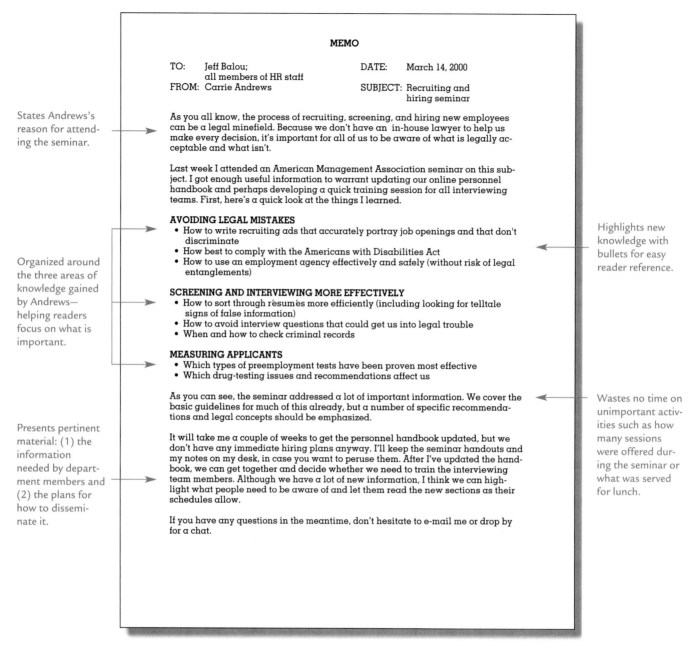

States Andrews's reason for attending the seminar.

Organized around the three areas of knowledge gained by Andrews—helping readers focus on what is important.

Presents pertinent material: (1) the information needed by department members and (2) the plans for how to disseminate it.

Highlights new knowledge with bullets for easy reader reference.

Wastes no time on unimportant activities such as how many sessions were offered during the seminar or what was served for lunch.

MEMO

TO: Jeff Balou;   DATE: March 14, 2000
        all members of HR staff
FROM: Carrie Andrews   SUBJECT: Recruiting and
                                                         hiring seminar

As you all know, the process of recruiting, screening, and hiring new employees can be a legal minefield. Because we don't have an in-house lawyer to help us make every decision, it's important for all of us to be aware of what is legally acceptable and what isn't.

Last week I attended an American Management Association seminar on this subject. I got enough useful information to warrant updating our online personnel handbook and perhaps developing a quick training session for all interviewing teams. First, here's a quick look at the things I learned.

AVOIDING LEGAL MISTAKES
- How to write recruiting ads that accurately portray job openings and that don't discriminate
- How best to comply with the Americans with Disabilities Act
- How to use an employment agency effectively and safely (without risk of legal entanglements)

SCREENING AND INTERVIEWING MORE EFFECTIVELY
- How to sort through résumés more efficiently (including looking for telltale signs of false information)
- How to avoid interview questions that could get us into legal trouble
- When and how to check criminal records

MEASURING APPLICANTS
- Which types of preemployment tests have been proven most effective
- Which drug-testing issues and recommendations affect us

As you can see, the seminar addressed a lot of important information. We cover the basic guidelines for much of this already, but a number of specific recommendations and legal concepts should be emphasized.

It will take me a couple of weeks to get the personnel handbook updated, but we don't have any immediate hiring plans anyway. I'll keep the seminar handouts and my notes on my desk, in case you want to peruse them. After I've updated the handbook, we can get together and decide whether we need to train the interviewing team members. Although we have a lot of new information, I think we can highlight what people need to be aware of and let them read the new sections as their schedules allow.

If you have any questions in the meantime, don't hesitate to e-mail me or drop by for a chat.

Figure 10–2
In-Depth Critique: Carrie Andrews's Personal Activity Report

Access policy is one example of a lasting guideline.

Case Study: William Lawson's Building Access Policy   William Lawson is in charge of security for a medical research lab. Many of the scientists employed there work irregular hours—especially when a deadline approaches or when experiments need constant monitoring. Employees who must work nights or weekends were issued a key to the outside door. However, the company recently won several new contracts and tripled its number of employees.

"In the past," explains Lawson, "we got by with a loose, informal policy. Everyone knew everyone else. But since we have so many new faces, it would be easy for an unauthorized person to walk right in. We need a formal policy for building access." See Figure 10–4 on page 278 for an excerpt from Lawson's policy report.

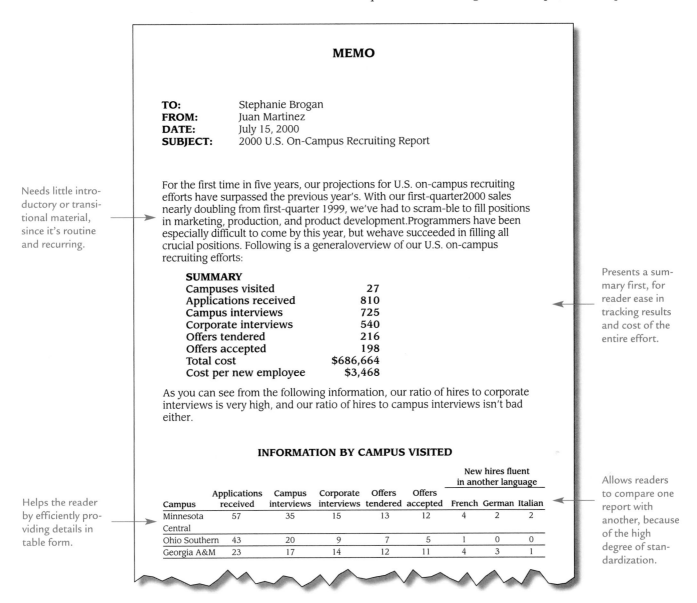

Needs little introductory or transitional material, since it's routine and recurring.

Presents a summary first, for reader ease in tracking results and cost of the entire effort.

Helps the reader by efficiently providing details in table form.

Allows readers to compare one report with another, because of the high degree of standardization.

Figure 10–3
In-Depth Critique: Juan Martinez's Recruiting Report (Excerpt)

Reports for Complying with Government Regulations All compliance reports are written in response to regulations of one sort or another, most of them imposed by government agencies. The regulatory agency issues instructions on how to write the necessary reports. The important thing is to be honest, thorough, and accurate.

Compliance reports explain what a company is doing to conform to government regulations.

Annual Compliance Reports Perhaps the most common examples of annual compliance reports are income tax returns, annual reports from corporations that have a pension plan, and annual shareholder reports. The second half of annual shareholder reports must conform to SEC requirements, but the first half serves a public relations function, giving corporations a forum for educating and persuading readers.

Many compliance reports are prepared on an annual basis.

Case Study: Tai Chen's Child-Care Facility Report Tai Chen operates a child-care facility in her home. To keep her state license current, she must submit regular reports on how her facility meets various state requirements. The report lists information such as the size

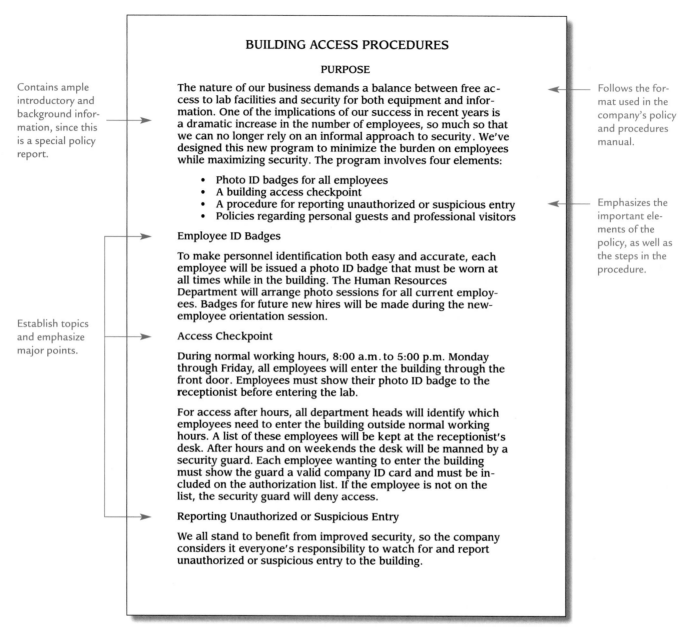

Contains ample introductory and background information, since this is a special policy report.

Establish topics and emphasize major points.

Follows the format used in the company's policy and procedures manual.

Emphasizes the important elements of the policy, as well as the steps in the procedure.

BUILDING ACCESS PROCEDURES

PURPOSE

The nature of our business demands a balance between free access to lab facilities and security for both equipment and information. One of the implications of our success in recent years is a dramatic increase in the number of employees, so much so that we can no longer rely on an informal approach to security. We've designed this new program to minimize the burden on employees while maximizing security. The program involves four elements:

- Photo ID badges for all employees
- A building access checkpoint
- A procedure for reporting unauthorized or suspicious entry
- Policies regarding personal guests and professional visitors

Employee ID Badges

To make personnel identification both easy and accurate, each employee will be issued a photo ID badge that must be worn at all times while in the building. The Human Resources Department will arrange photo sessions for all current employees. Badges for future new hires will be made during the new-employee orientation session.

Access Checkpoint

During normal working hours, 8:00 a.m. to 5:00 p.m. Monday through Friday, all employees will enter the building through the front door. Employees must show their photo ID badge to the receptionist before entering the lab.

For access after hours, all department heads will identify which employees need to enter the building outside normal working hours. A list of these employees will be kept at the receptionist's desk. After hours and on weekends the desk will be manned by a security guard. Each employee wanting to enter the building must show the guard a valid company ID card and must be included on the authorization list. If the employee is not on the list, the security guard will deny access.

Reporting Unauthorized or Suspicious Entry

We all stand to benefit from improved security, so the company considers it everyone's responsibility to watch for and report unauthorized or suspicious entry to the building.

Figure 10–4
In-Depth Critique: William Lawson's Building Access Policy (Excerpt)

of the facility, the number of bathrooms, whether the outdoor play area is fenced, and the number of staff members.

"I started my day-care center when I had my first child," Chen said. "That way I can stay home with my own children while still earning an income. Before I applied for my license, I had no idea how many regulations apply to child care and how much paperwork is involved." Figure 10–5 provides an excerpt from one of Chen's reports. It is straightforward and takes as little time as possible to prepare from the records that Chen keeps.

Reports documenting progress on a contract provide all the information the client needs.

Reports for Documenting Progress Reports that document progress vary in importance and complexity. Some are a mere formality; others are a vital element in a client relationship. Whether you're writing a progress report for a client or for your boss, it's important to anticipate your reader's needs and to provide the required information clearly and tactfully.

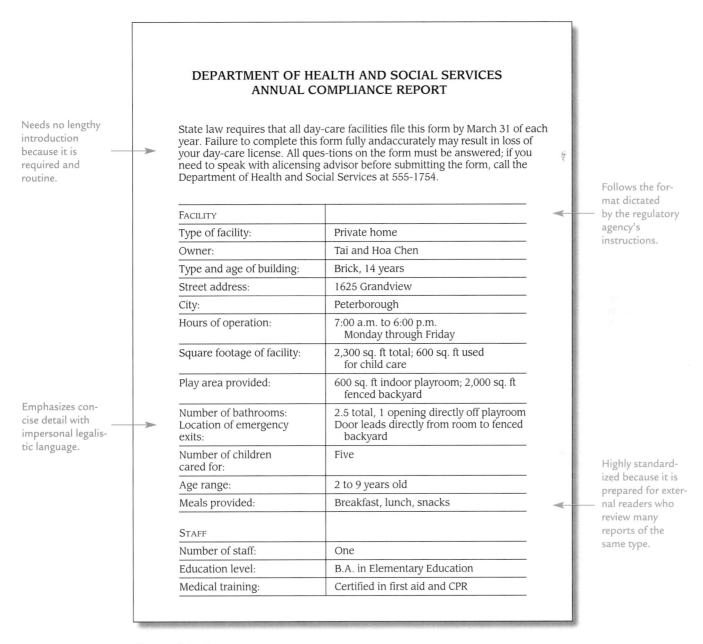

Needs no lengthy introduction because it is required and routine.

Emphasizes concise detail with impersonal legalistic language.

Follows the format dictated by the regulatory agency's instructions.

Highly standardized because it is prepared for external readers who review many reports of the same type.

**DEPARTMENT OF HEALTH AND SOCIAL SERVICES
ANNUAL COMPLIANCE REPORT**

State law requires that all day-care facilities file this form by March 31 of each year. Failure to complete this form fully and accurately may result in loss of your day-care license. All ques-tions on the form must be answered; if you need to speak with a licensing advisor before submitting the form, call the Department of Health and Social Services at 555-1754.

FACILITY	
Type of facility:	Private home
Owner:	Tai and Hoa Chen
Type and age of building:	Brick, 14 years
Street address:	1625 Grandview
City:	Peterborough
Hours of operation:	7:00 a.m. to 6:00 p.m. Monday through Friday
Square footage of facility:	2,300 sq. ft total; 600 sq. ft used for child care
Play area provided:	600 sq. ft indoor playroom; 2,000 sq. ft fenced backyard
Number of bathrooms: Location of emergency exits:	2.5 total, 1 opening directly off playroom Door leads directly from room to fenced backyard
Number of children cared for:	Five
Age range:	2 to 9 years old
Meals provided:	Breakfast, lunch, snacks
STAFF	
Number of staff:	One
Education level:	B.A. in Elementary Education
Medical training:	Certified in first aid and CPR

Figure 10–5
In-Depth Critique: Tai Chen's Compliance Report (Excerpt)

Progress reports are generally submitted on a regular basis. They may be required monthly or weekly, or they may be keyed to phases of the project. In many cases these interim progress reports are followed by a final report at the conclusion of the contract.

Interim Progress Reports *Interim progress reports* naturally vary in length, depending on the period covered and the complexity of the contract. They give others an idea of the work that has been accomplished to date. They are often keyed to the work plan that was established at the beginning of the contract or project. The writer states what tasks have been accomplished, identifies problems, outlines future steps, and summarizes important findings.

A long or complex project is documented with periodic updates on the progress that has been made.

Final Reports *Final reports* are generally more elaborate than interim reports because they serve as a permanent record of what was accomplished. They focus on results rather than on progress. So they report *what* was done, not *how* it was done.

At the end of the project, a final report provides a wrap-up of results.

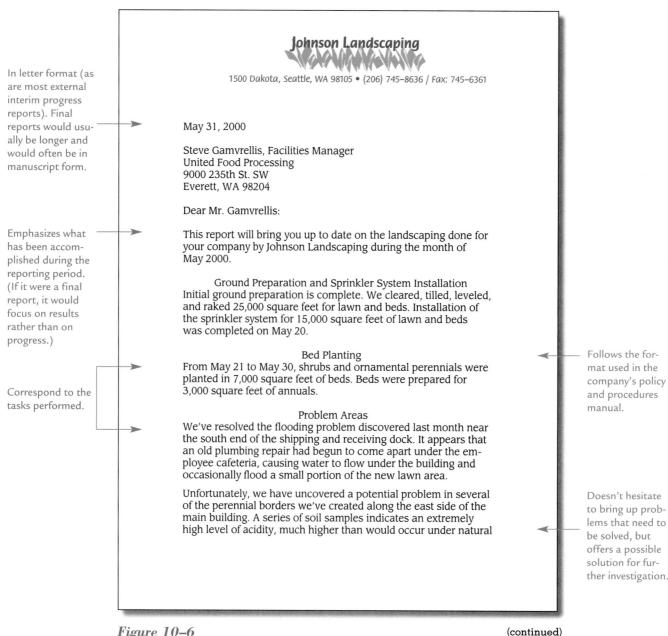

In letter format (as are most external interim progress reports). Final reports would usually be longer and would often be in manuscript form.

Emphasizes what has been accomplished during the reporting period. (If it were a final report, it would focus on results rather than on progress.)

Correspond to the tasks performed.

Follows the format used in the company's policy and procedures manual.

Doesn't hesitate to bring up problems that need to be solved, but offers a possible solution for further investigation.

Johnson Landscaping

1500 Dakota, Seattle, WA 98105 • (206) 745–8636 / Fax: 745–6361

May 31, 2000

Steve Gamvrellis, Facilities Manager
United Food Processing
9000 235th St. SW
Everett, WA 98204

Dear Mr. Gamvrellis:

This report will bring you up to date on the landscaping done for your company by Johnson Landscaping during the month of May 2000.

Ground Preparation and Sprinkler System Installation
Initial ground preparation is complete. We cleared, tilled, leveled, and raked 25,000 square feet for lawn and beds. Installation of the sprinkler system for 15,000 square feet of lawn and beds was completed on May 20.

Bed Planting
From May 21 to May 30, shrubs and ornamental perennials were planted in 7,000 square feet of beds. Beds were prepared for 3,000 square feet of annuals.

Problem Areas
We've resolved the flooding problem discovered last month near the south end of the shipping and receiving dock. It appears that an old plumbing repair had begun to come apart under the employee cafeteria, causing water to flow under the building and occasionally flood a small portion of the new lawn area.

Unfortunately, we have uncovered a potential problem in several of the perennial borders we've created along the east side of the main building. A series of soil samples indicates an extremely high level of acidity, much higher than would occur under natural

Figure 10–6   (continued)
In-Depth Critique: Carlyce Johnson's Interim Progress Report (Excerpt)

Projects or jobs that take place over time must provide regular updates in the form of progress reports.

Business summaries communicate and organize information that is needed in business.

Case Study: Carlyce Johnson's Progress Report   Carlyce Johnson runs the office for her family's landscaping business. The jobs vary from replanting a few beds for homes to installing thousands of square feet of new lawn and beds for businesses. Each customer must approve the design before installation can begin, and Johnson is responsible for monitoring and reporting progress on every job.

"Our landscaping jobs vary in length from part of a day to several months," explains Johnson. "Often the only report required is a short final report sent to the customer with our bill. For longer jobs, I send weekly or monthly progress reports. These reports can vary from 1 to 20 pages, depending on the complexity of the installation." For an excerpt from one of Johnson's interim progress reports, see Figure 10–6.

Reports for Summarizing Information   Businesspeople are bombarded with masses of information, and at one time or another, everyone in business relies on someone else's

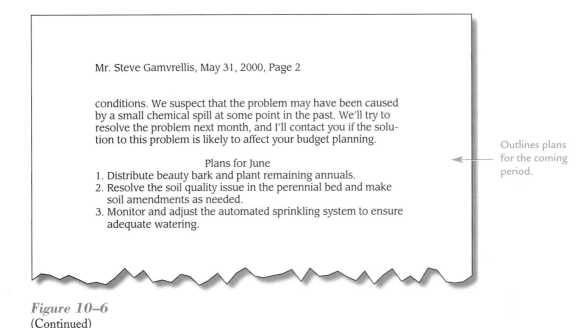

Mr. Steve Gamvrellis, May 31, 2000, Page 2

conditions. We suspect that the problem may have been caused by a small chemical spill at some point in the past. We'll try to resolve the problem next month, and I'll contact you if the solution to this problem is likely to affect your budget planning.

Plans for June
1. Distribute beauty bark and plant remaining annuals.
2. Resolve the soil quality issue in the perennial bed and make soil amendments as needed.
3. Monitor and adjust the automated sprinkling system to ensure adequate watering.

Outlines plans for the coming period.

Figure 10–6
(Continued)

summary of a situation, publication, or document. To write a summary report, gather the information (whether by reading, talking with others, or observing circumstances), organize that information, and then present it in your own words. Although summarizing may seem a simple skill, it's actually more complex than it appears. A well-written summary has at least three characteristics:

◆ **The content must be accurate.** If you're summarizing a report or a group of reports, make sure that you present the information without error. Check your references, then check for typos.

◆ **The summary must be comprehensive and balanced.** To help colleagues or supervisors make a decision, include all the information necessary for readers to understand the situation, problem, or proposal. Present all sides of the issue fairly and equitably, and include all the information necessary. Even though summaries are intended to be as brief as possible, your readers need a minimum amount of information to grasp the issue being presented.

◆ **The report structure must be clear.** Clear sentence structure and good transitions are essential.[7] Save your reader's time by making sure your sentences are uncluttered, contain well-chosen words, and proceed logically (see "Sharpening Your Career Skills—Seven Errors in Logic That Can Undermine Your Reports"). To help your readers move from one point to the next, make your transitions just as clear and logical. For a successful summary, identify the ideas that belong together, and organize them in a way that's easy to understand.[8]

Analytical Reports

When making major decisions, managers such as Michael Dell must rely on analytical reports for information, analysis, and recommendations. Analytical reports require a strong foundation of facts combined with good insight and excellent communication skills on the part of the writer. When you prepare one of these reports, you have the chance to present your skills to top management. Naturally, you'll want to give these assignments your best effort.

Although analytical reports vary greatly, all of them tend to ask "should we or shouldn't we" questions: Should we expand into this market? Should we reorganize the research department? Should we invest in new equipment? Some of the more common

Yahoo! cofounder Jerry Yang is in charge of the company's business development. Already one of the largest online navigational guide sites in the world, Yahoo! is involved in numerous subsidiary ventures, including city-guide sites and a print publication. Before making any decision to expand into a new market, Yang and his partner, David Filo, need to carefully prepare analytical reports.

Reports that help managers make decisions about problems and opportunities are especially interesting to write.

Sharpening Your Career Skills

Sharpening Your Career Skills

Seven Errors in Logic That Can Undermine Your Reports

For your report to be effective, it must be logical. If you learn how to think logically, you'll also write more logically. Here are some common errors to avoid.

1. **Lack of objectivity.** Seeing only the facts that support your views and ignoring any contradictory information:

   "Although half the survey population expressed dissatisfaction with our current product, a sizable portion finds it satisfactory." *(You may be tempted to ignore the dissatisfied half instead of investigating the reasons for their dissatisfaction.)*

2. **Hasty generalizations.** Forming judgments on the basis of insufficient evidence or special cases:

   "Marketing strategy Z increased sales 13 percent in Atlanta supermarkets. Let's try it in Fairbanks." *(Atlanta and Fairbanks are probably vastly different markets.)*

3. **Hidden assumptions.** Hiding a questionable major premise:

   "We are marketing product X in trade journals because we marketed product Y in trade journals." *(Who says product X and product Y should be marketed the same way?)*

4. **Either-or scenarios.** Setting up two alternatives and not allowing for others:

   "We must open a new plant by spring, or we will go bankrupt." *(Surely there are other ways to avoid bankruptcy.)*

5. **False causal relationships.** Assuming that event A caused event B merely because A preceded B:

   "Sales increased 42 percent as soon as we hired the new sales director." *(Something besides the new sales director might have been responsible for increased sales.)*

6. **Begged questions.** Assuming as proven what you are seeking to prove:

   "We need a standard procedure so that we will have standard results." *(But why is standardization important?)*

7. **Personal attacks or appeals to popular prejudice.** Sinking people or ideas you don't like by chaining them to irrelevant but unpopular actions or ideas:

   "Ellen mishandled the budget last year, so she can't be expected to motivate her staff." *(Ellen's accounting ability may have nothing to do with her ability to motivate a staff.)*

   "It's un-American to impose government regulations." *(Regulations are unpopular, but they do exist in the United States.)*

CAREER APPLICATIONS

1. Discuss some newsworthy business problem that arose from errors in logic. For example, Huffy tried to sell a combination mountain-and-racing bicycle through Kmart and other large stores that sold Huffy bicycles. Unfortunately, Huffy's logic was faulty. The company had no reason to assume that this special bike (which was priced higher than other Huffy models) could be sold by salespeople who weren't knowledgeable about bicycles. Huffy lost $5 million on the product.

2. Go through the "Letters to the Editor" columns in recent newspapers or newsmagazines. Examine the arguments made, and point out errors in logic.

---

examples of analytical reports are those for solving problems, justifying a project or a course of action, and obtaining new business or funding (usually called proposals).

Problem-solving reports provide management with background information and analysis of options.

Reports for Solving Problems   When making decisions, managers need both basic information and detailed analysis of the various options. Most problem-solving reports require research or internal information that may cover topics such as product demand, growth projections, competitor profiles, company strengths and weaknesses, and so on. If the report is prepared on a computer, it might include a financial model that allows managers to compare various scenarios by plugging in different assumptions and projections.

Troubleshooting reports are one type of problem-solving report. Whenever a problem exists, somebody has to investigate it and propose a solution. Regardless of the specific problem at hand, these troubleshooting reports deal with the same basic research questions: How did this problem arise, what's the extent of the damage, and what can we do about it? These reports usually start with some background information on the problem, then analyze alternative solutions, and finally recommend the best approach.

A justification report is a proposal to upper-level management from lower- or middle-level management.

Reports for Justifying a Project or Course of Action   Justification reports (or feasibility reports) are used to persuade top management to approve a project or course of action. These reports may be written about acquiring capital assets, reorganizing a department,

MEMO

TO: Jamie Engle
FROM: Shandel Cohen
DATE: July 8, 2000
SUBJECT: Proposed automatic mail-response system

THE PROBLEM:
SLOW RESPONSE TO CUSTOMER REQUESTS FOR INFORMATION

(Describes the problem carefully in a positive light (in terms of the company's success).)

Our new product line has been very well received, and orders have surpassed our projections. This very success, however, has created a shortage of printed catalogs and data sheets, as well as considerable overtime for people in the customer response center. As we introduce upgrades and new options, our printed materials quickly become outdated. If we continue to rely on printed materials for customer information, we have two choices: Distribute existing materials (even though they are incomplete or inaccurate) or discard existing materials and print new ones.

THE SOLUTION:
AUTOMATED MAIL-RESPONSE SYSTEM

With minor modifications to our current computer system and very little additional software, we can set up an automated mail-response system to respond to customer requests for information. This process can save us time and money and can keep our distributed information current.

Automated mail-response systems have been tested and proven effective. Many companies already use this method to respond to customer information requests, so we won't have to worry about relying on untested technology. Both customer and company responses have been positive.

Ever-Current Information

(Uses headings to highlight the benefits of the solution.)

Rather than discard and print new materials, we would need to update only the electronic files. We would be able to provide customers and our field sales organization with up-to-date, correct information as soon as the upgrades or options are available.

Instantaneous Delivery

Within a very short time of requesting information, customers would have that information in hand. Electronic delivery would

(continued)

Figure 10–7
In Depth Critique: Shandel Cohen's Justification Report

revising recruiting procedures, changing the company's training programs, or improving operations in hundreds of other ways.

A good justification report explains why a project or course of action is needed, what it will involve, how much it will cost, and what the benefits will be. Also, even if a justification report is intended to persuade others to do something, it must always be unbiased. For example, look at Shandel Cohen's report in Figure 10–7.

Cohen manages the customer-response section of the marketing department at a Midwest personal computer manufacturer. Her section sends out product information requested by customers and the field sales force. Cohen has observed that the demand for information increases when a new product is released and diminishes as a product matures. This fluctuating demand causes drastic changes in her section's workload.

"Either we have more work than we can possibly handle," says Cohen, "or we don't have enough to keep us busy. But I don't want to get into a hiring-and-firing cycle."

2

be especially advantageous for our international customers. Regular mail to remote locations sometimes takes weeks to arrive, by which time the information may already be out of date. Both customers and field salespeople will appreciate the automatic mail-response system.

Minimized Waste

With our current method of sending printed information, we discard virtually tons of obsolete catalogs, data sheets, and other materials.

By maintaining and distributing the information electronically, we would eliminate this waste. We would also free up a considerable amount of floor space and shelving that is required for storing printed materials.

Of course, some of our customers may still prefer to receive printed materials, or they may not have access to electronic mail. For these customers we could simply print copies of the files when we receive requests.

Lower Overtime Costs

Besides savings in paper and space, we would also realize considerable savings in wages. Because of the increased interest in our new products, we must continue to work overtime or hire new people to meet the demand. An automatic mail-response system would eliminate this need, allowing us to deal with fluctuating interest without a fluctuating work force.

Setup and Operating Costs

Carefully explains the costs of the proposal.

The necessary equipment and software costs approximately $15,000. System maintenance and upgrades are estimated at $5,000 per year.

We expect the following annual savings from eliminating printed information:

3

$100,000	Printing costs
25,000	Storage costs
5,000	Postage
20,000	Wages
$150,000	

Justifies the cost by detailing projected annual savings.

CONCLUSION

Closes by offering to answer any questions management may have, rather than trying to anticipate management's questions and including unnecessary detail.

I will be happy to answer any questions you have about this system. I believe that this system would greatly benefit our company, in terms of both cost and customer satisfaction. If you approve the system, we can have it installed and running in six weeks.

Figure 10–7
(Continued)

Cohen is also concerned about the amount of printed material that's discarded when products are upgraded or replaced.

Cohen's report proposes to install an automatic mail-response system. Because the company manufactures computers, she knows that her boss won't object to a computer solution. Also, since profits are always a concern, her report emphasizes the financial benefits of her proposal. Her report describes the problem, her proposed solutions, and the benefits to the company.

Proposals for Obtaining New Business or Funding   A **proposal** is a special type of analytical report designed to get products, plans, or projects accepted by outside business or government clients. Proposals to outsiders are similar to the justification reports that solicit approval of projects within an organization. However, proposals have some important differences:

Proposals are reports written to get products, plans, or projects accepted by outside business or government clients.

◆ **Proposals are legally binding.** Unlike justification reports, proposals form the basis of a contract, so they are prepared with extreme care. Proposals spell out precisely what your company will provide under specific terms and conditions. If you propose to sell 500 units at a price of $250 each, you are bound to deliver at that price, come what may.

◆ **Proposals often compete for a client's business.** Although justification reports may compete for company dollars, time, or resources, they don't compete for business. Proposals try to convince readers that your organization is the best source of a product. Thus, you devote considerable space to explaining your experience, qualifications, facilities, and equipment. Moreover, you show that you clearly understand your reader's problem or need.[9]

The two basic types of proposal are those invited by a prospective client and those sent without a specific invitation from a prospective client.

Solicited Proposals   Solicited proposals are prepared at the request of clients who need something done. The invitation to bid on the contract is called a *request for proposal* (RFP), and you respond by preparing a proposal that shows how you would meet the potential customer's needs. Say that the National Aeronautics and Space Administration (NASA) decides to develop a new satellite. The agency prepares an RFP that specifies exactly what the satellite should accomplish and sends it to several aerospace companies, inviting them to bid on the job.

A solicited proposal demonstrates that your organization is better qualified than competitors to handle a particular contract.

When a company gets an RFP, the managers decide whether they're interested in the job and whether they have a reasonable chance of winning the contract. When the proposal effort actually begins, the company reviews the requirements, defines the scope of the work, determines the methods and procedures to be used, and estimates time requirements, personnel requirements, and costs. Then the proposal writers put it all on paper—exactly as specified in the RFP, following the exact format it requires and responding meticulously to every point it raises.[10]

Most proposals begin with an introductory section that states the purpose of the proposal, defines the scope of the work, presents background information, and explains any restrictions that might apply to the contract. The body of the proposal gives details on the proposed effort and specifies what the anticipated results will be. The discussion covers the methods, schedule, facilities, equipment, personnel, and costs that will be involved in the contract. A final section generally summarizes the key points of the proposal and asks for a decision from the client.

Unsolicited Proposals   Unsolicited proposals are initiated by organizations attempting to obtain business or funding without a specific invitation from a potential client. Unsolicited proposals differ from solicited proposals in one important respect: The recipient has to be convinced of the benefits of buying (or funding) something. Unsolicited proposals generally spend considerable time explaining why the recipient should take action.

An unsolicited proposal establishes the value of funding your project.

Unsolicited proposals vary widely in form, length, and purpose. For example, a university seeking funding for a specific research project might submit an unsolicited proposal to a large local corporation. To be convincing, the proposal would show how the

When writing proposals, Don Lessem understands the importance of showing potential investors how they can make money. Through his company, Dinosaur Productions, Lessem creates traveling dinosaur exhibits, such as *Dinosaurs of Jurassic Park/The Lost World* and *Discovering Dinosaurs.* For *The Lost World* exhibit, Lessem raised some $1.8 million from private investors. Since 1997 the exhibit has been traveling from museum to museum, making the company about $100,000 for each three-month stay.

research could benefit the corporation, and it would demonstrate that the university has the resources and expertise to conduct the research.[11] Or an entrepreneur seeking funding for a new venture might modify a business plan to create a proposal showing potential investors the return they should expect in exchange for the use of their funds. Such a proposal would try to convince investors of the viability of the new business.

PLANNING BUSINESS REPORTS—ANALYSIS

As with other business messages, reports benefit from the three-step writing process (See Figure 10–8). In this chapter we focus on Step 1, "Planning Business Reports." Step 2 is discussed in Chapter 11, "Writing Business Reports and Proposals," and Step 3 is the subject of Chapter 12, "Completing Formal Business Reports and Proposals."

The planning tasks for reports fall into the three familiar categories: analysis, investigation, and adaptation. However, certain tasks have a special importance for business reports and proposals. For example, when analyzing your purpose, you'll want to put particular effort into defining the problem, limiting the scope of the study, outlining the issues for investigation, developing the statement of purpose, and preparing the work plan.

Objective **3**

Explain the difference between a problem statement and a statement of purpose, and then identify five other elements often included in a formal work plan.

When writing reports, pay special attention to analysis tasks such as the following:
- Defining the problem
- Limiting the scope
- Outlining the issues
- Developing the statement of purpose
- Preparing the work plan

One way to limit the scope of your study is to verify your assignment with the person authorizing your report.

Defining the Problem

If you're writing an informational report, your assignment may be as simple as gathering last month's sales figures and submitting them to management in a table format. Most informational reports don't go beyond submitting the facts. However, if you're writing an analytical report, your assignment will likely involve solving a problem, so begin by developing a **problem statement** that defines the problem you need to resolve.

This problem can be negative or positive—it may deal with shrinking sales or the need for more child-care facilities. Just be careful not to confuse a simple topic (campus parking) with a problem (the lack of enough campus parking). If you're the only person who thinks this issue is a problem, your audience won't be very interested in your solution, so be sure to focus on your audience, consider your company's perspective, and keep in mind the needs of the people who will read your report.[12] You may have to spend some time convincing your readers that a problem exists.

Limiting the Scope of Study

Linda Moreno is the cost accounting manager for Electrovision, a high-tech company based in Los Gatos, California. She was recently asked to find ways of reducing employee travel and entertainment costs (her complete report appears in Chapter 12). As in Moreno's case, the problem is often defined for the writer by the person who authorizes the report. To ensure that she understands exactly what is required of her, Moreno begins by discussing the objectives of her report with the person who requested and authorized the investigation. Specifically, she tries to answer the following questions:

◆ What needs to be determined?

◆ Why is this issue important?

◆ Who is involved in the situation?

◆ Where is the trouble located?

◆ When did it start?

◆ How did the situation originate?

1 Planning

Analyze: Study the audience and analyze your purpose: Define the problem, limit the scope, outline the investigation, write the statement of purpose, and prepare the work plan.

Investigate: Research secondary or primary sources.

Adapt: Establish a good audience relationship and choose the right medium.

2 Writing

Organize: Decide format, length, order, and structure. Prepare the final outline, and organize any visual aids.

Compose: Control your style through level of formality and tone. Establish a time perspective and help readers find their way with devices such as headings, lists, and transitions.

3 Completing

Revise: Evaluate content and review readability, editing and rewriting for conciseness and clarity.

Produce: Use effective design elements. Include all required formal components.

Proofread: Review text and visuals for errors in layout, spelling, and mechanics.

Figure 10–8
The Three-Step Writing Process for Reports

Not all these questions apply in every situation, but asking them helps limit the scope of the problem and clarify the boundaries of the investigation. You can then draft a written statement that will serve as a guide to whatever problem you're trying to solve or whatever question you're trying to answer in the report.[13]

Besides asking such general questions, you can also limit the scope of your study by breaking down the problem into a series of logical, connected questions that try to identify cause and effect. This process is sometimes called **problem factoring.** You probably subconsciously approach most problems this way. When your car's engine won't start, what do you do? You use the available evidence to organize your investigation, to start a search for cause-and-effect relationships. For example, if the engine doesn't turn over at all, you might suspect a dead battery. If the engine does turn over but won't fire, you can conclude that the battery is okay but perhaps you're out of gas. When you speculate on the cause of a problem, you're forming a **hypothesis,** a potential explanation that needs to be tested. By subdividing a problem and forming hypotheses based on available evidence, you can tackle even the most complex situations.

> Another way to limit the scope of your study is to factor the problem.

> Studies that focus on problem solving may be structured around hypotheses that the report writer plans to prove or disprove during the investigation.

Linda Moreno used the factoring process to structure her investigation into ways of reducing travel and entertainment costs at Electrovision. "I began with a two-part question," says Moreno. "Why have our travel costs grown so dramatically, and how can we reduce them? Then I factored that question into two subquestions: Do we have adequate procedures for tracking and controlling costs? Are these procedures being followed?

"Looking into cost-control procedures, I speculated that the right kind of information was not reaching the executives who were responsible for these costs. From there, the questioning naturally led to the systems and procedures for collecting this information. If we didn't have the right procedures in place or if people weren't following procedures, the information wouldn't reach the people in charge."

Once Moreno had determined what was wrong with Electrovision's cost-control system, she could address the second part of the main question: the problem of recommending improvements. This factoring process, or breaking a problem into a series of subproblems, enabled Moreno and her colleagues to approach the task methodically.

Outlining Issues for Investigation

As you go through the factoring process, you may want to use an outline format to represent your ideas. For example, if your problem is to determine why your company is having trouble hiring secretaries, you'll begin by speculating on the causes. Then you'll collect

> Use an outline format when factoring complex problems.

information to confirm or disprove each reason. Your outline of the major issues might look something like this:

Why are we having trouble hiring secretaries?

1. Are salaries too low?
a. What do we pay our secretaries?
b. What do comparable companies pay their secretaries?
c. How important is pay in influencing secretaries' job choices?

2. Is our location poor?
a. Are we accessible by public transportation and major roads?
b. Is the area physically attractive?
c. Are housing costs affordable?
d. Is crime a problem?

3. Is the supply of secretaries diminishing?
a. How many secretaries were available five years ago as opposed to now?
b. What was the demand for secretaries five years ago as opposed to now?

When writing headings for outlines, use the same grammatical form for items of the same level. Parallel construction shows that the ideas are related, of similar importance, and on the same level of generality. When wording outlines, you must also choose between descriptive (topical) and informative (talking) headings. Descriptive headings label the subject that will be discussed, whereas informative headings (in either question or summary form) suggest more about the meaning of the issues.

Informative outline headings are useful in guiding your work.

Although outlines with informative headings take a little longer to write, they're generally more useful in guiding your work, especially if written in terms of the questions you plan to answer during your investigation. They're also easier for others to review. If other people are going to comment on your outline, they may not have a very clear idea of what you mean by the descriptive heading "Advertising." However, they will get the main idea if you use the informative heading "Did Cuts in Ad Budget Cause Sales to Decline?"

The outline for investigation differs from the final outline of the report.

The way you outline your investigation may differ from the final outline of your resulting report. That's because solving a problem is one thing, and "selling" the solution is another. During your investigation, you might analyze five possible causes of a problem and discover that only two are relevant. In your report, you might not even introduce the three unrelated causes. (Chapter 4 discusses common outline forms, and Chapter 11 discusses the benefits of preparing a final outline.) If a few notes are enough to guide you through a short, informal report in memo form, an outline might not be necessary.

Developing the Statement of Purpose

The statement of purpose defines the objective of your report.

Once you've determined the problem and limited its scope, you're ready to develop a **statement of purpose,** which defines the objective of the report. In contrast to the problem statement, which defines *what* you are going to investigate, the statement of purpose defines *why* you are preparing the report (see Table 10–2).

The most useful way to phrase your purpose is to begin with an infinitive phrase. For instance, in an informational report, your statement of purpose can be as simple as these:

◆ To update clients on the progress of the research project (interim progress report)

◆ To develop goals and objectives for the coming year (strategic plan)

◆ To identify customers and explain how the company will service them (marketing plan)

◆ To submit monthly sales statistics to management (periodic operating report)

◆ To summarize what occurred at the annual sales conference (personal activity report)

◆ To explain the building access procedures (policy implementation report)

◆ To submit required information to the SEC (compliance report)

Using an infinitive phrase (*to* plus a verb) encourages you to take control and decide where you're going before you begin. When you choose an infinitive phrase—*to inform, to*

Table 10–2   Problem Statements Versus Purpose Statements

Problem Statement	Statement of Purpose
Our company's market share is steadily declining.	To explore different ways of selling our products and to recommend the ones that will most likely increase our market share.
Our current computer network system is inefficient and cannot be upgraded to meet our future needs.	To analyze various computer network systems and to recommend the system will best meet our company's current and future needs.
We need $2 million to launch our new product.	To convince investors that our new business would be a sound investment so that we can obtain desired financing.
Our current operations are too decentralized and expensive.	To justify the closing of the Newark plant and the transfer of East Coast operations to a single Midwest location in order to save the company money.

confirm, to analyze, to persuade, to recommend—you pin down your general goal in preparing the report.

The statement of purpose for analytical reports is often more comprehensive. Look at Linda Moreno's statement of purpose. Because she was supposed to suggest specific ways of reducing costs, she phrased her statement like this:

Statements of purpose for analytical reports are often more complex than are those for informational reports.

. . . to analyze the T&E [travel and entertainment] budget, evaluate the impact of recent changes in airfares and hotel costs, and suggest ways to tighten management's control over T&E expenses.

If Moreno had been given an informational assignment instead, she might have stated her purpose this way:

To summarize Electrovision's spending on travel and entertainment.

You can see from these two examples how much influence the purpose statement has on the scope of your report. If Moreno's manager had expected her to suggest ways to reduce costs but Moreno had collected only cost data, her report would have failed to meet expectations. Because she was assigned an analytical report rather than an informational report, Moreno had to go beyond merely collecting data to drawing conclusions and making recommendations.

Remember, the more specific your purpose, the more useful it will be as a guide to planning your report. Furthermore, always double-check your statement of purpose with the person who authorized the report. Seeing the purpose written down in black and white, the authorizer may decide that the report needs to go in a different direction.

Prepare a written statement of your purpose; then review it with the person who authorized the study.

Preparing the Work Plan

Once you've defined the problem and the purpose of your report, you are ready to establish a work plan. In business, most reports have a firm deadline and finite resources. You not only have to produce quality reports, you have to do so quickly and efficiently. A carefully thought-out work plan is the best way to make sure you produce quality work on schedule.

If you are preparing the work plan for yourself, it can be relatively informal: a simple list of the steps you plan to take, an estimate of their sequence and timing, and a list of the sources of information you plan to use. If you're conducting a lengthy, formal study, however, you'll want to develop a detailed work plan that can guide the performance of many

Whether you prepare an informal work plan for yourself or a detailed work plan for your team, be sure it identifies all the tasks that must be performed.

tasks over a span of time. Most proposals require a detailed work plan, which becomes the basis for a contract if the proposal is accepted. A formal work plan might include the following elements (especially the first two):

◆ **Statement of the problem.** The problem statement clarifies the challenge you face, helps you and anyone working with you to stay focused on the core problem, and helps everyone avoid the distractions that are likely to arise during report preparation.

◆ **Statement of the purpose and scope of your investigation.** The purpose statement describes what you plan to accomplish with this report and, thus, the boundaries of your work. Stating which issues you will cover and which issues you won't cover is especially important with complex, lengthy investigations.

◆ **Discussion of tasks to be accomplished.** Be sure to indicate your sources of information, the research necessary, and any constraints (on time, money, personnel, or data). For simple reports, the list of tasks to be accomplished will be short and probably obvious. However, longer reports and complex investigations require an exhaustive list so that you can reserve time with customers, with executives, or for outside services such as pollsters or print shops.

◆ **Description of any products that will result from your investigation.** In many cases, the only product of your efforts will be the report itself. In other cases, you'll need to produce something beyond a report, perhaps a new marketing plan or even a tangible product. Make these expectations clear at the outset, and be sure to schedule enough time and resources to get the job done.

◆ **Review of project assignments, schedules, and resource requirements.** Indicate who will be responsible for what, when tasks will be completed, and how much the investigation will cost. If more than one person will be involved, you may also want to include a brief section on coordinating report writing and production. (Collaborative writing is discussed in detail in Chapter 2. Also see "Give Others Specific, Constructive Criticism," in Chapter 6.)

◆ **Working outline.** Some work plans include a tentative outline of the report, as does the plan in Figure 10–9. This plan was developed for a report on whether to launch a company newsletter.

◆ **Plans for following up after delivering the report.** Follow-up can be as simple as making sure people received the information they needed or as complex as conducting additional research to evaluate the results of proposals included in your report. Even informal follow-up can help you improve your future reports and communicate that you care about your work's effectiveness and its impact on the organization.

With a plan in place, you're ready to get to work, which in some cases means starting with research.

PLANNING BUSINESS REPORTS—INVESTIGATION

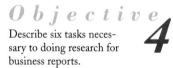

Objective

4

Describe six tasks necessary to doing research for business reports.

Sharpening your research strategy will help you find all the business information you need.

Like Michael Dell, you may someday need to gather information on specific companies, industries, trends, issues, or people. This may seem like an overwhelming task considering the amount of information available today. But if you sharpen your research strategy, you'll find that looking for business information can be a rewarding experience.

Over the years, your instructors have assigned carefully designed research projects to help you develop and practice good information literacy and library skills. We'll build on those skills in this chapter by explaining a research strategy that you can use for the remainder of your college business studies (including this course), on the job, or whenever you're looking for information. In addition, we'll introduce you to some popular resources that you'll need in business, and we'll explain where to find them, how to use them, and how to evaluate them.

When it comes to finding information, many people go to the library, log on to a database or the Internet, type in some key words, produce a bazillion resources, and immediately begin taking notes on whatever comes up under their topic. Resist the

Clear enough for anyone to understand without background research.

Lays out the tasks to be accomplished and does so in clear, simple terms.

A preliminary outline is presented for guidance, even though no description of the end product is included.

States the assignments and the schedules for completing them.

Delineates exactly what will be covered in the report.

Includes no plans for following up.

STATEMENT OF THE PROBLEM

The rapid growth of our company over the past five years has reduced the sense of community among our staff. People no longer feel like part of an intimate organization where they matter as individuals.

PURPOSE AND SCOPE OF WORK

The purpose of this study is to determine whether a company newsletter would help rebuild employee identification with the organization. The study will evaluate the impact of newsletters in other companies and will attempt to identify features that might be desirable in our own newsletter. Such variables as length, frequency of distribution, types of articles, and graphic design will be considered. Costs will be estimated for several approaches. In addition, the study will analyze the personnel and the procedures required to produce a newsletter.

SOURCES AND METHODS OF DATA COLLECTION

Sample newsletters will be collected from 50 companies similar to ours in size, growth rate, and types of employees. The editors will be asked to comment on the impact of their publications on employee morale. Our own employees will be surveyed to determine their interest in a newsletter and their preferences for specific features. Production procedures and costs will be analyzed through conversations with newsletter editors and printers.

PRELIMINARY OUTLINE

I. Do newsletters affect morale?
   A. Do people read them?
   B. How do employees benefit?
   C. How does the company benefit?
II. What are the features of good newsletters?
   A. How long are they?
   B. What do they contain?
   C. How often are they published?
   D. How are they designed?
III. How should a newsletter be produced?
   A. Should it be written, edited, and printed internally?
   B. Should it be written internally and printed outside?
   C. Should it be totally produced outside?
IV. What would a newsletter cost?
   A. What would the personnel costs be?
   B. What would the materials costs be?
   C. What would outside services cost?
V. Should we publish a company newsletter?
VI. If so, what approach should we take?

WORK PLAN

Collect/analyze newsletters	09/01-09/14
Interview editors by phone	09/16-09/20
Survey employees	09/14-09/28
Develop sample	09/28-10/05
Develop cost estimates	10/07-10/10
Prepare report	10/10-10/24
Submit final report	10/25

Figure 10–9
In-Depth Critique: Work Plan for a Formal Study

temptation. If your research strategy is weak, any business decisions based on your research will also be weak.

Adopt an organized approach to research by completing six tasks: (1) find and access secondary information, (2) gather any necessary primary information, (3) evaluate and finalize your sources, (4) process your information, (5) analyze your data, and (6) interpret your findings. In most cases you'll perform these tasks in order; however, the amount of time you spend on a single task will depend on the nature and volume of information you need, as well as on the purpose of your research. Conducting research often requires jumping around, branching off, or looping back; that is, your discoveries may lead you to additional questions, which require further research, and so on. What's important is to become competent in each task and to complete all six of them.

Complete six tasks to find, evaluate, and process information effectively and efficiently.

Find and Access Secondary Information[14]

You conduct secondary research by locating information that has already been collected, usually in the form of books, periodicals, and reports. In most cases, you'll be unfamiliar with your research topic, so you'll need to learn something about your subject before you begin your research in earnest.

The best way to learn about something new is to browse through materials on your topic. Leaf through some books and periodicals, conduct some loosely structured interviews, or log on to a database (either at the library or on the Internet) and see what comes up. You may even want to visit your favorite bookstore (whether physical or online, such as Amazon.com), gather some business books on your topic, and scan their table of contents. Once you have a better understanding of your topic, you're ready to begin your research in earnest.

Begin your research effort by becoming familiar with your topic.

Knowing What to Look For   If you're looking for information about a specific company, one of the first things you'll need to know is whether the company is public (sells shares of stock to the general public) or private. Public companies generally have more information available than private companies. You can find a list of public companies in the *Directory of Companies Required to File Annual Reports with the Securities and Exchange Commission.*

If you're looking for industry information, you'll need to know the Standard Industrial Classification (SIC) code of that particular industry. The U.S. government requires all companies, from sole proprietorships to corporations, to assign themselves a four-digit industry number when establishing their business. The North American Industry Classification System (NAICS) will eventually replace the SIC system. Both SIC and NAICS codes are available on the Internet and in business reference books.

You may need to find information on company and industry statistics, economic forecasts, business concerns, legal issues, competition, and industry performance ratios and averages. Figure 10–10 lists some of the more popular resources for company and industry information (many of which are available in both print and electronic database format). One of the best places to begin your search for secondary information is the nearest public or university library.

To research a company, first find out whether it's public or private. You can also look up the company's SIC (or NAICS) code to find information related to the industry.

Finding Information in the Library   Libraries are where you'll find business books, databases, periodicals, and other helpful materials. In addition, you'll find your most important resource: librarians. Reference librarians are trained in research techniques, and they spend their days managing information and helping people find materials. They can show you how to use the library's many databases, and they can help you find obscure information. Whether you're trying to locate information in printed materials, on databases, or on microfilm, each type of resource serves a specific function.

Reference librarians are there to assist you with your research efforts.

At the library, you can find most of the information you need either in print format, in databases or other electronic media, or on microfilm.

Business Books   Books are less timely than journal articles, but they provide in-depth coverage of a variety of business topics. Because of budgetary constraints, libraries must be selective about the books they put on their shelves; so you may have better luck finding specialized information at company libraries or at a college library (assuming the school offers courses in those subjects).

COMPANY, INDUSTRY, AND PRODUCT RESOURCES (PRINT)

- *Brands and Their Companies/Companies and Their Brands.* Data on over 281,000 consumer products and 51,000 manufacturers, importers, marketers, and distributors.
- *Corporate and Industry Research Reports (CIRR).* Collection of industry reports produced by industry analysts for investment purposes. Unique coverage includes industry profitability, comparative company sales, market share, profits, and forecasts.
- *Directory of Companies Required to File Annual Reports with the Securities and Exchange Commission.* Listing of U.S. publicly held firms.
- *Dun's Directory of Service Companies.* Information on 205,000 U.S. service companies.
- *Forbes.* Annual Report on American Industry published in first January issue of each year.
- *Hoover's Handbook of American Business.* Profiles of over 500 public and private corporations.
- *Manufacturing USA.* Data series listing nearly 25,000 companies, including detailed information on over 450 manufacturing industries.
- *Market Share Report.* Data covering products and service categories originating from trade journals, newsletters, and magazines.
- *Moody's Industry Review.* Data on 4,000 companies in about 150 industries. Ranks companies within industry by five financial statistics (revenue, net income, total assets, cash and marketable securities, and long-term debt) and includes key performance ratios.
- *Moody's Manuals.* Weekly manual of financial data in each of six business areas: industrials, transportation, public utilities, banks, finance, and over-the-counter (OTC) industrials.
- *Service Industries USA.* Comprehensive data on 2,100 services grouped into over 150 industries.
- *Standard & Poor's Industry Surveys.* Concise investment profiles for a broad range of industries. Coverage is extensive, with a focus on current situation and outlook. Includes some summary data on major companies in each industry.
- *Standard & Poor's Register of Corporations, Directors and Executives.* Index of major U.S. and international corporations. Lists officers, products, sales volume, and number of employees.
- *Thomas's Register of American Manufacturers.* Information on thousands of U.S. manufacturers indexed by company name and product.
- *U.S. Industrial Outlook.* Annual profiles of several hundred key U.S. industries. Each industry report covers several pages and includes tables, graphs, and charts that visually demonstrate how an industry compares with similar industries, including important component growth factors and other economic measures.

COMPANY, INDUSTRY, AND PRODUCT RESOURCES (ONLINE)

- **Hoover's Online** www.hoovers.com. Profiles of publicly listed U.S. companies traded on major stock exchanges and more than 1,200 large private companies. Search by ticker symbol, company name, location, industry, or sales.
- **NAICS Codes** www.census.gov/epcd/naics/naicstb2.txt. North American Industry Classification System.
- **SEC filings** www.sec.gov.edgarhp.htm. SEC filings including 10Ks, 10Qs, annual reports, and prospectuses for 35,000 U.S. public firms.
- **Fortune.com** www.fortune.com. Brief profiles of the 500 leading companies in the U.S.
- **Yahoo!** dir.yahoo.com/Business. More than 50 categories of information with dozens of links.

DIRECTORIES AND INDEXES (PRINT)

- *Books in Print.* Index of 425,000 books in 62,000 subject categories currently available from U.S. publishers. Indexed by author and title.
- *Directories in Print.* Information on over 16,000 business and industrial directories.
- *Encyclopedia of Associations.* Index of thousands of associations listed by broad subject category, specific subject, association, and location.
- *Reader's Guide to Periodical Literature.* Periodical index categorized by subject and author.
- *Ulrich's International Periodicals Directory.* Listings by title, publisher, editor, phone, and address of over 140,000 publications such as popular magazines, trade journals, government documents, and newspapers. Great for locating hard-to-find trade publications.

PEOPLE (PRINT)

- *Dun & Bradstreet's Reference Book of Corporate Management.* Professional histories of people serving as the principal officers and directors of more than 12,000 U.S. companies.
- *Who's Who in America.* Biographies of living U.S. citizens who have gained prominence in their fields. Related book, *Who's Who in the World*, covers global achievers.

Figure 10–10
Major Business Resources

(continued)

TRADEMARKS (PRINT/ONLINE)

- *Official Gazette of the United States Patent and Trademark Office.* Weekly publication (one for trademarks and one for patents) providing official record of newly assigned trademarks and patents, product descriptions and product names.
- **United States Patent and Trademark Office** www.uspto.gov. Trademark and patent information records.

STATISTICS AND FACTS (PRINT)

- *Industry Norms and Key Business Ratios (Dun & Bradstreet).* Industry, financial, and performance ratios.
- *Information Please Almanac.* Compilation of broad-range statistical data with strong focus on labor force.
- *Robert Morris Associates' Annual Statement Studies.* Industry, financial, and performance ratios.
- *Statistical Abstract of the United States.* U.S. economic, social, political, and industrial statistics.
- *The World Almanac and Book of Facts.* Facts on economic, social, educational, and political events for major countries.

STATISTICS AND FACTS (ONLINE)

- **Bureau of Economic Analysis** www.bea.doc.gov. Large collection of economic and government data.
- **FedStats** www.fedstats.gov. Access to full range of statistics and information from over 70 U.S. government agencies.
- **STAT-USA** www.stat-usa.gov. Large collection of economic and government data.
- **U.S. Census Bureau** www.census.gov. Demographic data on both consumers and businesses based on 1990 census.
- **U.S. Bureau of Labor Statistics** www.bls.gov. Extensive national and regional information on labor and business, including employment, industry growth, productivity, Consumer Price Index (CPI), and overall U.S. economy.

COMMERCIAL DATABASES (REQUIRE SUBSCRIPTIONS)

- **ABI Inform.** Database of over 1,500 scholarly and trade journals in business, management, industry, and economics (full text and abstracts).
- **Dialog.** Over 900 main databases that include areas such as business and finance, news and media, medicine, pharmaceuticals, reference, social sciences, government and regulation, science and technology, and more.
- **Electric Library.** Hundreds of full-text newspaper, magazine, newswire and articles, plus maps and photographs.
- **LEXIS-NEXIS.** More than 1.4 billion documents in more than 8,000 databases.
- **UMI ProQuest Direct.** More than 5,000 journals, magazines, newspapers, and other information sources.

Figure 10–10
(Continued)

Electronic databases contain journal articles that are more timely than books.

Electronic Databases   An **electronic database** is a computer-searchable collection of information, often categorized by subject areas such as business, law, science, technology, and education. When using an electronic database, try to get a list of the periodicals or publications it includes, as well as the time period it covers. Then fill in the gaps for any important resources not in the database.

Newspapers can be one of the more up-to-date resources.

Newspapers   Libraries subscribe to only a select number of newspapers and store only a limited number of back issues in print. However, they frequently subscribe to databases containing newspaper articles in full text (available online, on CD-ROM, or on microfilm). In addition, most newspapers today offer full-text or limited editions of their papers on the Internet.

Periodicals are another timely resource for business information.

Periodicals   Most periodicals fall into one of four categories: (1) popular magazines (not intended for business, professional, or academic use), (2) trade journals (providing news and other facts about particular professions, industries, and occupations), (3) business magazines (covering all major industries and professions), and (4) academic journals (publishing data from professional researchers and educators). To locate a certain periodical, check your library's database.

Directories offer basic information on organizations and companies.

Directories   More than 14,000 directories are published in the United States—covering everything from accountants to zoos. Many include membership information for all kinds of special-interest groups. For instance, business directories provide entries for companies, products, and individuals, and they include the name of key contact persons. Directories are considered invaluable for marketers, job seekers, and others who need to establish a prospect list.

Almanacs and Statistical Resources   Almanacs are handy guides to factual and statistical information about countries, politics, the labor force, and so on. Also check out the *Statistical Abstract of the United States* (published annually by the U.S. Department of Commerce). This resource contains statistics about life, work, government, population patterns, health issues, business, crime, and the environment.

> Almanacs offer statistics about countries, politics, and more.

Government Publications   For information on a law, a court decision, or current population patterns and business trends, consult government documents. A librarian can direct you to the information you want. You'll need the name of the government agency you're interested in and some identification for the specific information you need (Safe Drinking Water Act of 1974, *Price v. Shell Oil*, or latest census figures). If you know the date and name of a specific publication, the search will be easier.

> The government tracks legal, population, and business trends.

Finding Information on the Internet   The most popular source of company and industry information today is the Internet, with business information that ranges from current news and industry trends to company-related data on financial performance, products, goals, and employment. You must remember that anyone (including you) can post anything on a Web site. No one filters it, checks it for accuracy, or screens authors about why they are placing it on the Internet. Before you seriously surf the Web for business information, learn a bit about your topic from journals, books, and commercial databases. You'll be able to detect skewed or erroneous information, and you can be more selective about which Web sites and documents you choose to use as resources.

> When doing research on the Internet you need to be selective, because anyone can publish anything and no one checks the information for accuracy.

One good place to start on the Web is the Internet Public Library at www.ipl.org. Modeled after a real library, this site provides you with a carefully selected collection of links to high-quality business resources. If you are looking for specific company information, your best source may be the company's Web site (if it maintains one). Company sites generally include detailed information about the firm's products, services, history, mission, strategy, financial performance, and employment needs. Many sites provide links to related company information, such as SEC filings, press releases, and more.

> You can find all kinds of information about a company on its Web site.

You can obtain press releases and general company news from news release sites such as PRNewswire (www.prnewswire.com) and Business Wire (www.businesswire.com). These sites offer free databases of news releases from companies subscribing to their services. If you subscribe to a commercial online database system, you can also use the Internet to access information from the provider's database.

> Press releases and general news about companies are also available at news release sites and through online databases.

The Web doesn't have everything. There may be nothing about small organizations, or perhaps just their address and phone number. And even if the information exists on the Web, you may not be able to find it. Web pages number over 320 million, but even the best search engines index only 100 million of those pages.[15]

Searchers can get the most dependable results from well-known, commercially backed search engines, which are likely to be well maintained and upgraded (see Table 10–3). Most have simple or advanced search features, plus extras such as interactive maps and weather, travel information, phone and e-mail directories, and company profiles.

Searching a Database   Even if search engines turn up what you're looking for, they'll also turn up a mountain of stuff you don't need. Narrow your results by following these tips to conduct an effective database search[16]:

> By following a few guidelines, you can improve your database search results.

◆ **Select appropriate databases.** You'll want a good business database. However, journals on your topic may be in a database that also includes journals on psychology, computers, or medicine.

◆ **Use multiple search engines.** Not all search engines are the same. Don't limit yourself to a single search engine, especially if you're looking for less-popular topics. To improve your results, read the help file and learn how the search engine works.

Table 10–3 Major Search Engines	
Site	**Description**
Alta Vista	www.altavista.com **Indexes data from millions of Web pages and articles from thousands of Usenet newsgroups.**
Excite	www.excite.com **All-purpose site loaded with options.**
Fedstats	www.fedstats.gov/search.html **Simultaneously queries 14 federal agencies for specified statistics and numerical data.**
Google	www.google.com **A simple directory that is especially useful for finding homepages of companies and organizations.**
GoTo	www.goto.com **Companies can pay to be placed higher in this engine's search results.**
HotBot	www.hotbot.com ***Wired* magazine packs all kinds of searching possibilities into this site.**
LookSmart	www.looksmart.com **Closest rival to Yahoo! in terms of being a human-compiled directory. Choose "Your Town" for local directories.**
Lycos	www.lycos.com **One of the oldest of the major search engines, provides short abstracts for each match.**
Northern Light	www.northernlight.com **Categorizes returns by subject. Has "special collection" of over 2 million documents not readily accessible to search engine spiders.**
WebCrawler	www.webcrawler.com **Either search the entire site or browse any of the preselected categories.**
Yahoo!	www.yahoo.com **The oldest major Web site directory, listing over 500,000 sites.**

◆ **Translate concepts into key words and phrases.** For instance, if you want to determine the "effect of TQM on company profits," you should select the key words *TQM, total quality management, profits, sales, companies,* and *corporations.* Remember, use synonyms or word equivalents whenever possible, and use quotation marks around phrases to look for the entire phrase instead of separate words.

◆ **Use a short phrase or single term rather than a long phrase.** Search engines look for the words exactly as you key them in. If the words occur in an entry but not in the same order, you may miss relevant hits.

◆ **Do not use stopwords.** Stopwords are words the computer disregards and will not search for. Database documentation will identify any stopwords in addition to the common ones: *a, an, the, of, by, with, for,* and *to.*

◆ **Do not use words contained in the name of the database.** Using words such as *business* or *finance* in the ABI Inform database will work, but they appear so often that searching for them slows the processing time and adds no precision to your results.

◆ **Use variations of your terms.** Use abbreviations (*CEO, CPA*), synonyms (*man, male*), related terms (*child, adolescent, youth*), different spellings (*dialog, dialogue*), singular and plural forms (*man, men*), nouns and adjectives (*manager, management, managerial*), and open and compound forms (*online, on line, on-line*).

◆ **Specify a logical relationship between the key words.** Must the document contain both *companies* and *corporations,* or is either one fine? Must it contain both *profits* and *companies,* or should it contain *TQM* or *total quality management* and *profits* or *sales?*

Table 10–4 Improving Your Search Results

Search Operator	Effect	Strategy	Results
AND	Narrows results. Searches for records containing both the words it separates. Words separated by AND may be anywhere in the document—and far away from each other.	Rock AND roll	Music
OR	Broadens results. Searches for records containing either of the words it separates. A scattergun search that turns up a lot of matches. Not particularly precise.	Rock OR Roll	Igneous rocks; gemstones; crescent rolls; music
NOT	Limits results. Searches for records containing the first word(s) but not the second one.	Snow skiing NOT water skiing	Snow skiing; cross-country skiing
NEAR OR WITHIN	Proximity operator. Searches for words that all appear in a specified word range.	Snow NEAR 2 skiing	Results in which *skiing* is within 2 words of *snow*
ADJ	Adjacency operator. Searches for records in which second word immediately follows first word (two words are next to each other).	Ski ADJ Patrol	Ski patrol
?	Wildcard operator for single character. Matches any one character.	Ski?	Skit; skid; skin; skip
*	Wildcard operator for string of characters. Matches any number of characters.	Ski*	Ski; skiing; skies; skill; skirt; skit; skinny; skimpy
""	Exact match. Searches for string of words placed within quotation marks.	"1999 budget deficit"	1999 budget deficit

◆ **Evaluate the precision and quality of your results to refine your search if necessary.** If you end up with more than 60 to 100 links to sort through, refine your search. If your first page of results doesn't have something of interest, you've entered the wrong words or too few words. Also pay attention to whether you're searching in the title, subject, or document field of the database. Each will return different results.

◆ **Use Boolean operators.** Narrow or broaden your search by including AND, OR, or NOT (See Table 10–4). Many search engines automatically include Boolean operators in their strategies even though you can't see them on the screen, so either insert your own (which should override automatic operators) or review the instructions for your search engine.

◆ **Use proximity operators.** To specify how close one of your key words should be to another, use a proximity operator such as NEAR. For example, the search phrase "marketing NEAR/2 organizations" means that *marketing* must be within two words of *organizations*.

◆ **Use wildcards.** Wildcard characters help you find plurals and alternate spellings of your key words. For example, by using a question mark in the word *organi?ations*, you'll find documents with both *organisations* (British spelling) and *organizations*. Similarly, by using an asterisk at the end of *chair**, you'll find *chairman, chairperson, chairs,* and *chairlift*.

Keeping Track of Your Progress As you find and review your secondary source materials, take some brief notes to keep track of your progress. These are not the detailed notes you'll be taking later, but you'll need enough information to evaluate and finalize your

The goal of your initial note taking is to keep track of your sources so that you can select the best ones to use.

sources. For instance, write down enough information to distinguish one source from the next. Identify the main idea or theme of each source, and perhaps write a brief comment about which subquestion the article addresses and whether the information was helpful. For example: "Discusses current franchise trends with statistics on number of new franchises started each year," or "Chapter 3 gives itemized steps for investigating franchise opportunities."

When using the Internet, note relevant Web sites by bookmarking, downloading, or printing out the actual Web pages. If the library database you're using includes material in full text, print out helpful articles; otherwise print out a copy of your search results and ask the librarian for assistance in finding the articles listed.

To record your comments, use note cards or Post-It Notes, or write on a printout or photocopy of the actual material. Develop a system that works for you. In addition, prepare a detailed bibliography of each source you intend to use later. Adopt one of the systems explained in Appendix B, "Documentation of Report Sources." If you photocopy an article, be sure to record on the photocopy all the bibliographic material you'll need to properly cite that source later on.

Gather Primary Information

As Michael Dell can tell you, sometimes the information you need is not available from secondary sources, or you may need information beyond what is covered in secondary sources. In that case, you must go out into the real world to gather the necessary information yourself. Five methods of collecting primary data are examining documents, making observations, conducting experiments, surveying people, and conducting interviews.

Documents, Observations, and Experiments Often the most useful primary references are internal sources, such as company sales reports, memos, balance sheets, income statements, policy statements, brochures, newsletters, annual reports, correspondence with customers or suppliers, and contracts. A great deal of information is often stored in company databases; by scouring company files, you can often piece together an accurate, factual, historical record from the tidbits of evidence revealed in various letters, memos, and reports.

A single document may be both a secondary source and a primary source. For example, when citing summaries of financial and operational data from an annual report, you're using the report as a secondary source; that is, somebody has already summarized the information for you. However, the same annual report would be considered a primary source if you were analyzing its design features, comparing it with annual reports from other years, or comparing it with reports from other companies.

Making informal observations is another method of gathering primary information in business. For instance, you can observe people performing their jobs or observe other business operations. Observation is a useful technique when you're studying objects, physical activities, processes, the environment, or human behavior. However, it can be expensive and time consuming, and the value of the observation depends on the reliability of the observer.

Experiments can be an excellent source of primary information. This method is far more common in technical fields than in general business. That's because an experiment requires extensive, accurate, and measurable manipulation of the factors involved—not only tweaking those variables being tested but also controlling those variables that aren't being tested. This sort of experiment management is often expensive.

Surveys One of the best ways to get information is to ask people with relevant experience and opinions. Surveys include everything from the one-time, one-on-one interview to the distribution of thousands of questionnaires. When prepared and conducted properly, surveys will tell you what a cross section of people think about a given topic.

Surveys are only useful when they're reliable and valid. A survey is *reliable* if it produces identical results when repeated. A survey is *valid* if it measures what it's intended to measure. One of the most crucial elements of a survey is the questionnaire.

(margin notes)

Conduct primary research by collecting basic information yourself.

Documentary evidence and historical records are sources of primary data.

Observation applies your five senses and your judgment to the investigation.

Experiments can be effective, but they are expensive.

QUESTION TYPE	EXAMPLE
Open-ended	How would you describe the flavor of this ice cream?
Either-or	Do you think this ice cream is too rich? _____ Yes _____ No
Multiple choice	Which description best fits the taste of this ice cream? (Choose only one.) a. Delicious b. Too fruity c. Too sweet d. Too intensely flavored e. Bland f. Stale
Scale	Please mark an X on the scale to indicate how you perceive the texture of this ice cream. Too light Light Creamy Too creamy
Checklist	Which flavors of ice cream have you had in the past 12 months? (Check all that apply.) _____ Vanilla _____ Chocolate _____ Strawberry _____ Chocolate chip _____ Coffee
Ranking	Rank these flavors in order of your preference, from 1 (most preferred) to 5 (least preferred): _____ Vanilla _____ Cherry _____ Maple nut _____ Chocolate ripple _____ Coconut
Short-answer	In the past month how many times did you buy ice cream in the supermarket? _____ In the past month how many times did you buy ice cream in ice cream shops? _____

Figure 10–11
Types of Survey Questions

Begin developing your questionnaire by making a list of the points you need to determine. Then break these points into specific questions, choosing an appropriate type of question for each point. (Figure 10–11 shows various types of survey questions.) The following guidelines will help you produce results that are both valid and reliable[17]:

Developing an effective survey questionnaire requires care and skill.

◆ **Provide clear instructions.** Respondents need to know exactly how to fill out your questionnaire.

◆ **Keep the questionnaire short and easy to answer.** Ask only questions that are relevant to your research. Remember that people are most likely to respond if they can complete your questionnaire within 10 to 15 minutes.

◆ **Formulate questions that provide easily tabulated or analyzed answers.** Remember, numbers and facts are easier to summarize than opinions.

◆ **Avoid leading questions.** Questions that lead to a particular answer bias your survey. If you ask, "Do you prefer that we stay open in the evenings for customer convenience?" you'll get a "yes" answer. Instead, ask, "What time of day do you normally do your shopping?"

◆ **Ask only one thing at a time.** A compound question such as "Do you read books and magazines regularly?" doesn't allow for respondents who read one but not the other.

◆ **Pretest the questionnaire.** Have a sample group identify questions that are subject to misinterpretation.

If you're mailing your questionnaire rather than administering it in person, include a persuasive cover letter that explains why you're conducting the research. You must convince your readers that responding is important. Remember that even under the best of circumstances, you may get no more than a 10 to 20 percent response.

Interviews   Getting information straight from an expert can be a great way to research a report. **Interviews** are planned conversations with a predetermined purpose that involve asking and answering questions. Although they are frequently overlooked, interviews are an effective method of gathering information. However, before you decide to do one, ask yourself whether an interview is really the best way to get the information you need.

In a typical information interview, the interviewer seeks facts that bear on a decision or that contribute to basic understanding. The action is controlled by the interviewer, who asks a list of questions designed to elicit information from the interviewee. When you are conducting an interview, it's important to decide in advance what kind of information you want and how you will use it. This sort of planning saves you time and builds goodwill with the people you interview.

Planning Interviews   Planning an interview is similar to planning any other form of communication. You begin by analyzing your purpose, learning about the other person, and formulating your main idea. Then you decide on the length, style, and organization of the interview.

Good interviews have an opening, a body, and a close. The opening establishes rapport and orients the interviewee to the remainder of the session. You might begin by introducing yourself, asking a few polite questions, and then explaining the purpose and ground rules of the interview. The body of the interview is used for asking questions. In the close of the interview you summarize the outcome, preview what will come next, and underscore the rapport that has been established.

Preparing Interview Questions   The answers you receive are influenced by the types of questions you ask, by the way you ask them, and by your subject's cultural and language background. Race, gender, age, educational level, and social status are all influential factors, so know your subject before you start writing questions.[18] In addition, be aware of ethical implications. For example, asking someone to divulge personal information about a co-worker may be asking that person to make an unethical choice. Always be careful about confidentiality, politics, and other sensitive issues.

Consider providing a list of questions a day or two before the interview, especially if you'd like to quote your subject in writing or if your questions might require your subject to conduct research or think extensively about the answers. Receiving your questions early will give your subject time to prepare more complete (and therefore more helpful) answers. Consider tape-recording the interview if your topic is complex or if you plan to quote or paraphrase the interviewee in a written document.

Interview questions can be categorized into four types. **Open-ended questions** invite the interviewee to offer an opinion, not just a yes, a no, or a one-word answer: "What do you think your company wants most from suppliers?" Such questions help you learn the reasons behind a decision rather than just the facts. However, they diminish your control of the interview.

Objective

5

Define information interviews and list four types of interview questions.

An interview is any planned conversation that has a specific purpose and involves two or more people.

Effective interviewers develop a communication plan.

Organize an interview much as you would organize a written message.

Sometimes you'll want to provide a list of questions days before the interview.

Four basic types of interview questions:
• Open-ended questions
• Direct open-ended questions
• Closed-ended questions
• Restatement questions

Direct open-ended questions suggest a response: "What have you done about smoothing out the intercultural clashes in your department?" These questions give you more control while still giving the interviewee some freedom in framing a response.

Closed-ended questions require yes or no answers or call for short responses: "Did you meet your sales quota?" Such questions produce specific information, save time, require less effort from the interviewee, and eliminate bias and prejudice in answers. On the other hand, they also limit the respondent's initiative and may prevent important information from being revealed.

Restatement questions mirror a respondent's previous answer and invite the respondent to expand on that answer: "You said you dislike sales quotas. Is that correct?" They also signal to the interviewee that you're paying attention.

The following guidelines will help you come up with a great set of interview questions:[19]

◆ **Think about sequence.** Arrange your questions in a way that helps uncover layers of information or that helps the subject tell you a complete story.

◆ **Rate your questions and highlight the ones you really need answers to.** If you start to run out of time during the interview, you may have to skip less important questions.

◆ **Ask smart questions.** If you ask a question that your subject perceives to be less than intelligent, the interview could go downhill in a hurry.

◆ **Use a mix of question types.** Vary the pacing of your interview by using open-ended, direct open-ended, closed-ended, and restatement questions.

◆ **Limit the number of questions.** Don't try to cover more questions than you have time for. People can speak at a rate of about 125 to 150 words (about one paragraph) per minute. If you're using a mix of question types, you can probably handle about 20 questions in a half-hour. Remember that open-ended questions take longer to answer than other types do.

◆ **Edit your questions.** Try to make your questions as neutral and as easy to understand as possible. Then practice them several times to make sure you're ready for the interview.

Processing Interview Information   When you've concluded the interview, take a few moments to write down your thoughts, go over your notes, and organize your material. Look for important themes, helpful facts or statistics, and direct quotes. Fill in any blanks while the interview is fresh in your mind. If you made a tape recording, *transcribe* it (take down word for word what the person said) or take notes from the tape just as you would while listening to someone in person.

> Carefully review your interview notes immediately after the interview and fill in the gaps before you forget.

Interviews don't necessarily have to take place in person. As more and more people come online, e-mail interviews are becoming more common. Perhaps one of the biggest advantages of an e-mail interview is that it gives subjects a chance to think through their responses thoroughly, rather than rushing to fit the time constraints of an in-person interview.[20] (As a reminder of the tasks involved in interviews, see this chapter's "Checklist: Conducting Effective Information Interviews.")

> Conducting interviews by e-mail is becoming increasingly popular.

Evaluate and Finalize Your Sources

Be selective when choosing your actual sources from the piles of material you've just gathered. Avoid dated or biased material. If possible, check on who collected the data, the methods they used, their qualifications, and their professional reputations.[21] Common sense will help you judge the credibility of the sources you plan to use.

To make the best selections, ask yourself the following questions about each piece of material:

> Ask questions about the reference works you use, such as
> • Who collected the data? How?
> • What are the authors' qualifications and reputations?
> • Is the source up to date?
> • Is the information objective?

◆ **Does the source have a reputation for honesty and reliability?** Naturally, you'll feel more comfortable using information from a publication that has a reputation for accuracy. But don't let your guard down completely; even the finest reporters and editors make mistakes. Find out how the publication accepts articles and whether it has an editorial board.

Checklist: Conducting Effective Information Interviews

Preparing Your Interview

✓ Analyze your purpose, goals, and audience.
✓ Determine the needs of your interviewee and gather background information.
✓ Outline your interview on the basis of your goals, audience, and interview category.
✓ Set the level of formality.
✓ Choose a structured or an unstructured approach.
✓ Formulate questions as clearly and concisely as possible.
✓ Ask questions in an order that helps your subject tell you a complete story.
✓ Ask intelligent questions that show you've done your homework.
✓ Use a mix of question types.
✓ Select a time and a site.
✓ Inform the interviewee of the nature of the interview and the agenda to be covered.
✓ Provide a list of questions in advance if the interviewee will need time to research and formulate quality answers.

Conducting Your Interview

✓ Be on time for the interview appointment.
✓ Remind the interviewee of the purpose and format.
✓ Clear the taking of notes or the use of a tape recorder with the interviewee.
✓ Use your ears and eyes to pick up verbal and nonverbal cues.
✓ Follow the stated agenda, but be willing to explore relevant subtopics.
✓ Close the interview by restating the interviewee's key ideas and by reviewing the actions, goals, and tasks that each of you has agreed to.

Following Up

✓ Write a thank-you memo or letter that provides the interviewee with a record of the meeting.
✓ Review notes and revise them while the interview is fresh in your mind.
✓ Transcribe tape recordings.
✓ Monitor progress by keeping in touch with your interviewee.

◆ **Is the source potentially biased?** Depending on what an organization stands for, its messages may be written with a certain bias—which is neither bad nor unethical. The Tobacco Institute and the American Association of Retired Persons have their own points of view. In order to interpret an organization's information, you need to know its point of view. Its source of funding may also influence its information output.

◆ **Where did the source get its information?** Many secondary sources get their information from other sources, removing you even further from the original data. If a newspaper article says that pollutants in a local river dropped by 50 percent since last year, the reporter probably didn't measure those pollutants directly. That information was obtained from someone else.

◆ **Can you verify the material independently?** A good way to uncover bias or a mistake is to search for the same information from another source. Verification can be particularly important when the information goes beyond simple facts to include projections, interpretations, and estimates.

◆ **Is the material current?** Check the publication date of a source, and make sure you are using the most current information available. Timeliness is especially important if you are using statistics or citing law.

◆ **Is the author credible?** Find out whether the person or the publisher is well known in the field. Is the author an amateur? Merely someone with an opinion to air?

◆ **What is the purpose of the material?** Was the material designed to inform others of new research, summarize existing research, advocate for a position, or stimulate discussion? Was it designed to promote or sell a product? Be sure to distinguish between advertising and informing.

◆ **Is the material complete?** Determine whether the information you have is the entire text or a selection from another document. If it's a selection, which parts were excluded? Do you need more detail?

◆ **Do the source's claims stand up to scrutiny?** Step back and ask yourself whether the information makes sense. If a researcher claims that the market for a particular product will triple in the next five years, ask yourself what would have to happen for that prediction to come true. Will three times as many customers buy the product? Will existing customers buy three times more than they currently buy? Why? Is this information relevant to your needs?

You probably won't have time to conduct a thorough background check on all your sources, so focus your efforts on the most important or most suspicious pieces of information.

At the end of your evaluation, you should have two piles of information: those sources you want to use and those you have eliminated. Now review the pile of information you intend to use and ask yourself several questions: Do I have enough of the right kind of information to answer all my questions? Do I need more? What type of information am I missing?

How will you know when you have enough information? You have enough when (1) you can answer all the questions that began the research project and (2) you begin noticing that sources are becoming redundant.[22] Too much information can frustrate your note-taking and processing efforts.

Stop when you reach the point at which additional effort provides little new information.

Process Your Information

Once you have selected your sources, it's time to start using what you've found. In some cases you may only need to read the material carefully and meet with your boss to discuss your findings—for example, when you're looking for the answer to a simple question. However, in most cases, you'll be asked to submit a written report or give an oral presentation on your findings. That means you'll need to go through your research and take some extensive notes.

Reading the Material and Taking Notes   Before you start taking notes, organize your research into a logical order. For instance, you might divide the material by subquestions and then divide it chronologically within each grouping. This approach will enable you to focus on a specific topic and read the most current information first. Afterward you can read earlier documents to fill in the history, gather background material, or find older statistics to analyze trends.

When you read a document to take notes, you need not read every word. Read the topic sentences first (generally the first sentence of a business article) to decide whether the paragraph may contain useful information. If it does, then read the entire paragraph.

When your information is a computer printout or a photocopy, feel free to mark up these documents. Highlight key phrases, facts, or segments, and write comments in the margins. Then record your notes on cards or enter them directly into a computer.

The recording system that most students use (and many instructors recommend) is taking notes on three-by-five-inch index cards. Note cards are easy to use, carry, sort, and arrange. Until recently, people generally agreed that taking notes on computer was slower and more cumbersome than using index cards. Computers simply didn't have the tools to make this task easy, and they tended to get in the way more than they helped. However, the portability of laptops and advances in software make it easier today to take notes by computer. By recording notes in electronic format instead of on handwritten cards, the researcher can easily search for words (using the "find" function), sort the notes by column headings, and copy information directly into the document draft.

You may find that the best solution is using a combination of index cards (to capture information while you're reading it) and computer software (to manage the information once you've captured it or to take notes directly from the source). Whichever method you choose, be sure to take complete notes so that you can avoid backtracking to look up something you forgot.

On each note card write only one fact. Indicate whether the information is your own idea, a paraphrase of someone else's idea, or a direct quote (by using quotation marks, ellipses, and brackets as necessary). For your own reference and sorting purposes, write at the top of the card the general subject of the material (either a simple phrase or identifying numbers from your outline). Finally, carefully record bibliographic information so that you can cite the source later. If you are collecting several pieces of information from each source, you might prepare a bibliography card for each source, number the source,

Decide whether a document contains useful information before reading it carefully to take notes.

When deciding whether to use note cards or computer software for taking notes, select whichever system works best for you.

Each note card or computer entry should contain
• Only one fact
• A subject heading
• Complete source information or a cross-reference to bibliography cards

and then use the numbers to cross-reference your note cards. Thus notes taken from source 75 will be written on notecards numbered 75.1, 75.2, and so on.

Quoting and Paraphrasing   Use direct quotations when the original language will enhance your argument or when rewording the passage would lessen its impact. However, try not to quote sources at great length. Too much quoting creates a choppy patchwork of varying styles and gives the impression that you've lost control of your material.

One way to avoid such choppiness is to **paraphrase** material, or express it in your own words. When you paraphrase, you present information to your reader in a fresh, condensed manner that demonstrates your complete understanding of the material. In fact, paraphrasing may actually increase your comprehension of the source material, because when you recast a passage, you have to think carefully about its meaning—more carefully than if you merely copied it word for word.[23]

To paraphrase effectively, follow these tips:[24]

- Reread the original passage until you fully understand its meaning.
- Record your paraphrase on a note card or in an electronic format.
- Use business language and jargon that your audience is familiar with.
- Check your version with the original source to verify that you have not altered the meaning.
- Use quotation marks to identify any unique terms or phrases you have borrowed exactly from the source.
- Record the source (including the page number) on your note card so that you can give proper credit if you use this material in your report.

In short, good paraphrasing accomplishes three goals: (1) It's shorter than the original text, (2) it's presented in your own words, and (3) it does not alter or distort the meaning of the original text.[25]

Whether you paraphrase or use direct quotes, maintain your credibility and ethics by giving proper credit to the original source.

Documenting Sources and Giving Credit   Whenever you quote or paraphrase, you are using someone else's words or ideas. Doing so without proper credit is **plagiarism.** You can avoid plagiarism by documenting the original source using one of the systems explained in Appendix B, "Documentation of Report Sources." Documenting your sources through footnotes, endnotes, or some similar system is necessary for books, articles, tables, charts, diagrams, song lyrics, scripted dialogue, letters, speeches—anything that you take from someone else. Even if you paraphrase the material, it's best to give credit to the person you obtained the original information.

However, you do not have to cite a source for general knowledge or for specialized knowledge that's generally known among your readers. For example, everyone knows that Franklin Roosevelt was elected to the presidency of the United States four times. You can say so on your own authority, even if you've read an article in which the author says the same thing. Moreover, even though copyright law covers printed materials, audiovisual material, many forms of artistic expression, computer programs, maps, mailing lists, and even answering machine messages, it does not protect

- Titles, names, short phrases, and slogans
- Familiar symbols or designs
- Lists of ingredients or contents
- Ideas, procedures, methods, systems, processes, concepts, principles, discoveries, or devices (although it does cover their description, explanation, or illustration)

A work is considered copyrighted as soon as it's put into fixed form, even if it hasn't been registered.[26]

Merely crediting the source is not always enough. According to the *fair use doctrine* you can use other people's work only as long as you don't unfairly prevent them from ben-

(margin notes)

Express material in your own words unless quoting the original language will have a greater impact.

Always give proper credit when you use someone else's material or ideas.

It's not necessary to give source credit for material that is general knowledge.

The fair use doctrine offers guidelines for determining how copyrighted material may be used.

efiting as a result. For example, if you reproduce someone else's copyrighted questionnaire in a report you're writing, even if you identify the source thoroughly you're preventing the author from selling a copy of that questionnaire to your readers.

In general, avoid relying to such a great extent on someone else's work. However, when you can't avoid it, contact the copyright holder (usually the author or publisher) for permission to reprint. You'll usually be asked to pay a fee.

Analyze Your Data

By themselves, the data you've collected won't offer much meaning or insight. You'll need to search for relationships among the facts and the bits of evidence you've compiled. This analysis allows you to interpret your findings and thus answer the questions or solve the problem that instigated your report.

Much of the information you compile during the research phrase will be in numerical form. However, Michael Dell can tell you that such statistical information in its raw state is of little practical value. It must be manipulated so that you and your readers can interpret its significance. Look at the data from various angles and try to detect patterns by fitting pieces together to form tentative conclusions. This process enables you to answer the questions you generated when defining the problem. As you proceed with your analysis, either verify or reject your conclusions.

One useful way of looking at numerical data is to find the **average,** which is a number that represents a group of numbers. Three useful averages are shown in Table 10–5. The **mean** is the sum of all the items in the group divided by the number of items in that group. The **median** is the "middle of the road" average, or the midpoint of a series (with an equal number of items above and below). The **mode** is the number that occurs more often than any other in your sample. It's the best average for answering a question such as "What is the usual amount?"

It's also helpful to look for a **trend,** a steady upward or downward movement in a pattern of events taking place over time. Trend analysis is common in business. By looking at data over a period of time, you can detect patterns and relationships that will help you answer important questions.

Once you have identified a trend, you'll want to look for a cause. To do this, you could look for a **correlation,** a statistical relationship between two or more variables. For example, if the salespeople with the largest accounts consistently produced higher sales, you might assume that those two factors were related in a predictable way. However, your conclusion might be wrong. Correlations are useful evidence, but they do not necessarily prove a cause-and-effect relationship. To be certain that factors are correlated, you might have to collect more evidence.

Analyze your results by calculating statistics, drawing reasonable and logical conclusions, and, if appropriate, developing a set of recommendations.

The same set of data can be used to produce three kinds of averages: mean, median, and mode.

Trend analysis involves examining data over time in order to detect patterns and relationships.

A correlation is a statistical relationship between two or more variables.

Table 10–5 Three Types of Average: Mean, Median, and Mode		
Salesperson	**Sales**	
Wilson	$3,000	
Green	5,000	
Carrick	6,000	
Wimper	7,000	—— Mean
Keeble	7,500	—— Median
Kemble	8,500	
O'Toole	8,500	Mode
Mannix	8,500	
Caruso	9,000	
Total	$63,000	

Interpret Your Data

Now your data is in a form that both you and your readers can understand. But you're not finished yet. Once you have thoroughly analyzed your information, your next step is to draw conclusions and, if requested, develop recommendations.

Conclusions are interpretations of the facts.

Drawing Conclusions   A **conclusion** is a logical interpretation of the facts in your report. Reaching good conclusions based on the evidence at hand is one of the most important skills you can develop in your business career. A sound conclusion

- ◆ **Must fulfill the original statement of purpose.** After all, drawing a conclusion is why you took on the project in the first place.
- ◆ **Must be based strictly on the information included in the rest of the report.** Consider all the information in your report. Don't ignore anything—even if it doesn't support your conclusion. Moreover, don't introduce any new information in your conclusion. (After all, if something is that important, it should be in the body of your report.)
- ◆ **Must be logical.** A logical conclusion is one that follows accepted patterns of reasoning.

Check the logic that underlies your conclusions.

Even though conclusions need to be logical, they may not automatically flow from the evidence. Most business decisions require assumptions and judgment; relatively few are based strictly on the facts. Your personal values or the organization's values may also influence your conclusions; just be sure that you're aware of how these biases affect your judgment. Also, don't expect all team members to examine the evidence and arrive at the same conclusion. One of the reasons for bringing additional people into a decision is to gain their unique perspectives and experiences.

Recommendations are suggestions for action.

Developing Recommendations   Whereas a conclusion interprets the facts, a **recommendation** suggests what to do about the facts. The difference between a conclusion and a recommendation can be seen in the following example:

CONCLUSION	RECOMMENDATION
I conclude that, on the basis of its track record and current price, this company is an attractive buy.	I recommend that we write a letter to the president offering to buy the company at a 10 percent premium over the market value of its stock.

Good recommendations are
- Practical
- Acceptable to readers
- Explained in enough detail for readers to take action

When you've been asked to take the final step and translate your conclusions into recommendations, be sure to make the relationship between them clear. Remember, recommendations are inappropriate in a report when you're not expected to supply them. But when you do develop recommendations of your own, try not to let your assumptions and personal values influence them. To be credible, recommendations must be based on logical analysis and sound conclusions. They must also be practical and acceptable to your readers, the people who have to make the recommendations work. Finally, when making a recommendation, be certain that you have adequately described the steps that come next. Don't leave your readers scratching their heads and saying, "This all sounds good, but what do I do on Monday morning?"

PLANNING BUSINESS REPORTS—ADAPTATION

Objective 6

Clarify what it means to adapt your report to your audience.

Now you're ready to think about how you want to present your findings to others. In one respect, reports are no different from other business messages: You need to establish a good relationship with your audience, and you must select a channel and medium that are appropriate to your audience and your purpose.

Establish a Good Relationship with Your Audience

Establishing a good relationship with an audience is the same for reports as for other business messages.

Even though reports are meant to be factual, objective, and logical, you still need to focus on your audience to help your reports succeed. To help your audience accept what you're saying, remember the following advice:

✓ *Checklist:* **Planning Business Reports**

Analyzing Business Reports

✓ Define the problem and develop a problem statement.

✓ Limit the scope of your study by clarifying your assignment, factoring the problem, and forming a hypothesis.

✓ Outline issues for investigation, using informative headings in parallel construction.

✓ Develop a statement of purpose that specifically defines why you're preparing the report.

✓ Prepare a work plan to clarify the tasks to be accomplished; describe any products to result from the investigation; review all project assignments, schedules, and resource requirements; and plan for following up after the report has been delivered.

Investigating Business Reports

✓ Find and access secondary information by searching libraries, the Internet, and databases.

✓ Know what you're looking for and keep track of your progress.

✓ Gather primary information from company documents, casual observations, controlled experiments, surveys, and interviews.

✓ Evaluate and finalize your sources by avoiding dated or biased material and by using only credible and reliable sources.

✓ Fill in any information holes by conducting more research as necessary.

✓ Process your information by reading your final sources and taking careful notes.

✓ Document all quoted and paraphrased material.

✓ Analyze your data so that you can interpret your findings.

✓ Draw conclusions that fulfill your original statement of purpose, that are based strictly on the information in your report, and that are logical.

✓ Carefully develop recommendations about how to solve the problem in your report (only if requested to do so).

Adapting Business Reports

✓ Establish a good relationship with your audience, using the "you" attitude, emphasizing the positive, establishing your credibility, being polite, using bias-free language, and projecting the company image.

✓ Select the appropriate channel and medium for your report, whether printed, electronic, or oral.

◆ **Use the "you" attitude.** Show readers how your report answers *their* questions and solves *their* problems.

◆ **Emphasize the positive.** Even if your report recommends a negative action, remember to state the facts and make your recommendations positively. Instead of using a negative tone, "The only way we'll ever strengthen our cash position is to reduce employee spending," use a positive, forthright one: "Reducing employee spending will strengthen our cash position."

◆ **Establish your credibility.** One of the best ways to gain your audience's trust is to be thorough, research all sides of your topic, and document your findings with credible sources.

◆ **Be polite.** Earn your audience's respect by being courteous, kind, and tactful.

◆ **Use bias-free language.** Avoid unethical and embarrassing blunders in language related to gender, race, ethnicity, age, and disability.

◆ **Project the company's image.** Whether your report is intended for people inside or outside the company, be sure to plan how you will adapt your style and your language to reflect the image of your organization.

Select the Appropriate Channel and Medium

As with other business messages, you'll need to select the best format for conveying your report. In some cases a simple letter, memo, or e-mail message will do. At other times you'll need to write a formal report or discuss your findings in an oral presentation. Remember, the medium you choose may be dictated by your report's classification—whether it's authorized, routine, or internal.

See this chapter's "Checklist: Planning Business Reports" to review the tasks and concepts just discussed. Chapter 11 discusses how to organize and write reports and how to incorporate visuals. Chapter 12 explains how to assemble and format formal reports and proposals. Finally, Chapter 13 discusses how to present information orally.

When the San Diego Wild Animal Park's Deirdre Ballou and her colleagues promote a new idea, they carefully plan a comprehensive and convincing business report. In addition, before the team presents any new concept to potential sponsors, they analyze the type and amount of information required so that they can decide whether it would be more effective to convey their message in an oral presentation or in a formal written report.

SUMMARY OF LEARNING OBJECTIVES

1 **Discuss why businesses need reports and how these documents can be classified.** Business reports provide the information that allows internal and external users to make effective decisions and solve business problems. Business reports may travel up or down the organizational hierarchy to link managers with employees. Successful reports are accurate, complete, and unbiased. To be useful, they must present exactly the right kind and amount of information in a clear and convenient manner. Whether printed or electronic, business reports fall into six classifications. They may be (1) authorized or (2) voluntary (depending on their source); they may be (3) special or (4) routine (depending on their frequency); and they may be (5) internal or (6) external (depending on their destination). Reports may also be classified as short or long and as formal or informal.

2 **Distinguish between informational and analytical reports.** Informational reports focus on facts and are intended mainly to inform and educate readers, not to persuade them. Informational reports include those for monitoring and controlling operations (plans, operating reports, personal activity reports), implementing policies and procedures (lasting guidelines, position papers), complying with government regulations, documenting progress (interim progress reports, final reports), and summarizing information. On the other hand, analytical reports analyze and interpret data, summarize the data in logical conclusions, and sometimes make recommendations based on the data. Many analytical reports are intended to persuade readers to accept a decision, action, or recommendation, so information plays a supporting role in these documents. Analytical reports tend to ask "should we or shouldn't we" questions, and they include reports for solving problems, justifying a project or course of action, and obtaining new business or funding (proposals).

3 **Explain the difference between a problem statement and a statement of purpose, and then identify five other elements often included in a formal work plan.** A problem statement defines *what* you're going to investigate, whereas a statement of purpose defines *why* you are preparing your report. Other work plan elements include (1) the tasks to be accomplished and the sequence in which they should be performed; (2) a description

of any product that will result from your study; (3) a review of responsibilities, assignments, schedules, and resource requirements, (4) a working outline, and (5) plans for following up after delivering the report.

4 **Describe six tasks necessary to doing research for business reports.** When investigating business reports, you need to complete six basic tasks. (1) Find and access secondary information by knowing what to look for and where to look (in libraries, on the Internet, and in databases). (2) Gather primary information from company documents, casual observations, formal experiments, surveys, or interviews. (3) Evaluate and finalize your sources by judging their relevance and credibility. (4) Process your information by reading the materials you've gathered, quoting and paraphrasing your sources, and giving credit to those sources. (5) Analyze your data by searching for relationships among the facts and evidence you've gathered. (6) Interpret your data by drawing conclusions and developing recommendations when appropriate.

5 **Define information interviews, and list four types of interview questions.** Interviews are planned conversations with a predetermined purpose that involve asking and answering questions. The interviewer seeks information that may broaden understanding or aid decision-making. Interview questions are of four types: (1) open-ended questions (which invite the person being interviewed to offer an opinion), (2) direct open-ended questions (which suggest a response), (3) closed-ended questions (which require little more than yes or no answers), and restatement questions (which mirror a respondent's previous answer and invite the person to expand on that answer).

6 **Clarify what it means to adapt your report to your audience.** As with other business messages, adapting a report to an audience involves establishing a good relationship and selecting the appropriate channel and medium. When preparing business reports, plan to use the "you" attitude, emphasize the positive, establish your own credibility, be polite, use bias-free language, and project the company's image. Then decide whether to convey your report in a letter, memo, or e-mail message or whether you should emphasize formality with a report that's in the form of a manuscript or an oral presentation.

SOLVING A COMMUNICATION DILEMMA AT DELL COMPUTER CORPORATION

To maintain his company's leading edge in the computer industry, founder Michael Dell and his management team need mountains of information, much of it in the form of reports. These reports must be well planned, must define each problem, and must not only present carefully researched data but also analyze that data. Such reports greatly influence Dell Computer.

During the 1990s, Dell learned the value of gathering and examining information for establishing inventory procedures. He now analyzes average discount rates and inventory turnover, and

with the help of his managers, Dell sets up daily reports for suppliers to provide timely communication about orders and delivery times. In addition, to boost quality standards and limit the number of defective parts, Dell's managers provide regular progress reports to suppliers with quality evaluations.

Reports also play a key role in Dell's e-commerce efforts, selling directly to customers over the Internet. Before setting a goal of selling 50 percent of the company's products through the Web, Dell gathered and analyzed information on overall market growth, the potential of online purchases, and the potential for his company's products. Once he had completed his analysis, Dell was able to introduce customers to the idea of ordering custom-built computers online—and he quickly achieved his Internet sales goals.

Knowing the value of reports, Dell makes sure that his Web site now offers much more than an online ordering center for customers. Through dell.com, company managers can track customer satisfaction levels, measure customer responses, monitor complaint resolutions, and prepare performance reports. In addition, the site enables managers and customer service representatives to establish and maintain direct links with consumers. Consumers can obtain quick responses to e-mail queries and technical questions, find timely information on new products and new technology, and track the progress of their orders at Dell Premier Pages (an Internet-based system customized for each client).

Reports also influence Dell's decisions about entering new markets and offering new products. For example, before expanding into a new country, Dell examines his company's market share, country-by-country and product-by-product, and evaluates the growth potential of the market under consideration. By collecting and analyzing data on customers and products from countries around the world, Dell can forecast potential market penetration and sales force productivity.

Dell also analyzes employee needs to anticipate the company's demand for new workers. He depends on his human resources staff to produce reports that measure turnover and productivity, identify key job openings, define training needs, and map out organizational charts. Dell also analyzes the key qualities of successful employees so that he can spot similar qualities in prospective job candidates.

Overall, Dell depends on more than 4,000 types of analysis to keep his operation running smoothly and to keep his company at the top of the computer industry. "To say that we have become a data-driven company is almost an understatement," Dell says. "Data is the engine that keeps us on track."

Your Mission Michael Dell realizes that to stay on top, Dell Computer must continue to improve customer service at *dell.com*. You are vice president of customer relations, and Dell has asked you to plan a report that will outline ways to increase customer service and satisfaction. You'll need to conduct the necessary research, analyze the findings, and present your recommendations. From the following, choose the best responses, and be prepared to explain why your choices are best.

1. Which of the following represents the most appropriate statement of purpose for this study?
   a. The purpose of this study is to identify any customer service problems at dell.com.
   b. This study answers the following question: "What improvements in customer service can dell.com make in order to increase overall customer satisfaction?"
   c. This study identifies the dell.com customer service representatives who are most responsible for poor customer satisfaction.

   d. This study identifies steps that Dell's customer service representatives should take to change customer service practices at dell.com.

2. You have tentatively identified the following factors for analysis:
   I. To improve customer service, we need to hire more customer service representatives.
      A. Compute competitors' employee-to-sales ratio.
      B. Compute our employee-to-sales ratio.
   II. To improve customer service, we need to hire better customer service representatives.
      A. Assess skill level of competitors' customer service representatives.
      B. Assess skill level of our customer service representatives.
   III. To improve customer service, we need to retrain our customer service representatives.
      A. Review competitors' training programs.
      B. Review our training programs.
   IV. To improve customer service, we need to compensate and motivate our people differently.
      A. Assess competitors' compensation levels and motivational techniques.
      B. Assess our compensation levels and motivational techniques.

   Should you proceed with the investigation on the basis of this preliminary outline, or should you consider other approaches to factoring the problem?
   a. Proceed with this outline.
   b. Do not proceed. Factor the problem by asking customers how they perceive current customer service efforts at dell.com. In addition, ask customer service representatives what they think should be done differently.
   c. Do not proceed. Factor the problem by surveying nonbuyers to find out if current customer service efforts influenced their decision not to buy at dell.com. In addition, ask nonbuyers what they think should be done differently.
   d. Do not proceed. Factor the problem by asking customer service representatives for suggestions on how to improve customer service. In addition, ask nonbuyers and current customers what they think should be done differently.

3. Which of the following work plans is the best option for guiding your study of ways to improve customer service?
   a. Version One

      Statement of Problem: As part of Dell's continuing efforts to offer the most attractive computers in the world, Michael Dell wants to improve customer service at dell.com. The challenge here is to identify service improvements that are meaningful and valuable to the customer without being too expensive or time consuming.

      Purpose and Scope of Work: The purpose of this study is to identify ways to increase customer satisfaction by improving customer service at dell.com. A four-member study team, composed of the vice president of customer relations and three customer service representatives, has been appointed to prepare a written service-improvement plan. To accomplish this objective, this study will survey customers to learn what changes they'd like to see in terms of customer service at dell.com. The team will analyze these potential improvements in terms of cost and time requirements and then will design new service procedures that customer service representatives can use to better satisfy customers.

Sources and Methods of Data Collection and Analysis: The study team will assess current customer service efforts by (1) querying customer service representatives regarding their customer service, (2) observing representatives in action dealing with customers through e-mail responses and telephone calls, (3) surveying current Dell owners regarding their purchase experiences, and (4) surveying visitors to dell.com who decide not to purchase from Dell (by intercepting a sample of these people as they leave the Web site). The team will also visit competitive Web sites to determine firsthand how they treat customers, and the team will submit online questionnaires to a sample of computer owners and classify the results by brand name. Once all these data have been collected, the team will analyze them to determine where buyers and potential buyers consider customer service to be lacking. Finally, the team will design procedures to meet their expectations.

Schedule:

Jan 10–Jan 30:	Query customer service representatives. Observe representatives in action. Survey current Dell owners. Survey nonbuyers at dell.com.
Jan 31–Feb 15:	Visit competitive Web sites. Conduct online survey of computer owners.
Feb 15–Mar 15:	Analyze data. Draft new procedures.
Mar 16–Mar 25:	Prepare final report.
Mar 28:	Present to management/customer service committee.

b. Version Two

Statement of Problem: Dell's customer service representatives need to get on the ball in terms of customer service, and we need to tell them what to do in order to fix their customer service shortcomings.

Purpose and Scope of Work: This report will address how we plan to solve the problem. We'll design new customer service procedures and prepare a written report that customer service representatives can learn from.

Sources and Methods of Data Collection: We plan to employ the usual methods of collecting data, including direct observation and surveys.

Schedule:

Collect data	Jan 10–Feb 15
Analyze data	Feb 15–Mar 1
Draft new procedures	Mar 2–Mar 15
Prepare final report	Mar 16–Mar 25
Present to management/ customer service committee	Mar 28

c. Version Three

Task 1—Query customer service representatives: We will interview a sampling of customer service representatives to find out what steps they take to ensure customer satisfaction. Dates: Jan 10–Jan 20

Task 2—Observe representatives in action: We will observe a sampling of customer service representatives as they work with potential buyers and current owners, in order to learn firsthand what steps employees typically take. Dates: Jan 21–Jan 30

Task 3—Survey current Dell owners: Using a sample of names from Dell's database of current owners, we'll ask owners how they felt about the purchase process when they bought their computer and how they feel they've been treated since then. We'll also ask them to suggest steps we could take to improve service. Dates: Jan 15–Feb 15

Task 4—Survey nonbuyers at dell.com: While we are observing customer service representatives, we will also approach visitors at dell.com who leave the site without making a purchase. As visitors exit the site, we'll present a quick online survey, asking them what they think about Dell's customer service policies and practices and whether these had any bearing on their decisions not a buy a Dell product. Dates: Jan 21–Jan 30

Task 5—Visit competitive Web sites: Under the guise of shoppers looking for new computers, we will visit a selection of competitive Web sites to discover how they treat customers and whether they offer any special service that Dell doesn't. Dates: Jan 31–Feb 15

Task 6—Conduct online survey of computer owners: Using Internet-based technology, we will survey a sampling of computer owners (of all brands). We will then sort the answers by brand of computer owned to see which dealers are offering which services. Dates: Jan 15–Feb 15

Task 7—Analyze data: Once we've collected all these data, we'll analyze them to identify (1) services that customers would like to see Dell offer, (2) services offered by competitors that aren't offered by Dell, and (3) services currently offered by Dell that may not be all that important to customers. Dates: Feb 15–Mar 1

Task 8—Draft new procedures: From the data we've analyzed, we'll select new services that should be considered by dell.com. We'll also assess the time and money burdens that these services are likely to present, so that management can see whether each new service will yield a positive return on investment. Dates: Mar 2–Mar 15

Task 9—Prepare final report: This is essentially a documentation task, during which we'll describe our work, make our recommendations, and prepare a formal report. Dates: Mar 16–Mar 25

Task 10—Present to management/customer relations committee: We'll summarize our findings and recommendations and will make the full report available to dealers at the quarterly meeting. Date: Mar 28

d. Version Four

Problem: To identify meaningful customer service improvements that can be implemented by Dell Computer at dell.com.

Data Collection: Use direct observation and online surveys to gather details about customer service at dell.com and at competing Web sites. Have the study team survey current Dell owners and people who visited dell.com but did not buy, and send an online questionnaire to computer owners.

Schedule:

Step 1:   Data collection. Work will begin on January 10 and end on February 15.

Step 2:   Data analysis. Work will start on February 15 and end on March 1.

Step 3:   Drafting new procedures. Work will start on March 2 and end on March 15.

Step 4:   Preparation of the final report. Work will start on March 16 and end on March 25.

Step 5:   Presentation of the final report. The report will be presented to management and the customer service committee on March 28.[27]

TEST YOUR KNOWLEDGE

1. What are the six classifications of business reports?

2. How do informational reports differ from analytical reports?

3. What is a problem statement, and how does it differ from a statement of purpose?

4. What is included in a work plan for a report, and why is it important?

5. How does primary information differ from secondary information?

6. What four types of questions can be posed during an interview?

7. What is paraphrasing, and what is its purpose?

8. What are the characteristics of a sound conclusion?

9. How does a conclusion differ from a recommendation?

10. Why do writers use the "you" attitude in their reports?

INTERACTIVE LEARNING

USE THIS TEXT'S ONLINE RESOURCES

Visit the myPHLIP Web site at www.prenhall.com/thill. For Chapter 10, take advantage of the interactive "Study Guide" to test your chapter knowledge. Get instant feedback on whether you need additional studying. Read the "Current Events" articles to get the latest on chapter topics, and complete the exercises—as specified by your instructor.

This site's "Study Hall" helps you succeed in this course. "Talk in the Hall" lets you leave messages and meet new friends online. If you have a question, you can "Ask the Tutor." And to get a better grade in this course, you can find more help at "Writing Skills," "Study Skills," and "Study Tips."

The "Research Area" helps you locate a wealth of information to use in course assignments. Plus, you can send a message to online research experts, who will help you find exactly the information you need.

APPLY YOUR KNOWLEDGE

1. If your report includes only factual information, is it objective? Please explain.

2. After an exhaustive study of an important problem, you have reached a conclusion that you believe your company's management will reject. What will you do? Explain your answer.

3. Why do you need to evaluate your sources?

4. Put yourself in the position of a manager who is supervising an investigation but doing very little of the research personally. Why would a work plan be especially useful to the manager? To the researcher? Explain.

5. **Ethical Choices** If you want to make a specific recommendation in your report, should you include information that might support a different recommendation? Explain.

PRACTICE YOUR KNOWLEDGE

DOCUMENT FOR ANALYSIS

Assume that your college president has received many student complaints about campus parking problems. You are appointed to chair a student committee organized to investigate the problems and report on recommended solutions. The president gives you the file labeled "Parking: Complaints from Students," and you jot down the essence of the complaints as you inspect the contents. Your notes look like this:

- Inadequate student spaces at critical hours
- Poor night lighting near the computer center
- Inadequate attempts to keep resident neighbors from occupying spaces
- Dim marking lines
- Motorcycles taking up full spaces

- Discourteous security officers
- Spaces (usually empty) reserved for college officials
- Relatively high parking fees
- Full fees charged to night students even though they use the lots only during low-demand periods
- Vandalism to cars and a sense of personal danger
- Inadequate total space

- Resident harassment of students parking on the street in front of neighboring houses

Your first job is to organize these complaints into four or five general categories for your committee to discuss and analyze before preparing its report. Choose the main headings for your outline, and group these specific complaints under them.

EXERCISES

10–1. Planning Reports: Classification and Adaptation Using the information presented in this chapter, identify the type of report represented by each of the following examples. Then write a paragraph about each, explaining the general purpose, who the audience is likely to be, what type of data would be used, whether conclusions and recommendations would be appropriate, and what medium would be most appropriate.

a. A statistical study of the pattern of violent crime in a large city during the last five years

b. A report prepared by a seed company demonstrating the benefits of its seed corn for farmers

c. A report prepared by an independent testing agency evaluating various types of cold remedies sold without prescription

d. A trip report submitted at the end of a week by a traveling salesperson

e. A report indicating how 45 acres of undeveloped land could be converted into an industrial park

f. An annual report to be sent to the shareholders of a large corporation

g. A report from a U.S. National Park wildlife officer to Washington, D.C., headquarters showing the status of the California condor (an endangered species)

h. A formal report by a police officer who has just completed an arrest

10–2. Internet The county of El Paso, Texas, posts RFPs on its purchasing Web site at www.co.el-paso.tx.us/general/purchasing/bids.htm. Visit the site and read through one recent RFP. Does the RFP specify a particular format for company bids? Is any specialized language used in the RFP form? What restrictions are mentioned? What financial points must be covered in each bid?

10–3. Planning Reports: Procedures You're the vice president of operations for a Florida fast-food chain. In the aftermath of a major hurricane, you're drafting a report on the emergency procedures to be followed by personnel in each restaurant when storm warnings are in effect. Answer who, what, when, where, why, and how, and then prepare a one-page draft of your report.

10–4. Planning Reports: Secondary Information You're getting ready to write a research paper on a topic of your choice. You decide to search for information using both the library databases and the Internet. Develop a search strategy.

a. What are some key words and phrases you might use?

b. Which Boolean operators would you use to narrow your search?

c. Which wildcard operators might you use?

10–5. Planning Reports: Primary Information Deciding how to collect primary data is an important part of the research process. Which one or more of the five methods of data collection (examining documents, making observations, surveying people, conducting experiments, and performing interviews) would you use if you were researching these questions?

a. Has the litter problem on campus been reduced since the cafeteria began offering fewer take-out choices this year than in past years?

b. Has the school attracted more transfer students since it waived the formal application process and allowed students at other colleges to send in transcripts with a one-page letter of application?

c. Have the number of traffic accidents at the school's main entrance been reduced since a traffic light was installed?

d. Has student satisfaction with the campus bookstore improved now that students can order their books over the Internet and pick them up at several campus locations?

10–6. Planning Reports: Surveys You work for a movie studio that is producing a young director's first motion picture, the story of a group of unknown musicians building a reputation in a competitive industry. Unfortunately, some of the director's friends leave the first complete screening saying that the 132-minute movie is simply too long. Others can't imagine any more editing cuts. Your boss wants to test the movie on a regular audience and ask viewers to complete a questionnaire that will help the director decide whether edits are needed and, if so, where. Design a questionnaire you can use to solicit valid answers for a report to the director about the audience's reaction to the movie.

10–7. Planning Reports: Data Analysis Your boss has asked you to analyze and report on your division's sales for the first nine months of this year. Using the following data from company invoices, calculate the mean for each quarter and all averages for the year to date. Then identify and discuss the quarterly sales trends.

January	$24,600	April	$21,200	July	$29,900
February	25,900	May	24,600	August	30,500
March	23,000	June	26,800	September	26,600

10-8. **Planning Reports: Secondary Information** Using online, database, or printed sources, find the following information. Be sure to properly cite your source using the formats discussed in Appendix B. (*Hint:* Start with Figure 10–9, Major Business Resources.)
   a. Contact information for the American Management Association
   b. Median weekly earnings of men and women by occupation
   c. Current market share for Perrier water
   d. Performance ratios for office supply retailers
   e. Annual stock performance for Hewlett-Packard
   f. Number of franchise outlets in the United States
   g. Composition of the U.S. workforce by profession

10-9. **Planning Reports: Library Sources** Businesspeople have to know where to look for secondary information when they research a report. Prepare a list of the most important magazines and professional journals in the following fields:
   a. Marketing/advertising
   b. Insurance
   c. Communications
   d. Accounting

10-10. **Planning Reports: Industry Information** Locate the SIC and NAICS codes for the following industries:
   a. Hotels and motels
   b. Breakfast cereals
   c. Bottled water
   d. Automatic vending machines

10-11. **Planning Reports: Company Information** Select any public company and find the following information:
   a. Names of the company's current officers
   b. List of the company's products or services
   c. Current issues in the company's industry
   d. Outlook for the company's industry as a whole

10-12. **Planning Reports: Study Scope** Your boss has asked you to do some research on franchising. Actually, he's thinking about purchasing a few Subway franchises and he needs some information. Visit www.amazon.com and review the site. On the home page, perform a key word search on "franchise." Explore some of the books by clicking on "read more about this title."
   a. Use the information to develop a list of subquestions to help you narrow your focus.
   b. Write down the names of three books you might purchase for your boss.
   c. How can this Web site assist you with your research efforts?

10-13. **Planning Reports: Unsolicited Proposal** You're getting ready to launch a new lawn-care business that offers mowing, fertilizing, weeding, and other services. The lawn surrounding a nearby shopping center looks as if it could use better care, so you target that business for your first sales proposal. To help prepare this proposal, write your answers to these questions:
   a. What problem statement and statement of purpose would be most appropriate? (Think about the reader's viewpoint.)
   b. What questions will you need answered before you can write a proposal to solve the reader's problem? Be as specific as possible.
   c. What conclusions and recommendations might be practical, acceptable to the reader, and specific enough for the shopping center to take action? (Think about the purpose of the report.)

10-14. **Planning Reports: Work Plan** Now turn the situation around and assume that you're the shopping center's facilities manager. You report to the general manager, who must approve any new contracts for lawn service. Before you contract for lawn care, you want to prepare a formal study of the current state of your lawn's health. The report will include conclusions and recommendations for your boss's consideration. Draft a work plan, including the problem statement, the statement of purpose and scope, a description of what will result from your investigation, the sources and methods of data collection, and a preliminary outline.

10-15. **Teamwork** The college administration has asked you to head a student committee that will look into how the bookstore can ease the long lines during the first two weeks of every term, when students need to buy books. Select two other students to serve on your committee and help plan a feasibility study and an analytical report showing your recommendations. As a first step, your committee should prepare a brief memo to the administration. The memo should accomplish the following:
   a. Identify the problem (problem statement) and the purpose (statement of purpose).
   b. Identify two or three likely alternatives to be investigated.
   c. Clearly identify the criteria for selecting among the options.
   d. Identify the primary and secondary sources of information to be used in the study.

10-16. **Ethical Choices** Your company operates a Web site featuring children's games and puzzles. The vice president of marketing needs to know more about the children who visit the site so she can plan new products. She has asked you to develop an online survey questionnaire to collect the data. What ethical issues do you see in this situation? What should you do?

GOING ONLINE EXERCISES

Pointers for Business Plans, page 274

What are the components of a business plan? What do readers of a plan look for? What common mistakes should you avoid? For answers to these questions and advice for planning a business plan, log on to BizPlanIt.Com.

1. Why is the executive summary such an important section of a plan? What kind of information is contained in the executive summary?
2. What is the product/service section? What information should it contain? List some of the common errors to avoid when planning this part.
3. What type of business planning should you describe in the exit strategy section? Why?

To complete this exercise, log on to this text's Web site at www.prenhall.com/thill. Select Chapter 10, then select "Student Resources," click on the name of the featured Web site, and follow the detailed navigational directions.

WRITING BUSINESS REPORTS AND PROPOSALS

chapter

FACING A COMMUNICATION DILEMMA AT FEDEX

Delivering On Time, Every Time

www.fedex.com

Imagine collecting, transporting, and delivering more than three million letters and packages every day. Now imagine that every one of these parcels absolutely, positively has to arrive at its destination when expected. That's the standard against which FedEx managers—and customers—measure performance. Living up to this exacting standard day in and day out presents founder and CEO Frederick W. Smith and his entire management team with a variety of communication challenges.

When FedEx began operations in 1973, its services covered 22 U.S. cities. Today it delivers throughout the United States and to 212 countries around the world. To make those deliveries on time, every time, FedEx operates nearly 600 airplanes, maintains a fleet of 38,500 trucks and vans, and employs more than 137,000 people. Making sure that all these people have the information they need in the form they need it is tough enough, but the challenge doesn't stop there.

FedEx must also battle a host of rivals, including United Parcel Service (UPS), the U.S. Postal Service, Airborne Express, DHL, and other delivery companies. Competition is fierce, so FedEx is constantly on the lookout for information on competitors and on innovative ways to serve its own customers better. One important way that FedEx helps commercial and industrial customers is by taking over their warehouse and inventory chores. Instead of just acting as a shipping service, FedEx operates as part of the customer's organization, so in addition to gathering information, Smith and his team are also responsible for reporting information to customers.

Smith's newest service innovations involve electronic commerce in general and the Internet in particular. To get around the tedious work of filling out shipping forms and telephoning a pick-up request, FedEx now lets customers place orders online with a new service called FedEx interNetShip. Also, to help customers capitalize on the selling power of the World Wide Web, the FedEx VirtualOrder service can handle everything from setting up a product catalog on a Web site to the more traditional service of delivering the goods. Carson's Ribs, a Chicago company, now ships fully cooked, flash-frozen orders of ribs overnight via FedEx. Customers just visit Carson's Web site, and a FedEx driver delivers tomorrow's dinner.

With competitors offering more and customers expecting more, Smith and his management team have their work cut out for them. Monitoring and controlling company operations, training new employees, tracking competitor service and performance, making a host of decisions about how to serve customers better—all these activities require the communication of timely, accurate information, and much of that information comes in the form of reports. To keep the business running smoothly, maintain satisfied customers, and hold competitors at bay, FedEx managers receive and prepare reports of all kinds. So how do Smith and his managers use reports for internal communication? How can FedEx writers make their reports readable and convenient to use? What makes one report better than another?[1]

After studying this chapter, you will be able to

1 Discuss the structure of informational reports.

2 Explain the structure of analytical reports.

3 List the most popular types of visuals and discuss when to use them.

4 Clarify five principles of graphic design to remember when preparing visuals.

5 Identify and briefly describe five tools that writers can use in long reports to help readers stay on track.

At FedEx, reports of all kinds are used to track both system and employee performance, as well as to assemble information needed for making managerial decisions. Not only does Frederick Smith read innumerable reports, he wrote a very famous one, which detailed the idea of his air express delivery service and persuaded investors to fund him.

ORGANIZING BUSINESS REPORTS AND PROPOSALS

Organizing means arranging your material in an order that is logical and that meets your audience's needs.

Before you can compose a business report or proposal, you must organize the material you've collected, arranging it in a logical order that meets your audience's needs. Frederick Smith advises you to carefully choose the format, length, order, and structure for your report before drafting even the first word.

When Karla Brown applied to the Small Business Association (SBA) for a microloan, she was facing stiff competition for the agency's limited resources. Organizing her proposal to satisfy the SBA's needs, Brown obtained a microloan of $19,000 to start her business, Ashmont Flowers Plus.

Deciding on Format and Length

At times, the decision about format and length will be made for you by the person who requests the report. Such guidance is often the case with monitor/control reports, justification reports, proposals, progress reports, and compliance reports. The more routine the report, the less flexibility you have in deciding format and length. Monthly status reports, for example, are usually pretty routine, so they will have the same basic appearance and structure. Within that framework, however, there is room for flexibility, depending on the nature of the information being reported.

Periodic reports are usually written in memo format and don't need much of an introduction; a subject line on the memo is adequate. They should follow the same general format and organization from period to period. Personal activity reports are also written in memo format, but because they're nonrecurring documents, they require more introduction than periodic reports do.

Base your format decisions on your readers' needs.

When you do have some leeway in length and format, base your decisions on your readers' needs. As FedEx's Frederick Smith can attest, your goal is to tell your audience what they need to know in a format that is easy for them to use. So when selecting a format for your report, you have four options:

You may present a report in one of four formats: preprinted form, letter, memo, or manuscript.

◆ **Preprinted form.** Used for fill-in-the-blank reports. Most are relatively short (five or fewer pages) and deal with routine information, often mainly numerical. Use this format when it's requested by the person authorizing the report.

◆ **Letter.** Commonly used for reports of five or fewer pages that are directed to outsiders. These reports include all the normal parts of a letter, but they may also have headings, footnotes, tables, and figures.

◆ **Memo.** Commonly used for short (fewer than 10 pages) informal reports distributed within an organization. Like longer reports, they often have internal headings and sometimes include visual aids. Memos exceeding 10 pages are sometimes referred to as *memo reports* to distinguish them from their shorter cousins.

◆ **Manuscript.** Commonly used for reports that require a formal approach, whether a few pages or several hundred. As length increases, reports in manuscript format require more elements before (prefatory parts) and after (supplementary parts) the text. Chapter 12 explains these elements and includes a checklist for preparing formal reports.

Appendix A, "Format and Layout of Business Documents," contains more specific guidelines for physically preparing reports.

Length depends on
• Your subject
• Your purpose
• Your relationship with your audience

The length of your report obviously depends on your subject and purpose, but it's also affected by your relationship with your audience. If they are relative strangers, if they are skeptical or hostile, if the material is nonroutine or controversial, you usually have to explain your points in greater detail, which results in a longer document. You can afford to be brief if you are on familiar terms with your readers, if they are likely to agree with you, and if the information is routine or uncomplicated. Short reports are more common in business than long ones, and you'll probably write many more 5-page memos than 250-page formal reports.

EFFECTIVE E-BUSINESS COMMUNICATION

Reporting in Many Languages

Global companies often prepare legally required financial reports and other business reports in different languages for different audiences. On the Web, however, you can allow readers to select their preferred language with a quick click. For example, Microsoft's annual report is prepared for investors and posted on the company's Web site in 11 languages (including French for Canadian readers and Portuguese for Brazilian readers). Readers simply click on the link for the language they want—and then read on (see www.microsoft.com).

1. When offering readers a choice of languages, must a company post translated versions of the graphics and every other element of the report?
2. What kinds of reports might companies post on their Web sites for access by audiences in multiple languages?

Choosing the Direct or Indirect Approach

What order is best for your audience and purpose? As Chapter 5 explains, when an audience is considered either receptive or open-minded, use the direct approach: Lead off with a summary of your key findings, conclusions, and recommendations. This "up-front" arrangement is by far the most popular and convenient order for business reports. It saves time and makes the rest of the report easier to follow. For those who have questions or want more information, later parts of the report provide complete findings and supporting details. The direct approach also produces a more forceful report. You sound sure of yourself when you state your conclusions confidently at the outset.

> The direct approach saves time and makes the report easier to understand by giving readers the main idea first.

Confidence may sometimes be misconstrued as arrogance. If you're a junior member of a status-conscious organization or if your audience is skeptical or hostile, you may want to use the indirect approach: Introduce your complete findings and discuss all supporting details before presenting your conclusions and recommendations. The indirect approach gives you a chance to prove your points and gradually overcome your audience's reservations. By deferring the conclusions and recommendations, you imply that you've weighed the evidence objectively without prejudging the facts. You also imply that you're subordinating your judgment to that of the audience, whose members are capable of drawing their own conclusions when they have access to all the facts.

> The indirect approach helps overcome resistance by withholding the main idea until later in the report.

Although the indirect approach has its advantages, some report readers will always be in a hurry to get to "the answer" and will flip to the recommendations immediately, thus defeating your purpose. Therefore, consider length before choosing the direct or indirect approach. In general, the longer the message, the less effective an indirect approach is likely to be. Furthermore, an indirect argument is harder to follow than a direct one.

Because both direct and indirect approaches have merit, businesspeople often combine them. They reveal their conclusions and recommendations as they go along, rather than putting them either first or last. Figure 11–1 presents the introductions from two

> Businesspeople often combine the direct and indirect approaches.

Figure 11–1
Direct Approach versus Indirect
Approach in an Introduction

THE DIRECT APPROACH

Since the company's founding 25 years ago, we have provided regular repair service for all our electric appliances. This service has been an important selling point as well as a source of pride for our employees. However, we are paying a high price for our image. Last year, we lost $500,000 on our repair business.

Because of your concern over these losses, you have asked me to study the pros and cons of discontinuing our repair service. With the help of John Hudson and Susan Lefkowitz, I have studied the issue for the past two weeks and have come to the conclusion that we have been embracing an expensive, impractical tradition.

By withdrawing from the electric appliance repair business, we can substantially improve our financial performance without damaging our reputation with customers. This conclusion is based on three basic points that are covered in the following pages:

- It is highly unlikely that we will ever be able to make a profit in the repair business.
- Sevice is no longer an important selling point with customers.
- Closing down the service operation will create few internal problems.

THE INDIRECT APPROACH

Since the company's founding 25 years ago, we have provided repair service for all our electric appliances. This service has been an important selling point as well as a source of pride for our employees. However, the repair business itself has consistently lost money.

Because of your concern over these losses, you have asked me to study the pros and cons of discontinuing our repair service. With the help of John Hudson and Susan Lefkowitz, I have studied the issue for the past two weeks. The following pages present my findings for your review. Three basic questions are addressed:

- What is the extent of our losses, and what can we do to turn the business around?
- Would withdrawal hurt our sales of electrical appliances?
- What would be the internal repercussions of closing down the repair business?

reports with the same general outline. In the direct version, a series of statements summarize the conclusion reached in relation to each main topic on the outline. In the indirect version, the same topics are introduced (in the same order) without drawing any conclusions about them. The conclusions appear within the body of the report instead. So is this second report direct or indirect? Business reports are often difficult to classify.

Regardless of the format, length, or order you use, you must still deal with the question of how your ideas will be subdivided and developed. Suppose you're writing a controversial report recommending that your company revise its policy on who reports to whom. You know that some of your readers will object to your ideas, so you decide to use indirect order. How do you develop your argument? Your job is to choose the most logical structure—the one that suits your topic and goals and that makes the most sense to your audience.

Structuring Informational Reports

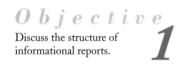

Discuss the structure of informational reports.

Reader reaction is rarely an issue in informational reports.

Topical organization is arranging material in order of importance, sequence, chronology, spatial relationships, location, or categories.

Informational reports are the easiest to organize because they provide nothing more than facts. When writing informational reports, reader reaction is not usually an issue. Most readers will presumably respond unemotionally to your material, so you can present it in the most direct fashion possible. What you do need to be concerned about, however, is reader comprehension. The information must be presented logically and accurately so that readers will understand exactly what you mean and be able to use your information in a practical way.

When writing an informational report, you can let the nature of whatever you're describing dictate your structure. For example, if you're describing a machine, each component can correspond to a part of your report. If you're describing an event, you can approach the discussion chronologically. And if you're explaining how to do something, you can describe the steps in a process. Informational reports use a **topical organization,** arranging material according to one of these following topics:

◆ **Importance.** If you're reviewing five product lines, you might organize your study according to the sales for each product line, beginning with the line that produces the most revenue and proceeding to the one that produces the least.

| | Conclusions or | Logical Argument | | |
Elements	Recommendations	2 + 2 = 4	Scientific	Yardstick
Readers	Are likely to accept	Are hostile or skeptical; need convincing	Need most convincing	Need most convincing
Order	Direct	Indirect	Indirect	Indirect
Writer credibility	High	Low	Low	Low
Advantages	Readers quickly grasp conclusions or recommendations	Readers follow writer's thinking process	Readers draw their own conclusions	Alternatives are all measured against same standards (criteria)
Drawbacks	Structure can make topic seem too simple	Structure can make report longer	Must discuss each alternative; very long	Must agree on criteria; can be boring; very long

Table 11–1   Common Ways to Structure Analytical Reports

◆ **Sequence.** If you're studying a process, discuss it step by step—1, 2, 3, and so on.

◆ **Chronology.** When investigating a chain of events, organize the study according to what happened in January, what happened in February, and so on.

◆ **Spatial orientation.** If you're explaining how a physical object works, describe it left to right (or right to left in some cultures), top to bottom, outside to inside.

◆ **Geography.** If location is important, organize your study according to geography, perhaps by region of the United States or by area of a city.

◆ **Category.** If you're asked to review several distinct aspects of a subject, look at one category at a time, such as sales, profit, cost, or investment.

There are other bases for organization. Because some informational reports, especially compliance reports and internal reports, are prepared on preprinted forms, they are organized according to instructions supplied by the person requesting the information. In addition, many proposals conform to an outline specified in the request for proposal that is issued by the client. The client's request might include a statement of the problem, some background information, the scope of work involved, applicable restrictions, recommended sources and methods, a work schedule, required personnel qualifications, available facilities, anticipated costs, and expected results.

Structuring Analytical Reports

It is more difficult to organize analytical reports that contain analyses and that are designed to lead the audience to specific conclusions and recommendations. Your choice of structural approach depends on the reaction you anticipate:

◆ **Receptive audiences.** When you expect your audience to agree with you, use a structure that focuses attention on conclusions and recommendations.

◆ **Skeptical audiences.** When you expect your audience to disagree with you or to be hostile, use a structure that focuses attention on the rationale behind your conclusions and recommendations.

The three most common structural approaches for analytical reports are (1) focusing on conclusions, (2) focusing on recommendations, and (3) focusing on logical argument (see Table 11–1).

Focusing on Conclusions: A Research and Analysis Report   When writing an analytical report for people from your own organization who have asked you to study something, you're writing for your most receptive readers. They may know from experience that you'll do a thorough job, and they may trust your judgment. If they're likely to accept

Objective **2**

Explain the structure of analytical reports.

The structure of analytical reports depends on audience reaction.

Three popular ways to organize analytical reports:
• By conclusions
• By recommendations
• By logical arguments

Analytical reports may be organized around conclusions and recommendations (direct approach) when the audience is receptive.

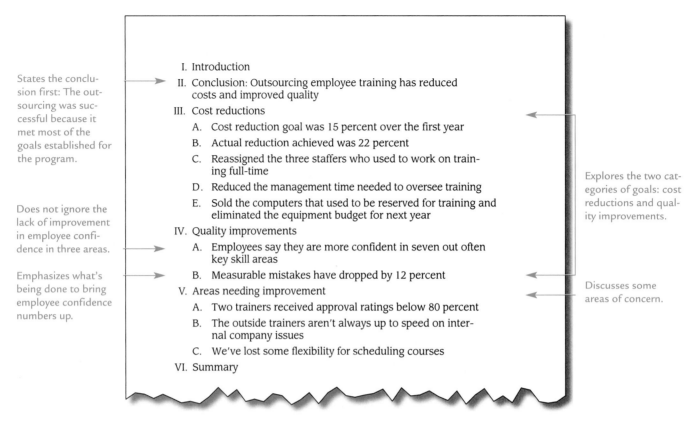

States the conclusion first: The outsourcing was successful because it met most of the goals established for the program.

Does not ignore the lack of improvement in employee confidence in three areas.

Emphasizes what's being done to bring employee confidence numbers up.

I. Introduction
II. Conclusion: Outsourcing employee training has reduced costs and improved quality
III. Cost reductions
   A. Cost reduction goal was 15 percent over the first year
   B. Actual reduction achieved was 22 percent
   C. Reassigned the three staffers who used to work on training full-time
   D. Reduced the management time needed to oversee training
   E. Sold the computers that used to be reserved for training and eliminated the equipment budget for next year
IV. Quality improvements
   A. Employees say they are more confident in seven out often key skill areas
   B. Measurable mistakes have dropped by 12 percent
V. Areas needing improvement
   A. Two trainers received approval ratings below 80 percent
   B. The outside trainers aren't always up to speed on internal company issues
   C. We've lost some flexibility for scheduling courses
VI. Summary

Explores the two categories of goals: cost reductions and quality improvements.

Discusses some areas of concern.

Figure 11–2
In-Depth Critique: Outline of a Research Report Focusing on Conclusions

your conclusions, you can structure your report around conclusions or recommendations using a direct approach.

However, the direct approach does have some drawbacks. If your readers have reservations either about you or about your material, strong statements at the beginning may intensify their resistance. Also, focusing on conclusions and recommendations may make everything seem too simple. Your readers could criticize your report as being superficial: "Why didn't you consider this option?" or "Where did you get this number?" You're generally better off taking the direct approach in a report only when your credibility is high—when your readers trust you and are willing to accept your conclusions and recommendations.

The direct approach has some drawbacks.

Cynthia Zolonka works on the human resources staff of a bank in Houston, Texas. Her company decided to have an outside firm handle its employee training, and a year after the outsourcing arrangement was established, Zolonka was asked to evaluate the results. She explains: "Moving our training programs to an outside supplier was a tough—and controversial—decision for the entire company. Some people were convinced outsourcing would never work; others thought it might save money but would hurt training quality. I took special care to do a thorough analysis of the data, and I supported my conclusion with objective answers, not personal opinions."

Figure 11–2 presents an outline of Zolonka's report. Her analysis shows that the outsourcing experiment was a success. She structured her report in three main sections, as the outline illustrates.

When the reader is concerned with conclusions, use them as the main points.

You can use a similar structure whenever you're asked to analyze a problem or an opportunity. Readers who are interested mainly in your conclusions can grasp them quickly, and readers who want to know more about your analysis can look at the data you provide.

Focusing on Recommendations: A Justification Report   A slightly different approach is useful when your readers want to know what they ought to do (as opposed to what they ought to conclude). You'll often be asked to solve a problem rather than just study it. So the actions you want your readers to take become the main subdivisions of your report.

When structuring a report around recommendations, follow five steps:

1. Establish the need for action in the introduction, generally by briefly describing the problem or opportunity.

2. Introduce the benefit that can be achieved, without providing any details.

3. List the steps (recommendations) required to achieve the benefit, using action verbs for emphasis.

4. Explain each step more fully, giving details on procedures, costs, and benefits.

5. Summarize the recommendations.

Alycia Jenn, the business development manager at a Chicago-based retail chain, was asked by the company's board of directors to suggest whether the company should set up a retailing site on the World Wide Web and, if so, how to implement the site. As Jenn noted, "Setting up shop on the Internet is a big decision for our company. We don't have the big computer staffs that our larger competitors have, and our business development team is stretched rather thin already. On the other hand, I know that more and more people are shopping online, and we don't want to be left out if this mode of retailing really takes off. After studying the issue for several weeks, I concluded that we should go ahead with a site, but we had to be careful about how we implement it."

Jenn's memo appears in Figure 11–3. She uses her recommendations to structure her thoughts. Because the directors wouldn't be interested in a lot of technical detail, she keeps her discussion at a pretty high level. She also maintains a formal and respectful tone for this audience.

Focusing on Logical Arguments   Focusing on conclusions or recommendations is the most forceful and efficient way to structure an analytical report, but it isn't the best solution for every situation. As FedEx's Fred Smith knows, you can sometimes achieve better results by encouraging readers to weigh all the facts before you present your conclusions or recommendations.

When your purpose is to collaborate with your audience and solve a problem or persuade them to take a definite action, your structural approach must highlight logical arguments or focus the audience's attention on what needs to be done. When you want your audience to concentrate on why your ideas make sense, use a **logical organization:** arrange your ideas around the reasoning behind your report's conclusions and recommendations. Organize your material to reflect the thinking process that will lead readers to your conclusions.

Three basic structural approaches may be used to argue your case: the 2 + 2 = 4 approach, the scientific method, and the yardstick approach. Bear in mind that these three approaches are not mutually exclusive. Essentially, you choose an approach that matches the reasoning process you used to arrive at your conclusions. This way you can lead readers along the same mental pathways you used in hopes they will follow you to the same conclusions.

In a long report, particularly, you may find it convenient to use differing organizational approaches for various sections. In general, however, simplicity of organization is a virtue. You need a clear, comprehensible argument in order to convince skeptical readers to accept your conclusions or recommendations.

The 2 + 2 = 4 Approach: A Troubleshooting Report   The 2 + 2 = 4 approach essentially convinces readers of your point of view by demonstrating that everything adds

When the reader is concerned about what action to take, use recommendations as the main points.

Supreme Court Justice Sandra Day O'Connor has held the deciding vote for several complicated decisions. In establishing a position and seeking an outcome to a case, Justice O'Connor must decide each case based on its specific facts. Her approach to the law must be consistent and logical in order for her recommendation to be persuasive.

Analytical reports may be organized around logical arguments (indirect approach) when the audience is unreceptive.

Three organizational approaches are useful for convincing skeptical readers that your conclusions and recommendations are well founded: the 2 + 2 = 4 approach, the scientific method, and the yardstick approach.

Clarifies the purpose and origin of the report in the introduction.

Logically and clearly presents reasons for recommending that the firm establish a Web site.

Recommendations include not only establishing a Web site but also hiring a consultant to implement it and integrate it with existing systems.

For clarity, the recommendations are simple and to the point.

MEMO

TO: Board of Directors, Executive Committee members
FROM: Alycia Jenn, Business Development Manager
DATE: July 6, 2000
SUBJECT: World Wide Web retailing site

In response to your request, my staff and I investigated the potential for establishing a retailing site on the World Wide Web. After analyzing the behavior of our customers and major competitors and studying the overall development of electronic retailing, we have three recommendations:

1. Yes, we should establish an online presence within the next six months.
2. We should engage a firm that specializes in online retailing to design and develop the Web site.
3. We must take care to integrate online retailing with our store-based and mail-order operations.

WE SHOULD SET UP A WEB SITE

First, does a Web site make financial sense today? Studies suggest that our competitors are not currently generating significant revenue from their Web sites. Stallini's is the leader so far, but its sales haven't broken the $1 million mark. Moreover, at least half of our competitors' online sales are from current customers who would have purchased the same items in-store or by mail order. The cost of setting up a retailing site is around $120,000, so it isn't possible to justify a site solely on the basis of current financial return.

Second, do we need to establish a presence now in order to remain competitive in the future? The online situation is too fluid and unpredictable to answer this question in a quantitative profit-and-loss way, but a qualitative view of strategy indicates that we should set up a site:

• As younger consumers (more comfortable with online shopping) reach their peak earning years (ages 35–54), they'll be more likely to buy online than today's peak spenders.
• The Web is erasing geographical shopping limits, presenting both a threat and an opportunity. Even though our customers can now shop Web sites anywhere in the world (so that we have thousands of competitors instead of a dozen), we can now target customers anywhere in the world.
• If the growth in online retailing continues, this will eventually be a viable market. Establishing a site now and working out any problems will prepare us for high-volume online business in the years ahead.

WE SHOULD ENGAGE A CONSULTANT TO IMPLEMENT THE SITE

Implementing a competitive retailing site can take anywhere from 1,000 to 2,500 hours of design and programming time. We have some of the expertise needed in-house, but the marketing and information systems departments have only 300 person-hours in the next six months. I recommend that we engage a Web-design consultant to help us with the design and to do all of the programming.

(continued)

Figure 11–3
In-Depth Critique: Sample Justification Report Focusing on Recommendations

up. The main points in your outline are the main reasons behind your conclusions and recommendations. You support each reason with the evidence you collected during your analysis.

As national sales manager of a New Hampshire sporting goods company, Binh Phan was concerned about his company's ability to sell to its largest customers. His boss, the vice president of marketing, shared these concerns and asked Phan to analyze the situation and recommend a solution. As Phan says, "We sell sporting goods to retail chains across the country. Large nationwide chains with superstores modeled after Toys "Я" Us have been revolutionizing the industry, but we haven't had as much success with these big customers as we've had with smaller companies that operate strictly on a local or regional basis. With more and more of the industry in the hands of the large chains, we knew we had to fix the situation."

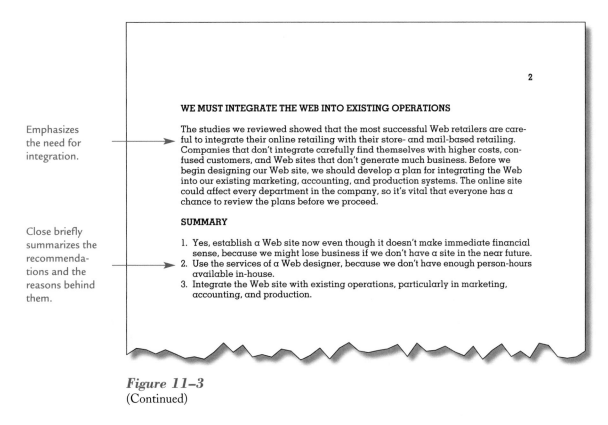

Emphasizes the need for integration.

WE MUST INTEGRATE THE WEB INTO EXISTING OPERATIONS

The studies we reviewed showed that the most successful Web retailers are careful to integrate their online retailing with their store- and mail-based retailing. Companies that don't integrate carefully find themselves with higher costs, confused customers, and Web sites that don't generate much business. Before we begin designing our Web site, we should develop a plan for integrating the Web into our existing marketing, accounting, and production systems. The online site could affect every department in the company, so it's vital that everyone has a chance to review the plans before we proceed.

Close briefly summarizes the recommendations and the reasons behind them.

SUMMARY

1. Yes, establish a Web site now even though it doesn't make immediate financial sense, because we might lose business if we don't have a site in the near future.
2. Use the services of a Web designer, because we don't have enough person-hours available in-house.
3. Integrate the Web site with existing operations, particularly in marketing, accounting, and production.

Figure 11–3
(Continued)

Phan's troubleshooting report appears in Figure 11–4. The main idea is that the company should establish separate sales teams for these major accounts, rather than continuing to service them through the company's four regional divisions. However, Phan knew his plan would be controversial because it required a big change in the company's organization and in the way sales reps are paid. His thinking had to be clear and easy to follow, so he used the 2 + 2 = 4 approach to focus on his reasons.

Because of its naturalness and versatility, the 2 + 2 = 4 approach is generally the most persuasive and efficient way to develop an analytical report for skeptical readers. When writing your own reports, try this structure first. You'll find that your arguments usually fall naturally into this pattern. However, not every problem or reporting situation can be handled with this organizational approach.

> The 2 + 2 = 4 approach works well when you have many reasons for your point of view but no single reason is overwhelming.

The Scientific Method: A Proposal   When you're trying to discover whether an explanation is true, whether an option will solve your problem, or which one of several solutions will work best, you're likely to find the scientific method useful. Every day hundreds of managers ask themselves, "What's wrong with this operation, and what should we do about it?" They approach the problem by coming up with one or several possible solutions (hypotheses) and then conducting experiments or gathering information to find the most effective one.

Reports based on the scientific method begin with a statement of the problem and a brief description of the hypothetical solution or a list of possible solutions. The body of the report discusses each alternative in turn and offers evidence that will either confirm the alternative or rule it out. Because many problems have multiple causes and complex solutions, several alternatives may be relevant. The final section of the report summarizes the findings and indicates which solution or solutions are valid. The report concludes with recommendations for solving the problem or eliminating the causes.

> When organizing a report to reflect the scientific method, you discuss, one by one, hypothetical solutions to the problem.

A proposal using a variation of the scientific method was prepared by Fredrik Swensen, an executive with a Miami restaurant management firm (see the outline in

MEMO

TO: Robert Mendoza, Vice President of Marketing
FROM: Binh Phan, National Sales Manager
DATE: September 12, 1999
SUBJECT: Major accounts sales problems

INTRODUCTION

This report outlines the results of my investigation into the recent slowdown in sales to major accounts and the accompanying rise in sales- and service-related complaints from some of our largest customers.

As we discussed at last quarter's management retreat, major account sales dropped 12 percent over the last four quarters, whereas overall sales were up 7 percent. During the same time, we've all noticed an increase in both formal and informal complaints from larger customers regarding how confusing and complicated it has become to do business with us.

My investigation started with in-depth discussions with the four regional sales managers, first as a group and then individually. The tension I felt in the initial meeting eventually bubbled to the surface during my meetings with each manager. Staff members in each region are convinced that other regions are booking orders they don't deserve, with one region doing all the legwork only to see another region get credited with the sale and, naturally, the commission and quota credit.

I followed up the sales manager discussions with informal talks and e-mail exchanges with several sales reps from each region. Virtually everyone who is involved with our major national accounts has a story to share. No one is happy with the situation, and I sense that some reps are walking away from major customers because the process is so frustrating.

ORGANIZATIONAL ISSUES

When we divided the national sales force into four geographical regions last year, the idea was to focus our sales efforts and clarify responsibilities for each prospective and current customer. The regional managers have gotten to know their market territories very well, and sales have increased beyond even our most optimistic projections.

Unfortunately, while solving one problem, we seem to have created another. In the past 12 to 18 months, several regional customers have grown to national status. In addition, a few national retailers have taken on (or expressed interest in) our products. As a result, a significant portion of both our current sales and our future opportunities lie with these large national accounts.

I uncovered more than a dozen cases in which sales reps from two or more regions found themselves competing with each other by pursuing the same customer from different locations.

Moreover, the complaints from our major accounts about overlapping or nonexistent account coverage are a direct result of the regional organization. In some

(continued)

Figure 11–4
In-Depth Critique: Sample Troubleshooting Report Using the 2 + 2 = 4 Approach

Figure 11–5 on page 326). The purpose of Swensen's proposal is to help his company decide which of four franchise operations to invest in. "We wanted to buy 45 or 50 more franchise outlets across the country," says Swensen, "so this was a major investment decision. Our company already owns several hundred fast-food franchises, so we have a good idea of how to evaluate which ones are right for us."

By analyzing each alternative, Swensen hoped to unify a divided audience. Your chances of bringing about a consensus are much better when you show the strengths and weaknesses of all the ideas. However, the main drawback is that many of the alternatives may turn out to be irrelevant or unproductive, but you still have to discuss them all. The more ideas you discuss, the more confused your readers may become and the more trouble they may have comparing pros and cons.

2

cases, customers aren't sure which of our reps they're supposed to call with problems and orders. In others, no one has been in contact with them for several months.

An example should help illustrate the problem. AmeriSport, with retail outlets across the lower tier of the country, was being pitched by reps from our West, South, and East regions. Because we give our regional offices a lot of negotiating freedom, the three reps were offering the client different prices. But all of AmeriSport's buying decisions are made at their headquarters in Tampa, so all we did was confuse the customer.

The irony of this situation is that we're often giving our weakest selling and support efforts to the largest customers in the country.

COMMISSION ISSUES

The regional organization issues are compounded because of the way we assign commissions and quota credit. Salespeople in one region can invest a lot of time in pursuing a sale, only to have the customer place the order in another region. So some sales rep in the second region ends up with the commission on a sale that was partly or even entirely earned by someone in the first region.

Also, sales reps sometimes don't pursue leads in their regions if they think that a rep in another region will get the commission. For example, Athletic Express, with outlets in 35 states spread across all four regions, finally got so frustrated with us that the company president called our headquarters. Athletic Express has been trying to place a large order for tennis and golf accessories, but none of our local reps seem interested in paying attention. I spoke with the rep responsible for Nashville, where the company is headquartered, and asked her why she wasn't working the account more actively. Her explanation was that last time she got involved with Athletic Express, the order was actually placed from their L.A. regional office, and she didn't get any commission after more than two weeks of selling time.

RECOMMENDATION

Our sales organization should reflect the nature of our customer base. To accomplish that goal, we need a group of reps who are free to pursue accounts across regional borders—and who are compensated fairly for their work. The most sensible answer is to establish a national accounts group. Any customers whose operations place them in more than one region would automatically be assigned to the national group.

Further, we need to modify our commission policy to reward people for team selling. I'll talk with the sales managers to work out the details, but in general, we'll need to split commissions whenever two or more reps help close a sale. This policy will also involve a "finder's fee" for a rep who pulls in leads at the regional level that are passed on to the national account team.

Each main point is supported with concrete evidence.

Saves recommendation for the fourth section, where writer adds up the reasons (2 + 2 = 4).

The recommendation is a logical culmination of the main points that have been presented so carefully.

3

SUMMARY

The regional sales organization is working at the regional and local levels but not at the national level. We should establish a national accounts group to handle sales that cross regional boundaries.

To make sure that the sales reps (at both the regional and national levels) are adequately motivated and fairly compensated, we need to devise a system of commission splitting and finders' fees. We'll then have one set of reps who are focused on the local and regional levels and another set who are pursuing national accounts. The two groups will have incentives to work together rather than against each other, as is now the case.

Clearly and succinctly recaps the recommendation and the reasons for it.

Figure 11–4
(Continued)

Main Idea: We should purchase the 45 franchises currently for sale in the Burger World chain.

I. Statement of problem and purpose of this proposal
II. Scope of the investigation
III. Method used to compare the business opportunities
    A. Establish decision criteria
    B. Get input from consultants
    C. Gather secondary research
    D. Conduct market surveys for primary research
    E. Meet with franchisor management teams
    F. Analyze quantitative and qualitative data
    G. Prioritize and select the best opportunity
IV. Analysis of the four franchise operations
    A. Wacky Taco
       1. Description: Low-fat Mexican food; most locations in malls
       2. Pros: 58 units available within a year; consultants believe the concept has significant growth potential; operations easy to manage
       3. Cons: Company recently hit with employment discrimination lawsuit; franchise fees are 30 percent above average
       4. Conclusion: Priority = 3; lawsuit may be indicative of mismanagement; fees too high
    B. Thai in the Sky
       1. Description: Thai food served in New Age settings
       2. Pros: Healthy and interesting food; unusual theme concept; no franchised competition
       3. Cons: Complexity of food preparation; only 40 franchises available; franchisor's top management team replaced only six months ago
       4. Conclusion: Priority = 4; too risky and not enough units available
    C. Dog Tower
       1. Description: Gourmet hot dogs
       2. Pros: No nationwide competition; more than 60 franchises available within a year; easy to manage; fees lower than average
       3. Cons: Limited market appeal; many stores need updating
       4. Conclusion: Priority = 2; needs too much investment
    D. Burger World
       1. Description: Mainstream competitor to McDonald's and Burger King

Covers two major steps: (1) establishing the decision criteria and (2) testing each of four alternatives against those criteria.

Assigns each of the four alternatives to an appropriate subdivision: description, pros, cons, and conclusion (priority).

---

       2. Pros: Aggressive franchisor willing to invest in national marketing; start-up costs are low; unique demographic target (teenagers and young adults; not a little kids' place)
       3. Cons: Fierce competition in burgers overall; some units in unproved locations
       4. Conclusion: Priority = 1; finances look good; research shows that teenagers will support a chain that doesn't cater to small children
V. Summary
VI. Appendixes
    A. Financial data
    B. Research results

Presents each alternative objectively—Swensen's task, even though the decision can never be black and white.

Figure 11–5
In-Depth Critique: Outline of a Proposal Using the Scientific Method

The Yardstick Approach: A Problem-Solving Report   One way to reduce the confusion presented by having a lot of alternatives is to establish a yardstick for evaluating them. You begin by discussing the problem, as with the scientific method, but then you set up the conditions that must be met to solve the problem. These are the criteria against which you evaluate all possible solutions. The body of the report evaluates those alternatives in relation to the criteria. The main points of the outline are either the criteria themselves or the alternatives.

With the yardstick approach, the report is organized around criteria; the solution is the alternative that best meets the criteria.

Yardstick reports are similar in some respects to those based on the scientific method, but in criteria-based reports, all the alternatives are reviewed against the same standards. Another distinction is that criteria-based reports can be used to prove the need for action: The current situation can be measured against the criteria and shown to be wanting.

The yardstick approach is useful for certain kinds of proposals because the client who requests the proposal often provides a list of criteria that the solution must meet. Say that your company has been asked to bid on a contract to install a computer for a large corporation. The client has listed the requirements (criteria) for the system, and you've developed a preliminary design to meet them. In the body of your proposal, you could use the client's list of requirements as the main headings and under each one explain how your preliminary design meets the requirement.

Some proposals are best organized by using the client's criteria as the main points.

Figure 11–6 is an outline of a yardstick report that was provided by J. C. Hartley, a market analyst for a large Sacramento company that makes irrigation equipment for farms and ranches. "We've been so successful in the agricultural market that we're starting to run out of customers to sell to," says Hartley. "To keep the company growing, we needed to find another market. Two obvious choices to consider were commercial buildings and residences." She was determined to make careful recommendations because, "even though I don't make the final decision, the information and the professional opinions that I provide in my report weigh heavily in the decision process."

If there is any disagreement on the decision criteria, you'll spin your wheels if you try to push forward to a decision. In Hartley's case, the criteria had been agreed to before she began her investigation, so she included the criteria in her report to remind her readers and make it easy for them to evaluate the options available.

For the yardstick approach to work, readers must accept your criteria.

The yardstick approach has one other drawback: It can be a little boring. You may find yourself saying the same things over and over again: "Opportunity A has high growth potential, opportunity B has high growth potential, opportunity C has high growth potential," and so on. One way to minimize the repetition is to compare the options in tables and then highlight the more unusual or important aspects of each alternative in the text so that you get the best of both worlds. This allows you to compare all the alternatives against the same yardstick but call attention to the most significant differences among them.

Tables are useful in the yardstick approach
- To avoid repetition
- To make the options easier to compare

Preparing the Final Outline

Once you've decided on the proper structure for your material, you can prepare a final report outline.[2] A final outline gives you a visual diagram of the report, its important points, the order in which they will be discussed, and the detail to be included. Sometimes you can use the preliminary outline that guided your research as a final blueprint for the report. More often, however, you have to rework the preliminary outline to take into account your purpose, your audience's probable reactions, and the things you learned during your study. Furthermore, you'll want to include only the items you plan to discuss in your report (your research outline may have additional topics).

Before you write your report, you may have to revise the outline you used to guide your research effort.

Aside from guiding you in the writing effort, preparing a final outline forces you to reevaluate the information you have selected to include and the order in which you present it. You may notice, once you look at the outline, that your discussion is too light in one area or too heavy in another. You may decide to use an indirect approach instead of a

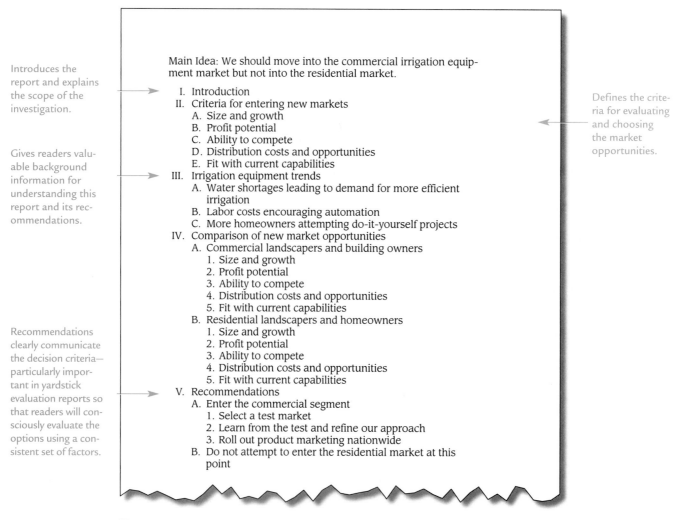

Introduces the report and explains the scope of the investigation.

Gives readers valuable background information for understanding this report and its recommendations.

Recommendations clearly communicate the decision criteria—particularly important in yardstick evaluation reports so that readers will consciously evaluate the options using a consistent set of factors.

Defines the criteria for evaluating and choosing the market opportunities.

Main Idea: We should move into the commercial irrigation equipment market but not into the residential market.

I. Introduction
II. Criteria for entering new markets
   A. Size and growth
   B. Profit potential
   C. Ability to compete
   D. Distribution costs and opportunities
   E. Fit with current capabilities
III. Irrigation equipment trends
   A. Water shortages leading to demand for more efficient irrigation
   B. Labor costs encouraging automation
   C. More homeowners attempting do-it-yourself projects
IV. Comparison of new market opportunities
   A. Commercial landscapers and building owners
      1. Size and growth
      2. Profit potential
      3. Ability to compete
      4. Distribution costs and opportunities
      5. Fit with current capabilities
   B. Residential landscapers and homeowners
      1. Size and growth
      2. Profit potential
      3. Ability to compete
      4. Distribution costs and opportunities
      5. Fit with current capabilities
V. Recommendations
   A. Enter the commercial segment
      1. Select a test market
      2. Learn from the test and refine our approach
      3. Roll out product marketing nationwide
   B. Do not attempt to enter the residential market at this point

Figure 11–6
In-Depth Critique: Outline of a Research Report Using the Yardstick Approach

A final outline is a work in progress.

direct one because now that you see your conclusions up front, you think it might be too forceful for your audience. Think of your final report outline as a working draft that you'll revise and modify as you go along.

As is often the case, you'll phrase your final outline so that the points on the outline can serve as headings that appear in the report (report headings are discussed later in this chapter). Bear in mind that the way you phrase outline headings will affect the tone of the report. If you want a hard-hitting, direct tone, use informative phrasing. If you prefer an objective, indirect tone, use descriptive phrasing. Be sure to use parallel construction when wording the points on the outline.

You can soften the force of controversial points by using descriptive (not informative) headings.

Once you've prepared a final outline, you can begin to identify which points should be illustrated with visual aids, such as tables, graphs, drawings, flowcharts, and so on.

ORGANIZING VISUAL AIDS FOR BUSINESS REPORTS

A visual aid is an illustration in tabular, graphic, schematic, or pictorial form.

Many report writers prefer to plan out and organize their visual aids before composing textual material.

Businesspeople such as FedEx's Frederick Smith include graphs and other visuals in their reports and proposals mainly to convey an important idea. But which would you prepare first, visuals or text? Although fitting visual aids to completed text makes some sense, many experienced businesspeople prefer to begin with the visual aids. Doing so has three advantages. First, much of the fact finding and analytical work is already in tabular or graphic form, so sorting through and refining your visuals will help you decide exactly what you're going to say. Second, by starting with the visual aids, you develop a graphic story line that

Table 11-2	When to Use Visuals
Purpose	*Application*
To clarify	Support text descriptions of "graphic" topics: quantitative or numerical information, explanations of trends, descriptions.
To simplify	Break complicated descriptions into components that can be depicted with conceptual models, flowcharts, organization charts, or diagrams.
To emphasize	Call attention to particularly important points by illustrating them with line, bar, and pie charts.
To summarize	Review major points in the narrative by providing a chart or table that sums up the data.
To reinforce	Present information in visual and written form to increase reader's retention.
To attract	Make material seem more interesting by decorating the cover or title page and by breaking up the text with visual aids.
To impress	Build credibility by putting ideas into visual form to convey the impression of authenticity and precision.
To unify	Depict the relationship among points—for example, with a flowchart.

can be used for your written report. Finally, because your text will explain and refer to any tables, charts, and graphs you include, you save time by having them ready before beginning to compose your text, particularly if you plan to use quite a few visuals.

Gaining an Advantage with Visuals

Carefully prepared visuals can make your report or presentation more interesting. But even more important, pictures are an effective way to communicate with the diverse audiences that are common in today's business environment. In addition, in the numbers-oriented world of work, people rely heavily on images. They think in terms of trend lines, distribution curves, and percentages. An upward curve means good news in any language. Finally, visual aids attract and hold people's attention.

Visual aids help communicators get through to an audience.

Despite their value, Frederick Smith recommends that you use visual aids selectively and include only those elements that support your primary message. Use visuals to supplement the written word, not to replace it. Restrict your use of visual aids to situations in which they do the most good. Table 11–2 helps you identify those situations.

"Visualizing" Information

When you begin to compose a report or a presentation, you usually have a lot of raw data that can be molded into any number of messages. As you sort through the information you compiled during the research phase, you begin to see relationships and draw conclusions. The following steps help you decide how many and what type of visuals to include in your report:

◆ **Decide on the message.** You must decide which interpretation of the data is most useful for your purpose and your audience. As you sort through your facts, looking at various interpretations, an outline of a message will begin to emerge. Some of these facts lend themselves to a prose presentation; others may be expressed more easily in graphic form.

When planning and organizing visual aids
- Decide what you want to say.
- Pick out the points that can best be made visually.
- Judge whether you have too many or too few graphics.

◆ **Identify the points requiring visual support.** Think of each main point as a separate scene in a movie, and picture a chart or graph that would visually dramatize that point and communicate it to your audience. Some elements are confusing and tedious in paragraph form. But tables and graphs conveniently organize and display facts and figures, and flowcharts, drawings, and photographs clarify detailed descriptions of physical relationships or procedures.

◆ **Maintain a balance between illustrations and words.** The ideal blend of words and pictures depends on the nature of your subject. Illustrating every point dilutes the effectiveness of your visuals and can confuse readers who assume that the amount of space allocated to a topic indicates its relative importance. Also, if you know that your audience prefers either words or pictures, you can adjust your balance accordingly.

◆ **Consider your production schedule.** If you're producing your report without the help of an art department or appropriate computer-graphics tools, you may want to restrict the number of visuals in your report. Making charts and tables takes time, particularly if you're inexperienced. In addition, constructing visual aids requires a good deal of imagination and attention to detail.

Deciding on the appropriate type of graph is always a challenge. Keep in mind that most types of graphs are not interchangeable. As we see in the next section, different types of graphs best depict different types of data.

Selecting the Right Graphic for the Job

O b j e c t i v e

List the most popular types of visuals and discuss when to use them.

3

Choose a type of graphic that best presents your message.

Once you've selected which points to illustrate graphically, your next step is to select the type of graph that will present your data most clearly and effectively to your audience:

◆ To present detailed, exact values, use tables.

◆ To illustrate trends over time, use a line chart or a bar chart.

◆ To show frequency or distribution, use a pie chart, segmented bar chart, or area chart.

◆ To compare one item with another, use a bar chart.

◆ To compare one part with the whole, use a pie chart.

◆ To show correlations, use a line chart, a bar chart, or a scatter (dot) chart.

◆ To show geographic relationships, use a map.

◆ To illustrate a process or a procedure, use a flowchart or a diagram.

Here's a closer look at each of these graphic types.

Use tables to help your audience understand detailed information.

Tables   When you have to present detailed, specific information, choose a **table,** a systematic arrangement of data in columns and rows. Tables are ideal when the audience needs the information that would be either difficult or tedious to handle in the main text.

Most tables contain the standard parts illustrated in Table 11–3. Every table includes vertical columns and horizontal rows, with useful headings along the top and side. Tables projected onto a screen during an oral presentation should be limited to three column heads and six row heads; tables presented on paper may include from one or two heads to a dozen or more. If the table has too many columns to fit comfortably between the margins of the page, turn the paper horizontally and insert it in the report with the top toward the binding.

Table 11–3 Parts of a Table				
		*Multicolumn Head**		
Stub Head	*Subhead*	*Subhead*	*Single-column head*	*Single-column head*
Row head	XXX	XXX	XX	XX
Row head				
Subhead	XX	XXX	XX	X
Subhead	XX	XXX	XX	XX
Total	XXX	XXX	XX	XX

Source: (In the same format as a text footnote; see Appendix B.)

*Footnote (for explanation of elements in the table; a superscript number or small letter may be used instead of a asterisk or other symbol.)

Although formal tables set apart from the text are necessary for complex information, you can present some data more simply within the text. You make the table, in essence, a part of the paragraph, typed in tabular format. Such text tables are usually introduced with a sentence that leads directly into the tabulated information. Here's an example:

However, we need to compare just how Amazon.com measures up against rival Barnes & Noble:

Feature	Amazon.com	Barnes & Noble
Number of stores	1 Web site	1,011
Titles per superstore	3.1 million	175,000
Book returns	2%	30%
Sales per employee (annual)	$375,000	$100,000
Inventory turnovers per year	24	3
Long-term capital requirements	Low	High
Cash flow	High	Low

Source: "Amazon.com the Wild World of E-Commerce," *Business Week,* 14 December 1998, 110.

Although many tables are strictly numerical, tables that also use words can be just as useful. Some tables contain no numbers at all. They are particularly appropriate for presenting survey findings or for comparing various items against a specific standard.

> Use word tables
> • To summarize survey results
> • To compare items with some standard

When preparing a numerical table, be sure to

♦ Use common, understandable units, and clearly identify the units you're using: dollars, percentages, price per ton, or whatever.

♦ Express all items in a column in the same unit, and round off for simplicity.

♦ Label column headings clearly, and use a subhead if necessary.

♦ Separate columns or rows with lines or extra space to make the table easy to follow.

♦ Provide column-to-row totals or averages when relevant.

♦ Document the source of the data below the table using the same format as a text footnote (see Appendix B).

Line and Surface Charts   A **line chart** illustrates trends over time or plots the relationship of two variables. In line charts showing trends, the vertical, or *y,* axis shows the amount, and the horizontal, or *x,* axis shows the time or the quantity being measured. Ordinarily, both scales begin at zero and proceed in equal increments; however, in Figure 11–7 the vertical axis is broken to show that some of the increments have been left out. A broken axis is appropriate when the data are plotted far above zero, but be sure to clearly indicate the omission of data points.

> Use line charts
> • To indicate changes over time
> • To plot the relationship of two variables

A simple line chart may be arranged in many ways. One of the most common is to plot several lines on the same chart for comparative purposes, as shown in Figure 11–8. Try to use no more than three lines on any given chart, particularly if the lines cross. Another variation of the simple line chart has a vertical axis with both positive and negative numbers (see Figure 11–9). This arrangement is handy when you have to illustrate losses.

A **surface chart,** also called an **area chart,** is a form of line chart with a cumulative effect; all the lines add up to the top line, which represents the total (see Figure 11–10). This form of chart helps you illustrate changes in the composition of something over time. When preparing a surface chart, put the most important segment against the baseline, and restrict the number of strata to four or five.

> A surface chart is a kind of line chart showing a cumulative effect.

Figure 11–7
Line Chart with Broken Axis

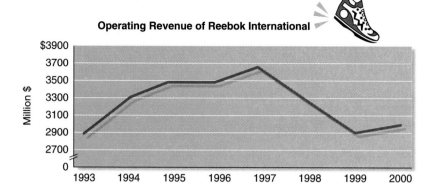

Figure 11–8
Line Chart with Multiple Lines

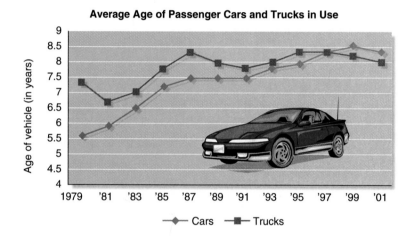

Figure 11–9
Line Chart with Positive and
Negative Values on Vertical Axis

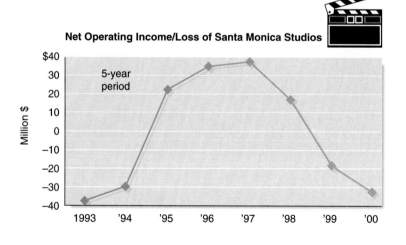

Bar charts, in which numbers are visually portrayed by rectangular bars, can take a variety of forms.

Bar Charts   A **bar chart** portrays numbers by the height or length of its rectangular bars, making a series of numbers easy to read or understand. Bar charts are particularly valuable when you want to

◆ Compare the size of several items at one time

◆ Show changes in one item over time

◆ Indicate the composition of several items over time

◆ Show the relative size of components of a whole

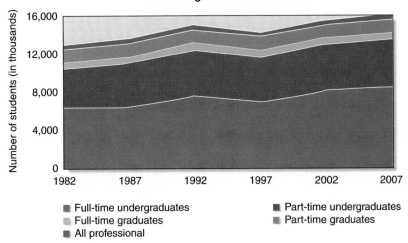

The College Market of Tomorrow

Full-time undergraduates

Full-time graduates

All professional

Part-time undergraduates

Part-time graduates

Figure 11–10
Surface Chart

As Figure 11–11 on pages 334–335 shows, bar charts can be singular (Where the College Students Are), grouped (Eating Occasions), segmented (Targeted Talk), or a combination of chart types (Commercial Superhighway—line and bar). Grouped bar charts compare more than one set of data (using a different color or pattern for each set). Segmented bar charts, also known as stacked bar charts, show how individual components contribute to a total number (using a different color or pattern for each component). Combination bar and line charts compare quantities that require different intervals.

You can be creative with bar charts in many ways. You might align the bars either vertically or horizontally or you might even use bar charts to show both positive and negative quantities. Be careful, however, to keep all the bars in the chart the same width; different widths could suggest a relative importance to the viewer. In addition, space the bars evenly and place them in a logical order, such as chronological or alphabetical. Keep in mind that most computer software (such as Microsoft Excel) will generate charts from data tables. The software will place the data in a graph based on the order that is used in the table. So plan ahead, and if you don't like the way the computer interprets your data graphically, go back to the data table and adjust the order there first.

Pie Charts   Like segmented bar charts and area charts, a **pie chart** shows how parts of a whole are distributed. Each segment represents a slice of a complete circle, or *pie*. As you can see in Figure 11–12 on page 336, pie charts are an effective way to show percentages or to compare one segment with another. You can combine pie charts with tables to expand the usefulness of such visuals.

> Use pie charts to show the relative sizes of the parts of a whole.

When composing pie charts, try to restrict the number of slices in the pie. Otherwise, the chart looks cluttered and is difficult to label. If necessary, lump the smallest pieces together in a "miscellaneous" category. Ideally, the largest or most important slice of the pie, the segment you want to emphasize, is placed at the twelve o'clock position; the rest are arranged clockwise either in order of size or in some other logical progression.

Use different colors or patterns to distinguish the various pieces. If you want to draw attention to the segment that is of the greatest interest to your readers, use a brighter color for that segment, draw an arrow to the segment, or explode it; that is, pull the segment away from the rest of the pie. In any case, label all the segments and indicate their value in either percentages or units of measure so that your readers will be able to judge the value of the wedges. Remember, the segments must add up to 100 percent if percentages are used or to the total number if numbers are used.

Flowcharts and Organization Charts   If you need to show physical or conceptual relationships rather than numerical ones, you might want to use a flowchart or an organization

Figure 11–11
The Versatile Bar Chart

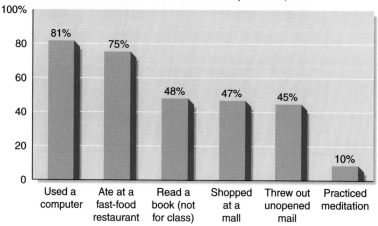

Where the College Students Are

Percentage of undergraduates enrolled full-time in four-year colleges and universities who did selected activities in the past week, 1997

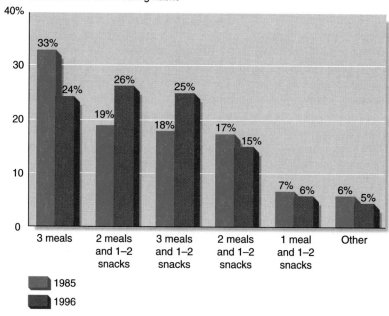

Eating Occasions

Percentage of adults aged 18 and older who say that selected patterns best describe their usual eating habits

Use flowcharts
• To show a series of steps from beginning to end
• To show sequential relationships

Use organization charts to depict the interrelationships among the parts of an organization.

Use maps
• To represent statistics by geographic area
• To show location relationships

chart. A **flowchart** illustrates a sequence of events from start to finish. It is indispensable when illustrating processes, procedures, and sequential relationships. The various elements in the process you want to portray may be represented by pictorial symbols or geometric shapes, as shown in Figure 11–13 on page 336.

An **organization chart,** as the name implies, illustrates the positions, units, or functions of an organization and the way they interrelate. An organization's normal communication channels are almost impossible to describe without the benefit of a chart like that in Chapter 1 (see Figure 1–5).

Maps   For certain applications, maps are ideal. One of the most common uses is to show concentrations of something by geographic area. In your own reports, you might use maps to show regional differences in variables such as your company's sales of a product, or you might indicate proposed plant sites and their relationship to key markets.

Figure 11–11
Continued

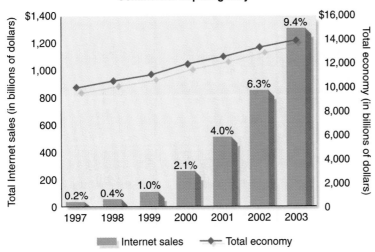

Most U.S. office-supply stores carry blank maps of various regions of the world, including all or part of the United States. You can illustrate these maps to suit your needs, using dots, shading, color, labels, numbers, and symbols. In addition, popular programs such as Excel and CorelDraw! come with regional, country, and world map templates. You just insert the columns of data and assign the data to a state or a country; the software will do the rest. Figure 11–14 (on page 337) was prepared using Excel's built-in map feature, the map template for the United States, and the projected state populations for 2025.

Drawings, Diagrams, and Photographs   Although less commonly used than other visual aids, drawings, diagrams, and photographs can also be valuable elements in business reports and presentations. Drawings and diagrams are most often used to show how something looks or operates. Figure 11–15 (on page 337) was prepared using Visio software and explains the benefits of converged communication networks over traditional networks. Diagrams can be much clearer than words alone when it comes to giving your audience an idea of how an item looks or can be used. In industries such as engineering and architecture, computer-aided design (CAD) systems produce detailed diagrams and

Use drawings and diagrams to show
• How something looks or works
• How something is made or used

Figure 11–12
Pie Chart

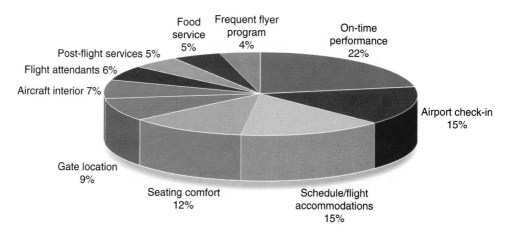

Ten Factors Drive Overall Airline Satisfaction

Percent of Contribution to Overall Satisfaction with the Flight

Figure 11–13
Flowchart

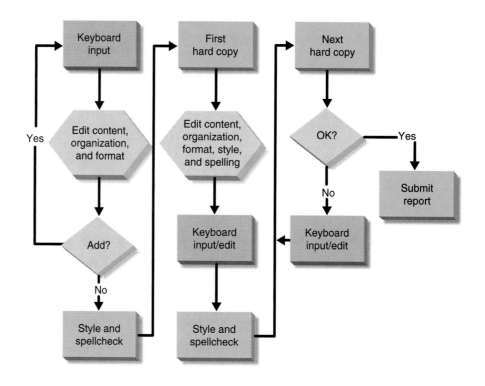

Use photographs
• For visual appeal
• To show exact appearance

drawings. A variety of widely available software programs for microcomputers provide a file of symbols and pictures of various types that can be used (sparingly) to add a decorative touch to reports and presentations.

Photographs have always been popular in certain types of business documents, such as annual reports, where their visual appeal is used to capture the interest of readers. As the technology for reproducing photographs improves and becomes less expensive, even analytical business reports for internal use are beginning to include more photographs. Digital cameras now make it easy to drop photographic images directly into a report or presentation. Furthermore, the collection of available photographs that you can import, crop, and clip grows daily. CD-ROMs provide an abundance of image libraries, and the Internet is another terrific resource for images. In most cases you can download pictures off the Internet for free; just be sure to give proper credit as you would for any material that you use from another source. To find specific photographs, images, or designs on the Internet, try the Web site AltaVista Photo Finder, image.altavista.com/cgi-bin/avncgi.

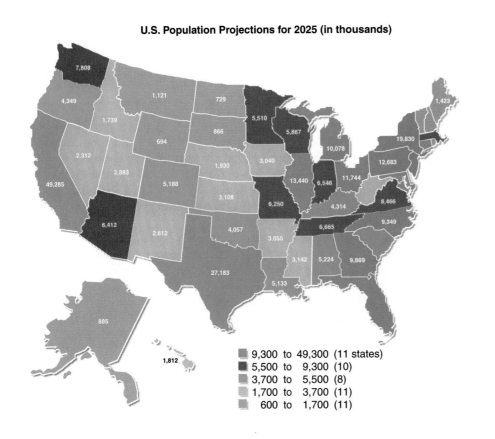

U.S. Population Projections for 2025 (in thousands)

Figure 11–14
Map

Traditional Networks versus Converged Networks

Figure 11–15
Diagram

Nothing can demonstrate the exact appearance of a new facility, a piece of property or equipment, or a new product the way a photograph can. However, in some situations a photograph may show too much detail. This is one of the reasons that repair manuals frequently use drawings instead of photos. With a drawing, you can select how much detail to show and focus the reader's attention on particular parts or places.

Although technology has made it easier to use photographs in reports and presentations, it also presents an important ethical concern. Software tools such as Photoshop and CorelDraw! make it easy for computer users to make dramatic changes to photos—without leaving a clue that they've been altered. Making small changes to photos has been possible for a long time (more than a few people have blemishes airbrushed out of

Today's technology for altering photos raises serious ethical questions.

their yearbook photos), but computers make drastic changes easy and undetectable. You can remove people from photographs, put Person A's head on Person B's body, and make products look more attractive than they really are. As you do when using other technological tools, stop and ask yourself where the truth lies before you start making changes.[3]

Designing Graphics for Reports

Professional-looking graphics used to be extremely expensive and time consuming to produce, but personal computer technology has changed all that. Graphics that used to cost hundreds of dollars and take several days to complete can now be done in minutes for little cost. Instead of relying on graphic designers, businesspeople are turning out their own professional-looking visual aids by turning to **computer graphics:** charts and graphs created and produced using a computer program.

Before you take advantage of any computer-graphics tools, think about the kind of image you want to project. The style of your visual aids communicates a subtle message about your relationship with the audience. A simple, hand-drawn diagram is fine for a working meeting but inappropriate for a formal presentation or report. On the other hand, elaborate, full-color visuals may be viewed as extravagant for an informal memo but may be entirely appropriate for a message to top management or influential outsiders. The image you want to project should determine the visual aid you create.

Understanding Graphic Design Principles   Few of us have studied the "language" of line, mass, space, size, color, pattern, and texture. When arranged in certain ways, these elements of visual design are pleasing to the eye. More important for the business communicator, as FedEx's Fred Smith can tell you, design elements have a meaning of their own. A thick line implies more power than a thin one; a bold color suggests strength; a solid mass seems substantial. To create effective visual aids, become aware of both the aesthetic and the symbolic aspects of graphic art so that you won't send the wrong message. Here are a few principles to remember:

Objective

4

Clarify five principles of graphic design to remember when preparing visuals.

◆ **Continuity.** Readers view a series of visual aids as a whole, assuming that design elements will be consistent from one page to the next. For instance, if your first chart shows results for division A in blue, readers will expect division A to be shown in blue throughout the report. You'll confuse people by arbitrarily changing color, shape, size, position, scale, or typeface.

◆ **Contrast.** Readers expect visual distinctions to match verbal ones. To emphasize differences, depict items in contrasting colors: red and blue, black and white. But to emphasize similarities, make color differences more subtle. In a pie chart, you might show two similar items in two shades of blue and a dissimilar item in yellow. Accent colors draw attention to key elements, but they lose their effect if you overdo them.

◆ **Emphasis.** Readers assume the most important point will receive the most visual emphasis. So present the key item on the chart in the most prominent way—through color, position, size, or whatever. Visually downplay less important items. Avoid using strong colors for unimportant data, and de-emphasize background features such as the grid lines on a chart.

◆ **Simplicity.** Limit the number of colors and design elements you use in reports. Also avoid *chartjunk,* the decorative elements that clutter documents (and confuse readers) without adding any relevant information.[4] Computers make it far too easy to add chartjunk, from clip art illustrations to three-dimensional bar charts that display only two dimensions of data.

◆ **Experience.** Culture and education condition people to expect things to look a certain way, including report visuals. For example, green may be associated with money in the United States, but not in countries whose currency is red or blue or yellow. A red cross on a white background stands for emergency medical care in many countries. But the cross is also a Christian symbol, so the International Red Cross uses a red crescent in Islamic countries.[5]

When designing visual aids, observe the principles of continuity, contrast, emphasis, simplicity, and experience.

The best time to think about the principles of good design is before preparing your visual aids; making changes after the fact increases the amount of time required to produce them.

Fitting Graphics into the Text   Your approach to integrating text and visuals depends on the type of report you're preparing. If you're working on a glossy public relations document, handle the visual aids as though they were illustrations in a magazine, positioning them to attract interest and tell a story of their own. However, in most business documents, the visuals clarify the text, so tie them closely to the discussion. Integrate your visuals into text in a manner that is convenient for your audience and practical from a production standpoint.

To tie visual aids to your text
- Introduce them in the text.
- Place them near the points they illustrate.
- Choose a meaningful title and legend for each one.

Introduce Visuals in the Text   Every visual you use should be clearly referred to by number in the text of your report. Some report writers refer to all visual aids as exhibits and number them consecutively throughout the report; many others number tables and figures separately (everything that isn't a table is regarded as a figure). In a long report with numbered chapters (as in this book), visuals may have a double number (separated by a period or a hyphen) representing the chapter number and the individual illustration number within that chapter.

Help your readers understand the significance of any visual aids by referring to them before they appear in the text. The reference helps readers understand why the table or chart is important. The following examples show how you can make this connection in the text:

Figure 1 summarizes the financial history of the motorcycle division over the past five years, with sales broken into four categories.

Total sales were steady over this period, but the mix of sales by category changed dramatically (see Figure 2).

The underlying reason for the remarkable growth in our sales of low-end fax machines is suggested by Table 4, which provides data on fax machine sales in the United States by region and model.

At Chapwell Marketing Resources, graphics play an important role not only in clients' projects but also in the company's own annual report. "It's worth the effort to learn how to incorporate effective visuals," says Ted Chapwell, founding partner (seated) along with Mark Wellington. "There's no better way to enhance a good report."

When describing the data shown in your visual aids, be sure to emphasize the main point you are trying to make. Don't make the mistake of simply repeating the data to be shown. Paragraphs like this are guaranteed to put the reader to sleep:

Among women who replied to the survey, 17.4 percent earn less than $5 per hour; 26.4 percent earn $5-$7; 25.7 percent, $8-$12; 18.0 percent, $13-$24; 9.6 percent, $25-$49; and 2.9 percent earn $50 and over.

The visual will provide these details; there is no need to repeat them in the text. Instead, use round numbers that sum up the message:

Over two-thirds of the women who replied earn less than $12 per hour.

Place Visual Aids near the Points They Illustrate   Try to position your visual aids so that your audience won't have to flip back and forth too much between the visuals and the text. Ideally, it is best to place each visual aid right beside or right after the paragraph it illustrates so that readers can consult the explanation and the visual at the same time. Make sure each visual is clearly and correctly referred to in the text. If you have four or more visual aids, prepare a separate list of them that can be placed with the table of contents at the front of the report. Some writers list tables separately from figures. The two lists should start on separate pages unless both lists will fit on the same page.

Put a visual aid as close as possible to its in-text reference to help readers understand the illustration's relevance.

Most word-processing programs and desktop publishing systems let you create layouts with artwork and text on the same page. If you don't have these programs, or choose not to integrate your visuals with text, then put the visual aids on separate pages and include them with the text after the report has been prepared. Having visual aids on separate pages raises the question of where to put them. Some writers prefer to cluster them at the end of the report, either as a separate section or as an appendix. Others group them at the end of each chapter. Still others prefer to place them as close as possible to the paragraphs they illustrate. Although a case can be made for each approach, the best one is generally to place the page with a visual aid right after the page referring to it. This arrangement encourages readers to look at the visual aids when you want them to, in the context you have prepared.

Titles and legends should
- *Reinforce the point you want to make*
- *Be specific*

Choose Titles and Legends with a Message   One of the best ways to tie your visual aids to the text is to choose titles (or captions) and descriptions (or legends) that reinforce the point you want to make. This precaution is especially necessary when the visual aids are widely separated from the text.

The title of a visual aid, when combined with labels and legends on the piece itself, should be complete enough to tell the reader what the content is. The title "Petroleum Tanks in the United States" is sufficient if it's the title of a line chart labeled "Year" along the horizontal axis and "Number (in thousands)" along the vertical axis. However, if the visual aid is a map overlaid with dots of different sizes, the title needs to explain a bit more: "Concentrations of Petroleum Tanks in the United States in 1999." A legend might then explain how many petroleum tanks each size of dot represents.

Legends identify specific content of visual aids.

When you place a visual aid next to the text discussion that pertains to it, clear labeling and a good title are usually enough; the text can explain the visual aid's significance and details. However, when you place a visual aid elsewhere or when the illustration requires considerable explanation that would disrupt the flow of the text, you may need to add a description (or legend). Legends are generally written as one or more complete sentences, and they do more than merely repeat what's already clear from the title and figure labels. It's better to be too specific than too general when you're identifying the content of an illustration. As a check, ask yourself whether you've covered the who, what, when, where, why, and how of the illustration.

If you're using informative headings in your report, carry this style over into the titles and legends. Instead of using a descriptive title, which identifies the topic of the illustration, call attention to the conclusion that ought to be drawn from the data by using an informative title. Here's the difference:

DESCRIPTIVE TITLE	INFORMATIVE TITLE
Relationship between Petroleum Demand and Refinery Capacity in the United States	Shrinking Refinery Capacity Results from Stagnant Petroleum Demand

Phrase titles and legends in a consistent manner.

Regardless of whether your titles and legends are informative or descriptive, phrase them consistently throughout the report. At the same time, be consistent in your format. If the title of the first visual aid is typed entirely in capital letters, type all the remaining titles that way as well. Although an employer may specify the placement of titles, as a general rule place all table titles at the top. Figure titles may be placed at the top or the bottom. When using legends, make them all roughly the same length. (For a review of the important points to remember when creating visual aids, see this chapter's "Checklist: Creating Effective Visual Aids.")

COMPOSING BUSINESS REPORTS AND PROPOSALS

Once you've organized the text and visuals for your report, you're nearly ready to begin composing it. However, to ensure your report's success, you need to make several deci-

Checklist: Creating Effective Visual Aids

Preparation

✓ Select the proper types of graphics for the data and for the objective of the message.
✓ Be sure the visual aid contributes to overall understanding of the subject.
✓ Depict data accurately.
✓ Portray information honestly.
✓ Give proper credit, if required, and follow proper bibliographic form.
✓ Make sure that the material is appropriate for the intended audience.

Design

✓ Make design elements consistent.
✓ Make sure that design elements meet audience expectations.
✓ Use color effectively.

✓ Emphasize important points.
✓ Make visuals simple and easy to understand.
✓ Make headings, labels, titles, and legends clear, whether descriptive or informative.
✓ Use space appropriately.
✓ Clearly identify data units so that they are easily understandable.
✓ Use typefaces and fonts that are clear and readable.
✓ Use clip art sparingly.

Layout

✓ Balance words and visuals.
✓ Clearly reference illustrations in text.
✓ Assign each illustration a number or letter.
✓ Place visuals close to the points they illustrate.
✓ Make sure that visuals appear balanced on the page.
✓ Make captions short, precise, and informative.

---

sions that will affect the way it's received and understood by readers. You must set the degree of formality, establish a consistent time perspective, and insert appropriate structural clues.

Choosing the Proper Degree of Formality

The issue of formality is closely related to considerations of format, length, and organization. If you know your readers reasonably well and if your report is likely to meet with their approval, you can generally adopt a fairly informal tone. You can speak to readers in the first person, referring to yourself as *I* and to your readers as *you*. This personal approach is often used in brief memo or letter reports, although there are many exceptions.

> For informal reports, adopt a personal style, using the pronouns *I* and *you*.

Longer reports, especially those dealing with controversial or complex information, are traditionally written using a more formal tone. You'll also write more formally when your report will be sent to other parts of the organization or to customers or suppliers. Communicating with people in other cultures often calls for more formality, for two reasons. First, the business environment outside the United States tends to be more formal in general, and that formality must be reflected in your communication style. Second, the things you do to make a document informal, such as using humor and idiomatic language, are the hardest to transfer from culture to culture. Reducing formality in these cases increases the risk of offending people and miscommunicating.

You achieve a formal tone by using the impersonal style, eliminating all references to *I* (including *we, us,* and *our*) and *you*. The style is borrowed from journalism, which stresses the reporter's objectivity. However, be careful that avoiding personal pronouns doesn't lead to overuse of phrases such as *there is* and *it is,* which are both dull and wordy. Also, avoiding personal pronouns makes it easier to slip into passive voice, which can be dull and wordy. Instead of saying "I think we should buy TramCo," you might end up saying "It is recommended that the company buy TramCo."

When you write in a formal style, you impose a certain distance between you and your readers. You remain businesslike, unemotional, and objective. You eliminate your own opinions and perceptions and retain only the provable facts (see "Promoting Workplace Ethics—Top Tips for Writing Reports That Mean Business"). You use no jokes, no similes or metaphors, and very few colorful adjectives or adverbs. You can easily

As chairman of the board of Computer Associates International, Charles B. Wang focuses on new business initiatives to compete in an expanding global market. To organize complex information for a culturally diverse audience, Wang makes sure that his company's reports adopt a formal tone to reduce the chance of miscommunication.

Promoting Workplace Ethics

Top Tips for Writing Reports That Mean Business

Put nothing in writing that you're unwilling to say in public, and write nothing that may embarrass or jeopardize your employer. Does this mean you should cover up problems? Of course not. However, when you're dealing with sensitive information, be discreet. Present the information in such a way that it will help readers solve a problem. Avoid personal gripes, criticisms, alibis, attempts to blame other people, sugar-coated data, and unsolicited opinions.

To be useful, the information must be accurate, complete, and honest. However, being honest is not always a simple matter. Each of us sees reality a little differently, and we describe what we see in our own way. To restrict the distortions introduced by differences in perception, follow these guidelines.

❏ **Describe facts or events in concrete terms.** Indicate quantities whenever you can. Say that "Sales have increased 17 percent," or that "Sales have increased from $40,000 to $43,000 in the past two months." Don't say, "Sales have skyrocketed."

❏ **Report all relevant facts.** Regardless of whether these facts support your theories or please your readers, they must be included. Omitting the details that undermine your position may be convenient, but it is misleading and inaccurate.

❏ **Put the facts in perspective.** Taken out of context, the most concrete facts are misleading. If you say "Stock values have doubled in three weeks," you offer an incomplete picture. Instead, say "Stock values have doubled in three weeks, rising from $2 to $4 per share."

❏ **Give plenty of evidence for your conclusions.** Statements such as "We have to reorganize the sales force or we'll lose market share" may or may not be true. Readers have no way of knowing unless you provide enough data to support your claim.

❏ **Present only verifiable conclusions.** Check facts, and use reliable sources. Don't draw conclusions too quickly (one rep may say that customers are unhappy, but that doesn't mean they all are). And don't assume that one event caused another (sales may have dipped right after you switched ad agencies, but that doesn't mean the new agency is at fault—the general state of the economy may be responsible).

❏ **Keep your personal biases in check.** Even if you feel strongly about your topic, keep those feelings from influencing your choice of words. Don't say, "Locating a plant in Kraymore is a terrible idea because the people there are mostly students who would rather play than work and who don't have the ability to operate our machines." Such language not only offends but also obscures the facts and provokes emotional responses.

CAREER APPLICATIONS

1. When would you use vague language instead of concrete detail? Would this action be unethical or merely one form of emphasizing the positive?
2. Recent budget cuts have endangered the day-care program at your local branch of a national company. You're writing a report for headquarters about the grave impact on employees. Describe the situation in a single sentence that reveals nothing about your personal feelings but that clearly shows your position.

---

destroy your credibility by exaggerating and using overblown language. Consider the following example:

> The catastrophic collapse in sales, precipitated by cutthroat pricing on the part of predatory and unscrupulous rivals, has jeopardized the very survival of the once-soaring hot-air balloon division.

Although this sentence contains no personal references, the colorful adjectives make its objectivity highly questionable.

Nor does the formal style guarantee objectivity of content. The selection of facts is far more important than the way they're phrased. If you omit crucial evidence, you're not being objective, even though you're using an impersonal style.

Despite its drawbacks, the impersonal style is a well-entrenched tradition in many business organizations. You can often tell what tone is appropriate for your readers by looking at other reports of a similar type in your company. If all the other reports on file are impersonal, you should probably adopt the same tone yourself, unless you're confident that your readers prefer a more personal style. However, most organizations expect an unobtrusive, impersonal writing style for business reports.

Establishing a Time Perspective

In what time frame will your report exist? Will you write in the past or present tense? The person who wrote this paragraph never decided:

> Of those interviewed 25 percent <u>report</u> that they <u>are</u> dissatisfied with their present brand. The wealthiest participants <u>complained</u> most frequently, but all income categories <u>are</u> interested in trying a new brand. Only 5 percent of the interviewees <u>say</u> they <u>had</u> no interest in alternative products.

By flipping from tense to tense when describing the same research results, you only confuse your readers. Is the shift significant, they wonder, or are you just being sloppy? Such confusion can be eliminated by using tense consistently.

Also be careful to observe the chronological sequence of events in your report. If you're describing the history or development of something, start at the beginning and cover each event in the order of its occurrence. If you're explaining the steps in a process, take each step in proper sequence.

Be consistent in the verb tense you use.

Follow a proper chronological sequence in your report.

Helping Readers Find Their Way

As you begin to compose the text for your report, remember that readers have no concept of how the various pieces of your report relate to one another. Because you have done the work, you have a sense of your document's wholeness and can see how each page fits into the overall structure. But readers see the report one page at a time. Report experts such as FedEx's Fred Smith know that good writers give their readers a preview or road map of a report's structure, clarifying how the various parts are related. These directions are particularly important for people from other cultures and countries, whose language skills and business expectations may differ from yours.

In a short report, readers are in little danger of getting lost. As the length of a report increases, however, so do readers' opportunities for becoming confused and losing track of the relationships among ideas. If you want readers to understand and accept your message, help them avoid confusion. Five tools are particularly useful for giving readers a sense of the overall structure of your document and for keeping them on track as they read along: the opening, headings and lists, smooth transitions, previews and reviews, and the ending.

O b j e c t i v e **5**

Identify and briefly describe five tools that writers can use in long reports to help readers stay on track.

Your readers' perspective differs from yours, so without help from you, they may not see your overall organization, and they may not understand how all the pieces fit together.

The Opening

As the name suggests, the **opening** is the first section in any report. A good opening accomplishes at least three things:

◆ Introduces the subject of the report.

◆ Indicates why the subject is important.

◆ Previews the main ideas and the order in which they'll be covered.

If you fail to provide readers with these clues to the structure of your report, they'll read aimlessly and miss important points, much like drivers trying to find their way through a strange city without a map.

If your audience is skeptical, the opening should downplay the controversial aspects of your message while providing the necessary framework for understanding your report. Here's a good example of an indirect opening, taken from the introduction of a memo on why a new line of luggage has failed to sell well. The writer's ultimate goal is to recommend a shift in marketing strategy.

In the opening, tell readers what to expect, tell them why your subject is important, and orient them toward your organizational approach.

> The performance of the Venturer line can be improved. In the two years since its introduction, this product line has achieved a sales volume lower than we expected, resulting in a drain on the company's overall earnings. The purpose of this report is to review the luggage-buying habits of consumers in all markets where the Venturer line is sold so that we can determine where to put our marketing emphasis.

Sharpening Your Career Skills

Writing Headings That Grab Your Reader

Headings help readers follow the main points of your report, but when carefully developed, they also do much more. By capturing interest, they make readers want to read your entire report. By showing how your document is organized, they save readers time. By labeling the parts of your document, they help readers find the most important or most relevant parts. Moreover, headings help you organize your writing.

Each heading offers you an opportunity to make an important point. For example, instead of "Introduction," your opening section might be called "An Insight into the Need for Better Communication." This heading gets attention and sparks interest. The heading "Chart of Proposed Organization" gains impact when reworded as "Organizing for Results." So does "Cost Considerations" when retitled "A New Way to Cut Costs."

Headings fall into two categories. Descriptive (topical) headings, such as "Cost Considerations," identify a topic but do little more. However, they are fine in routine reports and in controversial reports, where they may defuse emotional reactions. Informative (talking) headings, such as "A New Way to Cut Costs," convey more information about the main idea of the report. They help readers think about your topic in a certain way. For more effective reports, concentrate on

developing informative headings rather than descriptive ones. However, be aware that informative headings are more difficult to create.

Try to avoid vague headings. In a chronological history of your company, headings such as "The Dawning of a New Era" and "The Times They Are a-Changin'" may sound distinguished or cute, but readers will have no idea what period you are discussing. Preferable headings would be "The War Years: Gebco Outfits Our GIs" or "The 1990s See International Expansion."

Whatever headings you choose, try to keep them grammatically parallel. For example, this series of headings is parallel: "Cutting Costs," "Reducing Inventory," "Increasing Profits." This series of headings is not: "Cutting Costs," "Inventory Reduction," "How to Increase Profits."

CAREER APPLICATIONS

1. Think about newspaper headlines. What functions do they perform? How are they usually phrased? What can you learn from journalistic headlines that would apply to report writing?
2. For practice in writing headings, collect some brochures, newsletters, or similar items and rewrite the headings to convey more information about the theme or main idea.

This paragraph quickly introduces the subject (disappointing sales), tells why the problem is important (drain on earnings), and indicates the main points to be addressed in the body of the report (review of markets where the Venturer line is sold), without revealing what the conclusions and recommendations will be.

Headings and Lists

Use headings to give readers the gist of your report.

A **heading** is a brief title at the start of a subdivision within a report. Headings cue readers about the content of the section that follows. Headings are useful markers for clarifying the framework of a report. They visually indicate shifts from one idea to the next, and when *subheadings* (lower-level headings) and headings are both used, they help readers see the relationship between subordinate and main ideas. In addition, busy readers can quickly understand the gist of a document simply by scanning the headings. (See "Sharpening Your Career Skills—Writing Headings That Grab Your Reader.")

Phrase all same-level headings within a section in parallel terms.

Within a given section, headings of the same level should be phrased in parallel form, as they are in outlines. If one heading begins with a verb, all same-level headings in that section should begin with a verb. If one is a noun phrase, all should be noun phrases. Putting comparable ideas in similar terms tells readers that the ideas are related. The only exception might be descriptive headings such as "Introduction" at the beginning of a report and "Conclusions" and "Recommendations" at the end. Many companies specify a format for headings. If yours does, use that format. Otherwise, you can use the scheme shown in Figure 11–16.

Lists are another effective way to set off important ideas and provide the reader with clues. (Bullets and lists are discussed in detail in Chapter 5.) Like headings, lists are

TITLE

The title is centered at the top of the page in all capital letters, usually, bold-faced (or underlined if typewritten), often in a large font (type size), and often using a sans serif typeface. When the title runs to more than one line, the lines are usually double-spaced and arranged as an inverted pyramid (longer line on the top).

FIRST-LEVEL HEADING

A first-level heading indicates what the following section is about, perhaps by describing the subdivisions. All first-level headings are grammatically parallel, with the possible exception of such headings as "Introduction," "Conclusions," and "Recommendations." Some text appears between every two headings, regardless of their levels. Still boldfaced and sans serif, the font may be smaller than that used in the title but still larger than the typeface used in the text and still in all capital letters.

Second-Level Heading

Like first-level headings, second-level headings indicate what the following material is about. All second-level headings within a section are grammatically parallel. Still boldfaced and sans serif, the font may either remain the same or shrink to the size used in the text, and the style is now initial capitals with lower case. Never use only one second-level heading under a first-level heading. (The same is true for every other level of heading.)

Third-Level Heading

A third-level heading is worded to reflect the content of the material that follows. All third-level headings beneath a second-level heading should be grammatically parallel.

Fourth-Level Heading. Like all the other levels of heading, fourth-level headings reflect the subject that will be developed. All fourth-level headings within a subsection are parallel.

Fifth-level headings are generally the lowest level of heading used. However, you can indicate further breakdowns in your ideas by using a list:

1. *The first item in a list.* You may indent the entire item in block format to set it off visually. Numbers are optional.
2. *The second item in a list.* All lists have at least two items. An introductory phrase or sentence may be italicized for emphasis, as shown here.

Figure 11–16
Heading Format for Reports

phrased in parallel form. A list that uses bullets or letters instead of numbers indicates choices without implying order or hierarchy[6]:

A. Convert an existing conference room.

B. Build an add-on room.

C. Lease space in an existing day-care center.

When you use lists, introduce them clearly so that people know what they're about to read. You might want to consider using multilevel lists, with subentries below each major item (much like an outline). If necessary, add further discussion after the lists (as this paragraph is doing). Moving your readers smoothly into and out of lists requires careful use of transitions—the subject of the next section.

Use lists to set off important ideas and to show sequence.

Transitions   Phrases such as *to continue the analysis, on the other hand,* and *an additional concept* are another type of structural clue. These are examples of **transitions,** words or

Use transitions consisting of a single word, a few words, or a whole paragraph to provide additional structural clues.

phrases that tie ideas together within a report and keep readers moving along the right track. Good writers use transitions to help readers move from one section of a report to the next, from one paragraph to the next, and even from one sentence to the next. (For example, the last sentence in the previous paragraph was a transition to help you move from the subject of lists to the subject of transitions.) Here is a list of transitions frequently used to move readers smoothly between sentences and paragraphs:

Additional detail	moreover, furthermore, in addition, besides, first, second, third, finally
Causal relationship	therefore, because, accordingly, thus, consequently, hence, as a result, so
Comparison	similarly, here again, likewise, in comparison, still
Contrast	yet, conversely, whereas, nevertheless, on the other hand, however, but, nonetheless
Condition	although, if
Illustration	for example, in particular, in this case, for instance
Time sequence	formerly, after, when, meanwhile, sometimes
Intensification	indeed, in fact, in any event
Summary	in brief, in short, to sum up
Repetition	that is, in other words, as I mentioned earlier

Although transitional words and phrases are useful, they're not sufficient in themselves to overcome poor organization. Your goal is first to put your ideas in a strong framework and then to use transitions to link them together even more strongly.

Consider using a transition device whenever it might help readers understand your ideas and follow you from point to point. You can use transitions inside paragraphs to tie related points together and between paragraphs to ease the shift from one distinct thought to another. In longer reports, transitions that link major sections or chapters are often complete paragraphs that serve as mini-introductions to the next section or as summaries of the ideas presented in the section just ending. Here's an example:

Given the nature of this problem, the alternatives are limited. As the previous section indicates, we can stop making the product, improve it, or continue with the current model. Each of these alternatives has advantages and disadvantages. The following section discusses pros and cons of each of the three alternatives.

Previews and Reviews   You may have heard the old saying, "Tell 'em what you're going to tell 'em, tell 'em, then tell 'em what you just told 'em." In other words, use *preview sections* before and *review sections* after important material in your report. Using a preview section to introduce a topic helps readers get ready for new information. Previews are particularly helpful when the information is complex or unexpected. You don't want readers to get halfway into a section before figuring out what it's all about.

Throughout your report, introduce topics with previews, and summarize them with reviews.

Review sections come after a body of material and summarize the information for your readers. Reviews help readers absorb details while keeping track of the big picture. Long reports and reports dealing with complex subjects can often benefit from multiple review sections, not just a single review at the very end.

Swimming is a good analogy for using preview and review sections. Before you jump into the water, you look around, get your bearings, and get an idea of what you're about to dive into. A preview section serves the same purpose for your reader. After you dive in and swim for a few moments, you come back up for air. You look around and get your

Checklist: **Writing Business Reports and Proposals**

Format and Style

✓ For brief external reports, use letter format, including a title or a subject line after the reader's address that clearly states the subject of the document.

✓ For brief internal reports, use memo or manuscript format.

✓ Single-space the text.

✓ Double-space between paragraphs.

✓ Use headings where helpful, but try not to use more than three levels of headings.

✓ Call attention to significant information by setting it off visually with lists or indention.

✓ Include visual aids to emphasize and clarify the text.

✓ Use an informal style (*I* and *you*) for letter and memo reports (unless company prefers impersonal third person).

✓ Use an impersonal style for more formal short reports in manuscript format.

✓ Maintain a consistent time frame by writing in either the present or the past tense, using other tenses only to indicate prior or future events.

✓ Give each paragraph a topic sentence.

✓ Link paragraphs by using transitional words and phrases.

✓ Strive for readability by using short sentences, concrete words, and appropriate terminology.

✓ Be accurate, thorough, and impartial in presenting the material.

✓ Avoid including irrelevant and unnecessary details.

✓ Document for all material quoted or paraphrased from secondary sources.

Opening

✓ For short, routine memos, use the subject line of the memo form and the first sentence or two of the text as the introduction.

✓ For all other short reports, cover these topics in the introduction: purpose, scope, background, restrictions (in conducting the study), sources of information and methods of research, and organization of the report.

✓ If using direct order, place conclusions and recommendations in the opening.

Body (Direct or Indirect Order)

✓ Use direct order for informational reports to receptive readers, developing ideas around subtopics (chronologically, geographically, categorically).

✓ Use direct order for analytical reports to receptive readers, developing points around conclusions or recommendations.

✓ Use indirect order for analytical reports to skeptical or hostile readers, developing points around logical arguments.

Ending

✓ In informational reports summarize major findings at the end, if you wish.

✓ Summarize points in the same order in which they appear in the body.

✓ In analytical reports using indirect order, list conclusions and recommendations at the end.

✓ Be certain that conclusions and recommendations follow logically from facts presented in the text.

✓ Consider using a list format for emphasis.

✓ Avoid introducing new material in the summary, conclusions, or recommendations.

---

bearings again. This is like a review section. Whenever you've had your readers "swimming in details" for any length of time, bring them back to the surface with a review section so that they can get their bearings again.

The Ending   Research shows that the **ending** of the final section of a report, leaves a strong and lasting impression. That's why it's important to use the ending to emphasize the main points of your message. In a report written in direct order, you may want to remind readers once again of your key points or your conclusions and recommendations. If your report is written in indirect order, end with a summary of key points (except in short memos). In analytical reports, end with conclusions and recommendations as well as key points.

Reemphasize your main ideas in the ending.

Be sure to summarize the benefits to the reader in any report that suggests a change of course or some other action. In general, the ending refers back to all the pieces and reminds readers how those pieces fit together. It provides a final opportunity to emphasize the wholeness of your message. Furthermore, it gives you one last chance to make sure that your report says what you intended.[7] To review the tasks involved in writing reports, see this chapter's "Checklist: Writing Business Reports and Proposals."

SUMMARY OF LEARNING OBJECTIVES

1 Discuss the structure of informational reports. Because reader reaction is rarely an issue for informational reports, structure is dictated by the nature of your topic. Of utmost concern is reader comprehension, so informational reports must be both logical and accurate. Topical organization allows you to structure your report in six common arrangements. When basing your structure on importance, cover the most important facts first and the least important last. When using sequence, cover a process step-by-step. When basing your structure on chronology, cover facts as a chain of events occurring in time. When using spatial orientation, detail physical aspects from right to left, left to right, top to bottom, or outside to inside. To base your structure on geography, cover facts by location. And to use category as your structural basis, cover facts as distinct aspects that can be classified into groups.

2 Explain the structure of analytical reports. Because the structure of analytical reports depends on anticipated audience reaction, use either a structure that focuses attention on conclusions and recommendations (for receptive audiences) or one that focuses attention on the rationale behind your conclusions and recommendations (for skeptical or hostile audiences). Focusing directly on conclusions or recommendations can intensify resistance or even make your solution seem too simple. When you want your audience to focus on why your ideas will work, you need to draw attention to the logic of your argument. There are three popular approaches to a logical organization. The 2 + 2 = 4 approach demonstrates that everything in your report adds up. The scientific method reveals the most effective solution, or hypothesis, by showing evidence that either proves or disproves each alternative. The yardstick approach establishes conditions, or criteria, against which all possible solutions are measured.

3 List the most popular types of visuals, and discuss when to use them. Various types of information are best depicted in various types of visuals. For example, tables communicate facts and

detail in an easy-to-read format. Line charts illustrate trends over time or plot the relationships of two or more variables. Surface charts illustrate the cumulative effect of trends. Bar charts portray numbers by the height or length of their rectangular bars and facilitate comparisons of size in addition to showing changes over time. Pie charts show percentages or how the parts of a whole are distributed. Flowcharts illustrate a sequence of events. Organization charts illustrate positions and functions in an organization. Maps show concentrations by geographic area. Drawings and diagrams show how something looks or operates.

4 Clarify five principles of graphic design to remember when preparing visuals. To design the most effective visuals for business reports, keep five principles in mind. First, continuity: To avoid confusing readers, be consistent in your use of design elements such as color, shape, size, position, scale, and typeface. Second, contrast: Use contrasting colors to show difference and subtle colors to show similarity. Third, emphasis: Use design elements to draw attention to key points and to visually downplay less important ones. Fourth, simplicity: Avoid clutter and chartjunk. Fifth, experience: Take into account your audience's culture, education, and other background experiences.

5 Identify and briefly describe five tools that writers can use in long reports to help readers stay on track. Readers see reports one page at a time, so in long reports, they may have difficulty seeing the overall structure and just how various report sections fit together. To help readers navigate your long reports, five tools are available. The opening introduces the subject of the report, indicates why it's important, and previews the key points in the order they will be discussed. Headings and lists set off important ideas and provide the reader with clues. Transitions tie ideas together and keep readers moving along. Previews and reviews prepare readers for new information and summarize previously discussed information. The ending summarizes the key points, conclusions, or recommendations.

On the job:
SOLVING A COMMUNICATION DILEMMA AT FEDEX

In the beginning, entrepreneur Frederick Smith was sure that his idea for a new transportation network would increase efficiency and decrease the cost of moving packages from state to state. He would fly packages from around the country to a central hub in Memphis, where they would be sorted and flown to their final destinations. To raise money for this venture, Smith used business reports, and reports have remained important through the years as he and his managers have built FedEx into a global business with $12 billion in annual revenues.

For example, because of FedEx's heavy orientation toward customer satisfaction, the company has a strong emphasis on training. Since training costs money, reports are needed to justify training expenditures, such as purchasing computer-networking equipment to

support the company's interactive training program. Reports are also important to the company's internal auditors, who are charged with studying how the company controls its finances, operations, and legal compliance. These analytical reports contain recommendations as well as conclusions.

The human resources and internal audit departments are only two of the many FedEx departments that prepare and receive reports. As Frederick Smith and his managers strive against competitors, work toward customer satisfaction, and keep the business running smoothly, business reports continue to play a key role at FedEx.

Your Mission You have recently joined FedEx as Frederick Smith's administrative assistant. Your job is to help him with a variety of special projects. During an average week, he might ask you to handle three or four assignments and then report back to him in writing. In each of the following situations, choose the best communication alternative from among those listed, and be prepared to explain why your choice is best.

1. To keep tabs on the industry, Smith has asked you to research two services offered by FedEx's top three competitors: the online pickup request (scheduling a pickup online rather than over the telephone) and package tracking (entering a tracking number on a Web site to see where a packaging is during transit). How should you introduce your report? Choose the best introduction from the four shown below.

   a. Recognizing that FedEx no longer has the overnight delivery business to itself, management has decided to examine the effect of online pickup-request and package-tracking services offered by other companies. Specifically, management wants to review two issues:

      1. What online pickup-request and package-tracking services are offered by the top three competitors?
      2. How can FedEx use its own online services to compete more effectively?

      The following pages present the results of a two-week study of these questions.

   b. Major changes are occurring in the overnight delivery business. Our online pickup-request and package-tracking services have attracted a great deal of customer use since we introduced them. Not surprisingly, however, we are not the only express shipping company offering such services.

      With more shippers and receivers conducting more business online, the demand for such services will only increase. FedEx can capitalize on this market demand and compete more effectively if we (1) publicize our fast, easy online services more heavily and (2) introduce additional online services for time-pressured customers. These conclusions are examined in detail in the following pages.

   c. I am happy to report that FedEx is still ahead of all competitors. However, I have to point out that rivals are doing everything they can to keep up the pressure. The two-week study of competitors' online services that I recently conducted shows that UPS and others offer a variety of services similar to our own offerings.

      Let me stress that customers have already tracked millions of packages and placed millions of pickup requests using these online services. Although this is obviously an important service, I want to emphasize that customers are going to continue expecting more and more of these online conveniences. Because of this trend, I want to present two recommendations that FedEx might pursue.

   d. Since FedEx was founded nearly 35 years ago, the company has looked for ways to turn customer convenience into both a competitive advantage and a way to operate more efficiently (and therefore, more profitably). In the past few years, the Internet has proven to be a very effective way to expand our customer service options while decreasing the amount of time our customer service representatives need to spend on the phone.

      At the request of senior management, an examination of the online pickup-request and package-tracking services offered by competitors was conducted. The following pages present the findings of this study, which addressed the following questions:

      1. What online pickup-request and package-tracking services do competitors offer?
      2. How do FedEx's services compare?
      3. What challenges and opportunities do such services represent?

2. Smith wants to celebrate the company's thirty-fifth anniversary by creating a special advertising insert on FedEx history. He wants to distribute this insert inside the April issue of a national business magazine. The magazine's publisher is excited about the concept and has asked Smith to send her "something in writing." Smith asks you to draft the proposal, which should be no more than 10 pages long. Which of the following outlines should you use?

   a. First version

      I. An overview of FedEx's history

         A. How company was founded

         B. Overview of company services

         C. Overview of markets served

         D. Overview of transportation operations

      II. The FedEx magazine insert

         A. Historic events to be included

         B. Employees to be interviewed

         C. Customers to be discussed

         D. Production schedule

      III. Pros and cons of FedEx magazine insert

         A. Pros: Make money for magazine, draw new customers for FedEx

         B. Cons: Costs, questionable audience interest

   b. Second version

      I. Introduction: Overview of the FedEx special insert

         A. Purpose

         B. Content

         C. Timing

II. Description of the insert

    A. Text

        1. Message from CEO

        2. History of FedEx

        3. Interviews with employees

        4. Customer testimonials

    B. Advertising

        1. Inside front and back covers

        2. Color spreads

        3. Congratulatory ads placed by customers

III. Next steps

IV. Summary

c. Third version

Who:	FedEx
What:	Special magazine insert
When:	Inserted in April issue
Where:	Coordinated by magazine's editors
Why:	To celebrate FedEx's anniversary
How:	Overview of content, production responsibilities, and schedule

d. Fourth version

    I. Introduction: The rationale for producing a magazine insert promoting FedEx

        A. Insert would make money for magazine

        B. Insert would boost morale of FedEx employees

        C. Insert would attract new customers

    II. Insert description

        A. Interview with founder Frederick Smith

        B. Interviews with employees

        C. Description of historic moments

        D. Interviews with customers

        E. Advertisements

    III. Production plan

        A. Project organization

        B. Timing and sequence of steps

        C. FedEx's responsibilities

        D. Magazine's responsibilities

    IV. Detailed schedule

    V. Summary of benefits and responsibilities

3. Smith has asked you to think about ways of attracting new customers that need FedEx's expertise in managing international parts and parcel distribution. You have talked with executives at Laura Ashley and National Semiconductor, two current customers, and discovered that they are most concerned about the time needed to process orders and deliver parts to stores or factories. FedEx can cut the delivery time from as much as 21 days to as little as 4 days after ordering. You believe that an advertising campaign featuring testimonials from these two satisfied customers will give FedEx a tremendous advantage over other competitors, who haven't yet developed a track record with large global companies. As a relatively junior person at FedEx, you are a little apprehensive about suggesting your idea. You don't want to seem presumptuous, but on the other hand, you think your idea is good. You have decided to raise the issue with Smith. Which of the following approaches is preferable?

a. Instead of writing a report, arrange a meeting to discuss your ideas with Smith, the advertising manager, and an executive from the company's advertising agency. This allows you to address the issues and ideas firsthand in an informal setting.

b. You write the following short report:
You recently asked me to give some thought to how FedEx might attract new customers for its international parts distribution business. I decided to sound out two of our largest customers to get a feel for why they hired us to handle this operation. Interestingly, they didn't choose FedEx because they wanted to reduce their shipping costs. Rather, they were interested in reducing the time needed to process and ship orders to stores and factories.

Many companies are in the same situation as Laura Ashley and National Semiconductor. They're not just looking for the carrier with the lowest prices, they're looking for the carrier with the proven ability to process orders and get shipments to their destinations as quickly as possible. Instead of waiting as long as 21 days for shipments to reach their destination, these companies can promise delivery in 4 days.

Clearly, our track record with Laura Ashley and National Semiconductor is the key to capturing the attention of other global companies. After all, how many competitors can show they have the ability to cut as much as 17 days off the time needed to process and deliver an order? Of course, companies might be skeptical if we made this claim on our own, but they would be more likely to accept it if our customers told their own stories. That's why FedEx should ask executives from Laura Ashley and National Semiconductor to offer testimonials in an advertising campaign.

c. You write the following short report:
In response to your request, I have investigated ways in which FedEx might attract new customers for its international parts distribution business. In conducting this investigation, I have talked with executives at two of our largest customers, Laura Ashley and National Semiconductor, and discussed the situation with our advertising manager and our advertising agency. All agreed that companies are interested in more than merely saving money on international shipments.

Typically, a global company has to keep a lot of parts or materials on hand and be ready to ship these whenever a store or factory places an order. As soon as an order arrives, the company packages the parts and ships it out. The store or factory doesn't want to wait a long time because it, in turn, has to keep a lot of money tied up in parts to be sure it doesn't run out before the new shipment arrives. Thus, if the company can cut the time between ordering and delivery, it will save its stores or factories a lot of money and, at the same time, build a lot of customer loyalty.

As a result, shipping costs are less important than the need to process orders and get shipments to their destinations as quickly as possible. Instead of delivery in 21 days, these companies can promise deliveries in 4 days. If we can show global companies how to do this, we will attract many more customers.

d. You write the following short report:
This report was authorized by Frederick W. Smith on May 7. Its purpose is to analyze ways of attracting more customers to FedEx's international parts distribution business.

Laura Ashley and National Semiconductor are two large, global companies that use our international parts distribution service. Both companies are pleased with our ability to cut the time between ordering and parts delivery. Both are willing to give testimonials to that effect.

These testimonials will help attract new customers if they are used in newspaper, magazine, and television advertising. A company is more likely to believe a satisfied customer than someone who works for FedEx. If the advertising department and the advertising agency start working on this idea today, it could be implemented within two months.[8]

TEST YOUR KNOWLEDGE

1. What are your options for structuring an informational report?

2. What are your options for structuring an analytical report?

3. How does topical organization differ from logical organization?

4. When is it appropriate to use tables, line charts, surface charts, and pie charts in a report?

5. What five principles apply to effective visuals for business reports?

6. How does a flowchart differ from an organization chart?

7. What tools can you use to help readers follow the structure and flow of information in a long report?

8. What ethical issue is raised by the use of technology to alter photographs in reports?

9. What is the purpose of adding titles and legends to visual aids in reports?

10. How do writers use transitions in reports?

INTERACTIVE LEARNING

USE THIS TEXT'S ONLINE RESOURCES

Visit the myPHILIP Web site at www.prenhall.com/thill. For Chapter 11, take advantage of the interactive "Study Guide" to test your chapter knowledge. Get instant feedback on whether you need additional studying. Read the "Current Events" articles to get the latest on chapter topics, and complete the exercises—as specified by your instructor.

This site's "Study Hall" helps you succeed in this course. "Talk in the Hall" lets you leave messages and meet new friends online. If you have a question, you can "Ask the Tutor." And to get a better grade in this course, you can find more help at "Writing Skills," "Study Skills," and "Study Tips."

The "Research Area" helps you locate a wealth of information to use in course assignments. Plus, you can send a message to online research experts, who will help you find exactly the information you need.

APPLY YOUR KNOWLEDGE

1. Should a report always explain the writer's method of gathering evidence or solving a problem? Why or why not?

2. Would you use the direct or indirect approach to document inventory shortages at your manufacturing plant? To propose an employee stock-option plan? Why?

3. What tense is better for most business reports, past or present? Explain.

4. Besides telling readers why an illustration is important, why must you refer to it in the text of your document?

5. **Ethical Choices** What should you consider when using color to accentuate key points in visual aids?

PRACTICE YOUR KNOWLEDGE

DOCUMENTS FOR ANALYSIS

Document 11.A

Examine the pie charts in Figure 11–17 and point out any problems or errors you notice.

Figure 11–17
Pie Charts for Analysis
(Document 11.A)

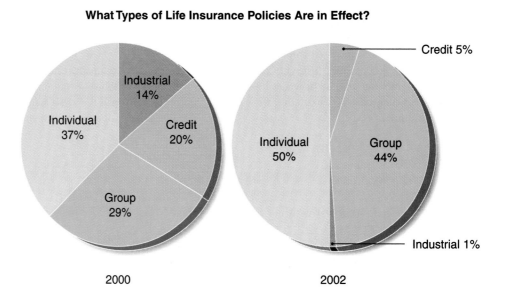

What Types of Life Insurance Policies Are in Effect?

Document 11.B

Examine the line chart in Figure 11–18 and point out any problems or errors you notice.

Figure 11–18
Line Chart for Analysis
(Document 11.B)

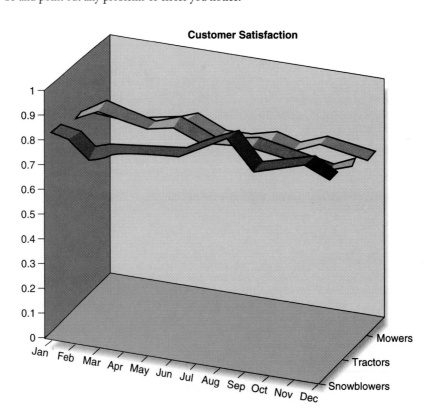

EXERCISES

11-1. Writing Reports: Organizational Approach Of the organizational approaches introduced in the chapter, which is best suited for reporting on each of the following problem statements? Briefly explain why.

a. In which market segment—root beer, cola, or lemon-lime—should Fizz Drinks, Inc., introduce a new soft drink to take advantage of its enlarged research and development budget?

b. Should Major Manufacturing, Inc., close down operations of its antiquated Bellville, Arkansas, plant despite the adverse economic impact on the town that has grown up around the plant?

c. Should you and your partner adopt a new accounting method to make your financial statements look better to potential investors?

d. Should Grand Canyon Chemicals buy disposable test tubes to reduce labor costs associated with cleaning and sterilizing reusable test tubes?

e. What are some reasons for the recent data loss at the college computer center, and how can we avoid similar problems in the future?

11-2. Writing Reports: Structure and Format Go to the library or visit the Internet site www.annualreport service.com and review the annual reports recently released by two corporations in the same industry. Analyze each report and be prepared to discuss the following questions in class:

a. What differences do you see in the way each corporation reports its financial data? Are the data presented clearly so that shareholders can draw conclusions about each corporation's financial results?

b. What goals, challenges, and plans do top managers emphasize in their discussion of results?

c. How do the format and organization of each report enhance or detract from the information being presented?

11-3. Writing Reports: Visual Aids As a market researcher for a statewide chain of car dealerships, you're examining car and truck ownership and lease patterns among single drivers in various age groups. By discovering which age groups have the highest percentages of owners, you will be better able to target advertising that promotes the leasing option. Using the following information, prepare a bar graph comparing the number of owners with the number of leasers in each age category. Be sure to label your graph, and include combined totals for owners and leasers ("total drivers"). Then prepare a pie chart showing the proportion of owners and leasers in the one age group that you think holds the most promise for leasing a new vehicle. Write a sentence that prepares your company's management for the information shown in the pie chart.

AGE GROUP	NUMBER OF OWNERS (IN 000S)	NUMBER OF LEASERS (IN 000S)
18–24	1,830	795
25–29	1,812	1,483
30–34	1,683	1,413
35–44	1,303	1,932
45–54	1,211	1,894
55–64	1,784	1,435
65–74	3,200	1,142
75+	3,431	854

11-4. Writing Reports: Pie Charts As director of new business development for a growing advertising agency, you're interested in how companies spend their advertising dollars. Create a pie chart based on the following information, which shows U.S. national advertising spending by media category. Summarize these findings (in two or three sentences) for publication in a report to top management.

MEDIA TYPE	EXPENDITURE (IN $BILLIONS)
Television	42.5
Newspaper	38.4
Direct mail	38.4
Miscellaneous	22.6
Radio	12.3
Yellow Pages	10.8
Magazines	9.0
Business papers	3.8
Outdoor	1.3
Total[9]	$179.1

11-5. Writing Reports: Line Charts The pet food manufacturer you work for is interested in the results of a recent poll of U.S. pet-owning households. Look at the statistics that follow and decide on the most appropriate scale for a chart; then create a line chart of the trends in cat ownership. What conclusions do you draw from the trend you've charted? Draft a paragraph or two discussing the results of this poll and the potential consequences for the pet food business. Support your conclusions by referring readers to your chart.

In 1980, 22 million U.S. households owned a cat. In 1985, 24 million households owned a cat. In 1990, 28 million households owned a cat. In 1995, 32 million households owned a cat.

11–6. **Writing Reports: Visual Aid Selection** You're preparing the annual report for FretCo Guitar Corporation. For each of the following types of information, what form of visual aid would you choose to illustrate the text? Explain your choices.

  a. Data on annual sales for the past 20 years
  b. Comparison of FretCo sales, product by product (electric guitars, bass guitars, amplifiers, acoustic guitars), for this year and last year
  c. Explanation of how a FretCo acoustic guitar is manufactured
  d. Explanation of how the FretCo Guitar Corporation markets its guitars
  e. Data on sales of FretCo products in each of 12 countries
  f. Comparison of FretCo sales figures with sales figures for three competing guitar makers over the past 10 years

11–7. **Teamwork** Team up with a classmate to design graphics based on a comparison of the total tax burden of the U.S. taxpayer with that of people in other nations. One teammate should sketch a horizontal bar chart and the other should sketch a vertical one from the estimates that follow. Then exchange visual aids and analyze how well each conveys the situation of the U.S. taxpayer. Would the bar chart look best with vertical or horizontal bars? Why? What scale is best? How does the direction used in the bar chart enhance or obscure the meaning or impact of the data? What suggestions can you make for improving your teammate's visual aid?

> Estimates show that Swedish taxpayers spend 51 percent of their incomes on taxes, British taxpayers spend 48 percent, French taxpayers spend 37 percent, Japanese taxpayers spend 28 percent, and U.S. taxpayers spend 27 percent.

11–8. **Writing Reports: Graphics Design** The following table shows last year's sales figures for the appliance and electronics megastore where you work. Construct visual aids based on these figures that will help you explain to the store's general manager how sales fluctuate by season in each department. Then write a title and legend for each visual aid.

Store Sales in 2001 (in $ thousands)

Month	Home Electronics	Computers	Appliances
January	$68	$39	$36
February	72	34	34
March	75	41	30
April	54	41	28
May	56	42	44
June	49	33	48
July	54	31	43
August	66	58	39
September	62	58	36
October	66	44	33
November	83	48	29
December	91	62	24

11–9. **Teamwork** With a team of three or four other students, brainstorm and then sketch at least three types of visual aids you can use to compare the populations of all 50 states in the United States. You can use any of the graphic ideas presented in this chapter, as well as any ideas or examples you find from other sources.

11–10. **Internet** One of the best places to see how data can be presented visually is in government statistical publications, which are often available on the Internet. For example, the International Trade Administration (ITA), a branch of the U.S. Department of Commerce, publishes monthly reports about U.S. trade with other countries. Visit the report page of its Web site at www.ita.doc.gov/td/industry/otea/ustrade.html and follow the link to the latest monthly trade update. Using what you learned in this chapter, evaluate the visual aids in the report. Do they present the data clearly? Are they missing any elements? What would you do to improve the visuals? Print out a copy of the report to turn in with your answers, and indicate which visuals you are evaluating.

11–11. **Ethical Choices** If you create a new visual aid using data drawn from a visual aid posted on a Web site or printed in a magazine, must you indicate the source of the original data? Explain your answer.

CASES

INFORMAL INFORMATIONAL REPORTS

1. My progress to date: Interim progress report on your academic career As you know, the bureaucratic process involved in getting a degree or certificate is nearly as challenging as any course you could take.

Your task: Prepare an interim progress report detailing the steps you've taken toward completing your graduation or certification requirements. After examining the requirements listed in your college catalog, indicate a realistic schedule for completing those that

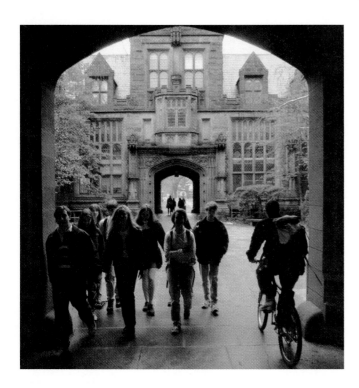

their new products, Sample U.S.A. offers supermarket shoppers bite-size samples of everything from cheese and ice cream to pretzels and cookies. This month Sample U.S.A. gave away a total of 12,800 samples of Cheezy sesame crackers in 11 New Orleans supermarkets. The Cheezy Company wants Sample U.S.A. to give away 14,000 sesame cracker samples in 13 Houston supermarkets during the coming month. However, one large supermarket chain hasn't yet agreed to let Sample U.S.A. set up a tasting booth.

Your task: As the Southwest regional manager for Sample U.S.A., you send your clients a monthly operating report on results and future sampling plans. Prepare this month's report to Jacques D'Aprix, the director of marketing at the Cheezy Company. Be sure to include future plans as well as any problems that may affect next month's activities.

INFORMAL ANALYTICAL REPORTS

5. My next career move: Justification report organized around recommendations If you've ever given yourself a really good talking-to, you'll be quite comfortable with this project.

Your task: Write a memo report directed to yourself and signed with a fictitious name. Indicate a possible job that your college education will qualify you for, mention the advantages of the position in terms of your long-range goals, and then outline the actions you must take to get the job.

6. Staying the course: Proposal using the 2 + 2 = 4 approach Think of a course you would love to see added to the core curriculum at your school. Conversely, if you would like to see a course offered as an elective rather than being required, write your e-mail report accordingly.

Your task: Write a short e-mail proposal using the 2 + 2 = 4 approach. Prepare your proposal to be submitted to the academic dean by e-mail. Be sure to include all the reasons supporting your idea.

7. Planning my program: Problem-solving report using the scientific method Assume that you will have time for only one course next term.

Your task: List the pros and cons of four or five courses that interest you, and use the scientific method to settle on the course that is best for you to take at this time. Write your report in memo format, addressing it to your academic adviser.

8. "Would you carry it?" Unsolicited sales proposal recommending a product to a retail outlet Select a product you are familiar with, and imagine that you are the manufacturer trying to get a local retail outlet to carry it.

remain. In addition to course requirements, include steps such as completing the residency requirement, filing necessary papers, and paying necessary fees. Use memo format for your report, and address it to anyone who is helping or encouraging you through school.

2. Gavel to gavel: Personal activity report of a meeting Meetings, conferences, and conventions abound in the academic world, and you have probably attended your share.

Your task: Prepare a personal activity report on a meeting, convention, or conference that you recently attended. Use memo format, and direct the report to other students in your field who were not able to attend.

3. Check that price tag: Informational report on trends in college costs Are tuition costs going up, going down, or remaining the same? Your college's administration has asked you to compare your college's tuition costs with those of a nearby college and determine which has risen more quickly. Research the trend by checking your college's annual tuition costs for each of the most recent four years. Then research the four-year tuition trends for a neighboring college. For both colleges, calculate the percentage change in tuition costs from year to year and between the first and fourth year.

Your task: Prepare an informal report (using the letter format) presenting your findings and conclusions to the president of your college. Include graphics to explain and support your conclusions.

4. Sampling success: Operating report on a program to promote a new cracker To help food manufacturers promote

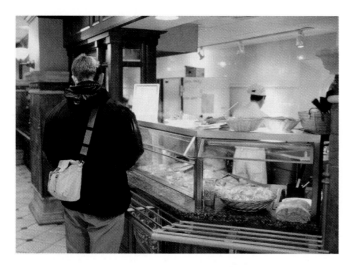

Your task: Write a sales proposal in letter format to the owner (or manager) of the store, proposing that the item be stocked. Making up some reasonable figures, tell what the item costs, what it can be sold for, and what services your company provides (return of unsold items, free replacement of unsatisfactory items, necessary repairs, and so on).

9. **Restaurant review: Troubleshooting report on a restaurant's food and operations** Visit any restaurant, possibly your school cafeteria. The workers and fellow customers will assume that you are an ordinary customer, but you are really a spy for the owner.

Your task: After your visit, write a short memo to the owner, explaining (a) what you did and what you observed, (b) any violations of policy that you observed, and (c) your recommendations for improvement. The first part of your report (what you did and what you observed) will be the longest. Include a description of the premises, inside and out. Tell how long it took for each step of ordering and receiving your meal. Describe the service and food thoroughly. You are interested in both the good and bad aspects of the establishment's décor, service, and food. For the second section (violations of policy), use some common sense. If all the servers but one have their hair covered, you may assume that policy requires hair to be covered; a dirty window or restroom obviously violates policy. The last section (recommendations for improvement) involves professional judgment. What management actions will improve the restaurant?

10. **On the books: Troubleshooting report on improving the campus bookstore** Imagine that you are a consultant hired to improve the profits of your campus bookstore.

Your task: Visit the bookstore and look critically at its operations. Then draft a memo offering recommendations to the bookstore manager that would make the store more profitable, perhaps suggesting products it should carry, hours that it should remain open, or added services that it should make available to students. Be sure to support your recommendations.

11. **Press one for efficiency: Unsolicited proposal on a telephone interviewing system** How can a firm be thorough yet efficient when considering dozens of applicants for each position? One tool that just may help is IntelliView, a 10-minute question-and-answer session conducted by Touch-Tone telephone. The company recruiter dials up the IntelliView computer and then leaves the room. The candidate punches in answers to roughly 100 questions about work attitudes and other issues. In a few minutes, the recruiter can call Pinkerton, which offers the service, and find out the results. On the basis of what the IntelliView interview revealed, the recruiter can delve more deeply into certain areas and, ultimately, have more information on which to base the hiring decision.

Your task: As a recruiter for Curtis Box and Crate, you think that IntelliView might help your firm. Write a brief memo to Wallace Jefferson, the director of human resources, in which you suggest a test of the IntelliView system. Your memo should tell your boss why you believe your firm should test the system before making a long-term commitment.[10]

12. **Day and night: Problem-solving report on stocking a 24-hour convenience store** When a store is open all day, every day, when's the best time to restock the shelves? That's the challenge at Store 24, a retail chain that never closes. Imagine you're the assistant manager of a Store 24 branch that just opened near your campus. You want to set up a restocking schedule that won't conflict with prime shopping hours. Think about the number of customers you're likely to serve in the morning, afternoon, evening, and overnight hours. Consider, too, how many employees you might have during these four periods.

Your task: Using the scientific approach, write a problem-solving report in letter form to the store manager (Isabel Chu) and the regional manager (Eric Angstrom), who must agree on a solution to this problem. Discuss the pros and cons of each of the four periods, and include your recommendation for restocking the shelves.

GOING ONLINE EXERCISES

Exploring Computer Graphics, page 338

How can you add effectively designed visual aids to a report or proposal to emphasize an important point, reinforce an idea, and create interest in the text? Computer graphics can create surprising, eye-catching visual information to supplement the written text. Log on to mambo and visit the Perceptual Science Lab and its many links to build on what you've learned in this chapter about computer graphics.

1. What type of computer graphics did you find? Tell how you could use these graphics (or ideas from them) to create a visual that would enhance a business report or proposal. If you did not get any ideas, explain why.

2. Describe what new information you learned about computer graphics at the PSL (or one of its links).

3. What new resources did you discover at the PSL (or one of its links)? If you didn't find the site or its links useful, explain why.

To complete this exercise, log onto this text's Web site at www.prenhall.com/thill. Select Chapter 11, then select "Student Resources," click on the name of the featured Web site, and follow the detailed navigational directions.

chapter 12

COMPLETING FORMAL REPORTS AND PROPOSALS

After studying this chapter, you will be able to

1 List the three tasks involved in completing business reports and proposals and briefly explain what's involved in revising them.

2 Explain the ten prefatory parts of a formal report.

3 Describe four important functions of a formal report's introduction and identify the possible topics it might include.

4 Discuss the four areas of specific information that must be covered in the body of a proposal.

5 Explain the four questions to ask when proofing visual aids.

Robert Haas isn't the only one in his company who places value on reports. Employees at Levi Strauss and Company know how important it is to produce reports that are easily understood, logical, attractive, persuasive, and thorough. So they include all the necessary components to accomplish these goals.

On the job:

FACING A COMMUNICATION DILEMMA AT LEVI STRAUSS

Placing a High Value on Reports

www.levistrauss.com

Robert Haas takes both business ethics and business communication seriously. As chairman of the board at Levi Strauss and Company, and as great-great-grandnephew of founder Levi Strauss, Haas defines the company's goal as "responsible commercial success." He envisions his company being run according to principles such as teamwork, trust, ethical management, environmental care, diversity, and individual respect.

Haas recognizes the importance of communicating his vision throughout the company, to customers, and in the community. Effective communication is one of his company's fundamental values, affecting everything from personal interactions to community relations. One way to communicate such a complex vision is through reports, so Haas has made sure he knows everything he can about developing reports that are clear, that are well organized, and that contain all the elements necessary to promote easy understanding.

Haas has not only helped create reports but also relies on them to make decisions and to set company policy. If you were Robert Haas, how would you approach the challenge of communicating complex ideas and issues? What steps would you take to make sure an audience gets what it needs from long reports? What features would you include to help readers find and understand the information in your reports? And how would you use reports in your own decision making?[1]

REVISING FORMAL REPORTS AND PROPOSALS

Experienced business communicators such as Robert Haas realize that writing a formal report or proposal is a demanding and time-consuming task. They also know that the process of writing a report or proposal doesn't end with a first draft. To complete a successful report, you still need to carefully edit and rewrite, produce, and then proofread your final version.

Just as you would do for any other business message, you revise formal reports and proposals by evaluating content and organization. You must make sure not only that you've said what you want to say but also that you've said it in the most logical order and in a way that responds to your audience's needs. Be sure to review your style and readability, editing and rewriting your message so that it is as concise and clear as possible. You can refresh your memory about revising business messages by referring back to Chapter 6. The revision process is basically the same for reports, but it may take longer, depending on the length of your report or proposal. However, important differences arise when it comes time to produce your formal reports and proposals.

PRODUCING FORMAL REPORTS AND PROPOSALS

How the final version of your report or proposal is actually produced depends on the nature of your organization. The traditional approach was usually a team effort, with secretaries or other support personnel handling the typing, formatting, and other tasks. For important, high-visibility reports, a graphics department would help with charts, drawings, covers, and other visual elements.

However, as personal computers have become commonplace in the business office, more and more employees are expected to handle most or even all of the formatting and production of their own reports. The good news is that computer tools are now generally easy enough for the average businessperson to use productively. A software "suite" such as Microsoft Office makes it easy to produce reports that incorporate graphics, tables, spreadsheet data, and even database records. Even advanced report features such as photography are relatively simple these days, with the advent of low-cost color desktop scanners and inexpensive color printers with near-photo-quality output.

No matter which tools you use, make sure you have scheduled enough time for formatting and production. Regardless of how the final product is produced, it will be up to you to make sure that all necessary components are included. Depending on the length and formality of your report, various prefatory and supplementary parts may be necessary. The more formal your report, the more components you'll include.

Components of a Formal Report

A formal report's manuscript format and impersonal tone convey an impression of professionalism. A formal report can be either short (fewer than 10 pages) or long (10 pages or more). It can be informational or analytical, direct or indirect. It may be directed to readers inside or outside the organization. What sets it apart from other reports is its polish.

The parts included in a report depend on the type of report you are writing, the requirements of your audience, the organization you're working for, and the length of your report. At Levi Strauss, Robert Haas pays close attention to his readers' needs, whether they are employees, customers, or members of the community. From the style of the report to the language used, Haas targets his readers' preferences and familiarity and includes only the parts that are appropriate for each one. The components listed in Figure 12–1 fall into three categories, depending on where they are found in a report: prefatory parts, text of the report, and supplementary parts. For an illustration of how the various parts fit together, see Linda Moreno's Electrovision report in "Sharpening

Objective

1

List the three tasks involved in completing business reports and proposals and briefly explain what's involved in revising them.

In organizations that produce many reports and proposals, the preparation process involves teamwork.

Personal computers can handle many of the mechanical aspects of report preparation.

The three basic divisions of a formal report:
- Prefatory parts
- Text
- Supplementary parts

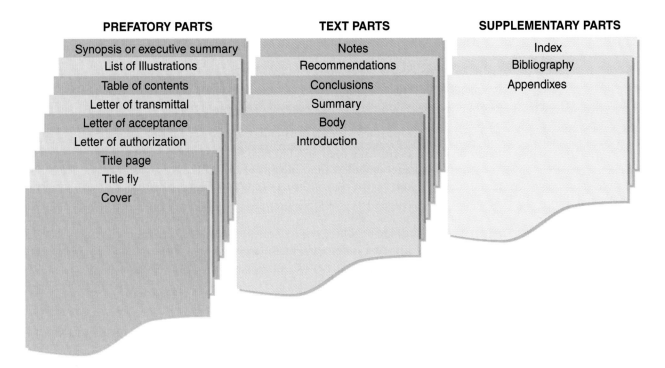

PREFATORY PARTS	TEXT PARTS	SUPPLEMENTARY PARTS
Synopsis or executive summary	Notes	Index
List of Illustrations	Recommendations	Bibliography
Table of contents	Conclusions	Appendixes
Letter of transmittal	Summary	
Letter of acceptance	Body	
Letter of authorization	Introduction	
Title page		
Title fly		
Cover		

Figure 12–1
Parts of a Formal Report

Steve Jobs is CEO of Apple, which he co-founded in 1976, and CEO of Pixar, the Academy-Award-winning computer animation studio, which he co-founded in 1986. Jobs revolutionized the computer hardware and software industry. Among other innovative ideas for software applications, Jobs developed the user-friendly interface with picture-like icons, giving any businessperson (even those lacking computer skills) the tools to design and the ability to produce professional-looking reports.

O b j e c t i v e **2**

Explain the 10 prefatory parts of a formal report.

Prefatory parts may be written after the text has been completed.

Put a title on the cover that is informative but not too long.

The title page usually includes four blocks of information.

A letter of authorization usually follows the direct-request plan.

Your Career Skills—In-Depth Critique: Analyzing a Formal Report," beginning on page 361.

Many of the components in a formal report start on a new page, but not always. Inserting page breaks consumes more paper and adds to the bulk of your report (which may be a significant financial concern if you plan to distribute many copies). On the other hand, starting a section on a new page helps your readers navigate the report and recognize transitions between major sections or features.

When a particular section is designed to stand apart, it generally starts on a new page, and the material after it also starts on a new page. Most prefatory parts (such as the table of contents) should be placed on their own pages. However, the various parts in the report text are often run together and seldom stand alone. If your introduction is only a paragraph long, don't bother with a page break before moving into the body of your report. If the introduction runs longer than a page, however, a page break can signal the reader that a major shift is about to occur in the flow of the report.

You can use this textbook as a model for deciding where to put page breaks. Each chapter starts on a new page, which provides a clear break between chapters. On the other hand, the opening vignettes, which come at the beginning of each chapter, flow right into the body of the chapter without a page break—because they are designed to lead readers into the chapter.

Prefatory Parts

Although the prefatory parts are placed before the text of the report, you may not want to write them until after you've written the text. Many of these parts—such as the table of contents, list of illustrations, and executive summary—are easier to prepare after the text has been completed because they directly reflect the contents. Other parts can be prepared at almost any time.

Cover   Many companies have standard covers for reports, made of heavy paper and imprinted with the company's name and logo. Report titles are either printed on these covers or attached with gummed labels. If your company has no standard covers, you can usually find something suitable in a good stationery store. Look for a cover that is attractive, convenient, and appropriate to the subject matter. Also, make sure it can be labeled with the report title, the writer's name (optional), and the submission date (also optional).

Think carefully about the title you put on the cover. A business report is not a mystery novel, so give your readers all the information they need: the who, what, when, where, why, and how of the subject. At the same time, try to be reasonably concise. You don't want to intimidate your audience with a title that's too long or awkward. You can reduce the length of your title by eliminating phrases such as *A Report of, A Study of,* or *A Survey of.*

Title Fly and Title Page   The **title fly** is a plain sheet of paper with only the title of the report on it. You don't really need one, but it adds a touch of formality.

The **title page** includes four blocks of information, as shown in Moreno's Electrovision report: (1) the title of the report; (2) the name, title, and address of the person, group, or organization that authorized the report (usually the intended audience); (3) the name, title, and address of the person, group, or organization that prepared the report; and (4) the date on which the report was submitted. On some title pages the second block of information is preceded by the words *Prepared for* or *Submitted to,* and the third block of information is preceded by *Prepared by* or *Submitted by.* In some cases the title page serves as the cover of the report, especially if the report is relatively short and intended solely for internal use.

Letter of Authorization and Letter of Acceptance   If you received written authorization to prepare the report, you may want to include that letter or memo in your report (and you may sometimes even include the letter or memo of acceptance). The **letter of authorization** (or *memo of authorization*) is a document requesting that a report be

(continued on page 380)

Report Writer's Notebook

In-Depth Critique: Analyzing a Formal Report

The report presented in the following pages was prepared by Linda Moreno, manager of the cost accounting department at Electrovision, a high-tech company based in Los Gatos, California. Electrovision's main product is optical character recognition equipment, which is used by the U.S. Postal Service for sorting mail. Moreno's job is to help analyze the company's costs. She has this to say about the background of the report:

> For the past three or four years, Electrovision has been on a roll. Our A-12 optical character reader was a real breakthrough, and the post office grabbed up as many as we could make. Our sales and profits kept climbing, and morale was fantastic. Everybody seemed to think that the good times would last forever. Unfortunately, everybody was wrong. When the Postal Service announced that it was postponing all new equipment purchases because of cuts in its budget, we woke up to the fact that we are essentially a one-product company with one customer. At that point, management started scrambling around looking for ways to cut costs until we could diversify our business a bit.
>
> The vice president of operations, Dennis McWilliams, asked me to help identify cost-cutting opportunities in the travel and entertainment area. On the basis of his personal observations, he felt that Electrovision was overly generous in its travel policies and that we might be able to save a significant amount by controlling these costs more carefully. My investigation confirmed his suspicion.
>
> I was reasonably confident that my report would be well received. I've worked with Dennis for several years and know what he likes: plenty of facts, clearly stated conclusions, and specific recommendations for what should be done next. I also knew that my report would be passed on to other Electrovision executives, so I wanted to create a good impression. I wanted the report to be accurate and thorough, visually appealing, readable, and appropriate in tone.

When writing the analytical report that follows, Moreno used an organization based on conclusions and recommendations, presented in direct order. The first two sections of the report correspond to Moreno's two main conclusions: That Electrovision's travel and entertainment costs are too high and that cuts are essential. The third section presents recommendations for achieving better control over travel and entertainment expenses. As you review the report, analyze both the mechanical aspects and the way Moreno presents her ideas. Be prepared to discuss the way the various components convey and reinforce the main message.

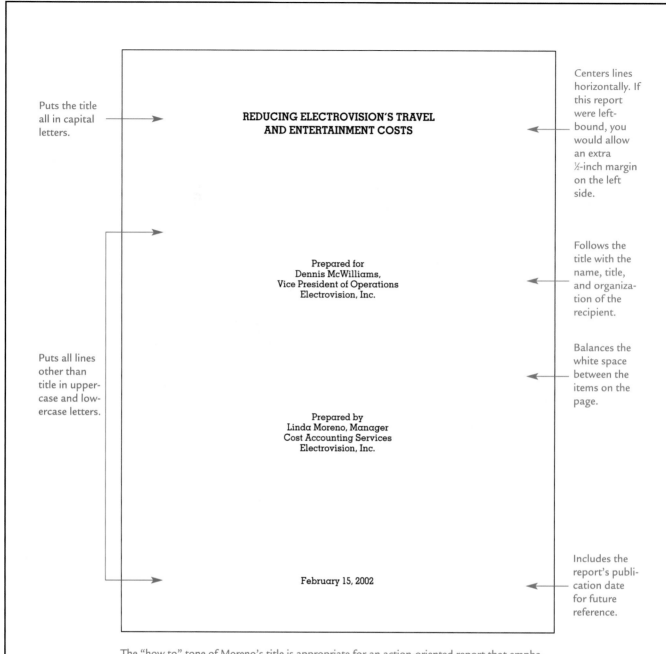

Puts the title all in capital letters.

Centers lines horizontally. If this report were left-bound, you would allow an extra ½-inch margin on the left side.

REDUCING ELECTROVISION'S TRAVEL AND ENTERTAINMENT COSTS

Prepared for
Dennis McWilliams,
Vice President of Operations
Electrovision, Inc.

Follows the title with the name, title, and organization of the recipient.

Puts all lines other than title in uppercase and lowercase letters.

Balances the white space between the items on the page.

Prepared by
Linda Moreno, Manager
Cost Accounting Services
Electrovision, Inc.

February 15, 2002

Includes the report's publication date for future reference.

The "how to" tone of Moreno's title is appropriate for an action-oriented report that emphasizes recommendations. A more neutral title, such as "An Analysis of Electrovision's Travel and Entertainment Costs," would be more suitable for an informational report.

Uses memo format for transmitting this internal report; otherwise, letter format would be used for transmitting external reports.

Presents the main conclusion right away (because Moreno expects a positive response).

Uses an informal, conversational style.

Acknowledges help that has been received.

Closes with thanks and an offer to discuss results. When appropriate, you could also include an offer to help with future projects.

MEMORANDUM

TO: Dennis McWilliams, Vice President of Operations

FROM: Linda Moreno, Manager of Cost Accounting Services

DATE: February 15, 2002

SUBJECT: Reducing Electrovision's Travel and Entertainment Costs

Here is the report you requested January 30 on Electrovision's travel and entertainment costs.

Your suspicion was right. We are spending far too much on business travel. Our unwritten policy has been "anything goes," leaving us with no real control over T&E expenses. Although this hands-off approach may have been understandable when Electrovision's profits were high, we can no longer afford the luxury of going first class.

The solutions to the problem seem rather clear. We need to have someone with centralized responsibility for travel and entertainment costs, a clear statement of policy, an effective control system, and a business-oriented travel service that can optimize our travel arrangements. We should also investigate alternatives to travel, such as videoconferencing. Perhaps more important, we need to change our attitude. Instead of viewing travel funds as a bottomless supply of money, all traveling employees need to act as though they were paying the bills themselves.

Getting people to economize is not going to be easy. In the course of researching this issue, I've found that our employees are exceedingly attached to their first-class travel privileges. I think they would almost prefer a cut in pay to a loss in travel status. We'll need a lot of top management involvement to sell people on the need for moderation. One thing is clear: People will be very bitter if we create a two-class system in which top executives get special privileges while the rest of the employees make the sacrifices.

I'm grateful to Mary Lehman and Connie McIlvain for their help in rounding up and sorting through five years' worth of expense reports. Their efforts were truly Herculean.

Thanks for giving me the opportunity to work on this assignment. It's been a real education. If you have any questions about the report, please give me a call.

In this report Moreno decided to write a brief memo of transmittal and include a separate executive summary. Short reports (fewer than 10 pages) often combine the synopsis or executive summary with the memo or letter of transmittal.

CONTENTS

Page

Includes no element that appears before the "Contents" page.

Words the headings exactly as they appear in the text.

Includes only the page numbers where sections begin.

iii

Moreno included only first- and second-level headings in her table of contents, even though the report contains third-level headings. She prefers a shorter table of contents that focuses attention on the main divisions of thought. She used informative titles, which are appropriate for a report to a receptive audience.

Numbers figures consecutively throughout the report.

LIST OF ILLUSTRATIONS

Numbers the contents pages with lowercase roman numerals centered at the bottom margin.

iv

Because figures and tables were numbered separately in the text, Moreno listed them separately here. If all were labeled as exhibits, a single list of illustrations would have been appropriate.

Begins by stating the purpose of the report.

EXECUTIVE SUMMARY

This report analyzes Electrovision's travel and entertainment (T&E) costs and presents recommendations for reducing those costs.

Travel and Entertainment Costs Are Too High

Travel and entertainment is a large and growing expense category for Electrovision. The company spends over $16 million per year on business travel, and these costs have been increasing by 12 percent annually. Company employees make roughly 3,390 trips each year at an average cost per trip of $4,720. Airfares are the biggest expense, followed by hotels, meals, and rental cars.

The nature of Electrovision's business does require extensive travel, but the company's costs appear to be excessive. Every year Electrovision employees spend more than twice as much on T&E as the average business traveler. Although the location of the company's facilities may partly explain this discrepancy, the main reason for Electrovision's high costs is the firm's philosophy and managerial style. Electrovision's tradition and its hands-off style almost invite employees to go first class and pay relatively little attention to travel costs.

Uses subheadings that summarize the content of the main sections of the report without repeating what appears in the text.

Presents the points in the executive summary in the same order as they appear in the report.

Cuts Are Essential

Although Electrovision has traditionally been casual about travel and entertainment expenses, management now recognizes the need to gain more control over this element of costs. The company is currently entering a period of declining profits, prompting management to look for every opportunity to reduce spending. At the same time, rising airfares and hotel rates are making travel and entertainment expenses more important to the bottom line.

Appears in the same typeface and type style as the text of the report. Uses single-spacing because the report is single-spaced, and follows the text's format for margins, paragraph indentions, and headings.

Electrovision Can Save $6 Million per Year

Fortunately, Electrovision has a number of excellent opportunities for reducing its travel and entertainment costs. Savings of up to $6 million per year should be achievable, judging by the experience of other companies. American Express suggests that a sensible travel-management program can save companies as much as 35 percent a year (Gilligan 39–40). Given that we purchase many more first-class tickets than the average company, we should be able to achieve even greater savings. The first priority should be to hire a director of travel and entertainment to assume overall responsibility for T&E spending. This individual should establish a written travel and entertainment policy and create a budget and a cost-control system. The director should also retain a nationwide travel agency to handle our reservations and should lead an investigation into electronic alternatives to travel.

v

Moreno decided to include an executive summary because her report was aimed at a mixed audience. She knew that some readers would be interested in the details of her report and some would prefer to focus on the big picture. The executive summary was aimed at the "big picture" group. Moreno wanted to give these readers enough information to make a decision without burdening them with the task of reading the entire report.

The hard-hitting tone of this executive summary is appropriate for a receptive audience. A more neutral approach would be better for hostile or skeptical readers.

At the same time, Electrovision should make employees aware of the need for moderation in travel and entertainment spending. People should be encouraged to forgo any unnecessary travel and to economize on airline tickets, hotels, meals, rental cars, and other expenses.

In addition to economizing on an individual basis, Electrovision should look for ways to reduce costs by negotiating preferential rates with travel providers. Once retained, a travel agency should be able to accomplish this.

Finally, we should look into alternatives to travel. Although we may have to invest money in videoconferencing systems or other equipment, we may be able to recover these costs through decreased travel expenses. I recommend that the new travel director undertake this investigation to make sure it is well integrated with the rest of the travel program.

These changes, although necessary, are likely to hurt morale, at least in the short term. Management will need to make a determined effort to explain the rationale for reduced spending. By exercising moderation in their own travel arrangements, Electrovision executives can set a good example and help other employees accept the changes. On the plus side, cutting back on travel with videoconferencing or other alternatives will reduce the travel burden on many employees and help them balance their business and personal lives much better.

Continue numbering the executive summary pages with lowercase roman numerals centered about 1 inch from the bottom of the page.

vi

This executive summary is written in an impersonal style, which adds to the formality of the report. Some writers prefer a more personal approach. You should gear your choice of style to your relationship with the readers. Moreno chose the formal approach because several members of her audience were considerably higher up in the organization. She did not want to sound too familiar. In addition, she wanted the executive summary and the text to be compatible, and her company prefers the impersonal style for formal reports.

Centers the title of the report on the first page of the text, 2 inches from the top of the page (2½ inches if top-bound).

REDUCING ELECTROVISION'S TRAVEL AND ENTERTAINMENT COSTS

INTRODUCTION

Electrovision has always encouraged a significant amount of business travel, believing that it is an effective way of operating. To compensate employees for the inconvenience and stress of frequent trips, management has authorized generous travel and entertainment (T&E) allowances. This philosophy has been good for morale, but the company has paid a price. Last year Electrovision spent $16 million on T&E—$7 million more than it spent on research and development.

This year the cost of travel and entertainment will have a bigger impact on profits, owing to changes in airfares and hotel rates. The timing of these changes is unfortunate because the company anticipates that profits will be relatively weak for a variety of other reasons. In light of these profit pressures, Dennis McWilliams, Vice President of Operations, has asked the accounting department to take a closer look at the T&E budget.

Begins the introduction by establishing the need for action.

Purpose, Scope, and Limitations

The purpose of this report is to analyze the T&E budget, evaluate the impact of recent changes in airfares and hotel costs, and suggest ways to tighten management's control over T&E expenses. Although the report outlines a number of steps that could reduce Electrovision's expenses, the precise financial impact of these measures is difficult to project. The estimates presented in the report provide a "best guess" view of what Electrovision can expect to save. Until the company actually implements these steps, however, we won't know exactly how much the travel and entertainment budget can be reduced.

Sources and Methods

In preparing this report, the accounting department analyzed internal expense reports for the past five years to determine how much Electrovision spends on travel and entertainment. These figures were then compared with average statistics compiled by Dow Jones (publisher of *The Wall Street Journal*) and presented as the Dow Jones Travel Index. We also analyzed trends and suggestions published in a variety of business journal articles to see how other companies are coping with the high cost of business travel.

Mentions sources and methods to increase credibility and to give readers a complete picture of the study's background.

1

Uses the arabic numeral 1 for the first page, centering the number about 1 inch from the bottom of the page.

In a brief introduction such as this one, some writers would omit the subheadings within the introduction and rely on topic sentences and on transitional words and phrases to indicate that they are discussing subjects such as the purpose, scope, and limitations of the study. Moreno decided to use headings because they help readers scan the document. Also, to conserve space, Moreno used single spacing and 1-inch side margins.

2

Uses arabic numerals to number the second and succeeding pages of the text in the upper right-hand corner, where the top and right-hand margins meet.

Report Organization

This report reviews the size and composition of Electrovision's travel and entertainment expenses, analyzes trends in travel costs, and recommends steps for reducing the T&E budget.

THE HIGH COST OF TRAVEL AND ENTERTAINMENT

Although many companies view travel and entertainment as an "incidental" cost of doing business, the dollars add up. At Electrovision the bill for airfares, hotels, rental cars, meals, and entertainment totaled $16 million last year. Our T&E budget has increased by 12 percent per year for the past five years. Compared with the average U.S. business's travel expenditures, Electrovision's expenditures are high, largely because of management's generous policy on travel benefits.

$16 Million per Year Spent on Travel and Entertainment

Electrovision's annual budget for travel and entertainment is only 8 percent of sales. Because this is a relatively small expense category compared with such things as salaries and commissions, it is tempting to dismiss T&E costs as insignificant. However, T&E is Electrovision's third-largest controllable expense, directly behind salaries and information systems.

Last year Electrovision personnel made about 3,390 trips at an average cost per trip of $4,720. The typical trip involved a round-trip flight of 3,000 miles, meals and hotel accommodations for two or three days, and a rental car. Roughly 80 percent of the trips were made by 20 percent of the staff—top management and sales personnel traveled most, averaging 18 trips per year.

Figure 1 illustrates how the travel and entertainment budget is spent. The largest categories are airfares and lodging, which together account for $7 out of every $10

Figure 1
Airfares and Lodging
Account for Over Two-Thirds
of Electrovision's Travel
and Entertainment Budget

Misc. 6%
Rental Cars 10%
Airfares 45%
Meals 14%
Lodging 25%

Places the visual aid as close as possible to the point it illustrates.

Makes placement of visual aid titles consistent throughout a report. Options for placement include above, below, or beside the visual.

Gives each visual aid a title that clearly indicates what it's about.

Moreno opened the first main section of the body with a topic sentence that introduces an important fact about the subject of the section. Then she oreinted the reader to the three major points developed in the section.

3

that employees spend on travel and entertainment. This spending breakdown has been relatively steady for the past five years and is consistent with the distribution of expenses experienced by other companies.

Although the composition of the T&E budget has been consistent, its size has not. As mentioned earlier, these expenditures have increased by about 12 percent per year for the past five years, roughly twice the rate of the company's growth in sales (see Figure 2). This rate of growth makes T&E Electrovision's fastest-growing expense item.

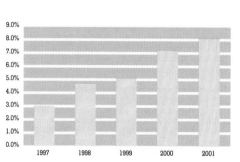

Percentage of Sales

▶ *Figure 2*
Travel and Entertainment Expenses Have Increased as a Percentage of Sales

Electrovision's Travel Expenses Exceed National Averages

Much of our travel budget is justified. Two major factors contribute to Electrovision's high travel and entertainment budget:

- With our headquarters on the West Coast and our major customer on the East Coast, we naturally spend a lot on cross-country flights.
- A great deal of travel takes place between our headquarters here on the West Coast and the manufacturing operations in Detroit, Boston, and Dallas. Corporate managers and division personnel make frequent trips to coordinate these disparate operations.

However, even though a good portion of Electrovision's travel budget is justifiable, our travelers spend considerably more on travel and entertainment than the average business traveler (see Figure 3).

Introduces visual aids before they appear and indicates what readers should notice about the data.

Numbers the visual aids consecutively and refers to them in the text by their numbers. If your report is a book-length document, you may number the visual aids by chapter: For example, Figure 4–2 would be the second figure in the fourth chapter.

Moreno originally drew the bar chart in Figure 2 as a line chart, showing both sales and T&E expenses in absolute dollars. However, the comparison was difficult to interpret because sales were so much greater than T&E expenses. Switching to a bar chart expressed in percentage terms made the main idea much easier to grasp.

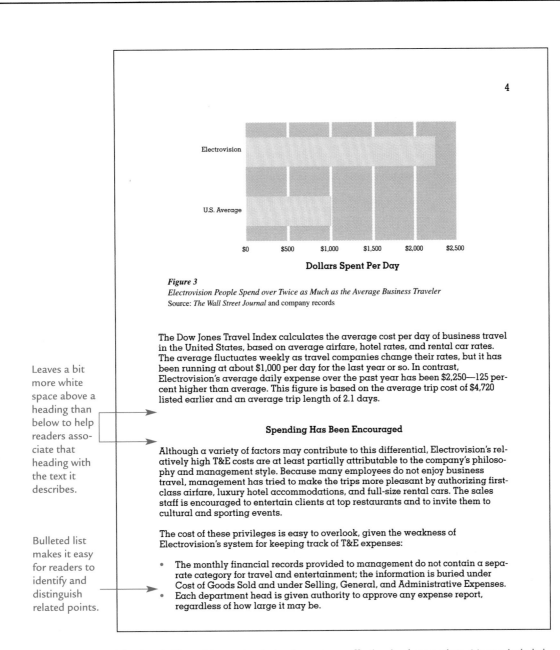

4

Dollars Spent Per Day

Figure 3
Electrovision People Spend over Twice as Much as the Average Business Traveler
Source: *The Wall Street Journal* and company records

The Dow Jones Travel Index calculates the average cost per day of business travel in the United States, based on average airfare, hotel rates, and rental car rates. The average fluctuates weekly as travel companies change their rates, but it has been running at about $1,000 per day for the last year or so. In contrast, Electrovision's average daily expense over the past year has been $2,250—125 percent higher than average. This figure is based on the average trip cost of $4,720 listed earlier and an average trip length of 2.1 days.

Spending Has Been Encouraged

Although a variety of factors may contribute to this differential, Electrovision's relatively high T&E costs are at least partially attributable to the company's philosophy and management style. Because many employees do not enjoy business travel, management has tried to make the trips more pleasant by authorizing first-class airfare, luxury hotel accommodations, and full-size rental cars. The sales staff is encouraged to entertain clients at top restaurants and to invite them to cultural and sporting events.

The cost of these privileges is easy to overlook, given the weakness of Electrovision's system for keeping track of T&E expenses:

- The monthly financial records provided to management do not contain a separate category for travel and entertainment; the information is buried under Cost of Goods Sold and under Selling, General, and Administrative Expenses.
- Each department head is given authority to approve any expense report, regardless of how large it may be.

Leaves a bit more white space above a heading than below to help readers associate that heading with the text it describes.

Bulleted list makes it easy for readers to identify and distinguish related points.

The chart in Figure 3 is very simple, but it creates an effective visual comparison. Moreno included just enough data to make her point. Moreno was as careful about the appearance of her report as she was about its content.

- Receipts are not required for expenditures of less than $100.
- Individuals are allowed to make their own travel arrangements.
- No one is charged with the responsibility for controlling the company's total spending on travel and entertainment.

Uses informative headings to focus reader attention on the main points. Such headings are appropriate when a report is in direct order and intended for a receptive audience. Descriptive headings are more effective when a report is in indirect order and readers are less receptive.

GROWING IMPACT ON THE BOTTOM LINE

During the past three years, the company's healthy profits have resulted in relatively little pressure to push for tighter controls over all aspects of the business. However, as we all know, the situation is changing. We're projecting flat to declining profits for the next two years, a situation that has prompted all of us to search for ways to cut costs. At the same time, rising airfares and hotel rates have increased the impact of T&E expenses on the company's financial results.

Lower Profits Underscore the Need for Change

The next two years promise to be difficult for Electrovision. After several years of steady increases in spending, the Postal Service is tightening procurement policies for automated mail-handling equipment. Funding for the A-12 optical character reader has been canceled. As a consequence, the marketing department expects sales to drop by 15 percent. Although Electrovision is negotiating several promising R&D contracts with nongovernment clients, the marketing department does not foresee any major procurements for the next two to three years.

At the same time, Electrovision is facing cost increases on several fronts. As we've known for several months, the new production facility now under construction in Salt Lake City, Utah, is behind schedule and over budget. Labor contracts in Boston and Dallas expire within the next six months, and plant managers there anticipate that significant salary and benefits concessions may be necessary to avoid strikes. Moreover, marketing and advertising costs are expected to increase as we attempt to strengthen these activities to better cope with competitive pressures. Given the expected decline in revenues and increase in costs, the Executive Committee's prediction that profits will fall by 12 percent in the coming fiscal year does not seem overly pessimistic.

Airfares and Hotel Rates Are Rising

Business travelers have grown accustomed to frequent fare wars and discounting in the travel industry in recent years. Excess capacity and aggressive price competition, particularly in the airline business, made travel a relative bargain.

However, that situation has changed, as weaker competitors have been forced out and the remaining players have grown stronger and smarter. Airlines and hotels

Because airfares represent Electrovision's biggest T&E expense, Moreno included a subsection that deals with the possible impact of trends in the airline industry. Airfares are rising, so it is especially important to gain more control over employees' air travel arrangements.

6

are better at managing inventory and keeping occupancy rates high, and high occupancy translates into higher prices because suppliers have less reason to compete on price. Last year saw some of the steepest rate hikes in years. Business airfares (tickets most likely to be purchased by business travelers) jumped over 40 percent in many markets. The trend is expected to continue, with rates increasing another 5 to 10 percent overall (Phillips 331; "Travel Costs Under Pressure" 30; Dahl B6).

Given the fact that airfare and hotel costs account for 70 percent of Electrovision's T&E budget, the trend toward higher prices in these two categories will have serious consequences on the company's expenses unless management takes action to control these costs.

METHODS FOR REDUCING TRAVEL AND ENTERTAINMENT COSTS

By implementing a number of reforms, management can expect to reduce Electrovision's T&E budget by as much as 40 percent. This estimate is based on the general assessment made by American Express (Gilligan 130–40) and the fact that we have an opportunity to significantly reduce air travel costs by reducing or eliminating first-class travel. However, these measures are likely to be unpopular with employees. To gain acceptance for such changes, management will need to sell employees on the need for moderation in travel and entertainment allowances.

Four Ways to Trim Expenses

By researching what other companies are doing to curb travel and entertainment expenses, the accounting department has identified four prominent opportunities that should enable Electrovision to save about $6 million annually in travel-related costs.

Institute Tighter Spending Controls

A single individual should be appointed director of travel and entertainment to spearhead the effort to gain control of the T&E budget. More than a third of all U.S. companies now employ travel managers in an effort to keep costs in line ("Businesses Use Savvy Managers" 4). The director should be familiar with the travel industry and should be well versed in both accounting and information technology. The director should also report to the vice president of operations. The director's first priorities should be to establish a written travel and entertainment policy and to implement a system for controlling travel and entertainment costs.

Documents the facts to add weight to Moreno's argument.

Points out both the benefits and the risks of taking action to give recommendations an objective flavor.

Moreno created a forceful tone by using action verbs in the third-level subheadings of this section. This approach is appropriate to the nature of the study and the attitude of the audience. However, in a status-conscious organization, the imperative verbs might sound a bit too presumptuous coming from a junior member of the staff.

7

Electrovision currently has no written policy on travel and entertainment, a step widely recommended by air travel experts (Smith D4). Creating a policy would clarify management's position and serve as a vehicle for communicating the need for moderation. At a minimum, the policy should include the following provisions:

- All travel and entertainment should be strictly related to business and should be approved in advance.
- Except under special circumstances to be approved on a case-by-case basis, employees should travel by coach and stay in mid-range business hotels.
- The travel and entertainment policy should apply equally to employees at all levels in the organization. No special benefits should be allowed for top executives.

To implement the new policy, Electrovision will need to create a system for controlling travel and entertainment expenses. Each department should prepare an annual T&E budget as part of its operating plan. These budgets should be presented in detail so that management can evaluate how travel and entertainment dollars will be spent and recommend appropriate cuts.

To help management monitor performance relative to these budgets, the director of travel should prepare monthly financial statements showing actual travel and entertainment expenditures by department. The system for capturing this information should be computerized and should be capable of identifying individuals who consistently exceed approved spending levels. The recommended average should range between $2,000 and $2,500 per month for each professional employee, depending on the individual's role in the company. Because they make frequent trips, sales and top management personnel can be expected to have relatively high travel expenses.

The director of travel should also be responsible for retaining a business-oriented travel service that will schedule all employee business trips and look for the best travel deals, particularly in airfares. In addition to centralizing Electrovision's reservation and ticketing activities, the agency will negotiate reduced group rates with hotels and rental car agencies. The agency selected should have offices nationwide so that all Electrovision facilities can channel their reservations through the same company. By consolidating its travel planning in this way, Electrovision can increase its control over costs and achieve economies of scale. This is particularly important in light of the dizzying array of often wildly different airfares available between some cities. It's not uncommon to find dozens of fares along commonly traveled routes (Rowe 30).

The director should also work with the agency to explore low-cost alternatives, such as buying tickets from airfare consolidators (the air travel equivalent of factory outlet malls). In addition, the director can help coordinate travel across the company to secure group discounts whenever possible (Barker 31; Miller B6).

Bulleted list format not only calls attention to important points but adds visual interest. You can also use visual aids, headings, and direct quotations to break up large, solid blocks of print.

Specifies the steps required to implement recommendations.

Moreno decided to single-space her report to create a formal, finished look; however, double-spacing can make the text of a long report somewhat easier to read and provide more space for readers to write comments.

8

Reduce Unnecessary Travel and Entertainment

One of the easiest ways to reduce expenses is to reduce the amount of traveling and entertaining that occurs. An analysis of last year's expenditures suggests that as much as 30 percent of Electrovision's travel and entertainment is discretionary. The professional staff spent $2.8 million attending seminars and conferences last year. Although some of these gatherings are undoubtedly beneficial, the company could save money by sending fewer representatives to each function and by eliminating some of the less valuable seminars.

Similarly, Electrovision could economize on trips between headquarters and divisions by reducing the frequency of such visits and by sending fewer people on each trip. Although there is often no substitute for face-to-face meetings, management could try to resolve more internal issues through telephone, electronic, and written communication.

Electrovision can also reduce spending by urging employees to economize. Instead of flying first class, employees can fly tourist class or take advantage of discount fares. Instead of taking clients to dinner, Electrovision personnel can hold breakfast meetings, which tend to be less costly. Rather than ordering a $50 bottle of wine, employees can select a less-expensive bottle or dispense with alcohol entirely. People can book rooms at moderately priced hotels and drive smaller rental cars. In general, employees should be urged to spend the company's money as though it were their own.

Obtain Lowest Rates from Travel Providers

Apart from urging individual employees to economize, Electrovision can also save money by searching for the lowest available airfares, hotel rates, and rental car fees. Currently, few Electrovision employees have the time or specialized knowledge to seek out travel bargains. When they need to travel, they make the most convenient and most comfortable arrangements. However, if Electrovision contracts with a professional travel service, the company will have access to professionals who can more efficiently obtain the lower rates from travel providers.

Judging by the experience of other companies, Electrovision may be able to trim as much as 30 to 40 percent from the travel budget by looking for bargains in airfares and negotiating group rates with hotels and rental car companies. Electrovision should be able to achieve these economies by analyzing its travel patterns, identifying frequently visited locations, and selecting a few hotels that are willing to reduce rates in exchange for guaranteed business. At the same time, the company should be able to save up to 40 percent on rental car charges by negotiating a corporate rate.

Note how Moreno made the transition from section to section. The first sentence under the second heading on this page refers to the subject of the previous paragraph and signals a shift in thought.

9

The possibilities for economizing are promising, but it's worth noting that making the best arrangements is a complicated undertaking, requiring many trade-offs such as the following:

- The best fares might not always be the lowest. Indirect flights are often less expensive than direct flights, but they take longer and may end up costing more in lost work time.
- The cheapest tickets may have to be booked 30 days in advance, often impossible for us.
- Discount tickets may be nonrefundable, which is a real drawback if the trip has to be canceled at the last minute.

Electrovision is currently ill-equipped to make these and other trade-offs. However, by employing a business-oriented travel service, the company will have access to computerized systems that can optimize its choices.

Replace Travel with Technological Alternatives

We might be able to replace a significant portion of our interdivisional travel with electronic meetings that utilize videoconferencing, real-time document sharing on PC screens, and other alternatives. Naturally, we don't want to reduce employee or team effectiveness, but many companies are using these new tools to cut costs and reduce wear and tear on employees.

Rather than make specific recommendations in this report, I suggest that the new travel director conduct an in-depth study of the company's travel patterns as part of an overall cost-containment effort. A thorough analysis of why employees travel and what they accomplish will highlight any opportunities for replacing face-to-face meetings. Part of this study should include limited-scope tests of various communication systems as a way of measuring their impact on both workplace effectiveness and overall costs.

The Impact of Reforms

By implementing tighter controls, reducing unnecessary expenses, negotiating more favorable rates, and exploring "electronic travel," Electrovision should be able to reduce its travel and entertainment budget significantly. As Table 1 illustrates, the combined savings should be in the neighborhood of $6 million, although the precise figures are somewhat difficult to project.

Note how Moreno calls attention in the last paragraph to items in the following table, without repeating the information in the table.

10

TABLE 1

**Electrovision Can Trim Travel and Entertainment Costs
by an Estimated $6 Million per Year**

Source of Savings	Amount Saved
Switching from first-class to coach airfare	$2,300,000
Negotiating preferred hotel rates	940,000
Negotiating preferred rental car rates	460,000
Systematically searching for lower airfares	375,000
Reducing interdivisional travel	675,000
Reducing seminar and conference attendance	1,250,000
TOTAL POTENTIAL SAVINGS	**$6,000,000**

To achieve the economies outlined in the table, Electrovision will incur expenses for hiring a director of travel and for implementing a T&E cost-control system. These costs are projected at $95,000: $85,000 per year in salary and benefits for the new employee and a one-time expense of $10,000 for the cost-control system. The cost of retaining a full-service travel agency is negligible because agencies normally receive a commission from travel providers rather than a fee from clients.

The measures required to achieve these savings are likely to be unpopular with employees. Electrovision personnel are accustomed to generous travel and entertainment allowances, and they are likely to resent having these privileges curtailed. To alleviate their disappointment

- Management should make a determined effort to explain why the changes are necessary.
- The director of corporate communication should be asked to develop a multi-faceted campaign that will communicate the importance of curtailing travel and entertainment costs.
- Management should set a positive example by adhering strictly to the new policies.
- The limitations should apply equally to employees at all levels in the organization.

Uses informative title in the table, which is consistent with the way headings are handled and is appropriate for a report to a receptive audience.

Uses complete sentence to help readers focus immediately on the point of the illustrations.

Includes dollar figures to help management envision the impact of the suggestions, even though estimated savings are difficult to project.

The table on this page puts Moreno's recommendations in perspective. Moreno calls attention to the most important sources of savings and also spells out the costs required to achieve those results.

11

Uses a descriptive heading for the last section of the text. In informational reports, this section is generally called "Summary"; in analytical reports, it is called "Conclusions" or "Conclusions and Recommendations."

Emphasizes the recommendations by presenting them in list format.

Summarizes conclusions in the first two paragraphs—a good approach because Moreno organized her report around conclusions and recommendations, so readers have already been introduced to them.

A simple list is enough to remind readers of the four main recommendations.

CONCLUSIONS AND RECOMMENDATIONS

Electrovision is currently spending $16 million per year on travel and entertainment. Although much of this spending is justified, the company's costs appear to be high relative to competitors', mainly because Electrovision has been generous with its travel benefits.

Electrovision's liberal approach to travel and entertainment was understandable during years of high profitability; however, the company is facing the prospect of declining profits for the next several years. Management is therefore motivated to cut costs in all areas of the business. Reducing T&E spending is particularly important because the impact of these costs on the bottom line will increase as a result of fare increases in the airline industry.

Electrovision should be able to reduce travel and entertainment costs by as much as 40 percent by taking four important steps:

1. *Institute tighter spending controls.* Management should hire a director of travel and entertainment who will assume overall responsibility for T&E activities. Within the next six months, this director should develop a written travel policy, institute a T&E budget and a cost-control system, and retain a professional, business-oriented travel agency that will optimize arrangements with travel providers.

2. *Reduce unnecessary travel and entertainment.* Electrovision should encourage employees to economize on travel and entertainment spending. Management can accomplish this by authorizing fewer trips and by urging employees to be more conservative in their spending.

3. *Obtain lowest rates from travel providers.* Electrovision should also focus on obtaining the best rates on airline tickets, hotel rooms, and rental cars. By channeling all arrangements through a professional travel agency, the company can optimize its choices and gain clout in negotiating preferred rates.

4. *Replace travel with technological alternatives.* With the number of computers already installed in our facilities, it seems likely that we could take advantage of desktop videoconferencing and other distance-meeting tools. This won't be quite as feasible with customer sites, since these systems require compatible equipment at both ends of a connection, but it is certainly a possibility for communication with Electrovision's own sites.

Because these measures may be unpopular with employees, management should make a concerted effort to explain the importance of reducing travel costs. The director of corporate communication should be given responsibility for developing a plan to communicate the need for employee cooperation.

Moreno introduces no new facts in this entire section. In a longer report she might have divided this section into subsections, labeled "Conclusions" and "Recommendations," to distinguish between the two. If the report has been organized around logical arguments, this section would have been the readers' first exposure to the conclusions and recommendations, and Moreno would have needed to develop them more fully.

12

WORKS CITED

Barker, Julie. "How to Rein in Group Travel Costs." *Successful Meetings* Feb. 2001: 31.

"Businesses Use Savvy Managers to Keep Travel Costs Down." *Christian Science Monitor* 17 July 2000: 4.

Dahl, Jonathan. "1998: The Year Travel Costs Took Off." *Wall Street Journal* 29 Dec. 2000: B6.

Gilligan, Edward P. "Trimming Your T&E Is Easier Than You Think." *Managing Office Technology* Nov. 2001: 39–40.

Miller, Lisa. "Attention, Airline Ticket Shoppers." *Wall Street Journal* 7 July 2001: B6.

Phillips, Edward H. "Airlines Post Record Traffic." *Aviation Week & Space Technology* 8 Jan. 2001: 331.

Rowe, Irene Vlitos. "Global Solution for Cutting Travel Costs." *European* 12 Oct. 2000: 30.

Smith, Carol. "Rising, Erratic Air Fares Make Company Policy Vital." *Los Angeles Times* 2 Nov. 2001: D4.

"Travel Costs Under Pressure." *Purchasing* 15 Feb. 2001: 30.

Lists references alphabetically by the author's last name, and when the author is unknown, by the title of the reference. See Appendix B for additional details on preparing reference lists.

Moreno's list of references follows the style recommended in *The MLA Style Manual*.

prepared. It normally follows the direct-request plan described in Chapter 5, and it typically specifies the problem, scope, time and money restrictions, special instructions, and due date.

The **letter of acceptance** (or *memo of acceptance*) acknowledges the assignment to conduct the study and to prepare the report. Following the good-news plan, the acceptance confirms time and money restrictions and other pertinent details. This document is rarely included in reports.

Letter of Transmittal   The **letter of transmittal** (or *memo of transmittal*) conveys your report to your audience. (In a book, this section is called the preface.) The letter of transmittal says what you'd say if you were handing the report directly to the person who authorized it, so the style is less formal than the rest of the report. For example, the letter would use personal pronouns (*you, I, we*) and conversational language. Moreno's Electrovision report includes a one-page transmittal memo from Moreno to her boss (the person who requested the report).

The transmittal letter usually appears right before the table of contents. If your report will be widely distributed, however, you may decide to include the letter of transmittal only in selected copies so that you can make certain comments to a specific audience. If your report discusses layoffs or other issues that affect people in the organization, you might want to discuss your recommendations privately in a letter of transmittal to top management. If your audience is likely to be skeptical of or even hostile to something in your report, the transmittal letter is a good opportunity to acknowledge their concerns and explain how the report addresses the issues they care about.

The letter of transmittal follows the routine and good-news plans described in Chapter 7. Begin with the main idea, officially conveying the report to the readers and summarizing its purpose. Such a letter typically begins with a statement such as "Here is the report you asked me to prepare on . . ." The rest includes information about the scope of the report, the methods used to complete the study, and the limitations that became apparent. In the middle section of the letter you may also highlight important points or sections of the report, make comments on side issues, give suggestions for follow-up studies, and offer any details that will help readers understand and use the report. You may also wish to acknowledge help given by others. The concluding paragraph is a note of thanks for having been given the report assignment, an expression of willingness to discuss the report, and an offer to assist with future projects.

If the report does not have a synopsis, the letter of transmittal may summarize the major findings, conclusions, and recommendations. This material would be placed after the opening of the letter.

Table of Contents   The table of contents indicates in outline form the coverage, sequence, and relative importance of the information in the report. The headings used in the text of the report are the basis for the table of contents. Depending on the length and complexity of the report, your contents page may show only the top two or three levels of headings or only first-level headings. The exclusion of some levels of headings may frustrate readers who want to know where to find every subject you cover. On the other hand, a simpler table of contents helps readers focus on the major points. No matter how many levels you include, make sure readers can easily distinguish between them (see Figure 11–16 for examples of various levels of headings).

The table of contents is prepared after the other parts of the report have been typed so that the beginning page numbers for each heading can be shown. The headings should be worded exactly as they are in the text of the report. Also listed on the contents page are the prefatory parts (only those that follow the contents page) and the supplementary parts. If you have fewer than four visual aids, you may wish to list them in the table of contents, too; but if you have four or more visual aids, create a separate list of illustrations.

List of Illustrations   For simplicity's sake, some reports refer to all visual aids as illustrations or exhibits. In other reports, as in Moreno's Electrovision report, tables are labeled

---

Margin notes:

Use the good-news plan for a letter of acceptance.

Use a less-formal style for the letter of transmittal than for the report itself.

Use the good-news plan for a letter of transmittal.

The synopsis of short reports is often included in the letter of transmittal.

The table of contents outlines the text and lists prefatory and supplementary parts.

Be sure the headings in the table of contents match up perfectly with the headings in the text.

separately from other types of visual aids, which are called figures. Regardless of the system used to label visual aids, the list of illustrations gives their titles and page numbers.

If you have enough space on a single page, include the list of illustrations directly beneath the table of contents. Otherwise, put the list on the page after the contents page. When tables and figures are numbered separately, they should also be listed separately. The two lists can appear on the same page if they fit; otherwise, start each list on a separate page.

Put the lists of figures and tables on separate pages if they won't fit on one page with the table of contents.

Synopsis or Executive Summary   A **synopsis** is a brief overview (one page or less) of a report's most important points, designed to give readers a quick preview of the contents. It's often included in long informational reports dealing with technical, professional, or academic subjects and can also be called an *abstract*. Because it's a concise representation of the whole report, it may be distributed separately to a wide audience; then interested readers can request a copy of the entire report.

Provide a brief overview of the report in a synopsis.

The phrasing of a synopsis can be either informative or descriptive, depending on whether the report is in direct or indirect order. In an informative synopsis, you present the main points of the report in the order in which they appear in the text. A descriptive synopsis, on the other hand, simply tells what the report is about, using only moderately greater detail than the table of contents; the actual findings of the report are omitted. Here are examples of statements from each type:

An informative synopsis summarizes the main ideas; a descriptive synopsis states what the report is about.

INFORMATIVE SYNOPSIS	DESCRIPTIVE SYNOPSIS
Sales of super-premium ice cream make up 11 percent of the total ice cream market.	This report contains information about super-premium ice cream and its share of the market.

The way you handle a synopsis reflects the approach you use in the text. If you're using an indirect approach in your report, you're better off with a descriptive synopsis. An informative synopsis, with its focus on conclusions and key points, may be too confrontational if you have a skeptical audience. You don't want to spoil the effect by providing a controversial beginning. No matter which type of synopsis you use, be sure to present an accurate picture of the report's contents.[2]

Use a descriptive synopsis for a skeptical or hostile audience, an informative synopsis for most other situations

Many business report writers prefer to include an **executive summary** instead of a synopsis or an abstract. Whereas a synopsis is a prose table of contents that outlines the main points of the report, an executive summary is a fully developed "mini" version of the report itself, intended for readers who lack the time or motivation to study the complete text. An executive summary is more comprehensive than a synopsis, often as much as 10 percent as long as the report itself.

Unlike a synopsis, an executive summary may contain headings, well-developed transitions, and even visual aids. It is often organized in the same way as the report, using a direct or an indirect approach, depending on the audience's receptivity. However, executive summaries can also deviate from the sequence of material in the remainder of the report.

Linda Moreno's Electrovision report provides one example of an executive summary. After reading the summary, audience members know the essentials of the report and are in a position to make a decision. Later, when time permits, they may read certain parts of the report to obtain additional detail. However, from daily newspapers to Web sites, businesspeople are getting swamped with more and more data and information. They are looking for ways to cut through all the clutter, and reading executive summaries is a popular shortcut. Because you can usually assume that many of your readers will not read the main text of your report, make sure you cover all your important points (along with significant supporting information) in the executive summary.

Put enough information in an executive summary so that an executive can make a decision without reading the entire report.

Many reports require neither a synopsis nor an executive summary. Length is usually the determining factor. Most reports of fewer than 10 pages either omit such a preview or combine it with the letter of transmittal. However, if your report is over 30 pages long, you'll probably include either a synopsis or an executive summary as a convenience for readers. Which one you'll provide depends on the traditions of your organization.

Text of the Report   Apart from deciding on the fundamental issues of content and organization, you must also make decisions about the design and layout of your report. You can use a variety of techniques to present your material effectively. Many organizations have format guidelines that make your decisions easier, but the goal is always to focus readers' attention on major points and on the flow of ideas. Headings, typographical devices (such as capital letters, italics, and boldface type), and white space are useful tools, as are visual aids. Also, as discussed in Chapter 11, you can use preview and review statements to frame sections of your text. This strategy keeps your audience informed and reinforces the substance of your message.

Aids to understanding the text of a report:
- Headings
- Typographical devices
- Visual aids
- Preview and summary statements

Introduction   The introduction of a report serves a number of important functions:

◆ Putting the report in a broader context by tying it to a problem or an assignment

◆ Telling readers the purpose of the report

◆ Previewing the contents and organization of the report

◆ Establishing the tone of the report and the writer's relationship with the audience

Objective

3

Describe four important functions of a formal report's introduction and identify the possible topics it might include.

The length of the introduction depends on the length of the report. In a relatively brief report, the introduction may be only a paragraph or two and may not be labeled with a heading of any kind. On the other hand, the introduction to a major formal report may extend to several pages and can be identified as a separate section by the first-level heading "Introduction." (See Linda Moreno's Electrovision report.)

An introduction has a number of functions and covers a wide variety of topics.

Here's a list of topics to consider covering in an introduction, depending on your material and your audience:

◆ **Authorization.** When, how, and by whom the report was authorized; who wrote it; and when it was submitted. This material is especially important when no letter of transmittal is included.

◆ **Problem/purpose.** The reason for the report's existence and what is to be accomplished as a result of the report's being written.

◆ **Scope.** What is and what isn't going to be covered in the report. The scope indicates the report's size and complexity.

◆ **Background.** The historical conditions or factors that led up to the report. This section enables readers to understand how the problem developed, and what has been done about it so far.

◆ **Sources and methods.** The primary and secondary sources of information used. This section explains how samples were selected, how questionnaires were constructed (which should be included in an appendix with any cover letters), what follow-up was done, and so on. This section builds reader confidence in the work and in the sources and methods used.

◆ **Definitions.** A brief statement introducing a list of terms and their definitions. This section is unnecessary if readers are familiar with the terms you've used in your report. Moreno's Electrovision report doesn't use unfamiliar terminology, so no list of definitions is included. However, if you have any question about reader knowledge, define any terms that might be misinterpreted. Terms may also be defined in the body, explanatory notes, or glossary.

◆ **Limitations.** Factors beyond your control that affect report quality, such as a budget too small to do needed work, a schedule too short to do needed research, and unreliable or unavailable data. Includes doubts about any aspect of your report. Such candor may lead

Noël Forgeard is CEO of Airbus, the consortium of European aerospace companies based in Toulouse, France. Foregard is now ramping up Airbus to produce by 2006 the A3XX (recently renamed the A380), the world's largest commercial aircraft, holding 600 passengers. To set priorities, focus on his goals, and maintain a strong team to achieve those goals, Forgeard must read a lot of reports. He expects a report's introduction to (1) give him perspective on where the report fits into the overall picture, (2) clearly state its purpose, (3) preview the contents, and (4) establish a tone that defines its relationship with its readers.

Linking from Introduction to Topic

A report's introduction gives readers just a brief overview of the main points covered. Readers who want more information must then flip back to the table of contents to locate the right page within the body. On the Web, however, your introduction can include links to bring readers directly to the report sections covering main points. For example, when the AT&T Foundation (www.att.com/foundation) posted an executive summary of its philanthropic activities on the Web, it added links labeled "more" to encourage readers to click for more details on each activity.

1. Besides the table of contents, in what other prefatory parts of an online report would readers appreciate seeing links to more information?
2. How could you use links in the bibliography of an online report?

readers to question results, but it also helps them assess those results, and it builds your report's integrity. Even so, limitations do not excuse a poor study or a bad report.

◆ **Report organization.** The organization of the report (what topics are covered and in what order), along with a rationale for following this plan. This section is a road map that helps readers understand what's coming at each turn of the report and why.

Some of these items may be combined in the introduction; some may not be included at all. You can decide what to include by figuring out what kind of information will help your readers understand and accept your report. Also give some thought to how the introduction relates to the prefatory parts of the report. In longer reports you may have a letter of transmittal, a synopsis or an executive summary, and an introduction—all of which cover essentially the same ground. To avoid redundancy, balance the various sections. For example, if the letter of transmittal and the synopsis are fairly detailed, you might make the introduction relatively brief.

Avoid repeating in the introduction the material that has already been covered in other prefatory parts.

However, because some people may barely glance at prefatory parts, be sure your introduction is detailed enough to provide an adequate preview of your report. If you believe that your introduction must repeat information that has already been covered in one of the prefatory parts, simply use different wording.

Body   The body of the report follows the introduction. It consists of the major sections or chapters (with various levels of headings) that present, analyze, and interpret the information gathered during your investigation. These chapters contain the "proof," the detailed information necessary to support your conclusions and recommendations. (See the body of Linda Moreno's Electrovision report.)

One of the decisions to make when writing the body of your report is how much detail to include. Your decision depends on the nature of your information, the purpose of your report, and the preferences of your audience. Some situations call for detailed

Restrict the body to those details necessary to prove your conclusions and recommendations.

coverage; others lend themselves to shorter treatment. Provide only enough detail in the body to support your conclusions and recommendations; put additional detail in tables, charts, and appendixes.

You can also decide whether to put your conclusions in the body or in a separate section or both. If the conclusions seem to flow naturally from the evidence, you'll almost inevitably cover them in the body. However, if you want to give your conclusions added emphasis, you can include a separate section to summarize them. Having a separate section is particularly appropriate in long reports; the reader may lose track of the conclusions if they're given only in the body.

Summary, Conclusions, and Recommendations   The final section of the report text tells readers what has been said. In a short report, this final wrap-up may be only a paragraph or two. A long report generally has separate sections labeled "Summary," "Conclusions," and "Recommendations." Here's how the three differ:

Summaries, conclusions, and recommendations serve different purposes.

◆ **Summary.** The key findings of your report, paraphrased from the body and stated or listed in the order in which they appear in the body.

◆ **Conclusions.** An analysis of what the findings mean. These are the answers to the questions that led to the report.

◆ **Recommendations.** Opinions about the course of action that should be taken—always based on reason and logic. In the Electrovision report, Moreno lists four specific steps the company should take to reduce travel costs.

If the report is organized in direct order, the summary, conclusions, and recommendations are presented before the body and are reviewed only briefly at the end. If the report is organized in indirect order, these sections are presented for the first time at the end and are covered in detail. Many report writers combine the conclusions and recommendations under one heading because it seems like the natural thing to do. It is often difficult to present a conclusion without implying a recommendation. (See Moreno's Electrovision report.)

In action-oriented reports, put all the recommendations in a separate section, and spell out precisely what should happen next.

Whether you combine them or not, if you have several conclusions and recommendations, you may want to number and list them. An appropriate lead-in to such a list might be, "The findings of this study lead to the following conclusions." A statement that could be used for a list of recommendations might be, "Based on the conclusions of this study, the following recommendations are made." New findings are not presented in the conclusions or in the recommendations section.

In reports that are intended to lead to action, the recommendations section is particularly important; it spells out exactly what should happen next. It brings all the action items together in one place and gives the details about who should do what, when, where, and how. Readers may agree with everything you say in your report but still fail to take any action if you're vague about what should happen next. Your readers must understand what's expected of them and must have some appreciation of the difficulties that are likely to arise. Providing a schedule and specific task assignments is helpful because concrete plans have a way of commanding action.

A. Barry Rand is chairman and CEO of Avis Rent A Car, Inc., and the third African American to head a *Fortune* 500 company. With reports that outlined his recommendations for sales and marketing and that spelled out exactly what actions would come next, Rand transformed Avis into a company that focuses on service and information, "providing a full array of business management solutions."

Give credit where credit is due.

Source Documentation   You have an ethical and a legal obligation to give other people credit for their work. Acknowledging your sources also enhances the credibility of your report. By citing references in the text, you demonstrate that you have thoroughly researched your topic. Mentioning the names of well-known or important authorities on the subject also helps build credibility for your message. It's often a good idea to mention a credible source's name several times if you need to persuade your audience.

On the other hand, you don't want to make your report read like an academic treatise, dragging along from citation to citation. The source references should be handled as conveniently and inconspicuously as possible. One approach, especially for internal reports, is simply to mention a source in the text:

According to Dr. Lewis Morgan of Northwestern Hospital hip replacement operations account for 7 percent of all surgery performed on women age 65 and over.

However, if your report will be distributed to outsiders, include additional information on where you obtained the data. Most college students are familiar with citation schemes suggested by the Modern Language Association (MLA) or the American Psychological Association (APA). *The Chicago Manual of Style* is a reference often used by typesetters and publishers. All of these encourage the use of in-text citations (inserting the author's last name and a year of publication or a page number directly into the text). An alternative is to use numbered footnotes (bottom of the page) or endnotes (end of the report). (Linda Moreno's Electrovision report uses the author-date system, whereas this textbook uses endnotes.) For more information on citing sources, see Appendix B, "Documentation of Report Sources."

Supplementary Parts   Supplementary parts follow the text of the report and include the appendixes, bibliography, and index. They are more common in long reports than in short ones.

An **appendix** contains materials related to the report but not included in the text because they're too lengthy or bulky or because they lack direct relevance. However, as Robert Haas warns, be sure not to include too much ancillary material. Keep your reports straightforward and concise.

Frequently included in appendixes are sample questionnaires and cover letters, sample forms, computer printouts, and statistical formulas; a glossary may be put in an appendix or may stand as a separate supplementary part. The best place to include visual aids is in the text body nearest the point of discussion. If any graphics are too large to fit on one page or are only indirectly relevant to your report, they too may be put in an appendix. Some organizations specify that all visual aids be placed in an appendix.

Each type of material deserves a separate appendix. Identify the appendixes by labeling them; for example, "Appendix A: Questionnaire," "Appendix B: Computer Printout of Raw Data," and so on. All appendixes should be mentioned in the text and listed in the table of contents.

A **bibliography** is a list of secondary sources consulted when preparing the report. Linda Moreno labeled her bibliography "Works Cited" in her Electrovision report because she listed only the works that were mentioned in the report. You might call this section "Sources" or "References" if it includes works consulted but not mentioned in your report. The construction of a bibliography is shown in Appendix B.

An **index** is an alphabetical list of names, places, and subjects mentioned in the report, along with the pages on which they occur (see the index for this book). An index is rarely included in unpublished reports.

> Put into an appendix materials that are
> • Bulky or lengthy
> • Not directly relevant to the text

Components of a Formal Proposal

As discussed in Chapter 13, certain analytical reports are called proposals, including bids to perform work under a contract and pleas for financial support from outsiders. Such bids and pleas are always formal. As Robert Haas knows only too well, the goal of a proposal is to impress readers with your professionalism and to make your service and your company stand out. This goal is best achieved through a structured and deliberate approach.

Formal proposals contain many of the same components as other formal reports (see Figure 12–2). The difference lies mostly in the text, although a few of the prefatory parts are also different. With the exception of an occasional appendix, most proposals have few supplementary parts.

Prefatory Parts   The cover, title fly, title page, table of contents, and list of illustrations are handled the same as in other formal reports. However, other prefatory parts are handled quite differently, such as the copy of the RFP, the letter of transmittal, and the synopsis or executive summary.

Copy of the RFP   Instead of having a letter of authorization, a formal proposal may have a copy of the **request for proposal (RFP),** which is a letter or memo soliciting a proposal

> *Going Online*
>
>
>
> **Research Reports and Learning by Example**
>
> *A good way to get ideas for the best style, organization, and format of a report is by looking at professional business reports. To find samples of different types of reports, you can use a metasearch engine, such as Ixquick Metasearch. Ixquick searches many engines simultaneously; in addition to searching in English, you can conduct your search in five other languages. See what Ixquick produces when you enter the phrase "business reports." Choose from various titles or descriptions to compare different kinds of reports. This research could result in your preparing better reports and proposals.*
>
> www.ixquick.com
>
> *To reach this Web site, go to* www.prenhall.com/thill *(the Web site for this text). Select Chapter 12, then select "Student Resources." There you'll find a current live link that will take you straight to the site.*

> Formal proposals contain most of the same prefatory parts as other formal reports.

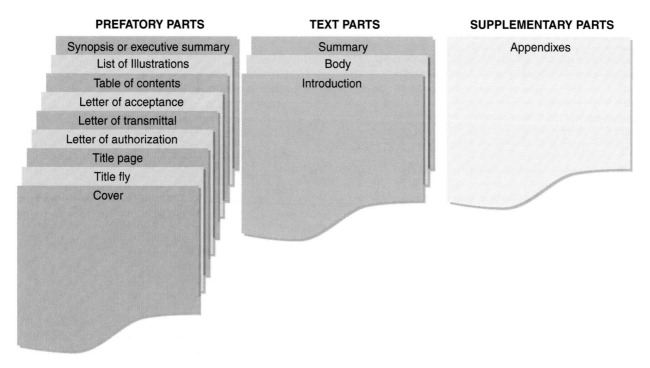

Figure 12–2
Parts of a Formal Proposal

Use a copy of the request for proposal in place of the letter of authorization.

or a bid for a particular project. The RFP is issued by the client to whom the proposal is being submitted, and it outlines what the proposal should cover. If the RFP includes detailed specifications, it may be too long to bind into the proposal; in that case, you may want to include only the introductory portion of the RFP. Another option is to omit the RFP and simply refer to it in your letter of transmittal.

Use the good-news pattern for the letter of transmittal if the proposal is solicited; use the persuasive plan if the proposal is unsolicited.

Letter of Transmittal   The way you handle the letter of transmittal depends on whether the proposal is solicited or unsolicited. If the proposal is solicited, the transmittal letter follows the pattern for good-news messages, highlighting those aspects of your proposal that may give you a competitive advantage. If the proposal is unsolicited, the transmittal letter takes on added importance; it may be all the client reads. The letter must persuade the reader that you have something worthwhile to offer, something that justifies the time required to read the entire proposal. The transmittal letter for an unsolicited proposal follows the pattern for persuasive messages (see Chapter 9).

Most proposals do not require a synopsis or an executive summary.

Synopsis or Executive Summary   Although you may include a synopsis or an executive summary for your reader's convenience if your proposal is quite long, these components are often less useful in a formal proposal than they are in a formal report. If your proposal is unsolicited, your transmittal letter will already have caught the reader's interest, making a synopsis or an executive summary pointless. It may also be pointless if your proposal is solicited, because the reader is already committed to studying your proposal to find out how you intend to satisfy the terms of a contract. The introduction to a solicited proposal would provide an adequate preview of the contents. However, in some cases, an executive summary can serve you well.

Bruce Rogow made good use of the executive summary in his *Suntrakker* proposal.

Bruce Rogow was a junior engineering major at San Diego State University when he was first struck by the idea of leading a team of students to design, build, and race a solar car at the World Solar Challenge Race across the Australian outback. The race itself would be the least of Rogow's challenges: First he had to convince students and faculty of the project's benefits; then he had to keep them motivated (and working long, hard hours) while he tackled administrative and engineering roadblocks that even he couldn't predict.

Ultimately, the SDSU Solar Car Project succeeded, and it drew involvement from various academic departments, dozens of student volunteers, several corporate benefactors, and many news organizations. Rogow challenged science, engineering, and computer students to design and test *Suntrakker* (as the car was named). But he also challenged SDSU's business students to come up with a proposal that would help him raise the support *Suntrakker* required.

"We needed to raise $145,000," Rogow recalls. "And since we had no faculty support in the beginning, we had to have something that would give us credibility. The proposal gave us much more than that."

Three students from an entrepreneurship class agreed to work with Rogow on a proposal that eventually filled over 70 pages. "The proposal mapped out every detail of our project, from start to finish, and made us look at things we had not considered. It also earned us respect from the faculty and was responsible for a $5,000 donation from our local power company." Rogow now believes that the proposal made the difference between "thriving and just surviving."

With the students' combined skills and Rogow's determined leadership, *Suntrakker* gave an impressive showing in Australia. The futuristic-looking solar car now tours schools as part of a university recruiting program. Moreover, both a book and a documentary film (*Warriors of the Sun*) have been produced about the project.

Figure 12–3 shows an excerpt from the executive summary that Rogow included in his unsolicited proposal. The proposal presents the benefits up front and the financial information at the close. Detailed and thorough, it includes sections describing the vehicle, the management team, and even "Critical Risks." Appendixes include an organization chart, résumé, design schematics, letters of support, lists of volunteers and contributors, and a telemarketing script.

Senior Vice President June Yee Felix solicited proposals from consultants and research firms when she needed to start a service for online bill payment at Chase Manhattan's Bank. The RFP stated her criteria and detailed requirements for selecting a service provider.

Text of the Proposal   The text of a proposal performs two essential functions: It persuades readers to award you a contract, and it spells out the terms of that contract. The trick is to sell your audience on your ideas without making promises that will haunt you later.

A proposal is both a selling tool and a contractual commitment.

If your proposal is unsolicited, you have some latitude in arranging the text. However, the organization of a solicited proposal is governed by the request for proposal. Most RFPs spell out precisely what you should cover, and in what order, so that all bids will be similar in form. This uniformity enables the client to evaluate the competing proposals in a systematic way. In many organizations a team of evaluators splits up the proposals and looks at various sections. An engineer might review the technical portions of all the proposals submitted, and an accountant might review the cost estimates.

Follow the instructions presented in the RFP.

Introduction   The introduction orients readers to the rest of your proposal. It identifies your organization and your purpose, and outlines the remainder of the text. If your proposal is solicited, the introduction should refer to the RFP; if not, it should mention any factors that led you to submit your proposal. You might mention mutual acquaintances, or you might refer to previous conversations you've had with readers. Subheadings in the introduction often include the following:

In the introduction, establish the need for action and summarize the key benefits of your proposal.

◆ **Background or statement of the problem.** Briefly reviews the reader's situation, and establishes a need for action. Readers may not perceive a problem or opportunity the same way you do. You must convince them that a problem or opportunity exists before you can convince them to accept your solution. In a way that is meaningful to your reader, discuss the current situation and explain how things could be better.

In some proposals, introductions include subheads.

◆ **Overview of approach.** Highlights your key selling points and their benefits, showing how your proposal will solve the reader's problem. The heading for this section might also be "Preliminary Analysis" or some other wording that will identify this section as a summary of your solution.

Answers questions about *who* (voluntary), *what* (business plan), *when* (special, nonrecurring), *where* (external), *why* (analytical), and *how* (receptive readers).

Subheads make it easy for readers to locate particular points.

Conveys a confident tone with thoughtful, well-developed paragraphs.

Uses the indirect approach to introduce objectives, justification, and benefits.

Motivates readers to invest or contribute.

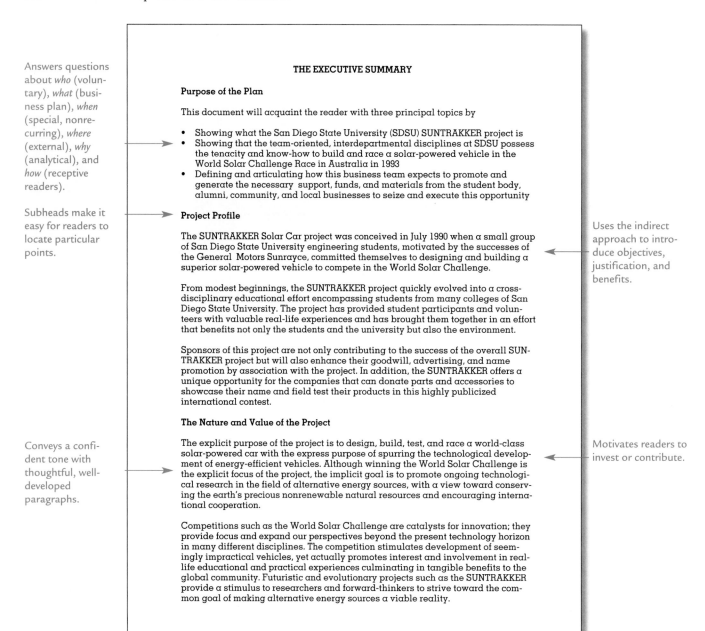

THE EXECUTIVE SUMMARY

Purpose of the Plan

This document will acquaint the reader with three principal topics by

- Showing what the San Diego State University (SDSU) SUNTRAKKER project is
- Showing that the team-oriented, interdepartmental disciplines at SDSU possess the tenacity and know-how to build and race a solar-powered vehicle in the World Solar Challenge Race in Australia in 1993
- Defining and articulating how this business team expects to promote and generate the necessary support, funds, and materials from the student body, alumni, community, and local businesses to seize and execute this opportunity

Project Profile

The SUNTRAKKER Solar Car project was conceived in July 1990 when a small group of San Diego State University engineering students, motivated by the successes of the General Motors Sunrayce, committed themselves to designing and building a superior solar-powered vehicle to compete in the World Solar Challenge.

From modest beginnings, the SUNTRAKKER project quickly evolved into a cross-disciplinary educational effort encompassing students from many colleges of San Diego State University. The project has provided student participants and volunteers with valuable real-life experiences and has brought them together in an effort that benefits not only the students and the university but also the environment.

Sponsors of this project are not only contributing to the success of the overall SUNTRAKKER project but will also enhance their goodwill, advertising, and name promotion by association with the project. In addition, the SUNTRAKKER offers a unique opportunity for the companies that can donate parts and accessories to showcase their name and field test their products in this highly publicized international contest.

The Nature and Value of the Project

The explicit purpose of the project is to design, build, test, and race a world-class solar-powered car with the express purpose of spurring the technological development of energy-efficient vehicles. Although winning the World Solar Challenge is the explicit focus of the project, the implicit goal is to promote ongoing technological research in the field of alternative energy sources, with a view toward conserving the earth's precious nonrenewable natural resources and encouraging international cooperation.

Competitions such as the World Solar Challenge are catalysts for innovation; they provide focus and expand our perspectives beyond the present technology horizon in many different disciplines. The competition stimulates development of seemingly impractical vehicles, yet actually promotes interest and involvement in real-life educational and practical experiences culminating in tangible benefits to the global community. Futuristic and evolutionary projects such as the SUNTRAKKER provide a stimulus to researchers and forward-thinkers to strive toward the common goal of making alternative energy sources a viable reality.

(continued)

Figure 12–3
In-Depth Critique: Bruce Rogow's Proposal (Executive Summary Excerpt)

Objective

4

Discuss the four areas of specific information that must be covered in the body of a proposal.

In the approach section, demonstrate the superiority of your ideas, products, or services.

- ◆ **Scope.** States the boundaries of the proposal—what you will and will not do. This brief section may also be labeled "Delimitations."

- ◆ **Report organization.** Orients the reader to the remainder of the proposal and calls attention to the major divisions of thought.

Body The core of the proposal is the body, which has the same purpose as the body of other reports. In a proposal, however, the body must cover some specific information:

- ◆ **Proposed approach.** May also be titled "Technical Proposal," "Research Design," "Issues for Analysis," or "Work Statement." This section describes what you have to offer: your concept, product, or service. To convince readers that your proposal has merit, focus on

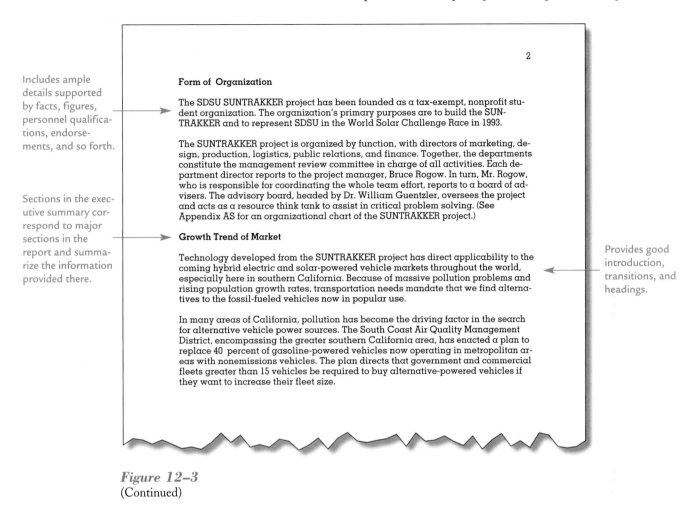

Includes ample details supported by facts, figures, personnel qualifications, endorsements, and so forth.

Sections in the executive summary correspond to major sections in the report and summarize the information provided there.

Provides good introduction, transitions, and headings.

Figure 12–3
(Continued)

the strengths of your offer in relation to reader needs. Point out any advantages that you have over your competitors.

◆ **Work plan.** Describes how you'll accomplish what must be done (unless you'll provide a standard, off-the-shelf item). Explain the steps you'll take, their timing, the methods or resources you'll use, and the person(s) responsible. Also indicate completion dates for critical portions of the work. If your proposal is accepted, the work plan is contractually binding, so don't promise to deliver more than you can realistically achieve within a given period.

Use the work plan to describe the tasks to be completed under the terms of the contract.

◆ **Statement of qualifications.** Describes your organization's experience, personnel, and facilities—all in relation to readers' needs. If you work for a large company that frequently submits proposals, you might borrow much of this section intact from previous proposals. However, be sure to tailor any boilerplate material to suit the situation. The qualifications section can be an important selling point, and it deserves to be handled carefully.

In the qualifications section, demonstrate that you have the personnel, facilities, and experience to do a competent job.

◆ **Costs.** Has few words and many numbers but can make or break your proposal. A high price can lose the bid; however, a low price could doom you to losing money on the project. Estimating costs is difficult, so prove that your costs are realistic—break them down in detail so that readers can see how you got your numbers: so much for labor, so much for materials, so much for overhead.

The more detailed your cost proposal is, the more credibility your estimates will have.

In a formal proposal it pays to be as thorough and accurate as possible. Carefully selected detail enhances your credibility, as does successful completion of any task you promise to perform.

Summary or Conclusion   You may want to include a summary or conclusion section because it's your last opportunity to persuade readers to accept your proposal. Summarize the merits of your approach, reemphasize why you and your firm are the ones to do the work, and stress the benefits. Make this section relatively brief, assertive, and confident.

PROOFREADING FORMAL REPORTS AND PROPOSALS

Don't forget to proofread everything one last time.

Finally, you have the final version of your report or proposal. You've revised the content for clarity and conciseness, and you've assembled all the various components. You've designed the document to please readers, and you've produced it in its final form. Now you need to review everything thoroughly one last time.

Checking Over Textual Materials

As you proofread your report, check for typos, spelling errors, and mistakes in punctuation. Make sure your text is laid out on the page in a clear, uncluttered fashion. Make sure that nothing has been left out or overlooked, and be certain that every word contributes to your report's purpose.

If you need specific tips on proofreading your report, look back at Chapter 6. Proofreading the textual part of your report is pretty much the same as proofreading any business message. However, reports often have elements that may not be included in other messages, so don't forget to proof your visual aids thoroughly.

Checking Over Visual Aids

O b j e c t i v e
5
Explain the four questions to ask when proofing visual aids.

Any visuals that you have included are present to help your readers absorb, understand, and accept your message. Their appearance is crucial to your message's success, so be sure to check visuals for mistakes such as typographical errors, inconsistent color treatment, and misaligned elements. Also take a few extra minutes to make sure that your visuals are necessary, absolutely accurate, properly documented, and honest.

Make sure the visual serves a specific purpose.

Is the Visual Necessary?   A few well-placed visual aids can clarify and dramatize your message, but an avalanche of illustrations may bury it. Avoid the temptation to overload your reports with unnecessary tables, graphs, and charts. Remember that your audience is busy. Don't give people information they don't need simply because you want to impress them or because you've fallen in love with your computer's graphics capabilities.

Proof visuals as carefully as you proof text.

Is the Visual Accurate?   Make sure that every number is correct. Verify that every line is plotted accurately and that every scale is drawn to reflect reality. Be sure that every bit of information included in a visual is consistent with what is said in the text. When you're proofreading, be sure to check each visual's source notes and content notes for accuracy.

Don't forget to document your visuals.

Is the Visual Properly Documented?   You may be the creator of the actual graphic design, but if you use someone else's data, you need to give credit by citing the source of any data you use in creating a visual. Identify the actual source of data (such as the name of the journal the information came from) or refer simply to the nature of the information (for example, "interviews with 50 soybean farmers"). If the data displayed in a visual are "primary" (you gathered the information for your own purposes), then say so. To avoid cluttering your graphic, you could use a shortened citation on the graphic itself and include a complete citation elsewhere in the report.

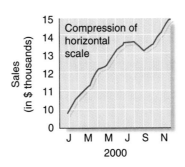

Figure 12–4
The Impact of Scale on
the Slope of a Curve

Is the Visual Honest?   In visuals, you can have all the numbers right and still give your audience a false impression; graphs and charts tend to oversimplify some numerical relationships. But deliberately leaving out important information is highly unethical. Don't leave out data points that don't fit your needs. And don't omit any outside influences on the data you're portraying.

The scale of a graph or chart can also introduce distortion. As Figure 12–4 illustrates, you can transform modest results into dramatic ones by compressing the horizontal scale or by expanding the vertical scale. But when you do so, you abandon good business ethics and mislead your audience in the process. So choose a scale that conveys a realistic picture of what's happening. Likewise, maintain the same scale in successive charts comparing the same factors.

Make your report ethical by keeping your visuals honest.

GETTING FEEDBACK FROM FORMAL REPORTS AND PROPOSALS

Once you've completed your formal report and sent it off to your audience, you'll naturally expect a positive response, and quite often you'll get one—but not always. You may get half-hearted praise or no action on your conclusions and recommendations. Even worse, you may get some serious criticism. Try to learn from these experiences. Sometimes you won't get any response at all. If you don't hear from your readers within a week or two, you might want to ask politely whether the report arrived. In hopes of stimulating a response, you might also offer to answer any questions or provide additional information. To review the ideas presented in this chapter, consult "Checklist: Producing Formal Reports and Proposals."

Ask for feedback, and learn from your mistakes.

Checklist: **Producing Formal Reports and Proposals**

Prepare Sturdy, Attractive Cover

✓ Label the cover clearly with the title of the document.
✓ Use a title that tells the audience exactly what the document is about.

Prepare Title Page

✓ List title; recipient's name, title, affiliation; author's name, title, affiliation; date of submission.
✓ Balance the information in blocks on the page.

Include Copy of Letter of Authorization or Request for Proposal, If Appropriate

Prepare Letter or Memo of Transmittal

✓ Include only in some copies if it contains sensitive information suitable for some but not all readers.
✓ Convey the document officially to the readers.
✓ Refer to authorization and discuss purpose, scope, background, source and methods, and limitations.
✓ Acknowledge everyone who was especially helpful in preparing the document.
✓ Close with thanks, offer to be of further assistance, and suggest future projects, if appropriate.

Prepare Table of Contents

✓ Include all first- and second-level headings (perhaps all third-level headings).
✓ Give the page number of each heading.
✓ Word all headings exactly as they appear in the text.
✓ Include the synopsis (if there is one) and supplementary parts.
✓ Number table of contents and all prefatory pages with lower-case roman numerals (bottom center).

Prepare List of Illustrations If You Have Four Visual Aids or More

✓ Put the list in the same format as the table of contents.
✓ Identify visuals either directly under table of contents or on a separate page under its own heading.

Develop Synopsis or Executive Summary (for Long, Formal Documents)

✓ Tailor the synopsis or executive summary to the document's length and tone.

✓ Condense the document's main points, using either the informative or the descriptive approach.
✓ Present the points in a synopsis in the same order as they appear in the document.
✓ An executive summary can deviate from the order of points appearing in the report.

Prepare Introduction to Text

✓ Leave a two-inch margin at the top of the page, and center the title of the document.
✓ In a long document, type the first-level heading "Introduction" three lines below title.
✓ In a short document, omit "Introduction" heading and begin typing three lines below title.
✓ Discuss the authorization (unless already covered in letter of transmittal), purpose, scope, background, sources and methods, definitions, limitations, and text organization.

Prepare Body of Document

✓ For left-bound documents, number all pages with arabic numerals in the upper right-hand corner (except for the first page, where the number is centered one inch from the bottom).
✓ For top-bound documents, number all pages with arabic numerals centered one inch from the bottom.

Prepare Conclusion of Document

✓ Wrap up the text of reports and proposals with a summary.
✓ If appropriate, include conclusions and recommendations.

Prepare Appendixes, If Necessary

✓ Give each appendix a title.
✓ For multiple appendixes, number or letter them consecutively in the order the text refers to them.

Prepare Reference List (Bibliography) Under Three Conditions

✓ If you used secondary sources that need to be identified.
✓ If it seems that readers would benefit.
✓ If the document would gain credibility.

SUMMARY OF LEARNING OBJECTIVES

1 **List the three tasks involved in completing business reports and proposals, and briefly explain what's involved in revising them.** To complete business reports and proposals, you need to revise, produce, and proofread the document, just as you would with any other business message. Revising reports and proposals involves evaluating content and organization, reviewing style and readability, and editing for conciseness and clarity.

2 **Explain the ten prefatory parts of a formal report.** Depending on readers' preferences and familiarity, formal reports may include as many as nine of the ten possible prefatory parts: (1) The cover includes at least the report's title and maybe the writer's name and submission date. (2) The title fly is a blank sheet of paper that adds a touch of formality. (3) The title page includes the report title; the name, title, and address of the person or group that authorized the report; the name, title, and address of the person or group that prepared the report; and the date of submission. (4) The letter (or memo) of authorization is the document requesting a report be written. (5) The letter (or memo) of acceptance acknowledges the assignment and is rarely included in reports. (6) The letter (or memo) of transmittal conveys the report to the audience and may appear in only selected copies of the report. (7) The table of contents lists report headings in outline form with page numbers. (8) The list of illustrations gives the titles and page numbers of visual aids. (9) A synopsis (or abstract) is a brief (one page or less) review of the report's most important points. (10) The executive summary is a fully developed "mini" version of the report that may contain headings and even visual aids. The executive summary would replace the synopsis, since both components would never be included in the same report.

3 **Describe four important functions of a formal report's introduction, and identify the possible topics it might include.** Four important functions of introductions are (1) putting the report in a broader context by tying it to a problem or an assignment, (2) telling readers the report's purpose, (3) previewing the report's contents and organization, and (4) establishing the tone of the report and the writer's relationship with the audience. To accomplish these functions, an introduction might address topics such as authorization, scope, background, sources and methods, definitions, limitations, and organization.

4 **Discuss the four areas of specific information that must be covered in the body of a proposal.** The body of a proposal must cover four specific areas of information. First, describe your proposed approach—your concept, product, or service. In this section, focus on how your approach satisfies reader needs and on any advantages you have over competitors. Second, describe your work plan—how you'll accomplish the task. Be clear about the steps you'll take, as well as when you'll take them and how. Clearly identify the person(s) responsible for the work and the completion dates for important portions of the work. Third, describe your qualifications to do the work. Include your organization's experience, personnel, and facilities, and make sure this material relates directly to the reader's particular situation. Fourth, describe the cost of the work. Break down all estimated costs so that readers can see how you arrived at your overall figure.

5 **Explain the four questions to ask when proofing visual aids.** As you check over visual aids, ask yourself four questions: (1) Is the visual necessary? Avoid overloading your report with unnecessary illustrations. Include as much information as readers need, but no more. (2) Is the visual accurate? Make sure that every number, word, and data point is consistent with the text of the report. Check carefully for typos, color inconsistencies, and misaligned elements. (3) Is the visual properly documented? Whether you include the full citation on the graphic or elsewhere in the report, you need to give credit for the information you include in your visual. (4) Is the visual honest? Make sure that your visual not only contains all the correct information but also projects the right impression. To ensure that your visual makes the right impression, be sure you haven't oversimplified data, omitted information, or chosen an unrealistic scale.

SOLVING A COMMUNICATION DILEMMA AT LEVI STRAUSS

Levi Strauss Chairman Robert Haas uses reports to communicate to employees, customers, and the community. He also uses them to make decisions. He believes strongly in good communication, even to the point of editing his staff's memos for grammar.

Haas relied on a report for the California Public Employees' Retirement System (CalPERS) to support his claim that employee empowerment leads to greater business success. That is, he concluded from this report that stock prices actually rise when people on the front lines are given greater authority to act and to make decisions that are in the best interest of both the customer and the company.

A key report at Levi Strauss is based on Haas's vision of an ethically driven business. Called the Aspiration Statement, this report helps guide the decisions and actions of all 37,500 Levi

Strauss employees. It clearly outlines the type of values and behaviors that the company expects from its employees. It covers issues ranging from trust to empowerment and even to good business communication skills—all of which help the company become the organization that it aspires to be. By laying out these complex issues clearly and presenting them in a way that all employees can understand, Haas's report helps ensure that everyone is "reading off the same page." It helps him lead the company forward.

Although most business reports are not accessible to the general public, anyone visiting the Levi Strauss corporate Web site (www. levistrauss.com) can see how much the company values the written word. The site makes a number of reports available to the public, from the Aspirations Statement to a complete history of the company. All of these reports are clear and concise, and all have the components necessary for making the material easily understandable.

Your Mission As manager of internal communication, you are responsible for maintaining the communication channels up, down, and across the organization. One of your most important tasks is updating 37,500 employees on the company's progress toward reaching the goals of the Aspirations Statement. Each year, you prepare a long report that is distributed both online and in printed form. Study the following questions, select the best answer in each case, and be prepared to support your choices.

1. From the boardroom to the warehouse, just about every employee in today's business world is overwhelmed with data and information. Because people have too much information to digest and too little time to read, the executive summary has become a particularly important part of corporate reports. Which of the following approaches would you take with the executive summary in this year's long report?

   a. Use the executive summary to provide a quick score card for the company's performance in each of the areas addressed by the Aspirations Statement. Readers may be tempted to skip the detail contained in the body of the report, but at least they'll get the highlights in the executive summary.

   b. Use the executive summary to highlight changes in the report from previous years. You believe that the report is widely read within the company every year, so people will need guidance to understand how this year's content and organization differ from that of past reports.

   c. Do not use an executive summary at all. This report is made available to everyone in the company, not just a handful of executives, so an executive summary is not appropriate.

2. One of your responsibilities in preparing this report is to recommend specific steps for improving on any area of concern that you uncover in your investigation. One of this year's areas of concern involves a Levi Strauss customer service center. Several customer service reps complained to your staff that the center's manager places so much emphasis on community service that the quality of the work is slipping. For example, employees who want to help out at AIDS awareness rallies or environmental clean-up projects are allowed to do so on company time, as often as they want. This frequently leaves the center short-handed, so employees who choose not to participate in these outside events are overloaded, and they are growing to resent both the volunteering program in general and particular employees who seem to be taking advantage of it. Remember that this report is distributed worldwide, so even though it's intended only for internal use, you must assume that people outside the company (including competitors and the news media) may gain access to it. How should you word your recommendation on this issue?

   a. Another concern we uncovered at a customer service center was a conflict between the company's desire to support the local community and the need to maintain a productive work environment. The specific problem involved too many employees taking too much volunteer time off work, leaving their co-workers overloaded. We've already discussed our concerns with the center manager involved, who is working with the next level of management to resolve the situation in a way that better balances these sometimes-conflicting needs. However, it seems possible that similar situations might develop at other locations. We recommend that all regional managers discuss the issue with their employees to see whether specific situations need to be resolved or whether the company's overall stance on volunteerism needs to be reviewed.

   b. Our investigation raised some concerns about the management style of Sarah Blackstone, manager of the Denver customer service center. Her commendable interest in supporting the local community through employee volunteerism is unfortunately in conflict with her responsibilities as a business manager. Too many employees are taking too much time off work to participate in community activities, leaving other employees behind to take up the slack. The result is both a decline in customer service and a growing resentment among the employees who stay in the office and have to work harder and longer to cover for their absent co-workers.

   c. Our investigation raised some concerns about the management style of Sarah Blackstone, manager of the Denver customer service center. Her commendable interest in supporting the local community through employee volunteerism is unfortunately in conflict with her responsibilities as a business manager. Too many employees are taking too much time off work to participate in community activities, leaving other employees behind to take up the slack. The result is both a decline in customer service and a growing resentment among the employees who stay in the office and have to work harder and longer to cover for their absent co-workers. We strongly recommend that Ms. Blackstone retake the standard LS&Co management-training program to help realign her priorities with the company's business priorities.

3. Much of the information you've collected from your interviews around the world is difficult or impossible to represent numerically. However, you believe that readers would appreciate a brief summary of the interview results. For one issue, you posed the following open-ended question to 153 employees and managers: "How would you describe our progress toward empowering front-line employees with the authority to make decisions and take actions that satisfy our customers quickly and completely?" The responses range from simple, one-sentence answers to long, involved essays complete with examples. All together, the responses fill 13 pages. What's the best way of summarizing your findings?

   a. Pick a half dozen responses that in your opinion represent the range of responses. For example, you might include one that says "we've made no progress at all," one that says "I believe we've been very successful at our empowerment efforts," and four more that fall between these two extremes.

b. Create a five-step measurement scale that ranges from "little or no progress" to "completely successful." Together with a few experienced members of your staff, review each response and decide in which of the five categories it belongs. Then create a chart that shows how the 153 responses are distributed among the five categories. Explain how you developed the chart, and offer to provide a complete listing of the responses to any reader who requests one.

c. Since the information is not quantitative, it's impossible to summarize and boil down to a few facts and figures. It would, therefore, be inappropriate to summarize the information at all. Simply include all 13 pages of responses as an appendix in your report.

4. One of the questions you asked 153 employees was to rate their feelings about the company's response to employee complaints. You provided a scale that included five choices: 1 (very satisfied), 2 (satisfied), 3 (no opinion), 4 (unsatisfied), and 5 (very unsatisfied). A staff member illustrated this data in a line chart, but during the revision process, you've realized that a line chart is not a good choice. (It attempts to show trends in the relationship between two variables, but you have five data points, and you need to show how many employees chose each one.) What would be the best visual to replace the original?

a. A bar chart with five bars that indicate the number of responses in each category.
b. A surface chart with one line for each choice, which shows the sum of all five lines.
c. A pie chart with five slices that indicate the number of responses in each category.[3]

TEST YOUR KNOWLEDGE

1. What are the tasks involved in revising a report or proposal?

2. What are the ten prefatory parts of a formal report?

3. How do writers use an introduction in a formal report?

4. What four questions do writers need to ask when checking visual aids for a report?

5. What information is included on the title page of a report?

6. What is a letter of transmittal, and where is it positioned within a report?

7. How does a synopsis differ from an executive summary?

8. How does the summary section of a report differ from the conclusions section?

9. What are three supplementary parts often included in formal reports?

10. Why is the work plan a key component of a proposal?

INTERACTIVE LEARNING

USE THIS TEXT'S ONLINE RESOURCES

Visit the myPHLIP Web site at www.prenhall.com/thill. For Chapter 12, take advantage of the interactive "Study Guide" to test your chapter knowledge. Get instant feedback on whether you need additional studying. Read the "Current Events" articles to get the latest on chapter topics, and complete the exercises—as specified by your instructor.

This site's "Study Hall" helps you succeed in this course. "Talk in the Hall" lets you leave messages and meet new friends online. If

you have a question, you can "Ask the Tutor." And to get a better grade in this course, you can find more help at "Writing Skills," "Study Skills," and "Study Tips."

The "Research Area" helps you locate a wealth of information to use in course assignments. Plus, you can send a message to online research experts, who will help you find exactly the information you need.

APPLY YOUR KNOWLEDGE

1. Under what circumstances would you include more than one index in a lengthy report?

2. If you were submitting a solicited proposal to build an indoor pool, would you include as references the names and addresses of other clients for whom you recently built similar pools? Would you include these references in an unsolicited pro-

posal? Where in either proposal would you include these references? Why?

3. If you were writing an analytical report about your company's advertising policies, where would you include your recommendations—in the beginning of the report or at the end? Why?

4. If you included a bibliography in your report, would you also need to include in-text citations? Please explain.

5. **Ethical Choices** How would you report on a confidential survey in which employees rated their managers' capabilities?

Both employees and managers expect to see the results. Would you give the same report to employees and managers? What components would you include or exclude for each audience? Explain your choices.

PRACTICE YOUR KNOWLEDGE

DOCUMENT FOR ANALYSIS

Visit the U.S. Department of Justice reports page at www.ins.usdoj. gov/graphics/aboutins/repsstudies/addition.html. Read the brief description of the department's Triennial Comprehensive Report on Immigration and follow the link to the executive summary. Using the information in this chapter, analyze the executive summary and offer specific suggestions for revising it.

EXERCISES

12–1. **Teamwork** You and a classmate are helping Linda Moreno prepare her report on Electrovision's travel and entertainment costs (see "Sharpening Your Career Skills," beginning on page 361). This time, however, the report is to be informational rather than analytical, so it will not include recommendations. Review the existing report and determine what changes would be needed to make it an informational report. Be as specific as possible. For example, if your team decides the report needs a new title, what title would you use? Now draft a transmittal memo for Moreno to use in conveying this informational report to Dennis McWilliams, Electrovision's vice president of operations.

12–2. **Producing Reports: Letter of Transmittal** You are president of the Friends of the Library, a nonprofit group that raises funds and provides volunteers to support your local library. Every February, you send a report of the previous year's activities and accomplishments to the County Arts Council, which provides an annual grant of $1,000 toward your group's summer reading festival. Now it's February 6, and you've completed your formal report. Here are the highlights:

- Back-to-school book sale raised $2,000.
- Holiday craft fair raised $1,100.
- Promotion and prizes for summer reading festival cost $1,450.
- Materials for children's program featuring local author cost $125.
- New reference databases for library's career center cost $850.
- Bookmarks promoting library's Web site cost $200.

Write a letter of transmittal to Erica Maki, the council's director. Because she is expecting this report, you can use the direct approach. Be sure to express gratitude for the council's ongoing financial support.

12–3. **Internet** Government reports vary in purpose and structure. Read through the Department of Education's report on how population growth is affecting school enrollment, posted online at www.ed.gov/pubs/bbecho00/index.html.

What is the purpose of this document? Does the title communicate this purpose? What type of report is this, and what is the report's structure? Which prefatory and supplementary parts are included? Now analyze the visuals. What types are included in this report? Are they all necessary? Are the titles and legends sufficiently informative? How does this report take advantage of the online medium to enhance readability?

12–4. **Ethical Choices** Your boss has asked you to proofread his yearly report on consumer accidents due to household chemicals. Chart A (Figure 12–5) catches your eye. Does the scale on this line graph leave the right impression about insecticide accident levels? What revisions, if any, would you suggest to ensure that this chart offers a realistic picture of the situation?

Figure 12–5

Chart A

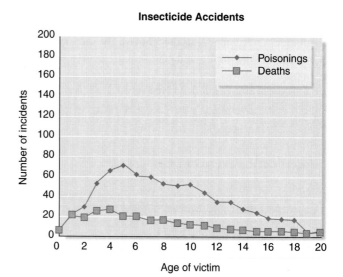

CASES

SHORT, FORMAL REPORT REQUIRING NO ADDITIONAL RESEARCH

1. Sailing past the sunsets: Report using statistical data to suggest a new advertising strategy As manager of Distant Dreams, a travel agency in Waco, Texas, you are interested in the information in Table 12–1. It seems that dollar income is shifting toward the 35–44 age group. Tables 12–2 and 12–3 are also broken down by age group.

Traditionally, your agency has concentrated its advertising on people nearing retirement, people who are closing out successful careers and now have the time and money to vacation abroad. After examining the three sets of data, however, you begin to think that a major shift in emphasis would be desirable.

Your task: Write a report to Mary Henderson, who writes your advertisements, explaining why future ads should still be directed to travelers who want to explore the far reaches of the world—but to people

besides those in their fifties and sixties. Justify your explanation by referring to the data you have examined.

SHORT, FORMAL REPORTS REQUIRING ADDITIONAL RESEARCH

2. Picking the better path: Research report assisting a client in a career choice You are employed by Open Options, a career-counseling firm, where your main function is to help clients make career choices. Today a client with the same name as yours (a truly curious coincidence!) came to your office and asked for help deciding between two careers, careers that you yourself had been interested in (an even greater coincidence!).

Your task: Do some research on the two careers and then prepare a short report that your client can study. Your report should compare at least five major areas, such as salary, working conditions, and education required. Interview the client to understand her or his personal preferences regarding each of the five areas. For example, what is the minimum salary the client will accept? By comparing the client's preferences with the research material you collect, such as salary data, you will have a basis for concluding which of the two careers is best. The report should end with a career recommendation.

3. Selling overseas: Research report on the prospects for marketing a product in another country Select (a) a product and (b) a country. The product might be a novelty item that you own (an inexpensive but accurate watch or clock, a desk organizer, or a coin bank). The country should be one that you are not now familiar with. Imagine that you are with the international sales department of the company that manufactures and sells the novelty item and that you are proposing to make it available in the country you have selected.

Table 12–1 Percentage of Total U.S. Household Income Earned by Various Age Groups

Age Group	1990	1995	2000
25–34	23%	24%	26%
35–44	22	25	28
45–54	22	21	19
55–64	19	17	15
65 and over	14	13	12

Table 12–2 Preferences in Travel Among Various Age Groups

Travel Interests	Age Group		
	18–34	35–54	55+
I prefer excitement and stimulation to rest and relaxation.	67%	42%	38%
I prefer to go where I haven't been before.	62	58	48
I prefer an adventure when traveling.	62	45	32
I prefer foreign and exotic things.	41	25	21
I prefer self-indulgence, regardless of cost.	31	16	14
I don't see the need for a travel agent.	67	63	52

Table 12–3 Basic Desire for Travel Among Various Age Groups

Attitude Toward Travel	Age Group		
	18–34	35–54	55+
Travel is one of the most rewarding and enjoyable things one can do.	71%	69%	66%
I love the idea of traveling and do so at every opportunity.	66	59	48
I often feel the need to get away from everything.	56	55	33

The first step is to learn as much as possible about the country in which you plan to market the product. Check almanacs and encyclopedias for the most recent information, paying particular attention to descriptions of the social life of the inhabitants and their economic conditions. If your library carries the *Yearbook of International Trade Statistics, Monthly Bulletin of Statistics,* or *Trade Statistics* (all put out by the United Nations), you may want to consult them. Check the card catalog and recent periodical indexes for sources of additional information; look for (among other matters) cultural traditions that would encourage or discourage use of the product. If you have online access, check both Web sites and any relevant databases you can find.

Your task: Write a short report that describes the product you plan to market abroad, briefly describes the country you have selected, indicates the types of people in this country who would find the product attractive, explains how the product would be transported into the country (or possibly manufactured there if materials and labor are available), recommends a location for a regional sales center, and suggests how the product should be sold. Your report is to be submitted to the chief operating officer of the company, whose name you can either make up or find in a corporate directory. The report should include your conclusions (how the product will do in this new environment) and your recommendations for marketing (steps the company should take immediately and those it should develop later).

4. The new way to advertise: Report summarizing Internet demographics   The number of Internet users continues to grow rapidly in the United States and around the world. For marketers, the Internet represents a veritable gold mine of potential customers. Unlike traditional print and broadcast media, an Internet site can be seen around the world at any time. The trick is to get your target customers to take the time to visit your page.

As marketing strategist for a specialty foods mail-order company, you have been toying with the idea of going online for quite some time. Your company, Martha's Kitchen, has been selling its cakes, cheeses, fruit, and candy in printed catalogs for a little over a decade and has built up a loyal clientele. Most of your customers are affluent adults age 30 and over, and 75 percent of them are women. Large portions of your sales come during the holidays.

As more and more customers ask about ordering on the Internet, you feel compelled to establish an Internet presence. Nevertheless, you have heard conflicting reports about whether companies actually make any money by selling over the Internet. Moreover, developing a top-notch Web site will likely cost a lot of money. How can you sort through the hype to find real answers?

Your task: Write a short formal report to the director of marketing explaining whether Martha's Kitchen should develop an Internet presence. You will need some solid figures about the demographics of Internet users, their surfing habits, the types of products they purchase online, and growth trends in online commerce. The following are good resources to help you get started.

- www.emarketer.com/estats/welcome.html
- www.cyberatlas.internet.com
- www.ad-guide.com

These sites also contain links to other sites with additional useful information. As background, you may also find it helpful to look at some competitors' sites, such as Harry and David (www.harryanddavid.com) and Norm Thompson (www.normthompson.com).

On the basis of your findings, how do you think an Internet site will improve the company's bottom line? Use your imagination to fill in the details about the company.

LONG, FORMAL REPORTS REQUIRING NO ADDITIONAL RESEARCH

5. Software in a hard market: Report on selling software in China   Breaking into the U.S. software market can be tough, especially when your product competes with well-known brands in established categories. As marketing director for a small (22 employees) developer of financial management software, you are keenly aware of how difficult it is to take on domestic market leaders such as Quicken and Microsoft Money. Fortunately, you also know that greater opportunities may exist for you in international markets.

Your company is considering marketing its product in China, where consumers are less brand loyal and more likely to try new products. The Chinese economy has boomed over the past decade, growing at a rate of 9 percent per year. Research also indicates that a growing percentage of China's 1.2 billion consumers make more money today than ever before. In addition, software sales in China totaled $1.35 billion in 1997, representing a 23 percent jump over the previous year, and analysts expect the growth to continue. Because your product can be used for both business and home financial management, China looks like a ripe market.

The Chinese market also has its problems. Economic growth slowed this past year to about 7 percent, and studies show that consumers are feeling a sense of uncertainty as a result of volatility in Asian markets. Consumer saving this year is up 17 percent over last year, while retail sales growth has slowed from almost 40 percent to just under 10 percent.

On the other hand, the new financial concerns of Chinese consumers might actually present an opportunity for your company. After all, you are marketing software to help consumers and businesses manage their money more wisely. Greater concerns may be adapting your product to the Chinese language and competing with local companies. For example, one Chinese firm, User Friend, markets an accounting software package that commands 40 percent of the market. Another concern is avoiding software piracy. China has a reputation for being lax about enforcing patent and copyright laws. According to a 1997 study by the Business Software Alliance and the Software Publisher's Association, 96 percent of all software units in use in China are pirated.

Your task: Write an analytical report on the current market conditions in China. Make a recommendation as to whether your company should attempt to sell its financial management software in China. You have already gathered a lot of data from different sources (see Tables 12–4 to 12–7 and Figures 12–6 to 12–8). Now you must interpret the data and make clear recommendations. Identify your target customer and make projections about how much software you think the company can sell over the next three years. Assuming that the product sells for the equivalent of $45, how much revenue do you expect the Chinese market to generate for your company?[4]

Table 12–4   Profile of China's Consumers

Market Segment	Nouveau Riche (Baofahu)	Yuppies (Dushi Yapishi)	Salary Men (Bongxin Jieceng)	Working Poor (Qionglaogong)
Size	200,000	60 million	330 million	800 million
Geographic location	Coastal urban areas	Major urban areas	Urban areas	Rural areas, small towns, urban areas
Average annual household income ($U.S.)	Over $5,000	$1,800–$5,000	$1,150–$1,799	Less than $1,150
Age	30–65	25–45	18–60	15–65
Highest level of education	Various levels	College	High school	Elementary school
Type of employment	Commercial/ entrepreneurial, entertainment, government	Managerial, professional, technical	Low-skilled office work, factory work, teaching	Manual labor, farming, migrant work
Lifestyle characteristics	Wheeling and dealing, wining and dining	Frequent travel and dining out	8-to-5 daily workweek, limited budget, few purchases	Struggling to make ends meet
Consumer readiness	High	Moderate	Low	Minimal
Innovativeness	Trend setters	Opinion leaders	Emulators	Laggards
Risk aversion	Low	Moderate	High	Very high

Table 12–5   Selected Responses to a Survey of 800 Urban Consumers in China

Purchase Practices of Respondents	Percent
Plan to buy or replace a personal computer in the next 3 years	26
Always look for new products when they shop	75
Try to cut down on expenses wherever they can	68
Saving more than they did a year ago	58
Try to buy Chinese brands whenever they can	71

Table 12–6   Key China Economic Sectors as a Percentage of GDP

Sector	1976	1986	1996	1997
Agriculture	33.2%	27.1%	20.2%	19.7%
Industry (all)	42.3	44.0	49.0	50.8
Manufacturing	30.1	35.5	38.1	39.5
Services	24.5	28.9	30.8	29.5

Table 12–7	Additional Economic Indicators for China			
Economic Indicators	*1976*	*1986*	*1996*	*1997*
($ U.S. billions)				
Gross domestic product (GDP)	148.8	295.7	825.0	935.0
Gross domestic investment/GDP	28.4	37.7	39.2	38.2
Gross domestic savings/GDP	29.0	35.2	41.3	42.2
($ U.S. millions)				
Exports of goods and services	7,383	29,583	171,700	207,800
Imports of goods and services	7,125	37,472	154,100	167,200

Figure 12–6
Percentage of Population That
Uses Selected Durable Products,
Beijing, Shanghai, Chengdu,
and Guangzhou (major urban
centers), 1998

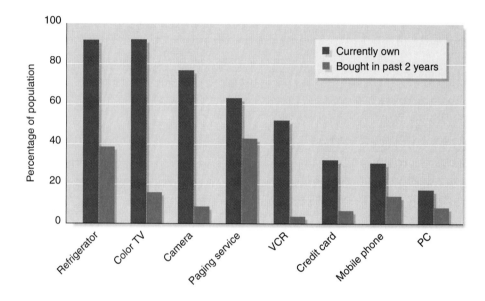

Figure 12–7
China's Retail-Sales
Growth Rate

Figure 12–8
Software Market in China, 1997 (total software sales $1.35 billion)

LONG, FORMAL REPORTS REQUIRING ADDITIONAL RESEARCH

6. Is there any justice? Report critiquing legislation Plenty of people complain about their state legislators, but few are specific about their complaints. Here's your chance.

Your task: Write a long formal report about a law that you believe should not have been enacted or should be enacted. Be objective. Write the report using specific facts to support your beliefs. Reach conclusions and offer your recommendation at the end of the report. As a final step, send a copy of the report to an appropriate state official or legislator.

7. Travel opportunities: Report comparing two destinations You are planning to take a two-week trip abroad sometime within the next year. Because there are a couple of destinations that appeal to you, you are going to have to do some research before you can make a decision.

Your task: Prepare a lengthy comparative study of two countries that you would like to visit. Begin by making a list of important questions you will need to answer. Do you want a relaxing vacation or an educational experience? What types of services will you require? What will your transportation needs be? Where will you have the least difficulty with the language? Using resources in your library, the Internet, and perhaps travel agencies, analyze the suitability of these two destinations with respect to your own travel criteria. At the end of the report, recommend the better country to visit this year.

8. Doing business abroad: Report summarizing the social and business customs of a foreign country Your company would like to sell their products overseas. Before they begin negotiating on the international horizon, however, management must have a clear understanding of the social and business customs of the foreign countries where they intend to do business.

Your task: Choose a non-English-speaking country, and write a long formal report summarizing the country's social and business customs. Review Chapter 3 and use that chapter's "Checklist: Doing Business Abroad" as a guide for the types of information you should include in your report.

FORMAL PROPOSALS

9. Brewing up sales: Proposal to supply coffee to Peter's Doughnuts You are the president of Lighthouse Roasters, a small but growing coffee-roasting company. The company has made a name for itself by offering fresh, dark-roasted gourmet coffees. Unlike Starbuck's and other competitors, Lighthouse Roasters does not operate its own stores. Instead, it sells roasted gourmet coffee beans to retailers such as restaurants, bakeries, and latte carts. These retailers then use the Lighthouse beans to make their coffee beverages.

Lighthouse's total cost to produce a pound of roasted gourmet coffee is $2.75. The company wholesales its roasted gourmet beans for an average price of $4.50 per pound. Competitors who sell nongourmet variety coffees typically charge about $3.00 per pound. However, the average price of a gourmet coffee beverage is $1.50, about $.50 more than beverages made with regular coffee (including both brewed coffee and espresso drinks). Each pound of coffee yields about 40 beverages.

Peter's Doughnuts, which owns 76 doughnut shops across 13 states, has seen its sales decline in recent months after Starbucks began opening stores in Peter's markets. Starbucks not only sells gourmet coffee but also carries a selection of delicious pastries that offer alternatives to doughnuts. Peter's management figures that by offering gourmet coffee, it will win back customers who like doughnuts but who also want darker-roasted coffees. Peter's has invited you to submit a proposal to be its exclusive supplier of coffee. Peter's anticipates that it will need 400 pounds of coffee a month during the colder months (October–March) and 300 pounds during the warmer months (April–September). The company has said it wants to pay no more than $3.75 per pound for Lighthouse coffee.

Your task: Using your imagination to supply the details, write a proposal describing your plan to supply the coffee. Considering your costs, will you meet Peter's pricing demands, or will you attempt to gain a higher price?

10. Competitive crisis: Proposal to win back customers
Willco is a multistate chain of large hardware stores whose once-loyal customers are migrating to newly opened Home Depot outlets. Your customer surveys show that customers are more impressed with Home Depot's service than with its prices and selection. Willco's board of directors already agrees that something must be done immediately to win back old customers and stop others from defecting. You believe that customer service is the answer.

Your task: As Willco's regional manager of operations, write a proposal to implement your strategy for ensuring that Willco offers the best customer service possible. Use your imagination to supply the facts that will back up your proposal. Focus on immediate measures to improve customer service as well as on a long-term plan. Consider all aspects of your solution, including changes in the company's culture, changes to daily operations, employee hiring and training, store design, and so on. Some library research will help you find examples of companies that have overcome challenges from tough competitors.

GOING ONLINE EXERCISES

Research Reports and Learning by Example, page 385

One way to learn how to write more skillfully and effectively is by reading other writers' work. Look at different examples of professional business reports, and skim their contents to reinforce what you've learned in this chapter about structure, style, and organization. Let ixquick.com work for you.

1. What is the purpose of the report you read? Who is its target audience? Explain why the structure and style of the report make it easy or difficult to follow the main idea.
2. What type of report did you read? Briefly describe the main message. Is the information well organized? If you answer "yes," explain how you can use the report as a guide for a report you might write. If you answer "no," explain why the report is not helpful.
3. Drawing on what you know about the qualities of a good business report, review a report and describe what features contribute to its readability.

To complete this exercise, log on to this text's Web site at www.prenhall.com/thill. Select Chapter 12, then select "Student Resources," click on the name of the featured Web site, and follow the detailed navigational directions.

GIVING SPEECHES AND ORAL PRESENTATIONS

chapter 13

On the job:

FACING A COMMUNICATION DILEMMA AT THE KEYS GROUP

The Key to Giving Speeches

"Acceptance in the community is the key," says Brady Keys. His company—the Keys Group—operates 11 KFC fast-food restaurants in Georgia. With annual sales of more than $7 million, the Keys Group ranks among the most well-respected African American business owners in the country.

When Keys started out in the restaurant business nearly 30 years ago, he realized that good food was only half the battle. Consumers have hundreds of fast-food outlets to choose from, all with similar menus. If you want the public to come to your restaurant rather than going to the one across the street, you have to do something extra.

For Brady Keys, the extra ingredient has been personal charisma. A former all-pro defensive halfback for the Pittsburgh Steelers, Keys has used his forceful personality along with expert speaking skills to inspire both investors and employees and to build a presence in the communities in which he does business. Today, he's a well-known and highly respected member of the business community, but winning acceptance hasn't been a fast or an easy process.

Keys realized that if he wanted to succeed in business, he'd have to gain people's respect. He'd have to persuade bankers to loan him money and big companies to do business with him. He'd have to convince employees to work hard and customers to trust him. But how? If you were Keys, whether you were addressing a large crowd or an audience of one, what would you need to know about preparing, developing, and delivering speeches? Can improving your speaking skills really lead to the success that Keys has realized?[1]

THE THREE-STEP ORAL PRESENTATION PROCESS

As Brady Keys will tell you, giving speeches and oral presentations can be an integral part of your business career. Chances are you'll have an opportunity to deliver a number of speeches and presentations throughout your career. You may not speak before large audiences of employees or the media, but you'll certainly be expected to present ideas to your colleagues, make sales presentations to potential customers, or engage in other kinds of spoken communication. The most common type of business presentation, by far, is one that occurs in a conference room in front of only a few people.[2]

When you address a U.S. or Canadian audience with few cultural differences—whether you're delivering a speech to associates, giving a formal presentation to clients, or simply explaining how to solve a business problem to your boss—follow three steps (see Figure 13–1):

1. Plan your speech or presentation.

2. Write your speech or presentation.

3. Complete your speech or presentation.

As president of the Keys Group, Brady Keys Jr. is responsible for addressing many different kinds of audiences. Whether he is explaining market trends to colleagues, motivating employees, or persuading investors, his speeches and presentations are successful because he focuses on his audiences and on making his ideas as clear and as interesting as possible.

Figure 13–1
The Three-Step Oral Presentation Process

Illustrate how planning
speeches differs from
planning written
documents.

STEP 1: PLANNING SPEECHES AND PRESENTATIONS

Planning speeches and oral presentations is much like planning any other business message. Because speeches and presentations are delivered orally under relatively public circumstances, they require a few special communication techniques. For one thing, a speech is a one-time event; your audience cannot leaf back through printed pages to review something you said earlier. You must make sure that audience members will hear what you say and remember it. To do so, you must capture their interest immediately. Otherwise, you'll lose them, and chances are, you won't get them back. So when you prepare your speech or presentation, be sure to define your purpose clearly and analyze your audience as thoroughly as possible.

Defining Your Purpose

Preparing speeches and
presentations requires some special
communication techniques to ensure
your audience hears what you say.

During your career you may be called on to give speeches and presentations for all sorts of reasons. If you're in the human resources department, you may give orientation briefings to new employees or explain company policies, procedures, and benefits at assemblies. If you're a department supervisor, you may conduct training programs. If you're a problem solver or consultant, you may give analytical presentations on the merits of various proposals.

The content and style of speeches
and presentations vary, depending
on your purpose.

These speeches and presentations can be categorized according to their purpose, which helps you determine your content and style. The four basic reasons for giving a speech or presentation are to inform, to persuade, to motivate, and to entertain. Here are sample statements of purpose for business speeches:

You usually give a speech for one of
four purposes.

◆ To inform the accounting department of the new remote data-access policy

◆ To explain to the executive committee the financial ramifications of OmniGroup's takeover offer

◆ To persuade potential customers that our bank offers the best commercial banking services for their needs

◆ To motivate the sales force to increase product sales by 10 percent

Many of your business speeches and presentations will be informative; if you're involved in a marketing or sales position, you'll need to give persuasive presentations as well. Motivational speeches tend to be more specialized. Many companies bring in outside speakers who specialize in motivational speaking. Entertainment speeches are per-

Achieving Intercultural Communication

Five Tips for Making Presentations Around the World

In any successful presentation, getting your message across to an audience requires clear communication. But how can you communicate successfully with members of an international audience—especially if their fluency in your language ranges from expert to novice?

1. **Speak slowly and distinctly.** The most common complaint of international audiences is that English speakers talk too fast. If you speak too rapidly, your less-fluent listeners will be lost. Articulate every word carefully. Emphasize consonants for clarity, and pause frequently so that the audience will have time to absorb each key point.
2. **Repeat key words and phrases.** When audiences are less familiar with your language, they need to hear important information more than once. In addition, they may not be familiar with synonyms, so refer to key points in the same way throughout your presentation. If you introduce the concept of *benefits*, for example, continue to use the same word. Don't refer to *advantages* later on.
3. **Aim for clarity.** Keep your message simple. Eliminate complex sentence structure, abbreviations, and acronyms. Avoid two-word verbs such as *look over* and *check out*. Such verbs are confusing because the definition of each separate word differs from the meaning of the two words combined. For clearer communication, use one specific term (substitute *review* for *look over; examine* for *check out; write* for *jot down; return* for *drop by*). Stay away from cultural idioms, such as "once in a blue moon," which may be unfamiliar to an international audience.

4. **Communicate with body language.** Establish a relationship with your audience through strong eye contact. And don't forget to smile! Smiles and other facial expressions are universally recognized. Moreover, multilingual audiences pay close attention to a speaker's body language to get clues about the meanings of unfamiliar words. For example, prepositions can often be confusing to multilingual listeners, so use gestures to illustrate the meaning of words such as *up, down,* or *under*.
5. **Support your oral message with visual aids.** For most audiences, visual messages support and clarify spoken words. Develop handouts, flip charts, or slides for your presentation, using simple words to describe your key points. To eliminate problems with rapid speech, unclear pronunciations, or strange accents, prepare captions both in English and in your audience's native language. Avoid confusion about quantities by presenting numbers in graphs or pie charts and by converting financial figures into local currency.

CAREER APPLICATIONS

1. As marketing director for an international corporation, you will be making a presentation to the company's marketing representatives in Germany. How will you communicate company goals and sales projections clearly?
2. Make a list of 10 two-word verbs. How does the meaning of each separate word differ from the definition of the combined words? Replace each two-word verb with a single, specific word that will be clearer to an international audience.

---

haps the rarest in the business world; they are usually limited to after-dinner speeches and to speeches at conventions or retreats. But no matter which kind of speech you plan to make, you need to understand your audience to be successful.

Developing an Audience Profile

Once you have your purpose firmly in mind, you can think about your audience. As Brady Keys points out, analyzing your audience is a particularly important element of your preparation because you'll be gearing the style and content of your speech to your audience's needs and interests (see "Achieving Intercultural Communication— Five Tips for Making Presentations Around the World"). Be sure to review the discussion of audience analysis presented in Chapter 4. For even more insight into audience evaluation (including emotional and cultural issues) consult a good public-speaking textbook.

In many cases, you'll be speaking to a group of people you know very little about. You'll have a much better chance of achieving your purpose if you investigate the audience's characteristics before showing up to speak. If you're involved in selecting the audience, you'll certainly have information about their characteristics. You can also ask your host or some other contact person for help with audience analysis, and you can supplement that information with some educated estimates of your own.

Gear the content, organization, and style of your message to your audience's size, background, attitudes, and interests.

O b j e c t i v e

Describe the five tasks that go into organizing speeches and presentations.

2

STEP 2: WRITING SPEECHES AND PRESENTATIONS

You may not ever actually write out a speech or presentation word for word. But that doesn't mean that preparing your speech will be any easier or quicker than preparing a written document. Speaking intelligently about a topic may actually involve more work and more time than writing about the same topic.

Organizing Your Speech or Presentation

Every facet of organizing your speech or presentation is driven by what you know about your audience. For example, if you're organizing a sales presentation, focus on how much your product will benefit the people in your audience, not on how great the product is. If you're explaining a change in medical benefits for company employees, address the concerns your audience is likely to have, such as cost and quality of care. You should organize an oral message just as you would organize a written message, by focusing on your audience as you define your main idea, limit your scope, choose your approach, prepare your outline, and decide on the most effective style for your presentation.

The main idea points out how the audience can benefit from your message.

Define the Main Idea   What is the one message you want your audience to walk away with? Look for a one-sentence generalization that links your subject and purpose to your audience's frame of reference, much as an advertising slogan points out how a product can benefit consumers. Here are some examples:

◆ Demand for low-calorie, high-quality frozen foods will increase because of basic social and economic trends.

◆ Reorganizing the data-processing department will lead to better service at a lower cost.

◆ We should build a new plant in Texas to reduce operating costs and to capitalize on growing demand in the Southwest.

◆ The new health plan reduces our costs by 12 percent while maintaining quality coverage.

Each of these statements puts a particular slant on the subject, one that is positive and directly related to the audience's interests. This sort of "you" attitude helps keep your audience's attention and convinces people that your points are relevant. For example, a group of new employees will be much more responsive to your discussion of plant safety procedures if you focus on how the procedures can save a life rather than on how the rules conform to Occupational Safety and Health Administration guidelines.

Limit Your Scope   You'll need to tailor your material to the time allowed, which is often strictly regulated. You can use your outline to estimate how much time your speech or presentation will take. The average speaker can deliver about 125 to 150 words a minute (or roughly 7,500 to 9,000 words an hour), which corresponds to 20 to 25 double-spaced, typed pages of text per hour. The average paragraph is about 125 to 150 words in length, so most of us can speak at a rate of about one paragraph per minute.

Say you want to make three basic points. In a 10-minute speech, you could take about 2 minutes to explain each point, using roughly two paragraphs for each. If you devoted a minute each to the introduction and the conclusion, you would have 2 minutes left over to interact with the audience. If you had an hour, however, you could spend the first 5 minutes introducing the presentation, establishing rapport with the audience, providing background information, and giving an overview of your topic. In the next 30 to 40 minutes, you could explain each of the three points, spending about 10 to 13 minutes on each one (the equivalent of 5 or 6 typewritten pages). Your conclusion might take another 3 to 5 minutes. The remaining 10 to 20 minutes would then be available for responding to questions and comments from the audience.

Which is better, the 10-minute speech or the hour-long presentation? If your speech doesn't have to fit into a specified time slot, the answer depends on your subject, your audience's attitude and knowledge, and the relationship you have with your audience. For a simple, easily accepted message, 10 minutes may be enough. On the other hand, if your

---

Going Online

Speak with Flair

◆

The Virtual Presentation Assistant offers abundant resources with related links. You can go to other public speaking sites that contain useful articles, reviews, or supplemental materials for planning presentations. You can also connect to popular media and library pages with worldwide research information. You'll find examples of speech types, suggestions for selecting and focusing your topic, tips on audience analysis, delivery, using visual aids, and various other guidelines to help you prepare and deliver an effective speech or presentation. If you need inspiration, check out this site.

www.ukans.edu/cwis/units/
coms2/vpa/vpa.htm

To reach this Web site, go to www.prenhall.com/thill *(the Web site for this text). Select Chapter 13, then select "Student Resources." There you'll find a current live link that will take you straight to the site.*

subject is complex or your audience is skeptical, you'll probably need more time. Don't squeeze a complex presentation into a period that is too brief, and don't spend any more time on a simple talk than necessary.

Choose Your Approach   With a well-defined main idea to guide you, and a clear idea about the scope of your speech, you can begin to arrange your message. If you have 10 minutes or less to deliver your message, organize your speech much as you would a letter or a brief memo: Use the direct approach if the subject involves routine information or good news, and use the indirect approach if the subject involves bad news or persuasion. Plan your introduction to arouse interest and to give a preview of what's to come. For the body of the presentation, be prepared to explain the who, what, when, where, why, and how of your subject. In the final paragraph or two, review the points you've made, and close with a statement that will help your audience remember the subject of your speech.

> Structure a short speech or presentation like a letter or a memo.

Longer speeches and presentations are organized like reports. If the purpose is to entertain, motivate, or inform, use direct order and a structure imposed naturally by the subject (importance, sequence, chronology, spatial orientation, geography, or category—as discussed in Chapter 11). If your purpose is to analyze, persuade, or collaborate, organize your material around conclusions and recommendations or around a logical argument. Use direct order if the audience is receptive and indirect if you expect resistance. Figure 13–2 is an outline for a 30-minute analytical presentation. It is organized around conclusions and presented in direct order. This outline is based on Chapter 12's Electrovision report, written by Linda Moreno.

> Organize longer speeches and presentations like formal reports.

You may have to adjust your organization in response to feedback from your audience, especially if your purpose is to collaborate. You can plan ahead by thinking of several organizational possibilities (based on "what if" assumptions about your audience's reactions). If someone says something that undercuts your planned approach, you can switch smoothly to another one.

Regardless of the length of your speech or presentation, bear in mind that simplicity of organization is especially valuable in oral communication. If listeners lose the thread of your comments, they'll have a hard time catching up and following the remainder of your message. They can't review a paragraph or flip pages back and forth, as they can when reading. So look for the most obvious and natural way to organize your ideas, using a direct order of presentation whenever possible. Explain at the beginning how you've organized your material, and try to limit the number of main points to three or four—even when the speech or presentation is rather long.

> Use a clear, direct organization to accommodate your listeners' limitations.

To keep the audience's attention, be sure to include only the most useful, interesting, and relevant supporting evidence. Brady Keys advises that you ask yourself whether this evidence is related to your core message. If it isn't, take it out. In addition, at the end of each section, reorient the audience by summarizing the point you've just made and explaining how it fits into your overall framework.

Prepare an Outline   A carefully prepared outline can be more than just the starting point for composing a speech or presentation—it will help you stay on task. You'll use it to make sure your message accomplishes its purpose. Your outline will help you keep your speech both audience centered and within the allotted time. If you plan to deliver your presentation from notes rather than from a written text, your outline can also become your final script.

> You'll use your outline for multiple tasks, including:
> - Composing your speech
> - Staying on task
> - Ensuring your speech accomplishes its purpose
> - Keeping your speech audience-centered
> - Keeping your speech within the allowed time
> - Serving as your final script

When your outline will serve as your speaking notes, the headings should be complete sentences or lengthy phrases, rather than one- or two-word topic headings. In addition, many speakers include notes that indicate where visual aids will be used. You might also want to write out the transitional sentences you'll use to connect main points. Or you may even want to jot down notes about using a certain tone or body language. Cues such as *pause here, speak slowly,* and *give extra emphasis* can be helpful when it comes to practicing and delivering your speech. Experienced speakers often use a two-column format that separates the "stage directions" from the content. Figure 13–3 on page 410 is an excerpt taken from a presentation that was made to persuade a company's marketing department to reassess its strategies.

> When you use your outline as speaking notes, you'll make some special alterations.

Includes the statement of purpose.

OUR TRAVEL AND ENTERTAINMENT COSTS ARE OUT OF CONTROL

Purpose: To explain why Electrovision's travel and entertainment (T&E) costs are so high and to propose a series of changes to bring them under control.

I. Introduction

Our T&E cost are way above average, and they pose a threat to the company's financial health; fortunately, we can fix the problem in four straightforward steps that could save as much as $6 million a year.

The introduction highlights the problem.

II. How we approached the investigation
   A. We analyzed internal expense reports.
   B. We compared our cost data with nationwide averages.
   C. We analyzed published information on trends and cost-control suggestions.

Explains the investigation process.

III. Analysis of spending patterns
   A. The amount we've been spending on T&E:
      1. Airfares, hotels, rental cars, restaurants, and entertainment totaled $16 million last year.
      2. T&E budget increased by 12 percent per year for the past five years.
   B. Where the money goes:
      1. We took 3,390 trips last year at an average cost per trip of $4,725.
      2. Airfares and lodging represent 70 percent of T&E expenses.
   C. How our spending compares with national averages:
      1. Facilities and customers spread from coast to coast force us to spend a lot on travel.
      2. However, we spend 125 percent more that the national average for every day travel.
   D. Why do we spend so much?
      1. First-class travel has been viewed as compensation for the demands of extensive travel.
      2. The sales staff is encouraged to entertain clients.
      3. T&E costs are hard for managers to view and study.
      4. No one has central responsibility for controlling costs.

The organization is logical and simple.

Explains why the problem exists.

(continued)

Figure 13–2
In-Depth Critique: Sample Outline for a 30-Minute Presentation

Decide on an Appropriate Style   Another important element in your preparation is style. Will you present a formal speech in an impressive setting, with professionally produced visual aids? Or will you lead a casual, roll-up-your-sleeves working session? Choose your style to fit the occasion. Your audience's size, your subject, your purpose, your budget, and the time available for preparation all influence your style.

Use a casual style for small groups; use a formal style for large groups and important events.

If you're speaking to a relatively small group, you can use a casual style that encourages audience participation. A small conference room, with your audience seated around a table, may be appropriate. Use simple visual aids, and invite your audience to interject comments. Deliver your remarks in a conversational tone, using notes to jog your memory if necessary.

In both formal and informal presentations, keep things simple.

If you're addressing a large audience and the event is an important one, you'll want to establish a more formal atmosphere. A formal style is well suited to announcements about mergers or acquisitions, new products, financial results, and other business mile-

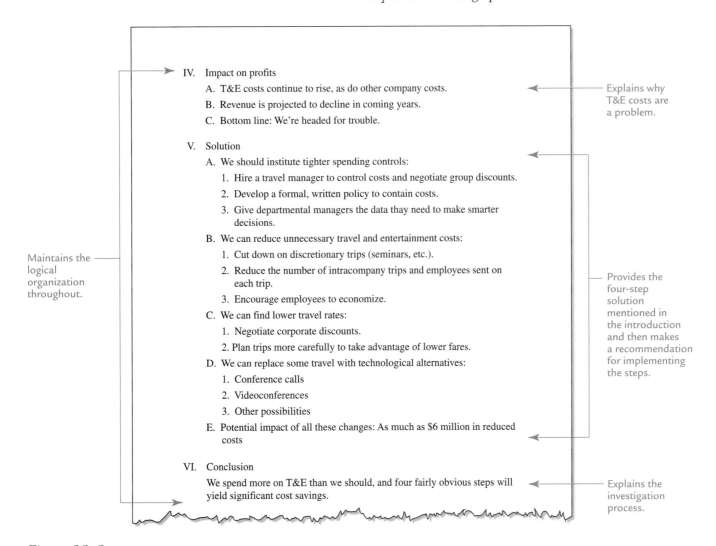

IV.   Impact on profits
    A.   T&E costs continue to rise, as do other company costs.   ← Explains why T&E costs are a problem.
    B.   Revenue is projected to decline in coming years.
    C.   Bottom line: We're headed for trouble.

V.   Solution
    A.   We should institute tighter spending controls: ← Provides the four-step solution mentioned in the introduction and then makes a recommendation for implementing the steps.
        1.   Hire a travel manager to control costs and negotiate group discounts.
        2.   Develop a formal, written policy to contain costs.
        3.   Give departmental managers the data thay need to make smarter decisions.
    B.   We can reduce unnecessary travel and entertainment costs:
        1.   Cut down on discretionary trips (seminars, etc.).
        2.   Reduce the number of intracompany trips and employees sent on each trip.
        3.   Encourage employees to economize.
    C.   We can find lower travel rates:
        1.   Negotiate corporate discounts.
        2.   Plan trips more carefully to take advantage of lower fares.
    D.   We can replace some travel with technological alternatives:
        1.   Conference calls
        2.   Videoconferences
        3.   Other possibilities
    E.   Potential impact of all these changes: As much as $6 million in reduced costs

VI.   Conclusion
We spend more on T&E than we should, and four fairly obvious steps will yield significant cost savings.   ← Explains the investigation process.

Maintains the logical organization throughout.

Figure 13–2
(Continued)

stones. During formal presentations, speakers are often located on a stage or platform, standing behind a lectern and using a microphone so that their remarks can be heard throughout the room. These speeches are often accompanied by multimedia presentations showcasing major products, technological breakthroughs, and other information that the speakers want audience members to remember.

Keep in mind that whether you're delivering a formal or an informal speech, you should always choose your words carefully. If you try to impress your audience with obscure or unfamiliar vocabulary, your message will be lost. Make sure you can define all the words you use. Keep things simple. If you repeatedly stumble over a word as you rehearse, use a different one.[4]

Developing Your Speech or Presentation

Developing a major speech or presentation is much like writing a formal report, with one important difference: You need to adjust your technique to an oral communication channel, which presents both opportunities and challenges. The major opportunity lies in the interaction that is possible between you and your audience. When you speak before a group, you can receive information as well as transmit it, which means you can adjust both the content and the delivery of your message as you go along to clarify or to be more compelling. Instead of simply expressing your ideas, you can draw ideas from your audience and then reach a mutually acceptable conclusion. Another opportunity is

Honored with many awards over the course of her 25-year career in TV journalism, Jane Pauley is currently anchor of NBC's *Dateline* and MSNBC's *Time and Again.* "Professionally," says Pauley, "I am absolutely wedded to the concept of objectivity and fairness." Her combination of candor and self-confidence helps her connect with audiences. Plus, whether she delivers a formal speech or an informal lecture, Pauley's style fits the occasion.

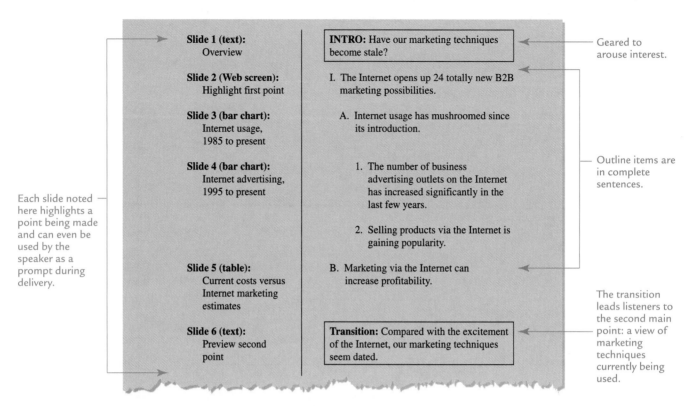

Figure 13–3
In-Depth Critique: Excerpt from Sample Outline with Delivery Notes

your ability to use nonverbal cues to reinforce your message. Audiences will receive much richer stimuli during a speech than they can while reading a written report.

The major challenge of using an oral communication channel is being able to control what happens. As you develop each part of your speech or presentation, think about how you will deliver the information. The more you expect to interact with your audience, the less control you'll have. Moreover, because listeners cannot refer back and forth to what has been or will be said, you must work harder to help them stay on track. Halfway through your presentation a comment from someone in the audience might force you to shift topics. If you can anticipate such shifts, you'll have a chance to prepare for them as you develop each part of your speech: the introduction, body, close, and question-and-answer period.

Introduction   You'll have a lot to accomplish during the first few minutes of your speech or presentation, including arousing your audience's interest in your topic, establishing your credibility, and preparing the audience for what will follow. That's why developing your introduction often requires a disproportionate amount of your attention.

Arousing Audience Interest   Some subjects are naturally more interesting than others. If you will be discussing a matter of profound significance that will personally affect the members of your audience, chances are they'll listen regardless of how you begin. All you really have to do is announce your topic ("Today I'm announcing the reorganization of our company").

Other subjects call for more imagination. How do you get people to listen if you're explaining the pension program to a group of new clerical employees, none of whom will be full participants for another five years and most of whom will probably leave the company within two? The best approach to dealing with an uninterested audience is to appeal to human nature and encourage people to take the subject personally. Show them how they'll be affected as individuals. For example, you might begin addressing the new clerical employees like this:

> If somebody offered to give you $200,000 in exchange for $5 per week, would you be interested? That's the amount you can expect to collect during your retirement years if you choose to contribute to the voluntary pension plan. During the next two weeks, you will have to decide whether you want to participate. Although retirement is many years away for most of you, it is an important financial decision. During the next 20 minutes, I hope to give you the information you need to make that decision intelligently.

Experienced speakers always make sure that the introduction matches the tone of the speech or presentation. If the occasion is supposed to be fun, you may begin with something light; but if you're talking business to a group of executives, don't waste their time with cute openings. Avoid jokes and personal anecdotes when you're discussing a serious problem. If you're giving a routine oral report, don't be overly dramatic. Most of all, be natural. Nothing turns off the average audience faster than a trite, staged beginning.

Match the introduction to the tone of your speech or presentation.

Building Your Credibility One of the chief drawbacks of overblown openings is that they damage a speaker's credibility, and building credibility is probably even more important than arousing interest. A speaker with high credibility is more persuasive than one with low credibility.[5] It's important to establish your credentials—and quickly; people will decide within a few minutes whether you're worth listening to.[6]

You have only a few minutes to establish your credibility.

You want your audience to like you as a person, but more important, you want them to respect your opinion. You have to prepare for that response while you're developing your speech. Establishing credibility is relatively easy if you're speaking to a familiar, open-minded audience. The difficulty comes when you try to earn the confidence of strangers, especially those predisposed to be skeptical or antagonistic.

One way to build credibility is to let someone else introduce you. That person can present your credentials so that you won't appear boastful. However, make sure that the person introducing you doesn't exaggerate your qualifications. Some members of the audience are likely to bristle if you're billed as being the world's greatest authority on your subject.

To build credibility, you can let someone else introduce you or you can introduce yourself—explaining (without boasting) why you are qualified to speak on the subject.

If you're introducing yourself, plan to keep your comments simple. At the same time, don't be afraid to mention your accomplishments. Your listeners will be curious about your qualifications, so tell them briefly who you are and why you're there. Generally, you need mention only a few aspects of your background: your position in an organization, your profession, and the name of your company. You might plan to say something like this:

> I'm Karen Whitney, a market research analyst with Information Resources Corporation. For the past five years, I've specialized in studying high technology markets. Your director of engineering, John LaBarre, has asked me to brief you on recent trends in computer-aided design so that you'll have a better idea of how to direct your research efforts.

This speaker established credibility by tying her credentials to the purpose of her presentation. By mentioning her company's name, her specialization and position, and the name of the audience's boss, she let her listeners know immediately that she was qualified to tell them something they needed to know. She connected her background to their concerns.

Previewing Your Presentation Giving your audience a preview of what's ahead adds to your authority and, more important, helps them understand your message. A reader can get an idea of the structure of a report by looking at the table of contents and scanning the headings. In an oral presentation, however, the speaker provides that framework. Without cues from the speaker, the audience may be unable to figure out how the main points of the message fit together.

Let the audience know what lies ahead.

In your introduction, summarize your main idea, identify the supporting points, and indicate the order in which you'll develop those points. Tell your listeners in so many words, "This is the subject, and these are the points I will cover." Once you've established the framework, you can be confident that the audience will understand how the individual facts and figures are related to your main idea as you move into the body of your presentation.

Body The bulk of your speech or presentation is devoted to a discussion of the three or four main points in your outline. Use the same organizational patterns you'd use in a letter, memo, or report, but keep things simple. As Brady Keys can tell you, your goals are to make sure that (1) the organization of your speech or presentation is clear and (2) your speech keeps your audience's attention.

Connecting Your Ideas To show how ideas are related, a written report uses typographical and formatting clues: headings, paragraph indentions, white space, and lists. However, an oral presentation relies on words to link various parts and ideas.

For the small links between sentences and paragraphs, use one or two transitional words: *therefore, because, in addition, in contrast, moreover, for example, consequently, nevertheless,* or *finally.* To link major sections of the speech or presentation, use complete sentences or paragraphs, such as "Now that we've reviewed the problem, let's take a look at some solutions." Every time you shift topics, be sure to stress the connection between ideas. Summarize what's been said, and then preview what's to come.

The longer your presentation, the more important transitions become. If you will be presenting many ideas, audience members may have trouble absorbing them and seeing the relationship among them. Your listeners need clear transitions to guide them to the most important points. Furthermore, they need transitions to pick up any ideas they may have missed. So if you plan to repeat key ideas in your transitions, you can compensate for lapses in your audience's attention. When you actually deliver your speech, you might also want to call attention to the transitions by using gestures, changing your tone of voice, or introducing a visual aid.

Holding Your Audience's Attention To communicate your points effectively, you must do more than connect your ideas with clear transitions. You also have to hold your audience's

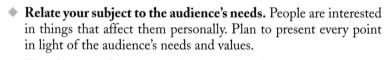

attention. Here are a few helpful tips for developing memorable speeches:

♦ **Relate your subject to the audience's needs.** People are interested in things that affect them personally. Plan to present every point in light of the audience's needs and values.

♦ **Use clear, vivid language.** People become bored quickly when they don't understand the speaker. If your presentation will involve abstract ideas, plan to show how those abstractions connect with everyday life. Use familiar words, short sentences, and concrete examples.

♦ **Explain the relationship between your subject and familiar ideas.** Plan to show how your subject is related to ideas that audience members already understand so that you give people a way to categorize and remember your points.[7]

As Brady Keys points out, another effective way to hold audience members' attention is to involve them. Ask their opinions or pause occasionally for questions or comments. Audience feedback helps you determine whether your listeners understand a key point before you launch into another section. Feedback also gives your audience a chance to switch for a time from listening to participating. Plan your pauses, even going so far as to note them in your outline so that you won't forget to pause once you're on stage.

Visual aids will also help clarify points and stimulate interest. (Visual aids are discussed in the next section, "Step 3: Completing Speeches and Presentations.") Be sure to include visual aids in your speeches or presentations whenever they're appropriate.

Limit the body to three or four main points.

Help your audience follow your presentation by using clear transitions between sentences and paragraphs, as well as between major sections.

Emphasize your transitions by repeating key ideas, using gestures, changing your tone of voice, or introducing a visual aid.

Make a special effort to capture wandering attention.

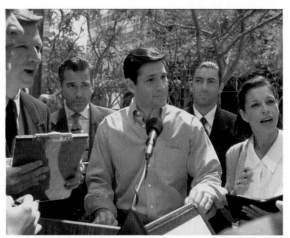

When attempting to hold an audience's attention, public speakers sometimes face challenging circumstances. As community relations director for AmTech, Ted Wilson often addresses large audiences on college campuses or even in public parks, where he has to battle crowd noises and other outdoor distractions. It takes a focused speaker to overcome such physical interruptions and get your message across.

Close   The close of a speech or presentation is almost as important as the beginning because audience attention peaks at this point. Plan to devote about 10 percent of your total time to the ending. When developing your conclusion, begin by telling listeners that you're about to finish so that they'll make one final effort to listen intently. Don't be afraid to sound obvious. Consider saying something like "in conclusion" or "to sum it all up." You want people to know that this is the home stretch.

The close should leave a strong and lasting impression.

Restating Your Main Points   Once you've decided how to announce your close, plan on repeating your main idea. Be sure to emphasize what you want your audience to do or think, and state the key motivating factor. Finally, reinforce your theme by repeating the three or four main supporting points. A few sentences are generally enough to refresh people's memories. Here's how one speaker ended a presentation on the company's executive compensation program:

Summarize the main idea and restate the main points.

> We can all be proud of the way our company has grown. If we want to continue that growth, however, we will have to adjust our executive compensation program to reflect competitive practices. If we don't, our best people will look for opportunities elsewhere.
>
> In summary, our survey has shown that we need to do four things to improve executive compensation:
>
> ◆ Increase the overall level of compensation
> ◆ Install a cash bonus program
> ◆ Offer a variety of stock-based incentives
> ◆ Improve our health insurance and pension benefits
>
> By making these improvements, we can help our company cross the threshold of growth into the major leagues.

The speaker repeated his four specific recommendations and then concluded with a memorable statement that would motivate the audience to take action.

Describing the Next Steps   Some speeches and presentations require the audience to reach a decision or to agree to take specific action. In such cases, the close provides a clear wrap-up. If the audience agrees on an issue covered in the presentation, plan to review the consensus in a sentence or two. If they don't agree, make the lack of consensus clear by saying something such as, "We seem to have some fundamental disagreement on this question." Then you'll be ready to suggest a method of resolving the differences.

Be certain that everyone agrees on the outcome and understands what should happen next.

If you expect any action to occur as a result of your speech, you must explain who is responsible for doing what. One effective technique is to list the action items, with an estimated completion date and the name of the person responsible. You can present this list in a visual aid, and ask each person on the list to agree to accomplish his or her assigned task by the target date. This public commitment to action is the best insurance that something will happen.

If the required action is likely to be difficult, make sure that everyone understands the problems involved. You don't want people to leave the presentation thinking their tasks will be easy, only to discover later that the jobs are quite demanding. You'll want everyone to have a realistic attitude and to be prepared to handle whatever arises. So when planning your presentation, use the close to alert people to potential difficulties or pitfalls.

Ending on a Positive Note   Make sure that your final remarks are encouraging and memorable. Even if parts of your speech are downbeat, plan to close on a positive note. You might stress the benefits of action or express confidence in the listeners' ability to accomplish the work ahead. An alternative is to end with a question or a statement that will leave your audience thinking.

Your audience will be more likely to remember your final words if those words are enthusiastic and upbeat.

Remember that your final words round out the presentation. Your task is to leave the audience with a satisfied feeling, a feeling of completeness. The close is not the place to introduce new ideas or to alter the mood of the presentation. And even though you want to close on a positive note, avoid using a staged finale. Keep it natural. As with everything else in your speech, plan your closing remarks carefully. You don't want to wind up on stage with nothing to say but, "Well, I guess that's it."

Question-and-Answer Period   Along with the introduction, body, and close, be sure to provide an opportunity for questions and answers. Otherwise, you might just as well write a report. If you don't expect to interact with the audience, you're wasting the chief advantage of an oral format.

Encourage questions throughout your speech if you are addressing a small group, but ask a large audience to defer questions until later.

Controlling the Situation   The important things to consider when developing your speech are the nature and timing of audience interaction. (Specifics about handling questions from the audience are discussed later in the chapter, under the heading "Mastering the Art of Delivery.") Responding to questions and comments during your presentation can interrupt the flow of your argument and reduce your control of the situation. If you're addressing a large group, particularly a hostile or an unknown group, questions could be dangerous. Your best bet in such cases is to ask people to hold their questions until after you have concluded your remarks. If you're working with a small group and need to draw out ideas, encourage comments from listeners throughout your presentation.

Anticipating questions will ensure a successful speech.

Anticipating Questions   Regardless of when you respond to questions, remember that they're one of the most important parts of your presentation. Questions give you a chance to obtain important information, to emphasize your main idea and supporting points, and to build enthusiasm for your point of view. Try to anticipate as many questions as you can beforehand, and rehearse your answers. You may even prepare some visuals in anticipation of your audience's needs for greater detail.

STEP 3: COMPLETING SPEECHES AND PRESENTATIONS

To complete your speech or presentation, you will need to revise it, being careful to evaluate the content and edit your remarks for clarity and conciseness. You will also need to carefully proof any handouts or other visuals for typos and for any errors in accuracy, alignment, scale, and so on—as you would for any other type of business message. But when completing your oral presentation, two areas require your special attention: designing and producing presentation visuals, and practicing actually delivering your speech.

Designing and Producing Visuals for Presentations

Just as with reports, you can help your audience get the picture by using visuals in oral presentations. When used effectively, visuals create interest and clarify important points. More important, however, visual aids dramatically increase the audience's ability to absorb and remember information. Keep in mind that audiences remember only 10 percent of a speaker's message when it's presented solely through words, but they remember 50 percent when the information is supported with visual aids such as slides and overhead transparencies.[8]

From a purely practical standpoint, visuals are a convenience for the speaker. They are an effective tool for remembering the details of the message (no small feat in a lengthy presentation). In addition, speakers who use presentation visuals often appear better prepared and more professional than speakers who do not use visuals.

Creating lively visual materials for oral presentations is not as hard as it used to be, thanks to popular computer software such as Microsoft's PowerPoint, Lotus's Freelance Graphics, Harvard Graphics, and CorelDraw! These products make it easy for you to

◆ Organize visuals in a logical manner and provide continuity throughout

◆ Repeat graphic elements on every visual (such as a border, a company logo, or a background)

◆ Select appropriate formats for your presentation (from paper handouts to computer-based presentations

◆ Incorporate multimedia such as sound and video into your presentation

◆ Modify or adapt your presentation for different audiences

Whether you use simple bar charts or complex multimedia in oral presentations, remember that the purpose of the visual is to *support* your message—not become the message itself.

Types of Presentation Visuals   Two types of visual aids are used to supplement speeches and presentations. First, text visuals consist of words and help the audience follow the flow of ideas. Because text visuals are simplified outlines of your presentation, you can use them to summarize and preview your message and to signal major shifts in thought. Second, graphic visuals illustrate your main points. They help the audience grasp numerical data and other information that would be hard to follow if presented orally.

As with all visual aids, the crucial factor is how you use presentation visuals. Properly integrated into an oral presentation, they can save time, create interest, add variety, make an impression, and illustrate points that are difficult to explain in words alone. Visual aids for documents are usually limited to paper. For speeches and presentations, however, you have a variety of media to choose from: handouts, boards, flip charts, overheads, slides, electronic presentations, and others.

Handouts   Use printed handouts to distribute an agenda, an outline of the program, an abstract, a written report, or supplementary materials such as tables, charts, and graphs. Listeners can refer to the handout while you're speaking. They can also keep the handout to later recall the subject and main ideas of your presentation. Handouts work especially well in informal situations where the audience takes an active role; participants often make their own notes on the handouts.

However, handouts can be distracting. People may be inclined to read the material rather than listen to you. So many speakers distribute handouts after the presentation.

Be sure to keep your handouts simple. Limit the amount of information you include to a single page. Try to summarize your key points without reproducing your entire presentation.

Chalkboards and Whiteboards   When you're addressing a small group of people and want to draw out their ideas, use a board to list points as they are mentioned. Because these visual aids are produced on the spot, the boards provide flexibility. However, they're too informal for some situations.

Flip charts   Large sheets of paper attached at the top like a tablet can be propped on an easel so that you can flip the pages as you speak, with each page illustrating or clarifying a point. You might have a few lines from your outline on one, a graph or diagram on another, and so on. By using felt-tip markers of various colors, you can also record ideas generated during a discussion. Remember, keep it simple: Try to limit each flip-chart page to three or four graphed lines or to five or six points in list format.

Overheads   One of the most common visual aids in business is the overhead transparency, which can be projected on a screen in full daylight. Because you don't have to dim the lights, you don't lose eye contact with your audience. Transparencies are easy to make using an original on regular paper, a copying machine, and a page-size sheet of plastic. Special markers can be used to write on transparencies. In that respect, they're similar to whiteboards and flip charts, but they have the added advantage of enabling you to face the audience.

Opaque projections are similar to transparencies, but require much less preparation. You could use an opaque projector to show the audience a photograph or an excerpt from a report or manual.

Slides   The content of 35-millimeter slides may be text, graphics, or pictures. If you're trying to create a polished, professional atmosphere, you might find this approach worthwhile, particularly if you'll be addressing a crowd and don't mind speaking in a darkened

---

Marginal notes:

Use visual aids to highlight your spoken words, not as a substitute for them.

Two kinds of visual aids:
• Text visuals help listeners follow the flow of ideas.
• Graphic visuals present and emphasize important facts.

In preparing visual aids for oral presentations, you have a variety of media to choose from.

Handouts can be both useful and distracting.

Chalkboards and whiteboards are informal.

Unlike boards, flip charts can be prepared in advance.

Overheads are one of the most common types of visual aids.

Slides look professional but may force you to speak from the dark.

room. Remember, however, that you may need someone to operate the projector and that you'll need to coordinate the slides with your speech. Take a few minutes before your speech to verify that the equipment works correctly and that your slides are positioned correctly in the tray.

Electronic presentations also look professional but can be used in a well-lit room.

Electronic Presentations   With special projection equipment, a personal computer can be turned into a large-screen "intelligent chalkboard" that allows you to create and modify your visual aids as the presentation unfolds. For live presentations, an increasing number of businesses now use LCD (liquid crystal display) projectors or display panels. These products grab the images from your computer screen and display them on the same projection screens used for viewing slides.

Electronic presentations have the advantage of including real-time manipulation of numbers, animation, video clips, and even sound. By using presentation software you can prepare a multimedia show that captures and involves your audience, replacing flip charts, cumbersome overheads, and chalkboards. Most presentation software packages today allow you to incorporate photos, sound, video, and animation into your multimedia presentations.[9]

Other visuals include product samples, models, audiotapes, film strips, and videotapes.

Other Visual Aids   In technical or scientific presentations, a sample of a product or material allows the audience to experience your subject directly. Models built to scale are convenient representations of an object. Audiotapes are often used to supplement a slide show or to present a precisely worded and timed message. Filmstrips and movies can capture the audience's attention with color and movement. Television and videotapes are good for showing demonstrations, interviews, and other events. In addition, filmstrips, movies, television, and videotapes can be used as stand-alone vehicles (independent of a speaker) to communicate with dispersed audiences at various times.

How to Build an Electronic Presentation   Whether you use Microsoft PowerPoint, Lotus Freelance Graphics, CorelDraw!, or another popular presentation program, you can create an effective **electronic presentation**—a series of computerized slides. Think of an electronic slide as a single page of information. When you build an electronic presentation, you design each slide to cover one point or one graph, much as you would when designing overhead transparencies.

An electronic presentation is a series of computer slides.

Templates   You begin by selecting a template or by preparing a custom design for your master slide. You'll use this master slide as the background for your entire presentation. Each time you call up a new slide to add text or graphs, a copy of this master slide will appear. The big advantage is that you can easily program the master slide for the font and color you'll use throughout your presentation as well as for items you want to appear on all the slides, such as a title or a company logo. Thus, having a master slide ensures that your slides are uniform and easy to follow (see Figure 13–4).

The master slide stores design elements that will appear on all presentation slides, ensuring uniformity and consistency.

Sorters   Once you've constructed all the slides to be included in your presentation, you organize them in a proper sequence so that your material flows in a logical order. Here again, the software makes it easy by allowing you to see all your slides in *slide sorter view* and to drag any slide to a different position in the presentation. (Figure 13–5 is a Microsoft PowerPoint presentation in slide sorter view.)

Sorters help you arrange your slides in proper sequence.

Automation   Next, you're ready to add some automation. In a simple slide show, you'll use special effects transitions between slides to make your presentation flow smoothly and to keep your audience's attention. These special effects include fading in and out, checkerboard motion, dissolving, and wiping or uncovering from different directions.

Special effects help your audience make the transition between slides, as well as giving your presentation a more professional look.

You can also select special features for your bullet points, called "builds." Rather than having all your bullet points appear on a slide at once (making it difficult to focus on a single point), you can make your bullet points appear one at a time, as if they were marching across the screen. You can even use special effects to have one bullet point disappear as another appears, or you can alter the intensity of the text's color for one bullet as you discuss it while fading the text of the others into the background.

Figure 13–4
Choosing Color for Master Slide

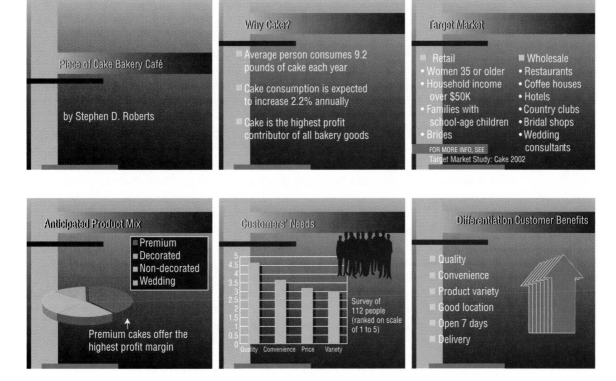

Figure 13–5
Slide Presentation for Piece of Cake Bakery Café

Multimedia   You can get fancy by adding sound effects, morphed graphics, video, and so on. You can even automate your program to move from one slide to the next without speaker intervention. Automation is especially useful for running the presentation on television monitors in large places such as conventions and trade shows, where the slide show is the only information presented.

You can add multimedia effects to your computer slides, including sound, graphics, and video.

Figure 13–6
Speaker's Notes with
Presentation Thumbnails

You can even insert links to Web pages into your computer slides.

Other useful features of electronic presentation software include:
• Handouts
• Speaker's notes
• Outlines

Objective

5

Discuss what is involved in designing effective presentation visuals and list five important guidelines.

Visual aids are most effective when they are simple.

Visuals are counterproductive if the audience cannot see them or understand them within a few moments.

Links   Another useful feature of presentation software is the ability to link your slide presentation to other files on your computer. Hypertext markup language (HTML) and integrated software packages such as Microsoft Office allow you to jump between files and software programs—even Web pages—so that you can illustrate fine details without having to incorporate each detail into a slide.

Handouts and Speaker's Notes   Once you've built your slide show, you can use additional presentation software features to create handouts, speaker's notes, outlines, and so on. Audience handouts can be actual copies of the slides with plenty of white space for note taking, or they can be scaled-down copies of the slides, fitting several slides on a page.

Speaker's notes are a helpful tool to use when delivering your presentation. You can input notes such as "Don't forget to explain the impact of last year's bad weather on sales" and coordinate these notes with a thumbnail sketch of the slide you'll show while delivering that message, as shown in Figure 13–6.

Tips for Designing Effective Presentation Visuals   Whether you're using presentation software or overheads, including too many visuals that are too complicated or too flashy will detract from your message. If your message is too complex or poorly written, you'll lose your audience's interest, no matter how glitzy your presentation looks. Technology has made snazzy special effects so accessible that some speakers rely on them too much, so audiences are increasingly underwhelmed by them.

Simplicity is the key to effectiveness when designing visual aids. People can't read and listen at the same time. Your presentation visuals must be simple enough for your audience to understand within a moment or two.

Text Visuals   As a rule, effective text visuals consist of no more than six lines, with a maximum of six words on each line. Produce them in large, clear type, using uppercase and lowercase letters, with extra white space between lines of text. Make sure the type is large enough to be seen from any place in the room. Avoid using script or decorative fonts that are hard to read from a distance, and limit the number of fonts you use. Phrase list

EFFECTIVE E-BUSINESS COMMUNICATION

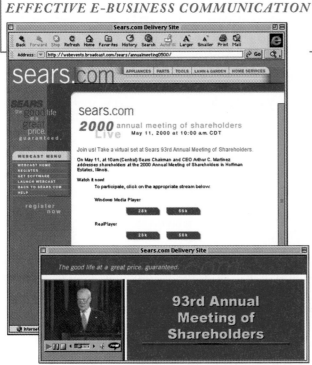

Speeches That Live On and On

Ordinarily, a speech is a one-time event that helps you connect with a particular audience at a particular time and place. However, a Webcast speech, accessed through the company's Web site, can reach thousands of people around the world. Companies such as Sears, Avon, Nike, and America Online use Webcast speeches to make live announcements of financial news, new products, and management changes, as shown on the Yahoo! Broadcast site (business.broad cast.com/apps.html). Webcast speeches are often available on the Web for later viewing, which increases the potential audience, and keeps the message alive long after the speakers have left the podium.

1. What changes might you make to the text of your speech if you know it will be available on the Web for later viewing?
2. Would you use the same kind of visual aids for a Webcast speech and for a speech that will not be Webcast? Explain your answer.

items in parallel grammatical form. Use telegraphic wording ("Profits Soar") without being cryptic ("Profits"); you are often better off including both a noun and a verb in each line item.

Many speeches and presentations begin with several text visuals. The first is usually the equivalent of a title page, announcing the subject and signaling the audience that the presentation is under way. The second typically lists the three or four major points you'll cover, providing a road map of what's to come. The remaining text visuals are used to cover the key points of your presentation.

Graphic Visuals   You can use any of the graphic visuals you might include in a formal report, such as charts, diagrams, maps, drawings, and tables. However, graphic visuals used in oral presentations must be simplified versions of those that appear in written documents. Eliminate anything that is not absolutely essential to the message. Too much graphic detail is difficult to read on a screen. To help your audience focus immediately on the point of each graphic visual, use headings that state the message in one clear phrase or sentence: "Earnings have increased by 15 percent."

> Graphic visuals must be simplified as much as possible.

Focus   Remember, you want the audience to listen to you, not study the visual aids. The visual aids are there to supplement your words—not the other way around. Visual aids are an excellent way to remind your audience of main points and to keep your presentation on track. But unless you maintain control, visuals will distract your listeners from your message. Furthermore, the more sophisticated the visuals, the stronger you must be, to keep them from upstaging you.[10] To design the most effective visuals, remember these five tips:

> Effective visuals do not distract the audience or upstage the speaker.

◆ Limit each visual to one idea.

◆ Illustrate your main points, not your entire presentation.

◆ Use borders, pointers, and boxes to highlight important information.

◆ Use clip art sparingly to add color and excitement to your presentation.

◆ Avoid visuals that conflict with your verbal message.

Mastering the Art of Delivery

Not all methods of delivery are ideal.

Once your visual aids are completed, you're ready to begin practicing your delivery. You have a variety of delivery methods to choose from, some of which are easier to handle than others.

◆ **Memorizing.** Unless you're a trained actor, avoid memorizing your speech, especially a long one. You're likely to forget your lines, and your speech will sound stilted. Besides, you'll often need to address audience questions during your speech, so you must be flexible enough to adjust your speech as you go. However, memorizing a quotation, an opening paragraph, or a few concluding remarks can bolster your confidence and strengthen your delivery.

◆ **Reading.** If you're delivering a technical or complex presentation, you may want to read it. Policy statements by government officials are sometimes read because the wording may be critical. If you choose to read your speech, practice enough so that you can still maintain eye contact with your audience. Triple-spaced copy, wide margins, and large type will help. You might even want to include stage cues, such as *pause, raise hands, lower voice.*

Speaking from notes is generally the best way to handle delivery.

◆ **Speaking from notes.** Making a presentation with the help of an outline, note cards, or visual aids is probably the most effective and easiest delivery mode. It gives you something to refer to and still allows for eye contact and interaction with the audience. If your listeners look puzzled, you can expand on a point or rephrase it. (Generally, note cards are preferable to sheets of paper, because nervousness is easier to see in shaking sheets of paper.)

◆ **Impromptu speaking.** You might have to give an impromptu, or unrehearsed, speech if you're called on to speak unexpectedly or if you've agreed to speak but neglected to prepare your remarks. Avoid speaking unprepared unless you've spoken countless times on the same topic or are an extremely good public speaker. When you're asked to speak "off the cuff," take a moment to think through what you'll say. Then avoid the temptation to ramble.

Regardless of which delivery mode you use, be sure that you're thoroughly familiar with your subject. Knowing what you're talking about is the best way to build your self-confidence. Also, knowing how to prepare yourself for successful speaking helps your confidence. Important factors include getting ready to speak, overcoming anxiety, presenting visual aids, and handling questions.

Microsoft Chairman Bill Gates is not intimidated in front of an audience. His ease as a public speaker results from being called on countless times not only to comment on his company's business but also to deliver formal speeches. Gates might take risks in his strategy for bringing new products to market, but he doesn't gamble when preparing to speak to an audience.

Before you speak:
• Practice.
• Prepare the location.
• Consider cultural differences.

Get Ready to Speak   In addition to knowing your material, you can build self-confidence as you get ready to give your presentation. Remember to get plenty of practice, to check the location, and to consider using an interpreter when addressing an audience that doesn't speak your language.

Practicing   That's right, practice makes perfect, especially if you haven't had much experience with public speaking. Even if you rehearse in front of a mirror, try to visualize the room filled with listeners. Put your talk on tape to check the sound of your voice, as well as your timing, phrasing, and emphasis. If possible, rehearse on videotape to see yourself as your audience will. Be sure to include your visual aids so that you get used to coordinating them with your talk.

Checking the Location   Whenever you can, check the location for your presentation in advance. Check the seating arrangements to ensure they're appropriate for your needs. If you want audience members to sit at tables, be sure tables are available. Check the room

Sharpening Your Career Skills

Nerves: The Secret Weapon of Polished Presenters

What do Barbra Streisand, Willard Scott, Sidney Poitier, and Liza Minelli have in common? All are professional performers, and all admit to being nervous about public speaking. If the pros can feel fear, it's no wonder beginners are sometimes scared speechless. Survey after survey has confirmed that public speaking is the number one fear in the United States—so if you're anxious about stepping in front of an audience, you're not alone.

Nervousness might make your hands tremble, your knees knock, your mouth feel dry, or your stomach churn. As bad as these symptoms can be, remember that nerves are a good indicator of your concern for the occasion, the topic, and the audience. If you didn't care, you wouldn't be anxious. A speaker who cares is more likely to seek out every method of communicating with the audience.

Remember also that you'll feel a little less nervous with every speech. Once you see how the audience responds to your first speech, you'll realize that you did better than you feared you would. Audience members can't see the butterflies fluttering; they're too busy paying attention and responding to your ideas. People in the audience want you to succeed; they're interested in learning from you or being inspired by your words, not in straining to hear the sound of your knees knocking together.

You can harness your nerves by focusing on what you want to accomplish. In the words of actress Carol Channing, "I don't call it nervousness—I prefer to call it concentration." Like Channing, you can concentrate your efforts on making that all-important connection with your audience. But don't make the mistake of expecting perfection. Put that nervous energy into planning, preparing, and practicing, and you'll be better equipped to face your audience, the first time and every time.

CAREER APPLICATIONS

1. Think of any speeches, lectures, or presentations you've recently attended. Have you ever noticed a speaker's level of anxiety? Were any of the speakers successful in overcoming this fear? As an informed observer, describe the ways in which a particular speaker visibly conquered his or her nervousness. If that speaker failed, what techniques might have helped?

2. As a member of the audience, what can you do to help a speaker overcome his or her nervousness? Briefly explain.

---

for outlets you may need for your projector or microphone. Locate light switches and dimmers. If you need a flip-chart easel or a chalkboard, be sure it's on hand. Check for chalk, an eraser, a pointer, extension cords, and any other small but crucial items you might need.

Considering an Interpreter   If you're addressing an audience that doesn't speak your language, consider using an interpreter. Working with an interpreter does constrain your presentation somewhat—you must speak slowly enough for the interpreter to keep up with you but not so slowly that the rest of your audience loses interest. Send your interpreter a copy of your speech and any visual aids as far in advance as possible.

Any time you make a speech or presentation to people from other cultures, you may need to adapt the content of your speech. It is also important to take into account any cultural differences in appearance, mannerisms, and other customs. Your interpreter will be able to suggest appropriate changes for a specific audience or particular occasion.

Overcome Anxiety   If you're nervous about facing an audience, you're not alone. Even speakers with years of experience feel some anxiety about getting up in front of an audience (see "Sharpening Your Skills—Nerves: The Secret Weapon of Polished Presenters"). Although you might not be able to make your nervous feelings disappear, you can learn to cope with your anxiety.

Feeling More Confident   Nervousness shows that you care about your audience, your topic, and the occasion. If your palms get wet or your mouth goes dry, don't think of nerves, think of excitement. Such stimulation can give you the extra energy you need to make your presentation sparkle. Harness your nervous energy to become a more confident speaker:[11]

◆ **Prepare more material than necessary.** Combined with a genuine interest in your topic, extra knowledge will reduce your anxiety.

Objective

6

Relate nine ways to overcome your anxiety and feel more confident.

Several techniques can help you become a more confident speaker.

◆ **Rehearse.** The more familiar you are with your material, the less panic you'll feel.

◆ **Think positively.** See yourself as polished and professional, and your audience will too.

◆ **Visualize your success.** Use the few minutes before you actually begin speaking to tell yourself you're on and you're ready.

◆ **Take a few deep breaths.** Before you begin to speak, remember that your audience is silently wishing you success.

◆ **Be ready.** Have your first sentence memorized and on the tip of your tongue.

◆ **Be comfortable.** If your throat is dry, drink some water.

◆ **Don't panic.** If you feel that you're losing your audience during your speech, try to pull them back by involving them in the action; ask for their opinions or pause for questions.

◆ **Keep going.** Things usually get better as you go.

> The best technique for overcoming your anxiety is to concentrate on your listeners and on their needs, rather than focusing on yourself.

Perhaps the best way to overcome stage fright and feel more confident is to concentrate on your message and on your audience, not on yourself. When you're busy thinking about your subject and observing your audience's response, you tend to forget your fears.

Appearing More Confident   As you deliver your presentation, try to be aware of the nonverbal signals you're transmitting. Regardless of how you feel inside, your effectiveness greatly depends on how you look and sound.

> Don't rush the opening.

Seamless presentations start with your first minute at the podium, so don't rush. As you approach the speaker's lectern, breathe deeply, stand up straight, and walk slowly. Face your audience, adjust the microphone, count to three slowly, and then survey the room. When you find a friendly face, make eye contact and smile. Count to three again, and then begin your presentation.[12] If you are nervous, this slow, controlled beginning will help you establish rapport and appear more confident.

> Use eye contact, posture, gestures, and voice to convey an aura of mastery and to keep your audience's attention.

Once your speech is under way, be particularly careful to maintain eye contact with your audience. Pick out several people positioned around the room, and shift your gaze from one to another. Looking directly at your listeners will make you appear sincere, confident, and trustworthy. It also helps you to get an idea of the impression you're creating.

Your posture is also important in projecting more confidence. Stand tall, with your weight on both feet and your shoulders back. Avoid gripping the lectern. In fact, you might step out from behind the lectern to help your audience feel more comfortable with you and to express your own comfort and confidence in what you're saying. Use your hands to emphasize your remarks with appropriate gestures. Meanwhile, vary your facial expressions to make the message more dynamic.

Finally, think about the sound of your voice. Studies indicate that people who speak with lower voice tones at a slightly faster than average rate are perceived as being more credible.[13] Speak in a normal, conversational tone but with enough volume for everyone to hear you. Try to sound poised and confident, varying your pitch and speaking rate to add emphasis. Don't ramble or use meaningless filler words such as *um, you know, okay,* and *like.* Speak clearly and crisply, articulating all the syllables, and sound enthusiastic about what you're saying.

> Visual aids help both the speaker and the audience.

Present Visuals Effectively   Use visuals to guide your speech and maintain audience interest. But be careful. Before you begin your presentation, make sure of a few things:

◆ Check the equipment in advance to make sure it's in good working order.

◆ Have a backup plan in case the technology fails.

◆ Be sure that all members of your audience can see your visual aids.

> Avoid simply reading your visuals.

Inexperienced speakers are often afraid of forgetting something, so they end up reading slides to the audience. When you read, you lose your voice inflection. As you focus on your visuals rather than on your audience, your listeners lose interest, perhaps missing your message altogether. Because you're simply reading instead of engaging your listeners, many members of the audience eventually stop paying attention.[14]

So keep your eyes on your audience. Don't talk to the screen. Visual aids don't need your attention, your audience does. If you know exactly what each slide contains, you'll find it easier to keep your eyes on your audience.[15] Don't put a visual up until you're ready to talk about it. When you've finished discussing the point illustrated, remove the visual from your audience's view. Also, try not to switch to the next visual right away.

When you put up a slide or a transparency, or as you turn to the next page on your flip chart, give your audience about five seconds to look at the visual before you start talking. Then introduce it, tell them what it represents, and direct them to the portion you want to talk about. Wait a few seconds for your audience to find your point of reference.

Give your audience a few seconds to view your visual before you begin to speak.

If you're using a pointer, remember that it's a tool meant to guide your audience to a specific part of a visual. It is not a riding crop, conductor's baton, leg scratcher, or walking stick. Use the pointer only at the time you need it, then fold it and remove it from sight. If you are using a laser pointer that puts a focused dot of light on the desired part of your visual, don't overdo it. A laser pointer is an excellent tool if used judiciously, but in the hands of the overzealous presenter, it can become a distraction.[16] If you must dim the lights to show your slides or transparencies, be sure to stand in a lighted area. Don't become the anonymous "offstage announcer."[17]

Minimize your use of a pointer and remove it from sight when you're not using it.

Handle Questions Responsively   The question-and-answer period is a valuable part of an oral presentation. In addition to giving you valuable feedback, this period gives you a chance to emphasize points you made earlier, work in material that didn't fit into the formal presentation, and identify and try to overcome audience resistance. Many speakers do well delivering their speech or presentation, only to falter during the question-and-answer period. But since you've already spent time anticipating these questions, you are ready with answers. Some experts recommend that you hold back some dramatic statistics as ammunition for the question-and-answer session.[18] If your message is unpopular, you should also be prepared for hostile questions. Treat them as legitimate requests for information. Maintaining your professionalism will improve your credibility.

Be ready with answers so that you can
- *Emphasize your most important points*
- *Refer to material that didn't fit in the formal presentation*
- *Overcome audience resistance*

Focusing on the Questioner   When someone poses a question, focus your attention on that individual. Pay attention to body language and facial expression to help determine what the person really means. Nod your head to acknowledge the question; then repeat it aloud to confirm your understanding and to ensure that the entire audience has heard it. If the question is vague or confusing, ask for clarification; then give a simple, direct answer. If you're asked to choose between two alternatives, don't feel you must do so. Offer your own choice instead, if that makes more sense.[19]

Use body language to emphasize the fact that you're listening to the questioner.

Responding Appropriately   Be sure to answer the question you're asked. Don't sidestep it, ignore it, or laugh it off. Furthermore, don't say more than you need to if you want to have enough time to cover all the questions. If giving an adequate answer would take too long, simply say, "I'm sorry, we don't have time to get into that issue right now, but if you'll see me after the presentation, I'll be happy to discuss it with you." If you don't know the answer, don't pretend that you do. Instead, say something like, "I don't have those figures. I'll get them for you as quickly as possible." Remember, you don't have to answer every question that is asked.

Keep your answers short and to the point.

Maintaining Control   Try to maintain control during the question-and-answer session by establishing some ground rules up front. Announce a time limit or question limit per person before you begin. Establishing limits will protect you from getting into a heated exchange with one member of the audience and from allowing one or two people to monopolize the question period. Give as many audience members as possible a chance to participate by calling on people from different parts of the room. If the same person keeps angling for attention, restate the question limit or say something like, "Several other people have questions; I'll get back to you if time permits."

During meetings at Tellme.com polished speakers use question-and-answer sessions to reinforce their ideas and credibility.

Checklist: **Speeches and Oral Presentations**

Planning Your Speech or Presentation

✓ Define your purpose.
✓ Analyze your audience.

Writing the Speech or Presentation

✓ Define your main idea.
✓ Limit your scope.
✓ Choose an appropriate approach.
✓ Prepare your outline.
✓ Decide on an appropriate style.
✓ Prepare the introduction: begin with an attention-getter, build credibility, preview the main points.
✓ Prepare the body by explaining who, what, when, where, why, and how.
✓ Tell listeners what's in it for them.
✓ Connect your ideas with transitions (use bridge words, ask questions, repeat key ideas).
✓ Reinforce your transitions with physical gestures.
✓ In longer presentations, include previews and summaries of major points as you go along.
✓ Include only necessary material.
✓ Prepare the close: review the main points, make a memorable statement, describe the next steps, assign responsibilities, and end on a positive note.

✓ Prepare for the question-and-answer period: figure out how to control the situation, and anticipate questions and objections.

Delivering the Speech or Presentation

✓ Practice delivery elements: (1) establish eye contact, (2) speak clearly, (3) speak distinctly (not too fast), (4) make sure everyone can hear, (5) speak in your own natural style, (6) stand up straight, (7) use gestures naturally and appropriately, (8) stress the important words and phrases.
✓ Check out the room ahead of time, and make sure the equipment works.
✓ Control your anxiety and use your nervousness as a tool.
✓ Use visual aids effectively.
✓ Build suspense before using a visual.
✓ Vary your transitions into visuals.
✓ Don't read your visuals; instead, editorialize and enlighten.
✓ Keep your eyes focused on your audience.
✓ Encourage questions.
✓ Respond to questions without getting sidetracked.
✓ Show sufficient knowledge to maintain credibility.
✓ Keep control of your audience and the situation.
✓ Maintain control of your feelings despite criticism.
✓ Use answers to refocus on your theme or message.

If audience members try to turn a question into an opportunity to mount their own soapboxes, it's up to you to stay in control. You might ask people to identify themselves before they ask questions. People are more likely to behave themselves when everyone present knows their name.[20] You might admit that you and the questioner have differing opinions and, before calling on someone else, offer to get back to the questioner once you've done more research. Or you might simply respond with a brief answer, avoiding a lengthy debate or additional questions.[21] Finally, you might thank the person for the comments and then remind everyone that you were looking for specific questions.

Respond unemotionally to tough questions.

Surviving the Hot Seat If a question ever puts you on the hot seat, remember to be honest, but keep your cool. Look the person in the eye, answer the question as well as you can, and try not to show your feelings. Don't get into an argument. Questioners who challenge your ideas, logic, or facts may be trying to push you into overreacting. Defuse hostility by paraphrasing the question and asking the questioner to confirm that you've understood it correctly. Break long, complicated questions into parts that you can answer simply. State your response honestly, accurately, and factually; then move on to the next question. Avoid postures or gestures that might seem antagonistic. Maintain a businesslike tone of voice and a pleasant expression.[22] Remember, don't indulge in put-downs. They may backfire and make the audience more sympathetic to the questioner.

Help audience members ask you questions.

Motivating Questions In case your audience is too timid or hostile to ask questions, you might want to plant some of your own. If a friend or the meeting organizer gets the ball rolling, other people in the audience will probably join in. You might ask a question yourself: "Would you like to know more about . . ." If someone in the audience answers, act as if the question came from that person in the first place. When all else fails, say something like, "I know from experience that most questions are asked after the question period. So I'll be around afterward to talk."[23]

Concluding Your Speech   When the time allotted for your presentation is up, call a halt to the question-and-answer session, even if more people want to talk. Prepare the audience for the end by saying: "Our time is almost up. Let's have one more question." After you've made your reply, summarize the main idea of the presentation and thank people for their attention. Conclude the way you opened: by looking around the room and making eye contact. Then gather your notes and leave the podium, shoulders straight, head up. (This chapter's "Checklist: Speeches and Oral Presentations" is a reminder of the tasks involved in oral communication.)

> Finish up on time—even if people are enthusiastic to continue.

SUMMARY OF LEARNING OBJECTIVES

1 Illustrate how planning speeches differs from planning written documents. Unlike a written document, a speech is a one-time event, so audience members cannot browse through the speaker's comments to verify something said earlier. Unlike document writers, speechwriters must find a way to capture audience attention and keep it so that readers will remember what is said. To capture attention, speechwriters must be especially careful to define the purpose of their speeches (to inform, explain, persuade, or motivate) and to develop accurate audience profiles (to specifically address audience needs and interests).

2 Describe the five tasks that go into organizing speeches and presentations. When you organize a speech or presentation, you need to complete five tasks: (1) When you define the main idea, you create a one-sentence generalization that first states the one message you want your audience to walk away with and then relates that message to your audience's needs. (2) When you limit your scope, you make sure that your speech or presentation fits into the time allowed for it and that the time allowed is enough for the complexity of your subject. (3) When you choose your approach, you arrange your speech in the order that is most appropriate for your audience's receptivity and for the purpose and duration of your speech. (4) When you prepare an outline of your speech, you use it to compose your speech, to stay on task as you proceed, to make sure your speech accomplishes your purpose, and sometimes to serve as speaking notes. (5) When you decide on an appropriate style, you match the occasion of your speech—anything from a formal presentation before a large audience to a casual working session around a conference table.

3 Delineate the tasks involved in developing the four main parts of your speech. As you develop each part of your speech, you must make sure that you accomplish specific tasks. In the introduction, you must arouse audience interest, build your credibility, and preview your presentation. In the body, you must connect your ideas and hold your audience's attention. In the close, you must restate your main points, describe the next steps, and end on a positive note. And in the question-and-answer period, you must plan how to control the situation and anticipate both questions and criticisms.

4 Explain why using visuals in a speech is a good idea, and list six types of visuals commonly used with oral presentations. When a speaker makes an oral presentation, visuals create interest and clarify important points. They help listeners absorb the information being presented. They help the speaker remember the details of a speech, and thus they help the speaker appear more professional and better prepared. Types of visuals commonly used in speeches include handouts, chalkboards and whiteboards, flip charts, overheads, slides, and electronic presentations.

5 Discuss what is involved in designing effective presentation visuals, and list five important guidelines. Simplicity is the key to effective visuals. Audiences need to be able to understand the visual in just a moment or two, so text visuals should have no more than six lines of text, with no more than six words per line. Graphic visuals must be simplified versions of what would appear in a written report. The most effective visuals adhere to five guidelines: (1) limit each visual to one idea; (2) illustrate your main points (not your entire presentation); (3) use borders, pointers, and boxes to highlight important information; (4) use clip art sparingly to add color and excitement; and (5) avoid visuals that conflict with your verbal message.

6 Relate nine ways to overcome your anxiety and feel more confident. To overcome anxiety and feel more confident as a speaker, prepare more material than necessary so that the extra knowledge will reduce your nervousness. Rehearse your speech to become as familiar as possible with your topic. Think positively and see yourself as a polished professional. Right before speaking, visualize your success and tell yourself you're ready. Take a few deep breaths and remember that your audience actually wants you to succeed. Be ready by memorizing your first sentence. Be comfortable by sipping some water. If you feel you're losing your audience, don't panic; instead, pull them back by asking for their opinions or questions and involving them in the action. Keep going no matter what because you'll get better as you go.

SOLVING A COMMUNICATION DILEMMA AT THE KEYS GROUP

When Brady Keys retired from professional football in the late 1960s, he pursued his dream of owning his own business. After noticing how well a friend's restaurant was doing, he decided on a fried-chicken business.

His first hurdle was raising enough money to launch the restaurant. Ten banks said "No thanks," but he finally persuaded his former team to loan him $10,000—enough to open his first All-Pro Fried Chicken store. Within three years, he'd presented himself and his ideas to banks and to the government, convincing them to loan him enough capital to open 35 more outlets in Pittsburgh, New York, and Cleveland. By that time, he was selling a million dollars' worth of fried chicken a year.

He decided it was time to try something new—hamburgers. Keys convinced Burger King to let him try turning around a struggling Burger King franchise in Detroit's inner city. Realizing that something had to spark sales, "We introduced a couple of themes that are now universal in the industry," says Keys. "We found that black people didn't want the Whopper fixed the usual way, so we made it to order." That concept eventually formed the basis for Burger King's successful "Have It Your Way" advertising campaign. As lines began to form for the new customized whopper, Keys stationed employees at the end of the lines to take orders and cut the waiting time—a practice that has become standard in many fast-food restaurants. These innovations transformed the struggling franchise into the top-selling U.S. Burger King outlet, which Keys eventually sold.

As Keys points out, "You don't get acceptance by going in and saying 'accept me.' You get it by engaging in worthy activities." For example, Keys has used his position to help other African Americans succeed in franchising: He founded both Burger King's and KFC's Minority Franchise associations; he talked Burger King's management into awarding the construction contract for the company's first inner-city outlet to an African American general contractor; and he convinced management to increase the number of minority people on Burger King's roster of franchisees, employees, and vendors.

After taking over the Burger King franchise, Keys sold his All-Pro Fried Chicken stores and became a KFC franchisee. Most of his new outlets were in Albany, Georgia, where worthy activities became even more important. Gaining acceptance in the predominantly white community was more of a challenge than it had been in either Detroit or Pittsburgh. Says Keys, "I became a philanthropist, I stressed my athletic background, and we brought in the Harlem Globetrotters as a benefit to the Special Olympics." He also served as chairman of the board of the Albany Civic Center Commission, and he is one of the largest individual contributors to the city's March of Dimes fund.

Keys's abilities to speak, to win friends, and to influence people help him deal with employees too. He believes in giving people a chance to live up to their potential. He promotes from within, and he rewards long-term employees with a piece of the business.

In return, his employees are loyal, so his turnover is low—which keeps costs down and service up. His restaurants actually serve as a "business school" for many young people who eventually move on to more challenging careers. A recent ad campaign featured distinguished former "graduates" of the Brady Keys school of practical experience.

Keys's current projects include real estate development, a video game company, a mining and brokering business, and a movie production company. In the process of selling these ideas, he uses his speaking skills to present his ideas to potential investors, to build goodwill in the communities where he operates, and to motivate his employees.

Your Mission As a member of the Keys Group's public relations department, you help Brady Keys plan some of the speeches he delivers to employees and to business, professional, and civic groups. For the following assignments, choose the best solution and be prepared to explain your choice.

1. Keys has agreed to give a 20-minute talk in Albany, Georgia, to a group of approximately 35 businesspeople who meet for lunch and networking on a monthly basis. The president of the group has suggested that Keys deal with the topic of franchising. Which of the following purposes do you think he should try to accomplish?

    a. To inform the audience about the history of franchising in America
    b. To inspire members of the audience to buy a franchise
    c. To entertain the audience with stories about Keys's franchising experiences
    d. To analyze the impact of national franchises on small, independently owned local businesses

2. Keys has asked you to help plan a 10-minute speech that he can give to his KFC employees during the annual summer picnic. He expects up to 1,000 employees to attend. His topic is "the state of the company." His purpose is to inspire employees to keep up the good work. His main idea is that the Keys Group is doing an excellent job in meeting the competition, thanks to the efforts of the workers. What general organizational scheme do you recommend for developing this idea?

a. Chronological: Highlights of company performance over the past year and outlook for the future

b. Geographical: Performance, problems, and opportunities in each of the 11 KFC outlets

c. Topical: Achievements of various types of employees such as store managers, kitchen workers, order takers, and maintenance workers

d. Comparison and contrast: KFC versus Boston Market and other fast-food competitors

3. Keys is trying to persuade a group of investors to put some money into his new movie production company. He has prepared a presentation that describes the company's goals, activities, and financial prospects. He is currently wrestling with the introduction to the presentation. Which of the following introductions would you recommend?

a. Years ago, when I opened my first restaurant, I knew I had to do something to attract business. So I said to myself, why not try some TV advertising? I was operating on a shoestring, so I decided to write, produce, direct, and star in the commercial myself. If I'd had more money and more sense, I probably wouldn't have taken on the job, but lacking both money and experience, I was willing to try anything. Anyway, once I got started, I discovered that making commercials isn't really all that tricky. All you need is a little money, a little equipment, a little imagination, and a little luck. And Bingo! You're in business. I've made a lot of my own commercials since then, and I've thoroughly enjoyed the process.

   That's one of the reasons I decided to get into the movie business. I said to myself, "Brady, if making commercials is fun, imagine what a ball you can have making movies." But fun is only one reason to start a movie production company. My principal motive is making money. And that's what I want to talk to you about today: how you can make money in the movie business.

b. In the last 10 years, the number of movie screens in the United States has increased by 50 percent, to nearly 25,000. Those screens are all designed to do one thing: show films. But the major studios cannot possibly provide enough films to fill all these new theaters. As a result, a new breed of independent film maker is springing up, many of whom are far more profitable than their larger rivals.

   I'd like to talk to you today about how you can participate in this exciting business opportunity. I think you will be intrigued by the potential payoff and the relatively limited risk involved. I'll begin by giving you a little background on the revolution currently under way in the movie industry. Then I'll describe the film production company that I'm forming in partnership with actor Leon Issac Kennedy. After you've heard our strategy and plans, I'll brief you on the returns that you could expect on your investment in my business.

c. When's the last time you went to the movies? And when did you last see a film on HBO or network TV? What about videocassettes? Have you rented any of them lately?

If you're like most people, you're hooked on movies, whether you see them in theaters or on TV. Somebody is making all those movies, and it isn't necessarily Paramount or Walt Disney. Many of the films you see are created by independent companies.

Starting an independent film production company requires relatively little capital, and the financial returns can be considerable. If you're careful, you can produce a low-budget film for as little as $2 million. Even if you don't do well at the box office, you can still clear perhaps $3 or $4 million from the TV rights and videocassette sales. Multiply that by 10 movies per year, and you have a $30- to $40-million business.

d. Who wouldn't jump at the chance to rub shoulders with box-office stars such as Sharon Stone, Spike Lee, Julia Roberts, Tom Cruise, Winona Ryder, Denzel Washington, Martin Lawrence, Russell Crowe, and Jennifer Lopez? Well, those are just some of the famous actors you'll meet when you visit the movie production company we're going to build together. Notice that I said "when" and not "if." After you've heard my speech today, you'll agree that there's no better place to invest your cash than in our movie production company.

Although you'll be happy you made this investment, we all know that money isn't everything. You'll also have the prestige of working on Hollywood's most exciting movies with the biggest names in the business. Give me your attention for a few minutes as I talk about the movies we're considering right now.

4. In his role as chairman of the board of the Albany Civic Center Commission, Keys must give a speech outlining the center's financial position. The audience will include other board members, the mayor and members of the city council, and a group of 15 to 20 influential business and professional people. How should he handle the quantitative financial details?

a. He should prepare handouts that summarize the financial data in tabular and graphic form. As the audience arrives, he should give everyone a copy of the handout and refer to it during the speech.

b. Keys should write the information on a blackboard while he delivers the speech.

c. He should prepare simple overhead transparencies to use during the speech. As he concludes his remarks, he should tell the audience that detailed financial statements are available at the door for those who are interested.

d. Given the size and importance of the audience, he should show full-color 35-mm slides that summarize the financial information in tabular and graphic format. The slides should be professionally prepared to ensure their quality.[24]

TEST YOUR KNOWLEDGE

1. What are the three steps in planning an oral presentation?

2. What is the purpose of defining the main idea of a speech?

3. Why do you have to limit your scope when planning a presentation?

4. What do you want to achieve with the introduction to your speech? With the close of your speech?

5. What six types of visuals are commonly used in presentations?

6. What are five key rules for designing effective presentation visuals?

7. How does the delivery method of impromptu speaking differ from the delivery method of speaking from notes?

8. As a speaker, what nonverbal signals can you send to appear more confident?

9. What can speakers do to maintain control during the question-and-answer period of a presentation?

10. Why is simplicity of organization important in oral communication?

INTERACTIVE LEARNING

USE THIS TEXT'S ONLINE RESOURCES

Visit the myPHLIP Web site at www.prenhall.com/thill. For Chapter 13, take advantage of the interactive "Study Guide" to test your chapter knowledge. Get instant feedback on whether you need additional studying. Read the "Current Events" articles to get the latest on chapter topics and complete the exercises—as specified by your instructor.

This site's "Study Hall" helps you succeed in this course. "Talk in the Hall" lets you leave messages and meet new friends online. If you have a question, you can "Ask the Tutor." And to get a better grade in this course, you can find more help at "Writing Skills," and "Study Tips."

The "Research Area" helps you locate a wealth of information to use in course assignments. Plus, you can send a message to online research experts, who will help you find exactly the information you need.

APPLY YOUR KNOWLEDGE

1. Would you rather (a) give a speech to an outside audience, (b) be interviewed for a news story, or (c) make a presentation to a departmental meeting? Why? How do the communication skills differ among those situations? Explain.

2. How might the audience's attitude affect the amount of audience interaction during or after a presentation? Explain your answer.

3. What are some of the advantages and disadvantages of distributing handouts before a presentation, and what can you do to minimize the disadvantages?

4. From the speaker's perspective, what are the advantages and disadvantages of responding to questions from the audience throughout a speech or presentation rather than just afterward? From the listener's perspective, which approach would you prefer? Why?

5. **Ethical Choices** What ethical concerns are raised by a speech that encourages audience members to take illegal or questionable actions?

PRACTICE YOUR KNOWLEDGE

DOCUMENT FOR ANALYSIS

Pick a speech from *Vital Speeches of the Day*, a publication containing recent speeches on timely and topical subjects. As an alternative, select a speech from an online source such as the speech archives of NASA (www.nasa.gov) or AT&T (www.att.com/speeches). Examine both the introduction and the close; then analyze how these two sections work together to emphasize the main idea. What action does the speaker want the audience to take?

Next, identify the transitional sentences or phrases that clarify the speech's structure for the listener, especially those that help the speaker shift between supporting points. Using these transitions as clues, list the main message and supporting points; then indicate how each transitional phrase links the current supporting point to the succeeding one. Now, prepare a brief (two- to three-minute) oral presentation summarizing your analysis for your class.

EXERCISES

13-1. **Internet** For many years, Toastmasters has been dedicated to helping its members give speeches. Instruction, good speakers as models, and practice sessions aim to teach members to convey information in lively and informative ways. Visit the Toastmasters Web site at www.toastmasters.org and carefully review the linked pages about listening, speaking, voice, and body. Evaluate the information and outline a three-minute presentation to your class telling why Toastmasters and its Web site would or would not help you and your classmates write and deliver an effective speech.

13-2. **Mastering Delivery: Analysis** Attend a speech at your school or in your area, or watch a speech on television. Categorize the speech as one that motivates or entertains, one that informs or analyzes, or one that persuades or urges collaboration. Then compare the speaker's delivery and use of visual aids with this chapter's "Checklist: Speeches and Oral Presentations." Write a two-page report analyzing the speaker's performance and suggesting improvements.

13-3. **Mastering Delivery: Nonverbal Signals** Observe and analyze the delivery of a speaker in a school, work, or other setting. What type of delivery did the speaker use? Was this delivery appropriate for the occasion? What nonverbal signals did the speaker use to emphasize key points? Were these signals effective? Which nonverbal signals would you suggest to further enhance the delivery of this speech—and why?

13-4. **Ethical Choices** Think again about the speech you observed and analyzed in 13.3. How could the speaker have used nonverbal signals to unethically manipulate the audience's attitudes or actions?

13-5. **Teamwork** You've been asked to give an informative 10-minute talk on vacation opportunities in your home state. Draft your introduction, which should last no more than 2 minutes. Then pair off with a classmate and analyze each other's introductions. How well do these two introductions arouse the audience's interest, build credibility, and preview the presentation? Suggest how these introductions might be improved.

13-6. **Completing Speeches: Visuals** Which types of visual aids would you use to accompany each of the following speeches? Explain your answers.

a. An informal 10-minute speech explaining the purpose of a new training program to 300 assembly-line employees

b. An informal 10-minute speech explaining the purpose of a new training program to five vice presidents

c. A formal five-minute presentation explaining the purpose of a new training program to the company's 12-member board of directors

d. A formal 5-minute speech explaining the purpose of a new company training program to 35 members of the press

13-7. **Completing Speeches: Self-Assessment** How good are you at planning, writing, and delivering speeches? Rate yourself on each of the following elements of the oral presentation process. Then examine your ratings to identify where you are strongest and where you can improve, using the tips in this chapter.

ELEMENT OF PRESENTATION PROCESS	ALWAYS	FREQUENTLY	OCCASIONALLY	NEVER
1. I start by defining my purpose.	___	___	___	___
2. I analyze my audience before writing a speech.	___	___	___	___
3. I match my speech length to the allotted time.	___	___	___	___
4. I begin my speeches with an attention-getting introduction.	___	___	___	___
5. I look for ways to build credibility as a speaker.	___	___	___	___
6. I cover only a few main points in the body of my speech.	___	___	___	___
7. I use transitions to help listeners follow my ideas.	___	___	___	___
8. I review main points and describe next steps in the close.	___	___	___	___
9. I choose visual aids appropriate for the audience and occasion.	___	___	___	___
10. I design simple visual aids to supplement my speech.	___	___	___	___
11. I practice my speech, with visuals, before the presentation.	___	___	___	___
12. I prepare in advance for questions and objections.	___	___	___	___
13. I conclude speeches by summarizing my main idea.	___	___	___	___

GOING ONLINE EXERCISES

Speak with Flair, page 406

Do you need new ideas for a speech that you're planning to deliver or material for an oral presentation? When you log on to the Virtual Presentation Assistant, you'll find examples of speeches, advice on delivery, and plentiful resources to help you prepare or improve a speech.

1. Suppose you have been asked to prepare a speaking project on a business issue currently in the news. How could you use what you've discovered at the VPA site to help you select a topic? How could you use this site to find additional information or supplementary materials related to your project?
2. List some reasons that visual aids are an important aspect of oral presentations. Describe two practical tips on preparing effective visual aids that you discovered using the VPA site or its links.
3. What topics or information will entice you to return to this site or its links? (If you don't find the Virtual Presentation Assistant useful, explain why.)

   To complete this exercise, log on to this text's Web Site at www.prenhall.com/thill. Select Chapter 13, then select "Student Resources," click on the name of the featured Web site, and follow the detailed navigational directions.

Employment Messages

part **V**

chapter 14

Writing Résumés and
Application Letters

chapter 15

Interviewing for
Employment and
Following Up

On the job:

FACING A COMMUNICATION DILEMMA AT PINKERTON

Keeping a Private Eye on Hiring

www.pinkertons.com

When you screen more than a million job applicants every year, you're sure to gain an in-depth knowledge of employment messages. That's the kind of expertise that Pinkerton has developed. Just one of the many security and protection services Pinkerton performs around the world is screening job applicants for clients (as well as for its own operations), but the company takes great pride in matching the right person to the right job.

Pinkerton clients range from General Motors, which spends roughly a hundred million dollars on Pinkerton's services every year, to the Academy of Motion Picture Arts and Sciences, which relies on Pinkerton to protect the rich and famous during the Academy Awards presentation in Los Angeles. Uniformed security services make up the bulk of Pinkerton's business, but the company is working to become a one-stop shop for asset-protection services. This includes electronic surveillance systems, undercover investigations, access control, insurance investigations, crisis management, ethics monitoring programs, and a wide variety of related services.

In charge of all this is CEO Denis Brown, whose background is even more diverse than Pinkerton's—his jobs range from helping develop the Global Positioning System to turning around a troubled supercomputer maker. Throughout his career, Brown has had the opportunity to review plenty of job applications for all kinds of positions.

If you were Brown, what qualities would you look for in a job applicant? How would you want Pinkerton to evaluate the résumés and application letters it receives? What would you think constitutes a good résumé? A good application letter? What steps would you take to screen job candidates?[1]

Like most companies today, Pinkerton is looking for applicants who are well educated, well trained, and well spoken. The process usually begins with a résumé and culminates with an interview.

BUILDING TOWARD A CAREER

Employers such as Denis Brown seek people who are able and willing to adapt to diverse situations, who thrive in an ever-changing workplace, and who continue to learn throughout their careers. Companies want team players with strong work records and leaders who are versatile. Many companies are encouraging their managers to get more varied job experience.[2] In some cases, your chances of being hired are better if you've studied abroad or learned another language. Most employers expect college graduates to be sensitive to intercultural differences and to have a sound understanding of international affairs.[3] Keep these things in mind as you build toward your career in the following ways:

◆ **Keep an employment portfolio.** Get a three-ring notebook and a package of plastic sleeves that open at the top. Collect anything that shows your ability to perform (classroom or work evaluations, certificates, awards, papers you've written). Your portfolio is a great resource for writing your résumé, and it gives employers tangible evidence of your professionalism.

◆ **Take interim assignments.** As you search for a permanent job, consider temporary or freelance work. Also gain a competitive edge by participating in an internship program. These temporary assignments not only help you gain valuable experience and relevant contacts but also provide you with important references and with items for your portfolio.[4]

◆ **Work on polishing and updating your skills.** Whenever possible, join networks of professional colleagues and friends who can help you keep up with your occupation and industry. While waiting for responses to your résumé, take a computer course, or seek out other educational or life experiences that would be hard to get while working full-time.

◆ **Learn about the services offered by your campus career center.** Placement offices offer individual counseling, credential services, job fairs, on-campus interviews, and job listings. They can give you advice on résumé-writing software and provide workshops in job-search techniques, résumé preparation, interview techniques, and more.[5]

◆ **Don't think the process is over once an employer hires you.** The best thing you can do for your long-term career is to continue learning. Listen to and learn from the experienced people around you. Be ready and willing to take on new responsibilities, and actively pursue new or better skills.

Not least important, when you send out employment messages, you need to showcase your communication skill. Write these messages carefully by following the Three-Step Writing Process (see Figure 14–1). Many of the employment messages you'll write depend on how carefully you plan, write, and complete your résumé. A well-written résumé can help you write other employment messages and can distinguish you from all the other people looking for work.

PLANNING YOUR RÉSUMÉ

As Denis Brown will tell you, analysis and research are important if you want to find a company that suits you. Before you limit your employment search to a particular industry or job, analyze what you have to offer and what you hope to get from your work. Only then can you identify employers who are likely to want you and vice versa. And only then will you be able to adapt your résumé to those employers.

Analyze Résumé Components

To be successful, your résumé must be more than a simple list of jobs you've held. As with other business messages, planning a résumé means analyzing your purpose and your audience. Plus, you'll need to take your analysis a bit further by looking at your own needs and talents.

Objective
1
Explain why companies are encouraging employees to get more varied job experience, and list five ways to build toward a career.

Your chances of getting a job are increased by career-building efforts.

As with other business messages, the three-step writing process can help you plan, write, and complete your résumé and other employment messages.

Objective
2
Delineate the three things that need to be analyzed when planning a résumé.

1 Planning

Analyze: Study your purpose, your employment skills and desires, and your audience.
Investigate: Gather relevant employment information to find the best job opportunities.
Adapt: Use audience focus to convey your qualifications honestly and to match your skills with each employer.

2 Writing

Organize: Identify the best type of résumé for conveying your particular educational and employment experience.
Compose: Adopt a style that is direct, brief, and crisp. Use action verbs to focus on your educational background, employment history, related extracurricular activities, and professional achievements.

3 Completing

Revise: Evaluate content, revising for both clarity and conciseness, and avoid known common mistakes.
Produce: Ensure a clean, sharp look when producing your traditional, electronic, or online version.
Proofread: Look for errors in spelling and mechanics.

Figure 14–1
Three-Step Writing Process for Employment Messages

Table 14–1   Fallacies and Facts about Résumés

Fallacy	Fact
⊗ The purpose of a résumé is to list all your skills and abilities.	☑ The purpose of a résumé is to kindle employer interest and generate an interview.
⊗ A good résumé will get you the job you want.	☑ All a résumé can do is get you in the door.
⊗ Your résumé will be read carefully and thoroughly by an interested employer.	☑ Your résumé probably has less than 45 seconds to make an impression.
⊗ The more good information you present about yourself in your résumé the better.	☑ Too much information on a résumé may actually kill the reader's appetite to know more.
⊗ If you want a really good résumé, have it prepared by a résumé service.	☑ Prepare your own résumé—unless the position is especially high-level or specialized. Even then, you should check carefully before using a service.

Your résumé is a structured, written summary of your educational and employment background, and it shows your qualifications for a job.

The purpose of the résumé is to get you an interview.

What you have to offer:
• Functional skills
• Education and experience
• Personality traits

Belinda Guadarrama is president and CEO of GC Micro Corporation, one of the 500 largest Hispanic-owned companies. She hopes that she can serve as an example of leadership to Hispanic youth and other women. "You can achieve any goal in life if you help enough other people reach their goals," says Guadarrama. She knows first-hand that being true to your own values helps you achieve your objective.

Envision the ideal "day at the office." What would you enjoy doing every day?

Know Your Purpose   A **résumé** is a structured, written summary of a person's education, employment background, and job qualifications. Although many people have some misconceptions about résumés (see Table 14–1), the fact is that a résumé is a form of advertising. It is intended to stimulate an employer's interest in you—in meeting you and learning more about you. A successful résumé inspires a prospective employer to pick up the phone and ask you to come in for an interview.

Your purpose in writing your résumé is to create interest—*not* to tell readers everything about you. In fact, it may be best to only hint at some things and leave the reader wanting more. The potential employer will then have even more reason to reach for the phone.[6]

Know Yourself   Before you can create a successful résumé, you have to know what talents and skills you have. Because you want to attract the interest of the right employers, you must also analyze what you want and expect from the people and organizations who will be receiving your résumé.

What Do You Have to Offer?   Get started by jotting down 10 achievements you're proud of, such as learning to ski, taking a prize-winning photo, tutoring a child, or editing your school paper. Think carefully about what specific skills these achievements demanded. For example, leadership skills, speaking ability, and artistic talent may have helped you coordinate a winning presentation to your school's administration. As you analyze your achievements, you'll begin to recognize a pattern of skills. Which of them might be valuable to potential employers?

Next, look at your educational preparation, work experience, and extracurricular activities. What do your knowledge and experience qualify you to do? What have you learned from volunteer work or class projects that could benefit you on the job? Have you held any offices, won any awards or scholarships, mastered a second language?

Take stock of your personal characteristics. Are you aggressive, a born leader? Or would you rather follow? Are you outgoing, articulate, great with people? Or do you prefer working alone? Make a list of what you believe are your four or five most important qualities. Ask a relative or friend to rate your traits as well.

If you're having trouble figuring out your interests, characteristics, or capabilities, consult your college placement office. Many campuses administer a variety of tests to help you identify interests, aptitudes, and personality traits. These tests won't reveal your "perfect" job, but they'll help you focus on the types of work best suited to your personality.

What Do You Want to Do?   Knowing what you *can* do is one thing. Knowing what you *want* to do is another. Don't lose sight of your own values. Discover the things that will bring you satisfaction and happiness on the job.

◆ **What would you like to do every day?** Talk to people in various occupations. You might consult relatives, local businesses, or former graduates (through your school's alumni relations office). Read about various occupations. Start with your college library or placement office.

◆ **How would you like to work?** Consider how much independence you want on the job, how much variety you like, and whether you prefer to work with products, machines, people, ideas, figures, or some combination thereof. Do you like physical work, mental work, or a mix? Constant change or a predictable role?

◆ **What specific compensation do you expect?** What do you hope to earn in your first year? What kind of pay increase do you expect each year? What's your ultimate earnings goal? Would you be comfortable getting paid on commission, or do you prefer a steady paycheck? Are you willing to settle for less money in order to do something you really love?

◆ **Can you establish some general career goals?** Consider where you'd like to start, where you'd like to go from there, and the ultimate position you'd like to attain. How soon after joining the company would you like to receive your first promotion? Your next one? What additional training or preparation will you need to achieve them?

◆ **What size company would you prefer?** Do you like the idea of working for a small, entrepreneurial operation? A small family business? Or would you prefer a large corporation?

◆ **What type of operation is appealing to you?** A profit-making company or a nonprofit organization? Are you attracted to service businesses or manufacturing operations? Do you want regular, predictable hours, or do you thrive on flexible, varied hours? Would you enjoy a seasonally varied job such as education (which may give you summers off) or retailing (with its selling cycles)?

◆ **What location would you like?** Would you like to work in a city, a suburb, a small town, an industrial area, or an uptown setting? Do you favor a particular part of the country? A country abroad? Do you like working indoors or outdoors?

◆ **What facilities do you envision?** Is it important to you to work in an attractive place, or will simple, functional quarters suffice? Do you need a quiet office to work effectively, or can you concentrate in a noisy, open setting? Is access to public transportation or freeways important?

◆ **What sort of corporate culture are you most comfortable with?** Would you be happy in a formal hierarchy with clear reporting relationships? Or do you prefer less structure? Are you looking for a paternalistic firm or one that fosters individualism? Do you like a competitive environment? One that rewards teamwork? What qualities do you want in a boss?

Know Your Audience   When searching for the job you want, you can save considerable time and effort by understanding how employers approach the recruiting process (see Figure 14–2). The quickest way to land a job is to get a referral from someone you know in the company. Personal contacts appear to be the prime source of jobs, regardless of whether applicants have just graduated from college or have been out of school for several years.[7] Many companies pay handsome referral bonuses to their employees for recommending a candidate who is hired and who stays for a designated period.[8]

But don't despair if you lack contacts. Many organizations send representatives to college campuses to interview students for job openings. These interviews are usually coordinated by the campus placement office, which keeps files of college records, data sheets, and recommendation letters for all students registered for the service.

Marginal notes:

How much do you want to earn, and how high do you hope to climb?

What type of industry and organization do you want to work in?

What type of corporate culture best suits you?

Employers find job candidates through
• Employee referrals
• On-campus interviews
• Placement agencies
• Unsolicited résumés
• Advertisements

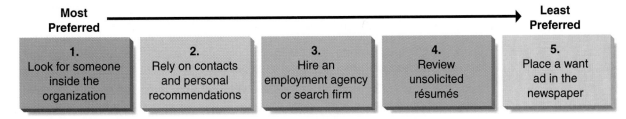

Most Preferred ——————————————→ **Least Preferred**

1.	2.	3.	4.	5.
Look for someone inside the organization	Rely on contacts and personal recommendations	Hire an employment agency or search firm	Review unsolicited résumés	Place a want ad in the newspaper

Figure 14–2
How Organizations Prefer to Find New Employees

Many companies accept unsolicited résumés. Growing companies like to maintain a steady influx of potential employees. In tight labor markets, companies probably have jobs for any good candidate they happen upon.[9] Most companies keep unsolicited résumés on file or in a database.

Employers also recruit candidates through employment agencies, state employment services, temporary staffing services, and the employment bureaus operated by some trade associations. They also post jobs through classified and display ads in newspapers, trade magazines, and campus publications. Some CEOs are even using nontraditional recruiting media, such as radio and television.[10] Many have begun advertising positions on the Internet.

Investigate Employment Opportunities and Information

If you haven't already committed yourself to a particular career field, first find out where the job opportunities are. Which industries are strong? Which parts of the country are booming, and which specific job categories offer the best prospects for the future?

Begin with Journals and Periodicals   In Chapter 11, we discuss how to research and find information on individual companies and industries, and we provide a list of popular business resources. Begin your job search by reviewing those sources, as well as professional and trade journals in the fields that interest you. Talk to people working in these fields. You may be able to network with executives in your field by joining or participating in student business organizations, especially those with ties to real-world organizations such as the American Marketing Association or the American Management Association.

Stay Abreast of Business and Financial News   If you don't already do so, subscribe to a major newspaper and scan the business pages every day. Watch some of the television programs that focus on business, such as *Wall Street Week.* You can find information about the future of specific jobs in the *Dictionary of Occupational Titles* (U.S. Employment Service), the *Occupational Outlook Handbook* (U.S. Bureau of Labor Statistics), and the employment publications of Science Research Associates.

Research Specific Companies   Once you've identified a promising industry and career field, compile a list of specific organizations that appeal to you (perhaps by consulting directories of employers at your college library or career center). Write to the organizations on your list, asking for an annual report and any descriptive brochures or newsletters. Find out whether a company maintains a Web site. Those that do generally include a company profile, press releases, financial information, and information on employment opportunities. If possible, visit some of the organizations on your list, contact their personnel departments, or talk with key employees. You can find ads for specific job openings by looking in local and major newspapers and by visiting your college placement office.

Use the Web   A source of growing importance to your job search is the Internet. An increasing number of large and small companies are posting job openings on the Internet. The Web offers an amazing amount of employment information, not only from employers seeking applicants but also from people seeking work. You can use the Web for a variety of job-seeking tasks:

◆ **Finding career counseling.** You can begin your self-assessment with the Keirsey Temperament Sorter, an online personality test at www.advisorteam.com/user/ktsintro. asp. For excellent job-seeking pointers and counseling, visit college- and university-run online career centers. Commercial career centers range from award winning to depressing, so make sure their advice is both useful and sensible.

◆ **Making contacts.** Locate and communicate with potential employers through discussion groups dedicated to your field. Usenet newsgroups provide an electronic bulletin board so that members can leave and retrieve messages whenever they visit. Listservs (Internet mailing lists) send each message to every member's e-mail address. Commercial systems (Prodigy, America Online, etc.) have their own discussion groups (and make a profit from

---

Margin notes:

Find out where the job opportunities are.

Make a list of desirable employers.

The Web offers valuable information and advice to job seekers.

the time users spend accessing their services). Once you locate a potential contact, use e-mail to request information or to state your interest in working for a company.

◆ **Researching companies.** Many companies include job listings on their Web site. Visit a company's Web site to find out about its mission, products, annual reports, employee benefits, and job openings. Locate company sites by knowing the URL (Web address), using links from other sites, or using a search engine such as Alta Vista, Lycos, or Excite.

◆ **Searching for job vacancies.** You can also find jobs at sites that list openings from multiple companies. See "Using the Power of Technology—Netting a Job on the Web" on page 438 for a list of popular online indexes (or job boards), many of which allow you to search by region, industry, job title, company, skills, or requirements. The Web offers no central, unified marketplace, so try to be selective in the sites you visit.

◆ **Posting your résumé online.** To post your résumé with an index service, you must convert it to an electronic format (see page 448) before transmitting it by mail, fax, modem, or e-mail. Once in the service's database, your résumé is sent to employers who match the key words you've listed. When posting your résumé on your home page, you can retain a nicer-looking format and make links to papers you've written, recommendations, and sound or video clips.

Using the Web to seek employment offers certain advantages. You can respond directly to job postings without going through recruiters, gain detailed information about your prospective employers, post tailor-made résumés (that match the qualifications required by a particular position), send résumés quickly and cheaply through e-mail, and send focused cover letters directly to the executives doing the hiring. In fact, most campus placement offices are retooling to help you take advantage of Web opportunities. Even so, at least 10 million U.S. employers don't think of the Internet when it's time to hire. So the Web doesn't replace other techniques for finding employment—it's just one more tool in your overall strategy.

> Despite the Web's obvious advantages, you must use other job-seeking tools to be successful.

Adapt Your Résumé to Your Audience

Your résumé has very little time to make an impression, so adopt a "you" attitude, and think about your résumé from the employer's perspective. Ask yourself: What key qualifications will this employer be looking for? Which of these qualifications are your greatest strengths? What quality would set you apart from other candidates in the eyes of a potential employer? What are three or four of your greatest accomplishments, and what resulted from these accomplishments?

A good résumé is flexible and can be customized for different situations and different employers. If you're applying for a marketing job at an international company such as Hewlett-Packard, the first skill on your list might be your ability to speak French. However, if you're applying for a sales position at Frito Lay, the first skill on your list will probably be your summer job building product displays at a local grocery store. It's perfectly fine to have several résumés, each tailored for a different type of position or company.

> Tailor your résumé to fit diverse situations and employers.

It's up to you to combine your experiences into a straightforward message that communicates what you can do for your potential employer.[11] Think in terms of an image or a theme you'd like to project. Are you academically gifted? A campus leader? A well-rounded person? A creative genius? A technical wizard? Don't exaggerate, and don't alter the past or claim skills you don't have. However, don't dwell on negatives, either. By knowing yourself and your audience, you'll focus successfully on the strengths that are needed by potential employers.

WRITING YOUR RÉSUMÉ

To interest potential employers in your résumé, call attention to your best features and downplay your weaknesses—without distorting or misrepresenting the facts.[12] A successful résumé conveys seven qualities that employers seek. It shows that a candidate (1) thinks in terms of results, (2) knows how to get things done, (3) is well rounded, (4) shows signs of progress, (5) has personal standards of excellence, (6) is flexible and

Using the Power of Technology

Netting a Job on the Web

Is the Web the answer to all your employment dreams? Perhaps . . . or perhaps not. As the Web grows, the employment information it provides is constantly expanding. And you're fortunate, because you don't have to start from scratch like some intrepid adventurer. For helpful hints and useful Web addresses, you can turn to books such as *What Color Is Your Parachute?* by Richard Nelson Bolles. Other places to check out online include the following:

❏ *America's Career InfoNet* (www.acinet.org). Good place to begin. Offers information on typical wages and employment trends. Gives education, knowledge, and skills requirements for most occupations. Includes links to multiple career resources on the Internet.

❏ *The Monster Board* (www.monster.com). Posts more than 25,000 openings and 300,000 résumés. Heavily marketed, it brings a flood of employers (many with under 500 employees).

❏ *America's Job Bank** (www.ajb.dni.us). State agencies post an average of 5,000 new openings each day on this government site. Companies contribute another 3,000.

❏ *HotJobs.Com* (www.hotjobs.com). This member-based site charges companies a hefty fee to post openings or search through résumés. Job seekers can create a personal page to manage their search and collect statistics on how many companies have retrieved their résumé.

❏ *Career Magazine* (www.careermag.com). Features topics such as interviewing, networking, and preparing résumés. Includes searchable index of job openings, employer profiles, résumé bank, news items, and calendars for job fairs and campus recruiting.

❏ *Nationjob Network* (www.nationjob.com). Posts more than 15,000 jobs nationwide, with an emphasis on those in the Midwest.

❏ *Headhunter* (www.headhunter.net). More then 70,000 jobs are updated daily on this site. Includes a career resources center.

❏ *4Work* (www.4work.com). One of the few sites that includes listings of internships and volunteer opportunities.

❏ *Net-Temps* (www.net-temps.com). Maintained by career consultants, this site offers several thousand updated listings and real-time seminars. Network forums help you develop new contacts and job leads. Includes chat room for online interviews.

❏ *Careerbuilder* (www.careerbuilder.com). Offers a network of career services, job-search information, and tips on how to succeed once you're hired. Includes a database of 20,000 openings.

❏ *Job Trak* (www.jobtrak.com). Has formed partnerships with 750 campuses nationwide and serves as a virtual career center for students and alumni. Many entry-level postings.

❏ *Yahoo! Classifieds* (classifieds.yahoo.com). Offers extensive listing of companies by city, in addition to a wealth of job-related information at the parent Web site, www.yahoo.com. Click on Business & Economy/Jobs/Company Job Listings.

CAREER APPLICATIONS

1. Surfing the Web can chew up a disproportionate amount of your job-seeking time. Explain how you can limit the amount of time you spend on the Web and still make it work for you.

2. When posting your résumé on the World Wide Web, you're revealing a lot of information about yourself that could be used by people other than employers (salespeople, people competing for similar positions, con artists). What sort of information might you leave off your Web résumé that would certainly appear on a traditional résumé?

*Direct links to this Web site can be accessed at the Riley Guide at www.dbm.com/jobguide.

---

willing to try new things, and (7) possesses strong communication skills. As you organize and compose your résumé, think about how you can convey those seven qualities.

O b j e c t i v e
3

Discuss how to choose the appropriate organization for your résumé and list the advantages or disadvantages of the three options.

Select an organizational pattern that focuses attention on your strengths.

Organize your Résumé Around Your Strengths

Although you may want to include a little information in all categories, emphasize the information that has a bearing on your career objective, and minimize or exclude any that is irrelevant or counterproductive. Focus attention on your strongest points by adopting an organizational approach—chronological, functional, or combination. The "right" choice depends on your background and goals.

The Chronological Résumé In a **chronological résumé,** the "Work Experience" section dominates and is placed in the most prominent slot, immediately after the name and address and the objective. You develop this section by listing your jobs sequentially in reverse order, beginning with the most recent position and working backward toward earlier jobs. Under each listing, describe your responsibilities and accomplishments, giving the most space to the most recent positions. If you're just graduating from college, you can vary this chronological approach by putting your educational qualifications before your experience, thereby focusing attention on your academic credentials.

The chronological approach is the most common way to organize a résumé, and many employers prefer it. This approach has three key advantages: (1) employers are familiar with it and can easily find information, (2) it highlights growth and career progression, and (3) it highlights employment continuity and stability.[13] As vice president with Korn/Ferry International, Robert Nesbit speaks for many recruiters: "Unless you have a really compelling reason, don't use any but the standard chronological format. Your résumé should not read like a treasure map, full of minute clues to the whereabouts of your jobs and experience. I want to be able to grasp quickly where a candidate has worked, how long, and in what capacities."[14]

Most recruiters prefer the chronological plan: a historical summary of your education and work experience.

The chronological approach is especially appropriate if you have a strong employment history and are aiming for a job that builds on your current career path. This is the case for Roberto Cortez, whose résumé appears in Figure 14–3.

The Functional Résumé A **functional résumé** emphasizes a list of skills and accomplishments, identifying employers and academic experience in subordinate sections. This pattern stresses individual areas of competence, so it's useful for people who are just entering the job market, want to redirect their careers, or have little continuous career-related experience. The functional approach also has three advantages: (1) without having to read through job descriptions, employers can see what you can do for them, (2) you can emphasize earlier job experience, and (3) you can de-emphasize any lack of career progress or lengthy unemployment.

A functional résumé focuses attention on your areas of competence.

Figure 14–4 illustrates how Glenda Johns uses the functional approach to showcase her qualifications for a career in retail. Although she has not held any paid, full-time positions in retail sales, Johns has participated in work-experience programs, and she knows a good deal about the profession from research and from talking with people in the industry. She organized her résumé in a way that demonstrates her ability to handle such a position. Bear in mind, however, that many seasoned employment professionals are suspect of this résumé style. They assume that candidates who use it are trying to hide something.[15]

The Combination Résumé A **combination résumé** includes the best features of the chronological and functional approaches. Nevertheless, it is not commonly used, and it has two major disadvantages: (1) it tends to be longer, and (2) it can be repetitious if you have to list your accomplishments and skills in both the functional section and the chronological job descriptions.[16] When Erica Vorkamp developed her résumé, she chose not to use a chronological pattern, which would focus attention on her lack of recent work experience. As Figure 14–5 shows, she used a combination approach to emphasize her abilities, skills, and accomplishments while also including a complete job history.

A combination résumé is a hybrid of the chronological and functional résumés.

Compose Your Résumé to Impress

To save your readers time and to state your information as forcefully as possible, write your résumé using a simple and direct style. Use short, crisp phrases instead of whole sentences, and focus on what your reader needs to know. Absolutely avoid using the word *I*. Instead, start your phrases with impressive action verbs such as these:[17]

To capture attention quickly, leave out the word *I*, and begin your phrases with strong, action verbs.

accomplished	coordinated	initiated	participated	set up
achieved	created	installed	performed	simplified
administered	demonstrated	introduced	planned	sparked
approved	developed	investigated	presented	streamlined
arranged	directed	joined	proposed	strengthened
assisted	established	launched	raised	succeeded
assumed	explored	maintained	recommended	supervised
budgeted	forecasted	managed	reduced	systematized
changed	generated	motivated	reorganized	targeted
chaired	identified	operated	resolved	trained
compiled	implemented	organized	saved	transformed
completed	improved	oversaw	served	upgraded

1 Planning

Analyze: Decide how best to combine accounting expertise with international experience.

Investigate: Gather information from contracts and research.

Adapt: Point out specific achievements to interest potential employers.

2 Writing

Organize: A chronological résumé will best emphasize years of work experience.

Compose: The style is direct, brief, and crisp, using action verbs to focus on employment history, professional achievements, and international abilities.

3 Completing

Revise: Make content clear and concise.

Produce: Give traditional résumé a clean, sharp look with dates set off in margin.

Proofread: Review for spelling and mechanical errors.

ROBERTO CORTEZ
5687 Crosswoods Drive
Falls Church, Virginia 22046
Home: (703) 987-0086   Office: (703) 549-6624

OBJECTIVE

Accounting management position requiring a knowledge of international finance

EXPERIENCE

March 1997 to present

Staff Accountant/Financial Analyst, Inter-American Imports (Alexandria, VA)
- Prepare accounting reports for wholesale giftware importer ($15 million annual sales)
- Audit financial transactions with suppliers in 12 Latin American countries
- Create a computerized model to adjust accounts for fluctuations in currency exchange rates
- Negotiate joint-venture agreements with major suppliers in Mexico and Colombia
- Implement electronic funds transfer for vendor dispursements, improving cash flow and eliminating payables clerk position

October 1993 to March 1997

Staff Accountant, Monsanto Agricultural Chemicals (Mexico City, Mexico)
- Handled budgeting, billing, and credit-processing functions for the Mexico City branch
- Audited travel/entertainment expenses for Monsanto's 30-member Latin American sales force
- Assisted in launching an online computer system to automate all accounting functions

EDUCATION

1991 to 1993

M.B.A. with emphasis on international business
George Mason University (Fairfax, Virginia)

1987 to 1991

B.B.A., Accounting
University of Texas, Austin

INTERCULTURAL AND TECHNICAL SKILLS

- Fluent in Spanish and German
- Traveled extensively in Latin America
- Excel • Access • HTML • Visual Basic

Highlights career progress with chronological organization.

Emphasizes achievements with an indented bulleted list.

Highlights foreign language and technological skills by presenting them in a special skills section.

Figure 14–3
In-Depth Critique: Chronological Résumé

Describes relevant skills first because Johns is a recent graduate.

Uses action verbs to enhance résumé effectiveness.

Describes but does not emphasize Johns' sketchy work history.

Calls attention to leadership abilities and experience by listing her leadership positions in a separate section.

The résumé content:

Glenda S. Johns

Home: 457 Mountain View Road
Clear Lake, IA 50428
(515) 633-5971

College: 1254 Main Street
Council Bluffs, IA 51505
(712) 438-5254

OBJECTIVE

Retailing position that utilizes my experience

RELEVANT SKILLS

- Personal Selling/Retailing
  - Led housewares department in employee sales for spring 1999
  - Created end-cap and shelf displays for special housewares promotions
  - Sold the most benefit tickets during college fund-raising drive for local community center
- Public Interaction
  - Commended by housewares manager for resolving customer complaints amicably
  - Performed in summer theater productions in Clear Lake, Iowa
- Managing
  - Trained part-time housewares employees in cash register operation and customer service
  - Reworked housewares employee schedules as assistant manager
  - Organized summer activities for children 6–12 years old for city of Clear Lake, Iowa—including reading programs, sports activities, and field trips

EDUCATION

- AA, Retailing Mid-Management (3.81 GPA / 4.0 scale), Iowa Western Community College, June 2000
- In addition to required retailing, buying, marketing, and merchandising courses, completed electives in visual merchandising, business information systems, principles of management, and business math

WORK EXPERIENCE

- Assistant manager, housewares, at Jefferson's Department Store during off-campus work experience program, Council Bluffs, Iowa (fall 1999–spring 2000)
- Sales clerk, housewares, at Jefferson's Department Store during off-campus work experience program, Council Bluffs, Iowa (fall 1998–spring 1999)
- Assistant director, Summer Recreation Program, Clear Lake, Iowa (summer 1998)
- Actress, Cobblestone Players, Clear Lake, Iowa (summer 1997)

LEADERSHIP EXPERIENCE

- Student Co-Chair for Clear Lake Women's Auxiliary Board Fashion Show 2000 (raised $45,000)
- President of Phi Kappa Phi Sorority 1999
- Student representative (high school) to Clear Lake Chamber of Commerce (2 years)

Figure 14–4
In-Depth Critique: Functional Résumé

For instance, you might say, "Coached a Little League team to the regional playoffs" or "Managed a fast-food restaurant and four employees."

AVOID WEAK STATEMENTS	USE ACTIVE STATEMENTS THAT SHOW RESULTS
Responsible for developing a new filing system	Developed a new filing system that reduced paperwork by 50 percent
I was in charge of customer complaints and all ordering problems	Handled all customer complaints and resolved all product order discrepancies

Erica Vorkamp

993 Church Street, Barrington, IL 60010
(847) 884-2153

OBJECTIVE

To obtain a position as a special events coordinator that will utilize my skills and experience

SKILLS AND CAPABILITIES

- Plan and coordinate large-scale public events
- Develop community support for concerts, festivals, and the arts
- Manage publicity for major events
- Coordinate activities of diverse community groups
- Establish and maintain financial controls for public events
- Negotiate contracts with performers, carpenters, electricians, and suppliers

SPECIAL EVENT EXPERIENCE

- Arranged 2001's week-long Arts and Entertainment Festival for the Barrington Public Library, involving performances by 25 musicians, dancers, actors, magicians, and artists
- Supervised the 2000 PTA Halloween Carnival, an all-day festival with game booths, live bands, contests, and food service that raised $7,600 for the PTA
- Organized the 1999 Midwestern convention for 800 members of the League of Women Voters, which extended over a three-day period and required arrangements for hotels, meals, speakers, and special tours
- Served as chairperson for the 1998 Children's Home Society Fashion Show, a luncheon for 400 that raised $5,000 for orphans and abused children

EDUCATION

- BA, Psychology, Northwestern University (Evanston, Illinois), Phi Beta Kappa

EMPLOYMENT HISTORY

- First National Bank of Chicago, 1988 to 1990, personnel counselor/campus recruiter; scheduled and conducted interviews with graduating MBA students on 18 Midwestern campuses; managed orientation program for recruits hired for bank's management trainee staff
- Northwestern University, 1996–1998, part-time research assistant for Professor Paul Harris (Science Department)

All capabilities and experience are related to the specific job objective, giving a selective picture of the candidate's abilities.

Includes event attendance statistics and fund-raising results to qualify accomplishments.

Includes work history (even though it has little bearing on job target) because Vorkamp believes recruiters want to see evidence that she's held a paying position.

Figure 14–5
In-Depth Critique: Combination Résumé

Won a trip to Europe for opening the most new customer accounts in my department

Generated the highest number of new customer accounts in my department

Member of special campus task force to resolve student problems with existing cafeteria assignments

Assisted in implementing new campus dining program allowing students to eat at any college dorm

Most potential employers expect to see certain items in any résumé. The bare essentials are name and address, academic credentials, and employment history.

Name and Address   The first thing an employer needs to know is who you are and where you can be reached: your name, address, and phone number (as well as your e-mail address or URL, if you have one). If you have contact information at school and at home, you can

Objective

4

List the major sections of a traditional résumé.

include both. Similarly, if you have a work phone and a home phone, list both and indicate which is which. Many résumé headings are nothing more than the name and address centered at the top of the page. You don't really need to include the word *résumé*. Just make sure the reader can tell in an instant who you are and how to communicate with you.

Career Objective or Summary of Qualifications   Experts disagree about the need to state a career objective on your résumé. Some argue that your objective is obvious from your qualifications. Some also maintain that such a statement only limits you as a candidate (especially if you want to be considered for a variety of openings) because it labels you as being interested in only one thing. Other experts argue that employers will try to categorize you anyway, so you might as well make sure they attach the right label. Remember, your goal is to generate interest immediately. If you decide to state your objective, make it effective by being as specific as possible about what you want to do:

Stating your objective or summarizing your qualifications helps the recruiter categorize you.

A software sales position in a growing company requiring international experience

Advertising assistance with print media emphasis requiring strong customer-contact skills

If you have different types of qualifications (such as a certificate in secretarial science and two years' experience in retail sales), prepare separate résumés, each with a different objective. If your immediate objective differs from your ultimate one, combine the two in a single statement:

A marketing position with an opportunity for eventual managerial status

Proposal writer, with the ultimate goal of becoming a contracts administrator

Instead of stating your objective, you might summarize your qualifications in a brief statement that highlights your strongest points, particularly if you have had a good deal of varied experience. Use a short, simple phrase:

Summary of qualifications: Ten years of experience in commission selling with track record of generating new customer leads through creative advertising and community leadership positions

The career objective or summary may be the only section read fully by the employer, so if you include either one, make it strong, concise, and convincing.

Education   If you're still in school, education is probably your strongest selling point. Present your educational background in depth, choosing facts that support your "theme." Give this section a heading such as "Education," "Professional College Training," or "Academic Preparation." Then, starting with the school you most recently attended, list the name and location of each one, the term of your enrollment (in months and years), your major and minor fields of study, significant skills and abilities you've developed in your course work, and the degrees or certificates you've earned. If you're working on an uncompleted degree, include in parentheses the expected date of completion. Showcase your qualifications by listing courses that have directly equipped you for the job you are seeking, and indicate any scholarships, awards, or academic honors you've received.

If education is your strongest selling point, discuss it thoroughly and highlight it visually.

The education section also includes off-campus training sponsored by business or government. Include any relevant seminars or workshops you've attended, as well as the certificates or other documents you've received. Mention high school or military training only if the associated achievements are pertinent to your career goals. Whether you list your grades depends on the job you want and the quality of your grades. If you choose to show a grade-point average, be sure to mention the scale, especially if a five-point scale is used instead of a four-point scale.

Education is usually given less emphasis in a résumé after you've worked in your chosen field for a year or more. If work experience is your strongest qualification, save the section on education for later in the résumé and provide less detail.

The work experience section lists all the related jobs you've had:
- Name and location of employer
- What the organization does (if not clear from its name)
- Your functional title
- How long you worked there
- Your duties and responsibilities
- Your significant achievements or contributions

As training coordinator for the FBI at its Phoenix Division, Jo Ann Sakato is also an experienced recruiter for the agency. The skills you've learned from other professional work experience can provide a suitable background for on-the-job training with the FBI. But it's important, advises Sakato, that you don't lie about yourself when answering questions or when submitting a résumé.

Include miscellaneous facts that are related to your career objective:
- Command of other languages
- Computer expertise
- Date you can start working

Nonpaid activities may provide evidence of work-related skills.

Work Experience, Skills, and Accomplishments Like the education section, the work experience section focuses on your overall theme. Tailor your description to highlight the relationship between your previous responsibilities and your target field. Call attention to skills you've developed and your progression from jobs of lesser to greater responsibility.

When describing your work experience, list your jobs in chronological order, with the current or last one first. Include any part-time, summer, or intern positions, even if unrelated to your current career objective. Employers will see that you have the ability to get and hold a job—an important qualification in itself. If you have worked your way through school, say so. Employers interpret this as a sign of character.

Each listing includes the name and location of the employer. If readers are unlikely to recognize the organization, briefly describe what it does. When you want to keep the name of your current employer confidential, identify the firm by industry only ("a large film-processing laboratory") or use the name but request confidentiality in the application letter or in an underlined note ("Résumé submitted in confidence") at the top or bottom of the résumé. If an organization's name or location has since changed, state the current name and location and then "formerly . . ."

Before or after each job listing, state your functional title, such as "clerk typist" or "salesperson." If you were a dishwasher, say so. Don't try to make your role seem more important by glamorizing your job title, functions, or achievements. Employers are checking on candidates' backgrounds more than they used to, so inaccuracies are likely to be exposed sooner or later (see "Promoting Workplace Ethics—Inflating Your Résumé: Is It Worth the Risk?"). Also state how long you worked on each job, from month/year to month/year. Use the phrase "to present" to denote current employment. If a job was part-time, say so.

Devote the most space to the jobs that are related to your target position. If you were personally responsible for something significant, be sure to mention it ("Devised a new collection system that accelerated payment of overdue receivables"). Facts about your skills and accomplishments are the most important information you can give a prospective employer, so quantify them whenever possible:

Designed a new ad that increased sales by 9 percent

Raised $2,500 in 15 days for cancer research

You may also include a section describing other aspects of your background that pertain to your career objective. If you were applying for a position with a multinational organization, you would mention your command of another language or your travel experience. Other skills you might mention include the ability to operate a computer, word processor, or other specialized equipment. You might title a special section "Computer Skills" or "Language Skills" and place it near your "Education" or "Work Experience" section.

If samples of your work might increase your chances of getting the job, insert a line at the end of your résumé offering to supply them on request. You may put "references available upon request" at the end of your résumé, but doing so is not necessary; the availability of references is usually assumed. Don't include actual names of references. List your references on a separate sheet and take them to your interview.

Activities and Achievements Your résumé should also describe any volunteer activities that demonstrate your abilities. List projects that require leadership, organization, teamwork, and cooperation. Emphasize career-related activities such as "member of the Student Marketing Association." List skills you learned in these activities, and explain how these skills are related to the job you're applying for. Include speaking, writing, or tutoring experience; participation in athletics or creative projects; fund-raising or community-service activities; and offices held in academic or professional organizations. (However, mention of political or religious organizations may be a red flag to someone with different views, so use your judgment.)

Note any awards you've received. Again, quantify your achievements whenever possible. Instead of saying that you addressed various student groups, state how many and the approx-

Promoting Workplace Ethics

Inflating Your Résumé: Is It Worth the Risk?

In an effort to put your best foot forward, you may be tempted to omit, enhance, or waltz around a few points that could raise questions about your résumé. Statistics on the prevalence of résumé inflation are difficult to gather, but most recruiters agree that distortion is common. The best guess is that up to 40 percent of all résumés either omit potentially damaging information or exaggerate the candidate's accomplishments. Some of the most frequent forms of deception include the following:

❏ *Claiming nonexistent educational credits.* Candidates may state (or imply) that they earned a degree when they never attended or did not complete the regular program.

❏ *Inflating grade-point averages.* Students feeling pressured to impress employers may claim a higher GPA than they actually achieved.

❏ *Stretching dates of employment to cover gaps.* Many candidates try to camouflage gaps in their work history by giving vague references to dates of employment.

❏ *Claiming to be self-employed.* Some candidates cover a period of unemployment by claiming to have operated an independent business during the time in question.

❏ *Leaving out any reference to jobs that might cause embarrassment.* To cover up a string of job losses, candidates may decide to drop a few positions, particularly if a reference check could prove embarrassing.

❏ *Exaggerating expertise or experience.* Candidates often inflate accomplishments by using verbs such as *supervised, managed, increased, improved,* and *created* to imply that the candidate was personally responsible for results that actually resulted from a group effort.

❏ *Claiming to have worked for companies that are out of business.* Candidates who need to fill a gap in their work record sometimes say they worked for a firm that has gone out of business.

Think twice before trying one of these ploys yourself. Experienced recruiters are familiar with the games that candidates play to look better. Many employers have a policy of firing people who lied on their résumés.

If your résumé raises suspicion, you may do yourself more harm than good by misrepresenting your background. Sure, it's fine to present your strongest, most impressive qualifications and to minimize your weaknesses. However, don't exaggerate, alter the past, or claim to have skills you don't have.

CAREER APPLICATIONS

1. You actually did quit your summer job as a door-to-door encyclopedia sales representative. Describe how you might handle that period on your résumé. Should you omit it? Can you mention it without revealing why you quit?

2. Consider one or two positions you've held (whether in a club, in a volunteer organization, or with a business). Write a realistic description of your responsibilities that doesn't inflate them but presents them in a positive light.

---

imate audience sizes. If your activities have been extensive, you may want to group them into divisions such as "College Activities," "Community Service," "Professional Associations," "Seminars and Workshops," and "Speaking Activities." An alternative is to divide them into two categories: "Service Activities" and "Achievements, Awards, and Honors."

Personal Data   Experts advise you to leave personal interests off your résumé—unless including them enhances the employer's understanding of why you would be the best candidate for the job.[18] For instance, candidates applying to Patagonia, maker of outdoor gear and apparel, may want to list outdoor activities as a personal interest. Someone applying for a bodyguard position with Pinkerton's security division may want to list martial arts achievements among their personal interests. According to Denis Brown, such information shows how a candidate will fit in with the organization's culture.

Some information is best excluded from your résumé. Civil rights laws prohibit employers from discriminating on the basis of gender, marital or family status, age (although only persons aged 40 to 70 are protected), race, color, religion, national origin, and physical or mental disability. So be sure to exclude any items that could encourage discrimination. Experts also recommend excluding salary information, reasons for leaving jobs, names of previous supervisors, your Social Security number, and other identification codes. Save these items for the interview, and offer them only if the employer specifically requests them.

If military service is relevant to the position, you may list it here (or under "Education" or "Work Experience"). List the date of induction, the branch of service, where you served, the highest rank you achieved, any accomplishments related to your career goals, and the date you were discharged.

Provide only the personal data that will help you get the job.

COMPLETING YOUR RÉSUMÉ

The last step in the Three-Step Writing Process is no less important than the other two. As with any other business message, you need to revise your résumé, produce it in an appropriate form, and proofread it for any errors.

Revise Your Résumé

The "perfect" résumé responds to the reader's needs and preferences and avoids some common faults.

The key to writing a successful résumé is to adopt the "you" attitude and focus on your audience. Think about what the prospective employer needs, and then tailor your résumé accordingly. People such as Denis Brown read thousands of résumés every year, and they complain about the following common problems:

◆ **Too long.** The résumé is not concise, relevant, and to the point.

◆ **Too short or sketchy.** The résumé does not give enough information for a proper evaluation of the applicant.

◆ **Hard to read.** A lack of "white space" and of devices such as indentions and boldfacing makes the reader's job more difficult.

◆ **Wordy.** Descriptions are verbose, with numerous words used for what could be said more simply.

◆ **Too slick.** The résumé appears to have been written by someone other than the applicant, which raises the question of whether the qualifications have been exaggerated.

◆ **Amateurish.** The applicant appears to have little understanding of the business world or of a particular industry, as revealed by including the wrong information or presenting it awkwardly.

◆ **Poorly reproduced.** The print is faint and difficult to read.

◆ **Misspelled and ungrammatical throughout.** Recruiters conclude that candidates who make such mistakes lack good verbal skills, which are important on the job.

◆ **Boastful.** The overconfident tone makes the reader wonder whether the applicant's self-evaluation is realistic.

◆ **Dishonest.** The applicant claims to have expertise or work experience that he or she does not possess.

◆ **Gimmicky.** The words, structure, decoration, or material used in the résumé depart so far from the usual as to make the résumé ineffective.

Guard against making these mistakes in your own résumé, and compare your final version with the suggestions in this chapter's "Checklist: Writing Résumés."

Produce Your Traditional Résumé

With less than a minute to make a good impression, your résumé needs to look sharp and grab a recruiter's interest in the first few lines. A typical recruiter devotes 45 seconds to each résumé before tossing it into either the "maybe" or the "reject" pile.[19] Most recruiters scan a résumé rather than read it from top to bottom. If yours doesn't stand out, chances are the recruiter won't look at it long enough to judge your qualifications.

The key characteristics of a good résumé are
• Neatness
• Simplicity
• Accuracy
• Honesty

To give your printed résumé the best appearance possible, use a clean typeface on high-grade, letter-size bond paper (in white or some light earth tone). Make sure that your stationery and envelope match. Leave ample margins all around, and make sure that any corrections are unnoticeable. Avoid italic typefaces, which are difficult to read, and use a quality laser printer.

Try to write a one-page résumé. If you have a great deal of experience and are applying for a higher-level position, you may wish to prepare a somewhat longer résumé. The important thing is to have enough space to present a persuasive, but accurate, portrait of your skills and accomplishments.

Lay out your résumé to make information easy to grasp.[20] Break up the text with headings that call attention to various aspects of your background, such as work experi-

Checklist: Writing Résumés

Organizational Approach

✓ Use the chronological approach unless you have a weak employment history.

✓ Use the functional approach if you are new to the job market, want to redirect your career, or have gaps in your employment history.

✓ Use the combined approach to maximize the advantages of both chronological and functional résumés, but only when neither of the other two formats will work.

Format and Style

✓ Use short noun phrases and action verbs, not whole sentences.

✓ Use facts, not opinions.

✓ Adopt a "you" attitude.

✓ Omit personal pronouns (especially *I*).

✓ Omit the date of preparation, desired salary, and work schedule.

✓ Use parallelism when listing multiple items.

✓ Use positive language and simple words.

✓ Use white space, quality paper, and quality printing.

Opening

✓ Include contact information (name, address).

✓ Include a career objective or skills summary if desired.

✓ Make your career objective specific and interesting.

✓ Prepare two separate résumés if you can perform two unrelated types of work.

✓ In a skills summary, present your strongest qualifications first.

Education

✓ List the name and location of every post-secondary school you've attended (with dates, and with degrees/certificates obtained).

✓ Indicate your college major (and minor).

✓ Indicate numerical scale (4.0 or 5.0) if you include your grade point average.

✓ List other experiences (seminars, workshops), with dates and certificates obtained.

Work Experience, Skills, and Accomplishments

✓ List all relevant work experience (paid employment, volunteer work, internships).

✓ List full-time and part-time jobs.

✓ Provide name and location of each employer (with dates of employment).

✓ List job title and describe responsibilities.

✓ Note on-the-job accomplishments and skills; quantify them whenever possible.

Activities and Achievements

✓ List all relevant offices and leadership positions.

✓ List projects you have undertaken.

✓ Show abilities such as writing or speaking, and list publications and community service.

✓ List other information, such as your proficiency in languages other than English.

✓ Mention ability to operate special equipment, including technical, computer, and software skills.

Personal Data

✓ Omit personal details that might be seen as negative or used to discriminate against you.

✓ Leave personal interests off unless they are relevant to the position being sought.

✓ List a reference only with permission to do so.

Modifications for an Electronic Résumé

✓ Eliminate graphics, boldface, underlines, italics, small print, tabs, and all format codes.

✓ Save file in plain-text (ASCII) format.

✓ Add blank spaces, align text, and use asterisks for bullets.

✓ Add a "Key Word Summary," listing nouns to define skills, experience, education, and professional attributes.

✓ Mirror the job description when possible.

✓ Add job-related jargon, but don't overdo it.

Modifications for an Online Résumé

✓ Provide your URL and e-mail address.

✓ Use a key word hyperlink to an ASCII version so that employers can download it.

✓ Use a key word hyerplink to a fully formatted résumé that can be read online and printed.

---

ence and education. Underline or capitalize key points, or set them off in the left margin. Use lists to itemize your most important qualifications, and leave plenty of white space, even if doing so forces you to use two pages rather than one.

Convert Your Résumé to an Electronic Format

You need to format your résumé in at least two and maybe three ways: as a traditional printed document, as a plain-text (or ASCII) document for scanning or submitting electronically, and as an HTML-coded document to post on a Web page (should you choose to).

Objective

5

Describe the process involved in adapting your résumé to an electronic format.

Doing an electronic version of your résumé is helpful if it will be scanned or if you will be posting it on the Internet or submitting it via e-mail.

Going Online

Post an Online Résumé

At CareerBuilder, you'll find sample résumés, tips on preparing different types of résumés (including scannable ones), links to additional articles, and expert advice on creating résumés that bring positive results. After you've polished your résumé-writing skills, you can search for jobs online using the site's numerous links to national and international industry-specific Web sites. You can access the information at CareerBuilder to develop your résumé and then post it with prospective employers—all free of charge. Take advantage of what this site offers, and get ideas for writing or improving a résumé.

www.careerbuilder.com/
gh-res-htg-tips.html

To reach this Web site, go to www.prenhall.com/thill *(the Web site for this text). Select Chapter 14, then select "Student Resources." There you'll find a current live link that will take you straight to the site.*

To make your résumé scannable
• Save it as an ASCII file
• Provide a list of key words
• Balance clear language with up-to-date jargon

Key words help potential employers sort through an entire database of résumés.

Understanding the Scanning Process   Overwhelmed by the number of résumés they receive, most *Fortune* 1,000 companies encourage applicants to submit electronic (scannable) résumés. By scanning these résumés into their electronic database, companies can quickly narrow the field of applicants. However, good scanning systems cost up to $100,000, so companies with fewer than 100 employees seldom use them.[21] If you're unsure whether an employer accepts scannable résumés, call and ask, or visit the company's Web site.

A scannable format differs from a traditional one—for good reason. Employers use special hardware and software to convert a traditional paper résumé into an image on the company's computer. Optical character recognition (OCR) software creates an electronic text document from the original by examining and reproducing every letter or number. This electronic document is then downloaded into a company database, which can be searched and sorted by key words, criteria, or almost anything the employer wants.

Say a manager wants to hire a marketing representative who is fluent in Spanish, has five years' sales experience, a background in new product marketing, and is experienced in cold calling. The employer enters these key words (plus others) into the database program and performs a sort function on all the résumés in the database. The computer then provides a list of candidates whose résumés include these key words. Next to the candidate's name is a percentage indicating how closely the résumé reflects the employer's requirements.[22]

Changing Format and Style   Scannable résumés convey the same information as traditional résumés, but the format and style must be computer friendly. That means eliminating any graphics, boldfacing, underlining, italics, small print, or other formatting codes (such as tab settings or tables) that were attached to your document when you saved your traditional résumé.[23] You no longer need to confine your electronic résumé to one page, but don't get carried away. To make your traditional résumé a scannable one, format it as plain text (ASCII) document, provide a list of key words, and balance common language with jargon.[24]

Format Your Résumé as an ASCII Document   ASCII is a common plain-text language that allows your résumé to be read by any scanner and accessed by any computer, regardless of the word-processing software you used to prepare the document. All word-processing programs allow you to save files as plain text. To convert your résumé to an ASCII plain-text file, open your document and remove all formatting (boldfacing, centering, bullets, graphic lines, etc.). Then highlight all text and select a popular typeface (such as Times, Helvetica, or Courier) with a 10- to 14-point font size. Finally, save your document under a different name by using your word processor's "save as" option and selecting "text only with line breaks."

To make your electronic résumé more readable, open your new document, align text by adding some blank spaces (rather than tabs), create headings and separate paragraphs by adding a few blank lines, and indicate bullets with an asterisk or the lowercase letter *o*. Use white space so that scanners and computers can tell when one topic ends and another begins. Also, make sure your name and address are the first lines on your résumé (with no text appearing above or beside your name). Your new electronic résumé is indeed plain, but it's now computer friendly.

Provide a List of Key Words   When converting your résumé to a scannable format, emphasize certain key words to help potential employers select your résumé from the thousands they scan. Employers generally search for nouns (since verbs tend to be generic rather than specific to a particular position or skill). To maximize the number of matches (or hits) include a key word summary of 20 to 30 words and phrases that define your skills, experience, education, professional affiliations, and so on. Place this list right after your name and address. Here's an example of a possible key word summary for an accountant:

Key Word Summary

Accountant, Corporate Controller, Fortune 1000, Receivables, Payables, Inventory, Cash Flow, Financial Analysis, Payroll Experience, Corporate Taxes, Activity-Based Accounting,

EFFECTIVE E-BUSINESS COMMUNICATION

Posting Your Résumé Online

Printing and mailing your résumé takes more time and effort offline than online. Instead of stuffing an envelope with each résumé, you can now post your résumé on the Web with a few keystrokes. On WorkAvenue.com (starnews.workavenue.com), for example, you can click to search the help-wanted ads of numerous local newspapers. When you're ready to apply for a listed job, simply open your electronic résumé file, copy the résumé, and paste it into your WorkAvenue profile. Then you can send it to the employer with a quick click—and leave it in the site's database for other employers to browse.

1. What role do key words play in résumés that are posted online for employers to browse?
2. What style and formatting changes should you make before pasting your résumé into an online database?

Problem Solving, Computer Skills, Excel, Access, Networks, HTML, Peachtree, Quick Books, BA Indiana University—Accounting, CPA, Dean's List, Articulate, Team Player, Flexible, Willing to Travel, Fluent Spanish.

One way to identify which key words to include in your electronic summary is to underline all the skills listed in ads for the types of jobs you're interested in. Make sure these ads match your qualifications and experience. Some job candidates try to beat the system by listing every conceivable skill and by guessing which words the computer is likely to be looking for. But that strategy seldom works. The computer may be looking for a Harvard Business School graduate who once worked at Netscape and now lives in Arizona. If you went to Yale, worked at Yahoo! and live in Maine, you're out of luck.[25]

Balance Common Language with Current Jargon   Another way to maximize hits on your résumé is to use words that potential employers will understand (for example, say *keyboard*, not *input device*). Also, use abbreviations sparingly (except for common ones such as B.A. or M.B.A.). At the same time, learn and use the important buzzwords in your field. Look for current jargon in the want ads of major newspapers such as the *Wall Street Journal* and in other résumés in your field that are posted online. Be careful to check and recheck the spelling, capitalization, and punctuation of any jargon you include, and use only those words you see most often.

> Use words your employer will understand by including some jargon specific to your field.

Roberto Cortez created an electronic résumé by changing his formatting and adding a list of key words. However, the information remains essentially the same and appears in the same order, as you can see in Figure 14–6. Now his target employers can scan his résumé into a database, and Cortez can submit his résumé via e-mail or post it on the Internet.

Submitting Electronic Résumés   If an employer gives you an option of submitting a scannable résumé by mail, by fax, or by e-mail, choose e-mail. E-mail puts your résumé directly into the employer's database, bypassing the scanning process. If you send your

> E-mail is the best way to transmit your plain-text résumé.

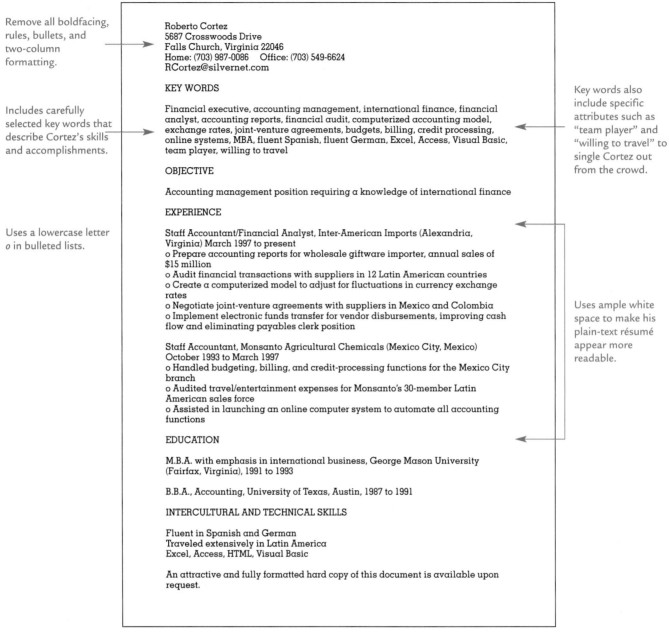

Remove all boldfacing, rules, bullets, and two-column formatting.

Includes carefully selected key words that describe Cortez's skills and accomplishments.

Uses a lowercase letter *o* in bulleted lists.

Key words also include specific attributes such as "team player" and "willing to travel" to single Cortez out from the crowd.

Uses ample white space to make his plain-text résumé appear more readable.

Roberto Cortez
5687 Crosswoods Drive
Falls Church, Virginia 22046
Home: (703) 987-0086   Office: (703) 549-6624
RCortez@silvernet.com

KEY WORDS

Financial executive, accounting management, international finance, financial analyst, accounting reports, financial audit, computerized accounting model, exchange rates, joint-venture agreements, budgets, billing, credit processing, online systems, MBA, fluent Spanish, fluent German, Excel, Access, Visual Basic, team player, willing to travel

OBJECTIVE

Accounting management position requiring a knowledge of international finance

EXPERIENCE

Staff Accountant/Financial Analyst, Inter-American Imports (Alexandria, Virginia) March 1997 to present
o Prepare accounting reports for wholesale giftware importer, annual sales of $15 million
o Audit financial transactions with suppliers in 12 Latin American countries
o Create a computerized model to adjust for fluctuations in currency exchange rates
o Negotiate joint-venture agreements with suppliers in Mexico and Colombia
o Implement electronic funds transfer for vendor disbursements, improving cash flow and eliminating payables clerk position

Staff Accountant, Monsanto Agricultural Chemicals (Mexico City, Mexico) October 1993 to March 1997
o Handled budgeting, billing, and credit-processing functions for the Mexico City branch
o Audited travel/entertainment expenses for Monsanto's 30-member Latin American sales force
o Assisted in launching an online computer system to automate all accounting functions

EDUCATION

M.B.A. with emphasis in international business, George Mason University (Fairfax, Virginia), 1991 to 1993

B.B.A., Accounting, University of Texas, Austin, 1987 to 1991

INTERCULTURAL AND TECHNICAL SKILLS

Fluent in Spanish and German
Traveled extensively in Latin America
Excel, Access, HTML, Visual Basic

An attractive and fully formatted hard copy of this document is available upon request.

Figure 14–6
In-Depth Critique: Electronic Résumé

résumé in a paper format by regular mail or by fax, you run the risk that an OCR scanning program will create an error when reading it.

When submitting your résumé by e-mail, don't attach it as a separate document. Most human resources departments won't accept attached files (they're concerned about computer viruses). Instead, paste your résumé into the body of your e-mail message. Whenever you know a reference number or a job ad number, include it in your e-mail subject line.

If you're posting your electronic résumé to an employer's online résumé builder, copy and paste the appropriate sections from your electronic file directly into the employer's form. This method avoids rekeying and eliminates errors.

If you fax your electronic résumé, set your machine to "fine" mode (to ensure a high-quality printout on the receiving end). If you're mailing your résumé, you may want to send both a well-designed traditional résumé and a scannable one. Simply attach Post-It notes, labeling one "visual résumé" and the other "scannable résumé."

Building an Online Résumé If you wish to post your résumé on your Web page, provide employers with your URL address; most recruiters won't take the time to use search engines to find your site.[26] As you design your Web-site résumé, think of important key words to use as hyperlinks—words that will grab an employer's attention and make the recruiter want to click on that hyperlink to learn more about you. Don't distract potential employers from your credentials by using hyperlinks to organizations or other Web sites.

One advantage of posting your résumé on your Web site is the opportunity to use hyperlinks.

Remember not to use photos and not to provide information that reveals your age, gender, race, marital status, or religion. Because a Web site is a public access area, you should also leave out the names of references and previous employers. Either mention that references are available on request, or say nothing. Also be sure not to name companies; simply refer to "a large accounting firm" or "a wholesale giftware importer." Finally, include an ASCII version of your résumé on your Web page so that prospective employers can download it into their company's database.

Proofread Your Résumé

Denis Brown cautions that your résumé is a concrete example of how you will prepare material on the job. So in every format, remember to pay close attention to mechanics and details. Check all headings and lists for parallelism, and be sure that your grammar, spelling, and punctuation are correct.

Once your résumé is complete, update it continuously. You'll need it whether you're applying for membership in a professional organization, working toward a promotion, or changing employers. People used to spend most of their career with one company. Today, however, the average person beginning a job in the United States will probably work in 10 or more jobs for five or more employers before retiring.[27] So keeping your résumé updated is a good idea.

Keep your résumé up to date.

WRITING OTHER TYPES OF EMPLOYMENT MESSAGES

You'll need to write more than one type of employment message. Your résumé will take the greatest amount of time and effort. But you'll also need to write application letters, send job-inquiry letters, fill out application forms, and follow up on your application.

Objective **6**

Define the purpose of application letters, and explain how to apply the AIDA organizational approach to them.

Application Letters

Whenever you submit your résumé, accompany it with a cover or application letter to let readers know what you're sending, why you're sending it, and how they can benefit from reading it. Because your application letter is in your own style (rather than the choppy, shorthand style of your résumé), it gives you a chance to make a good personal impression. Always send your résumé and application letter together, because each has a unique job to perform.

Application letters are intended to interest readers enough to read your résumé.

The purpose of your cover letter is to get the reader interested enough to read your résumé. Before you begin to write, learn something about the organization you're applying to. Then focus on your audience so that you can show you've done your homework. Imagine yourself in the recruiter's situation, and show how your background and talents will solve a particular problem or fill a specific need the company has. The more you can learn about the organization, the better you'll be able to capture the reader's attention and convey your desire to join the company.[28]

During your research, find out the name, title, and department of the person you're writing to. Reaching and addressing the right person is the most effective way to gain attention. Avoid phrases such as "To Whom It May Concern" and "Dear Sir."

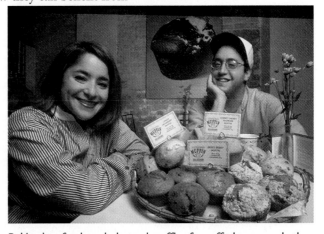

Baking low-fat, low-cholesterol muffins for coffeehouses and other clients in the Chicago area was a successful recipe for Little Miss Muffin founders Trisha and Barry Malone, brother and sister. Before you can make a muffin that people want, you have to know what people want in a muffin. Likewise, before you write an application letter that convinces an employer to read your résumé, you need to know what that employer is looking for.

States the reason for writing and links the writer's experience to stated qualifications.

Explains an achievement mentioned in the résumé and refers the reader to the enclosure.

Discusses how specific skills apply to the job sought, showing that Sawyer understands the job's responsibilities.

Asks for an interview and facilitates action.

Kenneth Sawyer

2893 Jack Pine Road, Chapel Hill, NC 27514

February 2, 2000

Ms. Angela Clair
Director of Administration
Cummings and Welbane, Inc.
770 Campus Point Drive
Chapel Hill, NC 27514

Dear Ms. Clair:

In the January 31 issue of the *Chapel Hill Post,* your ad mentioned "proven skills." I believe I have what you are looking for in an administrative assistant. In addition to experience in a variety of office settings, I am familiar with the computer software used in your office.

I recently completed a three-course sequence at Hamilton College on Microsoft Word and PowerPoint. I learned how to apply those programs to speed up letter- and report-writing tasks. A workshop on "Writing and Editing with the Unix Processor" gave me experience with other valuable applications such as composing and formatting sales letters, financial reports, and presentation slides.

These skills have been invaluable to me as assistant to the chief nutritionist at our campus cafeteria (please refer to my résumé). I'm particularly proud of the order-confirmation system I designed, which has sharply reduced the problems of late shipments and depleted inventories.

Because "proven skills" are best explained in person, I would appreciate an interview with you. Please phone me any afternoon between 3 and 5 p.m. at (919) 220-6139 to let me know the day and time most convenient for you.

Sincerely,

Kenneth Sawyer

Kenneth Sawyer

Enclosure: Résumé

Figure 14–7
In-Depth Critique: Sample Solicited Application Letter

You write a solicited application letter in response to an announced job opening.

You write an unsolicited application letter to an organization that has not announced a job opening.

If you're sending a **solicited application letter**—in response to an announced job opening—you'll usually know what qualifications the organization is seeking. You'll also have more competition because hundreds of other job seekers will have seen the listing and may be sending applications too. The letter in Figure 14–7 was written in response to a help-wanted ad. Kenneth Sawyer highlights his chief qualifications and mirrors the requirements specified in the ad. He actually grabs attention by focusing on the phrase "proven skills" used in the ad: he elaborates on his own proven skills throughout the letter, and even mentions the term in the closing paragraph.

In some respects, an **unsolicited letter**—sent to an organization that has not announced an opening—stands a better chance of being read and receiving individualized attention. In her unsolicited application letter in Figure 14–8, Glenda Johns manages to give a snapshot of her qualifications and skills without repeating what is said in her résumé (which appears in Figure 14–4). She gains attention by focusing on the needs of the employer.

Both solicited and unsolicited letters present your qualifications similarly. The main difference is in the opening paragraph. In a solicited letter, you need no special attention-

On the left side of the letter:

Gains attention in the first paragraph.

Interests reader with knowledge of the company's policy toward promotion.

On the right side of the letter:

Points out personal qualities that aren't specifically stated in her résumé.

Focuses on the audience and displays the "you" attitude, even though the last paragraph uses the word *I*.

The letter reads:

Glenda S. Johns

Home: 457 Mountain View Road, Clear Lake, IA 50428 (515) 633-5971
College: 1254 Main Street, Council Bluffs, IA 51505 (712) 438-5254

June 16, 2001

Ms. Patricia Downings, Store Manager
Wal-Mart
840 South Oak
Iowa Falls, Iowa 50126

Dear Ms. Downings:

You want retail clerks and managers who are accurate, enthusiastic, and experienced. You want someone who cares about customer service, who understands merchandising, and who can work with others to get the job done. When you're ready to hire a manager trainee or a clerk who is willing to work toward promotion, please consider me for the job.

Working as a clerk and then as an assistant department manager in a large department store has taught me how challenging a career in retailing can be. Moreover, my AA degree in retailing (including work in such courses as retailing, marketing, and business information systems) will provide your store with a well-rounded associate. Most important, I can offer Wal-Mart's Iowa Falls store more than my two years' of study and field experience. You'll find that I'm interested in every facet of retailing, eager to take on responsibility, and willing to continue learning throughout my career. Please look over my résumé to see how my skills can benefit your store.

I understand that Wal-Mart prefers to promote its managers from within the company, and I would be pleased to start out with an entry-level position until I gain the necessary experience. Do you have any associate positions opening up soon? Could we discuss my qualifications? I will phone you early next Wednesday to arrange a meeting at your convenience.

Sincerely,

Glenda Johns

Glenda Johns

Enclosure

Figure 14–8
In-Depth Critique: Sample Unsolicited Application Letter

getter because you have been invited to apply. In an unsolicited letter, you need to start by capturing the reader's attention and interest.

Getting Attention　Like your résumé, your application letter is a form of advertising, so organize it as you would a sales letter: Use the AIDA approach, focus on your audience, and emphasize reader benefits (as discussed in Chapter 9). Make sure your style projects confidence. To sell a potential employer on your merits, you must believe in them and sound as though you do. Table 14–2 highlights some important ways to spark interest and grab attention in your opening paragraph. All these openings demonstrate the "you" attitude, and many indicate how the applicant can serve the employer.

　The opening paragraph of your application letter must also state your reason for writing and the position you are applying for:

Please consider my application for an entry-level position in technical writing.
Your firm advertised a fleet sales position (on September 23, 2001, in the *Baltimore Sun*).
With my 16 months of new-car sales experience, won't you consider me for that position?

Follow the AIDA approach when writing your application letter: attention, interest, desire, action.

The opening of an application letter captures attention, gives the reason you're writing, and states which job you're applying for.

Open a solicited application letter by mentioning how you found out about the position.

Table 14–2   Tips for Getting Attention in Application Letters

Tip	Example
Unsolicited Application Letters	
· Show how your strongest skills will benefit the organization. A 20-year-old in her third year of college might begin like this:	When you need a secretary in your export division who can take shorthand at 125 words a minute and transcribe notes at 70—in English, Spanish, or Portuguese—call me.
· Describe your understanding of the job's requirements and then show how well your qualifications fit them:	Your annual report states that Mobil Corporation runs employee-training programs about workforce diversity. The difficulties involved in running such programs can be significant, as I learned while tutoring inner-city high school students last summer. My 12 pupils were enrolled in vocational training programs and came from diverse ethnic and racial backgrounds. The one thing they had in common was a lack of familiarity with the typical employer's expectations. To help them learn the "rules of the game," I developed exercises that cast them in various roles: boss, customer, new recruit, and coworker. Of the 12 students, 10 subsequently found full-time jobs and have called or written to tell me how much they gained from the workshop.
· Mention the name of a person known to and highly regarded by the reader:	When Janice McHugh of your franchise sales division spoke to our business communication class last week, she said you often need promising new marketing graduates at this time of year.
· Refer to publicized company activities, achievements, changes, or new procedures:	Today's issue of the *Detroit News* reports that you may need the expertise of computer programmers versed in robotics when your Lansing tire plant automates this spring.
· Use a question to demonstrate your understanding of the organization's needs:	Can your fast-growing market research division use an interviewer with 1½ years of field survey experience, a B.A. in public relations, and a real desire to succeed? If so, please consider me for the position.
· Use a catch-phrase opening if the job requires ingenuity and imagination:	Haut monde—whether said in French, Italian, or Arabic, it still means "high society." As an interior designer for your Beverly Hills showroom, not only could I serve and sell to your distinguished clientele, but I could do it in all these languages. I speak, read, and write them fluently.
Solicited Application Letters	
· Identify the publication in which the ad ran; then describe what you have to offer:	Your ad in the April issue of *Travel & Leisure* for a cruise-line social director caught my eye. My eight years of experience as a social director in the travel industry would allow me to serve your new Caribbean cruise division well.

Another way to state your reason for writing is to use a title at the opening of your letter:

Subject: Application for bookkeeper position

After getting your reader's attention, you can begin emphasizing how hiring you will benefit the organization.

Building Interest and Increasing Desire   The middle section of your application letter presents your strongest selling points in terms of their potential benefit to the organization, thereby building interest in you and creating a desire to interview you. If you already mentioned your selling points in the opening, don't repeat them. Simply give supporting evidence. Be careful not to repeat the facts presented in your résumé; simply interpret those facts for the reader. Otherwise, spell out a few of your key qualifications, and back up your assertions with some convincing evidence of your ability to perform:

The middle section of an application letter
• Summarizes your relevant qualifications
• Emphasizes your accomplishments
• Suggests desirable personal qualities
• Justifies salary requirements
• Refers to your résumé

Poor: I completed three college courses in business communication, earning an A in each course, and have worked for the past year at Imperial Construction.

Improved: Using the skills gained from three semesters of college training in business communication, I developed a collection system for Imperial Construction that reduced its 2001 bad-debt losses by 3.7 percent, or $9,902, over those of 2000. Instead of using timeworn terminology, the new system's collection letters offered discount incentives for speedy payment.

Improved: Experience in customer relations and college courses in public relations have taught me how to handle the problem-solving tasks that arise in a leading retail clothing firm like yours. Such important tasks include identifying and resolving customer complaints, writing letters that build good customer relations, and above all, promoting the organization's positive image.

When writing a solicited letter responding to an advertisement, be sure to discuss each requirement specified in the ad. If you are deficient in any of these requirements, stress other solid selling points to help strengthen your overall presentation.

The middle of your application letter also demonstrates a few significant job-related qualities, such as your diligence or your ability to work hard, learn quickly, handle responsibility, or get along with people:

While attending college full-time, I trained 3 hours a day with the varsity track team. In addition, I worked part-time during the school year and up to 60 hours a week each summer in order to be totally self-supporting while in college. I can offer your organization the same level of effort and perseverance.

Another matter you might bring up in this section is your salary requirements—but *only* if the organization has asked you to state them. Unless you know approximately what the job pays, suggest a salary range, or indicate that the salary is negotiable or open. You might consult the latest government "Area Wage Survey" at the library to get an idea of the salary range for various job classifications and geographic areas. If you do state a target salary, tie it to the benefits you would bring to the organization (much as you would handle price in a sales letter):

For the past two years, I have been helping a company similar to yours organize its database. I would therefore like to receive a salary in the same range (the mid-20s) for helping your company set up a more efficient customer database.

Toward the end of this section, refer the reader to your résumé by citing a specific fact or general point covered there:

You will find my people skills an asset. As you can see in the attached résumé, I've been working part-time with a local publisher since my sophomore year, and during that time, I have successfully resolved more than a few "client crises."

Motivating Action   The final paragraph of your application letter has two important functions: to ask the reader for a specific action and to make a reply easy. In almost all cases, the action you request is an interview. Don't demand it, however; try to sound natural and appreciative. Offer to come to the employer's office at a convenient time or, if the firm is some distance away, to meet with its nearest representative. Make the request easy to fulfill by stating your phone number and the best time to reach you—or, if you wish to be in control, by mentioning that you will follow up with a phone call in a few days. Refer again to your strongest selling point and, if desired, your date of availability:

Close by asking for an interview and making the interview easy to arrange.

After you have reviewed my qualifications, could we discuss the possibility of putting my marketing skills to work for your company? Because I will be on spring break the week of March 8, I would like to arrange a time to talk then. I will call in late February

Checklist: Writing Application Letters

Attention (Opening Paragraph)

✓ Open the letter by capturing the reader's attention in a businesslike way.
✓ Use a summary, name, source, question, news, personalized, or creative opening.
✓ State that you are applying for a job, and identify the position or the type of work you seek.

Interest and Desire, or Evidence of Qualifications (Next Several Paragraphs)

✓ Present your key qualifications for the job, highlighting what is on your résumé: job-related education and training; relevant work experience; and related activities, interests, and qualities.
✓ Adopt a mature, businesslike tone.
✓ Eliminate boasting and exaggeration.
✓ Back up your claims by citing specific achievements in educational, work, and outside settings.
✓ Demonstrate your knowledge of the organization by citing its operations or trends in the industry.
✓ Link your education, experience, and personal qualities to the job requirements.
✓ Relate aspects of your training or work experience to those of the target position.

✓ Outline your educational preparation for the job.
✓ Provide evidence that you can learn quickly, work hard, handle responsibility, and get along with others.
✓ Show that you possess personal qualities and work attitudes that are desirable for job performance.
✓ If asked to state salary requirements in your letter, state current salary or a desired salary range, and link it to the benefits of hiring you.
✓ Refer the reader to the enclosed résumé.

Action (Closing Paragraph)

✓ Request an interview at the reader's convenience.
✓ Request a screening interview with the nearest regional representative, if company headquarters is some distance away.
✓ Make it easy to comply with your request by providing your phone number (with area code) and stating the best time to reach you, or mention a time when you will be calling to set up an interview.
✓ Express your appreciation for an opportunity to have an interview.
✓ Repeat your strongest qualification to reinforce your claim that you can contribute to the organization.

---

to schedule a convenient time when we could discuss employment opportunities at your company.

Once you have edited and proofread your application letter, mail it and your résumé promptly, especially if they have been solicited.

Adapting Style and Approach to Culture   The AIDA approach isn't appropriate for job seekers in every culture. If you're applying for a job abroad or want to work with a subsidiary of an organization based in another country, you may need to adjust your tone. Blatant self-promotion is considered bad form in some cultures. Other cultures stress group performance over individual contributions. As for format, recruiters in some countries (including France) prefer handwritten letters to printed or typed ones. So research a company carefully before drafting your application letter.

For U.S. and Canadian companies, let your letter reflect your personal style. Be yourself, but be businesslike too; avoid sounding cute. Don't use slang or a gimmicky layout. The only time to be unusually creative in content or format is when the job you're seeking requires imagination, such as a position in advertising. Compare your own letters with the tasks in this chapter's "Checklist: Writing Application Letters."

> You may need to vary your approach according to your reader's culture.

Job-Inquiry Letters

> Use a job-inquiry letter to request an application form, which is a standardized data sheet that simplifies comparison of applicants' credentials.

Before considering you for a position, some organizations require you to fill out and submit an **application form,** a standardized data sheet that simplifies the comparison of applicants' qualifications. To request such a form, send a job-inquiry letter and include enough information about yourself in the letter to show that you have at least some of the requirements for the position you are seeking:

Please send me an application form for work as an interior designer in your home furnishings department. For my certificate in design, I took courses in retail merchandising and customer relations. I have also had part-time sales experience at Capwell's department store.

Instead of writing a letter of this kind, you may want to drop in at the office you're applying to. You probably won't be able to talk to anyone other than the receptionist or a human resources assistant, but you can pick up the form, get an impression of the organization, and demonstrate your initiative and energy.

Application Forms

Organizations will use your application form as a convenient one-page source for information about your qualifications. So try to be thorough and accurate when filling it out. Have your résumé with you to remind you of important information, and if you can't remember something and have no record of it, provide the closest estimate possible. If you cannot provide some information because you have no such background (military experience, for example), write "Not applicable." When filling out applications, use a pen (unless specifically requested to use a pencil) and print legibly.

Your care in filling out application forms suggests to the employer that you will be thorough and careful in your work.

Application forms rarely give you enough space or ask you the right questions to reflect your skills and abilities accurately. Nevertheless, show your cooperation by doing your best to fill out the form completely. If you get an interview, you'll have an opportunity to fill in the gaps. You might also ask whether you might submit a résumé and an application letter along with the application.

Application Follow-Ups

If your application letter and résumé fail to bring a response within a month or so, follow up with a second letter to keep your file active. This follow-up letter also gives you a chance to update your original application with any recent job-related information:

Use a follow-up letter to let the employer know you're still interested in the job.

Since applying to you on May 3 for an executive secretary position, I have completed a course in office management at South River Community College. I received straight A's in the course. I now am a proficient user of MS Word, including macros and other complex functions.

Please keep my application in your active file, and let me know when you need a skilled executive secretary.

Even if you've received a letter acknowledging your application and saying that it will be kept on file, don't hesitate to send a follow-up letter three months later to show that you are still interested:

Three months have elapsed since I applied to you for an underwriting position, but I want to let you know that I am still very interested in joining your company.

I recently completed a four-week temporary work assignment at a large local insurance agency. I learned several new verification techniques and gained experience in using the online computer system. This experience could increase my value to your underwriting department.

Please keep my application in your active file, and let me know when a position opens for a capable underwriter.

Unless you state otherwise, the human resources office is likely to assume that you've already found a job and are no longer interested in the organization. Moreover, requirements change. A follow-up letter can demonstrate that you're sincerely interested in working for the organization, that you're persistent in pursuing your goals, and that you're upgrading your skills to make yourself a better employee. And it might just get you an interview.

SUMMARY OF LEARNING OBJECTIVES

1 Explain why companies are encouraging employees to get more varied job experience, and list five ways to build toward a career. Employers want people who can adapt to various situations, who are not afraid of change, who continue to learn on the job, and who are sensitive to intercultural differences. To build toward a successful career, (1) keep an employment file, (2) take interim job assignments, (3) polish and update your skills, (4) learn about your campus career center, and (5) continue learning throughout your career.

2 Delineate the three things that need to be analyzed when planning a résumé. Before preparing a résumé, it's important to realize that its purpose is to get you an interview. With that knowledge, you can emphasize your positive points without including absolutely everything about you. Before you can emphasize your positive points, you must know what they are, so you need to analyze yourself—what you have to offer and what you want to do. Finally, you need to analyze your audience so that you know what potential employers are looking for, how they go about recruiting employees, and what skills and qualities are important to them.

3 Discuss how to choose the appropriate organization for your résumé, and list the advantages or disadvantages of the three options. Each organizational approach emphasizes different strengths. If you have a lot of employment experience, you would choose the chronological approach because it focuses on your work history. The advantages of the chronological résumé are (1) it helps employers easily locate necessary information, (2) it highlights your professional growth and career progress, and (3) it emphasizes continuity and stability in your employment background. The functional approach focuses on particular skills and competencies you've developed. The advantages of the functional résumé are (1) it helps employers easily see what you can do for them, (2) it allows you to emphasize earlier job experience, and (3) it lets you downplay any lengthy periods of unemployment or a lack of career progress. The combination approach uses the best features of the other two, but it has two disadvantages: (1) it tends to be longer, and (2) it can be repetitious if you must list accomplishments and skills in the functional section as well as in the individual job descriptions.

4 List the major sections of a traditional résumé. Your résumé must include three sections: (1) your name and address, (2) your education background (with related skills and accomplishments), and (3) your work experience (with related skills and accomplishments). Options include listing your career objective or summary of qualifications, describing related activities and achievements, and perhaps (although not necessarily recommended) explaining relevant personal data.

5 Describe the process involved in adapting your résumé to an electronic format. Begin by eliminating all fancy printing, graphics, and formatting such as boldface, italics, and tabs. Save the résumé as a plain-text (ASCII) document, adding some blank spaces, blank lines, and asterisks to make it more readable. Finally, provide a list of key words (nouns) that define your skills, experience, and education. Make sure it also includes important jargon that is characteristic of the language in your field.

6 Define the purpose of application letters, and explain how to apply the AIDA organizational approach to them. The purpose of an application letter is to convince readers to look at your résumé. This makes application letters a type of sales letter, so you'll want to use the AIDA organizational approach. Get attention in the opening paragraph by showing how your work skills could benefit the organization, by explaining how your qualifications fit the job, or by demonstrating an understanding of the organization's needs. Build interest and desire by showing how you can meet the job requirements, and be sure to refer your reader to your résumé near the end of this section. Finally, motivate action by making your request easy to fulfill and by including all necessary contact information.

On the job: SOLVING A COMMUNICATION DILEMMA AT PINKERTON

Whether safeguarding movie stars or making sure a multinational corporation hires the right people, it's all in a day's work for Pinkerton. Founded by Allan Pinkerton in 1850, the security company made its name with exploits such as tracking Butch Cassidy and the Sundance Kid and protecting Abraham Lincoln before his inauguration. Thomas Wathen bought Pinkerton in 1987 and began expanding it into a worldwide network that now encompasses more than 200 offices, 47,000 employees, and nearly $1 billion in annual revenue. Denis Brown took the reins in 1994 with the goal of continuing that growth while improving the company's profit margins.

With the company's services so dependent on the quality of people it hires, Brown must screen potential job seekers and pick only those individuals who have the experience, attitude, and talent to perform well in whatever unique and demanding situation the company assigns them to. These security officers also need excellent communication skills to interact with the public and handle troubles that might range from petty theft to terrorism.

Pinkerton follows the same five-step approach to screen, evaluate, and select employees, whether it's filling internal openings or helping clients evaluate job candidates. In the first step, each candidate fills out a job application and sits through an initial interview with Pinkerton personnel. Only candidates whose qualifications meet Pinkerton's job requirements move to the second step.

Next, prospective employees fill out questionnaires measuring attitudes toward honesty and willingness to follow company rules. Again, only people who meet Pinkerton's standards advance.

In the third step, candidates participate in a 10-minute interview session conducted over the telephone by a computerized voice system. They answer roughly 100 questions about job stability, career goals, work ethic, enthusiasm, and other aspects of their work history by pushing buttons on the telephone keypad. Just a few minutes after each candidate hangs up the phone, Pinkerton personnel can call the computer center and get the results.

This information helps the staff pinpoint topics to be addressed in the fourth step of the process, an in-depth personal interview. By this time, at least 30 percent of the applicants are weeded out. In the fifth step, Pinkerton investigators check the backgrounds of those candidates who have completed the personal interview successfully. Once they have the results of the investigation, Pinkerton personnel are then able to decide which candidates to hire.

Your Mission As a member of Pinkerton's human resources department, you regularly review unsolicited résumés. You're particularly on the lookout for recent college graduates who might be good candidates for management training positions in Pinkerton's comprehensive security operations for General Motors, which span the United States, Canada, and Mexico. Give Denis Brown your best advice about the following applicants, and be prepared to explain your recommendations.

1. You have received résumés from four people. Based only on the career objectives listed, which one of the candidates will you consider hiring as a management trainee?

   a. **Career Objective:** An entry-level management position in a large company

   b. **Career Objective:** To invest my management talent and business savvy and shepherd a business toward explosive growth

   c. **Career Objective:** A management position in which a degree in business administration and experience in managing personnel will be useful

   d. **Career Objective:** To learn all I can about personnel management in an exciting environment with a company whose reputation is outstanding

2. On the basis of only the education sections of another four résumés, which of the following candidates would you recommend?

   a. **Education**
   Morehouse College, Atlanta, GA, 1994–1998.
   Received B.A. degree with a major in Business Administration and a minor in Finance. Graduated with a 3.65 grade-point average. Played varsity football and basketball. Worked 15 hours per week in the library. Coordinated the local student chapter of the American Management Association. Member of Alpha Phi Alpha social fraternity.

   b. **Education**
   I attended Wayne State University in Detroit, Michigan, for two years and then transferred to the University of Michigan

at Ann Arbor, where I completed my studies. My major was economics, but I also took many business management courses, including employee motivation, leadership, history of management theory, and organizational behavior. I selected courses based on the professors' reputation for excellence, and I received mostly A's and B's. Unlike many college students, I viewed the acquisition of knowledge—rather than career preparation—as my primary goal. I believe I have received a well-rounded education that has prepared me to approach management situations as problem-solving exercises.

   c. **Academic Preparation**
   University of Connecticut, Storrs, Connecticut. Graduated with a B.A. degree in 1997. Majored in Physical Education. Minored in Business Administration. Graduated with a 2.85 average.

   d. **Education**
   North Texas State University and University of Texas at Tyler. Received B.A. and M.B.A. degrees. I majored in business as an undergraduate and concentrated in manufacturing management during my M.B.A. program. Received a special $2,500 scholarship offered by Rotary International recognizing academic achievement in business courses. I also won the MEGA award in 1995. Dean's list.

3. Which of the following four candidates would you recommend, based only on the experience sections?

   a. **Related Work Experience**
   McDonald's, Peoria, IL, 1992–1993. Part-time cook. Worked 15 hours per week while attending high school. Prepared hamburgers, chicken bits, and french fries. Received employee-of-the-month award for outstanding work habits.
   University Grill, Ames, IA, 1993–1996. Part-time cook. Worked 20 hours per week while attending college. Prepared hot and cold sandwiches. Helped manager purchase ingredients. Trained new kitchen workers. Prepared work schedules for kitchen staff.

   b. **Related Experience**
   Although I have never held a full-time job, I have worked part-time and during summer vacations throughout my high school and college years. During my freshman and sophomore years in high school, I bagged groceries at the A&P store three afternoons a week. The work was not terribly challenging, but I liked the customers and the other employees. During my junior and senior years, I worked at the YMCA as an after-school counselor for elementary school children. The kids were really sweet, and I still get letters from some of them. During summer vacations while I was in college, I did construction work for a local home builder. The job paid well, and I also learned a lot about carpentry. The guys I worked with were a mixed bag who expanded my vocabulary and knowledge of the world. I also worked part-time in college in the student cafeteria, where I scooped food onto plates. This did not require much talent, but it taught me a lot about how people behave when standing in line. I also learned quite a bit about life from my boss, Sam "the man" Benson, who has been managing the student cafeteria for 25 years.

c. **Previous Work Experience**

The Broadway Department Store, Sherman Oaks, CA, Summers, 1997–2000. Sales Consultant, Furniture Department. I interacted with a diverse group of customers, including suburban matrons, teenagers, career women, and professional couples. I endeavored to satisfy their individual needs and make their shopping experience memorable, efficient, and enjoyable. Under the direction of the sales manager, I helped prepare employee schedules and fill out departmental reports. I also helped manage the inventory, worked the cash register, and handled a variety of special orders and customer complaints with courtesy and aplomb. During the 1997 annual storewide sale, I sold more merchandise than any other salesperson in the entire furniture department.

d. **Experience Related to Management**

Belle Fleure, GA, Civilian Member of Public Safety Committee, January-December 2001.

- Organized and promoted a lecture series on vacation safety and home security for the residents of Belle Fleure, GA; recruited and trained seven committee members to help plan and produce the lectures; persuaded local businesses to finance the program; designed, printed, and distributed fliers; wrote and distributed press releases; attracted an average of 120 people to each of three lectures
- Developed a questionnaire to determine local residents' home security needs; directed the efforts of 10 volunteers working on the survey; prepared written report for city council and delivered oral summary of findings at town meeting; helped persuade city to fund new home security program
- Initiated the Business Security Forum as an annual meeting at which local business leaders could meet to discuss safety and security issues; created promotional flyers for the first forum; convinced 19 business owners to fund a business security survey; arranged press coverage of the first forum

4. You've received the following résumé. What action will you take?

Maria Martin
1124 2nd S.W., Rhinelander, WI 54501
(715) 369-0098

Career Objective: To build a management career in a growing U.S. company

Summary of Qualifications: As a student at the University of Wisconsin in Madison, carried out various assignments that have required skills related to a career in management. For example:

Planning Skills. As president of the university's foreign affairs forum, organized six lectures and workshops featuring 36 speakers from 16 foreign countries within a nine-month period. Identified and recruited the speakers, handled their travel arrangements, and scheduled the facilities.

Interpersonal Skills. As chairman of the parade committee for homecoming weekend, worked with the city of Madison to obtain approval, permits, and traffic control for the parade. Also encouraged local organizations such as the Lion's Club, the Kiwanis Club, and the Boy Scouts to participate in the parade. Coordinated the efforts of the 15 fraternities and 18 sororities that entered floats in the parade. Recruited 12 marching bands from surrounding communities and coordinated their efforts with the university's marching band. Also arranged for local auto dealers to provide cars for the 10 homecoming queen candidates.

Communication Skills. Wrote over 25 essays and term papers dealing with academic topics. Received an A on all but two of these papers. As a senior, wrote a 20-page analysis of the paper products industry, interviewing the five top executives at the Rhinelander paper company. Received an A+ on this paper.

a. Definitely recommend that Pinkerton take a look at this outstanding candidate.

b. Turn down the candidate. She doesn't give enough information about when she attended college, what she majored in, or where she has worked.

c. Call the candidate on the phone and ask for more information. If she sounds promising, send her an application form that requests more specific information about her academic background and employment history.

d. Consider the candidate's qualifications relative to those of other applicants. Recommend her if you do not have three or four other applicants with more directly relevant qualifications.[29]

TEST YOUR KNOWLEDGE

1. What is the purpose of maintaining an employment portfolio?

2. What is a résumé, and why is it important to adopt a "you" attitude when preparing one?

3. In what ways can job-seekers use the Internet during their career and employment search?

4. How does a chronological résumé differ from a functional résumé, and when is each appropriate?

5. What elements are commonly included in a résumé?

6. What are some of the most common problems with résumés?

7. Why is it important to provide a key word summary in a scannable or electronic résumé?

8. What advantages do résumés sent by e-mail have over résumés sent by fax or by mail?

9. How does a solicited application letter differ from an unsolicited letter?

10. How does the AIDA approach apply to an application letter?

INTERACTIVE LEARNING

USE THIS TEXT'S ONLINE RESOURCES

Visit the myPHLIP Web site at www.prenhall.com/thill. For Chapter 14, take advantage of the interactive "Study Guide" to test your chapter knowledge. Get instant feedback on whether you need additional studying. Read the "Current Events" articles to get the latest on chapter topics, and complete the exercises—as specified by your instructor.

This site's "Study Hall" helps you succeed in this course. "Talk in the Hall" lets you leave messages and meet new friends online. If you have a question, you can "Ask the Tutor." And to get a better grade in this course, you can find more help at "Writing Skills," "Study Skills," and "Study Tips."

The "Research Area" helps you locate a wealth of information to use in course assignments. Plus, you can send a message to online research experts, who will help you find exactly the information you need.

APPLY YOUR KNOWLEDGE

1. According to experts in the job-placement field, the average job seeker relies too heavily on the résumé and not enough on other elements of the job search. Which elements do you think are most important? Please explain.

2. One of the disadvantages of résumé scanning is that some qualified applicants will be missed because the technology isn't perfect. However, more companies are using this approach. Do you think that résumé scanning is a good idea? Please explain.

3. Stating your career objective on a résumé or application might limit your opportunities by labeling you too narrowly. Not stating your objective, however, might lead an employer to categorize you incorrectly. Which outcome is riskier? Do summaries of qualifications overcome such drawbacks? If so, how? Explain briefly.

4. When writing a solicited application letter and describing the skills requested in the employer's ad, how can you avoid using *I* too often? Explain and give examples.

5. **Ethical Choices** If your college grades are not spectacular, is it ethical to avoid mentioning your exact grade-point average on your résumé?

PRACTICE YOUR KNOWLEDGE

DOCUMENTS FOR ANALYSIS

Read the following documents; then (1) analyze the strengths or weaknesses of each document and (2) revise each document so that it follows the guidelines presented in this chapter.

Document 14.A: Writing a Résumé

Sylvia Manchester
765 Belle Fleur Blvd.
New Orleans, LA 70113
(504) 312-9504
smanchester@renmail.com

PERSONAL: Single, excellent health, 5'8", 116 lbs.; hobbies include cooking, dancing, and reading.

JOB OBJECTIVE: To obtain a responsible position in marketing or sales with a good company.

Education: B.A. degree in biology, University of Louisiana. Graduated with a 3.0 average. Member of the varsity cheerleading squad. President of Panhellenic League. Homecoming queen.

WORK EXPERIENCE

Fisher Scientific Instruments, 2000 to Present, Field Sales Representative. Responsible for calling on customers and explaining the features of Fisher's line of laboratory instruments. Also responsible for writing sales letters, attending trade shows, and preparing weekly sales reports.

Fisher Scientific Instruments, 1997–99, Customer Service Representative. Was responsible for handling incoming phone calls from customers who had questions about delivery, quality, or operation of Fisher's line of laboratory instruments. Also handled miscellaneous correspondence with customers.

Medical Electronics, Inc. 1994–97. Administrative Assistant to the Vice President of Marketing. In addition to handling typical secretarial chores for the vice president of marketing, I was in charge of compiling the monthly sales reports, using figures provided by members of the field sales force. I also was given responsibility for doing various market research activities.

New Orleans Convention and Visitors Bureau. 1991–94, Summers. Tour Guide. During the summers of my college years, I led tours of New Orleans for tourists visiting the city. My duties included greeting conventioneers and their spouses at hotels, explaining the history and features of the city during an all-day sight-seeing tour, and answering questions about New Orleans and its attractions. During my fourth summer with the bureau, I was asked to help train the new tour guides.

I prepared a handbook that provided interesting facts about the various tourist attractions and answers to the most commonly asked tourist questions. The Bureau was so impressed with the handbook they had it printed up so that it could be given as a gift to visitors.

University of Louisiana. 1991–94. Part-Time Clerk in Admissions Office. While I was a student in college, I worked 15 hours a week in the admissions office. My duties included filing, processing applications, and handling correspondence with high school students and administrators.

Document 14.B: Writing an Application Letter

I'm writing to let you know about my availability for the brand manager job you advertised. As you can see from my enclosed résumé, my background is perfect for the position. Even though I don't have any real job experience, my grades have been outstanding considering that I went to a top-ranked business school.

I did many things during my undergraduate years to prepare me for this job:

- Earned a 3.4 out of a 4.0 with a 3.8 in my business courses
- Elected representative to the student governing association
- Selected to receive the Lamar Franklin Award
- Worked to earn a portion of my tuition

I am sending my résumé to all the top firms, but I like yours better than any of the rest. Your reputation is tops in the industry, and I want to be associated with a business that can pridefully say it's the best.

If you wish for me to come in for an interview, I can come on a Friday afternoon or anytime on weekends when I don't have classes. Again, thanks for considering me for your brand manager position.

Document 14.C: Writing Application Follow-Up Messages

Did you receive my résumé? I sent it to you at least two months ago and haven't heard anything. I know you keep résumés on file, but I just want to be sure that you keep me in mind. I heard you are hiring health-care managers and certainly would like to be considered for one of those positions.

Since I last wrote you, I've worked in a variety of positions that have helped prepare me for management. To wit, I've become lunch manager at the restaurant where I work, which involved a raise in pay. I now manage a wait-staff of 12 girls and take the lunch receipts to the bank every day.

Of course, I'd much rather be working at a real job, and that's why I'm writing again. Is there anything else you would like to know about me or my background? I would really like to know more about your company. Is there any literature you could send me? If so, I would really appreciate it.

I think one reason I haven't been hired yet is that I don't want to leave Atlanta. So I hope when you think of me, it's for a position that wouldn't require moving. Thanks again for considering my application.

EXERCISES

14–1. **Teamwork** Working with another student, change the following statements to make them more effective for a traditional résumé by using active verbs.

   a. Have some experience with database design.

   b. Assigned to a project to analyze the cost accounting methods for a large manufacturer.

   c. I was part of a team that developed a new inventory control system.

   d. Am responsible for preparing the quarterly department budget.

   e. Was a manager of a department with seven employees working for me.

   f. Was responsible for developing a spreadsheet to analyze monthly sales by department.

   g. Put in place a new program for ordering supplies.

14–2. **Résumé Preparation: Work Accomplishments** Using your team's answers to Exercise 14–1, make the statements stronger by quantifying them (make up any numbers you need).

14–3. **Ethical Choices** Assume that you achieved all the tasks shown in Exercise 14–1 not as an individual employee, but as part of a team. In your résumé, must you mention other team members? Explain your answer.

14–4. **Résumé Preparation: Electronic Version** Using your revised version of Document for Analysis 14.A (on page 461), prepare a fully formatted print résumé. What formatting changes would Sylvia Manchester need to make if she were sending her résumé electronically? Develop a key-word summary and make all the changes needed to complete this electronic résumé.

14–5. **Work-Related Preferences: Self-Assessment** What work-related activities and situations do you prefer? Evaluate your preferences in each of the following areas. Use the results as a good start for guiding your job search.

ACTIVITY OR SITUATION	STRONGLY AGREE	AGREE	DISAGREE	NO PREFERENCE
1. I want to work independently.	_____	_____	_____	_____
2. I want variety in my work.	_____	_____	_____	_____
3. I want to work with people.	_____	_____	_____	_____
4. I want to work with products or machines.	_____	_____	_____	_____
5. I want physical work.	_____	_____	_____	_____
6. I want mental work.	_____	_____	_____	_____
7. I want to work for a large organization.	_____	_____	_____	_____
8. I want to work for a nonprofit organization.	_____	_____	_____	_____
9. I want to work for a small family business.	_____	_____	_____	_____
10. I want to work for a service business.	_____	_____	_____	_____
11. I want regular, predictable work hours.	_____	_____	_____	_____
12. I want to work in a city location.	_____	_____	_____	_____
13. I want to work in a small town or suburb.	_____	_____	_____	_____
14. I want to work in another country.	_____	_____	_____	_____
15. I want to work outdoors.	_____	_____	_____	_____
16. I want to work in a structured environment.	_____	_____	_____	_____

14–6. **Internet** Based on the preferences you identified in the self-assessment (Exercise 14–5) and the academic, professional, and personal qualities you have to offer, perform an Internet search for an appropriate career, using any of the Web sites listed in "Using the Power of Technology—Netting a Job on the Web." Draft a brief report indicating how the careers you select and job openings you find match your strengths and preferences.

CASES

THINKING ABOUT YOUR CAREER

1. Taking stock and taking aim: Application package for the right job Think about yourself. What are some things that come easily to you? What do you enjoy doing? In what part of the country would you like to live? Do you like to work indoors? Outdoors? A combination of the two? How much do you like to travel? Would you like to spend considerable time on the road? Do you like to work closely with others or more independently? What conditions make a job unpleasant? Do you delegate responsibility easily, or do you like to do things yourself? Are you better with words or numbers? Better at speaking or writing? Do you

like to work under fixed deadlines? How important is job security to you? Do you want your supervisor to state clearly what is expected of you, or do you like the freedom to make many of your own decisions?

Your task: After answering these questions, gather information about possible jobs that suit your profile by consulting reference materials (from your college library or placement center) and by searching the Internet (using some of the search strategies discussed in Chapter 11). Next, choose a location, a company, and a job that interests you. With guidance from your instructor, decide whether to apply for a job you're qualified for now or one you'll be qualified for with additional education. Then, as directed by your instructor, write one or more of the following: (a) a job-inquiry letter, (b) a résumé, (c) a letter of application, (d) a follow-up letter to your application letter.

2. Scanning the possibilities: Résumé for the Internet In your search for a position, you discover that Career Magazine is a Web site that lists hundreds of companies advertising on the Internet. Your chances of getting an interview with a leading company will be enhanced if you submit your résumé and cover letter electronically. On the Web, explore www. careermag.com.

Your task: Prepare a scannable résumé that could be submitted to the site that best fits your qualifications, experience, and education. Print out the résumé for your instructor.

3. Online application: Electronic cover letter introducing a résumé *Motley Fool* (www.fool.com) is a "Generation X" online magazine accessed via the World Wide Web. Although its founders and writers are extremely creative and motivated, they lack business experience and need a fellow "X'er" to help them manage the business. Among articles in a recent edition was one titled "The Soul of the Dead," about the influence of the Grateful Dead on more than one generation of concert-goers. Other articles deal with lifestyle issues, pop movies, music, and "trends for an old-young generation."

Your task: Write an e-mail message that will serve as your cover letter, and attach your résumé as a file to be downloaded. Address your message to Louis Corrigan, Managing Editor. Try to limit your message to one screen (about 23 lines). You'll need a creative "hook" and a reassuring approach that identifies you as the right person to help *Motley Fool* become financially viable.

WRITING A RÉSUMÉ AND AN APPLICATION LETTER

4. "Help wanted": Application for a job listed in the classified section Among the jobs listed in today's **Chicago Tribune** (435 N. Michigan Avenue, Chicago, IL 60641) are the following:

Accounting Assistant

Established leader in the vacation ownership industry has immediate opening in its Northbrook corp. accounting dept. for an Accounting Assistant. Responsibilities include: bank reconciliation, preparation of deposits, AP, and cash receipt posting. Join our fast-growing company and enjoy our great benefits package. Flex work hours, medical, dental insurance. Fax résumé to Lisa: 847-564-3876.

Administrative Assistant

Fast-paced Wood Dale office seeks professional with strong computer skills. Proficient in MS Word & Excel, PowerPoint a plus. Must be detail oriented, able to handle multiple tasks, and possess strong communication skills. Excellent benefits, salary, and work environment. Fax résumé to 630-350-8649.

Customer Service

A nationally known computer software developer has an exciting opportunity in customer service and inside sales support in its fast-paced downtown Chicago office. You'll help resolve customer problems over the phone, provide information, assist in account management, and administer orders. If you're friendly, self-motivated, energetic, and have 2 years of experience, excellent problem-solving skills, organizational, communication, and PC skills, and communicate well over the phone, send résumé to J. Haber, 233 North Lake Shore Drive, Chicago, IL 60641.

Sales-Account Manager

MidCity Baking Company is seeking an Account Manager to sell and coordinate our programs to major accounts in the Chicago market. The candidate should possess strong analytical and selling skills and demonstrate computer proficiency. Previous sales experience with major account level assignment desired. A degree in business or equivalent experience preferred. For confidential consideration please mail résumé to Steven Crane, Director of Sales, MidCity Baking Company, 133 N. Railroad Avenue, Northlake IL 60614.

Your task: Send a résumé and an application letter to one of these potential employers.

WRITING OTHER TYPES OF EMPLOYMENT MESSAGES

5. Crashing the last frontier: Letter of inquiry about jobs in Alaska Your friend can't understand why you would want to move to Alaska. So you explain: "What really decided it for me was that I'd never seen the northern lights."

"But what about the bears? The 60-degree-below winters? The permafrost?" asks your friend.

"No problem. Anchorage doesn't get much colder than Buffalo does. It is just windier and wetter. Anyhow, I want to live near Fairbanks, which is near the gold-mining area—and the university is there. Fairbanks has lots of small businesses, like a frontier town in the West about 150 years ago. I think it still has homesteading tracts for people who want to do their own building and are willing to stay for a certain number of years."

"Your plans seem a little hasty," your friend warns. "Maybe you should write for information before you just take off. How do you know you could get a job?"

Your task: Take your friend's advice and write to the Chamber of Commerce, Fairbanks, AK 99701. Ask what types of employment are available to someone with your education and experience, and ask who specifically is hiring year-round employees.

GOING ONLINE EXERCISES

Post an Online Résumé, page 448

Your résumé is like a letter of introduction: it should make a good first impression. It must be organized, error-free, and in an appropriate format. In today's electronic business world, you should know how to prepare a résumé to post on the Internet or to send by e-mail. Learn this and more by logging on to CareerBuilder.

1. Before writing a new résumé, make a list of action verbs that describe your skills and experience.
2. Describe the advantages and disadvantages of chronological and functional résumé formats. Do you think a combination résumé would be an appropriate format for your new résumé? Explain why or why not.
3. List some of the tips you learned for preparing an electronic résumé.

To complete this exercise, log on to this text's Web site at www.prenhall.com/thill. Select Chapter 14, then select "Student Resources," click on the name of the featured Web site, and follow the detailed navigational directions.

15

INTERVIEWING FOR EMPLOYMENT AND FOLLOWING UP

chapter

After studying this chapter, you will be able to

1 Define *employment interview* and explain its dual purpose.

2 Describe briefly what employers look for during an employment interview.

3 List six tasks you need to complete to prepare for a successful job interview.

4 Explain the three stages of a successful employment interview.

5 Name six common employment messages that follow an interview and state briefly when you would use each one.

Herman Miller's recruiters look at a candidate's education and experience, but even more important is the candidate's personality. It's a challenge to find people who can operate in the company's participative environment without regarding the culture as permissive.

On the job:

FACING A COMMUNICATION DILEMMA AT HERMAN MILLER, INC.

How to Tell a Good Dancer Before the Waltz Begins

www.hermanmiller.com

Looking for a company that cares about people? You might try Herman Miller, a highly successful establishment that manufactures office furniture in Zeeland, Michigan. Founded in 1923 by D. J. DePree, Herman Miller is justifiably famous for its corporate culture. It may be the only company on the *Fortune* 500 list that actually has a "vice president for people." Participation is the name of the game in this organization. Employees at all levels are consulted about important decisions and reap the rewards if the business does well.

When Herman Miller's recruiters interview a job candidate, they look at the person's education and experience, but they also look for something else: the ability to get along with others. If the candidate's personality is outstanding, the company may be willing to overlook a lack of relevant experience. A senior vice president of research was once a high school football coach. The senior vice president of marketing and sales used to be the dean of agriculture at Michigan State. And the vice president for people had been planning to become a prison warden but joined Herman Miller instead.

On the surface, these people didn't seem to be good candidates for management jobs in the office furniture business, but Herman Miller looked beyond the superficial to see their true potential. The most important quality in a Herman Miller employee is the capacity for teamwork. "To be successful here," says one Herman Miller executive, "you have to know how to dance."

How do you know whether someone is a good dancer before you actually begin the waltz? That's the challenge facing Herman Miller's recruiters when they interview job candidates. The challenge facing candidates is how to prepare for a job interview. What would you do? What can you do during an interview? Is there anything you could do after the interview?[1]

UNDERSTANDING THE INTERVIEWING PROCESS

As recruiters at Herman Miller will advise you, the best way to prepare for a job interview is to think carefully about the job itself. Job interviews have a dual purpose. The organization's main objective is to find the best person available for the job; the applicant's main objective is to find the job best suited to his or her goals and capabilities. While recruiters such as those at Herman Miller are trying to decide whether you are right for them, you must decide whether Herman Miller or any other company is right for you.

It takes an average of 10 interviews to get one job offer. If you hope to have several offers to choose from, you can expect to go through 20 or 30 interviews during your job search.[2] Because interviewing takes time, start seeking jobs well in advance of the date you want to start work. Some students start their job search as much as nine months before graduation. During downturns in the economy, early planning is even more crucial. Many employers become more selective and many corporations reduce their campus visits and campus hiring programs, so more of the job search burden falls on you.

But once you get your foot in the door, you must prepare to meet with a recruiter during an **employment interview,** a formal meeting during which both employer and applicant ask questions and exchange information to see whether the applicant and the organization are a good match. Applicants often face a series of interviews, each with a different purpose.

The Typical Sequence of Interviews

Most employers interview an applicant two or three times before deciding to make a job offer. First is the preliminary screening stage, which is generally held on campus and which helps employers screen out unqualified applicants. Those candidates who best meet the organization's requirements are invited to visit company offices for further evaluation. Interviews at the screening stage are fairly structured, so applicants are often asked roughly the same questions. Many companies use standardized evaluation sheets to "grade" the applicants so that all the candidates will be measured against the same criteria.

Your best approach to an interview at the screening stage is to follow the interviewer's lead. Keep your responses short and to the point. Time is limited, so talking too much can be a big mistake. However, to give the interviewer a way to differentiate you from other candidates and to demonstrate your strengths and qualifications, try to emphasize the "theme" you used in developing your résumé.

The next stage of interviews helps the organization narrow the field a little further. Typically, if you're invited to visit a company, you will talk with several people: a member of the human resources department, one or two potential colleagues, and your potential supervisor. You might face a panel of several interviewers who ask you questions during a single session. By noting how you listen, think, and express yourself, they can decide how likely you are to get along with colleagues. Your best approach during this selection stage of interviews is to show interest in the job, relate your skills and experience to the organization's needs, listen attentively, ask insightful questions, and display enthusiasm.

If the interviewers agree that you're a good candidate, you may receive a job offer, either on the spot or a few days later by phone or mail. In other cases, you may be invited back for a final evaluation by a higher-ranking executive who has the authority to make the hiring decision and to decide on your compensation. An underlying objective of the final stage is often to sell you on the advantages of joining the organization.

Types of Interviews

Organizations use different types of interviews to discover as much as possible about applicants. A **structured interview** is generally used in the screening stage. Here the employer controls the interview by asking a series of prepared questions in a set order. Working from a checklist, the interviewer asks candidates each question, staying within an allotted time period. All answers are noted. Although useful in gathering facts, the structured interview is generally regarded as a poor measure of an applicant's personal qualities. Nevertheless, some companies, such as Ameritech Cellular Services, use structured interviews to create uniformity in their hiring process.[3]

By contrast, the **open-ended interview** is less formal and unstructured, with a relaxed format. The interviewer poses broad, open-ended questions and encourages the applicant to talk freely. This type of interview is good for bringing out an applicant's personality and is used to test professional judgment. However, some candidates reveal too much, rambling on about personal or family problems that have nothing to do with their qualifications for employment, their ability to get along with co-workers, or any personal interests that could benefit their performance on the job. So be careful. You need to strike a delicate balance between being friendly and remembering that you're in a business situation.

Some organizations perform **group interviews,** meeting with several candidates simultaneously to see how they interact. This type of interview is useful for judging interpersonal skills. For example, the Walt Disney Company uses group interviews when hiring people for its theme parks. During a 45-minute session, the Disney recruiter watches how three candidates relate to one another. Do they smile? Are they supportive of one another's comments? Do they try to score points at each other's expense?[4]

Perhaps the most unnerving type of interview is the **stress interview,** which is set up to see how well a candidate handles stressful situations (an important qualification for certain jobs). During a stress interview you might be asked pointed questions designed to irk or unsettle you. You might be subjected to long periods of silence, criticisms of your appearance, deliberate interruptions, and abrupt or even hostile reactions by the interviewer.

As employers try to cut travel costs, the **video interview** is becoming more popular. Many large companies use videoconferencing systems to screen middle-management candidates or to interview new recruits at universities. Experts recommend that candidates prepare a bit differently for a video interview than for an in-person meeting:[5]

◆ Ask for a preliminary phone conversation to establish rapport with the interviewer.

◆ Arrive early enough to get used to the equipment and setting.

◆ During the interview, speak clearly but not more slowly than normal.

◆ Sit straight.

◆ Look up, not down.

◆ Try to show some animation, but not too much (since it will appear blurry to the interviewer).

Another modern twist is the **situational interview,** in which an interviewer describes a situation and asks, "How would you handle this?" Many companies have learned that no correlation exists between how well people interview and how well they perform on the job. So companies such as Kraft Foods, Delta Air Lines, AT&T, and Procter & Gamble rely on situational interviews. Proponents of this approach claim that interviewing is about the job, not about a candidate's five-year goals, weaknesses or strengths, challenging experiences, or greatest accomplishment. So the situational interview is a hands-on, at-work meeting between an employer who needs a job done and a worker who must be fully prepared to do the work.[6]

Regardless of the type of interview you may face, a personal interview is vital because your résumé can't show whether you're lively and outgoing or subdued and low-key, able to take direction or able to take charge. Each job requires a different mix of personality traits. The interviewer's task is to find out whether you will be effective on the job.

O b j e c t i v e

Describe briefly what employers look for during an employment interview.

2

What Employers Look For

Having the right personality traits for the job is important in today's workplace. Southwest Airlines CEO Herb Kelleher knows exactly what he's looking for in a potential employee. A sense of humor tops his list because he believes that people who don't take themselves too seriously are better able to cope with the stress of airline work. Kelleher also wants employees who are self-motivated, enthusiastic, not afraid to make decisions, willing to take risks, intelligent, good communicators, and considerate of others.[7]

When it comes down to it, every job has basic qualifications. Employers first look for two things: evidence that a candidate will fit in with the organization and proof that the person can handle a specific job.

A Good Fit with the Organization   Interviewers try to decide whether a candidate will be compatible with the other people in the organization. Some interviewers believe that personal background is an indication of how well the candidate will fit in, so they might ask about your interests, hobbies, awareness of world events, and so forth. You can expand your potential along these lines by reading widely, making an effort to meet new people, and participating in discussion groups, seminars, and workshops.

Some interviewers may also consider a candidate's personal style. You're likely to impress an employer by being open, enthusiastic, and interested. Some interviewers also look for courtesy, sincerity, willingness to learn, and a style that is positive and self-confident. All of these qualities help a new employee adapt to a new workplace and new responsibilities.

Qualifications for the Job   When you're invited to interview for a position, the interviewer may already have some idea of whether you have the right qualifications, based on a review of your résumé. But during the interview, you'll be asked to describe your education and previous jobs in more depth so that the interviewer can determine how well your skills match the requirements. In many cases, the interviewer will be seeking someone with the flexibility to apply diverse skills in several areas.[8] When describing your skills, be honest. If you don't know how to do something, say so. Given the high cost of hiring unsuitable employees, more and more companies are turning to preemployment testing to verify candidates' skills and to determine whether they have the necessary psychological characteristics to handle a particular job.

> Suitability for the specific job is judged on the basis of
> • Academic preparation
> • Work experience
> • Job-related personality traits

Preemployment Testing   Your chances of being asked to take some form of preemployment test are roughly one in six if you're applying for a managerial position and one in four if you're applying for a nonsupervisory job.[9] Even though many of the tests are related to specific job skills, the real growth is occurring in tests designed to weed out dishonest candidates and substance abusers.

Companies are concerned about these issues for good reason. Estimates are that white-collar crime costs U.S. businesses more than $400 billion a year and is increasing at a rate of 10 to 20 percent annually.[10] Moreover, substance abusers have two to four times as many accidents as other employees. Drug use can be linked to 40 percent of industrial fatalities.[11] Statistics such as these are enough to worry any employer, particularly given the threat of being held liable for negligent hiring practices if an employee harms an innocent party on the job.

To combat such problems, approximately 45 percent of all companies now require applicants to undergo drug and alcohol testing.[12] Some companies administer medical and psychological exams. Some of the larger firms are even using gene testing to screen out applicants who may develop expensive and debilitating diseases.[13]

Tests have their critics. Some employers prefer not to go to the extra expense of administering them or feel that educated judgment works just as well. Some applicants question the validity of honesty and drug tests or consider them an invasion of privacy. However, when used in conjunction with other evidence, such as reference checks, employment tests attempt to provide an objective, quantitative measure of an applicant's qualifications (see "Sharpening Your Career Skills—How to Check References and Stay within the Law"). To protect candidates' interests, employment tests must meet strict criteria of fairness set forth by the Equal Employment Opportunity Commission (EEOC).

PREPARING FOR A JOB INTERVIEW

For a successful interview, preparation is mandatory. Today's companies expect serious candidates to demonstrate an understanding of the company's operations, its market, and its strategic and tactical problems.[14] Candidates might be asked to collaborate on a decision or to develop a group presentation. Trained observers evaluate the candidates' performance using predetermined criteria and then advise management on how well each person is likely to handle the challenges normally faced on the job.[15]

It's perfectly normal to feel a little anxious before an interview. But preparation will help you perform well. Before the interview, do some follow-up research, think ahead about questions, bolster your confidence, polish your interview style, plan to look good, and be ready when you arrive. Be sure to consider any cultural differences when preparing for interviews, and base your approach on what your audience expects. The advice in this chapter is most appropriate for companies and employers in the United States and Canada.

O b j e c t i v e

3

List six tasks you need to complete to prepare for a successful job interview.

Just as written messages need planning, employment interviews need preparation.

Sharpening Your Career Skills

How to Check References and Stay within the Law

Employers who hire people without adequately checking their backgrounds face not only the possibility of expensive hiring mistakes but also legal action if problems arise. Some chilling examples include the building janitor with an unchecked criminal record who murdered a tenant, the school bus driver with an unchecked record of drunk driving arrests, and the "chemist" whose difficulties on his new job were finally explained by his forged college degree. More commonly, reference checks can reveal long employment gaps, inflated accomplishments, false claims about academic degrees, and potential interpersonal problems on the job.

Even though companies realize how much they need to share relevant information on employees, many executives are uncomfortable about committing their remarks to paper. Here's some advice from the most successful reference checkers. (Check references before making an offer; if you withdraw it, applicants won't blame references.)

❏ *Get applicants involved.* Ask candidates to provide a list of references to check. Have them sign a waiver releasing their references from legal liability for their statements, and ask each candidate to contact references beforehand to encourage them to speak freely.

❏ *Take your time, and don't delegate.* Take about two hours per candidate. Call early in the morning or after five, when executives are likely to answer the phone themselves.

❏ *Prepare your questions carefully.* Whether writing or calling, pose open-ended, job-related questions about *how* a candidate performed, not just what was accomplished. Ask similar questions for all applicants (don't ask whether a female executive fears traveling alone if you wouldn't ask the same question about a male executive). Also, ask for referrals to others who can comment on the candidate's performance.

❏ *Know the laws in your state.* State and federal laws on reference checks are constantly being updated. In most states, it's illegal to ask directly or indirectly about a candidate's age, sex, religion, race, marital status, sexual orientation, disabilities, politics, pregnancy, drug use, medical history, or arrest records (unless the candidate will be working with minors). But it's legal in most states to contact police departments and former employers to ask about arrest records or whether a person has ever been *convicted* of a crime. Also, you can (and should) contact schools, or have applicants request, to have course transcripts mailed directly to you.

CAREER APPLICATIONS

1. Think about who you would supply as references on an employment application. Now assume a potential employer's perspective, and prepare the questions you'd want those references to answer about you and your work.
2. You've interviewed a job candidate who has all the right answers and seems to have the right qualifications, but your intuition tells you something isn't quite right. What checking would you do to confirm or quell your concerns?

Do Some Follow-Up Research

When planning your employment search, you probably already researched the companies you sent your résumé to. But now that you've been invited for an interview, you'll want to fine-tune your research and brush up on the facts you've collected (see Table 15–1). You can review Chapter 14 for ideas on where to look for information.

Be prepared to relate your qualifications to the organization's needs.

Learning about the organization and the job enables you to show the interviewer just how you will meet the organization's particular needs. With a little research, for instance, you would discover that Microsoft plans on investing heavily in the technical and marketing support of software developers as well as making things simpler for all users and system administrators.[16] Knowing these facts might help you pinpoint aspects of your background (such as the ability to simplify processes) that would appeal to Microsoft's recruiters.

Think Ahead About Questions

Planning ahead for questions is one of the best ways to prepare. Planning will help you handle the interviewer's questions intelligently. (See "Sharpening Your Career Skills—Interview Strategies: Answering the 16 Toughest Questions.") Moreover, you'll be able to prepare intelligent questions of your own.

Planning for the Employer's Questions   Employers usually gear their interview questions to specific organizational needs.

In her efforts to find work, Marci Burkhart gets help from the Career Center at Syracuse University.

Table 15–1   Finding Out About the Organization and the Job

Where to Look for Information

• *Annual report*	Summarizes operations; describes products, lists events, names key personnel
• *In-house magazine or newspaper*	Reveals information about company operations, events, personnel
• *Product brochure or publicity release*	Gives insight into firm's operations and values (obtain from public relations office)
• *Stock research report*	Helps assess stability and growth prospects (obtain online or from stockbroker)
• *Newspapers business or financial pages*	Contain news items about organizations, current performance figures
• *Periodicals indexes*	Contain descriptive listings of magazine/newspaper articles about firms (obtain from library)
• *Better Business Bureau and Chamber of Commerce*	Distribute information about some local organizations
• *Former and current employees*	Have insight into job and work environment
• *College placement office*	Collects information on organizations that recruit and on job qualifications and salaries

What to Find Out About the Organization

• *Full Name*	How the firm is officially known (e.g., 3M is Minnesota Mining & Manufacturing Company)
• *Location*	Where the organization's headquarters, branch offices, and plants are
• *Age*	How long the organization has been in business
• *Products*	What goods and services the organization produces and sells
• *Industry position*	What the organization's current market share, financial position, and profit picture are
• *Earnings*	What the trends in the firm's stock prices and dividends are (if firm is publicly held)
• *Growth*	How the firm's earnings/holdings have changed in recent years and prospects for expansion
• *Organization*	What subsidiaries, divisions, and departments make up the whole

What to Find Out About the Job

• *Job title*	What you will be called
• *Job functions*	What the main tasks of the job are
• *Job qualifications*	What knowledge and skills the job requires
• *Career path*	What chances for ready advancement exist
• *Salary range*	What the firm typically offers and what is reasonable in this industry and geographic area
• *Travel opportunities*	How often, long, and far you'll be allowed (or required) to travel
• *Relocation opportunities*	Where you might be allowed (or required) to move and how often

You can expect to be asked about your skills, achievements, and goals, as well as about your attitude toward work and school, your relationships with others (work supervisors, colleagues, and fellow students), and occasionally, your hobbies and interests. For a look at the types of questions often asked, see Table 15–2 on page 473. Jot down a brief answer to each one. Then read the answers over until you feel comfortable with each of them. You may want to tape record your answers and then listen to make sure they sound clear and convincing.

Practice answering interview questions.

Although practicing your answers will help you feel prepared and confident, you don't want to memorize responses or sound over-rehearsed. You might also give a list of interview questions to a friend or relative and have that person ask you various questions at random. This method helps you learn to articulate answers and to look at the person as you answer.

Planning Questions of Your Own   In an interview the questions you ask are just as important as the answers you provide. By asking intelligent questions, you demonstrate your understanding of the organization, and you can steer the discussion into those areas that allow you to present your qualifications to peak advantage. Before the

Sharpening Your Career Skills

Interview Strategies: Answering the 16 Toughest Questions

The answers to challenging interview questions can reveal a lot about a candidate. You can expect to face several such questions during every interview. If you're prepared with thoughtful answers that are related to your specific situation, you're bound to make a good impression. Here are 16 tough questions and guidelines for planning answers that put your qualities in the best light.

1. **What was the toughest decision you ever had to make?** Be prepared with a good example, explaining why the decision was difficult and how you decided.

2. **Why do you want to work for this organization?** Show that you've done your homework, and cite some things going on in the company that appeal to you.

3. **Why should we employ you?** Emphasize your academic strengths, job skills, and enthusiasm for the firm. Tie specific skills to the employer's needs, and give examples of how you can learn and become productive quickly. Cite past activities to prove you can work with others as part of a team.

4. **If we hire you, what changes would you make?** No one can know what to change in a position before settling in and learning about the job and company operations. State that you would take a good hard look at everything the company is doing before making recommendations.

5. **Can we offer you a career path?** Reply that you believe so, but you need to know more about the normal progression within the organization.

6. **What are your greatest strengths?** Answer sincerely by summarizing your strong points: "I can see what must be done and then do it" or "I'm willing to make decisions" or "I work well with others."

7. **What are your greatest weaknesses?** Describe a weakness so that it sounds like a virtue—honestly revealing something about yourself while showing how it works to an employer's advantage. If you sometimes drive yourself too hard, explain that it has helped when you've had to meet deadlines.

8. **What didn't you like about previous jobs you've held?** State what you didn't like and discuss what the experience taught you. Avoid making slighting references to former employers.

9. **How do you spend your leisure time?** Rather than focusing on just one, mention a cross section of interests—active and quiet, social and solitary.

10. **Are there any weaknesses in your education or experience?** Take stock of your weaknesses before the interview, and practice discussing them in a positive light. You'll see they're minor when discussed along with the positive qualities you have to offer.

11. **Where do you want to be five years from now?** This question tests (1) whether you're merely using this job as a stopover until something better comes along and (2) whether you've given thought to your long-term goals. Saying that you'd like to be company president is unrealistic, and yet few employers want people who are content to sit still. Your answer should reflect your long-term goals and the organization's advancement opportunities.

12. **What are your salary expectations?** If you're asked this at the outset, say, "Why don't we discuss salary after you decide whether I'm right for the job?" If the interviewer asks this after showing real interest in you, speak up. Do your homework, but if you need a clue about salary levels, say, "Can you discuss the salary range with me?"

13. **What would you do if . . .** This question tests your resourcefulness. For example: "What would you do if your computer broke down during an audit?" Your answer is less important than your approach to the problem—and a calm approach is best.

14. **What type of position are you interested in?** Job titles and responsibilities vary from firm to firm. So state your skills ("I'm good with numbers") and the positions that require those skills ("accounts payable").

15. **Tell me something about yourself.** Answer that you'll be happy to talk about yourself, and ask what the interviewer wants to know. If this point is clarified, respond. If it isn't, explain how your skills can contribute to the job and the organization. This is a great chance to sell yourself.

16. **Do you have any questions about the organization or the job?** Employers like candidates who are interested in the organization. Convey your interest and enthusiasm.

Be sure that your answers are sincere, truthful, and positive. Take a moment to compose your thoughts before responding so that your answers are to the point.

CAREER APPLICATIONS

1. What makes an effective answer to an interviewer's question? Consider some of the ways answers can vary: specific versus general, assertive versus passive, informal versus formal.

2. Think of four additional questions that pertain specifically to your résumé. Practice your answers.

You are responsible for deciding whether the work and the organization are compatible with your goals and values.

interview, prepare a list of about a dozen questions you need answered in order to evaluate the organization and the job.

Don't limit your questions to those you think will impress the interviewer, or you won't get the information you'll need to make a wise decision if and when you're offered the job. Here's a list of some things you might want to find out:

◆ **Are these my kind of people?** Observe the interviewer, and if you can, arrange to talk with other employees.

Table 15–2   Twenty-Five Common Interview Questions

Questions About College

1. What courses in college did you like most? Least? Why?
2. Do you think your extracurricular activities in college were worth the time you spent on them? Why or why not?
3. When did you choose your college major? Did you ever change your major? If so, why?
4. Do you feel you did the best scholastic work you are capable of?
5. Which of your college years was the toughest? Why?

Questions About Employers and Jobs

6. What jobs have you held? Why did you leave?
7. What percentage of your college expenses did you earn? How?
8. Why did you choose your particular field of work?
9. What are the disadvantages of your chosen field?
10. Have you served in the military? What rank did you achieve? What jobs did you perform?
11. What do you think about how this industry operates today?
12. Why do you think you would like this particular type of job?

Questions About Personal Attitudes and Preferences

13. Do you prefer to work in any specific geographic location? If so, why?
14. How much money do you hope to be earning in 5 years? In 10 years?
15. What do you think determines a person's progress in a good organization?
16. What personal characteristics do you feel are necessary for success in your chosen field?
17. Tell me a story.
18. Do you like to travel?
19. Do you think grades should be considered by employers? Why or why not?

Questions About Work Habits

20. Do you prefer working with others or by yourself?
21. What type of boss do you prefer?
22. Have you ever had any difficulty getting along with colleagues or supervisors? With instructors? Other students?
23. Would you prefer to work in a large or a small organization? Why?
24. How do you feel about overtime work?
25. What have you done that shows initiative and willingness to work?

◆ **Can I do this work?** Compare your qualifications with the requirements described by the interviewer.

◆ **Will I enjoy the work?** Know yourself and what's important to you. Will you find the work challenging? Will it give you feelings of accomplishment, of satisfaction, and of making a real contribution?

◆ **Is the job what I want?** You may never find a job that fulfills all your wants, but the position you accept should satisfy at least your primary ones. Will it make use of your best capabilities? Does it offer a career path to the long-term goals you've set?

◆ **Does the job pay what I'm worth?** By comparing jobs and salaries before you're interviewed, you'll know what's reasonable for someone with your skills in your industry.

◆ **What kind of person would I be working for?** If the interviewer is your prospective boss, watch how others interact with that person, tactfully query other employees, or pose a careful question or two during the interview. If your prospective boss is someone else, ask for that person's name, job title, and responsibilities. Try to learn all you can.

◆ **What sort of future can I expect with this organization?** How healthy is the organization? Can you look forward to advancement? Does the organization offer insurance, pension, vacation, or other benefits?

Types of questions to ask during an interview:
• Warm-up
• Open-ended
• Indirect

Rather than bombarding the interviewer with these questions the minute you walk in the room, use a mix of formats to elicit this information. Start with a warm-up question to help break the ice. You might ask a Herman Miller recruiter, "What departments usually hire new graduates?" After that, you might build rapport by asking an open-ended question that draws out the interviewer's opinion ("How do you think Internet sales will affect Herman Miller's continued growth?"). Indirect questions can elicit useful information and show that you've prepared for the interview ("I'd really like to know more about Herman Miller's plans for expanding its corporate presence on the Web" or "That recent *Business Week* article about the company was very interesting"). Any questions you ask should be in your own words so that you don't sound like every other candidate. For a list of other good questions you might use as a starting point, see Table 15–3.

Take your list of questions to the interview on a notepad. If you need to, jot down brief notes during the meeting, and be sure to record answers in more detail afterward. Having a list of questions should impress the interviewer with your organization and thoroughness. It will also show that you're there to evaluate the organization and the job as well as to sell yourself.

Bolster Your Confidence

By building your confidence, you'll make a better impression. The best way to counteract any apprehension is to remove its source. You may feel shy or self-conscious because you think you have some flaw that will prompt others to reject you. Bear in mind, however, that you're much more conscious of your limitations than other people are.

If you feel shy or self-conscious, remember that recruiters are human too.

If some aspect of your appearance or background makes you uneasy, correct it or offset it by exercising positive traits such as warmth, wit, intelligence, or charm. Instead of dwelling on your weaknesses, focus on your strengths so that you can emphasize them to an interviewer. Make a list of your good points and compare them with what you see as your shortcomings.

Remember that you're not alone. All the other candidates for the job are just as nervous as you are. Even the interviewer may be nervous.

Table 15–3 Fifteen Questions to Ask the Interviewer	
Questions About the Job	*Questions About the Organization*
What are the job's major responsibilities?	What are the organization's major strengths? Weaknesses?
What qualities do you want in the person who fills this position?	Who are your organization's major competitors, and what are their strengths and weaknesses?
Do you want to know more about my related training?	What makes your organization different from others in the industry?
What is the first problem that needs the attention of the person you hire?	What are your organization's major markets?
Would relocation be required now or in the future?	Does the organization have any plans for new products? Acquisitions?
Why is this job now vacant?	How would you define your organization's managerial philosophy?
What can you tell me about the person I would report to?	What additional training does your organization provide?
	Do employees have an opportunity to continue their education with help from the organization?

Figure 15–1
Marks Against Applicants (in General Order of Importance)

WHAT EMPLOYERS DON'T LIKE TO SEE IN CANDIDATES

- ☑ Poor personal appearance
- ☑ Overbearing, overaggressive, conceited demeanor; a "superiority complex"; "know it all" attitude
- ☑ Inability to express ideas clearly; poor voice, diction, grammar
- ☑ Lack of knowledge or experience
- ☑ Poor preparation for the interview
- ☑ Lack of interest in the job
- ☑ Lack of planning for career; lack of purpose, goals
- ☑ Lack of enthusiasm; passive and indifferent demeanor
- ☑ Lack of confidence and poise; appearance of being nervous and ill at ease
- ☑ Insufficient evidence of achievement
- ☑ Failure to participate in extracurricular activities
- ☑ Overemphasis on money; interest only in the best dollar offer
- ☑ Poor scholastic record; just got by
- ☑ Unwillingness to start at the bottom; expecting too much too soon
- ☑ Tendency to make excuses
- ☑ Evasive answers; hedges on unfavorable factors in record
- ☑ Lack of tact
- ☑ Lack of maturity
- ☑ Lack of courtesy; ill-mannered
- ☑ Condemnation of past employers
- ☑ Lack of social skills
- ☑ Marked dislike for schoolwork
- ☑ Lack of vitality
- ☑ Failure to look interviewer in the eye
- ☑ Limp, weak handshake

Polish Your Interview Style

Confidence helps you walk into an interview, but once you're there, you want to give the interviewer an impression of poise, good manners, and good judgment. One way to develop an adept style is to stage mock interviews with a friend. After each practice session, try to identify opportunities for improvement. Have your friend critique your performance, using the list of interview faults shown in Figure 15–1. You can even videotape these mock interviews and then evaluate them yourself. The taping process can be intimidating, but it helps you work out any problems before you begin actual job interviews.

Staging mock interviews with a friend is a good way to hone your style.

As you stage your mock interviews, pay particular attention to your nonverbal behavior. In the United States, you are more likely to have a successful interview if you maintain eye contact, smile frequently, sit in an attentive position, and use frequent hand gestures. These nonverbal signals convince the interviewer that you're alert, assertive, dependable, confident, responsible, and energetic.[17] Some companies based in the United States are owned and managed by people from other cultures, so during your research, find out about the company's cultural background and preferences regarding nonverbal behavior.

Nonverbal behavior has a significant effect on the interviewer's opinion of you.

The sound of your voice can also have a major impact on your success in a job interview.[18] You can work with a tape recorder to overcome voice problems. If you tend to speak too rapidly, practice speaking more slowly. If your voice sounds too loud or too soft, practice adjusting it. Work on eliminating speech mannerisms such as *you know*, *like*, and *um*, which might make you sound inarticulate.

The way you speak is almost as important as what you say.

Plan To Look Good

Physical appearance is important because clothing and grooming reveal something about a candidate's personality and professionalism. When it comes to clothing, the best policy

To look like a winner
- Dress conservatively
- Be well groomed
- Smile when appropriate

is to dress conservatively. Wear the best-quality businesslike clothing you can, preferably in a dark, solid color. Avoid flamboyant styles, colors, and prints. Even in companies where interviewers may dress casually, it's important to show good judgment by dressing (and acting) in a professional manner.

Good grooming makes any style of clothing look better. Make sure your clothes are clean and unwrinkled, your shoes unscuffed and well shined, your hair neatly styled and combed, your fingernails clean, and your breath fresh. If possible, check your appearance in a mirror before entering the room for the interview. Finally, remember that one of the best ways to look good is to smile at appropriate moments.

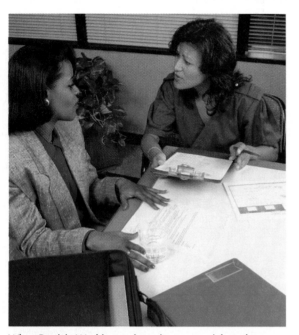

When Patricia Washington interviews potential employees, she looks for people who communicate well. Part of good communication is being prepared with résumés and work samples; another part is knowing how to look. Applicants show more than their job skills. They also demonstrate their ability to communicate and their concern for a professional appearance.

Be prepared for the interview by
- Taking proof of your accomplishments
- Arriving on time
- Waiting graciously

Be Ready When You Arrive

Plan to take a small notebook, a pen, a list of the questions you want to ask, two copies of your résumé (protected in a folder), an outline of what you have learned about the organization, and any past correspondence about the position. You may also want to take a small calendar, a transcript of your college grades, a list of references, and a portfolio containing samples of your work, performance reviews, and certificates of achievement. In an era when many people exaggerate their qualifications, visible proof of your abilities carries a lot of weight.[19]

Be sure you know when and where the interview will be held. The worst way to start any interview is to be late. Check the route you will take, even if it means phoning the interviewer's secretary to ask. Find out how much time it takes to get there; then plan to arrive early. Allow a little extra time in case you run into a problem on the way.

Once you arrive, relax. You may have to wait a little while, so bring along something to read or occupy your time (the less frivolous or controversial, the better). If company literature is available, read it while you wait. In any case, be polite to the interviewer's assistant. If the opportunity presents itself, ask a few questions about the organization or express enthusiasm for the job. Refrain from smoking before the interview (nonsmokers can smell smoke on the clothing of interviewees), and avoid chewing gum in the waiting room. Anything you do or say while you wait may well get back to the interviewer, so make sure your best qualities show from the moment you enter the premises. That way you'll be ready for the interview itself once it actually begins.

Objective **4**

Explain the three stages of a successful employment interview.

Present a memorable "headline" during an interview at the screening stage.

Cover all your strengths during an interview at the selection stage.

Emphasize your personality during a final interview.

INTERVIEWING FOR SUCCESS

How you handle a particular interview depends on where you stand in the interview process. If you're being interviewed for the first time, your main objective is to differentiate yourself from the many other candidates who are also being screened. Without resorting to gimmicks, call attention to one key aspect of your background so that the recruiter can say, "Oh yes, I remember Jones—the one who sold used Toyotas in Detroit." Just be sure the trait you accentuate is relevant to the job in question. In addition, you'll want to be prepared in case an employer expects you to demonstrate a particular skill (perhaps problem solving) during the screening interview.

If you progress to the initial selection interview, broaden your sales pitch. Instead of telegraphing the "headline," give the interviewer the whole story. Touch briefly on all your strengths, but explain three or four of your best qualifications in depth. At the same time, probe for information that will help you evaluate the position objectively. As important as it is to get an offer, it's also important to learn whether the job is right for you.

If you're asked back for a final visit, your chances of being offered a position are quite good. At this point, you'll talk to a person who has the authority to make an offer and negotiate terms. This individual may have already concluded that your background is right for the job and may be more concerned with sizing up your personality. Both you and the employer need to find out whether there is a good psychological fit. Be honest about your motivations and values. If the interview goes well, your objective should be to clinch the deal on the best possible terms.

Regardless of where you are in the interview process, every interview will proceed through three stages: the warm-up, the question-and-answer session, and the close.

The Warm-Up

Of the three stages, the warm-up is the most important, even though it may account for only a small fraction of the time you spend in the interview. Psychologists say that 50 percent of an interviewer's decision is made within the first 30 to 60 seconds, and another 25 percent is made within 15 minutes. If you get off to a bad start, it's extremely difficult to turn the interview around.[20]

The first minute of the interview is crucial.

Body language is important at this point. Because you won't have time to say much in the first minute or two, you must sell yourself nonverbally. Begin by using the interviewer's name if you're sure you can pronounce it correctly. If the interviewer extends a hand, respond with a firm but gentle handshake, then wait until you are asked to be seated. Let the interviewer start the discussion, and listen for cues that tell you what he or she is interested in knowing about you as a potential employee.

The Question-and-Answer Stage

Questions and answers will consume the greatest part of the interview. The interviewer will ask you about your qualifications and discuss many of the points mentioned in your résumé. You'll also be asked whether you have any questions of your own.

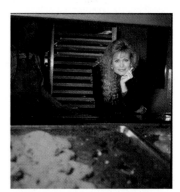

Debbie Fields, founder of Mrs. Fields, the famous chain of cookie stores, looks for enthusiasm in a potential employee. Fields hires "attitude and ability." She sometimes asks an applicant to sing "Happy Birthday" during a job interview. Says Fields, "The important thing is not being afraid to take a chance . . . the greatest failure is to not try."

Dealing with Questions   Remember, let the interviewer lead the conversation, and never answer a question before he or she has finished asking it. Surprisingly, the last few words of the question might alter how you respond. As questions are asked, tailor your answers to make a favorable impression. Don't limit yourself to yes or no answers. If you're asked a difficult question, be sure you pause to think before responding.

If you periodically ask a question or two from the list you've prepared, you'll not only learn something but also demonstrate your interest. Probe for what the company is looking for in its new employees so that you can show how you meet the firm's needs. Also try to zero in on any reservations the interviewer might have about you so that you can dispel them.

Tailor your answers to emphasize your strengths.

Listening to the Interviewer   Paying attention when the interviewer speaks can be as important as giving good answers or asking good questions. The recruiters at Herman Miller agree that listening should make up about half the time you spend in an interview. For tips on becoming a better listener, read Chapter 2.

Paying attention to both verbal and nonverbal messages can help you turn the question-and-answer stage to your advantage.

The interviewer's facial expressions, eye movements, gestures, and posture may tell you the real meaning of what is being said. Be especially aware of how your comments are received. Does the interviewer nod in agreement or smile to show approval? If so, you're making progress. If not, you might want to introduce another topic or modify your approach.

Fielding Discriminatory Questions   Remember that employers cannot legally discriminate against a job candidate on the basis of race, color, gender, age (from 40 to 70), marital status, religion, national origin, or disability. Although federal law does not specifically prohibit questions that touch on these areas, the Equal Employment Opportunity Commission considers such questions with "extreme disfavor." In general, the following topics should not be directly or indirectly introduced by an interviewer:[21]

Some questions should not be asked by interviewers.

◆ Your religious affiliation or organizations and lodges you belong to

◆ Your national origin, age, marital status, or former name

◆ Your spouse, spouse's employment or salary, dependents, children, or child-care arrangements

◆ Your height, weight, gender, pregnancy, or any health conditions or disabilities that are not reasonably related to job performance

◆ Arrests or criminal convictions that are not related to job performance

How to Respond   If your interviewer asks these personal questions, how you respond depends on how badly you want the job, how you feel about revealing the information asked for, what you think the interviewer will do with the information, and whether you want to work for a company that asks such questions. If you don't want the job, you can tell the interviewer that you think a particular question is unethical or simply refuse to answer—responses that will leave an unfavorable impression.[22] If you do want the job, you might (1) ask how the question is related to your qualifications, (2) explain that the information is personal, (3) respond to what you think is the interviewer's real concern, or (4) answer both the question and the concern. If you answer an unethical or unlawful question, you run the risk that your answer may hurt your chances, so think carefully before answering.[23]

Where to File a Complaint   When a business can show that the safety of its employees or customers is at stake, it may be allowed to ask questions that would seem discriminatory in another context. Despite this exception, if you believe an interviewer's questions are unreasonable, unrelated to the job, or an attempt to discriminate, you may complain to the Equal Employment Opportunity Commission or to the state agency that regulates fair employment practices. To report discrimination on the basis of age or physical disability, contact the employer's equal opportunity officer or the U.S. Department of Labor. If you file a complaint, be prepared to spend a lot of time and effort—and remember that you may not win.[24]

The Close

Like the opening, the end of the interview is more important than its duration would indicate. In the last few minutes, you need to evaluate how well you've done. You also need to correct any misconceptions the interviewer might have.

Concluding Gracefully   You can generally tell when the interviewer is trying to conclude the session. The interviewer may ask whether you have any more questions, sum up the discussion, change position, or indicate with a gesture that the interview is over. When you get the signal, respond promptly, but don't rush. Be sure to thank the interviewer for the opportunity and express an interest in the organization. If you can do so comfortably, try to pin down what will happen next, but don't press for an immediate decision.

If this is your second or third visit to the organization, the interview may culminate with an offer of employment. You have two options: Accept it or request time to think it over. The best course is usually to wait. If no job offer is made, the interviewer may not have reached a decision yet, but you may tactfully ask when you can expect to know the decision.

Discussing Salary   If you do receive an offer during the interview, you'll naturally want to discuss salary. However, let the interviewer raise the subject. If asked your salary requirements, say that you would expect to receive the standard salary for the job in question. If you have added qualifications, point them out: "With my 18 months of experience in the field, I would expect to start in the middle of the normal salary range." Some applicants find the Internet a terrific resource for salary information.

When to Negotiate   If you don't like the offer, you might try to negotiate, provided you're in a good bargaining position and the organization has the flexibility to accommodate you. You'll be in a fairly strong position if your skills are in short supply and you have several other offers. It also helps if you're the favorite candidate and the organization is booming. However, many organizations are relatively rigid in their salary practices, particularly at the entry level. In the United States and some European countries, it is perfectly acceptable to ask, "Is there any room for negotiation?"

What to Negotiate   Even if you can't bargain for more money, you may be able to win some concessions on benefits and perquisites. The value of negotiating can be significant because benefits often cost the employer 25 to 45 percent of your salary. In other words, if you're offered an annual salary of $20,000, you'll ordinarily get an additional $5,000 to $9,000 in benefits: life, health, and disability insurance; pension and savings plans; vacation time; or even tuition reimbursement.[25]

If you can trade one benefit for another, you may be able to enhance the value of the total package. For example, life insurance may be relatively unimportant to you if you're single, whereas extra vacation time might be very valuable indeed. Don't inquire about benefits, however, until you know you have a job offer.

Interview Notes

If yours is a typical job search, you'll have many interviews before you accept an offer. For that reason, keeping a notebook or binder of interview notes can help you refresh your memory of each conversation. As soon as the interview ends, jot down the names and titles of the people you met. Briefly summarize the interviewer's answers to your questions. Then quickly evaluate your performance during the interview, listing what you handled well and what you didn't. Going over these notes can help you improve your performance in the future.[26] In addition to improving your performance during interviews, interview notes will help you keep track of any follow-up messages you'll need to send. Whenever you need to review important tips, consult this chapter's "Checklist: Succeeding with Job Interviews."

FOLLOWING UP AFTER THE INTERVIEW

Touching base with the prospective employer after the interview, either by phone or in writing, shows that you really want the job and are determined to get it. As Herman Miller recruiters point out, following up brings your name to the interviewer's attention once again and reminds him or her that you're waiting for the decision.

The two most common forms of follow-up are the thank-you message and the inquiry. These messages are generally handled by letter, but a phone call is often just as effective, particularly if the employer seems to favor a casual, personal style. Other types of follow-up messages are sent only in certain cases—letter requesting a time extension, letter of acceptance, letter declining a job offer, and letter of resignation. These four employment messages are best handled in writing to document any official actions relating to your employment.

Thank-You Message

Express your thanks within two days after the interview, even if you feel you have little chance for the job. Acknowledge the interviewer's time and courtesy, and be sure to restate the specific job you're applying for. Convey your continued interest, then ask politely for a decision.

Keep your thank-you message brief (less than five minutes for a phone call or only one page for a letter), and organize it like a routine message. Demonstrate the "you" attitude, and sound positive without sounding overconfident. The following sample thank-you letter shows how to achieve all this in three brief paragraphs:

After talking with you yesterday, touring your sets, and watching the television commercials being filmed, I remain very enthusiastic about the possibility of joining your staff as a television/film production assistant. Thanks for taking so much time to show me around.

Negotiating benefits may be one way to get more value from an employment package.

Objective **5**

Name six common employment messages that follow an interview and state briefly when you would use each one.

Six types of follow-up messages:
- Thank-you message
- Inquiry
- Request for a time extension
- Letter of acceptance
- Letter declining a job offer
- Letter of resignation

Herman Cain is President and CEO of the Washington, D.C.–based National Restaurant Association, and he's also a member of the Board of Directors of Godfathers Pizza. His own winning combination of people skills and analytical ability has made him an influential business leader. For a successful thank-you message, advises Cain, be specific and refer to points discussed in the interview.

A note or phone call thanking the interviewer
- Is organized like a routine message
- Closes with a request for a decision or future consideration

Reminds the interviewer of the reasons for the meeting and graciously acknowledges the consideration shown to the applicant.

Checklist: **Succeeding with Job Interviews**

Preparation

✓ Determine the requirements and general salary range of the job.
✓ Research the organization's products, structure, financial standing, and prospects for growth.
✓ Determine the interviewer's name, title, and status in the firm.
✓ Prepare (but don't over-rehearse) answers for the questions you are likely to be asked.
✓ Develop relevant questions to ask.
✓ Dress in a businesslike manner, regardless of the mode of dress preferred within the organization.
✓ Take a briefcase or portfolio—with pen, paper, list of questions, two résumés, work samples.
✓ Double-check the location and time of the interview, mapping out the route beforehand.
✓ Plan to arrive 10 to 15 minutes early; allow 10 to 15 minutes for possible problems en route.

Initial Stages of the Interview

✓ Greet the interviewer by name, with a smile and direct eye contact.
✓ Offer a firm (not crushing) handshake if the interviewer extends a hand.
✓ Take a seat only after the interviewer invites you to be seated or has taken his or her own seat.
✓ Listen for cues about what the questions are trying to reveal about you and your qualifications.
✓ Assume a calm and poised attitude (avoid gum chewing, smoking, and other signs of nerves).

Body of the Interview

✓ Display a genuine (not artificial) smile, when appropriate.
✓ Convey interest and enthusiasm.
✓ Listen attentively so that you can give intelligent responses (taking few notes).
✓ Relate your knowledge and skills to the position and stress your positive qualities.
✓ Keep responses, brief, clear, and to the point.
✓ Avoid exaggeration, and convey honesty and sincerity.
✓ Avoid slighting references to former employers.
✓ Avoid alcoholic drinks if you are interviewed over lunch or dinner.

Salary Discussions

✓ Let the interviewer initiate the discussion of salary, but put it off until late in the interview, if possible.
✓ If asked, state that you would like to receive the standard salary for the position.

Closing Stages of the Interview

✓ Watch for signs that the interview is about to end.
✓ Tactfully ask when you will be advised of the decision of your application.
✓ If you're offered the job, either accept or ask for time to consider the offer.
✓ With a warm smile and a handshake, thank the interviewer for meeting with you.

Indicates the writer's flexibility and commitment to the job if hired. →

During our meeting, I said that I would prefer not to relocate, but I've reconsidered the matter. I would be pleased to relocate wherever you need my skills in set decoration and prop design.

Reminds the recruiter of special qualifications. →

Closes on a confident, "you"-oriented noted. →

Ends with a request for decision. →

Now that you've explained the details of your operation, I feel quite strongly that I can make a contribution to the sorts of productions you're lining up. You can also count on me to be an energetic employee and a positive addition to your crew. Please let me know your decision as soon as possible.

Even if the interviewer has said that you are unqualified for the job, a thank-you message may keep the door open.

Letter of Inquiry

An inquiry about a hiring decision follows the plan for a direct request.

If you're not advised of the interviewer's decision by the promised date or within two weeks, you might make an inquiry. A letter of inquiry is particularly appropriate if you've received a job offer from a second firm and don't want to accept it before you have an answer from the first. The following letter follows the general plan for a direct request; the writer assumes that a simple oversight, and not outright rejection, is the reason for the delay:

Identifies the position and introduces the main idea. →

When we talked on April 7 about the fashion coordinator position in your Park Avenue showroom, you said you would let me know your decision before May 1. I would still like the position very much, so I'm eager to know what conclusion you've reached.

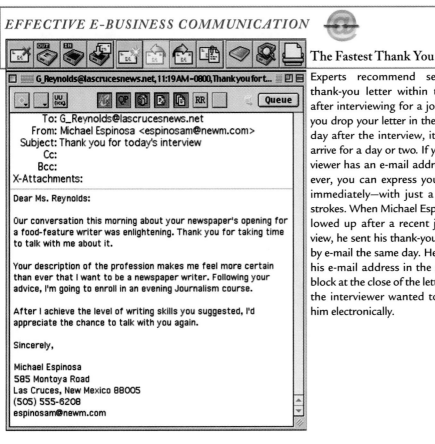

Experts recommend sending a thank-you letter within two days after interviewing for a job. Even if you drop your letter in the mail one day after the interview, it may not arrive for a day or two. If your interviewer has an e-mail address, however, you can express your thanks immediately—with just a few keystrokes. When Michael Espinosa followed up after a recent job interview, he sent his thank-you message by e-mail the same day. He included his e-mail address in the signature block at the close of the letter in case the interviewer wanted to contact him electronically.

1. Why is there no inside address in this thank-you e-mail?
2. How else could a candidate make productive use of a thank-you e-mail?

To complicate matters, another firm has now offered me a position and has asked that I reply within the next two weeks.

Places the reason for the request second.

Because your company seems to offer a greater challenge, I would appreciate knowing about your decision by Thursday, May 12. If you need more information before then, please let me know.

Makes a courteous request for specific action last, while clearly stating a preference for this organization.

Request for a Time Extension

If you receive a job offer while other interviews are still pending, you'll probably want more time to decide, so write to the offering organization and ask for a time extension. Employers understand that candidates often interview with several companies. They want you to be sure you're making the right decision, so most are happy to accommodate you with a reasonable extension.

Preface your request with a friendly opening. Ask for more time, stressing your enthusiasm for the organization. Conclude by allowing for a quick decision if your request for additional time is denied. Ask for a prompt reply confirming the time extension if the organization grants it. This type of letter is, in essence, a direct request. However, because the recipient may be disappointed, be sure to temper your request for an extension with statements indicating your continued interest. The letter in Figure 15–2 is a good example.

A request for a time extension follows the plan for a direct request but pays extra attention to easing the reader's disappointment.

Letter of Acceptance

When you receive a job offer that you want to accept, reply within five days. Begin by accepting the position and expressing thanks. Identify the job that you're accepting. In

A letter of acceptance follows the good-news plan.

Begins with a strong statement of interest in the job.

Emphasizes specific reasons for preferring the first job offer to help reassure the reader of sincerity.

Stresses professional obligations, not the desire to learn what the other company may offer.

Closes with expression of willingness to yield or compromise, conveying continued interest in the position.

Figure 15–2
In-Depth Critique: Request for a Time Extension

the next paragraph, cover any necessary details. Conclude by saying that you look forward to reporting for work. As always, a good-news letter should convey your enthusiasm and eagerness to cooperate:

Confirms the specific terms of the offer with a good-news statement at the beginning.

I'm delighted to accept the graphic design position in your advertising department at the salary of $1,575 a month.

Covers miscellaneous details in the middle.

Enclosed are the health insurance forms you asked me to complete and sign. I've already given notice to my current employer and will be able to start work on Monday, January 18.

Closes with another reference to the good news and a look toward the future.

The prospect of joining your firm is very exciting. Thank you for giving me this opportunity for what I'm sure will be a challenging future.

Written acceptance of a job offer is legally binding.

Be aware that a job offer and a written acceptance of that offer constitute a legally binding contract, for both you and the employer. Before you write an acceptance letter, be sure you want the job.

Letter Declining a Job Offer

After all your interviews, you may find that you need to write a letter declining a job offer. The bad-news plan is ideally suited to this type of letter. Open warmly, state the reasons for refusing the offer, decline the offer explicitly, and close on a pleasant note, expressing gratitude. By taking the time to write a sincere, tactful letter, you leave the door open for future contact.

A letter declining a job offer follows the bad-news plan.

One of the most interesting interviews I have ever had was the one last month at your Durham textile plant. I'm flattered that you would offer me the computer analyst position that we talked about.

Makes the opening paragraph a buffer.

During my job search, I applied to five highly rated firms like your own, each one a leader in its field. Both your company and another offered me a position. Because my desire to work abroad can more readily be satisfied by the other company, I have accepted that job offer.

Precedes the bad news with tactfully phrased reasons from the applicant's unfavorable decision, and leaves the door open.

I deeply appreciate the hour you spent talking with me. Thank you again for your consideration and kindness.

Lets the reader down gently with a sincere and cordial ending.

Letter of Resignation

If you get a job offer and are currently employed, you can maintain good relations with your current employer by writing a letter of resignation to your immediate supervisor. Follow the bad-news plan, and make the letter sound positive, regardless of how you feel. Say something favorable about the organization, the people you work with, or what you've learned on the job. Then state your intention to leave and give the date of your last day on the job. Be sure you give your current employer at least two weeks' notice.

A letter of resignation also follows the bad-news plan.

My sincere thanks to you and to all the other Emblem Corporation employees for helping me learn so much about serving the public these past 11 months. You have given me untold help and encouragement.

Appreciative opening serves as a buffer.

You may recall that when you first interviewed me, my goal was to become a customer relations supervisor. Because that opportunity has been offered to me by another organization, I am submitting my resignation. I regret leaving all of you, but I can't pass up this opportunity.

States reasons before the bad news itself, using tactful phrasing to help keep the relationship friendly, should the writer later want letters of recommendation.

I would like to terminate my work here two weeks from today but can arrange to work an additional week if you want me to train a replacement.

Discusses necessary details in an extra paragraph.

My sincere thanks and best wishes to all of you.

Tempers any disappointment with a cordial close.

Compare your messages with the suggestions in this chapter's "Checklist: Writing Follow-up Messages" on the next page.

Checklist: Writing Follow-up Messages

Thank-You Messages

✓ Write a thank-you letter within two days of the interview (keeping it to one page).

✓ If you have no alternative, thank the interviewer by phone (in less than five minutes).

✓ In the opening, express thanks and identify the job and the time and place of the interview.

✓ Use the middle section for supporting details.

✓ Express your enthusiasm about the organization and the job.

✓ Add any new facts that may help your chances.

✓ Try to repair any negative impressions you may have left during the interview.

✓ Use an action ending.

Inquiries

✓ Phone or write an inquiry if you aren't informed of the decision by the promised date.

✓ Follow the plan for direct requests: main idea, necessary details, specific request.

Requests for a Time Extension

✓ Request an extension if you have pending interviews and need time to decide about an offer.

✓ Open with an expression of warmth.

✓ In the middle, explain why you need more time and express continued interest in the company.

✓ In the close, promise a quick decision if your request is denied, and ask for a confirmation if your request is granted.

Letters Accepting a Job Offer

✓ Send this message within five days of receiving the offer.

✓ State clearly that you accept the offer, identify the job you're accepting, and include vital details.

✓ Conclude with a statement that you look forward to reporting for work.

Letters Rejecting a Job Offer

✓ Open a letter of rejection warmly.

✓ Explain why you are refusing the offer, and express your appreciation.

✓ End on a sincere, positive note.

Letters of Resignation

✓ Send a letter of resignation to your current employer as soon as possible.

✓ Begin with an appreciative buffer.

✓ In the middle section, state your reasons for leaving, and actually state that you are resigning.

✓ Close cordially.

SUMMARY OF LEARNING OBJECTIVES

1 Define *employment interview*, and explain its dual purpose. An employment interview is a formal meeting during which an employer and an applicant ask questions and exchange information to see whether the two are a good match. The purpose of an employment interview is twofold: (1) to help the organization find the best person for the job, and (2) to help the applicant find the job best suited to his or her goals and capabilities.

2 Describe briefly what employers look for during an employment interview. Employers look for two things during an employment interview. First, they seek evidence that an applicant will be compatible with the other people in the organization. Whether interviewers focus on personal background or personal style, they are interested in finding someone who will easily adapt to a new workplace and new responsibilities. Second, employers seek evidence that an applicant is qualified for the position. Even though interviewers have already reviewed your résumé, they want to see how well your skills match their requirements and perhaps even get a sense of your ability to be flexible and apply diverse skills in more than one area. Sometimes, interviewers will use preemployment tests to help them gather the evidence they need to make a decision.

3 List six tasks you need to complete to prepare for a successful job interview. To prepare for a successful job interview, begin by (1) refining the research you did when planning your résumé. Knowing as much as you can about the company and its needs helps you highlight the aspects of your background and qualifications that will appeal to the organization. (2) Next, think ahead about questions—both those you'll need to answer and those you'll want to ask. (3) Bolster your confidence by focusing on your strengths to overcome any apprehension. (4) Polish your style by staging mock interviews and paying close attention to nonverbal behaviors, including voice problems. (5) Plan to look your best with businesslike clothing and good grooming. And (6) arrive on time and ready to begin.

4 Explain the three stages of a successful employment interview. All employment interviews have three stages. The warm-up stage is the most important because first impressions greatly influence an interviewer's decision. The question-and-answer stage is the longest, during which you will answer and ask questions. Listening carefully and watching the interviewer's nonverbal clues help you determine how the interview is going. The close is also important because you need to evaluate your performance to see whether the interviewer has any misconceptions that you must correct.

5 **Name six common employment messages that follow an interview, and state briefly when you would use each one.** The two most common types of follow-up messages are usually in letter form but can also be effective by phone or e-mail. You send the *thank-you* message within two days after your interview to show appreciation, express your continued interest in the job, and politely ask for a decision. You send an *inquiry* if you haven't received the interviewer's decision by the date promised or within

two weeks of the interview—especially if you've received a job offer from another firm. The remaining four employment messages are best sent in letter form, to document any official action. You request a *time extension* if you receive a job offer while other interviews are pending and you want more time to complete those interviews before making a decision. You send a *letter of acceptance* within five days of receiving a job offer that you want to take. You send a *letter declining a job offer* when you want to refuse an offer tactfully and leave the door open for future contact. You send a *letter of resignation* when you receive a job offer that you want to accept while you are currently employed.

SOLVING A COMMUNICATION DILEMMA AT HERMAN MILLER, INC.

Herman Miller's corporate culture reflects the philosophy of Max DePree, son of the firm's founder and, until recently, chairman of the board. DePree based his management style on his assumptions about human nature. In his view, the idea of motivating people is nonsense. "Employees bring their own motivation," he said. "What people need from work is to be liberated, to be involved, to be accountable, and to reach their potential."

DePree believes that good management consists of establishing an environment in which people can unleash their creativity. "My goal for Herman Miller is that when people both inside and outside the company look at all of us, they'll say, 'Those folks have a gift of the spirit.'" He wanted the organization, like its products, to be a work of art. To carry out his philosophy, DePree created an employee bill of rights, which includes: "The right to be needed, the right to understand, the right to be involved, the right to affect one's own destiny, the right to be accountable, and the right to appeal."

The company's organizational structure, now in the hands of president and CEO Michael Volkema, reinforces DePree's philosophy. All employees are assigned to work teams. The team leader evaluates the workers every six months, and the workers voluntarily evaluate the leader as well. Teams elect representatives to caucuses that meet periodically to discuss operations and problems. Through the team structure, employees have a say in decisions that affect them. They also have a vehicle for dealing with grievances. If a problem isn't resolved by the team supervisor, employees can go directly to the next executive level—all the way to Volkema, if needed.

But like all good things, Herman Miller's corporate culture has its downside. Teamwork takes time, and an egalitarian approach to decision making can be frustrating if you value efficiency. Although today's business environment requires decisive action, it takes a special kind of talent to draw the line between participation and permissiveness. Finding people who appreciate the distinction—and who can operate effectively in this climate— is a real challenge.

To identify people who have the right mix of attitudes, Herman Miller uses what it calls "value-based" interviewing. During an initial job interview, the staffing department probes the

candidate's work style, likes, and dislikes by posing "what if" questions. By evaluating how the candidate would handle a variety of scenarios, the recruiter gets a good idea of how well the individual would fit into the company. If the fit seems good, the candidate is invited back for follow-up interviews with members of the department where he or she would be working. During these follow-up interviews, the candidate's functional expertise is evaluated along with his or her psychological makeup. By the end of the interview process, Herman Miller has a good idea of whether the candidate "knows how to dance."

Your Mission As a member of Herman Miller's staffing department, you are responsible for screening job candidates and arranging for candidates to interview with members of Herman Miller's professional staff. Your responsibilities include the development of interview questions and evaluation forms for use by company employees involved in the interview process. You also handle all routine correspondence with job candidates. In each of the following situations, choose the best alternative, and be prepared to explain why your choice is best.

1. Herman Miller has decided to establish a management-training program for recent college graduates. The program will groom people for careers in finance, strategic planning, marketing, administration, and general management. To recruit people for the program, the firm will conduct on-campus interviews at several colleges—something it has not generally done. You and the other Herman Miller interviewers will be talking with 30 or 40 applicants on campus. You will have 20 minutes for each interview. Your goal is to identify the candidates who will be invited to come to the office for evaluation interviews. You want the preliminary screening process to be as fair and objective as possible, so how will you approach the task?

   a. Meet with all the Herman Miller interviewers to discuss the characteristics that successful candidates will exhibit. Allow each interviewer to use his or her individual approach to identify these characteristics in applicants. Encourage the interviewers to ask whatever questions seem most useful in light of the individual characteristics of each candidate.

b. Develop a list of 10 to 15 questions that will be posed to all candidates. Instruct the Herman Miller interviewers to adhere strictly to the list so that all applicants will respond to the same questions and be evaluated on the same basis.

c. Develop a written evaluation form for measuring all candidates against criteria such as academic performance, relevant experience, capacity for teamwork, and communication skills. For each criterion, suggest four or five questions that interviewers might use to evaluate the candidate. Instruct the interviewers to cover all the criteria and to fill out the written evaluation form for each applicant immediately after the interview.

d. Design a questionnaire for candidates to complete prior to their interviews. Then ask the interviewers to outline the ideal answers they would like to see a candidate offer for each item on this questionnaire. These ideal answers give you a standard against which to measure actual candidate answers.

2. During the on-campus screening interviews, you ask several candidates, "Why do you want to work for this organization?" Of the following responses, which would you rank the highest?

a. "I'd like to work here because I'm interested in the office furniture business. I've always been fascinated by industrial design and the interaction between people and their environment. In addition to studying business, I have taken courses in industrial design and industrial psychology. I also have some personal experience in building furniture. My grandfather is a cabinet maker and an antique restorer, and I have been his apprentice since I was 12 years old. I've paid for college by working as a carpenter during summer vacations."

b. "I'm an independent person with a lot of internal drive. I do my best work when I'm given a fairly free reign to use my creativity. From what I've read about your corporate culture, I think my working style would fit very well with your management philosophy. I'm also the sort of person who identifies very strongly with my job. For better or worse, I define myself through my affiliation with my employer. I get a great sense of pride from being part of a first-rate operation, and I think Herman Miller is first-rate. I've read about the design awards you've won and about your selection as one of America's most admired companies. The articles say that Herman Miller is a well-managed

company. I think I would learn a lot working here, and I think my drive and creativity would be appreciated."

c. "There are several reasons why I'd like to work for Herman Miller. For one thing, I have family and friends in Zeeland, and I'd like to stay in the area. Also, I have friends who work for Herman Miller, and they both say it's terrific. I've also heard good things about your compensation and benefits."

d. "My ultimate goal is to start my own company, but first I need to learn more about managing a business. I read in *Fortune* that Herman Miller is one of America's most admired corporations. I think I could learn a lot by joining your management training program and observing your operations."

3. You are preparing questions for the professional staff to use when conducting follow-up interviews at Herman Miller's headquarters. You want a question that will reveal something about the candidates' probable loyalty to the organization. Which of the following questions is the best choice?

a. If you knew you could be one of the world's most successful people in a single occupation, such as music, politics, medicine, or business, what occupation would you choose? If you knew you had only a 10 percent chance of being so successful, would you still choose the same occupation?

b. We value loyalty among our employees. Tell me something about yourself that demonstrates your loyalty as a member of an organization.

c. What would you do if you discovered that a co-worker routinely made personal, unauthorized long-distance phone calls from work?

d. What other companies are you interviewing with?

4. In concluding an evaluation interview, you ask the candidate, "Do you have any questions?" Which of the following answers would you respond most favorably to?

a. "No. I can't think of anything. You've been very thorough in describing the job and the company. Thank you for taking the time to talk with me."

b. "Yes. I have an interview with one of your competitors, Steelcase, next week. How would you sum up the differences between your two firms?"

c. "Yes. If I were offered a position here, what would my chances be of getting promoted within the next 12 months?"

d. "Yes. Do you think Herman Miller will be a better or worse company 15 years from now?"[27]

TEST YOUR KNOWLEDGE

1. How does a structured interview differ from an open-ended interview and a situational interview?

2. What typically occurs during a stress interview?

3. Why do employers conduct preemployment testing?

4. Why are the questions you ask during an interview as important as the answers you give to the interviewer's questions?

5. What are the three stages of every interview, and which is the most important?

6. How should you respond if an interviewer at a company where you want to work asks you a question that seems too personal or unethical?

7. What should you say in a thank-you message after an interview?

8. What is the purpose of sending a letter of inquiry after an interview?

9. What is the legal significance of a letter of acceptance?

10. What organization plan is appropriate for a letter of resignation, and why?

INTERACTIVE LEARNING

USE THIS TEXT'S ONLINE RESOURCES

Visit the myPHLIP Web site at www.prenhall.com/thill. For Chapter 15, take advantage of the interactive "Study Guide" to test your chapter knowledge. Get instant feedback on whether you need additional studying. Read the "Current Events" articles to get the latest on chapter topics, and complete the exercises—as specified by your instructor.

This site's "Study Hall" helps you succeed in this course. "Talk in the Hall" lets you leave messages and meet new friends online. If you have a question, you can "Ask the Tutor." And to get a better grade in this course, you can find more help at "Writing Skills," "Study Skills," and "Study Tips."

The "Research Area" helps you locate a wealth of information to use in course assignments. Plus, you can send a message to online research experts, who will help you find exactly the information you need.

APPLY YOUR KNOWLEDGE

1. How can you distinguish yourself from other candidates in a screening interview and still keep your responses short and to the point? Explain.

2. What can you do to make a favorable impression when you discover that an open-ended interview has turned into a stress interview? Briefly explain your answer.

3. If you want to switch jobs because you can't work with your supervisor, how can you explain this situation to a prospective employer? Give an example.

4. During a group interview you notice that one of the other candidates is trying to monopolize the conversation. He's always the first to answer, his answer is the longest, and he even interrupts the other candidates while they are talking. The interviewer doesn't seem to be concerned about his behavior, but you are. You would like to have more time to speak so that the interviewer could get to know you better. What should you do?

5. **Ethical Choices** Why is it important to distinguish unethical or illegal interview questions from acceptable questions? Explain.

PRACTICE YOUR KNOWLEDGE

DOCUMENTS FOR ANALYSIS

Read the following documents; then (1) analyze the strengths or weaknesses of each document and (2) revise each document so that it follows this chapter's guidelines.

Document 15.A: Thank-You Message

Thank you for the really marvelous opportunity to meet you and your colleagues at Starret Engine Company. I really enjoyed touring your facilities and talking with all the people there. You have quite a crew! Some of the other companies I have visited have been so rigid and uptight that I can't imagine how I would fit in. It's a relief to run into a group of people who seem to enjoy their work as much as all of you do.

I know that you must be looking at many other candidates for this job, and I know that some of them will probably be more experienced than I am. But I do want to emphasize that my two-year hitch in the Navy involved a good deal of engineering work. I don't think I mentioned all my shipboard responsibilities during the interview.

Please give me a call within the next week to let me know your decision. You can usually find me at my dormitory in the evening after dinner (phone: 877-9080).

Document 15.B: Letter of Inquiry

I have recently received a very attractive job offer from the Warrington Company. But before I let them know one way or another, I would like to consider any offer that your firm may extend. I was quite impressed with your company during my recent interview, and I am still very interested in a career there.

I don't mean to pressure you, but Warrington has asked for my decision within 10 days. Could you let me know by Tuesday whether you plan to offer me a position? That would give me enough time to compare the two offers.

Document 15.C: Letter Declining a Job Offer

I'm writing to say that I must decline your job offer. Another company has made me a more generous offer, and I have decided to accept. However, if things don't work out for me there, I will let you know. I sincerely appreciate your interest in me.

EXERCISES

15-1. **Teamwork** Divide the class into two groups. Half the class will be recruiters for a large chain of national department stores looking to fill manager trainee positions (there are 15 openings). The other half of the class will be candidates for the job. The company is specifically looking for candidates who demonstrate these three qualities: initiative, dependability, and willingness to assume responsibility.

a. Have each recruiter select and interview an applicant for 10 minutes.

b. Have all the recruiters discuss how they assessed the applicant against each of the three desired qualities. What questions did they ask or what did they use as an indicator to determine whether the candidate possessed the quality?

c. Have all the applicants discuss what they said to convince the recruiters that they possessed each of these qualities.

15-2. **Internet** Select a large company (one that you can easily find information on) where you might like to work. Use Internet sources to gather some preliminary research on the company.

a. What did you learn about this organization that would help you during an interview there?

b. What Internet sources did you use to obtain this information?

c. Armed with this information, what aspects of your background do you think might appeal to this company's recruiters?

d. If you choose to apply for a job with this company, what key words would you include on your résumé, and why?

15-3. **Interviews: Being Prepared** Prepare written answers to 10 of the questions listed in Table 15–2, "Twenty-Five Common Interview Questions" (see page 473).

15-4. **Ethical Choices** You have decided to accept a new position with a competitor of your company. Write a letter of resignation to your supervisor announcing your decision.

a. Will you notify your employer that you are joining a competing firm? Please explain.

b. Will you use the direct or the indirect approach? Please explain.

c. Will you send your letter by e-mail, send it by regular mail, or place it on your supervisor's desk?

15-5. **Interviews: Understanding Qualifications** Write a short memo to your instructor discussing what you believe are your greatest strengths and weaknesses from an employment perspective. Next, explain how these strengths and weaknesses would be viewed by interviewers evaluating your qualifications.

CASES

INTERVIEWING WITH POTENTIAL EMPLOYERS

1. Interviewers and interviewees: Classroom exercise in interviewing Interviewing is clearly an interactive process involving at least two people. The best way to practice for interviews is to work with others.

Your task: You and all other members of your class are to write letters of application for an entry-level or management-trainee position requiring a pleasant personality and intelligence but a minimum of specialized education or experience. Sign your letter with a fictitious name that conceals your identity. Next polish (or prepare) a résumé that accurately identifies you and your educational and professional accomplishments.

Now, three members of the class who volunteer as interviewers divide among themselves all the anonymously written application letters. Then each interviewer selects a candidate who seems the most pleasant and convincing in his or her letter. At this time the selected candidates identify themselves and give the interviewers their résumés.

Each interviewer then interviews his or her chosen candidate in front of the class, seeking to understand how the items on the résumé qualify the candidate for the job. At the end of the interviews, the class may decide who gets the job and discuss why this candidate was successful. Afterward, retrieve your letter, sign it with the right name, and submit it to the instructor for credit.

2. Internet interview: Exercise in interviewing Using the Web 100 site at www.web100.com, locate the home page of a company you would like to work for. Then identify a position within the company for which you would like to apply. Study the company using any of the online business resources discussed in Chapter 11, and prepare for an interview with that company.

Your task: Working with a classmate, take turns interviewing each other for your chosen positions. Interviewers should take notes during the interview. Once the interview is complete, critique each other's performance (interviewers should critique how well candidates prepared for the interview and answered the questions; interviewees should critique the quality of the questions asked). Write a follow-up letter thanking your interviewer and submit the letter to your instructor.

FOLLOWING UP AFTER THE INTERVIEW

3. A slight error in timing: Letter asking for delay of an employment decision You botched your timing and applied for your third-choice job before going after what you really wanted. What you want to do is work in retail marketing with Neiman Marcus in Dallas; what you have been offered is a similar job with Longhorn Leather and Lumber, 55 dry and dusty miles away in Commerce, just south of the Oklahoma panhandle.

You review your notes. Your Longhorn interview was three weeks ago with the human resources manager, R. P. Bronson, a congenial person who has just written to offer you the position. The store's address is 27 Sam Rayburn Dr., Commerce, TX 75428. Mr. Bronson notes that he can hold the position open for 10 days. You have an interview scheduled with Neiman Marcus next week, but it is unlikely that you will know the store's decision within this 10-day period.

Your task: Write to R. P. Bronson, requesting a reasonable delay in your consideration of his job offer.

4. Job hunt: Set of employment-related letters to a single company Where would you like to work? Pick a real or an imagined company, and assume that a month ago you sent your résumé and application letter. Not long afterward, you were invited to go in for an interview, which seemed to go very well.

Your task: Use your imagination to write the following: (a) a thank-you letter for the interview, (b) a note of inquiry, (c) a request for more time to decide, (d) a letter of acceptance, and (e) a letter declining the job offer.

GOING ONLINE EXERCISES

Planning for a Successful Interview, page 469

If you have not interviewed recently (or ever) for a job, do you have an idea of the kind of questions you might be asked? How can you prepare for an interview so that you'll appear knowledgeable about the job and confident in your skills? At Job-interview.net you'll get advice and ideas to make your next interview successful.

1. What are some awkward questions you might be asked during a job interview? How would you handle these questions?
2. Choose a job title from the list and read more about it. What did you learn that could help during an actual interview for the job you selected?
3. Developing an "interview game plan" ahead of time helps you make a strong, positive impression during an interview. What are some of the things you can practice to help make everything you do during an interview seem to come naturally?

To complete this exercise, log onto this text's Web site at www.prenhall.com/thill. Select Chapter 15, then select "Student Resources," click on the name of the featured Web site and follow the detailed navigational directions.

APPENDIX A

FORMAT AND LAYOUT OF BUSINESS DOCUMENTS

An effective letter, memo, or report does more than store words on paper. It communicates with the right person, makes an impression, and tells the recipient who wrote it and when it was written. It may even carry responses back to the sender, if only to relate how and by whom it was received and processed.

Over the centuries certain conventions have developed for the format and layout of business documents. Conventions vary from country to country, and, even within the United States, few hard-and-fast rules exist. Many organizations develop variations of standard styles to suit their own needs, adopting the style that's best for the types of messages they send and for the kinds of audiences that receive them. The conventions described here are more common than others. Whether you handle all your own communication on your computer or rely on someone else to handle it for you, knowing the proper form for your documents and knowing how to make them attractive to your readers are crucial.

FIRST IMPRESSIONS

A letter or other written document is often the first (sometimes the only) contact you have with an external audience. Memos and other documents used within an organization represent you to supervisors, colleagues, and employees. So it's important that your documents look neat and professional and that they're easy to read. Your audience's first impressions come from the paper you use, the way you customize it, and the general appearance of your document. These elements tell readers a lot about you and about your company's professionalism.

Paper

From your own experience, you know that a flimsy, see-through piece of paper gives a much less favorable impression than a richly textured piece. Paper quality is measured in two ways: The first measure of quality is weight, specifically the weight of four reams (each a 500-sheet package) of letter-size paper. The quality most commonly used by U.S. business organizations is 20-pound paper, but 16- and 24-pound versions are also used. The second measure of quality is the percentage of cotton in the paper. Cotton doesn't yellow over time the way wood pulp does, and it's both strong and soft. Paper with a 25 percent cotton content is an appropriate quality for letters and outside reports. For memos and other internal documents, lighter-weight paper and paper with a lower cotton content may be used. Also, airmail-weight paper may be more cost effective for international correspondence, but make sure it isn't too flimsy.[1]

In the United States the standard size of paper for business documents is 8½ by 11 inches. Standard legal documents are 8½ by 14 inches. Executives sometimes have heavier 7-by-10-inch paper on hand (with matching envelopes) for such personal messages as congratulations and recommendations.[2] They may also have a box of correspondence note cards imprinted with their initials and a box of plain folded notes for condolences or for acknowledging formal invitations.

Stationery may vary in color. White is standard for business purposes, although neutral colors such as gray and ivory are sometimes used. Memos are sometimes produced on pastel-colored paper so that internal correspondence can be more easily distinguished from external, and memos are sometimes printed or typed on various colors of paper for routing to separate departments. Light-colored papers are distinctive and often appropriate; bright or dark colors make reading difficult and may appear too frivolous.

Customization

For letters to outsiders, U.S. businesses commonly use letterhead stationery printed with the company's name and address, usually at the top of the page but sometimes along the left side or even at the bottom of the page. Other information may be included in the letterhead as well: the company's telephone number, fax number, cable address, Web site address, product lines, date of establishment, officers and directors, slogan, and symbol (logo). The idea is to give the recipient pertinent reference data and a good idea not only of what the company does but also of the company's image.[3] Nevertheless, the letterhead should be as simple as possible; too much information gives the page a cluttered look, cuts into the space needed for the letter, and may become outdated before all the letterhead has been used. If you correspond frequently with people in foreign countries, your letterhead can be misleading. If you do a lot of business abroad, be sure your letterhead is intelligible to foreigners, and make sure it includes the name of your country as well as your cable, telex, e-mail address, or fax information.

In the United States, company letterhead is always used for the first page of a letter. Successive pages are plain sheets of paper that match the letterhead in color and quality, or some companies use a specially printed second-page letterhead bearing only the company's name. Other countries have other conventions. For example, Latin American companies use a cover page with their printed seal in the center.

Many companies also design and print standardized forms for memos and for reports that are written frequently and always require the same sort of information (such as sales reports and expense reports). These forms may be printed in sets for use with carbon paper or in carbonless copy sets that produce multiple copies automatically with the original. More and more, organizations are using computers to generate their standardized forms. These electronic forms can save money and time.[4]

Appearance

Most business documents are produced using either a letter-quality (not a dot matrix) printer or a typewriter. Some short informal memos are handwritten, and it's appropriate to handwrite a note of condolence to a close business associate. The envelope is handwritten, printed, or typed to match the document. However, even a letter on the best-quality paper with the best-designed letterhead may look unprofessional if it's poorly produced.

Companies in the United States make sure that documents (especially external ones) are centered on the page, with margins of at least an inch all around (unlike documents produced in Latin America, which use much wider margins and thus look much longer). Using word-processing or desktop publishing software, you can achieve this balanced appearance simply by defining the format parameters. If you are using a typewriter, such balance can be achieved either by establishing a standard line length or by establishing a "picture frame."

The most common line length is about six inches. Lines aren't usually right-hand justified because the resulting text can be hard to read, even with proportional spacing, and because the document generally looks too much like a form letter. Varying line length makes the document look more personal and interesting. The larger, pica type will give you 60 characters in a line; the smaller, elite type will give you 72 characters in a line. The number of lines between elements of the document (such as between the date line and inside address in a letter) can be adjusted to ensure that a short document fills the page vertically or that a longer document extends to at least three lines of body on the last page.

Another important aspect of a professional-looking document is the proper spacing after punctuation. For example, U.S. conventions include (1) leaving one space after commas and semicolons and (2) leaving two spaces after periods at the ends of sentences and after colons (unless your typeface is proportional, requiring only one space). Each letter in a person's initials is followed by a period and a single space. Abbreviations for organizations, such as P.T.A., may or may not have periods, but they never have internal spaces. On computers and typewriters that have no special characters for dashes, use two hyphens with no space before, between, or after. Other details of this sort are provided in your company's style book or in most secretarial handbooks.

Finally, messy corrections are dreadfully obvious and unacceptable in business documents. Be sure that any letter, report, or memo requiring a lot of corrections is reprinted or retyped. Word-processing software and self-correcting typewriters can produce correction-free documents at the push of a button.

LETTERS

For a long time, letters have begun with some kind of phrase in greeting and have ended with some sort of polite expression before the writer's signature. Books printed in the sixteenth century prescribed letter formats for writers to follow. Styles have changed some since then, but all business letters still have certain elements in common. Several of these elements appear in every letter; others appear only when desirable or appropriate. In addition, these letter parts are usually arranged in one of three basic formats.

Standard Letter Parts

All business letters typically include seven elements, in the following order: (1) heading, (2) date, (3) inside address, (4) salutation, (5) body, (6) complimentary close, and (7) signature block. The letter in Figure A–1 shows the placement of these standard letter parts. The writer of this business letter had no letterhead available but correctly included a heading.

Heading   Letterhead (the usual heading) shows the organization's name, full address, and (almost always) telephone number. Executive letterhead also bears the name of an individual within the organization. Computers allow you to design your own letterhead (either one to use for all correspondence or a new one for each piece of correspondence). If letterhead stationery is not available, the heading consists of a return address (but not a name) starting 13 lines from the top of the page, which leaves two inches between the return address and the top of the page.

Date   If you're using letterhead, place the date at least one blank line beneath the lowest part of the letterhead. Without letterhead, place the date immediately below the return address. The standard method of writing the date in the United States uses the full name of the month (no abbreviations), followed by the day (in numerals, without *st*, *rd*, or *th*), a comma, and then the year: July 14, 2002 (7/14/02). The U.S. government and some U.S. industries place the day (in numerals) first, followed by the month (unabbreviated), followed by the year—with no comma: 14 July 2002 (14/7/02). This convention is similar to the one used in Europe, except that European convention replaces the U.S. solidus (diagonal line) with periods when the date appears all in numerals: 14 July 2002 (14.7.2002). The international standard places the year first, followed by the month and the day, separated by

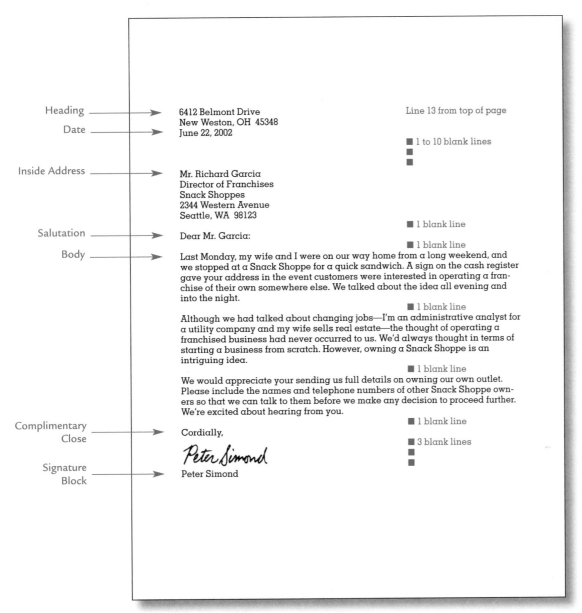

Figure A–1
In-Depth Critique: Standard Letter Parts

commas in the all-numeral form: 2002 July 14 (2002,7,14). To maintain the utmost clarity, always spell out the name of the month in dates for international correspondence.[5]

When communicating internationally, you may also experience some confusion over time. Some companies in the United States refer to morning (A.M.) and afternoon (P.M.), dividing a 24-hour day into 12-hour blocks so that they refer to four o'clock in the morning (4:00 A.M.) or four o'clock in the afternoon (4:00 P.M.). The U.S. military and European companies refer to one 24-hour period so that 0400 hours (4:00 A.M.) is always in the morning and 1600 hours (4:00 P.M.) is always in the afternoon.[6] Make sure your references to time are as clear as possible, and be sure you clearly understand your audience's time references.

Inside Address   The inside address identifies the recipient of the letter. For U.S. correspondence, begin the inside address one or more lines below the date, depending on how long the letter is. Precede the addressee's name with a courtesy title, such as *Dr., Mr.,* or *Ms.* The accepted courtesy title for women in business is Ms., although a woman known to prefer the title *Miss* or *Mrs.* is always accommodated. If you don't know whether a person is a man or a woman (and you have no way of finding out), do not use a courtesy title. For example, Terry Smith could be either a man or a woman. The first line of the inside address would be just Terry Smith, and the salutation would be Dear Terry Smith. The same is true if you know only a person's initials, as in S. J. Adams.

Table A-1 Forms of Address

PERSON	IN ADDRESS	IN SALUTATION
	Personal Titles	
Man	Mr. [first & last name]	Dear Mr. [last name]:
Woman (marital status unknown)	Ms. [first & last name]	Dear Ms. [last name]:
Woman (single)	Ms. *or* Miss [first & last name]	Dear Ms. *or* Miss [last name]:
Woman (married)	Ms. *or* Mrs. [wife's first & last name] or Mrs. [husband's first & last name]	Dear Ms. *or* Mrs. [last name]:
Woman (widowed)	Ms. or Mrs. [wife's first name & last name]	Dear Ms. *or* Mrs. [last name]:
Woman (separated or divorced)	Ms. or Mrs. [first & last name]	Dear Ms. *or* Mrs. [last name]:
Two men (or more)	Mr. [first & last name] and Mr. [first & last name]	Dear Mr. [last name] and Mr. [last name] *or* Messrs. [last name] and [last name]:
Two women (or more)	Ms. [first & last name] and Ms. [first & last name] *or*	Dear Ms. [last name] and Ms. [last name] *or* Mses. [last name] and [last name]:
	Mrs. [first & last name] and Mrs. [first & last name]	Dear Mrs. [last name] and Mrs. [last name]: *or* Dear Mesdames [last name] and [last name] *or* Mesdames:
	Miss [first & last name] and Mrs. [first & last name]	Dear Miss [last name] and Mrs. [last name]:
One woman and one man	Ms. [first & last name] and Mr. [first & last name]	Dear Ms. [last name] and Mr. [last name]:
Couple (married)	Mr. and Mrs. [husband's first & last name]	Dear Mr. and Mrs. [last name]:
Couple (married with different last names)	[title] [first & last name of husband] [title] [first & last name of wife]	Dear [title] [husband's last name] and [title] [wife's last name]:
Couple (married professionals with same title & same last name)	[title in plural form] [husband's first name] and [wife's first name] [last name]	Dear [title in plural form] [last name]:
Couple (married professionals with different titles & same last name)	[title] [first & last name of husband] [title] [first & last name of wife]	Dear [title] and [title] [last name]:

(continued)

Spell out and capitalize titles that precede a person's name, such as *Professor* or *General* (see Table A–1 for the proper forms of address). The person's organizational title, such as *Director,* may be included on this first line (if it is short) or on the line below; the name of a department may follow. In addresses and signature lines, don't forget to capitalize any professional title that follows a person's name:

Mr. Ray Johnson, Dean

Ms. Patricia T. Higgins
Assistant Vice President

However, professional titles not appearing in an address or signature line are capitalized only when they directly precede the name.

President Kenneth Johanson will deliver the speech.

Maria Morales, president of ABC Enterprises, will deliver the speech.

The Honorable Helen Masters, senator from Arizona, will deliver the speech.

If the name of a specific person is unavailable, you may address the letter to the department or to a specific position

Table A–1   Continued

PERSON	IN ADDRESS	IN SALUTATION
Professional Titles		
President of a college or university (doctor)	Dr. [first & last name], President	Dear Dr. [last name]:
Dean of a school of college	Dean [first & last name] *or* Dr., Mr., Mrs., or Miss [first & last name] Dean of (title)	Dear Dean [last name]: Dear Dr., Mr., Ms., Mrs., *or* Miss [last name]:
Professor	Professor [first & last name]	Dear Professor [last name]:
Physician	[first & last name], M.D.	Dear Dr. [last name]:
Lawyer	Mr., Ms., Mrs., *or* Miss [first & last name]	Dear Mr., Ms., Mrs., *or* Miss [last name]:
Service personnel	[full rank, first & last name, abbreviation of service designation] (add *Retired* if applicable)	Dear [rank] [last name]:
Company or corporation	[name of organization]	Ladies and Gentlemen *or* Gentlemen and Ladies
Governmental Titles		
President of the United States	The President	Dear Mr. *or* Madam President:
Senator of the United States	Honorable [first & last name]	Dear Senator [last name]:
Cabinet member Postmaster General Attorney General	Honorable [first & last name]	Dear Mr. *or* Madam Secretary: Dear Mr. *or* Madam Postmaster General: Dear Mr. *or* Madam Attorney General:
Mayor	Honorable [first & last name] Mayor of [name of city]	Dear Mayor [last name]:
Judge	The Honorable [first and last name]	Dear Judge [last name]:
Religious Titles		
Priest	The Reverend [first & last name], [initials of order, if any]	Reverend Sir: (formal) *or* Dear Father [last name]: (informal)
Rabbi	Rabbi [first & last name]	Dear Rabbi [last name]:
Minister	The Reverend [first & last name] [title, if any]	Dear Reverend [last name]:

within the department. Also, be sure to spell out company names in full, unless the company itself uses abbreviations in its official name.

Other address information includes the treatment of buildings, house numbers, and compass directions. Capitalize the names of buildings, and if you specify a location within a building (suite, room, and so on), capitalize it and use a comma to separate it from the building name.

Empire State Building, Suite 1073

Use numerals for all house or building numbers, except the number *one.*

One Trinity Lane
637 Adams Avenue, Apt. 7

Spell out compass directions that fall within a street address, but abbreviate compass directions that follow the street address:

1074 West Connover Street
783 Main Street, N.E., Apt. 27

Also remember that apartment, suite, and room numbers always appear in numerals (as in the examples already listed in this paragraph). The following example shows all the information that may be included in the inside address and its proper order for U.S. correspondence:

Ms. Linda Coolidge, Vice President
Corporate Planning Department
Midwest Airlines
Kowalski Building, Suite 21-A
7279 Bristol Avenue
Toledo, OH 43617

Canadian addresses are similar, except that the name of the province is usually spelled out:

Dr. H. C. Armstrong
Research and Development
Commonwealth Mining Consortium
The Chelton Building, Suite 301
585 Second Street SW
Calgary, Alberta T2P 2P5

When addressing correspondence for other countries, follow the format and information that appear in the company's letterhead.[7] You want to be especially careful about the format of international correspondence because you want everything to be as clear as possible.[8] The order and layout of address information vary from country to country, so follow the conventions of the country of the recipient. When you're sending mail from the United States, however, be sure that the name of the destination country appears on the last line of the address in capital letters. Also, use the English version of the country name so that your mail is routed from the United States to the right country. Then, to be sure your mail is routed correctly within the destination country, use the foreign spelling of the city name (using the characters and diacritical marks that would be commonly used in the region). For example, the following address uses Köln, instead of Cologne:

H. R. Veith, Director	Addressee
Eisfieren Glaswerk	Company Name
Blaubachstraße 13	Street address
Postfach 10 80 07	Post office box
D-5000 Köln I	District, city
GERMANY	Country

Additional addresses might look similar to the following:

Mr. Toru Hasegawa
7-35 Kitashinagawa
6 Chrome—141 Shinagawa-ku
Tokyo
JAPAN

Cairo
Cleopatra
165 El Corniche Road
Mrs. Ahmed Abbas Zaki
EGYPT

Crédit Lyonnais
c/o Claude Rubinowicz
19, Boulevard des Italiens
75002 Paris
FRANCE

Sr. Ari Matos Cardoso
Superintendent of Human Resources and Personnel
Av. República do Chile, 65
Centro-Rio de Janeiro, RJ
CEP 20035
BRAZIL

Be sure to get organizational titles right when addressing international correspondence. Job designations vary around the world. In England, for example, a managing director is often what a U.S. company would call its chief executive officer or president, and a British deputy is the equivalent of a vice president. In France, responsibilities are assigned to individuals without regard to title or organizational structure, and in China the title *project manager* has meaning, but the title *sales manager* may not. To make matters worse, businesspeople in some countries sign correspondence without their names typed below. In Germany, for example, the belief is that employees represent the company, so it's inappropriate to emphasize personal names.[9]

Salutation   In the salutation of your letter, follow the first line of the inside address. That is, if the first line is a person's name, the salutation is *Dear Mr.* or *Ms. Name*. Base the formality of the salutation on your relationship with the addressee. If in conversation you would say "Mary," your letter's salutation should be *Dear Mary,* followed by a colon. In letters to people you don't know well enough to address personally, include the courtesy title and last name, followed by a colon. Presuming to write *Dear Lewis* instead of *Dear Professor Chang* demonstrates a disrespectful familiarity that a stranger will probably resent. If the first line is a position title such as Director of Personnel, then use *Dear Director;* if the addressee is unknown, use a polite description, such as *Dear Alumnus, Dear SPCA Supporter,* or *Dear Voter.* If the first line is plural (a department or company), then use *Ladies and Gentlemen* (look again at Table A–1). When you do not know whether you're writing to an individual or a group (for example, when writing a reference or a letter of recommendation), use *To whom it may concern.*

In the United States some letter writers use a salutopening on the salutation line. A salutopening omits *Dear* but includes the first few words of the opening paragraph along with the recipient's name. After this line, the sentence continues a double space below as part of the body of the letter, as in these examples:

Thank you, Mr. Brown,	Salutopening
for your prompt payment of your bill.	Body
Congratulations, Ms. Lake!	Salutopening
Your promotion is well deserved.	Body

Don't overlook an especially important point with personalized salutations: Whether they're informal or formal, make sure names are spelled right. A misspelled name is glaring evidence of carelessness, and it belies the personal interest you're trying to express.

Body The body of the letter is your message. Almost all letters are single-spaced, with double spacing (one blank line) before and after the salutation or salutopening, between paragraphs, and before the complimentary close. The body may include indented lists, entire paragraphs indented for emphasis, and even subheadings. If it does, all similar elements should be treated in the same way. Your department or company may select a format to use for all letters.

Complimentary Close The complimentary close begins on the second line below the body of the letter. Alternatives for wording are available, but currently the trend seems to be toward using one-word closes, such as *Sincerely* and *Cordially*. In any case, the complimentary close reflects the relationship between you and the person you're writing to. Avoid cute closes, such as *Yours for bigger profits*. If your audience doesn't know you well, your sense of humor may be misunderstood.

Signature Block Leave three blank lines for a written signature below the complimentary close, and then include the sender's name (unless it appears in the letterhead). The person's title may appear on the same line as the name or on the line below:

Cordially,

Raymond Dunnigan
Director of Personnel

Your letterhead indicates that you're representing your company. However, if your letter is on plain paper or runs to a second page, you may want to emphasize that you're speaking legally for the company. The accepted way of doing that is to place the company's name in capital letters a double space below the complimentary close and then include the sender's name and title four lines below that:

Sincerely,

WENTWORTH INDUSTRIES

(Mrs.) Helen B. Taylor
President

If your name could be taken for either a man's or a woman's, a courtesy title indicating gender should be included, with or without parentheses. Also, women who prefer a particular courtesy title should include it:

Mrs. Nancy Winters
(Miss) Juana Flores

Ms. Pat Li
(Mr.) Jamie Saunders

Additional Letter Parts

Letters vary greatly in subject matter and thus in the identifying information they need and the format they adopt. The following elements may be used in any combination, depending on the requirements of the particular letter, but generally in this order:

1. Addressee notation
2. Attention line
3. Subject line
4. Second-page heading
5. Company name
6. Reference initials
7. Enclosure notation
8. Copy notation
9. Mailing notation
10. Postscript

The letter in Figure A–2 shows how these additional parts should be arranged.

Addressee Notation Letters that have a restricted readership or that must be handled in a special way should include such addressee notations as *Personal, Confidential,* or *Please Forward*. This sort of notation appears a double space above the inside address, in all capital letters.

Attention Line Although an attention line is not commonly used today, you may find it useful if you know only the last name of the person you're writing to. An attention line can also be used to direct a letter to a position title or department. An attention line may take any of the following forms or variants of them: *Attention Dr. McHenry, Attention Director of Marketing,* or *Attention Marketing Department*. You may place the attention line on the first line and use the company name as the second line of the inside address.[10] The address on the envelope should always match the style of the inside address shown in Figure A–2, which includes many of the elements often appearing in business letters.

Subject Line The subject line lets the recipient know at a glance what the letter is about; it also indicates where to file the letter for future reference. It usually appears below the salutation—against the left margin, indented as the paragraphs in the body of the letter, or centered on the line. Sometimes the subject line is placed above the salutation or at the very top of the page. The subject line may take a variety of forms, including the following:

Subject: RainMaster Sprinklers
About your February 2, 2002, order
FALL 1998 SALES MEETING
Reference Order No. 27920

Sometimes the subject line (or the last line of a long subject "line") is underscored. Some writers omit the word *Subject* and put the other information all in capitals to distinguish it from the other letter parts. Organizations such as insurance

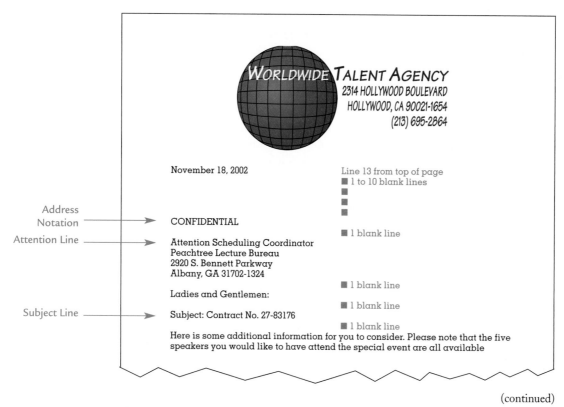

Figure A–2
In-Depth Critique: Additional Letter Parts

and financial institutions, attorneys, and government offices may use the words *Re:* or *In re:* (meaning "concerning" or "in the matter of") rather than using the word *Subject.*

Second-Page Heading   If the letter is long and an additional page is required, use a second-page heading. Some companies have second-page letterhead, with the company name and address on one line and in a smaller typeface than on the regular letterhead. In any case, the second-page heading bears the name that appears in the first line of the inside address (the person or organization receiving the letter), the page number, and the date of the letter; you can also include a reference number. All the following are acceptable:

Ms. Melissa Baker
May 10, 1998
Page 2

Ms. Melissa Baker, May 10, 2002, Page 2

Ms. Melissa Baker   -2-   May 10, 2002

Triple-space (leave two blank lines) between the second-page heading and the body. If a paragraph must be continued on a second page, make sure at least two lines of that paragraph appear on the first page and on the second page. Also, the closing lines of a business letter must never appear alone on a continued page. At least two lines of the body

must precede the complimentary close or signature lines. And finally, don't hyphenate the last word on a page.

Company Name   If you include the company's name in the signature block, put it all in capital letters a double space below the complimentary close. You usually include the company's name in the signature block only when the writer is serving as the company's official spokesperson or when letterhead has not been used.

Reference Initials   Because it can happen in business that one person may dictate or write a letter and another person may produce it, reference initials are used to show who helped prepare the letter. Reference initials appear at the left margin, a double space below the last line of the signature block. When the writer's name has been included in the signature block, only the preparer's initials are necessary. If only the department appears in the signature block, both sets of initials should appear, usually in one of the following forms:

RSR/sm

RSR:sm

RSR:SM

The first set of initials is the writer's; the second set is the preparer's.

Sometimes the writer and the signer of a letter are different people. In that case, at least the file copy of a letter

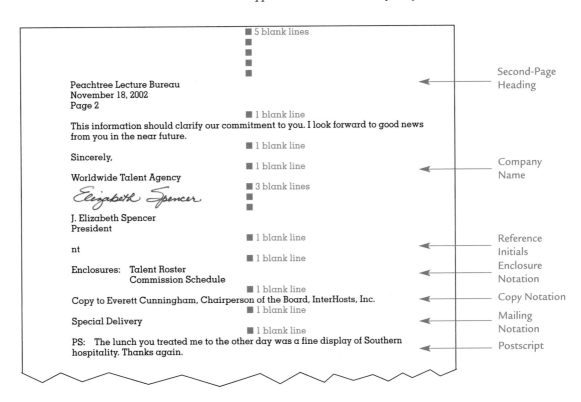

Figure A–2
(Continued)

should bear both their initials as well as those of the typist: JFS/RSR/sm (signer, writer, preparer). When businesspeople keyboard their own letters, reference initials are not included, so such initials are becoming more and more rare.

Enclosure Notation   Enclosure notations also appear at the bottom of a letter, one or two lines below the reference initials. Some common forms:

Enclosure

Enclosures (2)

Enclosures: Résumé
              Photograph

Attachment

Copy Notation   Copy notations may follow reference initials or enclosure notations. They indicate who's receiving a *courtesy copy* (*cc*). Some companies indicate copies made on a photocopier (*pc*), or they simply use *copy* (*c*). Recipients are listed in order of rank or (rank being equal) in alphabetical order. Among the forms used:

cc: David Wentworth

pc: Martha Littlefield

Copy to Hans Vogel

c: Joseph Martinez

In addition to the name of an individual, copy notations may include any combination of that person's courtesy title, position, department, company, and complete address, along with notations about any enclosures being sent with the copies.

On occasion, copies are sent to benefit readers other than the person who receives the original letter. In that case, place the notation *bc, bcc,* or *bpc* (for blind copy, blind courtesy copy, or blind photocopy) with the name where the copy notation would normally appear—but only on the copy, not on the original.

Mailing Notation   You may place a mailing notation (such as *Special Delivery* or *Registered Mail*) at the bottom of the letter, after reference initials or enclosure notations (whichever one is last) and before copy notations. Or you may place it at the top of the letter, either above the inside address on the left-hand side or just below the date on the right-hand side. For greater visibility, mailing notations may appear in capital letters.

Postscript   Letters may also bear postscripts: afterthoughts to the letter, messages that require emphasis, or personal notes. The postscript is usually the last thing on any letter and may be preceded by *P.S., PS., PS:*, or nothing at all. A second afterthought would be designated *P.P.S.,* meaning "post postscript."

Postscripts usually indicate poor planning, so generally avoid them. However, they're commonly used in sales letters, not as an afterthought but as a punch line to remind the reader of a benefit for taking advantage of the offer.

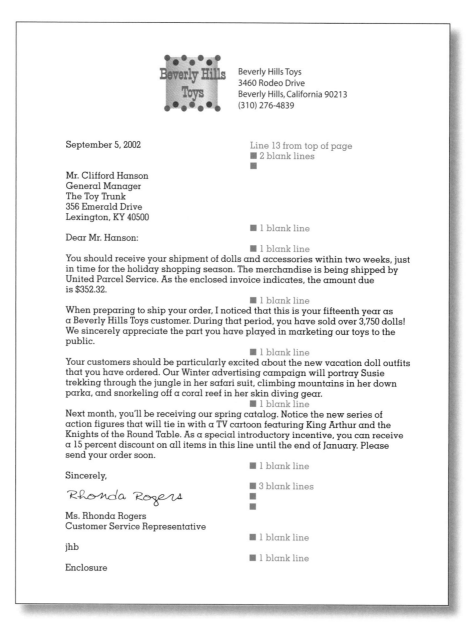

Figure A–3
In-Depth Critique: Block Letter Format

Letter Formats

Although the basic letter parts have remained the same for centuries, ways of arranging them do change. Sometimes a company adopts a certain format as its policy; sometimes the individual letter writer or preparer is allowed to choose the format most appropriate for a given letter or to settle on a personal preference. In the United States, three major letter formats are commonly used:

- *Block format.* Each letter part begins at the left margin. The main advantage is quick and efficient preparation (see Figure A–3).

- *Modified block format.* Same as block format, except the date, complimentary close, and signature block start near

the center of the page (see Figure A–4). The modified block format does permit indentions as an option. This format mixes preparation speed with traditional placement of some letter parts. It also looks more balanced on the page than the block format does.

- *Simplified format.* Instead of using a salutation, this format often works the audience's name into the first line or two of the body and often includes a subject line in capital letters (see Figure A–5). It also omits the complimentary close, so you sign your name after the body of the letter, followed by the printed (or typewritten) name (customarily in all capital letters). The advantages include convenience when you don't know your audience's name. However, some people object to this format because it

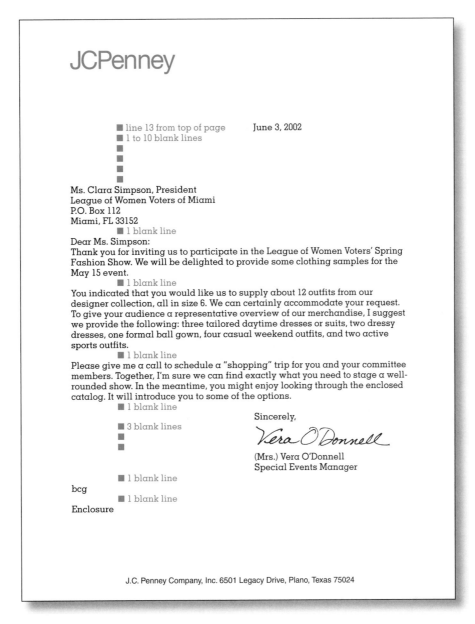

JCPenney

■ line 13 from top of page   June 3, 2002
■ 1 to 10 blank lines
■
■
■
■

Ms. Clara Simpson, President
League of Women Voters of Miami
P.O. Box 112
Miami, FL 33152
■ 1 blank line
Dear Ms. Simpson:
Thank you for inviting us to participate in the League of Women Voters' Spring
Fashion Show. We will be delighted to provide some clothing samples for the
May 15 event.
■ 1 blank line
You indicated that you would like us to supply about 12 outfits from our
designer collection, all in size 6. We can certainly accommodate your request.
To give your audience a representative overview of our merchandise, I suggest
we provide the following: three tailored daytime dresses or suits, two dressy
dresses, one formal ball gown, four casual weekend outfits, and two active
sports outfits.
■ 1 blank line
Please give me a call to schedule a "shopping" trip for you and your committee
members. Together, I'm sure we can find exactly what you need to stage a well-
rounded show. In the meantime, you might enjoy looking through the enclosed
catalog. It will introduce you to some of the options.
■ 1 blank line

■ 3 blank lines   Sincerely,
■
■   *Vera O'Donnell*
                  (Mrs.) Vera O'Donnell
                  Special Events Manager
■ 1 blank line
bcg
■ 1 blank line
Enclosure

J.C. Penney Company, Inc. 6501 Legacy Drive, Plano, Texas 75024

Figure A–4
In-Depth Critique: Modified Block Letter Format

seems mechanical and impersonal (a drawback that may be overcome with a warm writing style). In this format, the elimination of certain letter parts changes some of the spacing between lines.

These formats differ in the way paragraphs are indented, in the way letter parts are placed, and in some punctuation. However, the elements are always separated by at least one blank line, and the printed (or typewritten) name is always separated from the line above by at least three blank lines to allow space for a signature. If paragraphs are indented, the indention is normally five spaces.

The most common formats for intercultural business letters are the block style and the modified block style. Use either the U.S. or the European format for dates. For the salutation, use *Dear (Title/Last name)*. Close the letter with *Sincerely* or *Cordially,* and sign it.

In addition to these three letter formats, letters may also be classified according to the style of punctuation they use. *Standard,* or *mixed, punctuation* uses a colon after the salutation (a comma if the letter is social or personal) and a comma after the complimentary close. *Open punctuation* uses no colon or comma after the salutation or the complimentary close. Although the most popular style in business communication is mixed punctuation, either style of punctuation may be used with block or modified block letter formats. Because the simplified letter format has no salutation or complimentary close, the style of punctuation is irrelevant.

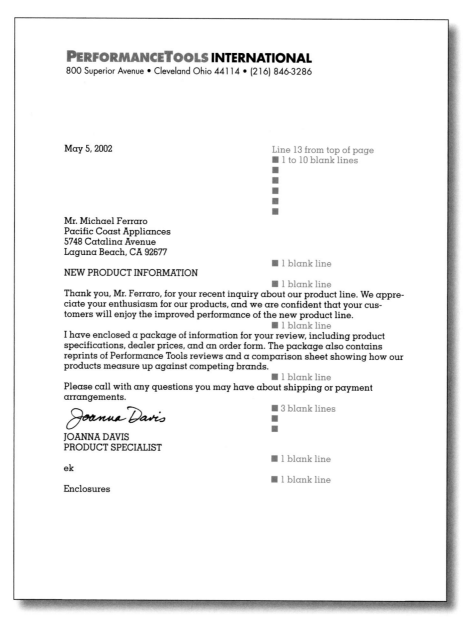

Figure A–5
In-Depth Critique: Simplified Letter Format

ENVELOPES

The quality of the envelope is just as important for first impressions as the quality of the stationery. In fact, letterhead and envelopes should be of the same paper stock, have the same color ink, and be imprinted with the same address and logo. Most envelopes used by U.S. businesses are No. 10 envelopes (9½ inches long), which are sized to contain an 8½-by-11-inch piece of paper folded in thirds. Some occasions call for a smaller, No. 6¾, envelope or for envelopes proportioned to fit special stationery. Figure A–6 shows the two most common sizes.

Addressing the Envelope

No matter what size the envelope, the address is always single-spaced and in block form—that is, with all lines aligned on the left. The address on the envelope is in the same style as the inside address and presents the same information. The order to follow is from the smallest division to the largest:

1. Name and title of recipient
2. Name of department or subgroup
3. Name of organization
4. Name of building

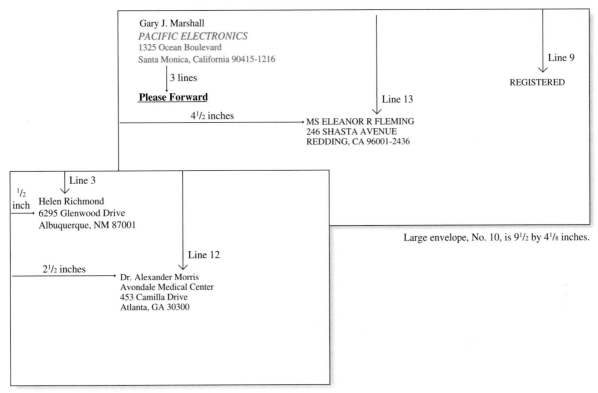

Gary J. Marshall
PACIFIC ELECTRONICS
1325 Ocean Boulevard
Santa Monica, California 90415-1216

| 3 lines

Please Forward

4½ inches

Line 13

MS ELEANOR R FLEMING
246 SHASTA AVENUE
REDDING, CA 96001-2436

Line 9

REGISTERED

Line 3

½ inch

Helen Richmond
6295 Glenwood Drive
Albuquerque, NM 87001

2½ inches

Line 12

Dr. Alexander Morris
Avondale Medical Center
453 Camilla Drive
Atlanta, GA 30300

Large envelope, No. 10, is 9½ by 4⅛ inches.

Small envelope, No. 6¾, is 6½ by 3⅝ inches.

Figure A–6
Prescribed Envelope Format

5. Street address and suite number, or post office box number

6. City, state or province, and ZIP code or Postal Code

7. Name of country (if the letter is being sent abroad)

Because the U.S. Postal Service uses optical scanners to sort mail, envelopes for quantity mailings, in particular, should be addressed in the prescribed format. As in the mailing address on the No. 10 envelope in Figure A–6, everything is in capital letters, no punctuation is included, and all mailing instructions of interest to the post office are placed above the address area. Canada Post requires a similar format, except that only the city is all in capitals and the Postal Code is placed on the line below the name of the city. The post office scanners read addresses from the bottom up, so if a letter is to be sent to a post office box rather than to a street address, the street address should appear on the line above the box number. Figure A–6 also shows the proper spacing for addresses and return addresses.

The U.S. Postal Service and the Canada Post Corporation have published lists of two-letter mailing abbreviations for states, provinces, and territories (see Table A–2), to be used without periods or commas. Nevertheless, some executives prefer that state and province names be spelled out in full and that a comma be used to separate the city and state or province names. Thus the use of a comma

between the name of the city and the state or province name is an unresolved issue. Most commonly, the comma is included; sometimes, however, the comma is eliminated to conform with post office standards.

Quantity mailings follow post office requirements. For letters that aren't mailed in quantity, a reasonable compromise is to use traditional punctuation and uppercase and lowercase letters for names and street addresses but two-letter state or province abbreviations, as shown here:

Mr. Kevin Kennedy
2107 E. Packer Drive
Amarillo, TX 79108

For all out-of-office correspondence, use ZIP codes and Postal Codes, assigned to speed mail delivery. The U.S. Postal Service has divided the United States and its territories into 10 zones, each represented by a digit from 0 to 9; this digit comes first in the ZIP code. The second and third digits represent smaller geographical areas within a state, and the last two digits identify a "local delivery area." Canadian Postal Codes are alphanumeric, with a three-character "area code" and a three-character "local code" separated by a single space (K2P 5A5). ZIP codes and Postal Codes should be separated from state and province names by one space. As an alternative, a Canadian Postal Code may be put on the bottom line of the address all by itself.

Table A–2   Two-Letter Mailing Abbreviations for the United States and Canada

State/Territory/Province	Abbreviation	State/Territory/Province	Abbreviation	State/Territory/Province	Abbreviation
UNITED STATES					
Alabama	AL	Michigan	MI	Utah	UT
Alaska	AK	Minnesota	MN	Vermont	VT
Arizona	AZ	Mississippi	MS	Virginia	VA
Arkansas	AR	Missouri	MO	Virgin Islands	VI
American Samoa	AS	Montana	MT	Washington	WA
California	CA	Nebraska	NE	West Virginia	WV
Canal Zone	CZ	Nevada	NV	Wisconsin	WI
Colorado	CO	New Hampshire	NH	Wyoming	WY
Connecticut	CT	New Jersey	NJ		
Delaware	DE	New Mexico	NM	CANADA	
District of Columbia	DC	New York	NY	Alberta	AB
		North Carolina	NC	British Columbia	BC
Florida	FL	North Dakota	ND	Labrador	LB
Georgia	GA	Northern Mariana Is.	CM	Manitoba	MB
Guam	GU			New Brunswick	NB
Hawaii	HI	Ohio	OH	Newfoundland	NF
Idaho	ID	Oklahoma	OK	Northwest Territories	NT
Illinois	IL	Oregon	OR		
Indiana	IN	Pennsylvania	PA	Nova Scotia	NS
Iowa	IA	Puerto Rico	PR	Ontario	ON
Kansas	KS	Rhode Island	RI	Prince Edward Island	PE
Kentucky	KY	South Carolina	SC		
Louisiana	LA	South Dakota	SD	Quebec	PQ
Maine	ME	Tennessee	TN	Saskatchewan	SK
Maryland	MD	Trust Territories	TT	Yukon Territory	YT
Massachusetts	MA	Texas	TX		

The U.S. Postal Service has added ZIP + 4 codes, which add a hyphen and four more numbers to the standard ZIP codes. The first two of the new numbers may identify an area as small as a single large building, and the last two digits may identify one floor in a large building or even a specific department of an organization. The ZIP + 4 codes are especially useful for business correspondence. The Canada Post Corporation achieves the same result with special postal codes assigned to buildings and organizations that receive a large volume of mail.

Folding to Fit

The way a letter is folded also contributes to the recipient's overall impression of your organization's professionalism. When sending a standard-size piece of paper in a No. 10 envelope, fold it in thirds, with the bottom folded up first and the top folded down over it (see Figure A–7); the open end should be at the top of the envelope and facing out. Fit smaller stationery neatly into the appropriate envelope simply by folding it in half or in thirds. When sending a standard-size letterhead in a No. 6¾ envelope, fold it in half from top to bottom and then in thirds from side to side.

International Mail

When sending mail internationally, remember that postal service differs from country to country. For example, street addresses are uncommon in India, and the mail there is unreliable.[11] It's usually a good idea to send international correspondence by air mail and to ask that responses be sent that way as well. Also, remember to check the postage; rates for sending mail to most other countries aren't the same as the rates for sending mail within your own country.

Three main categories of international mail are the following:

◆ *LC mail.* An abbreviation of the French *Lettres et Cartes* ("letters and cards"), this category consists of letters, letter packages, aerograms, and postcards.

◆ *AO mail.* An abbreviation of the French *Autres Objets* ("other articles"), this category includes regular printed matter, books and sheet music, matter for the blind, small packets, and publishers' periodicals (second class).

◆ *CP mail.* An abbreviation of the French *Colis Postaux* ("parcel post"), this category resembles fourth-class mail, including packages of merchandise or any other articles not required to be mailed at letter postage rates.

Figure A–7
Letter Folds for Standard-Size
Letterhead

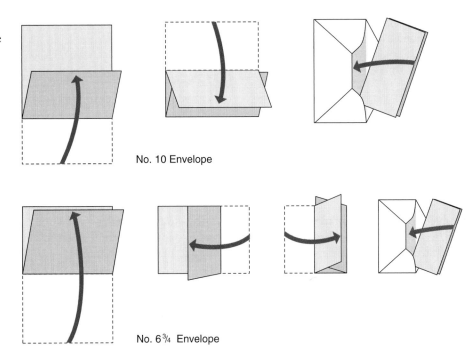

No. 10 Envelope

No. 6¾ Envelope

The U.S. Postal Service also offers Express Mail International Service (EMS), a high-speed mail service to many countries; International Priority Airmail (IPA), an international service that's as fast as or faster than regular airmail service; International Surface Air Lift (ISAL), a service providing quicker delivery and lower cost for all kinds of printed matter; Bulk Letter Service to Canada, an economical airmail service for letters weighing 1 ounce or less; VALUEPOST/CANADA, a reduced postage rate for bulk mailings; International Electronic Post (INTELPOST), a service offering same- or next-day delivery of fax documents; International Postal Money Orders, a service for transferring funds to other countries; and several optional special services.

To prepare your mail for international delivery, follow the instructions in the U.S. Postal Service Publication 51, *International Postal Rates and Fees.* Be sure to note instructions for the address, return address, and size limits. Envelopes and wrappers must be clearly marked to show their classification (letter, small packet, printed matter, air mail). All registered letters, letter packages, and parcel post packages must be securely sealed. Printed matter may be sealed only if postage is paid by permit imprint, postage meter, precanceled stamps, or second-class imprint. Otherwise, prepare contents so that they're protected but in such a way that they won't hinder inspection. Finally, because international mail is subject to customs examination in the country of destination, the contents and value must be declared on special forms.

MEMOS

Interoffice memos aren't distributed outside the organization, so they may not need the best-quality paper. However, they still convey important information, so clarity, careful arrange-

ment, and neatness are important. As do those for letters, the guidelines for formatting memos help recipients understand at a glance what they've received and from whom.

Many organizations have memo forms printed, with labeled spaces for the recipient's name (or sometimes a checklist of all departments in an organization or all persons in a department), the sender's name, the date, and the subject (see Figure A–8). If such forms don't exist, you can use plain paper.

Include a title such as *Memo* or *Interoffice Correspondence* (all in capitals) centered at the top of the page or aligned with the left margin. Also include the words *To, From, Date,* and *Subject*—followed by the appropriate information—at the top with a blank line between, as shown here:

MEMO

TO:

FROM:

DATE:

SUBJECT:

Sometimes the heading is organized like this:

MEMO

TO:	DATE:
FROM:	SUBJECT:

You can arrange these four pieces of information in almost any order. The date sometimes appears without the heading

Date. The subject may be presented with the letters *Re:* (in place of *SUBJECT:*) or may even be presented without any heading (but put it in capital letters so that it stands out clearly). You may want to include a file or reference number, introduced by the word *File.*

If you send a memo to a long list of people, include the notation *See distribution list* or *See below* in the *To* position at the top; then list the names at the end of the memo. Arranging such a list alphabetically is usually the most diplomatic course, although high-ranking officials may deserve more prominent placement. You can also address memos to groups of people—*All Sales Representatives, Production Group, Assistant Vice Presidents.*

You don't need to use courtesy titles anywhere in a memo; first initials and last names, first names, or even initials alone are often sufficient. As a general rule, however, use a courtesy title if you would use one in face-to-face encounters with the person.

The subject line of a memo helps busy colleagues find out quickly what your memo is about. Although the subject "line" may overflow onto a second line, it's most helpful when it's short (but still informative).

Start the body of the memo on the second or third line below the heading. Like the body of a letter, it's usually single-spaced. Separate paragraphs with blank lines. Indenting them is optional. Handle lists, important passages, and subheadings as you do in letters. If the memo is very short, you may double-space it.

If the memo carries over to a second page, head the second page just as you head the second page of a letter.

Unlike a letter, a memo doesn't require a complimentary close or a signature, because your name is already prominent at the top. However, you may initial the memo—either beside the name appearing at the top of the memo or at the bottom of the memo—or you may even sign your name at the bottom, particularly if the memo deals with money or confidential matters. Treat all other elements—reference initials, enclosure notations, and copy notations—as you would in a letter.

Memos may be delivered by hand, by the post office (when the recipient doesn't work at the same location as the memo writer), or through interoffice mail. Interoffice mail may require the use of special reusable envelopes that have spaces for the recipient's name and department or room number; the name of the previous recipient is simply crossed out. If a regular envelope is used, the words *Interoffice Mail* appear where the stamp normally goes so that it won't accidentally be stamped and mailed with the rest of the office correspondence.

Informal, routine, or brief reports for distribution within a company are often presented in memo form (see Chapter 10). Don't include such report parts as a table of contents and appendixes, but write the body of the memo report just as carefully as you'd write a formal report.

E-MAIL

Because e-mail messages can act both as memos (carrying information within your company) and as letters (carrying information outside your company and around the world), their format depends on your audience and purpose. You may choose to have your e-mail resemble a formal letter or a detailed report, or you may decide to keep things as simple as an interoffice memo. A modified memo format is appropriate for most e-mail messages.[12] All e-mail programs include two major elements: the header and the body (see Figure A–9).

Header

The e-mail header depends on the particular program you use. Some programs even allow you to choose between a shorter and a longer version. However, most headers contain similar information.

The *To:* line contains your audience's e-mail address. The most common e-mail addresses are Internet addresses, like the following:

◆ NMAA.BETSY@C.SI.EDU (Smithsonian Institute's National Museum of American Art)

◆ webwsj@dowjones.com (*Wall Street Journal*'s home page)

◆ mailto: cc131@iway.fr (Chamber of Commerce and Industry in Toulouse, France)

On the Internet, everything on the left side of the @ symbol is the user name; everything on the right side describes the computer where that user has an account. This machine name usually ends with a country code (such as fr for France, dk for Denmark, hk for Hong Kong, ca for Canada). But within the United States, the country code is

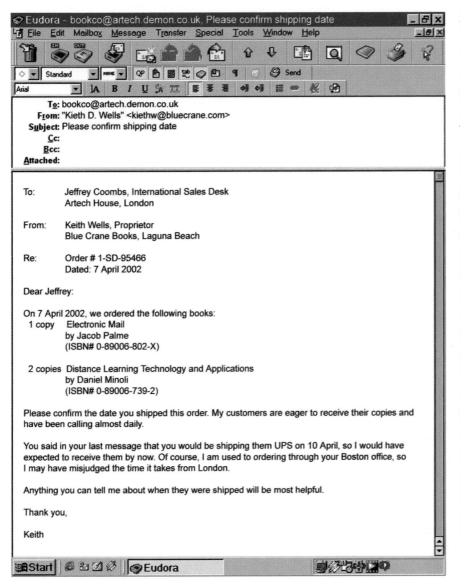

HEADER (May vary from program to program)
Date: Includes the day, date, time, and time zone on printout
To: Includes the recipient's address (perhaps addressee's proper name)
From: Includes your address (perhaps your proper name)
Subject (Re): Describes what your message concerns (an opportunity to gain interest)
Cc: Includes the address of anyone you want to receive a copy of the message
Bcc: Includes the address of anyone you want to receive a copy of the message but don't want listed as a receiver
Attachments: Includes the name of any files you have attached to your message
Greeting: Makes the message more personal
Message: Format depends on your audience and purpose. Can include headings, lists, and other common devices used in letters and memos
Closing: Personalizes your message and resembles simple closings in letters
Signature: Can be simply your name typed or can be a signature file

replaced with the type of organization that operates that particular computer:[13]

- .com   business and commercial users
- .edu   educational institutions
- .gov   nonmilitary government and related groups
- .mil   military-related groups
- .net   network providers
- .org   organizations and nonprofit groups

Most e-mail programs will also allow you to send mail to an entire group of people all at once. First, you create a distribution list. Then you type the name of the list in the *To:* line instead of typing the addresses of every person in the group.[14]

The *From:* line contains your e-mail address. The *Date:* line contains the day of the week, date (day, month, year), time, and time zone. The *Subject:* line describes the content of the message and presents an opportunity for you to build

interest in your message. The *cc:* line allows you to send copies of a message to more than one person at a time. It also allows everyone on the list to see who else received the same message. The *Bcc:* line lets you send copies to people without the other recipients knowing—a practice considered unethical by some.[15] The *Attachments:* line contains the name(s) of the file(s) you attach to your e-mail message. The file can be a word-processing document, a digital image, an audio or video message, a spreadsheet, or a software program.[16]

Other lines containing more detailed information can be listed in your e-mail's header, including *Message-Id* (the exact location of this e-mail message on the sender's system), *X-mailer:* (the version of the e-mail program being used), and *Content type:* (a description of what kind of text and character set is contained in the message). Also, the *Received:* lines include information about each of the systems your e-mail passed through en route to your mailbox.[17] Most e-mail programs now allow you the choice of hiding or revealing this sort of detailed information.

Body

You might consider your mail program's header to be something like letterhead, because the rest of the space below the header is for the body of your message. In the *To:* and *From:* lines, some headers actually print out the names of the sender and the receiver (in addition to the e-mail addresses). Other headers do not. If your mail program includes only the e-mail addresses, you might consider including your own memo-type header, as was done in Figure A–9. The writer even included a subject line in his memo-type header that is more specific than the one in the mail program header. Although some may applaud the clarity such a second header provides, others may criticize the space it takes. Your decision depends on how formal you want to be.

Do include a greeting in your e-mail. As pointed out in Chapter 5, greetings personalize your message. Leave one line space above and below your greeting to set it off from the rest of your message. Again, depending on the level of formality you want, you may choose to end your greeting with a colon (most formal), a comma (conversational), or even two hyphens (informal).

Your message begins one blank line space below your greeting. Just as in memos and letters, skip one line space between paragraphs and include headings, numbered lists, bulleted lists, and embedded lists when appropriate. Limit your line lengths to a maximum of 80 characters by inserting a hard return at the end of each line.

One blank line space below your message, include a simple closing, often just one word. A blank line space below that, include your signature. Whether you type your name or use a signature file, including your signature personalizes your message.

TIME-SAVING MESSAGES

If there's a way to speed up the communication process, the organization stands to gain. Telephones and electronic mail systems are quick, as are mailgrams, telegrams, faxes, and the like. In addition, organizations have developed special formats to reduce the amount of time spent writing and typing short messages:

◆ *Fax cover sheets.* When faxing messages, you may use a fax cover sheet, which includes the recipient's name, company, fax number, and city; the sender's name, complete address, fax number, and telephone number; the number of pages being sent; a phone number to call if the faxed transmission isn't successful; and enough space for any brief message.[18] The format for this information varies widely. When a document is self-explanatory, a cover sheet may be unnecessary, so be sure not to waste paper or transmission time.

◆ *Memo-letters.* Printed with a heading somewhat like a memo's, memo-letters provide a space for an inside address so that the message may be sent outside the company (see Figure A–10). When the memo is folded properly, the address shows through a window in the envelope, thereby eliminating the need to address the envelope separately. Memo-letters often include a space for a reply message so that the recipient doesn't have to print out or type a whole new letter in response; carbonless copy sets allow sender and recipient to keep on file a copy of the entire correspondence. Although convenient, memo-letters are much less formal than business letters for outside correspondence.

◆ *Short-note reply technique.* Popular in many organizations, this technique can be used even without a special form. The recipient of a memo (or sometimes a letter) simply handwrites a response on the original document, makes a copy for the files, and sends the annotated original back to the person who wrote it.

◆ *Letterhead postcards.* Ideal for short, impersonal messages, letterhead postcards are preprinted with a list of responses so that the "writer" merely checks the appropriate response(s) and slips the postcard into the mail. Organizations such as mail-order companies and government agencies use these time-saving devices to communicate frequently with individuals by mail.

The important thing to realize about these and all other message formats is that they've developed over time to meet the need for clear communication and to speed responses to the needs of customers, suppliers, and associates.

REPORTS

You can enhance your report's effectiveness by paying careful attention to its appearance and layout. Follow whatever guidelines your organization prefers, but remember to be neat and consistent throughout. If it's up to you to decide formatting questions, the following conventions may help you decide how to handle margins, headings, spacing and indention, and page numbers.

Margins

All margins on a report page are at least 1 inch wide. Margins of 1 inch are customary for double-spaced pages, and margins of between $1\frac{1}{4}$ and $1\frac{1}{2}$ inches are customary for single-spaced pages. The top, left, and right margins are usually the same, but the bottom margins can be $1\frac{1}{2}$ times as deep as the others. Some special pages also have deeper top margins. Set top margins as deep as 2 inches for pages that contain major titles: prefatory parts such as the table of contents or the executive summary, supplementary parts such as the reference notes or bibliography, and textual parts such as the first page of the text or the first page of each chapter.

If you're going to bind your report at the left or at the top, add half an inch to the margin on the bound edge (see Figure A–11). Because of the space taken by the binding on left-bound reports, make the center point of the page a quarter inch to the right of the center of the paper. Be sure

MEMO

TO: Green Ridge Gifts
           1786 Century Road
           Nashua, NH 03060
           USA

FROM: Whiteside Import/Export, Ltd.
           1601 Ronson Drive
           Toronto, Ontario M9W 3E3
           CANADA

SUBJECT: Order for Royal Dorchester china
           completer sets

DATE: October 11, 2002

MESSAGE:

The six Wellington pattern completer sets that you ordered by telephone
October 9 are on their way and should reach your shop by October 18.

The three Mayfield pattern completer sets are coming from the factory, however, and will not arrive here until October 26 or 27. That means you will get
them around November 2 or 3.

Do you still want the Mayfield sets? Would you like us to bill you for the
Wellington sets only so that you can pay for the Mayfield order separately?
Please add your reply below, retain the yellow copy for your records, and send
us the white and pink copies.

SIGNED: *Barbara Hutchins*

REPLY: *PLEASE SEND THE MAYFIELD SETS AS SOON*
       AS POSSIBLE. YOU MAY BILL FOR BOTH
       MAYFIELD AND WELLINGTON SETS.

DATE: *OCT. 15, 2002*

SIGNED:

Figure A–10
In-Depth Critique: Memo-Letter

that centered headings are centered between the margins,
not centered on the paper. Computers can do this for you
automatically. Other guidelines for formatting a report can
be found in the sample in Chapter 12.

Headings

Headings of various levels provide visual clues to a report's
organization. Figure 11–16, on page 345, illustrates one good
system for showing these levels, but many variations exist. No
matter which system you use, be sure to be consistent.

Spacing and Indentions

The spacing and indention of most elements of a report are
relatively easy. If your report is double-spaced (perhaps to
ease comprehension of technical material), indent all paragraphs five character spaces (or about $\frac{1}{2}$ inch). In single-
spaced reports, you can block the paragraphs (no indentions), leaving one blank line between them.

When using a typewriter, properly spacing the material
on the title page is more complicated. For reports that will
be bound on the left, start a quarter inch to the right of center. From that point, backspace once for each two letters in
the line so that the line will appear centered once the report
is bound.

To correctly place lines of type on the title page, first
count the number of lines in each block of copy, including
blank lines. Subtract the total from 66 (the total number of
lines on an 11-inch page) to get the number of unused lines.
To allocate these unused lines equally among the spaces

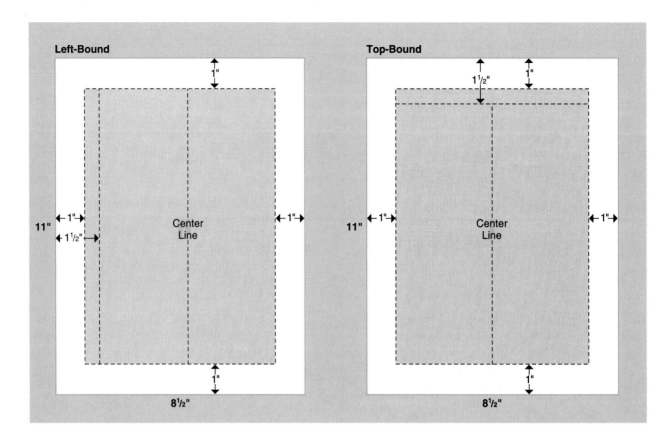

Figure A–11
Margins for Formal Reports

between the blocks of copy, divide the number of unused lines by the number of blank areas (always one more than the number of blocks of copy). The result is the number of blank lines to devote to each section. A computer with a good word-processing program will do these calculations for you at the click of a mouse. As the title page of the sample report in Chapter 12 shows, the title page should look well balanced.

Page Numbers

Remember that every page in the report is counted but that not all pages have numbers shown on them. The first page of the report, normally the title page, is not numbered. All other pages in the prefatory section are numbered with a lowercase roman numeral, beginning with ii and continuing with iii, iv, v, and so on. The unadorned (no dashes, no period) page number is centered at the bottom margin.

Number the first page of the text of the report with the unadorned arabic numeral 1, centered at the bottom margin (double- or triple-spaced below the text). In left-bound reports, number the following pages (including the supplementary parts) consecutively with unadorned arabic numerals (2, 3, and so on), placed at the top right-hand margin (double- or triple-spaced above the text). For top-bound reports and for special pages having 2-inch top margins, center these page numbers at the bottom margin.

Meeting Documents

The success of any meeting depends on the preparation of the participants and on the follow-up measures they take to implement decisions or to seek information after the meeting. Meeting documents—agendas and minutes—aid this process by putting the meeting plan and results into permanent, written form. Although small informal meetings may not require a written agenda, any meeting involving a relatively large number of people or covering a lot of ground will run more smoothly if an agenda is distributed in advance. A written agenda helps participants prepare by telling them what will be discussed, and it helps keep them on track once the meeting begins. The typical agenda format (shown in Figure A–12) may seem stiff and formal, but it helps structure a meeting so that as little time as possible is wasted. It also provides opportunities for discussion, if that's what is called for.

The presentation, a special form of meeting that allows for relatively little group interaction, may also require an agenda or a detailed outline. Special visual aids such as flip charts help attendees grasp the message, and copies of the charts are often provided for future reference.

After a meeting the secretary who attended prepares a set of minutes for distribution to all attendees and to any other interested parties. The minutes are prepared in much

AGENDA

PLANNING COMMITTEE MEETING

Monday, August 21, 2001
10:00 A.M.

Executive Conference Room

   I. Call to Order

  II. Roll Call

 III. Approval of Agenda

 IV. Approval of Minutes from Previous Meeting

  V. Chairperson's Report

 VI. Subcommittee Reports
     A. New Markets
     B. New Products
     C. Finance

VII. Unfinished Business

VIII. New Business
     A. Carson and Canfield Data
     B. Reassignments

 IX. Announcements

  X. Adjournment

the same format as a memo or letter, except for the heading, which takes this form:

MINUTES
PLANNING COMMITTEE MEETING
MONDAY, AUGUST 21, 2001

Present: [All invited attendees who were present are listed here, generally by rank, in alphabetical order, or in some combination.]

Absent: [All invited attendees who were not present are listed here, in similar order.]

The body of the minutes follows the heading, and it notes the times the meeting started and ended, all major decisions reached at the meeting, all assignments of tasks to meeting participants, and all subjects that were deferred to a later meeting. In addition, the minutes objectively summarize important discussions, noting the names of those who contributed major points. Outlines, subheadings, and lists help organize the minutes, and additional documentation (such as tables or charts submitted by meeting participants) are noted in the minutes and attached.

At the end of the minutes, the words *Submitted by* should be added, followed by a couple of blank lines for a signature and then the signer's printed (or typed) name and title (if appropriate). If the minutes have been written by one person and prepared by another, the preparer's initials should be added, as in the reference initials on a letter or memo.

An informal meeting may not require minutes. Attendees simply pencil their own notes onto their copies of the agenda. Follow-up is then their responsibility, although the meeting leader may need to remind them through a memo, phone call, or face-to-face talk.

APPENDIX B

DOCUMENTATION OF REPORT SOURCES

Documenting a report is too important a task to undertake haphazardly. By providing information about your sources, you improve your own credibility as well as the credibility of the facts and opinions you present. Documentation gives readers the means for checking your findings and pursuing the subject further. Also, documenting your report is the accepted way to give credit to the people whose work you have drawn from.

What style should you use to document your report? Experts recommend various forms, depending on your field or discipline. Moreover, your employer or client may use a form different from those the experts suggest. Don't let this discrepancy confuse you. If your employer specifies a form, use it; the standardized form is easier for colleagues to understand. However, if the choice of form is left to you, adopt one of the styles described here. Whatever style you choose, be consistent within any given report, using the same order, punctuation, and format from one reference citation or bibliography entry to the next.

A wide variety of style manuals provide detailed information on documentation:

♦ American Psychological Association. *Publication Manual of the American Psychological Association.* 4th ed. Washington, D.C.: American Psychological Association, 1994. Details the author-date system, which is preferred in the social sciences and often in the natural sciences as well.

♦ *The Chicago Manual of Style.* 14th ed. Chicago: University of Chicago Press, 1993. Often referred to only as *Chicago* and widely used in the publishing industry; provides detailed treatment of documentation in Chapters 15, 16, and 17.

♦ Gibaldi, Joseph. *MLA Style Manual and Guide to Scholarly Publishing.* 2d ed. New York: Modern Language Association, 1998. Serves as the basis for the note and bibliography style used in much academic writing and is recommended in many college textbooks on writing term papers; provides a lot of examples in the humanities.

♦ Harnack, Andrew, and Eugene Kleppinger. *Online! A Reference Guide to Using Internet Sources.* New York: St. Martin's Press, 1997. Offers an approach to style for citing online references.

♦ Slade, Carol. *Form and Style: Research Papers, Reports, Theses.* 10th ed. Boston: Houghton Mifflin, 1997. Presents a comprehensive review of *Chicago, MLA,* and *APA* styles.

♦ Turabian, Kate L. *A Manual for Writers of Term Papers, Theses, and Dissertations.* 6th ed. Revised and expanded by Bonnie Birtwhistle Honigsblum. Chicago: University of Chicago Press, 1995. Based on the *Chicago Manual* but smaller and limited to matters of concern to report writers; contains many examples of documenting nonstandard references.

♦ Warren, Thomas L. *Words into Type.* 3d ed. Englewood Cliffs, N.J.: Prentice Hall, 1992. Presents useful information on the classic approach to scholarly notes and bibliographies.

Although many schemes have been proposed for organizing the information in source notes, all of them break the information into parts: (1) information about the author (name), (2) information about the work (title, edition, volume number), (3) information about the publication (place, publisher), (4) information about the date, and (5) information on relevant page ranges.

In the following sections, we summarize the major conventions for documenting sources in three styles: *The Chicago Manual of Style (Chicago),* the *Publication Manual of the American Psychological Association (APA),* and *The MLA Style Manual (MLA).*

CHICAGO STYLE

The Chicago Manual of Style recommends two types of documentation systems. The *documentary-note,* or *humanities,* style gives bibliographic citations in notes—either footnotes (when printed at the bottom of a page) or endnotes (when printed at the end of the report). The humanities system is often used in literature, history, and the arts. The other system strongly recommended by *Chicago* is the *author-date* system, which cites the author's last name and the date of publication in the text, usually in parentheses, reserving full documentation for the reference list (or bibliography). For the purpose of comparing styles, we will concentrate on the humanities system, which is described in detail in *Chicago.*

In-Text Citation—Chicago Style

To document report sources in text, the humanities system relies on superscripts—arabic numerals placed just above the line of type at the end of the reference:

Toward the end of his speech, Myers sounded a note of caution, saying that even though the economy is expected to grow, it could easily slow a bit.[10]

Figure B–1
Major Reference Works

Journal article with volume and issue numbers	
Brochure	
Newspaper article, no author	
Annual report	
Magazine article	
Television broadcast	
Internet, World Wide Web	
Book, component part	
Dissertation or thesis	
Paper presented at a meeting	
Online magazine article	
CD-ROM encyclopedia article, one author	
Newspaper article, one author	
Interview	
Book, two authors	
Government publication	

Endnotes

1. James Assira, "Are They Speaking English in Japan?" *Journal of Business Communication* 36, no. 4 (Fall 1999): 72.

2. BestTemp Staffing Services, *An Employer's Guide to Staffing Services.* 2d ed. (Denver: BestTemp Information Center, 1997), 31.

3. "Buying Asian Supplies on the Net," *Los Angeles Times.* 12 February 1997. sec. D, p. 3.

4. Eurotec, *1998 Annual Report* (New York: Eurotec, Inc., 1998), 48.

5. Holly Graves, "Prospecting Online," *Business Week,* 17 November 1999, 43–45.

6. Daniel Han, "Trade Wars Heating Up Around the Globe." *CNN Headline News* (Atlanta: CNN, 5 March 1999).

7. "Intel—Company Capsule," Hoover's Online [cited 8 March 1999], 3 screens, available online from World Wide Web at www.hoovers.com/capsules/13787.html.

8. Sonja Kuntz, "Moving Beyond Benefits," in *Our Changing Workforce,* ed. Randolf Jacobson (New York: Citadel Press, 1998), 213-227.

9. George H. Morales, "The Economic Pressures on Industrialized Nations in a Global Economy" (Ph.D. diss., University of San Diego, 1998), abstract in *Dissertation Abstracts International* 52 (1998): 5436C-5437C.

10. Charles Myers, "HMOs in Today's Environment" (paper presented at the Conference on Medical Insurance Solution, Chicago, Ill., August 1998), 16–17.

11. Preston Norwalk, "Training Managers to Help Employees Accept Change," in *Business Line* [online] (San Francisco, 1999 [updated 17 September 1999; cited 3 October 1999]); available from www.busline.com/news; INTERNET.

12. Robert Parkings, "George Eastman," *The Concise Columbia Encyclopedia* (New York: Columbia University Press, 1995) [CD-ROM].

13. Evelyn Standish, "Global Market Crushes OPEC's Delicate Balance of Interests," *Wall Street Journal,* 19 January 1999, sec. A, p. 1.

14. Georgia Stainer, communications manager, Day Cable and Communications, interview by author, Topeka, Kansas, 2 March 1997.

15. Miriam Toller and Jay Fielding, *Global Business for Smaller Companies* (Rocklin, Calif: Prima Publishing, 1998), 102-103.

16. U.S. Department of Defense, *Stretching Research Dollars: Survival Advice for Universities and Government Labs* (Washington, D.C.: GPO, 1999), 126.

The superscript lets the reader know how to look for source information in either a footnote or an endnote (see Figure B–1). Some readers prefer footnotes so that they can simply glance at the bottom of the page for information. Others prefer endnotes so that they can read the text without a clutter of notes on the page. Also, endnotes relieve the writer from worrying about how long each note will be and how much space it will take away from the page. Both footnotes and endnotes are handled automatically by today's word-processing software.

For the reader's convenience, you can use footnotes for **content notes** (which may supplement your main text with asides about a particular issue or event, provide a cross-reference to another section of your report, or direct the reader to a related source). Then you can use endnotes for

source notes (which document direct quotations, paraphrased passages, and visual aids). Consider which type of note is most common in your report, and then choose whether to present these notes all as endnotes or all as footnotes. Regardless of the method you choose for referencing textual information in your report, both content notes and source notes are placed on the same page as visual aids.

Bibliography—Chicago Style

The humanities system may or may not be accompanied by a bibliography (because the notes give all the necessary bibliographic information). However, endnotes are arranged in order of appearance in the text, so an alphabetical bibliography can be valuable to your readers. The bibliography may

Bibliography

Assira, James. "Are They Speaking English in Japan?" *Journal of Business Communication* 36, no. 4 (Fall 1999): 72.

BestTemp Staffing Services. *An Employer's Guide to Staffing Services.* 2d ed. Denver: BestTemp Information Center, 1997.

"Buying Asian Supplies on the Net." *Los Angeles Times.* 12 February 1997, Sec. D. p. 3.

Eurotec, 1998 *Annual Report.* New York: Eurotec, Inc., 1998.

Graves, Holly. "Prospecting Online." *Business Week,* 17 November 1999, 43-45.

Han, Daniel. "Trade Wars Heating Up Around the Globe." *CNN Headline News.* Atlanta: CNN, 5 March 1999).

"Intel—Company Capsule." *Hoover's Online* [cited 8 March 1999]. 3 screens. Available online from World Wide Web at www.hoovers.com/capsules/13787.html.

Kuntz, Sonja. "Moving Beyond Benefits." In *Our Changing Workforce,* edited by Randolf Jacobson, 213-227. New York: Citadel Press, 1998.

Morales, George H. "The Economic Pressures on Industrialized Nations in a Global Economy" Ph.D. diss., University of San Diego, 1998. Abstract in *Dissertation Abstracts International* 52 (1998): 5436C-5437C.

Myers, Charles. "HMOs in Today's Environment." Paper presented at the Conference on Medical Insurance Solutions, Chicago, Ill., August 1998.

Norwalk, Preston. "Training Managers to Help Employees Accept Change." In *Business Line* [online]. San Francisco, 1999 [updated 17 September 1999; cited 3 October 1999]. Available from www.busline.com/news; INTERNET.

Parkings, Robert. "George Eastman." *The Concise Columbia Encyclopedia.* New York: Columbia University Press, 1995. [CD-ROM].

Standish, Evelyn. "Global Market Crushes OPEC's Delicate Balance of Interests." *Wall Street Journal,* 19 January 1999, sec. A, p. 1.

Stainer, Georgia, communications manager, Day Cable and Communications. Interview by author. Topeka, Kansas, 2 March 1997.

Toller, Miriam, and Jay Fielding, *Global Business for Smaller Companies.* Rocklin, Calif.: Prima Publishing, 1998.

U.S. Department of Defense. *Stretching Research Dollars: Survival Advice for Universities and Government Labs* Washington, D.C.: GPO, 1999.

Figure B–2
Sample Reference List

Journal article with volume and issue numbers

Brochure

Newspaper article, no author

Annual report

Magazine article

Television broadcast

Internet, World Wide Web

Book, component part

Dissertation or thesis

Paper presented at a meeting

Online magazine article

CD-ROM encyclopedia article, one author

Newspaper article, one author

Interview

Book, two authors

Government publication

be titled *Bibliography, Reference List, Sources, Works Cited* (if you include only those sources you actually cited in your report), or *Works Consulted* (if you include uncited sources as well). This list of sources may also serve as a reading list for those who want to pursue the subject of your report further, so you may want to annotate each entry—that is, comment on the subject matter and viewpoint of the source, as well as on its usefulness to readers. Annotations may be written in either complete or incomplete sentences. (See the annotated list of style manuals early in this component chapter.) A bibliography may also be more manageable if you subdivide it into categories (a classified bibliography), either by type of reference (such as books, articles, and unpublished material) or by subject matter (such as government regulation, market forces, and so on). Following are the major conventions for developing a bibliography according to *Chicago* style (see Figure B–2):

◆ Exclude any page numbers that may be cited in source notes.

◆ Alphabetize entries by the last name of the lead author (listing last name first). The names of second and succeeding authors are listed in normal order. Entries without an author name are alphabetized by the first important word in the title.

◆ Format entries as hanging indents (indent second and succeeding lines three to five spaces).

◆ Arrange entries in the following general order: (1) author name, (2) title information, (3) publication information, (4) date, (5) periodical page range.

◆ Use quotation marks around the titles of articles from magazines, newspapers, and journals—capitalizing the first and last words, as well as all other important words (except prepositions, articles, and coordinating conjunctions).

◆ Use italics to set off the names of books, newspapers, journals, and other complete publications—capitalizing the first and last words, as well as all other important words.

◆ For journal articles, include the volume number and the issue number (if necessary). Include the year of publication inside parentheses and follow with a colon and the page range of the article: *Journal of Business Communication 36, no. 4 (1999): 72.* (In this source, the volume is 36, the number is 4, and the page is 72.)

◆ Use brackets to identify all electronic references: [Online database] or [CD-ROM].

◆ Explain how electronic references can be reached: Available from CompuServe.

◆ Give the citation date for online references: Cited 23 August 1999.

APA STYLE

The American Psychological Association (APA) recommends the author-date system of documentation, which is popular in the physical, natural, and social sciences. When using this system, you simply insert the author's last name and the year of publication within parentheses following the text discussion of the material cited. Include a page number if you use a direct quote. This approach briefly identifies the source so that readers can locate complete information in the alphabetical reference list at the end of the report. The author-date system is both brief and clear, saving readers time and effort.

In-Text Citation—APA Style

To document report sources in text using the *APA* style, insert the author's surname and the date of publication at the end of a statement. Enclose this information in parentheses. If the author's name is referred to in the text itself, then the number can be omitted from parenthetical material.

Some experts recommend both translation and back-translation when dealing with any non-English-speaking culture (Assira, 1999).

Toller and Fielding (1998) make a strong case for small companies succeeding in global business.

Personal communications and interviews conducted by the author would not be listed in the reference list at all. Such citations would appear in the text only.

Increasing the role of cable companies is high on the list of Georgia Stainer, communications manager at Day Cable and Communications (personal communication, March 2, 1999).

List of References—APA Style

The *APA* style recommends listing only those works actually cited in the text (so you would not include works for background or for further reading). Report writers must choose their references judiciously. Following are the major conventions for developing a reference list according to *APA* style (see Figure B–3):

◆ Format entries for publication by indenting the first line five to seven spaces. Students may wish to format entries as hanging indents to conform to the requirements of their university.

◆ List all author names in reversed order (last name first), and use only initials for the first and middle names.

◆ Arrange entries in the following general order: (1) author name, (2) date, (3) title information, (4) publication information, (5) periodical page range.

◆ Follow the author name with the date of publication in parentheses.

◆ List titles of articles from magazines, newspapers, and journals without underlines or quotation marks. Capitalize only the first word of the title and the first word to follow an internal colon.

◆ Italicize titles of books, capitalizing only the first word, any proper nouns, and the first word to follow a colon.

◆ Italicize names of magazines, newspapers, journals, and other complete publications—capitalizing all the important words.

◆ For journal articles, include the volume number (in italic) and, if necessary, the issue number (in parentheses). Finally, include the page range of the article: *Journal of Business Communication, 36*(4), 72. (In this example, the volume is 36, the number is 4, and the page number is 72.)

◆ Include personal communications (such as letters, memos, e-mail, conversations) only in text, *not* in reference lists.

◆ Electronic references include author, date of publication, title of article, name of publication, electronic medium (*online* or *CD-ROM*), volume, series, page, and path.

◆ For electronic references, indicate the actual year of publication, the most recent update, or the exact date of your search.

◆ For electronic references, specify the method used to find the material (Telnet, FTP, Internet, etc.), the directory, and the file name. Leave periods off URLs (because stray punctuation in a path will hinder retrieval).

MLA STYLE

The style recommended by Modern Language Association of America is used widely in the humanities, especially in the study of language and literature. Like *APA* style, *MLA* style uses brief parenthetical citations in the text. However,

References

Assira, J. (1999) "Are They Speaking English in Japan?" *Journal of Business Communication 36*(4), 72.

BestTemp Staffing Services. *An employer's guide to staffing services.* (2d ed.) [Brochure]. Denver: BestTemp Information Center.

Buying Asian supplies on the net. (1997, February 12). *Los Angeles Times,* p. D3.

Eurotec, (1998). *1998 annual report.* New York: Author

Graves, H. (1999, November 17). Prospecting Online. *Business Week,* 43-45.

Han, D. (1999, March 5). Trade wars heating up around the globe." *CNN Headline News.* Atlanta, GA: CNN.

"Intel—Company Capsule. (1999). *Hoover's Online* [Online]. Available: http://www.hoovers.com/capsules/13787.html Cited 1999, March 8.

Kuntz, S. (1998). Moving beyond benefits." In Randolph Jacobson (Ed.), *Our changing workforce* (pp. 213-227). New York: Citadel Press.

Morales, G. H. (1998). The economic pressures on industrialized nations in a global economy. (Doctoral dissertation, University of San Diego, 1998.) *Dissertation Abstracts International,* 52, 5436C-5437C.

Myers, C. (1998, August). *HMOs in today's environment.* Paper presented at the Conference on Medical Insurance Solutions, Chicago, IL

Norwalk, P. (1999, July 17). Training managers to help employees accept change. *Business Line* [On-line]. Available http://www.busline.com/news

Parkings, R. (1995) George Eastman. *The concise Columbia encyclopedia.* [CD-ROM]. New York: Columbia University Press.

Standish, E. (1999, January 19). Global market crushes OPEC's delicate balance of interests. *Wall Street Journal,* p. A1.

Cited in text only, not in the list of references.

Toller, M., & Fielding J. (1998) *Global business for smaller companies.* Rocklin, CA: Prima Publishing.

U.S. Department of Defense. (1999). *Stretching research dollars: Survival advice for universities and government labs.* Washington, DC: Government Publishing Office, 1999.

Figure B–3
Sample References—APA Style

Journal article with volume and issue numbers

Brochure

Newspaper article, no author

Annual report

Magazine article

Television broadcast

Internet, World Wide Web

Book, component part

Dissertation or thesis

Paper presented at a meeting

Online magazine article

CD-ROM encyclopedia article, one author

Newspaper article, one author

Interview

Book, two authors

Government publication

---

instead of including author name and year, *MLA* citations include author name and page reference.

Toller and Fielding make a strong case for small companies succeeding in global business (102–103).

In-Text Citation—MLA Style

To document report sources in text using *MLA* style, insert the author's last name and a page reference inside parentheses following the cited material: (Matthews 63). If the author's name is mentioned in the text reference, the name can be omitted from the parenthetical citation: (63). The citation indicates that the reference came from page 63 of a work by Matthews. With the author's name, readers can find complete publication information in the alphabetically arranged list of works cited that comes at the end of the report.

Some experts recommend both translation and back-translation when dealing with any non-English-speaking culture (Assira 72).

List of Works Cited—MLA Style

The *MLA Style Manual* recommends preparing your list of works cited first so that you will know what information to give in the parenthetical citation (for example, whether to add a short title if you're citing more than one work by the same author, or whether to give an initial or first name if you're citing two authors who have the same last name). Your list of works cited appears at the end of your report, contains all the works that you cite in your text, and lists them in alphabetical order. Following are the major conventions for developing a reference list according to *MLA* style (see Figure B–4):

◆ Format entries as hanging indents (that is, indent second and succeeding lines by three to five character spaces).

Figure B–4
Sample References—MLA Style

Journal article with volume and issue numbers	
Brochure	
Newspaper article, no author	
Annual report	
Magazine article	
Television broadcast	
Internet, World Wide Web	
Book, component part	
Dissertation or thesis	
Paper presented at a meeting	
Online magazine article	
CD-ROM encyclopedia article, one author	
Newspaper article, one author	
Interview	
Book, two authors	
Government publication	

Works Cited

Assira, James. "Are They Speaking English in Japan?" *Journal of Business Communication* 36.4 (1999): 72.

BestTemp Staffing Services. *An Employer's Guide to Staffing Services.* 2d ed. Denver: BestTemp Information Center, 1997.

"Buying Asian Supplies on the Net." *Los Angeles Times.* 12 Feb. 1997: D3.

Eurotec, *1998 Annual Report.* New York: Eurotec, Inc., 1998.

Graves, Holly. "Prospecting Online." *Business Week* 17 November 1999, 43-45.

Han, Daniel. "Trade Wars Heating Up Around the Globe." *CNN Headline News.* CNN Atlanta. 5 Mar. 1999.

"Intel—Company Capsule." *Hoover's Online* 1999. Hoover's Company Information. 8 Mar. 1999 <http://www.hoovers.com/capsules/13787.html>.

Kuntz, Sonja. *Moving Beyond Benefits. Our Changing Workforce,* Ed. Randolf Jacobson. New York: Citadel Press, 1998. 213–227.

Morales, George H. "The Economic Pressures on Industrialized Nations in a Global Economy" Diss. U of San Diego, 1998. *DAI 52* (1998): 5436C-5437C.

Myers, Charles. "HMOs in Today's Environment." Conference on Medical Insurance Solutions. Chicago. 13 August 1998.

Norwalk, Preston. "Training Managers to Help Employees Accept Change." *Business Line* 17 July 1999 <http://www.busline.com/news>.

Parkings, Robert. "George Eastman." *The Concise Columbia Encyclopedia.* CD-ROM. New York: Columbia UP, 1995.

Standish, Evelyn. "Global Market Crushes OPEC's Delicate Balance of Interests." *Wall Street Journal,* 19 Jan. 1999, p. A1.

Stainer, Georgia, communications manager, Day Cable and Communications. Telephone interview. Topeka. 2 Mar. 1997.

Toller, Miriam, and Jay Fielding, *Global Business for Smaller Companies.* Rocklin: Prima Publishing, 1998.

United States. Department of Defense. *Stretching Research Dollars: Survival Advice for Universities and Government Labs.* Washington: GPO, 1999.

♦ Arrange entries in the following general order: (1) author name, (2) title information, (3) publication information, (4) date, (5) periodical page range.

♦ List the lead author's name in reverse order (last name first), using either full first names or initials. List second and succeeding author names in normal order.

♦ Use quotation marks around the titles of articles from magazines, newspapers, and journals—capitalize all important words.

♦ Italicize the names of books, newspapers, journals and other complete publications, capitalizing all main words in the title.

♦ For journal articles, include the volume number and the issue number (if necessary). Include the year of publication inside parentheses and follow with a colon and the page range of the article: *Journal of Business Communication* 36.4

(1999): 72. (In this source, the volume is 36, the number is 4, and the page is 72.)

♦ Electronic sources are less fixed than print sources, and they may not be readily accessible to readers. So citations for electronic sources must provide more information. Always try to be as comprehensive as possible, citing whatever information is available.

♦ The date for electronic sources must contain both the date assigned in the source and the date accessed by the researcher.

♦ The URL for electronic sources must be as accurate and complete as possible, from access-mode identifier (http, ftp, gopher, telnet) to all relevant directory and file names. Be sure to enclose this path inside angle brackets: <http://www.hoovers.com/capsules/13787.html>.

Appendix C

Fundamentals of Grammar and Usage

Grammar is nothing more than the way words are combined into sentences, and usage is the way words are used by a network of people—in this case, the community of businesspeople who use English. You'll find it easier to get along in this community if you know the accepted standards of grammar and usage. What follows is a review of the basics of grammar and usage, things you've probably learned but may have forgotten. Without a firm grasp of these basics, you risk not only being misunderstood but also damaging your company's image, losing money for your company, and possibly even losing your job.

1.0 Grammar

The sentence below looks innocent, but is it really?

We sell tuxedos as well as rent.

You might sell rent, but it's highly unlikely. Whatever you're selling, some people will ignore your message because of a blunder like this. The following sentence has a similar problem:

Vice President Eldon Neale told his chief engineer that he would no longer be with Avix, Inc., as of June 30.

Is Eldon or the engineer leaving? No matter which side the facts are on, the sentence can be read the other way. You may have a hard time convincing either person that your simple mistake was not a move in a game of office politics. Now look at this sentence:

The year before we budgeted more for advertising sales were up.

Confused? Perhaps this is what you meant:

The year before, we budgeted more for advertising. Sales were up.

Maybe you meant this:

The year before we budgeted more for advertising, sales were up.

The meaning of language falls into bundles called sentences. A listener or reader can take only so much meaning before filing a sentence away and getting ready for the next one. So, as a writer, you have to know what a sentence is. You need to know where one ends and the next one begins.

If you want to know what a thing is, you have to find out what goes into it, what its ingredients are. Luckily, the basic ingredients of an English sentence are simple. They're called the parts of speech, and the content-bearing ones are nouns, pronouns, verbs, adjectives, and adverbs. They combine with a few functional parts of speech to convey meaning. Meaning is also transmitted by punctuation, mechanics, and vocabulary.

1.1 Nouns

A noun names a person, place, or thing. Anything you can see or detect with one of your other senses has a noun to name it. Some things you can't see or sense are also nouns—ions, for example, or space. So are things that exist as ideas, such as accuracy and height. (You can see that something is accurate or that a building is tall, but you can't see the idea of accuracy or the idea of height.) These names for ideas are known as abstract nouns. The simplest nouns are the names of things you can see or touch: car, building, cloud, brick.

1.1.1 Proper Nouns and Common Nouns
So far, all the examples of nouns have been common nouns, referring to general classes of things. The word *building* refers to a whole class of structures. Common nouns such as *building* are not capitalized.

If you want to talk about one particular building, however, you might refer to the Glazier Building. The name is capitalized, indicating that *Glazier Building* is a proper noun.

Here are three sets of common and proper nouns for comparison:

Common	Proper
city	Kansas City
company	Blaisden Company
store	Books Galore

1.1.2 Plural Nouns
Nouns can be either singular or plural. The usual way to make a plural noun is to add *s* to the singular form of the word:

Singular	Plural
rock	rocks
picture	pictures
song	songs

519

Many nouns have other ways of forming the plural. Letters, numbers, and words used as words are sometimes made plural by adding an apostrophe and an *s*. Very often, *'s* is used with abbreviations that have periods, lowercase letters that stand alone, and capital letters that might be confused with words when made into plurals:

Spell out all *St.*'s and *Ave.*'s.

He divided the page with a row of *x*'s.

Sarah will register the *A*'s through the *I*'s at the convention.

In other cases, however, the apostrophe may be left out:

They'll review their ABCs.

The stock market climbed through most of the 1980s.

Circle all *thes* in the paragraph.

In some of these examples, the letters used as letters and words used as words *are italicized* (discussed later).

Other nouns, such as those below, are so-called irregular nouns; they form the plural in some way other than simply adding *s*:

SINGULAR	PLURAL
tax	taxes
specialty	specialties
cargo	cargoes
shelf	shelves
child	children
woman	women
tooth	teeth
mouse	mice
parenthesis	parentheses
son-in-law	sons-in-law
editor-in-chief	editors-in-chief

Rather than memorize a lot of rules about forming plurals, use a dictionary. If the dictionary says nothing about the plural of a word, it's formed the usual way: by adding *s*. If the plural is formed in some irregular way, the dictionary shows the plural or has a note something like this: *ples*.

1.1.3 Possessive Nouns

A noun becomes possessive when it's used to show the ownership of something. Then you add *'s* to the word:

the man's car   the woman's apartment

However, ownership does not need to be legal:

the secretary's desk   the company's assets

Also, ownership may be nothing more than an automatic association:

a day's work   a job's prestige

An exception to the rule about adding *'s* to make a noun possessive occurs when the word is singular and already has two *s* sounds at the end. In cases like the following, an apostrophe is all that's needed:

crisis' dimensions   Mr. Moses' application

When the noun has only one *s* sound at the end, however, retain the *'s*:

Chris's book   Carolyn Nuss's office

With hyphenated nouns (compound nouns), add *'s* to the last word:

HYPHENATED NOUN	POSSESSIVE NOUN
mother-in-law	mother-in-law's
mayor-elect	mayor-elect's

To form the possessive of plural nouns, just begin by following the same rule as with singular nouns: add *'s*. However, if the plural noun already ends in an *s* (as most do), drop the one you've added, leaving only the apostrophe:

the clients' complaints   employees' benefits

1.2 Pronouns

A pronoun is a word that stands for a noun; it saves repeating the noun:

Drivers have some choice of weeks for vacation, but *they* must notify this office of *their* preference by March 1.

The pronouns *they* and *their* stand in for the noun *drivers*. The noun that a pronoun stands for is called the antecedent of the pronoun; *drivers* is the antecedent of *they* and *their*.

When the antecedent is plural, the pronoun that stands in for it has to be plural; *they* and *their* are plural pronouns because *drivers* is plural. Likewise, when the antecedent is singular, the pronoun has to be singular:

We thought the *contract* had been signed, but we soon learned that *it* had not been.

1.2.1 Multiple Antecedents

Sometimes a pronoun has a double (or even a triple) antecedent:

Kathryn Boettcher and Luis Gutierrez went beyond *their* sales quotas for January.

Kathryn Boettcher, if taken alone, is a singular antecedent. So is *Luis Gutierrez*. However, when together they are the antecedent of a pronoun, they're plural and the pronoun has to be plural. Thus the pronoun is *their* instead of *her* or *his*.

1.2.2 Unclear Antecedents
In some sentences the pronoun's antecedent is unclear:

Sandy Wright sent Jane Brougham *her* production figures for the previous year. *She* thought they were too low.

To which person does the pronoun *her* refer? Someone who knew Sandy and Jane and knew their business relationship might be able to figure out the antecedent for *her*. Even with such an advantage, however, a reader might receive the wrong meaning. Also, it would be nearly impossible for any reader to know which name is the antecedent of *she*.

The best way to clarify an ambiguous pronoun is usually to rewrite the sentence, repeating nouns when needed for clarity:

Sandy Wright sent her production figures for the previous year to Jane Brougham. *Jane* thought they were too low.

The noun needs to be repeated only when the antecedent is unclear.

1.2.3 Gender-Neutral Pronouns
The pronouns that stand for males are *he, his,* and *him.* The pronouns that stand for females are *she, hers,* and *her.* However, you'll often be faced with the problem of choosing a pronoun for a noun that refers to both females and males:

Each manager must make up (his, her, his or her, its, their) own mind about stocking this item and about the quantity that (he, she, he or she, it, they) can sell.

This sentence calls for a pronoun that's neither masculine nor feminine. The issue of gender-neutral pronouns responds to efforts to treat females and males evenhandedly. Here are some possible ways to deal with this issue:

Each manager must make up *his* . . .

(Not all managers are men.)

Each manager must make up *her* . . .

(Not all managers are women.)

Each manager must make up *his or her* . . .

(This solution is acceptable but becomes awkward when repeated more than once or twice in a document.)

Each manager must make up *her* . . . Every manager will receive *his* . . . A manager may send *her* . . .

(A manager's gender does not alternate like a windshield wiper!)

Each manager must make up *their* . . .

(The pronoun can't be plural when the antecedent is singular.)

Each manager must make up *its* . . .

(*It* never refers to people.)

The best solution is to make the noun plural or to revise the passage altogether:

Managers must make up *their* minds . . .

Each manager must decide whether . . .

Be careful not to change the original meaning.

1.2.4 Case of Pronouns
The case of a pronoun tells whether it's acting or acted upon:

She sells an average of five packages each week.

In this sentence *she* is doing the selling. Because *she* is acting, *she* is said to be in the nominative case. Now consider what happens when the pronoun is acted upon:

After six months Ms. Browning promoted *her.*

In this sentence the pronoun *her* is acted upon. The pronoun *her* is thus said to be in the objective case.

Contrast the nominative and objective pronouns in this list:

NOMINATIVE	OBJECTIVE
I	me
we	us
he	him
she	her
they	them
who	whom
whoever	whomever

Objective pronouns may be used as either the object of a verb (such as *promoted*) or the object of a preposition (such as *with*):

Rob worked with *them* until the order was filled.

In this example *them* is the object of the preposition *with* because Rob acted upon—worked with—them.

Here's a sample sentence with three pronouns, the first one nominative, the second the object of a verb, and the third the object of a preposition:

He paid *us* as soon as the check came from *them.*

He is nominative; *us* is objective because it's the object of the verb *paid; them* is objective because it's the object of the preposition *from.*

Every writer sometimes wonders whether to use *who* or *whom:*

(Who, Whom) will you hire?

Because this sentence is a question, it's difficult to see that *whom* is the object of the verb *hire*. You can figure out which pronoun to use if you rearrange the question and temporarily try *she* and *her* in place of *who* and *whom*: "Will you hire *she?*" or "Will you hire *her?*" *Her* and *whom* are both objective, so the correct choice is "*Whom* will you hire?" Here's a different example:

(Who, Whom) logged so much travel time?

Turning the question into a statement, you get:

He logged so much travel time.

Therefore, the correct statement is:

Who logged so much travel time?

1.2.5 Possessive Pronouns

Possessive pronouns are like possessive nouns in the way they work: They show ownership or automatic association.

her job	their preferences
his account	its equipment

However, possessive pronouns are different from possessive nouns in the way they are written. That is, possessive pronouns never have an apostrophe.

Possessive Noun	Possessive Pronoun
the woman's estate	her estate
Roger Franklin's plans	his plans
the shareholders' feelings	their feelings
the vacuum cleaner's attachments	its attachments

The word *its* is the possessive of *it*. Like all other possessive pronouns, *its* doesn't have an apostrophe. Some people confuse *its* with *it's*, the contraction of *it is*. Contractions are discussed later.

1.3 Verbs

A verb describes an action:

They all *quit* in disgust.

It may also describe a state of being:

Working conditions *were* substandard.

The English language is full of action verbs. Here are a few you'll often run across in the business world:

verify	perform	fulfill
hire	succeed	send
leave	improve	receive
accept	develop	pay

You could undoubtedly list many more.

The most common verb describing a state of being instead of an action is *to be* and all its forms:

I *am, was,* or *will be;* you *are, were,* or *will be*

Other verbs also describe a state of being:

It *seemed* a good plan at the time.

She *sounds* impressive at a meeting.

These verbs link what comes before them in the sentence with what comes after; no action is involved. (See Section 1.7.5 for a fuller discussion of linking verbs.)

1.3.1 Verb Tenses

English has three simple verb tenses: present, past, and future.

Present:	Our branches in Hawaii *stock* other items.
Past:	When we *stocked* Purquil pens, we received a great many complaints.
Future:	Rotex Tire Stores *will stock* your line of tires when you begin a program of effective national advertising.

With most verbs (the regular ones), the past tense ends in *ed*; the future tense always has *will* or *shall* in front of it. But the present tense is more complex:

Singular	Plural
I stock	we stock
you stock	you stock
he, she, it stocks	they stock

The basic form, *stock*, takes an additional *s* when *he, she,* or *it* precedes it.

In addition to the three simple tenses, there are three perfect tenses using forms of the helping verb *have*. The present perfect tense uses the past participle (regularly the past tense) of the main verb, *stocked*, and adds the present-tense *have* or *has* to the front of it:

(I, we, you, they) *have stocked*.

(He, she, it) *has stocked*.

The past perfect tense uses the past participle of the main verb, *stocked*, and adds the past-tense *had* to the front of it:

(I, you, he, she, it, we, they) *had stocked*.

The future perfect tense also uses the past participle of the main verb, *stocked*, but adds the future-tense *will have*:

(I, you, he, she, it, we, they) *will have stocked*.

Keep verbs in the same tense when the actions occur at the same time:

When the payroll checks *came* in, everyone *showed* up for work.

We have *found* that everyone *has pitched* in to help.

When the actions occur at different times, you may change tense accordingly:

A shipment *came* last Wednesday, so when another one *comes* in today, please return it.

The new employee *had been* ill at ease, but now she *has become* a full-fledged member of the team.

1.3.2 Irregular Verbs

Many verbs don't follow in every detail the patterns already described. The most irregular of these verbs is *to be:*

TENSE	SINGULAR	PLURAL
Present:	I *am*	we *are*
	you *are*	you *are*
	he, she, it *is*	they *are*
Past:	I *was*	we *were*
	you *were*	you *were*
	he, she, it *was*	they *were*

The future tense of *to be* is formed in the same way that the future tense of a regular verb is formed.

The perfect tenses of *to be* are also formed as they would be for a regular verb, except that the past participle is a special form, *been*, instead of just the past tense:

Present perfect:	you *have been*
Past perfect:	you *had been*
Future perfect:	you *will have been*

Here's a sampling of other irregular verbs:

PRESENT	PAST	PAST PARTICIPLE
begin	began	begun
shrink	shrank	shrunk
know	knew	known
rise	rose	risen
become	became	become
go	went	gone
do	did	done

Dictionaries list the various forms of other irregular verbs.

1.3.3 Transitive and Intransitive Verbs

Many people are confused by three particular sets of verbs:

lie/lay	sit/set	rise/raise

Using these verbs correctly is much easier when you learn the difference between transitive and intransitive verbs.

Transitive verbs convey their action to an object; they "transfer" their action to an object. Intransitive verbs do not. Here are some sample uses of transitive and intransitive verbs:

INTRANSITIVE	TRANSITIVE
We should include in our new offices a place to *lie* down for a nap.	The workers will be here on Monday to *lay* new carpeting.
Even the way an interviewee *sits* is important.	That crate is full of stemware, so *set* it down carefully.
Salaries at Compu-Link, Inc., *rise* swiftly.	They *raise* their level of production every year.

The workers *lay* carpeting, you *set* down the crate, they *raise* production; each action is transferred to something. In the intransitive sentences, one *lies* down, an interviewee *sits*, and salaries *rise* without (at least grammatically) affecting anything else. Intransitive sentences are complete with only a subject and a verb; transitive sentences are not complete unless they also include an object, or something to transfer the action to.

Tenses are a confusing element of the *lie/lay* problem:

PRESENT	PAST	PAST PARTICIPLE
I *lie*	I *lay*	I have *lain*
I *lay* (something down)	I *laid* (something down)	I have *laid* (something down)

The past tense of *lie* and the present tense of *lay* look and sound alike, even though they're different verbs.

1.3.4 Voice of Verbs

Verbs have two voices, active and passive:

Active: The buyer paid a large amount.
Passive: A large amount was paid by the buyer.

The passive voice uses a form of the verb *to be.*

Also, the passive-voice sentence uses eight words, whereas the active-voice sentence uses only six words to say the same thing. The words *was* and *by* are unnecessary to convey the meaning of the sentence. In fact, extra words usually clog meaning. So be sure to opt for the active voice when you have a choice.

At times, however, you have no choice:

Several items *have been taken,* but so far we don't know who took them.

The passive voice becomes necessary when you don't know (or don't want to say) who performed the action; the active voice is bolder and more direct.

1.3.5 Mood of Verbs

You have three moods to choose from, depending on your intentions. Most of the time you use the indicative mood to make a statement or to ask a question:

The secretary *mailed* a letter to each supplier.

Did the secretary *mail* a letter to each supplier?

When you wish to command or request, use the imperative mood:

Please mail a letter to each supplier.

Sometimes, especially in business, a courteous request is stated like a question; in that case, however, no question mark is required:

Would you *mail* a letter to each supplier.

The subjunctive mood, most often used in formal writing or in presenting bad news, expresses a possibility or a recommendation. The subjunctive is usually signaled by a word such as *if* or *that*. In these examples, the subjunctive mood uses special verb forms:

If the secretary *were* to *mail* a letter to each supplier, we might save some money.

I suggested that the secretary *mail* a letter to each supplier.

Although the subjunctive mood is not used as often as it once was, it's still found in such expressions as *Come what may* and *If I were you*. In general, it is used to convey an idea that is contrary to fact: If iron *were* lighter than air.

1.4 Adjectives

An adjective modifies (tells something about) a noun or pronoun:

an *efficient* staff	a *heavy* price
brisk trade	*poor* you

Each of these phrases says more about the noun or pronoun than the noun or pronoun would say alone.

Adjectives always tell us something we wouldn't know without them. So you don't need to use adjectives when the noun alone, or a different noun, will give the meaning:

a *company* employee

(An employee ordinarily works for a company.)

a *crate-type* container

(Crate gives the entire meaning.)

At times, adjectives pile up in a series:

It was a *long*, and *active* workday.

Such strings of adjectives are acceptable as long as they all convey a different part of the phrase's meaning.

Verbs in the *ing* (present participle) form can be used as adjectives:

A *boring* job can sometimes turn into a *fascinating* career.

So can the past participle of verbs:

A freshly *painted* house is a *sold* house.

Adjectives modify nouns more often than they modify pronouns. When adjectives do modify pronouns, however, the sentence usually has a linking verb:

They were *attentive*.	It looked *appropriate*.
He seems *interested*.	You are *skillful*.

Most adjectives can take three forms: simple, comparative, and superlative. The simple form modifies a single noun or pronoun. Use the comparative form when comparing two items. When comparing three or more items, use the superlative form.

SIMPLE	COMPARATIVE	SUPERLATIVE
hard	harder	hardest
safe	safer	safest
dry	drier	driest

The comparative form adds *er* to the simple form, and the superlative form adds *est*. (The *y* at the end of a word changes to *i* before the *er* or *est* is added.)

A small number of adjectives are irregular, including these:

SIMPLE	COMPARATIVE	SUPERLATIVE
good	better	best
bad	worse	worst
little	less	least

When the simple form of an adjective is two or more syllables, you usually add *more* to form the comparative and *most* to form the superlative:

SIMPLE	COMPARATIVE	SUPERLATIVE
useful	more useful	most useful
exhausting	more exhausting	most exhausting
expensive	more expensive	most expensive

The most common exceptions are two-syllable adjectives that end in *y:*

SIMPLE	COMPARATIVE	SUPERLATIVE
happy	happier	happiest
costly	costlier	costliest

If you choose this option, change the *y* to *i,* and tack *er* or *est* onto the end.

1.5 Adverbs

An adverb modifies a verb, an adjective, or another adverb:

Modifying a verb: Our marketing department works *efficiently.*

Modifying an adjective: She was not dependable, although she was *highly* intelligent.

Modifying another adverb: His territory was *too* broadly diversified, so he moved *extremely* cautiously.

Most of the adverbs mentioned are adjectives turned into adverbs by adding *ly,* which is how many adverbs are formed:

ADJECTIVE	ADVERB
efficient	efficiently
high	highly
extreme	extremely
special	specially
official	officially
separate	separately

Some adverbs are made by dropping or changing the final letter of the adjective and then adding *ly:*

ADJECTIVE	ADVERB
due	duly
busy	busily

Other adverbs don't end in *ly* at all. Here are a few examples of this type:

often	fast	too
soon	very	so

1.6 Other Parts of Speech

Nouns, pronouns, verbs, adjectives, and adverbs carry most of the meaning in a sentence. Four other parts of speech link them together in sentences: prepositions, conjunctions, articles, and interjections.

1.6.1 Prepositions
Prepositions are words like these:

of	to	for	with
at	by	from	about

They most often begin prepositional phrases, which function like adjectives and adverbs by telling more about a pronoun, noun, or verb:

of a type	*by* Friday
to the point	*with* characteristic flair

1.6.2 Conjunctions, Articles, and Interjections
Conjunctions are words that usually join parts of a sentence. Here are a few:

and	but	because
yet	although	if

Using conjunctions is discussed in sections 1.7.3 and 1.7.4.

Only three articles exist in English: *the, a,* and *an.* These words are used, like adjectives, to specify which item you are talking about.

Interjections are words that express no solid information, only emotion:

Wow!	Well, well!
Oh, no!	Good!

Such purely emotional language has its place in private life and advertising copy, but it only weakens the effect of most business writing.

1.7 Sentences

Sentences are constructed with the major building blocks, the parts of speech.

Money talks.

This two-word sentence consists of a noun (*money*) and a verb (*talks*). When used in this way, the noun works as the first requirement for a sentence, the subject, and the verb works as the second requirement, the predicate. Now look at this sentence:

They merged.

The subject in this case is a pronoun (*they*), and the predicate is a verb (*merged*). This is a sentence because it has a subject and a predicate. Here is yet another kind of sentence:

The plans are ready.

This sentence has a more complicated subject, the noun *plans* and the article *the;* the complete predicate is a state-of-being verb (*are*) and an adjective (*ready*).

Without these two parts, the subject (who or what does something) and the predicate (the doing of it), no collection of words is a sentence.

1.7.1 Commands

In commands, the subject (always *you*) is only understood, not stated:

(You) Move your desk to the better office.

(You) Please try to finish by six o'clock.

1.7.2 Longer Sentences

More complicated sentences have more complicated subjects and predicates, but they still have a simple subject and a predicate verb. In the following examples, the subject is underlined once, the predicate verb twice:

<u>Marex</u> and <u>Contron</u> <u>enjoy</u> higher earnings each quarter.

(*Marex* [and] *Contron* did something; *enjoy* is what they did.)

My <u>interview,</u> coming minutes after my freeway accident, <u>did</u> not <u>impress</u> or <u>move</u> anyone.

(*Interview* is what did something. What did it do? It *did* [not] *impress* [or] *move*.)

In terms of usable space, a steel <u>warehouse,</u> with its extremely long span of roof unsupported by pillars, <u>makes</u> more sense.

(*Warehouse* is what *makes*.)

These three sentences demonstrate several things. First, in all three sentences the simple subject and predicate verb are the "bare bones" of the sentence, the parts that carry the core idea of the sentence. When trying to find the subject and predicate verb, disregard all prepositional phrases, modifiers, conjunctions, and articles.

Second, in the third sentence the verb is singular (*makes*) because the subject is singular (*warehouse*). Even though the plural noun *pillars* is closer to the verb, *warehouse* is the subject. So *warehouse* determines whether the verb is singular or plural. Subject and predicate must agree.

Third, the subject in the first sentence is compound (*Marex* [and] *Contron*). A compound subject, when connected by *and*, requires a plural verb (*enjoy*). Also in the second sentence, compound predicates are possible (*did* [not] *impress* [or] *move*).

Fourth, the second sentence incorporates a group of words—*coming minutes after my freeway accident*—containing a form of a verb (*coming*) and a noun (*accident*). Yet this group of words is not a complete sentence for two reasons:

◆ *Accident* is not the subject of *coming*. Not all nouns are subjects.

◆ A verb that ends in *ing* can never be the predicate of a sentence (unless preceded by a form of *to be*, as in *was coming*). Not all verbs are predicates.

Because they don't contain a subject and a predicate, the words *coming minutes after my freeway accident* (called a phrase) can't be written as a sentence. That is, the phrase can't stand alone; it can't begin with a capital letter and end with a period. So a phrase must always be just one part of a sentence.

Sometimes a sentence incorporates two or more groups of words that do contain a subject and a predicate; these word groups are called clauses:

My <u>interview,</u> because it <u>came</u> minutes after my freeway accident, <u>did</u> not <u>impress</u> or <u>move</u> anyone.

The independent clause is the portion of the sentence that could stand alone without revision:

My <u>interview</u> <u>did</u> not <u>impress</u> or <u>move</u> anyone.

The other part of the sentence could stand alone only by removing *because:*

(because) It <u>came</u> minutes after my freeway accident.

This part of the sentence is known as a dependent clause; although it has a subject and a predicate (just as an independent clause does), it's linked to the main part of the sentence by a word (*because*) showing its dependence.

In summary, the two types of clauses—dependent and independent—both have a subject and a predicate. Dependent clauses, however, do not bear the main meaning of the sentence and are therefore linked to an independent clause. Nor can phrases stand alone, because they lack both a subject and a predicate. Only independent clauses can be written as sentences without revision.

1.7.3 Sentence Fragments

An incomplete sentence (a phrase or a dependent clause) that is written as though it were a complete sentence is called a fragment. Consider the following sentence fragments:

Marilyn Sanders, having had pilferage problems in her store for the past year. Refuses to accept the results of our investigation.

This serious error can easily be corrected by putting the two fragments together:

Marilyn Sanders, having had pilferage problems in her store for the past year, refuses to accept the results of our investigation.

Not all fragments can be corrected so easily. Here's more information on Sanders's pilferage problem.

Employees a part of it. No authority or discipline.

Only the writer knows the intended meaning of those two phrases. Perhaps the employees are taking part in the pilferage. If so, the sentence should read:

Some employees are part of the pilferage problem.

On the other hand, it's possible that some employees are helping with the investigation. Then the sentence would read:

Some employees are taking part in our investigation.

It's just as likely, however, that the employees are not only taking part in the pilferage but are also being analyzed:

Those employees who are part of the pilferage problem will accept no authority or discipline.

Even more meanings could be read into these fragments. Because fragments can mean so many things, they mean nothing. No well-written memo, letter, or report ever demands the reader to be an imaginative genius.

One more type of fragment exists, the kind represented by a dependent clause. Note what *because* does to change what was once a unified sentence:

Our stock of sprinklers is depleted.

Because our stock of sprinklers is depleted.

Although the second version contains a subject and a predicate, adding *because* makes it a fragment. Words such as *because* form a special group of words called subordinating conjunctions. Here's a partial list:

since	though	whenever
although	if	unless
while	even if	after

When a word of this type begins a clause, the clause is dependent and cannot stand alone as a sentence. However, if a dependent clause is combined with an independent clause, it can convey a complete meaning. The independent clause may come before or after the dependent clause:

We are unable to fill your order because our stock of sprinklers is depleted.

Because our stock of sprinklers is depleted, we are unable to fill your order.

Another remedy for a fragment that is a dependent clause is to remove the subordinating conjunction. That solution leaves a simple but complete sentence:

Our stock of sprinklers is depleted.

The actual details of a transaction will determine the best way to remedy a fragment problem.

The ban on fragments has one exception. Some advertising copy contains sentence fragments, written knowingly to convey a certain rhythm. However, advertising is the only area of business in which fragments are acceptable.

1.7.4 Fused Sentences and Comma Splices

Just as there can be too little in a group of words to make it a sentence, there can also be too much:

All our mail is run through a postage meter every afternoon someone picks it up.

This example contains two sentences, not one, but the two have been blended so that it's hard to tell where one ends and the next begins. Is the mail run through a meter every afternoon? If so, the sentences should read:

All our mail is run through a postage meter every afternoon. Someone picks it up.

Perhaps the mail is run through a meter at some other time (morning, for example) and is picked up every afternoon:

All our mail is run through a postage meter. Every afternoon someone picks it up.

The order of words is the same in all three cases; sentence division makes all the difference. Either of the last two cases is grammatically correct. The choice depends on the facts of the situation.

Sometimes these so-called fused sentences have a more obvious point of separation:

Several large orders arrived within a few days of one another, too many came in for us to process by the end of the month.

Here the comma has been put between two independent clauses in an attempt to link them. When a lowly comma separates two complete sentences, the result is called a comma splice. A comma splice can be remedied in one of three ways:

- Replace the comma with a period and capitalize the next word: "... one another. Too many ..."
- Replace the comma with a semicolon and do not capitalize the next word: "... one another; too many ..." This remedy works only when the two sentences have closely related meanings.
- Change one of the sentences so that it becomes a phrase or a dependent clause. This remedy often produces the best writing, but it takes more work.

The third alternative can be carried out in several ways. One is to begin the blended sentence with a subordinating conjunction:

Whenever several large orders arrived within a few days of one another, too many came in for us to process by the end of the month.

Another way is to remove part of the subject or the predicate verb from one of the independent clauses, thereby creating a phrase:

Several large orders arrived within a few days of one another, too many for us to process by the end of the month.

Finally, you can change one of the predicate verbs to its *ing* form:

Several large orders arrived within a few days of one another, too many coming in for us to process by the end of the month.

At other times a simple coordinating conjunction (such as *or, and,* or *but*) can separate fused sentences:

You can fire them, *or* you can make better use of their abilities.

Margaret drew up the designs, *and* Matt carried them out.

We will have three strong months, *but* after that sales will taper off.

Be careful using coordinating conjunctions: Use them only to join simple sentences that express similar ideas.

Also, because they say relatively little about the relationship between the two clauses they join, avoid using coordinating conjunctions too often: *and* is merely an addition sign; *but* is just a turn signal; *or* only points to an alternative. Subordinating conjunctions such as *because* and *whenever* tell the reader a lot more.

1.7.5 Sentences with Linking Verbs

Linking verbs were discussed briefly in the section on verbs (Section 1.3). Here you can see more fully the way they function in a sentence. The following is a model of any sentence with a linking verb:

A (verb) B.

Although words such as *seems* and *feels* can also be linking verbs, let's assume that the verb is a form of *to be:*

A *is* B.

In such a sentence, A and B are always nouns, pronouns, or adjectives. When one is a noun and the other is a pronoun, or when both are nouns, the sentence says that one is the same as the other:

She is president.

Rachel is president.

When one is an adjective, it modifies or describes the other:

She is forceful.

Remember that when one is an adjective, it modifies the other as any adjective modifies a noun or pronoun, except that a linking verb stands between the adjective and the word it modifies.

1.7.6 Misplaced Modifiers

The position of a modifier in a sentence is important. The movement of *only* changes the meaning in the following sentences:

Only we are obliged to supply those items specified in your contract.

We are obliged *only* to supply those items specified in your contract.

We are obliged to supply *only* those items specified in your contract.

We are obliged to supply those items specified *only* in your contract.

In any particular set of circumstances, only one of those sentences would be accurate. The others would very likely cause problems. To prevent misunderstanding, place modifiers such as *only* as close as possible to the noun or verb they modify.

For similar reasons, whole phrases that are modifiers must be placed near the right noun or verb. Mistakes in placement create ludicrous meanings.

Antia Information Systems has bought new computer chairs for the programmers *with more comfortable seats.*

The anatomy of programmers is not normally a concern of business writers. Obviously, the comfort of the chairs was the issue:

Antia Information Systems has bought new computer chairs *with more comfortable seats* for the programmers.

Here is another example:

I asked him to file all the letters in the cabinet *that had been answered.*

In this ridiculous sentence the cabinet has been answered, even though no cabinet in history is known to have asked a question.

That had been answered is too far from *letters* and too close to *cabinet.* Here's an improvement:

I asked him to file in the cabinet all the letters *that had been answered.*

In some cases, instead of moving the modifying phrase closer to the word it modifies, the best solution is to move the word closer to the modifying phrase.

2.0 PUNCTUATION

On the highway, signs tell you when to slow down or stop, where to turn, when to merge. In similar fashion, punctuation helps readers negotiate your prose. The proper use of punctuation keeps readers from losing track of your meaning.

2.1 Periods

Use a period (1) to end any sentence that is not a question, (2) with certain abbreviations, and (3) between dollars and cents in an amount of money.

2.2 Question Marks

Use a question mark after any direct question that requests an answer:

Are you planning to enclose a check, or shall we bill you?

Don't use a question mark with commands phrased as questions for the sake of politeness:

Will you send us a check today.

2.3 Exclamation Points

Use exclamation points after highly emotional language. Because business writing almost never calls for emotional language, you will seldom use exclamation points.

2.4 Semicolons

Semicolons have three main uses. One is to separate two closely related independent clauses:

The outline for the report is due within a week; the report itself is due at the end of the month.

A semicolon should also be used instead of a comma when the items in a series have commas within them:

Our previous meetings were on November 11, 1998; February 20, 1999; and April 28, 2000.

Finally, a semicolon should be used to separate independent clauses when the second one begins with a word such as *however, therefore,* or *nevertheless* or a phrase such as *for example* or *in that case:*

Our supplier has been out of part D712 for 10 weeks; however, we have found another source that can ship the part right away.

His test scores were quite low; on the other hand, he has a lot of relevant experience.

Section 4.4 has more information on using transitional words and phrases.

2.5 Colons

Use a colon after the salutation in a business letter. You also use a colon at the end of a sentence or phrase introducing a list or (sometimes) a quotation:

Our study included the three most critical problems: insufficient capital, incompetent management, and inappropriate location.

In some introductory sentences, phrases such as *the following* or *that is* are implied by using a colon.

A colon should not be used when the list, quotation, or idea is a direct object or part of the introductory sentence:

We are able to supply

staples
wood screws
nails
toggle bolts

This shipment includes 9 videotapes, 12 CDs, and 14 cassette tapes.

Another way you can use a colon is to separate the main clause and another sentence element when the second explains, illustrates, or amplifies the first:

Management was unprepared for the union reps demands: this fact alone accounts for their arguing well into the night.

However, in contemporary usage, such clauses are frequently separated by a semicolon.

2.6 Commas

Commas have many uses; the most common is to separate items in a series:

He took the job, learned it well, worked hard, and succeeded.

Put paper, pencils, and paper clips on the requisition list.

Company style often dictates omitting the final comma in a series. However, if you have a choice, use the final comma; it's often necessary to prevent misunderstanding.

A second place to use a comma is between independent clauses that are joined by a coordinating conjunction (*and, but,* or *or*) unless one or both are very short:

She spoke to the sales staff, and he spoke to the production staff.

I was advised to proceed and I did.

A third use for the comma is to separate a dependent clause at the beginning of a sentence from an independent clause:

Because of our lead in the market, we may be able to risk introducing a new product.

However, a dependent clause at the end of a sentence is separated from the independent clause by a comma only when the dependent clause is unnecessary to the main meaning of the sentence:

We may be able to introduce a new product, although it may involve some risk.

A fourth use for the comma is after an introductory phrase or word:

Starting with this amount of capital, we can survive in the red for one year.

Through more careful planning, we may be able to serve more people.

Yes, you may proceed as originally planned.

However, with short introductory prepositional phrases and some one-syllable words (such as *hence* and *thus*), the comma is often omitted:

Before January 1 we must complete the inventory.

Thus we may not need to hire anyone.

In short the move to Tulsa was a good idea.

Fifth, commas are used to surround nonrestrictive phrases or words (expressions that can be removed from the sentence without changing the meaning):

The new owners, the Kowacks, are pleased with their purchase.

Sixth, commas are used between adjectives modifying the same noun (coordinate adjectives):

She left Monday for a long, difficult recruiting trip.

To test the appropriateness of such a comma, try reversing the order of the adjectives: *a difficult, long recruiting trip.* If the order cannot be reversed, leave out the comma (*a good old friend* isn't the same as *an old good friend*). A comma is also not used when one of the adjectives is part of the noun. Compare these two phrases:

a distinguished, well-known figure
a distinguished public figure

The adjective-noun combination of *public* and *figure* has been used together so often that it has come to be considered a single thing: *public figure.* So no comma is required.

Seventh, commas should precede *Inc., Ltd.,* and the like:

Cloverdell, Inc.   Beamer, Ltd.

In a sentence, a comma also follows such abbreviations:

Belle Brown, Ph.D., is the new tenant.

Eighth, commas are used both before and after the year in sentences that include month, day, and year:

It will be sent by December 15, 1999, from our Cincinnati plant.

Some companies write dates in another form: 15 December 2000. No commas should be used in that case. Nor is a comma needed when only the month and year are present (December 2000).

Ninth, a comma may be used after an informal salutation in a letter to a personal friend. (In business letters, however, the salutation is followed by a colon.)

Tenth, a comma is used to separate a quotation from the rest of the sentence:

Your warranty reads, "These conditions remain in effect for one year from date of purchase."

However, the comma is left out when the quotation as a whole is built into the structure of the sentence:

He hurried off with an angry "Look where you're going."

Finally, a comma should be used whenever it's needed to avoid confusion or an unintended meaning. Compare the following:

Ever since they have planned new ventures more carefully.

Ever since, they have planned new ventures more carefully.

2.7 Dashes

Use a dash to surround a comment that is a sudden turn in thought:

Membership in the IBSA—it's expensive but worth it—may be obtained by applying to our New York office.

A dash can also be used to emphasize a parenthetical word or phrase:

Third-quarter profits—in excess of $2 million—are up sharply.

Finally, use dashes to set off a phrase that contains commas:

All our offices—Milwaukee, New Orleans, and Phoenix—have sent representatives.

Don't confuse a dash with a hyphen. A dash separates and emphasizes words, phrases, and clauses more strongly than a comma or parentheses can; a hyphen ties two words so tightly that they almost become one word.

When typing a dash, type two hyphens with no space before, between, or after.

2.8 Hyphens

Hyphens are mainly used in three ways. The first is to separate the parts of compound words beginning with such prefixes as self-, ex-, quasi-, and all:

self-assured   quasi-official
ex-wife   all-important

However, hyphens are usually left out and the words closed up in words that have such prefixes as *pro, anti, non, un, inter,* and *extra:*

prolabor   nonunion
antifascist   interdepartmental

Exceptions occur when (1) the prefix occurs before a proper noun or (2) the vowel at the end of the prefix is the same as the first letter of the root word:

pro-Republican   anti-American
anti-inflammatory   extra-atmospheric

When in doubt, consult your dictionary.

Hyphens are also used in some compound adjectives, which are adjectives made up of two or more words. Specifically, you should use hyphens in compound adjectives that come before the noun:

an interest-bearing account   well-informed executives

However, you need not hyphenate when the adjective follows a linking verb:

This account is interest bearing.

Their executives are well informed.

You can shorten sentences that list similar hyphenated words by dropping the common part from all but the last word:

Check the costs of first-, second-, and third-class postage.

Finally, hyphens may be used to divide words at the end of a typed line. Such hyphenation is best avoided, but when you have to divide words at the end of a line, do so correctly (see Section 3.4). A dictionary will show how words are divided into syllables.

2.9 Apostrophes

Use an apostrophe in the possessive form of a noun (but not in a pronoun):

On *his* desk was a reply to Bette *Ainsley's* application for the *manager's* position.

Apostrophes are also used in place of the missing letter(s) of a contraction:

WHOLE WORDS	CONTRACTION
we will	we'll
do not	don't
they are	they're

2.10 Quotation Marks

Use quotation marks to surround words that are repeated exactly as they were said or written:

The collection letter ended by saying, "This is your third and final notice."

Remember: (1) When the quoted material is a complete sentence, the first word is capitalized. (2) The final comma or period goes inside the closing quotation marks.

Quotation marks are also used to set off the title of a newspaper story, magazine article, or book chapter:

You should read "Legal Aspects of the Collection Letter" in *Today's Credit.*

The book title is shown here in italics. When typewritten, the title is underlined. The same treatment is proper for newspaper and magazine titles. (Appendix B explains documentation style in more detail.)

Quotation marks may also be used to indicate special treatment for words or phrases, such as terms that you're using in an unusual or ironic way:

Our management "team" spends more time squabbling than working to solve company problems.

When using quotation marks, take care to put in both sets, the closing marks as well as the opening ones.

Although periods and commas go inside any quotation marks, colons and semicolons go outside them. A question mark goes inside the quotation marks only if the quotation is a question:

All that day we wondered, "Is he with us?"

If the quotation is not a question but the entire sentence is, the question mark goes outside:

What did she mean by "You will hear from me"?

2.11 Parentheses

Use parentheses to surround comments that are entirely incidental:

Our figures do not match yours, although (if my calculations are correct) they are closer than we thought.

Parentheses are also used in legal documents to surround figures in arabic numerals that follow the same amount in words:

Remittance will be One Thousand Two Hundred Dollars ($1,200).

Be careful to put punctuation (period, comma, and so on) outside the parentheses unless it is part of the statement in parentheses.

2.12 Ellipses

Use ellipsis points, or dots, to indicate that material has been left out of a direct quotation. Use them only in direct quotations and only at the point where material was left out. In the following example, the first sentence is quoted in the second:

The Dow Jones Industrial Average, which skidded 38.17 points in the previous five sessions, gained 4.61 to end at 2213.84.

According to the Honolulu *Star Bulletin*, "The Dow Jones Industrial Average . . . gained 4.61" on June 10.

The number of dots in ellipses is not optional; always use three. Occasionally, the points of ellipsis come at the end of a sentence, where they seem to grow a fourth dot. Don't be fooled: One of the dots is a period.

2.13 Underscores and Italics

Usually a line typed underneath a word or phrase either provides emphasis or indicates the title of a book, magazine, or newspaper. If possible, use italics instead of an underscore. Italics (or underlining) should also be used for defining terms and for discussing words as words:

In this report *net sales* refers to after-tax sales dollars.

The word *building* is a common noun and should not be capitalized.

3.0 Mechanics

The most obvious and least tolerable mistakes that a business writer makes are probably those related to grammar and punctuation. However, a number of small details, known as writing mechanics, demonstrate the writer's polish and reflect on the company's professionalism.

3.1 Capitals

You should capitalize words that begin sentences:

Before hanging up, he said, "*We'll* meet here on Wednesday at noon."

A quotation that is a complete sentence should also begin with a capitalized word.

Capitalize the names of particular persons, places, and things (proper nouns):

We sent *Ms. Larson* an application form, informing her that not all *applicants* are interviewed.

Let's consider opening a branch in the *West,* perhaps at the *west* end of *Tucson, Arizona.*

As *office buildings* go, the *Kinney Building* is a pleasant setting for *TDG Office Equipment.*

Ms. Larson's name is capitalized because she is a particular applicant, whereas the general term *applicant* is left uncapitalized. Likewise, *West* is capitalized when it refers to a particular place but not when it means a direction. In the same way, *office* and *building* are not capitalized when they are general terms (common nouns), but they are capitalized when they are part of the title of a particular office or building (proper nouns).

Titles within families, governments, or companies may also be capitalized:

My *Uncle David* offered me a job, but I wouldn't be comfortable working for one of my uncles.

We've never had a *president* quite like *President Sweeney.*

In addition, always capitalize the first word of the salutation and complimentary close of a letter:

Dear Mr. Andrews: *Yours* very truly,

Finally, capitalize the first word after a colon when it begins a complete sentence:

Follow this rule: *When* in doubt, leave it out.

Otherwise, the first word after a colon should not be capitalized (see Section 2.5).

3.2 Abbreviations

Abbreviations are used heavily in tables, charts, lists, and forms. They're used sparingly in prose paragraphs, however. Here are some abbreviations often used in business writing:

ABBREVIATION	FULL TERM
b/l	bill of lading
ca.	circa (about)
dol., dols.	dollar, dollars
etc.	et cetera (and so on)
FDIC	Federal Deposit Insurance Corporation
Inc.	Incorporated
L.f.	Ledger folio
Ltd.	Limited
mgr.	manager
NSF or N/S	not sufficient funds
P&L or P/L	profit and loss
reg.	regular
whsle.	wholesale

Because *etc.* contains a word meaning "and," never write *and etc.*

3.3 Numbers

Numbers may be correctly handled many ways in business writing, so follow company style. In the absence of a set style, however, generally spell out all numbers from one to nine and use arabic numerals for the rest.

There are some exceptions to this general rule. First, never begin a sentence with a numeral:

Twenty of us produced *641* units per week in the first *12* weeks of the year.

Second, use numerals for the numbers one through ten if they're in the same list as larger numbers:

Our weekly quota rose from *9* to *15* to *27*.

Third, use numerals for percentages, time of day (except with *o'clock*), dates, and (in general) dollar amounts.

Our division is responsible for *7* percent of total sales.

The meeting is scheduled for *8:30* A.M. on August *2*.

Add *$3* for postage and handling.

Use a comma in numbers with four digits (*1,257*) unless the company specifies another style.

When writing dollar amounts, use a decimal point only if cents are included. In lists of two or more dollar amounts, use the decimal point either for all or for none:

He sent two checks, one for *$67.92* and one for *$90.00*.

3.4 Word Division

In general, avoid dividing words at the ends of lines. When you must, follow these rules:

◆ Don't divide one-syllable words (such as *since, walked,* and *thought*); abbreviations (*mgr.*); contractions (*isn't*); or numbers expressed in numerals (*117,500*).

◆ Divide words between syllables, as specified in a dictionary or word-division manual.

◆ Make sure that at least three letters of the divided word are moved to the second line: *sin-cerely* instead of *sincere-ly*.

◆ Do not end a page or more than three consecutive lines with hyphens.

◆ Leave syllables consisting of a single vowel at the end of the first line (*impedi-ment* instead of *imped-iment*), except when the single vowel is part of a suffix such as *-able,* *-ible, -ical,* or *-ity* (*re-spons-ible* instead of *re-sponsi-ble*).

◆ Divide between double letters (*tomor-row*), except when the root word ends in double letters (*call-ing* instead of *cal-ling*).

◆ Wherever possible, divide hyphenated words at the hyphen only: instead of *anti-inde-pendence*, use *anti-independence*.

4.0 VOCABULARY

Using the right word in the right place is a crucial skill in business communication. However, many pitfalls await the unwary.

4.1 Frequently Confused Words

Because the following sets of words sound similar, be careful not to use one when you mean to use the other:

WORD	MEANING
accede	to comply with
exceed	to go beyond
accept	to take
except	to exclude
access	admittance
excess	too much
advice	suggestion
advise	to suggest
affect	to influence
effect	the result
allot	to distribute
a lot	much or many
all ready	completely prepared
already	completed earlier
born	given birth to
borne	carried
capital	money; chief city
capitol	a government building
cite	to quote
sight	a view
site	a location
complement	complete amount; to go well with
compliment	to flatter
corespondent	party in a divorce suit
correspondent	letter writer
council	a panel of people
counsel	advice; a lawyer
defer	to put off until later
differ	to be different
device	a mechanism
devise	to plan
die	to stop living; a tool
dye	to color
discreet	careful
discrete	separate

WORD	MEANING	WORD	MEANING
envelop	to surround	precedence	priority
envelope	a covering for a letter	precedents	previous events
forth	forward	principal	sum of money; chief; main
fourth	number four	principle	general rule
holey	full of holes	rap	to knock
holy	sacred	wrap	to cover
wholly	completely		
		residence	home
human	of people	residents	inhabitants
humane	kindly		
		right	correct
incidence	frequency	rite	ceremony
incidents	events	write	to form words on a surface
instance	example	role	a part to play
instants	moments	roll	to tumble; a list
interstate	between states	root	part of a plant
intrastate	within a state	rout	to defeat
		route	a traveler's way
later	afterward		
latter	the second of two	shear	to cut
		sheer	thin, steep
lead	a metal		
led	guided	stationary	immovable
		stationery	paper
lean	to rest at an angle		
lien	a claim	than	as compared with
		then	at that time
levee	embankment		
levy	tax	their	belonging to them
		there	in that place
loath	reluctant	they're	they are
loathe	to hate		
		to	a preposition
loose	free; not tight	too	excessively; also
lose	to mislay	two	the number
material	substance	waive	to set aside
materiel	equipment	wave	a swell of water; a gesture
miner	mineworker	weather	atmospheric conditions
minor	underage person	whether	if
moral	virtuous; a lesson		
morale	sense of well-being		

moral	virtuous; a lesson
morale	sense of well-being
ordinance	law
ordnance	weapons
overdo	to do in excess
overdue	past due
peace	lack of conflict
piece	a fragment
pedal	a foot lever
peddle	to sell
persecute	to torment
prosecute	to sue
personal	private
personnel	employees

In the preceding list only enough of each word's meaning is given to help you distinguish between the words in each group. Several meanings are left out entirely. For more complete definitions, consult a dictionary.

4.2 Frequently Misused Words

The following words tend to be misused for reasons other than their sound. Reference books (including the *Random House College Dictionary*, revised edition; Follett's *Modern American Usage;* and Fowler's *Modern English Usage*) can help you with similar questions of usage.

a lot: When the writer means "many," *a lot* is always two separate words, never one.

correspond with: Use this phrase when you are talking about exchanging letters. Use *correspond to* when you mean "similar to." Use either *correspond with* or *correspond to* when you mean "relate to."

disinterested: This word means "fair, unbiased, having no favorites, impartial." If you mean "bored" or "not interested," use *uninterested.*

etc.: This is the abbreviated form of a Latin phrase, *et cetera.* It means "and so on" or "and so forth." The current tendency among business writers is to use English rather than Latin.

imply/infer: Both refer to hints. Their great difference lies in who is acting. The writer *implies;* the reader *infers,* sees between the lines.

lay: This is a transitive verb. Never use it for the intransitive *lie.* (See Section 1.3.3.)

less: Use *less* for uncountable quantities (such as amounts of water, air, sugar, and oil). Use *fewer* for countable quantities (such as numbers of jars, saws, words, pages, and humans). The same distinction applies to *much* and *little* (uncountable) versus *many* and *few* (countable).

like: Use *like* only when the word that follows is just a noun or a pronoun. Use *as* or *as if* when a phrase or clause follows:

> She looks *like* him.
> She did just *as* he had expected.
> It seems *as if* she had plenty of time.

many/much: See *less.*

regardless: The *less* ending is the negative part. No word needs two negative parts, so it is illiterate to add *ir* (a negative prefix) at the beginning.

to me/personally: Use these phrases only when personal reactions, apart from company policy, are being stated (not often the case in business writing).

try: Always follow with *to,* never *and.*

verbal: People in the business community who are careful with language frown on those who use *verbal* to mean "spoken" or "oral." Many others do say "verbal agreement." Strictly speaking, *verbal* means "of words" and therefore includes both spoken and written words. Be guided in this matter by company usage.

4.3 Frequently Misspelled Words

All of us, even the world's best spellers, sometimes have to check a dictionary for the spelling of some words. People who have never memorized the spelling of commonly used words must look up so many that they grow exasperated and give up on spelling words correctly.

Don't expect perfection, and don't surrender. If you can memorize the spelling of just the words listed here, you'll need the dictionary far less often and you'll write with more confidence.

absence	dissatisfied
absorption	dissipate
accessible	
accommodate	eligible
accumulate	embarrassing
achieve	endorsement
advantageous	exaggerate
affiliated	exceed
aggressive	exhaust
alignment	existence
aluminum	extraordinary
ambience	
analyze	fallacy
apparent	familiar
appropriate	flexible
argument	fluctuation
asphalt	forty
assistant	
asterisk	gesture
auditor	grievous
bankruptcy	haphazard
believable	harassment
brilliant	holiday
bulletin	
	illegible
calendar	immigrant
campaign	incidentally
category	indelible
ceiling	independent
changeable	indispensable
clientele	insistent
collateral	intermediary
committee	irresistible
comparative	
competitor	jewelry
concede	judgment
congratulations	judicial
connoisseur	
consensus	labeling
convenient	legitimate
convertible	leisure
corroborate	license
criticism	litigation
definitely	maintenance
description	mathematics
desirable	mediocre
dilemma	minimum
disappear	
disappoint	necessary
disbursement	negligence
discrepancy	negotiable

newsstand
noticeable

occurrence
omission

parallel
pastime
peaceable
permanent
perseverance
persistent
personnel
persuade
possesses
precede
predictable
preferred
privilege
procedure
proceed
pronunciation
psychology
pursue

questionnaire

receive
recommend

repetition
rescind
rhythmical
ridiculous

salable
secretary
seize
separate
sincerely
succeed
suddenness
superintendent
supersede
surprise

tangible
tariff
technique
tenant
truly

unanimous
until

vacillate
vacuum
vicious

4.4 Transitional Words and Phrases

The following sentences don't communicate as well as they might because they lack a transitional word or phrase:

Production delays are inevitable. Our current lag time in filling orders is one month.

A semicolon between the two sentences would signal a close relationship between their meanings, but it wouldn't even hint at what that relationship is. Here are the sentences, now linked by means of a semicolon, with a space for a transitional word or phrase:

Production delays are inevitable; _____ , our current lag time in filling orders is one month.

Now read the sentence with *nevertheless* in the blank space. Now try *therefore, incidentally, in fact,* and *at any rate* in the blank. Each substitution changes the meaning of the sentence.

Here are some transitional words (called conjunctive adverbs) that will help you write more clearly:

accordingly	furthermore	moreover
anyway	however	otherwise
besides	incidentally	still
consequently	likewise	therefore
finally	meanwhile	

The following transitional phrases are used in the same way:

as a result	in other words
at any rate	in the second place
for example	on the other hand
in fact	to the contrary

When one of these words or phrases joins two independent clauses, it should be preceded by a semicolon and followed by a comma, as shown here:

The consultant recommended a complete reorganization; moreover, she suggested that we drop several products.

APPENDIX D

CORRECTION SYMBOLS

Instructors often use these short, easy-to-remember correction symbols and abbreviations when evaluating students' writing. You can use them too, to understand your instructor's suggestions and to revise and proofread your own letters, memos, and reports. Refer to Appendix C for information on grammar and usage.

CONTENT AND STYLE

Acc	Accuracy. Check to be sure information is correct.
ACE	Avoid copying examples.
ACP	Avoid copying problems.
Adp	Adapt. Tailor message to reader.
App	Follow proper organization approach. (Refer to Chapter 5.)
Assign	Assignment. Review instructions for assignment.
AV	Active verb. Substitute active for passive.
Awk	Awkward phrasing. Rewrite.
BC	Be consistent.
BMS	Be more sincere.
Chop	Choppy sentences. Use longer sentences and more transitional phrases.
Con	Condense. Use fewer words.
CT	Conversational tone. Avoid using overly formal language.
Depers	Depersonalize. Avoid attributing credit or blame to any individual or group.
Dev	Develop. Provide greater detail.
Dir	Direct. Use direct approach; get to the point.
Emph	Emphasize. Develop this point more fully.
EW	Explanation weak. Check logic; provide more proof.
Fl	Flattery. Avoid compliments that are insincere.
FS	Figure of speech. Find a more accurate expression.
GNF	Good news first. Use direct order.
GRF	Give reasons first. Use indirect order.
GW	Goodwill. Put more emphasis on expressions of goodwill.

H/E	Honesty/ethics. Revise statement to reflect good business practices.
Imp	Imply. Avoid being direct.
Inc	Incomplete. Develop further.
Jar	Jargon. Use less specialized language.
Log	Logic. Check development of argument.
Neg	Negative. Use more positive approach or expression.
Obv	Obvious. Do not state point in such detail.
OC	Overconfident. Adopt humbler language.
OM	Omission.
Org	Organization. Strengthen outline.
OS	Off the subject. Close with point on main subject.
Par	Parallel. Use same structure.
Pom	Pompous. Rephrase in down-to-earth terms.
PV	Point of view. Make statement from reader's perspective rather than your own.
RB	Reader benefit. Explain what reader stands to gain.
Red	Redundant. Reduce number of times this point is made.
Ref	Reference. Cite source of information.
Rep	Repetitive. Provide different expression.
RS	Resale. Reassure reader that he or she has made a good choice.
SA	Service attitude. Put more emphasis on helping reader.
Sin	Sincerity. Avoid sounding glib or uncaring.
SL	Stereotyped language. Focus on individual's characteristics instead of on false generalizations.

Spec	Specific. Provide more specific statement.	UAS	Use appropriate salutation.
SPM	Sales promotion material. Tell reader about related goods or services.	UAV	Use active voice.
		Unc	Unclear. Rewrite to clarify meaning.
Stet	Let stand in original form.	UPV	Use passive voice.
Sub	Subordinate. Make this point less important.	USS	Use shorter sentences.
SX	Sexist. Avoid language that contributes to gender stereotypes.	V	Variety. Use different expression or sentence pattern.
Tone	Tone needs improvement.	W	Wordy. Eliminate unnecessary words.
Trans	Transition. Show connection between points.	WC	Word choice. Find a more appropriate word.
UAE	Use action ending. Close by stating what reader should do next.	YA	"You" attitude. Rewrite to emphasize reader's needs.

GRAMMAR, USAGE, AND MECHANICS

Ab	Abbreviation. Avoid abbreviations in most cases; use correct abbreviation.	M	Margins. Improve frame around document.
Adj	Adjective. Use adjective instead.	MM	Misplaced modifier. Place modifier close to word it modifies.
Adv	Adverb. Use adverb instead.	NRC	Nonrestrictive clause (or phrase). Separate from rest of sentence with commas.
Agr	Agreement. Make subject and verb or noun and pronoun agree.		
Ap	Appearance. Improve appearance.	P	Punctuation. Use correct punctuation.
Apos	Apostrophe. Check use of apostrophe.	Par	Parallel. Use same structure.
Art	Article. Use correct article.	PH	Place higher. Move document up on page.
BC	Be consistent.	PL	Place lower. Move document down on page.
Cap	Capitalize.	Prep	Preposition. Use correct preposition.
Case	Use cases correctly.	RC	Restrictive clause (or phrase). Remove commas that separate clause from rest of sentence.
CoAdj	Coordinate adjective. Insert comma between coordinate adjectives; delete comma between adjective and compound noun.		
		RO	Run-on sentence. Separate two sentences with comma and coordinating conjunction or with semicolon.
CS	Comma splice. Use period or semicolon to separate clauses.		
DM	Dangling modifier. Rewrite so that modifier clearly relates to subject of sentence.	SC	Series comma. Add comma before *and*.
		SI	Split infinitive. Do not separate *to* from rest of verb.
Exp	Expletive. Avoid expletive beginnings, such as it is, there are, there is, this is, and these are.	Sp	Spelling error. Consult dictionary.
		Stet	Let stand in original form.
F	Format. Improve layout of document.	S-V	Subject-verb pair. Do not separate with comma.
Frag	Fragment. Rewrite as complete sentence.		
Gram	Grammar. Correct grammatical error.	Syl	Syllabification. Divide word between syllables.
HCA	Hyphenate compound adjective.	WD	Word division. Check dictionary for proper end-of-line hyphenation.
lc	Lowercase. Do not use capital letter.	WW	Wrong word. Replace with another word.

PROOFREADING MARKS

Symbol	Meaning	Symbol Used in Content	Corrected Copy
═	Align horizontally	meaningful ᵣₑsult	meaningful result
‖	Align vertically	1. Power cable 2. Keyboard	1. Power cable 2. Keyboard
(ac)	Capitalize	(ac) Do not immerse.	DO NOT IMMERSE.
≡	Capitalize	Pepsico, Inc.	PepsiCo, Inc.
◡	Close up	self- confidence	self-confidence
～	Delete	harrassment and abuse	harassment
(STET)	Restore to original	none of the (STET)	none of the
∧	Insert	*a* *and white* tirquoise shirts	turquoise and white shirts
⟨	Insert comma	a, b and c	a, b, and c
⊙	Insert period	Harrigan et al ⊙	Harrigan et al.
/	Lowercase	TULSA, South of here	Tulsa, south of here
⊏	Move left	Attention: ⊏ Security	Attention: Security
⊐	Move right	February 2, 2000 ⊐	February 2, 2000
⊔	Move down	Sincerely,	Sincerely,
⊓	Move up	⌐THIRD-QUARTER SALES⌐	THIRD-QUARTER SALES
⊐ ⊏	Center	⊐Awards Banquet ⊏	Awards Banquet
⌐⌐	Start new line	Marla Fenton, Manager, Distri-bution	Marla Fenton Manager, Distribution
⌐	Run lines together	Manager, Distribution	Manager, Distribution
¶	Start paragraph	¶The solution is easy to determine but difficult to implement in a competitive environment like the one we now face.	The solution is easy to determine but difficult to implement in a competitive environment like the one we now face.
#	Leave space	# # real estate testcase	real estate test case
◯	Spell out	(COD)	cash on delivery
(SP)	Spell out	(SP) Assn. of Biochem. Engrs.	Association of Biochemical Engineers
∿	Transpose	airy, light, casaul tone	light, airy, casual tone

REFERENCES

Chapter 1

1. Adapted from Doug Glass, "Escaping the Rut Is Good Idea for Hallmark Artists, Writers," Orange County Edition, *Los Angeles Times*, 6 June 1996, D-7; Gillian Flynn, "Sending a Quality of Life Message: Hallmark Cares," *Personnel Journal*, March 1996, 56; Karen Matthes, "Greeting from Hallmark," *HR Focus*, Vol. 70 (1 August 1993): 12.

2. Raymond M. Olderman, *10 Minute Guide to Business Communication* (New York: Simon & Schuster, 1997), 1–2.

3. Ted Pollock, "9 Ways to Improve Your Communication," *Supervision*, February 1999, 24–26.

4. Stephanie Armour, "Failure to Communicate Costly for Companies," *USA Today*, 30 September 1998, 1A.

5. "Interpersonal Skills Are Key in Office of the Future," *TMA Journal* 19, no. 4 (July–August 1999): 53.

6. Shari Caudron, "Workers' Ideas for Improving Alternative Work Situations," *Workforce*, December 1998, 42–46; Carol Leonetti Dannhauser, "Who's in the Home Office?" *American Demographics*, June 1999, 50–56.

7. "Interpersonal Skills Are Key in Office of the Future," 53.

8. Katrina Brooker, "First: The Nightmare Before Christmas," *Fortune*, 24 January 2000, 24–25.

9. Lillian H. Chaney and Jeanette S. Martin, *Intercultural Business Communications*, (Upper Saddle River, N.J.: Prentice Hall, 2000), 1–2.

10. Chaney and Martin, *Intercultural Business Communications*, 1–2.

11. Timothy Aeppel, "A 3Com Factory Hires a Lot of Immigrants, Gets Mix of Languages," *Wall Street Journal*, 30 March 1999, A1, A12.

12. Fernando Bartolome, *The Articulate Executive* (Boston: Harvard Business Review, 1993), xi.

13. Paula Jacobs, "Strong Writing Skills Essential for Success, Even in IT," *InfoWorld*, 6 July 1998, 86.

14. James M. Citrin and Thomas J. Neff, "Digital Leadership," *Strategy and Business*, First Quarter 2000, 42–50; Gary L. Neilson, Bruce A. Pasternack, and Albert J. Viscio, "Up the E-Organization," *Strategy and Business*, First Quarter 2000, 52–61.

15. "How to Improve Communications," *Control Engineering* 45, no. 12 (September 1998): 23.

16. Donald O. Wilson, "Diagonal Communication Links with Organizations," *Journal of Business Communication* 29, no. 2 (Spring 1992): 129–143.

17. Carol Hymowitz, "Spread the Word: Gossip Is Good," *Wall Street Journal*, 4 November 1988, B1; Donald B. Simmons, "The Nature of the Organizational Grapevine," *Supervisory Management*, November 1985, 40.

18. J. David Johnson, William A. Donohoe, Charles K. Atkin, and Sally Johnson, "Differences Between Formal and Informal Communication Channels," *Journal of Business Communication*, 31, no. 2 (1994): 111–122.

19. "Presumed Guilty: Managing When Your Company's Name Is Mud," *Working Woman*, November 1991, 31; Judy A. Smith, "Crisis Communications: The War on Two Fronts," *Industry Week*, 20 May 1996, 136.

20. Some material adapted from Courtland L. Bovée, John V. Thill, Marian Burk Wood, and George P. Dovel, *Management* (New York: McGraw-Hill, 1993), 537–538.

21. Gillian Flynn, "Pillsbury's Recipe Is Candid Talk," *Workforce*, February 1998, 56–57+.

22. "Information Deluge Clogging Workplace," *Honolulu Advertiser*, 25 May 1998, B6; Stephen Barr, "Message Madness," *CFO*, May 1998, 25.

23. Alice La Plante, "Still Drowning!" *Computerworld*, 10 March 1997, 69–70.

24. Bruce W. Speck, "Writing Professional Codes of Ethics to Introduce Ethics in Business Writing," *Bulletin of the Association for Business Communication* 53, no. 3 (September 1990): 21–26; H. W. Love, "Communication, Accountability and Professional Discourse: The Interaction of Language Values and Ethical Values," *Journal of Business Ethics* 11 (1992): 883–892; Kathryn C. Rentz and Mary Beth Debs, "Language and Corporate Values: Teaching Ethics in Business Writing Courses," *Journal of Business Communication* 24, no. 3 (Summer 1987): 37–48.

25. J. Michael Sproule, *Communication Today* (Glenview, Ill.: Scott Foresman, 1981), 329.

26. Louis Hecht, corporate secretary of Molex, personal communication, May 1997; Matt Krantz, "Molex Inc.'s Fred Krehbiel," *Investor's Business Daily*, 7 January 1997, 1; Paul Conley, "Molex Sets Record-Breaking Global Pace," *Chicago Tribune*, 2 August 1996; Dave Savona, "The Billion-Dollar Globetrotter," *International Business*, November 1995, 52–56; Robert Knight, "How Molex, Inc. Connected in World Markets," *Chicago Enterprise*, July–August 1994, 24–27; Ronald E. Yates, "Firm's Growth Tied to Global Connections," *Chicago Tribune*, 6 February 1994, 8.

27. Carol Hymowitz, "If the Walls Had Ears You Wouldn't Have Any Less Privacy," *Wall Street Journal*, 19 May 1998, B1.

28. Kenneth Hein, "Hungry for Feedback," *Incentive*, September 1997, 9+.

29. John A. Byrne, "Jack," *Business Week*, 8 June 1998, 92–111.

30. Michael H. Mescon, Courtland L. Bovée, and John V. Thill, *Business Today*, 9th ed. (Upper Saddle River: Prentice Hall, 1999), 214.

31. A. Thomas Young, "Ethics in Business: Business of Ethics," *Vital Speeches*, 15 September 1992, 725–730.

32. David Grier, "Confronting Ethical Dilemmas: The View from Inside—A Practitioner's Perspective," *Vital Speeches*, 1 December 1989, 100–104.

33. Joseph L. Badaracco Jr., "Business Ethics: Four Spheres of Executive Responsibility," *California Management Review*, Spring 1992, 64–79; Kenneth Blanchard and Norman Vincent Peale, *The Power of Ethical Management* (New York: Ballantine Books, 1996) 7–17.

34. Blanchard and Peale, *The Power of Ethical Management*, 7–17; Badaracco, "Business Ethics: Four Spheres of Executive Responsibility," 64–79.

35. Jules Harcourt, "Developing Ethical Messages: A Unit of Instruction for the Basic Business Communication Course,"

Bulletin of the Association for Business Communication 53, no. 3 (September 1990): 17–20; John D. Pettit, Bobby Vaught, and Kathy J. Pulley, "The Role of Communication in Organizations," *Journal of Business Communication* 27, no. 3 (Summer 1990): 233–249; Kenneth R. Andrews, "Ethics in Practice," *Harvard Business Review,* September–October 1989, 99–104; Priscilla S. Rogers and John M. Swales, "We the People? An Analysis of the Dana Corporation Policies Document," *Journal of Business Communication* 27, no. 3 (Summer 1990): 293–313; Larry Reynolds, "The Ethics Audit," *Business Ethics,* July–August 1991, 120–122.

36. See note 1.

37. "When Rumors Disrupt Your Staff," *Working Woman,* October 1992, 36.

Chapter 2

1. Adapted from the American Express Web site: www.americanexpress.com, accessed 29 February 2000; Mahlon Apgar IV, "The Alternative Workplace: Changing Where and How People Work," *Harvard Business Review,* May/June 1998, 121–130; "How Senior Executives at American Express View the Alternative Workplace," *Harvard Business Review,* May/June 1998, 132–133; Michelle Marchetti, "Master Motivators," *Sales and Marketing Management,* April 1998, 38–44; Sally Richards, "Make the Most of Your First Job," *Informationweek,* 21 June 1999, 183–186; Carrie Shook, "Leader, Not Boss," *Forbes,* 1 December 1997, 52–54.

2. Michael H. Mescon, Courtland L. Bovée, and John V. Thill, *Business Today* (Upper Saddle River, N.J.: Prentice Hall, 1999), 203.

3. Richard L. Daft, *Management,* 4th ed. (Fort Worth: Dryden, 1997), 338.

4. "Teamwork Translates Into High Performance," *HR Focus,* July 1998, 7.

5. Ellen Neuborne, "Companies Save, But Workers Pay," *USA Today,* 25 February 1997, B2; Charles L. Parnell, "Teamwork: Not a New Idea, But It's Transforming the Workplace," *Vital Speeches of the Day,* 1 November 1996, 46.

6. Neuborne, "Companies Save, But Workers Pay," B1; Daft, *Management,* 594–595; Robbins and De Cenzo, *Fundamentals of Management,* 336–338; Robbins, *Managing Today!* 309–310.

7. Richard Moderow, "Teamwork Is the Key to Cutting Costs," *Modern Healthcare,* 29 April 1996, 138.

8. "Sharing Knowledge Through BP's Virtual Team Network," *Harvard Business Review,* September/October 1997, 152–153.

9. Daft, *Management,* 612–615.

10. Stephen P. Robbins, *Essentials of Organizational Behavior,* 4th ed. (Upper Saddle River, N.J.: Prentice Hall, 2000), 98.

11. Mike Verespej, "Drucker Sours on Teams," *Industry Week,* 6 April 1998, 16+.

12. B. Aubrey Fisher, *Small Group Decision Making: Communication and the Group Process,* 2nd ed. (New York: McGraw-Hill, 1980), 145–149; Robbins and De Cenzo, *Fundamentals of Management,* 334–335; Daft, *Management,* 602–603.

13. Lynda McDermott, Bill Waite, and Nolan Brawley, "Executive Teamwork," *Executive Excellence,* May 1999, 15.

14. Larry Cole and Michael Cole, "Why Is the Teamwork Buzz Word Not Working?" *Communication World,* February/March 1999, 29; Patricia Buhler, "Managing in the 90s: Creating Flexibility in Today's Workplace," *Supervision,* January 1997, 24+; Allison W. Amason, Allen C. Hochwarter, Wayne A. Thompson, and Kenneth R. Harrison, "Conflict: An Important Dimension in Successful Management Teams," *Organizational Dynamics,* Autumn 1995, 20+.

15. "Team Players," *Executive Excellence,* May 1999, 18.

16. Thomas K. Capozzoli, "Conflict Resolution—A Key Ingredient in Successful Teams," *Supervision,* November 1999, 14–16.

17. Daft, *Management,* 609–612.

18. Amason, Hochwarter, Thompson, and Harrison, "Conflict: An Important Dimension in Successful Management Teams."

19. Jesse S. Nirenberg, *Getting Through to People* (Paramus, N.J.: Prentice Hall, 1973), 134–142.

20. Nirenberg, *Getting Through to People,* 134–142.

21. Nirenberg, *Getting Through to People,* 134–142.

22. Julia Lawlor, "Videoconferencing: From Stage Fright to Stage Presence," *New York Times,* 27 August 1998, D6.

23. Heath Row, "The Joys of Togetherness," *Webmaster,* June 1997, 44–48.

24. William P. Galle Jr., Beverly H. Nelson, Donna W. Luse, and Maurice F. Villere, *Business Communication: A Technology-Based Approach* (Chicago: Irwin, 1996), 260.

25. Mary Beth Debs, "Recent Research on Collaborative Writing in Industry," *Technical Communication* (November 1991), 476–484.

26. Ruth G. Newman, "Communication: Collaborative Writing with Purpose and Style," *Personnel Journal,* April 1988, 37–38; Galle, Nelson, Luse, and Villere, *Business Communication,* 256.

27. Jon Hanke, "Presenting as a Team," *Presentations,* January 1998, 74–82.

28. Robyn D. Clarke, "Do You Hear What I Hear?" *Black Enterprise,* May 1998, 129; Dot Yandle, "Listening to Understand," *Pryor Report Management Newsletter Supplement* 15, no. 8 (August 1998): 13.

29. Clarke, "Do You Hear What I Hear?"

30. Augusta M. Simon, "Effective Listening: Barriers to Listening in a Diverse Business Environment," *Bulletin of the Association for Business Communication* 54, no. 3 (September 1991): 73–74.

31. Bob Lamons, "Good Listeners Are Better Communicators," *Marketing News,* 11 September 1995, 13+; Phillip Morgan and H. Kent Baker, "Building a Professional Image: Improving Listening Behavior," *Supervisory Management,* November 1985, 35–36.

32. "An Added Joy of E-Mail: Fewer Face-to-Face Meetings," *Wall Street Journal,* 14 July 1998, A1.

33. "Listening: Hearing Better at Meetings," *Communication Briefings* 18, no. 11 (September 1999): 2.

34. J. Michael Sproule, *Communication Today* (Glenview, Ill.: Scott, Foresman, 1981), 69.

35. Sproule, *Communication Today,* 69.

36. Sproule, *Communication Today,* 69.

37. Sherwyn P. Morreale and Courtland L. Bovée, *Excellence in Public Speaking* (Orlando, Fla.: Harcourt Brace, 1998), 72–76; Lyman K. Steil, Larry L. Barker, and Kittie W. Watson, *Effective Listening: Key to Your Success* (Reading, Mass.: Addison-Wesley, 1983), 21–22.

38. Patrick J. Collins, *Say It with Power and Confidence* (Upper Saddle River, N.J.: Prentice Hall, 1997), 40–45.

39. Collins, *Say It with Power and Confidence,* 40–45.

40. David Lewis, *The Secret Language of Success* (New York: Carroll & Graf, 1989), 67, 170.

41. Nido Qubein, *Communicate Like a Pro* (New York: Berkeley Books, 1986), 97.

42. Dale G. Leathers, *Successful Nonverbal Communication: Principles and Applications* (New York: Macmillan, 1986), 19.

43. Gerald H. Graham, Jeanne Unrue, and Paul Jennings, "The Impact of Nonverbal Communication in Organizations: A Survey of Perceptions," *Journal of Business Communication* 28, no. 1 (Winter 1991): 45–62.

44. Brenda Park Sundo, "Are You Noticing Too Many Yawns?" *Workforce,* April 1998, 16–17.

45. "Better Meetings Benefit Everyone: How to Make Yours More Productive," *Working Communicator Bonus Report,* July 1998.

46. William C. Waddell and Thomas A. Rosko, "Conducting an Effective Off-Site Meeting," *Management Review,* February 1993, 40–44.

47. "Better Meetings Benefit Everyone."

48. Kathy E. Gill, "Board Primer: Parliamentary Procedure," *Association Management,* 1993, L-39.

49. See note 1.

Chapter 3

1. Adapted from Target Stores Web site (www.targetstores.com/TargetWWW/html/ about01.htm), accessed 21 March 2001; D. R. Barnes, "Company Plans to Establish Community Partnerships," *Washington Informer,* 13 December 1995, PG; Susan Moffat, "Work Force Diversity; The Young and the Diverse; The Next Generation May Be Better Equipped to Deal with Cultural Complexities at Work," Home Edition, *Los Angeles Times,* 16 May 1994, 2–15.

2. N. Hed Seelye and Alan Seelye-James, *Culture Clash* (Chicago: NTC Business Books, 1995), xv, xviii.

3. Sari Kalin, "The Importance of Being Multiculturally Correct," *Computerworld,* 6 October 1997, G16–G17; Lawrence M. Fisher, "REI Climbs Online," *Strategy and Business,* First Quarter 2000, 116–129.

4. Rona Gindin, "Dealing with a Multicultural Workforce," *Nation's Restaurant News,* September/October 1998, 31, 83; Howard Gleckman, "A Rich Stew in the Melting Pot," *Business Week,* 31 August 1998, 76+.

5. Joan Crockett, "Winning Competitive Advantage Through a Diverse Workforce," *HRFocus,* May 1999, 9–10.

6. Philip R. Harris and Robert T. Moran, *Managing Cultural Differences,* 3d ed. (Houston: Gulf, 1991), 394–397, 429–430.

7. Lillian H. Chaney and Jeanette S. Martin, *Intercultural Business Communication,* (Upper Saddle River, N.J.: Prentice Hall, 2000), 6.

8. Stephanie Strom, "Breaking from Tradition: Change Trickles Down the Ranks as Workers Rethink Benefit Plans," *Chicago Tribune,* 5 July 1998, sec. G, 1, 3; Carley H. Dodd, *Dynamics of Intercultural Communication,* 3d ed. (Dubuque, Ia.: Brown, 1991), 50; Philip R. Harris and Robert T. Moran, *Managing Cultural Differences,* 3d ed. (Houston: Gulf, 1991), 140.

9. Larry A. Samovar and Richard E. Porter, "Basic Principles of Intercultural Communication," in *Intercultural Communication: A Reader,* 6th ed., edited by Larry A. Samovar and Richard E. Porter (Belmont, Calif.: Wadsworth, 1991), 12.

10. Chaney and Martin, *Intercultural Business Communication,* 11.

11. Gus Tyler, "Tokyo Signs the Paychecks," *New York Times Book Review,* 12 August 1990, 7.

12. Chaney and Martin, *Intercultural Business Communication,* 159.

13. Otto Kreisher, "Annapolis Has a New Attitude Toward Sexual Harassment," *San Diego Union,* 30 July 1990, A-6.

14. Linda Beamer, "Teaching English Business Writing to Chinese-Speaking Business Students," *Bulletin of the Association for Business Communication* 57, no. 1 (1994): 12–18.

15. Edward T. Hall, "Context and Meaning," in *Intercultural Communication,* edited by Samovar and Porter, 46–55.

16. Beamer, "Teaching English Business Writing to Chinese-Speaking Business Students."

17. Dodd, *Dynamics of Intercultural Communication,* 69–70.

18. Chaney and Martin, *Intercultural Business Communication,* 206–211.

19. James Wilfong and Toni Seger, *Taking Your Business Global* (Franklin Lakes, N.J.: Career Press, 1997), 277–278.

20. Harris and Moran, *Managing Cultural Differences,* 260.

21. Skip Kaltenheuser, "Bribery Is Being Outlawed Virtually Worldwide," *Business Ethics,* May–June 1998, 11; Thomas Omestad, "Bye-bye to Bribes," *U.S. News & World Report,* 22 December 1997, 39, 42–44.

22. Kaltenheuser, "Bribery Is Being Outlawed Virtually Worldwide"; Omestad, "Bye-bye to Bribes."

23. Guo-Ming Chen and William J. Starosta, *Foundations of Intercultural Communication* (Boston: Allyn & Bacon, 1998), 288–289.

24. Sharon Ruhly, *Intercultural Communication,* 2d ed., MODCOM (Modules in Speech Communication) (Chicago: Science Research Associates, 1982), 14.

25. Robert O. Joy, "Cultural and Procedural Differences That Influence Business Strategies and Operations in the People's Republic of China," *SAM Advanced Management Journal,* Summer 1989, 29–33.

26. Chaney and Martin, *Intercultural Business Communication,* 122–123.

27. Chaney and Martin, *Intercultural Business Communication,* 110–111.

28. Laray M. Barna, "Stumbling Blocks in Intercultural Communication," in *Intercultural Communication,* edited by Samovar and Porter, 345–352; Jean A. Mausehund, Susan A. Timm, and Albert S. King, "Diversity Training: Effects of an Intervention Treatment on Nonverbal Awareness," *Business Communication Quarterly* 38, no. 1 (1995): 27–30.

29. Chaney and Martin, *Intercultural Business Communication,* 9.

30. Chen and Starosta, *Foundations of Intercultural Communication,* 39–40.

31. Richard W. Brislin, "Prejudice in Intercultural Communication," in *Intercultural Communication,* edited by Samovar and Porter, 366–370.

32. Chaney and Martin, *Intercultural Business Communication,* 130.

33. Stephen Dolainski, "Are Expats Getting Lost in the Translation?" *Workforce,* February 1997, 32–39.

34. "Less Yiddish, More Tagalog," *U.S. News & World Report,* 10 May 1993, 16; Gary Levin, "Marketers Learning New Languages for Ads," *Advertising Age,* 10 May 1993, 33.

35. Doreen Mangan, "What's New in Language Translation: A Tool for Examining Foreign Patents and Research," *New York Times,* 19 November 1989, sec. 3, 15.

36. Wilfong and Seger, *Taking Your Business Global,* 232.

37. Vern Terpstra, *The Cultural Environment of International Business* (Cincinnati: South-Western, 1979), 19.

38. David A. Victor, *International Business Communication* (New York: HarperCollins, 1992), 36.

39. James S. O'Rourke IV, "International Business Communication: Building a Course from the Ground Up," *Bulletin of the Association for Business Communication* 56, no. 4 (1993): 22–27.

40. Jensen J. Zhao and Calvin Parks, "Self-Assessment of Communication Behavior: An Experiential Learning Exercise for Intercultural Business Success," *Business Communication Quarterly* 58, no. 1 (1995): 20–26; Dodd, *Dynamics of Intercultural Communication,* 142–143, 297–299; Stephen P. Robbins, *Organizational Behavior,* 6th ed. (Paramus, N.J.: Prentice Hall, 1993), 345.

41. Mona Casady and Lynn Wasson, "Written Communication Skills of International Business Persons," *Bulletin of the Association for Business Communication* 57, no. 4 (1994): 36–40.

42. See note 1.

43. Michael Copeland, specialist, international training, personal communication, January 1990.

Chapter 4

1. Adapted from Home Depot's Web site [accessed 8 March 2000] www.homedepot.com; Bernie Marcus and Arthur Blank with Bob Andelman, *Built from Scratch* (New York: Random House, 1999), 105, 110, 125, 135–137, 142, 149, 155–161, 178, 205, 216, 240–241, 255–258, 280, 287–289, 313; Carlton P. McNamara, "Making Human Capital More Productive," *Business and Economic Review,* October–December 1999, 10–13; Sarah Rose, "Building a Powerhouse," *Money,* December 1999, 62–64; Chris Roush, *Inside Home Depot* (New York: McGraw-Hill, 1999), 5–6, 12, 29, 31–35; 89, 101–108, 115, 141, 213–215, 221; Robert S. Salomon, Jr., "Reinventing Retail," *Forbes,* 19 October 1998, 171; and Bruce Upin, "Profit in a Big Orange Box," *Forbes,* 24 January 2000, 122–127.

2. Sanford Kaye, "Writing Under Pressure," *Soundview Executive Book Summaries* 10, no. 12, part 2 (December 1988): 1–8.

3. Peter Bracher, "Process, Pedagogy, and Business Writing," *Journal of Business Communication* 24, no. 1 (Winter 1987): 43–50.

4. Mahalingham Subbiah, "Adding a New Dimension to the Teaching of Audience Analysis: Cultural Awareness," *IEEE Transactions on Professional Communication* 35, no. 1 (March 1992): 14–19; Ronald E. Dulek, John S. Fielden, and John S. Hill, "International Communication: An Executive Primer," *Business Horizons,* January–February 1991, 20–25; Dwight W. Stevenson, "Audience Analysis Across Cultures," *Journal of Technical Writing and Communication* 13, no. 4 (1983): 319–330.

5. Iris I. Varner, "Internationalizing Business Communication Courses," *Bulletin of the Association for Business Communication* 50, no.4 (December 1987): 7–11.

6. Laurey Berk and Phillip G. Clampitt, "Finding the Right Path in the Communication Maze," *IABC Communication World,* October 1991, 28–32.

7. Berk and Clampitt, "Finding the Right Path in the Communication Maze."

8. Berk and Clampitt, "Finding the Right Path in the Communication Maze."

9. Raymond M. Olderman, *10 Minute Guide to Business Communication* (New York: Alpha Books, 1997), 19–20.

10. Mohan R. Limaye and David A. Victor, "Cross-Cultural Business Communication Research: State of the Art and Hypotheses for the 1990s," *Journal of Business Communication* 28, no. 3 (Summer 1991): 277–299.

11. Berk and Clampitt, "Finding the Right Path in the Communication Maze."

12. Berk and Clampitt, "Finding the Right Path in the Communication Maze."

13. Mike Bransby, "Voice Mail Makes a Difference," *Journal of Business Strategy,* January–February 1990, 7–10.

14. Tim McCollum, "The Net Result of Computer Links," *Nation's Business,* March 1998, 55–58.

15. Elizabeth Blackburn and Kelly Belanger, "You-Attitude and Positive Emphasis: Testing Received Wisdom in Business Communication," *Bulletin of the Association for Business Communication* 56, no. 2 (June 1993): 1–9.

16. Annette N. Shelby and N. Lamar Reinsch, Jr., "Positive Emphasis and You Attitude: An Empirical Study," *Journal of Business Communication* 32, no. 4 (1995): 303–322.

17. Judy E. Pickens, "Terms of Equality: A Guide to Bias-Free Language," *Personnel Journal,* August 1985, 24.

18. Lisa Taylor, "Communicating About People with Disabilities: Does the Language We Use Make a Difference?" *Bulletin of the Association for Business Communication* 53, no. 3 (September 1990): 65–67.

19. See note 1.

Chapter 5

1. Adapted from U.S. Mint's Web site [accessed 14 April 2000] www.usmint.gov; Christy Harris, "Government Improves Its Image," *Federal Times,* 10 May 1999, S3–5; Bill Landauer, "U.S. Mint Is Awash in Flood of Online Coin Sales," *Federal Times,* 27 September 1999, 8; "Mint Chief Has Golden Day as Dollar Coins Gain Favor," *American Banker,* 28 February 2000, 2–4; Anna Muoio, "Mint Condition," *Fast Company,* December 1999, 330–338, 342–348.

2. Carol S. Mull, "Orchestrate Your Ideas," *The Toastmaster,* February 1987, 19.

3. Susan Hall and Theresa Tiggeman, "Getting the Big Picture: Writing to Learn in a Finance Class," *Business Communication Quarterly* 58, no. 1 (1995): 12–15.

4. Bruce B. MacMillan, "How to Write to Top Management," *Business Marketing,* March 1985, 138.

5. Ernest Thompson, "Some Effects of Message Structure on Listener's Comprehension," *Speech Monographs* 34 (March 1967): 51–57.

6. Based on the Pyramid Model developed by Barbara Minto of McKinsey & Company, management consultants.

7. Philip Subanks, "Messages, Models, and the Messy World of Memos," *Bulletin of the Association for Business Communication* 57, no. 1 (1994): 33–34.

8. Mary A. DeVries, *Internationally Yours* (Boston: Houghton Mifflin, 1994), 61.

9. Randolph H. Hudson, Gertrude M. McGuire, and Bernard J. Selzler, *Business Writing: Concepts and Applications* (Los Angeles: Roxbury, 1983), 79–82.

10. William M. Bulkeley, "Software Writers Try to Speak a Language Users Understand," *Wall Street Journal,* 30 June 1992, B6.

11. Peter Crow, "Plain English: What Counts Besides Readability?" *Journal of Business Communication* 25, no. 1 (Winter 1988): 87–95.

12. Portions of this section are adapted from Courtland L. Bovée, *Techniques of Writing Business Letters, Memos, and Reports* (Sherman Oaks, Calif.: Banner Books International, 1978), 13–90.

13. Robert Hartwell Fiske, *Thesaurus of Alternatives to Worn-Out Words and Phrases* (Cincinnati: Writer's Digest Books, 1994), 171.

14. Iris I. Varner, "Internationalizing Business Communication Courses," *Bulletin of the Association for Business Communication* 50, no. 4 (December 1987): 7–11.

15. Alinda Drury, "Evaluating Readability," *IEEE Transactions on Professional Communication* PC-28 (December 1985): 12.

16. DeVries, *Internationally Yours,* 168; Susan Benjamin, *Words at Work* (Reading, Mass.: Addison-Wesley, 1997), 61, 140–141.

17. William Zinsser, *On Writing Well,* 5th ed. (New York: HarperCollins, 1994), 117.

18. Jill H. Ellsworth and Matthew V. Ellsworth, *The Internet Business Book* (New York: Wiley, 1994), 91.

19. Lance Cohen, "How to Improve Your E-Mail Messages," galaxy.einet/galaxy/Business-and-Commerce/Management/Communications/How_to_Improve_Your Email.html.

20. Angell and Heslop, *The Elements of E-Mail Style,* 24.

21. Angell and Heslop, *The Elements of E-Mail Style,* 18–19.

22. Renee B. Horowitz and Marian G. Barchilon, "Stylistic Guidelines for E-mail," *IEEE Transactions on Professional Communication* 37, no. 4 (December 1994): 207–212; Cohen, "How to Improve Your E-Mail Messages."

23. Most of the material in this section is adapted from Angell and Heslop, *The Elements of E-Mail Style,* 21, 30, 117; Ellsworth and Ellsworth, The Internet Business Book, 99; William Eager, Using

the Internet (Indianapolis: Que Corporation, 1994), 99; Cohen, "How to Improve Your E-Mail Messages"; William Eager, Larry Donahue, David Forsyth, Kenneth Mitton, and Martin Waterhouse, Net.Search (Indianapolis: Que Corporation, 1995), 225.

24. Angell and Heslop, *The Elements of E-Mail Style,* 20.

25. Horowitz and Barchilon, "Stylistic Guidelines for E-Mail"; Angell and Heslop, *The Elements of E-Mail Style,* 22.

26. Jack Powers, "Writing for the Web, Part I," Electric Pages [accessed 28 June 2000] www.electric-pages.com/articles/wftw1.htm.

27. Kaye Vivian, "Writing for Webs" [accessed 28 June 2000, updated 4 January 1999] www.users.cloud9.net/~kvivian/html/web_readers.html.

28. Jakob Nielson, "Be Succinct! (Writing for the Web)," Alterbox [accessed 28 June 2000] www.useit.com/alertbox/9703b.html.

29. See note 1.

30. Milton Moskowitz, Michael Katz, and Robert Levering, eds., *Everybody's Business: An Almanac* (San Francisco: Harper & Row, 1980), 131.

31. Randolph H. Hudson, Gertrude M. McGuire, and Bernard J. Selzler, *Business Writing: Concepts and Applications* (Los Angeles: Roxbury, 1983), 27.

32. Benjamin, Words at Work, 121.

Chapter 6

1. Adapted from Brian Bremmer, "The Burger Wars Were Just a Warmup for McDonald's," *Business Week,* 8 May 1989, 67, 70; Richard Gibson and Robert Johnson, "Big Mac Plots Strategy to Regain Sizzle; Besides Pizza, It Ponders Music and Low Lights," *Wall Street Journal,* 29 September 1989, B1; Dyan Machan, "Great Hash Browns, but Watch Those Biscuits," *Forbes,* 19 September 1988, 192–196; Penny Moser, "The McDonald's Mystique," *Fortune,* 4 July 1988, 112–116; Thomas N. Cochran "McDonald's Corporation," *Barron's,* 16 November 1987, 53–55; Lenore Skenazy, "McDonald's Colors Its World," *Advertising Age,* 9 February 1987, 37.

2. Iris I. Varner, "Internationalizing Business Communication Courses," *Bulletin of the Association for Business Communication* 50, no. 4 (December 1987): 7–11.

3. Kevin T. Stevens, Kathleen C. Stevens, and William P. Stevens, "Measuring the Readability of Business Writing: The Cloze Procedure versus Readability Formulas," *Journal of Business Communication* 29, no. 4 (1992): 367–382; Alinda Drury, "Evaluating Readability," *IEEE Transactions on Professional Communication* PC-28 (December 1985): 11.

4. Susan Benjamin, *Words at Work* (Reading, Mass.: Addison-Wesley, 1997), 71.

5. William Zinsser, *On Writing Well,* 5th ed. (New York: HarperCollins, 1994), 126.

6. "Message Lost in Some Memos," *USA Today,* 25 March 1987, 1A.

7. Zinsser, *On Writing Well,* 7, 17.

8. Mary A. DeVries, *Internationally Yours* (Boston: Houghton Mifflin, 1994), 160.

9. Zinsser, *On Writing Well,* vii–12.

10. Zinsser, *On Writing Well,* 9.

11. Joel Haness, "How to Critique a Document," *IEEE Transactions on Professional Communication* PC-26, no. 1 (March 1983): 15–17.

12. Charles E. Risch, "Critiquing Written Material," *Manage* 35, no. 4 (1983): 4–6.

13. Risch, "Critiquing Written Material."

14. Portions of the following sections are adapted from Roger C. Parker, *Looking Good in Print,* 2d ed. (Chapel Hill, N.C.: Ventana Press, 1990).

15. Raymond W. Beswick, "Designing Documents for Legibility," *Bulletin of the Association for Business Communication* 50, no. 4 (December 1987): 34–35.

16. Patsy Nichols, "Desktop Packaging," *Bulletin of the Association for Business Communication* 54, no. 1 (March 1991): 43–45; Beswick, "Designing Documents for Legibility."

17. Beswick, "Designing Documents for Legibility."

18. "The Process Model of Document Design," *IEEE Transactions on Professional Communication* PC-24, no. 4 (December 1981): 176–178.

19. William Wresch, Donald Pattow, and James Gifford, *Writing for the Twenty-First Century: Computers and Research Writing* (New York: McGraw-Hill, 1988), 192–211; Melissa E. Barth, *Strategies for Writing with the Computer* (New York: McGraw-Hill, 1988), 108–109, 140, 172–177.

20. Eric J. Adams, "The Fax of Global Business," *World Trade,* August–September 1991, 34–39.

21. "A Misspelling Proves Costly," *New York Times,* 23 November 1991, 29.

22. See note 1.

Chapter 7

1. Adapted from Campbell Soup Web site, [accessed 13 October 1997], www.campbellsoup.com; "Campbell Soup Company," Hoover's Online [accessed 23 January 1997] www.hoovers.com; 1993 Campbell Soup Annual Report; Joseph Weber, "Campbell: Now It's M-M-Global," *Business Week,* 15 March 1993, 52–54; Pete Engardio, "Hmm. Could Use A Little More Snake," *Business Week,* 15 March 1993, 53; Joseph Weber, "Campbell Is Bubbling, But for How Long?" *Business Week,* 17 June 1991, 56–57; Joseph Weber, "From Soup to Nuts and Back to Soup," *Business Week,* 5 November 1990, 114, 116; Alix Freedman and Frank Allen, "John Dorrance's Death Leaves Campbell Soup with Cloudy Future," *Wall Street Journal,* 19 April 1989, A1, A14; Claudia H. Deutsch, "Stirring up Profits at Campbell," *New York Times,* 20 November 1988, sec. 3, 1, 22; Bill Saporito, "The Fly in Campbell's Soup," *Fortune,* 9 May 1988, 67–70.

2. Courtland L. Bovée and John V. Thill, *Business Communication Today,* 6th ed. (Upper Saddle River, N.J.: Prentice Hall, 2000), 202.

3. Daniel P. Finkelman and Anthony R. Goland, "Customers Once Can Be Customers for Life," *Information Strategy: The Executive's Journal,* Summer 1990, 5–9.

4. Susan Stobaugh, "Watch Your Language," *Inc.,* May 1985, 156.

5. *Techniques for Communicators* (Chicago: Lawrence Ragan Communication, 1995), 34, 36.

6. John A. Byrne, "Jack," *Business Week,* 8 June 1998, 91–112.

7. Donna Larcen, "Authors Share the Words of Condolence," *Los Angeles Times,* December 20, 1991, E11.

8. See note 1.

9. Adapted from Robirda's A Place for Canaries Web site [accessed 21 August 2000] www.robirda.com; Herman Brothers Pet Products Web site [accessed 21 August 2000] www.ddc.com/hermanbros.

10. Eben Shapiro, "Blockbuster Rescue Bid Stars Viacom Top Guns," *Wall Street Journal,* 7 May 1997, B1, B10.

11. *Red Herring News* 13, no. 2 [accessed 3 September 1998] www.RedHerringProductions.com.

12. Adapted from Bruce Frankel and Alex Tresniowski, "Stormy Skies," *People Weekly,* 31 July 2000, 112–115.

13. Adapted from George Anders, "Voyage to the New Economy," *Fast Company,* 36, 142 [accessed 11 July 2000] wysiwyg://22/http://fastcompany.com/online/36/stopinsanity.html; Anna

Muoio, "Should I Go.Com?" *Fast Company*, 36, 164 [accessed 11 July 2000]wysiwyg://46/http://www.fastcompany.com/online/36/stein.html.

14. "Entrepreneurs across America," *Entrepreneur Magazine Online* [accessed 12 June 1997] www.entrepreneurmag.com/entmag/50states5.hts.

15. Adapted from Barbara Carton, "Farmers Begin Harvesting Satellite Data to Boost Yields," *Wall Street Journal*, 11 July 1996, B4.

16. Adapted from LifeSketch.com Web site [accessed 24 July 2000] www.lifesketch.com.

17. "Entrepreneurs across America," *Entrepreneur Magazine Online* [accessed 12 June 1997] www.entrepreneurmag.com/entmag/50states5.hts#top.

18. Sal D. Rinalla and Robert J. Kopecky, "Recruitment: Burger King Hooks Employees with Educational Incentives," *Personnel Journal*, October 1989, 90–99.

19. Adapted from Bernard Weinraub, "New Harry Potter Book Becoming a Publishing Phenomenon," *New York Times*, 3 July 2000 [accessed on 12 July 2000] www.nytimes.com/library/books/070300potter-parties.html; Laura Miller, "Pottermania at Midnight," *Salon.com*, 8 July 2000 [accessed 12 July 2000] http://www.salon.com/books/features/2000/07/08/potter/; David D. Kirkpatrick, "Harry Potter Magic Halts Bedtime for Youngsters," *New York Times*, 9 July 2000 [accessed 12 July 2000] www.nytimes.com/library/books/070900potter-goblet.html; David D. Kirkpatrick, "Vanishing Off the Shelves," *New York Times*, 10 July 2000 [accessed 10 July 2000] http://www.nytimes.com/library/books/071000rowling-goblet.html.

20. Adapted from Keith H. Hammonds, "Difference Is Power," *Fast Company*, 36, 258 [accessed 11 July 2000] wysiwyg://19/http://www.fastcompany.com/online/36/power.html; Terri Morrison, Wayne A. Conaway, George A. Borden, Ph.D., *Kiss, Bow, or Shake Hands* (Holbrook, Mass.: Adams Media Corporation, April 1995).

Chapter 8

1. "Purchasing: Professional Profile, American Airlines," *Purchasing*, 17 October 1996, 32; "AMR Corporation," *Hoover's Online*, [accessed 22 January 1997] www.hoovers.com; Carole A. Shifrin, "American Commits to All-Boeing Jet Fleet," *Aviation Week & Space Technology*, 25 November 1996, 34.

2. Mark H. McCormack, *On Communicating* (Los Angeles: Dove Books, 1998), 87.

3. James Calvert Scott and Diana J. Green, "British Perspectives on Organizing Bad-News Letters: Organizational Patterns Used by Major U.K. Companies," *Bulletin of the Association for Business Communication* 55, no. 1 (March 1992): 17–19.

4. Ram Subramanian, Robert G. Insley, and Rodney D. Blackwell, "Performance and Readability: A Comparison of Annual Reports of Profitable and Unprofitable Corporations," *Journal of Business Communication* 30, no. 2 (1993): 49–61.

5. *Techniques for Communicators* (Chicago: Lawrence Ragan Communication, 1995), 18.

6. Maura Dolan and Stuart Silverstein, "Court Broadens Liability for Job References," *Los Angeles Times*, 28 January 1997, A1, A11; Frances A. McMorris, "Ex-Bosses Face Less Peril Giving Honest Job References," *Wall Street Journal*, 8 July 1996, B1, B8.

7. Thomas S. Brice and Marie Waung, "Applicant Rejection Letters: Are Businesses Sending the Wrong Message?" *Business Horizons*, March–April 1995, 59–62.

8. Gwendolyn N. Smith, Rebecca F. Nolan, and Yong Dai, "Job-Refusal Letters: Readers' Affective Responses to Direct and Indirect

Organizational Plans," *Business Communication Quarterly* 59, no. 1 (1996): 67–73; Brice and Waung, "Applicant Rejection Letters."

9. Judi Brownell, "The Performance Appraisal Interviews: A Multipurpose Communication Assignment," *Bulletin of the Association for Business Communication* 57, no. 2 (1994): 11–21.

10. Brownell, "The Performance Appraisal Interviews."

11. Stephanie Gruner, "Feedback from Everyone," *Inc.*, February 1997, 102–103.

12. Howard M. Bloom, "Performance Evaluations," *New England Business,* December 1991, 14.

13. David I. Rosen, "Appraisals Can Make–or Break–Your Court Case," *Personnel Journal*, November 1992, 113.

14. Patricia A. McLagan, "Advice for Bad-News Bearers: How to Tell Employees They're Not Hacking It and Get Results," *Industry Week*, 15 February 1993, 42; Michael Lee Smith, "Give Feedback, Not Criticism," *Supervisory Management*, 1993, 4; "A Checklist for Conducting Problem Performer Appraisals," *Supervisory Management,* December 1993, 7–9.

15. Jane R. Goodson, Gail W. McGee, and Anson Seers, "Giving Appropriate Performance Feedback to Managers: An Empirical Test of Content and Outcomes," *Journal of Business Communication* 29, no. 4 (1992): 329–342.

16. Craig Cox, "On the Firing Line," *Business Ethics*, May–June 1992, 33–34.

17. Cox, "On the Firing Line."

18. See note 1.

19. "Swimmer Invents Pool Tool," *The Coast News*, 13 August 1998, A-15.

20. Adapted from Craftopia.com print advertisement, 31 July 2000; Craftopia.com Web site [accessed 24 August 2000] www.craftopia.com/shop/promo/martha3.asp; Claire Furia Smith, "West Chester Start-up Tries to Become a Crafters' Utopia," *Philadelphia Inquirer*, 26 June 2000 [accessed 24 August 2000] www.craftopia.com/shop/features/about_us_mc_6_26_00_inquirer.asp; Laura M. Naughton, "Crafting a Niche," *Daily Local News*, 8 March 2000 [accessed 24 August 2000] www.craftopia.com/shop/features/about_us_mc_3_8_00_dailylocal.asp.

21. Adapted from Wolf Blitzer, "More Employers Taking Advantage of New Cyber-Surveillance Software," *CNN.com*, 10 July 2000 [accessed 11 July 2000] www.cnn.com/2000/US/07/10/workplace.eprivacy/index.html .

22. Adapted from Dan McSwain, "Consumers Could Owe $1.4B for Cuts," *North County Times*, 20 August 2000, A1; R. J. Ignelzi, "Now, Bill Can Be Clearer than Mud/But that Won't Ease Baseline Frustration," *San Diego Union-Tribune*, 15 August 2000, E-1 [accessed 29 August 2000] www.uniontrib.com/news/utarchives/cgi/idoc.cgi?589762+unix++www.uniontrib.com..80+Union-Tribune+Union-Tribune+Library+Library++%28sdge%29; Craig D. Rose, "Power Industry Politics: Ominous signs point to higher electricity bills," *San Diego Union-Tribune*, 22 July 2000, A-1 [accessed 29 August 2000] www.uniontrib.com/news/utarchives/cgi/idoc.cgi?585891+unix++www.uniontrib.com..80+Union-Tribune+Union-Tribune+Library+Library++%28sdge%29.

23. Associated Press, "Is the Boss Watching? Surveillance Common at Work," *CNN Interactive*, cnn.com/US/9705/23/watching.workers.ap/index/html, [accessed 30 May 1997].

24. Michelle Higgins, "The Ballet Shoe Gets a Makeover, But Few Yet See the Pointe," *Wall Street Journal*, 8 August 1998, A1, A6.

25. Pascal Zachary, "Sun Microsystems Apologizes in Letter for Late Payments," *Wall Street Journal*, 11 October 1989, B4.

26. Peter Fritsch, "It's Lighter Than Glass and Hurts Less When Thrown, But Can Plastic Stack Up?" *Wall Street Journal,* 24 July 1996, B1.

27. Adapted from Ty Holland, "Vision Quest," *TV Guide,* 22 July 2000, 3.

28. "Entrepreneurs across America," *Entrepreneur Magazine Online,* www.enterpreneurmag.com/entmag/50states2.hts, [accessed 25 June 1997].

29. Patti Bond, "Hispanics Display Growing Muscle in Entrepreneurship," *Atlanta Journal-Constitution,* 11 July 1996, B1.

Chapter 9

1. Adapted from Andrea Adelson, "Wedded to Its Moral Imperatives: Patagonia Weaves Sales and Advocacy," *New York Times,* 17 May 1999, 9; Jim Collins, "The Foundation for Doing Good," *Inc.,* December 1997, 41–42; Stan Friedman, "Apparel with Conscience: The Givers," *Apparel Industry Magazine,* June 1999, 78–79; Paul C. Judge, "It's Not Easy Being Green," *Business Week,* 24 November 1997, 180; Jacquelyn Ottman, "Proven Environmental Commitment Helps Create Committed Customers," *Marketing News,* 2 February 1998, 5–6; Roger Rosenblatt, "The Root of All Good: Reaching the Top by Doing the Right Thing," *Time,* 18 October 1999, 88–91; John Steinbreder, "Yvon Chouinard, founder and owner of the Patagonia Outdoor. . .," *Sports Illustrated,* 11 February 1991, 200.

2. Jay A. Conger, "The Necessary Art of Persuasion," *Harvard Business Review,* May–June 1998, 84–95; Jeanette W. Gilsdorf, "Write Me Your Best Case for . . ." *Bulletin of the Association for Business Communication* 54, no. 1 (March 1991): 7–12.

3. Anne Fisher, "Success Secret: A High Emotional IQ," *Fortune,* 16 October 1998, 293–298.

4. Mary Cross, "Aristotle and Business Writing: Why We Need to Teach Persuasion," *Bulletin of the Association for Business Communication* 54, no. 1 (March 1991): 3–6.

5. Abraham H. Maslow, *Motivation and Personality* (New York: Harper & Row, 1954), 12, 19.

6. Robert T. Moran, "Tips on Making Speeches to International Audiences," *International Management,* April 1980, 58–59.

7. Conger, "The Necessary Art of Persuasion."

8. Gilsdorf, "Write Me Your Best Case for . . ."

9. Raymond M. Olderman, *10-Minute Guide to Business Communication* (New York: Macmillan Spectrum/Alpha Books, 1997), 57–61.

10. Gilsdorf, "Write Me Your Best Case for . . ."

11. John D. Ramage and John C. Bean, *Writing Arguments: A Rhetoric with Readings,* 3d ed. (Boston: Allyn & Bacon, 1995), 430–442.

12. Conger, "The Necessary Art of Persuasion."

13. Dianna Booher, *Communicate with Confidence* (New York: McGraw-Hill, 1994), 110.

14. Tamra B. Orr, "Persuasion without Pressure," *Toastmaster,* January 1994, 19–22; William Friend, "Winning Techniques of Great Persuaders," *Association Management,* February 1985, 82–86; Patricia Buhler, "How to Ask For—and Get—What You Want!" *Supervision,* February 1990, 11–13.

15. Booher, *Communicate with Confidence,* 102.

16. Conger, "The Necessary Art of Persuasion."

17. Robert L. Hemmings, "Think Before You Write," *Fund Raising Management,* February 1990, 23–24.

18. William North Jayme, quoted in Albert Haas Jr., "How to Sell Almost Anything by Direct Mail," *Across the Board,* November 1986, 50.

19. Teri Lammers, "The Elements of Perfect Pitch," *Inc.,* March 1992, 53–55.

20. Kimberly Paterson, "The Writing Process—Sales Letters That Work," *Rough Notes,* April 1998, 59–60.

21. Paterson, "The Writing Process."

22. Hemmings, "Think Before You Write."

23. Hemmings, "Think Before You Write."

24. Conrad Squires, "How to Write a Strong Letter, Part Two: Choosing a Theme," *Fund Raising Management,* November 1991, 65–66.

25. Conrad Squires, "Getting the Compassion out of the Box," *Fund Raising Management,* September 1992, 55, 60.

26. Squires, "Getting the Compassion out of the Box."

27. Constance L. Clark, "25 Steps to Better Direct Mail Fundraising," *Nonprofit World,* July–August 1989, 11–13; Squires, "How to Write a Strong Letter."

28. Squires, "How to Write a Strong Letter."

29. Clark, "25 Steps to Better Direct Mail Fundraising."

30. Conrad Squires, "Why Some Letters Outpull Others," *Fund Raising Management,* January 1991, 67, 72.

31. Squires, "Why Some Letters Outpull Others"; Clark, "25 Steps to Better Direct Mail Fundraising"; Jerry Huntsinger, "My First 29½ Years in Direct-Mail Fund Raising: What I've Learned," *Fund Raising Management,* January 1992, 40–43.

32. See note 1.

33. Adapted from Goosehead Teen Entertainment Network [accessed 29 August 2000] www.goosehead.com; Samantha Miller, "Home Work," *People Weekly,* 31 July 2000, 23.

34. Monty Roberts and Lawrence Scanlan, with contributor Lucy Grealy, *The Man Who Listens to Horses* (New York. Random House, 1997); www.MontyRoberts.com/farm/fiuf.html, [accessed 26 August 1998].

35. Kevin M. Savetz, "Preventive Medicine for the Computer User," *Multimedia Online* 2, no. 2 (June 1996): 58–60.

36. John Case and Jerry Useem, "Six Characters in Search of a Strategy," *Inc.,* March 1996, 46–49.

37. "US West Labor Strike Ends," CNNfn, CNN Interactive cnnfn.com:80/hotsotreis/companies/9808/31/uswest/, [accessed 31 August 1998].

38. Steve Bass, "ISDN Not; The Agony, the Ecstasy, the Migraines," *Computer Currents,* 7 May 1996, 43.

39. Adapted from advertisement, *The Atlantic Monthly,* January 2000, 119; Endless Pools, Inc. Web site [accessed 31 August 2000] www.endlesspools.com/.

40. Adapted from "Tobacco Smoke and the Nonsmoker," Americans for Nonsmokers' Rights, 1988, revised 1994; "Nuisance/Real Property" case citation and abstract, "Contract Management Services, Inc., et al. v. Kuykendahl Joint, Inc., and Kamen Management, Inc., Dist. Ct. Harris County (TX), 61st Jud. Dist., No. 93-006228 (1993)," Tobacco Control Resource Center, 1998, 39.

41. "Down These Aisles Is Matrimonial Bliss," *Los Angeles Times,* 22 March 1996, D3.

42. Adapted from Charles Fishman, "The Greener Cleaners," *Fast Company,* 36, 54 [accessed 11 July 2000] http://fastcompany.com/online/36/greenclean.html; Micell Technologies Web site [accessed 1 September 2000] www.micell. com/08142000.htm; Hangers Cleaners Web site [accessed 1 September 2000] www.hangersdrycleaners.com/about/corp/triplebottomline.htm.

43. Adapted from Quotesmith.com Web site, Investor Overview and FAQ [accessed 31 August 2000] investor.quotesmith.com/ireye/ir_site.zhtml?ticker=QUOT&script=2100.

Chapter 10

1. Adapted from Dell Computer Corporation's Web site [accessed 22 March 2000] www.dell.com; Neel Chowdhury, "Dell Cracks China," *Fortune,* 21 June 1999, 120–124; Michael Dell with Catherine Fredman, *Direct from Dell* (New York: HarperCollins Publishers, 1999), 8–15, 36–38, 66–80, 92–101, 133, 144, 175–182, 186, 196–197, 208; Louise Fickel, "Know Your Customer," *CIO,* 15 August 1999, 62–72; "Interview: E-commerce Drives Dell Computer's Success," *IT Cost Management Strategies,* June 1999, 4–6; Carla Joinson, "Moving at the Speed of Dell," *HRMagazine,* April 1999, 50–56; and Daniel Roth, "Dell's Big New Act," *Fortune,* 6 December 1999, 152–156.

2. Susan L. Leach, "SEC Takes Next Leap into Computer Age," *Christian Science Monitor,* 7 June 1994, 8.

3. Stephan Manes, "E-Mail Troubles? You Have No Idea!" *PC World,* July 1996, 39.

4. Dan Steinhoff and John F. Burgess, *Small Business Management Fundamentals,* 5th ed. (New York: McGraw-Hill, 1989), 37.

5. Joan F. Vesper and Karl H. Vesper, "Writing a Business Plan: The Total Term Assignment," *Bulletin of the Association for Business Communication* 56, no. 2 (June 1993): 29–32.

6. Tom Peters, "Don't Send Memos!" *Washington Monthly,* November 1987, 13.

7. Claudia Mon Pere McIsaac, "Improving Student Summaries through Sequencing," *Bulletin of the Association for Business Communication* (September 1987): 17–20.

8. David A. Hayes, "Helping Students GRASP the Knack of Writing Summaries," *Journal of Reading* (November 1989): 96–101.

9. Tom Sant, *Persuasive Business Proposals* (New York: American Management Association, 1992), summarized in *Soundview Executive Book Summaries* 14, no. 10, pt. 2 (October 1992), 3.

10. Iris I. Varner, *Contemporary Business Report Writing,* 2d ed. (Chicago: Dryden Press, 1991), 170.

11. Varner, *Contemporary Business Report Writing,* 178.

12. Bruce McComiskey, "Defining Institutional Problems: A Heuristic Procedure," *Business Communication Quarterly* 58, no. 4 (1995): 21–24.

13. Varner, *Contemporary Business Report Writing,* 135.

14. Information for this section was obtained from "Finding Industry Information" [accessed 3 November 1998] www.pitt.edu/~buslibry/industries.htm. Thomas P. Bergman, Stephen M. Garrison, and Gregory M. Scott, *The Business Student Writer's Manual and Guide to the Internet* (Upper Saddle River, N.J.: Prentice Hall, 1998), 67–80; Ernest L. Maier, Anthony J. Faria, Peter Kaatrude, and Elizabeth Wood, *The Business Library and How to Use It* (Detroit: Omnigraphics, 1996), 53–76; Sherwyn P. Morreale and Courtland L. Bovée, *Excellence in Public Speaking* (Fort Worth: Harcourt Brace College Publishers, 1998), 166–171.

15. "The Research Sites Fairy Godmother Report," What Color Is Your Parachute Online [accessed 10 October 1998] www.washingtonpost.com/wp~adv/classifieds/careerpost/parachute/reseajhg.htm.

16. Maier, Faria, Kaatrude, and Wood, *The Business Library and How to Use It,* 84–97; Matt Lake, "Desperately Seeking Susan OR Suzie NOT Sushi," *New York Times,* 3 September 1998, D1, D7.

17. "How to Design and Conduct a Study," *Credit Union Magazine,* October 1983, 36–46.

18. Morreale and Bovée, *Excellence in Public Speaking,* 177.

19. Morreale and Bovée, *Excellence in Public Speaking,* 178–180.

20. Morreale and Bovée, *Excellence in Public Speaking,* 182.

21. David A. Aaker and George S. Day, *Marketing Research,* 2d ed.

22. (New York: Wiley, 1983), 88–89.

23. Robert E. Cason, *Writing for the Business World* (Upper Saddle River, N.J.: Prentice Hall, 1997), 102.

24. Bergman, Garrison, and Scott, *The Business Student Writer's Manual and Guide to the Internet,* 65.

25. "How to Paraphrase Effectively: 6 Steps to Follow," Research paper.com [accessed 26 October 1998] www.researchpaper.com/writing_center/30.html.

26. Cason, *Writing for the Business World,* 71–72.

27. Dorothy Geisler, "How to Avoid Copyright Lawsuits," *IABC Communication World,* June 1984, 34–37.

28. See note 1.

Chapter 11

1. Adapted from FedEx Web site [accessed 27 October 1997] www.fedex.com; UPS Web site [accessed 27 October 1997] www.ups.com; DHL Web site [accessed 27 October 1997] www.dhl.com; Airborne Express Web site [accessed 27 October 1997] www.airborne.com; Hoover's Online [accessed 27 October 1997] www.hoovers.com; "All Strung Up," *The Economist,* 17 April 1993, 70; Gary M. Stern, "Improving Verbal Communications," *Internal Auditor,* August 1993, 49–54; Gary Hoover, Alta Campbell, and Patrick J. Spain, *Hoover's Handbook of American Business 1994* (Austin, Tex.: Reference Press, 1993), 488–489; "Pass the Parcel," *The Economist,* 21 March 1992, 73–74; "Federal Express," *Personnel Journal,* January 1992, 52.

2. This section is based on John V. Thill and Courtland L. Bovée, *Excellence in Business Communication,* 4th ed. (Upper Saddle River, N.J.: Prentice Hall, 1999), 314.

3. Sheri Rosen, "What Is Truth?" *IABC Communication World,* March 1995, 40.

4. Edward R. Tufte, *The Visual Display of Quantitative Information* (Cheshire, Conn.: Graphic Press, 1983), 113.

5. Courtland L. Bovée, Michael J. Houston, and John V. Thill, *Marketing,* 2d ed. (New York: McGraw-Hill, 1995), 250.

6. Eleanor Rizzo, "Document Design Basics," *Technical Communication,* Fourth Quarter 1992, 645.

7. A. S. C. Ehrenberg, "Report Writing—Six Simple Rules for Better Business Documents," *Admap,* June 1992, 39–42.

8. See note 1.

9. *Advertising Age,* 29 September 1997, S63.

10. Adapted from Bob Smith, "The Evolution of Pinkerton," *Management Review,* September 1993, 54–58.

Chapter 12

1. "Responsible Commercial Success," "A Unique Company Culture at Levi Strauss & Co.," "Levi Strauss & Co. Global Sourcing & Operating Guidelines," and "Levi Strauss & Co. General Information," Levi Strauss and Company Web site [accessed 29 September 1997] www.levistrauss.com; " Charlene Marmer Solomon, "Put Your Ethics to the Test," *Personnel Journal* 75, no. 1 (January 1996): 66–74; Russell Mitchell and Michael Oneal, "Managing by Values," *BusinessWeek,* 1 August 1994, 46–52.

2. Oswald M. T. Ratteray, "Hit the Mark with Better Summaries," *Supervisory Management,* September 1989, 43–45.

3. See note 1.

4. Gina Fraone, "China's Challenge," *Electronic Business* 24, no. 12 (1998): 24, downloaded from ABI/INFORM database, 1 December 1998; Trish Saywell, "Preparing for Take-Off," *Far Eastern Economic Review* 161, no. 48 (1998): 38, downloaded from ABI/INFORM database, 1 December 1998; Colin Bates, "The Many China Markets," *China Business Review* 25, no. 5 (1998):

26–29, downloaded from ABI/INFORM database, 1 December 1998; U.S. Department of Commerce, *Big Emerging Markets Information Resource Page,* 28 August 1998, [accessed 1 December 1998] www.ita.doc.gov/bems/index.html; Trish Saywell, "Curious in China," *Far Eastern Economic Review* 161, no. 28 (1998): 74–76, downloaded from ABI/INFORM database, 1 December 1998; Catherine Gelb, "Installing a Software Sector," *China Business Review* 24, no. 5 (1997): 28–36, downloaded from ABI/INFORM database, 1 December 1998; Geng Cui, "The Different Faces of the Chinese Consumer," *China Business Review* 24, no. 4 (1997): 34–38, downloaded from ABI/INFORM database 1 December 1998.

Chapter 13

1. Adapted from Trudy Gallant-Stokes, "Brady Keys Does Franchising Right," *Black Enterprise,* September 1988, 56–62; Cynthia Legette, "The New Entrepreneur: Nobody Does It Better," *Black Enterprise* 19 (December 1988): 56–60; Bill Carlino, "Keys Opens Doors for Minorities," *Nation's Restaurant News* 22 (10 October 1988): 1; Marsha Westbrook, "Burger King Honors a Pioneering Food Franchisee," *Black Enterprise* 18 (February 1988): 40.
2. Edward P. Bailey, *Writing and Speaking at Work* (Paramus, N.J.: Prentice Hall, 1999), 124.
3. Sherwyn P. Morreale and Courtland L. Bovée, *Excellence in Public Speaking* (Fort Worth: Harcourt Brace, 1998), 309.
4. "Choose and Use Your Words Deliberately," *Soundview Executive Book Summaries,* 20, no. 6, pt. 2 (June 1998): 3.
5. Sherron B. Kenton, "Speaker Credibility in Persuasive Business Communication: A Model Which Explains Gender Differences," *Journal of Business Communication* 26, no. 2 (Spring 1989): 143–157.
6. Walter Kiechel III, "How to Give a Speech," *Fortune,* 8 June 1987, 180.
7. *Communication and Leadership Program* (Santa Ana, Calif.: Toastmasters International, 1980), 44, 45.
8. The staff of *Presentation Products Magazine,* "Better Presentations for a Better Bottom Line," *Fortune,* 9 October 1989, 24–25.
9. Kathleen K. Weigner, "Visual Persuasion," *Forbes,* 16 September 1991, 176; Kathleen K. Weigner, "Showtime!" *Forbes,* 13 May 1991, 118.
10. Kevin Daley, "Presentation Skills: How to Be Focused, Forceful, Passionate and Persuasive," *Information Executive,* September 1998, 7+.
11. Morreale and Bovée, *Excellence in Public Speaking,* 24–25.
12. Judy Linscott, "Getting On and Off the Podium," *Savvy,* October 1985, 44.
13. Iris R. Johnson, "Before You Approach the Podium," *MW,* January–February 1989, 7.
14. Bailey, *Writing & Speaking at Work,* 162.
15. Pauline Gravier, "How to Speak So People Will Listen," *Planning,* December 1992, 15+.
16. Patrick J. Collins, *Say It with Power and Confidence* (Upper Saddle River, N.J.: Prentice Hall, 1997), 122–124.
17. Collins, *Say It with Power and Confidence,* 122–124.
18. Sandra Moyer, "Braving No Woman's Land," *The Toastmaster,* August 1986, 13.
19. "Control the Question-and-Answer Session," *Soundview Executive Book Summaries* 20, no. 6, pt. 2 (June 1998): 4.
20. "Control the Question-and-Answer Session."
21. Teresa Brady, "Fielding Abrasive Questions During Presentations," *Supervisory Management,* February 1993, 6.
22. Robert L. Montgomery, "Listening on Your Feet," *The Toastmaster,* July 1987, 14–15.
23. Adapted from Ronald L. Applebaum and Karl W. E. Anatol, *Effective Oral Communication: For Business and the Professions* (Chicago: Science Research Associates, 1982), 240–244.
24. See note 1.

Chapter 14

1. Adapted from U.S. Securities and Exchange Commission EDGAR data-base, [accessed 7 November 1997] www.sec.gov/Archives/edgar/data/78666/0000898430-97-001002.txt; Pinkerton Web site [accessed 7 November 1997] www.pinkertons.com; Seth Lubove, "High-Tech Cobs," *Forbes,* 25 September 1995, 44–45; Hoover's Online [accessed 23 January 1997] www.hoovers.com; Bob Smith, "The Evolution of Pinkerton," *Management Review,* September 1993, 54–58; Bob Smith, "Pinkerton Keeps Its Eye on Recruitment," *HR Focus,* 6 September 1993, 1, 6; "Oscar's News," *Security Management,* 14 June 1993, 14; Pinkerton 1993 Annual Report.
2. Amanda Bennett, "GE Redesigns Rungs of Career Ladder," *Wall Street Journal,* 15 March 1993, B1, B3.
3. Robin White Goode, "International and Foreign Language Skills Have an Edge," *Black Enterprise,* May 1995, 53.
4. Nancy M. Somerick, "Managing a Communication Internship Program," *Bulletin of the Association for Business Communication* 56, no. 3 (1993): 10–20.
5. Cheryl L. Noll, "Collaborating with the Career Planning and Placement Center in the Job-Search Project," *Business Communication Quarterly* 58, no. 3 (1995): 53–55.
6. Rockport Institute, "How to Write a Masterpiece of a Résumé" [accessed 16 October 1998] www.rockportinstitute.com/résumés.html.
7. Robert J. Gerberg, *Robert Gerberg's Job Changing System,* summarized by Macmillan Book Clubs, Inc., in the "Macmillan Executive Summary Program," April 1987, 4.
8. Christoper Caggiano, "Recruiting Secrets," *Inc.,* October 1998, 29–42; Donna Fenn, "The Right Fit," *Inc. 500,* 1997, 104+.
9. Caggiano, "Recruiting Secrets," 29–42.
10. Caggiano, "Recruiting Secrets," 29–42.
11. Sal Divita, "If You're Thinking Résumé, Think Creatively," *Marketing News,* 14 September 1992, 29.
12. Pam Stanley-Weigand, "Organizing the Writing of Your Resume," *Bulletin of the Association for Business Communication* 54, no. 3 (September 1991): 11–12.
13. Richard H. Beatty and Nicholas C. Burkholder, *The Executive Career Guide for MBAs* (New York: Wiley, 1996), 133.
14. Adapted from Burdette E. Bostwick, *How to Find the Job You've Always Wanted* (New York: Wiley, 1982), 69–70.
15. Beatty and Burkholder, *The Executive Career Guide for MBAs,* 151.
16. Rockport Institute, "How to Write a Masterpiece of a Résumé."
17. Rockport Institute, "How to Write a Masterpiece of a Résumé."
18. Rockport Institute, "How to Write a Masterpiece of a Résumé."
19. Beverly Culwell-Block and Jean Anna Sellers, "Résumé Content and Format—Do the Authorities Agree?" *Bulletin of the Association for Business Communication* 57, no. 4 (1994): 27–30.
20. Janice Tovey, "Using Visual Theory in the Creation of Résumés: A Bibliography," *Bulletin of the Association for Business Communication* 54, no. 3 (September 1991): 97–99.
21. Regina Pontow, "Electronic Résumé Writing Tips" [accessed 18 October 1998] www.provenresumes.com/reswkshps/electronic/scnres.html.

22. Ellen Joe Pollock, "Sir: Your Application for a Job Is Rejected; Sincerely, Hal 9000," *Wall Street Journal,* 30 July 1998, A1, A12.

23. William H. Baker, Kristen DeTienne, and Karl L. Smart, "How Fortune 500 Companies Are Using Electronic Résumé Management Systems," *Business Communication Quarterly* 61, no. 3, September 1998, 8–19.

24. Bronwyn Fryer, "Job Hunting the Electronic Way," *Working Woman,* March 1995, 59–60, 78; Joyce Lane Kennedy and Thomas J. Morrow, *Electronic Resume Revolution,* 2d ed. (New York: Wiley, 1995), 30–33; Mary Goodwin, Deborah Cohn, and Donna Spivey, *Netjobs: Use the Internet to Land Your Dream Job* (New York: Michael Wolff, 1996), 149–150; Zane K. Quible, "Electronic Résumés: Their Time Is Coming," *Business Communication Quarterly* 58, no. 3 (1995): 5–9; Alfred Glossbrenner and Emily Glossbrenner, *Finding a Job on the Internet* (New York: McGraw-Hill, 1995), 194–197; Pam Dixon and Silvia Tiersten, *Be Your Own Headhunter Online* (New York: Random House, 1995), 80–83.

25. Pollock, "Sir: Your Application for a Job Is Rejected."

26. Pontow, "Electronic Résumé Writing Tips."

27. Louis S. Richman, "How to Get Ahead," *Fortune,* 16 May 1994, 46–51; Bruce Nussbaum, "I'm Worried about My Job," *Business Week,* 7 October 1991, 94–97.

28. William J. Banis, "The Art of Writing Job-Search Letters," *CPC Annual, 36th Edition* 2 (1992): 42–50.

Chapter 15

1. Adapted from On Call Plus Company News, PRNewswire, www.prnewswire.com/cgi-bin/liststory?4063251> [accessed 9 November 1997]; Herman-Miller Web site, www.herman-miller.com [accessed 9 November 1997]; Hoover's Online [accessed 23 January 1997] www.hoovers.com; A. J. Vogl, "Risky Work," *Across the Board,* July–August 1993, 27–31; Kenneth Labich, "Hot Company, Warm Culture," *Fortune,* 27 February 1989, 74–78; George Melloan, "Herman Miller's Secrets of Corporate Creativity," *Wall Street Journal,* 3 May 1988, A31; Beverly Geber, "Herman Miller: Where Profits and Participation Meet," *Training,* November 1987, 62–66; Robert J. McClory, "The Creative Process at Herman Miller," *Across the Board,* May 1985, 8–22; Tom Peters and Nancy Austin, *A Passion for Excellence,* (New York: Random House, 1985), 204–205.

2. Sylvia Porter, "Your Money: How to Prepare for Job Interviews," *San Francisco Chronicle,* 3 November 1981, 54.

3. Samuel Greengard, "Are You Well Armed to Screen Applicants?" *Personnel Journal,* December 1995, 84–95.

4. Charlene Marmer Solomon, "How Does Disney Do It?" *Personnel Journal,* December 1989, 53.

5. Marcia Vickers, "Don't Touch That Dial: Why Should I Hire You?" *New York Times,* 13 April 1997, F11.

6. Nancy K. Austin, "Goodbye Gimmicks," *Incentive,* May 1996, 24+.

7. "Southwest Is Picky," *Soundview Executive Book Summaries,* September 1998, 5.

8. Joel Russell, "Finding Solid Ground," *Hispanic Business,* February 1992, 42–44, 46.

9. Holly Rawlinson, "Pre-Employment Testing," *Small Business Reports,* April 1989, 20.

10. Josh Martin, "An HR Guide to White Collar Crime," *HR Focus,* September 1998, 1, 14+.

11. "Substance Abuse in the Workplace," *HR Focus,* February 1997, 1, 4+.

12. Tyler D. Hartwell, Paul D. Steele, and Nathaniel F. Rodman, "Workplace Alcohol-Testing Programs: Prevalence and Trends," *Monthly Labor Review,* June 1998, 27–34.

13. Michael P. Cronin, "This Is a Test," *Inc.,* August 1993, 64–68.

14. Austin, "Goodbye Gimmicks."

15. Peter Rea, Julie Rea, and Charles Moonmaw, "Training: Use Assessment Centers in Skill Development," *Personnel Journal,* April 1990, 126–131; Greengard, "Are You Well Armed to Screen Applicants?"

16. Microsoft 1997 Annual Report [accessed 23 October 1998] www.microsoft.com.

17. Robert Gifford, Cheuk Fan Ng, and Margaret Wilkinson, "Nonverbal Cues in the Employment Interview: Links between Applicant Qualities and Interviewer Judgments," *Journal of Applied Psychology* 70, no. 4 (1985): 729.

18. Dale G. Leathers, *Successful Nonverbal Communication* (New York: Macmillan, 1986), 225.

19. Shirley J. Shepherd, "How to Get That Job in 60 Minutes or Less," *Working Woman,* March 1986, 119.

20. Shepherd, "How to Get That Job in 60 Minutes or Less," 118.

21. H. Anthony Medley, *Sweaty Palms: The Neglected Art of Being Interviewed* (Berkeley, Calif.: Ten Speed Press, 1993), 179.

22. Gerald L. Wilson, "Preparing Students for Responding to Illegal Selection Interview Questions," *Bulletin of the Association for Business Communication* 54, no. 2 (1991): 44–49.

23. Jeff Springston and Joann Keyton, "Interview Response Training," *Bulletin of the Association for Business Communication* 54, no. 3 (1991): 28–30; Gerald L. Wilson, "An Analysis of Instructional Strategies for Responding to Illegal Selection Interview Questions," *Bulletin of the Association for Business Communication* 54, no. 3 (1991): 31–35.

24. Stephen J. Pullum, "Illegal Questions in the Selection Process: Going Beyond Contemporary Business and Professional Communication Textbooks," *Bulletin of the Association for Business Communication* 54, no. 3 (1991): 36–43; Alicia Kitsuse, "Have You Ever Been Arrested?'" *Across the Board,* November 1992, 46–49; Christina L. Greathouse, "10 Common Hiring Mistakes," *Industry Week,* 20 January 1992, 22–23, 26.

25. Marilyn Moats Kennedy, "Are You Getting Paid What You're Worth?" *New Woman,* November 1984, 110.

26. Harold H. Hellwig, "Job Interviewing: Process and Practice," *Bulletin of the Association for Business Communication* 55, no. 2 (1992): 8–14.

27. See note 1.

Appendix A

1. Mary A. DeVries, *Internationally Yours* (Boston: Houghton Mifflin, 1994), 9.

2. Patricia A. Dreyfus, "Paper That's Letter Perfect," *Money,* May 1985, 184.

3. "When Image Counts, Letterhead Says It All," The Advocate and Greenwich Time, 10 January 1993, F4.

4. Mel Mandell, "Electronic Forms Are Cheap and Speedy," *D&B Reports,* July–August 1993, 44–45.

5. Linda Driskill, Business & Managerial Communication: New Perspectives (Orlando, Fla.: Harcourt Brace Jovanovich, 1992), 470.

6. Driskill, Business & Managerial Communication, 470.

7. Lennie Copeland and Lewis Griggs, Going International: How to Make Friends and Deal Effectively in the Global Marketplace, 2d ed. (New York: Random House, 1985), 24–27.

8. DeVries, Internationally Yours, 8.

9. Copeland and Griggs, Going International, 24–27.

10. U.S. Postal Service, Postal Addressing Standards (Washington, D.C.: GPO, 1992).

11. Copeland and Griggs, Going International, 24–27.

12. Renee B. Horowitz and Marian G. Barchilon, "Stylistic Guidelines for E-Mail," IEEE Transactions on Professional Communications 37, no. 4 (1994): 207–12.

13. Jill H. Ellsworth and Matthew V. Ellsworth, The Internet Business Book (New York: Wiley, 1994), 93.

14. Bill Eager, Using the Internet (Indianapolis, Ind.: Que, 1994), 11.

15. Eager, Using the Internet, 10.

16. William Eager, Larry Donahue, David Forsyth, Kenneth Mitton, and Martin Waterhouse, net.Search (Indianapolis, Ind.: Que, 1995), 221.

17. Rosalind Resnick and Dave Taylor, Internet Business Guide (Indianapolis, Ind.: Sams.net Publishing, 1995), 117.

18. James L. Clark and Lyn R. Clark, How 7: A Handbook for Office Workers, 7th ed. (Cincinnati: South-Western, 1995), 431–32.

ACKNOWLEDGMENTS

Text

4 (Is Telecommuting Right For You?) Adapted from Bronwyn Fryer, "Workshop," *Working Woman*, April 1997, 59–60; Lisa Chadderdon, "Merrill Lynch Works—at Home," *Fast Company*, April/May 1998, 70–72; Peg Verone, "House Rules," *Success*, July 1998, 22–23. **17 (Ethical Boundaries: Where Would You Draw the Line?)** Adapted from Ben Stein, "An Employer's Bill of Rights," *Business Month*, April 1990, 55; Thomas A. Young, "Ethics in Business: Business of Ethics," *Vital Speeches*, 15 September 1992, 725–730; "Business Ethics: What Are Your Personal Standards?" *Working Woman*, February 1990, 61–62; Kyle Herger, "One Communicator's Gold Star Is Another's Scarlet Letter," *IABC Communication World*, September 1989, 34–36; Barbara D. Langham, "Ethics: Where Do You Stand?" *IABC Communication World*, May 1989, 21–22, 24–25; Frank Yanacek, "A Question of Ethics," *Transportation and Distribution*, December 1988, 48–50. **39 (Actions Speak Louder Than Words All Around the World)** Adapted from David A. Victor, *International Business Communication* (New York: HarperCollins, 1992); David Wallace, "Mind Your Manners," *World Trade*, October 1992, 52, 54–55; Hannele Duvfa, "Innocents Abroad: The Politics of Cross-Cultural Communication," *Communication and Discourse Across Cultures and Languages*, 1991, 73–89; M. Katherine Glover, "Do's & Taboos: Cultural Aspects of International Business," *Business America*, 13 August 1990, 2–6; C. Barnum and N. Woniansky, "Taking Cues from Body Language," *Management Review*, June 1989, 59–60. **32 (Electronic Meetings: Work Together—Wherever You Are—to Get the Results You Want)** Adapted from Elizabeth Niendorf, "High-Tech Meetings Help Timid Give Voice to Ideas," *Nashville Business Journal*, 18 November 1996, 20; Jim Clark and Richard Koonce, "Meetings Go High-Tech," *Training and Development*, 1 November 1995, 32+; Joseph G. Donelan, "Using Electronic Tools to Improve Meetings," *Management Accounting*, March 1993, 42–45; Brent Gallupe and George Fox, "Facilitated Electronic Meetings: Higher Quality, Less Time," *CMA Magazine*, April 1992, 29–32; Rosemary Hamilton, "Electronic Meetings: No More ZZZZ's," *Computerworld*, 14 September 1992, 109, 113; Michael Finley, "The Best of All Possible Meetings?" *Across the Board*, September 1991, 40–45; Michael Finley, "The New Meaning of Meetings," *IABC Communication World*, March 1991, 25–27; Stephen F. Friedman, "The Electronic Alternative," *Small Business Reports*, July 1991, 68–72; Robert Moskowitz, "Electronic Meetings Raise Effectiveness," *Office Systems*, August 1991, 30–36; Shawn Hartley Hancock, "Electronic Meetings: Ready for Prime Time," *Successful Meetings*, October 1988, 32–37; Ellen Muraskin, "Electronic Meetings," *Meetings & Conventions*, November 1988, 138; Sam Dickey, "Electronic Meetings: Substitutes with Substance?" *Today's Office*, July 1986, 40–46. **88 (Spin Cycle: Deciphering Corporate Doublespeak):** Adapted from William Lutz, "Life Under the Chief Doublespeak Officer," *USA Today*, 17 October 1996, 15A. **113 (No Need to Explain It—Just Say It in Plain English)** Adapted from Toddi Gutner, "At Last, the Readable Prospectus," *Business Week*, 13 April 1998, 11; Philip Maher, "One for the Writers," *Investment Dealers' Digest*, 17 November 1997, 41; Ronald G. Shafer, "Government Bureaucrats to Learn a New Language: Simple English," *Wall Street Journal*, 2 June 1998, B1; Peder Zane, "For Investors, an Initial Public Offering of English," *New York Times*, 25 August 1996, 7; Dan Seligman, "The Gobbledygook Profession," *Forbes*, 7 September 1998, 174–175; Michael Weiss and James Hildebrandt, "Art of Clear Writing Lost in Sea of Legalese," *San Antonio Business Journal*, 28 October 1996 [accessed September 1998], www.amcity.com/sanantonio/stories/102896/editorial2.html. **126 (Checklist: Writing for the Web)** Adapted from John S. Rhodes, "Writing for the Web and Creating Effective Online Content: An Interview with Online Writing Expert, Amy Gahran," WebWord.com [accessed 28 June 2000] www.webword.com/interviews/gahran.html; Joe Landsberger, "Writing Effective Web Pages," University of St. Thomas' ISS Learning Center [accessed 28 June 2000] www.iss.stthomas.edu/studyguides/writing_content.htm; Kaye Vivian, "Writing for Webs" [accessed 28 June 2000, updated 4 January 1999] www.users.cloud9.net/~kvivian/html/web_readers.html; Nathan Wallace, "Web Writing for Many Interest Levels," e-gineer.com [18 May 1999, accessed 28 June 2000] www.e-gineer.com/articles/web-writing-for-many-interest-levels.html. **152 (How to Proofread Like a Pro)** Adapted from Philip C. Kolin, *Successful Writing at Work*, 2d ed., 102. Used with permission of D. C. Heath and Company; Dennis Hensley, "A Way with Words: Proofreading Can Save Cash and Careers," *Dallas Magazine*, May 1986, 57–58. Reprinted with permission. **147 (Warding Off Digital Disaster)** Adapted from Marcia Stepanek, "From Digits to Dust," *Business Week*, 20 April 1998, 128–130; Stephan H. Wildstrom, "Don't Be a Crash Dummy," *Business Week*, 13 April 1998, 15; Gary Sutton, "Backing Up Onsite—or Online: 25 Smart Ways to Protect Your PC from Data Disaster," *Computer Technology Review*, February 1998, 38, 42+; Deborah Branscum and Jennifer Lach, "E-mail Scare," *Newsweek*, 10 August 1998, 10; Brooks Talley, "Killing Viruses Dead," *InfoWorld*, 10 August 1998, 1, 66+; Stan Miastkowski, "Virus Killers," *PC World Online*, 1 March 1998; Philip Elmer-DeWitt, Scott Brown, and Thomas McCarroll, "Invasion of the Data Snatchers," *Time*, 26 September 1998, 62+; James E. Hunton, "Facts and Fables about Computer Viruses," *Journal of Accountancy*, May 1998, 39–42. **162 (How Direct is Too Direct?)** Source: Adapted from Mary A. DeVries, *Internationally Yours* (Boston: Houghton Mifflin, 1994), 195; Myron W. Lustig and Jolene Koester, *Intercultural Competence* (New York: HarperCollins, 1993), 66–72; Mary Munter, "Cross-Cultural Communication for Managers," *Business Horizons*, May–June 1993, 69–78; David A. Victor, *International Business Communication* (New York: HarperCollins, 1992), 137–168; Larry A. Samovar and Richard E. Porter, *Intercultural Communication: A Reader*, 6th ed. (Belmont, Calif.: Wadsworth, 1991), 109–110; Larry A. Samovar and Richard E. Porter, *Communication between Cultures* (Belmont, Calif.: Wadsworth, 1991), 235–244; Carley H. Dodd, *Dynamics of Intercultural Communication*, 3d ed. (Dubuque, Iowa: Wm. C. Brown, 1989), 69–73. **179 (Recommendation Letters: What's Right to Write?)** Source: Adopted from Maura Dolan and Stuart Silverstein, "Court Broadens Liability for Job References," *Los Angeles Times*, 28 January 1997, A1, A11; David A. Price, "Good References Pave Road to Court," *USA Today*, 13 February 1997, 11A; Frances A. McMorris,

"Ex-Bosses Face Less Peril Giving Honest Job References," *Wall Street Journal,* 8 July 1996, B1, B8; Dawn Gunsch, "Gray Matters: Centralize Control of Giving References," *Personnel Journal,* September 1992, 114, 116–117; Betty Southard Murphy, Wayne E. Barlow, and D. Diane Hatch, "Manager's Newsfront: Job Reference Liability of Employees," *Personnel Journal,* September 1991, 22, 26; Ross H. Fishman, "When Silence Is Golden," *Nation's Business,* July 1991, 48–49. **201 (Good Ways to Send Bad News Around the World)** Adapted from James Calvert Scott and Diana J. Green, "British Perspectives on Organizing Bad-News Letters: Organizational Patterns Used by Major U.K. Companies," *Bulletin of the Association for Business Communication* 55, no. 1 (March 1992): 17–19; Iris I. Varner, "A Comparison of American and French Business Correspondence," *Journal of Business Communication* 24, no. 4 (Fall 1988): 55–65; Susan Jenkins and John Hinds, "Business Letter Writing: English, French, and Japanese," *TESOL Quarterly* 21, no. 2 (June 1987): 327–349; Saburo Haneda and Hiosuke Shima, "Japanese Communication Behavior As Reflected in Letter Writing," *Journal of Business Communication* 19, no. 1 (1982): 19–32. **216 (Mastering the Art of Constructive Criticism)** Adapted from Les Giblin, *How to Have Confidence and Power in Dealing with People* (New York: Prentice Hall, 1956), 132–133. **253 (Spam: Putting a Lid on It)** Adapted from Rebecca Quick, "Sick of Junk E-Mail? Here Are Some Tips for Fighting Back," *Wall Street Journal,* 23 May 1998, B7; Jeri Clausing, "New Plan for Junk E-Mail is Dividing Internet Camps," *New York Times,* 18 May 1998, C4; Rebecca Quick, "Measures to Rid Cyberspace of 'Spam' Run into Snags," *Wall Street Journal,* 18 May 1998, B1, B10. **282 (Seven Errors in Logic That Can Undermine Your Reports)** Adapted from Christopher Power, "Flops," *Business Week,* 16 August 1993, 79; Mary Munter, *Guide to Managerial Communication,* 2d ed. (Upper Saddle River, N.J.: Prentice Hall, 1982), 31. Adapted by permission of Prentice Hall, Inc., Upper Saddle River, NJ. **271 (Minding Your Business with Online Reporting)** Adapted from the FedEx home page [accessed 14 June 1996] (www.fedex.com/svcs_online.html); Jack Schember, "Mrs. Fields' Secret Weapon," *Personnel Journal,* September 1991, 56–58; Paul Konstadt, "Ship 54—Where Are You?" *CIO,* May 1990, 80–81, 84, 86; Bruce G. Posner and Bo Burlingham, "The Hottest Entrepreneur in America," *Inc.,* January 1988, 44–48. **342 (Top Tips for Writing Business Reports that Mean Business)** *Source:* Adapted from Joan Minninger, The Perfect Memo (New York: Doubleday, 1990), 169–170. Copyright © 1990 by Joan Minninger. Used by permission of Doubleday, a division of Bantam Doubleday Dell Publishing Group, Inc. **405 (Five Tips for Making Presentations Around the World)** Adapted from Eric J. Adams, "Management Focus: User-Friendly Presentation Software," *World Trade,* March 1995, 92. **421 (Nerves: The Secret Weapon of Polished Presenters)** Adapted from Sherwyn P. Morreale and Courtland L. Bovée, *Excellence in Public Speaking* (Forth Worth: Harcourt Brace, 1998), 7; Leon Fletcher, "A Remedy for Stage Fright," *The Toastmaster,* June 1994, 8–10; Greg Dahl, "Fear of Fear," *The Toastmaster,* June 1994, 10–11; "A Survival Guide to Public Speaking," *Training & Development Journal,* September 1990, 15–16, 18–25. **438 (Netting a Job on the Web)** Adapted from Richard Nelson Bolles, *The 1997 What Color Is Your Parachute?* (Berkeley, Calif. Ten Speed Press, 1996), 129–166; Karen W. Arenson, "Placement Offices Leave Old Niches to Become Computerized Job Bazaars," *New York Times,* 17 July 1996; B12; Lawrence J. Magid, "Job Hunters Cast Wide Net Online," *Los Angeles Times,* 26 February 1996, 20; Richard Von Doren, "On-Line Career Advice Speeds Search for Jobs," *Network Word,* 4 March 1996; 54; Alex Markels, "Job Hunting Takes Off in Cyberspace," *Wall Street Journal,* 20 September 1996; B1, B2; Michael Chorost, "Jobs on the Web," *Hispanic,* October 1995, 50–53; Zane K. Quible, "Electronic Résumés: Their Time Is Coming," *Business Communication Quarterly* 58, no. 3 (1995): 5–9; Margaret Mannix, "The Home-Page Help Wanteds," *U.S. News & World Report,* 30 October 1995, 88, 90; Pam Dixon and Silivia Tiersten, *Be Your Own Headhunter Online* (New York: Random House, 1995), 53–69; Michele Himmelberg, "Internet an Important Tool in Employment Search," *San Diego Union-Tribune,* 7 September 1998, D2; Richard N. Bolles, "Career Strategizing, or What Color Is Your Parachute?" *Yahoo! Internet Life,* May 1998, 116–122; Valerie Frazee, "Online Job Services Explode," *Personnel Journal,* August 1996, 21. **445 (Inflating Your Résumé: Is It Worth the Risk?)** Adapted from Joan E. Rigdon, "Deceptive Résumés Can Be Door-Openers but Can Become an Employee's Undoing," *Wall Street Journal,* 17 June 1992; B1; Diane Cole, "Ethics: Companies Crack Down on Dishonesty," *Managing Your Career,* Spring 1981, 8–11; Nancy Marx Better, "Résumé Liars," *Savvy,* December 1990–January 1991, 26–29. **470 (How to Check References and Stay Within the Law)** Adapted from James Krohe, Jr., "Why Traditional Screening Doesn't Work," *Across the Board,* December 1997, 22+; Frances A. McMorris, "Ex-Bosses Face Less Peril Giving Honest Job References," *Wall Street Journal,* 8 July 1996, B1, B8; Michael Kinsman, "Firm's Cost Cutting Left This Job-Seeker out in the Cold," *San Diego Union-Tribune,* 21 June 1996, C1; Samuel Greengard, "Are You Well Armed to Screen Applicants?" *Personnel Journal,* December 1995, 84–95; "Employers Find It More Difficult to Check References," *Personnel Journal,* May 1993, 20; Time Weiner, "Fearing Suits, Companies Avoid Giving Job References," *New York Times,* 8 May 1993, 17, 29; David B. Kern, "Handling References Requests on Fired Employees," *Supervisory Management,* January 1993, 6; Paul W. Barada, "Check References with Care," *Nation's Business,* May 1993, 54, 56; Max Messmer, "Nothing But the Truth," *Small Business Reports,* March 1993, 11–14; "Managing People: Reference-Checking Tips," *Inc.,* November 1992; 38; James W. Fenton Jr. and Kay W. Lawrimore, "Employment Reference Checking, Firm Size, and Defamation Liability," *Journal of Small Business Management,* October 1992, 88–95; George D. Webster, "Background and Reference Checks," *Agency Sales Magazine,* October 1992, 26–28; Emily Leinfuss, "Reference Checks: The Truth Be Known," *Computerworld,* 22 April 1991, 88; Lois Vander Waerdt, "Take Nothing for Granted," *Management World,* November 1990, 68, 70, 73; James Braham, "Hiring Mr. Wrong," *Industry Week,* 7 March 1988, 31–34; Robert Half, "Reference Checking: A Critical Part of the Hiring Process," *Journal of Accountancy,* August 1988, 130–134. **472 (Interview Strategies: Answering the 16 Toughest Questions)** Adapted from "Career Strategies," *Black Enterprise,* February 1986, 122. Copyright © 1986, *Black Enterprise* Magazine, The Earl Graves Publishing Company, Inc., New York, NY. All rights reserved.

Figures and Tables

5 (Figure 1.2) Data from Richard W. Judy and Carol D'Amico, *Workforce 2020* (Indianapolis: Hudson Institute, 1997), 109. **8** (Figure 1.4) Adapted from David J. Rachman and Michael H. Mescon, *Business Today,* 5th ed. (New York: McGraw-Hill, 1987), 127. **13** (Figure 1.7) Adapted from Allan D. Frank, *Communicating on the Job* (Glenview, Ill.: Scott Foresman, 1982), 20. **14** (Figure 1.8) "Information Deluge Clogging Workplace," *The Honolulu Advertiser,* 25 May 1998, B6. **28** (Table 2.1) Adapted from Phillip Morgan and H. Kent Baker, "Building a Professional Image: Improving Listening Behavior." Reprinted by permission of the publisher, from *Supervisory Management,* November 1985, 34. © 1987 McGraw-Hill, Inc. **33** (Figure 2.1) Copyright, Dr. Lyman K. Steil, president, Communication Development, Inc., St. Paul, Minn. Prepared for the

Sperry Corporation. Reprinted with permission of Dr. Steil and Unisys Corporation. **36** (Table 2.3) Adapted from J. Michael Sproule, *Communication Today* (Glenview, Ill.: Scott, Foresman, 1981), by permission of J. Michael Sproule. Copyright J. Michael Sproule. **38** (Figure 2.2) S. E. Taylor, L. A. Peplan, and D. O. Sears, Social Psucology, 9th ed. (Upper Saddle River, N. J.: Prentice Hall, 1997), 98. Photographs by Paul Ekman, Ph.D. Used with permission. **49** (Figure 3.1) Steffano Korper and Juanita Ellis, *The E-Commerce Book: Building the E-Empire* (San Diego, California: Academic Press, 2000), 56. **53** (Table 3.1) Mary O'Hara-Devereaux and Robert Johansen, *Global Work: Bridging Distance, Culture, and Time* (San Francisco: Jossey-Bass, 1994), 55, 59. **55** (Figure 3.2) Lillian H. Chaney and Jeanette S. Martin, *Intercultural Business Communication,* 2d edition (Upper Saddle River, N. J.: Prentice Hall, 2000), 50. **57** (Table 3.2) Guo-Ming Chen and William J. Starosta, *Foundations of Intercultural Communication* (Boston, Mass: Allyn and Bacon, 1998), 66. **79** (Figure 4.3) Scott DeGraeve, president, Scotty's Home Market, personal communication, August 1998. **81** (Figure 4.4) Courtesy of General Mills, Inc. **149** (Figure 6.6) Grammatik 5, © 1986–93, Reference Software International, a wholly owned subsidiary of WordPerfect Corporation. All rights reserved. Used with permission. **231** (Figure 9.1) Adapted from Abraham H. Maslow, *Motivation and Personality* (New York: Harper & Row, 1954), 12, 19, Copyright © 1970 by Abraham H. Maslow. Reprinted by permission of HarperCollins Publishers. **293** (Figure 10.10) Adapted from "Finding Industry Information," University of Pittsburg Web site [accessed 3 November 1998] www.pitt.edu/~buslibry/industries.htm; Thomas P. Bergman, Stephen M. Garrison, and Gregory M. Scott, *The Business Student Writer's Manual and Guide to the Internet* (Paramus, N. J.: Prentice Hall, 1998), 67–80; Ernest L. Maier, Anthony J. Faria, Peter Kaatrude, and Elizabeth Wood, *The Business Library and How to Use It* (Detroit: Omnigraphics, 1996), 53–76. **296** (Table 10.3) Search Engines Fact and Fun [accessed 11 March 1998] searchenginewatch.com/facts/major.html; Getting Started—What You Need to Know to Begin Using the Internet," *Fortune Technology Buyer's Guide,* Winter 1998, 232–240; Matt Lake, "Desperately Seeking Susan OR Suzie NOT Sushi," *New York Times,* 3 September 1998, D1, D7; "Notable Websites," *Fortune Technology Buyer's Guide,* Winter 1999, 238, 240. **332** (Figure 11.7) *Standard & Poor's Industry Surveys—Footware,* 1 December 1998, 26. **332** (Figure 11.8) *Standard & Poor's Industry Surveys—Autos,* 5 March 1998, 16. **332** (Figure 11.9) *Standard & Poor's Industry Surveys—Movies,* 12 November 1998, 30. **333** (Figure 11.10) *American Demographics,* March 1998, 42. **334** (Figure 11.11) F11.11–a, (Where the College Students Are): *American Demographics,* March 1998, 47; F11.11–b (Eating Occasions): *American Demographics,* January 1998, 58; F11.11–c (Targeted Talks): *American Demographics,* February 1998, 52; F11.11–d (Commercial Superhighway): *Wall Street Journal,* 7 December 1998, R4. **336** (Figure 11.12) *Frequent Flyer Magazine* and J. D. Power and Associates, 1998, Airline Customer Satisfaction Study—U.S. Flights. **336** Figure (11.13) Iris I. Varner, *Contemporary Business Report Writing,* 2d ed. (Chicago: Dryden Press, 1991), 75. **337** (Figure 11.14) www.census.gov/statab/ranks/pg05.txt **337** (Figure 11.15) "How the Networks Deliver the Goods," *Business Week,* 6 April 1998, 91–92. **396** (Figure 12.5) Adapted from A. S. C. Ehrenberg, "The Problem of Numeracy," *Admap,* February 1992, 37–40; Mary S. Auvil and Kenneth W. Auvil, *Introduction to Business Graphics: Concepts and Applications* (Cincinnati: South-Western, 1992), 40, 192–193; Peter H. Selby, *Using Graphs and Tables: A Self-Teaching Guide* (New York: Wiley, 1979), 8–9. **397** (Table 12.1) Adapted from Robert Lefferts, *How to Prepare Charts and Graphs for Effective Reports* (New York: Harper & Row, Publishers, Inc., 1981). **397** (Table 12.2) Adapted

from Robert Lefferts, *How to Prepare Charts and Graphs for Effective Reports* (New York: Harper & Row, Publishers, Inc., 1981). **399** (Table 12.4) Geng Cui, "The Different Faces of the Chinese Consumer," *China Business Review* 24, no. 4 (1997): 34–38, downloaded from ABI/INFORM database 1 December 1998. **399** (Table 12.5) Grey China, *The Grey ChinaBase Annual Consumer Study,* 1998, cited in Colin Bates, "The Many China Markets," *China Business Review* 25, no. 5 (1998): 26–29, downloaded from ABI/INFORM database 1 December 1998. **399** (Table 12.6) U.S. Department of Commerce, *Big Emerging Markets Information Resource Page,* [28 August 1998; accessed 1 December 1998] www.ita.doc.gov/bems/index.html. **400** (Table 12.7) U.S. Department of Commerce, *Big Emerging Markets Information Resource Page,* 28 August 1998; accessed 1 December 1998: www.ita.doc.gov/bems/index.html. **400** (Figure 12.6) Grey China, *The Grey China Base Annual Consumer Study,* 1998, cited in Colin Bates, "The Many China Markets," *China Business Review* 25, no. 5 (1998): 26–29, downloaded from ABI/INFORM database 1 December 1998. **400** (Figure 12.7) China Economic Information Center, cited in Trish Saywell, "Preparing for Take-Off," *Far Eastern Economic Review* 161, no. 48 (1998): 38, downloaded from ABI/INFORM database 1 December 1998. **401** (Figure 12.8) IGI Consulting, cited in Gina Fraone, "China's Challenge," *Electronic Business* 24, no. 12 (1998): 24, downloaded from ABI/INFORM database 1 December 1998. **435** (Figure 14.2) Adapted from Richard Nelson Bolles, *What Color Is Your Parachute?* (Berkeley, Calif.: Ten Speed Press, 1997), 67. **471** (Table 15.1) Adapted from *The Northwestern Endicott Report* (Evanston: Ill.: Northwestern University Placement Center). **473** (Table 15.2) Adapted from The Northwestern *Endicott Report* (Evanston, Ill.: Northwestern University Placement Center). **474** (Table 15.3) Adapted from H. Lee Rust, *Job Search: The Completion Manual for Jobseekers* (New York: American Management Association, 1979), 56. **475** (Figure 15.1) Adapted from *The Northwestern Endicott Report* (Evanston: Ill.: Northwestern University Placement Center). **494** (Table A.1) Adapted from James L. Clark and Lyn R. Clark, *How 7: A Handbook for Office Workers,* 7th ed. (Cincinnati, Oh.: South-Western, 1995), 257–264. **500** (Figure A.3) Letterhead courtesy of J.C. Penney.

Photo Credits

v Churchhill Klehr Photography **v** Cindy Karp/Black Star **vi** James Leynse/Corbis/SABA Press Photos, Inc. **vii** Gary I. Rothstein/Corbis/Sygma **vii viii** APWide World Photos **viii** Campbell Soup Company **ix** David Weintraub/Stock Boston **ix** Alan Levenson **x** Bob Daemmrich Photography, Inc. **xi** George Disario/Corbis/Stock Market **xi** Najlah Feanny/Corbis/SABA/Press Photos, Inc. **xii** Courtesy of Keys Group **xii** Pinketon Security and Investigation Services **xiii** Herman Miller, Inc. **1** George B. Diebold, Corbis/Stock Market **2** Churchill & Klehr Photography **4** Alan Levenson **6** Jamie Tanaka Photography **13** Spencer Grant, PhotoEdit **15** NBC Photo **20** Churchill & Klehr Photography **25** Cindy Karp, Black Star **27** Andes Chemical Corporation **31** Andy Freeberg Photography **34** Bob Daemmrich, Stock Boston **38** (fig. 02) Paul Ekman, Ph.D. Professor of Psychology **40** Susan Shacter, Corbis/Outline **44** Cindy Karp, Black Star **48** James Leynse, Corbis/SABA Press Photos, Inc. **49** John Abbott, John Abbott Photography **51** Cheryl Gerber, AP/Wide World Photos **57** Eddie Adams, Corbis/Outline **58** Charles Gupton, Stock Boston **66** James Leynse, Corbis/SABA Press Photos, Inc. **72** Gary I. Rothstein, Corbis/Sygma **71** William Whitehurst, Corbis/Stock Market **74** Suzanne Opton **76** Mark Richards **86** Patrick Pagnano, CBS Photo Archive **92** Chip Williams Inc. ©2000Chip

Williams **93** Gary I. Rothstein, Corbis/Sygma **99** Reuters/Beverly Schaefer, Hulton/Archive **100** E. J. Camp Photography, Inc., Corbis/Outline **105** I. Uimonen, Corbis/Sygma **108** Churchill & Klehr Photography **119** Ariel Skelley, Corbis/Stock Market **127** Reuters/Beverly Schaefer, Hulton/Archive **133** AP/Wide World Photos **136** E. J. Camp, Corbis/Outline **141** Starbucks Coffee Company **148** John R. Fulton, Jr. **150** Caldwell Photography **153** AP/Wide World Photos **159** Michael Waine, Corbis/Stock Market **160** Campbell Soup Company **161** Philip Saltonstall **166** Charley Shin **172** Corbis/Sygma **182** Jeff Greenberg, The Image Works **185** Campbell Soup Company **191** D. Young Wolff, PhotoEdit **193** Deere & Company **195** The Blue Marble **197** David Weintraub, Stock Boston **198** Yla Eason **200** Michael Paras, International Stock Photography Ltd. **204** The Chicago Reporter **213** Gary C. Caskey/REUTERS Hulton/Archive **219** David Weintraub, Stock Boston **224** Suzanne Plunkett, AP/Wide World Photos **226** Victor Pobedinsky, AP/Wide World Photos **228** Tom Bean Stone **230** Alan Levenson **232** Christopher Pillitz, Matrix International, Inc. **236** The Children's Defense Fund **244** Felix Adamo **246** Kim Kulish, Corbis/SABA Press Photos, Inc. **257** Alan Levenson **262** Westlight/Bill Ross Corbis **263** ML Sinibaldi, Corbis/Stock Market **265** Clarksburg Exponent Telegram, Bob Shaw, AP/Wide World Photos **269** George B. Diebold, Corbis/Stock Market **270** Bob Daemmrich Photography, Inc. **273** Cambridge Technology Partners **273** Urban City Foods **281** Reglain Frederic Liaison Agency, Inc. **286** William Polo Copyright Photo By Bill Polo **307** Rob Crandall, Stock Boston **308** Bob Daemmrich, Photography, Inc. **315** George Disario, Corbis/Stock Market **316** Richard Howard Photography **321** Chris Carroll, Corbis/Outline **339** Steve Niedorf, The Image Bank **341** Computer Associates **348** George Disario, Corbis/Stock Market **355** Charles Rex Arbogast, AP/Wide World Photos **356** Churchill & Klehr Photography **358** Najlah Feanny, Corbis/SABA Press Photos, Inc. **360** Kim Kulish, Corbis/SABA Press Photos, Inc. **361** SuperStock, Inc. **382** ©2001 Brad Trent **384** Avis Rent-A-Car System **387** Peter Gregoire **393** Najlah Feanny, Corbis/SABA Press Photos, Inc. **398** Miwako Ikeda, International Stock Photography Ltd. **401** Frank Oberle, ImageQuest **403** Courtesy of Keys Group **409** Deborah Feingold, Corbis/Outline **412** Tom & Dee Ann McCarthy, Corbis/Stock Market **420** Waggner Edstrom Courtesy of Microsoft Corporation **423** Mark Richards **426** Courtesy of Keys Group **431** George B. Diebold, Corbis/Stock Market **432** Pinkerton Security and Investigation Services **434** GC Micro **444** FBI Phoenix Division **451** Todd Buchanan **458** Pinkerton Security and Investigation Services **466** Courtesy of Herman Miller, Inc. **470** The Image Works **476** Bob Daemmrich, The Image Works **477** Darryl Estrine, Corbis/Outline **479** Godfather's Pizza, Inc. **485** Courtesy of Herman Miller, Inc.

NAME/ORGANIZATION/ BRAND/COMPANY INDEX

SUBJECT INDEX